KEY TO WORLD MAP PAGES

...EX

Country	Page	Country	Page
Afghanistan	36	Laos	34
Albania	21	Latvia	22
Algeria	44	Lebanon	41
Angola	46–47	Lesotho	47
Argentina	80	Liberia	44
Armenia	23	Libya	44–45
Australia	52–55	Lithuania	22
Austria	16	Luxembourg	15
Azerbaijan	23		
		Macedonia	21
Bahamas	75	Madagascar	47
Bahrain	39	Malawi	46–47
Bangladesh	37	Malaysia	32–34
Barbados	75	Mali	44
Belgium	15	Malta	20
Belize	74	Mauritania	44
Belorussia	22	Mauritius	43
Benin	44	Mexico	74
Bhutan	37	Moldavia	23
Bolivia	78	Mongolia	30–31
Bosnia-Herzegovina	20–21	Morocco	44
Botswana	47	Mozambique	46–47
Brazil	78–80		
Brunei	32	Namibia	47
Bulgaria	21	Nepal	37
Burkina Faso	44	Netherlands	15
Burma	37	New Zealand	51
Burundi	46	Nicaragua	74–75
		Niger	44–45
Cambodia	34	Nigeria	44–45
Cameroon	46	Northern Ireland	13
Canada	60–65	Norway	8–9
Central African			
Republic	46	Oman	40
Chad	45		
Chile	78, 80	Pakistan	36
China	30–31	Panama	75
Colombia	78	Papua New Guinea	50
Congo	46	Paraguay	78, 80
Costa Rica	74–75	Peru	78
Croatia	20–21	Philippines	33
Cuba	75	Poland	16–17
Cyprus	23	Portugal	19
Czech Republic	16–17	Puerto Rico	75
Denmark	9	Qatar	39
Djibouti	40		
Dominican Republic	75	Romania	17
		Russia	22–25
Ecuador	78	Rwanda	46
Egypt	45		
El Salvador	74	Saudi Arabia	40
England	10–11	Scotland	12
Equatorial Guinea	46	Senegal	44
Eritrea	40	Sierra Leone	44
Estonia	22	Singapore	34
Ethiopia	40	Slovak Republic	17
		Slovenia	20
Fiji	51	Somali Republic	40
Finland	8–9	South Africa	47
France	18	Spain	19
French Guiana	79	Sri Lanka	36
		Sudan	45
Gabon	46	Surinam	78–79
Gambia	44	Swaziland	47
Georgia	23	Sweden	8–9
Germany	16	Switzerland	16
Ghana	44	Syria	38, 41
Greece	21		
Greenland	4	Taiwan	31
Guatemala	74	Tajikistan	24
Guinea	44	Tanzania	46
Guinea-Bissau	44	Thailand	34
Guyana	78	Togo	44
		Trinidad and	
Haiti	75	Tobago	75
Honduras	74–75	Tunisia	44–45
Hong Kong	31	Turkey	23
Hungary	16–17	Turkmenistan	24
Iceland	8	Uganda	46
India	36–37	Ukraine	22–23
Indonesia	32–33	United Arab	
Iran	38–39	Emirates	39
Iraq	38–39	United Kingdom	10–14
Irish Republic	13	USA	66–73
Israel	41	Uruguay	80
Italy	20–21	Uzbekistan	24
Ivory Coast	44		
		Venezuela	78
Jamaica	75	Vietnam	34
Japan	28–29		
Jordan	41	Wales	10–11
Kazakhstan	24	Yemen	40
Kenya	46	Yugoslavia	21
Kirghizia	24		
Korea, North	31	Zaïre	46–47
Korea, South	31	Zambia	46–47
Kuwait	38–39	Zimbabwe	47

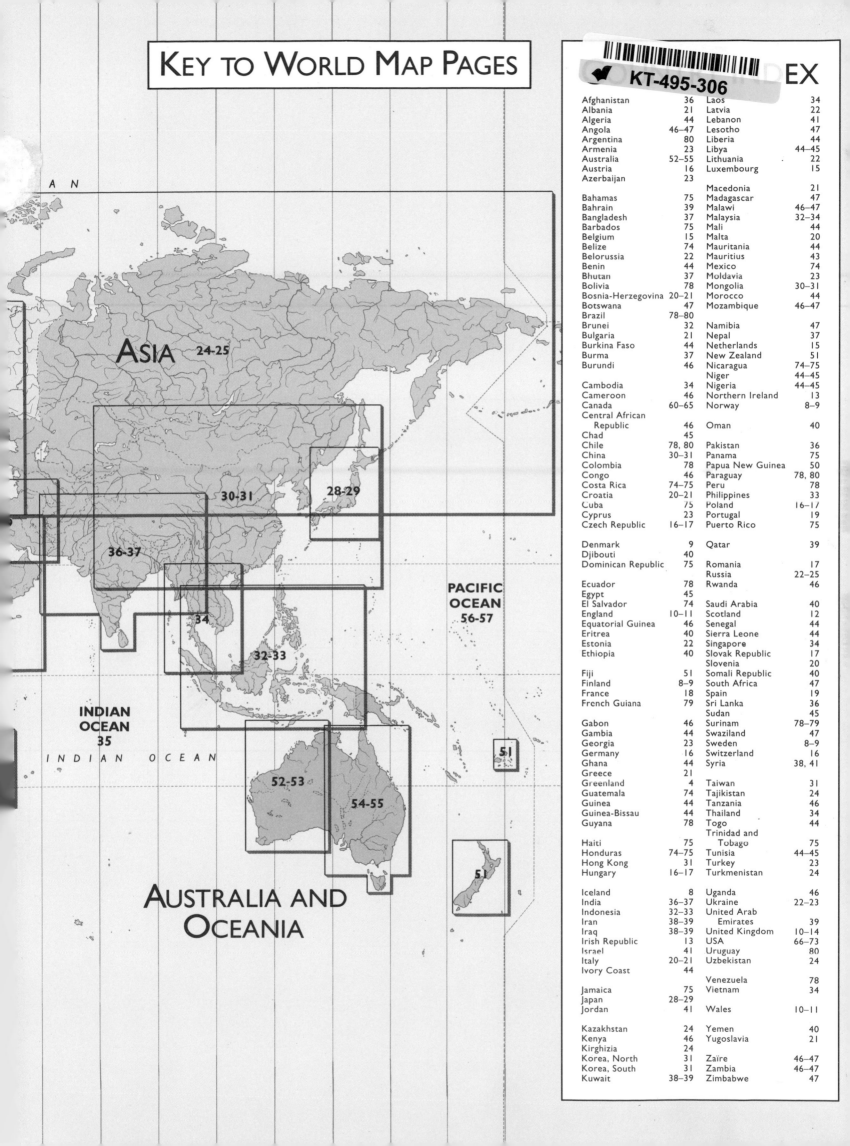

ASIA 24-25

30-31

28-29

36-37

34

32-33

INDIAN OCEAN 35

INDIAN OCEAN

PACIFIC OCEAN 56-57

51

52-53

54-55

51

AUSTRALIA AND OCEANIA

PHILIP'S

WORLD
ATLAS

Published in Great Britain in 1994
by George Philip Limited,
an imprint of Reed Consumer Books Limited,
Michelin House, 81 Fulham Road, London SW3 6RB,
and Auckland, Melbourne, Singapore and Toronto

Cartography by Philip's

Copyright © 1994 Reed International Books Limited

ISBN 0-540-05827-0

A CIP catalogue record for this book is available
from the British Library

Printed in Hong Kong

PHILIP'S

WORLD ATLAS

CONTENTS

WORLD STATISTICS

Countries vi
Physical
Dimensions vii
Philip's
World Maps viii

INTRODUCTION TO

WORLD GEOGRAPHY

Planet Earth 2–3
Restless Earth 4–5
Landscape 6–7
Oceans 8–9
Climate 10–11
Water 12–13
Environment 14–15
Population 16–17
The Human
Family 18–19
Wealth 20–21
Quality of Life 22–23
Energy 24–25
Production 26–27
Trade 28–29
Travel and
Tourism 30–31
Subject Index 32

WORLD MAPS

Map Symbols
I

The World: Political
1:80 000 000
2–3

Arctic Ocean
1:35 000 000
4

Antarctica
1:35 000 000
5

EUROPE

Europe: Physical
1:20 000 000
6

Europe: Political
1:20 000 000
7

Scandinavia and the
Baltic Lands 1:5 000 000

8–9

England and Wales
1:2 000 000

10–11

Scotland 1:2 000 000

12

Ireland 1:2 000 000

13

British Isles 1:4 000 000

14

Netherlands, Belgium
and Luxembourg
1:2 500 000

15

Central Europe
1:5 000 000

16–17

France 1:5 000 000

18

Spain and Portugal
1:5 000 000

19

Italy and the Balkan
States 1:5 000 000

20–21

Eastern Europe and
Turkey 1:10 000 000

22–23

ASIA

Russia and Central
Asia 1:20 000 000

24–25

Asia: Physical
1:50 000 000
26

Asia: Political
1:50 000 000
27

Japan 1:5 000 000

28–29

China and Korea
1:15 000 000

30–31

Indonesia and the
Philippines 1:12 500 000

32–33

Mainland South-East
Asia 1:10 000 000

34

Indian Ocean
1:50 000 000
35

South Asia 1:10 000 000

36–37

The Middle East
1:7 000 000

38–39

Arabia and the Horn
of Africa 1:15 000 000

40

The Near East
1:2 500 000

41

AFRICA

Africa: Physical
1:40 000 000
42

Africa: Political
1:40 000 000
43

Northern Africa
1:15 000 000

44–45

Central and Southern Africa 1:15 000 000

46–47

Southern Africa
1:8 000 000
Madagascar 1:8 000 000

48–49

AUSTRALIA AND OCEANIA

Australia and Oceania: Physical and Political 1:40 000 000
50

New Zealand
1:6 000 000

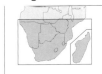

51

Western Australia
1:8 000 000

52–53

Eastern Australia
1:8 000 000

54–55

Pacific Ocean
1:54 000 000
56–57

NORTH AMERICA

North America: Physical 1:35 000 000
58

North America: Political 1:35 000 000
59

Canada 1:15 000 000
Alaska 1:30 000 000

60–61

Eastern Canada
1:7 000 000

62–63

Western Canada
1:7 000 000

64–65

United States
1:12 000 000
Hawaii 1:10 000 000

66–67

Eastern United States
1:6 000 000

68–69

Middle United States
1:6 000 000

70–71

Western United States
1:6 000 000

72–73

Mexico, Central America and the West Indies
1:15 000 000

74–75

SOUTH AMERICA

South America: Physical 1:30 000 000
76

South America: Political 1:30 000 000
77

South America – North
1:16 000 000

78–79

South America – South
1:16 000 000

80

INDEX TO WORLD MAPS
81–128

WORLD STATISTICS: COUNTRIES

This alphabetical list includes the principal countries and territories of the world. If a territory is not completely independent, then the country it is associated with is named. The area figures give the total area of land, inland water and ice. Units for areas and populations are thousands. The annual income is the Gross National Product per capita in US dollars. The figures are the latest available, usually 1993.

Country/Territory	Area km² Thousands	Area miles² Thousands	Population Thousands	Capital	Annual Income US $
Afghanistan	648	250	19,062	Kabul	450
Albania	28.8	11.1	3,363	Tirana	1,000
Algeria	2,382	920	26,346	Algiers	1,980
American Samoa (US)	0.20	0.08	50	Pago Pago	6,000
Andorra	0.45	0.17	58	Andorra la Vella	–
Angola	1,247	481	10,609	Luanda	620
Anguilla (UK)	0.09	0.04	9	The Valley	–
Antigua & Barbuda	0.44	0.17	66	St John's	4,770
Argentina	2,767	1,068	33,101	Buenos Aires	2,790
Armenia	29.8	11.5	3,677	Yerevan	2,150
Aruba (Neths)	0.19	0.07	62	Oranjestad	6,000
Australia	7,687	2,968	17,529	Canberra	17,050
Austria	83.9	32.4	7,884	Vienna	20,140
Azerbaijan	86.6	33.4	7,398	Baku	1,670
Azores (Port.)	2.2	0.87	260	Ponta Delgada	–
Bahamas	13.9	5.4	262	Nassau	11,750
Bahrain	0.68	0.26	533	Manama	7,130
Bangladesh	144	56	119,288	Dacca	200
Barbados	0.43	0.17	259	Bridgetown	6,630
Belau (US)	0.46	0.18	16	Koror	–
Belgium	30.5	11.8	9,998	Brussels	18,950
Belize	23	8.9	198	Belmopan	2,010
Belorussia	207.6	80.1	10,297	Minsk	3,110
Benin	113	43	4,889	Porto-Novo	380
Bermuda (UK)	0.05	0.02	62	Hamilton	25,000
Bhutan	47	18.1	1,612	Thimphu	180
Bolivia	1,099	424	7,832	La Paz/Sucre	650
Bosnia-Herzegovina	51.2	19.8	4,366	Sarajevo	–
Botswana	582	225	1,373	Gaborone	2,590
Brazil	8,512	3,286	156,275	Brasilia	2,940
Brit. Antarctic Terr. (UK)	1,709	660	0.3	Stanley	–
Brit. Ind. Ocean Terr. (UK)	0.08	0.03	3	–	–
Brunei	5.8	2.2	270	Bandar Seri Begawan	6,000
Bulgaria	111	43	8,963	Sofia	1,840
Burkina Faso	274	106	9,490	Ouagadougou	290
Burma (Myanmar)	679	262	43,668	Rangoon	500
Burundi	27.8	10.7	5,786	Bujumbura	210
Cambodia	181	70	9,054	Phnom Penh	300
Cameroon	475	184	12,198	Yaoundé	850
Canada	9,976	3,852	27,562	Ottawa	20,440
Canary Is. (Spain)	7.3	2.8	1,700	Las Palmas/Santa Cruz	–
Cape Verde Is.	4	1.6	384	Praia	750
Cayman Is. (UK)	0.26	0.10	29	Georgetown	–
Central African Republic	623	241	3,173	Bangui	390
Chad	1,284	496	5,961	Ndjamena	220
Chile	757	292	13,599	Santiago	2,160
China	9,597	3,705	1,187,997	Beijing (Peking)	370
Colombia	1,139	440	33,424	Bogotá	1,260
Comoros	2.2	0.86	585	Moroni	500
Congo	342	132	2,368	Brazzaville	1,120
Costa Rica	51.1	19.7	3,099	San José	1,850
Croatia	56.5	21.8	4,764	Zagreb	1,800
Cuba	111	43	10,822	Havana	3,000
Cyprus	9.3	3.6	716	Nicosia	8,640
Czech Republic	78.9	30.4	10,299	Prague	2,370
Denmark	43.1	16.6	5,170	Copenhagen	23,700
Djibouti	23.2	9	467	Djibouti	1,000
Dominica	0.75	0.29	72	Roseau	2,440
Dominican Republic	48.7	18.8	7,471	Santo Domingo	950
Ecuador	284	109	10,741	Quito	1,020
Egypt	1,001	387	55,163	Cairo	620
El Salvador	21	8.1	5,396	San Salvador	1,070
Equatorial Guinea	28.1	10.8	369	Malabo	330
Eritrea	94	36	3,500	Asmera	–
Estonia	44.7	17.3	1,542	Tallinn	3,830
Ethiopia	1,128	436	55,117	Addis Ababa	120
Falkland Is. (UK)	12.2	4.7	2	Stanley	–
Faroe Is. (Den.)	1.4	0.54	47	Tórshavn	23,660
Fiji	18.3	7.1	739	Suva	1,930
Finland	338	131	5,042	Helsinki	23,980
France	552	213	57,372	Paris	20,380
French Guiana (Fr.)	90	34.7	104	Cayenne	2,500
French Polynesia (Fr.)	4	1.5	207	Papeete	6,000
Gabon	268	103	1,237	Libreville	3,780
Gambia, The	11.3	4.4	878	Banjul	360
Georgia	69.7	26.9	5,471	Tbilisi	1,640
Germany	357	138	80,569	Berlin	23,650
Ghana	239	92	15,400	Accra	400
Gibraltar (UK)	0.007	0.003	31	–	4,000
Greece	132	51	10,300	Athens	6,340
Greenland (Den.)	2,176	840	57	Godthåb	6,000
Grenada	0.34	0.13	91	St George's	2,180
Guadeloupe (Fr.)	1.7	0.66	400	Basse-Terre	7,000
Guam (US)	0.55	0.21	139	Agana	6,000
Guatemala	109	42	9,745	Guatemala City	930
Guinea	246	95	6,116	Conakry	450
Guinea-Bissau	36.1	13.9	1,006	Bissau	190
Guyana	215	83	808	Georgetown	430
Haiti	27.8	10.7	6,764	Port-au-Prince	370
Honduras	112	43	5,462	Tegucigalpa	570
Hong Kong (UK)	1.1	0.40	5,801	–	13,430
Hungary	93	35.9	10,313	Budapest	2,720
Iceland	103	40	260	Reykjavik	23,170
India	3,288	1,269	879,548	Delhi	330
Indonesia	1,905	735	191,170	Jakarta	610
Iran	1,648	636	56,964	Tehran	2,170
Iraq	438	169	19,290	Baghdad	2,000
Ireland	70.3	27.1	3,547	Dublin	11,120
Israel	27	10.3	4,946	Jerusalem	11,950
Italy	301	116	57,782	Rome	18,580
Ivory Coast	322	125	12,910	Abidjan	690
Jamaica	11	4.2	2,469	Kingston	1,480
Japan	378	146	124,336	Tokyo	26,920
Jordan	89.2	34.4	4,291	Amman	1,060
Kazakhstan	2,717	1,049	17,038	Alma Ata	7,570
Kenya	580	224	26,985	Nairobi	340
Kirghizia	198.5	76.6	4,472	Bishkek	4,000
Kiribati	0.72	0.28	74	Tarawa	750
Korea, North	121	47	22,618	Pyongyang	900
Korea, South	99	38.2	43,663	Seoul	6,340
Kuwait	17.8	6.9	1,970	Kuwait City	16,380

Country/Territory	Area km² Thousands	Area miles² Thousands	Population Thousands	Capital	Annual Income US $
Laos	237	91	4,469	Vientiane	230
Latvia	65	25	2,632	Riga	3,410
Lebanon	10.4	4	2,838	Beirut	2,000
Lesotho	30.4	11.7	1,836	Maseru	580
Liberia	111	43	2,580	Monrovia	500
Libya	1,760	679	4,875	Tripoli	5,800
Liechtenstein	0.16	0.06	28	Vaduz	33,000
Lithuania	65.2	25.2	3,759	Vilnius	2,710
Luxembourg	2.6	1	390	Luxembourg	31,780
Macau (Port.)	0.02	0.006	374	–	2,000
Macedonia	25.3	9.8	2,174	Skopje	–
Madagascar	587	227	12,827	Antananarivo	210
Malawi	118	46	8,823	Lilongwe	230
Malaysia	330	127	18,181	Kuala Lumpur	2,520
Maldives	0.30	0.12	231	Malé	460
Mali	1,240	479	9,818	Bamako	280
Malta	0.32	0.12	359	Valletta	6,630
Martinique (Fr.)	1.1	0.42	368	Fort-de-France	4,000
Mauritania	1,025	396	2,143	Nouakchott	510
Mauritius	1.9	0.72	1,084	Port Louis	2,420
Mexico	1,958	756	89,538	Mexico City	3,030
Micronesia, Fed. States	0.70	0.27	110	Palikir	–
Moldavia	33.7	13	4,458	Kishinev	2,170
Monaco	0.002	0.0001	30	–	20,000
Mongolia	1,567	605	2,310	Ulan Bator	400
Montserrat (UK)	0.10	0.04	11	Plymouth	–
Morocco	447	172	26,318	Rabat	1,030
Mozambique	802	309	14,872	Maputo	80
Namibia	825	318	1,562	Windhoek	1,460
Nauru	0.02	0.008	10	Yaren	–
Nepal	141	54	20,577	Katmandu	180
Netherlands	41.5	16	15,178	Amsterdam	18,780
Neths Antilles (Neths)	0.99	0.38	175	Willemstad	6,000
New Caledonia (Fr.)	19	7.3	173	Nouméa	4,000
New Zealand	269	104	3,414	Wellington	12,350
Nicaragua	130	50	4,130	Managua	460
Niger	1,267	489	8,252	Niamey	300
Nigeria	924	357	88,515	Lagos/Abuja	340
Norway	324	125	4,286	Oslo	24,220
Oman	212	82	1,637	Muscat	6,120
Pakistan	796	307	115,520	Islamabad	400
Panama	77.1	29.8	2,515	Panama City	2,130
Papua New Guinea	463	179	4,056	Port Moresby	820
Paraguay	407	157	4,519	Asunción	1,270
Peru	1,285	496	22,454	Lima	1,070
Philippines	300	116	64,259	Manila	740
Poland	313	121	38,356	Warsaw	1,790
Portugal	92.4	35.7	9,846	Lisbon	5,930
Puerto Rico (US)	9	3.5	3,580	San Juan	6,470
Qatar	11	4.2	453	Doha	15,860
Réunion (Fr.)	2.5	0.97	624	St-Denis	4,000
Romania	238	92	23,185	Bucharest	1,390
Russia	17,075	6,592	149,527	Moscow	3,220
Rwanda	26.3	10.2	7,526	Kigali	260
St Christopher & Nevis	0.36	0.14	42	Basseterre	3,960
St Lucia	0.62	0.24	137	Castries	2,500
St Pierre & Miquelon (Fr.)	0.24	0.09	6	St-Pierre	–
St Vincent & Grenadines	0.39	0.15	109	Kingstown	1,730
San Marino	0.06	0.02	23	San Marino	–
São Tomé & Príncipe	0.96	0.37	124	São Tomé	350
Saudi Arabia	2,150	830	15,922	Riyadh	7,820
Senegal	197	76	7,736	Dakar	720
Seychelles	0.46	0.18	72	Victoria	5,110
Sierra Leone	71.7	27.7	4,376	Freetown	210
Singapore	0.62	0.24	2,812	Singapore	14,210
Slovak Republic	49	18.9	5,297	Bratislava	1,650
Slovenia	20.3	7.8	1,996	Ljubljana	–
Solomon Is.	28.9	11.2	342	Honiara	690
Somalia	638	246	9,204	Mogadishu	150
South Africa	1,219	471	39,790	Pretoria	2,560
Spain	505	195	39,085	Madrid	12,460
Sri Lanka	65.6	25.3	17,405	Colombo	500
Sudan	2,506	967	26,656	Khartoum	310
Surinam	163	63	438	Paramaribo	3,610
Swaziland	17.4	6.7	792	Mbabane	1,060
Sweden	450	174	8,678	Stockholm	25,110
Switzerland	41.3	15.9	6,905	Bern	33,610
Syria	185	71	12,958	Damascus	1,160
Taiwan	36	13.9	20,659	Taipei	6,600
Tajikistan	143.1	55.2	5,465	Dushanbe	2,980
Tanzania	945	365	27,829	Dar es Salaam	100
Thailand	513	198	57,760	Bangkok	1,580
Togo	56.8	21.9	3,763	Lomé	410
Tokelau (NZ)	0.01	0.005	2	Nukunonu	–
Tonga	0.75	0.29	97	Nuku'alofa	1,100
Trinidad & Tobago	5.1	2	1,265	Port of Spain	3,620
Tunisia	164	63	8,410	Tunis	1,510
Turkey	779	301	58,775	Ankara	1,820
Turkmenistan	488.1	188.5	3,714	Ashkhabad	1,700
Turks & Caicos Is. (UK)	0.43	0.17	13	Grand Turk	–
Tuvalu	0.03	0.01	12	Funafuti	600
Uganda	236	91	18,674	Kampala	160
Ukraine	603.7	233.1	52,200	Kiev	2,340
United Arab Emirates	83.6	32.3	1,629	Abu Dhabi	20,140
United Kingdom	243.3	94	57,848	London	16,550
United States of America	9,373	3,619	255,020	Washington	22,240
Uruguay	177	68	3,131	Montevideo	2,860
Uzbekistan	447.4	172.7	21,627	Tashkent	1,350
Vanuatu	12.2	4.7	157	Port Vila	1,120
Vatican City	0.0004	0.0002	1	–	–
Venezuela	912	352	20,249	Caracas	2,730
Vietnam	332	127	69,306	Hanoi	200
Virgin Is. (UK)	0.15	0.06	17	Road Town	–
Virgin Is. (US)	0.34	0.13	107	Charlotte Amalie	12,000
Western Sahara	266	103	250	El Aaiún	–
Western Samoa	2.8	1.1	161	Apia	960
Yemen	528	204	11,282	Sana	540
Yugoslavia	102.3	39.5	10,469	Belgrade	2,940
Zaire	2,345	906	39,882	Kinshasa	230
Zambia	753	291	8,638	Lusaka	460
Zimbabwe	391	151	10,583	Harare	650

World Statistics: Physical Dimensions

Each topic list is divided into continents and within a continent the items are listed in size order. The order of the continents is as in the atlas, Europe through to South America. The bottom part of many of the lists are selective. The world top ten are shown in square brackets; in the case of mountains this has not been done because the world top 30 are all in Asia. The figures are rounded as appropriate.

World, Continents, Oceans

	km²	miles²	%
The World	509,450,000	196,672,000	–
Land	149,450,000	57,688,000	29.3
Water	360,000,000	138,984,000	70.7
Asia	44,500,000	17,177,000	29.8
Africa	30,302,000	11,697,000	20.3
North America	24,241,000	9,357,000	16.2
South America	17,793,000	6,868,000	11.9
Antarctica	14,100,000	5,443,000	9.4
Europe	9,957,000	3,843,000	6.7
Australia & Oceania	8,557,000	3,303,000	5.7
Pacific Ocean	179,679,000	69,356,000	49.9
Atlantic Ocean	92,373,000	35,657,000	25.7
Indian Ocean	73,917,000	28,532,000	20.5
Arctic Ocean	14,090,000	5,439,000	3.9

Mountains

		m	ft
Europe			
Mont Blanc	*France/Italy*	4,807	15,771
Monte Rosa	*Italy/Switzerland*	4,634	15,203
Dom	*Switzerland*	4,545	14,911
Weisshorn	*Switzerland*	4,505	14,780
Matterhorn/Cervino	*Italy/Switzerland*	4,478	14,691
Mt Maudit	*France/Italy*	4,465	14,649
Finsteraarhorn	*Switzerland*	4,274	14,022
Aletschhorn	*Switzerland*	4,182	13,720
Jungfrau	*Switzerland*	4,158	13,642
Barre des Ecrins	*France*	4,103	13,461
Schreckhorn	*Switzerland*	4,078	13,380
Gran Paradiso	*Italy*	4,061	13,323
Piz Bernina	*Italy/Switzerland*	4,049	13,284
Ortles	*Italy*	3,899	12,792
Monte Viso	*Italy*	3,841	12,602
Grossglockner	*Austria*	3,797	12,457
Mulhacén	*Spain*	3,478	11,411
Pico de Aneto	*Spain*	3,404	11,168
Etna	*Italy*	3,340	10,958
Galdhöpiggen	*Norway*	2,469	8,100
Hvannadalshnúkur	*Iceland*	2,119	6,952
Ben Nevis	*UK*	1,343	4,406
Asia			
Everest	*China/Nepal*	8,848	29,029
Godwin Austen (K2)	*China/Kashmir*	8,611	28,251
Kanchenjunga	*India/Nepal*	8,598	28,208
Lhotse	*China/Nepal*	8,516	27,939
Makalu	*China/Nepal*	8,481	27,824
Cho Oyu	*China/Nepal*	8,201	26,906
Dhaulagiri	*Nepal*	8,172	26,811
Manaslu	*Nepal*	8,156	26,758
Nanga Parbat	*Kashmir*	8,126	26,660
Annapurna	*Nepal*	8,078	26,502
Gasherbrum	*China/Kashmir*	8,068	26,469
Broad Peak	*India*	8,051	26,414
Gosainthan	*China*	8,012	26,286
Disteghil Sar	*Kashmir*	7,885	25,869
Nuptse	*Nepal*	7,879	25,849
Elbrus	*Russia*	5,633	18,481
Fuji-san	*Japan*	3,776	12,388
Pidurutalagala	*Sri Lanka*	2,524	8,281
Africa			
Kilimanjaro	*Tanzania*	5,895	19,340
Mt Kenya	*Kenya*	5,199	17,057
Ruwenzori	*Uganda/Zaïre*	5,109	16,762
Ras Dashan	*Ethiopia*	4,620	15,157
Meru	*Tanzania*	4,565	14,977
Karisimbi	*Rwanda/Zaïre*	4,507	14,787
Mt Elgon	*Kenya/Uganda*	4,321	14,176
Batu	*Ethiopia*	4,307	14,130
Guna	*Ethiopia*	4,231	13,882
Toubkal	*Morocco*	4,165	13,665
Oceania			
Puncak Jaya	*Indonesia*	5,029	16,499
Puncak Trikora	*Indonesia*	4,750	15,584
Puncak Mandala	*Indonesia*	4,702	15,427
Mt Wilhelm	*Papua New Guinea*	4,508	14,790
Mauna Kea	*USA (Hawaii)*	4,205	13,796
Mauna Loa	*USA (Hawaii)*	4,170	13,681
Mt Cook	*New Zealand*	3,753	12,313
Mt Kosciusko	*Australia*	2,237	7,339
North America			
Mt McKinley	*USA (Alaska)*	6,194	20,321
Mt Logan	*Canada*	5,959	19,551
Citlaltepetl	*Mexico*	5,700	18,701
Mt St Elias	*USA/Canada*	5,489	18,008
Popocatepetl	*Mexico*	5,452	17,887
Mt Foraker	*USA (Alaska)*	5,304	17,401
Ixtaccihuatl	*Mexico*	5,286	17,342
Lucania	*Canada*	5,227	17,149
Mt Steele	*Canada*	5,073	16,644
Mt Bona	*USA (Alaska)*	5,005	16,420
South America			
Aconcagua	*Argentina*	6,960	22,834
Illimani	*Bolivia*	6,882	22,578
Bonete	*Argentina*	6,872	22,546
Ojos del Salado	*Argentina/Chile*	6,863	22,516
Tupungato	*Argentina/Chile*	6,800	22,309
Pissis	*Argentina*	6,779	22,241
Mercedario	*Argentina/Chile*	6,770	22,211
Huascaran	*Peru*	6,768	22,204
Llullaillaco	*Argentina/Chile*	6,723	22,057
Nudo de Cachi	*Argentina*	6,720	22,047
Antarctica			
Vinson Massif		4,897	16,066

Ocean Depths

	m	ft
Atlantic Ocean		
Puerto Rico (Milwaukee) Deep [7]	9,220	30,249
Cayman Trench [10]	7,680	25,197
Gulf of Mexico	5,203	17,070
Mediterranean Sea	5,121	16,801
Black Sea	2,211	7,254
North Sea	660	2,165
Baltic Sea	463	1,519
Hudson Bay	258	846
Indian Ocean		
Java Trench	7,450	24,442
Red Sea	2,635	8,454
Persian Gulf	73	239
Pacific Ocean		
Mariana Trench [1]	11,022	36,161
Tonga Trench [2]	10,882	35,702
Japan Trench [3]	10,554	34,626
Kuril Trench [4]	10,542	34,587
Mindanao Trench [5]	10,497	34,439
Kermadec Trench [6]	10,047	32,962
Peru-Chile Trench [8]	8,050	26,410
Aleutian Trench [9]	7,822	25,662
Middle American Trench	6,662	21,857
Arctic Ocean		
Molloy Deep	5,608	18,399

Land Lows

		m	ft
Caspian Sea	*Europe*	–28	–92
Dead Sea	*Asia*	–400	–1,312
Lake Assal	*Africa*	–156	–512
Lake Eyre North	*Oceania*	–16	–52
Death Valley	*N. America*	–86	–282
Valdés Peninsula	*S. America*	–40	–131

Rivers

		km	miles
Europe			
Volga	*Caspian Sea*	3,700	2,300
Danube	*Black Sea*	2,850	1,770
Ural	*Caspian Sea*	2,535	1,574
Dnepr	*Volga*	2,285	1,420
Kama	*Volga*	2,030	1,260
Don	*Volga*	1,990	1,240
Petchora	*Arctic Ocean*	1,790	1,110
Dnestr	*Black Sea*	1,400	870
Rhine	*North Sea*	1,320	820
Elbe	*North Sea*	1,145	710
Vistula	*Baltic Sea*	1,090	675
Loire	*Atlantic Ocean*	1,020	635
W. Dvina	*Baltic Sea*	1,019	633
Asia			
Yangtze [3]	*Pacific Ocean*	6,380	3,960
Yenisey-Angara [5]	*Arctic Ocean*	5,550	3,445
Huang He [6]	*Pacific Ocean*	5,464	3,395
Ob-Irtysh [7]	*Arctic Ocean*	5,410	3,360
Mekong [9]	*Pacific Ocean*	4,500	2,795
Amur [10]	*Pacific Ocean*	4,400	2,730
Lena	*Arctic Ocean*	4,400	2,730
Irtysh	*Ob*	4,250	2,640
Yenisey	*Arctic Ocean*	4,090	2,540
Ob	*Arctic Ocean*	3,680	2,285
Indus	*Indian Ocean*	3,100	1,925
Brahmaputra	*Indian Ocean*	2,900	1,800
Syr Darya	*Aral Sea*	2,860	1,775
Salween	*Indian Ocean*	2,800	1,740
Euphrates	*Indian Ocean*	2,700	1,675
Vilyuy	*Lena*	2,650	1,645
Kolyma	*Arctic Ocean*	2,600	1,615
Amu Darya	*Aral Sea*	2,540	1,575
Ural	*Caspian Sea*	2,535	1,575
Ganges	*Indian Ocean*	2,510	1,560
Si Kiang	*Pacific Ocean*	2,100	1,305
Irrawaddy	*Indian Ocean*	2,010	1,250
Tigris	*Indian Ocean*	1,900	1,180
Africa			
Nile [1]	*Mediterranean Sea*	6,670	4,140
Zaïre/Congo [8]	*Atlantic Ocean*	4,670	2,900
Niger	*Atlantic Ocean*	4,180	2,595
Zambezi	*Indian Ocean*	3,540	2,200
Oubangi/Uele	*Zaïre*	2,250	1,400
Kasai	*Zaïre*	1,950	1,210
Shaballe	*Indian Ocean*	1,930	1,200
Orange	*Atlantic Ocean*	1,860	1,155
Australia			
Murray-Darling	*Indian Ocean*	3,750	2,330
Darling	*Murray*	3,070	1,905
Murray	*Indian Ocean*	2,575	1,600
Murrumbidgee	*Murray*	1,690	1,050
North America			
Mississippi-Missouri [4]	*Gulf of Mexico*	6,020	3,740
Mackenzie	*Arctic Ocean*	4,240	2,630
Mississippi	*Gulf of Mexico*	3,780	2,350
Missouri	*Mississippi*	3,780	2,350
Yukon	*Pacific Ocean*	3,185	1,980
Rio Grande	*Gulf of Mexico*	3,030	1,880
Arkansas	*Mississippi*	2,340	1,450
Colorado	*Pacific Ocean*	2,330	1,445
Red	*Mississippi*	2,040	1,270
Columbia	*Pacific Ocean*	1,950	1,210
Saskatchewan	*Lake Winnipeg*	1,940	1,205
Snake	*Columbia*	1,670	1,040
South America			
Amazon [2]	*Atlantic Ocean*	6,450	4,010
Paraná-Plate	*Atlantic Ocean*	4,500	2,800
Purus	*Amazon*	3,350	2,080
Madeira	*Amazon*	3,200	1,990
São Francisco	*Atlantic Ocean*	2,900	1,800
Paraná	*Plate*	2,800	1,740
Tocantins	*Atlantic Ocean*	2,750	1,710
Paraguay	*Paraná*	2,550	1,580
Orinoco	*Atlantic Ocean*	2,500	1,550
Pilcomayo	*Paraná*	2,500	1,550

Lakes

		km²	miles²
Europe			
Lake Ladoga	*Russia*	17,700	6,800
Lake Onega	*Russia*	9,700	3,700
Saimaa system	*Finland*	8,000	3,100
Asia			
Caspian Sea [1]	*Asia*	371,800	143,550
Aral Sea [6]	*Kazakh./Uzbek.*	36,000	13,900
Lake Baykal [9]	*Russia*	30,500	11,780
Tonlé Sap	*Cambodia*	20,000	7,700
Lake Balkhash	*Kazakhstan*	18,500	7,100
Africa			
Lake Victoria [3]	*E. Africa*	68,000	26,000
Lake Tanganyika [7]	*C. Africa*	33,000	13,000
Lake Malawi [10]	*E. Africa*	29,600	11,430
Lake Chad	*C. Africa*	25,000	9,700
Australia			
Lake Eyre	*Australia*	8,900	3,400
North America			
Lake Superior [2]	*Canada/USA*	82,350	31,800
Lake Huron [4]	*Canada/USA*	59,600	23,010
Lake Michigan [5]	*USA*	58,000	22,400
Great Bear Lake [8]	*Canada*	31,800	12,280
Great Slave Lake	*Canada*	28,500	11,000
Lake Erie	*Canada/USA*	25,700	9,900
Lake Winnipeg	*Canada*	24,400	9,400
Lake Ontario	*Canada/USA*	19,500	7,500
South America			
Lake Titicaca	*Bolivia/Peru*	8,300	3,200

Islands

		km²	miles²
Europe			
Great Britain [8]	*UK*	229,880	88,700
Iceland	*Atlantic Ocean*	103,000	39,800
Ireland	*Ireland/UK*	84,400	32,600
Asia			
Borneo [3]	*S. E. Asia*	744,360	287,400
Sumatra [6]	*Indonesia*	473,600	182,860
Honshu [7]	*Japan*	230,500	88,980
Celebes	*Indonesia*	189,000	73,000
Java	*Indonesia*	126,700	48,900
Luzon	*Philippines*	104,700	40,400
Mindanao	*Philippines*	101,500	39,200
Hokkaido	*Japan*	78,400	30,300
Sakhalin	*Russia*	74,060	28,600
Sri Lanka	*Indian Ocean*	65,600	25,300
Africa			
Madagascar [4]	*Indian Ocean*	587,040	226,660
Oceania			
New Guinea [2]	*Indonesia/Pap. NG*	821,030	317,000
New Zealand (S.)	*New Zealand*	150,500	58,100
New Zealand (N.)	*New Zealand*	114,700	44,300
Tasmania	*Australia*	67,800	26,200
North America			
Greenland [1]	*Greenland*	2,175,600	839,800
Baffin Is. [5]	*Canada*	508,000	196,100
Victoria Is. [9]	*Canada*	212,200	81,900
Ellesmere Is. [10]	*Canada*	212,000	81,800
Cuba	*Cuba*	110,860	42,800
Newfoundland	*Canada*	110,680	42,700
Hispaniola	*Atlantic Ocean*	76,200	29,400
South America			
Tierra del Fuego	*Argentina/Chile*	47,000	18,100

PHILIP'S WORLD MAPS

The reference maps which form the main body of this atlas have been prepared in accordance with the highest standards of international cartography to provide an accurate and detailed representation of the Earth. The scales and projections used have been carefully chosen to give balanced coverage of the world, while emphasizing the most densely populated and economically significant regions. A hallmark of Philip's mapping is the use of hill shading and relief colouring to create a graphic impression of landforms: this makes the maps exceptionally easy to read. However, knowledge of the key features employed in the construction and presentation of the maps will enable the reader to derive the fullest benefit from the atlas.

Map sequence

The atlas covers the Earth continent by continent: first Europe; then its land neighbour Asia (mapped north before south, in a clockwise sequence), then Africa, Australia and Oceania, North America and South America. This is the classic arrangement adopted by most cartographers since the 16th century. For each continent, there are maps at a variety of scales. First, physical relief and political maps of the whole continent; then a series of larger-scale maps of the regions within the continent, each followed, where required, by still larger-scale maps of the most important or densely populated areas. The governing principle is that by turning the pages of the atlas, the reader moves steadily from north to south through each continent, with each map overlapping its neighbours. A key map showing this sequence, and the area covered by each map, can be found on the endpapers of the atlas.

Map presentation

With very few exceptions (e.g. for the Arctic and Antarctic), the maps are drawn with north at the top, regardless of whether they are presented upright or sideways on the page. In the borders will be found the map title; a locator diagram showing the area covered and the page numbers for maps of adjacent areas; the scale; the projection used; the degrees of latitude and longitude; and the letters and figures used in the index for locating place names and geographical features. Physical relief maps also have a height reference panel identifying the colours used for each layer of contouring.

Map symbols

Each map contains a vast amount of detail which can only be conveyed clearly and accurately by the use of symbols. Points and circles of varying sizes locate and identify the relative importance of towns and cities; different styles of type are employed for administrative, geographical and

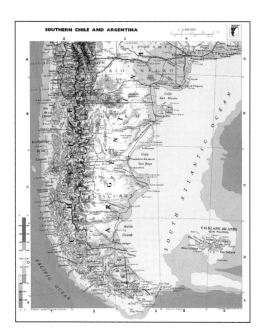

regional place names. A variety of pictorial symbols denote landscape features such as glaciers, marshes and reefs, and man-made structures including roads, railways, airports, canals and dams. International borders are shown by red lines. Where neighbouring countries are in dispute, for example in the Middle East, the maps show the *de facto* boundary between nations, regardless of the legal or historical situation. The symbols are explained on the first page of the World Maps section of the atlas.

Map scales

The scale of each map is given in the numerical form known as the 'representative fraction'. The first figure is always one, signifying one unit of distance on the map; the second figure, usually in millions, is the number by which the map unit must be multiplied to give the equivalent distance on the Earth's surface. Calculations can easily be made in centimetres and kilometres, by dividing the Earth units figure by 100 000 (i.e. deleting the last five 0s). Thus 1:1 000 000 means 1 cm = 10 km. The calculation for inches and miles is more laborious, but 1 000 000 divided by 63 360 (the number of inches in a mile) shows that 1:1 000 000 means approximately 1 inch = 16 miles. The table below provides distance equivalents for scales down to 1:50 000 000.

LARGE SCALE		
1:1 000 000	1 cm = 10 km	1 inch = 16 miles
1:2 500 000	1 cm = 25 km	1 inch = 39.5 miles
1:5 000 000	1 cm = 50 km	1 inch = 79 miles
1:6 000 000	1 cm = 60 km	1 inch = 95 miles
1:8 000 000	1 cm = 80 km	1 inch = 126 miles
1:10 000 000	1 cm = 100 km	1 inch = 158 miles
1:12 000 000	1 cm = 120 km	1 inch = 189 miles
1:15 000 000	1 cm = 150 km	1 inch = 237 miles
1:20 000 000	1 cm = 200 km	1 inch = 316 miles
1:50 000 000	1 cm = 500 km	1 inch = 790 miles
SMALL SCALE		

Measuring distances

Although each map is accompanied by a scale bar, distances cannot always be measured with confidence because of the distortions involved in portraying the curved surface of the Earth on a flat page. As a general rule, the larger the map scale (i.e. the lower the number of Earth units in the representative fraction), the more accurate and reliable will be the distance measured. On small-scale maps such as those of the world and of entire continents, measurement may only be accurate along the 'standard parallels', or central axes, and should not be attempted without first considering the map projection used.

Latitude and longitude

Accurate positioning of individual points on the Earth's surface is made possible by reference to the geometrical system of latitude and longitude. Latitude *parallels* are drawn west–east around the Earth and numbered by degrees north and south of the Equator, which is designated 0° of latitude. Longitude *meridians* are drawn north–south and numbered by degrees east and west of the *prime meridian*, 0° of longitude, which passes through Greenwich in England. By referring to these co-ordinates and their subdivisions of minutes (¹⁄₆₀th of a degree) and seconds (¹⁄₆₀th of a minute), any place on Earth can be located to within a few hundred yards. Latitude and longitude are indicated by blue lines on the maps; they are straight or curved according to the projection employed. Reference to these lines is the easiest way of determining the relative positions of places on different large-scale maps, and for plotting compass directions.

Name forms

For ease of reference, both English and local name forms appear in the atlas. Oceans, seas and countries are shown in English throughout the atlas; country names may be abbreviated to their commonly accepted form (e.g. Germany, not The Federal Republic of Germany). Conventional English forms are also used for place names on the smaller-scale maps of the continents. However, local name forms are used on all large-scale and regional maps, with the English form given in brackets only for important cities – the large-scale map of Eastern Europe and Turkey thus shows Moskva (Moscow). For countries which do not use a Roman script, place names have been transcribed according to the systems adopted by the British and US Geographic Names Authorities. For China, the Pin Yin system has been used, with some more widely known forms appearing in brackets, as with Beijing (Peking). Both English and local names appear in the index to the world maps.

INTRODUCTION TO WORLD GEOGRAPHY

**Planet Earth 2, Restless Earth 4, Landscape 6, Oceans 8,
Climate 10, Water 12, Environment 14,
Population 16, The Human Family 18, Wealth 20,
Quality of Life 22, Energy 24, Production 26, Trade 28,
Travel and Tourism 30**

PLANET EARTH

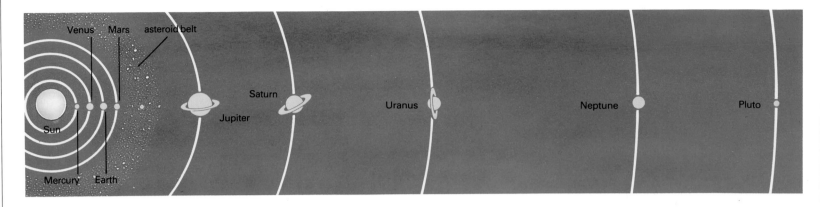

THE SOLAR SYSTEM

A minute part of one of the billions of galaxies (collections of stars) that comprise the Universe, the Solar System lies some 27,000 light-years from the centre of our own galaxy, the 'Milky Way'. Thought to be over 4,700 million years old, it consists of a central sun with nine planets and their moons revolving around it, attracted by its gravitational pull. The planets orbit the Sun in the same direction – anti-clockwise when viewed from the Northern Heavens – and almost in the same plane. Their orbital paths, however, vary enormously.

The Sun's diameter is 109 times that of Earth, and the temperature at its core – caused by continuous thermonuclear fusions of hydrogen into helium – is estimated to be 15 million degrees Celsius. It is the Solar System's only source of light and heat.

PROFILE OF THE PLANETS

	Mean distance from Sun (million km)	Mass (Earth = 1)	Period of orbit	Period of rotation (in days)	Diameter (km)	Number of known satellites
Mercury	58.3	0.06	88 days	58.67	4,878	0
Venus	107.7	0.8	224.7 days	243.0	12,104	0
Earth	149.6	1.0	365.24 days	0.99	12,756	1
Mars	227.3	0.1	1.88 years	1.02	6,794	2
Jupiter	777.9	317.8	11.86 years	0.41	142,800	16
Saturn	1427.1	95.2	29.63 years	0.42	120,000	17
Uranus	2872.3	14.5	83.97 years	0.45	52,000	15
Neptune	4502.7	17.2	164.8 years	0.67	48,400	8
Pluto	5894.2	0.002	248.63 years	6.38	2,400	1

All planetary orbits are elliptical in form, but only Pluto and Mercury follow paths that deviate noticeably from a circular one. Near Perihelion – its closest approach to the Sun – Pluto actually passes inside the orbit of Neptune, an event that last occurred in 1983. Pluto will not regain its station as outermost planet until February 1999.

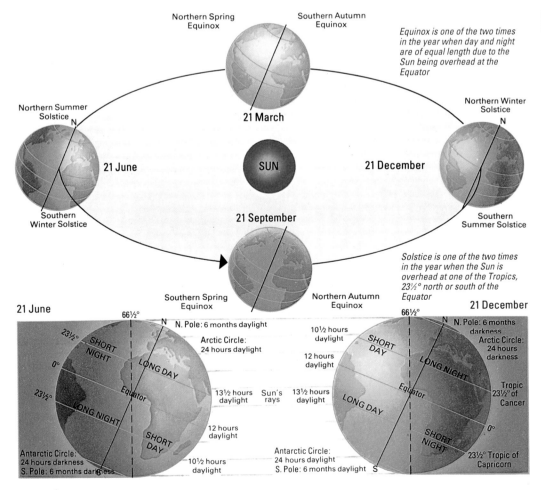

Equinox is one of the two times in the year when day and night are of equal length due to the Sun being overhead at the Equator

Solstice is one of the two times in the year when the Sun is overhead at one of the Tropics, 23½° north or south of the Equator

THE SEASONS

The Earth revolves around the Sun once a year in an 'anti-clockwise' direction, tilted at a constant angle 66½°. In June, the northern hemisphere is tilted towards the Sun: as a result it receives more hours of sunshine in a day and therefore has its warmest season, summer. By December, the Earth has rotated halfway round the Sun so that the southern hemisphere is tilted towards the Sun and has its summer; the hemisphere that is tilted away from the Sun has winter. On 21 June the Sun is directly overhead at the Tropic of Cancer (23½° N), and this is midsummer in the northern hemisphere. Midsummer in the southern hemisphere occurs on 21 December, when the Sun is overhead at the Tropic of Capricorn (23½° S).

DAY AND NIGHT

The Sun appears to rise in the east, reach its highest point at noon, and then set in the west, to be followed by night. In reality it is not the Sun that is moving but the Earth revolving from west to east. Due to the tilting of the Earth the length of day and night varies from place to place and month to month.

At the summer solstice in the northern hemisphere (21 June), the Arctic has total daylight and the Antarctic total darkness. The opposite occurs at the winter solstice (21 December). At the Equator, the length of day and night are almost equal all year, at latitude 30° the length of day varies from about 14 hours to 10 hours, and at latitude 50° from about 16 hours to about 8 hours.

Year: The time taken by the Earth to revolve around the Sun, or 365.24 days.

Month: The approximate time taken by the Moon to revolve around the Earth. The 12 months of the year in fact vary from 28 (29 in a Leap Year) to 31 days.

Week: An artificial period of 7 days, not based on astronomical time.

Day: The time taken by the Earth to complete one rotation on its axis.

Hour: 24 hours make one day. Usually the day is divided into hours AM (ante meridiem or before noon) and PM (post meridiem or after noon), although most timetables now use the 24-hour system, from midnight to midnight.

SUNRISE

SUNSET

THE MOON

Distance from Earth: 356,410 km – 406,685 km; Mean diameter: 3,475.1 km; Mass: approx. 1/81 that of Earth;
Surface gravity: one-sixth of Earth's; Daily range of temperature at lunar equator: 200°C; Average orbital speed: 3,683 km/h

PHASES OF THE MOON

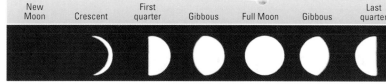

| New Moon | Crescent | First quarter | Gibbous | Full Moon | Gibbous | Last quarter | Crescent | New Moon |

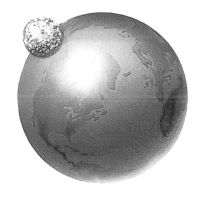

The Moon rotates more slowly than the Earth, making one complete turn on its axis in just over 27 days. Since this corresponds to its period of revolution around the Earth, the Moon always presents the same hemisphere or face to us, and we never see 'the dark side'. The interval between one Full Moon and the next (and between New Moons) is about 29$\frac{1}{2}$ days – a lunar month. The apparent changes in the shape of the Moon are caused by its changing position in relation to the Earth; like the planets, it produces no light of its own and shines only by reflecting the rays of the Sun.

ECLIPSES

When the Moon passes between the Sun and the Earth it causes a partial eclipse of the Sun (1) if the Earth passes through the Moon's outer shadow (P), or a total eclipse (2) if the inner cone shadow crosses the Earth's surface. In a lunar eclipse, the Earth's shadow crosses the Moon and, again, provides either a partial or total eclipse. Eclipses of the Sun and the Moon do not occur every month because of the 5° difference between the plane of the Moon's orbit and the plane in which the Earth moves. In the 1990s only 14 lunar eclipses are possible, for example, seven partial and seven total; each is visible only from certain, and variable, parts of the world. The same period witnesses 13 solar eclipses – six partial (or annular) and seven total.

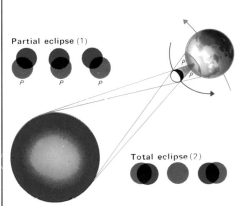

Partial eclipse (1)

Total eclipse (2)

Lunar eclipse

TIDES

The daily rise and fall of the ocean's tides are the result of the gravitational pull of the Moon and that of the Sun, though the effect of the latter is only 46.6% as strong as that of the Moon. This effect is greatest on the hemisphere facing the Moon and causes a tidal 'bulge'. When lunar and solar forces pull together, with Sun, Earth and Moon in line (near New and Full Moons), higher 'spring tides' (and lower low tides) occur; when lunar and solar forces are least coincidental with the Sun and Moon at an angle (near the Moon's first and third quarters), 'neap tides' occur, which have a small tidal range.

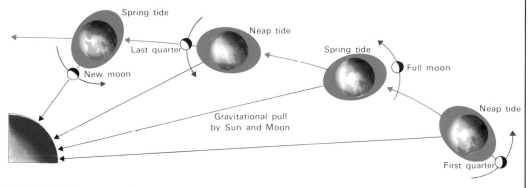
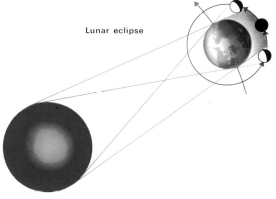

Spring tide

Neap tide

Last quarter

New moon

Spring tide

Full moon

Neap tide

Gravitational pull by Sun and Moon

First quarter

RESTLESS EARTH

THE EARTH'S STRUCTURE

Upper mantle (*c*. 370 km)
Crust (average 5–50 km)
Transitional zone (600 km)
Outer core (2,100 km)
Lower mantle (1,700 km)
Inner core (2,700 km)

CONTINENTAL DRIFT

About 200 million years ago the original Pangaea landmass began to split into two continental groups, which further separated over time to produce the present-day configuration.

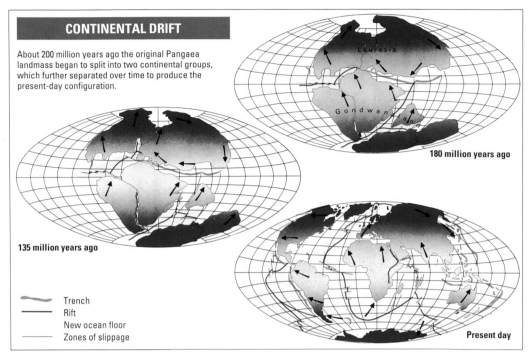

Laurasia

Gondwanaland

180 million years ago

135 million years ago

Present day

Trench
Rift
New ocean floor
Zones of slippage

EARTHQUAKES

Earthquake magnitude is usually rated according to either the Richter or the Modified Mercalli scale, both devised by seismologists in the 1930s. The Richter scale measures absolute earthquake power with mathematical precision: each step upwards represents a tenfold increase in shockwave amplitude. Theoretically, there is no upper limit, but the largest earthquakes measured have been rated at between 8.8 and 8.9. The 12–point Mercalli scale, based on observed effects, is often more meaningful, ranging from I (earthquakes noticed only by seismographs) to XII (total destruction); intermediate points include V (people awakened at night; unstable objects overturned), VII (collapse of ordinary buildings; chimneys and monuments fall) and IX (conspicuous cracks in ground; serious damage to reservoirs).

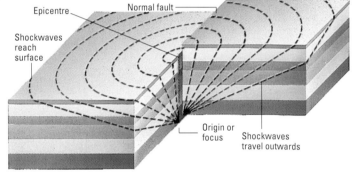

Epicentre
Normal fault
Shockwaves reach surface
Origin or focus
Shockwaves travel outwards

NOTABLE EARTHQUAKES SINCE 1900

Year	Location	Mag.	Deaths
1906	San Francisco, USA	8.3	503
1906	Valparaiso, Chile	8.6	22,000
1908	Messina, Italy	7.5	83,000
1915	Avezzano, Italy	7.5	30,000
1920	Gansu (Kansu), China	8.6	180,000
1923	Yokohama, Japan	8.3	143,000
1927	Nan Shan, China	8.3	200,000
1932	Gansu (Kansu), China	7.6	70,000
1934	Bihar, India/Nepal	8.4	10,700
1935	Quetta, India*	7.5	60,000
1939	Chillan, Chile	8.3	28,000
1939	Erzincan, Turkey	7.9	30,000
1960	Agadir, Morocco	5.8	12,000
1962	Khorasan, Iran	7.1	12,230
1963	Skopje, Yugoslavia**	6.0	1,000
1964	Anchorage, Alaska	8.4	131
1968	N.E. Iran	7.4	12,000
1970	N. Peru	7.7	66,794
1972	Managua, Nicaragua	6.2	5,000
1974	N. Pakistan	6.3	5,200
1976	Guatemala	7.5	22,778
1976	Tangshan, China	8.2	650,000
1978	Tabas, Iran	7.7	25,000
1980	El Asnam, Algeria	7.3	20,000
1980	S. Italy	7.2	4,800
1985	Mexico City, Mexico	8.1	4,200
1988	N.W. Armenia	6.8	55,000
1990	N. Iran	7.7	36,000
1993	Maharashtra, India	6.4	30,000

The highest magnitude recorded on the Richter scale was 8.9, in Japan on 2 March 1933 (2,990 deaths). The most devastating quake ever was in Shaanxi (Shensi) province, central China, on 24 January 1566, when an estimated 830,000 people were killed.

* now Pakistan   ** now Macedonia

DISTRIBUTION OF EARTHQUAKES

Major earthquake zones
Areas experiencing frequent earthquakes

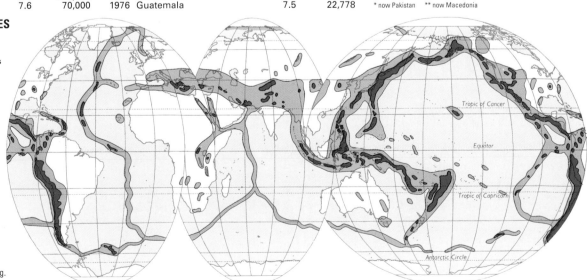

Tropic of Cancer
Equator
Tropic of Capricorn
Antarctic Circle

Earthquakes are a series of rapid vibrations originating from the slipping or faulting of parts of the Earth's crust when stresses within build up to breaking point. They usually happen at depths varying from 8 km to 30 km. Severe earthquakes cause extensive damage when they take place in populated areas, destroying structures and severing communications. Most initial loss of life occurs due to secondary causes such as falling masonry, fires and flooding.

4

PLATE TECTONICS

The drifting of the continents is a feature that is unique to Planet Earth. The complementary, almost jigsaw-puzzle fit of the coastlines on each side of the Atlantic Ocean inspired Alfred Wegener's theory of continental drift in 1915. The theory suggested that an ancient super-continent, which Wegener named Pangaea, incorporated all of the Earth's landmasses and gradually split up to form today's continents.

The original debate about continental drift was a prelude to a more radical idea: plate tectonics. The basic theory is that the Earth's crust is made up of a series of rigid plates which float on a soft layer of the mantle and are moved about by continental convection currents within the Earth's interior. These plates diverge and converge along margins marked by earthquakes, volcanoes and other seismic activity. Plates diverge from mid-ocean ridges where molten lava pushes upwards and forces the plates apart at a rate of up to 40 mm a year; converging plates form either a trench (where the oceanic plate sinks below the lighter continental rock) or mountain ranges (where two continents collide).

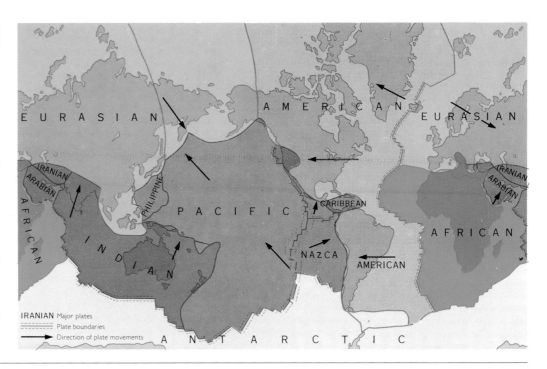

IRANIAN Major plates
‑‑‑‑‑‑‑ Plate boundaries
⟶ Direction of plate movements

VOLCANOES

The word 'volcano' derives from the island of Vulcano off Sicily, in the Mediterranean Sea. In classical times the people of this area thought that Vulcano was the chimney of the forge of Vulcan, blacksmith of the Roman gods. Today volcanoes might be the subject of scientific study but they remain both dramatic and unpredictable, if not exactly supernatural: in 1991 Mount Pinatubo, 100 kilometres north of the Philippines capital Manila, suddenly burst into life after more than six centuries of lying dormant.

Most of the world's active volcanoes occur in a belt around the Pacific Ocean, on the edge of the Pacific plate, called the 'ring of fire'. Indonesia has the greatest concentration with 90 volcanoes, 12 of which are active. The most famous, Krakatau, erupted in 1883 with such force that the resulting tidal wave killed 36,000 people and tremors were felt as far away as Australia.

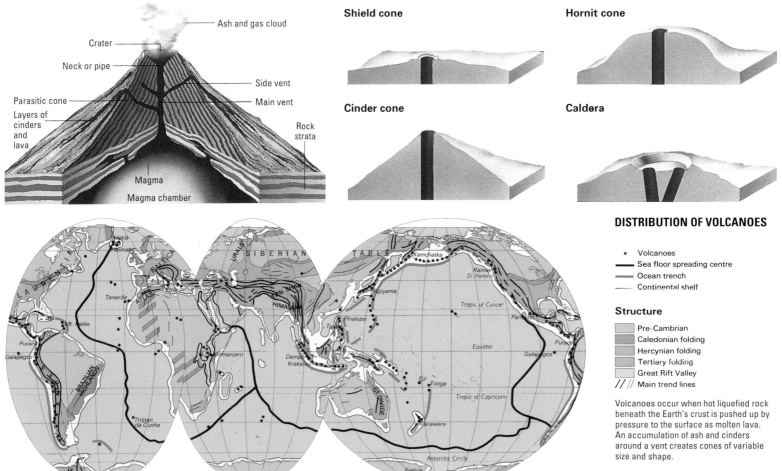

DISTRIBUTION OF VOLCANOES

- • Volcanoes
- ▬▬ Sea floor spreading centre
- ▬▬ Ocean trench
- ── Continental shelf

Structure

- Pre-Cambrian
- Caledonian folding
- Hercynian folding
- Tertiary folding
- Great Rift Valley
- // /// Main trend lines

Volcanoes occur when hot liquefied rock beneath the Earth's crust is pushed up by pressure to the surface as molten lava. An accumulation of ash and cinders around a vent creates cones of variable size and shape.

LANDSCAPE

Above and below the surface of the oceans, the features of the Earth's crust are constantly changing. The phenomenal forces generated by convection currents in the molten core of our planet carry the vast segments or 'plates' of the crust across the globe in an endless cycle of creation and destruction. A continent may travel little more than 25 millimetres [one inch] per year, yet in the vast span of geological time this process throws up giant mountain ranges and creates new land.

Destruction of the landscape, however, begins as soon as it is formed. Wind, water, ice and sea, the main agents of erosion, mount a constant assault that even the hardest rocks can not withstand. Mountain peaks may dwindle by as little as a few millimetres each year, but if they are not uplifted by further movements of the crust they will eventually be reduced to rubble. Water is the most powerful destroyer – it has been estimated that 100 billion tonnes of rock is washed into the oceans every year.

Rivers and glaciers, like the sea itself, generate much of their effect through abrasion – pounding the landscape with the debris they carry with them. But as well as destroying they also create new landscapes, many of them spectacular: vast deltas like the Mississippi and the Nile, or the fjords cut by glaciers in British Columbia, Norway and New Zealand.

THE SPREADING EARTH

The vast ridges that divide the Earth's crust beneath each of the world's oceans mark the boundaries between tectonic plates which are moving gradually in opposite directions. As the plates shift apart, molten magma rises from the Earth's core to seal the rift and the sea floor slowly spreads towards the continental landmasses. The rate of spreading has been calculated by magnetic analysis of the rock at 40 mm [1.5 in] a year in the North Atlantic. Underwater volcanoes mark the line where the continental rise begins. As the plates meet, much of the denser ocean crust dips beneath the continental plate and melts back to the magma.

THE SPREADING EARTH

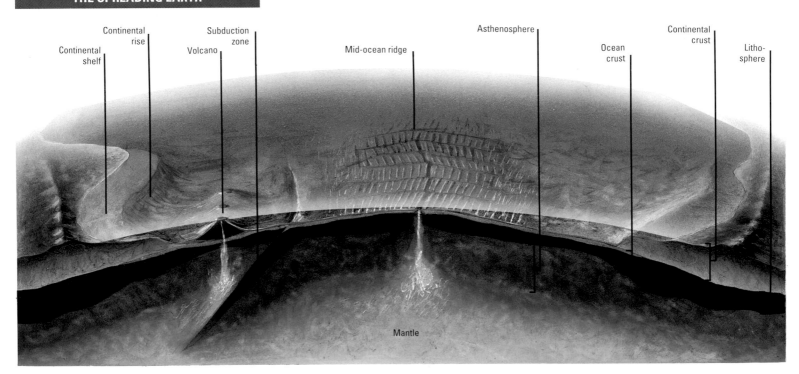

Continental shelf — Continental rise — Volcano — Subduction zone — Mid-ocean ridge — Asthenosphere — Ocean crust — Continental crust — Litho-sphere — Mantle

MOUNTAIN BUILDING

Mountains are formed when pressures on the Earth's crust caused by continental drift become so intense that the surface buckles or cracks. This happens most dramatically where two tectonic plates collide: the Rockies, Andes, Alps, Urals and Himalayas resulted from such impacts. These are all known as fold mountains, because they were formed by the compression of the rocks, forcing the surface to bend and fold like a crumpled rug.

The other main building process occurs when the crust fractures to create faults, allowing rock to be forced upwards in large blocks; or when the pressure of magma within the crust forces the surface to bulge into a dome, or erupts to form a volcano. Large mountain ranges may reveal a combination of those features; the Alps, for example, have been compressed so violently that the folds are fragmented by numerous faults and intrusions of molten rock.

Over millions of years, even the greatest mountain ranges can be reduced by erosion to a rugged landscape known as a peneplain.

Types of fold: Geographers give different names to the degrees of fold that result from continuing pressure on the rock strata. A simple fold may be symmetric, with even slopes on either side, but as the pressure builds up, one slope becomes steeper and the fold becomes asymmetric. Later, the ridge or 'anticline' at the top of the fold may slide over the lower ground or 'syncline' to form a recumbent fold. Eventually, the rock strata may break under the pressure to form an overthrust and finally a nappe fold.

Symmetric — Asymmetric — Recumbent — Overthrust — Nappe

Types of faults: Faults are classified by the direction in which the blocks of rock have moved. A normal fault results when a vertical movement causes the surface to break apart; compression causes a reverse fault. Sideways movement causes shearing, known as a strike-slip fault. When the rock breaks in two places, the central block may be pushed up in a horst fault, or sink in a graben fault.

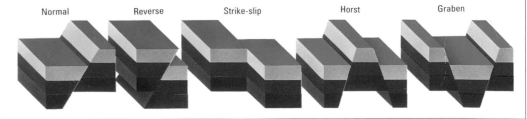

Normal — Reverse — Strike-slip — Horst — Graben

SHAPING FORCES: GLACIERS

Many of the world's most dramatic landscapes have been carved by glaciers. During the Ice Ages of the Pleistocene Epoch (over 10,000 years ago) up to a third of the land surface was glaciated; even today a tenth is covered in ice. Glaciers are formed from compressed snow, called *névé*, accumulating in a valley head or cirque. Slowly the glacier moves downhill scraping away debris from the mountains and valleys through which it passes. The debris, or moraine, adds to the abrasive power of the ice.

The rate of movement can vary from a few centimetres to several metres a day, but the end of the glacier may not reach the bottom of the valley – the position of the snout depends on the rate at which the ice melts. Glaciers create numerous distinctive landscape features from arête ridges and pyramidal peaks to ice-dammed lakes and truncated spurs, with the U-shape distinguishing a glacial valley from one cut by a river.

SHAPING FORCES: RIVERS

From their origins as upland rills and streams channelling rainfall, or as springs releasing water that has seeped into the ground, all rivers are incessantly at work cutting and shaping the landscape on their way to the sea. In highland regions their flow may be rapid, pounding rocks and boulders with enough violence to cut deep gorges and V-shaped valleys through softer rocks, or tumble as waterfalls over harder ones.

As they reach more gentle slopes, rivers release some of the pebbles they have carried downstream and flow more slowly, broadening out and raising levees or ridges along their banks by depositing mud and sand. In lowland plains, where the gradient is minimal, the river drifts into meanders, depositing deep layers of sediment especially on the inside of each bend, where the flow is weakest. Here farmers may dig drainage ditches and artificial levees to keep the floodplain dry.

As the river finally reaches the sea, it deposits all its remaining sediments, and estuaries are formed where the tidal currents are strong enough to remove them; if not, the debris creates a delta, through which the river cuts outlet streams known as distributaries.

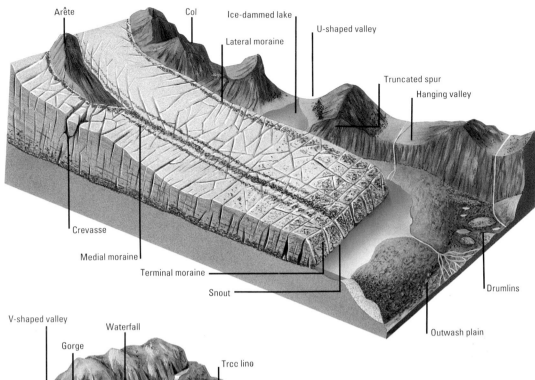

Arête   Col   Ice-dammed lake   U-shaped valley
Lateral moraine
Truncated spur
Hanging valley
Crevasse
Medial moraine
Terminal moraine
Snout
Drumlins
Outwash plain

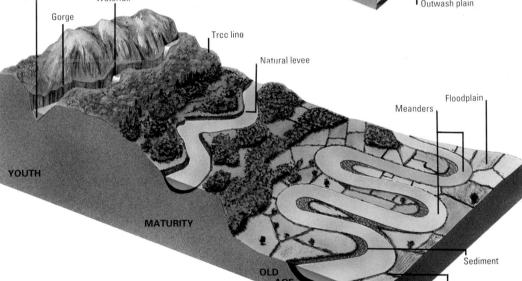

V-shaped valley   Waterfall
Gorge
Tree line
Natural levee
Meanders   Floodplain
YOUTH
MATURITY
Sediment
OLD AGE
Man-made levee

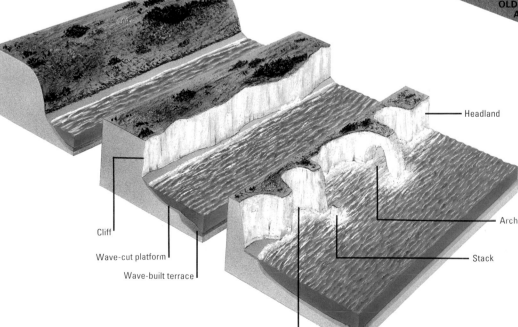

Headland
Cliff
Wave-cut platform
Wave-built terrace
Arch
Stack
Cove

SHAPING FORCES: THE SEA

Under the constant assault from tides and currents, wind and waves, coastlines change faster than most landscape features, both by erosion and by the build-up of sand and pebbles carried by the sea. In severe storms, giant waves pound the shoreline with rocks and boulders, and frequently destroy concrete coastal defences; but even in much quieter conditions, the sea steadily erodes cliffs and headlands, creating new land in the form of sand-dunes, spits and salt marshes.

Where the coastline is formed from soft rocks such as sandstones, debris may fall evenly and be carried away by currents from shelving beaches. In areas with harder rock, the waves may cut steep cliffs and form underwater platforms; eroded debris is deposited as a terrace. Bays are formed when sections of soft rock are carved away between headlands of harder rock. These are then battered by waves from both sides, until the headlands are eventually reduced to rock arches and stacks.

OCEANS

THE GREAT OCEANS

Relative sizes of the world's oceans

Pacific
Atlantic
Indian
Arctic

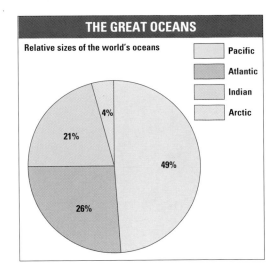

4%
21%
49%
26%

In a strict geographical sense there are only three true oceans – the Atlantic, Indian and Pacific. The legendary 'Seven Seas' would require these to be divided at the Equator and the addition of the Arctic Ocean – which accounts for less than 4% of the total sea area. The International Hydrographic Bureau does not recognize the Antarctic Ocean (even less the 'Southern Ocean') as a separate entity.

The Earth is a watery planet: more than 70% of its surface – over 360,000,000 square kilometres – is covered by the oceans and seas. The mighty Pacific alone accounts for nearly 36% of the total, and 49% of the sea area. Gravity holds in around 1,400 million cubic kilometres of water, of which over 97% is saline.

The vast underwater world starts in the shallows of the seaside and plunges to depths of more than 11,000 metres. The continental shelf, part of the landmass, drops gently to around 200 metres; here the seabed falls away suddenly at an angle of 3° to 6° – the continental slope. The third stage, called the continental rise, is more gradual with gradients varying from 1 in 100 to 1 in 700. At an average depth of 5,000 metres there begins the aptly-named abyssal plain – massive submarine depths where sunlight fails to penetrate and few creatures can survive.

From these plains rise volcanoes which, taken from base to top, rival and even surpass the biggest continental mountains in height. Mount Kea, on Hawaii, reaches a total of 10,203 metres, some 1,355 metres more than Mount Everest, though only 4,205 is visible above sea level.

In addition there are underwater mountain chains up to 1,000 kilometres across, whose peaks sometimes appear above sea level as islands such as Iceland and Tristan da Cunha.

THE OCEAN DEPTHS

Average and maximum depths of the world's great oceans, in metres

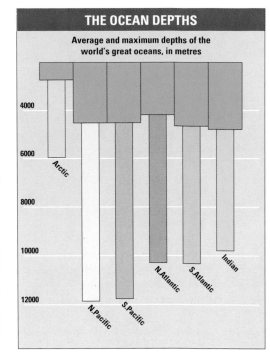

4000
6000
8000
10000
12000

Arctic
N.Pacific
S.Pacific
N.Atlantic
S.Atlantic
Indian

OCEAN CURRENTS

[Cold currents are shown in blue, warm currents in red]

WINTER IN NORTHERN HEMISPHERE

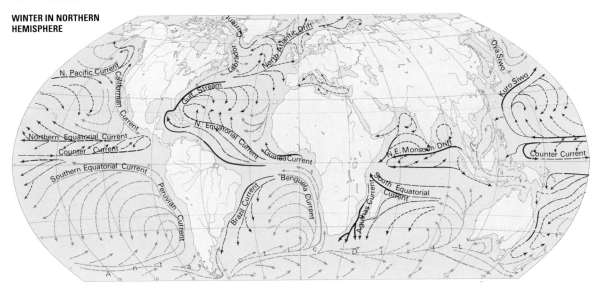

N. Pacific Current
Labrador
North Atlantic Drift
Oya Siwo
Kuro Siwo
Gulf Stream
Californian Current
N. Equatorial Current
Northern Equatorial Current
Counter Current
N. E. Monsoon Drift
Counter Current
Southern Equatorial Current
Guinea Current
Benguela Current
South Equatorial Current
Brazil Current
Peruvian Current
Agulhas Current
Antarctic Drift

SUMMER IN NORTHERN HEMISPHERE

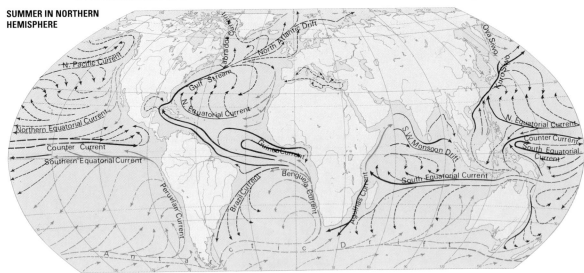

N. Pacific Current
Labrador Current
North Atlantic Drift
Oya Siwo
Gulf Stream
N. Equatorial Current
N. Equatorial Current
Northern Equatorial Current
Counter Current
Counter Current
Southern Equatorial Current
Guinea Current
S.W. Monsoon Drift
South Equatorial Current
Benguela Current
South Equatorial Current
Brazil Current
Peruvian Current
Agulhas Current
Antarctic Drift

Moving immense quantities of energy as well as billions of tonnes of water every hour, the ocean currents are a vital part of the great heat engine that drives the Earth's climate. They themselves are produced by a twofold mechanism. At the surface, winds push huge masses of water before them; in the deep ocean, below an abrupt temperature gradient that separates the churning surface waters from the still depths, density variations cause slow vertical movements.

The pattern of circulation of the great surface currents is determined by the displacement known as the Coriolis effect. As the Earth turns beneath a moving object – whether it is a tennis ball or a vast mass of water – it appears to be deflected to one side. The deflection is most obvious near the Equator, where the Earth's surface is spinning eastwards at 1,700 km/h; currents moving polewards are curved clockwise in the northern hemisphere and anti-clockwise in the southern.

The result is a system of spinning circles known as gyres. The Coriolis effect piles up water on the left of each gyre, creating a narrow, fast-moving stream that is matched by a slower, broader returning current on the right. North and south of the Equator, the fastest currents are located in the west and in the east respectively. In each case, warm water moves from the Equator and cold water returns to it. Cold currents often bring an upwelling of nutrients with them, supporting the world's most economically important fisheries.

Depending on the prevailing winds, some currents on or near the Equator may reverse their direction in the course of the year – a seasonal variation on which Asian monsoon rains depend, and whose occasional failure can bring disaster to millions.

FISHING

Main commercial fishing areas

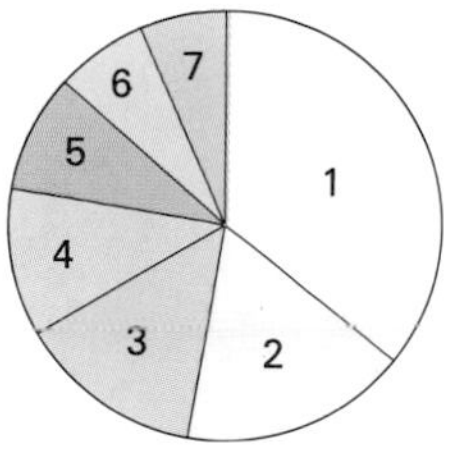
1
2
3
4
5
6
7

Percentage of world catch

1. North Pacific 36%
2. North Atlantic 17%
3. South Pacific 14%
4. Central Pacific 11%
5. Central Atlantic 9%
6. South Atlantic 7%
7. Indian 6%

Leading fishing nations

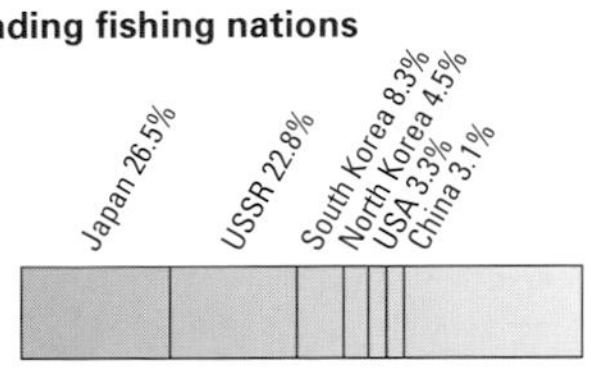
Japan 26.5%
USSR 22.8%
South Korea 8.3%
North Korea 4.5%
USA 3.3%
China 3.1%

World total (1989): 14,143,923 tonnes*

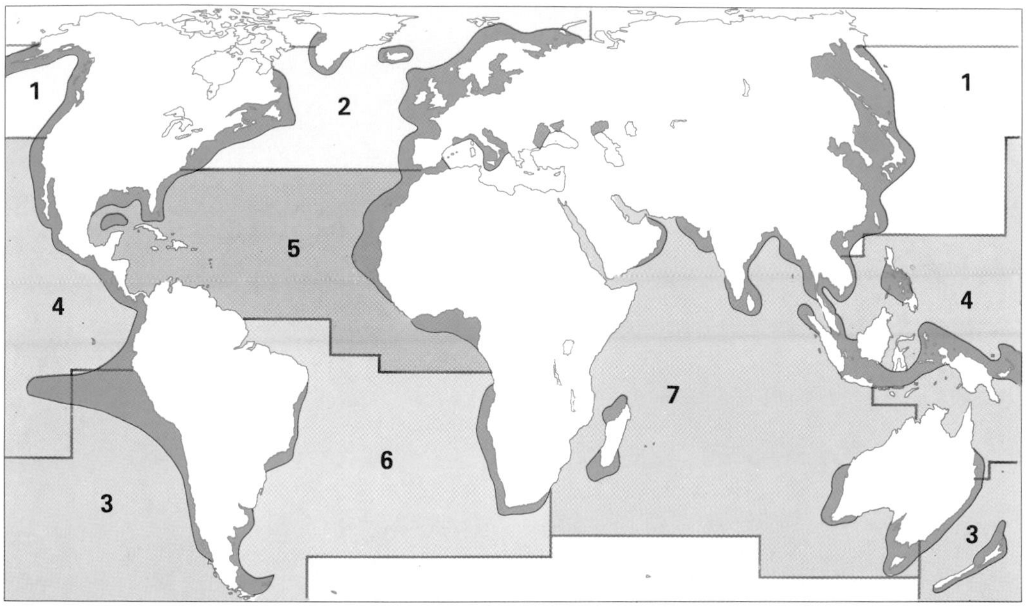
1
2
5
4
7
6
3
1
4
3

MARINE POLLUTION

Sources of marine oil pollution (1980s)

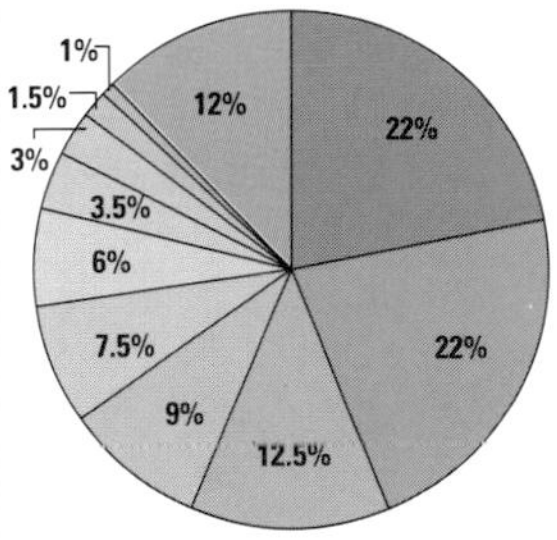
1%
1.5%
3%
12%
22%
3.5%
6%
7.5%
9%
12.5%
22%

Tanker operations
Municipal wastes
Tanker accidents
Bilge and fuel oils
Natural seeps
Industrial waste
Urban runoff
Coastal oil refining
Offshore oil rigs
River runoffs
Other

OIL SPILLS

Major oil spills from tankers and combined carriers

Year	Vessel	Location	Spill (barrels)**	Cause
1979	Atlantic Empress	West Indies	1,890,000	collision
1983	Castillo De Bellver	South Africa	1,760,000	fire
1978	Amoco Cadiz	France	1,628,000	grounding
1988	Odyssey	Canada	1,000,000	fire
1967	Torrey Canyon	UK	909,000	grounding
1972	Sea Star	Gulf of Oman	902,250	collision
1977	Hawaiian Patriot	Hawaiian Is.	742,500	fire
1979	Independenta	Turkey	696,350	collision
1976	Urquiola	Spain	670,000	grounding
1980	Irenes Serenade	Greece	600,000	fire
1989	Khark V	Morocco	560,000	fire
Other sources of major oil spills				
1983	Nowruz oilfield	Persian Gulf	4,250,000†	war
1979	Ixtoc 1 oilwell	Gulf of Mexico	4,200,000	blow-out
1991	Kuwait	Persian Gulf	2,500,000	war

** 1 barrel = 0.136 tonnes/159 lit./35 Imperial gal./42 US gal. † estimated

RIVER POLLUTION

Sources of river pollution, USA (1987)

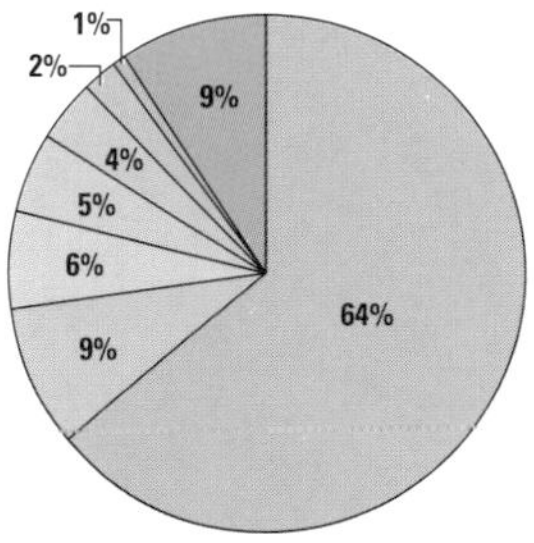
1%
2%
9%
4%
5%
6%
9%
64%

Agriculture
Mining
Forestry
Urban runoff
Hydro-engineering
Construction
Land disposal
Other

WATER POLLUTION

Severely polluted sea areas and lakes
Less polluted sea areas and lakes
Areas of frequent oil pollution by shipping
Major oil tanker spills
Major oil rig blow-outs
Offshore dumpsites for industrial and municipal waste
Severely polluted rivers and estuaries

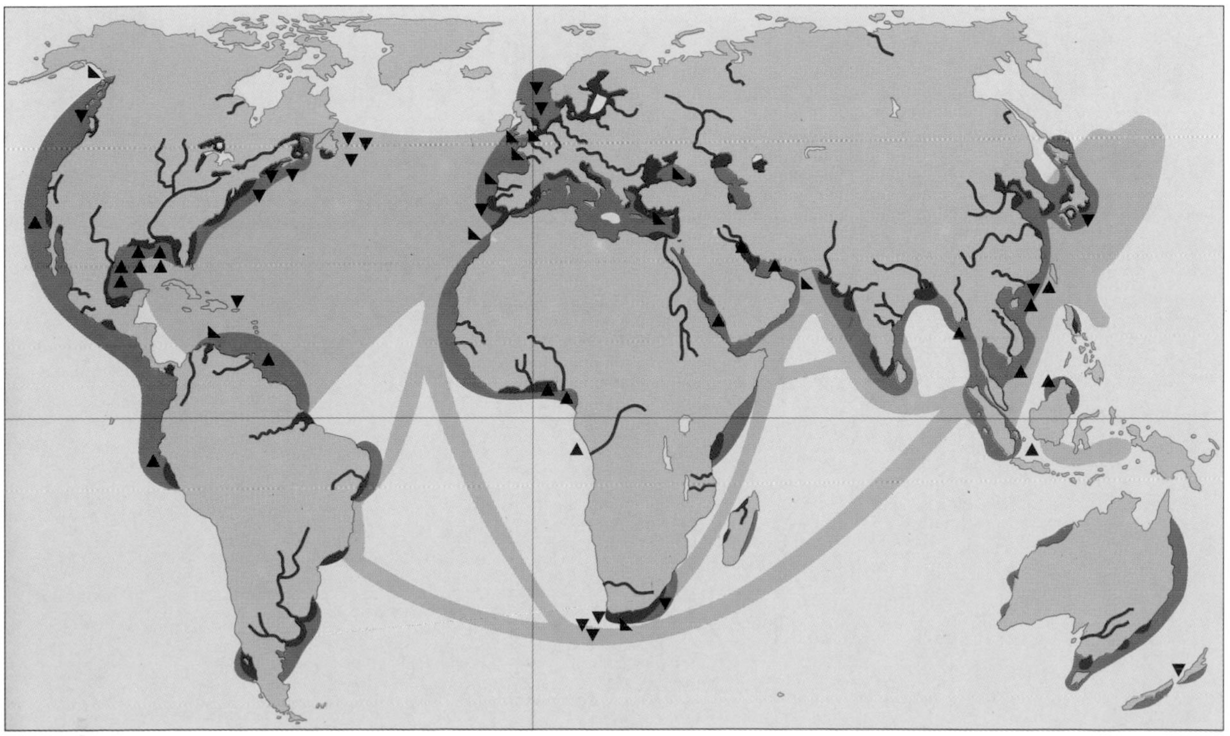

The most notorious tanker spillage of the 1980s occurred when the *Exxon Valdez* ran aground in Prince William Sound, Alaska, in 1989, spilling 267,000 barrels of crude oil close to shore in a sensitive ecological area. This rates as the world's 28th worst spill in terms of volume.

**Statistics for the new republics of the former USSR, Czechoslovakia and Yugoslavia are not yet available.*

CLIMATE

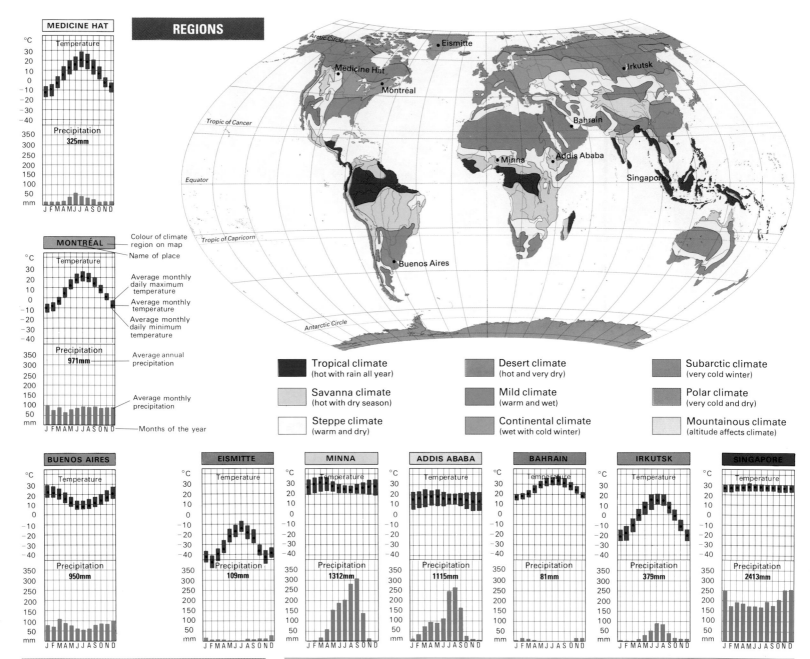

MEDICINE HAT

°C
30
20
10
0
-10
-20
-30
-40

Temperature

Precipitation
325mm

350
300
250
200
150
100
50
mm

J F M A M J J A S O N D

MONTRÉAL

°C
30
20
10
0
-10
-20
-30
-40

Temperature

— Colour of climate region on map
— Name of place
— Average monthly daily maximum temperature
— Average monthly temperature
— Average monthly daily minimum temperature

Precipitation
971mm

350
300
250
200
150
100
50
mm

J F M A M J J A S O N D

— Average annual precipitation
— Average monthly precipitation
— Months of the year

Tropical climate (hot with rain all year)

Savanna climate (hot with dry season)

Steppe climate (warm and dry)

Desert climate (hot and very dry)

Mild climate (warm and wet)

Continental climate (wet with cold winter)

Subarctic climate (very cold winter)

Polar climate (very cold and dry)

Mountainous climate (altitude affects climate)

BUENOS AIRES — Precipitation 950mm
EISMITTE — Precipitation 109mm
MINNA — Precipitation 1312mm
ADDIS ABABA — Precipitation 1115mm
BAHRAIN — Precipitation 81mm
IRKUTSK — Precipitation 379mm
SINGAPORE — Precipitation 2413mm

Temperature

Highest recorded temperature: Al Aziziyah, Libya, 58°C [136.4°F], 13 September 1922.

Highest mean annual temperature: Dallol, Ethiopia, 34.4°C [94°F], 1960–66.

Longest heatwave: Marble Bar, W. Australia, 162 days over 38°C [100°F], 23 October 1923 to 7 April 1924.

Lowest recorded temperature (outside poles): Verkhoyansk, Siberia, -68°C [-90°F], 6 February 1933. Verkhoyansk also registered the greatest annual range of temperature: -70°C to 37°C [-94°F to 98°F].

Lowest mean annual temperature: Polus Nedostupnosti, Pole of Cold, Antarctica, -57.8°C [-72°F].

Precipitation

Driest place: Arica, N. Chile, 0.8mm [0.03 in] per year (60-year average).

Longest drought: Calama, N. Chile: no recorded rainfall in 400 years to 1971.

Wettest place (average): Tututendo, Colombia: mean annual rainfall 11,770 mm [463.4 in].

Wettest place (12 months): Cherrapunji, Meghalaya, N.E. India, 26,470 mm [1,040 in], August 1860 to August 1861. Cherrapunji also holds the record for rainfall in one month: 930 mm [37 in], July 1861.

Wettest place (24 hours): Cilaos, Réunion, Indian Ocean, 1,870 mm [73.6 in], 15–16 March 1952.

Heaviest hailstones: Gopalganj, Bangladesh, up to 1.02 kg [2.25 lb], 14 April 1986 (killed 92 people).

Heaviest snowfall (continuous): Bessans, Savoie, France, 1,730 mm [68 in] in 19 hours, 5–6 April 1969.

Heaviest snowfall (season/year): Paradise Ranger Station, Mt Rainier, Washington, USA, 31,102 mm [1,224.5 in], 19 February 1971 to 18 February 1972.

Pressure and winds

Highest barometric pressure: Agata, Siberia, 1,083.8 mb [32 in] at altitude 262 m [862 ft], 31 December 1968.

Lowest barometric pressure: Typhoon Tip, 480 km [300 mls] west of Guam, Pacific Ocean, 870 mb [25.69 in], 12 October 1979.

Highest recorded wind speed: Mt Washington, New Hampshire, USA, 371 km/h [231 mph], 12 April 1934. This is three times as strong as hurricane force on the Beaufort Scale.

Windiest place: Commonwealth Bay, George V Coast, Antarctica, where gales reach over 320 km/h [200 mph].

In sub-zero weather, even moderate winds significantly reduce effective temperatures. The chart below shows the windchill effect across a range of speeds. Figures in the pink zone are not dangerous to well-clad people; in the blue zone, the risk of serious frostbite is acute.

	Wind speed (km/h)				
	16	32	48	64	80
0°C	-8	-14	-17	-19	-20
-5°C	-14	-21	-25	-27	-28
-10°C	-20	-28	-33	-35	-36
-15°C	-26	-36	-40	-43	-44
-20°C	-32	-42	-48	-51	-52
-25°C	-38	-49	-56	-59	-60
-30°C	-44	-57	-63	-66	-68
-35°C	-51	-64	-72	-74	-76
-40°C	-57	-71	-78	-82	-84
-45°C	-63	-78	-86	-90	-92
-50°C	-69	-85	-94	-98	-100

BEAUFORT WIND SCALE

Named after the 19th-century British naval officer who devised it, the Beaufort Scale assesses wind speed according to its effects. It was originally designed as an aid for sailors, but has since been adapted for use on land.

Scale	Wind speed km/h	mph	Effect
0	0-1	0-1	**Calm** Smoke rises vertically
1	1-5	1-3	**Light air** Wind direction shown only by smoke drift
2	6-11	4-7	**Light breeze** Wind felt on face; leaves rustle; vanes moved by wind
3	12-19	8-12	**Gentle breeze** Leaves and small twigs in constant motion; wind extends small flag
4	20-28	13-18	**Moderate** Raises dust and loose paper; small branches move
5	29-38	19-24	**Fresh** Small trees in leaf sway; crested wavelets on inland waters
6	39-49	25-31	**Strong** Large branches move; difficult to use umbrellas; overhead wires whistle
7	50-61	32-38	**Near gale** Whole trees in motion; difficult to walk against wind
8	62-74	39-46	**Gale** Twigs break from trees; walking very difficult
9	75-88	47-54	**Strong gale** Slight structural damage
10	89-102	55-63	**Storm** Trees uprooted; serious structural damage
11	103-117	64-72	**Violent storm** Widespread damage
12	118+	73+	**Hurricane**

Conversions
°C = (°F −32) x 5/9; °F = (°C x 9/5) + 32; 0°C = 32°F
1 in = 25.4 mm; 1 mm = 0.0394 in; 100 mm = 3.94 in

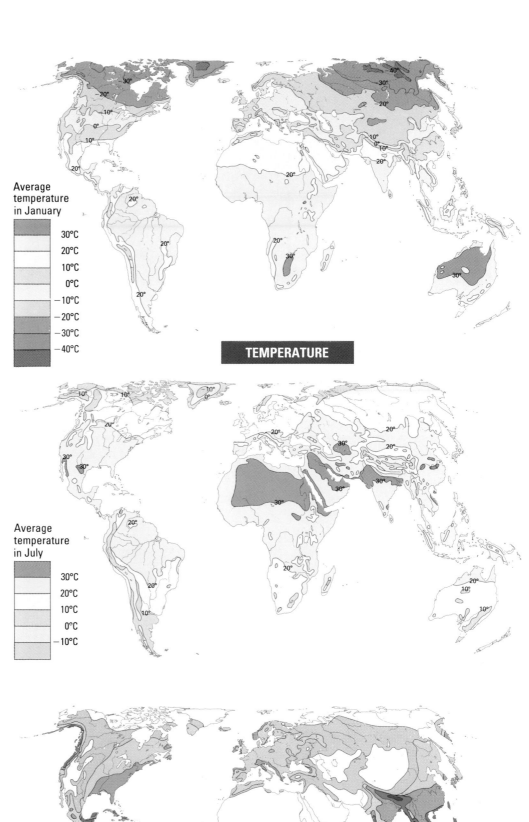

Average temperature in January

- 30°C
- 20°C
- 10°C
- 0°C
- −10°C
- −20°C
- −30°C
- −40°C

TEMPERATURE

Average temperature in July

- 30°C
- 20°C
- 10°C
- 0°C
- −10°C

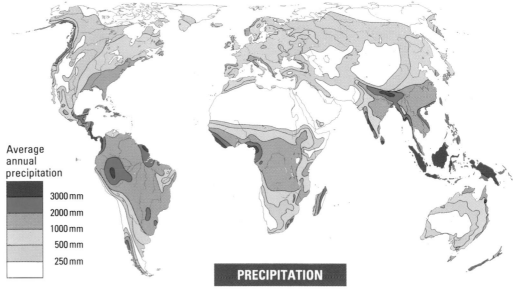

Average annual precipitation

- 3000 mm
- 2000 mm
- 1000 mm
- 500 mm
- 250 mm

PRECIPITATION

WATER

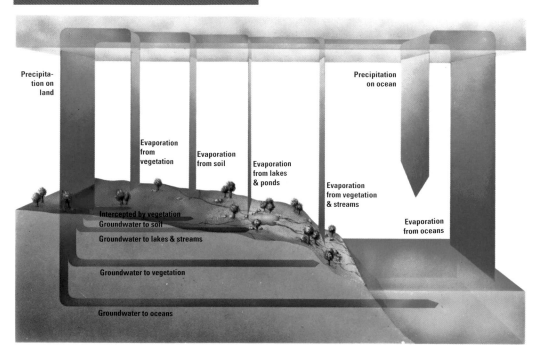

Precipitation on land

Precipitation on ocean

Evaporation from vegetation

Evaporation from soil

Evaporation from lakes & ponds

Evaporation from vegetation & streams

Evaporation from oceans

Intercepted by vegetation
Groundwater to soil
Groundwater to lakes & streams
Groundwater to vegetation
Groundwater to oceans

WATER DISTRIBUTION

The distribution of planetary water, by percentage. Oceans and ice-caps together account for more than 99% of the total; the breakdown of the remainder is estimated.

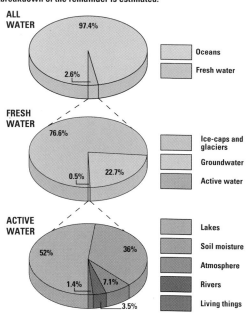

ALL WATER
- 97.4%
- 2.6%

Oceans
Fresh water

FRESH WATER
- 76.6%
- 0.5%
- 22.7%

Ice-caps and glaciers
Groundwater
Active water

ACTIVE WATER
- 52%
- 36%
- 1.4%
- 7.1%
- 3.5%

Lakes
Soil moisture
Atmosphere
Rivers
Living things

WATER RUNOFF

Annual freshwater runoff by continent in cubic kilometres

Asia | Australasia
North America | Europe
South America | Africa

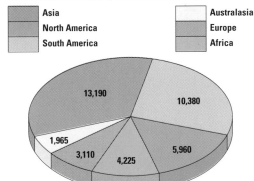

- 13,190
- 10,380
- 1,965
- 3,110
- 4,225
- 5,960

WATER UTILIZATION

The percentage breakdown of water usage by sector, selected countries (latest available year)*

Domestic | Industrial | Agriculture

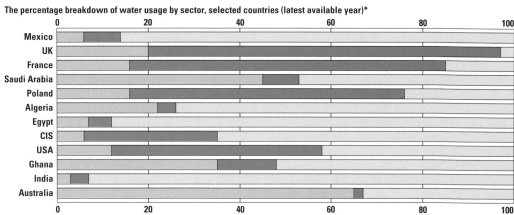

Mexico
UK
France
Saudi Arabia
Poland
Algeria
Egypt
CIS
USA
Ghana
India
Australia

WATER SUPPLY

Percentage of total population with access to safe drinking water (latest available year)*

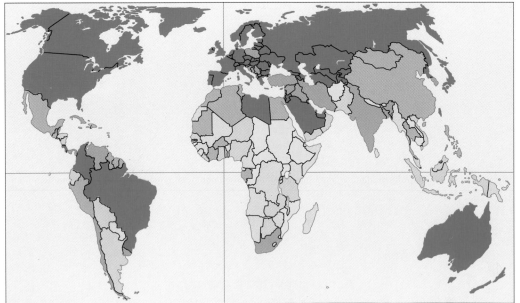

- Over 90% with safe water
- 75 – 90% with safe water
- 60 – 75% with safe water
- 45 – 60% with safe water
- 30 – 45% with safe water
- Under 30% with safe water

Least well-provided countries

Cambodia	3%	Afghanistan	21%
Central Africa	12%	Congo	21%
Ethiopia	19%	Guinea-Bissau	21%
Uganda	20%	Sudan	21%

*Statistics for the new republics of the former USSR, Czechoslovakia and Yugoslavia are not yet available.
The map shows the statistics for the entire USSR, Czechoslovakia and Yugoslavia.

NATURAL VEGETATION

Regional variation in vegetation

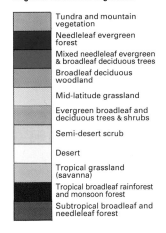

- Tundra and mountain vegetation
- Needleleaf evergreen forest
- Mixed needleleaf evergreen & broadleaf deciduous trees
- Broadleaf deciduous woodland
- Mid-latitude grassland
- Evergreen broadleaf and deciduous trees & shrubs
- Semi-desert scrub
- Desert
- Tropical grassland (savanna)
- Tropical broadleaf rainforest and monsoon forest
- Subtropical broadleaf and needleleaf forest

The map shows the natural 'climax vegetation' of regions, as dictated by climate and topography. In most cases, however, agricultural activity has drastically altered the vegetation pattern. Western Europe, for example, lost most of its broadleaf forest many centuries ago, while irrigation has turned some natural semi desert into productive land.

LAND USE BY CONTINENT

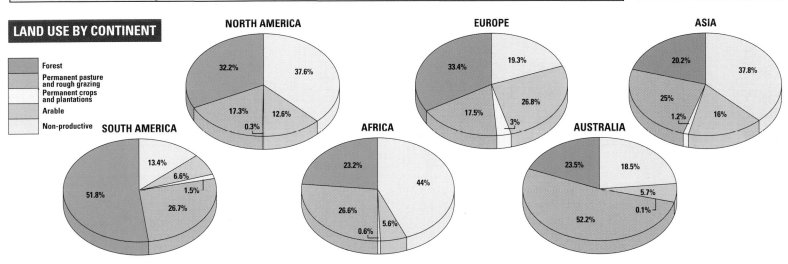

- Forest
- Permanent pasture and rough grazing
- Permanent crops and plantations
- Arable
- Non-productive

NORTH AMERICA
37.6%, 32.2%, 17.3%, 0.3%, 12.6%

EUROPE
19.3%, 33.4%, 17.5%, 3%, 26.8%

ASIA
37.8%, 20.2%, 25%, 1.2%, 16%

SOUTH AMERICA
13.4%, 6.6%, 1.5%, 51.8%, 26.7%

AFRICA
44%, 23.2%, 26.6%, 0.6%, 5.6%

AUSTRALIA
18.5%, 23.5%, 5.7%, 0.1%, 52.2%

FORESTRY: PRODUCTION

	Forest & woodland (million hectares)	Annual production (1980s average, million cubic metres)	
		Fuelwood & charcoal	Industrial roundwood
World	*4,121.4*	*1,646.1*	*1,534.8*
USSR (1988)	928.6	85.6	284.9
S. America	867.1	217.0	91.7
N. America	806.6	154.4	538.7
Africa	705.3	384.7	53.4
Asia	497.2	739.1	245.7
Europe	159.1	56.5	292.1
Australasia	158.8	8.8	28.3

PAPER AND BOARD

Top producers (1988)**

USA	69,477
Japan	24,624
Canada	16,638
China	12,645
USSR	10,750

Top exporters (1988)**

Canada	11,420
Finland	7,185
Sweden	6,377
USA	4,294
Germany	3,780

** in thousand tonnes

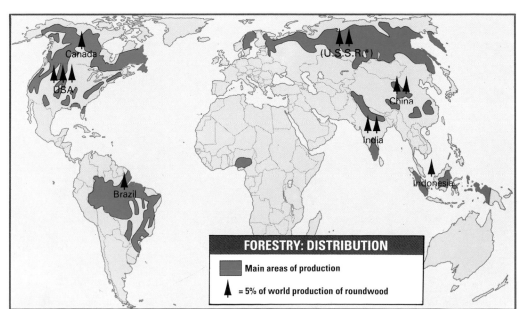

FORESTRY: DISTRIBUTION

- Main areas of production
- = 5% of world production of roundwood

Statistics for the new republics of the former USSR, Czechoslovakia and Yugoslavia are not yet available. The map shows the statistics for the entire USSR, Czechoslovakia and Yugoslavia.

CARTOGRAPHY BY PHILIP'S. COPYRIGHT REED INTERNATIONAL BOOKS LTD

ENVIRONMENT

Humans have always had a dramatic effect on their environment, at least since the invention of agriculture almost 10,000 years ago. Generally, the Earth has accepted human interference without obvious ill effects: the complex systems that regulate the global environment have been able to absorb substantial damage while maintaining a stable and comfortable home for the planet's trillions of lifeforms. But advancing human technology and the rapidly-expanding populations it supports are now threatening to overwhelm the Earth's ability to compensate.

Industrial wastes, acid rainfall, desertification and large-scale deforestation: all combine to create environmental change at a rate far faster than the slow cycles of planetary evolution can accommodate. Equipped with chain-saws and flamethrowers, humans can now destroy more forest in a day than their ancestors could in a century, upsetting the balance between plant and animal, carbon dioxide and oxygen, on which all life ultimately depends.

The fossil fuels that power industrial civilization have pumped enough carbon dioxide and other so-called greenhouse gases into the atmosphere to make climatic change a near-certainty. Chlorofluorocarbons – CFCs – and other man-made chemicals are rapidly eroding the ozone layer, the atmosphere's screen against ultra-violet radiation.

As a result, the Earth's average temperature has risen by approximately 0.5°C since the beginning of the 20th century, and is still rising.

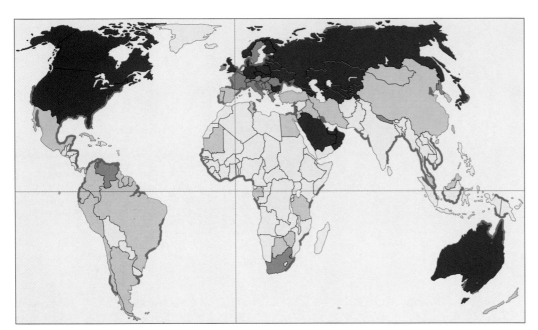

GLOBAL WARMING

Carbon dioxide emissions in tonnes per person per year (1980s)

High atmospheric concentrations of heat-absorbing gases, especially carbon dioxide, appear to be causing a steady rise in average temperatures worldwide – up to 1.5°C by the year 2020, according to some estimates. Global warming is likely to bring with it a rise in sea levels that may flood some of the Earth's most densely populated coastlines.

- Over 10 tonnes of CO_2
- 5 – 10 tonnes of CO_2
- 1 – 5 tonnes of CO_2
- Under 1 tonne of CO_2
- Coastal areas in danger of flooding from rising sea levels caused by global warming

GREENHOUSE POWER

Relative contributions to the Greenhouse Effect by the major heat-absorbing gases in the atmosphere

The chart combines greenhouse potency and volume. Carbon dioxide has a greenhouse potential of only 1, but its concentration of 350 parts per million makes it predominate. CFC 12, with 25,000 times the absorption capacity of CO_2, is present only as 0.00044 ppm.

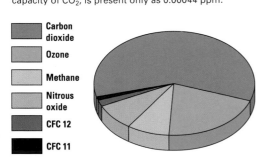

- Carbon dioxide
- Ozone
- Methane
- Nitrous oxide
- CFC 12
- CFC 11

CARBON DIOXIDE

Carbon dioxide released in millions of tonnes (1980s)

Although most of the net increase in atmospheric carbon dioxide comes from fossil fuel combustion, deforestation and changing land use also contribute.

- Fuel burning
- Deforestation

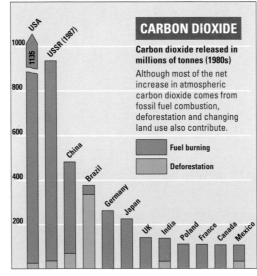

GLOBAL WARMING

The rise in average temperatures caused by carbon dioxide and other greenhouse gases (1960–2020)

- assumes present trends continue
- assumes drastic emissions cuts in the 1990s

Recorded change

Projected changes

THE GREENHOUSE EFFECT

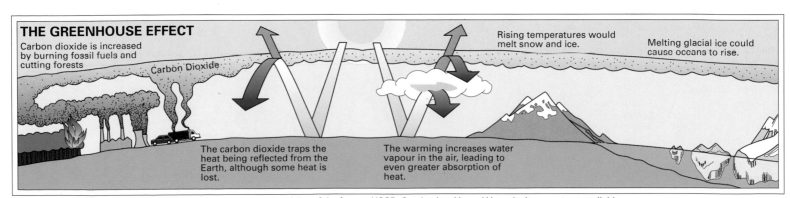

Carbon dioxide is increased by burning fossil fuels and cutting forests

Carbon Dioxide

Rising temperatures would melt snow and ice.

Melting glacial ice could cause oceans to rise.

The carbon dioxide traps the heat being reflected from the Earth, although some heat is lost.

The warming increases water vapour in the air, leading to even greater absorption of heat.

Statistics for the new republics of the former USSR, Czechoslovakia and Yugoslavia are not yet available.
The map shows the statistics for the entire USSR, Czechoslovakia and Yugoslavia.

Existing deserts

Areas with a high risk of
desertification

Areas with a moderate
risk of desertification

Former areas of
rainforest

Existing rainforest

DEFORESTATION

5200

1.5

Thousands of
hectares of forest
cleared annually,
tropical countries
surveyed 1981–85
and 1987–90. Loss
as a percentage
of remaining
stocks is shown
in figures on each
column.

3000

2000

1000

0

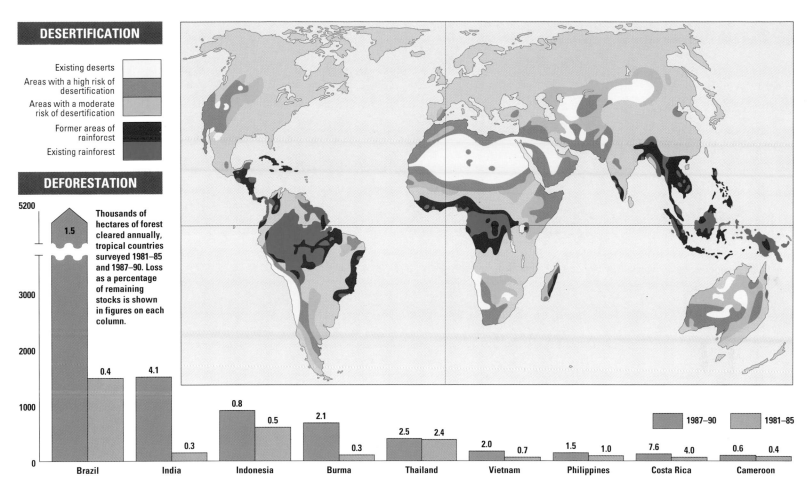

	1987–90	1981–85

Brazil 1.5 / 0.4
India 4.1 / 0.3
Indonesia 0.8 / 0.5
Burma 2.1 / 0.3
Thailand 2.5 / 2.4
Vietnam 2.0 / 0.7
Philippines 1.5 / 1.0
Costa Rica 7.6 / 4.0
Cameroon 0.6 / 0.4

DESERTIFICATION

The result of overcultivation, overgrazing and overcutting of ground cover for firewood, desertification is also caused by faulty irrigation techniques that leave land too saline or alkaline to support viable crops. Changing rainfall patterns or prolonged droughts exacerbate the process. As much as 60% of the world's croplands and rangelands are in some danger, with 6 million hectares lost altogether every year and a further 21 million rendered agriculturally worthless. Africa is especially badly hit: in Mali, the Sahara advanced 350 kilometres southwards in only 20 years.

DEFORESTATION

The Earth's remaining forests are under attack from three directions: expanding agriculture, logging, and growing consumption of fuelwood, often in combination. Sometimes deforestation is the direct result of government policy, as in the efforts made to resettle the urban poor in some parts of Brazil; just as often, it comes about despite state attempts at conservation. Loggers, licensed or unlicensed, blaze a trail into virgin forest, often destroying twice as many trees as they harvest. Landless farmers follow, burning away most of what remains to plant their crops, completing the destruction.

ACID RAIN

Killing trees, poisoning lakes and rivers and eating away buildings, acid rain is mostly produced by sulphur dioxide emissions from industry, although the burning of savanna lands by African farmers has also caused acid downpours on tropical rainforests. By the late 1980s, acid rain had sterilized 4,000 or more of Sweden's lakes and left 45% of Switzerland's alpine conifers dead or dying, while the monuments of Greece were dissolving in Athens' smog. Prevailing wind patterns mean that the acids often fall many hundred kilometres from where the original pollutants were discharged.

ACID RAIN

Acid rainfall and sources of acidic emissions (1980s)

Acid rain is caused when sulphur and nitrogen oxides in the air combine with water vapour to form sulphuric, nitric and other acids.

Regions where sulphur and nitrogen oxides are released in high concentrations, mainly from fossil fuel combustion.

• Major cities with high levels of air pollution (including nitrogen and sulphur emissions)

Areas of heavy acid deposition

pH numbers indicate acidity, decreasing from a neutral 7. Normal rain, slightly acid from dissolved carbon dioxide, never exceeds a pH of 5.6.

pH less than 4.0 (most acidic)

pH 4.0 to 4.5

pH 4.5 to 5.0

Areas where acid rain is a potential problem

POPULATION

Developed nations such as the UK have populations evenly spread across age groups and, usually, a growing proportion of elderly people. Developing nations fall into a pattern somewhere between that of Kenya and the world model: the great majority of their people are in the younger age groups, about to enter their most fertile years. In time, even Kenya's population profile should resemble the world profile, but the transition will come about only after a few more generations of rapid population growth.

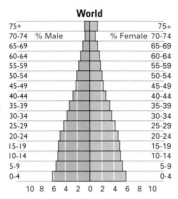

World

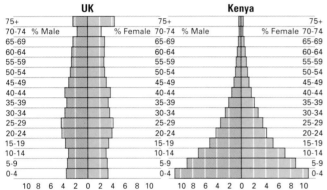

UK   Kenya

India   Saudi Arabia

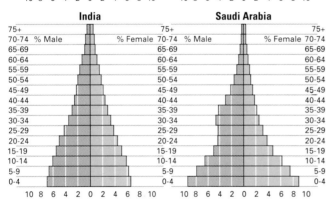

USA   China

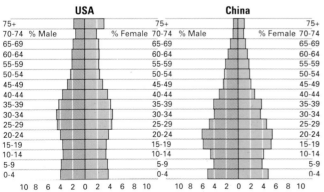

MOST POPULOUS NATIONS [in millions (1993)]

1. China	1,187	9. Pakistan	115	17. Italy	57
2. India	879	10. Mexico	89	18. Thailand	57
3. USA	255	11. Nigeria	88	19. France	57
4. Indonesia	191	12. Germany	80	20. Iran	56
5. Brazil	156	13. Vietnam	69	21. Egypt	55
6. Russia	149	14. Philippines	64	22. Ethiopia	55
7. Japan	124	15. Turkey	58	23. Ukraine	52
8. Bangladesh	119	16. UK	57	24. S. Korea	43

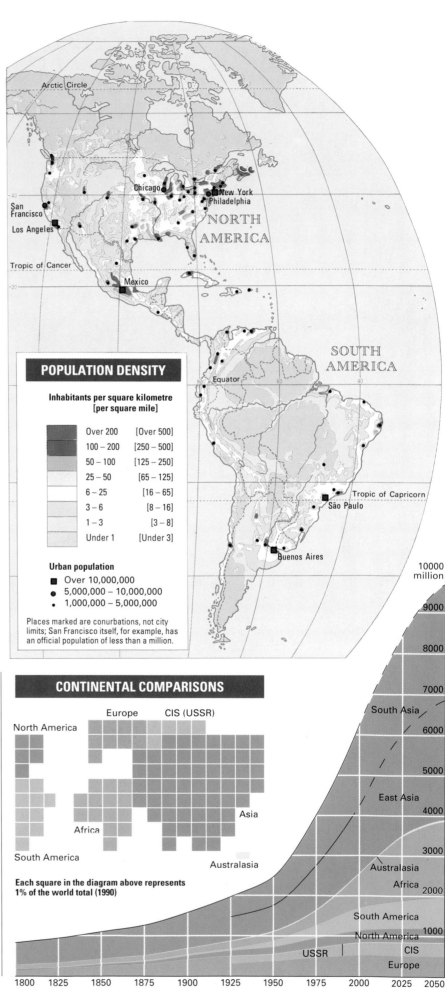

POPULATION DENSITY

Inhabitants per square kilometre [per square mile]

Over 200	[Over 500]
100 – 200	[250 – 500]
50 – 100	[125 – 250]
25 – 50	[65 – 125]
6 – 25	[16 – 65]
3 – 6	[8 – 16]
1 – 3	[3 – 8]
Under 1	[Under 3]

Urban population
- ■ Over 10,000,000
- ● 5,000,000 – 10,000,000
- • 1,000,000 – 5,000,000

Places marked are conurbations, not city limits; San Francisco itself, for example, has an official population of less than a million.

CONTINENTAL COMPARISONS

Each square in the diagram above represents 1% of the world total (1990)

North America Europe CIS (USSR) Africa Asia South America Australasia

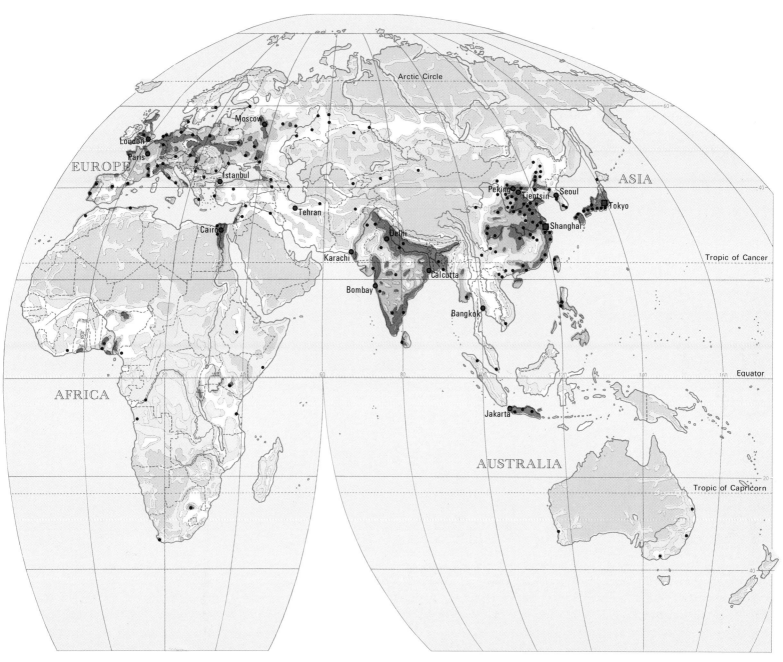

Arctic Circle

EUROPE

Moscow
London
Paris
Istanbul

ASIA

Tehran

Cairo

Peking   Seoul
Tientsin   Tokyo
Shanghai

Delhi

Karachi   Tropic of Cancer

Calcutta

Bombay

Bangkok

AFRICA

Equator

Jakarta

AUSTRALIA

Tropic of Capricorn

URBAN POPULATION

Percentage of total population living in towns and cities (1990)

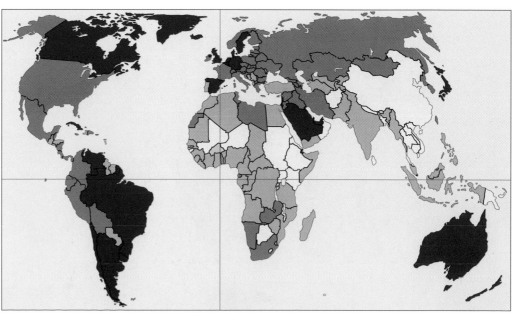

Over 75%
50 – 75%
25 – 50%
10 – 25%
Under 10%

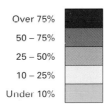

Most urbanized		Least urbanized	
Singapore	100%	Bhutan	5%
Belgium	97%	Burundi	7%
Kuwait	96%	Rwanda	8%
Hong Kong	93%	Burkina Faso	9%
UK	93%	Nepal	10%

THE HUMAN FAMILY

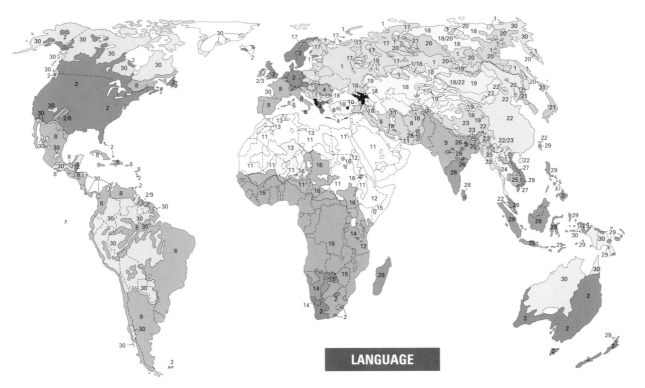

MOTHER TONGUES
Chinese 1,069 million (Mandarin 864), English 443, Hindi 352, Spanish 341, Russian 293, Arabic 197, Bengali 184, Portuguese 173, Malay-Indonesian 142, Japanese 125, French 121, German 118, Urdu 92, Punjabi 84, Korean 71

OFFICIAL LANGUAGES
English 27% of world population, Chinese 19%, Hindi 13.5%, Spanish 5.4%, Russian 5.2%, French 4.2%, Arabic 3.3%, Portuguese 3%, Malay 3%, Bengali 2.9%, Japanese 2.3%

Language can be classified by ancestry and structure. For example, the Romance and Germanic groups are both derived from an Indo-European language believed to have been spoken 5,000 years ago.

LANGUAGE

INDO-EUROPEAN FAMILY

1	Balto-Slavic group (incl. Russian, Ukrainian)
2	Germanic group (incl. English, German)
3	Celtic group
4	Greek
5	Albanian
6	Iranian group
7	Armenian
8	Romance group (incl. Spanish, Portuguese, French, Italian)
9	Indo-Aryan group (incl. Hindi, Bengali, Urdu, Punjabi, Marathi)
10	CAUCASIAN FAMILY

AFRO-ASIATIC FAMILY

11	Semitic group (incl. Arabic)
12	Kushitic group
13	Berber group
14	KHOISAN FAMILY
15	NIGER-CONGO FAMILY
16	NILO-SAHARAN FAMILY
17	URALIC FAMILY

ALTAIC FAMILY

18	Turkic group
19	Mongolian group
20	Tungus-Manchu group
21	Japanese and Korean

SINO-TIBETAN FAMILY

22	Sinitic (Chinese) languages
23	Tibetic-Burmic languages
24	TAI FAMILY

AUSTRO-ASIATIC FAMILY

25	Mon-Khmer group
26	Munda group
27	Vietnamese
28	DRAVIDIAN FAMILY (incl. Telugu, Tamil)
29	AUSTRONESIAN FAMILY (incl. Malay-Indonesian)
30	OTHER LANGUAGES

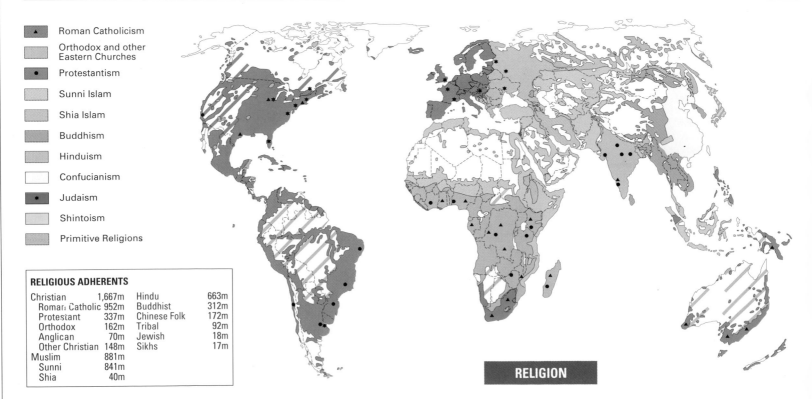

- ▲ Roman Catholicism
- Orthodox and other Eastern Churches
- • Protestantism
- Sunni Islam
- Shia Islam
- Buddhism
- Hinduism
- Confucianism
- ★ Judaism
- Shintoism
- Primitive Religions

RELIGIOUS ADHERENTS

Christian	1,667m	Hindu	663m
Roman Catholic	952m	Buddhist	312m
Protestant	337m	Chinese Folk	172m
Orthodox	162m	Tribal	92m
Anglican	70m	Jewish	18m
Other Christian	148m	Sikhs	17m
Muslim	881m		
Sunni	841m		
Shia	40m		

RELIGION

CARTOGRAPHY BY PHILIP'S. COPYRIGHT REED INTERNATIONAL BOOKS LTD

UNITED NATIONS

Created in 1945 to promote peace and co-operation and based in New York, the United Nations is the world's largest international organization, with 184 members and an annual budget of US $2.6 billion (1994–95). Each member of the General Assembly has one vote, while the permanent members of the 15-nation Security Council – USA, Russia, China, UK and France – hold a veto. The 54 members of the Economic and Social Council are responsible for economic, social, cultural, educational, health and related matters. The Secretariat is the UN's principal administrative arm; the only territory now administered by the Trusteeship Council is Belau (by the USA). The UN has 16 specialized agencies – based in Canada, France, Switzerland and Italy as well as the USA – which help members in fields such as education (UNESCO), agriculture (FAO), medicine (WHO) and finance (IFC).

[The International Court of Justice is based in The Hague]

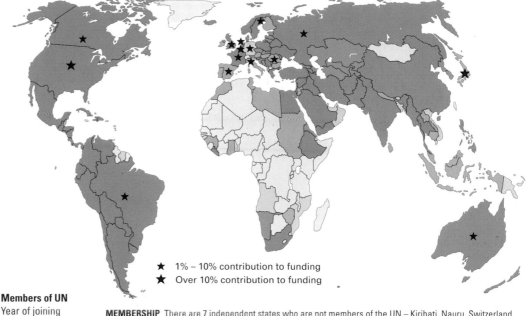

★ 1% – 10% contribution to funding
★ Over 10% contribution to funding

Members of UN
Year of joining

▨	1940s
▨	1950s
▨	1960s
▨	1970s
▨	1980s
▨	1990s
	Non-members

MEMBERSHIP There are 7 independent states who are not members of the UN – Kiribati, Nauru, Switzerland, Taiwan, Tonga, Tuvalu and Vatican City. By the end of 1992, all the successor states of the former USSR had joined. There were 51 members in 1945. Official languages are Chinese, English, French, Russian, Spanish and Arabic.

FUNDING The UN budget for 1994–95 is US $2.6 billion. Contributions are assessed by the members' ability to pay, with the maximum 25% of the total, the minimum 0.01%. Contributions for 1992–94 were: USA 25%, Japan 12.45%, Germany 8.93%, Russia 6.71%, France 6%, UK 5.02%, Italy 4.29%, Canada 3.11% (others 28.49%).

PEACEKEEPING The UN has been involved in 33 peacekeeping operations worldwide since 1948 and there are currently 17 areas of UN patrol. In July 1993 there were 80,146 'blue berets' from 74 countries.

EC As from December 1993 the European Union (EU) refers to matters of foreign policy, security and justice. The European Community (EC) refers to all other matters. The 12 members – Belgium, Denmark, France, Germany, Greece, Ireland, Italy, Luxembourg, Netherlands, Portugal, Spain and the UK – aim to integrate economies, co-ordinate social developments and bring about political union. These members of what is now the world's biggest market share agricultural and industrial policies and tariffs on trade.

EFTA European Free Trade Association (formed in 1960). Portugal left the 'Seven' in 1989 to join the EC.

ACP African-Caribbean-Pacific (1963).

NATO North Atlantic Treaty Organization (formed in 1949). It continues after 1991 despite the winding up of the Warsaw Pact.

OAS Organization of American States (1949). It aims to promote social and economic co-operation between developed countries of North America and developing nations of Latin America.

ASEAN Association of South-east Asian Nations (1967).

OAU Organization of African Unity (1963). Its 52 members represent over 90% of Africa's population.

LAIA Latin American Integration Association (1980).

OECD Organization for Economic Co-operation and Development (1961). The 24 major Western free-market economies. 'G7' is its 'inner group' of USA, Canada, Japan, UK, Germany, Italy and France.

COMMONWEALTH The Commonwealth of Nations evolved from the British Empire; it comprises 18 nations recognizing the British monarch as head of state and 32 with their own heads of state.

OPEC Organization of Petroleum Exporting Countries (1960). It controls about three-quarters of the world's oil supply.

ARAB LEAGUE (1945) The League's aim is to promote economic, social, political and military co-operation.

COLOMBO PLAN (1951) Its 26 members aim to promote economic and social development in Asia and the Pacific.

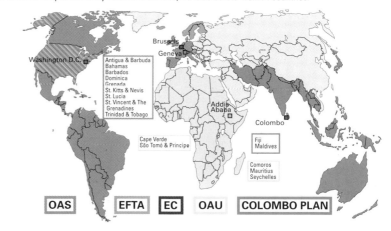

OAS EFTA EC OAU COLOMBO PLAN

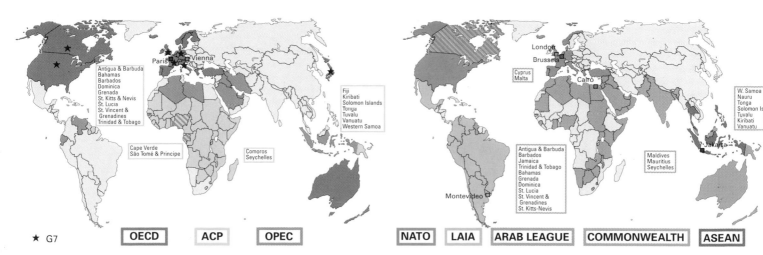

★ G7

OECD ACP OPEC

NATO LAIA ARAB LEAGUE COMMONWEALTH ASEAN

WEALTH

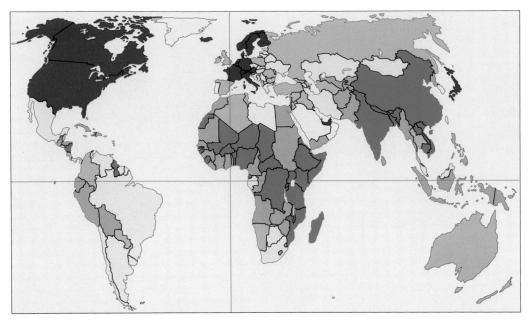

LEVELS OF INCOME

Gross National Product per capita: the value of total production divided by the population (1991)

- Over 400% of world average
- 200 – 400% of world average
- 100 – 200% of world average

[World average wealth per person US $4,210]

- 50 – 100% of world average
- 25 – 50% of world average
- 10 – 25% of world average
- Under 10% of world average

Richest countries		Poorest countries	
Switzerland	$33,510	Mozambique	$70
Luxembourg	$31,080	Tanzania	$100
Japan	$26,920	Ethiopia	$120
Sweden	$25,490	Somalia	$150

WEALTH CREATION

The Gross National Product (GNP) of the world's largest economies, US $ billion (1991)

1.	USA	5,686,038	21.	Austria	157,538
2.	Japan	3,337,191	22.	Iran	127,366
3.	Germany	1,516,785	23.	Finland	121,982
4.	France	1,167,749	24.	Denmark	121,695
5.	Italy	1,072,198	25.	Ukraine	121,458
6.	UK	963,696	26.	Indonesia	111,409
7.	Canada	568,765	27.	Saudi Arabia	105,133
8.	Spain	486,614	28.	Turkey	103,388
9.	Russia	479,546	29.	Norway	102,885
10.	Brazil	447,324	30.	Argentina	91,211
11.	China	424,012	31.	South Africa	90,953
12.	Australia	287,765	32.	Thailand	89,548
13.	India	284,668	33.	Hong Kong	77,302
14.	Netherlands	278,839	34.	Poland	70,640
15.	South Korea	274,464	35.	Greece	65,504
16.	Mexico	252,381	36.	Israel	59,128
17.	Switzerland	225,890	37.	Portugal	58,451
18.	Sweden	218,934	38.	Venezuela	52,775
19.	Belgium	192,370	39.	Algeria	52,239
20.	Taiwan	161,000	40.	Pakistan	46,725

THE WEALTH GAP

The world's richest and poorest countries, by Gross National Product per capita in US $ (1991)

1.	Switzerland	33,510	1.	Mozambique	70
2.	Liechtenstein	33,000	2.	Tanzania	100
3.	Luxembourg	31,080	3.	Ethiopia	120
4.	Japan	26,920	4.	Somalia	150
5.	Sweden	25,490	5.	Uganda	160
6.	Bermuda	25,000	6.	Bhutan	180
7.	Finland	24,400	7.	Nepal	180
8.	Norway	24,160	8.	Guinea-Bissau	190
9.	Denmark	23,660	9.	Cambodia	200
10.	Germany	23,650	10.	Burundi	210
11.	Iceland	22,580	11.	Madagascar	210
12.	USA	22,560	12.	Sierra Leone	210
13.	Canada	21,260	13.	Bangladesh	220
14.	France	20,600	14.	Chad	220
15.	Austria	20,380	15.	Zaire	220
16.	UAE	19,500	16.	Laos	230
17.	Belgium	19,300	17.	Malawi	230
18.	Italy	18,580	18.	Rwanda	260
19.	Netherlands	18,560	19.	Mali	280
20.	UK	16,750	20.	Guyana	290

GNP per capita is calculated by dividing a country's Gross National Product by its population.

CONTINENTAL SHARES

Shares of population and of wealth (GNP) by continent

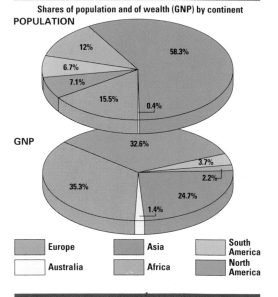

POPULATION
- 58.3%
- 12%
- 6.7%
- 7.1%
- 15.5%
- 0.4%

GNP
- 32.6%
- 35.3%
- 1.4%
- 3.7%
- 2.2%
- 24.7%

Europe	Asia
Australia	Africa

South America
North America

INFLATION

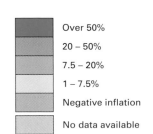

Average annual rate of inflation (1980–91)*

- Over 50%
- 20 – 50%
- 7.5 – 20%
- 1 – 7.5%
- Negative inflation
- No data available

Highest average inflation		Lowest average inflation	
Nicaragua	584%	Oman	–3.1%
Argentina	417%	Kuwait	–2.7%
Brazil	328%	Saudi Arabia	–2.4%
Peru	287%	Equatorial Guinea	–0.9%
Bolivia	263%	Albania	–0.4%
Israel	89%	Bahrain	–0.3%
Mexico	66%	Libya	0.2%

*Statistics for the new republics of the former USSR, Czechoslovakia and Yugoslavia are not yet available.
The map shows the statistics for the entire USSR, Czechoslovakia and Yugoslavia.

INTERNATIONAL AID

Aid provided or received, divided by total population in US $ (1990)*

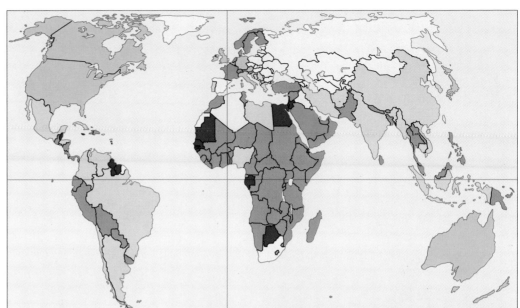

PROVIDERS

Over $100 per person	
$10 – $100 per person	
$0 – $10 per person	
No aid given or received	
$0 – $10 per person	
$10 – $100 per person	
Over $100 per person	

RECEIVERS

Top 5 providers

Kuwait	$793
UAE	$555
Norway	$287
Saudi Arabia	$248
Sweden	$234

Top 5 receivers

Israel	$295
Djibouti	$293
Jordan	$221
Dominica	$185
Surinam	$135

DEBT AND AID

International debtors and the aid they receive (1989)

Although aid grants make a vital contribution to many of the world's poorer countries, they are usually dwarfed by the burden of debt that developing economies are expected to repay. In the case of Mozambique, aid amounted to more than 70% of GNP. In 1990, the World Bank rated Mozambique as the world's poorest country; yet debt interest payments came to almost 75 times its entire export earnings.

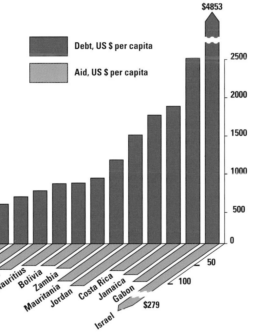

- Debt, US $ per capita
- Aid, US $ per capita

$4853

Lesotho, Central African R., Niger, Mali, Mozambique, Somalia, Togo, El Salvador, Botswana, Senegal, Papua New Guinea, Honduras, Mauritius, Bolivia, Zambia, Mauritania, Jordan, Costa Rica, Jamaica, Gabon, Israel $279

DISTRIBUTION OF SPENDING

Percentage share of household spending

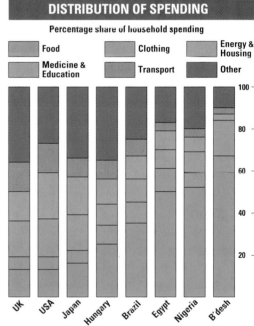

- Food
- Clothing
- Energy & Housing
- Medicine & Education
- Transport
- Other

UK, USA, Japan, Hungary, Brazil, Egypt, Nigeria, B'desh

HIGH INCOME

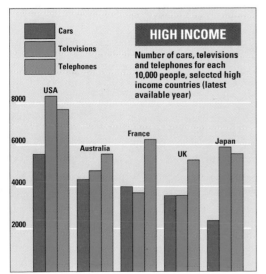

- Cars
- Televisions
- Telephones

Number of cars, televisions and telephones for each 10,000 people, selected high income countries (latest available year)

USA, Australia, France, UK, Japan

MIDDLE INCOME

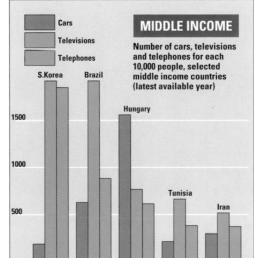

- Cars
- Televisions
- Telephones

Number of cars, televisions and telephones for each 10,000 people, selected middle income countries (latest available year)

S.Korea, Brazil, Hungary, Tunisia, Iran

LOW INCOME

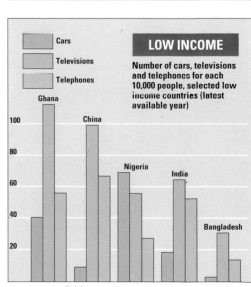

- Cars
- Televisions
- Telephones

Number of cars, televisions and telephones for each 10,000 people, selected low income countries (latest available year)

Ghana, China, Nigeria, India, Bangladesh

*Statistics for the new republics of the former USSR, Czechoslovakia and Yugoslavia are not yet available. The map shows the statistics for the entire USSR, Czechoslovakia and Yugoslavia.

QUALITY OF LIFE

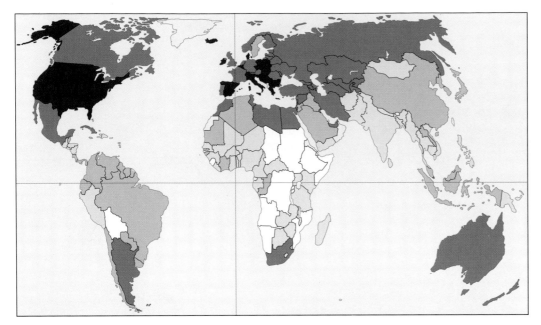

FOOD CONSUMPTION

Average daily food intake in calories per person (1989)*

- Over 3,500 calories per person
- 3,000 – 3,500 calories per person
- 2,500 – 3,000 calories per person
- 2,000 – 2,500 calories per person
- Under 2,000 calories per person
- No available data

Top 5 countries		Bottom 5 countries	
Belgium	3,902 cal.	Ethiopia	1,666 cal.
Greece	3,825 cal.	Mozambique	1,679 cal.
Ireland	3,778 cal.	Chad	1,742 cal.
Bulgaria	3,707 cal.	Sierra Leone	1,799 cal.
USA	3,650 cal.	Angola	1,806 cal.

[UK 3,148]

HOSPITAL CAPACITY

Hospital beds available for each 1,000 people (latest available year)

Highest capacity		Lowest capacity	
Finland	14.9	Bangladesh	0.2
Sweden	13.2	Nepal	0.2
France	12.9	Ethiopia	0.3
USSR	12.8	Mauritania	0.4
Netherlands	12.0	Mali	0.5
North Korea	11.7	Burkina Faso	0.6
Switzerland	11.3	Pakistan	0.6
Austria	10.4	Niger	0.7
Czechoslovakia	10.1	Haiti	0.8
Hungary	9.1	Chad	0.8

[USA 5.9] [UK 8]

Although the ratio of people to hospital beds gives a good approximation of a country's health provision, it is not an absolute indicator. Raw numbers may mask inefficiency and other weaknesses: the high availability of beds in North Korea, for example, has not prevented infant mortality rates almost three times as high as in the United Kingdom.

LIFE EXPECTANCY

Years of life expectancy at birth, selected countries (1988–89)

The chart shows combined data for both sexes. On average, women live longer than men worldwide, even in developing countries with high maternal mortality rates. Overall, life expectancy is steadily rising, though the difference between rich and poor nations remains dramatic.

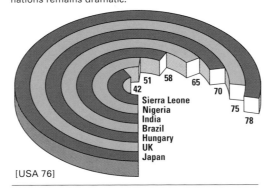

42 — 51 — 58 — 65 — 70 — 75 — 78

Sierra Leone
Nigeria
India
Brazil
Hungary
UK
Japan

[USA 76]

INFECTIOUS DISEASE

Deaths from infectious disease, per 100,000 people, selected countries (latest available year)

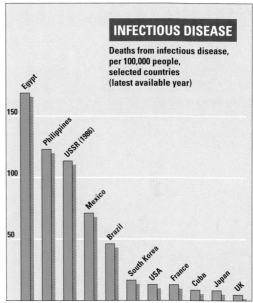

Egypt — Philippines — USSR (1986) — Mexico — Brazil — South Korea — USA — France — Cuba — Japan — UK

CHILD MORTALITY

Number of babies who will die before the age of one year, per 1,000 live births (average 1990–95)*

- Over 150 deaths per 1,000 births
- 100 – 150 deaths per 1,000 births
- 50 – 100 deaths per 1,000 births
- 20 – 50 deaths per 1,000 births
- 10 – 20 deaths per 1,000 births
- Under 10 deaths per 1,000 births

Highest child mortality		Lowest child mortality	
Afghanistan	162	Hong Kong	6
Mali	159	Denmark	6
Sierra Leone	143	Japan	5
Guinea-Bissau	140	Iceland	5
Malawi	138	Finland	5

[USA 9] [UK 8]

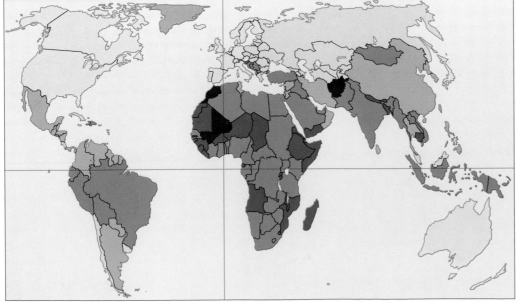

*Statistics for the new republics of the former USSR, Czechoslovakia and Yugoslavia are not yet available.
The map shows the statistics for the entire USSR, Czechoslovakia and Yugoslavia.

ILLITERACY

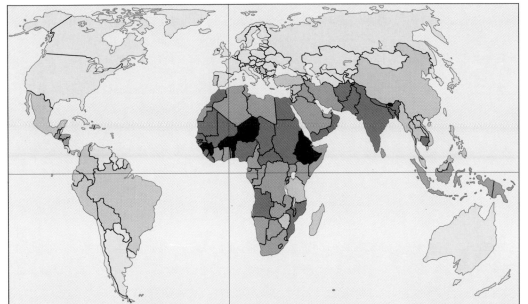

Percentage of the total population unable to read or write (latest available year)*

- Over 75% of population illiterate
- 50 – 75% of population illiterate
- 25 – 50% of population illiterate
- 10 – 15% of population illiterate
- Under 10% of population illiterate

Educational expenditure per person (latest available year)

Top 5 countries		Bottom 5 countries	
Sweden	$997	Chad	$2
Qatar	$989	Bangladesh	$3
Canada	$983	Ethiopia	$3
Norway	$971	Nepal	$4
Switzerland	$796	Somalia	$4

EDUCATION

Percentage of age group in secondary school, selected countries (latest available year)

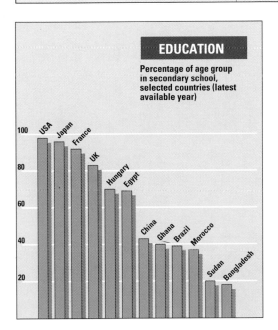

FERTILITY AND EDUCATION

Fertility rates compared with female education, selected countries (latest available year)

- Fertility rate: number of children borne by average woman
- Percentage of female age group in secondary education

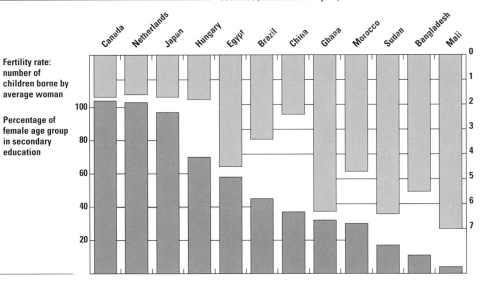

WOMEN IN THE WORKFORCE

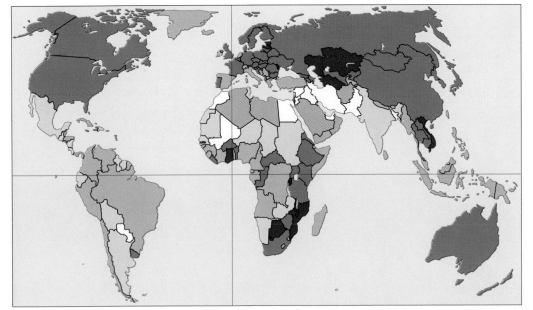

Women in paid employment as a percentage of the total workforce (latest available year)

- Over 50% are women
- 40 – 50% are women
- 30 – 40% are women
- 20 – 30% are women
- 10 – 20% are women
- Under 10% are women

Most women in the workforce		Fewest women in the workforce	
Kazakhstan	54%	Guinea-Bissau	3%
Rwanda	54%	Oman	6%
Botswana	53%	Afghanistan	8%
Burundi	53%	Libya	8%
Mozambique	52%	Algeria	9%

*Statistics for the new republics of the former USSR, Czechoslovakia and Yugoslavia are not yet available.
The map shows the statistics for the entire USSR, Czechoslovakia and Yugoslavia.*

ENERGY

[Each square represents 1% of world energy production]

[Each square represents 1% of world energy consumption]

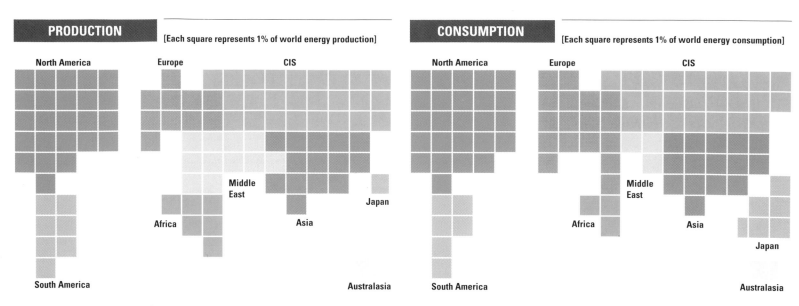

PRODUCTION

North America | Europe | CIS | Middle East | Japan | Africa | Asia | South America | Australasia

CONSUMPTION

North America | Europe | CIS | Middle East | Japan | Africa | Asia | South America | Australasia

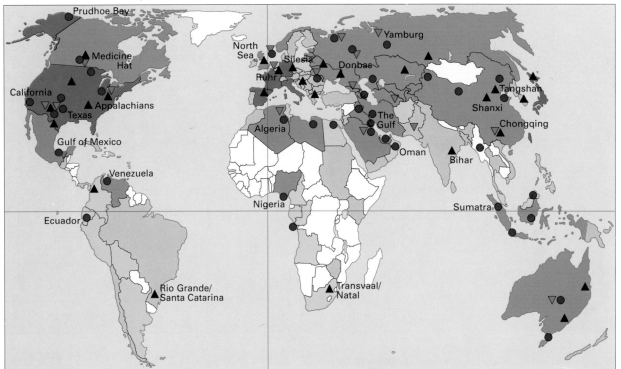

Prudhoe Bay · Medicine Hat · California · Appalachians · Texas · Gulf of Mexico · Venezuela · Ecuador · Rio Grande/Santa Catarina · North Sea · Ruhr · Silesia · Donbas · Yamburg · Algeria · The Gulf · Oman · Nigeria · Transvaal/Natal · Bihar · Shanxi · Tangshan · Chongqing · Sumatra

ENERGY BALANCE

Difference between energy production and consumption in millions of tonnes of oil equivalent (1989)

Energy deficit ↑

Over 35 MtOe

1 – 35 MtOe

Approx. balance

1 – 35 MtOe

Over 35 MtOe

Energy surplus ↓

● Major oilfields

▽ Major gasfields

▲ Major coalfields

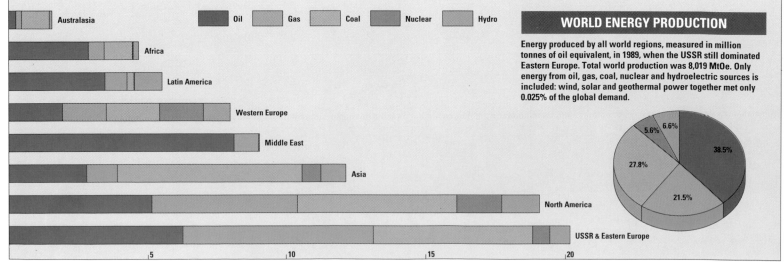

Oil · Gas · Coal · Nuclear · Hydro

Australasia · Africa · Latin America · Western Europe · Middle East · Asia · North America · USSR & Eastern Europe

WORLD ENERGY PRODUCTION

Energy produced by all world regions, measured in million tonnes of oil equivalent, in 1989, when the USSR still dominated Eastern Europe. Total world production was 8,019 MtOe. Only energy from oil, gas, coal, nuclear and hydroelectric sources is included: wind, solar and geothermal power together met only 0.025% of the global demand.

6.6% · 38.5% · 21.5% · 27.8% · 5.6%

Statistics for the new republics of the former USSR, Czechoslovakia and Yugoslavia are not yet available.
The map shows the statistics for the entire USSR, Czechoslovakia and Yugoslavia.

NUCLEAR POWER

Percentage of electricity generated by nuclear power stations, leading nations (1988)

1.	France 70%	11.	Germany (W) 34%
2.	Belgium 66%	12.	Japan 28%
3.	Hungary 49%	13.	Czechoslovakia .. 27%
4.	South Korea 47%	14.	UK 18%
5.	Sweden 46%	15.	USA 17%
6.	Taiwan 41%	16.	Canada 16%
7.	Switzerland 37%	17.	Argentina 12%
8.	Finland 36%	18.	USSR (1989) 11%
9.	Spain 36%	19.	Yugoslavia 6%
10.	Bulgaria 36%	20.	Netherlands 5%

The decade 1980–90 was a bad time for the nuclear power industry. Major projects regularly ran vastly over-budget, and fears of long-term environmental damage were heavily reinforced by the 1986 Soviet disaster at Chernobyl. Although the number of reactors in service continued to increase throughout the period, orders for new plant shrank dramatically, and most countries cut back on their nuclear programmes.

HYDROELECTRICITY

Percentage of electricity generated by hydroelectrical power stations, leading nations (1988)

1.	Paraguay 99.9%	11.	Laos 95.5%
2.	Zambia 99.6%	12.	Nepal 95.2%
3.	Norway............ 99.5%	13.	Iceland 94.0%
4.	Congo 99.1%	14.	Uruguay 93.0%
5.	Costa Rica 98.3%	15.	Brazil 91.7%
6.	Uganda 98.3%	16.	Albania 87.2%
7.	Rwanda 97.7%	17.	Fiji 81.4%
8.	Malawi 97.6%	18.	Ecuador 80.7%
9.	Zaïre 97.4%	19.	C. African Rep. 80.4%
10.	Cameroon 97.2%	20.	Sri Lanka 80.4%

Countries heavily reliant on hydroelectricity are usually small and non-industrial: a high proportion of hydroelectric power more often reflects a modest energy budget than vast hydroelectric resources. The USA, for instance, produces only 8% of power requirements from hydroelectricity; yet that 8% amounts to more than three times the hydro-power generated by all of Africa.

ALTERNATIVE ENERGY SOURCES

Solar: Each year the sun bestows upon the Earth almost a million times as much energy as is locked up in all the planet's oil reserves, but only an insignificant fraction is trapped and used commercially. In some experimental installations, mirrors focus the sun's rays on to boilers, whose steam generates electricity by spinning conventional turbines. Solar cells turn sunlight into electricity directly. Efficiencies are still low, but advancing technology could make the sun a major electricity source by 2100.
Wind: Caused by the uneven heating of the spinning Earth, winds are themselves the product of solar energy. Traditional windmills turn wind power into mechanical work; recent models usually generate electricity. But efficient windmills are expensive to build, and suitable locations are few.
Tidal: The energy from tides is potentially enormous, although only a few installations have been built to exploit it. In theory, at least, waves and currents could also provide almost unimaginable power, and the thermal differences in the ocean depths are another huge well of potential energy.

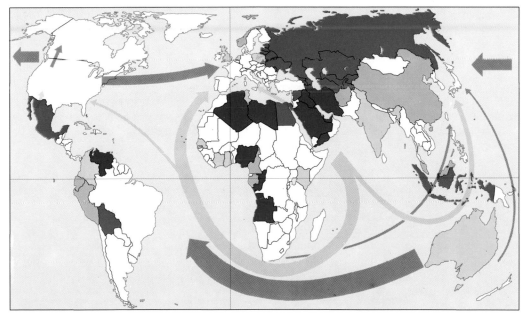

FUEL EXPORTS

Fuels as a percentage of total value of all exports (1986)

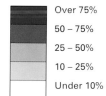

- Over 75%
- 50 – 75%
- 25 – 50%
- 10 – 25%
- Under 10%

Direction of trade

→ Major movements of coal
Major movements of oil

CONVERSIONS

For historical reasons, oil is still traded in 'barrels'. The weight and volume equivalents shown below are all based on average-density 'Arabian light' crude oil.

The energy equivalents given for a tonne of oil are also somewhat imprecise: oil and coal of different qualities will have varying energy contents, a fact usually reflected in their price on world markets.

1 barrel: 0.136 tonnes/159 litres/35 Imperial gallons/42 US gallons. **1 tonne:** 7.33 barrels/1,185 litres/256 Imperial gallons/261 US gallons. **1 tonne oil:** 1.5 tonnes hard coal/3.0 tonnes lignite/12,000 kWh.

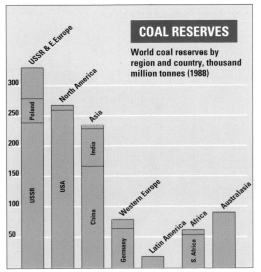

COAL RESERVES

World coal reserves by region and country, thousand million tonnes (1988)

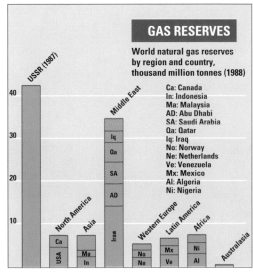

GAS RESERVES

World natural gas reserves by region and country, thousand million tonnes (1988)

Ca: Canada
In: Indonesia
Ma: Malaysia
AD: Abu Dhabi
SA: Saudi Arabia
Qa: Qatar
Iq: Iraq
No: Norway
Ne: Netherlands
Ve: Venezuela
Mx: Mexico
Al: Algeria
Ni: Nigeria

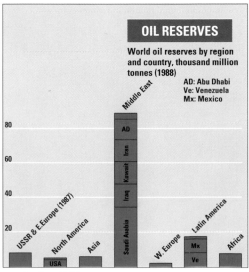

OIL RESERVES

World oil reserves by region and country, thousand million tonnes (1988)

AD: Abu Dhabi
Ve: Venezuela
Mx: Mexico

Statistics for the new republics of the former USSR, Czechoslovakia and Yugoslavia are not yet available.
The map shows the statistics for the entire USSR, Czechoslovakia and Yugoslavia.

PRODUCTION

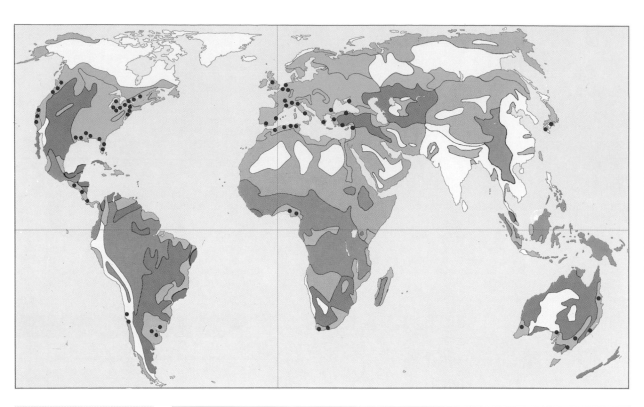

STAPLE CROPS

Separate figures for Russia, Ukraine and the other successors of the former USSR are not yet available

Wheat
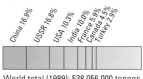
China 16.9% USSR 16.8% USA 10.3% India 10.0% France 5.9% Canada 4.5% Turkey 2.9%

World total (1989): 538,056,000 tonnes

Rice
China 35.4% India 21.2% Indonesia 8.6% Bangladesh 5.3% Thailand 4.2% Vietnam 3.6%

World total (1989): 506,291,000 tonnes

Maize
USA 40.7% China 16.1% Brazil 5.6% USSR 3.6% France 2.7%

World total (1989): 470,318,000 tonnes

Potatoes
USSR 26.0% Poland 12.4% China 10.9% Germany 6.1% USA 6.0% India 5.2%

World total (1989): 276,740,000 tonnes

Millet
India 32.8% China 18.7% USSR 13.1% Nigeria 11.5% Niger 4.2%

World total (1989): 30,512,000 tonnes

Rye
USSR 53.9% Poland 17.8% Germany 11.2% China 2.9% Canada 2.4%

World total (1989): 34,893,000 tonnes

Soya
USA 48.9% Brazil 22.4% China 10.1% Argentina 5.8%

World total (1989): 107,350,000 tonnes

Cassava
Thailand 15.9% Brazil 15.8% Indonesia 11.24% Nigeria 11.19% Zaire 11.1% Tanzania 4.3% India 3.6%

World total (1989): 147,500,000 tonnes

SUGARS

Sugar cane
Brazil 22.4% India 19.7% Cuba 7.3% China 5.5% Mexico 4.0% Pakistan 3.7% Thailand 3.6%

World total (1989): 1,007,184,000 tonnes

Sugar beet
USSR 31.9% Germany 8.8% USA 7.7% France 7.6% Italy 4.9% Poland 4.7% Turkey 4.0%

World total (1989): 305,882,000 tonnes

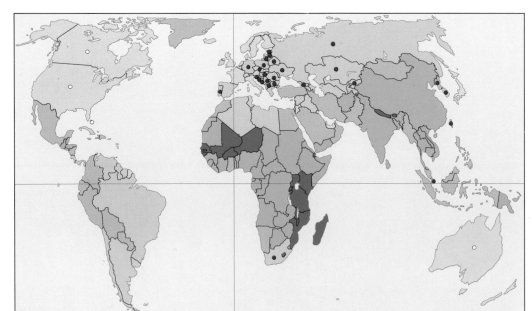

BALANCE OF EMPLOYMENT

Percentage of total workforce employed in agriculture, including forestry and fishing (latest available year)*

- Over 75% in agriculture
- 50 – 75% in agriculture
- 25 – 50% in agriculture
- 10 – 25% in agriculture
- Under 10% in agriculture

- Over 25% of total workforce employed in manufacturing
- Over 75% of total workforce employed in service industries (work in offices, shops, tourism, transport, construction and government)

*Statistics for the new republics of the former USSR, Czechoslovakia and Yugoslavia are not yet available.
The map shows the statistics for the entire USSR, Czechoslovakia and Yugoslavia.

Separate figures for Russia, Ukraine and the other successors of the former USSR are not yet available

Copper
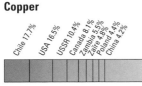
Chile 17.7% | USA 16.5% | USSR 10.4% | Canada 8.1% | Zambia 5.5% | Zaire 4.8% | Poland 4.4% | China 4.2%

World total (1989): 9,100,000 tonnes

Iron
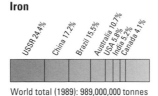
USSR 24.4% | China 17.2% | Brazil 15.5% | Australia 10.7% | USA 5.8% | India 5.2% | Canada 4.1%

World total (1989): 989,000,000 tonnes

Chromium
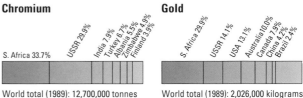
S. Africa 33.7% | USSR 29.9% | India 7.9% | Turkey 6.7% | Albania 5.5% | Zimbabwe 4.9% | Finland 3.9%

World total (1989): 12,700,000 tonnes

Gold
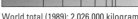
S. Africa 29.9% | USSR 14.1% | USA 13.1% | Australia 10.0% | Canada 7.9% | China 4.2% | Brazil 2.4%

World total (1989): 2,026,000 kilograms

Uranium
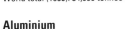
Canada 33.1% | USA 15.6% | Australia 10.8% | France 9.5% | Namibia 9.1% | Niger 8.8% | S. Africa 8.6%

World total (1989): 34,000 tonnes

Lead

USSR 14.7% | Australia 14.6% | USA 12.3% | China 10.1% | Canada 8.1% | Peru 5.1% | Mexico 4.8%

World total (1989): 3,400,000 tonnes

Tin
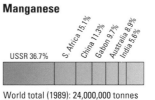
Brazil 22.5% | China 14.6% | Malaysia 14.4% | Indonesia 14.2% | Bolivia 7.1% | Thailand 6.6% | USSR 6.3%

World total (1989): 223,000 tonnes

Manganese
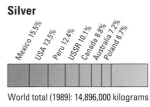
USSR 36.7% | S. Africa 15.1% | China 11.3% | Gabon 9.7% | Australia 8.9% | India 5.6%

World total (1989): 24,000,000 tonnes

Silver
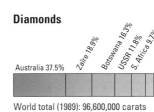
Mexico 15.5% | USA 13.5% | Peru 12.4% | USSR 10.1% | Canada 8.8% | Australia 7.2% | Poland 6.7%

World total (1989): 14,896,000 kilograms

Aluminium
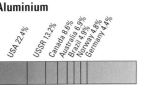
USA 22.4% | USSR 13.2% | Canada 8.6% | Australia 6.9% | Brazil 4.9% | Norway 4.8% | Germany 4.4%

World total (1989): 18,000,000 tonnes

Mercury
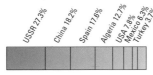
USSR 27.3% | China 18.2% | Spain 17.6% | Algeria 12.7% | USA 7.8% | Mexico 6.3% | Turkey 3.7%

World total (1989): 5,500,000 kilograms

Zinc
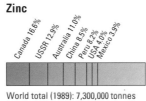
Canada 16.6% | USSR 12.9% | Australia 11.0% | China 8.5% | Peru 8.2% | USA 4.0% | Mexico 3.9%

World total (1989): 7,300,000 tonnes

Nickel
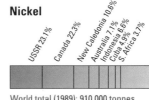
USSR 23.1% | Canada 22.3% | New Caledonia 10.6% | Australia 7.1% | Indonesia 6.6% | Cuba 4.9% | S. Africa 3.7%

World total (1989): 910,000 tonnes

Diamonds

Australia 37.5% | Zaire 18.9% | Botswana 16.3% | USSR 11.8% | S. Africa 9.7%

World total (1989): 96,600,000 carats

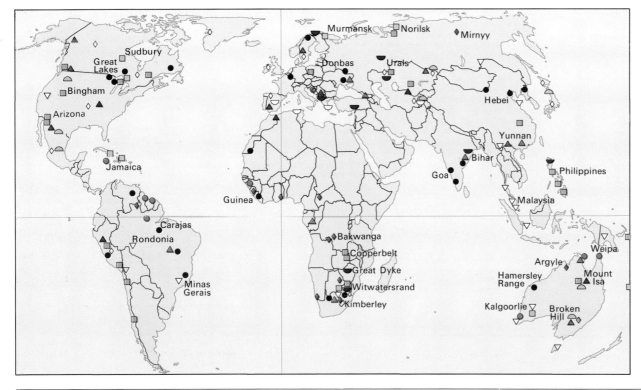

MINERAL DISTRIBUTION

Light metals
- ● Bauxite

Base metals
- ■ Copper
- ▲ Lead
- ▽ Mercury
- ▽ Tin
- ◇ Zinc

Iron and ferro-alloys
- ● Iron
- ◗ Chrome
- ▲ Manganese
- ■ Nickel

Precious metals
- ▽ Gold
- ◠ Silver

Precious stones
- ◆ Diamonds

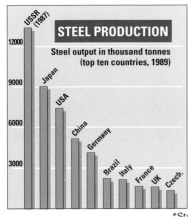

STEEL PRODUCTION
Steel output in thousand tonnes (top ten countries, 1989)

(USSR (1987), Japan, USA, China, Germany, Brazil, Italy, France, UK, Czech.)

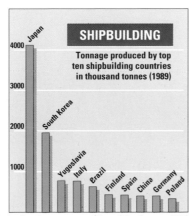

SHIPBUILDING
Tonnage produced by top ten shipbuilding countries in thousand tonnes (1989)

(Japan, South Korea, Yugoslavia, Italy, Brazil, Finland, Spain, China, Germany, Poland)

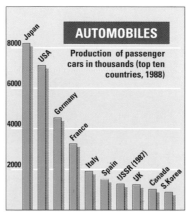

AUTOMOBILES
Production of passenger cars in thousands (top ten countries, 1988)

(Japan, USA, Germany, France, Italy, Spain, USSR (1987), UK, Canada, S.Korea)

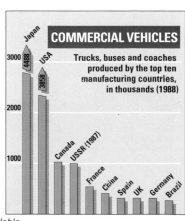

COMMERCIAL VEHICLES
Trucks, buses and coaches produced by the top ten manufacturing countries, in thousands (1988)

(Japan 4488, USA 3858, Canada, USSR (1987), France, China, Spain, UK, Germany, Brazil)

Statistics for the new republics of the former USSR, Czechoslovakia and Yugoslavia are not yet available. The map shows the statistics for the entire USSR, Czechoslovakia and Yugoslavia.

TRADE

SHARE OF WORLD TRADE

Percentage share of total world exports by value (1990)*

Over 10% of world trade

5 – 10% of world trade

1 – 5% of world trade

0.5 – 1% of world trade

0.25 – 0.5% of world trade

Under 0.25% of world trade

International trade is dominated by a handful of powerful maritime nations. The members of 'G7', the inner circle of OECD and the top seven countries listed in the diagram below, account for more than half the total. The majority of nations – including all but four in Africa – contribute less than one quarter of one per cent to the worldwide total of exports; the EC countries account for 40%, the Pacific Rim nations over 35%.

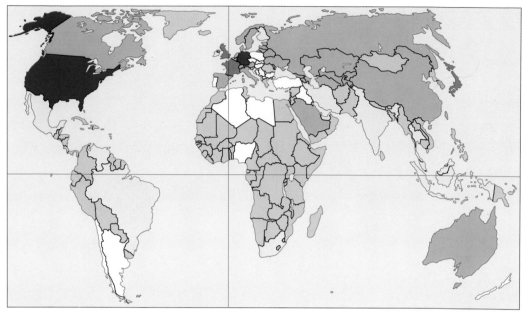

THE GREAT TRADING NATIONS

The imports and exports of the top ten trading nations as a percentage of world trade (latest available year). Each country's trade in manufactured goods is shown in orange.

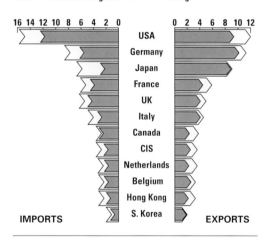

16 14 12 10 8 6 4 2 0   0 2 4 6 8 10 12

USA
Germany
Japan
France
UK
Italy
Canada
CIS
Netherlands
Belgium
Hong Kong
S. Korea

IMPORTS   EXPORTS

PATTERNS OF TRADE

Thriving international trade is the outward sign of a healthy world economy, the obvious indicator that some countries have goods to sell and others the wherewithal to buy them. Despite local fluctuations, trade throughout the 1980s grew consistently faster than output, increasing in value by almost 50% in the decade 1979–89. It remains dominated by the rich, industrialized countries of the Organization for Economic Development: between them, OECD members account for almost 75% of world imports and exports in most years. OECD dominance is just as marked in the trade in 'invisibles' – a column in the balance sheet that includes among other headings the export of services, interest payments on overseas investments, tourism and even remittances from migrant workers abroad. In the UK, invisibles account for more than half all trading income.

However, the size of these great trading economies means that imports and exports usually make up only a fraction of their total wealth: in the case of the famously export-conscious Japanese, trade in goods and services amounts to less than 18% of GDP. In poorer countries, trade – often in a single commodity – may amount to 50% GDP or more.

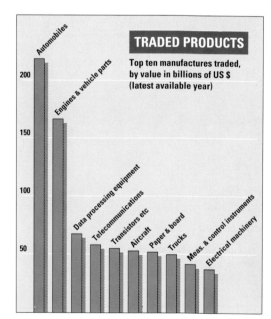

TRADED PRODUCTS

Top ten manufactures traded, by value in billions of US $ (latest available year)

BALANCE OF TRADE

Value of exports in proportion to the value of imports (latest available year)

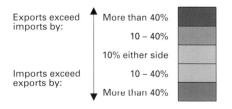

Exports exceed imports by:

More than 40%

10 – 40%

10% either side

Imports exceed exports by:

10 – 40%

More than 40%

The total world trade balance should amount to zero, since exports must equal imports on a global scale. In practice, at least $100 billion in exports go unrecorded, leaving the world with an apparent deficit and many countries in a better position than public accounting reveals. However, a favourable trade balance is not necessarily a sign of prosperity: many poorer countries must maintain a high surplus in order to service debts, and do so by restricting imports below the levels needed to sustain successful economies.

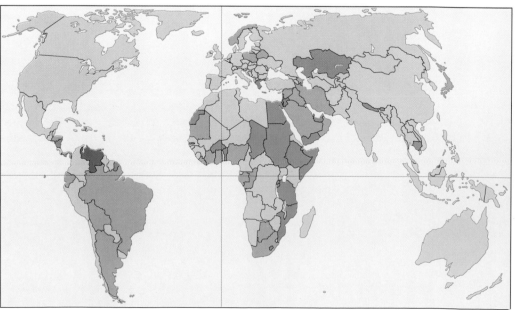

*Statistics for the new republics of the former USSR, Czechoslovakia and Yugoslavia are not yet available.
The map shows the statistics for the entire USSR, Czechoslovakia and Yugoslavia.

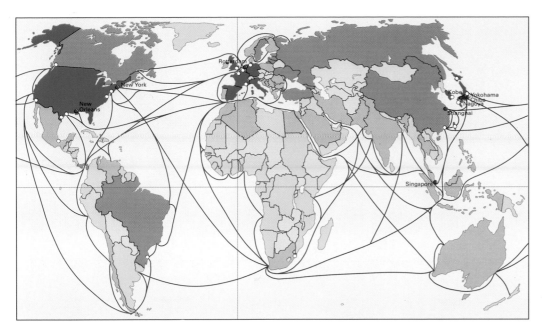

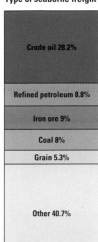

FREIGHT

Freight unloaded in millions of tonnes (latest available year)*

- Over 100
- 50 – 100
- 10 – 50
- 5 – 10
- Under 5
- Landlocked countries

Major seaports

- ● Over 100 million tonnes per year
- ○ 50 – 100 million tonnes per year

CARGOES

Type of seaborne freight

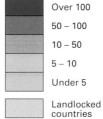

- Crude oil 28.2%
- Refined petroleum 8.8%
- Iron ore 9%
- Coal 8%
- Grain 5.3%
- Other 40.7%

MERCHANT FLEETS

National merchant fleets in thousand deadweight tonnes (1989). The chart records national ownership, not necessarily registry. The countries listed account for 83% of world shipping. The division of the former Soviet fleet among the USSR's successor republics was still incomplete in 1992.

France
Cyprus
Singapore
Iran
Taiwan
Denmark
India
Brazil
Italy
Germany
South Korea
China
UK
Hong Kong
USSR (1988)
Norway
USA
Japan
Greece

20,000   40,000   60,000   80,000

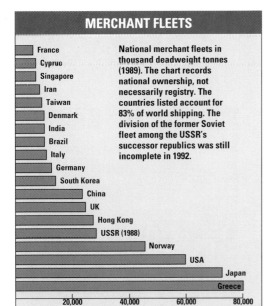

WORLD SHIPPING

World merchant fleet by type of vessel and deadweight tonnage (1989)

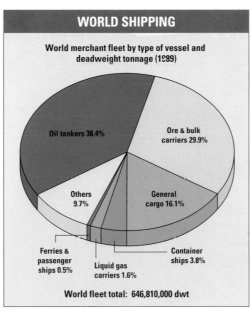

- Oil tankers 38.4%
- Ore & bulk carriers 29.9%
- General cargo 16.1%
- Others 9.7%
- Container ships 3.8%
- Liquid gas carriers 1.6%
- Ferries & passenger ships 0.5%

World fleet total: 646,810,000 dwt

THE GREAT PORTS

The world's ten busiest ports by million tonnes of shipping arrivals (late 1980s)

Singapore
Rotterdam
Yokohama
Los Angeles
Antwerp
Hong Kong
Europoort
New Orleans
Hamburg
Kobe

30
25
20
15
10
5

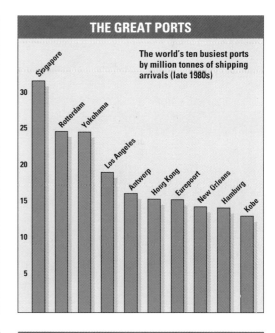

DEPENDENCE ON TRADE

Value of exports as a percentage of Gross Domestic Product (1991)

- Over 50% GDP
- 40 – 50% GDP
- 30 – 40% GDP
- 20 – 30% GDP
- 10 – 20% GDP
- Under 10% GDP
- ● Most dependent on industrial exports (over 75% of total exports)
- ● Most dependent on fuel exports (over 75% of total exports)
- ○ Most dependent on mineral and metal exports (over 75% of total exports)

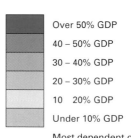

*Statistics for the new republics of the former USSR, Czechoslovakia and Yugoslavia are not yet available.
The map shows the statistics for the entire USSR, Czechoslovakia and Yugoslavia.

CARTOGRAPHY BY PHILIP'S. COPYRIGHT REED INTERNATIONAL BOOKS LTD

TRAVEL AND TOURISM

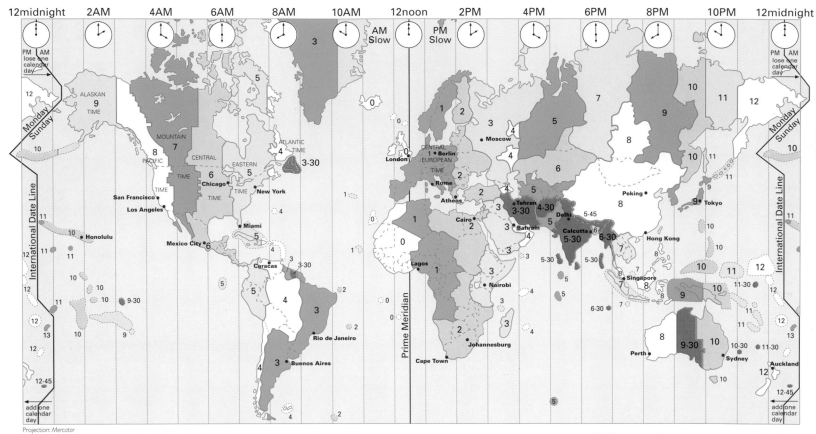

Projection: Mercator

TIME ZONES

Zones slow or fast of Greenwich Mean Time

Half-hour zones

The time when it is 12 noon at Greenwich

RAIL AND ROAD: THE LEADING NATIONS

Total rail network ('000 km)		Passenger km per head per year		Total road network ('000 km)		Vehicle km per head per year		Vehicle km per head per year per km road network	
1. USSR (1986)	247.2	Japan	2,745	1. USA	623.3	USA	12,505	Hong Kong	4,705.7
2. USA	225.4	Switzerland	1,523	2. Brazil	167.4	Luxembourg	7,989	Kuwait	3,433.4
3. Canada	65.8	Germany (E:'87)	1,353	3. USSR (1986)	158.6	Kuwait	7,251	Jordan	1,321.4
4. India	61.8	Czech'vakia	1,286	4. India	155.4	France	7,142	UK	929.6
5. China	52.6	Poland	1,282	5. Japan	110.4	Sweden	6,991	Italy	923.4
6. Germany	41.4	USSR	1,276	6. China	98.2	Germany	6,806	Germany	843.8
7. Australia	39.3	France	1,074	7. Australia	85.3	Denmark	6,764	Netherlands	761.4
8. France	34.6	Austria	971	8. Canada	84.4	Austria	6,518	Tunisia	726.4
9. Argentina	34.1	Denmark	937	9. France	80.5	Netherlands	5,984	Iraq	657.2
10. Poland	24.2	Hungary	906	10. Germany	49.4	UK	5,738	Luxembourg	581.3
11. South Africa	23.8	Bulgaria	897	11. Poland	36.1	Canada	5,493	Japan	497.0
12. Brazil	22.1	South Africa	873	12. UK	35.2	Italy	4,852	USA	494.2
13. Mexico	20.0	Italy	722	13. Turkey	32.1	Belgium	4,821	Denmark	491.0
14. Japan	19.9	Sweden	716	14. Spain	31.8	Japan	4,476	Austria	464.9
15. UK	16.6	Germany (W:'88)	640	15. Italy	30.2	South Africa	2,776	France	459.6

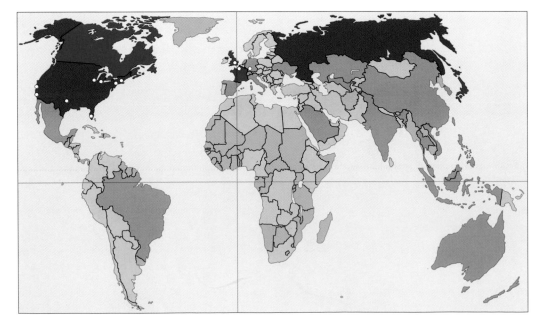

AIR TRAVEL

Passenger kilometres [the number of passengers, international and domestic, multiplied by the distance flown by each passenger from the airport of origin] (latest available year)

Over 100,000 million

50,000 – 100,000 million

10,000 – 50,000 million

1,000 – 10,000 million

500 – 1,000 million

Under 500 million

○ Major airports (handling over 20 million passengers in 1991)

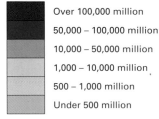

World's busiest airports (total passengers)		World's busiest airports (international passengers)	
1. Chicago	(O'Hare)	1. London	(Heathrow)
2. Atlanta	(Hatsfield)	2. London	(Gatwick)
3. Los Angeles	(Intern'l)	3. Frankfurt	(International)
4. Dallas	(Dallas/Ft Worth)	4. New York	(Kennedy)
5. London	(Heathrow)	5. Paris	(De Gaulle)

DESTINATIONS

- ■ Cultural & historical centres
- □ Coastal resorts
- □ Ski resorts
- ▨ Centres of entertainment
- ▨ Places of pilgrimage
- ▨ Places of great natural beauty

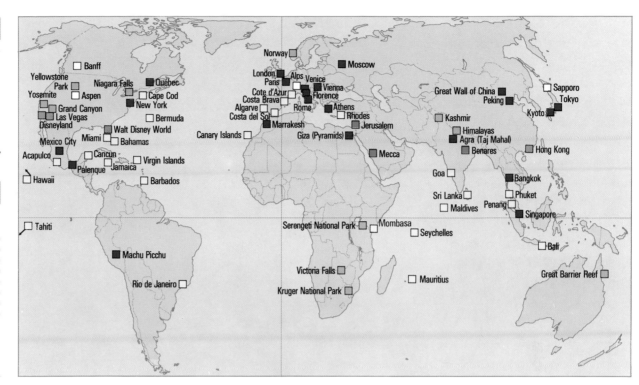

Norway · Moscow · London · Paris · Alps · Venice · Vienna · Cote d'Azur · Florence · Costa Brava · Rome · Athens · Rhodes · Algarve · Costa del Sol · Marrakesh · Jerusalem · Canary Islands · Giza (Pyramids) · Mecca · Great Wall of China · Peking · Sapporo · Tokyo · Kyoto · Kashmir · Himalayas · Agra (Taj Mahal) · Benares · Hong Kong · Goa · Bangkok · Sri Lanka · Phuket · Penang · Maldives · Singapore · Bali · Great Barrier Reef · Serengeti National Park · Mombasa · Seychelles · Mauritius · Victoria Falls · Kruger National Park

Banff · Yellowstone Park · Yosemite · Niagara Falls · Québec · Cape Cod · Aspen · New York · Grand Canyon · Las Vegas · Bermuda · Disneyland · Walt Disney World · Mexico City · Miami · Bahamas · Acapulco · Cancun · Virgin Islands · Palenque · Jamaica · Barbados · Hawaii · Tahiti · Machu Picchu · Rio de Janeiro

VISITORS TO THE USA

International visitors spending in US $ million (1989)

1. Japan 7,480
2. Canada 6,020
3. Mexico 4,170
4. UK 4,130
5. Germany..................... 2,450
6. France 1,290
7. Australia 1,120
8. All others....................16,380

A record 38.3 million foreigners visited the US in 1989, about 70% of them on vacation. Between them they spent $43 billion.

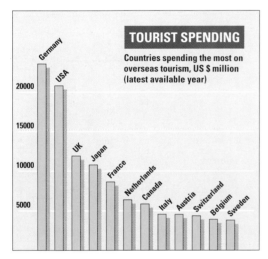

TOURIST SPENDING

Countries spending the most on overseas tourism, US $ million (latest available year)

Germany · USA · UK · Japan · France · Netherlands · Canada · Italy · Austria · Switzerland · Belgium · Sweden

IMPORTANCE OF TOURISM

	Arrivals from abroad (1987)	Receipts as % of GDP (1987)
1. France	36,820,000	1.4%
2. Spain	32,900,000	5.1%
3. USA	28,790,000	0.4%
4. Italy	25,750,000	1.6%
5. Austria	15,760,000	6.5%
6. UK	15,445,000	1.5%
7. Canada	15,040,000	0.9%
8. Germany	12,780,000	0.7%
9. Hungary	11,830,000	3.2%
10. Switzerland	11,600,000	3.1%
11. China	10,760,000	0.7%
12. Greece	7,564,000	4.7%

Small economies in attractive areas are often completely dominated by tourism: in some West Indian islands, tourist spending provides over 90% of total income. In cash terms the USA is the world leader: its 1987 earnings exceeded $15 billion, though that sum amounted to only 0.4% of GDP.

TOURIST EARNING

Countries receiving the most from overseas tourism, US $ million (latest available year)

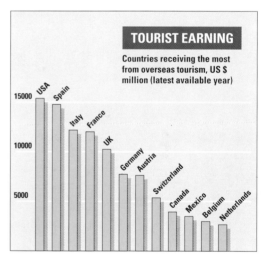

USA · Spain · Italy · France · UK · Germany · Austria · Switzerland · Canada · Mexico · Belgium · Netherlands

TOURISM

Receipts from tourism as a percentage of Gross National Product (1990)*

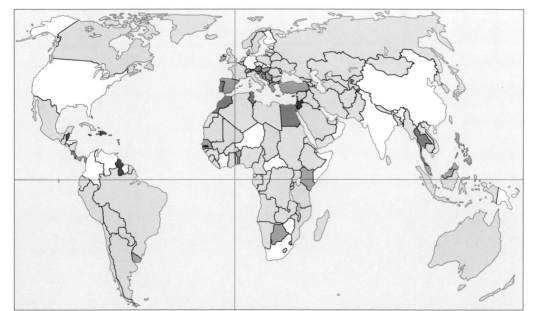

- ■ Over 10% of GNP from tourism
- ▨ 5 – 10% of GNP from tourism
- ▨ 2.5 – 5% of GNP from tourism
- ▨ 1 – 2.5% of GNP from tourism
- □ 0.5 – 1% of GNP from tourism
- ▨ Under 0.5% of GNP from tourism

Largest percentage share of total spending on tourism (1991)

USA	16%
Germany	13%
Japan	10%
UK	7%
Italy	6%

Largest percentage share of total world receipts from tourism (1991)

USA	16%
France	8%
Italy	8%
Spain	7%
UK	6%

Statistics for the new republics of the former USSR, Czechoslovakia and Yugoslavia are not yet available. The map shows the statistics for the entire USSR, Czechoslovakia and Yugoslavia.

SUBJECT INDEX

Acid Rain, 15
Agricultural Employment, 26
Agriculture, 26
Air Travel, 30
Alternative Energy Sources, 25
Automobiles, 27
Beaufort Scale, 11
Child Mortality, 22
Climate, 10–11
Climatic Change, 14
Coal, 25
Commercial Vehicles, 27
Continental Drift, 4
Day and Night, 2
Deforestation, 15
Demographic Profiles, 16
Desertification, 15
Earth's Structure, 4
Earthquakes, 4
Eclipses, 3
Education, 23
Energy, 24–25
Erosion, 7
Faults, 6
Female Employment, 23
Fertility, 23
Fishing, 9
Folds, 6
Food Consumption, 22
Foreign Aid, 21
Forestry, 13
Freight, 29
Fuel Exports, 25
Gas, 25
Glaciers, 7
Global Warming, 14
Greenhouse Effect, 14
Gross National Product, 20
Holiday Destinations, 31
Hospital Beds, 22
Household Spending, 21
Hydroelectricity, 25
Hydrological Cycle, 12
Illiteracy, 23
Infectious Disease, 22

Inflation, 20
International Aid, 21
International Debt, 21
International Organizations, 19
Land Use, 13
Language, 18
Life Expectancy, 22
Mercalli Scale, 4
Merchant Fleets, 29
Minerals, 27
Moon, 3
Mountain Building, 6
Natural Vegetation, 13
Nuclear Power, 25
Oceans, 8
Ocean Currents, 8
Oil, 25
Planets, 2
Plate Tectonics, 5
Pollution, 9
Population Density, 16–17
Ports, 29
Railways, 30
Richter Scale, 4
Religion, 18
Rivers, 7
Roads, 30
Sea-floor Spreading, 6
Seaborne Freight, 29
Seasons, 2
Shipbuilding, 27
Solar System, 2
Staple Crops, 26
Steel Production, 27
Sugar, 26
Tides, 3
Time Zones, 30
Tourism, 31
Trade, 28–29
Travel, 30
United Nations, 19
Urban Population, 17
Volcanoes, 5
Water, 12
Windchill Factor, 11

WORLD
MAPS

SETTLEMENTS

◻ PARIS   ▪ Berne   ◉ Livorno   ● Brugge   ◉ Algeciras   ○ Fréjus   ○ Oberammergau   ○ Thira

Settlement symbols and type styles vary according to the scale of each map and indicate the importance
of towns on the map rather than specific population figures

∴   Ruins or Archæological Sites   ⌣   Wells in Desert

───── ADMINISTRATION ─────

───── International Boundaries

─ ─ ─ International Boundaries
(Undefined or Disputed)

⎯·⎯· Internal Boundaries

National Parks

Country Names

NICARAGUA

Administrative
Area Names

K E N T

CALABRIA

International boundaries show the *de facto* situation where there are rival claims to territory

───── COMMUNICATIONS ─────

───── Principal Roads

⌣⌣ Other Roads

·─·─· Trails and Seasonal Roads

≍ Passes

✿ Airfields

⌣ Principal Railways

·⌣· Railways
Under Construction

⌣ Other Railways

╕---╘ Railway Tunnels

⫴⫴⫴ Principal Canals

───── PHYSICAL FEATURES ─────

⌣ Perennial Streams

·⌣· Intermittent Streams

⬭ Perennial Lakes

⬭ Intermittent Lakes

⬭ Swamps and Marshes

▱ Permanent Ice
and Glaciers

▴ 8848   Elevations in metres

▾ 8050   Sea Depths in metres

1134   Height of Lake Surface
Above Sea Level
in metres

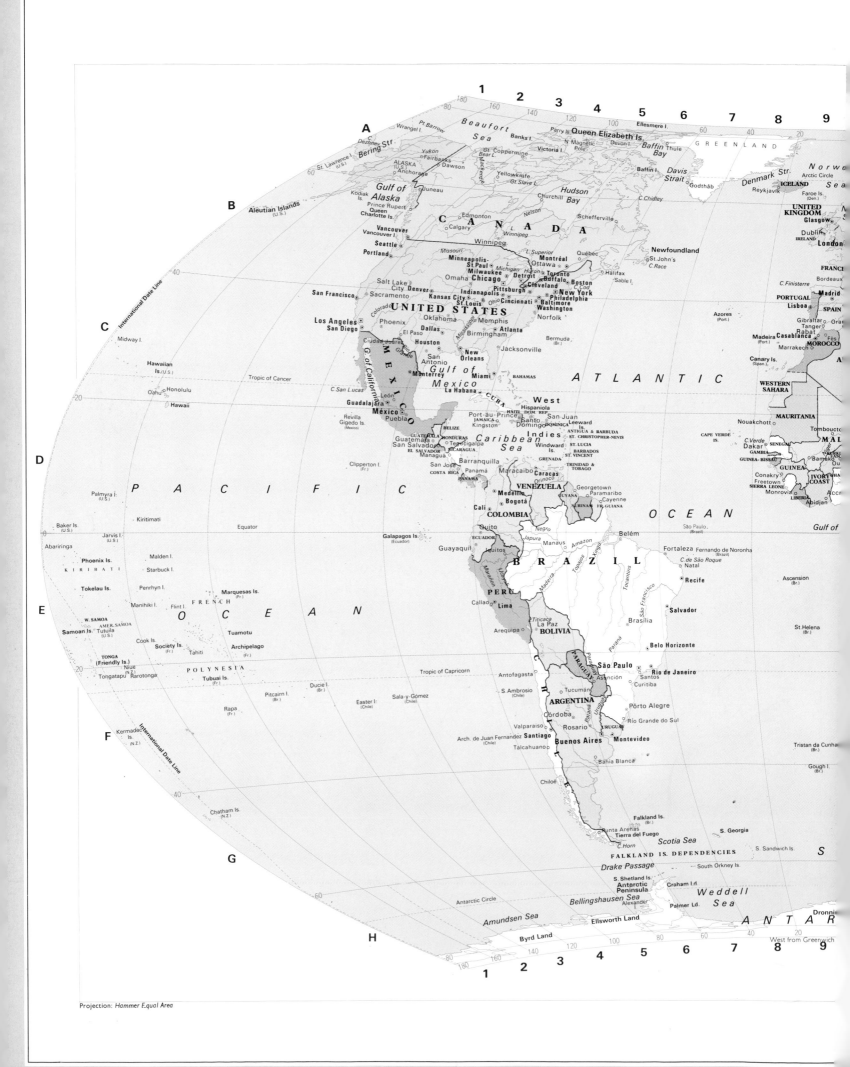

1 2 3 4 5 6 7 8 9

A

Beaufort
Sea

Pt.Barrow
Wrangel I.
St.Lawrence I.
(U.S.)
Dezhnev Str.
Bering Str.
Yukon
Fairbanks
ALASKA
(U.S.)
Anchorage
Dawson

Banks I.
Parry Is.
Queen Elizabeth Is.
N.Magnetic
Pole
Victoria I.
Gt.Coppermine
Bear L.
Mackenzie
Yellowknife
Gt.Slave L.

Devon I.
Ellesmere I.
Baffin I.
Baffin
Bay
C.Chidley

GREENLAND
Arctic Circle
Thule
Godthåb
Davis
Strait
Denmark Str.
ICELAND
Reykjavik
Faroe Is.
(Den.)

Norwe
Sea

B

Aleutian Islands
(U.S.)
Gulf of
Alaska
Juneau
Kodiak
Is.
Prince Rupert
Queen
Charlotte Is.
Vancouver
Vancouver I.
Seattle
Portland

CANADA
Edmonton
Calgary
Winnipeg
Winnipeg
Missouri
Nelson
Churchill
Hudson
Bay
Schefferville

UNITED
KINGDOM
Glasgow
Dublin
IRELAND
London
FRANCE

C

San Francisco
Sacramento
Salt Lake
City
Denver
Los Angeles
San Diego
Phoenix
El Paso
Ciudad Juárez
Rio Grande
G. of California

Minneapolis
St.Paul
Milwaukee
Chicago
L.Superior
L.Michigan
L.Huron
Detroit
Omaha
Indianapolis
L.Ontario
Ohio
Cincinnati
Kansas City
St.Louis
Pittsburgh
UNITED STATES
Oklahoma
Colorado
Missouri
Mississippi
Memphis
Dallas
Houston
San
Antonio
Monterrey
New
Orleans

Montréal
Ottawa
Québec
Toronto
Buffalo
Cleveland
Boston
New York
Philadelphia
Baltimore
Washington
Norfolk
C.Cod
Halifax
Sable I.
St.John's
C.Race
Newfoundland

Bermuda
(Br.)

Atlanta
Birmingham
Jacksonville
Miami
Gulf of
Mexico
BAHAMAS
La Habana
CUBA
West

C.Finisterre
Bordeaux
Azores
(Port.)
PORTUGAL
Lisboa
Madeira
(Port.)
Gibraltar
Tanger
Rabat
SPAIN
MADRID
Oran
Casablanca
Fès
Marrakech
MOROCCO

D

PACIFIC
Midway I.
Hawaiian
Is.(U.S.)
Oahu Honolulu
Hawaii
Tropic of Cancer

Revilla
Gigedo Is.
(Mexico)
C.San Lucas
León
Guadalajara
México
Puebla
MEXICO
BELIZE
GUATEMALA
Guatemala
HONDURAS
San Salvador
EL SALVADOR Tegucigalpa
Managua
NICARAGUA
COSTA RICA
San José
Panamá
PANAMA

Clipperton I.
(Fr.)

Hispaniola
HAITI DOM.REP.
Port-au-Prince
Santo
Domingo
San Juan
JAMAICA
Kingston
Indies
DOMINICA
Leeward
Is.
ANTIGUA & BARBUDA
ST.CHRISTOPHER-NEVIS
ST.LUCIA
Windward
Is.
BARBADOS
ST.VINCENT
GRENADA
TRINIDAD &
TOBAGO
Caribbean
Sea
Barranquilla
Maracaibo
Caracas
Cartagena
VENEZUELA
Georgetown
GUYANA
Paramaribo
SURINAM
Cayenne
FR.GUIANA

ATLANTIC
WESTERN
SAHARA
Canary Is.
(Span.)
Nouakchott
MAURITANIA
Tombouctou
CAPE VERDE
IS.
C.Verde
Dakar
SENEGAL
GAMBIA
GUINEA-BISSAU
Conakry
GUINEA
Freetown
SIERRA LEONE
Monrovia
LIBERIA
MALI
NIGER
Bamako
Ou
IVORY
COAST
Abidjan

OCEAN
Gulf of

E

Palmyra I.
(U.S.)
Baker Is.
(U.S.)
Jarvis I.
(U.S.)
Abariringa
Kiritimati
Phoenix Is.
Malden I.
KIRIBATI
Starbuck I.
Tokelau Is.
Penrhyn I.
Manihiki I.
Marquesas Is.
(Fr.)
Flint I.
FRENCH
W.SAMOA
AMER.SAMOA
Samoan Is.
(U.S.)
Tutuila
Equator

Quito
ECUADOR
Galapagos Is.
(Ecuador)
Guayaquil
Iquitos
Medellín
Bogotá
Cali
COLOMBIA
Negro
Japurá
Manaus
Amazon
Marañón
Ucayali
Madeira
BRAZIL
Juruá
Purus
Tapajós
Xingu
Belém
São Paulo
(Brazil)
Fortaleza
Fernando de Noronha
(Brazil)
C.de São Roque
Natal
Recife
Tocantins

OCEAN
Ascension
(Br.)

F

Society Is.
(Fr.)
Cook Is.
Tahiti
Archipelago
TONGA
(Friendly Is.)
Tongatapu
(N.Z.)
Niue
(N.Z.)
Rarotonga
POLYNESIA
Tubuai Is.
(Fr.)
Tropic of Capricorn
Tuamotu

Antofagasta
S.Ambrosio
(Chile)
S.Félix
(Chile)
Tucumán
Easter I.
(Chile)
Sala-y-Gómez
(Chile)
Pitcairn I.
(Br.)
Ducie I.
(Br.)
Rapa
(Fr.)
Kermadec
Is.
(N.Z.)
International Date Line
Valparaíso
Santiago
Arch.de Juan Fernández
(Chile)
Talcahuano
Córdoba
Rosario
ARGENTINA
PERU
Callao
Lima
Arequipa
Titicaca
La Paz
BOLIVIA
Brasília
São Francisco
Paraguay
PARAGUAY
Asunción
Paraná
Belo Horizonte
São Paulo
Santos
Curitiba
Rio de Janeiro
Pôrto Alegre
Río Grande do Sul
URUGUAY
Uruguay
Montevideo
Buenos Aires
Bahía Blanca

Salvador
Brasília
St.Helena
(Br.)
Tristan da Cunha
(Br.)
Gough I.
(Br.)

G

CHILE
Chiloé
Falkland Is.
(Br.)
S.Georgia
Punta Arenas
Tierra del Fuego
C.Horn
Scotia Sea
S.Sandwich Is.
FALKLAND IS.DEPENDENCIES
Drake Passage
South Orkney Is.

S

H

Antarctic Circle
Byrd Land
Amundsen Sea
Ellsworth Land
S.Shetland Is.
Antarctic
Peninsula
Graham Ld.
Bellingshausen Sea
Alexander
Palmer Ld.
Weddell
Sea
ANTAR
Dronni

West from Greenwich

1 2 3 4 5 6 7 8 9

Projection: *Hammer Equal Area*

ARCTIC   OCEAN
10   11   12   13   14   15   16   17   18   180
60   20   40   80   100   120   140   160
Svalbard   Zemlya Frantsa Iosifa   Severnaya   Laptev Sea   New Siberian Is.   East Siberian
(Norway)   Novaya Zemlya   Zemlya   Tiksi   Sea
Barents Sea   Kara   Ust-Port   Verkhoyansk   Nizhne-Kolymsk   Arctic Circle   A
Nord Kapp   Sea   Yenisey   Lena   Anadyr
Narvik   Murmansk   Arkhangelsk   Salekhard   Vilyuysk   Yakutsk   Bering
NORWAY   R   U   S   S   I   A   Okhotsk   Sea
SWEDEN   FINLAND   Perm   Tomsk   Kamchatka   B
Helsinki   Yekaterinburg   Krasnoyarsk   L. Baykal   Petropavlovsk-
Oslo   Stockholm   EST   Yaroslavl   Kazan   Novosibirsk   Ulan   Okhotsk   Sakhalin   Kamchatskiy
København   Moskva   Chelyabinsk   Omsk   Novokuznetsk   Ude   Irkutsk   C.Lopatka
DENMARK   LATVIA   Samara   Ufa   Irtysh   Ulaanbaatar   Komsomolsk
Hamburg   LITH   BELO   Saratov   Orenburg   Barnaul   Khabarovsk
Amsterdam   Berlin   POLAND   Warszawa   Minsk   Voronezh   KAZAKHSTAN   MONGOLIA   Amur   Kuril Is.
Brussel   GERM   Praha   Kiyev   Volga   Volgograd   Karaganda   L.Balkhash   Harbin   Vladivostok   Sapporo
Paris   Budapest   UKRAINE   Kharkov   Rostov   Astrakhan   Alma Ata   Changchun   N.KOREA   Hakodate
AUSTRIA   Lvov   Shenyang   Sea of
Torino   Beograd   ROMANIA   Odessa   Caspian   Aral   Beijing   Tianjin   Dalian   KOREA   Japan   Tōkyō
Milano   YUG   Bucuresti   Black   Grozny   Sea   Sea   UZBEKISTAN   CHINA   Pyŏngyang   JAPAN   Yokohama
Roma   Sofiya   BULGARIA   Sea   Tbilisi   Samarkand   Tashkent   Taiyuan   Jinan   Qingdao   Sŏul   Kyoto
Marseille   ITALY   GREECE   Istanbul   GEO   Yerevan   Baku   TURKMENISTAN   Lanzhou   Xi'an   Pusan   Kōbe   Nagoya
Barcelona   Sardinia   Izmir   TURKEY   Ankara   AZ.   Ashkhabad   TA   Huang   Kitakyūshū   Ōsaka
Napoli   Sicily   Athinai   Tabriz   Mashhad   Srinagar   Chengdu   Wuhan   Shanghai   C
Valencia   MALTA   Crete   CYPRUS   SYRIA   Halab   Tehrān   AFGHANISTAN   Kabul   Lahore   XIZANG   Lhasa   Chongqing   Changsha   East China
Alger   Tunis   TUNISIA   Dimashq   Baghdad   Rawalpindi   (TIBET)   NEPAL   Kunming   Fuzhou   Sea
Tarābulus   Bayrūt   El   Tel Aviv-Yafo   Amman   IRAQ   Ābādān   IRAN   Esfahan   Delhi   KATH   BHU   Guangzhou   Taibei
Banghāzī   Iskandarīya   Jerusalem   Būr Sa'īd   KWT   Shiraz   PAKISTAN   Agra   Kanpur   Lucknow   BANGLA   Dhaka   Hong Kong   TAIWAN   Tropic of Cancer
ERIA   Ain Salah   El Qāhira   The Gulf   Karachi   INDIA   Ganga   Calcutta   BURMA   Mandalay   Hainan   PACIFIC   20
LIBYA   EGYPT   Ar Riyād   QATAR   BAHRAIN   Ahmadābād   Nagpur   Bay of   (MYANMAR)   Hanoi   South   NORTHERN   Wake I.
Aswân   SAUDI   U.A.E.   Arabian   Bombay   Pune   Bengal   Rangoon   VIET-   China   MARIANAS   (U.S.)
Makkah   ARABIA   OMAN   Sea   Hyderabad   THAILAND   NAM   Sea   OCEAN
NIGER   CHAD   Omdurmân   El Khartûm   YEMEN   Bangalore   Madras   Andaman Is.   Bangkok   Manila   Guam   D
Niamey   Red   SUDAN   Gulf of Aden   Socotra   Lakshadweep Is.   Nicobar Is.   CAMBODIA   PHILIPPINES   (U.S.)
Kano   L.Chad   Ndjamena   Asmera   ERITREA   (Yemen)   (India)   Phanh Bho   Cebu   FEDERATED STATES
NIGERIA   DJIBOUTI   SRI LANKA   Nicobar Is.   Ho Chi Minh   Yap   Truk   MARSHALL IS.
Ibadan   CENTRAL   Addis Abeba   SOMALI REP.   (CEYLON)   (India)   Ponape   OF MICRONESIA
Lagos   CAMEROON   AFRICAN   Bangui   ETHIOPIA   Colombo   MALAYSIA   BELAU   Caroline Is.
Douala   REPUBLIC   Yaoundé   MALDIVES   Dondra Hd.   Kuala Lumpur   SABAH   Ponape
EQUATORIAL   Libreville   Zaïre   Kisangani   UGANDA   KENYA   Medan   PEN.MALAYSIA   GABON   NAURU   Gilbert Is.
Guinea   SÃO TOMÉ   (Congo)   Kampala   Equator   Singapore   Borneo   Kuching   KIRIBATI
& PRINCIPE   GABON   ZAÏRE   Victoria   Nairobi   INDIAN   Banjarmasin   Sulawesi   Maluku   Irian
Brazzaville   (CONGO)   Mombasa   SEYCHELLES   Palembang   INDONESIA   Jaya   PAPUA   New Ireland   E
CABINDA   Kinshasa   Kasai   L.   Zanzibar   Amirante   Chagos Arch.   Ujung Pandang   NEW   Rabaul
Luanda   Kananga   Tanganyika   Dar es Salaam   Is.   (Br.)   Jakarta   Jawa   Surabaya   GUINEA   New   SOLOMON
TANZANIA   Aldabra   Diego Garcia   Bandung   Port   Britain   IS.   TUVALU
Benguela   Kubumbashi   (Br.)   Moresby   Louisiade
ANGOLA   COMORO   Cocos   Timor   Arafura Sea   Arch.   Santa Cruz Is.
ZAMBIA   IS.   Christmas I.   Sea   C.York   Timor
Lusaka   Malawi   (Keeling Is.)   (Australia)   Darwin   VANUATU
ZIMBABWE   MOZAMBIQUE   MADAGASCAR   (Australia)   NORTHERN   Cairns   Vanua Levu   20
NAMIBIA   Bulawayo   Zomba   Antananarivo   Rodriguez   TERRITORY   Townsville   FIJI   Viti Levu   Suva
Harare   Tropic of Capricorn   North West C.   WESTERN   QUEENSLAND   New   F
Windhoek   MAURITIUS   Réunion   AUSTRALIA   Alice Springs   Caledonia
BOTSWANA   (Fr.)   AUSTRALIA   (Fr.)
WEST   Gaborone   SWZ   Pretoria   Amsterdam   Perth   Kalgoorlie-   SOUTH   Rockhampton   Norfolk I.
SOUTH   Johannesburg   Maputo   (Fr.)   Fremantle   Boulder   AUSTRALIA   Brisbane   (Australia)
AFRICA   LES   Durban   St.Paul   C.Leeuwin   Darling   NEW SOUTH   Lord Howe
Cape Town   Port Elizabeth   (Fr.)   Great   Adelaide   WALES   Newcastle   (Australia)
C.of Good Hope   Australian   VICTORIA   Sydney   North C.
Bight   Canberra   Auckland
SOUTHERN   OCEAN   TASMANIA   Melbourne   Tasman   NEW   North I.
Pr.Edward Is.   Crozet Is.   Hobart   Sea   ZEALAND
(South Africa)   (Fr.)   C.Farewell   Wellington
Kerguelen   Stewart I.   Christchurch
(Fr.)   Dunedin   South I.
Bouvet I.   Antipodes Is.
(Norway)   McDonald I.   Heard I.   (N.Z.)   40
(Australia)   (Australia)   Bounty Is.
(N.Z.)
ud Land   Macquarie I.   Campbell I.   G
CTICA   (Australia)   (N.Z.)
East from Greenwich   Antarctic Circle   Balleny Is.
Enderby   Wilkes Land   S.Magnetic Pole   60
Land   Ross Sea   H
10   11   12   13   14   15   16   17   18
20   40   60   80   100   120   140   160   180

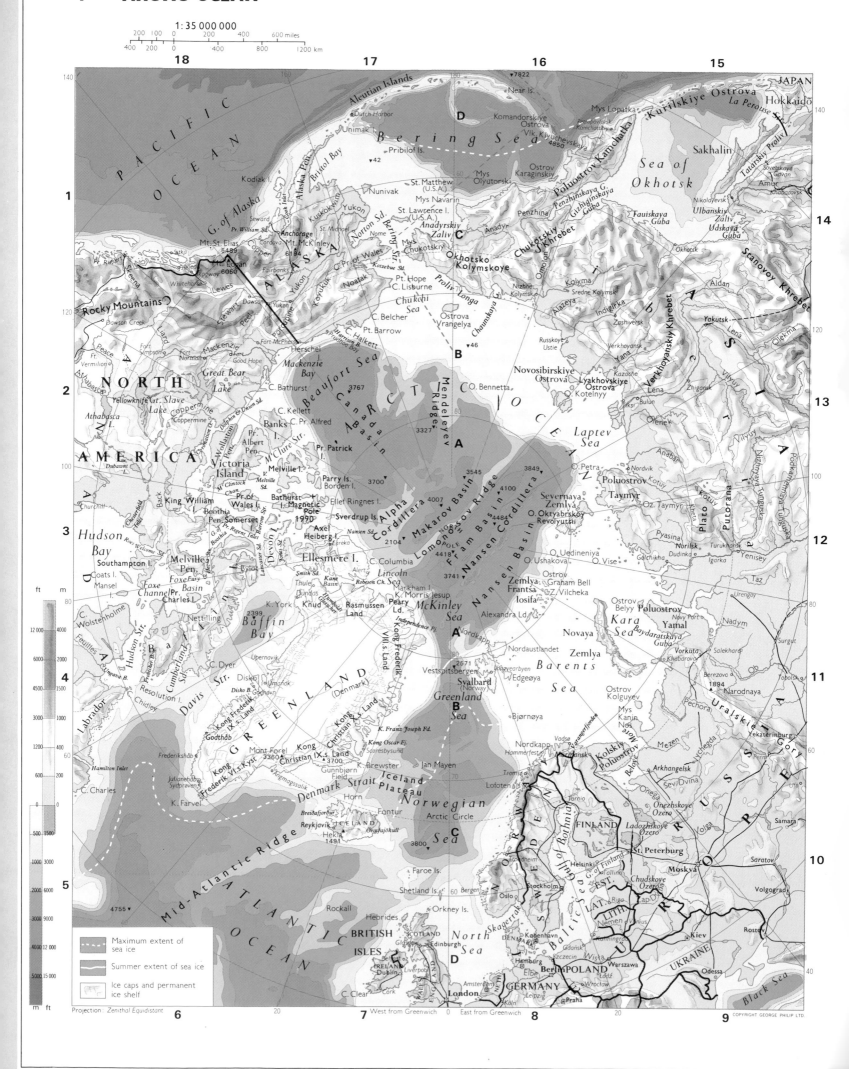

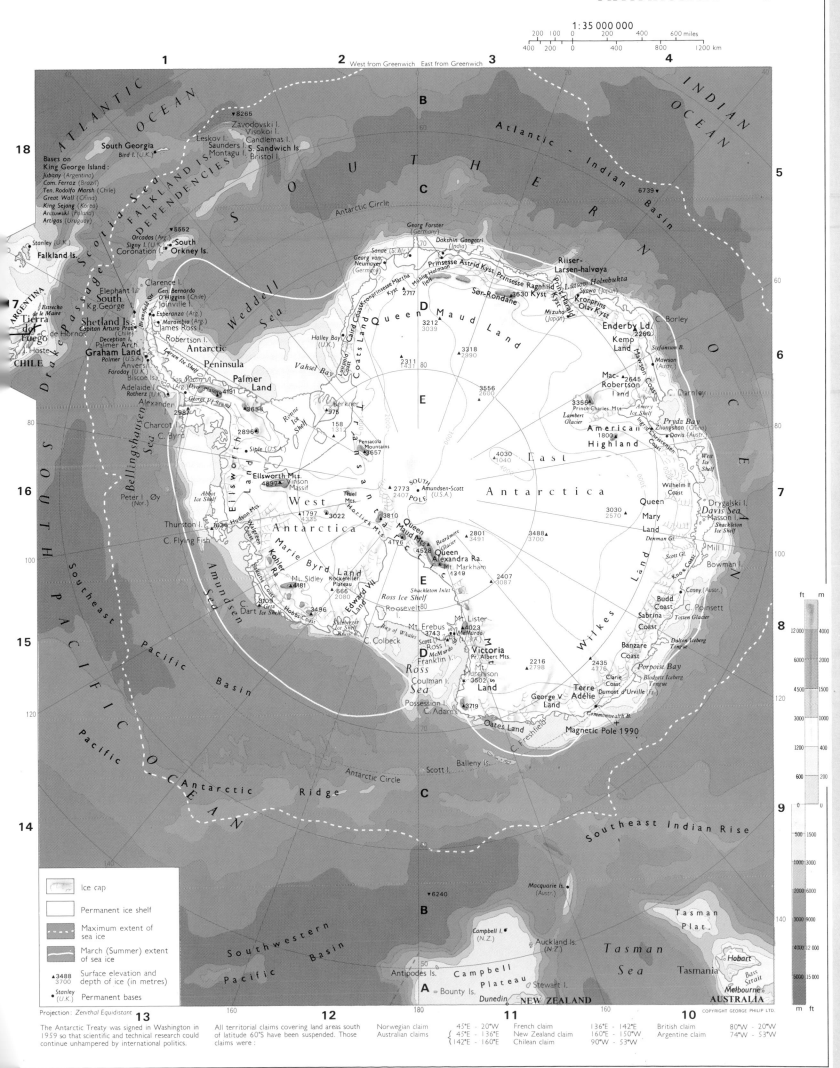

1 : 35 000 000

```
200  100   0        200        400        600 miles
400  200   0    200   400       800       1200 km
```

1   2   West from Greenwich   East from Greenwich   3   4

ATLANTIC OCEAN

INDIAN OCEAN

SOUTHERN

Atlantic - Indian Basin

▼8265

Zavodovski I.
Visokoi I.
Leskov I.
Saunders I.
Candlemas I.
Montagu I.
S. Sandwich Is.
Bristol I.

South Georgia
Bird I. (U.K.)

6739▼

Bases on King George Island:
Jubany (Argentina)
Com. Ferraz (Brazil)
Ten. Rodolfo Marsh (Chile)
Great Wall (China)
King Sejong (Korea)
Arctowski (Poland)
Artigas (Uruguay)

Antarctic Circle

Georg Forster (Germany)
Dakshin Gangotri (India)

FALKLAND IS. DEPENDENCIES

Stanley (U.K.)

▼5552
Orcadas (Arg.)
Signy I. (U.K.)
Coronation I.
South Orkney Is.

Sande (S. Afr.)
Georg von Neumayer (Germany)
Prinsesse Astrid Kyst
Prinsesse Ragnhild Kyst
Riiser-Larsen-halvøya
Lützow-Holmbukta
Syowa (Japan)

Falkland Is.

Prinsesse Martha Kyst
Mühlig Hofmann
2717
Kronprins Olav Kyst
Mizuho (Japan)

ARGENTINA
Estrecho de le Maire
Tierra del Fuego
C. de Hornos
I. Hoste

Elephant I.
South Kg. George I.
Shetland Is.
Deception I.
Palmer Arch.
Graham Land
Anvers I.
Faraday (U.K.)
Biscoe Is.
Adelaide I.
Rothera (U.K.)

Gen. Bernardo O'Higgins (Chile)
Joinville I.
Esperanza (Arg.)
Marambio (Arg.)
Capitan Arturo Prat (Chile)
James Ross I.
Robertson I.
Antarctic Peninsula
Palmer (U.S.A.)
Larsen Ice Shelf

Halley Bay (U.K.)

3630 Kyst

Sør-Rondane

Queen Maud Land

Enderby Ld.

C. Borley

CHILE

Coats Land
Luitpold Coast
Vahsel Bay

3212
3039

3318
2990

Kemp Land
2260
Stefansson B.
Mawson (Austr.)

Palmer Land

2311
1431

Mac-Robertson Land
2645
Prince Charles Mts.
3355
Amery Ice Shelf
Lambert Glacier

C. Darnley

Alexander I.

4191

Berkner I.
Ronne Ice Shelf

3556
2600

American Highland
1800

Zhongshan (China)
Prydz Bay
Davis (Austr.)

2987
3658

George VI Sound

975

158
1311

East Antarctica

Ingrid Christensen Coast

Charcot I.
C. Byrd

2896

Pensacola Mountains
3657

West Ice Shelf

Siple (U.S.A.)

4030
1040

Wilhelm II Coast

Drygalski I.
Davis Sea
Masson I.
Shackleton Ice Shelf

Peter I. Øy (Nor.)

Ellsworth Mts.
4897
Vinson Massif

2773
2407

SOUTH POLE

Amundsen-Scott (U.S.A.)

Queen Mary Land

3030
2570

Thurston I.

Abbot Ice Shelf

Thiel Mts.

West Antarctica

1797
4335

3022

Horlick Mts.

3810

Queen Maud Mts.

3488
3700

Bowman I.

C. Flying Fish

1036

4176
4528

2801
3491

Denman Gl.

Scott Gl.
Knox Coast
Casey (Austr.)

Marie Byrd Land
Kohler Ra.
4181
Mt. Sidley

Hudson Mts.

Beardmore Glacier
Queen Alexandra Ra.
Mt. Markham 4319

2407
3087

Budd Coast
C. Poinsett

3109
3496

Rockefeller Plateau
666
2080

Shackleton Inlet

Sabrina Coast
Totten Glacier

Gretz Ice Shelf
Hobbs Coast

Edward VII Land

Ross Ice Shelf

Banzare Coast

Sulzberger Ice Shelf
Bay of Whales

Roosevelt I.

Mt. Erebus
4023
3743
Scott (N.Z.)
McMurdo (U.S.A.)

Mt. Lister

Dalton Iceberg Tongue

C. Colbeck

Ross I.
Franklin I.

Victoria
Pr. Albert Mts.

Clarie Coast

Porpoise Bay

Blodgett Iceberg Tongue

Ross Sea

Coulman I.

Murchison
3502

2216
2798

2435
4776

Magnetic Pole 1990

George V Land

Dumont d'Urville (Fr.)

Possession I.
3719
C. Adare

Terre Adélie

Commonwealth B.

Oates Land

C. Freshfield

Balleny Is.
Scott I.

Antarctic Circle

▼6240

Macquarie Is. (Austr.)

Tasman Plat.

Southeast Indian Rise

Campbell I. (N.Z.)

Tasman Sea

Southwestern Pacific Basin

Auckland Is. (N.Z.)

Hobart

Tasmania

Bass Strait

Antipodes Is.

Campbell Plateau

Bounty Is.
Dunedin

Stewart I.

Melbourne

NEW ZEALAND

AUSTRALIA

COPYRIGHT GEORGE PHILIP LTD.

Drake Passage
Scotia Sea
Weddell Sea
Bellingshausen Sea
SOUTH
SOUTHEAST PACIFIC
Pacific Basin
Pacific Antarctic Ridge
Amundsen Sea
Ellsworth Land

Legend:

	Ice cap
	Permanent ice shelf
	Maximum extent of sea ice
	March (Summer) extent of sea ice
▲3488 / 3700	Surface elevation and depth of ice (in metres)
● Stanley (U.K.)	Permanent bases

Projection: Zenithal Equidistant

ft m
12 000 / 4000
6000 / 2000
4500 / 1500
3000 / 1000
1200 / 400
600 / 200
0 / 0
500 / 1500
1000 / 3000
2000 / 6000
3000 / 9000
4000 / 12 000
5000 / 15 000
m ft

The Antarctic Treaty was signed in Washington in 1959 so that scientific and technical research could continue unhampered by international politics.

All territorial claims covering land areas south of latitude 60°S have been suspended. Those claims were:

Norwegian claim	45°E – 20°W
Australian claims	45°E – 136°E
	142°E – 160°E
French claim	136°E – 142°E
New Zealand claim	160°E – 150°W
Chilean claim	90°W – 53°W
British claim	80°W – 20°W
Argentine claim	74°W – 53°W

1:20 000 000

100   0   100   200   300   400 miles
100   0 100 200 300 400 500 600 km

CASPIAN SEA

Ural Mountains
Obshchisyrt
Ural'sk
Pechora
Volga Uplands
Caucasus
Elbrus 5633
Ararat 5165
Kurdistan
Tundra
Anatolia

Kanin Peninsula
Kola Peninsula
White Sea
Mezen
N. Dvina
Onega
L. Onega
Central Russian Uplands
Don
Sea of Azov
Crimea
BLACK SEA
Cyprus 1951

Nordkinn
North Cape
Lofoten
Vesterålen
Lapland
Finland
L. Ladoga
Neva
L. Chudskoye
Pripyat
Pripyat Marshes
Ukraine
Bug
Danube
Prut
Carpathians
Transylvanian Alps
Wallachia
Balkans
Balkan Peninsula
Crete

NORWEGIAN SEA
Scandinavia
Galdhøpiggen 2469
Gulf of Bothnia
Gotland
Öland
BALTIC SEA
Vistula (Wisła)
Odra (Oder)
Sudetes
Tatra 2655
Plain of Hungary
Tisza
Dinaric Alps
Apennines
ADRIATIC SEA
Pindus
Morea
C. Matapan
Ionian Is.

Iceland
Faroe Is.
Fisher Bank
Shetland Is.
Orkney Is.
Hebrides
Skagerrak
Kattegat
Jutland
Lindesnes
Elbe
Weser
Harz 1142
Erz Geb.
Bohemian For.
Alps
Mont Blanc 4807
Po
Corsica
Sardinia
Ligurian Sea
Gran Sasso
Vesuvius 1277
Tyrrhenian Sea
Str. of Messina
Etna 3263
Sicily
Malta

NORTH SEA
Dogger Bank
Great Britain
English Channel
Land's End
Irish Sea
Ireland
Netherlands
Rhine
Vosges
Jura
Thames
Seine
Brittany
Loire
Garonne
Gironde
Central Massif
Cévennes
G. of Lions
Pyrenees
Balearic Is.

ATLANTIC OCEAN
Rockall
Valentia
C. Clear
Finisterre
Bay of Biscay
Cantabrian Mts.
Old Castile
New Castile
Iberian Peninsula
Sierra Morena
Andalusia
Sa. Nevada 3478
Str. of Gibraltar
C. Trafalgar
C. St. Vincent
Maritime Atlas
Plateau of the Shotts
MEDITERRANEAN SEA

Projection: Bonne West from Greenwich 0 East from Greenwich

ft   m
12 000 4000
6000   2000
3000   1000
      600
      200
   0
      200
      600
2000 6000
4000 12 000
m   ft

1:20 000 000

100   0   100   200   300   400 miles
100   0   100 200 300 400 500 600 km

COPYRIGHT GEORGE PHILIP & SON LTD

Projection Bonne   West from Greenwich 0 East from Greenwich

LONDON Capital Cities

ICELAND

ATLANTIC OCEAN

Reykjavik

Faroe Is. (Den.)

Shetland Is.

Orkney Is.

Hebrides

UNITED KINGDOM

IRELAND   Dublin

SCOTLAND   Aberdeen   Dundee
Glasgow   Edinburgh   Newcastle
Belfast   I. of Man
ENGLAND   Leeds   Hull
Liverpool   Manchester   Sheffield
WALES   Birmingham
Cardiff   LONDON
Bristol   Southampton
Plymouth   Portsmouth   Dover
Swansea
Is. of Scilly   C. Clear

English Channel

BAY OF BISCAY

FRANCE   PARIS
Nantes   Rouen   Le Havre
Limoges   Dijon   St. Étienne
Lyons   Bordeaux   Toulouse
Marseilles   Nice
Loire   Seine   Garonne   Rhône

SPAIN   MADRID
La Coruña   Oporto   Valladolid   Zaragoza
Barcelona   Valencia   Alicante   Murcia
Bilbao   Ebro   Guadiana
Córdoba   Sevilla   Málaga   Granada
Guadalquivir   Cádiz   Gibraltar (Br.)
Andorra   Menorca   Mallorca (Majorca)
Balearic Is.   Palma   Ibiza

PORTUGAL   Lisbon   Tagus   Douro   Vigo

MOROCCO   Rabat   Fes   Meknes   Tanger
Str. of Gibraltar

ALGERIA   Algiers   Oran   Constantine   Annaba

TUNISIA   Tunis   Sousse

MEDITERRANEAN SEA

NORWAY   Oslo   Bergen   Stavanger   Trondheim   Tromsø   Hammerfest
Sogne Fd.   Hardanger Fd.   Skagerrak

SWEDEN   Stockholm   Göteborg   Malmö   Uppsala   Jönköping   Gävle   Luleå   Umeå
Vänern   Vättern

FINLAND   Helsinki   Tampere   Turku   Vaasa   Oulu
L. Inari

DENMARK   COPENHAGEN   Aarhus   Kiel   Kattegat

NORTH SEA   BALTIC SEA   G. of Bothnia

Arctic Circle

White Sea   N. Dvina   Onega   L. Ladoga   L. Onega   Murmansk   Arkhangelsk   Kotlas

R U S S I A   MOSCOW   St. Petersburg
Novgorod   Nizhniy Novgorod   Ivanovo   Kostroma   Yaroslavl   Rybinsk Res.
Kazan   Samara   Saratov   Penza   Tambov   Tula   Orel   Kursk   Voronezh
Smolensk   Volgograd   Astrakhan   Rostov   Krasnodar
Perm   Yekaterinburg   Chelyabinsk   Nizhniy Tagil   Orenburg   Ufa   Magnitogorsk
Ob   Volga   Ural   Don   Kama

KAZAKHSTAN   Guryev

CASPIAN SEA

GERMANY   BERLIN   Hamburg   Bremen   Hanover   Cologne   Essen   Dortmund   Frankfurt   Munich   Nuremberg   Stuttgart   Leipzig   Dresden   Chemnitz   Halle   Magdeburg   Bonn   Elbe   Weser
Kiel

NETHERLANDS   Amsterdam   The Hague   Rotterdam
BELGIUM   Brussels   Antwerp   Liège   Lille
LUX.

SWITZERLAND   Bern   Zürich   Basle   Geneva
LIECH.
AUSTRIA   VIENNA   Graz   Linz   Innsbruck   Salzburg

POLAND   WARSAW   Łódź   Kraków   Wrocław   Poznań   Gdańsk   Szczecin   Bydgoszcz   Lublin   Katowice   Vistula   Oder

CZECH REP.   PRAGUE   Brno   Ostrava
SLOVAK REP.   Bratislava

HUNGARY   BUDAPEST   Miskolc   Debrecen   Szeged

SLOVENIA   Ljubljana
CROATIA   Zagreb
BOSNIA-HERZ.   Sarajevo
YUGOSLAVIA   Belgrade   SERBIA   Niš   MONTENEGRO
MACEDONIA   Skopje
ALBANIA   Tiranë

ITALY   Rome   Milan   Turin   Genoa   Naples   Florence   Bologna   Venice   Trieste   Bari   Palermo   Catania   Messina
Tiber   Corsica   Sardinia   Sicily   Elba
Tyrrhenian Sea   ADRIATIC SEA   Ionian Sea
MALTA   Valletta   Pantelleria (Italy)

ROMANIA   BUCHAREST   Cluj-Napoca   Timișoara   Brașov   Ploiești   Constanța   Galați   Iași
Danube
MOLDAVIA   Kishinev

BULGARIA   Sofia   Plovdiv   Varna   Ruse

GREECE   ATHENS   Thessaloníki   Pátrai   Piraeus   Larisa   Vólos
AEGEAN SEA   Crete

BLACK SEA

BELORUSSIA   Minsk
LATVIA   Riga
LITHUANIA   Kaunas   Vilnius   Kaliningrad
ESTONIA   Tallinn
L. Chudskoye   L. Peipus

UKRAINE   Kiev   Kharkov   Donetsk   Dnepropetrovsk   Odessa   Krivoy Rog   Zaporozhye   Nikolayev   Kherson   Lvov   Zhitomir   Chernigov   Gomel   Vitebsk   Mogilev   Sevastopol
Dnepr (Dnieper)   Dnestr (Dniester)   Bug   Pripet   Donets   Volga
S. of Azov

TURKEY   Ankara   Istanbul   Izmir   Bursa   Adana   Konya   Antalya   Kayseri   Samsun   Erzurum   Diyarbakir   Gaziantep
CYPRUS   Nicosia   Limassol

GEORGIA   Tbilisi
ARMENIA   Yerevan
AZERBAIJAN   Baku

IRAN   Tabriz

IRAQ   Baghdad   Mosul   Euphrates

SYRIA   Aleppo (Halab)   Homs

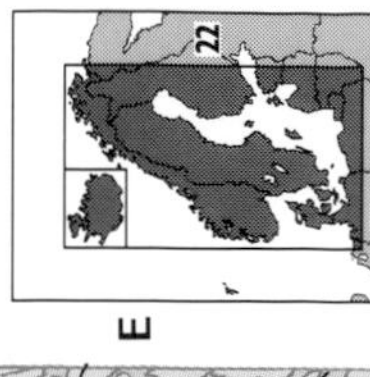

ICELAND
on the same scale
as general map

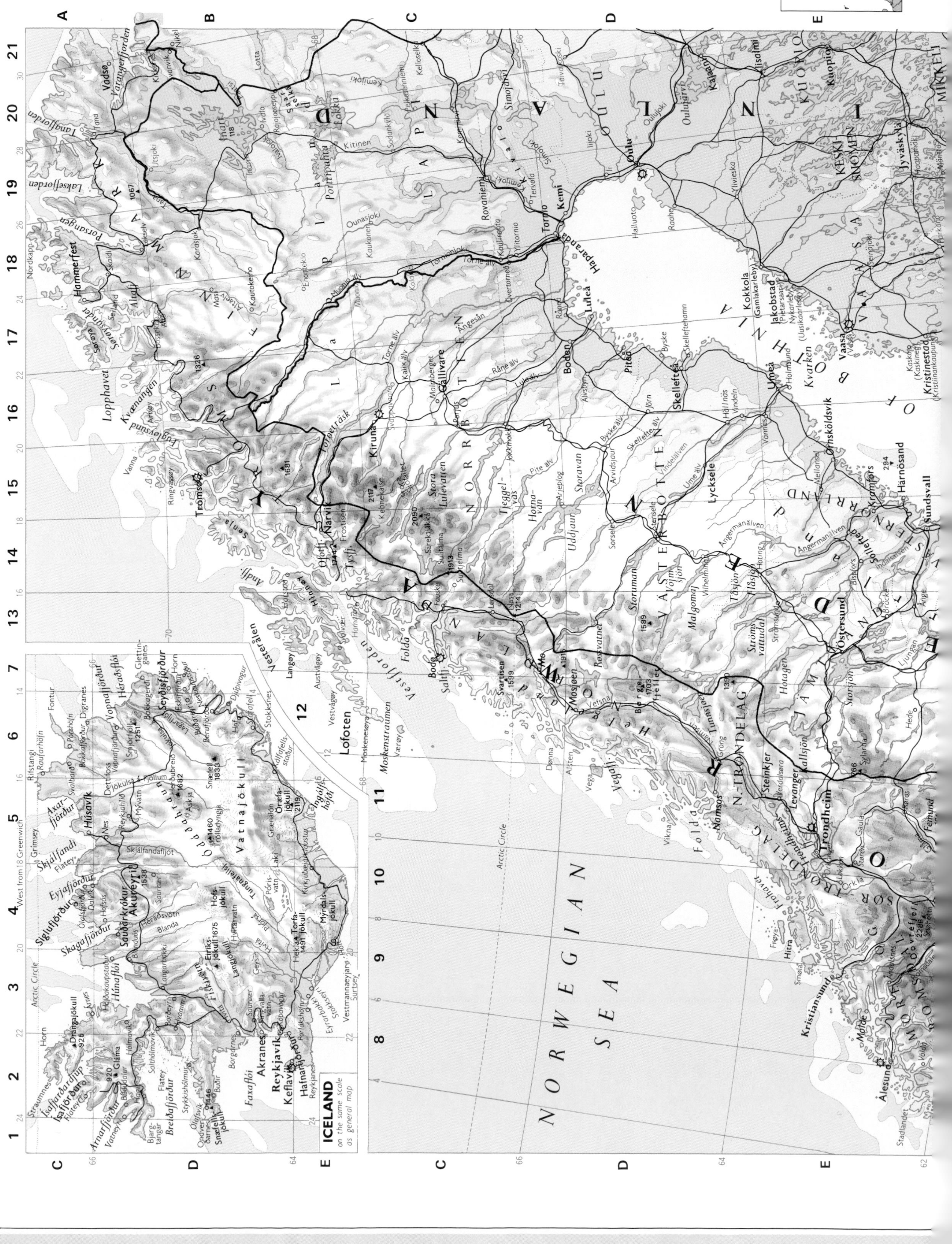

NORWEGIAN SEA

LAPLAND

NORRBOTTEN

VÄSTERBOTTEN

GULF OF BOTHNIA

N-TRÖNDELAG

SØR-TRÖNDELAG

Arctic Circle

Vadsø
Hammerfest
Tromsø
Narvik
Bodø
Mosjøen
Steinkjer
Levanger
Trondheim
Kristiansund
Ålesund

Kiruna
Gällivare
Luleå
Piteå
Skellefteå
Umeå
Härnösand
Sundsvall
Lycksele
Storuman
Östersund

Rovaniemi
Kemi
Torneå
Haparanda
Oulu
Kokkola
Jakobstad
Vaasa
Kristinestad

Reykjavík
Keflavík
Akranes
Akureyri
Húsavik
Siglufjörður
Sauðárkrókur

Vatnajökull
Lofoten
Vesterålen

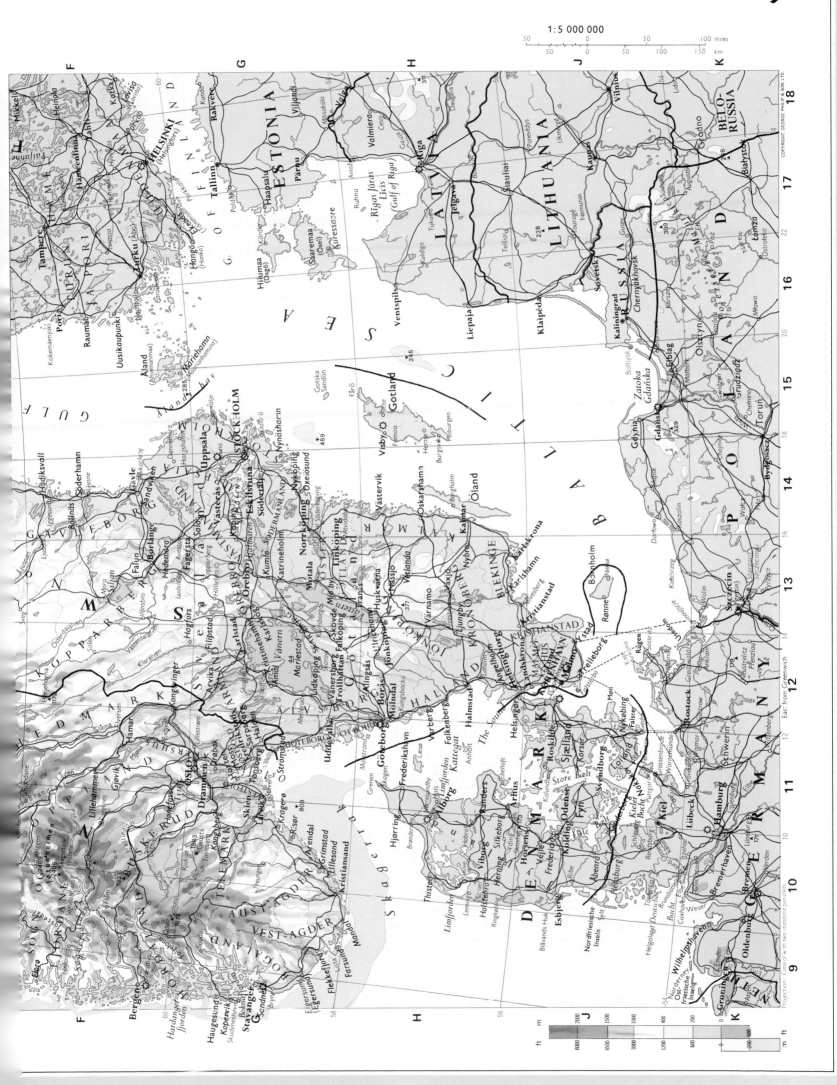

1:5 000 000

50   50   100 miles
50   0   50   100   150 km

F   G   H   J   K

18

17

16

15

14

13

12

11

10

9

FINLAND

HELSINKI (Helsingfors)

ESTONIA

Tallinn

LATVIA

Rīgas Jūras Līcis (Gulf of Riga)

Rīga

LITHUANIA

Vilnius

Kaunas

Klaipėda

Kaliningrad

RUSSIA

Chernyakhovsk

BELO-RUSSIA

Grodno

Białystok

POLAND

Gdańsk

Gdynia

Szczecin

BALTIC SEA

Gotland

Visby

Öland

Kalmar

BLEKINGE

Karlskrona

Karlshamn

Kristianstad

Bornholm

Rønne

Rügen

GERMANY

Rostock

Lübeck

Hamburg

Kiel

Bremen

Bremerhaven

Wilhelmshaven

Oldenburg

NETH.

Groningen

DENMARK

København

Malmö

Helsingør

Helsingborg

Ålborg

Århus

Odense

Esbjerg

Skagen

Kattegat

Skagerrak

NORWAY

OSLO

Bergen

Stavanger

Kristiansand

STOCKHOLM

Uppsala

Västerås

Örebro

Norrköping

Linköping

Jönköping

GÖTEBORG

Borås

Halmstad

Gävle

Sundsvall

Hudiksvall

Trollhättan

SWEDEN

Vänern

Vättern

GULF OF BOTHNIA

Åland (Ahvenanmaa)

Mariehamn

Tampere

Turku (Åbo)

Pori

J

K

ft   m
6000 2000
4500 1500
3000 1000
1200 400
600   200
0
200-600
m   ft

East from Greenwich

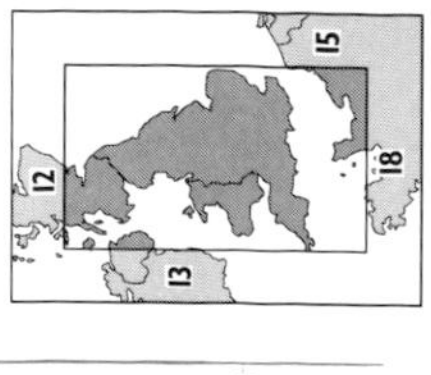
12
13
15
18

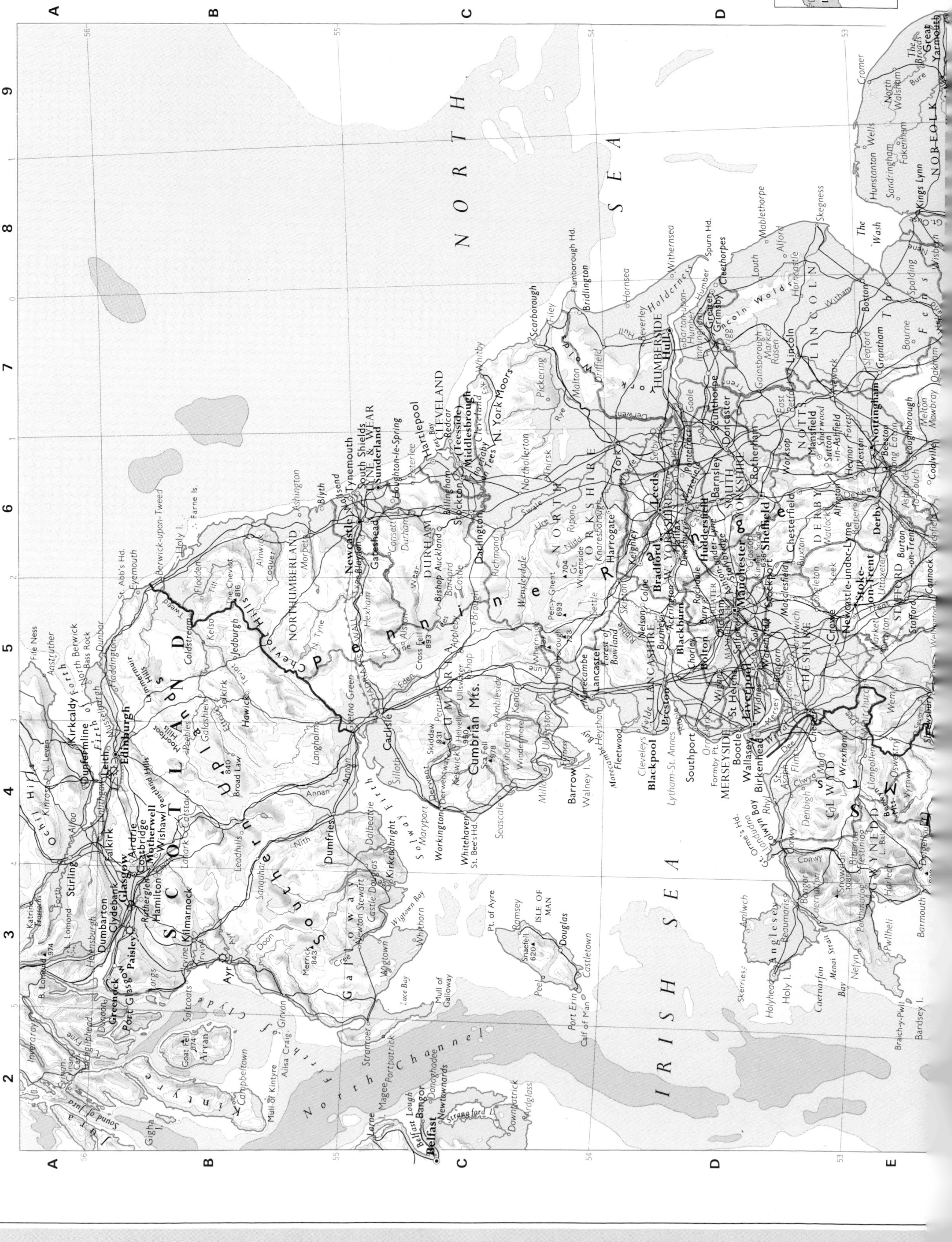
NORTH SEA
IRISH SEA
North Channel
SCOTLAND
NORTHUMBERLAND
DURHAM
CLEVELAND
TYNE & WEAR
CUMBRIA
NORTH YORKSHIRE
WEST YORKSHIRE
SOUTH YORKSHIRE
HUMBERSIDE
LANCASHIRE
GREATER MANCHESTER
MERSEYSIDE
CHESHIRE
CLWYD
GWYNEDD
DERBY
NOTTS
LINCOLN
NORFOLK
STAFFORD
ISLE OF MAN
Pennines
Cheviot Hills
Cumbrian Mts.
Southern Uplands
N. York Moors
Newcastle
Sunderland
Middlesbrough
Carlisle
Leeds
Bradford
York
Hull
Sheffield
Manchester
Liverpool
Preston
Blackpool
Lancaster
Nottingham
Derby
Lincoln
Edinburgh
Glasgow
Belfast
Douglas

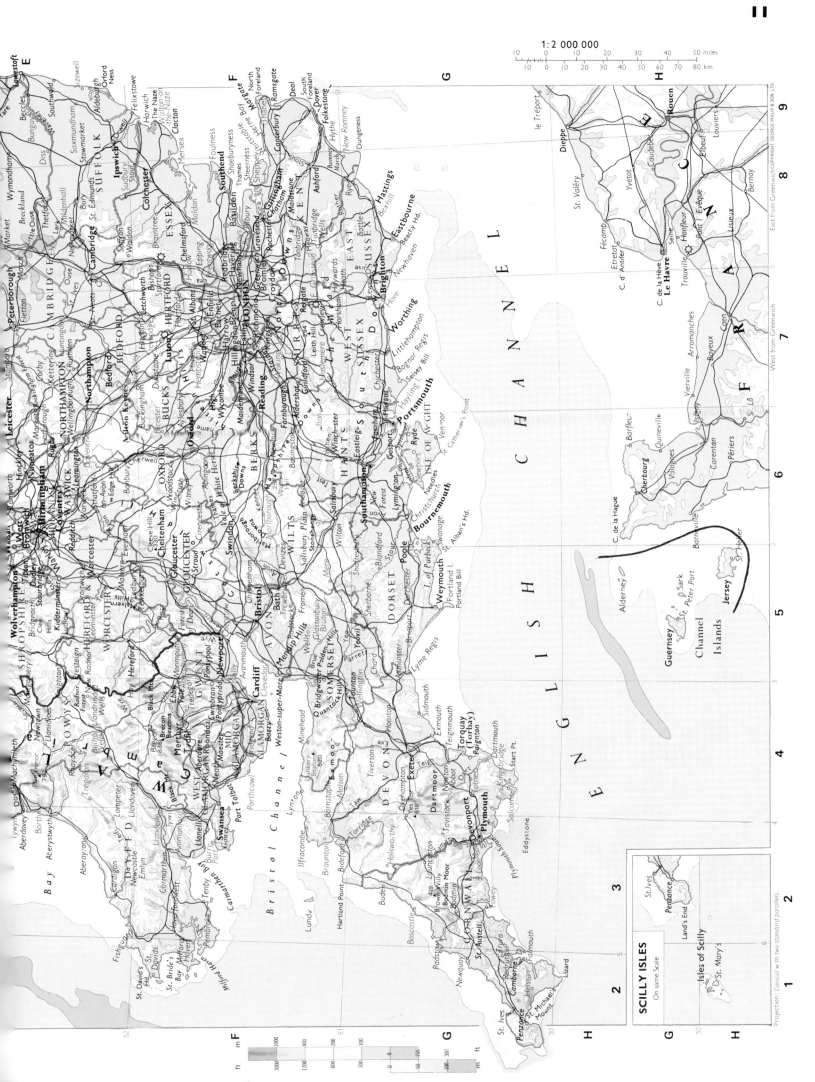

II

1:2 000 000

SCILLY ISLES
On same Scale

Projection Conical with two standard parallels.

COPYRIGHT GEORGE PHILIP & SON LTD.

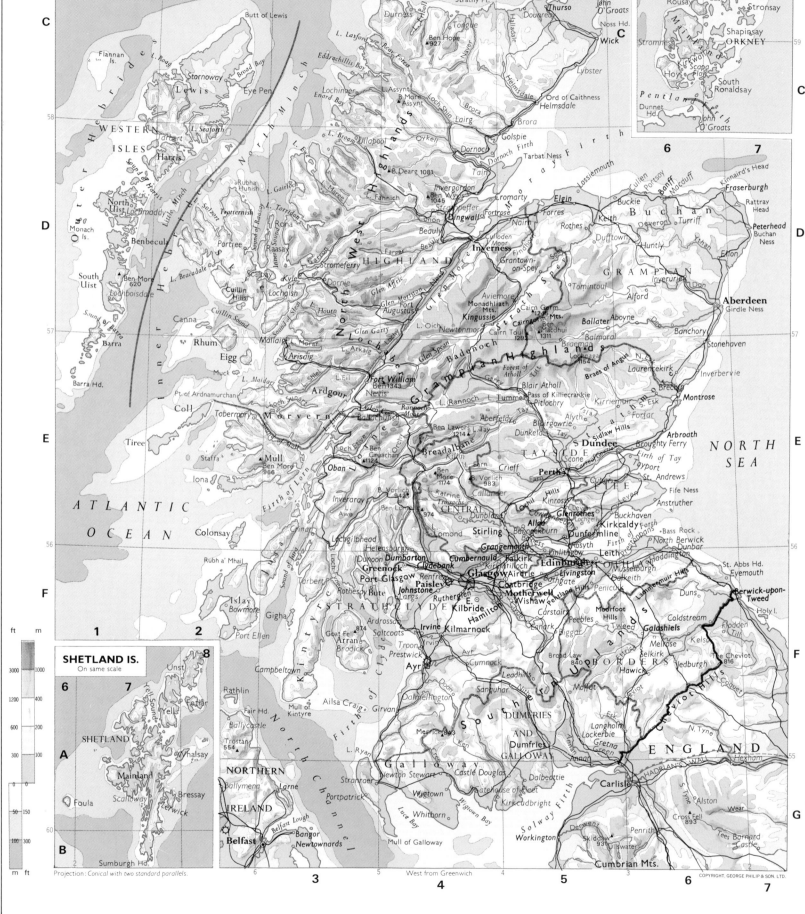

1 : 2 000 000

ORKNEY IS.
On same scale

SHETLAND IS.
On same scale

Projection : Conical with two standard parallels.

West from Greenwich

COPYRIGHT. GEORGE PHILIP & SON. LTD.

1:2 000 000

10 0 10 20 30 40 50 miles
10 0 10 20 30 40 50 60 70 80 km

Towns underlined in Northern Ireland give their names to the Districts in which they stand

The remaining Districts are:—

1 Fermanagh   5 Castlereagh
2 Moyle   6 Ards
3 Newtownabbey   7 Down
4 North Down   8 Newry & Mourne

Projection: Conical with two standard parallels.

8 West from Greenwich

COPYRIGHT. GEORGE PHILIP & SON LTD.

ft   m
3000 1000
1200 400
600   200
300   100
0   0
100   300
200   600
m   ft

ATLANTIC OCEAN

NORTH CHANNEL

IRISH SEA

St. George's Channel

DONEGAL
SLIGO
LEITRIM
MAYO
ROSCOMMON
CONNACHT
LONGFORD
CAVAN
MONAGHAN
LOUTH
MEATH
WESTMEATH
GALWAY
IRELAND
OFFALY
KILDARE
DUBLIN
LAOIS
WICKLOW
LEINSTER
CLARE
TIPPERARY
KILKENNY
CARLOW
WEXFORD
LIMERICK
KERRY
MUNSTER
WATERFORD
CORK

NORTHERN IRELAND
Londonderry
Coleraine
Ballymoney
Ballymena
Larne
Belfast
Lisburn
Armagh
Newry
Dundalk
Dublin (Baile Atha Cliath)
Dun Laoghaire
Bray
Wicklow
Arklow
Wexford
Rosslare
Waterford
Dungarvan
Youghal
Cork
Cobh
Kinsale
Bantry
Killarney
Tralee
Limerick
Ennis
Galway
Sligo
Donegal
Letterkenny
Enniskillen
Omagh
Monaghan
Cavan
Longford
Mullingar
Athlone
Roscommon
Castlebar
Westport
Ballina

1 : 4 000 000

20   0   20   40   60 miles

20   0   20   40   60   80   km

The DISTRICTS of Northern Ireland have been numbered and can be identified by reference to this table.

1 Londonderry	14 Craigavon
2 Limavady	15 Armagh
3 Coleraine	16 Newry & Mourne
4 Ballymoney	17 Banbridge
5 Moyle	18 Down
6 Larne	19 Lisburn
7 Ballymena	20 Antrim
8 Magherafelt	21 Newtownabbey
9 Cookstown	22 Carrickfergus
10 Strabane	23 North Down
11 Omagh	24 Ards
12 Fermanagh	25 Castlereagh
13 Dungannon	26 Belfast

ORKNEY

SHETLAND

HIGHLAND

WESTERN ISLES

HIGHLAND

GRAMPIAN

SCOTLAND

TAYSIDE

FIFE

CENTRAL

LOTHIAN

STRATHCLYDE

BORDERS

DUMFRIES AND GALLOWAY

NORTHUMBERLAND

TYNE AND WEAR

CUMBRIA

DURHAM

CLEVELAND

ISLE OF MAN

NORTH YORKSHIRE

HUMBERSIDE

LANCASHIRE

WEST YORKSHIRE

GREATER MANCHESTER

MERSEYSIDE

SOUTH YORKSHIRE

CHESHIRE

DERBYSHIRE

NOTTINGHAMSHIRE

LINCOLNSHIRE

ENGLAND

GWYNEDD

CLWYD

STAFFORDSHIRE

LEICESTERSHIRE

NORFOLK

SHROPSHIRE

WEST MIDLANDS

WARWICKSHIRE

NORTHAMPTONSHIRE

CAMBRIDGESHIRE

SUFFOLK

WALES

POWYS

HEREFORD AND WORCESTER

BEDFORDSHIRE

BUCKINGHAMSHIRE

HERTFORDSHIRE

ESSEX

DYFED

GLOUCESTERSHIRE

OXFORDSHIRE

GREATER LONDON

WEST GLAMORGAN

MID GLAMORGAN

GWENT

AVON

BERKSHIRE

SURREY

KENT

SOUTH GLAMORGAN

WILTSHIRE

HAMPSHIRE

WEST SUSSEX

EAST SUSSEX

SOMERSET

DORSET

DEVON

ISLE OF WIGHT

CORNWALL

WESTERN

ISLES

NORTHERN IRELAND

DONEGAL

Tyrone

Fermanagh

LEITRIM

SLIGO

MAYO

ROSCOMMON

LONGFORD

WESTMEATH

MEATH

GALWAY

OFFALY

KILDARE

DUBLIN

IRELAND

LAOIS

WICKLOW

CLARE

CARLOW

LIMERICK

TIPPERARY

KILKENNY

WEXFORD

KERRY

WATERFORD

CORK

Monaghan

Cavan

CAVAN

MONAGHAN

LOUTH

ATLANTIC

OCEAN

NORTH SEA

IRISH SEA

St George's Channel

North Channel

CELTIC

SEA

ENGLISH CHANNEL

FRANCE

Stornoway

Inverness

Aberdeen

Dundee

Glenrothes

Stirling

Edinburgh

Glasgow

Newtown St. Boswells

Morpeth

Newcastle

Dumfries

Carlisle

Durham

Middlesbrough

Northallerton

Beverley

Preston

Wakefield

Barnsley

Manchester

Liverpool

Lincoln

Nottingham

Matlock

Chester

Caernarfon

Mold

Stafford

Leicester

Norwich

Shrewsbury

Birmingham

Warwick

Northampton

Cambridge

Ipswich

Llandrindod Wells

Hereford

Worcester

Bedford

Hertford

Chelmsford

Carmarthen

Gloucester

Oxford

Aylesbury

Kingston

Maidstone

Swansea

Cardiff

Bristol

Reading

Trowbridge

Winchester

Lewes

Chichester

Newport

Taunton

Dorchester

Exeter

Truro

Cwmbran

Lifford

Londonderry

Antrim

Belfast

Down

Sligo

Carrick-on-Shannon

Dundalk

Castlebar

Roscommon

Longford

An Uaimh (Navan)

Mullingar

Tullamore

Naas

Dublin

Galway

Port Laoise

Wicklow

Ennis

Carlow

Limerick

Kilkenny

Tralee

Clonmel

Wexford

Waterford

Cork

Kirkwall

Lerwick

Douglas

o Norwich   Administrative headquarters

MERSEYSIDE   Metropolitan counties

Antrim   Former Northern Ireland counties

Projection: Conical with two standard parallels

West from Greenwich   East from Greenwich

COPYRIGHT. GEORGE PHILIP & SON, LTD.

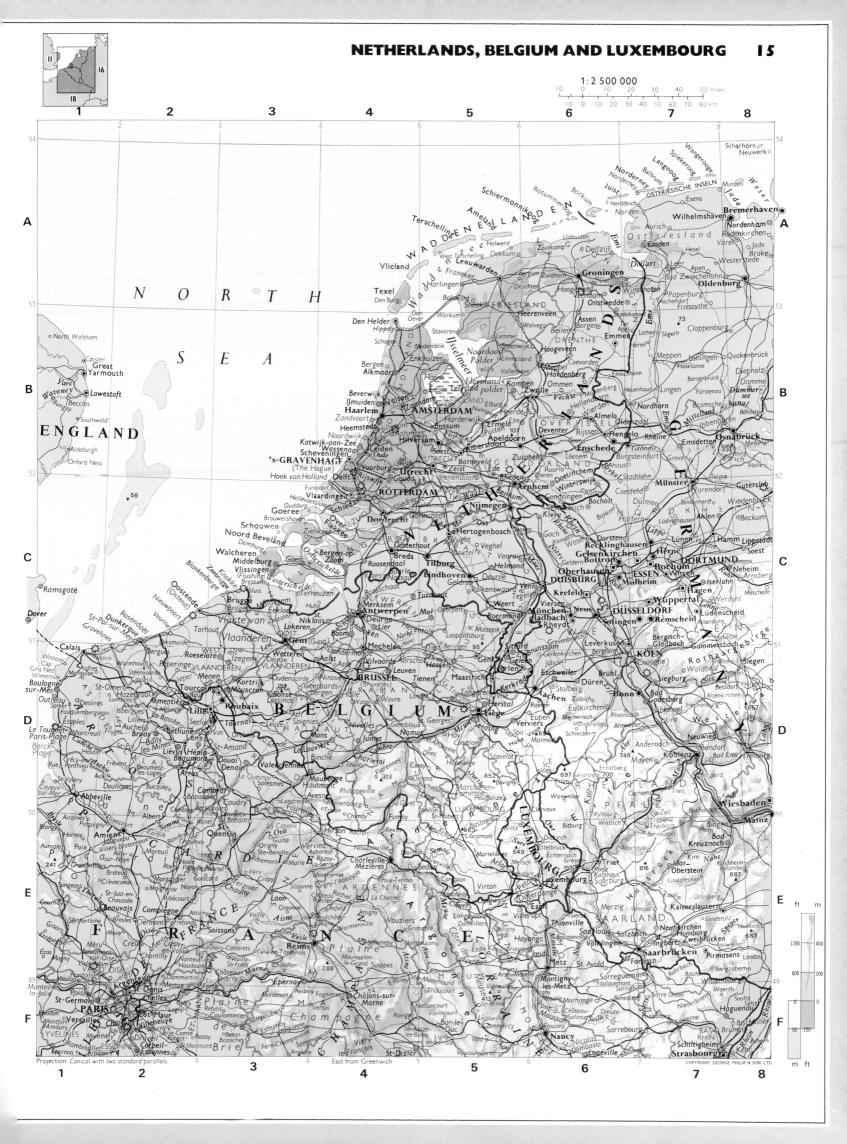

1 : 2 500 000

NORTH

SEA

ENGLAND

NORTH WALSHAM
Great Yarmouth
Lowestoft
Southwold
Aldeburgh
Orford Ness

Ramsgate
Dover
Calais

ENGLAND

WADDEN EILANDEN

Schiermonnikoog
Ameland
Terschelling
Vlieland
Texel
Den Burg

Leeuwarden
Harlingen
Franeker
Dokkum
Holwerd
Zoutkamp

Ostfriesische Inseln
Norderney
Borkum
Juist

Wilhelmshaven
Bremerhaven
Nordenham

Ostfriesland
Emden
Aurich
Leer
Oldenburg

Groningen
Assen
Emmen
DRENTHE

Den Helder
Alkmaar
Hoorn
Amsterdam
Haarlem
IJmuiden

NETHERLANDS

'S-GRAVENHAGE
(The Hague)
ROTTERDAM
Delft
Dordrecht

Utrecht
Amersfoort
Apeldoorn
Arnhem
Nijmegen

GELDERLAND
Enschede
OVERIJSSEL
Zwolle

Münster
DORTMUND
ESSEN
DUISBURG
DÜSSELDORF
KÖLN (Cologne)
Bonn

GERMANY

Antwerpen
Brugge
Gent (Gand)
Oostende (Ostend)

BRUSSEL
(Bruxelles)
Leuven
BELGIUM
Liège
Namur
Maastricht
Aachen

LUXEMBOURG
Luxembourg

Lille
Roubaix
Tournai
Mons
Charleroi

Calais
Boulogne-sur-Mer
Abbeville
Amiens
Arras
Cambrai
St Quentin

FRANCE

Reims
PARIS
Versailles
Châlons-sur-Marne
Épernay
Nancy
Strasbourg

SAARLAND
Saarbrücken
Mainz
Wiesbaden
Koblenz

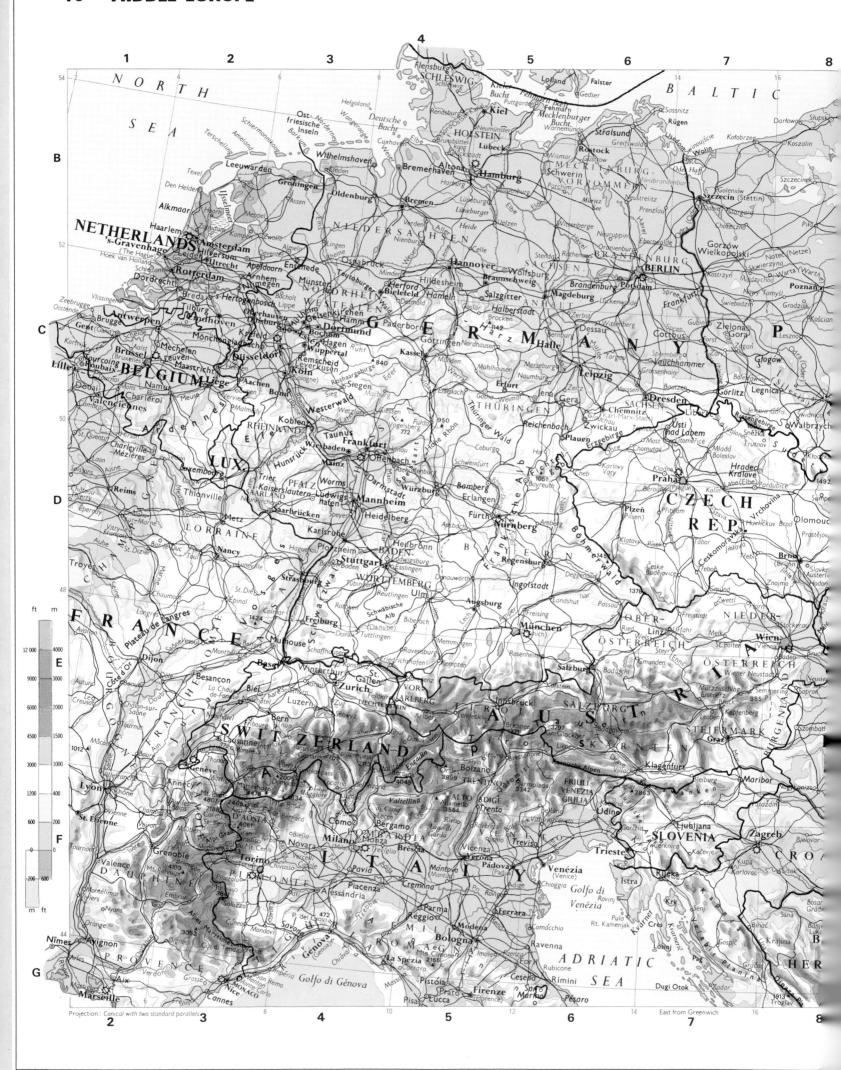

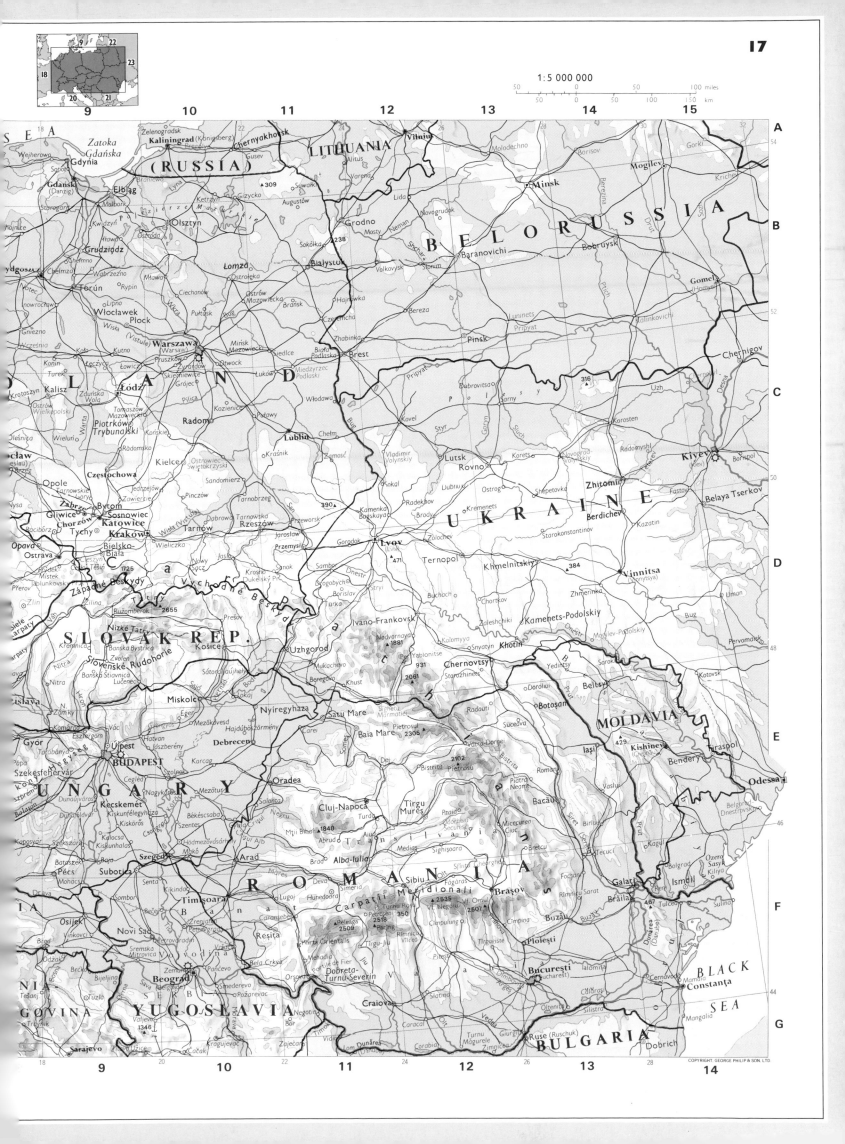

1:5 000 000

FRENCH DEPARTMENTS

A.	01	Ain
Ai.	02	Aisne
A.H.P.	04	Alpes-de-Haute-Provence
H.A.	05	Hautes-Alpes
A.M.	06	Alpes-Maritimes
Ard.	07	Ardèche
Ar.	08	Ardennes
Ar.	09	Ariège
Aub.	10	Aube
Aud.	11	Aude
Av.	12	Aveyron
B.Rh.	13	Bouches-du-Rhône
C.	14	Calvados
Ca.	15	Cantal
Ch.	16	Charente
Ch.M.	17	Charente-Maritime
Che	18	Cher
Co.	19	Corrèze
C.Q.	20	Corse a) Haute-Corse b) Corse du Sud
C.d'Or	21	Côte-d'Or
C.A.	22	Côtes d'Armor
Cr.	23	Creuse
D.	24	Dordogne
Do.	25	Doubs
Dr.	26	Drôme
E.	27	Eure
E.L.	28	Eure-et-Loir
F.	29	Finistère
G.	30	Gard
H.G.	31	Haute-Garonne
Ge.	32	Gers
Gi.	33	Gironde
H.	34	Hérault
I.V.	35	Ille-et-Vilaine
I.	36	Indre
I.L.	37	Indre-et-Loire
Is.	38	Isère
Ju.	39	Jura
La.	40	Landes
L.C.	41	Loir-et-Cher
Loi.	42	Loire
H.L.	43	Haute-Loire
L.A.	44	Loire-Atlantique
Loi.	45	Loiret
Lo.	46	Lot
L.G.	47	Lot-et-Garonne
Loz.	48	Lozère
M.L.	49	Maine-et-Loire
Ma.	50	Manche
Mar.	51	Marne
H.M.	52	Haute-Marne
May.	53	Mayenne
M.M.	54	Meurthe-et-Moselle
Me.	55	Meuse
Mo.	56	Morbihan
Mos.	57	Moselle
N.	58	Nièvre
No.	59	Nord
O.	60	Oise
Or.	61	Orne
P.C.	62	Pas-de-Calais
P.D.	63	Puy-de-Dôme
P.A.	64	Pyrénées-Atlantiques
H.P.	65	Hautes Pyrénées
P.O.	66	Pyrénées-Orientales
B.R.	67	Bas Rhin
H.R.	68	Haut Rhin
Rh.	69	Rhône
H.S.	70	Haute Saône
S.L.	71	Saône-et-Loire
Sa.	72	Sarthe
Sav.	73	Savoie
H.Sa.	74	Haute-Savoie
	75	Paris
S.Me.	76	Seine-Maritime
S.M.	77	Seine-et-Marne
Y.M.	78	Yvelines
D.S.	79	Deux-Sèvres
So.	80	Somme
T.	81	Tarn
T.G.	82	Tarn-et-Garonne
Va.	83	Var
Vau.	84	Vaucluse
Ve.	85	Vendée
Vi.	86	Vienne
H.V.	87	Haute-Vienne
Vo.	88	Vosges
Y.	89	Yonne
B.	90	Belfort
Es.	91	Essonne
H.Se.	92	Hauts-de-Seine
S.S.D.	93	Seine-St-Denis
V.M.	94	Val-de-Marne
V.O.	95	Val-d'Oise

CORSICA
On same scale

Projection: Conical with two standard parallels

1:5 000 000

50   0   50   100 miles
50   0   50   100   150 km

COPYRIGHT GEORGE PHILIP & SON LTD

East from Greenwich

West from Greenwich

Projection: Conical with two standard parallels

ft   m   5000   3000   2000   1500   1000   400   200   0
m   ft
9000   6000   4500   3000   1200   600   200   600

FRANCE — Montpellier, Béziers, Narbonne, Golfe du Lion, Perpignan, Toulouse, Bayonne, Biarritz, Carcassonne

Golfe de Rosos, C. Creus, Gerona, Barcelona, Badalona, Sabadell, Tarrasa, Tarragona, Costa Dorada, Lérida, Huesca, Zaragoza

Pyrénées, ANDORRA, NAVARRA, Pamplona, Logroño, San Sebastián, Bilbao, PAÍS VASCO, Baracaldo, Vitoria

BALEARES, Menorca, Mallorca, Palma, Ibiza, Formentera, Cabrera

ARAGÓN, CATALUÑA, Teruel, Cuenca, Serranía de Cuenca, Guadalajara, Castellón de la Plana, Golfo de Valencia, Valencia, Albufera de Valencia, Sagunto

SPAIN, CASTILLA Y LEÓN, Burgos, Soria, Sierra de la Demanda, Valladolid, Salamanca, Ávila, Sierra de Gredos, Segovia, MADRID, Alcalá de Henares, Getafe, Leganés, Toledo, Montes de Toledo, CASTILLA — LA MANCHA, Ciudad Real, Albacete, Alicante, Elche, MURCIA, Murcia, Cartagena, Lorca, Almería, ANDALUCÍA, Granada, Sierra Nevada, Jaén, Linares, Úbeda, Sierra Morena, Córdoba, Sevilla, Huelva, Cádiz, Jerez, Gibraltar (Br.), La Línea de la Concepción, Ceuta (Sp.), Tánger, Tetouan, Málaga, Marbella, Gulfo de Cádiz

CANTÁBRICA, Santander, Oviedo, Gijón, Mieres, León, ASTURIAS, GALICIA, La Coruña, El Ferrol, Lugo, Santiago de Compostela, Pontevedra, Vigo, Orense, C. Ortegal, C. Finisterre

PORTUGAL, MINHO, DOURO, Porto, Braga, BEIRA ALTA, BEIRA BAIXA, BEIRA LITORAL, Coimbra, ESTREMADURA, RIBATEJO, Lisboa, Setúbal, ALTO ALENTEJO, BAIXO ALENTEJO, Évora, ALGARVE, C. de S. Vicente, Cabo de Sta. María, TRÁS OS MONTES, Bragança, Zamora

EXTREMADURA, Cáceres, Badajoz, Mérida, Sierra Morena

ALGERIA, Alger, Blida, Boufarik, Koléa, Khemis Miliana, Ech Cheliff, Mostaganem, Oran, MOROCCO

BALEARIC SEA, MEDITERRANEAN SEA, Bay of Biscay, ATLANTIC OCEAN, Strait of Gibraltar

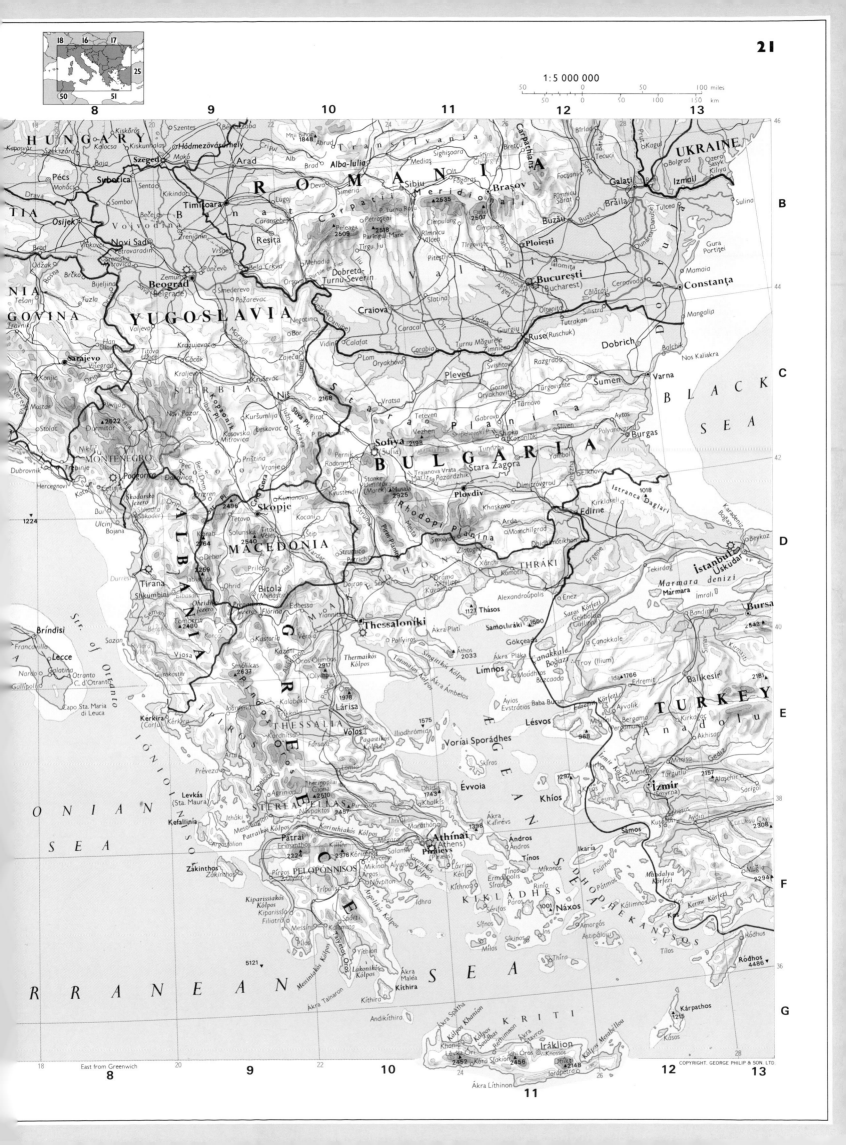

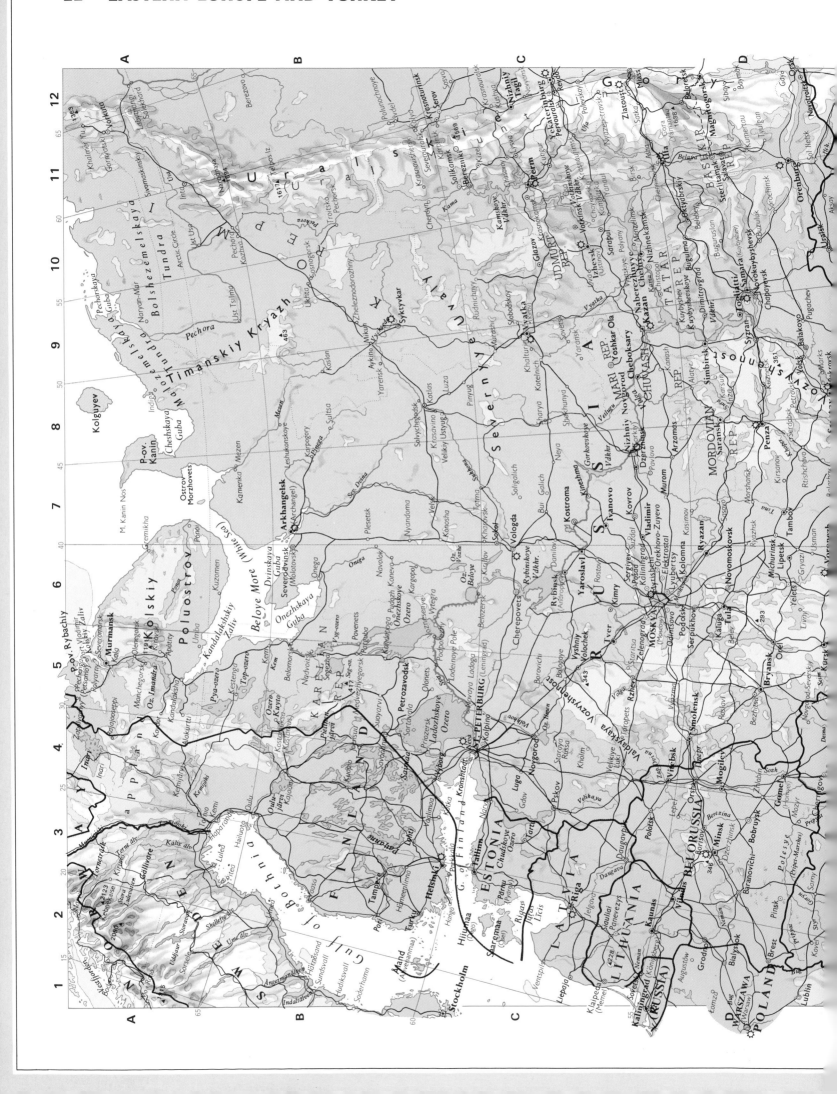

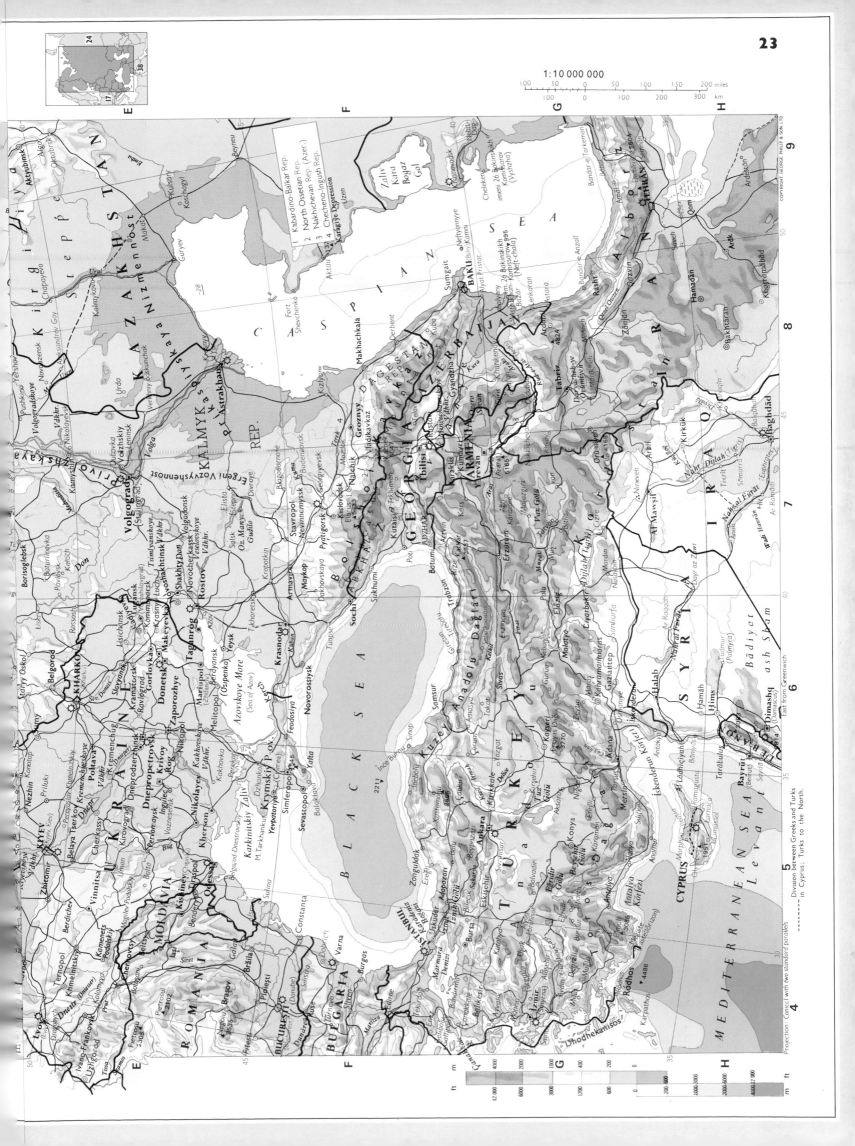

1:50 000 000

PACIFIC OCEAN

ARCTIC OCEAN

INDIAN OCEAN

S t e p p e

West Siberian Plain

North European Plain

Ural Mountains

Plateau of Tibet

Himalaya

Kunlun Shan

Tien Shan

Altai

Plateau of Mongolia

Central Siberian Plateau

Great Plains of China

China

Yellow Sea

East China Sea

South China Sea

Bay of Bengal

Arabian Sea

Red Sea

Mediterranean Sea

Black Sea

Caspian Sea

Caucasus

Arabia

Plateau of Iran

Mesopotamia

Borneo

Sumatra

Java Sea

Celebes Sea

Sulu Sea

Philippine Is.

Luzon

Mindanao

Formosa

Sunda Is.

Malay Peninsula

G. of Thailand

Str. of Malacca

Andaman Is.

Nicobar Is.

Ceylon

Western Ghats

Eastern Ghats

Deccan

India

Ganges

Mekong

Irrawaddy

Chao Phraya

Salween

Si-kiang

Hwang-ho

Yangtze

Amur

Lena

Yenisei

Ob

Volga

Danube

Tigris

Euphrates

Nile

Libyan Desert

Syrian Desert

Dead Sea

Suez Canal

Cyprus

Anatolia

Taurus Mts.

Carpathians

Adriatic Sea

North Sea

Baltic Sea

British Isles

Iceland

Greenland

Scandinavia

Finland

Kola Pen.

Novaya Zemlya

Svalbard

Barents Sea

Kara Sea

Laptev Sea

Taimyr Peninsula

New Siberian Is.

Wrangel I.

Kamchatka Peninsula

Bering Sea

Sea of Okhotsk

Sakhalin

Kuril Is.

Hokkaido

Honshu

Kyushu

Korea

Japan

Sikhote Alin Ra.

Verkhoyansk Range

Stanovoy Ra.

Yablonovy Ra.

Sayan Mts.

Great Khingan Mts.

Manchurian Plain

Turan Lowland

Aral Sea

Lake Balkhash

Pamir

Hindu Kush

Karakoram

Tarim Basin

Takla Makan

Turfan Basin

Koko Nor

Gydan Ra. (Kolyma)

Elburz Mts.

Zagros Mts.

Arafura Sea

Banda Sea

Molucca

Halmahera

Celebes

Ceram

Flores

Timor

Bali

Java

New Guinea

Australia

Caroline Is.

Palau Is.

Marianas Is.

Bonin Is.

Aleutian Is.

Seychelles

Amirantes

Socotra

Somali Peninsula

Madagascar (Lake Rezerva)

Maldive Is.

Laccadive Is.

Chagos Arch.

Equator

Tropic of Cancer

Arctic Circle

Projection: Bonne

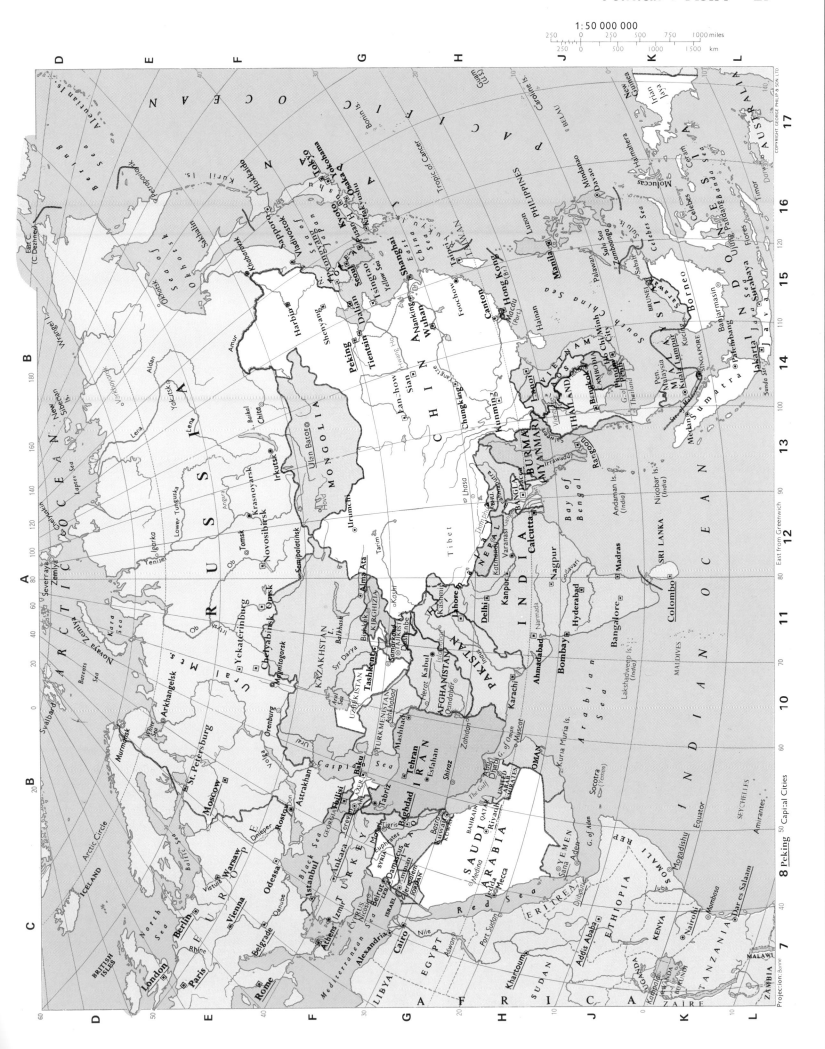

1 : 50 000 000

250   0   250   500   750   1000 miles
500   0   500   1000   1500   km

COPYRIGHT GEORGE PHILIP & SON LTD

Projection: Bonne

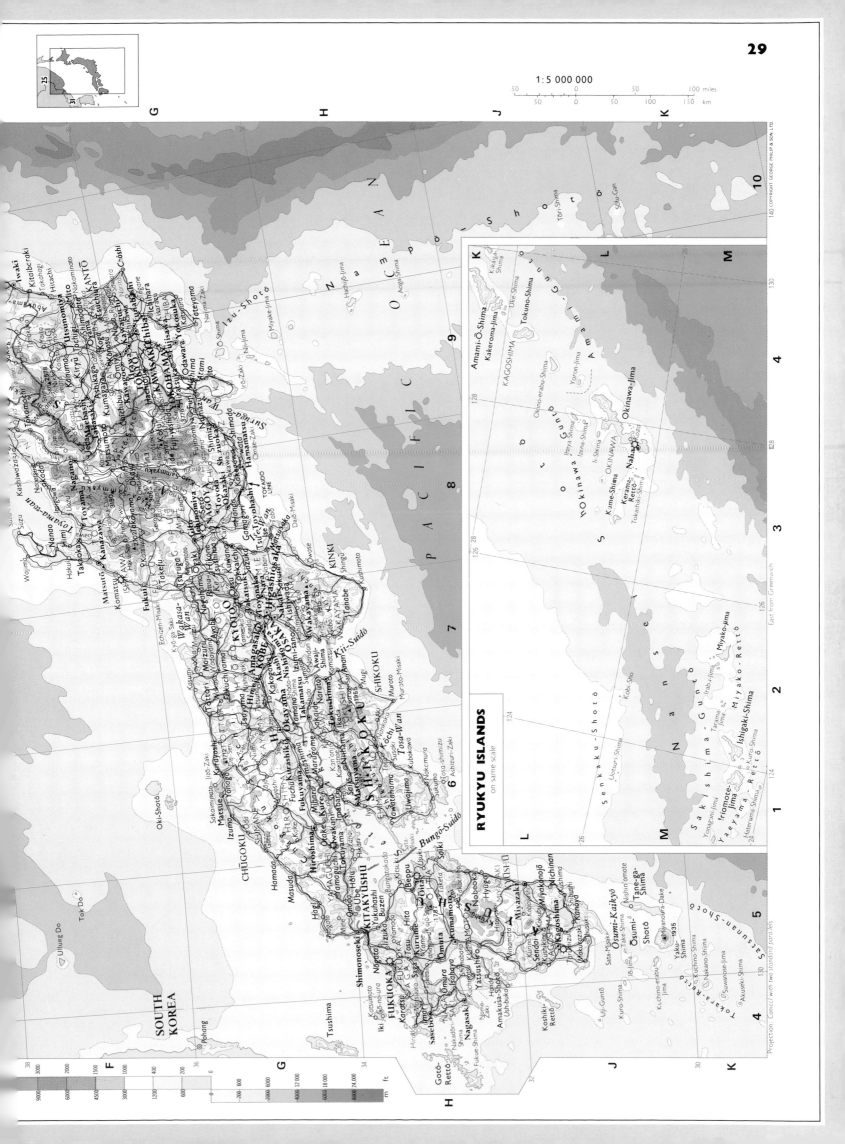

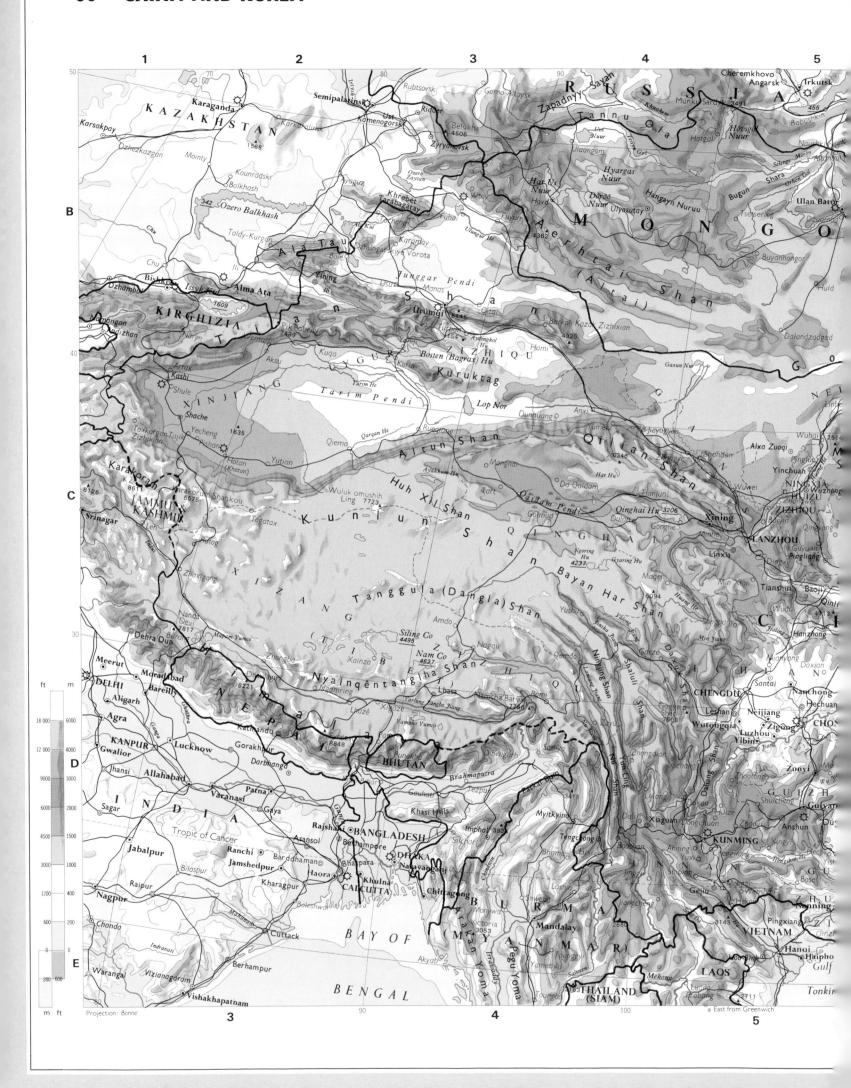

Projection: Bonne

East from Greenwich

A

B

C

D

E

F

1   2   3   4   5

BURMA (MYANMAR)
RANGOON
G. of Martaban
Moulmein
Thaton
Tavoy
Mergui
Tenasserim

THAILAND
BANGKOK
Nakhon Ratchasima (Khorat)
Phra Nakhon Si Ayutthaya
Kanchanaburi
Phitsanulok
Uttaradit
Tak
Chon Buri
Samut Prakan
Samut Songkhram
Phetchaburi
Chumphon
Surat Thani
Nakhon Si Thammarat
Phuket
Trang
Thale Luang
Songkhla (Singora)
Pattani
Yala
Narathiwat
Phnom Dangrek

LAOS
Vientiane
Savannakhet
Thakhek
Pakse

CAMBODIA
Phnom Penh
Battambang
Siem Reap
Tonle Sap
Pursat
Kompong Cham
Kompong Som
Kampot
Takeo

VIET-NAM
Hue
Da Nang (Tourane)
Qui Nhon
An Nhon (Binh Dinh)
Nha Trang
Phan Rang
Mui Ca Na
B. Me Thuot
Da Lat
Bien Hoa
PHANH BHO HO CHI-MINH (Saigon)
Ba Ria
Vung Tau
Can Tho
Ca Mau

Hanoi
Nong Khai
Udon Thani
Sakon Nakhon
Quang Tri
Quang Ngai
Binh Son
Pleiku
Kontum
Cheo Reo

Gulf of Thailand
Ko Samui
Ko Phangan
Phu Quoc
Con Son
Mui Bai Bung

SOUTH CHINA SEA

Pei Chiao
Hsisha
Howu Tao
Chuntao
P. Triton
Flat Nanshan
Laoita I.
Itu Aba
Palawan
C. Buliluyan
Bugsuk
Balabac I.
Balabac Strait
Spratly I.
Amboyna I.
Sin Crowe I.
Islands (Philippines)

ANDAMAN SEA

Strait of Malacca

Sabang (Kutaraja)
Banda Aceh
Sigli
Meureudu
Bireuen
Lhokseumawe
Langsa
Medan
Belawan
Pematangsiantar
Tanjungbalai
Pangkalansusu
ACEH
Leuser △3466
Meulaboh
Tapaktuan
Simeulue
Sinabang
Sibolga
UTARA
Tarutung
Gunungsitoli
Nias
Kepulauan Banyak
Telukdalem
Padangsidempuan
Kepulauan Batu
Tanahbala
Lubuksikaping
Bukittinggi
BARAT
Payakumbuh
Padang
Pariaman
Solok
Kerinci △3800
Muarabungo
Sungaipenuh
Siberut
Sipora
Pulau Pagai Utara
Pulau Pagai Selatan
Mukomuko
JAMBI
Jambi
Muaratembesi
Muaratebo
BENGKULU
Bengkulu
Lahat
Muaraenim
Lubuklinggau
Manna
Dempo △3159
Baturaja
Kotabumi

PENINSULAR MALAYSIA
KUALA LUMPUR
George Town
Pinang
Butterworth
Bukit Mertajam
Taiping
Ipoh
Teluk Anson
Port Weld
Port Dickson
Kelang
Melaka
Segamat
Labis
Mersing
Kluang
Johor Baharu
Kota Tinggi
Batu Pahat
Muar
Gemas
Kuala Dungun
Kuala Terengganu
Kota Baharu
Kuantan
Temerloh
Jerantut
Tapah
Kuala Lipis
G. Tahan △2190
Pasir Mas
Kuala Kubu
Kota Baharu
Perhentian
Redang
Kemaman

SINGAPORE
Bintan
Tanjungpinang
Kepulauan Riau

Kepulauan Natuna Besar
Telukbutun
Natuna Besar
Kepulauan Natuna Selatan
Kepulauan Anambas
Matak
Siantan
Midai
Serasan
Kepulauan Tambelan
Kepulauan Badas

MALAYSIA

SARAWAK
Kuching
Sibu
Kapit
Bintulu
Tubau
Niah
Miri
Lutong
Bintangor
Sri Aman
Serian
Simanggang
Betong
Sambas
Singkawang
Pontianak
BARAT
Mempawah
Sanggau
Sintang
Putussibau
Sekadau
Nangapinoh

SABAH
KOTA KINABALU (Jesselton)
Kota Belud
Kudat
Victoria
Beaufort
Keningau
Pulau Labuan
Papar
Kinabalu △4101
Tenom
Melalap △1346
Lawas

BRUNEI
Bandar Seri Begawan
Serasa
Tutong

BORNEO
KALIMANTAN
TENGAH
Pegunungan Muller
Pegunungan Schwaner
Gunung Hose
Gunung Raya
Banjaran Iran
Pangkalanbun
Sampit
Kualakapuas
Palangkaraya
Kotawaringin
Kumai
Pembuang
Seruyan
SELATAN
Banjarmasin
Martapura
Pelaihari
Amuntai
Kandangan
Barabai
Tanjung
Kotabaru
Pulau Laut

TIMUR
Tanjungredeb
Tanjungselor
Numeh
Tarakan
Samarinda
Balikpapan
Tanahgrogot
Muarakaman
Muarawahau
Longiram
Muaratewe
Sangkulirang

SUMATERA
Danau Toba
Pekanbaru
RIAU
Rengat
Dumai
Rupat
Bengkalis
Siak Sri Inderapura
Tanjungpinang
Selatpanjang

INDONESIA

Bangka
Belitung (Billiton)
Pangkalpinang
Muntok
Tanjungpandan
Manggar
Pulau Bangka
Pulau Belitung
Kepulauan Karimata
Kepulauan Lingga
Lingga
Singkep
Berhala

Palembang
SELATAN
Tebingtinggi
Sekayu
Menggala
LAMPUNG
Tanjungkarang
Telukbetung
Kotaagung
Kalianda

Greater Sunda Islands

JAVA SEA
Kepulauan Karimunjawa
Bawean
Kepulauan Masalembo
Kepulauan Kangean
Kepulauan Paternoster
Laut Ketil
Tg. Selatan

INDIAN OCEAN
△6073
Enggano
△6650
Java Trench

JAKARTA
Serang
Bogor
BANDUNG
Purwakarta
Cirebon
Tegal
Brebes
Pekalongan
Semarang
Kudus
Kendal
Pemalang
Tasikmalaya
Garut
Pelabuhan Ratu
Pengalengan
Pulau Rakata (Krakatau)
Selat Sunda
Tanjungpriok
Purwokerto
Pekalongan
Magelang
Surakarta
Yogyakarta
Madiun
Kediri
Blitar
Surabaya
Madura
Bangkalan
Pasuruan
Probolinggo
Situbondo
Malang
Tulungagung
TIMUR
△3265
△3342
△2568
△3676
△3726
△3142
Slamet △3428
Bali
Denpasar
Lombok
Rinjani △3726
Sumbawa
Singaraja

NUSA TENGGARA

J A W A (JAVA)
TENGAH

Projection: Mercator

East from Greenwich

ft | m
12 000 | 4000
9000 | 3000
6000 | 2000
4500 | 1500
3000 | 1000
1200 | 400
600 | 200
0 | 0
−200 | 600
2000 | 6000
4000 | 12 000
6000 | 18 000
8000 | 24 000
m | ft

100   105   110   115

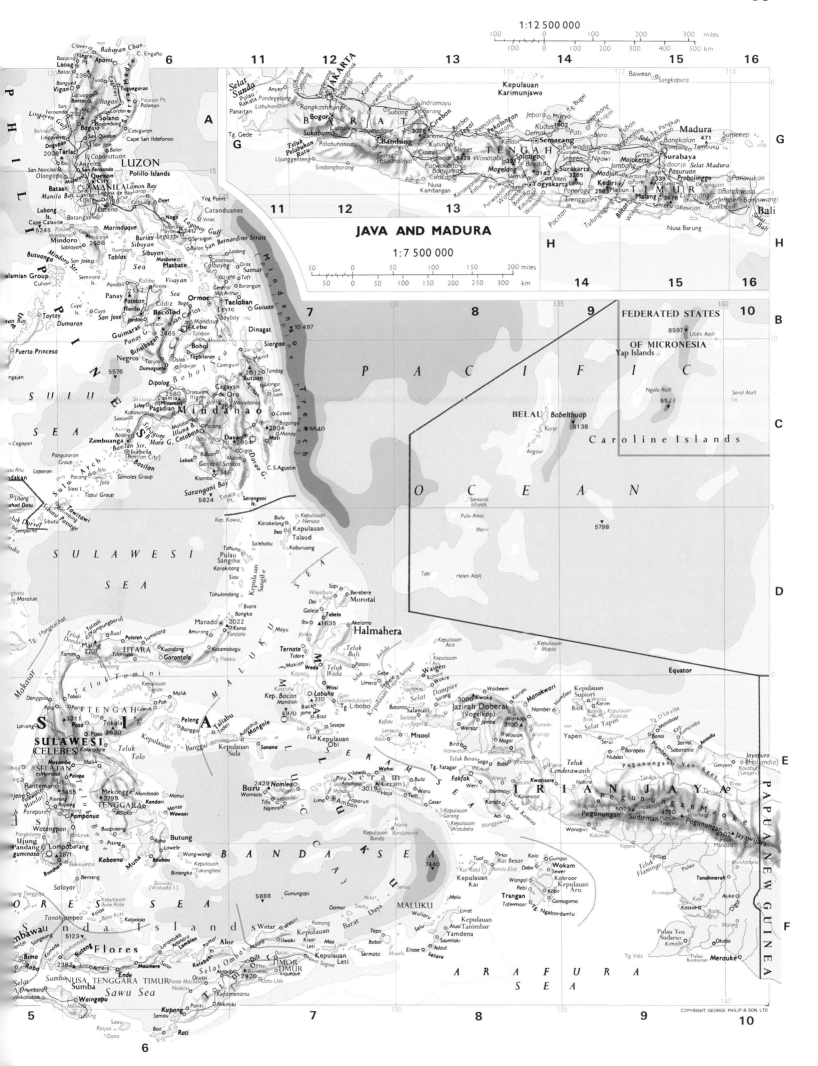

JAVA AND MADURA

1:7 500 000

1:12 500 000

1:10 000 000

100   50   0   50   100   150   200 miles
100   0   100   200   300 km

BANGLADESH

BURMA (MYANMAR)

CHIN

KAYAH

KAWTHULE

TENASSERIM

Mandalay
Sagaing
Myinmu
Meiktila
Yenangyaung
Magwe
Minbu
Prome
Henzada
Rangoon
Bassein
Pegu
Moulmayaing
Martaban

Arakan Coast

Andaman Sea

Andaman (India) Islands

North Andaman
Middle Andaman
South Andaman
Port Blair

Preparis North Channel
Preparis South Channel
Koko Kyunzu (Burma)
Coco Channel

Moscos
Maungmagan Islands
Tavoy
Mergui
Myeik Kyunzu (Mergui)

Archipelago

G. of Thailand

Gulf of Martaban

THAILAND

Chiengmai
Lampang
Uttaradit
Phitsanulok
Sukhothai
Nakhon Sawan
Uthai Thani
Suphan Buri
Bangkok
Thon Buri
Samut Prakan
Chon Buri
Nakhon Ratchasima (Khorat)
Surin

Khorat

Chumphon
Surat Thani
Nakhon Si Thammarat
Phuket
Songkhla
Pattani
Yala
Alor Setar

Kho Khot Kra (Isthmus of Kra)
Ko Samui
Ko Phangan

CHINA

Nanning
Pinxiang
Beihai
Hainan Dao
Leizhou Bandao
Gejiu
Mengzi

Gulf of Tongking

LAOS

Luang Prabang
Vientiane
Vang Vieng
Savannakhet
Pakse

VIETNAM

Hanoi
Haiphong
Nam Dinh
Ninh Binh
Thanh Hoa
Vinh
Ha Tinh
Dong Hoi
Quang Tri
Hue
Da Nang (Tourane)
Quang Ngai
Qui Nhon
An Nhon

CAMBODIA

Battambang
Siem Reap
Tanlé Sap
Phnom Penh
Kompong Cham
Pursat
Kompong Som (Sihanoukville)
Kampot
Kratie
Stung Treng

Phanh Bho Ho Chi Minh (Saigon)
Bien Hoa
Vung Tau
My Tho
Long Xuyen
Can Tho
Rach Gia
Phu Quoc
Con Dao
Mui Ca Mau

SOUTH CHINA SEA

Phnom Dang Rek

Gulf of Tongking (Bac Phan)

PENINSULAR MALAYSIA AND SINGAPORE
1:6 000 000

50   0   50 miles
50   0   50 km

PERLIS
Alor Setar
KEDAH
George Town
Butterworth
Bukit Mertajam
PINANG
Taiping
PERAK
Ipoh
Kampar
Teluk Anson
KELANTAN
Kota Baharu
TERENGGANU
Kuala Terengganu
Kuala Dungun
Kuantan
PAHANG
Raub
SELANGOR
Kuala Lumpur
Shah Alam
Kelang
NEGERI SEMBILAN
Seremban
MELAKA
Melaka
Bandar Maharani (Muar)
Bandar Penggaram
JOHOR
Johor Baharu
SINGAPORE

G. Tahan 2182
Cameron Highlands

Strait of Malacca

SUMATERA INDONESIA

PENINSULAR MALAYSIA

George Town
Pulau Pinang
Butterworth
Taiping
Ipoh
Kuala Lipis
Kuantan
Kuala Lumpur
Kelang
Seremban
Melaka
Johor Baharu

Gunong Tahan 2190
Cameron Highlands

Kepulauan Anambas
Kepulauan Natuna Besar
Kepulauan Natuna Selatan
Kepulauan Tambelan

INDONESIA

Strait of Malacca

Projection: Conical with two standard parallels

East from Greenwich

COPYRIGHT GEORGE PHILIP & SON LTD.

ft   m
9000   3000
6000   2000
4500   1500
3000   1000
1200   400
600   200
0   0
200   600
2000   6000
m ft

Equatorial Scale 1:50 000 000

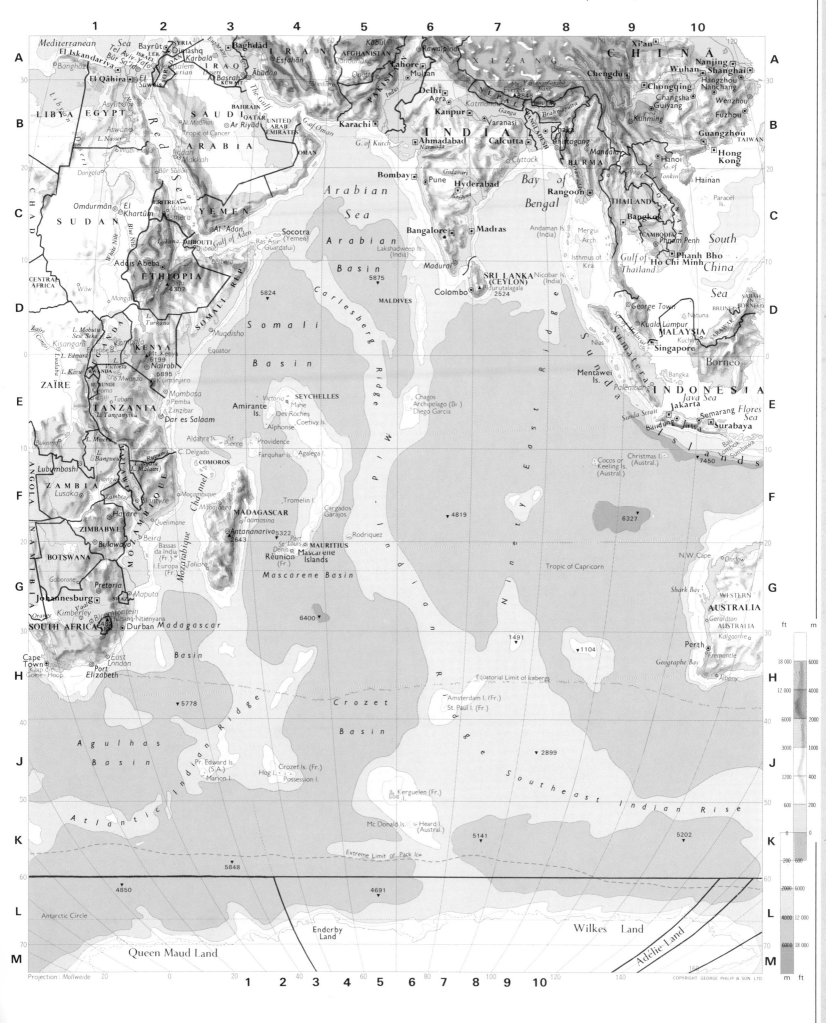

Projection: Mollweide

COPYRIGHT GEORGE PHILIP & SON LTD.

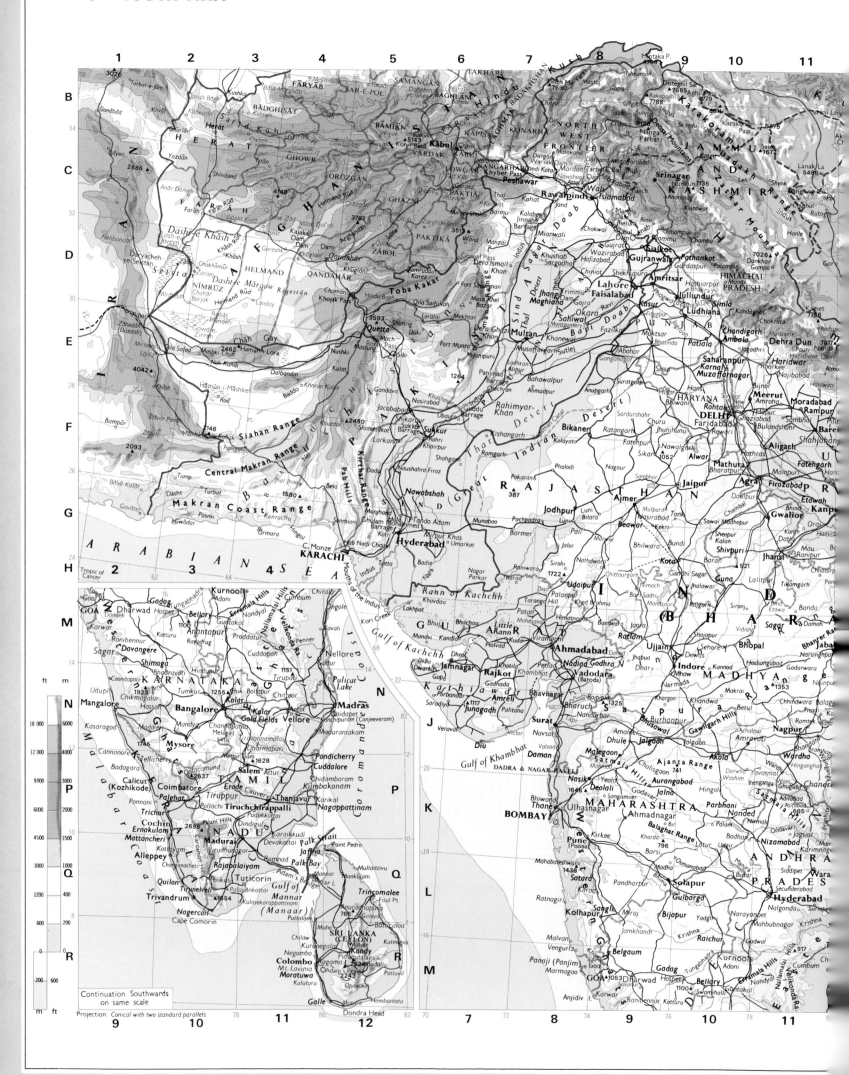

Continuation Southwards
on same scale

Projection: Conical with two standard parallels

1:10 000 000

100 50 0 50 100 150 200 miles
100 0 100 200 300 km

B

XINJIANG UYGUR

CHINA

QINGHAI

Kun lun Shan Shan

Xil Shan

Gyaring Hu
Ngoring Hu
Maqên Gangri
Darlag

Dogai Coring

Bayan Har Shan

Yushu

C

CHINA

Ngangglong Kangri ▲7315

XIZANG

(TIBET)

Tanggula (Dangla) Shan

Tanggula Shankou ✕5180

Gangri

Kangri

Siling Co

Dêngqên

Baiyu

SICHUAN

D

Nam Co

Nagqu

Dorong

Zhaxze

Nu Jiang (Salween)

Litang
▲4959

Mustang

7059

Nyainqêntanglha Shan

Lhunzhub

7088

Lhasa

Gongbo'gyamda

Yushu

E

Simikot

Mugu ▲4944

Maquan He (Tsangpo)

Xigaze

Lhaze Gyangze

Yarlung Zangbo Jiang (Brahmaputra)

✕7766

ARUNACHAL PRADESH

YUNNAN

Dhaulagiri ▲8221

5602

Xixabangma Feng ▲8013

NEPAL

Katmandu

7554

7314

7089

Saikhoa Ghat

3072 Putao (Ft. Hertz)

5500

F

Everest 8848

Kanchenjunga 8598

SIKKIM

Thimphu Punakha

BHUTAN

Taga-Dzong

Rupa

Dibrugarh

North Lakhimpur

Hpungan La

Kawngum 2432

KACHIN

Myitkyina

Gorakhpur

Darbhanga

Taga

WEST

Tura 1412 1961

MEGHALAYA

Shillong

Barail Range

NAGALAND

Kohima 3824

Singkaling Hkamti

2424

Kumon Bum

Mogaung

G

Lucknow
Rae Bareli
Faizabad

Deoria

BENGAL

Cherrapunji

Sylhet

Hoflong

Barakhola

MANIPUR

Imphal

Homalin

Katha

Shwegu

Bhamo

H

Allahabad
Varanasi (Benares)
Mirzapur

Patna

BIHAR

Gaya

Deoghar

Bhagalpur

Rajshahi

Bogra

EAST BENGAL

Mymensingh

Silchar

Aijal

Churachandpur

Tamu

Kalewa

Shwebo

Mandalay

Bhagalpur

ORISSA

Cuttack
Bhubaneswar
Puri

BAY OF BENGAL

BURMA (MYANMAR)

THAILAND
Chiengmai

INDIAN OCEAN

Rangoon

Gulf of Martaban

Preparis North Channel

Pariparit Kyun (Burma)

Preparis South Channel

Koko Kyunzu (Burma)

Tavoy

COPYRIGHT GEORGE PHILIP & SON, LTD

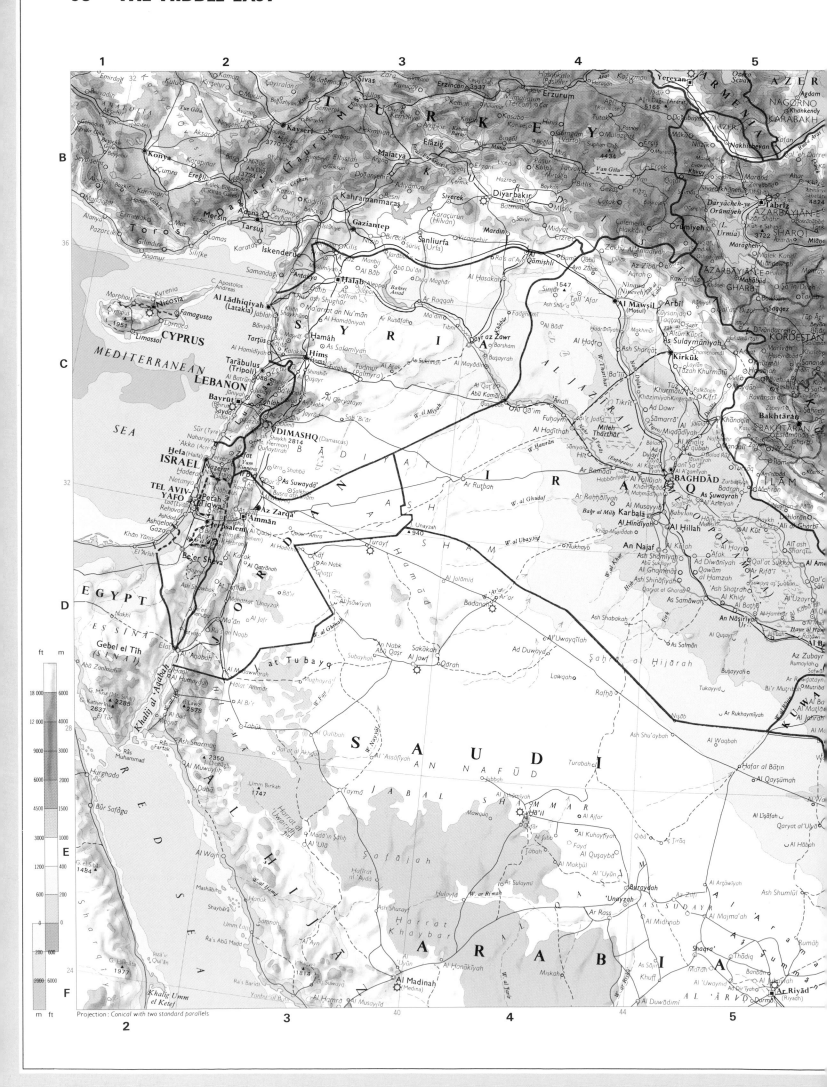

Projection: Conical with two standard parallels

1:7 000 000

50 0 50 100 150 200 miles
50 0 50 100 150 200 250 300 km

23
23   36
45
40

6   7   8   9   10

TURKMENISTAN

KARA KUM

Baku
Krasnovodsk
Nebit Dag
Kizyl Arvat
Kazandzhik
Chardzhou
Amudarya

CASPIAN SEA

Ashkhabad (Ashgabat)
Mary
Bayram-Ali
Jolotan
Tedzhen
Serakhs
Tashkepri

Ardabil
Āstārā
Bandar-e Anzali
Rasht
Fowman

GĪLĀN
MĀZANDARĀN

Reshteh-ye Kūhhā-ye Alborz

Qazvin
Karaj
Tajrish
TEHRĀN
Rey

MARKAZĪ

SEMNĀN

KHORĀSĀN

Mashhad (Meshed)
Neyshābūr
Sabzevār
Kāshmar
Torbat-e Heydarīyeh
Torbat-e Jām

Kūh-e Binālūd

HERĀT
Herāt

BADGHISAT

Safīd Kūh

Qom
HAMADĀN
Hamadān
Arāk

DASHT-E KAVĪR

Chāh Kavīr

IRAN

AFGHANISTAN

Borūjerd
Khorramābād
Golpāyegān
Nā'īn

EŞFAHĀN
Eşfahān

Dezfūl
Najafābād
Shahr-e Kord

CHAHĀR MAHĀLL VA BAKHTĪARĪ

Āhvāz
KHŪZESTĀN

YAZD
Yazd

Bīrjand

KŌHKILŪYEH VA BŪYER AHMADĪ

Kūh-e Dīnār

Khorramshahr
Ābādān
Shatt al Arab

Rafsanjān

KERMĀN
Kermān

Bam

Kūh-e Jebal Barez

SĪSTĀN VA BALŪCHESTĀN

Zāhedān
(Duzdab)
Mīrjāveh

PAKISTAN

Shīrāz

FĀRS

Dasht-e Margow

NĪMRŪZ

Daryāche-ye Sīstān

Būshehr
(Bushire)

Kāzerūn
Fīrūzābād

HORMOZGĀN

Kūhhā-ye Bashākerd

Bandar-e Lengeh

Qeshm

Str. of Hormuz

Ra's al Khaymah
Dībā

BAHRAIN
Al Manāmah

Ad Dawḩah (Doha)
QATAR

Dubayy (Dubai)
Ash Shāriqah (Sharjah)

Abū Zaby (Abu Dhabi)

OMAN

Gulf of Oman

THE GULF

Ad Dammām
Az Zahrān (Dhahran)
Al Hufūf

Al Wakrah

East from Greenwich

UNITED ARAB EMIRATES

60 COPYRIGHT GEORGE PHILIP & SON LTD.

6   7   8   9

B

C

D

E

F

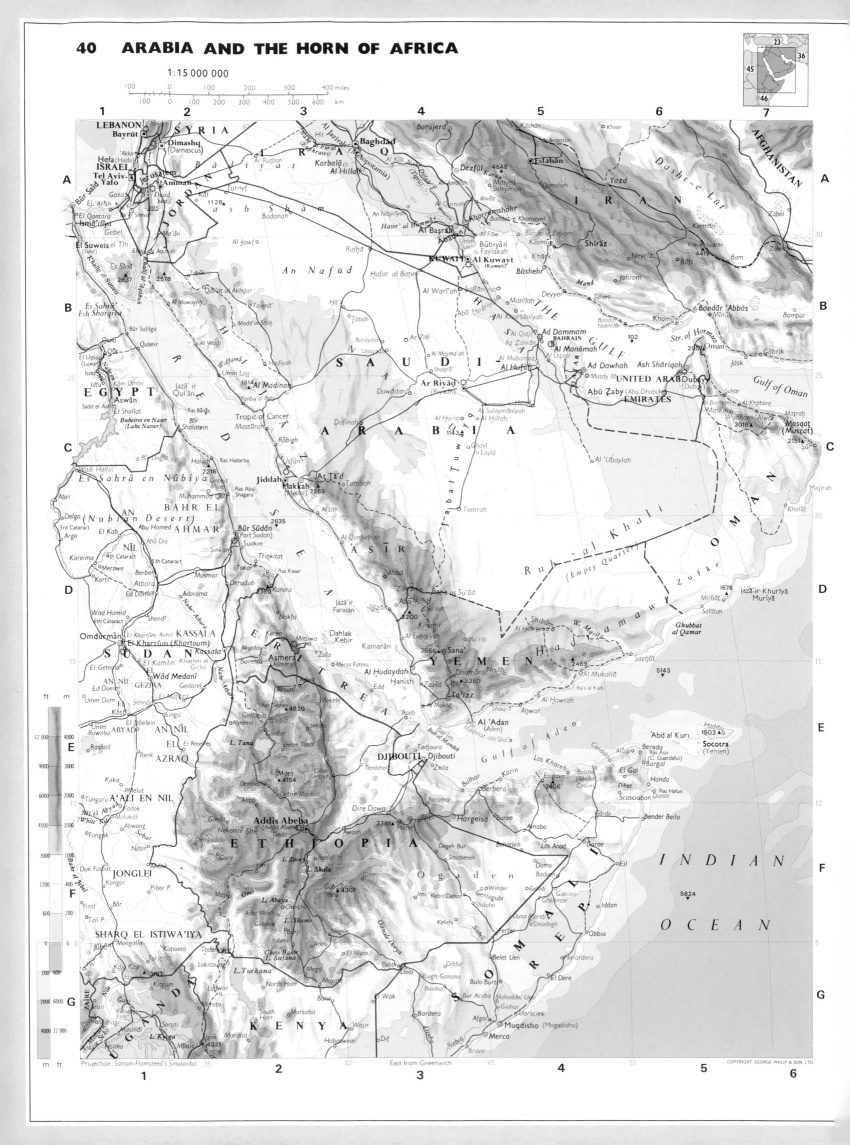

1:15 000 000

100   0   100   200   300   400 miles
100   0   100   200   300   400   600 km

1   2   3   4   5   6   7

LEBANON
Bayrût   SYRIA   Al Jazíra   Borujerd   Kāshān   Khvor   AFGHANISTAN
Hefa (Haifa)   Dimashq   Al Furāt   Baghdad   Ardeston
ISRAEL   (Damascus)   Karbalā   Dezful   4548   Eşfahān   Dasht-e Lut   A
Tel Aviv-   Al Hillah   Masjed   Yazd
Yafo   'Ammān   IRAQ   Soleyman   Qomsheh   Zabol
Gaza   JORDAN   Al Kūt   Ahvāz   Kermān

El 'Arîsh   Ma'ān   An Nāsirîyah   Khorramshahr   Būshehr   Shīrāz   Neyriz   Koh   4419   Bam
Ismâ'îlya   Badanah   Hawr al Hammār   Al Başrah   Abādān   Bandar-e Khomeyni   Bandar 'Abbās
El Suweis   el Tih   1128   Turayf   Al Qurnah   Būbiyān   Kāzerūn   Devan
(Suez)   2637   2578   Rafhā   KUWAIT   Faylakah   Khārk   Jahrom   Bāft
Es Sinâ   Tabūk   An Nafūd   Hafar al Bāţin   AL Kuwayt   (Kuwait)   Deyyer   Maşule
Gebel   Qal'at al Akhdar   Hā'il   Saffānîyah   Tôherí   Mand
'Aqaba

B   Es Sahrâ   Al Muwayliḥ   Taymā'   Burydah   Al Majma'ah   Az Zilfî   Al Warî'ah   Manîfah   Khamīr   Str. of Hormuz   Oman   Bampūr
Esh Sharqîya   Madâ'in Sâliḥ   Tūbah   Abū Haḍrîyah   THE   Bandar   Gābrik
Bûr Safâga   Tūbah   'Unayzah   Al Kharsānîyah   S'Al Qaţif   Nakhilû
Qena   Al Wajh   GULF   2997
Quseir   Hadîyah   Ad Dammam   Ad Dawḥah   Mînāb
Umm Lajj   1814   Al Madinah   Az Zahrān   BAHRAIN   Ash Shāriqah

C   El Uqsur   Ras Bânâs   SAUDI-   Ar Riyad   Al Majma'ah   Al Hufūf   Al Manāmah   Dubayy   Gulf of Oman
(Luxor)   Aswân   Bîr   (Riyadh)   Al Qaţr   Al Uqayr   UNITED ARAB   (Dubai)
Kôm Ombo   Shalatein   Tropic of Cancer   Duwādimi   As Sulaymānīyah   Abū Zaby (Abu Dhabi)   Suḥār
Idfu   Sadd el Aali   Rābigh   Al Hillah   EMIRATES   Al Khābūra
EGYPT   El Shallal   Mastūrah   Dafinah   As Sulaymānīyah   Al Buraymī   Maskīn   Matrah
Buheiret en Naser   ARABIA   Al Hariq   Al Buraymī   3019   Masqaṭ
(Lake Nasser)   1143   Ghayl   Wushāḥ   (Muscat)
Halaib   Ras Hadarba   2216   Jiddah   Makkah   2565   Al 'Ubaylah   2151   Şūr

Ras Abu   Usfān   Ghayl   Khalūf
Shagara   Ar Ţā'if   al Laylā

D   Muhammad Qol   At Tā'if   Turabah   OMAN
Abri   Gebeit   Mine   Al Lith   Tamrah
Wadi Halfa   Es Sahrâ en Nûbiya   BAHR EL   2635   Al Qunfudhah   Ruḥ 'al Khali   Jazā'ir Khurlyā   1678
Delgo   (Nubian Desert)   AHMAR   Bûr Sûdân   (Empty Quarter)   Mirbāţ   Muriyā
3rd Cataract   El Kab   Abu Hamed   (Port Sudan)   'ASĪR   Jaza'ir   Ghubbat   Salāla
Argo   Suakin   Farasān   Jizān   al Qamar
Kareima   NÎL   Sinkat   Abha   'Abs as Su'ūd
4th Cataract   Abū Dis   Trinkitat   W. Masila   Sayhūt
Merowe   Berber   Tokar   Ras Kasar   3200   Şa'dah   Shibām   5143
Korti   Atbara   Ras Kasar   Jizān   Khamir   Ma'rib   2469 Al Mukallā
5th Cataract   Musmar   Derudub   2780   Karora   3666   Sana'   Ra's al Kalb   1503
Wad Hamid   Adarama   Nakfa   Al Luḥayyah   Dhamār   3350   Hadibu
Shendi   KASSALA   ERITREA   Mitsiwa   Dahlak   Zabīd   Ibb   Ta'izz   'Abd al Kuri   Socotra

E   Omdurmân   Kassala   Keren   Kebir   Kamarān   Al Mukhā   Shaqra   Ahwar   Al Hawrah   (Yemen)   Bereda
El Khartûm (Khartoum)   Aksum   Asmera   Zula   Al Hudaydah   YEMEN   Las Khoreh   Ras Asir
SUDAN   El Kamlin   Kassala   Barentu   Mecsa Fatma   Haniish   Bāb el   Ma'dīnat ush Sha'b   Alula   (C. Guardafui)
AN NÎL   Khashm el Girba   Adwa   Edd   Mandeb   Al 'Adan   Candala   Bargal
El Geteina   Gedaref   Aksum   4620   Mekele   Aseb   (Aden)   Bosaso   El Gal   Handa
Ed Dueim   El Manâqil   Ras Dashen   Gondar   Todjoura   Gulf of Aden   (Bender)   Dhut   Ras Hafun
GEZIRA   Dabat   Sekota   Tendaho   Cassim   2406   Scusciuban   Dante
Umm Dam   Wâd Medanî   DJIBOUTI Djibouti   Zeila   Karin
Sennâr   Debre Tabor   Berbera   Bender Beila

F   Umm   El   L. Tana   Mâta   Zeila   Barama
Ruwaba   Jebelein   Dese (Dessye)   Dire Dawa   Bulhar   Hargeisa   Buao   Ainabo
Rashad   ABYAD   Dembecha   4154   Buao   Garoe
Renk   Er Roseires   Alibo   Dire Dawa   Degeh Bur   Las Anod
A'ALI EN NIL   Debre Markos   Awash   3381 Harer   Gardo
Nîl el Abyad   L. Zima   Nekemte   Addis Ababa)   Bohotleh   Obbia
(White Nil)   EL   Sire   ETHIOPIA   Domo   INDIAN
Tungaru   Kaka   AZRAQ   Geda   Ogaden   Badaweyn
Fangak   Gimbi   Addis Abeba   Sebeli   Werder   OCEAN
Malakâl   Gore   Imi   Kebri Dehar   Galcaio   5824
JONGLEI   Abwong   Nâsir   L. Abaya   Sodo   Gobā   Ginir   Ghensor   Iddan
Duk Fadiat   Sobat   Dembidollo   Chencha   4307 Batu   Kelafo   Dusa Mareb   Sinadogo
Pibor P.   Majī   Omo   Negele   Sebel   Eil
Kongor   L. Abaya   Arba Minch   Arero   Dinsor   El Dere   El Dere

G   Tirol   Bôr   L. Shamo   Burjī   Dolo   Lugh Ganana   Belet Uen   Hararadera
SHARQ EL ISTIWA'IYA   Gidole   Chew Bahir   El Niybo   Baidoa   Bur Acaba   Mahaddei Ueu   Giohar
Juba   Mongalla   Kapoeta   Todenyang   (L. Stefanie)   Dif   Bardera   Afgoi   Uarsciek
Kajo Kaji   Torit   Lokitaung   Mega   Mayale   Bulo Burti   Muqdisho (Mogadishu)
Yei   ZAIRE   North Horr   Buna   Dusa Mareb   Merca
UGANDA   1321   L. Turkana   Marsabit   Wajir   Bur Acaba   Brava   SOMALI REP.
KENYA   Habaswein

ft   m
12 000   4000
9000   3000
6000   2000
4500   1500
3000   1000
1200   400
600   200
0   0
200   600
2000   6000
4000   12000
m   ft

Projection: Sanson-Flamsteed's Sinusoidal   35   2   East from Greenwich   3   45   4   50   5   6   COPYRIGHT GEORGE PHILIP & SON, LTD.

1   2   3   4   5   6

1:2 500 000

10 0 10 20 30 40 50 miles
10 0 10 20 30 40 50 60 70 80 km

38
45
45 38

CYPRUS
Paphos
Limassol
Akrotiri Bay
Episkopi Bay
C. Gata

M E D I T E R R A N E A N   S E A

Al Hamidiyah
Tall Kalakh
Hims (Homs)
1075
Shinshār
Furqlus
Al Qusayr
Halbā
ASH SHAMĀL
Tarābulus (Tripoli)
Al Minā'
Zgharta
Qurnat as Sawdā' 3088
Al Hirmil
HIMS
Al Batrūn
Dūmā
Qartaba
Al Buray'
Al Qaryatayn
Jubayl
Ibrāhīm
2464
Bi'r Ghadīr
Al Labwah
2616
Ba'labakk
BIQĀ Al 'Āṣī Beqaa Valley
Shaqlāwī
Yabrūd
An Nabk
Jūniyah
Bikfāyā
2628
Sannīn
BAYRŪT (Beirut)
Ash Shuwayfāt
Zahlah
Tāz Zubdāniyah
1406
Al Qutayfah
Khān Abu Shāmāt
LEBANON
2420
Az Zabdānī
DIMASHQ (Damascus)
S Y R I A
Saydā (Sidon)
Jazzin
Khirbat Qanāfār
Qadas
1942
AL LĪTĀNĪ
Jabal Ash Sharqī
Dūmā
Qaṭanā
DIMASHQ
An Nabatiyah at Tahta
AL JANŪB
Khiyām
Jabal ash Shaykh (Mt. Hermon) 2814
Al A'waj
Daraya
Al Hijānah
Sūr (Tyre)
Qiryat Shemona
Burāq
As Sanamayn
Al Kiswah
Nahariyya
1197
Al Qunaytirah
DARĀ
Shahba
AS SUWAYDĀ'
Me'ona
Golan Hts.
Rafid
W. al Harīr
'Akko (Acre)
HAZOR (Hazor)
Jabal ad Durūz
Mifraz Hefa
HAGALIL
Zefat
Qiryat Yam
Sakhnin
Migdal
Soham al Jawlān
As Suwayda
Hefa (Haifa)
Qiryat Ata
Teverya (Tiberias)
Dar'ā
Shahba
1800
Tirat Karmel
Nazerat (Nazareth)
Yam Kinneret
Salkhad
Dāliyat el Karmel
HAZAFON
'Afula
Jisr
IRBID
HEFA'
TEL MEGIDDO
Bet She'an
Irbid
Umm al Qittayn
Umm el Fahm
Jenin
'Ar Ramthā
Jusra ash Sham
CAESAREA
Hadera
'Ajlūn
'Ajlun ad Dara'
Al Mafruq
Hadera
SHOMRON
ISRAEL
Netanya
'Anabta
Tulkarm
NABULUS SAMARIA
Jarash
1247
Zarqa
Herzliyya
Nābulus
Benē Beraq
Under Israeli Administration
Tel Aviv-Yafo
Petah Tiqwa
SHILO
AL BALQĀ'
As Salt
Az Zarqā'
Ramat Gan
West Bank
Tel Aviv
Bat Yam
1016
AL ARDAN
AMMĀN
Rishon le Ziyyon
AL 'UDS
249
N. Soreq
Ramla
Ram Allāh
Wādi as Sir
Ashdod
Rehovot
'Arūb (Jericho)
Lod
At Tunayb
Yavne
Qiryat Mal'akhi
Jerusalem (Yerushalayim) (Al Quds)
Ma'daba
AL 'ASIMAH
Ashqelon
Bet Lehem (Bethlehem)
Qiryat Gat
Bet Shemesh
LAKHISH
HAR YEHUDA
Al Khalil (Hebron)
W. al Haydān
Gaza
N. Shiqma
Az Zāhiriya
AL KHALIL
W. al Mūjib
Sederot
Dhibān
Gaza Strip
Khān Yūnis
1065
Rafah
'Arad
Al Qatrānah
Be'er Sheva
Bor Mashash
1305 Al Mazār
981
W. al Ghadaf
Bûr Sa'îd (Port Said)
Bûr Fu'âd
El Daheir
333
Al Karak
Dimona
1682
At Tafilah
AL KARAK
Khalīg el Tīna
Râs Burûn
Sabkhet el Bardawil
El 'Arîsh
AL KARAK
W. al Hasa
Qanã el Suweis (Suez Canal)
Români
Bîr el Garârât
HADAROM
ft m
Bîr Qatia
Bîr el 'Abd
Bîr Kaseiba
Bîr el Garârât
Bîr el Jafir
Bîr Lahfân
Qezi'ot
9000 3000
Ismâ'ilîya
Wâhid
Bîr el Duweidar
W. el 'Arîsh
Bîr Madkûr
Birein
1072 W. ash Shawmarī
6000 2000
El Qantara
892
Mizpe Ramon
Ma'ān
Khamsa
Bîr Hasana
HANEGEV (Negev Desert)
Bi'r ad Dabbaghāt
W. Abu Safar
Qa'el Jafr
El Buheirat el Murrat el Kubra (Gt. Bitter L.)
1094
G. Yi 'Allâq
Bîr Beida
Ruim Tal'at al Jamā'ah 1736
4500 1500
PETRA
3000 1000
G. el Kabrît
W. Qirâtya
W. el Agrûd
N. Paran
N. Hiyyon
MA'ĀN
Al Jafr
EL SUWEIS
875
El Suweis (Suez)
E G Y P T
Bîr Gebel Hasa
Bîr Thamâda
W. el Brûk
W. Mahasham
Mahattat 'Unayzah
Nijil
1200 400
Râs el Naqb
Mahattat ash Shidīyah
600 200
Bîr Taufiq
Uyûn Mûsa
SINAI
Nakhl
W. el Jaqaba
W. el Tamarūni
Bîr Abu Muhammad
En Avrona
1435
Ra's an Naqb
0 0
'Ain Sudr
W. el Saheira
W. Ruag
El Thamad
Bîr al Mōri
Bi'r al Qattar
Bîr Bad
948
El Wabeira
Gebel el Tîh
1592
Al 'Aqabah
Bi'r al Butayyin
200 600
Ghubbet el Bûs
G. el Kabrît
Bîr el Biarât
SAUDI
Bîr Abu Sandia
Khalîg el Suweis
1272
S i n a i   P e n i n s u l a
Bîr Taba
Khalīj al 'Aqaba
952
Jal Tubayq
2000 6000
W. Wariq
W. Abu el Gairi
Matarma
W. Abu Ga'da
Bîr el Hassi
1165
W. an Nuqra'
ARABIA

J O R D A N

ft m

East from Greenwich
COPYRIGHT. GEORGE PHILIP & SON LTD.
m ft
-------- 1949 Armistice Line, 1967 and 1974 Cease Fire Lines

1 : 40 000 000

200   0   200   400   600   800   1000 miles
200   0   200   400   600   800 1000 1200 1400 1600 km

1   2   3   4   5   6   7   8   9   10

ATLANTIC

OCEAN

British Isles

Bay of Biscay

Carpathians

Black Sea

Caucasus   Elbrus 5633

Caspian Sea

Aral Sea

Mt Blanc 4807   Alps

Pyrenees   Dinaric Alps   Apennines   Adriatic Sea

Iberian   Corsica

Peninsula   Sardinia

6578

Madeira

Str. of Gibraltar   C. Bon   Sicily   Crete   Cyprus   Levant

Malta   5121

Anatolia

Mediterranean Sea

Mesopotamia   Tigris

Middle Atlas   High Plateaus   Saharan Atlas

High Atlas   G. of Gabes   Syrian Desert   Euphrates

Canary Is.   Anti Atlas   Toubkal   Chott Djerid   G. of Sidra   The Gull

3718   4165   Dra   Tripolitania   Cyrenaica   Bahrain

Tenerife   I g i d i   Siwa   Tropic of Cancer

Tasili   Fezzan   Egypt   Arabian Desert   Sinai 2643

Plateau   Kufra   Libyan Desert   El Kharga

Ras   Tuat   Hoggar   S a h a r a   Nubia   Nubian Desert   Rub' al Khali

Nouadhibou   El Djouf   Tibesti   Khali

Adrar   Air   3415   Pelim I.

Bilma   Str. of Bab el Mandeb   Gulf of Aden   Socotra

Cape Verde Is.   Ras Dashan   Ras Asir

C. Vert   Senegal (Joliba)   Niger   L. Chad   W a d a i   Darfur   Kordofan   White Nile   Blue Nile   4620   L. Tana

Senegambia   S   Atbara   Ethiopian

Gambia   Fouta   u   d   a   n   Highlands   Somali

Djalon   Volta   Niger   Chari   Peninsula

G u i n   Benue   Dar Banda   Bahr el   Shabelle

Grain Coast   e   a   Adamawa   Uele   Ghazal

Gold Coast   Slave Coast   Highlands   Bahr el Jebel   Turkana

Ivory Coast   Bight of Benin   Cameroon   Congo   L. Mobuto   Elgon   Kenya

C. Palmas   6363   Peak   Bioko   Sese Seko   4321   5199   Equator

4070   Bight of Bonny   Chutes Ruwenzori

Gulf of Guinea   Príncipe   Boyoma   5109   L. Edward

São Tomé   B a s i n   L. Kivu   Victoria   INDIAN

Annobón   C. Lopez   Ogooué   Kilimanjaro

Zaïre (Congo)   Kasai   5895   Pemba   OCEAN

Pool   Sankuru   Luluaba   Zanzibar

Malebo   L.

Ascension   Kasai   Tanganyika

Cuanza   Luena   Rungwe

Mweru   2961   L. Nyasa

St. Helena   Shaba   L.   Ruvuma   C. Delgado

Bangweulu   L.   Comores Is.

Bié   Luapula   Malawi   Aldabra Is.

Plateau   Cuando   Zambezi   Shire   Mulanje

ATLANTIC   Cubango   3000

Cunene   Mozambique Channel

OCEAN   Victoria Falls

Madagascar

C. Fria   Limpopo   2643   Maur

Namib Desert   Tropic of Capricorn   Réunion

Walvis Bay   Kalahari   Delagoa Bay

Orange   High Veld   3482   Drakensberg

Compass B.   Algoa Bay

2505   Oranje

Nineveldberge   Gt. Karoo   Swartberg

C. of Good Hope   C. Agulhas   Agulhas Bank

ft   m
12 000   4000
9000   3000
6000   2000
4500   1500
3000   1000
1200   400
600   200
0   0
200   600
2000   6000
4000   12 000
6000   18 000
m   ft

Projection: Zenithal Equidistant.   West from Greenwich   East from Greenwich

COPYRIGHT. GEORGE PHILIP & SON LTD.

1   2   3   4   5   6   7   8   9

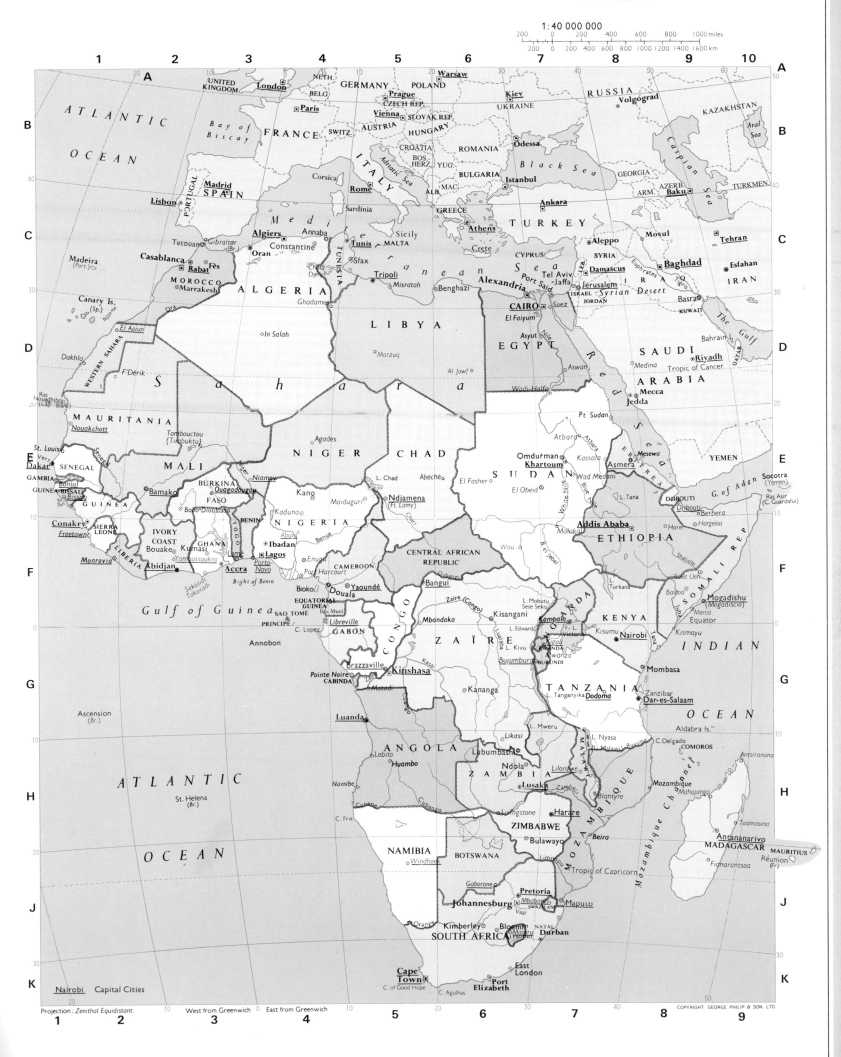

1:40 000 000

200 0 200 400 600 800 1000 miles
200 0 200 400 600 800 1000 1200 1400 1600 km

A

ATLANTIC

OCEAN

UNITED KINGDOM London NETH. GERMANY POLAND Warsaw RUSSIA
BELG. Prague KAZAKHSTAN
B Paris CZECH REP. Kiev Volgograd
FRANCE Vienna SLOVAK REP. UKRAINE
Bay of Biscay SWITZ. AUSTRIA HUNGARY Odessa Aral Sea
CROATIA ROMANIA Black Sea GEORGIA Caspian Sea
PORTUGAL Madrid BOS. YUG. BULGARIA Istanbul AZERB. Baku TURKMEN.
SPAIN HERZ. MAC. ARM.
Lisbon ITALY Rome ALB. GREECE Ankara TURKEY Aleppo Mosul Tehran
C Corsica Athens CYPRUS SYRIA Damascus Baghdad Esfahan
Madeira Algiers Annaba Sardinia Crete Tel Aviv Euphrates IRAQ IRAN
(Port.) Casablanca Constantine Tunis MALTA Port Said Jaffa Jerusalem Basra
Tetouan Gibraltar Oran Sicily Tripoli Alexandria ISRAEL Syrian JORDAN KUWAIT Bahrain
Rabat Fès TUNISIA Sfax Misratah CAIRO Suez Desert QATAR The Gulf
MOROCCO Chott Benghazi El Faiyum SAUDI Riyadh
D Marrakesh Djerid Asyut Aswan Medina ARABIA Tropic of Cancer
Canary Is. Ghadames LIBYA Al Jawf Mecca
(Sp.) ALGERIA Marzuq Wadi Halfa Jedda
Dakhla In Salah Pt. Sudan
WESTERN SAHARA F'Dérik S a h a r a Atbara Atbara YEMEN
Ras Nouadhibou Agades Abéché Omdurman Kassala Mesewa G. of Aden Socotra
(C. Blanc) MAURITANIA Khartoum ERITREA Asmera (Yemen)
E Nouakchott NIGER CHAD El Fasher SUDAN Wad Medani DJIBOUTI Ras Asir
St. Louis Tombouctou Niamey L. Chad El Obeid White Nile Blue Nile L. Tana Djibouti (C. Guardafui)
Senegal (Timbuktu) MALI Kano Maiduguri Wau Malakal Berbera
Dakar BURKINA Ndjamena Bel Jebel Addis Ababa Harer Hargeisa
GAMBIA Bamako Ouagadougou (Ft. Lamy) Kaduna Chari ETHIOPIA SOMALI REP.
Banjul FASO Abuja CENTRAL AFRICAN Wau Shabelle
GUINEA-BISSAU GUINEA Bobo-Dioulasso NIGERIA REPUBLIC Baidoa
F Conakry SIERRA BENIN Ibadan Benue Bangui Balei Ueh Mogadishu
Freetown LEONE IVORY GHANA TOGO Lagos Enugu CAMEROON Oubangui L. Mobutu (Mogadiscio)
COAST Kumasi Porto Port Harcourt Yaoundé Zaïre (Congo) Sese Seko KENYA
Monrovia Bouake Yamoussoukro Novo Douala Kisangani Juba L. Turkana Kismayu
LIBERIA Abidjan Accra Bioko ZAÏRE Mbandaka L. Edward UGANDA Nairobi INDIAN
Sekondi EQUATORIAL GABON CONGO L. Kivu Kampala Equator Tana
Takoradi GUINEA Rio Muni Kasai Bujumbura RWANDA Mwanza Kisumu Mombasa
G Gulf of Guinea SAO TOMÉ & Libreville Brazzaville Matadi BURUNDI L. Victoria TANZANIA OCEAN
PRINCIPE C. Lopez Kinshasa Kananga L. Tanganyika Dodoma Zanzibar Aldabra Is.
Annobon Pointe Noire Kasai Dar-es-Salaam
CABINDA Luanda Likasi L. Mweru MALAWI C. Delgado
H Ascension Lobito ANGOLA Lubumbashi L. Nyasa Ruvuma COMOROS Antsiranana
(Br.) Huambo Ndola ZAMBIA Lilongwe (L. Malawi) Mozambique Mahajanga
St. Helena Namibe Lusaka Blantyre Beira MOZAMBIQUE MADAGASCAR MAURITIUS
(Br.) Cunene Cubango Livingstone Harare Zambezi Mozambique Channel Antananarivo Réunion
J ATLANTIC NAMIBIA Windhoek BOTSWANA ZIMBABWE Bulawayo Tropic of Capricorn Fianarantsoa (Fr)
Namibe C. Fria Gaborone Limpopo Maputo
Pretoria Mbabane Toamasina
Johannesburg SWAZILAND
OCEAN Orange Vaal Kimberley Bloemfontein NATAL Durban
K SOUTH AFRICA Maseru LESOTHO
Cape Town East London
C. of Good Hope C. Agulhas Port Elizabeth

Nairobi Capital Cities

Projection: Zenithal Equidistant.   West from Greenwich   East from Greenwich   COPYRIGHT. GEORGE PHILIP & SON. LTD

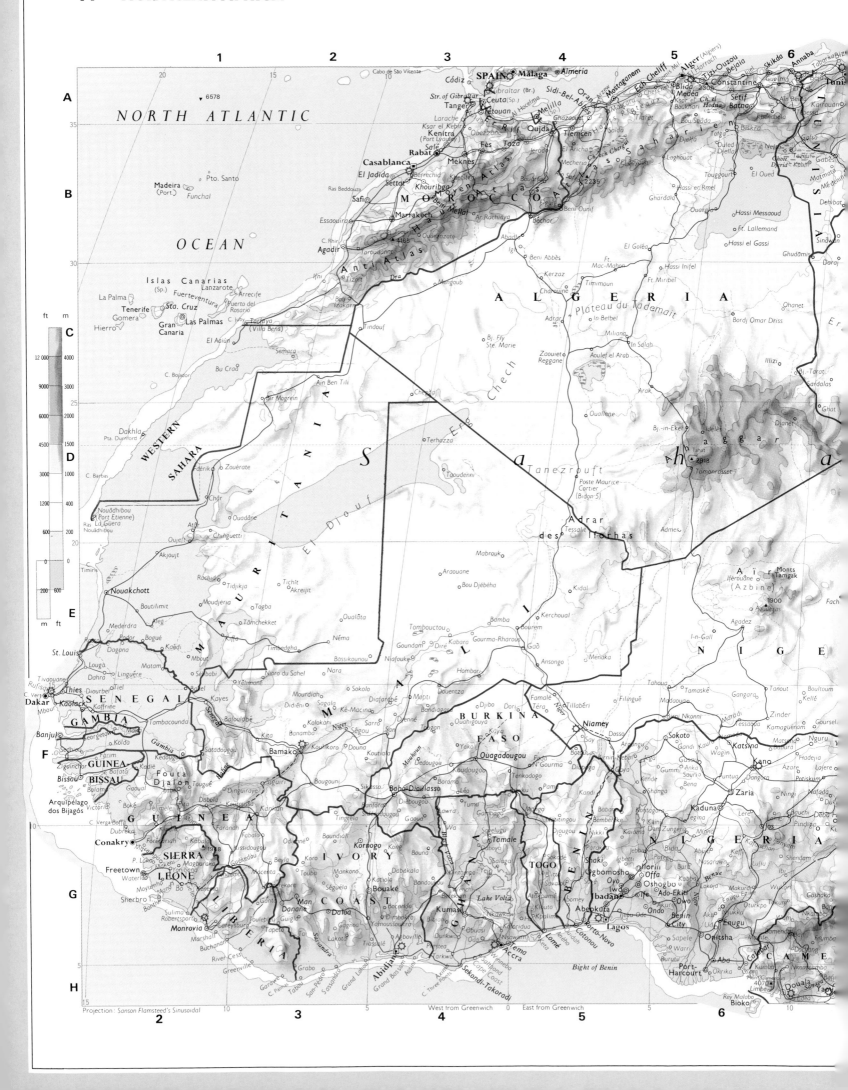

NORTH ATLANTIC

OCEAN

SPAIN

Cabo de São Vicente

Cádiz · Málaga · Almería

Gibraltar (Br.)

Str. of Gibraltar · Ceuta (Sp.) · Melilla · Sidi-Bel-Ab

Tanger · Tetouan · Al Hoceima · Oran · Mostaganem · Ech Cheliff · Alger (Algers) · Tizi-Ouzou · Bejaïa · Skikda · Annaba

Larache · Ghazaouet · Blida · Médéa · Constantine · Guelma · Tuni

Ksar el Kebir · Rif · Oujda · Tlemcen · Ksar el Chel · Sétif · Batna · Aïn Bei

Kenitra (Port Lyautey) · Fes · Toza · Saïda · Tiaret · Bou Khari · Hodna · TUNI

Rabat · Salé · Meknès · Jerada · El Aricha · Djelfa · Tolga · Ouled el Ne

Casablanca · Berrechid · Khenifra · Mecheria · Laghouat · Biskra · Chott

El Jadida · Settat · Khouribga · Béchar · Touggourt · El Oued · Matma

Ras Beddouza · Safi · Moyen Atlas · Beni Mellal · Ar Rachidya · Beni Ounif · Gharðaïa · Hassi er Rmel · Ouargla · Hassi Messaoud · Sindwan

Essaouira · MOROCCO · Haut Atlas · Bou Arfa · 2235 · Ghardaïa · Ft. Lallemand · Déhib

Marrakech · Ouarzazate · Abadla · Igli · El Goléa · Hassi el Gassi

C. Rhir · Haut Atlas · 4165 · Ouarzazate · Kerzaz · Ghudāmis

Agadir · Taroudannt · Anti Atlas · Dra · Mengoub · Fort · Mac-Mahon · Hassi Inifel · Ohanet · Daraj

Ifni · Tizint · Bj. Fly · Charouine · Timimoun · In Belbel · Bordj Omar Driss · Er

Goulimine · Tata · Bou · Izakarn · Ste. Marie · Miliana · In Salah · Bj.-Tarat

WESTERN · C. Juby · Tarfaya (Villa Bens) · Tindouf · Adrar · Zaouiet · Reggane · Aoulef el Arab · Illizi · Sardalas

El Aiún · Semara · Chegga · **ALGERIA** · Plateau du Tademait

SAHARA · Bir Mogrein · Aïn Ben Tili · Chech · Arak · Bj.-in-Eket · Idelès · Djanet · Ghat

Dakhla · Pta. Durnford · Terhazza · a · **Tanezrouft** · Ahaggar · Tamanrasset · 2918

C. Barbas · Fderîk · Zouérate · Taoudenni · Poste Maurice Cortier (Bidon 5) · Admer

Nouâdhibou (Port Étienne) · Châr · Ouadâne · **MAURITANIA** · El Djouf · Adrar des Iforhas · Tessalit

Ras La Güera · Nouâdhibou · Atâr · Mabrouk · Aïr (Azbine) · Monts Tamgak · Fach

Timiris · Akjoujt · Chinguetti · Araouane · Kidal · 1900 · Iferouâne

OuJeft · Rachid · Tidjikja · Tichît · Bou Djébéha · Agadez

Nouakchott · Moudjéria · Akreijit · **MALI** · I-n-Gall

Boutilimit · Togba · Oualâta · Tombouctou · Bamba · Kerchoual · Meńaka · **NIGER**

Mederdra · Aleg · Tâmchekket · Goundam · Diré · Kabara · Gourma-Rharous · Gaô · Arlit · Agadez

St. Louis · Podor · Bogué · Kaédi · Kiffa · Néma · Timbedgha · Bassikounou · Niafouke · Ansongo · Tahoua · Tamaské

Louga · Dagana · Matam · Mbout · Sé
labi · Nioro du Sahel · Nara · Hombori · Dori · Filingué · Madaoua · Zinder

Tivouane · Dahra · Linguère · Sélibabi · Yélimané · Mourdiah · Sokolo · Douentza · Téra · Tillabéri · Niamey · Dosso · Birni Nkonni · Maradi

Thies · Diourbel · Tiel · Bakel · Kayes · Didiéni · Diafarabé · Mopti · Djibo · Kaya · Say · Gaya · Sokoto · Gusau · Katsina

Dakar · Kaolack · **SENEGAL** · Bafoulabé · Banamba · Ségou · Sarro · Djenné · Bandiagara · Ouahigouya · **BURKINA** · Tillabéri · Gandi · Zaria

Mbour · **GAMBIA** · Tambacounda · Kita · Koulikoro · Douna · Niger · **FASO** · Kaduna

Banjul · Georgetown · Kolda · Gambia · **MALI** · Bamako · Sikasso · Bobo-Dioulasso · Ouagadougou · Fada N'Gourma · Kano · Hadeja · Azare

GUINEA-BISSAU · Satadougou · Siguiri · Bougouni · Banfora · Diébougou · Léo · Tenkodogo · **NIGERIA**

Bissau · Ziguinchor · Bafatá · Fouta · Kankan · Tingréla · Kadiogo · Bawku · **BENIN** · Kaduna · Jos

Bolama · Gaoual · Djalon · Tougué · Dinguiraye · Kouroussa · Gaoua · Bobo · **GHANA** · **TOGO** · Kaina · Zungeru · Bida

Arquipélago dos Bijagós · Boké · Telimele · Dabola · Faranah · Odienné · Kong · Bouna · Wa · Tamale · Nikki · Kainji · Kontagora

C. Verga · **GUINEA** · Dubréka · Kindia · Kissidougou · Mankono · Katiola · Bondoukou · Sunyani · Salaga · Parakou · Ilorin · Offa · Makurdi

Conakry · Forécariah · Beyla · Touba · Dabakala · **IVORY** · Kintampo · Yendi · Shaki · Ogbomosho · Kabba · Enugu

SIERRA LEONE · Macenta · Séguéla · Bouaké · Lake Volta · Oyo · Iwa · Oshogbo · Ado-Ekiti · Owo · Onitsha

Freetown · Mano · Bo · Kenema · Man · **COAST** · Bouaflé · Kumasi · Abomey · Ibadan · Ondo · Benin City · Sapele

Waterloo · Moyamba · Danané · Guiglo · Daloa · Yamoussoukro · Dimbokro · Kumasi · Kpalimé · Abeokuta · Ijebu-Ode · Warri · **CAME**

Sherbro · Bonthe · Sulima · Tapeta · **LIBERIA** · Bocanda · Agboville · Nsawam · Lomé · Cotonou · Porto-Novo · Lagos · Sapele · Port-Harcourt · Aba · Calabar · Douala

Monrovia · Careysburg · Toulepleu · Gagnoa · Abengourou · Dunkwa · Keta · Cotonou · Ikeja · Owerri · Bioko

Marshall · Buchanan · Tabou · Sassandra · San-Pédro · Divo · Axim · Accra · Tema · Bight of Benin · Rey Malabo · Yao · Limbe · 4070

River Cess · Greenville · Garraway · C. Palmas · Grand Bassam · Takoradi · Sekondi-Takoradi · C. Three Points · Cape Coast

Cabo de São Vicente

Madeira (Port.) · Pto. Santo · Funchal

Islas Canarias (Sp.) · Lanzarote · Fuerteventura · Arrecife

La Palma · Tenerife · Gomera · Sta. Cruz · Gran Canaria · Las Palmas · Puerto del Rosario

Hierro

6578

ft m

12 000 · 4000
9000 · 3000
6000 · 2000
4500 · 1500
3000 · 1000
1200 · 400
600 · 200
0 · 0
200 · 600
m ft

West from Greenwich · 0 · East from Greenwich

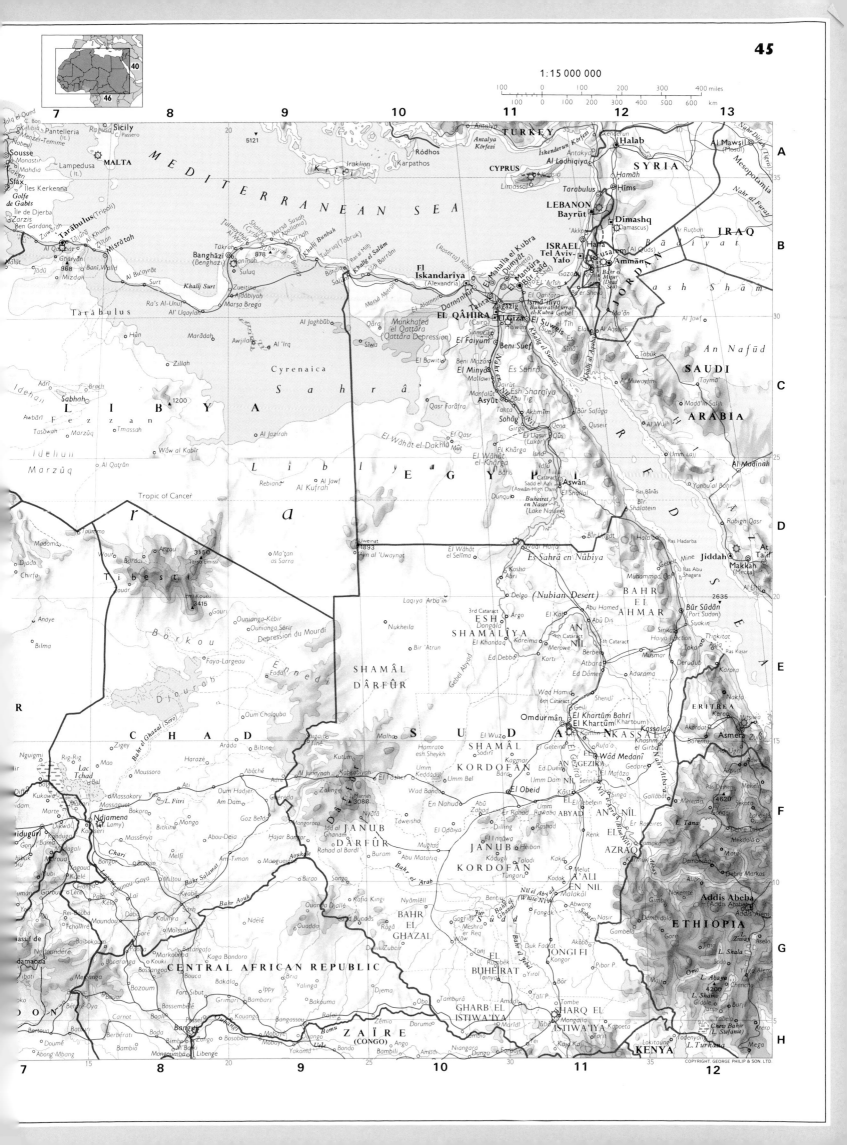

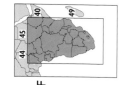

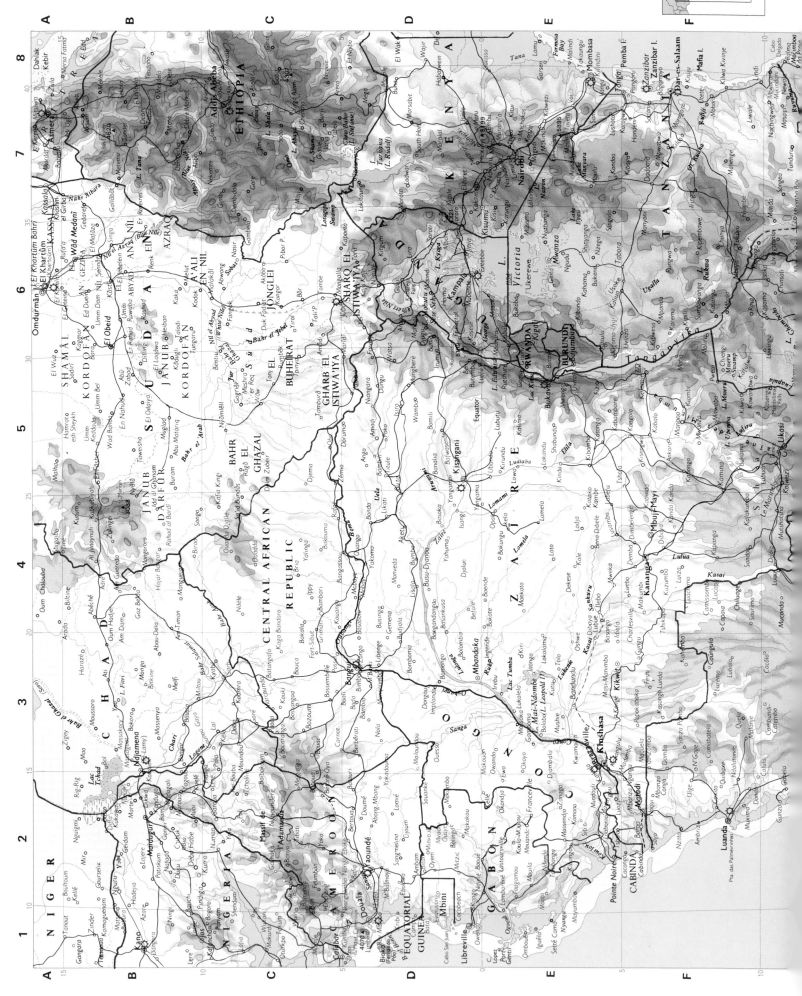

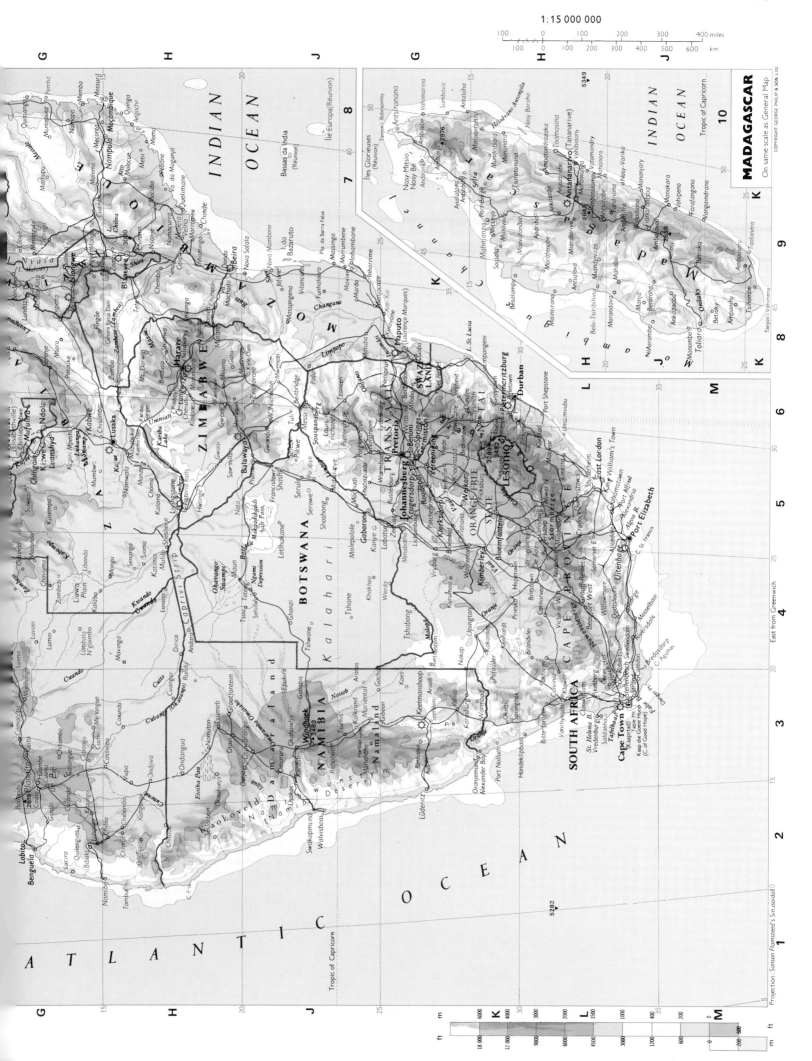

47

1   2   3   4

ANGOLA

CUANDO CUBANGO

WESTERN ZAMBIA

SOUTH

Livingstone

Victoria Falls

Caprivi Strip

Chobe Nat. Park

Hwange

Hwange Nat. Park

Okavango Swamps

NAMIBIA

Etosha Pan

Ovamboland

Tsumeb
Grootfontein
Otavi 2148
Uchab

Outjo
Okaputa
Otjiwarongo

Kaukauveld

Sandveld

Ghanzi

BOTSWANA

Serowe
Palapye

Khama's Country

Windhoek
Okahandja
Khomas Hochland
2483

Rehoboth
2351

Mariental

Kalahari

Mahalapye

Molepolole
Gaborone
Kanye
Lobatse

BOPHUTHATSWANA

Keetmanshoop

Kalahari Gemsbok National Park

Mafikeng
Krugersdorp
Vereeniging
Potchefstroom
Klerksdorp

Lüderitz
Lüderitzbaai

Upington
Augrabies Falls
Keimoes

Kuruman

Kimberley

Bloemhof
Kroonstad
Welkom
Virginia

ORANGE FREE STATE

Bloemfontein

Karasburg

Alexander Bay
Oranjemund

Port Nolleth

Springbok
Namaqualand

SOUTH AFRICA

De Aar

Hopetown

ATLANTIC OCEAN

Tropic of Capricorn

Kareeberg

CAPE PROVINCE

Great Karoo

Graaff-Reinet

Beaufort West

Cradock
2369

CISKEI

Fort Beaufort

Grahamstown

Vredenburg
Saldanha
Moorreesburg
Malmesbury

Worcester

Swartberg
Little Karoo
Oudtshoorn
George

Kougaberg
Uitenhage

PORT ELIZABETH

Algoa Bay

CAPE TOWN (Kaapstad)
Table Mt. 1086
Stellenbosch
Simonstown
Kaap die Goeie Hoop (Cape of Good Hope)
C. Agulhas

Mosselbaai

Projection: Lambert's Equivalent Azimuthal

ft / m scale:
9000 / 3000
6000 / 2000
4500 / 1500
3000 / 1000
1200 / 400
600 / 200
0 / 0
200 / 600
2000 / 6000
4000 / 12,000
m ft

This map shows the four provinces in South Africa prior to the April 1994 elections. A map at the end of the index shows the proposed nine new provinces.

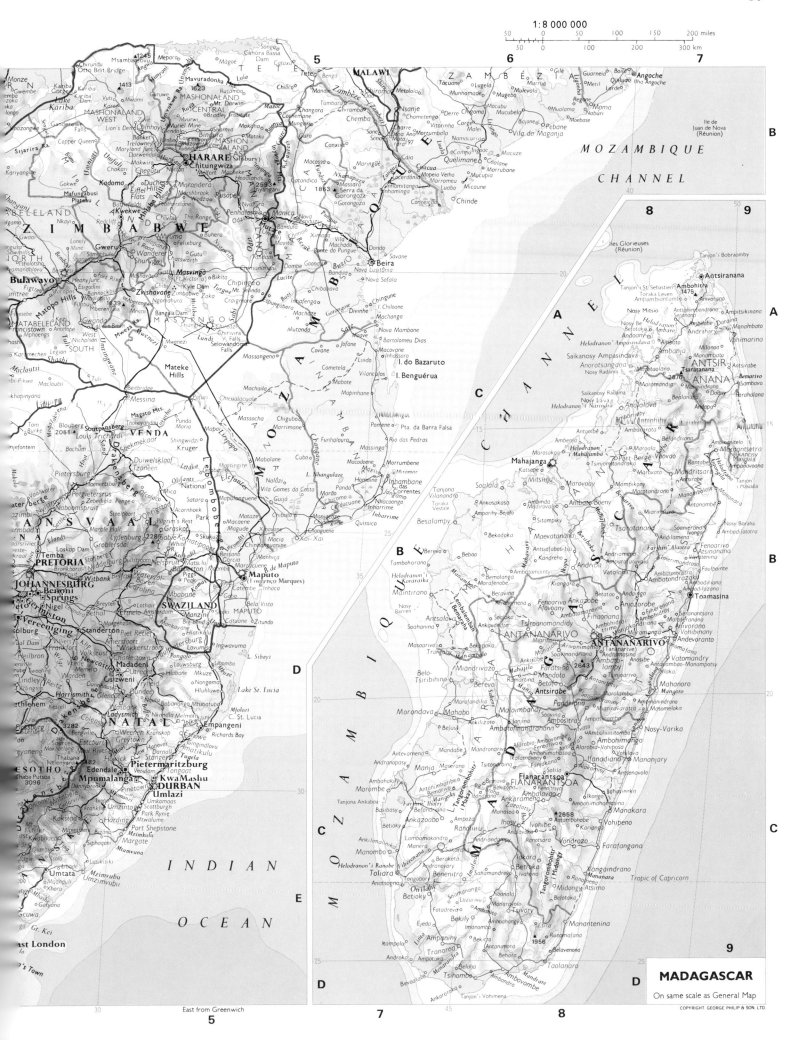

49

MADAGASCAR

On same scale as General Map

COPYRIGHT GEORGE PHILIP & SON, LTD.

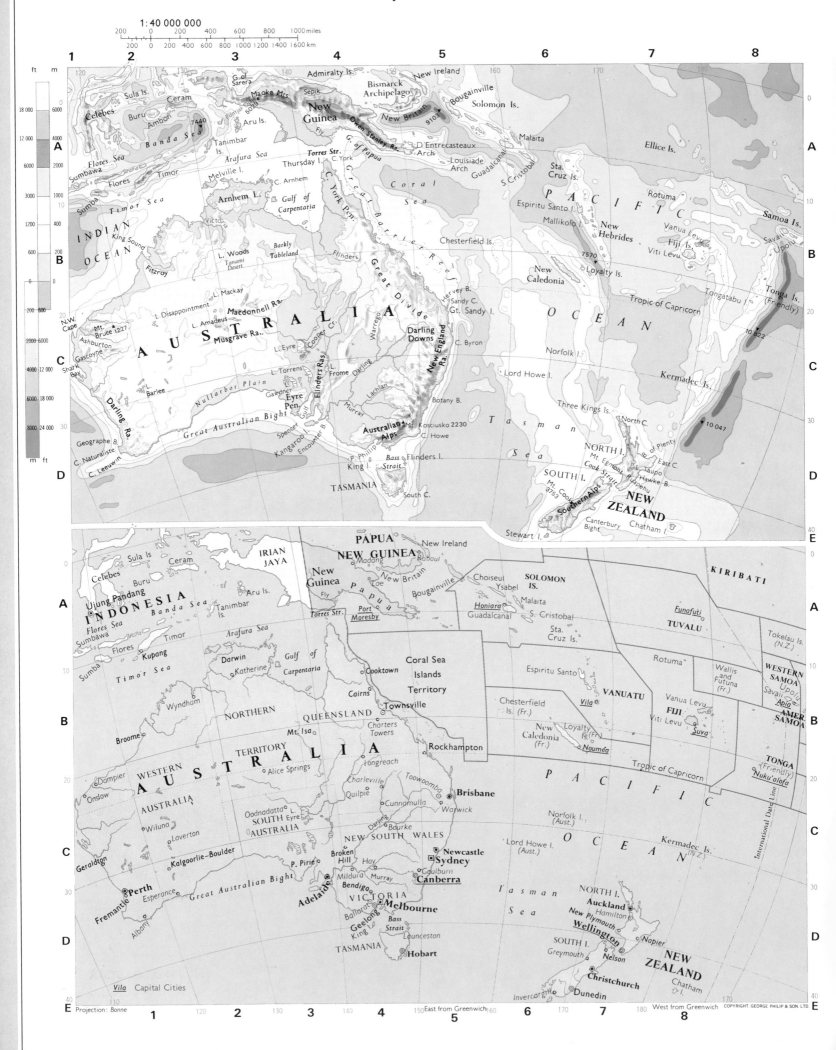

1:40 000 000

1:6 000 000

20 0   20 40 60 80   100 miles
20 0   40   80   120   160 km

KIRIBATI

TUVALU (Ellice Is.)

Tokelau Is.(N.Z.)

WESTERN SAMOA
Savai'i Upolu

WALLIS & FUTUNA (Fr.)

Rotuma

FIJI
Vanua Levu
Viti Levu

VAN-UATU

AMER. SAMOA (U.S.)
Tutuila

TONGA (Friendly Is.)

Niue (N.Z.)

Pukapuka Nassau Manihiki
Northern Group
Suwarrow

Rakahanga
Tongareva (Penrhyn) I.

Palmerston Atoll

Cook Is.(N.Z.)

Aitutaki
Mitiaro Atiu Mauke
Lower Group
Rarotonga Mangaia

Îles de la Société

FRENCH POLYNESIA

Tropic of Capricorn

PACIFIC OCEAN

Macauley
Raoul (Sunday) I.
Kermadec Is. (N.Z.)
Curtis

Three Kings Is.

Auckland
NORTH I.
Cook Strait
NEW ZEALAND
Wellington
SOUTH I.
Christchurch
Dunedin
Tasman Sea

Chatham I.
Chatham Is.
Pitt I.

Bounty Is.
Stewart I.
Snares
Antipodes Is.
Campbell I.
Macquarie I. (Austl.)
Auckland Is.

SOUTHERN OCEAN

NEW ZEALAND & S.W. PACIFIC
1:60 000 000

200 0   200 400 600 800 miles
200 0   400 800   1200 km

NORTH ISLAND

Three Kings Is.
C. Reinga
C. Maria van Diemen
North C.
Houhora
Rangaunu Bay
Doubtless Bay
Ahipara B.
Mangonui Whangaroa Bay
Kaitaia
Tauroa Pt.
B. of Islands
Rawene
C. Brett
Hokianga Harb.
Donnelly's Crossing
Opua
Kaikohe Hikurangi
Whangarei
Whangarei Harb.
Dargaville
Bream Hd.
Waipu
Bream Bay
Lit. Barrier I.
Kaipara Harb.
C. Rodney
Gt. Barrier I.
Helensville
Warkworth
Cuvier I.
C. Colville
Takapuna
Hauraki Gulf
Coromandel
AUCKLAND
Devonport
Whitianga
Onehunga Manukau
Papakura
Thames
Mayor I.
Waiuku Pukekohe
Waihi
Tauranga Harb.
Waikato
Mercer
Paeroa
Tauranga
White I. Runaway
Huntly
Morrinsville
Te Aroha
Te Puke
Bay of Plenty
Raglan
Cambridge
Mt. Maunganui
Whakatane
Hamilton
Kawhia Harb.
Kawerau
Opotiki
Raukumara Ra.
Kawhia
Putaruru
Rotorua
Hikurangi
Awamutu Otorohanga
Te Kuiti
Murupara
Waipiro
Te Karaka
Mokai
Kinleith
Taupo
Motu
Tolaga Bay
North Taranaki Bight
Ongarue
Kaimanawa Mts.
Ormond
Waitara
Taumarunui
Mokau
Waikaremoana
Gisborne
New Plymouth
Whangamomona
Poverty Bay
Mt. Egmont (Taranaki)
Inglewood
Wairoa
Opunake
Stratford
Raetihi Ruapehu
Wai-iti View
Mahia Peninsula
Eltham
Ohakune
Napier
Kapuni
Hawera
Waiouru
Hastings
Waverley
Taihape
C. Kidnappers
South Taranaki Bight
Hawke Bay
Patea
Mangaweka
Waipawa
Ruahine Ra.
Waipukurau
Wanganui
Hunterville
Marton
Halcombe
Palmerston N.
Bulls
Feilding
Dannevirke
Foxton Sanson
Woodville
Shannon
Pahiatua
Levin
Eketahuna
C. Turnagain
Otaki
Paraparaumu
Kapiti I.
Tararua Ra.
Masterton
Featherston Carterton
Pelorus Sd.
Blenheim
Greytown
Martinborough

SOUTH ISLAND

C. Farewell
Golden Bay
D'Urville I.
Collingwood
Tasman Bay
Takaka
Tasman Mts.
Motueka
Richmond
Picton
Nelson
Wakefield
Havelock
Tadmor
Waitohi
Wairau
WELLINGTON
Up. Hutt
Petone
Lr. Hutt
Eastbourne
Cook Strait

Karamea Bight
Matiri Ra.
Murchison
Renwick
Seddon
Seddonville
Inangahua Junction
Ward
Granity
Lyell
Westport
Reefton
Maruia
Tapuaenuku 2885
Spenser Mts.
Hanmer
Kaikoura Ra.
Blackball
Kaikoura
Runanga
Greymouth
Stillwater
Kumara
L. Brunner
Hokitika
Jacksons
Arthur's Pass
Waiau
Culverden
Ross
Waikari
Hurunui
Amberley
Waipara
Oxford
Rangiora
Pegasus Bay
Kaiapoi
New Brighton
Springfield
Whitecliffs
Christchurch
Riccarton
Lincoln
Lyttelton
Methven
Banks Peninsula
Staveley
Little River
Akaroa
Mt. Cook 3764
Rakaia
Southbridge
Westland Bight
Okarito
Abut Hd.
Rolleston
Temuka
Timaru
Fairlie
St. Andrews
Tekapo
Canterbury Bight
Jackson
Haast
Pukaki
Waimate
Mt. Aspiring 3027
L. Wanaka
Hawea
Kurow
Ngapara
Milford Sd.
Cromwell
Naseby
Maheno
Oamaru
Bligh Sd.
Queenstown
Arrowtown
Kakanui Mts.
George Sd.
Alexandra
Hampden
Secretary I.
Kingston
Roxburgh
Palmerston
Doubtful Sd.
Eyre Mts.
Ranfurly
Dunback
Breaksea Sd.
Te Anau
Garvie Mts.
Clyde
Port Chalmers
Resolution I.
Mossburn
Umbrella Mts.
Dunedin
Manapouri
Lumsden
Clinton
Mosgiel
St. Kilda
Dusky Sd.
Edievale
Otago Harbour
Lawrence
C. Saunders
Clifden
Nightcaps
Kelso
Fairfield
Milton
Orepuki
Otautau
Waikouaiti
Te Waewae B.
Riverton
Winton
Gore
Balclutha
Chalky Inlet
Invercargill
Mataura
Kaitangata
Preservation Inlet
Lokanui
Wyndham
Owaka
Bluff
Awarua
Nugget Pt.
Ruapuke I.
Foveaux Str.
Halfmoon B.
Invercargill
Stewart I.
S.W. Cape
Port Pegasus

TASMAN SEA

SOUTH ISLAND

PACIFIC OCEAN

SAMOA ISLANDS
1:12 000 000

WESTERN SAMOA
Savai'i Upolu
Apia
AMERICAN SAMOA
Pago Pago
Tutuila
Manua Is.
Rose I.

WESTERN SAMOA
Wallis & Futuna (Fr.)
Futuna

FIJI AND TONGA ISLANDS
1:12 000 000

50 0   50   100   150 miles
50 0 50 100 150 200 250 km

Thikombia
Lambasa
Niuafo'ou (Tonga)
Vanua Levu
Taveuni
Koro
Vanua Balavu
Lau or Eastern Group
FIJI
Yasawa Group
Levuka
Ovalau
Nandi
Viti Levu
Koro Sea
Lakemba
Suva
Ngau
Moala
TONGA (Friendly Is.)
Kandavu
Vatoa
Vava'u
Tofua
Tongatapu
Noku'alofa
Vava'u

Projection: Conical with two standard parallels

ft m
12 000 4000
9000 3000
6000 2000
3000 1000
1200 400
600 200
0
200 600
m ft

NORTHERN TERRITORY

INDONESIA

TIMOR SEA

INDIAN OCEAN

Tanami Desert

Great Sandy Desert

Gibson Desert

King Leopold Ranges

Hamersley Range

Joseph Bonaparte Gulf

Bonaparte Archipelago

Timor

Lombok
Sumbawa
Sumba
Roti
Semau
Sawa
Raidjoea
Danu

C. Croker
C. Grant
McCluer I.
Croker I.
Cobourg Pen.
P. Essington
Van Diemen
C. Don
Dundas Str.
C. Van Diemen
Bathurst I.
Melville I.
Darwin
C. Gambier
Clarence Str.
Port Darwin
Gordon B.
Pt. Fawcett
Pt. Blaze
Anson B.
Peron Is.
C. Scott
C. Hay
C. Ford

Onpelly
Jabiru
480
Oenpelli
Nooranboh
C. Hotham
Field Is.
Margahello
Murganella
Bim Jungle
Bachelor
Adelaide River
Pine Creek
Tiddal
Marandboy
Marankboy
Birdum Creek
Birdum
Katherine
Daly River
Daly
Willeroo
Larrimah
Mataranka
Fitzmaurice
Daly Waters
Victoria
Victoria River Downs
Humbert River
Wave Hill
Top Springs
Montejinnie
Hooker Creek
Winnecke Cr.
Lander
Willowra
Yuendumu
Anningie
Mt. Singleton
808
Reynolds Ra.
Stuart Bluff Ra.
Mt. Zeil
1510
Mt. Liebig
1524
Papunya
Macdonnell Ranges
Hermannsburg
Missionb
George Gill Ra.
Haast Bluff
Palmer
James Ranges
Tempe Downs
Mt. Leisler
901
L. Bennett
L. Macdonald
Lake Mackay
Kintore Ra.
L. Macdonald
Baron Ra.
Bonython Hills
Angus Hills
Hopkins

Wingate Mts.
Mt. Greenwood
152
Quees Chan.
Kununurra
Auvergnie
Rosewood
Rebecca
Stokes Ra.
Newcastle Ra.
Limbunya
Nicholson
Gordon Downs
Sturt Creek
Corongie
Billiluna
Gregory Lake
Stansmore Ra.
L. Wills
L. Hazlett
L. White
L. Naak

Wyndham
Carr Boyd Ra.
Ord
Ivanhoe
E. Argyle
Turkey Creek
Kimberley
Black Range
Margaret
Fitzroy
Bohemia Downs
Christmas Creek
L. Tobin
L. Dora
L. Auld
L. George
L. Blanche
L. Waukarlycarly
McKay

Cockburn Ra.
Durack
Durack River
Gibb River
Bedford Downs
Springvale
Mount Amhurst
Alice Downs
Hall's Creek
Mount House
Mueller Ra.
McClintock Ra.
Albert Edward Ra.
Chamberlain Ra.
Hann
Tableland
Mornington
St. George Ra.
Leopold Downs
Noonkanbah
Myroodah

Kulumburu
Drysdale
Mount Elizabeth
King Edward
Mt. Hann
716
Mt. Ord
1007
Napier Downs
Kimberley Downs
Fitzroy Crossing
Margaret River
Mt. Anderson
Liveringa
Noonkanbah
Fitzroy

Lesley I.
Londonderry
Napier Broome B.
Vansittart B.
Graham Moore Is.
Talbot
Rulhieres
Eclipse Is.
Bigge
York Sd.
Prince Regent
Harding Ra.
St. Georges
Bain
Camden Sd.
Hall Pt.
Adele I.
Derby
Myroodah
Noonkanboh

C. Bougainville
Long Reef
Admiralty Gulf
Montague Sd.
C. Voltaire
Coronation
Brunswick B.
Adieu Pt.
Augustus I.
C. Leveque
C. Borda
Sunday I.
King Sound
Greenull

C. Londonderry
Browse I.
Vampi Sd.
Pender B.
Beagle Bay
Carnot B.
C. Boileau
Broome
Roebuck B.
Thangoo
Roebuck Plains
Anna Plains
Wallal Downs
Frazier Downs
Lagrange B.
Lagrange
Eighty Mile Beach

Hibernia Reef
Ashmore Reef
Cartier I.
Seringapatam Reef
Scott Reef
Lynher Reef
Mermaid Reef
Clerke Reef
Imperieuse Reef
Rowley Shoals

Poissonnier Pt.
C. Keraudren
Pope Grey
C. Thouin
Port Hedland
Goldsworthy
DeGrey
Wallarigang
Shay Gap
Isabella Ra.
Gregory Ra.
Oakover
Robertson Ra.
Poisonbush Ra.
Broadhurst Ra.
Throssell Ra.
Paterson Ra.

Legendre I.
Delambre I.
Dampier Archipelago
Enderby
Roebourne
Karratha
Cossack
Whim Creek
Marble Bar
Hillside
Woodstock
Nullagine
Bonnie Downs
Roy Hill
Ethel Creek
Newman
1053
Ophthalmia Ra.

North West C.
Exmouth
Exmouth Gulf
Learmonth
Onslow
Barrow I.
Monte Bello Is.
Peak I.
Nickol B.
C. Preston
Yardie
Yanrey
Yarraloola
Mardie
Pyramid
Robe
Peedamullah
Wyloo
Ashburton
Hardey
Duck Cr.
Turee Cr.
Mt. Bruce
1235
Mt. Meharry
1251
Mt. Florrie
Price
Wittenoom
Hamersley
Chichester Ra.
Paraburdoo
Tom Price
Mt. McRae

Tropic of Capricorn

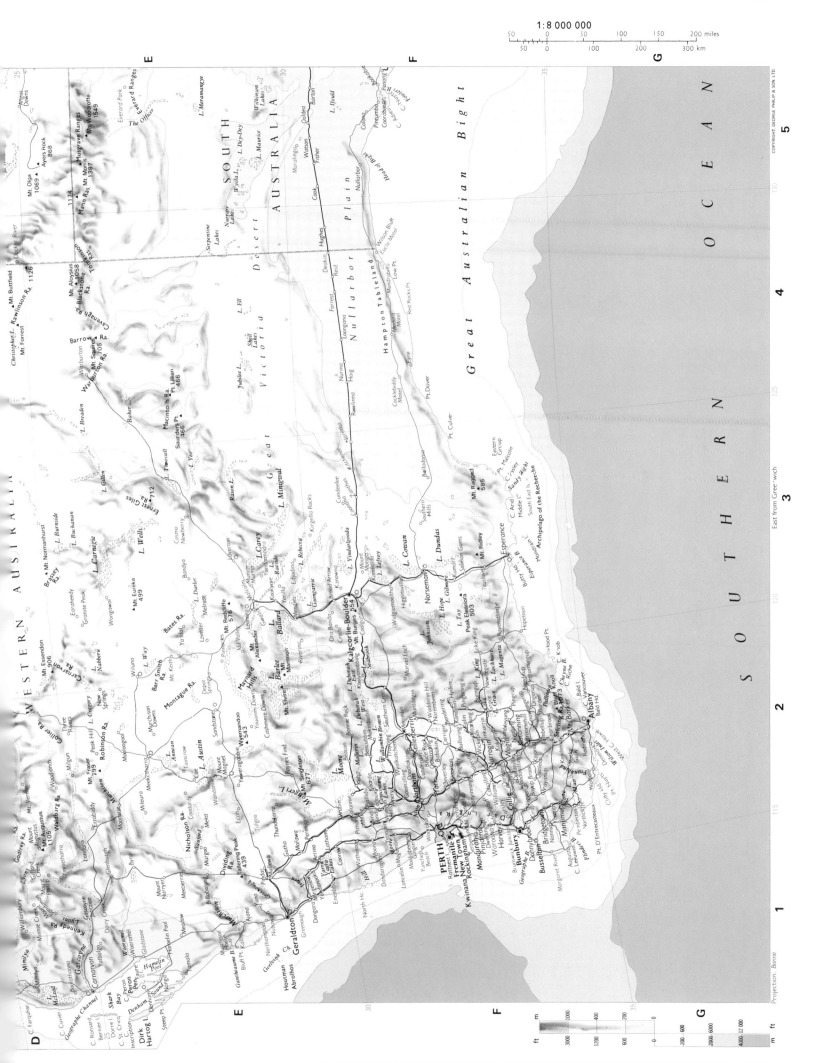

1 : 8 000 000

50 0 50 100 150 200 miles
50 0 100 200 300 km

D

E

F

G

WESTERN AUSTRALIA

SOUTH AUSTRALIA

C. Cuvier
C. Farquhar
Williambury
Minnie Creek
Kennedy Ra.
Lyndon
Minilya
L. McLeod
C. Ronsard
Berner I.
C. St. Cross
Inscription Pt.
Dirk Hartog
Shark Bay
Denham
C. Peron
Peron Pen.
Steep Pt.
Useless Loop
Hamelin Pool
Carnarvon
Babbage I.
Boologooro
Yalbalgo
Gladstone
Wooramel
Woorarel
Meadow

Godfrey Ra.
Mt. Vernon
Mount Augustus
1105 Waldburg Ra.
Gifford Cr.
Landor
Errabiddy
Bangemall
Mt. Padbury
Meekatharra
Peak Hill
Murchison Downs

Everard Ranges
The Officer
Ayers Rock
868
Mt. Olga
1069
Musgrave Ranges
Mt. Woodroffe
1549
Mann Ra.
Mt. Morris
1387
1174
Wyola L.
L. Maurice
L. Dey-Dey
L. Meramangye

Oscar River
Mt. Butfield
Mt. Butfield Rawlinson Ra.
Christopher I.
Mt. Forest
Cavenagh Ra.
Mt. Aloysius
1058
Blackstone Ra.
Tomkinson Ra. 1126
Barrow Mt. Squires 705
Warburton Ra.
Warburton Ra.
Pt. Lillian
Macintosh Ra.
466
Saunders Pt.
466

Great Victoria Desert

Nurseries Lakes
Serpentine Lakes

Cook
Hughes
Deakin
Reid
Forrest
Nurina
Haig
Loongana
Naretha
Rawlinna
Zanthus
Naretha

Coorabie
Penong
C. Nuyts
Fowlers B.
Coorabie
Bookabie
Yalata
Colona

Ooldea
Watson
Fisher
Barton
Ooldea
Maralinga
Pintumba

Nullarbor Plain

Hampton Tableland

Wilson Bluff
Eucla Motel
Mundrabilla Motel
Madura Motel
Nullarbor
Low Pt.
Pt. Dover
Red Rocks Pt.
Pt. Culver
Eyre

Head of Bight

Great Australian Bight

SOUTHERN OCEAN

Archipelago of the Recherche

East from Greenwich

Projection: Bonne
Bonne

ft m
3000 1000
1200 400
600 200
0 0
m ft
200 600
2000 6000
4000 12000

PERTH
Fremantle
New Town
Rockingham
Kwinana
Mandurah
Harvey
Bunbury
Busselton
Bridgetown
Manjimup
Augusta
C. Leeuwin
Pt. D'Entrecasteaux
Geographe B.
Margaret River

Geraldton
Houtman Abrolhos
Greenough
Dongara
Mingenew
Three Springs
Moora
Gingin
Lancelin
North Hd.
Yanchep

Kalgoorlie-Boulder
Mt. Burges 554
Coolgardie
Kambalda
Norseman
Widgiemooltha
L. Cowan
L. Dundas
L. Lefroy
Mt. Ridley
Esperance

Albany
Mt. Barker
Stirling Ra.
Bluff Knoll 1073
C. Vancouver
Bald Hd.
C. Riche
King George Sd.
Denmark
West C. Howe
C. Knob

Northam
York
Merredin
Southern Cross
Coolgardie
Moora
Wongan Hills

L. Moore
Moore
Morawa
Perenjori
Wubin
Dalwallinu
Koorda
Mukinbudin
Bencubbin
Beacon
Bonnie Rock

L. Carnegie
L. Wells
L. Nabberu
Mt. Eureka 499
Carnarvon Ra.
Mt. Essendon 906
Earaheedy
Granite Peak
L. Burnside
Mt. Normanhurst
Brassey Ra.
Bates Ra.

Wiluna
Lake Way
Yakabindie
Sandstone
Leonora
Laverton
Mt. Redcliffe 576
L. Carey
L. Raeside
Leonora
Menzies
Gwalia
Kookynie
Niagara

L. Austin
Mt. Magnet
Cue
Tuckanarra
Nannine
L. Annean
Meekatharra

Montague Ra.
Robinson Ra. Mt. Fraser 799
Nicholson Ra.
Byro
Glenburgh
Murgoo
Yalgoo
Mullewa
Morawa
Perenjori

Mount Magnet
Sandstone
Yeelirrie
Youanmi Downs
L. Barlee
Barlee
Diemals
Marmion
Mt. Elvire
Maynard Hills
Menzies

L. Ballard
Mt. Alexander
Mt. Marmion

Wongan Hills
Goomalling
Dowerin
Wyalkatchem
Kellerberrin
Merredin
Bruce Rock
Corrigin
Narembeen
Hyden
Kondinin
Kulin
Lake King
L. King

Southern Cross
Marvel Loch
Bullfinch
Westonia
Nungarin

Cunderdin
Kellerberrin
Tammin
Doodlakine
Northam
York
Beverley
Brookton
Pingelly
Wagin
Katanning
Kojonup
Gnowangerup
Ongerup
Jerramungup
Ravensthorpe
Hopetoun

Boddington
Wandering
Williams
Narrogin
Wickepin
Dumbleyung
Lake Grace
Newdegate

Collie
Darkan
Donnybrook
Greenbushes
Boyup Brook
Kojonup
Cranbrook
Tambellup
Mount Barker
Frankland
Denmark
Walpole
Nornalup

L. Grace
L. Magenta
L. King

Esperance
Grass Patch
Salmon Gums
Norseman
Peak Eleanora 503
L. Hope
L. Tay
C. Arid
Middle I.
Sandy Bight
South East I.
C. Le Grand
C. Pasley

Mt. Ragged 585

Eastern Group
Middle I.

Balladonia
Coolgardie
Cundeelee
Kirgella Rocks
Southern Hills
Karonie
Zanthus

Meekatharra
Murchison
Mt. Gould
Yalgoo
Paynes Find
Dalwallinu
Wongan Hills

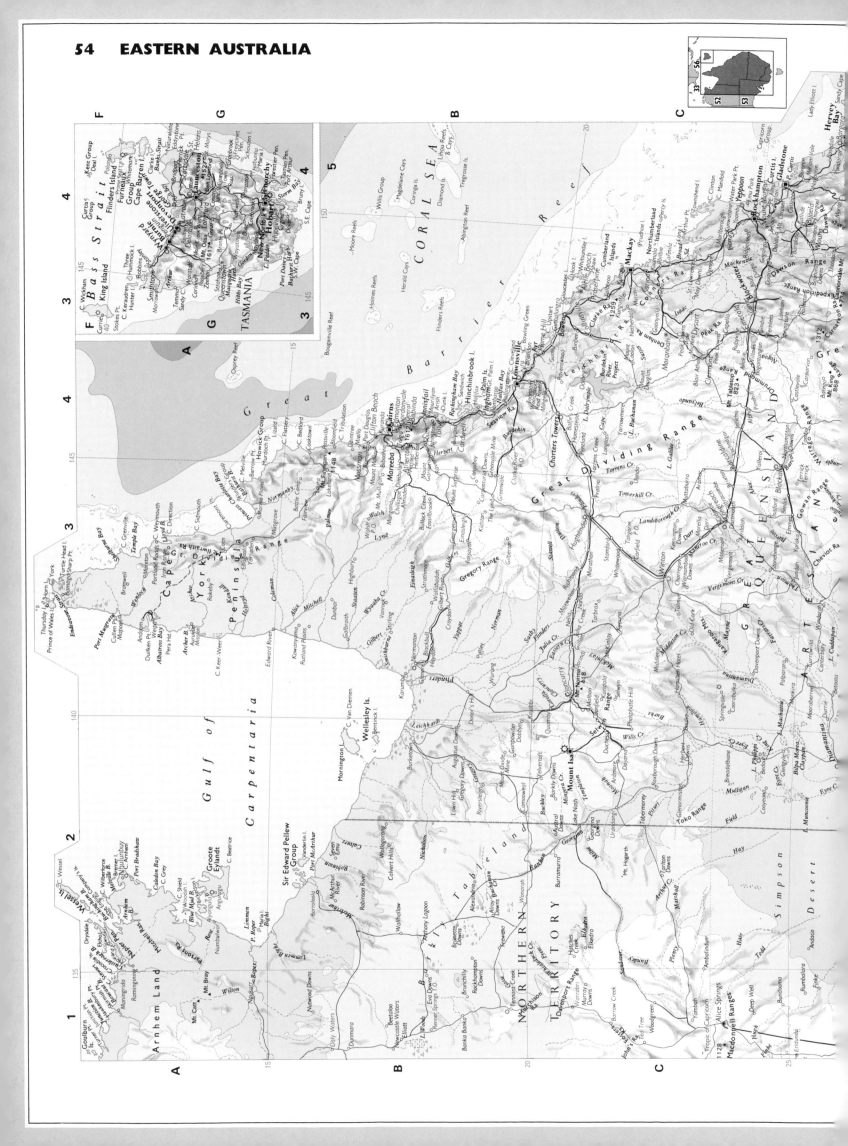

1:8 000 000

50 0 50 100 150 200 miles
50 0 100 200 300 km

Projection: Bonne

East from Greenwich

T A S M A N   S E A

S O U T H   A U S T R A L I A

N E W   S O U T H   W A L E S

BRISBANE

Gold Coast

Coffs Harbour

Newcastle

SYDNEY

Wollongong

CANBERRA

COMMONWEALTH TERR.

MELBOURNE

ADELAIDE

Broken Hill

Bass Strait

Flinders Island

Furneaux Group

Cape Barren I.

King Island

Great Dividing Range

Darling Downs

Liverpool Plains

Lake Eyre North

Lake Eyre South

Lake Torrens

Lake Frome

Lake Gairdner

Spencer Gulf

Gulf St. Vincent

Kangaroo I.

Eyre Peninsula

Yorke Peninsula

Port Augusta

Port Pirie

Whyalla

Port Lincoln

Mount Gambier

Geelong

Ballarat

Bendigo

Warrnambool

Mildura

Wagga Wagga

Albury

Wodonga

Goulburn

Dubbo

Tamworth

Armidale

Grafton

Lismore

Toowoomba

Ipswich

Warwick

Maryborough

Bundaberg

Gympie

Fraser Island

Darling R.

Murray R.

Murrumbidgee R.

D   E

E   F

D   E   F   G

1   2   3   4   5

m   ft
4500
3000
1500
1200
600
400
200
0

ft   m
12 000
6000
4000
2000
600
0

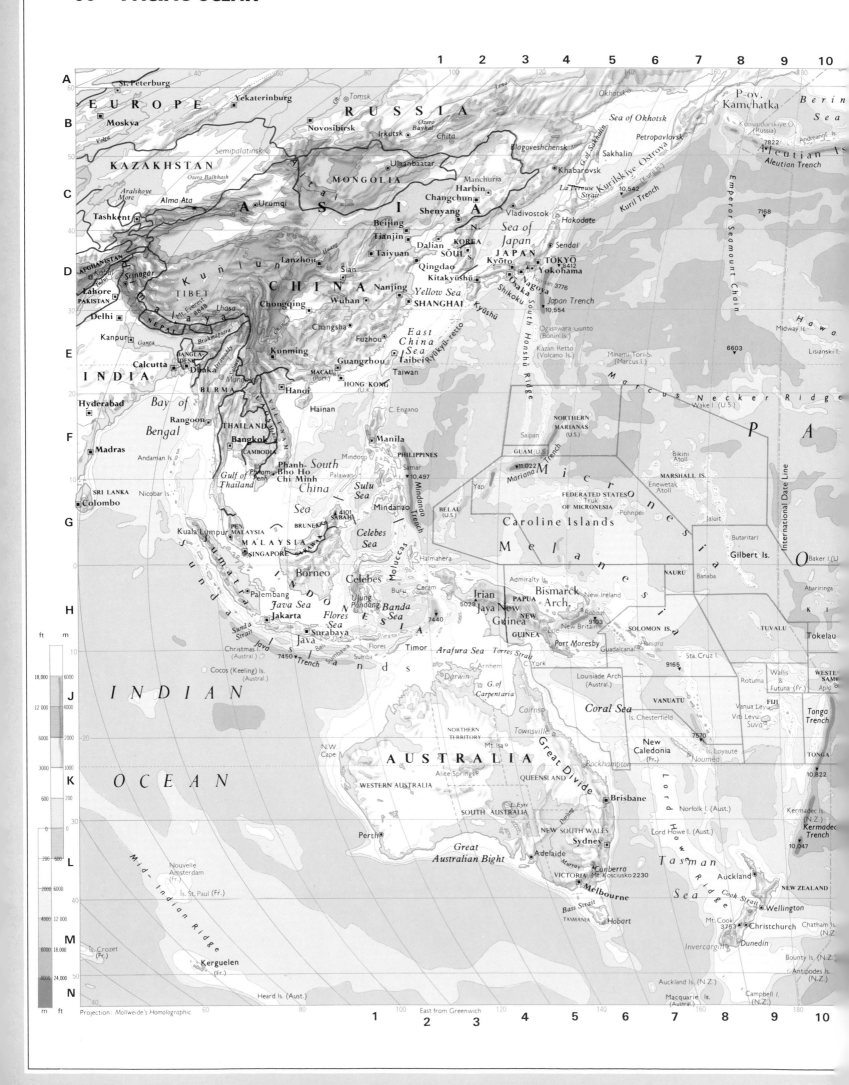

1 2 3 4 5 6 7 8 9 10

A
St. Peterburg
EUROPE
Yekaterinburg
RUSSIA
Ob
Tomsk
Okhotsk
P-ov.
Kamchatka
Berin

B
Moskva
Novosibirsk
Irkutsk
Ozero
Baykal
Chita
Sea of Okhotsk
Komandorskiye O.
(Russia)
Andreanof Is.
Volga
Semipalatinsk
Blagoveshchensk
Amur
Petropavlovsk
7822
Aleutian Is.
Aleutian Trench

KAZAKHSTAN
Ozero Balkhash
MONGOLIA
Ulaanbaatar
Manchuria
Khabarovsk
G. of Sakhalin
Sakhalin
La Perouse
Strait
Kuril'skiye Ostrova
(Kurils)
10,542
Kuril Trench

C
Aralskoye
More
Alma Ata
Urumqi
Altai
ASIA
Harbin
Changchun
Shenyang
Vladivostok
Hakodate
Kuril Trench
7168
Emperor Seamount Chain

Tashkent
Beijing
Tianjin
Dalian
KOREA
Sea of
Japan
Sendai
Indus
N.

D
AFGHANISTAN
Kabul
Srinagar
Kunlun
Lanzhou
Sian
Taiyuan
Qingdao
SOUL
S.
Kyoto
Nagoya
TOKYO
Yokohama
JAPAN
Osaka
Fujisan 3776
Japan Trench
10,554

Lahore
PAKISTAN
Mt.Everest 8848
TIBET
Lhasa
CHINA
Nanjing
Chongqing
Wuhan
SHANGHAI
Kitakyushu
Kyushu
Shikoku
Honshu Ridge
South

Delhi
Himalaya
NEPAL
Brahmaputra
Changsha
Yellow Sea
Taibei
Ogasawara Gunto
(Bonin Is.)

Kanpur
Ganga
E
Kunming
Guangzhou
Fuzhou
East
China
Sea
Taiwan
Ryukyu-retto
Kazan Retto
(Volcano Is.)
Minami-Tori-S.
(Marcus I.)
6603
Midway Is.
Hawa
Lisianski I.

Calcutta
BANGLA-
DESH
Dhaka
Irrawaddy
MACAU
(Port.)
HONG KONG
(U.K.)
Marcus
Necker
Ridge
Wake I. (U.S.)

INDIA
BURMA
Hanoi
Hainan
C. Engano

F
Hyderabad
Bay of
Bengal
Rangoon
THAILAND
Bangkok
VIETNAM
Mindoro
Manila
PHILIPPINES
Samar
NORTHERN
MARIANAS
(U.S.)
Saipan
Bikini
Atoll
PA

Madras
CAMBODIA
Andaman Is.
Phanh-
Phnom
Penh
Bho Ho
Chi Minh
South
China
Sea
Palawan
Sulu
Sea
10,497
GUAM (U.S.)
11,022
Mariana Trench
Mi
Yap
MARSHALL IS.
Enewetak
Atoll

Gulf of
Thailand
Nicobar Is.
Mindanao
SABAH
4101
FEDERATED STATES
OF MICRONESIA
Truk
Pohnpei
Jaluit
c
r
o
n
e
s
i
a

SRI LANKA
Colombo
PEN.
MALAYSIA
Kuala Lumpur
BRUNEI
Celebes
Sea
Mindanao
Trench
BELAU
(U.S.)
Caroline Islands
O
Butaritari
International Date Line

G
Sumatra
MALAYSIA
SINGAPORE
SARAWAK
Borneo
Celebes
Moluccas
Ceram
Halmahera
Me
l
a
n
e
NAURU
Banaba
Gilbert Is.
Baker I. (U
O

Palembang
Sunda
INDO
Buru
5029
Irian
Jaya
New
Guinea
PAPUA
NEW
GUINEA
Admiralty Is.
Bismarck
Arch.
New Ireland
New Britain
9103
Rabaul
s
i
a
Abariringa

H
Jakarta
Java Sea
Flores
Sea
Banda
Sea
7440
NESIA
Ujung
Pandang
Flores
Timor
Lae
Port Moresby
SOLOMON IS.
Guadalcanal
Honiara
TUVALU
KI
Tokelau

Surabaya
Bali
Sumbawa
Sumba
Arafura Sea
Torres Strait
C. York
9165
Sta. Cruz Is.
Rotuma
Wallis
&
Futuna (Fr.)
WESTE
SAM
Api

Christmas I.
(Austral.)
7450
Java
Trench
Sunda
Strait
Islands
Darwin
Arnhem
G. of
Carpentaria
Louisiade Arch.
(Austral.)
VANUATU
Vanua Levu
Viti Levu
Suva
FIJI

J
Cocos (Keeling) Is.
(Austral.)
INDIAN
NORTHERN
TERRITORY
Cairns
Coral Sea
Is. Chesterfield
7570
Tonga
Trench

Townsville
Mt. Isa
Rockhampton
New
Caledonia
(Fr.)
Noumea
Is. Loyaute
TONGA

K
OCEAN
Nouvelle
Amsterdam
(Fr.)
N.W.
Cape
AUSTRALIA
Alice Springs
QUEENSLAND
Great
Divide
Brisbane
Norfolk I. (Aust.)
Lord Howe I. (Aust.)
Kermadec Is.
(N.Z.)
Kermadec
Trench
10,047
10,822

WESTERN AUSTRALIA
SOUTH AUSTRALIA
L. Eyre
NEW SOUTH WALES
Sydney
Lord Howe Ridge
Tasman

L
Is. St. Paul
(Fr.)
Perth
Great
Australian Bight
Adelaide
Murray
Canberra Mt. Kosciusko 2230
VICTORIA
Melbourne
Sea
Auckland
NEW ZEALAND

M
Is. Crozet
(Fr.)
Mid-Indian Ridge
Bass Strait
TASMANIA
Hobart
Mt. Cook
3753
Christchurch
Chatham Is.
(N.Z.)
Cook Strait
Wellington
Invercargill
Dunedin
Bounty Is. (N.Z.)
Antipodes Is.
(N.Z.)

N
Kerguelen
(Fr.)
Heard Is. (Aust.)
Auckland Is. (N.Z.)
Macquarie Is.
(Austral.)
Campbell I.
(N.Z.)

Projection: Mollweide's Homographic
East from Greenwich

ft m
18,000 6000
12,000 4000
6000 2000
3000 1000
600 200
0
200 600
2000 6000
4000 12,000
6000 18,000
8000 24,000
m ft

1 2 3 4 5 6 7 8 9 10

1:54 000 000

ALASKA (U.S.)
Bristol Bay
Gulf of Alaska
Prince of Wales I.
Queen Charlotte Is.
Prince Rupert
Kitimat
Juneau
5959

GREENLAND
C. Farewell
U.K.

NORTH

CANADA
NORTH AMERICA
Edmonton
Vancouver
Victoria
Vancouver I.
Calgary
Seattle
Portland
Regina
Winnipeg
L. Winnipeg
Labrador
Newfoundland
St. Lawrence
Montréal
Québec
Ottawa
Toronto
L. Superior
L. Huron
L. Michigan
Erie
L. Ontario
Pr. Edward I.
Saint John
C. Sable

Rocky Mountains
Boise
Snake
Minneapolis
CHICAGO
Detroit
Buffalo
Boston
Pittsburgh
NEW YORK
Philadelphia
Baltimore
Washington

ATLANTIC

C. Mendocino
Salt Lake City
Denver
Kansas City
St. Louis
Cincinnati
UNITED STATES
Colorado
4418
San Francisco
Oklahoma
Memphis
Appalachian Mts.
Atlanta
C. Hatteras

OCEAN

6741
Los Angeles
San Diego
Ciudad Juarez
6225
Dallas
San Antonio
Houston
New Orleans
Mississippi
Jacksonville
Bermuda (U.K.)

Hawaiian Is. (U.S.)
Tropic of Cancer
Sierra Madre
MEXICO
Monterrey
Gulf of Mexico
Miami
Florida Strait
BAHAMAS

Honolulu
Oahu
Hawaii
Gulf of California
Is. Revilla Gigedo (Mexico)
México
Guadalajara
Puebla 5700
Acapulco
La Habana
Mérida
Yucatan Channel
CUBA
West Indies
Hispaniola
HAITI
DOM. REP.
9200
Leeward Is.

PACIFIC

Johnston I. (U.S.)
Christmas Island Ridge
BELIZE
GUATEMALA
Guatemala
San Salvador
EL SALVADOR
HONDURAS
NICARAGUA
Managua
7680
JAMAICA
Kingston
PUERTO RICO (U.S.)
Caribbean Sea
BARBADOS
Windward Is.
TRINIDAD & TOBAGO

OCEAN

Palmyra Is. (U.S.)
Teraina
Tabuaeran
Kiritimati
Jarvis I. (U.S.)
CENTRAL AMERICA
COSTA RICA
San José
Colón
Panama
PANAMA
Canal
I. Clipperton (Fr.)
Barranquilla
Maracaibo
Caracas
Orinoco
VENEZUELA

Canterbury I.
Phoenix Is.
Malden I.
Starbuck I.
Equator
Galápagos (Ecuador)
Guayaquil
Quito
ECUADOR
I. del Coco (Costa Rica)
Medellín
Bogota
Cali
COLOMBIA

Tongareva
Penrhyn Is.
Manihiki
Suwarrow Is.
Vostok I.
Flint I.
Caroline I.
Île Marquises
C. Pariñas
Iquitos
Amazonas
Manaus
BRAZIL
SOUTH

Kapuka
Cook Islands (N.Z.)
Îs. de la Société
Îs. Tuamotu
Tahiti
Manuae
Trujillo
PERU
Lima
6369
AMERICA

Austral
Rarotonga
FRENCH POLYNESIA
East Pacific Ridge
Cuzco
Arequipa
L. Titicaca
Illampu & Ancohuma 6550
La Paz
BOLIVIA

Îs. Tubuai (Îs. Australes)
Rapa
Seamount Chain
Pitcairn I. (U.K.)
Ducie I. (U.K.)
Tropic of Capricorn
Iquique Chile
Peru 6866
Antofagasta Trench
8050
PARAGUAY
Asunción

I. de Pascua (Easter I.) (Chile)
Sala-y-Gomez (Chile)
San Félix (Chile)
San Ambrosio (Chile)
Arch. de Juan Fernández (Chile)
6960
Córdoba
Rosario
Pto. Alegre
URUGUAY

Pacific-Antarctic Ridge
Chile Rise
Valparaíso
Santiago
Concepción
Buenos Aires
Montevideo
ARGENTINA
Rio de la Plata

SOUTH
ATLANTIC
6212
OCEAN

Patagonia
Str. of Magellan
Punta Arenas
Tierra del Fuego
C. Horn
Falkland Is. (U.K.)
South Georgia

West from Greenwich

COPYRIGHT. GEORGE PHILIP & SON. LTD.

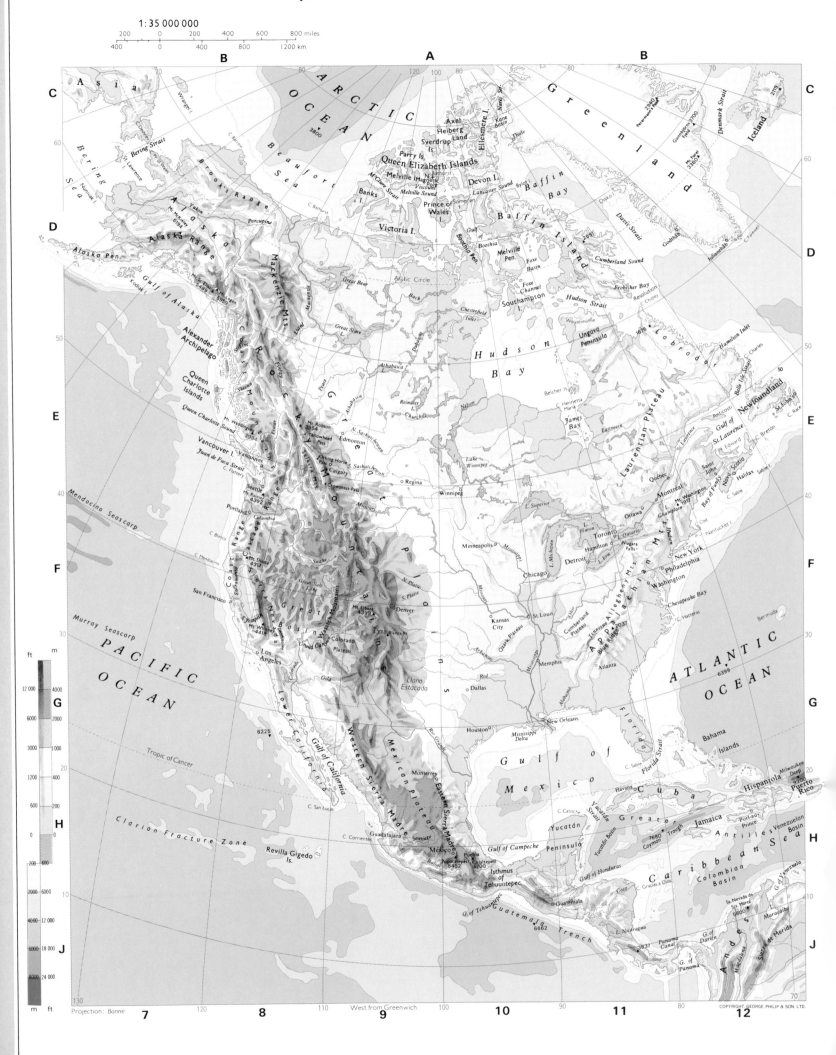

1:35 000 000

Projection: Bonne

West from Greenwich

1:35 000 000

200   0   200   400   600   800 miles
400   0   400   800   1200 km

B   **A**   **B**

C RUSSIA   ARCTIC OCEAN   GREENLAND (Denmark)   ICELAND **C**

Bering Strait
Bering Sea
Beaufort Sea
Queen Elizabeth Is.
Ellesmere I.
Baffin Bay
Reykjavik

D ALASKA   Victoria I.   Baffin I.   Denmark Strait **D**
Arctic Circle
Fairbanks
Porcupine
Anchorage
YUKON TERRITORY
INUVIK
KITIKMEOT
NORTHWEST TERRITORIES
BAFFIN
Godthaab

Whitehorse
Mackenzie
FORT SMITH
Yellowknife
Great Bear L.
KEEWATIN
Hudson Strait
NEWFOUNDLAND

E Juneau   Great Slave L.   Hudson Bay   Labrador **E**
Gulf of Alaska
Liard
BRITISH COLUMBIA
Peace
Athabasca
CANADA
Churchill
Nelson
Finlay
Skeena
Fraser
ALBERTA
Edmonton
N. Saskatchewan
MANITOBA
L. Winnipeg
Eastmain
QUÉBEC
St. Lawrence
St. John's

Calgary
S. Saskatchewan
SASKATCHEWAN
Regina
ONTARIO
Québec
PR. EDWARD I.
Charlottetown
NOVA SCOTIA

F Victoria   Winnipeg   L. Superior   Montréal   Halifax **F**
Vancouver
WASHINGTON
Seattle
Olympia
Portland
Salem
Columbia
OREGON
MONTANA
Helena
IDAHO
Boise
Snake
NORTH DAKOTA
Bismarck
Missouri
MINNESOTA
St. Paul
Minneapolis
WISCONSIN
Madison
L. Michigan
L. Huron
Toronto
L. Ontario
Buffalo
NEW YORK
Ottawa
MAINE
Montpelier
Augusta
VER. N.H.
Concord
Boston
MASS.
Providence
R.I.
Hartford
Albany
CONN.

SOUTH DAKOTA
Pierre
MICHIGAN
Lansing
Detroit
Cleveland
PENNSYLVANIA
Harrisburg
NEW YORK
Trenton
Philadelphia
N.J.
Dover

Sacramento
San Francisco
San Jose
CALIFORNIA
Carson City
NEVADA
Salt Lake City
UTAH
WYOMING
Cheyenne
NEBRASKA
Lincoln
N. Platte
Des Moines
IOWA
Chicago
ILLINOIS
Springfield
INDIANA
Indianapolis
Columbus
OHIO
Pittsburg
WEST VIRGINIA
MARYLAND
Annapolis
Washington D.C.
Richmond

G Denver   Kansas City   Cincinnati   Raleigh   Bermuda(Br.) **G**
COLORADO
Topeka
Jefferson City
St. Louis
MISSOURI
KENTUCKY
Frankfort
Charleston
VIRGINIA
PACIFIC OCEAN
Las Vegas
LOS ANGELES
San Diego
ARIZONA
Phoenix
Tucson
Colorado
Gila
Santa Fe
Albuquerque
NEW MEXICO
Oklahoma City
OKLAHOMA
KANSAS
Arkansas
Red River
Little Rock
ARKANSAS
Memphis
TENNESSEE
Nashville
Tennessee
NORTH CAROLINA
Columbia
SOUTH CAROLINA
ATLANTIC OCEAN

El Paso
Rio Grande
Dallas
TEXAS
Austin
LOUISIANA
Baton Rouge
MISSISSIPPI
Jackson
Birmingham
ALABAMA
Montgomery
GEORGIA
Atlanta
Jacksonville
FLORIDA

H UNITED STATES   Houston   New Orleans   Tallahassee   Tampa **H**
Tropic of Cancer
Monterrey
Gulf of Mexico
Miami
Nassau
BAHAMAS
Turks & Caicos (Br.)
C. Sable
Str. of Florida

MEXICO
Guadalajara
MEXICO
Revilla Gigedo Is. (Mexico)
Havana
CUBA
Cayman Is. (Br.)
JAMAICA
Kingston
HAITI
Port-au-Prince
DOMINICAN REP.
Santo Domingo
PUERTO RICO
San Juan

J BELIZE   Caribbean Sea   Maracaibo   VENEZUELA **J**
Belmopan
GUATEMALA
Guatemala
HONDURAS
Tegucigalpa
San Salvador
EL SALVADOR
NICARAGUA
Managua
Nicaragua
COSTA RICA
San José
PANAMA
Panamá
Barranquilla
Medellin
COLOMBIA
Bogotá
SOUTH AMERICA

7 Capital Cities
Washington
U.S. State Capitals and
Canadian Provincial Capitals

C.	CONNECTICUT	N.H.	NEW HAMPSHIRE
D.	DELAWARE	N.J.	NEW JERSEY
D.C.	DISTRICT OF COLUMBIA	R.I.	RHODE ISLAND
M.	MARYLAND	VER.	VERMONT
MASS.	MASSACHUSETTS	SPM	ST. PIERRE ET MIQUELON

Projection: Bonne

West from Greenwich

COPYRIGHT GEORGE PHILIP & SON. LTD.

8   **9**   **10**   **11**   **12**

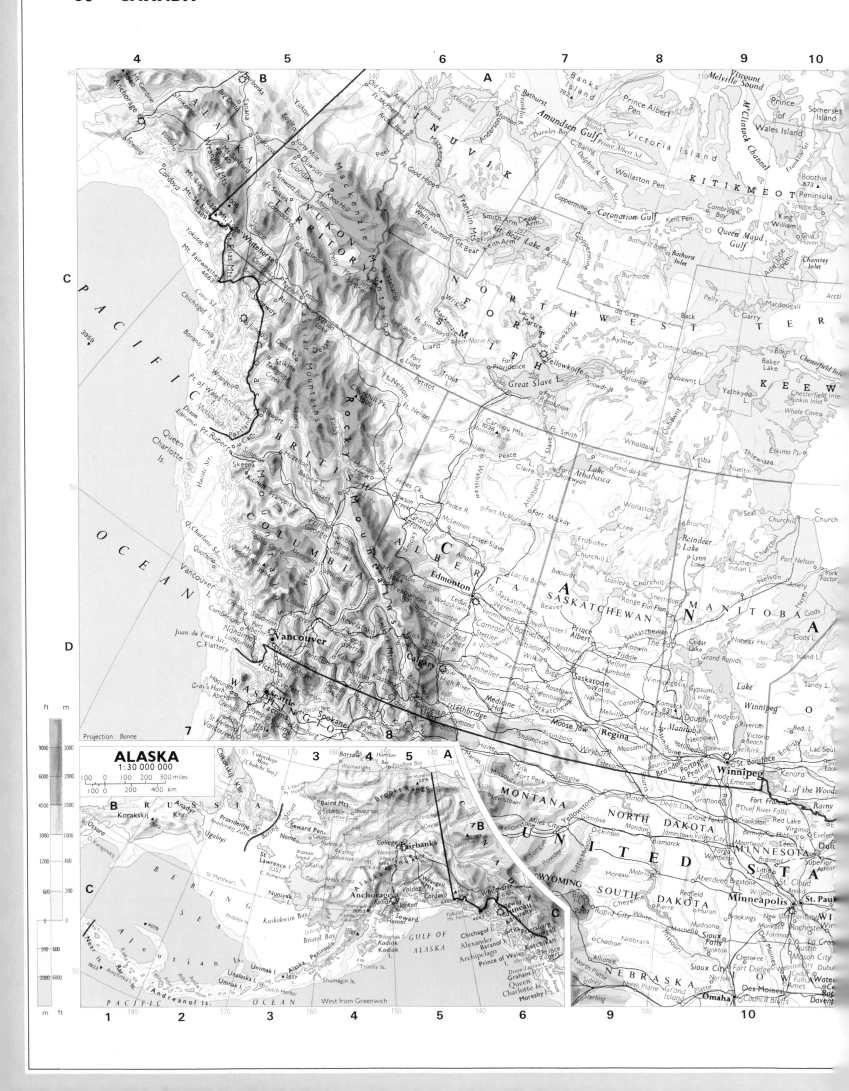

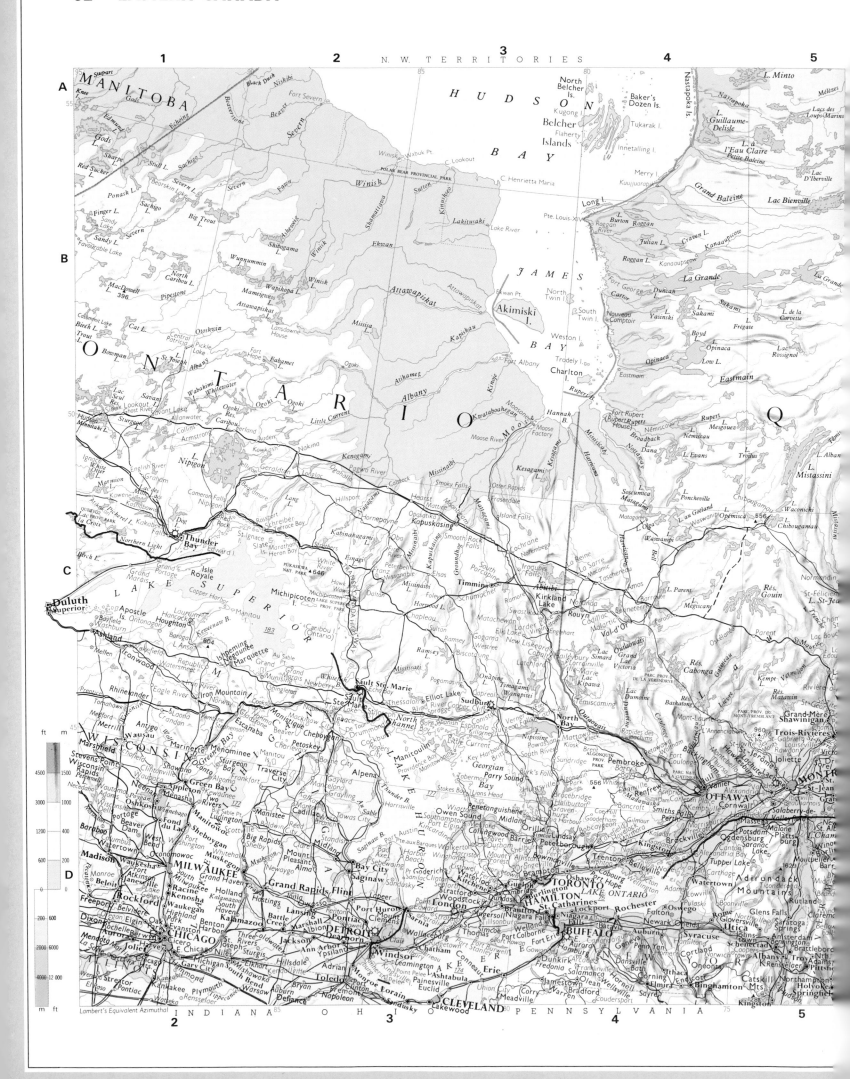

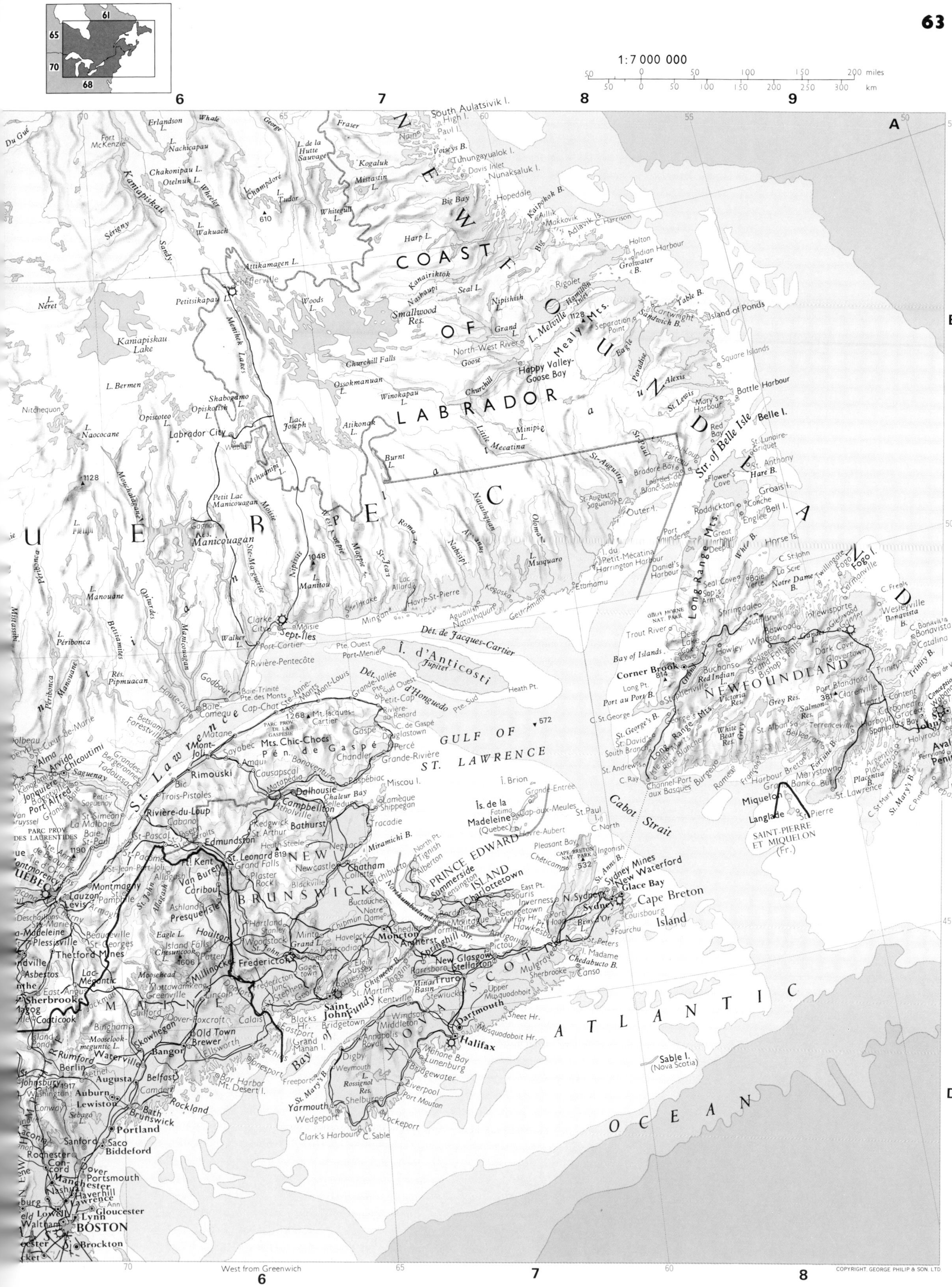

1:7 000 000

50 0 50 100 150 200 miles
50 0 50 100 150 200 250 300 km

West from Greenwich

COPYRIGHT GEORGE PHILIP & SON LTD

COAST OF LABRADOR

QUEBEC

NEWFOUNDLAND

NEW BRUNSWICK

NOVA SCOTIA

PRINCE EDWARD ISLAND

MAINE

GULF OF ST. LAWRENCE

ATLANTIC OCEAN

Cabot Strait

Str. of Belle Isle

Cape Breton Island

Avalon Peninsula

SAINT-PIERRE ET MIQUELON (Fr.)

Halifax
Dartmouth
Boston
Portland
Bangor
Augusta
Fredericton
Saint John
Moncton
Charlottetown
Summerside
Sydney
New Glasgow
Truro
Yarmouth
Corner Brook
Sept-Îles
Labrador City
Happy Valley-Goose Bay
Churchill Falls
Gaspé
Rimouski
Matane
Edmundston
Sherbrooke
Thetford Mines
Lévis
Québec

Î. d'Anticosti

Î. de la Madeleine (Quebec)

Sable I. (Nova Scotia)

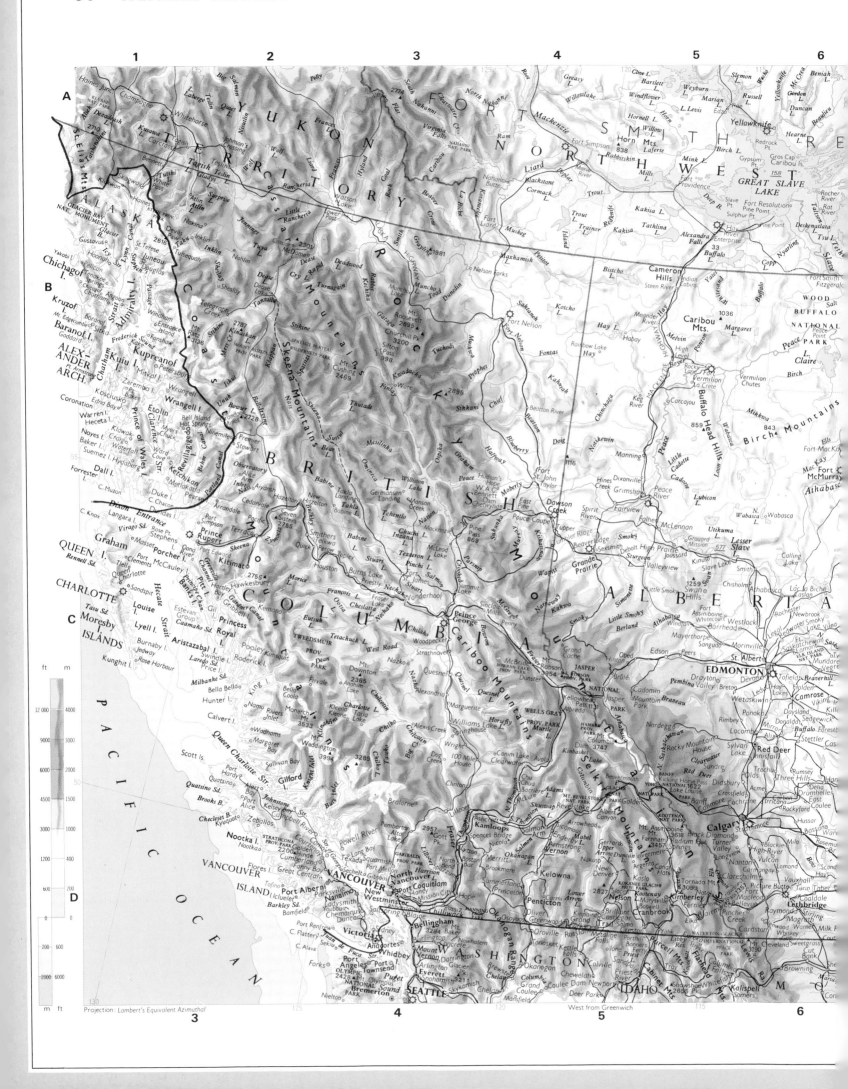

Projection: Lambert's Equivalent Azimuthal

West from Greenwich

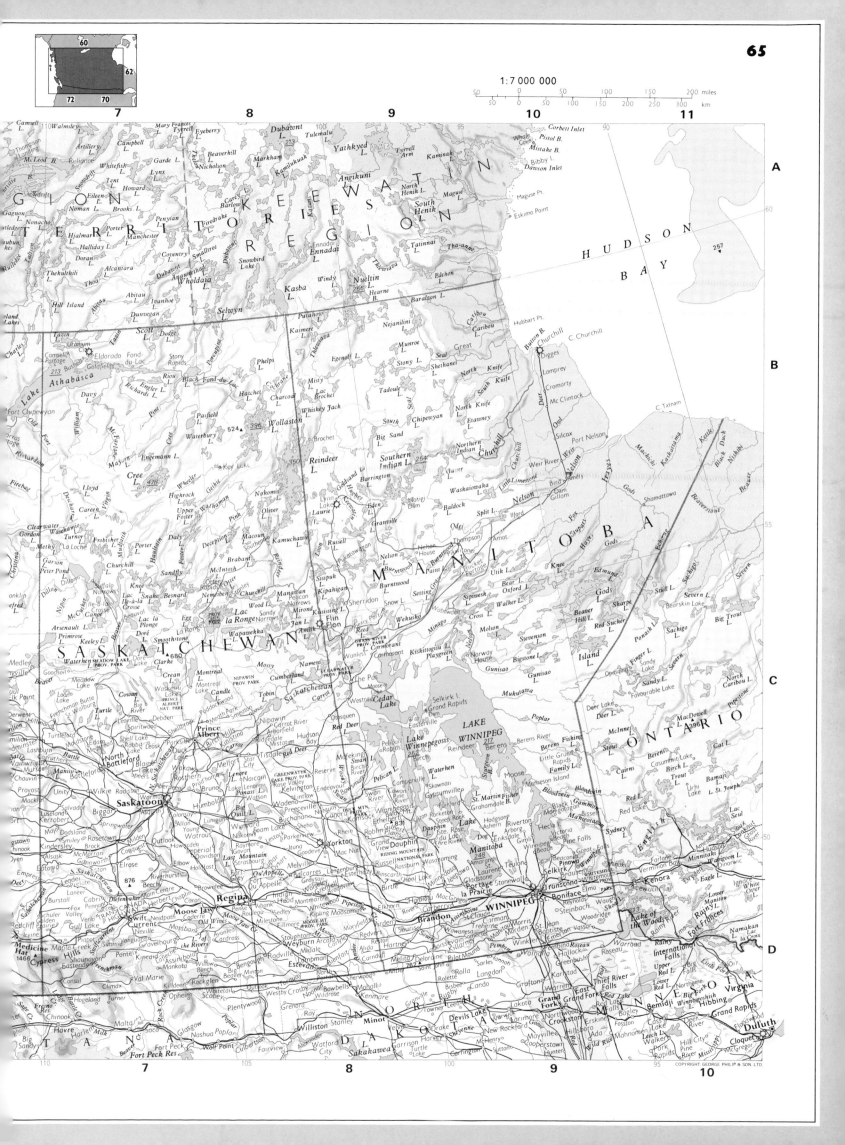

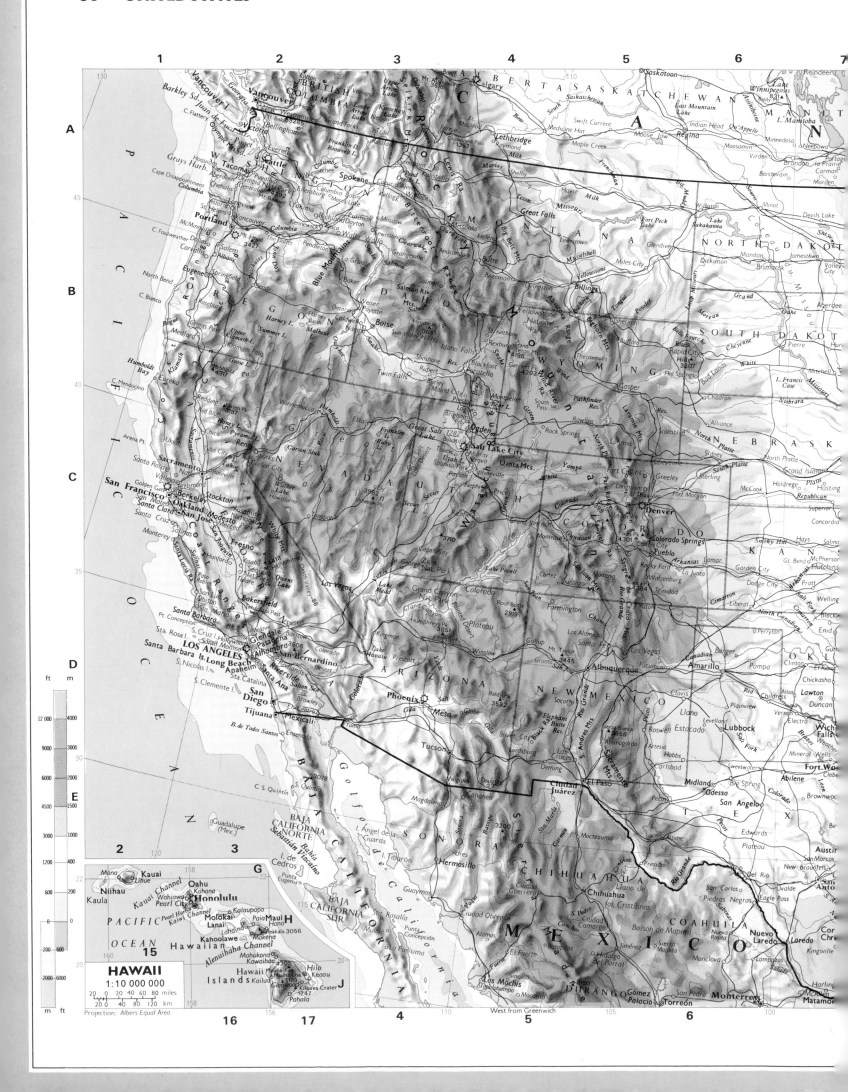

HAWAII
1:10 000 000

20 0 20 40 60 80 miles
20 0 40 80 120 km

Projection: Albers Equal Area

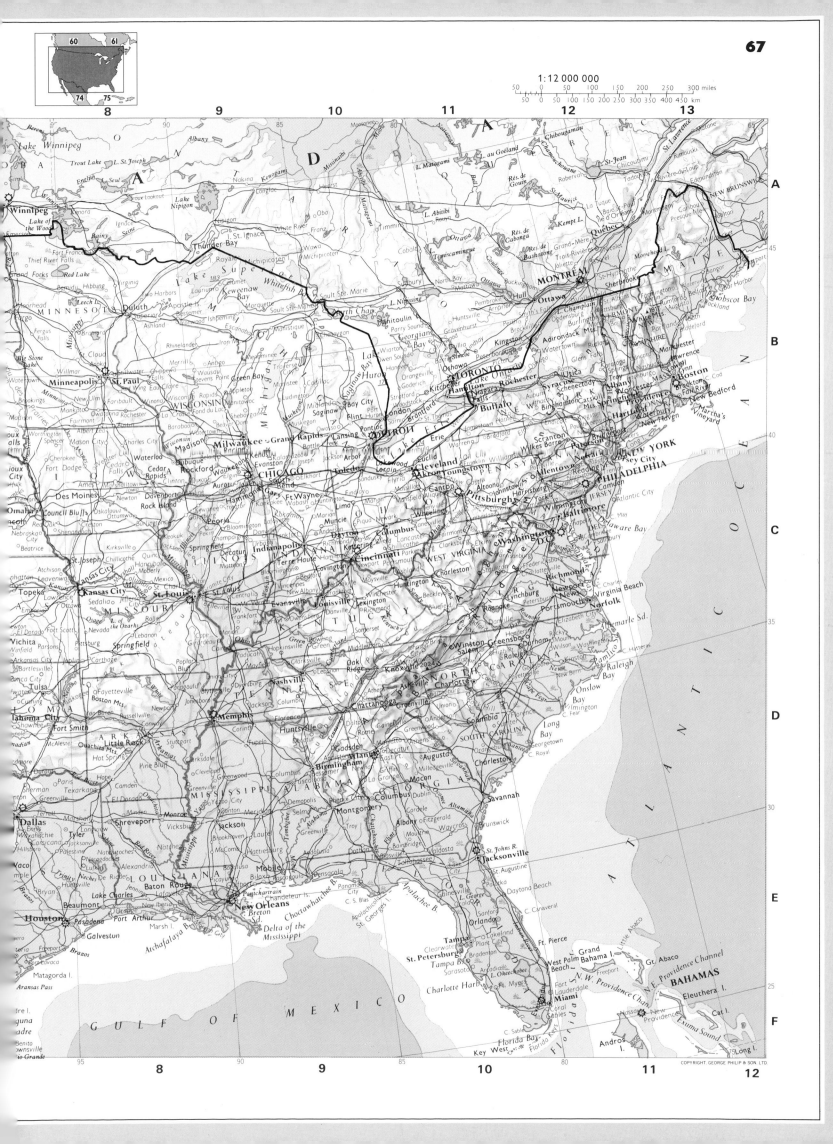

QUEBEC

ONTARIO

MICHIGAN

WISCONSIN

ILLINOIS

INDIANA

OHIO

KENTUCKY

WEST VIRGINIA

VIRGINIA

PENNSYLVANIA

MARYLAND

DELAWARE

NEW JERSEY

NEW YORK

VERMONT

NEW HAMPSHIRE

MASS.

CONN.

R.I.

WASHINGTON D.C.

MONTREAL

OTTAWA

TORONTO

MILWAUKEE

CHICAGO

DETROIT

CLEVELAND

COLUMBUS

CINCINNATI

PITTSBURGH

PHILADELPHIA

BALTIMORE

NEW YORK

BOSTON

INDIANAPOLIS

LOUISVILLE

LAKE SUPERIOR

LAKE HURON

LAKE ONTARIO

LAKE ERIE

Georgian Bay

Chesapeake Bay

1:6 000 000

50   0   50   100   150 miles
50 0 50 100 150 200 km

COPYRIGHT GEORGE PHILIP & SON, LTD

Continuation Eastwards
On same scale.

CANADA

Edmundston St-Leonard Grand Falls Plaster Rock Woodstock
Eagle Lake Fort Kent Caribou Presque Isle Houlton
Allagash Ashland Millinocket Lincoln Old Town
Moosehead Greenville Dover-Foxcroft Brewer Bangor Ellsworth Mt. Desert I.
Mt. Katahdin Skowhegan Waterville Belfast Rockland
Rangeley Farmington Augusta Gardiner Bath Rockport
Berlin Lewiston Auburn Brunswick Casco B. Portland
Mt. Washington Conway Laconia Biddeford Saco Westbrook
Colebrook Dover Portsmouth Newburyport Haverhill

MAINE
NEW HAMPSHIRE

ATLANTIC OCEAN

BAHAMAS
Little Abaco I. Great Abaco I. Hope Town Gt. Guana Cay
Grand Cays Settlement Pt. Grand Bahama I. Freeport West End

NORTH CAROLINA
Currituck Sd. Elizabeth City Manteo Roanoke I. Albemarle Sd.
Edenton Plymouth Washington Pamlico Sound C. Hatteras
Raleigh Rocky Mount Wilson Goldsboro Kinston New Bern Morehead City C. Lookout
Durham Chapel Hill Smithfield Dunn Clinton Jacksonville Wilmington C. Fear
Winston-Salem Greensboro High Point Asheboro Fayetteville
Charlotte Salisbury Lexington Concord Albemarle Lumberton
Asheville Mt. Mitchell 2037 Hickory Statesville Gastonia

SOUTH CAROLINA
Rock Hill Chester Lancaster Cheraw Bennettsville Dillon Marion Conway Myrtle Beach
Columbia Sumter Florence Georgetown
Greenville Spartanburg Union Newberry Orangeburg Aiken
Charleston Beaufort Parris I. Summerville

GEORGIA
Augusta Savannah Brunswick Jekyll I. Cumberland I.
Athens Gainesville Macon Warner Robins Dublin Statesboro
ATLANTA Marietta Decatur East Point Griffin Columbus
Americus Albany Tifton Moultrie Valdosta Waycross Fitzgerald Cordele
Rome Dalton Cartersville

ALABAMA
Huntsville Decatur Sheffield Florence Gadsden Anniston
Birmingham Bessemer Tuscaloosa Jasper
Montgomery Selma Troy Dothan Ozark Enterprise Andalusia
Mobile Dauphin I.

TENNESSEE
Nashville Clarksville Gallatin Murfreesboro Lebanon Columbia
Knoxville Chattanooga Cleveland Johnson City Kingsport Bristol

MISSISSIPPI
Tupelo Columbus Aberdeen Starkville West Point
Meridian Laurel Hattiesburg Biloxi Pascagoula Gulfport

FLORIDA
JACKSONVILLE Jacksonville Beach St. Augustine Palatka Gainesville
Daytona Beach Ocala Leesburg Sanford Orlando Winter Park Cocoa C. Canaveral
Tampa St. Petersburg Clearwater Lakeland Winter Haven Sebring Melbourne
Bradenton Sarasota Punta Gorda Ft. Myers Vero Beach Ft. Pierce
Lake Okeechobee West Palm Beach Pompano Beach Ft. Lauderdale Hollywood
Miami Miami Beach Hialeah Coral Gables Biscayne B. Homestead
Naples EVERGLADES NAT. PARK Big Cypress Swamp

GULF OF MEXICO

Tallahassee Apalachicola Panama City Pensacola Warrington
Apalachee B. C. St. George C. San Blas Port St. Joe

West from Greenwich

Projection: Albers' Equal Area with two standard parallels

m ft
6000
4500
3000
1500
1200
600
200
0

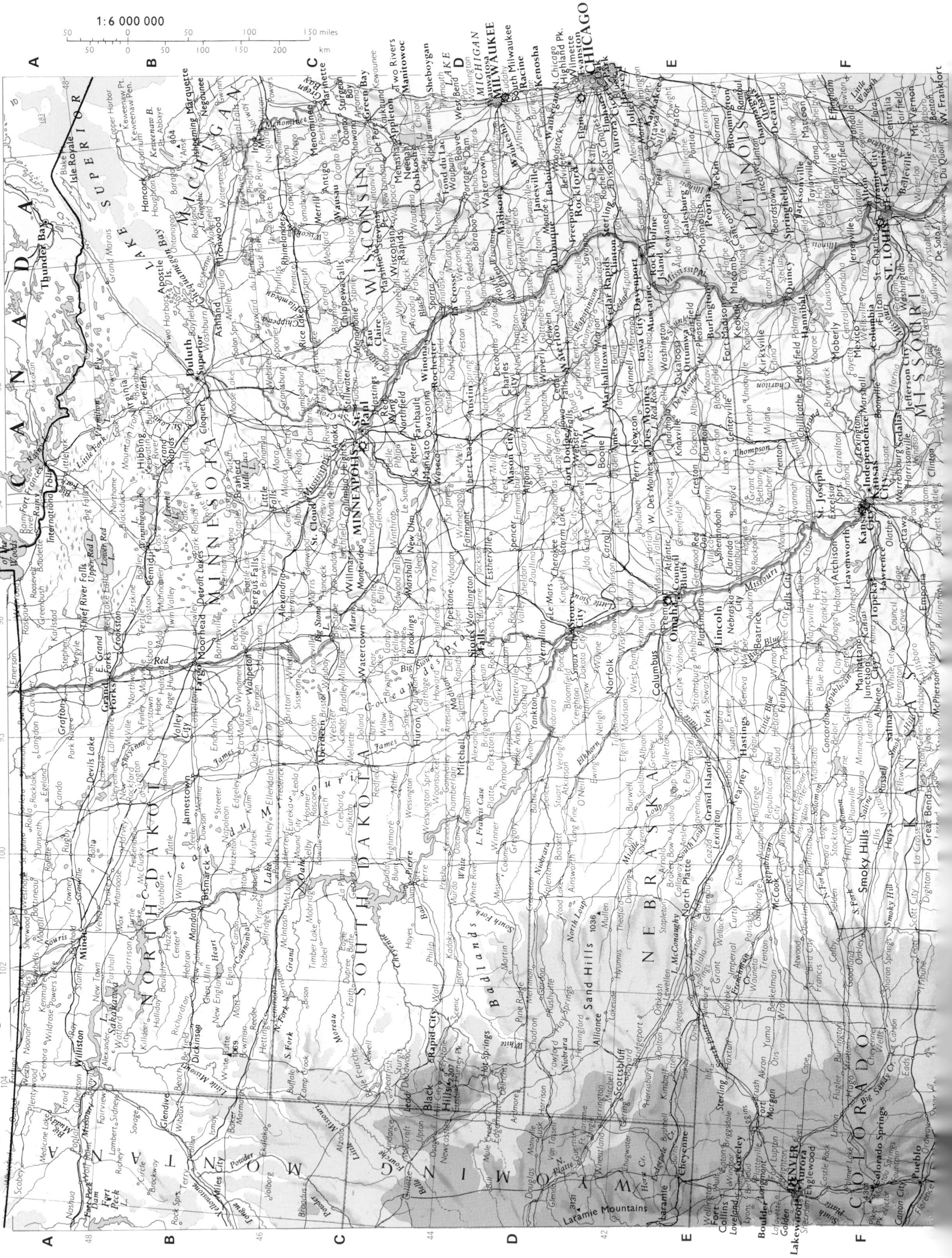

1:6 000 000

50   0   50   100   150 miles
50   0   50   100   150   200 km

CANADA

LAKE SUPERIOR

MICHIGAN

WISCONSIN

MINNESOTA

NORTH DAKOTA

SOUTH DAKOTA

NEBRASKA

KANSAS

IOWA

ILLINOIS

MISSOURI

MONTANA

WYOMING

COLORADO

LAKE MICHIGAN

CHICAGO
MILWAUKEE
MINNEAPOLIS
ST. LOUIS
DENVER

Missouri

Mississippi

Badlands

Black Hills

Sand Hills

Laramie Mountains

65 68 69
72 73 74
G H

10
9

Continuation Southwards on same scale

MEXICO
Laguna Madre
Mirando City · Kingsville
Hebbronville · Premont
San Ygnacio · Falfurrias
Zapata · Falcon Dam
Rio Grande
Roma · McAllen
Mier · Edinburg
Reynosa · Harlingen
Matamoros · San Benito
Brownsville
Padre I.

J K

TENNESSEE
Memphis · West Memphis
Forrest City
Muscle Shoals · Iuka
Corinth · Booneville
Tupelo · Fulton
Aberdeen · Columbus
West Point · Starkville
MISSISSIPPI
Greenwood · Winona
Grenada · Oxford · New Albany
Clarksdale · Batesville
Cleveland · Greenville
Leland · Indianola · Greenwood
Yazoo City
Jackson · Philadelphia · Meridian
Vicksburg · Canton
Natchez · Brookhaven
McComb · Hattiesburg · Laurel
Baton Rouge · Hammond
LOUISIANA
New Orleans
Metairie
Houma

GULF OF MEXICO

ARKANSAS
Little Rock
Pine Bluff
Hot Springs
Fort Smith
Fayetteville
Springdale · Harrison
Batesville · Newport
Jonesboro · Blytheville
Forrest City · Helena
El Dorado · Magnolia
Camden · Hope · Texarkana

OKLAHOMA
Oklahoma City
Tulsa
Muskogee
Enid · Stillwater
Norman · Ada
Lawton · Ardmore
Duncan · Frederick
Durant

KANSAS
Wichita
Wellington · Arkansas City
Winfield · Eureka
El Dorado

MISSOURI
Springfield
Poplar Bluff
Cape Girardeau
Joplin

TEXAS
DALLAS · Fort Worth
Arlington · Irving
Houston
SAN ANTONIO
Austin
Waco · Temple
Corpus Christi
Galveston
Beaumont · Port Arthur · Orange
Tyler · Longview · Marshall
Shreveport
Texarkana
Wichita Falls
Abilene
San Angelo
Amarillo
Lubbock
Midland · Odessa
Big Spring · Sweetwater
Brownwood · Eastland
Del Rio
Laredo
Nuevo Laredo
Piedras Negras
Eagle Pass
Kingsville
Alice
Victoria

NEW MEXICO
Roswell
Carlsbad
Hobbs
Clovis · Portales
Tucumcari
Las Vegas
Raton · Trinidad

Sangre de Cristo Mts.

Llano Estacado
Edwards Plateau
Stockton Plateau
Chisos Mts.
Davis Mts.
Alpine · Marfa · Marathon
Fort Davis · Presidio

COAHUILA
Ciudad Acuña
Nueva Rosita
Sabinas

CHIHUAHUA

Rio Bravo del Norte
Rio Grande
Pecos

Projection: Albers' Equal Area with two standard parallels

ft · m
12,000 · 4000
9,000 · 3000
6,000 · 1500
4500 · 600
400 · 200
0

West from Greenwich
102 · 100 · 98 · 96 · 94 · 92 · 90
28

G H J K M L M
6 5 8 7 6 5 4 3 2

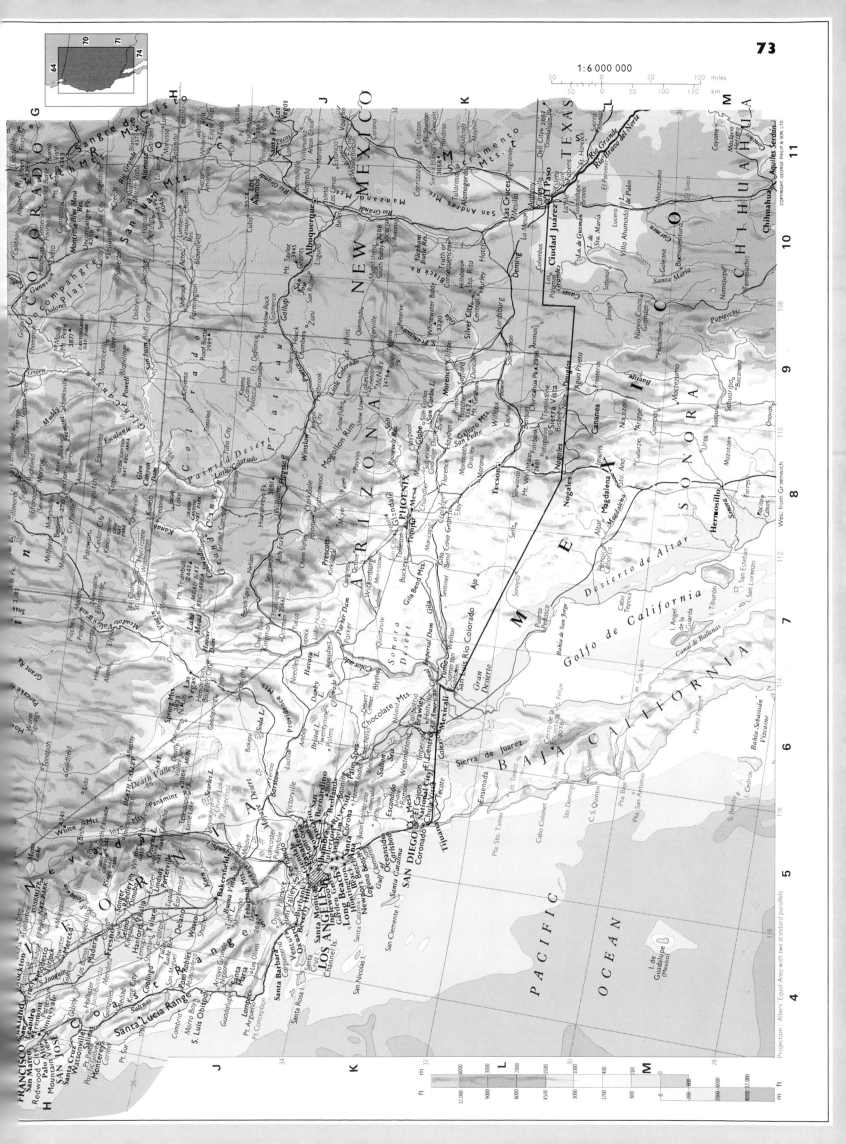

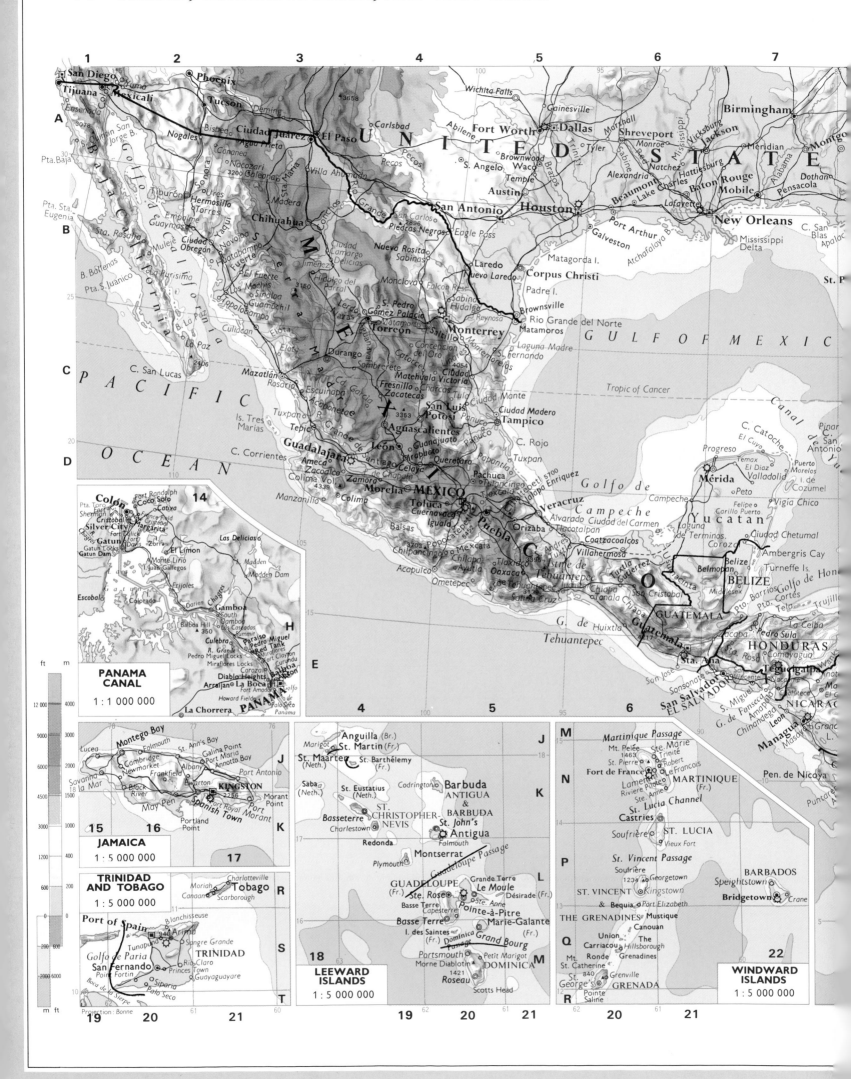

PANAMA CANAL
1 : 1 000 000

JAMAICA
1 : 5 000 000

TRINIDAD
AND TOBAGO
1 : 5 000 000

LEEWARD
ISLANDS
1 : 5 000 000

WINDWARD
ISLANDS
1 : 5 000 000

1 : 30 000 000

100 0 100 200 300 400 500 miles
100 0 200 400 600 800 km

Projection: Lambert's Equivalent Azimuthal

COPYRIGHT. GEORGE PHILIP & SON. LTD

1 : 30 000 000

100 0 100 200 300 400 500 miles
100 0 200 400 600 800 km

COSTA RICA
San José
PANAMA
Panamá
Golfo de Darién
Golfo de Panamá

Barranquilla
Cartagena
Maracaibo
Barquisimeto
Valencia
Caracas
Port of Spain
TRINIDAD AND TOBAGO

Cúcuta
San Cristóbal
Bucaramanga
Medellín
Bogotá
Cali
COLOMBIA

VENEZUELA
Orinoco
Ciudad Guayana
Georgetown
Paramaribo
Cayenne
GUYANA
SURINAM
FRENCH GUIANA
C. Orange

NORTH ATLANTIC OCEAN

C. de San Francisco
Quito
ECUADOR
Guayaquil
G. de Guayaquil
Iquitos
Pta. Aguja
Chiclayo
Trujillo
Chimbote
PERU
Callao
Lima
Cuzco
Arequipa

Napo
Putumayo
Marañón
Ucayali
Madre de Dios
Titicaca
La Paz
Cochabamba
BOLIVIA
Sucre
Santa Cruz

Negro
Japurá
Amazon
Manaus
Santarem
Juruá
Purus
Madeira
Tapajós
Pôrto Velho
Mamoré
Guaporé
Iquique

Equator
Ilha de Marajó
Belém
São Luis
Teresina
Fortaleza (Ceara)
C. de São Roque
Natal
João Pessoa
Recife (Pernambuco)
Maceió
Aracaju

B R A Z I L
Xingu
Araguaia
Tocantins
Parnaiba
São Francisco

Cuiabá
Brasília
Goiânia
Salvador

Belo Horizonte
Campo Grande
Ribeirão Prêto
Vitória
Campos

P A C I F I C   O C E A N
Tropic of Capricorn
Antofagasta
Isla San Felix (Chile)
Isla San Ambrosio (Chile)

PARAGUAY
Paraguay
Pilcomayo
Asunción
Londrina
Campinas
Niterói
SÃO PAULO
Santos
RIO DE JANEIRO
Curitiba
Juiz de Fora
Paraná

C H I L E
Salta
San Miguel de Tucumán
Resistencia
Corrientes
Uruguay
Pôrto Alegre
Lagoa dos Patos
Pelotas

SOUTH

ARGENTINA
Córdoba
San Juan
Santa Fe
Paraná
Rosario
URUGUAY
Salado
Viña del Mar
Valparaíso
Mendoza
Santiago
BUENOS AIRES
La Plata
Montevideo
Mar del Plata
Rio de la Plata

ATLANTIC

Talca
Concepción
Bahía Blanca
Colorado
Negro
Valdivia
Viedma
Puerto Montt
Chubut

OCEAN

Golfo Comodoro Rivadavia
San Jorge
G. de Penas
Arch de Juan Fernández (Chile)

FALKLAND ISLANDS
West Falkland
Stanley
East Falkland
(U.K.)
Punta Arenas
Strait of Magellan
Cape Horn
Tierra del Fuego

Projection : Lambert's Equivalent Azimuthal
West from Greenwich
COPYRIGHT. GEORGE PHILIP & SON. LTD.

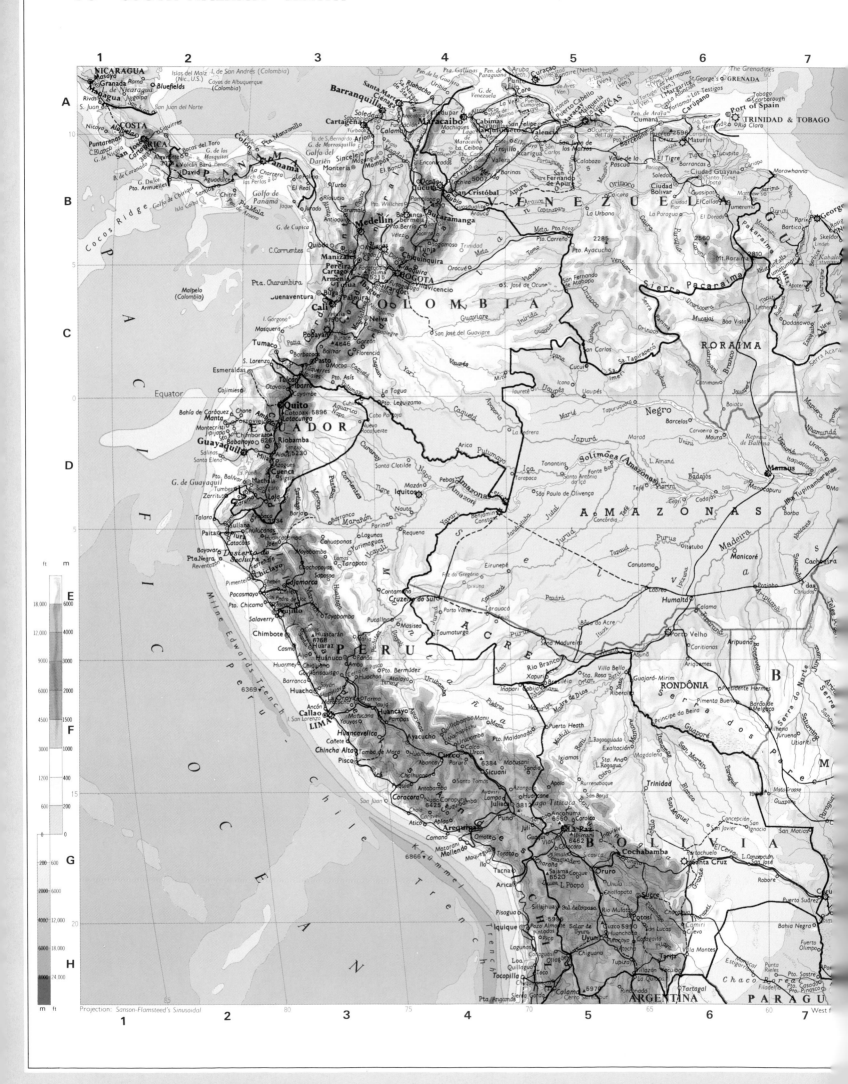

1 : 16 000 000

100 50 0 100 200 300 miles
100 0 100 200 300 400 km

78 | 79

Projection: Sanson-Flamsteed's Sinusoidal

COPYRIGHT GEORGE PHILIP & SON, LTD

West from Greenwich

ft m
18 000 — 6000
12 000 — 4000
9000 — 3000
6000 — 2000
4500 — 1500
3000 — 1000
1200 — 400
600 — 200
0 — 0
200 — 600
2000 — 6000
4000 — 12 000
6000 — 18 000
8000 — 24 000
m ft

MATO GROSSO DO SUL
PARAGUAY
PARANÁ
BRASIL
SANTA CATARINA
RIO GRANDE DO SUL
URUGUAY
SÃO PAULO
RIO DE JANEIRO

Asunción
Curitiba
Pôrto Alegre
MONTEVIDEO
BUENOS AIRES
Rosario
Córdoba
Mendoza
SANTIAGO
Valparaíso
Viña del Mar
Antofagasta
Concepción
Talcahuano
Valdivia
Puerto Montt
Bahía Blanca
Mar del Plata
Comodoro Rivadavia
Río Gallegos
Punta Arenas

SOUTH ATLANTIC OCEAN
Perú–Chile Trench
Richard's Deep

Tropic of Capricorn

FALKLAND ISLANDS (ISLAS MALVINAS) (Br.)
West Falkland
East Falkland
Stanley
Tierra del Fuego
Estrecho de Magallanes (Magellan's Str.)
Cabo de Hornos (C. Horn)
South Georgia (Br.)
I. de Chiloé
Archipiélago de los Chonos
Pen. de Taitao
I. Wellington
Golfo San Jorge
Golfo San Matías
Península Valdés
Golfo Nuevo

INDEX

The index contains the names of all the principal places and features shown on the World Maps. Each name is followed by an additional entry in italics giving the country or region within which it is located. The alphabetical order of names composed of two or more words is governed primarily by the first word and then by the second. This is an example of the rule:

Mīr Kūh, *Iran*	**39**	**E8**
Mīr Shahdād, *Iran*	**39**	**E8**
Miraj, *India*	**36**	**L9**
Miram Shah, *Pakistan*	**36**	**C7**
Miramar, *Mozam.*	**49**	**C6**

Physical features composed of a proper name (Erie) and a description (Lake) are positioned alphabetically by the proper name. The description is positioned after the proper name and is usually abbreviated:

Erie, L., *N. Amer.*	**68**	**D5**

Where a description forms part of a settlement or administrative name however, it is always written in full and put in its true alphabetic position:

Mount Morris, *U.S.A.*	**68**	**D7**

Names beginning with M' and Mc are indexed as if they were spelled Mac. Names beginning St. are alphabetised under Saint, but Sankt, Sint, Sant', Santa and San are all spelt in full and are alphabetised accordingly. If the same place name occurs two or more times in the index and all are in the same country, each is followed by the name of the administrative subdivision in which it is located. The names are placed in the alphabetical order of the subdivisions. For example:

Jackson, *Ky., U.S.A.*	**68**	**G4**
Jackson, *Mich., U.S.A.*	**68**	**D3**
Jackson, *Minn., U.S.A.*	**70**	**D7**

The number in bold type which follows each name in the index refers to the number of the map page where that feature or place will be found. This is usually the largest scale at which the place or feature appears. The letter and figure which are in bold type immediately after the page number give the grid square on the map page, within which the feature is situated. The letter represents the latitude and the figure the longitude.

In some cases the feature itself may fall within the specified square, while the name is outside. This is usually the case only with features which are larger than a grid square. Rivers are indexed to their mouths or confluences, and carry the symbol ➔ after their names. A solid square ■ follows the name of a country while, an open square □ refers to a first order administrative area.

Abbreviations used in the index

A.C.T. — Australian Capital Territory
Afghan. — Afghanistan
Ala. — Alabama
Alta. — Alberta
Amer. — America(n)
Arch. — Archipelago
Ariz. — Arizona
Ark. — Arkansas
Atl. Oc. — Atlantic Ocean
B. — Baie, Bahía, Bay, Bucht, Bugt
B.C. — British Columbia
Bangla. — Bangladesh
Barr. — Barrage
C. — Cabo, Cap, Cape, Coast
C.A.R. — Central African Republic
C. Prov. — Cape Province
Calif. — California
Cent. — Central
Chan. — Channel
Colo. — Colorado
Conn. — Connecticut
Cord. — Cordillera
Cr. — Creek
Czech. — Czech Republic
D.C. — District of Columbia
Del. — Delaware
Dep. — Dependency
Des. — Desert
Dist. — District
Dj. — Djebel
Domin. — Dominica
Dom. Rep. — Dominican Republic
E. — East
El Salv. — El Salvador

Eq. Guin. — Equatorial Guinea
Fla. — Florida
Falk. Is. — Falkland Is.
G. — Golfe, Golfo, Gulf, Guba, Gebel
Ga. — Georgia
Gt. — Great, Greater
Guinea-Biss. — Guinea-Bissau
H.K. — Hong Kong
H.P. — Himachal Pradesh
Hants. — Hampshire
Harb. — Harbor, Harbour
Hd. — Head
Hts. — Heights
I.(s). — Île, Ilha, Insel, Isla, Island, Isle
Ill. — Illinois
Ind. — Indiana
Ind. Oc. — Indian Ocean
Ivory C. — Ivory Coast
J. — Jabal, Jebel, Jazira
Junc. — Junction
K. — Kap, Kapp
Kans. — Kansas
Kep. — Kepulauan
Ky. — Kentucky
L. — Lac, Lacul, Lago, Lagoa, Lake, Limni, Loch, Lough
La. — Louisiana
Liech. — Liechtenstein
Lux. — Luxembourg
Mad. P. — Madhya Pradesh
Madag. — Madagascar
Man. — Manitoba
Mass. — Massachusetts

Md. — Maryland
Me. — Maine
Medit. S. — Mediterranean Sea
Mich. — Michigan
Minn. — Minnesota
Miss. — Mississippi
Mo. — Missouri
Mont. — Montana
Mozam. — Mozambique
Mt.(e). — Mont, Monte, Monti, Montaña, Mountain
N. — Nord, Norte, North, Northern, Nouveau
N.B. — New Brunswick
N.C. — North Carolina
N. Cal. — New Caledonia
N. Dak. — North Dakota
N.H. — New Hampshire
N.I. — North Island
N.J. — New Jersey
N. Mex. — New Mexico
N.S. — Nova Scotia
N.S.W. — New South Wales
N.W.T. — North West Territory
N.Y. — New York
N.Z. — New Zealand
Nebr. — Nebraska
Neths. — Netherlands
Nev. — Nevada
Nfld. — Newfoundland
Nic. — Nicaragua
O. — Oued, Ouadi
Occ. — Occidentale
O.F.S. — Orange Free State
Okla. — Oklahoma

Ont. — Ontario
Or. — Orientale
Oreg. — Oregon
Os. — Ostrov
Oz. — Ozero
P. — Pass, Passo, Pasul, Pulau
P.E.I. — Prince Edward Island
Pa. — Pennsylvania
Pac. Oc. — Pacific Ocean
Papua N.G. — Papua New Guinea
Pass. — Passage
Pen. — Peninsula, Péninsule
Phil. — Philippines
Pk. — Park, Peak
Plat. — Plateau
P-ov. — Poluostrov
Prov. — Province, Provincial
Pt. — Point
Pta. — Ponta, Punta
Pte. — Pointe
Qué. — Québec
Queens. — Queensland
R. — Rio, River
R.I. — Rhode Island
Ra.(s). — Range(s)
Raj. — Rajasthan
Reg. — Region
Rep. — Republic
Res. — Reserve, Reservoir
S. — San, South, Sea
Si. Arabia — Saudi Arabia
S.C. — South Carolina
S. Dak. — South Dakota
S.I. — South Island
S. Leone — Sierra Leone

Sa. — Serra, Sierra
Sask. — Saskatchewan
Scot. — Scotland
Sd. — Sound
Sev. — Severnaya
Sib. — Siberia
Sprs. — Springs
St. — Saint, Sankt, Sint
Sta. — Santa, Station
Ste. — Sainte
Sto. — Santo
Str. — Strait, Stretto
Switz. — Switzerland
Tas. — Tasmania
Tenn. — Tennessee
Tex. — Texas
Tg. — Tanjung
Trin. & Tob. — Trinidad & Tobago
U.A.E. — United Arab Emirates
U.K. — United Kingdom
U.S.A. — United States of America
Ut. P. — Uttar Pradesh
Va. — Virginia
Vdkhr. — Vodokhranilishche
Vf. — Vîrful
Vic. — Victoria
Vol. — Volcano
Vt. — Vermont
W. — Wadi, West
W. Va. — West Virginia
Wash. — Washington
Wis. — Wisconsin
Wlkp. — Wielkopolski
Wyo. — Wyoming
Yorks. — Yorkshire

A Coruña

A

A Coruña = La Coruña, Spain 19 A1
Aachen, Germany 16 C3
Aalborg = Ålborg, Denmark 9 H10
A'âli en Nîl □, Sudan 45 G11
Aalsmeer, Neths. 15 B4
Aalst, Belgium 15 D4
Aalten, Neths. 15 C6
Aarau, Switz. 16 E4
Aare →, Switz. 16 E4
Aarhus = Århus, Denmark 9 H11
Aarschot, Belgium 15 D4
Aba, Nigeria 44 G6
Ābādān, Iran 39 D6
Ābādeh, Iran 39 D7
Abadla, Algeria 44 B4
Abaetetuba, Brazil 79 D9
Abakan, Russia 25 D10
Abancay, Peru 78 F4
Abariringa, Kiribati 56 H10
Abarqū, Iran 39 D7
Abashiri, Japan 28 B12
Abashiri-Wan, Japan 28 B12
Abay, Kazakhstan 24 E8
Abaya, L., Ethiopia 45 G12
Abaza, Russia 24 D10
'Abbāsābād, Iran 39 C8
Abbay = Nîl el Azraq →, Sudan 45 E11
Abbaye, Pt., U.S.A. 68 B1
Abbeville, France 18 A4
Abbeville, La., U.S.A. 71 K8
Abbeville, S.C., U.S.A. 69 H4
Abbieglassie, Australia 55 D4
Abbot Ice Shelf, Antarctica 5 D16
Abbotsford, Canada 64 D4
Abbotsford, U.S.A. 70 C9
Abbottabad, Pakistan 36 B8
Abd al Kūrī, Ind. Oc. 40 E5
Ābdar, Iran 39 D7
'Abdolābād, Iran 39 C8
Abéché, Chad 45 F9
Åbenrå, Denmark 9 J10
Abeokuta, Nigeria 44 G5
Aberaeron, U.K. 11 E3
Aberayron = Aberaeron, U.K. 11 E3
Abercorn = Mbala, Zambia 46 F6
Abercorn, Australia 55 D5
Aberdare, U.K. 11 F4
Aberdeen, Australia 55 E5
Aberdeen, Canada 65 C7
Aberdeen, S. Africa 48 E3
Aberdeen, U.K. 12 D6
Aberdeen, Ala., U.S.A. 69 J1
Aberdeen, Idaho, U.S.A. 72 E7
Aberdeen, S. Dak., U.S.A. 70 C5
Aberdeen, Wash., U.S.A. 72 C2
Aberdovey = Aberdyfi, U.K. 11 E3
Aberdyfi, U.K. 11 E3
Aberfeldy, U.K. 12 E5
Abergavenny, U.K. 11 F4
Abernathy, U.S.A. 71 J4
Abert, L., U.S.A. 72 E3
Aberystwyth, U.K. 11 E3
Abhar, Iran 39 B6
Abidjan, Ivory C. 44 G4
Abilene, Kans., U.S.A. 70 F6
Abilene, Tex., U.S.A. 71 J5
Abingdon, U.K. 11 F6
Abingdon, Ill., U.S.A. 70 E9
Abingdon, Va., U.S.A. 69 G5
Abington Reef, Australia 54 B4
Abitau →, Canada 65 B7
Abitau L., Canada 65 A7
Abitibi L., Canada 62 C4
Abkhaz Republic □, Georgia 23 F7
Abkit, Russia 25 C16
Abminga, Australia 55 D1
Abohar, India 36 D9
Abomey, Benin 44 G5
Abong-Mbang, Cameroon 46 D2
Abou-Deïa, Chad 45 F8
Aboyne, U.K. 12 D6
Abrantes, Portugal 19 C1
Abri, Sudan 45 D11
Abrolhos, Banka, Brazil 79 G11
Abrud, Romania 17 E11
Abruzzi □, Italy 20 C5
Absaroka Ra., U.S.A. 72 D9
Abū al Khaşīb, Iraq 39 D6
Abū 'Alī, Si. Arabia 39 E6
Abū 'Alī →, Lebanon 41 A4
Abu 'Arīsh, Si. Arabia 40 D3
Abu Dhabi = Abū Ẓāby, U.A.E. 39 E7
Abū Dis, Sudan 45 E11
Abū Du'ān, Syria 38 B3
Abu el Gairi, W. →, Egypt 41 F2
Abu Ga'da, W. →, Egypt 41 F1
Abū Ḩadrīyah, Si. Arabia 39 E6
Abu Hamed, Sudan 45 E11
Abū Kamāl, Syria 38 C4
Abū Madd, Ra's, Si. Arabia 38 E3
Abu Matariq, Sudan 45 F10
Abu Şafāt, W. →, Jordan 41 E5
Abū Şukhayr, Iraq 38 D5
Abu Tig, Egypt 45 C11
Abû Zabad, Sudan 45 F10
Abū Ẓāby, U.A.E. 39 E7
Abū Zeydābād, Iran 39 C6
Abuja, Nigeria 44 G6
Abukuma-Gawa →, Japan 28 E10
Abukuma-Sammyaku, Japan 28 F10
Abunã, Brazil 78 E5
Abunã →, Brazil 78 E5
Abut Hd., N.Z. 51 K3
Abwong, Sudan 45 G11
Acaponeta, Mexico 74 C3
Acapulco, Mexico 74 D5
Acarigua, Venezuela 78 B5
Accomac, U.S.A. 68 G8
Accra, Ghana 44 G4
Accrington, U.K. 10 D5
Aceh □, Indonesia 32 D1
Achalpur, India 36 J10
Achill, Ireland 13 C2
Achill Hd., Ireland 13 C1
Achill I., Ireland 13 C1
Achill Sd., Ireland 13 C2
Achinsk, Russia 25 D10
Ackerman, U.S.A. 71 J10
Acklins I., Bahamas 75 C10
Acme, Canada 64 C6
Aconcagua, Cerro, Argentina 80 C3
Aconquija, Mt., Argentina 80 B3
Açores, Is. dos = Azores, Atl. Oc. 2 C8
Acraman, L., Australia 55 E2
Acre = 'Akko, Israel 41 C4
Acre □, Brazil 78 E4
Acre →, Brazil 78 E5
Ad Dammām, Si. Arabia 39 E6
Ad Dawhah, Qatar 39 E6
Ad Dawr, Iraq 38 C4
Ad Dir'īyah, Si. Arabia 38 E5
Ad Dīwānīyah, Iraq 38 D5
Ad Dujayl, Iraq 38 C5
Ad Durūz, J., Jordan 41 C5
Ada, Minn., U.S.A. 70 B6
Ada, Okla., U.S.A. 71 H6
Adaja →, Spain 19 B3
Adamaoua, Massif de l', Cameroon 45 G7
Adamawa Highlands = Adamaoua, Massif de l', Cameroon 45 G7
Adamello, Mt., Italy 20 A4
Adaminaby, Australia 55 F4
Adams, N.Y., U.S.A. 68 D7
Adams, Wis., U.S.A. 70 D10
Adams, Mt., U.S.A. 72 C3
Adam's Bridge, Sri Lanka 36 Q11
Adams L., Canada 64 C5
Adam's Peak, Sri Lanka 36 R12
Adana, Turkey 23 G6
Adapazarı, Turkey 23 F5
Adarama, Sudan 45 E11
Adare, C., Antarctica 5 D11
Adaut, Indonesia 33 F8
Adavale, Australia 55 D3
Adda →, Italy 20 B3
Addis Ababa = Addis Abeba, Ethiopia 45 G12
Addis Abeba, Ethiopia 45 G12
Addis Alem, Ethiopia 45 G12
Addo, S. Africa 48 E4
Ādeh, Iran 38 B5
Adel, U.S.A. 69 K4
Adelaide, Australia 55 E2
Adelaide, S. Africa 48 E4
Adelaide I., Antarctica 5 C17
Adelaide Pen., Canada 60 B10
Adelaide River, Australia 52 B5
Adele I., Australia 52 C3
Adélie, Terre, Antarctica 5 C10
Adélie Land = Adélie, Terre, Antarctica 5 C10
Aden = Al 'Adan, Yemen 40 E4
Aden, G. of, Asia 40 E4
Adendorp, S. Africa 48 E3
Adh Dhayd, U.A.E. 39 E7
Adi, Indonesia 33 E8
Adi Ugri, Eritrea 45 F12
Adieu, C., Australia 53 F5
Adieu Pt., Australia 52 C3
Adige →, Italy 20 B5
Adilabad, India 36 K11
Adin, U.S.A. 72 F3
Adin Khel, Afghan. 36 C6
Adirondack Mts., U.S.A. 68 D8
Adlavik Is., Canada 63 B8
Admer, Algeria 44 D6
Admiralty G., Australia 52 B4
Admiralty I., U.S.A. 60 C6
Admiralty Inlet, U.S.A. 72 C2
Admiralty Is., Papua N. G. 56 H6
Ado Ekiti, Nigeria 44 G6
Adonara, Indonesia 33 F6
Adoni, India 36 M10
Adour →, France 18 E3
Adra, Spain 19 D4
Adrano, Italy 20 F6
Adrar, Algeria 44 C4
Adré, Chad 45 F9
Adrī, Libya 45 C7
Adrian, Mich., U.S.A. 68 E3
Adrian, Tex., U.S.A. 71 H3
Adriatic Sea, Europe 20 C6
Adua, Indonesia 33 E7
Adwa, Ethiopia 45 F12
Adzhar Republic □, Georgia 23 F7
Ægean Sea, Europe 21 E11
Æolian Is. = Eólie, Is., Italy 20 E6
Aerhtai Shan, Mongolia 30 B4
'Afak, Iraq 38 C5
Afars & Issas, Terr. of = Djibouti ■, Africa 40 E3
Afghanistan ■, Asia 36 C4
Afgoi, Somali Rep. 40 G3
Afognak I., U.S.A. 60 C4
Africa 42 E6
'Afrīn, Syria 38 B3
Afuá, Brazil 79 D8
Afula, Israel 41 C4
Afyonkarahisar, Turkey 23 G5
Agadès = Agadez, Niger 44 E6
Agadez, Niger 44 E6
Agadir, Morocco 44 B3
Agapa, Russia 25 B9
Agartala, India 37 H17
Agassiz, Canada 64 D4
Agats, Indonesia 33 F9
Agboville, Ivory C. 44 G4
Agde, France 18 E5
Agen, France 18 D4
Āgh Kand, Iran 39 B6
Aginskoye, Russia 25 D12
Agra, India 36 F10
Agri →, Italy 20 D7
Ağrı Dağı, Turkey 23 G7
Ağrı Karakose, Turkey 23 G7
Agrigento, Italy 20 F5
Agrinion, Greece 21 E9
Água Clara, Brazil 79 H8
Agua Prieta, Mexico 74 A3
Aguadas, Colombia 78 B3
Aguadilla, Puerto Rico 75 D11
Aguanish, Canada 63 B7
Aguanus →, Canada 63 B7
Aguarico →, Ecuador 78 D3
Aguas Blancas, Chile 80 A3
Aguascalientes, Mexico 74 C4
Aguilas, Spain 19 D5
Agulhas, C., S. Africa 48 E3
Agung, Indonesia 32 F5
Agusan →, Phil. 33 C7
Aha Mts., Botswana 48 B3
Ahaggar, Algeria 44 D6
Ahar, Iran 38 B5
Ahipara B., N.Z. 51 F4
Ahiri, India 36 K12
Ahmadabad, India 36 H8
Aḩmadābād, Khorāsān, Iran 39 C9
Aḩmadābād, Khorāsān, Iran 39 C8
Aḩmadī, Iran 39 E8
Ahmadnagar, India 36 K9
Ahmadpur, Pakistan 36 E7
Ahmedabad = Ahmadabad, India 36 H8
Ahmednagar = Ahmadnagar, India 36 K9
Ahram, Iran 39 D6
Āhū, Iran 39 C6
Ahvāz, Iran 39 D6
Ahvenanmaa = Åland, Finland 9 F16
Aḩwar, Yemen 40 E4
Aichi □, Japan 29 G8
Aigues-Mortes, France 18 E6
Aihui, China 31 A7
Aija, Peru 78 E3
Aikawa, Japan 28 E9
Aiken, U.S.A. 69 J5
Aillik, Canada 63 A8
Ailsa Craig, U.K. 12 F3
'Ailūn, Jordan 41 C4
Aim, Russia 25 D14
Aimere, Indonesia 33 F6
Aimorés, Brazil 79 G10
Ain □, France 18 C6
Aïn Beïda, Algeria 44 A6
Aïn Ben Tili, Mauritania 44 C3
Aïn-Sefra, Algeria 44 B4
'Ain Sudr, Egypt 41 F2
Ainabo, Somali Rep. 40 F4
Ainsworth, U.S.A. 70 D5
Aïr, Niger 44 E6
Airdrie, U.K. 12 F5
Aire →, U.K. 10 D7
Airlie Beach, Australia 54 C4
Aisne □, France 18 B5
Aisne →, France 18 B5
Aitkin, U.S.A. 70 B8
Aiud, Romania 17 E11
Aix-en-Provence, France 18 E6
Aix-la-Chapelle = Aachen, Germany 16 C3
Aiyansh, Canada 64 B3
Aiyina, Greece 21 F10
Aiyion, Greece 21 E10
Aizawl, India 37 H18
Aizuwakamatsu, Japan 28 F9
Ajaccio, France 18 F8
Ajanta Ra., India 36 J9
Ajari Rep. = Adzhar Republic □, Georgia 23 F7
Ajdâbiyah, Libya 45 B9
'Ajmān, U.A.E. 39 E7
Ajmer, India 36 F9
Ajo, U.S.A. 73 K7
Akabira, Japan 28 C11
Akaroa, N.Z. 51 K4
Akashi, Japan 29 G7
Akelamo, Indonesia 33 D7
Akershus fylke □, Norway 9 G11
Aketi, Zaïre 46 D4
Akhelóös →, Greece 21 E9
Akhmîm, Egypt 45 C11
Aki, Japan 29 H6
Akimiski I., Canada 62 B3
Akita, Japan 28 E10
Akita □, Japan 28 E10
Akjoujt, Mauritania 44 E2
Akkeshi, Japan 28 C12
'Akko, Israel 41 C4
Akkol, Kazakhstan 24 E8
Aklavik, Canada 60 B6
Akmolinsk = Tselinograd, Kazakhstan 24 D8
Akō, Japan 29 G7
Akobo →, Ethiopia 45 G11
Akola, India 36 J10
Akordat, Eritrea 45 E12
Akpatok I., Canada 61 B13
Akranes, Iceland 8 D3
Akreïjit, Mauritania 44 E3
Akron, Colo., U.S.A. 70 E3
Akron, Ohio, U.S.A. 68 E5
Aksai Chih, India 36 B11
Aksarka, Russia 24 C7
Aksay, Kazakhstan 22 D9
Aksenovo Zilovskoye, Russia 25 D12
Aksu, China 30 B3
Aksum, Ethiopia 45 F12
Aktogay, Kazakhstan 24 E8
Aktyubinsk, Kazakhstan 23 D10
Aku, Nigeria 44 G6
Akure, Nigeria 44 G6
Akureyri, Iceland 8 D4
Akuseki-Shima, Japan 29 K4
Akyab = Sittwe, Burma 37 J18
Al 'Adan, Yemen 40 E4
Al Aḩsā, Si. Arabia 39 E6
Al Ajfar, Si. Arabia 38 E4
Al Amādīyah, Iraq 38 B4
Al Amārah, Iraq 38 D5
Al 'Aqabah, Jordan 41 F4
Al Arak, Syria 38 C3
Al 'Aramah, Si. Arabia 38 E5
Al Arţāwīyah, Si. Arabia 38 E5
Al 'Āşimah □, Jordan 41 D5
Al' Assāfīyah, Si. Arabia 38 D3
Al 'Ayn, Oman 39 E7
Al 'Ayn, Si. Arabia 38 E3
Al A'ẓamīyah, Iraq 38 C5
Al 'Azīzīyah, Iraq 38 C5
Al Bāb, Syria 38 B3
Al Bad', Si. Arabia 38 D2
Al Bādī, Iraq 38 C4
Al Baḩrah, Kuwait 38 D5
Al Balqā' □, Jordan 41 C4
Al Bārūk, J., Lebanon 41 B4
Al Başrah, Iraq 38 D5
Al Baţḩā, Iraq 38 D5
Al Batrūn, Lebanon 41 A4
Al Bi'r, Si. Arabia 38 D3
Al Bu'ayrāt, Libya 45 B8
Al Burayj, Syria 41 A5
Al Fallūjah, Iraq 38 C4
Al Fāw, Iraq 39 D6
Al Fujayrah, U.A.E. 39 E8
Al Ghadaf, W. →, Jordan 41 D5
Al Ghammās, Iraq 38 D5
Al Ḩābah, Si. Arabia 38 E5
Al Ḩadīthah, Iraq 38 C4
Al Ḩadīthah, Si. Arabia 38 D3
Al Ḩājānah, Syria 41 B5
Al Ḩāmad, Si. Arabia 38 D3
Al Hamdānīyah, Syria 38 C3
Al Ḩamīdīyah, Syria 41 A4
Al Ḩammār, Iraq 38 D5
Al Ḩarīr, W. →, Syria 41 C4
Al Ḩasā, W. →, Jordan 41 D4
Al Ḩasakah, Syria 38 B4
Al Ḩawrah, Yemen 40 E4
Al Ḩaydān, W. →, Jordan 41 D4
Al Ḩayy, Iraq 38 C5
Al Ḩijāz, Si. Arabia 40 B2
Al Ḩillah, Iraq 38 C5
Al Ḩillah, Si. Arabia 40 C4
Al Hirmil, Lebanon 41 A5
Al Hoceïma, Morocco 44 A4
Al Ḩudaydah, Yemen 40 E3
Al Ḩufūf, Si. Arabia 39 E6
Al Ḩumaydah, Si. Arabia 38 D2
Al Ḩunayy, Si. Arabia 39 E6
Al Irq, Libya 45 C9
Al Īsāwīyah, Si. Arabia 38 D3
Al Ittihad = Madīnat ash Sha'b, Yemen 40 E3
Al Jafr, Jordan 41 E5
Al Jaghbūb, Libya 45 C9
Al Jahrah, Kuwait 38 D5
Al Jalāmīd, Si. Arabia 38 D3
Al Jamalīyah, Qatar 39 E6
Al Janūb □, Lebanon 41 B4
Al Jawf, Libya 45 D9
Al Jawf, Si. Arabia 38 D3
Al Jazirah, Iraq 38 C5
Al Jazirah, Libya 45 C9
Al Jithāmīyah, Si. Arabia 38 E4
Al Jubayl, Si. Arabia 39 E6
Al Jubaylah, Si. Arabia 38 E5
Al Jubb, Si. Arabia 38 E4
Al Junaynah, Sudan 45 F9
Al Kabā'ish, Iraq 38 D5
Al Karak, Jordan 41 D4
Al Karak □, Jordan 41 E5
Al Kāzim Tyah, Iraq 38 C5
Al Khalīl, Jordan 41 D4
Al Khalīl □, Jordan 41 D4
Al Khawr, Qatar 39 E6
Al Khiḑr, Iraq 38 D5
Al Khiyām, Lebanon 41 B4
Al Kiswah, Syria 41 B5
Al Kufrah, Libya 45 D9
Al Kuhayfīyah, Si. Arabia 38 E4
Al Kūt, Iraq 38 C5
Al Kuwayt, Kuwait 38 D5
Al Labwah, Lebanon 41 A5
Al Lādhiqīyah, Syria 38 C2
Al Līwā', Oman 39 E8
Al Luḩayyah, Yemen 40 D3
Al Madīnah, Iraq 38 D5
Al Madīnah, Si. Arabia 40 C2
Al-Mafraq, Jordan 41 C5
Al Maḩmūdīyah, Iraq 38 C5
Al Majma'ah, Si. Arabia 38 E5
Al Makhruq, W. →, Jordan 41 D6
Al Makḩūl, Si. Arabia 38 E4
Al Manāmah, Bahrain 39 E6
Al Maqwa', Kuwait 38 D5
Al Marj, Libya 45 B9
Al Maţlā, Kuwait 38 D5
Al Mawjib, W. →, Jordan 41 D4
Al Mawşil, Iraq 38 B4
Al Mayādin, Syria 38 C4
Al Mazār, Jordan 41 D4
Al Midhnab, Si. Arabia 38 E5
Al Minā', Lebanon 41 A4
Al Miqdādīyah, Iraq 38 C5
Al Mubarraz, Si. Arabia 39 E6
Al Mughayrā', U.A.E. 39 E7
Al Muḩarraq, Bahrain 39 E6
Al Mukallā, Yemen 40 E4
Al Mukhā, Yemen 40 E3
Al Musayjīd, Si. Arabia 38 E3
Al Musayyib, Iraq 38 C5
Al Muwaylih, Si. Arabia 38 E2
Al Qā'im, Iraq 38 C4
Al Qalibah, Si. Arabia 38 D3
Al Qaryatayn, Syria 41 A6
Al Qaşabát, Libya 45 B7
Al Qaţ'ā, Syria 38 C4
Al Qaţīf, Si. Arabia 39 E6
Al Qatrānah, Jordan 41 D5
Al Qaţrūn, Libya 45 D8
Al Qayşūmah, Si. Arabia 38 D5
Al Quds = Jerusalem, Israel 41 D4
Al Quds □, Jordan 41 D4
Al Qunaytirah, Syria 41 C4
Al Qurnah, Iraq 38 D5
Al Quşayr, Iraq 38 D5
Al Quşayr, Syria 41 A5
Al Qutayfah, Syria 41 B5
Al' Uḑaylīyah, Si. Arabia 39 E6
Al 'Ulā, Si. Arabia 38 E3
Al Uqaylah ash Sharqīgah, Libya 45 B8
Al Uqayr, Si. Arabia 39 E6
Al 'Uwaynid, Si. Arabia 38 E5
Al' 'Uwayqīlah, Si. Arabia 38 D4
Al 'Uyūn, Si. Arabia 38 E4
Al 'Uyūn, Si. Arabia 38 E3
Al Wajh, Si. Arabia 38 E3
Al Wakrah, Qatar 39 E6
Al Wannān, Si. Arabia 39 E6
Al Waqbah, Si. Arabia 38 D5
Al Wari'āh, Si. Arabia 38 E5
Al Wusayl, Qatar 39 E6
Ala Tau Shankou = Dzhungarskiye Vorota, Kazakhstan 30 B3
Alabama □, U.S.A. 69 J2
Alabama →, U.S.A. 69 K2
Alagoa Grande, Brazil 79 E11
Alagoas □, Brazil 79 E11
Alagoinhas, Brazil 79 F11
Alajuela, Costa Rica 75 E8
Alakamisy, Madag. 49 C8
Alakurtti, Russia 22 A5
Alameda, U.S.A. 73 J10
Alamo, U.S.A. 73 H6
Alamogordo, U.S.A. 73 K11
Alamosa, U.S.A. 73 H11
Åland, Finland 9 F16
Ålands hav, Sweden 9 G15
Alandur, India 36 N12
Alanya, Turkey 23 G5
Alaotra, Farihin', Madag. 49 B8
Alapayevsk, Russia 24 D7
Alaşehir, Turkey 23 G4
Alaska □, U.S.A. 60 B5
Alaska, G. of, Pac. Oc. 60 C5
Alaska Highway, Canada 64 B3
Alaska Pen., U.S.A. 60 C4
Alaska Range, U.S.A. 60 B4
Alatyr, Russia 22 D8
Alausi, Ecuador 78 D3
Alava, C., U.S.A. 72 B1
Alawoona, Australia 55 E3
'Alayh, Lebanon 41 B4
Alba, Italy 20 B3
Alba Iulia, Romania 21 A10
Albacete, Spain 19 C5
Albacutya, L., Australia 55 F3
Albania ■, Europe 21 D9
Albany, Australia 53 G2
Albany, Ga., U.S.A. 69 K3
Albany, Minn., U.S.A. 70 C7
Albany, N.Y., U.S.A. 68 D9
Albany, Oreg., U.S.A. 72 D2
Albany, Tex., U.S.A. 71 J5
Albany →, Canada 62 B3
Albardón, Argentina 80 C3
Albarracín, Sierra de, Spain 19 B5
Albatross B., Australia 54 A3
Albemarle, U.S.A. 69 H5
Albemarle Sd., U.S.A. 69 H7
Alberche →, Spain 19 C3
Albert, L. = Mobutu Sese Seko, L., Africa 46 D6
Albert, L., Australia 55 F2
Albert Canyon, Canada 64 C5
Albert Edward Ra., Australia 52 C4
Albert Lea, U.S.A. 70 D8
Albert Nile →, Uganda 46 D6
Alberta □, Canada 64 C6
Albertinia, S. Africa 48 E3
Alberton, Canada 63 C7
Albertville = Kalemie, Zaïre 46 F5
Albi, France 18 E5
Albia, U.S.A. 70 E8
Albina, Surinam 79 B8
Albina, Ponta, Angola 48 B1
Albion, Idaho, U.S.A. 72 E7
Albion, Mich., U.S.A. 68 D3
Albion, Nebr., U.S.A. 70 E5
Ålborg, Denmark 9 H10
Alborz, Reshteh-ye Kūhhā-ye, Iran 39 C7
Albreda, Canada 64 C5
Albuquerque, U.S.A. 73 J10
Alburquerque, Spain 19 C2
Albury, Australia 55 F4
Alcalá de Henares, Spain 19 B4
Alcalá la Real, Spain 19 D4
Alcamo, Italy 20 F5
Alcaníz, Spain 19 B5
Alcântara, Brazil 79 D10
Alcántara, Spain 19 C2
Alcantara L., Canada 65 A7
Alcaraz, Sierra de, Spain 19 C4
Alcaudete, Spain 19 D3
Alcázar de San Juan, Spain 19 C4
Alchevsk = Kommunarsk, Ukraine 23 E6
Alcira, Spain 19 C5
Alcoa, U.S.A. 69 H4
Alcobaça, Portugal 19 C1
Alcova, U.S.A. 72 E10
Alcoy, Spain 19 C5
Aldabra Is., Seychelles 43 G8
Aldan, Russia 25 D13
Aldan →, Russia 25 C13
Aldeburgh, U.K. 11 E9
Alder, U.S.A. 72 D7
Alderney, Chan. Is. 11 H5
Aldershot, U.K. 11 F7
Aledo, U.S.A. 70 E9
Aleg, Mauritania 44 E2
Alegrete, Brazil 80 B5
Aleisk, Russia 24 D9
Aleksandrovsk-Sakhalinskiy, Russia 25 D15
Aleksandrovskiy Zavod, Russia 25 D12
Aleksandrovskoye, Russia 24 C8
Alemania, Argentina 80 B3
Alençon, France 18 B4
Alenuihaha Chan., U.S.A. 66 H17
Aleppo = Ḩalab, Syria 38 B3
Aléria, France 20 C3
Alert Bay, Canada 64 C3
Alès, France 18 D6
Alessándria, Italy 20 B3
Ålesund, Norway 8 E9
Aleutian Is., Pac. Oc. 60 C2
Aleutian Trench, Pac. Oc. 56 B10
Alexander, U.S.A. 70 B3
Alexander, Mt., Australia 53 E3
Alexander Arch., U.S.A. 64 B2
Alexander B., S. Africa 48 D2
Alexander Bay, S. Africa 48 D2
Alexander City, U.S.A. 69 J3
Alexander I., Antarctica 5 C17
Alexandra, Australia 55 F4
Alexandra, N.Z. 51 L2
Alexandra Falls, Canada 64 A5
Alexandretta = İskenderun, Turkey 23 G6

Alexandria = El
  Iskandarîya, Egypt . 45 B10
Alexandria, Australia . 54 B2
Alexandria, B.C.,
  Canada 64 C4
Alexandria, Ont.,
  Canada 62 C5
Alexandria, S. Africa . 48 E4
Alexandria, Ind., U.S.A. 68 E3
Alexandria, La., U.S.A. 71 K8
Alexandria, Minn.,
  U.S.A. 70 C7
Alexandria, S. Dak.,
  U.S.A. 70 D6
Alexandria, Va., U.S.A. 68 F7
Alexandria Bay, U.S.A. 68 C8
Alexandrina, L.,
  Australia 55 F2
Alexandroúpolis,
  Greece 21 D11
Alexis →, Canada . . . 63 B8
Alexis Creek, Canada . 64 C4
Alford, U.K. 12 D6
Alfreton, U.K. 10 D6
Alga, Kazakhstan . . . 23 E10
Algarve, Portugal . . . 19 D1
Algeciras, Spain 19 D3
Algemesí, Spain 19 C5
Alger, Algeria 44 A5
Algeria ■, Africa . . . 44 C4
Alghero, Italy 20 D3
Algiers = Alger,
  Algeria 44 A5
Algoa B., S. Africa . . 48 E4
Algoma, U.S.A. 68 C2
Algona, U.S.A. 70 D7
Alhama de Murcia,
  Spain 19 D5
Alhambra, U.S.A. . . . 73 J4
Alhucemas = Al
  Hoceïma, Morocco . 44 A4
'Alī al Gharbī, Iraq . . 38 C5
'Alī ash Sharqī, Iraq . 38 C5
'Alī Khēl, Afghan. . . . 36 C4
'Alī Shāh, Iran 38 B5
'Alīābād, Khorāsān,
  Iran 39 C8
'Alīābād, Kordestān,
  Iran 38 C5
'Alīābād, Yazd, Iran . . 39 D7
Aliákmon →, Greece . 21 D10
Alibo, Ethiopia 45 G12
Alicante, Spain 19 C5
Alice, S. Africa 48 E4
Alice, U.S.A. 71 M5
Alice →, Queens.,
  Australia 54 C3
Alice →, Queens.,
  Australia 54 B3
Alice Arm, Canada . . 64 B3
Alice Downs, Australia 52 C4
Alice Springs, Australia 54 C1
Alicedale, S. Africa . . 48 E4
Aliceville, U.S.A. . . . 69 J1
Alick Cr. →, Australia 54 C3
Alida, Canada 65 D8
Aligarh, India 36 F11
Alīgūdarz, Iran 39 C6
Alingsås, Sweden . . . 9 H12
Alipur, Pakistan 36 E7
Alipur Duar, India . . . 37 F16
Aliquippa, U.S.A. . . . 68 E5
Aliwal North, S. Africa 48 E4
Alix, Canada 64 C6
Aljustrel, Portugal . . . 19 D1
Alkmaar, Neths. 15 B4
All American Canal,
  U.S.A. 73 K6
Allahabad, India 37 G12
Allakh-Yun, Russia . . 25 C14
Allan, Canada 65 C7
Allanmyo, Burma . . . 37 K19
Allanridge, S. Africa . 48 D4
Allanwater, Canada . . 62 B1
Allegan, U.S.A. 68 D3
Allegheny →, U.S.A. . 68 E6
Allegheny Plateau,
  U.S.A. 68 G6
Allen, Bog of, Ireland 13 C4
Allen, L., Ireland . . . 13 B3
Allentown, U.S.A. . . . 68 E8
Alleppey, India 36 Q10
Alliance, Nebr., U.S.A. 70 D3
Alliance, Ohio, U.S.A. 68 E5
Allier □, France 18 C5
Allier →, France 18 C5
Alliston, Canada 62 D4
Alloa, U.K. 12 E5
Allora, Australia 55 D5
Alluitsup Paa =
  Sydprøven,
  Greenland 4 C5
Alma, Canada 63 C5
Alma, Ga., U.S.A. . . . 69 K4
Alma, Kans., U.S.A. . . 70 F6
Alma, Mich., U.S.A. . . 68 D3
Alma, Nebr., U.S.A. . . 70 E5
Alma, Wis., U.S.A. . . 70 C9
Alma Ata, Kazakhstan 24 E8
Almada, Portugal . . . 19 C1
Almaden, Australia . . 54 B3
Almadén, Spain 19 C3
Almanor, L., U.S.A. . . 72 F3
Almansa, Spain 19 C5
Almanzor, Pico de,
  Spain 19 B3
Almanzora →, Spain . 19 D5
Almaty = Alma Ata,
  Kazakhstan 24 E8
Almazán, Spain 19 B4
Almeirim, Brazil 79 D8
Almelo, Neths. 15 B6

Almendralejo, Spain . 19 C2
Almería, Spain 19 D4
Almora, India 36 E11
Alnwick, U.K. 10 B6
Alon, Burma 37 H19
Alor, Indonesia 33 F6
Alor Setar, Malaysia . 34 N13
Alpena, U.S.A. 68 C4
Alpes-de-Haute-
  Provence □, France 18 D7
Alpes-Maritimes □,
  France 18 E7
Alpha, Australia 54 C4
Alphonse, Seychelles . 35 E4
Alpine, Ariz., U.S.A. . 73 K9
Alpine, Tex., U.S.A. . . 71 K3
Alps, Europe 16 E4
Alroy Downs, Australia 54 B2
Alsace, France 18 B7
Alsask, Canada 65 C7
Alsásua, Spain 19 A4
Alsten, Norway 8 D12
Alta, Norway 8 B17
Alta Gracia, Argentina 80 C4
Alta Lake, Canada . . . 64 C4
Altaelva →, Norway . 8 B17
Altafjorden, Norway . 8 A17
Altagracia, Venezuela 78 A4
Altai = Aerhtai Shan,
  Mongolia 30 B4
Altai = Aerhtai Shan,
  Mongolia 30 B4
Altamaha →, U.S.A. . 69 K5
Altamira, Brazil 79 D8
Altanbulag, Mongolia 30 A5
Altavista, U.S.A. 68 G6
Altay, China 30 B3
Altdorf, Switz. . . . . .
Alto Adige = Trentino-
  Alto Adige □, Italy . 20 A4
Alto-Alentejo, Portugal 19 C2
Alto Araguaia, Brazil . 79 G8
Alto Molocue, Mozam. 47 H7
Alton, U.S.A. 70 F9
Alton Downs, Australia 55 D2
Altoona, U.S.A. 68 E6
Altūn Kūprī, Iraq . . . 38 C5
Altun Shan, China . . . 30 C3
Alturas, U.S.A. 72 F3
Altus, U.S.A. 71 H5
Alūla, Somali Rep. . . 40 E5
Alusi, Indonesia 33 F8
Al'Uzayr, Iraq 38 D5
Alva, U.S.A. 71 G5
Alvarado, Mexico . . . 74 D5
Alvarado, U.S.A. 71 J6
Alvear, Argentina . . . 80 B5
Alvesta, Sweden 9 H13
Alvie, Australia 55 F3
Alvin, U.S.A. 71 L7
Álvkarleby, Sweden . . 9 F14
Älvsborgs län □,
  Sweden 9 G12
Älvsbyn, Sweden . . . 8 D16
Alwar, India 36 F10
Alxa Zuoqi, China . . . 30 C5
Alyaskitovyy, Russia . 25 C15
Alyata, Azerbaijan . . 23 G8
Alyth, U.K. 12 E5
Alzada, U.S.A. 70 C2
Am Dam, Chad 45 F9
Am-Timan, Chad . . . 45 F9
Amadeus, L., Australia 53 D5
Amâdi, Sudan 45 G11
Amadi, Zaïre 46 D5
Amadjuak, Canada . . 61 B12
Amadjuak L., Canada . 61 B12
Amagasaki, Japan . . . 29 G7
Amakusa-Shotō, Japan 29 H5
Amalner, India 36 J9
Amambay, Cordillera
  de, S. Amer. 80 A5
Amami-Guntō, Japan . 29 L4
Amami-Ō-Shima,
  Japan 29 L4
Amangeldy,
  Kazakhstan 24 D7
Amapá, Brazil 79 C8
Amapá □, Brazil 79 C8
Amarante, Brazil 79 E10
Amaranth, Canada . . 65 C9
Amargosa, Brazil . . . 79 F11
Amarillo, U.S.A. 71 H4
Amaro, Mt., Italy . . . 20 C6
Amatikulu, S. Africa . 49 D5
Amazon =
  Amazonas →,
  S. Amer. 79 C9
Amazonas □, Brazil . . 78 E6
Amazonas →,
  S. Amer. 79 C9
Ambahakily, Madag. . 49 C7
Ambala, India 36 D10
Ambalavao, Madag. . . 49 C8
Ambalindum, Australia 54 C2
Ambam, Cameroon . . 46 D2
Ambanja, Madag. . . . 49 A8
Ambarchik, Russia . . 25 C17
Ambarijeby, Madag. . 49 A8
Ambaro, Helodranon',
  Madag. 49 A8
Ambartsevo, Russia . 24 D9
Ambato, Ecuador . . . 78 D3
Ambato Boeny,
  Madag. 49 B8
Ambatofinandrahana,
  Madag. 49 C8
Ambatolampy, Madag. 49 B8
Ambatondrazaka,
  Madag. 49 B8
Ambatosoratra,
  Madag. 49 B8

Ambenja, Madag. . . . 49 B8
Amberg, Germany . . . 16 D5
Ambergris Cay, Belize 74 D7
Amberley, N.Z. 51 K4
Ambikapur, India . . . 37 H13
Ambilobé, Madag. . . . 49 A8
Ambinanindrano,
  Madag. 49 C8
Ambleside, U.K. 10 C5
Ambo, Peru 78 F3
Ambodifototra, Madag. 49 B8
Ambodilazana, Madag. 49 B8
Ambohimahasoa,
  Madag. 49 C8
Ambohimanga,
  Madag. 49 C8
Ambohitra, Madag. . . 49 A8
Ambon, Indonesia . . . 33 E7
Ambositra, Madag. . . 49 C8
Ambovombé, Madag. . 49 D8
Amboy, U.S.A. 73 J6
Amboyna I.,
  S. China Sea 32 C4
Ambriz, Angola 46 F2
Amby, Australia 55 D4
Amchitka I., U.S.A. . . 60 C1
Amderma, Russia . . . 24 C7
Ameca, Mexico 74 C4
Ameland, Neths. 15 A5
Amen, Russia 25 C18
American Falls, U.S.A. 72 E7
American Falls Res.,
  U.S.A. 72 E7
American Highland,
  Antarctica 5 D6
American Samoa ■,
  Pac. Oc. 51 B13
Americus, U.S.A. 69 J3
Amersfoort, Neths. . . 15 B5
Amersfoort, S. Africa . 49 D4
Amery, Australia 53 F2
Amery, Canada 65 B10
Amery Ice Shelf,
  Antarctica 5 C6
Ames, U.S.A. 70 E8
Amga, Russia 25 C14
Amga →, Russia . . . 25 C14
Amgun →, Russia . . 25 D14
Amherst, Burma 37 L20
Amherst, Canada . . . 63 C7
Amherst, U.S.A. 71 H3
Amherstburg, Canada 62 D3
Amherstdale, U.S.A. . 68 G5
Amiata, Mte., Italy . . 20 C4
Amiens, France 18 B5
Amindra, Iran 38 C5
Amirante Is.,
  Seychelles 35 E4
Amisk L., Canada . . . 65 C8
Amite, U.S.A. 71 K9
Amlwch, U.K. 10 D3
'Ammān, Jordan 41 D4
Ammanford, U.K. . . . 11 F3
Ammassalik =
  Angmagssalik,
  Greenland 4 C6
Åmol, Iran 39 B7
Amorgós, Greece . . . 21 F11
Amory, U.S.A. 69 J1
Amos, Canada 62 C4
Amoy = Xiamen,
  China 31 D6
Ampanihy, Madag. . . 49 C7
Ampasimanolotra =
  Helodranon', Madag. 49 A8
Ampasindava,
  Saikanosy, Madag. . 49 A8
Ampenan, Indonesia . 32 F5
Ampotaka, Madag. . . 49 D7
Ampoza, Madag. . . . 49 C7
Amqui, Canada 63 C6
Amravati, India 36 J10
Amreli, India 36 J7
Amritsar, India 36 D9
Amroha, India 36 E11
Amsterdam, Neths. . . 15 B4
Amsterdam, U.S.A. . . 68 D8
Amsterdam, I., Ind. Oc. 35 H6
Amudarya →,
  Uzbekistan 24 E6
Amundsen Gulf,
  Canada 60 A7
Amundsen Sea,
  Antarctica 5 D15
Amuntai, Indonesia . . 32 E5
Amur →, Russia . . . 25 D15
Amurang, Indonesia . 33 D6
Amuri Pass, N.Z. . . . 51 K4
Amursk, Russia 25 D14
Amurzet, Russia 25 E14
Amyderya =
  Amudarya →,
  Uzbekistan 24 E6
An Nabk at Tahta,
  Lebanon 41 B4
An Nabk, Si. Arabia . 38 D3
An Nabk, Syria 41 A5
An Nabk Abū Qaşr,
  Si. Arabia 38 D3
An Nafūd, Si. Arabia . 38 D4
An Najaf, Iraq 38 C5
An Nāşirīyah, Iraq . . 38 D5
An Nhon, Vietnam . . 34 F10
An Nîl □, Sudan 45 E11
An Nîl el Abyad □,
  Sudan 45 F11
An Nîl el Azraq □,
  Sudan 45 F11
An Nu'ayrīyah,
  Si. Arabia 39 E6
An Nuwaybi', W. →,
  Si. Arabia 41 F3

An Uaimh, Ireland . . 13 C5
Anabar →, Russia . . 25 B12
'Anabtā, Jordan 41 C4
Anaconda, U.S.A. . . . 72 C7
Anacortes, U.S.A. . . . 72 B2
Anadarko, U.S.A. . . . 71 H5
Anadolu, Turkey 23 G5
Anadyr, Russia 25 C18
Anadyr →, Russia . . 25 C18
Anadyrskiy Zaliv,
  Russia 25 C19
'Ānah, Iraq 38 C4
Anaheim, U.S.A. 73 K5
Anahim Lake, Canada 64 C3
Anakapalle, India . . . 37 L13
Anakie, Australia . . . 54 C4
Analalava, Madag. . . 49 A8
Anambas, Kepulauan,
  Indonesia 32 D3
Anambas Is. =
  Anambas,
  Kepulauan,
  Indonesia 32 D3
Anamoose, U.S.A. . . . 70 B4
Anamosa, U.S.A. 70 D9
Anamur, Turkey 23 G5
Anan, Japan 29 H7
Anantnag, India 36 C9
Anápolis, Brazil 79 G9
Anār, Iran 39 D7
Anārak, Iran 39 C7
Anatolia = Anadolu,
  Turkey 23 G5
Anatone, U.S.A. 72 C5
Añatuya, Argentina . . 80 B4
Anaye, Niger 45 E7
Anchorage, U.S.A. . . . 60 B5
Ancohuma, Nevada,
  Bolivia 78 G5
Ancón, Peru 78 F3
Ancona, Italy 20 C5
Ancud, Chile 80 E2
Ancud, G. de, Chile . . 80 E2
Anda, China 31 B7
Andalgalá, Argentina . 80 B3
Andalucía □, Spain . . 19 D3
Andalusia, U.S.A. . . . 69 K2
Andalusia □ =
  Andalucía □, Spain . 19 D3
Andaman Is., Ind. Oc. 34 F2
Andaman Sea, Ind. Oc. 34 F3
Andara, Namibia 48 B3
Andenne, Belgium . . . 15 D5
Anderson, Calif.,
  U.S.A. 72 F2
Anderson, Ind., U.S.A. 68 E3
Anderson, Mo., U.S.A. 71 G7
Anderson, S.C., U.S.A. 69 H4
Anderson →, Canada 60 B7
Anderson, Mt.,
  S. Africa 49 D5
Andes, Cord. de los, S. Amer. 78 F4
Andes, S. Amer. 78 F3
Andes, Cord. de los,
  S. Amer. 78 F4
Andfjorden, Norway . 8 B14
Andhra Pradesh □,
  India 36 L11
Andijon = Andizhan,
  Uzbekistan 24 E8
Andikithira, Greece . . 21 G10
Andimeshk, Iran 39 C6
Andizhan, Uzbekistan 24 E8
Andoany, Madag. . . . 49 A8
Andorra ■, Europe . . 19 A6
Andorra La Vella,
  Andorra 19 A6
Andover, U.K. 11 F6
Andrahary, Mt.,
  Madag. 49 A8
Andramasina, Madag. 49 B8
Andranopasy, Madag. 49 C7
Andreanof Is., U.S.A. . 60 C2
Andrewilla, Australia . 55 D2
Andrews, S.C., U.S.A. 69 J6
Andrews, Tex., U.S.A. 71 J3
Ándria, Italy 20 D7
Andriba, Madag. 49 B8
Androka, Madag. . . . 49 C7
Andropov = Rybinsk,
  Russia 22 C6
Ándros, Greece 21 F11
Andros I., Bahamas . . 75 C9
Andújar, Spain 19 C3
Andulo, Angola 46 G3
Anéfis, Mali 44 E5
Aného, Togo 44 G5
Aneto, Pico de, Spain 19 A6
Ang Thong, Thailand . 34 E6
Angamos, Punta, Chile 80 A2
Angara →, Russia . . 25 D10
Angarsk, Russia 25 D11
Angas Downs,
  Australia 53 E5
Angas Hills, Australia 52 D4
Angaston, Australia . . 55 E2
Ånge, Sweden 8 E13
Angel, Salto, Venezuela 78 B6
Angeles, Phil. 33 A6
Ängelholm, Sweden . 9 H12
Angels Camp, U.S.A. . 73 G3
Angermanälven →,
  Sweden 8 E14
Angers, France 18 C3
Ångesån →, Sweden . 8 C17
Angikuni L., Canada . 65 A9
Angkor, Cambodia . . 34 F7
Antonibé, Madag. . . . 49 B8

Anglesey, U.K. 10 D3
Angleton, U.S.A. 71 L7
Angmagssalik,
  Greenland 4 C6
Ango, Zaïre 46 D5
Angola, U.S.A. 68 E3
Angola ■, Africa . . . 47 G3
Angoon, U.S.A. 64 B2
Angoulême, France . . 18 D4
Angoumois, France . . 18 D4
Angra dos Reis, Brazil 80 A8
Angren, Uzbekistan . . 24 E8
Angu, Zaïre 46 D4
Anguang, China 31 B7
Anguilla ■, W. Indies . 74 J18
Angurugu, Australia . 54 A2
Angus, Braes of, U.K. 12 E5
Anholt, Denmark . . . 9 H11
Anhui □, China 31 C6
Anhwei □ = Anhui □,
  China 31 C6
Anichab, Namibia . . . 48 C1
Animas, U.S.A. 73 L9
Anin, Burma 34 E4
Anivorano, Madag. . . 49 B8
Anjidiv I., India 36 M9
Anjou, France 18 C3
Anjozorobe, Madag. . 49 B8
Anka, Nigeria 44 F6
Ankaboa, Tanjona,
  Madag. 49 C7
Ankang, China 31 C5
Ankara, Turkey 23 G5
Ankaramena, Madag. . 49 C8
Ankazoabo, Madag. . 49 C7
Ankazobe, Madag. . . 49 B8
Ankisabe, Madag. . . . 49 B8
Ankoro, Zaïre 46 F5
Ann, C., U.S.A. 68 D10
Ann Arbor, U.S.A. . . . 68 D4
Anna, U.S.A. 71 G10
Anna Plains, Australia 52 C3
Annaba, Algeria 44 A6
Annalee →, Ireland . 13 B4
Annam = Trung-Phan,
  Vietnam 34 D10
Annamitique, Chaîne,
  Asia 34 D9
Annan, U.K. 12 G5
Annan →, U.K. 12 G5
Annapolis, U.S.A. . . . 68 F7
Annapolis Royal,
  Canada 63 D6
Annean, L., Australia . 53 E2
Annecy, France 18 D7
Anning, China 30 D5
Anningie, Australia . . 52 D5
Anniston, U.S.A. 69 J3
Annobón, Atl. Oc. . . . 43 G4
Annotto Bay, Jamaica 74 J17
Annuello, Australia . . 55 E3
Anoka, U.S.A. 70 C8
Anorotsangana,
  Madag. 49 A8
Anqing, China 31 C6
Ansbach, Germany . . 16 D5
Anshan, China 31 B7
Anshun, China 30 D5
Ansirabe, Madag. . . . 49 B8
Ansley, U.S.A. 70 E5
Anson, U.S.A. 71 J5
Anson B., Australia . . 52 B5
Ansongo, Mali 44 E5
Anstruther, U.K. 12 E6
Ansudu, Indonesia . . 33 E9
Antabamba, Peru . . . 78 F4
Antakya, Turkey 23 G6
Antalaha, Madag. . . . 49 A9
Antalya, Turkey 23 G5
Antalya Körfezi, Turkey 23 G5
Antananarivo, Madag. 49 B8
Antananarivo □,
  Madag. 49 B8
Antanimbaribe,
  Madag. 49 C7
Antarctic Pen.,
  Antarctica 5 C18
Antarctica 5 E3
Antequera, Spain . . . 19 D3
Antero, Mt., U.S.A. . . 73 G10
Anthony, Kans., U.S.A. 71 G5
Anthony, N. Mex.,
  U.S.A. 73 K10
Anthony Lagoon,
  Australia 54 B2
Anti Atlas, Morocco . 44 C3
Anti-Lebanon = Ash
  Sharqi, Al Jabal,
  Lebanon 41 B5
Anticosti, I. d', Canada 63 C7
Antigo, U.S.A. 70 C10
Antigonish, Canada . . 63 C7
Antigua, W. Indies . . 74 L20
Antigua & Barbuda ■,
  W. Indies 74 K20
Antilla, Cuba 75 C9
Antimony, U.S.A. . . . 73 G8
Antioch, U.S.A. 72 G3
Antioquia, Colombia . 78 B3
Antipodes Is., Pac. Oc. 56 M9
Antler, U.S.A. 70 A4
Antler →, Canada . . 65 D8
Antlers, U.S.A. 71 H7
Antofagasta, Chile . . 80 A2
Antofagasta de la
  Sierra, Argentina . . 80 B3
Anton, U.S.A. 71 J3
Anton Chico, U.S.A. . 73 J11
Antongila, Helodrano,
  Madag. 49 B8
Antonibé, Madag. . . . 49 B8

Antonibé, Presqu'île d',
  Madag. 49 A8
Antonina, Brazil 80 B7
Antonito, U.S.A. 73 H10
Antrim, U.K. 13 B5
Antrim □, U.K. 13 B5
Antrim, Mts. of, U.K. . 13 B5
Antrim Plateau,
  Australia 52 C4
Antsalova, Madag. . . 49 B7
Antsiranana, Madag. . 49 A8
Antsohihy, Madag. . . 49 A8
Antsohimbondrona
  Seranana, Madag. . 49 A8
Antwerp = Antwerpen,
  Belgium 15 C4
Antwerpen, Belgium . 15 C4
Antwerpen □, Belgium 15 C4
Anupgarh, India 36 E8
Anuradhapura,
  Sri Lanka 36 Q12
Anveh, Iran 39 E7
Anvers = Antwerpen,
  Belgium 15 C4
Anvers I., Antarctica . 5 C17
Anxi, China 30 B4
Anxious B., Australia . 55 E1
Anyang, China 31 C6
Anzhero-Sudzhensk,
  Russia 24 D9
Ánzio, Italy 20 D5
Aoga-Shima, Japan . . 29 H9
Aomori, Japan 28 D10
Aomori □, Japan 28 D10
Aosta, Italy 20 B2
Aoudéras, Niger 44 E6
Aoulef el Arab, Algeria 44 C5
Apache, U.S.A. 71 H5
Apalachee B., U.S.A. . 69 L3
Apalachicola, U.S.A. . 69 L3
Apalachicola →,
  U.S.A. 69 L3
Apaporis →,
  Colombia 78 D5
Aparri, Phil. 33 A6
Apatity, Russia 22 A5
Apeldoorn, Neths. . . 15 B5
Apennines =
  Appennini, Italy . . . 20 C4
Apia, W. Samoa 51 A13
Apiacás, Serra dos,
  Brazil 78 E7
Aplao, Peru 78 G4
Apo, Mt., Phil. 33 C7
Apollonia = Marsá
  Susah, Libya 45 B9
Apolo, Bolivia 78 F5
Apostle Is., U.S.A. . . . 70 B9
Apostolos Andreas, C.,
  Cyprus 38 C2
Apoteri, Guyana 78 C7
Appalachian Mts.,
  U.S.A. 68 G6
Appennini, Italy 20 C4
Appleby, U.K. 10 C5
Appleton, U.S.A. 68 C1
Approuague →,
  Fr. Guiana 79 C8
Apucarana, Brazil . . . 80 A6
Apulia = Púglia □,
  Italy 20 D7
Apure →, Venezuela 78 B5
Apurimac →, Peru . . 78 F4
Aqaba = Al 'Aqabah,
  Jordan 41 F4
'Aqaba, Khalîj al,
  Red Sea 38 D2
'Aqdā, Iran 39 C7
Aqiq, Sudan 45 E12
Aqmola = Tselinograd,
  Kazakhstan 24 D8
Aqrah, Iraq 38 B4
Aqtöbe = Aktyubinsk,
  Kazakhstan 23 D10
Aquidauana, Brazil . . 79 H7
Ar Rachidiya, Morocco 44 B4
Ar Rafid, Syria 41 C4
Ar Raḩḩālīyah, Iraq . 38 C4
Ar Ramādī, Iraq 38 C4
Ar Ramthā, Jordan . . 41 C5
Ar Raqqah, Syria . . . 38 C3
Ar Rass, Si. Arabia . . 38 E4
Ar Rifā'i, Iraq 38 D5
Ar Riyāḍ, Si. Arabia . 40 C4
Ar Ru'ays, Qatar . . . 39 E6
Ar Rukhaymīyah, Iraq 38 D5
Ar Ruqayyidah,
  Si. Arabia 39 E6
Ar Rusāfah, Syria . . . 38 C3
Ar Ruţbah, Iraq 38 C4
Ara, India 37 G14
'Arab, Bahr el →,
  Sudan 45 G10
'Arabābād, Iran 39 C8
Arabia, Asia 40 C4
Arabian Desert = Es
  Sahrâ' Esh Sharqîya,
  Egypt 45 C11
Arabian Gulf = Gulf,
  The, Asia 39 E6
Arabian Sea, Ind. Oc. 26 H10
Aracaju, Brazil 79 F11
Aracataca, Colombia . 78 A4
Aracati, Brazil 79 D11
Araçatuba, Brazil . . . 79 H8
Aracena, Spain 19 D2
Araçuaí, Brazil 79 G10
'Arad, Israel 41 D4
Arad, Romania 17 E10
Arada, Chad 45 F9
Arafura Sea, E. Indies 33 F8
Aragón □, Spain 19 B5

Aragón

Aragón →, *Spain* 19 A5
Araguacema, *Brazil* 79 E9
Araguaia →, *Brazil* 79 E9
Araguari, *Brazil* 79 G9
Araguari →, *Brazil* 79 C9
Arak, *Algeria* 44 C5
Arāk, *Iran* 39 C6
Arakan Coast, *Burma* 37 K19
Arakan Yoma, *Burma* 37 K19
Araks = Aras, Rūd-e →, *Iran* 38 B5
Aral Sea = Aralskoye More, *Asia* 24 E7
Aralsk, *Kazakhstan* 24 E7
Aralskoye More, *Asia* 24 E7
Aramac, *Australia* 54 C4
Aran I., *Ireland* 13 B3
Aran Is., *Ireland* 13 C2
Arandān, *Iran* 38 C5
Aranjuez, *Spain* 19 B4
Aranos, *Namibia* 48 C2
Aransas Pass, *U.S.A.* 71 M6
Araouane, *Mali* 44 E4
Arapahoe, *U.S.A.* 70 E5
Arapiraca, *Brazil* 79 E11
Arapongas, *Brazil* 80 A6
Ar'ar, *Si. Arabia* 38 D4
Araranguá, *Brazil* 80 B7
Araraquara, *Brazil* 79 H9
Ararat, *Australia* 55 F3
Ararat, Mt. = Ağrı Dağı, *Turkey* 23 G7
Araripe, Chapada do, *Brazil* 79 E11
Aras, Rūd-e →, *Iran* 38 B5
Arauca, *Colombia* 78 B4
Arauca →, *Venezuela* 78 B5
Arauco, *Chile* 80 D2
Araxá, *Brazil* 79 G9
Araya, Pen. de, *Venezuela* 78 A6
Arbat, *Iraq* 38 C5
Arbatax, *Italy* 20 E3
Arbaza, *Russia* 25 D10
Arbīl, *Iraq* 38 B5
Arborfield, *Canada* 65 C8
Arborg, *Canada* 65 C9
Arbroath, *U.K.* 12 E6
Arbuckle, *U.S.A.* 72 G2
Arcachon, *France* 18 D3
Arcadia, *Fla., U.S.A.* 69 M5
Arcadia, *La., U.S.A.* 71 J8
Arcadia, *Nebr., U.S.A.* 70 E5
Arcadia, *Wis., U.S.A.* 70 C9
Arcata, *U.S.A.* 72 F1
Archangel = Arkhangelsk, *Russia* 22 B7
Archer →, *Australia* 54 A3
Archer B., *Australia* 54 A3
Arcila = Asilah, *Morocco* 44 A3
Arckaringa, *Australia* 55 D1
Arckaringa Cr. →, *Australia* 55 D2
Arco, *U.S.A.* 72 E7
Arcola, *Canada* 65 D8
Arcos, *Spain* 19 B4
Arcot, *India* 36 N11
Arcoverde, *Brazil* 79 E11
Arctic Bay, *Canada* 61 A11
Arctic Ocean, *Arctic* 4 B18
Arctic Red River, *Canada* 60 B6
Arda →, *Bulgaria* 21 D12
Ardabīl, *Iran* 39 B6
Ardakān = Sepīdān, *Iran* 39 D7
Ardèche □, *France* 18 D6
Ardee, *Ireland* 13 C5
Ardenne, *Belgium* 15 E5
Ardennes = Ardenne, *Belgium* 15 E5
Ardennes □, *France* 18 B6
Ardestān, *Iran* 39 C7
Ardgour, *U.K.* 12 E3
Ardlethan, *Australia* 55 E4
Ardmore, *Australia* 54 C2
Ardmore, *Okla., U.S.A.* 71 H6
Ardmore, *S. Dak., U.S.A.* 70 D3
Ardnacrusha, *Ireland* 13 D3
Ardnamurchan, Pt. of, *U.K.* 12 E2
Ardrossan, *Australia* 55 E2
Ardrossan, *U.K.* 12 F4
Ards □, *U.K.* 13 B6
Ards Pen., *U.K.* 13 B6
Arecibo, *Puerto Rico* 75 D11
Areia Branca, *Brazil* 79 D11
Arendal, *Norway* 9 G10
Arequipa, *Peru* 78 G4
Arero, *Ethiopia* 45 H12
Arévalo, *Spain* 19 B3
Arezzo, *Italy* 20 C4
Argamakmur, *Indonesia* 32 E2
Argentário, Mte., *Italy* 20 C4
Argentia, *Canada* 63 C9
Argentina ■, *S. Amer.* 80 D3
Argentina Is., *Antarctica* 5 C17
Argentino, L., *Argentina* 80 G2
Argeş →, *Romania* 17 F13
Arghandab →, *Afghan.* 36 D4
Argo, *Sudan* 45 E11
Argolikós Kólpos, *Greece* 21 F10
Argonne, *France* 18 B6
Árgos, *Greece* 21 F10
Argostólion, *Greece* 21 E9
Arguello, Pt., *U.S.A.* 73 J3
Argun →, *Russia* 25 D13
Argungu, *Nigeria* 44 F5
Argyle, *U.S.A.* 70 A6
Argyle, L., *Australia* 52 C4
Århus, *Denmark* 9 H11
Ariadnoye, *Russia* 28 B7
Ariamsvlei, *Namibia* 48 D2
Arica, *Chile* 78 G4
Arica, *Colombia* 78 D4
Arid, C., *Australia* 53 F3
Arida, *Japan* 29 G7
Ariège □, *France* 18 E4
Arīḥā, *Syria* 38 C3
Arima, *Trin. & Tob.* 74 S20
Arinos →, *Brazil* 78 F7
Aripuanã, *Brazil* 78 E6
Aripuanã →, *Brazil* 78 E6
Ariquemes, *Brazil* 78 E6
Arisaig, *U.K.* 12 E3
Aristazabal I., *Canada* 64 C3
Arivaca, *U.S.A.* 73 L8
Arivonimamo, *Madag.* 49 B8
Arizona, *Argentina* 80 D3
Arizona □, *U.S.A.* 73 J8
Arjeplog, *Sweden* 8 C15
Arjona, *Colombia* 78 A3
Arjuno, *Indonesia* 33 G15
Arka, *Russia* 25 C15
Arkadelphia, *U.S.A.* 71 H8
Arkaig, L., *U.K.* 12 E3
Arkalyk, *Kazakhstan* 24 D7
Arkansas □, *U.S.A.* 71 H8
Arkansas →, *U.S.A.* 71 J9
Arkansas City, *U.S.A.* 71 G6
Arkhangelsk, *Russia* 22 B7
Arklow, *Ireland* 13 D5
Arkticheskiy, Mys, *Russia* 25 A10
Arlanzón →, *Spain* 19 A3
Arlberg Pass, *Austria* 16 E5
Arlee, *U.S.A.* 72 C6
Arles, *France* 18 E6
Arlington, *S. Africa* 49 D4
Arlington, *Oreg., U.S.A.* 72 D3
Arlington, *S. Dak., U.S.A.* 70 C6
Arlington, *Va., U.S.A.* 68 F7
Arlington, *Wash., U.S.A.* 72 B2
Arlon, *Belgium* 15 E5
Armagh, *U.K.* 13 B5
Armagh □, *U.K.* 13 B5
Armagnac, *France* 18 E4
Armavir, *Russia* 23 E7
Armenia, *Colombia* 78 C3
Armenia ■, *Asia* 23 F7
Armidale, *Australia* 55 E5
Armour, *U.S.A.* 70 D5
Armstrong, *B.C., Canada* 64 C5
Armstrong, *Ont., Canada* 62 B2
Armstrong, *U.S.A.* 71 M6
Armstrong →, *Australia* 52 C5
Arnarfjörður, *Iceland* 8 D2
Arnaud →, *Canada* 61 B12
Arnauti, C., *Cyprus* 38 C2
Arnes, *Iceland* 8 C3
Arnett, *U.S.A.* 71 G5
Arnhem, *Neths.* 15 C5
Arnhem, C., *Australia* 54 A2
Arnhem B., *Australia* 54 A2
Arnhem Land, *Australia* 54 A1
Arno →, *Italy* 20 C4
Arno Bay, *Australia* 55 E2
Arnold, *U.S.A.* 70 E4
Arnot, *Canada* 65 B9
Arnøy, *Norway* 8 A16
Arnprior, *Canada* 62 C4
Aroab, *Namibia* 48 D2
Arrabury, *Australia* 55 D3
Arrah = Ara, *India* 37 G14
Arraiján, *Panama* 74 H14
Arran, *U.K.* 12 F3
Arrandale, *Canada* 64 C3
Arras, *France* 18 A5
Arrecife, *Canary Is.* 44 C2
Arrée, Mts. d', *France* 18 B2
Arrilalah P.O., *Australia* 54 C3
Arrino, *Australia* 53 E2
Arrow, L., *Ireland* 13 B3
Arrow Rock Res., *U.S.A.* 72 E6
Arrowhead, *Canada* 64 C5
Arrowtown, *N.Z.* 51 L2
Arroyo Grande, *U.S.A.* 73 J3
Ars, *Iran* 38 B5
Arsenault L., *Canada* 65 B7
Arsenev, *Russia* 28 B6
Árta, *Greece* 21 E9
Artem, *Russia* 28 C6
Artemovsk, *Russia* 25 D10
Artesia = Mosomane, *Botswana* 48 C4
Artesia, *U.S.A.* 71 J2
Artesia Wells, *U.S.A.* 71 L5
Artesian, *U.S.A.* 70 C6
Arthur →, *Australia* 54 G3
Arthur Cr. →, *Australia* 54 C2
Arthur Pt., *Australia* 54 C5
Arthur's Pass, *N.Z.* 51 K3
Artigas, *Uruguay* 80 C5
Artillery L., *Canada* 65 A7
Artois, *France* 18 A5
Artvin, *Turkey* 23 F7
Aru, Kepulauan, *Indonesia* 33 F8
Aru Is. = Aru, Kepulauan, *Indonesia* 33 F8
Arua, *Uganda* 46 D6
Aruanã, *Brazil* 79 F8
Aruba ■, *W. Indies* 75 E11
Arumpo, *Australia* 55 E3
Arunachal Pradesh □, *India* 37 E19
Arusha, *Tanzania* 46 E7
Aruwimi →, *Zaïre* 46 D4
Arvada, *U.S.A.* 72 D10
Arvida, *Canada* 63 C5
Arvidsjaur, *Sweden* 8 D15
Arvika, *Sweden* 9 G12
Arxan, *China* 31 B6
Arys, *Kazakhstan* 24 E7
Arzamas, *Russia* 22 C7
Arzew, *Algeria* 44 A4
Aş Şadr, *U.A.E.* 39 E7
Aş Şafā, *Syria* 41 B6
'As Saffānīyah, *Si. Arabia* 39 D6
As Safīrah, *Syria* 38 B3
Aş Şahm, *Oman* 39 E8
As Sājir, *Si. Arabia* 38 E5
As Salamīyah, *Syria* 38 C3
As Salt, *Jordan* 41 C4
As Sal'w'a, *Qatar* 39 E6
As Samāwah, *Iraq* 38 D5
As Sanamayn, *Syria* 41 B5
As Sukhnah, *Syria* 38 C3
As Sulaymānīyah, *Iraq* 38 C5
As Sulaymī, *Si. Arabia* 38 E4
As Summān, *Si. Arabia* 38 E5
As Suwaydā', *Syria* 41 C5
As Suwaydā' □, *Syria* 41 C5
As Şuwayrah, *Iraq* 38 C5
Asab, *Namibia* 48 D2
Asahi-Gawa →, *Japan* 29 G6
Asahigawa, *Japan* 28 C11
Asansol, *India* 37 H15
Asbesberge, *S. Africa* 48 D3
Asbestos, *Canada* 63 C5
Asbury Park, *U.S.A.* 68 E8
Ascension I., *Atl. Oc.* 2 E9
Aschaffenburg, *Germany* 16 D4
Áscoli Piceno, *Italy* 20 C5
Ascope, *Peru* 78 E3
Aseb, *Eritrea* 40 E3
Asela, *Ethiopia* 45 G12
Ash Fork, *U.S.A.* 73 J7
Ash Grove, *U.S.A.* 71 G8
Ash Shamāl □, *Lebanon* 41 A5
Ash Shāmīyah, *Iraq* 38 D5
Ash Shāriqah, *U.A.E.* 39 E7
Ash Sharmah, *Si. Arabia* 38 D2
Ash Sharqāt, *Iraq* 38 C4
Ash Sharqi, Al Jabal, *Lebanon* 41 B5
Ash Shaṭrah, *Iraq* 38 D5
Ash Shawbak, *Jordan* 38 D2
Ash Shawmari, J., *Jordan* 41 E5
Ash Shaykh, J., *Lebanon* 41 B4
Ash Shināfīyah, *Iraq* 38 D5
Ash Shu'aybah, *Si. Arabia* 38 E5
Ash Shumlūl, *Si. Arabia* 38 E5
Ash Shūr'a, *Iraq* 38 C4
Ash Shurayf, *Si. Arabia* 38 E3
Ash Shuwayfāt, *Lebanon* 41 B4
Asha, *Russia* 22 D10
Ashburn, *U.S.A.* 69 K4
Ashburton, *N.Z.* 51 K3
Ashburton →, *Australia* 52 D1
Ashburton Downs, *Australia* 52 D2
Ashby de la Zouch, *U.K.* 11 E6
Ashcroft, *Canada* 64 C4
Ashdod, *Israel* 41 D3
Asheboro, *U.S.A.* 69 H6
Asherton, *U.S.A.* 71 L5
Asheville, *U.S.A.* 69 H4
Asheweig →, *Canada* 62 B2
Ashford, *Australia* 55 D5
Ashford, *U.K.* 11 F8
Ashford, *U.S.A.* 72 C2
Ashgabat = Ashkhabad, *Turkmenistan* 24 F6
Ashibetsu, *Japan* 28 C11
Ashikaga, *Japan* 29 F9
Ashizuri-Zaki, *Japan* 29 H6
Ashkhabad, *Turkmenistan* 24 F6
Ashland, *Kans., U.S.A.* 71 G5
Ashland, *Ky., U.S.A.* 68 F4
Ashland, *Maine, U.S.A.* 63 C6
Ashland, *Mont., U.S.A.* 72 D10
Ashland, *Nebr., U.S.A.* 70 E6
Ashland, *Ohio, U.S.A.* 68 E4
Ashland, *Oreg., U.S.A.* 72 E2
Ashland, *Va., U.S.A.* 68 G7
Ashland, *Wis., U.S.A.* 70 B9
Ashley, *U.S.A.* 70 B5
Ashmont, *Canada* 64 C6
Ashmore Reef, *Australia* 52 B3
Ashq'elon, *Israel* 41 D3
Ashtabula, *U.S.A.* 68 E5
Ashton, *S. Africa* 48 E3
Ashton, *U.S.A.* 72 D8
Ashton under Lyne, *U.K.* 10 D5
Ashuanipi, L., *Canada* 63 B6
Asia 26 E11
Asia, Kepulauan, *Indonesia* 33 D8
Āsīā Bak, *Iran* 39 C6
Asifabad, *India* 36 K11
Asike, *Indonesia* 33 F10
Asilah, *Morocco* 44 A3
Asinara, *Italy* 20 D3
Asinara, G. dell', *Italy* 20 D3
Asino, *Russia* 24 D9
'Asīr □, *Si. Arabia* 40 D3
Asir, Ras, *Somali Rep.* 40 E5
Askersund, *Sweden* 9 G13
Askham, *S. Africa* 48 D3
Askja, *Iceland* 8 D5
Asmara = Asmera, *Eritrea* 45 E12
Asmera, *Eritrea* 45 E12
Asotin, *U.S.A.* 72 C5
Aspen, *U.S.A.* 73 G10
Aspermont, *U.S.A.* 71 J4
Aspiring, Mt., *N.Z.* 51 L2
Asquith, *Canada* 65 C7
Assam □, *India* 37 F18
Asse, *Belgium* 15 D4
Assen, *Neths.* 15 B6
Assini, *Ivory C.* 44 G4
Assiniboia, *Canada* 65 D7
Assiniboine →, *Canada* 65 D9
Assis, *Brazil* 80 A6
Assisi, *Italy* 20 C5
Assynt, L., *U.K.* 12 C3
Astara, *Azerbaijan* 23 G8
Asti, *Italy* 20 B3
Astipálaia, *Greece* 21 F12
Astorga, *Spain* 19 A2
Astoria, *U.S.A.* 72 C2
Astrakhan, *Russia* 23 E8
Astrakhan-Bazàr, *Azerbaijan* 23 G8
Asturias □, *Spain* 19 A2
Asunción, *Paraguay* 80 B5
Aswân, *Egypt* 45 D11
Aswân High Dam = Sadd el Aali, *Egypt* 45 D11
Asyût, *Egypt* 45 C11
At Ṭafilah, *Jordan* 41 E4
At Tā'if, *Si. Arabia* 40 C3
Aṭ Ṭirāq, *Si. Arabia* 38 E5
Atacama, Desierto de, *Chile* 80 A3
Atacama, Salar de, *Chile* 80 A3
Atakpamé, *Togo* 44 G5
Atalaya, *Peru* 78 F4
Atami, *Japan* 29 G9
Atapupu, *Indonesia* 33 F6
Atâr, *Mauritania* 44 D2
Atara, *Russia* 25 C13
Atascadero, *U.S.A.* 73 J3
Atasu, *Kazakhstan* 24 E8
Atauro, *Indonesia* 33 F7
Atbara, *Sudan* 45 E11
'Atbara →, *Sudan* 45 E11
Atbasar, *Kazakhstan* 24 D7
Atchafalaya B., *U.S.A.* 71 L9
Atchison, *U.S.A.* 70 F7
Ath, *Belgium* 15 D3
Athabasca, *Canada* 64 C6
Athabasca →, *Canada* 65 B6
Athabasca, L., *Canada* 65 B7
Athboy, *Ireland* 13 C5
Athenry, *Ireland* 13 C3
Athens = Athínai, *Greece* 21 F10
Athens, *Ala., U.S.A.* 69 H2
Athens, *Ga., U.S.A.* 69 J4
Athens, *Ohio, U.S.A.* 68 F4
Athens, *Tenn., U.S.A.* 69 H3
Athens, *Tex., U.S.A.* 71 J7
Atherton, *Australia* 54 B4
Athínai, *Greece* 21 F10
Athlone, *Ireland* 13 C4
Atholl, Forest of, *U.K.* 12 E5
Atholville, *Canada* 63 C6
Áthos, *Greece* 21 D11
Athy, *Ireland* 13 D5
Ati, *Chad* 45 F8
Atico, *Peru* 78 G4
Atikokan, *Canada* 62 C1
Atikonak L., *Canada* 63 B7
Atka, *Russia* 25 C16
Atkinson, *U.S.A.* 70 D5
Atlanta, *Ga., U.S.A.* 69 J3
Atlanta, *Tex., U.S.A.* 71 J7
Atlantic, *U.S.A.* 70 E7
Atlantic City, *U.S.A.* 68 F8
Atlantic Ocean 2 E9
Atlas Mts. = Haut Atlas, *Morocco* 44 B3
Atlin, *Canada* 64 B2
Atlin, L., *Canada* 64 B2
Atmore, *U.S.A.* 69 K2
Atoka, *U.S.A.* 71 H6
Atrak →, *Iran* 39 B8
Atsuta, *Japan* 28 C10
Attalla, *U.S.A.* 69 H2
Attawapiskat, *Canada* 62 B3
Attawapiskat →, *Canada* 62 B3
Attawapiskat, L., *Canada* 62 B2
Attica, *U.S.A.* 68 E2
Attikamagen L., *Canada* 63 A6
Attleboro, *U.S.A.* 68 E10
Attock, *Pakistan* 36 C8
Attopeu, *Laos* 34 E9
Attur, *India* 36 P11
Atuel →, *Argentina* 80 D3
Åtvidaberg, *Sweden* 9 G14
Atwater, *U.S.A.* 73 H3
Atwood, *U.S.A.* 70 F4
Atyrau, *Kazakhstan* 23 E9
Au Sable →, *U.S.A.* 68 C4
Au Sable Pt., *U.S.A.* 62 C2
Aube □, *France* 18 B6
Aube →, *France* 18 B5
Auburn, *Ala., U.S.A.* 69 J3
Auburn, *Calif., U.S.A.* 72 G3
Auburn, *Ind., U.S.A.* 68 E3
Auburn, *N.Y., U.S.A.* 68 D7
Auburn, *Nebr., U.S.A.* 70 E7
Auburn Ra., *Australia* 55 D5
Auburndale, *U.S.A.* 69 L5
Aubusson, *France* 18 D5
Auch, *France* 18 E4
Auckland, *N.Z.* 51 G5
Auckland Is., *Pac. Oc.* 56 N8
Aude □, *France* 18 E5
Aude →, *France* 18 E5
Auden, *Canada* 62 B2
Audubon, *U.S.A.* 70 E7
Augathella, *Australia* 55 D4
Augrabies Falls, *S. Africa* 48 D3
Augsburg, *Germany* 16 D5
Augusta, *Italy* 20 F6
Augusta, *Ark., U.S.A.* 71 H9
Augusta, *Ga., U.S.A.* 69 J5
Augusta, *Kans., U.S.A.* 71 G6
Augusta, *Maine, U.S.A.* 63 D6
Augusta, *Mont., U.S.A.* 72 C7
Augusta, *Wis., U.S.A.* 70 C9
Augustów, *Poland* 17 B11
Augustus, Mt., *Australia* 52 D2
Augustus Downs, *Australia* 54 B2
Augustus I., *Australia* 52 C3
Auld, L., *Australia* 52 D3
Ault, *U.S.A.* 70 E2
Aunis, *France* 18 C3
Auponhia, *Indonesia* 33 E7
Aurangabad, *Bihar, India* 37 G14
Aurangabad, *Maharashtra, India* 36 K9
Aurillac, *France* 18 D5
Aurora, *S. Africa* 48 E2
Aurora, *Colo., U.S.A.* 70 F2
Aurora, *Ill., U.S.A.* 68 E1
Aurora, *Mo., U.S.A.* 71 G8
Aurora, *Nebr., U.S.A.* 70 E6
Aurukun Mission, *Australia* 54 A3
Aus, *Namibia* 48 D2
Aust-Agder fylke □, *Norway* 9 G9
Austerlitz = Slavkov, *Czech.* 16 D8
Austin, *Minn., U.S.A.* 70 D8
Austin, *Nev., U.S.A.* 72 G5
Austin, *Tex., U.S.A.* 71 K6
Austin, L., *Australia* 53 E2
Austral Downs, *Australia* 54 C2
Austral Is. = Tubuai Is., *Pac. Oc.* 57 K12
Austral Seamount Chain, *Pac. Oc.* 57 K13
Australia ■, *Oceania* 56 K5
Australian Alps, *Australia* 55 F4
Australian Capital Territory □, *Australia* 55 F4
Austria ■, *Europe* 16 E6
Austvågøy, *Norway* 8 B13
Autun, *France* 18 C6
Auvergne, *Australia* 52 C5
Auvergne, *France* 18 D5
Auvergne, Mts. d', *France* 18 D5
Auxerre, *France* 18 C5
Avallon, *France* 18 C5
Avalon Pen., *Canada* 63 C9
Aveiro, *Brazil* 79 D7
Aveiro, *Portugal* 19 B1
Āvej, *Iran* 39 C6
Avellaneda, *Argentina* 80 C5
Avellino, *Italy* 20 D6
Aversa, *Italy* 20 D6
Avery, *U.S.A.* 72 C6
Avesta, *Sweden* 9 F14
Aveyron □, *France* 18 D5
Aviá Terai, *Argentina* 80 B4
Avignon, *France* 18 E6
Ávila, *Spain* 19 B3
Avilés, *Spain* 19 A3
Avoca, *Ireland* 13 D5
Avoca →, *Australia* 55 F3
Avola, *Canada* 64 C5
Avon, *U.S.A.* 70 D5
Avon □, *U.K.* 11 F5
Avon →, *Australia* 53 F2
Avon →, *Avon, U.K.* 11 F5
Avon →, *Hants., U.K.* 11 G6
Avon →, *Warks., U.K.* 11 F5
Avonlea, *Canada* 65 D7
Avonmouth, *U.K.* 11 F5
Avranches, *France* 18 B3
A'waj →, *Syria* 41 B5
Awaji-Shima, *Japan* 29 G7
'Awālī, *Bahrain* 39 E6
Awash, *Ethiopia* 40 F3
Awatere →, *N.Z.* 51 J5
Awbārī, *Libya* 45 C7
Awe, L., *U.K.* 12 E3
Awjilah, *Libya* 45 C9
Axarfjörður, *Iceland* 8 C5
Axel Heiberg I., *Canada* 4 B3
Axim, *Ghana* 44 H4
Axminster, *U.K.* 11 G4
Ayabaca, *Peru* 78 D3
Ayabe, *Japan* 29 G7
Ayacucho, *Argentina* 80 D5
Ayacucho, *Peru* 78 F4
Ayaguz, *Kazakhstan* 24 E9
Ayamonte, *Spain* 19 D2
Ayan, *Russia* 25 D14
Ayaviri, *Peru* 78 F4
Ayeritam, *Malaysia* 34 P13
Ayers Rock, *Australia* 53 E5
Ayios Evstrátios, *Greece* 21 E11
Aykin, *Russia* 22 B8
Aylesbury, *U.K.* 11 F7
Aylmer, L., *Canada* 60 B8
Ayon, Ostrov, *Russia* 25 C17
Ayr, *Australia* 54 B4
Ayr, *U.K.* 12 F4
Ayr →, *U.K.* 12 F4
Ayre, Pt. of, *U.K.* 10 C3
Aytos, *Bulgaria* 21 C12
Ayu, Kepulauan, *Indonesia* 33 D8
Ayutla, *Mexico* 74 D5
Ayvalık, *Turkey* 23 G4
Az Zabdānī, *Syria* 41 B5
Aẓ Ẓāhirīyah, *Jordan* 41 D3
Aẓ Ẓahrān, *Si. Arabia* 39 E6
Az Zarqā, *Jordan* 41 C5
Az Zībār, *Iraq* 38 B5
Az-Zilfī, *Si. Arabia* 38 E5
Az Zubayr, *Iraq* 38 D5
Azamgarh, *India* 37 F13
Āzār Shahr, *Iran* 38 B5
Azärbayjan = Azerbaijan ■, *Asia* 23 F8
Āzarbāyjān-e Gharbī □, *Iran* 38 B5
Āzarbāyjān-e Sharqī □, *Iran* 38 B5
Azare, *Nigeria* 44 F7
A'zāz, *Syria* 38 B3
Azbine = Aïr, *Niger* 44 E6
Azerbaijan ■, *Asia* 23 F8
Azerbaijchan = Azerbaijan ■, *Asia* 23 F8
Azogues, *Ecuador* 78 D3
Azores, *Atl. Oc.* 2 C8
Azov, *Russia* 23 E6
Azov, Sea of = Azovskoye More, *Europe* 23 E6
Azovskoye More, *Europe* 23 E6
Azovy, *Russia* 24 C7
Aztec, *U.S.A.* 73 H10
Azúa, *Dom. Rep.* 75 D10
Azuaga, *Spain* 19 C3
Azuero, Pen. de, *Panama* 75 F8
Azul, *Argentina* 80 D5
'Azzūn, *Jordan* 41 C4

B

Ba Don, *Vietnam* 34 D9
Ba Ngoi = Cam Lam, *Vietnam* 34 G10
Ba Ria, *Vietnam* 34 G9
Baa, *Indonesia* 33 F6
Baarle Nassau, *Belgium* 15 C4
Baarn, *Neths.* 15 B5
Bab el Mandeb, *Red Sea* 40 E3
Bābā Kalū, *Iran* 39 D6
Babadayhan = Kirovsk, *Turkmenistan* 24 F7
Babahoyo, *Ecuador* 78 D3
Babakin, *Australia* 53 F2
Babana, *Nigeria* 44 F5
Babar, *Indonesia* 33 F7
Babb, *U.S.A.* 72 B7
Babinda, *Australia* 54 B4
Babine, *Canada* 64 B3
Babine →, *Canada* 64 B3
Babine L., *Canada* 64 C3
Babo, *Indonesia* 33 E8
Bābol, *Iran* 39 B7
Bābol Sar, *Iran* 39 B7
Baboua, *C.A.R.* 46 C2
Babruysk = Bobruysk, *Belorussia* 22 D4
Babura, *Nigeria* 44 F6
Babuyan Chan., *Phil.* 33 A6
Babylon, *Iraq* 38 C5
Bac Kan, *Vietnam* 34 A8
Bac Ninh, *Vietnam* 34 B9
Bac Phan, *Vietnam* 34 A8
Bac Quang, *Vietnam* 34 A8
Bacabal, *Brazil* 79 D10
Bacan, *Indonesia* 33 F7
Bacan, Kepulauan, *Indonesia* 33 E7
Bacan, Pulau, *Indonesia* 33 E7
Bacarra, *Phil.* 33 A6
Bacău, *Romania* 17 E13
Bachelina, *Russia* 24 D7
Back →, *Canada* 60 B9
Backstairs Passage, *Australia* 55 F2
Bacolod, *Phil.* 33 B6
Bād, *Iran* 39 C7
Bad →, *U.S.A.* 70 C4

Bawku

Bad Axe, U.S.A. 68 D4
Bad Ischl, Austria 16 E6
Bad Lands, U.S.A. 70 D3
Badagara, India 36 P9
Badajoz, Spain 19 C2
Badalona, Spain 19 B7
Badalzai, Afghan. 36 E4
Badampahar, India 37 H15
Badanah, Si. Arabia 38 D4
Badarinath, India 36 D11
Badas, Brunei 32 D4
Badas, Kepulauan, Indonesia 32 D3
Baddo →, Pakistan 36 F4
Bade, Indonesia 33 F9
Baden, Austria 16 D8
Baden-Baden, Germany 16 D4
Baden-Württemberg □, Germany 16 D4
Badenoch, U.K. 12 E4
Badgastein, Austria 16 E6
Badger, Canada 63 C8
Bādghīsāt □, Afghan. 36 B3
Badin, Pakistan 36 G6
Baduen, Somali Rep. 40 F4
Badulla, Sri Lanka 36 R12
Baeza, Spain 19 D4
Bafatá, Guinea-Biss. 44 F2
Baffin B., Canada 4 B4
Baffin I., Canada 61 B12
Bafia, Cameroon 44 H7
Bafing →, Mali 44 F2
Bafliyūn, Syria 38 B3
Bafoulabé, Mali 44 F2
Bāfq, Iran 39 D7
Bāft, Iran 39 D8
Bafwasende, Zaïre 46 D5
Bagamoyo, Tanzania 46 F7
Baganga, Phil. 33 C7
Bagani, Namibia 48 B3
Bagansiapiapi, Indonesia 32 D2
Bagdarin, Russia 25 D12
Bagé, Brazil 80 C6
Bagenalstown = Muine Bheag, Ireland 13 D5
Baggs, U.S.A. 72 F10
Baghdād, Iraq 38 C5
Baghlān, Afghan. 36 A6
Bagley, U.S.A. 70 B7
Bagotville, Canada 63 C5
Baguio, Phil. 33 A6
Bahamas ■, N. Amer. 75 C10
Baharampur, India 37 G16
Bahau, Malaysia 34 S15
Bahawalpur, Pakistan 36 E7
Bahía = Salvador, Brazil 79 F11
Bahía □, Brazil 79 F10
Bahía Blanca, Argentina 80 D4
Bahía de Caráquez, Ecuador 78 D2
Bahía Laura, Argentina 80 F3
Bahía Negra, Paraguay 78 H7
Bahmanzād, Iran 39 D6
Bahr Aouk →, C.A.R. 46 C3
Bahr el Ahmar □, Sudan 45 E12
Bahr el Ghazâl □, Sudan 45 G10
Bahr Salamat →, Chad 45 G8
Bahraich, India 37 F12
Bahrain ■, Asia 39 E6
Bahret Assad, Syria 38 C3
Bāhū Kalāt, Iran 39 E9
Bai Bung, Mui, Vietnam 34 H8
Baia Mare, Romania 17 E11
Baïbokoum, Chad 45 G8
Baidoa, Somali Rep. 40 G3
Baie Comeau, Canada 63 C6
Baie-St-Paul, Canada 63 C5
Baie Trinité, Canada 63 C6
Baie Verte, Canada 63 C8
Ba'ījī, Iraq 38 C4
Baikal, L. = Baykal, Oz., Russia 25 D11
Baile Atha Cliath = Dublin, Ireland 13 C5
Bailundo, Angola 47 G3
Bainbridge, U.S.A. 69 K3
Baing, Indonesia 33 F6
Bainville, U.S.A. 70 A2
Bā'ir, Jordan 41 E5
Baird, U.S.A. 71 J5
Baird Mts., U.S.A. 60 B3
Bairnsdale, Australia 55 F4
Baitadi, Nepal 37 E12
Baixo-Alentejo, Portugal 19 D1
Baiyin, China 30 C5
Baja, Hungary 17 E9
Baja, Pta., Mexico 74 B1
Baja California, Mexico 74 B2
Bājgīrān, Iran 39 B8
Bajimba, Mt., Australia 55 D5
Bajool, Australia 54 C5
Bakala, C.A.R. 45 G9
Bakchar, Russia 24 D9
Bakel, Senegal 44 F2
Baker, Calif., U.S.A. 73 J5
Baker, Mont., U.S.A. 70 B2
Baker, Oreg., U.S.A. 72 D5
Baker, L., Canada 60 B10
Baker I., Pac. Oc. 56 G10
Baker L., Australia 53 E4
Baker Lake, Canada 60 B10
Baker Mt., U.S.A. 72 B3
Bakers Creek, Australia 54 C4
Baker's Dozen Is., Canada 62 A4
Bakersfield, U.S.A. 73 J4
Bākhtarān, Iran 38 C5
Bākhtarān □, Iran 38 C5
Bakkafjörður, Iceland 8 C6
Bakkagerði, Iceland 8 D7
Bakony Forest = Bakony Hegyseg, Hungary 17 E8
Bakony Hegyseg, Hungary 17 E8
Bakouma, C.A.R. 45 G9
Baku, Azerbaijan 23 F8
Bakutis Coast, Antarctica 5 D15
Baky = Baku, Azerbaijan 23 F8
Bala, L., U.K. 10 E4
Balabac I., Phil. 32 C5
Balabac Str., E. Indies 32 C5
Balabakk, Lebanon 41 A5
Balabalangan, Kepulauan, Indonesia 32 E5
Balad, Iraq 38 C5
Balad Rūz, Iraq 38 C5
Bālādeh, Fārs, Iran 39 D6
Bāladeh, Māzandaran, Iran 39 B6
Balaghat, India 36 J12
Balaghat Ra., India 36 K10
Balaguer, Spain 19 B6
Balaklava, Australia 55 E2
Balaklava, Ukraine 23 F5
Balakovo, Russia 22 D8
Balashov, Russia 22 D7
Balasore = Baleshwar, India 37 J15
Balaton, Hungary 17 E8
Balboa, Panama 74 H14
Balboa Hill, Panama 74 H14
Balbriggan, Ireland 13 C5
Balcarce, Argentina 80 D5
Balcarres, Canada 65 C8
Balchik, Bulgaria 21 C13
Balclutha, N.Z. 51 M2
Bald Hd., Australia 53 G2
Bald I., Australia 53 F2
Bald Knob, U.S.A. 71 H9
Baldock L., Canada 65 B9
Baldwin, Fla., U.S.A. 69 K4
Baldwin, Mich., U.S.A. 68 D3
Baldwinsville, U.S.A. 68 D7
Baldy Peak, U.S.A. 73 K9
Baleares, Is., Spain 19 C7
Balearic Is. = Baleares, Is., Spain 19 C7
Baler, Phil. 33 A6
Baleshwar, India 37 J15
Balfe's Creek, Australia 54 C4
Balfour, S. Africa 49 D4
Bali, Cameroon 44 G7
Bali, Indonesia 32 F5
Bali □, Indonesia 32 F5
Bali, Selat, Indonesia 33 H16
Balikeşir, Turkey 23 G4
Balikpapan, Indonesia 32 E5
Balimbing, Phil. 33 C5
Baling, Malaysia 34 P13
Balipara, India 37 F18
Baliza, Brazil 79 G8
Balkan Mts. = Stara Planina, Bulgaria 21 C10
Balkan Peninsula, Europe 6 G10
Balkhash, Kazakhstan 24 E8
Balkhash, Ozero, Kazakhstan 24 E8
Balla, Bangla. 37 G17
Ballachulish, U.K. 12 E3
Balladonia, Australia 53 F3
Ballarat, Australia 55 F3
Ballard, L., Australia 53 E3
Ballater, U.K. 12 D5
Balleny Is., Antarctica 5 C11
Ballidu, Australia 53 F2
Ballina, Australia 55 D5
Ballina, Mayo, Ireland 13 B2
Ballina, Tipp., Ireland 13 D3
Ballinasloe, Ireland 13 C3
Ballinger, U.S.A. 71 K5
Ballinrobe, Ireland 13 C2
Ballinskelligs B., Ireland 13 E1
Ballycastle, U.K. 13 A5
Ballymena, U.K. 13 B5
Ballymena □, U.K. 13 B5
Ballymoney, U.K. 13 A5
Ballymoney □, U.K. 13 A5
Ballyshannon, Ireland 13 B3
Balmaceda, Chile 80 F2
Balmoral, Australia 55 F3
Balmoral, U.K. 12 D5
Balmorhea, U.S.A. 71 K3
Balonne →, Australia 55 D4
Balqash Kol = Balkhash, Ozero, Kazakhstan 24 E8
Balrampur, India 37 F13
Balranald, Australia 55 E3
Balsas →, Mexico 74 D4
Balta, Ukraine 23 E4
Balta, U.S.A. 70 A4
Bălţi = Beltsy, Moldavia 23 E4
Baltic Sea, Europe 9 H15
Baltimore, Ireland 13 E2
Baltimore, U.S.A. 68 F7
Baluchistan □, Pakistan 36 F4
Balygychan, Russia 25 C16
Bam, Iran 39 D8
Bama, Nigeria 45 F7
Bamako, Mali 44 F3
Bamba, Mali 44 E4
Bambari, C.A.R. 45 G9
Bambaroo, Australia 54 B4
Bamberg, Germany 16 D5
Bamberg, U.S.A. 69 J5
Bambili, Zaïre 46 D5
Bamenda, Cameroon 44 G7
Bamfield, Canada 64 D3
Bāmīān □, Afghan. 36 B5
Bampūr, Iran 39 E9
Ban Aranyaprathet, Thailand 34 F7
Ban Ban, Laos 34 C7
Ban Bua Chum, Thailand 34 E6
Ban Don = Surat Thani, Thailand 34 H5
Ban Houei Sai, Laos 34 B6
Ban Khe Bo, Vietnam 34 C8
Ban Khun Yuam, Thailand 34 C4
Ban Mê Thuôt = Buon Me Thuot, Vietnam 34 F10
Ban Phai, Thailand 34 D7
Ban Thateng, Laos 34 E9
Banaba, Kiribati 56 H8
Banalia, Zaïre 46 D5
Banam, Cambodia 34 G8
Banamba, Mali 44 F3
Banana, Australia 54 C5
Bananal, I. do, Brazil 79 F8
Banaras = Varanasi, India 37 G13
Banbān, Si. Arabia 38 E5
Banbridge, U.K. 13 B5
Banbridge □, U.K. 13 B5
Banbury, U.K. 11 E6
Banchory, U.K. 12 D6
Bancroft, Canada 62 C4
Band Bonī, Iran 39 E8
Band Qīr, Iran 39 D6
Banda, India 36 G12
Banda, Kepulauan, Indonesia 33 E7
Banda Aceh, Indonesia 32 C1
Banda Banda, Mt., Australia 55 E5
Banda Elat, Indonesia 33 F8
Banda Is. = Banda, Kepulauan, Indonesia 33 E7
Banda Sea, Indonesia 33 F7
Bandai-San, Japan 28 F10
Bandān, Iran 39 D9
Bandanaira, Indonesia 33 E7
Bandar = Machilipatnam, India 37 L12
Bandār 'Abbās, Iran 39 E8
Bandar-e Anzalī, Iran 39 B6
Bandar-e Chārak, Iran 39 E7
Bandar-e Deylam, Iran 39 D6
Bandar-e Khomeyni, Iran 39 D6
Bandar-e Lengeh, Iran 39 E7
Bandar-e Maqām, Iran 39 E7
Bandar-e Ma'shur, Iran 39 D6
Bandar-e Nakhīlū, Iran 39 E7
Bandar-e Rīg, Iran 39 D6
Bandar-e Torkeman, Iran 39 B7
Bandar Maharani = Muar, Malaysia 34 S15
Bandar Penggaram = Batu Pahat, Malaysia 34 T15
Bandar Seri Begawan, Brunei 32 C4
Bandawe, Malawi 47 G6
Bandeira, Pico da, Brazil 79 H10
Bandera, Argentina 80 B4
Bandera, U.S.A. 71 L5
Bandiagara, Mali 44 F4
Bandırma, Turkey 23 F4
Bandon, Ireland 13 E3
Bandon →, Ireland 13 E3
Bandundu, Zaïre 46 E3
Bandung, Indonesia 33 G12
Bandya, Australia 53 E3
Bāneh, Iran 38 C5
Banff, Canada 64 C5
Banff, U.K. 12 D6
Banff Nat. Park, Canada 64 C5
Banfora, Burkina Faso 44 F4
Bang Hieng →, Laos 34 D8
Bang Lamung, Thailand 34 F6
Bang Saphan, Thailand 34 G5
Bangalore, India 36 N10
Bangassou, C.A.R. 46 D4
Banggai, Kepulauan, Indonesia 33 E6
Banggi, P., Malaysia 32 C5
Banghāzī, Libya 45 B9
Bangil, Indonesia 33 G15
Bangka, P., Sulawesi, Indonesia 33 D7
Bangka, P., Sumatera, Indonesia 32 E3
Bangka, Selat, Indonesia 32 E3
Bangkalan, Indonesia 33 G15
Bangkinang, Indonesia 32 D2
Bangko, Indonesia 32 E2
Bangkok, Thailand 34 F6
Bangladesh ■, Asia 37 H17
Bangong Co, India 36 B11
Bangor, Down, U.K. 13 B6
Bangor, Gwynedd, U.K. 10 D3
Bangor, U.S.A. 63 D6
Bangued, Phil. 33 A6
Bangui, C.A.R. 46 D3
Bangweulu, L., Zambia 46 G6
Bani, Dom. Rep. 75 D10
Banī Sa'd, Iraq 38 C5
Banī Walīd, Libya 45 B7
Banīnah, Libya 45 B9
Bāniyās, Syria 38 C3
Banja Luka, Bos.-H. 20 B7
Banjar, Indonesia 33 G13
Banjarmasin, Indonesia 32 E4
Banjarnegara, Indonesia 33 G13
Banjul, Gambia 44 F1
Banka Banka, Australia 54 B1
Bankipore, India 37 G14
Banks I., B.C., Canada 64 C3
Banks I., N.W.T., Canada 60 A7
Banks Pen., N.Z. 51 K4
Banks Str., Australia 54 G4
Bankura, India 37 H15
Bann →, Down, U.K. 13 B5
Bann →, L'derry., U.K. 13 A5
Banning, U.S.A. 73 K5
Banningville = Bandundu, Zaïre 46 E3
Bannockburn, U.K. 12 E5
Bannu, Pakistan 36 C7
Banská Bystrica, Slovak Rep. 17 D9
Banská Štiavnica, Slovak Rep. 17 D9
Banswara, India 36 H9
Banten, Indonesia 33 G12
Bantry, Ireland 13 E2
Bantry B., Ireland 13 E2
Bantul, Indonesia 33 G14
Banu, Afghan. 36 B6
Banyak, Kepulauan, Indonesia 32 D1
Banyo, Cameroon 44 G7
Banyumas, Indonesia 33 G13
Banyuwangi, Indonesia 33 H16
Banzare Coast, Antarctica 5 C9
Banzyville = Mobayi, Zaïre 46 D4
Baoding, China 31 C6
Baoji, China 30 C5
Baoshan, China 30 D4
Baotou, China 31 B6
Bapatla, India 37 M12
Bāqerābād, Iran 39 C6
Ba'qūbah, Iraq 38 C5
Bar, Montenegro 21 C8
Bar Harbor, U.S.A. 63 D6
Bar-le-Duc, France 18 B6
Barabai, Indonesia 32 E5
Barabinsk, Russia 24 D8
Baraboo, U.S.A. 70 D10
Baracaldo, Spain 19 A4
Baracoa, Cuba 75 C10
Baraga, U.S.A. 70 B10
Barahona, Dom. Rep. 75 D10
Barail Range, India 37 G18
Barakhola, India 37 G18
Barakpur, India 37 H16
Barakula, Australia 55 D5
Baralaba, Australia 54 C4
Baralzon L., Canada 65 B9
Baramula, India 36 B9
Baran, India 36 G10
Baranavichy = Baranovichi, Belorussia 22 D4
Baranof I., U.S.A. 64 B1
Baranovichi, Belorussia 22 D4
Barão de Melgaço, Brazil 78 F6
Barapasi, Indonesia 33 E9
Barat Daya, Kepulauan, Indonesia 33 F7
Barataria B., U.S.A. 71 L10
Barbacena, Brazil 79 H10
Barbacoas, Colombia 78 C3
Barbados ■, W. Indies 74 P22
Barberton, S. Africa 49 D5
Barberton, U.S.A. 68 E5
Barbourville, U.S.A. 69 G4
Barbuda, W. Indies 74 K20
Barcaldine, Australia 54 C4
Barcelona, Spain 19 B7
Barcelona, Venezuela 78 A6
Barcelos, Brazil 78 D6
Barcoo →, Australia 54 D3
Bardai, Chad 45 D8
Barddhaman, India 37 H15
Bardera, Somali Rep. 40 G3
Bardia, Libya 45 B9
Bardsey I., U.K. 10 E3
Bardstown, U.S.A. 68 G3
Bareilly, India 36 E11
Barents Sea, Arctic 4 B9
Barentu, Eritrea 45 E12
Bargal, Somali Rep. 40 E5
Bargara, Australia 54 C5
Barguzin, Russia 25 D11
Barhi, India 37 G14
Bari, Italy 20 D7
Bari Doab, Pakistan 36 D8
Barīm, Yemen 40 E3
Barinas, Venezuela 78 B4
Baring, C., Canada 60 B8
Bâris, Egypt 45 D11
Barisal, Bangla. 37 H17
Barisan, Bukit, Indonesia 32 E2
Barito →, Indonesia 32 E4
Barkley Sound, Canada 64 D3
Barkly Downs, Australia 54 C2
Barkly East, S. Africa 48 E4
Barkly Tableland, Australia 54 B2
Barkly West, S. Africa 48 D3
Barkol, China 30 B4
Barksdale, U.S.A. 71 L4
Barlee, L., Australia 53 E2
Barlee, Mt., Australia 53 D4
Barletta, Italy 20 D7
Barlow L., Canada 65 A8
Barmedman, Australia 55 E4
Barmer, India 36 G7
Barmera, Australia 55 E3
Barmouth, U.K. 10 E3
Barnard Castle, U.K. 10 C6
Barnato, Australia 55 E3
Barnaul, Russia 24 D9
Barnesville, U.S.A. 69 J3
Barnet, U.K. 11 F7
Barneveld, Neths. 15 B5
Barngo, Australia 54 D4
Barnhart, U.S.A. 71 K4
Barnsley, U.K. 10 D6
Barnstaple, U.K. 11 F3
Barnsville, U.S.A. 70 B6
Baro, Nigeria 44 G6
Baroda = Vadodara, India 36 H8
Baroe, S. Africa 48 E3
Baron Ra., Australia 52 D4
Barpeta, India 37 F17
Barques, Pte. aux, U.S.A. 68 C4
Barquisimeto, Venezuela 78 A5
Barra, Brazil 79 F10
Barra, U.K. 12 E1
Barra, Sd. of, U.K. 12 D1
Barra do Corda, Brazil 79 E9
Barra do Piraí, Brazil 79 H10
Barra Falsa, Pta. da, Mozam. 49 C6
Barra Hd., U.K. 12 E1
Barraba, Australia 55 E5
Barrackpur = Barakpur, India 37 H16
Barranca, Lima, Peru 78 F3
Barranca, Loreto, Peru 78 D3
Barrancabermeja, Colombia 78 B4
Barrancas, Venezuela 78 B6
Barrancos, Portugal 19 C2
Barranqueras, Argentina 80 B5
Barranquilla, Colombia 78 A4
Barras, Brazil 79 D10
Barraute, Canada 62 C4
Barre, Mass., U.S.A. 67 B12
Barre, Vt., U.S.A. 68 C9
Barreiras, Brazil 79 F10
Barreirinhas, Brazil 79 D10
Barreiro, Portugal 19 C1
Barreiros, Brazil 79 E11
Barren, Nosy, Madag. 49 B7
Barren I., India 34 F2
Barretos, Brazil 79 H9
Barrhead, Canada 64 C6
Barrie, Canada 62 D4
Barrier Ra., Australia 55 E3
Barrière, Canada 64 C4
Barrington L., Canada 65 B8
Barrington Tops, Australia 55 E5
Barringun, Australia 55 D4
Barrow, U.S.A. 60 A4
Barrow →, Ireland 13 D4
Barrow, C., U.S.A. 58 B4
Barrow Creek, Australia 54 C1
Barrow I., Australia 52 D2
Barrow-in-Furness, U.K. 10 C4
Barrow Pt., Australia 54 A3
Barrow Ra., Australia 53 E4
Barrow Str., Canada 4 B3
Barry, U.K. 11 F4
Barry's Bay, Canada 62 C4
Barsham, Syria 38 C4
Barsi, India 36 K9
Barsoi, India 37 G15
Barstow, Calif., U.S.A. 73 J5
Barstow, Tex., U.S.A. 71 K3
Bartica, Guyana 78 B7
Bartlesville, U.S.A. 71 G7
Bartlett, U.S.A. 71 K6
Bartlett, L., Canada 64 A5
Barton, Australia 53 F5
Barton upon Humber, U.K. 10 D7
Bartow, U.S.A. 69 M5
Barysaw = Borisov, Belorussia 22 D4
Barzān, Iraq 38 B5
Bas-Rhin □, France 18 B7
Bāsa'idū, Iran 39 E7
Basankusa, Zaïre 46 D3
Basel, Switz. 16 E3
Bāshī, Iran 39 D6
Bashkir Republic □, Russia 22 D10
Bashkortostan = Bashkir Republic □, Russia 22 D10
Basilan, Phil. 33 C6
Basilan Str., Phil. 33 C6
Basildon, U.K. 11 F8
Basilicata □, Italy 20 D7
Basim = Washim, India 36 J10
Basin, U.S.A. 72 D9
Basingstoke, U.K. 11 F6
Baskatong, Rés., Canada 62 C4
Basle = Basel, Switz. 16 E3
Basoka, Zaïre 46 D4
Basongo, Zaïre 46 E4
Basque Provinces = País Vasco □, Spain 19 A4
Basra = Al Başrah, Iraq 38 D5
Bass Rock, U.K. 12 E6
Bass Str., Australia 54 F4
Bassano, Canada 64 C6
Bassano del Grappa, Italy 20 B4
Bassas da India, Ind. Oc. 47 J7
Basse-Terre, Guadeloupe 74 M20
Bassein, Burma 37 L19
Basseterre, St. Christopher-Nevis 74 K19
Bassett, Nebr., U.S.A. 70 D5
Bassett, Va., U.S.A. 69 G6
Bassigny, France 18 C6
Bassikounou, Mauritania 44 E3
Bastak, Iran 39 E7
Baştām, Iran 39 B7
Bastar, India 37 K12
Basti, India 37 F13
Bastia, France 18 E9
Bastogne, Belgium 15 D5
Bastrop, U.S.A. 71 K6
Bat Yam, Israel 41 C3
Bata, Eq. Guin. 46 D1
Bataan, Phil. 33 B6
Batabanó, Cuba 75 C8
Batabanó, G. de, Cuba 75 C8
Batac, Phil. 33 A6
Batagoy, Russia 25 C14
Batalha, Portugal 19 C1
Batamay, Russia 25 C13
Batang, Indonesia 33 G13
Batangafo, C.A.R. 45 G8
Batangas, Phil. 33 B6
Batanta, Indonesia 33 E8
Batavia, U.S.A. 68 D6
Batchelor, Australia 52 B5
Bateman's B., Australia 55 F5
Batemans Bay, Australia 55 F5
Bates Ra., Australia 53 E3
Batesburg, U.S.A. 69 J5
Batesville, Ark., U.S.A. 71 H9
Batesville, Miss., U.S.A. 71 H10
Batesville, Tex., U.S.A. 71 L5
Bath, U.K. 11 F5
Bath, Maine, U.S.A. 63 D6
Bath, N.Y., U.S.A. 68 D7
Bathgate, U.K. 12 F5
Bathurst = Banjul, Gambia 44 F1
Bathurst, Australia 55 E4
Bathurst, Canada 63 C6
Bathurst, S. Africa 48 E4
Bathurst, C., Canada 60 A7
Bathurst B., Australia 54 A3
Bathurst Harb., Australia 54 G4
Bathurst I., Australia 52 B5
Bathurst I., Canada 4 B2
Bathurst Inlet, Canada 60 B9
Batlow, Australia 55 F4
Batna, Algeria 44 A6
Baton Rouge, U.S.A. 71 K9
Batouri, Cameroon 46 D2
Battambang, Cambodia 34 F7
Batticaloa, Sri Lanka 36 R12
Battle, U.K. 11 G8
Battle →, Canada 65 C7
Battle Camp, Australia 54 B3
Battle Creek, U.S.A. 68 D3
Battle Harbour, Canada 63 B8
Battle Lake, U.S.A. 70 B7
Battle Mountain, U.S.A. 72 F5
Battleford, Canada 65 C7
Batu, Ethiopia 40 F2
Batu, Kepulauan, Indonesia 32 E1
Batu Gajah, Malaysia 34 Q14
Batu Is. = Batu, Kepulauan, Indonesia 32 E1
Batu Pahat, Malaysia 34 T15
Batuata, Indonesia 33 F6
Batumi, Georgia 23 F7
Baturaja, Indonesia 32 E2
Baturité, Brazil 79 D11
Bau, Malaysia 32 D4
Baubau, Indonesia 33 F6
Bauchi, Nigeria 44 F6
Baudette, U.S.A. 70 A7
Bauer, C., Australia 55 E1
Bauhinia Downs, Australia 54 C4
Bauru, Brazil 79 H9
Baús, Brazil 79 G8
Bautzen, Germany 16 C7
Bavānāt, Iran 39 D7
Bavaria = Bayern □, Germany 16 D5
Bawdwin, Burma 37 H20
Bawean, Indonesia 32 F4
Bawku, Ghana 44 F4

Bawlake

Bawlake, *Burma* 37 K20
Baxley, *U.S.A.* 69 K4
Baxter Springs, *U.S.A.* . 71 G7
Bay, L. de, *Phil.* 33 B6
Bay Bulls, *Canada* 63 C9
Bay City, *Mich., U.S.A.* . 68 D4
Bay City, *Oreg., U.S.A.* . 72 D2
Bay City, *Tex., U.S.A.* .. 71 L7
Bay de Verde, *Canada* . 63 C9
Bay Minette, *U.S.A.* ... 69 K2
Bay St. Louis, *U.S.A.* .. 71 K10
Bay Springs, *U.S.A.* ... 71 K10
Bay View, *N.Z.* 51 H6
Bayamo, *Cuba* 75 C9
Bayan Har Shan, *China* 30 C4
Bayan Hot = Alxa
Zuoqi, *China* 30 C5
Bayanaul, *Kazakhstan* . 24 D8
Bayanhongor,
Mongolia 30 B5
Bayard, *U.S.A.* 70 E3
Baybay, *Phil.* 33 B6
Bayern □, *Germany* ... 16 D5
Bayeux, *France* 18 B3
Bayfield, *U.S.A.* 70 B9
Baykal, Oz., *Russia* .. 25 D11
Baykit, *Russia* 25 C10
Baykonur, *Kazakhstan* 24 E7
Baymak, *Russia* 22 D10
Baynes Mts., *Namibia* 48 B1
Bayombong, *Phil.* ... 33 A6
Bayonne, *France* 18 E3
Bayovar, *Peru* 78 E2
Bayram-Ali,
Turkmenistan 24 F7
Bayreuth, *Germany* .. 16 D5
Bayrūt, *Lebanon* 41 B4
Bayt Lahm, *Jordan* ... 41 D4
Baytown, *U.S.A.* 71 L7
Baza, *Spain* 19 D4
Bazaruto, I. do,
Mozam. 49 C6
Bazmān, Kūh-e, *Iran* . 39 D9
Beach, *U.S.A.* 70 B3
Beachport, *Australia* .. 55 F2
Beachy Hd., *U.K.* 11 G8
Beacon, *Australia* 53 F2
Beacon, *U.S.A.* 68 E9
Beaconia, *Canada* ... 65 C9
Beagle, Canal,
S. Amer. 80 G3
Beagle Bay, *Australia* . 52 C3
Bealanana, *Madag.* .. 49 A8
Bear I., *Ireland* 13 E2
Bear L., *B.C., Canada* . 64 B3
Bear L., *Man., Canada* 65 B9
Bear L., *U.S.A.* 72 E8
Bearcreek, *U.S.A.* ... 72 D9
Beardmore, *Canada* .. 62 C2
Beardmore Glacier,
Antarctica 5 E11
Beardstown, *U.S.A.* .. 70 F9
Béarn, *France* 18 E3
Bearpaw Mts., *U.S.A.* . 72 B9
Bearskin Lake, *Canada* 62 B1
Beatrice, *U.S.A.* 70 E6
Beatrice, C., *Australia* 54 A2
Beatton →, *Canada* . 64 B4
Beatton River, *Canada* 64 B4
Beatty, *U.S.A.* 73 H5
Beauce, Plaine de la,
France 18 B4
Beauceville, *Canada* . 63 C5
Beaudesert, *Australia* 55 D5
Beaufort, *Malaysia* .. 32 C5
Beaufort, *N.C., U.S.A.* . 69 H7
Beaufort, *S.C., U.S.A.* . 69 J5
Beaufort Sea, *Arctic* .. 4 B1
Beaufort West,
S. Africa 48 E3
Beauharnois, *Canada* . 62 C5
Beaulieu →, *Canada* . 64 A6
Beauly, *U.K.* 12 D4
Beauly →, *U.K.* 12 D4
Beaumaris, *U.K.* 10 D3
Beaumont, *U.S.A.* ... 71 K7
Beauséjour, *Canada* . 65 C9
Beauvais, *France* 18 B5
Beauval, *Canada* 65 B7
Beaver, *Alaska, U.S.A.* 60 B5
Beaver, *Okla., U.S.A.* . 71 G4
Beaver, *Utah, U.S.A.* . 73 G7
Beaver →, *B.C.,*
Canada 64 B4
Beaver →, *Ont.,*
Canada 62 A2
Beaver →, *Sask.,*
Canada 65 B7
Beaver City, *U.S.A.* .. 70 E5
Beaver Dam, *U.S.A.* .. 70 D10
Beaver Falls, *U.S.A.* .. 68 E5
Beaver Hill L., *Canada* 65 C10
Beaver I., *U.S.A.* 68 C3
Beaverhill L., *Alta.,*
Canada 64 C6
Beaverhill L., *N.W.T.,*
Canada 65 A8
Beaverlodge, *Canada* . 64 B5
Beavermouth, *Canada* 64 C5
Beaverstone →,
Canada 62 B2
Beawar, *India* 36 F9
Beboa, *Madag.* 49 B7
Beccles, *U.K.* 11 E9
Bečej, *Serbia, Yug.* .. 21 B9
Béchar, *Algeria* 44 B4
Beckley, *U.S.A.* 68 G5
Bedford, *Canada* 62 C5
Bedford, *S. Africa* ... 48 E4
Bedford, *U.K.* 11 E7
Bedford, *Ind., U.S.A.* . 68 F2

Bedford, *Iowa, U.S.A.* . 70 E7
Bedford, *Ohio, U.S.A.* . 68 E5
Bedford, *Va., U.S.A.* .. 68 G6
Bedford, C., *Australia* 54 B4
Bedford Downs,
Australia 52 C4
Bedfordshire □, *U.K.* . 11 E7
Bedourie, *Australia* .. 54 C2
Beech Grove, *U.S.A.* . 68 F2
Beechy, *Canada* 65 C7
Beenleigh, *Australia* . 55 D5
Be'er Menuha, *Israel* . 38 D2
Be'er Sheva', *Israel* .. 41 D3
Beersheba = Be'er
Sheva', *Israel* 41 D3
Beeston, *U.K.* 10 E6
Beetaloo, *Australia* .. 54 B1
Beeville, *U.S.A.* 71 L6
Befale, *Zaïre* 46 D4
Befandriana, *Madag.* . 49 C7
Befotaka, *Madag.* ... 49 C8
Bega, *Australia* 55 F4
Behābād, *Iran* 39 C8
Behara, *Madag.* 49 C8
Behbehān, *Iran* 39 D6
Behshahr, *Iran* 39 B7
Bei Jiang →, *China* .. 31 D6
Bei'an, *China* 31 B7
Beihai, *China* 31 D5
Beijing, *China* 31 C6
Beilen, *Neths.* 15 B6
Beilpajah, *Australia* .. 55 E3
Beira, *Mozam.* 47 H6
Beira-Alta, *Portugal* .. 19 B2
Beira-Baixa, *Portugal* . 19 B2
Beira-Litoral, *Portugal* 19 B1
Beirut = Bayrūt,
Lebanon 41 B4
Beitbridge, *Zimbabwe* 47 J6
Beja, *Portugal* 19 C2
Béja, *Tunisia* 44 A6
Bejaia, *Algeria* 44 A6
Béjar, *Spain* 19 B3
Bejestān, *Iran* 39 C8
Bekasi, *Indonesia* ... 33 G12
Békéscsaba, *Hungary* 17 E10
Bekily, *Madag.* 49 C8
Bekok, *Malaysia* 34 S16
Bela, *India* 37 G13
Bela, *Pakistan* 36 F5
Bela Crkva,
Serbia, Yug. 21 B9
Bela Vista, *Brazil* ... 80 A5
Bela Vista, *Mozam.* .. 49 D5
Belarus =
Belorussia ■, *Europe* 22 D4
Belau ■, *Pac. Oc.* ... 56 G5
Belavenona, *Madag.* . 49 C8
Belawan, *Indonesia* .. 32 D1
Belaya →, *Russia* ... 22 C9
Belaya Tserkov,
Ukraine 23 E5
Belcher Is., *Canada* .. 61 C12
Belebey, *Russia* 22 D9
Belém, *Brazil* 79 D9
Belén, *Paraguay* 80 A5
Belet Uen, *Somali Rep.* 40 G4
Belev, *Russia* 22 D6
Belfast, *S. Africa* ... 49 D5
Belfast, *U.K.* 13 B6
Belfast, *U.S.A.* 63 D6
Belfast □, *U.K.* 13 B6
Belfast L., *U.K.* 13 B6
Belfield, *U.S.A.* 70 B3
Belfort, *France* 18 C7
Belfort, Territoire de □,
France 18 C7
Belfry, *U.S.A.* 72 D9
Belgaum, *India* 36 M9
Belgium ■, *Europe* .. 15 C4
Belgorod, *Russia* ... 23 D6
Belgorod-Dnestrovskiy,
Ukraine 23 E5
Belgrade = Beograd,
Serbia, Yug. 21 B9
Belgrade, *U.S.A.* 72 D8
Belhaven, *U.S.A.* ... 69 H7
Beli Drim →, *Europe* 21 C9
Belinga, *Gabon* 46 D2
Belinyu, *Indonesia* .. 32 E3
Beliton Is. = Belitung,
Indonesia 32 E3
Belitung, *Indonesia* . 32 E3
Belize ■, *Cent. Amer.* 74 D7
Belize City, *Belize* ... 74 D7
Belkovskiy, Ostrov,
Russia 25 B14
Bell →, *Canada* 62 C4
Bell Bay, *Australia* .. 54 G4
Bell-Irving →, *Canada* 64 B3
Bell Peninsula, *Canada* 61 B11
Bell Ville, *Argentina* . 80 C4
Bella Bella, *Canada* . 64 C3
Bella Coola, *Canada* . 64 C3
Bella Unión, *Uruguay* 80 C5
Bella Vista, *Argentina* 80 B5
Bellaire, *U.S.A.* 68 E5
Bellary, *India* 36 M10
Bellata, *Australia* ... 55 D4
Belle Fourche, *U.S.A.* 70 C3
Belle Fourche →,
U.S.A. 70 C3
Belle Glade, *U.S.A.* .. 69 M5
Belle-Ile, *France* 18 C2
Belle Isle, Str. of,
Canada 63 B8
Belle Plaine, *Iowa,*
U.S.A. 70 E8
Belle Plaine, *Minn.,*
U.S.A. 70 C8

Belledune, *Canada* .. 63 C6
Bellefontaine, *U.S.A.* 68 E4
Bellefonte, *U.S.A.* ... 68 E7
Belleoram, *Canada* .. 63 C8
Belleville, *Canada* ... 62 D4
Belleville, *Ill., U.S.A.* . 70 F10
Belleville, *Kans., U.S.A.* 70 F6
Bellevue, *Canada* ... 64 D6
Bellevue, *U.S.A.* 72 E6
Bellin, *Canada* 61 B13
Bellingen, *Australia* . 55 E5
Bellingham, *U.S.A.* .. 72 B2
Bellingshausen Sea,
Antarctica 5 C17
Bellinzona, *Switz.* ... 16 E4
Bellows Falls, *U.S.A.* . 68 D9
Belluno, *Italy* 20 A5
Bellville, *U.S.A.* 71 L6
Bélmez, *Spain* 19 C3
Belmont, *Australia* .. 55 E5
Belmont, *S. Africa* .. 48 D3
Belmonte, *Brazil* ... 79 G11
Belmopan, *Belize* ... 74 D7
Belmullet, *Ireland* .. 13 B2
Belo Horizonte, *Brazil* 79 G10
Belo-sur-Mer, *Madag.* 49 C7
Belo-Tsiribihina,
Madag. 49 B7
Belogorsk, *Russia* .. 25 D13
Beloha, *Madag.* 49 D8
Beloit, *Kans., U.S.A.* . 70 F5
Beloit, *Wis., U.S.A.* .. 70 D10
Belomorsk, *Russia* .. 22 B5
Belonia, *India* 37 H17
Beloretsk, *Russia* ... 22 D10
Belorussia ■, *Europe* 22 D4
Belovo, *Russia* 24 D9
Beloye, Oz., *Russia* . 22 B6
Beloye More, *Russia* . 22 A6
Belozersk, *Russia* ... 22 B6
Beltana, *Australia* ... 55 E2
Belterra, *Brazil* 79 D8
Belton, *S.C., U.S.A.* .. 69 H4
Belton, *Tex., U.S.A.* .. 71 K6
Belton Res., *U.S.A.* .. 71 K6
Beltsy, *Moldavia* ... 23 E4
Belturbet, *Ireland* ... 13 B4
Belukha, *Russia* 24 E9
Beluran, *Malaysia* ... 32 C5
Belvidere, *U.S.A.* ... 70 D10
Belyando →,
Australia 54 C4
Belyy, Ostrov, *Russia* 24 B8
Belyy Yar, *Russia* ... 24 D9
Belzoni, *U.S.A.* 71 J9
Bemaraha,
Lembalemban' i,
Madag. 49 B7
Bemarivo, *Madag.* .. 49 C7
Bemarivo →, *Madag.* 49 B8
Bemavo, *Madag.* ... 49 C8
Bembéréke, *Benin* .. 44 F5
Bemidji, *U.S.A.* 70 B7
Ben, *Iran* 39 C6
Ben Cruachan, *U.K.* . 12 E3
Ben Dearg, *U.K.* 12 D4
Ben Gardane, *Tunisia* 45 B7
Ben Hope, *U.K.* 12 C4
Ben Lawers, *U.K.* ... 12 E4
Ben Lomond, *N.S.W.,*
Australia 55 E5
Ben Lomond, *Tas.,*
Australia 54 G4
Ben Lomond, *U.K.* .. 12 E4
Ben Macdhui, *U.K.* .. 12 D5
Ben Mhor, *U.K.* 12 D1
Ben More, *Central,*
U.K. 12 E4
Ben More, *Strath., U.K.* 12 E2
Ben More Assynt, *U.K.* 12 C4
Ben Nevis, *U.K.* 12 E3
Ben Vorlich, *U.K.* ... 12 E4
Ben Wyvis, *U.K.* 12 D4
Bena, *Nigeria* 44 F6
Bena Dibele, *Zaïre* .. 46 E4
Benagerie, *Australia* . 55 E3
Benalla, *Australia* ... 55 F4
Benambra, Mt.,
Australia 55 F4
Benares = Varanasi,
India 37 G13
Benavides, *U.S.A.* ... 71 M5
Benbecula, *U.K.* 12 D1
Benbonyathe, *Australia* 55 E2
Bencubbin, *Australia* 53 F2
Bend, *U.S.A.* 72 D3
Bender Beila,
Somali Rep. 40 F5
Bendering, *Australia* . 53 F2
Bendery, *Moldavia* .. 23 E4
Bendigo, *Australia* .. 55 F3
Benē Beraq, *Israel* .. 41 C3
Benenitra, *Madag.* .. 49 C8
Benevento, *Italy* 20 D6
Bengal, Bay of,
Ind. Oc. 37 K16
Bengbu, *China* 31 C6
Benghazi = Banghāzī,
Libya 45 B9
Bengkalis, *Indonesia* . 32 D2
Bengkulu, *Indonesia* . 32 E2
Bengkulu □, *Indonesia* 32 E2
Bengough, *Canada* .. 65 D7
Benguela, *Angola* ... 47 G2
Benguérua, I., *Mozam.* 49 C6
Beni, *Zaïre* 46 D5
Beni →, *Bolivia* 78 F5
Beni Abbès, *Algeria* . 44 B4
Beni Mazâr, *Egypt* .. 45 C11
Beni Mellal, *Morocco* 44 B3
Beni Ounif, *Algeria* .. 44 B4
Beni Suef, *Egypt* 45 C11

Beniah L., *Canada* ... 64 A6
Benidorm, *Spain* ... 19 C5
Benin ■, *W. Afr.* 44 G5
Benin, Bight of, *W. Afr.* 44 H5
Benin City, *Nigeria* .. 44 G6
Benjamin Constant,
Brazil 78 D4
Benkelman, *U.S.A.* .. 70 E4
Benlidi, *Australia* ... 54 C3
Bennett, *Canada* 64 B2
Bennett, L., *Australia* 52 D5
Bennett, Ostrov, *Russia* 25 B15
Bennettsville, *U.S.A.* 69 H6
Bennington, *U.S.A.* . 68 D9
Benoni, *S. Africa* 49 D4
Benson, *U.S.A.* 73 L8
Bent, *Iran* 39 E8
Benteng, *Indonesia* . 33 F6
Bentinck I., *Australia* 54 B2
Benton, *Ark., U.S.A.* . 71 H8
Benton, *Ill., U.S.A.* .. 70 F10
Benton Harbor, *U.S.A.* 68 D2
Bentung, *Malaysia* .. 34 R14
Benue →, *Nigeria* .. 44 G6
Benxi, *China* 31 B7
Beo, *Indonesia* 33 D7
Beograd, *Serbia, Yug.* 21 B9
Beowawe, *U.S.A.* ... 72 F5
Beppu, *Japan* 29 H5
Berau, Teluk, *Indonesia* 33 E8
Berber, *Sudan* 45 E11
Berbera, *Somali Rep.* 40 E4
Berbérati, *C.A.R.* ... 46 D3
Berbice →, *Guyana* . 78 B7
Berdichev, *Ukraine* . 23 E4
Berdsk, *Russia* 24 D9
Berdyansk, *Ukraine* . 23 E6
Berdyanskiy =
Berdichev, *Ukraine* 23 E4
Berea, *U.S.A.* 68 G3
Berebere, *Indonesia* . 33 D7
Bereda, *Somali Rep.* . 40 E5
Berekum, *Ghana* 44 G4
Berens →, *Canada* . 65 C9
Berens I., *Canada* ... 65 C9
Berens River, *Canada* 65 C9
Berevo, Mahajanga,
Madag. 49 B7
Berevo, Toliara,
Madag. 49 B7
Berezina →,
Belorussia 22 D5
Berezniki, *Russia* ... 24 D6
Berezovo, *Russia* ... 22 B11
Bérgamo, *Italy* 20 B3
Bergen, *Neths.* 15 B4
Bergen, *Norway* 9 F8
Bergen-op-Zoom,
Neths. 15 C4
Bergerac, *France* ... 18 D4
Bergum, *Neths.* 15 A5
Bergville, *S. Africa* .. 49 D4
Berhala, Selat,
Indonesia 32 E2
Berhampore =
Baharampur, *India* . 37 G16
Berhampur, *India* ... 37 K14
Bering Sea, *Pac. Oc.* . 60 C1
Bering Str., *U.S.A.* ... 60 B3
Beringen, *Belgium* .. 15 C5
Beringovskiy, *Russia* . 25 C18
Berja, *Spain* 19 D4
Berkeley, *U.S.A.* 72 H2
Berkeley Springs,
U.S.A. 68 F6
Berkner I., *Antarctica* 5 D18
Berkshire □, *U.K.* ... 11 F6
Berland →, *Canada* . 64 C5
Berlin, *Germany* 16 B6
Berlin, *Md., U.S.A.* .. 68 F8
Berlin, *N.H., U.S.A.* .. 68 C10
Berlin, *Wis., U.S.A.* .. 68 D1
Bermejo →, *Formosa,*
Argentina 80 B5
Bermejo →,
San Juan, Argentina 80 C3
Bermuda ■, *Atl. Oc.* . 75 A12
Bern, *Switz.* 16 E3
Bernado, *U.S.A.* 73 J10
Bernalillo, *U.S.A.* ... 73 J10
Bernam →, *Malaysia* 34 R14
Bernardo de Irigoyen,
Argentina 80 B6
Bernburg, *Germany* . 16 C5
Berne = Bern, *Switz.* 16 E3
Bernier I., *Australia* .. 53 D1
Beroroha, *Madag.* .. 49 C8
Beroun, *Czech.* 16 D7
Berrechid, *Morocco* . 44 B3
Berri, *Australia* 55 E3
Berry, *Australia* 55 E5
Berry, *France* 18 C5
Berryville, *U.S.A.* ... 71 G8
Berthold, *U.S.A.* 70 A4
Berthoud, *U.S.A.* ... 70 E2
Bertoua, *Cameroon* . 46 D2
Bertrand, *U.S.A.* 70 E5
Berufjörður, *Iceland* . 8 D6
Berwick, *U.S.A.* 68 E7
Berwick-upon-Tweed,
U.K. 10 B5
Berwyn Mts., *U.K.* .. 10 E4
Besalampy, *Madag.* . 49 B7
Besançon, *France* ... 18 C7
Besar, *Indonesia* 32 E5
Beserah, *Malaysia* .. 34 R16
Besnard L., *Canada* .. 65 B7
Besor, N. →, *Egypt* . 41 D3
Bessarabiya, *Moldavia* 17 E14
Bessemer, *Ala., U.S.A.* 69 J2

Bessemer, *Mich.,*
U.S.A. 70 B9
Bet She'an, *Israel* ... 41 C4
Bet Shemesh, *Israel* . 41 D3
Betafo, *Madag.* 49 B8
Bétaré Oya, *Cameroon* 46 C2
Bethal, *S. Africa* 49 D4
Bethanien, *Namibia* . 48 D2
Bethany, *S. Africa* ... 48 D4
Bethany, *U.S.A.* 70 E7
Bethel, *U.S.A.* 60 B3
Bethlehem = Bayt
Lahm, *Jordan* 41 D4
Bethlehem, *S. Africa* . 49 D4
Bethlehem, *U.S.A.* .. 68 E8
Bethulie, *S. Africa* ... 48 E4
Béthune, *France* 18 A5
Betioky, *Madag.* 49 C7
Betong, *Thailand* ... 34 P14
Betoota, *Australia* ... 54 D3
Betroka, *Madag.* 49 C8
Betsiamites, *Canada* . 63 C6
Betsiamites →,
Canada 63 C6
Betsiboka →, *Madag.* 49 B8
Betsjoeanaland,
S. Africa 48 D3
Bettiah, *India* 37 F14
Betul, *India* 36 J10
Beulah, *U.S.A.* 70 B4
Beverley, *Australia* .. 53 F2
Beverley, *U.K.* 10 D7
Beverly, *U.S.A.* 72 C4
Beverly Hills, *U.S.A.* . 73 J4
Beverwijk, *Neths.* ... 15 B4
Beyānlū, *Iran* 38 C5
Beyla, *Guinea* 44 G3
Beyneu, *Kazakhstan* . 23 E10
Beypazarı, *Turkey* ... 23 F5
Beyşehir Gölü, *Turkey* 23 G5
Bezhitsa, *Russia* 22 D5
Béziers, *France* 18 E5
Bezwada =
Vijayawada, *India* . 37 L12
Bhachau, *India* 36 H7
Bhadrakh, *India* 37 J15
Bhadravati, *India* 36 N9
Bhagalpur, *India* 37 G15
Bhakra Dam, *India* .. 36 D10
Bhamo, *Burma* 37 G20
Bhandara, *India* 36 J11
Bhanrer Ra., *India* .. 36 H11
Bharat = India ■, *Asia* 36 K11
Bharatpur, *India* 36 F10
Bhatpara, *India* 37 H16
Bhaunagar =
Bhavnagar, *India* .. 36 J8
Bhavnagar, *India* ... 36 J8
Bhawanipatna, *India* 37 K12
Bhilsa = Vidisha, *India* 36 H10
Bhilwara, *India* 36 G9
Bhima →, *India* 36 L10
Bhimavaram, *India* .. 37 L12
Bhind, *India* 36 F11
Bhiwandi, *India* 36 K8
Bhiwani, *India* 36 E10
Bhola, *Bangla.* 37 H17
Bhopal, *India* 36 H10
Bhubaneshwar, *India* 37 J14
Bhuj, *India* 36 H6
Bhusaval, *India* 36 J9
Bhutan ■, *Asia* 37 F17
Biafra, B. of = Bonny,
Bight of, *Africa* ... 46 D1
Biak, *Indonesia* 33 E9
Biała Podlaska, *Poland* 17 B11
Białystok, *Poland* ... 17 B11
Biărjmand, *Iran* 39 B7
Biaro, *Indonesia* 33 D7
Biarritz, *France* 18 E3
Bibai, *Japan* 28 C10
Bibala, *Angola* 47 G2
Bibby I., *Canada* 65 A10
Biberach, *Germany* . 16 D4
Bibiani, *Ghana* 44 G4
Bic, *Canada* 63 C6
Bickerton I., *Australia* 54 A2
Bicknell, *Ind., U.S.A.* 68 F2
Bicknell, *Utah, U.S.A.* 73 G8
Bida, *Nigeria* 44 G6
Bidar, *India* 36 L10
Biddeford, *U.S.A.* ... 63 D5
Bideford, *U.K.* 11 F3
Bidon 5 = Poste
Maurice Cortier,
Algeria 44 D5
Bidor, *Malaysia* 34 Q14
Bié, Planalto de,
Angola 47 G3
Bieber, *U.S.A.* 72 F3
Biel, *Switz.* 16 E3
Bielé Karpaty, *Europe* 17 D8
Bielefeld, *Germany* . 16 B4
Biella, *Italy* 20 B3
Bielsko-Biała, *Poland* 17 D9
Bien Hoa, *Vietnam* .. 34 G9
Bienfait, *Canada* 65 D8
Bienne = Biel, *Switz.* 16 E3
Bienville, L., *Canada* . 62 A5
Biesiesfontein,
S. Africa 48 E2
Big →, *Canada* 63 B8
Big B., *Canada* 63 A7
Big Beaver, *Canada* . 65 D7
Big Belt Mts., *U.S.A.* 72 C8

Big Bend, *Swaziland* . 49 D5
Big Bend Nat. Park,
U.S.A. 71 L3
Big Black →, *U.S.A.* . 71 J9
Big Blue →, *U.S.A.* .. 70 F6
Big Cr. →, *Canada* .. 64 C4
Big Cypress Swamp,
U.S.A. 69 M5
Big Falls, *U.S.A.* 70 A8
Big Fork →, *U.S.A.* .. 70 A8
Big Horn Mts. =
Bighorn Mts., *U.S.A.* 72 D10
Big Lake, *U.S.A.* 71 K4
Big Muddy →, *U.S.A.* 70 A2
Big Pine, *U.S.A.* 73 H4
Big Piney, *U.S.A.* ... 72 E8
Big Quill L., *Canada* . 65 C8
Big Rapids, *U.S.A.* .. 68 D3
Big River, *Canada* ... 65 C7
Big Sable Pt., *U.S.A.* 68 C2
Big Sand L., *Canada* . 65 B9
Big Sandy, *U.S.A.* ... 72 B8
Big Sandy Cr. →,
U.S.A. 70 F3
Big Sioux →, *U.S.A.* 70 D6
Big Spring, *U.S.A.* ... 71 J4
Big Springs, *U.S.A.* . 70 E3
Big Stone City, *U.S.A.* 70 C6
Big Stone Gap, *U.S.A.* 69 G4
Big Stone L., *U.S.A.* . 70 C6
Big Timber, *U.S.A.* .. 72 D9
Big Trout L., *Canada* 62 B1
Bigfork, *U.S.A.* 72 B6
Biggar, *Canada* 65 C7
Biggar, *U.K.* 12 F5
Bigge I., *Australia* ... 52 B4
Biggenden, *Australia* 55 D5
Bighorn →, *U.S.A.* .. 72 C10
Bighorn →, *U.S.A.* .. 72 C10
Bighorn Mts., *U.S.A.* 72 D10
Bigorre, *France* 18 E4
Bigstone L., *Canada* . 65 C9
Bihać, *Bos.-H.* 20 B6
Bihar, *India* 37 G14
Bihar □, *India* 37 G14
Bijagós, Arquipélago
dos, *Guinea-Biss.* . 44 F1
Bijapur, *Karnataka,*
India 36 L9
Bijapur, *Mad. P., India* 37 K12
Bījār, *Iran* 38 C5
Bijeljina, *Bos.-H.* ... 21 B8
Bijnor, *India* 36 E11
Bikaner, *India* 36 E8
Bikfayyā, *Lebanon* .. 41 B4
Bikin, *Russia* 25 E14
Bikin →, *Russia* 28 A7
Bikini Atoll, *Pac. Oc.* 56 F8
Bila Tserkva = Belaya
Tserkov, *Ukraine* .. 23 E5
Bilara, *India* 36 F8
Bilaspur, *India* 37 H13
Bilauk Taungdan,
Thailand 34 F5
Bilbao, *Spain* 19 A4
Bilbo = Bilbao, *Spain* 19 A4
Bildudalur, *Iceland* .. 8 D2
Bilecik, *Turkey* 23 F5
Bilibino, *Russia* 25 C17
Bilir, *Russia* 25 C14
Bill, *U.S.A.* 70 D2
Billabalong, *Australia* 53 E2
Billiluna, *Australia* .. 52 C4
Billingham, *U.K.* 10 C6
Billings, *U.S.A.* 72 D9
Billiton Is. = Belitung,
Indonesia 32 E3
Bilma, *Niger* 45 E7
Biloela, *Australia* ... 54 C5
Biloxi, *U.S.A.* 71 K10
Bilpa Morea Claypan,
Australia 54 D2
Biltine, *Chad* 45 F9
Bilyana, *Australia* ... 54 B4
Bima, *Indonesia* 33 F5
Bimbo, *C.A.R.* 46 D3
Bina-Etawah, *India* .. 36 G11
Binalbagan, *Phil.* ... 33 B6
Binalong, *Australia* .. 55 E4
Bīnālūd, Kūh-e, *Iran* 39 B8
Binatang, *Malaysia* . 32 D4
Binbee, *Australia* ... 54 C4
Binche, *Belgium* 15 D4
Binda, *Australia* 55 D4
Bindle, *Australia* 55 D4
Bindura, *Zimbabwe* . 47 H6
Bingara, *N.S.W.,*
Australia 55 D5
Bingara, *Queens.,*
Australia 55 D3
Bingham, *U.S.A.* 63 C6
Bingham Canyon,
U.S.A. 72 F7
Binghamton, *U.S.A.* . 68 D8
Binh Dinh = An Nhon,
Vietnam 34 F10
Binh Son, *Vietnam* .. 34 E10
Binjai, *Indonesia* 32 D1
Binnaway, *Australia* . 55 E4
Binongko, *Indonesia* 33 F6
Binscarth, *Canada* .. 65 C8
Bintan, *Indonesia* ... 32 D2
Bintulu, *Malaysia* ... 32 D4
Bintuni, *Indonesia* .. 33 E8
Binzert = Bizerte,
Tunisia 44 A6
Bioko, Eq. Guin. 44 H6
Bir, *India* 36 K9
Bîr Abu Muḥammad,
Egypt 41 F3

Brazzaville

Bi'r ad Dabbāghāt, Jordan 41 E4
Bi'r al Butayyihāt, Jordan 41 F4
Bi'r al Mārī, Jordan 41 E4
Bi'r al Qattār, Jordan 41 F4
Bir Autrun, Sudan 45 E10
Bîr Beiḍa, Egypt 41 E3
Bîr el 'Abd, Egypt 41 D2
Bîr el Biarât, Egypt 41 F3
Bîr el Duweidar, Egypt 41 E1
Bîr el Garârât, Egypt 41 D2
Bîr el Heisi, Egypt 41 F3
Bîr el Jafir, Egypt 41 E1
Bîr el Mâlḥi, Egypt 41 E2
Bîr el Thamâda, Egypt 41 E2
Bîr Gebeil Ḥiṣn, Egypt 41 E2
Bi'r Ghadīr, Syria 41 A6
Bîr Ḥasana, Egypt 41 E2
Bi'r Jadīd, Iraq 38 C4
Bîr Kaseiba, Egypt 41 E2
Bîr Lahfân, Egypt 41 D2
Bîr Madkûr, Egypt 41 E1
Bir Mogreïn, Mauritania 44 C2
Bi'r Muṭribah, Kuwait 38 D5
Bîr Qaṭia, Egypt 41 E1
Bîr Ungât, Egypt 45 D11
Bira, Indonesia 33 E8
Birao, C.A.R. 45 F9
Birch Hills, Canada 65 C7
Birch I., Canada 65 C9
Birch L., N.W.T., Canada 64 A5
Birch L., Ont., Canada 62 B1
Birch L., U.S.A. 62 C1
Birch Mts., Canada 64 B6
Birch River, Canada 65 C8
Birchip, Australia 55 F3
Bird, Canada 65 B10
Bird City, U.S.A. 70 F4
Bird I., S. Africa 48 E2
Birdlip, U.K. 11 F5
Birdsville, Australia 54 D2
Birdum, Australia 52 C5
Birein, Israel 41 E3
Bireuen, Indonesia 32 C1
Birkenhead, U.K. 10 D4
Bîrlad, Romania 17 E13
Birmingham, U.K. 11 E6
Birmingham, U.S.A. 69 J2
Birmitrapur, India 37 H14
Birni Nkonni, Niger 44 F6
Birnin Kebbi, Nigeria 44 F5
Birobidzhan, Russia 25 E14
Birr, Ireland 13 C4
Birrie →, Australia 55 D4
Birsk, Russia 22 C10
Birtle, Canada 65 C8
Birur, India 36 N9
Bisa, Indonesia 33 E7
Bisbee, U.S.A. 73 L9
Biscay, B. of, Atl. Oc. 18 F4
Biscayne B., U.S.A. 69 N5
Biscoe Bay, Antarctica 5 D13
Biscoe Is., Antarctica 5 C17
Biscostasing, Canada 62 C3
Bishkek, Kirghizia 24 E8
Bisho, S. Africa 49 E4
Bishop, Calif., U.S.A. 73 H4
Bishop, Tex., U.S.A. 71 M6
Bishop Auckland, U.K. 10 C6
Bishop's Falls, Canada 63 C8
Bishop's Stortford, U.K. 11 F8
Biskra, Algeria 44 B6
Bislig, Phil. 33 C7
Bismarck, U.S.A. 70 B4
Bismarck Arch., Papua N. G. 56 H6
Bison, U.S.A. 70 C3
Bīsotūn, Iran 38 C5
Bispfors, Sweden 8 E14
Bissagos = Bijagós, Arquipélago dos, Guinea-Biss. 44 F1
Bissau, Guinea-Biss. 44 F1
Bissett, Canada 65 C9
Bistcho L., Canada 64 B5
Bistriţa, Romania 17 E12
Bistriţa →, Romania 17 E13
Bitam, Gabon 46 D2
Bitkine, Chad 45 F8
Bitlis, Turkey 23 G7
Bitola, Macedonia 21 D9
Bitolj = Bitola, Macedonia 21 D9
Bitter Creek, U.S.A. 72 F9
Bitter L. = Buheirat-Murrat-el-Kubra, Egypt 45 B11
Bitterfontein, S. Africa 48 E2
Bitterroot →, U.S.A. 72 C6
Bitterroot Range, U.S.A. 72 D6
Biu, Nigeria 45 F7
Biwa-Ko, Japan 29 G8
Biwabik, U.S.A. 70 B8
Biysk, Russia 24 D9
Bizana, S. Africa 49 E4
Bizen, Japan 29 G7
Bizerte, Tunisia 44 A6
Bjargtangar, Iceland 8 D1
Bjelovar, Croatia 20 B7
Bjørnøya, Arctic 4 B8
Black = Da →, Vietnam 34 B8
Black →, Ark., U.S.A. 71 H9
Black →, Wis., U.S.A. 70 D9
Black Diamond, Canada 64 C6
Black Forest = Schwarzwald, Germany 16 E4
Black Hills, U.S.A. 70 C3
Black I., Canada 65 C9
Black L., Canada 65 B7
Black L., U.S.A. 68 C3
Black Mesa, U.S.A. 71 G3
Black Mt. = Mynydd Du, U.K. 11 F4
Black Mts., U.K. 11 F4
Black Range, U.S.A. 73 K10
Black River, Jamaica 74 K16
Black River Falls, U.S.A. 70 C9
Black Sea, Europe 23 F6
Black Volta →, Africa 44 G4
Black Warrior →, U.S.A. 69 J2
Blackall, Australia 54 C4
Blackball, N.Z. 51 K3
Blackbull, Australia 54 B3
Blackburn, U.K. 10 D5
Blackduck, U.S.A. 70 B7
Blackfoot, U.S.A. 72 E7
Blackfoot →, U.S.A. 72 C7
Blackfoot Res., U.S.A. 72 E8
Blackie, Canada 64 C6
Blackpool, U.K. 10 D4
Blacks Harbour, Canada 63 C6
Blacksburg, U.S.A. 68 G5
Blacksod B., Ireland 13 B2
Blackstone, U.S.A. 68 G6
Blackstone →, Canada 64 A4
Blackstone Ra., Australia 53 E4
Blackville, Canada 63 C6
Blackwater, Australia 54 C4
Blackwater →, Ireland 13 E4
Blackwater →, U.K. 13 B5
Blackwater Cr. →, Australia 55 D3
Blackwell, U.S.A. 71 G6
Blaenau Ffestiniog, U.K. 10 E4
Blagodarnoye, Russia 23 E7
Blagoveshchensk, Russia 25 D13
Blaine, U.S.A. 72 B2
Blaine Lake, Canada 65 C7
Blair, U.S.A. 70 E6
Blair Athol, Australia 54 C4
Blair Atholl, U.K. 12 E5
Blairgowrie, U.K. 12 E5
Blairmore, Canada 64 D6
Blake Pt., U.S.A. 70 A10
Blakely, U.S.A. 69 K3
Blanc, Mont, Alps 18 D7
Blanca, B., Argentina 80 D4
Blanca Peak, U.S.A. 73 H11
Blanchard, U.S.A. 71 H6
Blanche, C., Australia 55 E1
Blanche, L., S. Austral., Australia 55 D2
Blanche, L., W. Austral., Australia 52 D3
Blanco, S. Africa 48 E3
Blanco, U.S.A. 71 K5
Blanco, C., U.S.A. 72 E1
Blanda →, Iceland 8 D4
Blandford Forum, U.K. 11 G5
Blanding, U.S.A. 73 H9
Blankenberge, Belgium 15 C3
Blantyre, Malawi 47 H6
Blarney, Ireland 13 E3
Blåvands Huk, Denmark 9 J10
Blaydon, U.K. 10 C6
Blayney, Australia 55 E4
Blaze, Pt., Australia 52 B5
Blednaya, Gora, Russia 24 B7
Bleiburg, Austria 16 E7
Blekinge län □, Sweden 9 H13
Blenheim, N.Z. 51 J4
Bletchley, U.K. 11 F7
Blida, Algeria 44 A5
Bligh Sound, N.Z. 51 L1
Blind River, Canada 62 C3
Blitar, Indonesia 33 H15
Blitta, Togo 44 G5
Block I., U.S.A. 68 E10
Blodgett Iceberg Tongue, Antarctica 5 C9
Bloemfontein, S. Africa 48 D4
Bloemhof, S. Africa 48 D4
Blois, France 18 C4
Blönduós, Iceland 8 D3
Bloodvein →, Canada 65 C9
Bloody Foreland, Ireland 13 A3
Bloomer, U.S.A. 70 C9
Bloomfield, Australia 54 B4
Bloomfield, Iowa, U.S.A. 70 E8
Bloomfield, N. Mex., U.S.A. 73 H10
Bloomfield, Nebr., U.S.A. 70 D6
Bloomington, Ill., U.S.A. 70 E10
Bloomington, Ind., U.S.A. 68 F2
Bloomsburg, U.S.A. 68 E7
Blora, Indonesia 33 G14
Blouberg, S. Africa 49 C4
Blountstown, U.S.A. 69 K3
Blue Island, U.S.A. 68 E2
Blue Lake, U.S.A. 72 F2
Blue Mesa Res., U.S.A. 73 G10
Blue Mts., Oreg., U.S.A. 72 D4
Blue Mts., Pa., U.S.A. 68 E7
Blue Mud B., Australia 54 A2
Blue Nile = An Nîl el Azraq □, Sudan 45 F11
Blue Nile = Nîl el Azraq →, Sudan 45 E11
Blue Rapids, U.S.A. 70 F6
Blue Ridge Mts., U.S.A. 69 G5
Blue Stack Mts., Ireland 13 B3
Blueberry →, Canada 64 B4
Bluefield, U.S.A. 68 G5
Bluefields, Nic. 75 E8
Bluff, Australia 54 C4
Bluff, N.Z. 51 M2
Bluff, U.S.A. 73 H9
Bluff Knoll, Australia 53 F2
Bluff Pt., Australia 53 E1
Bluffton, U.S.A. 68 E3
Blumenau, Brazil 80 B7
Blunt, U.S.A. 70 C4
Bly, U.S.A. 72 E3
Blyth, U.K. 10 B6
Blyth Bridge, U.K. 10 E5
Blythe, U.S.A. 73 K6
Bo, S. Leone 44 G2
Bo Duc, Vietnam 34 G9
Bo Hai, China 31 C6
Boa Vista, Brazil 78 C6
Boatman, Australia 55 D4
Bobadah, Australia 55 E4
Bobbili, India 37 K13
Bobcaygeon, Canada 62 D4
Bobo-Dioulasso, Burkina Faso 44 F4
Bóbr →, Poland 16 B7
Bobraomby, Tanjon' i, Madag. 49 A8
Bobruysk, Belorussia 22 D4
Bôca do Acre, Brazil 78 E5
Boca Raton, U.S.A. 69 M5
Bocaiúva, Brazil 79 G10
Bocanda, Ivory C. 44 G4
Bocaranga, C.A.R. 45 G8
Bocholt, Germany 16 C3
Bochum, Germany 16 C3
Boda, C.A.R. 46 D3
Bodaybo, Russia 25 D12
Boddington, Australia 53 F2
Boden, Sweden 8 D16
Bodensee, Europe 16 E4
Bodhan, India 36 K10
Bodmin, U.K. 11 G3
Bodmin Moor, U.K. 11 G3
Bodrog →, Hungary 17 D10
Boegoebergdam, S. Africa 48 D3
Boende, Zaïre 46 E4
Boerne, U.S.A. 71 L5
Boffa, Guinea 44 F2
Bogalusa, U.S.A. 71 K10
Bogan Gate, Australia 55 E4
Bogantungan, Australia 54 C4
Bogata, U.S.A. 71 J7
Boggabilla, Australia 55 D5
Boggabri, Australia 55 E5
Boggeragh Mts., Ireland 13 D3
Bognor Regis, U.K. 11 G7
Bogo, Phil. 33 B6
Bogong, Mt., Australia 55 F4
Bogor, Indonesia 33 G12
Bogorodskoye, Russia 25 D15
Bogotá, Colombia 78 C4
Bogotol, Russia 24 D9
Bogra, Bangla. 37 G16
Boguchany, Russia 25 D10
Bogué, Mauritania 44 E2
Bohemia Downs, Australia 52 C4
Bohemian Forest = Böhmerwald, Germany 16 D6
Bohena Cr. →, Australia 55 E4
Böhmerwald, Germany 16 D6
Bohol, Phil. 33 C6
Bohol Sea, Phil. 33 C6
Bohotleh, Somali Rep. 40 F4
Boileau, C., Australia 52 C3
Boise, U.S.A. 72 E5
Boise City, U.S.A. 71 G3
Boissevain, Canada 65 D8
Bojador C., W. Sahara 44 C2
Bojana →, Albania 21 D8
Bojnūrd, Iran 39 B8
Bojonegoro, Indonesia 33 G14
Boké, Guinea 44 F2
Bokhara →, Australia 55 D4
Boknafjorden, Norway 9 G8
Bokoro, Chad 45 F8
Bokote, Zaïre 46 E4
Bokpyin, Burma 34 G5
Bokungu, Zaïre 46 E4
Bol, Chad 45 F7
Bolama, Guinea-Biss. 44 F1
Bolan Pass, Pakistan 36 E5
Bolbec, France 18 B4
Boldājī, Iran 39 D6
Bole, China 30 B3
Bolesławiec, Poland 16 C7
Bolinao C., Phil. 33 A5
Bolívar, Argentina 80 D4
Bolívar, Colombia 78 C3
Bolivar, Mo., U.S.A. 71 G8
Bolivar, Tenn., U.S.A. 71 H10
Bolivia ■, S. Amer. 78 G6
Bolivian Plateau, S. Amer. 76 D3
Bollnäs, Sweden 9 F14
Bollon, Australia 55 D4
Bolobo, Zaïre 46 E3
Bologna, Italy 20 B4
Bologoye, Russia 22 C5
Bolomba, Zaïre 46 D3
Bolong, Phil. 33 C6
Boloven, Cao Nguyen, Laos 34 E9
Bolsena, L. di, Italy 20 C4
Bolshereche, Russia 24 D8
Bolshevik, Ostrov, Russia 25 B11
Bolshezemelskaya Tundra, Russia 22 A10
Bolshoi Kavkas, Asia 23 F7
Bolshoy Anyuy →, Russia 25 C17
Bolshoy Atlym, Russia 24 C7
Bolshoy Begichev, Ostrov, Russia 25 B12
Bolshoy Lyakhovskiy, Ostrov, Russia 25 B15
Bolsward, Neths. 15 A5
Bolton, U.K. 10 D5
Bolu, Turkey 23 F5
Bolvadin, Turkey 23 G5
Bolzano, Italy 20 A4
Bom Despacho, Brazil 79 G9
Bom Jesus da Lapa, Brazil 79 F10
Boma, Zaïre 46 F2
Bomaderry, Australia 55 E5
Bombala, Australia 55 F4
Bombay, India 36 K8
Bomboma, Zaïre 46 D3
Bomili, Zaïre 46 D5
Bomongo, Zaïre 46 D3
Bomu →, C.A.R. 46 D4
Bon, C., Tunisia 45 A7
Bonaire, Neth. Ant. 75 E11
Bonang, Australia 55 F4
Bonaparte Arch., Australia 52 B3
Bonaventure, Canada 63 C6
Bonavista, Canada 63 C9
Bonavista, C., Canada 63 C9
Bondo, Zaïre 46 D4
Bondoukou, Ivory C. 44 G4
Bondowoso, Indonesia 33 G15
Bone, Teluk, Indonesia 33 E6
Bone Rate, Indonesia 33 F6
Bone Rate, Kepulauan, Indonesia 33 F6
Bo'ness, U.K. 12 E5
Bong Son = Hoai Nhon, Vietnam 34 E10
Bongandanga, Zaïre 46 D4
Bongor, Chad 45 F8
Bonham, U.S.A. 71 J6
Bonifacio, France 18 F9
Bonifacio, Bouches de, Medit. S. 20 D3
Bonifacio, Str. of, Medit. S. 20 D3
Bonin Is. = Ogasawara Gunto, Pac. Oc. 56 E6
Bonn, Germany 16 C3
Bonne Terre, U.S.A. 71 G9
Bonners Ferry, U.S.A. 72 B5
Bonney, L., Australia 55 F3
Bonnie Downs, Australia 54 C3
Bonnie Rock, Australia 53 F2
Bonny, Bight of, Africa 46 D1
Bonnyville, Canada 65 C6
Bonoi, Indonesia 33 E9
Bontang, Indonesia 32 D5
Bonthain, Indonesia 33 F5
Bonthe, S. Leone 44 G2
Bontoc, Phil. 33 A6
Bonython Ra., Australia 52 D4
Bookabie, Australia 53 F5
Booker, U.S.A. 71 G4
Boolaboolka L., Australia 55 E3
Booligal, Australia 55 E3
Boom, Belgium 15 C4
Boonah, Australia 55 D5
Boone, Iowa, U.S.A. 70 D8
Boone, N.C., U.S.A. 69 G5
Booneville, Ark., U.S.A. 71 H8
Booneville, Miss., U.S.A. 69 H1
Boonville, Ind., U.S.A. 68 F2
Boonville, Mo., U.S.A. 70 F8
Boonville, N.Y., U.S.A. 68 D8
Boorindal, Australia 55 E4
Boorowa, Australia 55 E4
Boothia, Gulf of, Canada 61 A11
Boothia Pen., Canada 60 A10
Bootle, Cumb., U.K. 10 C4
Bootle, Mersey., U.K. 10 D4
Booué, Gabon 46 E2
Bophuthatswana □, S. Africa 48 D4
Bor, Serbia, Yug. 21 B10
Bôr, Sudan 45 G11
Bor Mashash, Israel 41 D3
Boradā →, Syria 41 B5
Borah Pk., U.S.A. 72 D7
Borama, Somali Rep. 40 F3
Borås, Sweden 9 H12
Borāzjān, Iran 39 D6
Borba, Brazil 78 D7
Bord Khūn-e Now, Iran 39 D6
Borda, C., Australia 55 F2
Bordeaux, France 18 D3
Borden, Australia 53 F2
Borden, Canada 63 C7
Borden I., Canada 4 B2
Borders □, U.K. 12 F6
Bordertown, Australia 55 F3
Borðeyri, Iceland 8 D3
Bordj Fly Ste. Marie, Algeria 44 C4
Bordj-in-Eker, Algeria 44 D6
Bordj Omar Driss, Algeria 44 C6
Bordj-Tarat, Algeria 44 C6
Borgå, Finland 9 F18
Borgarnes, Iceland 8 D3
Børgefjellet, Norway 8 D12
Borger, Neths. 15 B6
Borger, U.S.A. 71 H4
Borgholm, Sweden 9 H14
Borisoglebsk, Russia 23 D7
Borisov, Belorussia 22 D4
Borja, Peru 78 D3
Borkou, Chad 45 E8
Borkum, Germany 16 B3
Borlänge, Sweden 9 F13
Borley, C., Antarctica 5 C5
Borneo, E. Indies 32 D5
Bornholm, Denmark 9 J13
Borobudur, Indonesia 33 G14
Borogontsy, Russia 25 C14
Boromo, Burkina Faso 44 F4
Borongan, Phil. 33 B7
Bororen, Australia 54 C5
Borovichi, Russia 22 C5
Borroloola, Australia 54 B2
Borth, U.K. 11 E3
Borujerd, Iran 39 C6
Borzya, Russia 25 D12
Bosa, Italy 20 D3
Bosanska Gradiška, Bos.-H. 20 B7
Bosaso, Somali Rep. 40 E4
Boscastle, U.K. 11 G3
Boshoek, S. Africa 48 D4
Boshof, S. Africa 48 D4
Boshrūyeh, Iran 39 C8
Bosna →, Bos.-H. 21 B8
Bosna i Hercegovina = Bosnia-Herzegovina ■, Europe 20 B7
Bosnia-Herzegovina ■, Europe 20 B7
Bosnik, Indonesia 33 E9
Bosobolo, Zaïre 46 D3
Bosporus = Karadeniz Boğazı, Turkey 21 D13
Bossangoa, C.A.R. 45 G8
Bossekop, Norway 8 B17
Bossembélé, C.A.R. 45 G8
Bossier City, U.S.A. 71 J8
Bosso, Niger 45 F7
Bostānābād, Iran 38 B5
Bosten Hu, China 30 B3
Boston, U.K. 10 E7
Boston, U.S.A. 68 D10
Boston Bar, Canada 64 D4
Boswell, Canada 64 D5
Boswell, U.S.A. 71 H7
Botany B., Australia 55 E5
Bothaville, S. Africa 48 D4
Bothnia, G. of, Europe 8 E16
Bothwell, Australia 54 G4
Botletle →, Botswana 48 C3
Botoşani, Romania 17 E13
Botswana ■, Africa 48 C3
Bottineau, U.S.A. 70 A4
Bottrop, Germany 15 C6
Botucatu, Brazil 80 A7
Botwood, Canada 63 C8
Bou Djébéha, Mali 44 E4
Bou Izakarn, Morocco 44 C3
Bouaké, Ivory C. 44 G3
Bouar, C.A.R. 46 C3
Bouârfa, Morocco 44 B4
Bouca, C.A.R. 45 G8
Boucaut B., Australia 54 A1
Bouches-du-Rhône □, France 18 E6
Bougainville, C., Australia 52 B4
Bougainville Reef, Australia 54 B4
Bougie = Bejaia, Algeria 44 A6
Bougouni, Mali 44 F3
Bouillon, Belgium 15 E5
Boulder, Colo., U.S.A. 70 E2
Boulder, Mont., U.S.A. 72 C7
Boulder City, U.S.A. 73 J6
Boulder Dam = Hoover Dam, U.S.A. 73 J6
Boulia, Australia 54 C2
Boulogne-sur-Mer, France 18 A4
Boultoum, Niger 44 F7
Bouna, Ivory C. 44 G4
Boundiali, Ivory C. 44 G3
Bountiful, U.S.A. 72 F8
Bounty Is., Pac. Oc. 56 M9
Bourbonnais, France 18 C5
Bourem, Mali 44 E4
Bourg-en-Bresse, France 18 C6
Bourges, France 18 C5
Bourgogne, France 18 C6
Bourke, Australia 55 E4
Bournemouth, U.K. 11 G6
Bousso, Chad 45 F8
Boutilimit, Mauritania 44 E2
Bouvet I. = Bouvetøya, Antarctica 3 G10
Bouvetøya, Antarctica 3 G10
Bovigny, Belgium 15 D5
Bovill, U.S.A. 72 C5
Bow Island, Canada 64 D6
Bowbells, U.S.A. 70 A3
Bowdle, U.S.A. 70 C5
Bowelling, Australia 53 F2
Bowen, Australia 54 C4
Bowen Mts., Australia 55 F4
Bowie, Ariz., U.S.A. 73 K9
Bowie, Tex., U.S.A. 71 J6
Bowkān, Iran 38 B5
Bowland, Forest of, U.K. 10 D5
Bowling Green, Ky., U.S.A. 68 G2
Bowling Green, Ohio, U.S.A. 68 E4
Bowling Green, C., Australia 54 B4
Bowman, U.S.A. 70 B3
Bowman I., Antarctica 5 C8
Bowmans, Australia 55 E2
Bowmanville, Canada 62 D4
Bowmore, U.K. 12 F2
Bowral, Australia 55 E5
Bowraville, Australia 55 E5
Bowron →, Canada 64 C4
Bowser L., Canada 64 B3
Bowsman, Canada 65 C8
Boxtel, Neths. 15 C5
Boyce, U.S.A. 71 K8
Boyer →, Canada 64 B5
Boyle, Ireland 13 C3
Boyne →, Ireland 13 C5
Boyne City, U.S.A. 68 C3
Boynton Beach, U.S.A. 69 M5
Boyup Brook, Australia 53 F2
Bozeman, U.S.A. 72 D8
Bozen = Bolzano, Italy 20 A4
Bozoum, C.A.R. 45 G8
Brabant □, Belgium 15 D4
Brabant L., Canada 65 B8
Brač, Croatia 20 C7
Bracadale, L., U.K. 12 D2
Bracciano, L. di, Italy 20 C5
Bracebridge, Canada 62 C4
Brach, Libya 45 C7
Bracke, Sweden 8 E13
Brackettville, U.S.A. 71 L4
Brad, Romania 17 E11
Bradenton, U.S.A. 69 M4
Bradford, U.K. 10 D6
Bradford, U.S.A. 68 E6
Bradley, Ark., U.S.A. 71 J8
Bradley, S. Dak., U.S.A. 70 C6
Bradore Bay, Canada 63 B8
Bradshaw, Australia 52 C5
Brady, U.S.A. 71 K5
Braemar, Australia 55 E2
Braga, Portugal 19 B1
Bragança, Brazil 79 D9
Bragança, Portugal 19 B2
Brahmanbaria, Bangla. 37 H17
Brahmani →, India 37 J15
Brahmaputra →, India 37 H16
Braich-y-pwll, U.K. 10 E3
Braidwood, Australia 55 F4
Brăila, Romania 21 B12
Brainerd, U.S.A. 70 B7
Braintree, U.K. 11 F8
Brak →, S. Africa 48 D3
Brakwater, Namibia 48 C2
Bralorne, Canada 64 C4
Brampton, Canada 62 D4
Bramwell, Australia 54 A3
Branco →, Brazil 78 D6
Brandenburg = Neubrandenburg, Germany 16 B6
Brandenburg, Germany 16 B6
Brandfort, S. Africa 48 D4
Brandon, Canada 65 D9
Brandon B., Ireland 13 D1
Brandon Mt., Ireland 13 D1
Brandvlei, S. Africa 48 E3
Braniewo, Poland 17 A9
Bransfield Str., Antarctica 5 C18
Brańsk, Poland 17 B11
Branson, Colo., U.S.A. 71 G3
Branson, Mo., U.S.A. 71 G8
Brantford, Canada 62 D3
Branxholme, Australia 55 F3
Bras d'Or, L., Canada 63 C7
Brasil, Planalto, Brazil 79 G9
Brasiléia, Brazil 78 F5
Brasília, Brazil 79 G9
Braşov, Romania 21 B11
Brasschaat, Belgium 15 C4
Brassey, Banjaran, Malaysia 32 D5
Brassey Ra., Australia 53 E3
Brasstown Bald, U.S.A. 69 H4
Bratislava, Slovakia 16 D8
Bratsk, Russia 25 D11
Brattleboro, U.S.A. 68 D9
Braunschweig, Germany 16 B5
Braunton, U.K. 11 F3
Brava, Somali Rep. 40 G3
Brawley, U.S.A. 73 K6
Bray, Ireland 13 C5
Bray, Mt., Australia 54 A1
Bray-sur-Seine, France 18 B5
Brazeau →, Canada 64 C5
Brazil, U.S.A. 68 F2
Brazil ■, S. Amer. 79 F9
Brazilian Highlands = Brasil, Planalto, Brazil 79 G9
Brazos →, U.S.A. 71 L7
Brazzaville, Congo 46 E3

Brčko, Bos.-H. 21 B8
Breadalbane, Australia 54 C2
Breadalbane, U.K. 12 E4
Breaden, L., Australia 53 E4
Breaksea Sd., N.Z. 51 L1
Bream B., N.Z. 51 F5
Bream Hd., N.Z. 51 F5
Brebes, Indonesia 33 G13
Brechin, U.K. 12 E6
Breckenridge, Colo., U.S.A. 72 G10
Breckenridge, Minn., U.S.A. 70 B6
Breckenridge, Tex., U.S.A. 71 J5
Breckland, U.K. 11 E8
Brecon, U.K. 11 F4
Brecon Beacons, U.K. 11 F4
Breda, Neths. 15 C4
Bredasdorp, S. Africa 48 E3
Bredbo, Australia 55 F4
Bregenz, Austria 16 E4
Breiðafjörður, Iceland 8 D2
Brejo, Brazil 79 D10
Bremen, Germany 16 B4
Bremer I., Australia 54 A2
Bremerhaven, Germany 16 B4
Bremerton, U.S.A. 72 C2
Brenham, U.S.A. 71 K6
Brenner Pass, Austria 16 E5
Brent, Canada 62 C4
Brent, U.K. 11 F7
Brentwood, U.K. 11 F8
Bréscia, Italy 20 B4
Breskens, Neths. 15 C3
Breslau = Wrocław, Poland 16 C8
Bressanone, Italy 20 A4
Bressay, U.K. 12 A7
Bresse, France 18 C6
Brest, Belorussia 22 D3
Brest, France 18 B1
Brest-Litovsk = Brest, Belorussia 22 D3
Bretagne, France 18 B2
Breţcu, Romania 17 E13
Breton, Canada 64 C6
Breton Sd., U.S.A. 71 L10
Brett, C., N.Z. 51 F5
Brevard, U.S.A. 69 H4
Brewarrina, Australia 55 D4
Brewer, U.S.A. 63 D6
Brewster, U.S.A. 72 B4
Brewster, Kap, Greenland 4 B6
Brewton, U.S.A. 69 K2
Breyten, S. Africa 49 D4
Brezhnev = Naberezhnyye Chelny, Russia 24 D6
Bria, C.A.R. 45 G9
Briançon, France 18 D7
Bribie I., Australia 55 D5
Bridgend, U.K. 11 F4
Bridgeport, Calif., U.S.A. 73 G4
Bridgeport, Conn., U.S.A. 68 E9
Bridgeport, Nebr., U.S.A. 70 E3
Bridgeport, Tex., U.S.A. 71 J6
Bridger, U.S.A. 72 D9
Bridgeton, U.S.A. 68 F8
Bridgetown, Australia 53 F2
Bridgetown, Barbados 74 P22
Bridgetown, Canada 63 D6
Bridgewater, Canada 63 D7
Bridgewater, U.S.A. 70 D6
Bridgewater, C., Australia 55 F3
Bridgnorth, U.K. 11 E5
Bridgwater, U.K. 11 F4
Bridlington, U.K. 10 C7
Bridport, Australia 54 G4
Bridport, U.K. 11 G5
Brie, Plaine de la, France 18 B5
Brig, Switz. 16 E3
Brigg, U.K. 10 D7
Briggsdale, U.S.A. 70 E2
Brigham City, U.S.A. 72 F7
Bright, Australia 55 F4
Brighton, Australia 55 E2
Brighton, Canada 62 D4
Brighton, U.K. 11 G7
Brighton, U.S.A. 70 F2
Brilliant, Canada 64 D5
Bríndisi, Italy 21 D7
Brinkley, U.S.A. 71 H9
Brinkworth, Australia 55 E2
Brion, I., Canada 63 C7
Brisbane, Australia 55 D5
Brisbane →, Australia 55 D5
Bristol, U.K. 11 F5
Bristol, Conn., U.S.A. 68 E9
Bristol, S. Dak., U.S.A. 70 C6
Bristol, Tenn., U.S.A. 69 G4
Bristol B., U.S.A. 60 C4
Bristol Channel, U.K. 11 F3
Bristol I., Antarctica 5 B1
Bristol L., U.S.A. 73 J5
Bristow, U.S.A. 71 H6
British Columbia □, Canada 64 C3
British Guiana = Guyana ■, S. Amer. 78 C7
British Honduras = Belize ■, Cent. Amer. 74 D7
British Isles, Europe 6 E5

Brits, S. Africa 49 D4
Britstown, S. Africa 48 E3
Britt, Canada 62 C3
Brittany = Bretagne, France 18 B2
Britton, U.S.A. 70 C6
Brixton, Australia 54 C3
Brlik, Kazakhstan 24 E8
Brno, Czech. 16 D8
Broad →, U.S.A. 69 J5
Broad Arrow, Australia 53 F3
Broad B., U.K. 12 C2
Broad Haven, Ireland 13 B2
Broad Law, U.K. 12 F5
Broad Sd., Australia 54 C4
Broadhurst Ra., Australia 52 D3
Broads, The, U.K. 10 E9
Broadus, U.S.A. 70 C2
Broadview, Canada 65 C8
Brochet, Canada 65 B8
Brochet, L., Canada 65 B8
Brock, Canada 65 C7
Brocken, Germany 16 C5
Brockport, U.S.A. 68 D7
Brockville, Canada 62 D4
Brockway, U.S.A. 70 B2
Brodeur Pen., Canada 61 A11
Brodick, U.K. 12 F3
Brogan, U.S.A. 72 D5
Broken Bow, Nebr., U.S.A. 70 E5
Broken Bow, Okla., U.S.A. 71 H7
Broken Hill = Kabwe, Zambia 47 G5
Broken Hill, Australia 55 E3
Bromfield, U.K. 11 E5
Bromley, U.K. 11 F8
Brønderslev, Denmark 9 H10
Bronkhorstspruit, S. Africa 49 D4
Bronte, U.S.A. 71 K4
Bronte Park, Australia 54 G4
Brookfield, U.S.A. 70 F8
Brookhaven, U.S.A. 71 K9
Brookings, Oreg., U.S.A. 72 E1
Brookings, S. Dak., U.S.A. 70 C6
Brookmere, Canada 64 D4
Brooks, Canada 64 C6
Brooks B., Canada 64 C3
Brooks L., Canada 65 A7
Brooks Ra., U.S.A. 60 B5
Brooksville, U.S.A. 69 L4
Brookville, U.S.A. 68 F3
Broom, L., U.K. 12 D3
Broome, Australia 52 C3
Broomehill, Australia 53 F2
Brora, U.K. 12 C5
Brora →, U.K. 12 C5
Brosna →, Ireland 13 C4
Brothers, U.S.A. 72 E3
Brough, U.K. 10 C5
Broughton Island, Canada 61 B13
Broughty Ferry, U.K. 12 E6
Brouwershaven, Neths. 15 C3
Browerville, U.S.A. 70 B7
Brown, Pt., Australia 55 E1
Brown Willy, U.K. 11 G3
Brownfield, U.S.A. 71 J3
Browning, U.S.A. 72 B7
Brownlee, Canada 65 C7
Brownsville, Oreg., U.S.A. 72 D2
Brownsville, Tenn., U.S.A. 71 H10
Brownsville, Tex., U.S.A. 71 N6
Brownwood, U.S.A. 71 K5
Brownwood, L., U.S.A. 71 K5
Browse I., Australia 52 B3
Bruas, Malaysia 34 Q13
Bruay-en-Artois, France 18 A5
Bruce, Mt., Australia 52 D2
Bruce Rock, Australia 53 F2
Bruck an der Leitha, Austria 16 D8
Brue →, U.K. 11 F5
Bruges = Brugge, Belgium 15 C3
Brugge, Belgium 15 C3
Brûlé, Canada 64 C5
Brumado, Brazil 79 F10
Brunchilly, Australia 54 B1
Brundidge, U.S.A. 69 K3
Bruneau, U.S.A. 72 E6
Bruneau →, U.S.A. 72 E6
Brunei = Bandar Seri Begawan, Brunei 32 C4
Brunei ■, Asia 32 D4
Brunette Downs, Australia 54 B2
Brunner, L., N.Z. 51 K3
Bruno, Canada 65 C7
Brunsbüttel, Germany 16 B4
Brunswick = Braunschweig, Germany 16 B5
Brunswick, Ga., U.S.A. 69 K5
Brunswick, Maine, U.S.A. 63 D6
Brunswick, Md., U.S.A. 68 F7
Brunswick, Mo., U.S.A. 70 F8
Brunswick, Pen. de, Chile 80 G2
Brunswick B., Australia 52 C3

Brunswick Junction, Australia 53 F2
Bruny I., Australia 54 G4
Brush, U.S.A. 70 E3
Brusque, Brazil 80 B7
Brussel, Belgium 15 D4
Brussels = Brussel, Belgium 15 D4
Bruthen, Australia 55 F4
Bruxelles = Brussel, Belgium 15 D4
Bryan, Ohio, U.S.A. 68 E3
Bryan, Tex., U.S.A. 71 K6
Bryan, Mt., Australia 55 E2
Bryansk, Russia 22 D5
Bryant, U.S.A. 70 C6
Bryne, Norway 9 G9
Bryson City, U.S.A. 69 H4
Bsharri, Lebanon 41 A5
Bū Baqarah, U.A.E. 39 E8
Bu Craa, W. Sahara 44 C2
Bū Ḩasā, U.A.E. 39 F7
Bua Yai, Thailand 34 E7
Buapinang, Indonesia 33 E6
Buayan, Phil. 33 C7
Bucaramanga, Colombia 78 B4
Buccaneer Arch., Australia 52 C3
Buchan, U.K. 12 D6
Buchan Ness, U.K. 12 D7
Buchanan, Canada 65 C8
Buchanan, Liberia 44 G2
Buchanan, L., Queens., Australia 54 C4
Buchanan, L., W. Austral., Australia 53 E3
Buchanan, L., U.S.A. 71 K5
Buchanan Cr. →, Australia 54 B2
Buchans, Canada 63 C8
Bucharest = București, Romania 21 B12
Buckeye, U.S.A. 73 K7
Buckhannon, U.S.A. 68 F5
Buckhaven, U.K. 12 E5
Buckie, U.K. 12 D6
Buckingham, Canada 62 C4
Buckingham, U.K. 11 F7
Buckingham B., Australia 54 A2
Buckinghamshire □, U.K. 11 F7
Buckle Hd., Australia 52 B4
Buckleboo, Australia 55 E2
Buckley, U.S.A. 72 C2
Buckley →, Australia 54 C2
Bucklin, U.S.A. 71 G5
Buctouche, Canada 63 C7
București, Romania 21 B12
Bucyrus, U.S.A. 68 E4
Budalin, Burma 37 H19
Budapest, Hungary 17 E9
Budd Coast, Antarctica 5 C8
Bude, U.K. 11 G3
Budennovsk, Russia 23 F7
Budgewoi, Australia 55 E5
Búðareyri, Iceland 8 D6
Búðir, Iceland 8 D2
Budjala, Zaïre 46 D3
Buena Vista, Colo., U.S.A. 73 G10
Buena Vista, Va., U.S.A. 68 G6
Buena Vista L., U.S.A. 73 J4
Buenaventura, Colombia 78 C3
Buenos Aires, Argentina 80 C5
Buenos Aires, L., Chile 80 F2
Buffalo, Mo., U.S.A. 71 G8
Buffalo, N.Y., U.S.A. 68 D6
Buffalo, Okla., U.S.A. 71 G5
Buffalo, S. Dak., U.S.A. 70 C3
Buffalo, Wyo., U.S.A. 72 D10
Buffalo →, Canada 64 A5
Buffalo Head Hills, Canada 64 B5
Buffalo L., Canada 64 C6
Buffalo Narrows, Canada 65 B7
Buffels →, S. Africa 48 D2
Buford, U.S.A. 69 H4
Bug →, Poland 17 B10
Bug →, Ukraine 23 E5
Buga, Colombia 78 C3
Bugel, Tanjung, Indonesia 32 F4
Bugsuk, Phil. 32 C5
Bugulma, Russia 22 D9
Bugun Shara, Mongolia 30 B5
Bugun Shara, Mongolia 30 B5
Buguruman, Russia 22 D9
Buheirat-Murrat-el-Kubra, Egypt 45 B11
Buhl, Idaho, U.S.A. 72 E6
Buhl, Minn., U.S.A. 70 B8
Buick, U.S.A. 71 G9
Builth Wells, U.K. 11 E4
Buir Nur, Mongolia 31 B6
Bujumbura, Burundi 46 E5
Bukachacha, Russia 25 D12
Bukama, Zaïre 46 F5
Bukavu, Zaïre 46 E5
Bukene, Tanzania 46 E6
Bukhara = Bukhoro, Uzbekistan 24 F7
Bukhoro, Uzbekistan 24 F7
Bukittinggi, Indonesia 32 E2

Bukoba, Tanzania 46 E6
Bula, Indonesia 33 E8
Bulahdelah, Australia 55 E5
Bulan, Phil. 33 B6
Bulandshahr, India 36 E10
Bulawayo, Zimbabwe 47 J5
Bulgaria ■, Europe 21 C11
Bulgroo, Australia 55 D3
Bulgunnia, Australia 55 E1
Bulhar, Somali Rep. 40 E3
Buli, Teluk, Indonesia 33 D7
Buliluyan, C., Phil. 32 C5
Bulkley →, Canada 64 B3
Bull Shoals L., U.S.A. 71 G8
Bullara, Australia 52 D1
Bullaring, Australia 53 F2
Bulli, Australia 55 E5
Bullock Creek, Australia 54 B3
Bulloo →, Australia 55 D3
Bulloo Downs, Queens., Australia 55 D3
Bulloo Downs, W. Austral., Australia 52 D2
Bulloo L., Australia 55 D3
Bulls, N.Z. 51 J5
Bulo Burti, Somali Rep. 40 G4
Bulsar = Valsad, India 36 J8
Bultfontein, S. Africa 48 D4
Bulu Karakelong, Indonesia 33 D7
Bulukumba, Indonesia 33 F6
Bulun, Russia 25 B13
Bumba, Zaïre 46 D4
Bumhpa Bum, Burma 37 F20
Buna, Kenya 46 D7
Bunbah, Khalīj, Libya 45 B9
Bunbury, Australia 53 F2
Buncrana, Ireland 13 A4
Bundaberg, Australia 55 C5
Bundey →, Australia 54 C2
Bundi, India 36 G9
Bundooma, Australia 54 C1
Bundoran, Ireland 13 B3
Bungatakada, Japan 29 H5
Bungil Cr. →, Australia 54 D4
Bungo-Suidō, Japan 29 H6
Bunia, Zaïre 46 D6
Bunji, Pakistan 36 B9
Bunkie, U.S.A. 71 K8
Bunnell, U.S.A. 69 L5
Buntok, Indonesia 32 E4
Bunyu, Indonesia 32 D5
Buol, Indonesia 33 D6
Buon Me Thuot, Vietnam 34 F10
Buorkhaya, Mys, Russia 25 B14
Buqayq, Si. Arabia 39 E6
Bur Acaba, Somali Rep. 40 G3
Bûr Safâga, Egypt 45 C11
Bûr Sa'îd, Egypt 45 B11
Bûr Sûdân, Sudan 45 E12
Burao, Somali Rep. 40 F4
Burãq, Syria 41 B5
Buras, U.S.A. 71 L10
Buraydah, Si. Arabia 38 E5
Burbank, U.S.A. 73 J4
Burcher, Australia 55 E4
Burdekin →, Australia 54 B4
Burdett, Canada 64 D6
Burdur, Turkey 23 G5
Burdwan = Barddhaman, India 37 H15
Bure →, U.K. 10 E9
Bureya →, Russia 25 E13
Burgas, Bulgaria 21 C12
Burgenland □, Austria 16 E8
Burgeo, Canada 63 C8
Burgersdorp, S. Africa 48 E4
Burges, Mt., Australia 53 F3
Burgos, Spain 19 A4
Burgsvik, Sweden 9 H15
Burgundy = Bourgogne, France 18 C6
Burhanpur, India 36 J10
Burias, Phil. 33 B6
Burin, Canada 63 C8
Buriram, Thailand 34 E7
Burji, Ethiopia 45 G12
Burkburnett, U.S.A. 71 H5
Burke, U.S.A. 72 C6
Burke →, Australia 54 C2
Burketown, Australia 54 B2
Burkina Faso ■, Africa 44 F4
Burk's Falls, Canada 62 C4
Burley, U.S.A. 72 E7
Burlington, Colo., U.S.A. 70 F3
Burlington, Iowa, U.S.A. 70 E9
Burlington, Kans., U.S.A. 70 F7
Burlington, N.C., U.S.A. 69 G6
Burlington, N.J., U.S.A. 68 E8
Burlington, Vt., U.S.A. 68 C9
Burlington, Wash., U.S.A. 72 B2
Burlington, Wis., U.S.A. 68 D1
Burlyu-Tyube, Kazakhstan 24 E8
Burma ■, Asia 37 J20
Burnaby I., Canada 64 C2
Burnet, U.S.A. 71 K5
Burney, U.S.A. 72 F3
Burngup, Australia 53 F2
Burnie, Australia 54 G4

Burnley, U.K. 10 D5
Burns, Oreg., U.S.A. 72 E4
Burns, Wyo., U.S.A. 70 E2
Burns Lake, Canada 64 C3
Burnside →, Canada 60 B9
Burnside, L., Australia 53 E3
Burntwood →, Canada 65 B9
Burntwood L., Canada 65 B8
Burqān, Kuwait 38 D5
Burra, Australia 55 E2
Burramurra, Australia 54 C2
Burren Junction, Australia 55 E4
Burrendong Dam, Australia 55 E4
Burrinjuck Res., Australia 55 F4
Burruyacú, Argentina 80 B4
Burry Port, U.K. 11 F3
Bursa, Turkey 23 F4
Burstall, Canada 65 C7
Burton L., Canada 62 B4
Burton upon Trent, U.K. 10 E6
Burtundy, Australia 55 E3
Buru, Indonesia 33 E7
Burûn, Râs, Egypt 41 D2
Burundi ■, Africa 46 E5
Burutu, Nigeria 44 G6
Burwell, U.S.A. 70 E5
Bury, U.K. 10 D5
Bury St. Edmunds, U.K. 11 E8
Buryat Republic □, Russia 25 D11
Buşayrah, Syria 38 C4
Buşayyah, Iraq 38 D5
Büshehr, Iran 39 D6
Büshehr □, Iran 39 D6
Bushell, Canada 65 B7
Bushire = Büshehr, Iran 39 D6
Bushnell, Ill., U.S.A. 70 E9
Bushnell, Nebr., U.S.A. 70 E3
Businga, Zaïre 46 D4
Bussum, Neths. 15 B5
Busto Arsízio, Italy 20 B3
Busu-Djanoa, Zaïre 46 D4
Busuanga, Phil. 33 B5
Buta, Zaïre 46 D4
Butare, Rwanda 46 E5
Butaritari, Kiribati 56 G9
Bute, U.K. 12 F3
Bute Inlet, Canada 64 C4
Butembo, Zaïre 46 D5
Butha Qi, China 31 B7
Butler, Mo., U.S.A. 70 F7
Butler, Pa., U.S.A. 68 E6
Butte, Mont., U.S.A. 72 C7
Butte, Nebr., U.S.A. 70 D5
Butterworth = Gcuwa, S. Africa 49 E4
Butterworth, Malaysia 34 P13
Buttfield, Mt., Australia 53 D4
Button B., Canada 65 B10
Butty Hd., Australia 53 F3
Butuan, Phil. 33 C7
Butung, Indonesia 33 E6
Buturlinovka, Russia 23 D7
Buxton, S. Africa 48 D3
Buxton, U.K. 10 D6
Buy, Russia 22 C7
Buyaga, Russia 25 D13
Buzău, Romania 21 B12
Buzău →, Romania 17 F13
Buzen, Japan 29 H5
Buzi →, Mozam. 47 H6
Buzuluk, Russia 22 D9
Buzzards Bay, U.S.A. 68 E10
Bydgoszcz, Poland 17 B8
Byelarus = Belorussia ■, Europe 22 D4
Byelorussia = Belorussia ■, Europe 22 D4
Byers, U.S.A. 70 F2
Byhalia, U.S.A. 71 H10
Bylas, U.S.A. 73 K8
Bylot I., Canada 61 A12
Byro, Australia 53 E2
Byrock, Australia 55 E4
Byron Bay, Australia 55 D5
Byrranga, Gory, Russia 25 B11
Byrranga Mts. = Byrranga, Gory, Russia 25 B11
Byske, Sweden 8 D16
Byske älv →, Sweden 8 D16
Bytom, Poland 17 C9

C

C.I.S. = Commonwealth of Independent States ■, Eurasia 25 D11
Ca Mau = Quan Long, Vietnam 34 H8
Ca Mau, Mui = Bai Bung, Mui, Vietnam 34 H8

Cabedelo, Brazil 79 E12
Cabimas, Venezuela 78 A4
Cabinda, Angola 46 F2
Cabinda □, Angola 46 F2
Cabinet Mts., U.S.A. 72 C6
Cabo Blanco, Argentina 80 F3
Cabo Frio, Brazil 79 H10
Cabo Pantoja, Peru 78 D3
Cabonga, Réservoir, Canada 62 C4
Cabool, U.S.A. 71 G8
Caboolture, Australia 55 D5
Cabora Bassa Dam = Cahora Bassa Dam, Mozam. 47 H6
Cabot Str., Canada 63 C8
Cabrera, I., Spain 19 C7
Cabri, Canada 65 C7
Cabriel →, Spain 19 C5
Čačak, Serbia, Yug. 21 C9
Cáceres, Brazil 78 G7
Cáceres, Spain 19 C2
Cache Bay, Canada 62 C4
Cachimbo, Serra do, Brazil 79 E7
Cachoeira, Brazil 79 F11
Cachoeira de Itapemirim, Brazil 79 H10
Cachoeira do Sul, Brazil 80 C6
Cacólo, Angola 46 G3
Caconda, Angola 47 G3
Cacongo, Angola 46 F2
Caddo, U.S.A. 71 H6
Cadell Cr. →, Australia 54 C3
Cader Idris, U.K. 10 E4
Cadibarrawiracanna, L., Australia 55 D2
Cadillac, Canada 62 C4
Cadillac, U.S.A. 68 C3
Cadiz, Phil. 33 B6
Cádiz, Spain 19 D2
Cádiz, G. de, Spain 19 D2
Cadney Park, Australia 55 D1
Cadomin, Canada 64 C5
Cadotte →, Canada 64 B5
Cadoux, Australia 53 F2
Caen, France 18 B3
Caernarfon, U.K. 10 D3
Caernarfon B., U.K. 10 D3
Caernarvon = Caernarfon, U.K. 10 D3
Caerphilly, U.K. 11 F4
Caesarea, Israel 41 C3
Caeté, Brazil 79 G10
Caetité, Brazil 79 F10
Cafu, Angola 48 B2
Cagayan →, Phil. 33 A6
Cagayan de Oro, Phil. 33 C6
Cágliari, Italy 20 E3
Cágliari, G. di, Italy 20 E3
Caguas, Puerto Rico 75 D11
Caha Mts., Ireland 13 E2
Cahama, Angola 48 B1
Caher, Ireland 13 D4
Cahersiveen, Ireland 13 E1
Cahora Bassa Dam, Mozam. 47 H6
Cahore Pt., Ireland 13 D5
Cahors, France 18 D4
Cahuapanas, Peru 78 E3
Caia, Mozam. 47 H7
Caibarién, Cuba 75 C9
Caicara, Venezuela 78 B5
Caicó, Brazil 79 E11
Caicos Is., W. Indies 75 C10
Caird Coast, Antarctica 5 D1
Cairn Gorm, U.K. 12 D5
Cairn Toul, U.K. 12 D5
Cairngorm Mts., U.K. 12 D5
Cairns, Australia 54 B4
Cairo = El Qâhira, Egypt 45 B11
Cairo, Ga., U.S.A. 69 K3
Cairo, Ill., U.S.A. 71 G10
Caithness, Ord of, U.K. 12 C5
Caiundo, Angola 47 H3
Caiza, Bolivia 78 H5
Cajamarca, Peru 78 E3
Cajàzeiras, Brazil 79 E11
Calabar, Nigeria 44 H6
Calábria □, Italy 20 E7
Calafate, Argentina 80 G2
Calahorra, Spain 19 A5
Calais, France 18 A4
Calais, U.S.A. 63 C6
Calama, Brazil 78 E6
Calama, Chile 80 A3
Calamar, Bolívar, Colombia 78 A4
Calamar, Vaupés, Colombia 78 C4
Calamian Group, Phil. 33 B5
Calamocha, Spain 19 B5
Calang, Indonesia 32 D1
Calapan, Phil. 33 B6
Calatayud, Spain 19 B5
Calauag, Phil. 33 B6
Calavite, C., Phil. 33 B6
Calbayog, Phil. 33 B6
Calca, Peru 78 F4
Calcasieu L., U.S.A. 71 L8
Calcutta, India 37 H16
Calder →, U.K. 10 D6
Caldera, Chile 80 B2
Caldwell, Idaho, U.S.A. 72 E5
Caldwell, Kans., U.S.A. 71 G6
Caldwell, Tex., U.S.A. 71 K6
Caledon, S. Africa 48 E2
Caledon →, S. Africa 48 E4

Cha Pa

Caledon B., Australia 54 A2
Calella, Spain 19 B7
Calemba, Angola 48 B2
Calexico, U.S.A. 73 K6
Calf of Man, U.K. 10 C3
Calgary, Canada 64 C6
Calhoun, U.S.A. 69 H3
Cali, Colombia 78 C3
Calicut, India 36 P9
Caliente, U.S.A. 73 H6
California, U.S.A. 70 F8
California □, U.S.A. 73 H4
California, G. de, Mexico 74 B2
Calingasta, Argentina 80 C3
Calipatria, U.S.A. 73 K6
Calistoga, U.S.A. 72 G2
Calitzdorp, S. Africa 48 E3
Callabonna, L., Australia 55 D3
Callan, Ireland 13 D4
Callander, U.K. 12 E4
Callao, Peru 78 F3
Callaway, U.S.A. 70 E5
Callide, Australia 54 C5
Calling Lake, Canada 64 B6
Calliope, Australia 54 C5
Calola, Angola 48 B2
Caloundra, Australia 55 D5
Calstock, Canada 62 C3
Caltagirone, Italy 20 F6
Caltanissetta, Italy 20 F6
Calulo, Angola 46 G2
Calumet, U.S.A. 68 B1
Calunda, Angola 47 G4
Calvados □, France 18 B3
Calvert, U.S.A. 71 K6
Calvert →, Australia 54 B2
Calvert Hills, Australia 54 B2
Calvert I., Canada 64 C3
Calvert Ra., Australia 52 D3
Calvi, France 18 E8
Calvinia, S. Africa 48 E2
Cam →, U.K. 11 E8
Cam Lam, Vietnam 34 G10
Cam Ranh, Vietnam 34 G10
Camabatela, Angola 46 F3
Camacupa, Angola 47 G3
Camagüey, Cuba 75 C9
Camaná, Peru 78 G4
Camaret, France 18 B1
Camargo, Bolivia 78 H5
Camarones, Argentina 80 E3
Camas, U.S.A. 72 D2
Camas Valley, U.S.A. 72 E2
Cambay = Khambhat, India 36 H8
Cambay, G. of = Khambat, G. of, India 36 J8
Cambodia ■, Asia 34 F8
Camborne, U.K. 11 G2
Cambrai, France 18 A5
Cambria, U.S.A. 73 J3
Cambrian Mts., U.K. 11 E4
Cambridge, Canada 62 D3
Cambridge, N.Z. 51 G5
Cambridge, U.K. 11 E8
Cambridge, Idaho, U.S.A. 72 D5
Cambridge, Mass., U.S.A. 68 D10
Cambridge, Md., U.S.A. 68 F7
Cambridge, Minn., U.S.A. 70 C8
Cambridge, Nebr., U.S.A. 70 E4
Cambridge, Ohio, U.S.A. 68 E5
Cambridge Bay, Canada 60 B9
Cambridge G., Australia 52 B4
Cambridgeshire □, U.K. 11 E8
Cambundi-Catembo, Angola 46 G3
Camden, Ala., U.S.A. 69 K2
Camden, Ark., U.S.A. 71 J8
Camden, Maine, U.S.A. 63 D6
Camden, N.J., U.S.A. 68 F8
Camden, S.C., U.S.A. 69 H5
Camden Sd., Australia 52 C3
Camdenton, U.S.A. 71 F8
Cameron, Ariz., U.S.A. 73 J8
Cameron, La., U.S.A. 71 L8
Cameron, Mo., U.S.A. 70 F7
Cameron, Tex., U.S.A. 71 K6
Cameron Falls, Canada 62 C2
Cameron Highlands, Malaysia 34 Q14
Cameron Hills, Canada 64 B5
Cameroon ■, Africa 45 G7
Cameroun, Mt., Cameroon 44 H6
Cametá, Brazil 79 D9
Caminha, Portugal 19 B1
Camino, U.S.A. 72 G3
Camira Creek, Australia 55 D5
Camissombo, Angola 46 F4
Camocim, Brazil 79 D10
Camooweal, Australia 54 B2
Camopi →, Fr. Guiana 79 C8
Camp Crook, U.S.A. 70 C3
Camp Wood, U.S.A. 71 L4
Campana, I., Chile 80 F1
Campania □, Italy 20 D6
Campbell, S. Africa 48 D3
Campbell I., Pac. Oc. 56 N8
Campbell L., Canada 65 A7
Campbell River, Canada 64 C3
Campbell Town, Australia 54 G4
Campbellsville, U.S.A. 68 G3
Campbellton, Canada 63 C6
Campbelltown, Australia 55 E5
Campbeltown, U.K. 12 F3
Campeche, Mexico 74 D6
Campeche, B. de, Mexico 74 D6
Camperdown, Australia 55 F3
Camperville, Canada 65 C8
Campina Grande, Brazil 79 E11
Campinas, Brazil 80 A7
Campo, Cameroon 46 D1
Campo Belo, Brazil 79 H9
Campo Formoso, Brazil 79 F10
Campo Grande, Brazil 79 H8
Campo Maíor, Brazil 79 D10
Campo Mourão, Brazil 79 H8
Campoalegre, Colombia 78 C3
Campobasso, Italy 20 D6
Campos, Brazil 79 H10
Campos Belos, Brazil 79 F9
Campuya →, Peru 78 D4
Camrose, Canada 64 C6
Camsell Portage, Canada 65 B7
Can Tho, Vietnam 34 G8
Canada ■, N. Amer. 60 C10
Cañada de Gómez, Argentina 80 C4
Canadian, U.S.A. 71 H4
Canadian →, U.S.A. 71 H7
Canadian Shield, Canada 61 C10
Çanakkale, Turkey 23 F4
Çanakkale Boğazı, Turkey 21 D12
Canal Flats, Canada 64 C5
Canandaigua, U.S.A. 68 D7
Cananea, Mexico 74 A2
Canarias, Is., Atl. Oc. 44 C1
Canary Is. = Canarias, Is., Atl. Oc. 44 C1
Canaveral, C., U.S.A. 69 L5
Canavieiras, Brazil 79 G11
Canbelego, Australia 55 E4
Canberra, Australia 55 F4
Canby, Calif., U.S.A. 72 F3
Canby, Minn., U.S.A. 70 C6
Canby, Oreg., U.S.A. 72 D2
Candala, Somali Rep. 40 E4
Candelo, Australia 55 F4
Candia = Iráklion, Greece 21 G11
Candle L., Canada 65 C7
Candlemas I., Antarctica 5 B1
Cando, U.S.A. 70 A5
Canea = Khaniá, Greece 21 G11
Canelones, Uruguay 80 C5
Cañete, Chile 80 D2
Cañete, Peru 78 F3
Cangas, Spain 19 A1
Canguaretama, Brazil 79 E11
Canguçu, Brazil 80 C6
Canim Lake, Canada 64 C4
Canipaan, Phil. 32 C5
Çankırı, Turkey 23 F5
Canmore, Canada 64 C5
Cann River, Australia 55 F4
Canna, U.K. 12 D2
Cannanore, India 36 P9
Cannes, France 18 E7
Cannock, U.K. 10 E5
Cannon Ball →, U.S.A. 70 B4
Cannondale Mt., Australia 54 D4
Canoas, Brazil 80 B6
Canoe L., Canada 65 B7
Canon City, U.S.A. 70 F2
Canora, Canada 65 C8
Canowindra, Australia 55 E4
Canso, Canada 63 C7
Cantabria □, Spain 19 A4
Cantabrian Mts. = Cantábrica, Cordillera, Spain 19 A3
Cantábrica, Cordillera, Spain 19 A3
Cantal □, France 18 D5
Canterbury, Australia 54 D3
Canterbury, U.K. 11 F9
Canterbury □, N.Z. 51 K3
Canterbury Bight, N.Z. 51 L3
Canterbury Plains, N.Z. 51 K3
Canton = Guangzhou, Guangdong, China 31 D6
Canton = Guangzhou, Guangdong, China 31 D6
Canton, Ga., U.S.A. 69 H3
Canton, Ill., U.S.A. 70 E9
Canton, Miss., U.S.A. 71 J9
Canton, Mo., U.S.A. 70 E9
Canton, N.Y., U.S.A. 68 C8
Canton, Ohio, U.S.A. 68 E5
Canton, Okla., U.S.A. 71 G5
Canton, S. Dak., U.S.A. 70 D6
Canton L., U.S.A. 71 G5
Canudos, Brazil 78 E7
Canutama, Brazil 78 E6
Canutillo, U.S.A. 73 L10
Canyon, Tex., U.S.A. 71 H4
Canyon, Wyo., U.S.A. 72 D8
Canyonlands Nat. Park, U.S.A. 73 G9
Canyonville, U.S.A. 72 E2
Cap-aux-Meules, Canada 63 C7
Cap-Chat, Canada 63 C6
Cap-de-la-Madeleine, Canada 62 C5
Cap-Haïtien, Haiti 75 D10
Cap St.-Jacques = Vung Tau, Vietnam 34 G9
Capaia, Angola 46 F4
Capanaparo →, Venezuela 78 B5
Cape →, Australia 54 C4
Cape Barren I., Australia 54 G4
Cape Breton Highlands Nat. Park, Canada 63 C7
Cape Breton I., Canada 63 C7
Cape Charles, U.S.A. 68 G8
Cape Coast, Ghana 44 G4
Cape Dorset, Canada 61 B12
Cape Dyer, Canada 61 B13
Cape Fear →, U.S.A. 69 H6
Cape Girardeau, U.S.A. 71 G10
Cape Jervis, Australia 55 F2
Cape May, U.S.A. 68 F8
Cape May Pt., U.S.A. 67 C12
Cape Province □, S. Africa 48 E3
Cape Tormentine, Canada 63 C7
Cape Town, S. Africa 48 E2
Cape Verde Is. ■, Atl. Oc. 2 D8
Cape York Peninsula, Australia 54 A3
Capela, Brazil 79 F11
Capella, Australia 54 C4
Capim →, Brazil 79 D9
Capitan, U.S.A. 73 K11
Capraia, Italy 20 C3
Capreol, Canada 62 C3
Caprera, Italy 20 D3
Capri, Italy 20 D6
Capricorn Group, Australia 54 C5
Capricorn Ra., Australia 52 D2
Caprivi Strip, Namibia 48 B3
Captain's Flat, Australia 55 F4
Caquetá →, Colombia 78 D5
Caracal, Romania 17 F12
Caracas, Venezuela 78 A5
Caracol, Brazil 79 E10
Caradoc, Australia 55 E3
Carajás, Serra dos, Brazil 79 E8
Carangola, Brazil 79 H10
Carani, Australia 53 F2
Caransebeş, Romania 17 F11
Caratasca, L., Honduras 75 D8
Caratinga, Brazil 79 G10
Caraúbas, Brazil 79 E11
Caravaca, Spain 19 C5
Caravelas, Brazil 79 G11
Caraveli, Peru 78 G4
Carballo, Spain 19 A1
Carberry, Canada 65 D9
Carbon, Canada 64 C6
Carbonara, C., Italy 20 E3
Carbondale, Colo., U.S.A. 72 G10
Carbondale, Ill., U.S.A. 71 G10
Carbondale, Pa., U.S.A. 68 E8
Carbonear, Canada 63 C9
Carbonia, Italy 20 E3
Carcajou, Canada 64 B5
Carcassonne, France 18 E5
Carcross, Canada 60 B6
Cardabia, Australia 52 D1
Cardamon Hills, India 36 Q10
Cárdenas, Cuba 75 C8
Cardiff, U.K. 11 F4
Cardigan, U.K. 11 E3
Cardigan B., U.K. 11 E3
Cardona, Spain 19 B6
Cardross, Canada 65 D7
Cardston, Canada 64 D6
Cardwell, Australia 54 B4
Careen L., Canada 65 B7
Carei, Romania 17 E11
Careme, Indonesia 33 G13
Carey, Idaho, U.S.A. 72 E7
Carey, Ohio, U.S.A. 68 E4
Carey, L., Australia 53 E3
Carey L., Canada 65 A8
Careysburg, Liberia 44 G2
Cargados Garajos, Ind. Oc. 35 F4
Carhué, Argentina 80 D4
Cariacica, Brazil 79 H10
Caribbean Sea, W. Indies 75 E10
Cariboo Mts., Canada 64 C4
Caribou, U.S.A. 63 C6
Caribou →, Man., Canada 65 B10
Caribou →, N.W.T., Canada 64 A3
Caribou I., Canada 62 C2
Caribou Is., Canada 64 A6
Caribou L., Man., Canada 65 B9
Caribou L., Ont., Canada 62 B2
Caribou Mts., Canada 64 B5
Carinda, Australia 55 E4
Carinhanha, Brazil 79 F10
Carinthia □ = Kärnten □, Austria 16 E6
Caripito, Venezuela 78 A6
Caritianas, Brazil 78 E6
Carleton Place, Canada 62 C4
Carletonville, S. Africa 48 D4
Carlin, U.S.A. 72 F5
Carlingford, L., Ireland 13 B5
Carlinville, U.S.A. 70 F10
Carlisle, U.K. 10 C5
Carlisle, U.S.A. 68 E7
Carlow, Ireland 13 D5
Carlow □, Ireland 13 D5
Carlsbad, Calif., U.S.A. 73 K5
Carlsbad, N. Mex., U.S.A. 71 J2
Carlyle, Canada 65 D8
Carlyle, U.S.A. 70 F10
Carmacks, Canada 60 B6
Carman, Canada 65 D9
Carmangay, Canada 64 C6
Carmanville, Canada 63 C9
Carmarthen, U.K. 11 F3
Carmarthen B., U.K. 11 F3
Carmel-by-the-Sea, U.S.A. 73 H3
Carmelo, Uruguay 80 C5
Carmen, Colombia 78 B3
Carmen de Patagones, Argentina 80 E4
Carmi, U.S.A. 68 F1
Carmila, Australia 54 C4
Carmona, Spain 19 D3
Carnarvon, Queens., Australia 54 C4
Carnarvon, W. Austral., Australia 53 D1
Carnarvon, S. Africa 48 E3
Carnarvon Ra., Queens., Australia 54 D4
Carnarvon Ra., W. Austral., Australia 53 E3
Carndonagh, Ireland 13 A4
Carnduff, Canada 65 D8
Carnegie, L., Australia 53 E3
Carnic Alps = Karnische Alpen, Europe 20 A5
Carniche Alpi = Karnische Alpen, Europe 20 A5
Carnot, C.A.R. 46 D3
Carnot, C., Australia 55 E2
Carnot B., Australia 52 C3
Carnsore Pt., Ireland 13 D5
Caro, U.S.A. 68 D4
Carol City, U.S.A. 69 N5
Carolina, Brazil 79 E9
Carolina, S. Africa 49 D5
Caroline I., Kiribati 57 H12
Caroline Is., Pac. Oc. 56 G6
Caron, Canada 65 C7
Caroni →, Venezuela 78 B6
Caroona, Australia 55 E5
Carpathians, Europe 17 D10
Carpaţii Meridionali, Romania 17 F12
Carpentaria, G. of, Australia 54 A2
Carpentaria Downs, Australia 54 B3
Carpinteria, U.S.A. 73 J4
Carpolac = Morea, Australia 55 F3
Carr Boyd Ra., Australia 52 C4
Carrabelle, U.S.A. 69 L3
Carranya, Australia 52 C4
Carrara, Italy 20 B4
Carrauntoohill, Ireland 13 E2
Carrick-on-Shannon, Ireland 13 C3
Carrick-on-Suir, Ireland 13 D4
Carrickfergus, U.K. 13 B6
Carrickfergus □, U.K. 13 B6
Carrickmacross, Ireland 13 C5
Carrieton, Australia 55 E2
Carrington, U.S.A. 70 B5
Carrizal Bajo, Chile 80 B2
Carrizo Cr. →, U.S.A. 71 G3
Carrizo Springs, U.S.A. 71 L5
Carrizozo, U.S.A. 73 K11
Carroll, U.S.A. 70 D7
Carrollton, Ga., U.S.A. 69 J3
Carrollton, Ill., U.S.A. 70 F9
Carrollton, Ky., U.S.A. 68 F3
Carrollton, Mo., U.S.A. 70 F8
Carron →, U.K. 12 D3
Carron, L., U.K. 12 D3
Carrot →, Canada 65 C8
Carrot River, Canada 65 C8
Carruthers, Canada 65 C7
Carse of Gowrie, U.K. 12 E5
Carson, U.S.A. 70 B4
Carson City, U.S.A. 72 G4
Carson Sink, U.S.A. 72 G4
Carstairs, U.K. 12 F5
Cartagena, Colombia 78 A3
Cartagena, Spain 19 D5
Cartago, Colombia 78 C3
Cartago, Costa Rica 75 F8
Cartersville, U.S.A. 69 H3
Carterton, N.Z. 51 J5
Carthage, Ark., U.S.A. 71 H8
Carthage, Ill., U.S.A. 70 E9
Carthage, Mo., U.S.A. 71 G7
Carthage, S. Dak., U.S.A. 70 C6
Carthage, Tex., U.S.A. 71 J7
Cartier I., Australia 52 B3
Cartwright, Canada 63 B8
Caruaru, Brazil 79 E11
Carúpano, Venezuela 78 A6
Caruthersville, U.S.A. 71 G10
Carvoeiro, Brazil 78 D6
Casa Grande, U.S.A. 73 K8
Casablanca, Morocco 44 B3
Casale Monferrato, Italy 20 B3
Cascade, Idaho, U.S.A. 72 D5
Cascade, Mont., U.S.A. 72 C8
Cascade Locks, U.S.A. 72 D3
Cascade Ra., U.S.A. 72 C3
Cascavel, Brazil 80 A6
Caserta, Italy 20 D6
Cashel, Ireland 13 D4
Cashmere, U.S.A. 72 C3
Cashmere Downs, Australia 53 E2
Casiguran, Phil. 33 A6
Casilda, Argentina 80 C4
Casino, Australia 55 D5
Casiquiare →, Venezuela 78 C5
Caslan, Canada 64 C6
Casma, Peru 78 E3
Caspe, Spain 19 B5
Casper, U.S.A. 72 E10
Caspian Sea, Asia 23 F9
Cass City, U.S.A. 68 D4
Cass Lake, U.S.A. 70 B7
Casselton, U.S.A. 70 B6
Cassiar, Canada 64 B3
Cassiar Mts., Canada 64 B2
Cassinga, Angola 47 H3
Cassville, U.S.A. 71 G8
Castellammare del Golfo, Italy 20 E5
Castellammare di Stábia, Italy 20 D6
Castellón de la Plana, Spain 19 C5
Castelo Branco, Portugal 19 C2
Castelvetrano, Italy 20 F5
Casterton, Australia 55 F3
Castilla La Mancha □, Spain 19 C4
Castilla La Nueva = Castilla La Mancha □, Spain 19 C4
Castilla La Vieja = Castilla y Leon □, Spain 19 B3
Castilla y Leon □, Spain 19 B3
Castle Dale, U.S.A. 72 G8
Castle Douglas, U.K. 12 G5
Castle Rock, Colo., U.S.A. 70 F2
Castle Rock, Wash., U.S.A. 72 C2
Castlebar, Ireland 13 C2
Castleblaney, Ireland 13 B5
Castlegar, Canada 64 D5
Castlemaine, Australia 55 F3
Castlereagh, Ireland 13 C3
Castlereagh □, U.K. 13 B6
Castlereagh →, Australia 55 E4
Castlereagh B., Australia 54 A2
Castletown, I. of Man 10 C3
Castletown Bearhaven, Ireland 13 E2
Castlevale, Australia 54 C4
Castor, Canada 64 C6
Castres, France 18 E5
Castries, St. Lucia 74 N21
Castro, Chile 80 E2
Castro Alves, Brazil 79 F11
Castro del Río, Spain 19 D3
Castroville, U.S.A. 71 L5
Casummit Lake, Canada 62 B1
Cat I., Bahamas 75 C9
Cat I., U.S.A. 71 K10
Cat L., Canada 62 B1
Catacáos, Peru 78 E2
Catahoula L., U.S.A. 71 K8
Catalão, Brazil 79 G9
Catalina, Canada 63 C9
Catalonia = Cataluña □, Spain 19 B6
Cataluña □, Spain 19 B6
Catamarca, Argentina 80 B3
Catanduanes, Phil. 33 B6
Catanduva, Brazil 79 H9
Catánia, Italy 20 F6
Catanzaro, Italy 20 E7
Catarman, Phil. 33 B6
Cateel, Phil. 33 C7
Cathcart, S. Africa 48 E4
Cathlamet, U.S.A. 72 C2
Cativa, Panama 74 H14
Catlettsburg, U.S.A. 68 F4
Catoche, C., Mexico 74 C7
Catrimani, Brazil 78 C6
Catskill, U.S.A. 68 D9
Catskill Mts., U.S.A. 68 D8
Catt, Mt., Australia 54 A1
Catuala, Angola 48 B2
Cauca →, Colombia 78 B4
Caucaia, Brazil 79 D11
Caucasus = Bolshoi Kavkas, Asia 23 F7
Caungula, Angola 46 F3
Cauquenes, Chile 80 D2
Caura →, Venezuela 78 B6
Causapscal, Canada 63 C6
Cauvery →, India 36 P11
Caux, Pays de, France 18 B4
Cavalier, U.S.A. 70 A6
Cavan, Ireland 13 C4
Cavan □, Ireland 13 C4
Cave City, U.S.A. 68 G3
Cavenagh Ra., Australia 53 E4
Cavendish, Australia 55 F3
Caviana, I., Brazil 79 C8
Cavite, Phil. 33 B6
Cawndilla L., Australia 55 E3
Cawnpore = Kanpur, India 36 F12
Caxias, Brazil 79 D10
Caxias do Sul, Brazil 80 B6
Caxito, Angola 46 F2
Cayambe, Ecuador 78 C3
Cayenne, Fr. Guiana 79 B8
Cayuga L., U.S.A. 68 D7
Cazombo, Angola 47 G4
Ceanannus Mor, Ireland 13 C5
Ceará = Fortaleza, Brazil 79 D11
Ceará □, Brazil 79 E11
Ceará Mirim, Brazil 79 E11
Cebollar, Argentina 80 B3
Cebu, Phil. 33 B6
Cecil Plains, Australia 55 D5
Cedar →, U.S.A. 70 E9
Cedar City, U.S.A. 73 H7
Cedar Creek Res., U.S.A. 71 J6
Cedar Falls, U.S.A. 70 D8
Cedar Key, U.S.A. 69 L4
Cedar L., Canada 65 C8
Cedar Rapids, U.S.A. 70 E9
Cedartown, U.S.A. 69 H3
Cedarvale, Canada 64 B3
Cedarville, S. Africa 49 E4
Cedarville, U.S.A. 72 F3
Cedro, Brazil 79 E11
Ceduna, Australia 55 E1
Cefalù, Italy 20 E6
Cegléd, Hungary 17 E9
Cehegín, Spain 19 C5
Celaya, Mexico 74 C4
Celbridge, Ireland 13 C5
Celebes = Sulawesi □, Indonesia 33 E6
Celebes Sea = Sulawesi Sea, Indonesia 33 D6
Celina, U.S.A. 68 E3
Celje, Slovenia 20 A6
Celle, Germany 16 B5
Cement, U.S.A. 71 H5
Center, N. Dak., U.S.A. 70 B4
Center, Tex., U.S.A. 71 K7
Centerfield, U.S.A. 73 G8
Centerville, Iowa, U.S.A. 70 E8
Centerville, S. Dak., U.S.A. 70 D6
Centerville, Tenn., U.S.A. 69 H2
Centerville, Tex., U.S.A. 71 K7
Central, U.S.A. 73 K9
Central □, U.K. 12 E4
Central, Cordillera, Colombia 78 C4
Central African Rep. ■, Africa 45 G9
Central City, Ky., U.S.A. 68 G2
Central City, Nebr., U.S.A. 70 E5
Central Makran Range, Pakistan 36 F4
Central Patricia, Canada 62 B1
Central Russian Uplands, Europe 6 E13
Central Siberian Plateau, Russia 26 C14
Centralia, Ill., U.S.A. 70 F10
Centralia, Mo., U.S.A. 70 F8
Centralia, Wash., U.S.A. 72 C2
Centreville, Ala., U.S.A. 69 J2
Centreville, Miss., U.S.A. 71 K9
Cephalonia = Kefallinía, Greece 21 E9
Cepu, Indonesia 33 G14
Ceram = Seram, Indonesia 33 E7
Ceram Sea = Seram Sea, Indonesia 33 E7
Ceres, Argentina 80 B4
Ceres, S. Africa 48 E2
Cerignola, Italy 20 D6
Cerigo = Kíthira, Greece 21 F11
Cerknica, Slovenia 20 B6
Cernavodă, Romania 17 F14
Cervera, Spain 19 B6
Cervera del Río Alhama, Spain 19 A5
Cesena, Italy 20 B5
České Budějovice, Czech. 16 D7
Ceskomoravská Vrchovina, Czech. 16 D7
Český Těšín, Czech. 17 D9
Cessnock, Australia 55 E5
Cetinje, Montenegro, Yug. 21 C8
Ceuta, Morocco 44 A3
Cévennes, France 18 D5
Ceyhan →, Turkey 23 G6
Ceylon = Sri Lanka ■, Asia 36 R12
Cha Pa, Vietnam 34 A7

Chablais

Chablais, *France* 18 C7
Chachapoyas, *Peru* .. 78 E3
Chachran, *Pakistan* .. 36 E7
Chad ■, *Africa* 45 E8
Chad, L. = Tchad, L.,
Chad 45 F7
Chadan, *Russia* 25 D10
Chadileuvú →,
Argentina 80 D3
Chadron, *U.S.A.* 70 D3
Chagai Hills, *Afghan.* . 36 E3
Chagda, *Russia* 25 D14
Chagos Arch., *Ind. Oc.* 26 K11
Chágres →, *Panama* 74 H14
Chāh Ākhvor, *Iran* ... 39 C8
Chāh-e-Malek, *Iran* ... 39 D8
Chāh Bahār, *Iran* ... 39 E9
Chāh Kavīr, *Iran* 39 D7
Chahar Burjak, *Afghan.* 36 D3
Chaibasa, *India* 37 H14
Chakhānsūr, *Afghan.* .. 36 D3
Chakonipau, L.,
Canada 63 A6
Chakradharpur, *India* . 37 H14
Chakwal, *Pakistan* ... 36 C8
Chala, *Peru* 78 G4
Chalcis = Khalkís,
Greece 21 E10
Chaleur B., *Canada* .. 63 C6
Chalhuanca, *Peru* ... 78 F4
Chalisgaon, *India* ... 36 J9
Chalky Inlet, *N.Z.* ... 51 M1
Challapata, *Bolivia* .. 78 G5
Challis, *U.S.A.* 72 D6
Châlons-sur-Marne,
France 18 B6
Chama, *U.S.A.* 73 H10
Chaman, *Pakistan* ... 36 D5
Chamba, *India* 36 C10
Chamba, *Tanzania* ... 47 G7
Chambal →, *India* ... 36 F11
Chamberlain, *U.S.A.* .. 70 D5
Chamberlain →,
Australia 52 C4
Chambers, *U.S.A.* ... 73 J9
Chambersburg, *U.S.A.* 68 F7
Chambéry, *France* ... 18 D6
Chambord, *Canada* .. 63 C5
Chamchamal, *Iraq* ... 38 C5
Chamical, *Argentina* . 80 C3
Chamonix-Mont-Blanc,
France 18 D7
Champagne, *Canada* . 64 A1
Champagne, Plaine de,
France 18 B6
Champaign, *U.S.A.* .. 68 E1
Champlain, *Canada* .. 68 B9
Champlain, *U.S.A.* ... 68 C9
Champlain, L., *U.S.A.* 68 C9
Chañaral, *Chile* 80 B2
Chanārān, *Iran* 39 B8
Chandeleur Is., *U.S.A.* 71 L10
Chandeleur Sd., *U.S.A.* 71 L10
Chandigarh, *India* ... 36 D10
Chandler, *Australia* .. 55 D1
Chandler, *Canada* ... 63 C7
Chandler, *Ariz., U.S.A.* 73 K8
Chandler, *Okla., U.S.A.* 71 H6
Chandpur, *Bangla.* ... 37 H17
Chandrapur, *India* ... 36 K11
Chānf, *Iran* 39 E9
Ch'ang Chiang =
Chang Jiang →,
China 31 C7
Chang Jiang →,
China 31 C7
Changanacheri, *India* . 36 Q10
Changane →, *Mozam.* 49 C5
Changchiak'ou =
Zhangjiakou, *China* 31 B6
Ch'angchun =
Changchun, *China* . 31 B7
Changchun, *China* ... 31 B7
Changde, *China* 31 D6
Changhai = Shanghai,
China 31 C7
Changsha, *China* 31 D6
Changzhi, *China* 31 C6
Changzhou, *China* ... 31 C6
Chanhanga, *Angola* .. 48 B1
Channapatna, *India* .. 36 N10
Channel Is., *U.K.* 11 H5
Channel Is., *U.S.A.* .. 73 K4
Channel-Port aux
Basques, *Canada* . 63 C8
Channing, *Mich.,*
U.S.A. 68 B1
Channing, *Tex., U.S.A.* 71 H3
Chantada, *Spain* 19 A2
Chanthaburi, *Thailand* 34 F7
Chantrey Inlet, *Canada* 60 B10
Chanute, *U.S.A.* 71 G7
Chao Phraya →,
Thailand 34 F6
Chao'an, *China* 31 D6
Chapala, L. de, *Mexico* 74 C4
Chapayevo,
Kazakhstan 23 D9
Chapayevsk, *Russia* .. 22 D8
Chapel Hill, *U.S.A.* .. 69 H6
Chapleau, *Canada* ... 62 C3
Chaplin, *Canada* 65 C7
Chapra = Chhapra,
India 37 G14
Châr, *Mauritania* 44 D2
Chara, *Russia* 25 D12
Charadai, *Argentina* . 80 B5
Charagua, *Bolivia* ... 78 G6
Charaña, *Bolivia* 78 G5
Charcoal L., *Canada* . 65 B8
Chard, *U.K.* 11 G5
Chardara, *Kazakhstan* 24 E7

Chardzhou,
Turkmenistan 24 F7
Charente □, *France* .. 18 D4
Charente-Maritime □,
France 18 D3
Chari →, *Chad* 45 F7
Chārīkār, *Afghan.* ... 36 B6
Chariton →, *U.S.A.* . 70 F8
Chärjew = Chardzhou,
Turkmenistan 24 F7
Charleroi, *Belgium* ... 15 D4
Charles, C., *U.S.A.* .. 68 G8
Charles City, *U.S.A.* . 70 D8
Charles L., *Canada* .. 65 B6
Charles Town, *U.S.A.* 68 F7
Charleston, *Ill., U.S.A.* 68 F1
Charleston, *Miss.,*
U.S.A. 71 H9
Charleston, *Mo., U.S.A.* 71 G10
Charleston, *S.C.,*
U.S.A. 69 J6
Charleston, *W. Va.,*
U.S.A. 68 F5
Charlestown, *S. Africa* 49 D4
Charlestown, *U.S.A.* . 68 F3
Charlesville, *Zaïre* ... 46 F4
Charleville = Rath
Luirc, *Ireland* 13 D3
Charleville, *Australia* . 55 D4
Charleville-Mézières,
France 18 B6
Charlevoix, *U.S.A.* ... 68 C3
Charlotte, *Mich., U.S.A.* 68 D3
Charlotte, *N.C., U.S.A.* 69 H5
Charlotte Amalie,
Virgin Is. 75 D12
Charlotte Harbor,
U.S.A. 69 M4
Charlottesville, *U.S.A.* 68 F6
Charlottetown, *Canada* 63 C7
Charlton, *Australia* ... 55 F3
Charlton, *U.S.A.* 70 E8
Charlton I., *Canada* .. 62 B4
Charny, *Canada* 63 C5
Charolles, *France* 18 C6
Charouine, *Algeria* ... 44 C4
Charters Towers,
Australia 54 C4
Chartres, *France* 18 B4
Chascomús, *Argentina* 80 D5
Chasovnya-
Uchurskaya, *Russia* 25 D14
Chāt, *Iran* 39 B7
Château-Salins, *France* 18 B7
Châteaubriant, *France* 18 C3
Châteauroux, *France* . 18 C4
Châtellerault, *France* . 18 C4
Chatfield, *U.S.A.* 70 D9
Chatham, *N.B., Canada* 63 C6
Chatham, *Ont., Canada* 62 D3
Chatham, *U.K.* 11 F8
Chatham, *U.S.A.* 71 J8
Chatham, *Pac. Oc.* .. 56 M10
Chatham Str., *U.S.A.* 64 B2
Chatrapur, *India* 37 K14
Chattahoochee →,
U.S.A. 69 K3
Chattanooga, *U.S.A.* . 69 H3
Chauk, *Burma* 37 J19
Chaukan La, *Burma* . 37 F20
Chaumont, *France* ... 18 B6
Chauvin, *Canada* 65 C6
Chaves, *Brazil* 79 D9
Chaves, *Portugal* 19 B2
Chavuma, *Zambia* ... 47 G4
Chaykovskiy, *Russia* . 22 C9
Cheb, *Czech.* 16 C6
Cheboksary, *Russia* .. 22 C8
Cheboygan, *U.S.A.* .. 68 C3
Chech, Erg, *Africa* .. 44 D4
Checheno-Ingush
Republic □, *Russia* . 23 F8
Checleset B., *Canada* . 64 C3
Checotah, *U.S.A.* 71 H7
Chedabucto B., *Canada* 63 C7
Cheduba I., *Burma* ... 37 K18
Cheepie, *Australia* ... 55 D4
Chegdomyn, *Russia* .. 25 D14
Chegga, *Mauritania* .. 44 C3
Chegutu, *Zimbabwe* . 47 H6
Chehalis, *U.S.A.* 72 C2
Cheju Do, *S. Korea* . 31 C7
Chekiang =
Zhejiang □, *China* . 31 D7
Chela, Sa. da, *Angola* 48 B1
Chelan, *U.S.A.* 72 C4
Chelan, L., *U.S.A.* ... 72 C3
Cheleken,
Turkmenistan 23 G9
Chelforó, *Argentina* .. 80 D3
Chelkar, *Kazakhstan* . 24 E6
Chelkar Tengiz,
Solonchak,
Kazakhstan 24 E7
Chelm, *Poland* 17 C11
Chełmno, *Poland* 17 B9
Chelmsford, *U.K.* 11 F8
Chelmsford Dam,
S. Africa 49 D4
Chełmża, *Poland* 17 B9
Chelsea, *U.S.A.* 71 G7
Cheltenham, *U.K.* ... 11 F5
Chelyabinsk, *Russia* . 24 D7
Chemainus, *Canada* . 64 D4
Chemnitz, *Germany* .. 16 C6
Chemult, *U.S.A.* 72 E3
Chen, Gora, *Russia* . 25 C15
Chenab →, *Pakistan* 36 D7
Chencha, *Ethiopia* ... 45 G12
Cheney, *U.S.A.* 72 C5

Chengchou =
Zhengzhou, *China* . 31 C6
Chengde, *China* 31 B6
Chengdu, *China* 30 C5
Chengjiang, *China* ... 30 D5
Ch'engtu = Chengdu,
China 30 C5
Cheo Reo, *Vietnam* .. 34 F10
Cheom Ksan,
Cambodia 34 E8
Chepén, *Peru* 78 E3
Chepes, *Argentina* ... 80 C3
Chequamegon B.,
U.S.A. 70 B9
Cher □, *France* 18 C5
Cher →, *France* 18 C4
Cheraw, *U.S.A.* 69 H6
Cherbourg, *France* ... 18 B3
Cherchell, *Algeria* ... 44 A5
Cherdyn, *Russia* 22 B10
Cheremkhovo, *Russia* 25 D11
Cherepanovo, *Russia* 24 D9
Cherepovets, *Russia* . 22 C6
Chergui, Chott ech,
Algeria 44 B5
Cherkassy, *Ukraine* .. 23 E5
Cherkasy = Cherkassy,
Ukraine 23 E5
Cherlak, *Russia* 24 D8
Chernihiv =
Chernigov, *Ukraine* 22 D5
Chernigov, *Ukraine* .. 22 D5
Chernikovsk, *Russia* . 22 D10
Chernivtsi =
Chernovtsy, *Ukraine* 23 E4
Chernogorsk, *Russia* . 25 D10
Chernovtsy, *Ukraine* . 23 E4
Chernoye, *Russia* ... 25 B9
Chernyakhovsk, *Russia* 24 D3
Chernyshovskiy,
Russia 25 C12
Cherokee, *Iowa, U.S.A.* 70 D7
Cherokee, *Okla., U.S.A.* 71 G5
Cherokees, L. O'The,
U.S.A. 71 G7
Cherquenco, *Chile* ... 80 D2
Cherrapunji, *India* ... 37 G17
Cherry Creek, *U.S.A.* 72 G6
Cherryvale, *U.S.A.* ... 71 G7
Cherskiy, *Russia* 25 C17
Cherskogo Khrebet,
Russia 25 C15
Cherwell →, *U.K.* ... 11 F6
Chesapeake, *U.S.A.* .. 68 G7
Chesapeake B., *U.S.A.* 68 F7
Cheshire □, *U.K.* 10 D5
Cheshskaya Guba,
Russia 22 A8
Cheslatta L., *Canada* . 64 C3
Chester, *U.K.* 10 D5
Chester, *Calif., U.S.A.* 72 F3
Chester, *Ill., U.S.A.* .. 71 G10
Chester, *Mont., U.S.A.* 72 B8
Chester, *Pa., U.S.A.* .. 68 F8
Chester, *S.C., U.S.A.* . 69 H5
Chesterfield, *U.K.* 10 D6
Chesterfield, Is., *N. Cal.* 56 J7
Chesterfield Inlet,
Canada 60 B10
Chesterton Ra.,
Australia 55 D4
Chesuncook L., *U.S.A.* 63 C6
Chéticamp, *Canada* .. 63 C7
Chetwynd, *Canada* .. 64 B4
Cheviot, The, *U.K.* ... 10 B5
Cheviot Hills, *U.K.* ... 10 B5
Cheviot, *Australia* ... 55 K3
Chew Bahir, *Ethiopia* 45 H12
Chewelah, *U.S.A.* 72 B5
Cheyenne, *Okla.,*
U.S.A. 71 H5
Cheyenne, *Wyo.,*
U.S.A. 70 E2
Cheyenne →, *U.S.A.* 70 C4
Cheyenne Wells,
U.S.A. 70 F3
Cheyne B., *Australia* . 53 F2
Chhapra, *India* 37 G14
Chhatarpur, *India* 36 G11
Chhindwara, *India* ... 36 H11
Chhlong, *Cambodia* .. 34 F8
Chi →, *Thailand* 34 E8
Chiai, *Taiwan* 31 D7
Chiamis, *Indonesia* .. 33 G13
Chiamussu = Jiamusi,
China 31 B8
Chiang Mai, *Thailand* 34 C5
Chiange, *Angola* 47 H2
Chiapa →, *Mexico* .. 74 D6
Chiba, *Japan* 29 G10
Chibabava, *Mozam.* .. 49 C5
Chibatu, *Indonesia* .. 33 G12
Chibemba, Cunene,
Angola 47 H2
Chibemba, Huila,
Angola 48 B2
Chibia, *Angola* 47 H2
Chibougamau, *Canada* 62 C5
Chibougamau L.,
Canada 62 C5
Chibuk, *Nigeria* 45 F7
Chic-Chocs, Mts.,
Canada 63 C6
Chicacole =
Srikakulam, *India* . 37 K13
Chicago, *U.S.A.* 68 E2
Chicago Heights,
U.S.A. 68 E2
Chichagof I., *U.S.A.* .. 64 B1
Chichester, *U.K.* 11 G7
Chichibu, *Japan* 29 F9

Ch'ich'ihaerh =
Qiqihar, *China* 25 E13
Chickasha, *U.S.A.* ... 71 H5
Chiclana de la
Frontera, *Spain* ... 19 D2
Chiclayo, *Peru* 78 E3
Chico, *U.S.A.* 72 G3
Chico →, *Chubut,*
Argentina 80 E3
Chico →, *Santa Cruz,*
Argentina 80 G3
Chicomo, *Mozam.* ... 49 C5
Chicopee, *U.S.A.* 68 D9
Chicoutimi, *Canada* .. 63 C5
Chicualacuala, *Mozam.* 49 C5
Chidambaram, *India* . 36 P11
Chidenguele, *Mozam.* 49 C5
Chidley, C., *Canada* .. 61 B13
Chiede, *Angola* 48 B2
Chiengi, *Zambia* 46 F5
Chiengmai = Chiang
Mai, *Thailand* 34 C5
Chiese →, *Italy* 20 B4
Chieti, *Italy* 20 C6
Chignecto B., *Canada* 63 C7
Chiguana, *Bolivia* 78 H5
Chihli, G. of = Bo Hai,
China 31 C6
Chihuahua, *Mexico* .. 74 B3
Chiili, *Kazakhstan* ... 24 E7
Chik Ballapur, *India* . 36 N10
Chikmagalur, *India* ... 36 N9
Chilako →, *Canada* . 64 C4
Chilapa, *Mexico* 74 D5
Chilas, *Pakistan* 36 B9
Chilaw, *Sri Lanka* ... 36 R11
Chilcotin →, *Canada* 64 C4
Childers, *Australia* ... 55 D5
Childress, *U.S.A.* 71 H4
Chile ■, *S. Amer.* ... 80 D2
Chile Rise, *Pac. Oc.* . 57 L18
Chilete, *Peru* 78 E3
Chililabombwe,
Zambia 47 G5
Chilin = Jilin, *China* . 31 B7
Chilka L., *India* 37 K14
Chilko →, *Canada* .. 64 C4
Chilko, L., *Canada* ... 64 C4
Chillagoe, *Australia* .. 54 B3
Chillán, *Chile* 80 D2
Chillicothe, *Ill., U.S.A.* 70 E10
Chillicothe, *Mo., U.S.A.* 70 F8
Chillicothe, *Ohio,*
U.S.A. 68 F4
Chilliwack, *Canada* .. 64 D4
Chiloane, I., *Mozam.* . 49 C5
Chiloé, I. de, *Chile* ... 80 E2
Chilpancingo, *Mexico* 74 D5
Chiltern Hills, *U.K.* ... 11 F7
Chilton, *U.S.A.* 68 C1
Chiluage, *Angola* 46 F4
Chilung, *Taiwan* 31 D7
Chilwa, L., *Malawi* ... 47 H7
Chimay, *Belgium* 15 D4
Chimbay, *Uzbekistan* 24 E6
Chimborazo, *Ecuador* 78 D3
Chimbote, *Peru* 78 E3
Chimkent, *Kazakhstan* 24 E7
Chimoio, *Mozam.* 47 H6
Chin □, *Burma* 37 J18
China ■, *Asia* 31 C6
Chinan = Jinan, *China* 31 C6
Chinandega, *Nic.* 74 E7
Chinati Pk., *U.S.A.* .. 71 K2
Chincha Alta, *Peru* .. 78 F3
Chinchilla, *Australia* . 55 D5
Chinchón, *Spain* 19 B4
Chinchou = Jinzhou,
China 31 B7
Chincoteague, *U.S.A.* 68 G8
Chinde, *Mozam.* 47 H7
Chindwin →, *Burma* 37 J19
Chingola, *Zambia* 47 G5
Ch'ingtao = Qingdao,
China 31 C7
Chinguetti, *Mauritania* 44 D2
Chingune, *Mozam.* ... 49 C5
Chinhanguanine,
Mozam. 49 D5
Chinhoyi, *Zimbabwe* . 47 H6
Chiniot, *Pakistan* 36 D8
Chinle, *U.S.A.* 73 H9
Chino, *Japan* 29 G9
Chino Valley, *U.S.A.* . 73 J7
Chinon, *France* 18 C4
Chinook, *Canada* 65 C6
Chinook, *U.S.A.* 72 B9
Chinsali, *Zambia* 46 G6
Chióggia, *Italy* 20 B5
Chíos = Khíos, *Greece* 21 E12
Chipata, *Zambia* 47 G6
Chipewyan L., *Canada* 65 B9
Chipley, *U.S.A.* 69 K3
Chipman, *Canada* ... 63 C6
Chippenham, *U.K.* ... 11 F5
Chippewa →, *U.S.A.* 70 C8
Chippewa Falls, *U.S.A.* 70 C9
Chiquián, *Peru* 78 F3
Chiquinquira,
Colombia 78 B4
Chirala, *India* 36 M12
Chirchik, *Uzbekistan* . 24 E7
Chiricahua Pk., *U.S.A.* 73 L9
Chirmiri, *India* 37 H13
Chiromo, *Malawi* 47 H7
Chisamba, *Zambia* ... 47 G5
Chisapani Garhi, *Nepal* 37 F14
Chisholm, *Canada* ... 64 C6
Chişinău = Kishinev,
Moldavia 23 E4
Chisos Mts., *U.S.A.* .. 71 L3
Chistopol, *Russia* 22 C9

Chita, *Russia* 25 D12
Chitado, *Angola* 47 H2
Chitembo, *Angola* ... 47 G3
Chitose, *Japan* 28 C10
Chitral, *Pakistan* 36 B7
Chitré, *Panama* 75 F8
Chittagong, *Bangla.* .. 37 H17
Chittagong □, *Bangla.* 37 G17
Chittaurgarh, *India* ... 36 G9
Chittoor, *India* 36 N11
Chiusi, *Italy* 20 C4
Chivasso, *Italy* 20 B2
Chivilcoy, *Argentina* . 80 D4
Chkalov = Orenburg,
Russia 22 D10
Chobe National Park,
Botswana 48 B3
Choctawhatchee B.,
U.S.A. 67 D9
Choele Choel,
Argentina 80 D3
Chojnice, *Poland* 17 B8
Chōkai-San, *Japan* ... 28 E10
Chokurdakh, *Russia* . 25 B15
Cholet, *France* 18 C3
Choluteca, *Honduras* . 74 E7
Choma, *Zambia* 47 H5
Chomutov, *Czech.* ... 16 C6
Chon Buri, *Thailand* . 34 F6
Chone, *Ecuador* 78 D2
Chongjin, *N. Korea* .. 31 B7
Chongqing, *China* ... 30 D5
Chonos, Arch. de los,
Chile 80 F2
Chorley, *U.K.* 10 D5
Chorregon, *Australia* . 54 C3
Chorzów, *Poland* 17 C9
Chos-Malal, *Argentina* 80 D2
Choszczno, *Poland* .. 16 B7
Choteau, *U.S.A.* 72 C7
Chotila, *India* 36 H7
Chowchilla, *U.S.A.* ... 73 H3
Choybalsan, *Mongolia* 31 B6
Christchurch, *N.Z.* ... 51 K4
Christchurch, *U.K.* ... 11 G6
Christiana, *S. Africa* . 48 D4
Christie B., *Canada* .. 65 A6
Christina →, *Canada* 65 B6
Christmas Cr. →,
Australia 52 C4
Christmas Creek,
Australia 52 C4
Christmas I. =
Kiritimati, *Kiribati* . 57 G12
Christmas I., *Ind. Oc.* 35 F9
Christopher L.,
Australia 53 D4
Chu, *Kazakhstan* 24 E8
Chu →, *Vietnam* 34 C8
Chu Chua, *Canada* .. 64 C4
Ch'uanchou =
Quanzhou, *China* . 31 D6
Chūbu □, *Japan* 29 F8
Chubut →, *Argentina* 80 E3
Chuchi L., *Canada* ... 64 B4
Chudskoye, Oz.,
Estonia 22 C4
Chūgoku □, *Japan* .. 29 G6
Chūgoku-Sanchi,
Japan 29 G6
Chugwater, *U.S.A.* ... 70 E2
Chukotskiy Khrebet,
Russia 25 C18
Chukotskoye More,
Russia 25 C19
Chula Vista, *U.S.A.* .. 73 K5
Chulman, *Russia* 25 D13
Chulucanas, *Peru* ... 78 E2
Chulym →, *Russia* .. 24 D9
Chumbicha, *Argentina* 80 B3
Chumikan, *Russia* ... 25 D14
Chumphon, *Thailand* . 34 G5
Chuna →, *Russia* ... 25 D10
Chungking =
Chongqing, *China* . 30 D5
Chunya, *Tanzania* ... 46 F6
Chuquibamba, *Peru* . 78 G4
Chuquicamata, *Chile* . 80 A3
Chur, *Switz.* 16 E4
Churachandpur, *India* 37 G18
Churchill, *Canada* ... 65 B10
Churchill →, *Man.,*
Canada 65 B10
Churchill →, *Nfld.,*
Canada 63 B7
Churchill, C., *Canada* 65 B10
Churchill Falls, *Canada* 63 B7
Churchill L., *Canada* . 65 B7
Churchill Pk., *Canada* 64 B3
Churu, *India* 36 E9
Chushal, *India* 36 C11
Chusovoy, *Russia* ... 22 C10
Chuvash Republic □,
Russia 22 C8
Chuwārtah, *Iraq* 38 C5
Cianjur, *Indonesia* ... 33 G12
Cibadak, *Indonesia* .. 33 G12
Cibatu, *Indonesia* ... 33 G12
Cicero, *U.S.A.* 68 E2
Ciechanów, *Poland* .. 17 B10
Ciego de Avila, *Cuba* 75 C9
Ciénaga, *Colombia* .. 78 A4
Cienfuegos, *Cuba* ... 75 C8
Cieszyn, *Poland* 17 D9
Cieza, *Spain* 19 C5
Cijulang, *Indonesia* .. 33 G13
Cikajang, *Indonesia* .. 33 G12
Cikampek, *Indonesia* 33 G12
Cilacap, *Indonesia* ... 33 G13
Cimahi, *Indonesia* ... 33 G12

Cimarron, *N. Mex.,*
U.S.A. 71 G2
Cimarron →, *U.S.A.* 71 G6
Cimone, Mte., *Italy* .. 20 B4
Cîmpina, *Romania* ... 17 F12
Cîmpulung, *Romania* 17 F12
Cinca →, *Spain* 19 B6
Cincinnati, *U.S.A.* 68 F3
Ciney, *Belgium* 15 D5
Cinto, Mte., *France* .. 18 E8
Circle, *Alaska, U.S.A.* 60 B5
Circle, *Mont., U.S.A.* . 70 B2
Circleville, *Ohio, U.S.A.* 68 F4
Circleville, *Utah, U.S.A.* 73 G7
Cirebon, *Indonesia* ... 33 G13
Cirencester, *U.K.* 11 F6
Cisco, *U.S.A.* 71 J5
Ciskei □, *S. Africa* ... 49 E4
Citlaltépetl, *Mexico* .. 74 D5
Citrusdal, *S. Africa* ... 48 E2
Ciudad Bolívar,
Venezuela 78 B6
Ciudad Chetumal,
Mexico 74 D7
Ciudad del Carmen,
Mexico 74 D6
Ciudad Delicias =
Delicias, *Mexico* .. 74 B3
Ciudad Guayana,
Venezuela 78 B6
Ciudad Juárez, *Mexico* 74 A3
Ciudad Madero,
Mexico 74 C5
Ciudad Mante, *Mexico* 74 C5
Ciudad Obregón,
Mexico 74 B3
Ciudad Real, *Spain* .. 19 C4
Ciudad Rodrigo, *Spain* 19 B2
Ciudad Trujillo =
Santo Domingo,
Dom. Rep. 75 D11
Ciudad Victoria,
Mexico 74 C5
Civitanova Marche,
Italy 20 C5
Civitavécchia, *Italy* ... 20 C4
Cizre, *Turkey* 23 G7
Clacton-on-Sea, *U.K.* 11 F9
Claire, L., *Canada* ... 64 B6
Clairemont, *U.S.A.* ... 71 J4
Clanton, *U.S.A.* 69 J2
Clanwilliam, *S. Africa* 48 E2
Clara, *Ireland* 13 C4
Clara →, *Australia* .. 54 B3
Clare, *Australia* 55 E2
Clare, *U.S.A.* 68 D3
Clare □, *Ireland* 13 D3
Clare →, *Ireland* 13 C2
Clare I., *Ireland* 13 C1
Claremont, *U.S.A.* ... 68 D9
Claremont Pt.,
Australia 54 A3
Claremore, *U.S.A.* ... 71 G7
Claremorris, *Ireland* . 13 C3
Clarence →, *Australia* 55 D5
Clarence →, *N.Z.* ... 51 K4
Clarence, I., *Chile* ... 80 G2
Clarence I., *Antarctica* 5 C18
Clarence Str., *Australia* 52 B5
Clarence Str., *U.S.A.* . 64 B2
Clarendon, *Ark., U.S.A.* 71 H9
Clarendon, *Tex., U.S.A.* 71 H4
Clarenville, *Canada* .. 63 C9
Claresholm, *Canada* . 64 C6
Clarie Coast, *Antarctica* 5 C9
Clarinda, *U.S.A.* 70 E7
Clarion, *U.S.A.* 70 D8
Clark, *U.S.A.* 70 C6
Clark Fork, *U.S.A.* ... 72 B5
Clark Fork →, *U.S.A.* 72 B5
Clark Hill Res., *U.S.A.* 69 J4
Clarkdale, *U.S.A.* 73 J7
Clarke City, *Canada* .. 63 B6
Clarke I., *Australia* ... 54 G4
Clarke L., *Canada* ... 65 C7
Clarke Ra., *Australia* . 54 C4
Clark's Fork →, *U.S.A.* 72 D9
Clark's Harbour,
Canada 63 D6
Clarksburg, *U.S.A.* ... 68 F5
Clarksdale, *U.S.A.* ... 71 H9
Clarkston, *U.S.A.* 72 C5
Clarksville, *Ark., U.S.A.* 71 H8
Clarksville, Tenn.,
U.S.A. 69 G2
Clarksville, *Tex., U.S.A.* 71 J7
Clatskanie, *U.S.A.* ... 72 C2
Claude, *U.S.A.* 71 H4
Claveria, *Phil.* 33 A6
Clay Center, *U.S.A.* .. 70 F6
Claypool, *U.S.A.* 73 K8
Clayton, *Idaho, U.S.A.* 72 D6
Clayton, *N. Mex.,*
U.S.A. 71 G3
Cle Elum, *U.S.A.* 72 C3
Clear, C., *Ireland* 13 E2
Clear I., *Ireland* 13 E2
Clear L., *U.S.A.* 72 G2
Clear Lake, *S. Dak.,*
U.S.A. 70 C6
Clear Lake, *Wash.,*
U.S.A. 72 B2
Clear Lake Res., *U.S.A.* 72 F3
Clearfield, *U.S.A.* 68 E6
Clearfield, *Utah, U.S.A.* 72 F7
Clearmont, *U.S.A.* ... 72 D10
Clearwater, *Canada* .. 64 C4
Clearwater, *U.S.A.* ... 69 M4
Clearwater →, *Alta.,*
Canada 64 C6
Clearwater →, *Alta.,*
Canada 65 B6

90

Clearwater Cr. →,
  Canada 64 A3
Clearwater Mts., U.S.A. 72 C6
Clearwater Prov. Park,
  Canada 65 C8
Cleburne, U.S.A. 71 J6
Cleethorpes, U.K. . . . 10 D7
Cleeve Hill, U.K. 11 F6
Clerke Reef, Australia 52 C2
Clermont, Australia . . 54 C4
Clermont-Ferrand,
  France 18 D5
Clervaux, Lux. 15 D6
Cleveland, Australia . . 55 D5
Cleveland, Miss.,
  U.S.A. 71 J9
Cleveland, Ohio, U.S.A. 68 E5
Cleveland, Okla.,
  U.S.A. 71 G6
Cleveland, Tenn.,
  U.S.A. 69 H4
Cleveland, Tex., U.S.A. 71 K7
Cleveland □, U.K. . . . 10 C9
Cleveland, C., Australia 54 B4
Clew B., Ireland 13 C2
Clewiston, U.S.A. . . . 69 M5
Clifden, Ireland 13 C1
Clifden, N.Z. 51 M1
Clifton, Australia 55 D5
Clifton, Ariz., U.S.A. . 73 K9
Clifton, Tex., U.S.A. . . 71 K6
Clifton Beach, Australia 54 B4
Clifton Forge, U.S.A. . 68 G6
Clifton Hills, Australia 55 D2
Climax, Canada 65 D7
Clinch →, U.S.A. . . . 69 H3
Clingmans Dome,
  U.S.A. 69 H4
Clint, U.S.A. 73 L10
Clinton, B.C., Canada . 64 C4
Clinton, Ont., Canada . 62 D3
Clinton, N.Z. 51 M2
Clinton, Ark., U.S.A. . 71 H8
Clinton, Ill., U.S.A. . . 70 E10
Clinton, Ind., U.S.A. . 68 F2
Clinton, Iowa, U.S.A. . 70 E9
Clinton, Mass., U.S.A. 68 D10
Clinton, Mo., U.S.A. . 70 F8
Clinton, N.C., U.S.A. . 69 H6
Clinton, Okla., U.S.A. 71 H5
Clinton, S.C., U.S.A. . 69 H5
Clinton, Tenn., U.S.A. 69 G3
Clinton C., Australia . . 54 C5
Clinton Colden L.,
  Canada 60 B9
Clintonville, U.S.A. . . 70 C10
Clipperton, I., Pac. Oc. 57 F17
Clive L., Canada 64 A5
Cloates, Pt., Australia 52 D1
Clocolan, S. Africa . . 49 D4
Clonakilty, Ireland . . . 13 E3
Clonakilty B., Ireland . 13 E3
Cloncurry, Australia . . 54 C3
Cloncurry →,
  Australia 54 B3
Clones, Ireland 13 B4
Clonmel, Ireland 13 D4
Cloquet, U.S.A. 70 B8
Cloud Peak, U.S.A. . . 72 D10
Cloudcroft, U.S.A. . . . 73 K11
Cloverdale, U.S.A. . . . 72 G2
Clovis, Calif., U.S.A. . 73 H4
Clovis, N. Mex., U.S.A. 71 H3
Cluj-Napoca, Romania 17 E11
Clunes, Australia 55 F3
Cluny, France 18 C6
Clutha →, N.Z. 51 M2
Clwyd □, U.K. 10 D4
Clwyd →, U.K. 10 D4
Clyde, N.Z. 51 L2
Clyde →, U.K. 12 F4
Clyde, Firth of, U.K. . 12 F3
Clyde River, Canada . 61 A13
Clydebank, U.K. 12 F4
Coachella, U.S.A. . . . 73 K5
Coahoma, U.S.A. . . . 71 J4
Coal →, Canada . . . 64 B3
Coaldale, Canada . . . 64 D6
Coalgate, U.S.A. 71 H6
Coalinga, U.S.A. 73 H3
Coalville, U.K. 10 E6
Coalville, U.S.A. 72 F8
Coari, Brazil 78 D6
Coast Mts., Canada . . 64 C3
Coast Ranges, U.S.A. 72 F2
Coatbridge, U.K. 12 F4
Coatesville, U.S.A. . . 68 F8
Coaticook, Canada . . 63 C5
Coats I., Canada 61 B11
Coats Land, Antarctica 5 D1
Coatzacoalcos, Mexico 74 D6
Cobalt, Canada 62 C4
Cobar, Australia 55 E4
Cóbh, Ireland 13 E3
Cobham, Australia . . 55 E3
Cobija, Bolivia 78 F5
Cobleskill, U.S.A. . . . 68 D8
Cobourg, Canada . . . 62 D4
Cobourg Pen.,
  Australia 52 B5
Cobram, Australia . . . 55 F4
Cobre, U.S.A. 72 F6
Cóbué, Mozam. 47 G6
Coburg, Germany . . . 16 C5
Cocanada = Kakinada,
  India 37 L13
Cochabamba, Bolivia . 78 G5
Cochin, India 36 Q10
Cochin China = Nam-
  Phan, Vietnam . . . 34 G9
Cochise, U.S.A. 73 K9
Cochran, U.S.A. 69 J4

Cochrane, Alta.,
  Canada 64 C6
Cochrane, Ont.,
  Canada 62 C3
Cochrane →, Canada 65 B8
Cochrane, L., Chile . . 80 F2
Cockburn, Australia . . 55 E3
Cockburn, Canal, Chile 80 G2
Cockburn I., Canada . 62 C3
Cockburn Ra., Australia 52 C4
Cockenbiddy Motel,
  Australia 53 F4
Coco →, Cent. Amer. 75 E8
Coco Chan., India . . . 34 F2
Coco Solo, Panama . . 74 H14
Cocoa, U.S.A. 69 L5
Cocobeach, Gabon . . 46 D1
Cocos, I. del, Pac. Oc. 57 G19
Cocos Is., Ind. Oc. . . 35 H8
Cod, C., U.S.A. 67 B13
Codajás, Brazil 78 D6
Coderre, Canada . . . 65 C7
Codó, Brazil 79 D10
Cody, U.S.A. 72 D9
Coe Hill, Canada . . . 62 D4
Coen, Australia 54 A3
Coetivy Is., Seychelles 35 E4
Cœur d'Alene, U.S.A. 72 C5
Cœur d'Alene L.,
  U.S.A. 72 C5
Coevorden, Neths. . . 15 B6
Coffeyville, U.S.A. . . 71 G7
Coffin B., Australia . . 55 E2
Coffin Bay Peninsula,
  Australia 55 E2
Coffs Harbour,
  Australia 55 E5
Coghinas →, Italy . . 20 D3
Cognac, France 18 D3
Cohagen, U.S.A. 72 C10
Cohoes, U.S.A. 68 D9
Cohuna, Australia . . . 55 F3
Coiba, I., Panama . . . 75 F8
Coig →, Argentina . . 80 G3
Coihaique, Chile 80 F2
Coimbatore, India . . . 36 P10
Coimbra, Brazil 78 G7
Coimbra, Portugal . . 19 B1
Coin, Spain 19 D3
Cojimies, Ecuador . . 78 C2
Cokeville, U.S.A. 72 E8
Colac, Australia 55 F3
Colatina, Brazil 79 G10
Colbeck, C., Antarctica 5 D13
Colbinabbin, Australia 55 F3
Colby, U.S.A. 70 F4
Colchester, U.K. 11 F8
Coldstream, U.K. . . . 12 F6
Coldwater, U.S.A. . . . 71 G5
Colebrook, Australia . 54 G4
Colebrook, U.S.A. . . . 68 C10
Coleman, Canada . . . 64 D6
Coleman, U.S.A. 71 K5
Coleman →, Australia 54 B3
Colenso, S. Africa . . 49 D4
Coleraine, Australia . . 55 F3
Coleraine, U.K. 13 A5
Coleraine □, U.K. . . . 13 A5
Coleridge, L., N.Z. . . 51 K3
Colesberg, S. Africa . 48 E4
Colfax, La., U.S.A. . . 71 K8
Colfax, Wash., U.S.A. 72 C5
Colhué Huapi, L.,
  Argentina 80 F3
Coligny, S. Africa . . . 49 D4
Colima, Mexico 74 D4
Colima, Colima,
  Mexico 74 D4
Colinas, Brazil 79 E10
Coll, U.K. 12 E2
Collaguasi, Chile . . . 78 H5
Collarenebri, Australia 55 D4
Collbran, U.S.A. 73 G10
College Park, U.S.A. . 69 J3
Collette, Canada . . . 63 C6
Collie, Australia 53 F2
Collier B., Australia . . 52 C3
Collier Ra., Australia . 52 D2
Collingwood, Canada 62 D3
Collingwood, N.Z. . . 51 J4
Collins, Canada 62 B2
Collinsville, Australia . 54 C4
Collooney, Ireland . . 13 B3
Colmar, France 18 B7
Colne, U.K. 10 D5
Colo →, Australia . . 55 E5
Cologne = Köln,
  Germany 16 C3
Colomb-Béchar =
  Béchar, Algeria . . 44 B4
Colômbia, Brazil . . . 79 H9
Colombia ■, S. Amer. 78 C4
Colombo, Sri Lanka . 36 R11
Colome, U.S.A. 70 D5
Colón, Cuba 75 C8
Colón, Panama 74 H14
Colona, Australia . . . 53 F5
Colonia, Uruguay . . . 80 C5
Colonia Dora,
  Argentina 80 B4
Colonial Heights,
  U.S.A. 68 G7
Colonsay, Canada . . 65 C7
Colonsay, U.K. 12 E2
Colorado □, U.S.A. . . 73 G10
Colorado →,
  Argentina 80 D4
Colorado →,
  N. Amer. 73 L6
Colorado →, U.S.A. . 71 L7
Colorado, I., Panama . 74 H14
Colorado City, U.S.A. 71 J4

Colorado Desert,
  U.S.A. 66 D3
Colorado Plateau,
  U.S.A. 73 H8
Colorado River
  Aqueduct, U.S.A. . 73 J6
Colorado Springs,
  U.S.A. 70 F2
Colton, U.S.A. 72 C5
Columbia, La., U.S.A. 71 J8
Columbia, Miss.,
  U.S.A. 71 K10
Columbia, Mo., U.S.A. 70 F8
Columbia, Pa., U.S.A. 68 E7
Columbia, S.C., U.S.A. 69 H5
Columbia, Tenn.,
  U.S.A. 69 H2
Columbia →,
  N. Amer. 72 C1
Columbia, C., Canada 4 A4
Columbia, District
  of □, U.S.A. 68 F7
Columbia, Mt., Canada 64 C5
Columbia Basin, U.S.A. 72 C4
Columbia Falls, U.S.A. 72 B6
Columbia Heights,
  U.S.A. 70 C8
Columbretes, Is., Spain 19 C6
Columbus, Ga., U.S.A. 69 J3
Columbus, Ind., U.S.A. 68 F3
Columbus, Kans.,
  U.S.A. 71 G7
Columbus, Miss.,
  U.S.A. 69 J1
Columbus, Mont.,
  U.S.A. 72 D9
Columbus, N. Dak.,
  U.S.A. 70 A3
Columbus, N. Mex.,
  U.S.A. 73 L10
Columbus, Nebr.,
  U.S.A. 70 E6
Columbus, Ohio,
  U.S.A. 68 F4
Columbus, Tex., U.S.A. 71 L6
Columbus, Wis., U.S.A. 70 D10
Colusa, U.S.A. 72 G2
Colville, U.S.A. 72 B5
Colville →, U.S.A. . . 60 A4
Colville, C., N.Z. 51 G5
Colwyn Bay, U.K. . . . 10 D4
Comácchio, Italy . . . 20 B4
Comallo, Argentina . . 80 E2
Comanche, Okla.,
  U.S.A. 71 H6
Comanche, Tex.,
  U.S.A. 71 K5
Combahee →, U.S.A. 69 J5
Comblain-au-Pont,
  Belgium 15 D5
Comeragh Mts.,
  Ireland 13 D4
Comet, Australia 54 C4
Comilla, Bangla. 37 H17
Comino, Malta 20 F6
Commerce, Ga., U.S.A. 69 H4
Commerce, Tex.,
  U.S.A. 71 J7
Committee B., Canada 61 B11
Commonwealth B.,
  Antarctica 5 C10
Commonwealth of
  Independent
  States ■, Eurasia . 25 D11
Commoron Cr. →,
  Australia 55 D5
Communism Pk. =
  Kommunizma, Pik,
  Tajikistan 24 F8
Como, Italy 20 B3
Como, L. di, Italy . . . 20 A3
Comodoro Rivadavia,
  Argentina 80 F3
Comorin, C., India . . 36 Q10
Comoro Is. =
  Comoros ■, Ind. Oc. 43 H8
Comoros ■, Ind. Oc. 43 H8
Comox, Canada 64 D4
Compiègne, France . . 18 B5
Compton Downs,
  Australia 55 E4
Côn Dao, Vietnam . . 34 H9
Conakry, Guinea . . . 44 G2
Conara Junction,
  Australia 54 G4
Concarneau, France . 18 C2
Conceição da Barra,
  Brazil 79 G11
Conceição do
  Araguaia, Brazil . . 79 E9
Concepción, Bolivia . 78 G6
Concepción, Chile . . 80 D2
Concepción, Paraguay 80 A5
Concepción □, Bolivia 78 G6
Concepción del Oro,
  Mexico 74 C4
Concepción del
  Uruguay, Argentina 80 C5
Conception, Pt., U.S.A. 73 J3
Conception B.,
  Namibia 48 C1
Conchas Dam, U.S.A. 71 H2
Conche, Canada 63 B8
Concho, U.S.A. 73 J9
Concho →, U.S.A. . . 71 K5
Conchos →, Mexico 74 B3
Concord, Calif., U.S.A. 72 H2
Concord, N.C., U.S.A. 69 H5
Concord, N.H., U.S.A. 68 D10
Concordia, Argentina 80 C5
Concórdia, Brazil . . . 80 D5

Concordia, U.S.A. . . 70 F6
Concrete, U.S.A. . . . 72 B3
Conde, U.S.A. 70 C5
Condeúba, Brazil . . . 79 F10
Condobolin, Australia 55 E4
Condon, U.S.A. 72 D3
Confuso →, Paraguay 80 B5
Congleton, U.K. 10 D5
Congo = Zaïre →,
  Africa 46 F2
Congo (Kinshasa) =
  Zaïre ■, Africa . . . 46 E4
Congo ■, Africa . . . 46 E3
Congo Basin, Africa . 42 G6
Congress, U.S.A. . . . 73 J7
Coniston, Canada . . 62 C3
Conjeeveram =
  Kanchipuram, India 36 N11
Conjuboy, Australia . 54 B3
Conklin, Canada . . . 65 B6
Conlea, Australia . . . 55 E3
Conn, L., Ireland . . . 13 B2
Connacht, Ireland . . 13 C3
Conneaut, U.S.A. . . . 68 E5
Connecticut □, U.S.A. 68 E9
Connecticut →,
  U.S.A. 68 E9
Connell, U.S.A. 72 C4
Connellsville, U.S.A. . 68 E6
Connemara, Ireland . 13 C2
Connersville, U.S.A. . 68 F3
Connors Ra., Australia 54 C4
Conoble, Australia . . 55 E3
Cononaco →,
  Ecuador 78 D3
Cononbridge, U.K. . . 12 D4
Conquest, Canada . . 65 C7
Conrad, U.S.A. 72 B8
Conran, C., Australia 55 F4
Conroe, U.S.A. 71 K7
Conselheiro Lafaiete,
  Brazil 79 H10
Consort, Canada . . . 65 C6
Constance = Konstanz,
  Germany 16 E4
Constance, L. =
  Bodensee, Europe . 16 E4
Constanţa, Romania . 21 B13
Constantine, Algeria . 44 A6
Constitución, Chile . . 80 D2
Consul, Canada 65 D7
Contact, U.S.A. 72 F6
Contai, India 37 J15
Contamana, Peru . . . 78 E4
Contas →, Brazil . . 79 F11
Contra Costa, Mozam. 49 D5
Conway = Conwy,
  U.K. 10 D4
Conway = Conwy →,
  U.K. 10 D4
Conway, Ark., U.S.A. 71 H8
Conway, N.H., U.S.A. 68 D10
Conway, S.C., U.S.A. 69 J6
Conway, L., Australia 55 D2
Conwy, U.K. 10 D4
Conwy →, U.K. 10 D4
Coober Pedy, Australia 55 D1
Cooch Behar = Koch
  Bihar, India 37 F16
Coodardy, Australia . 53 E2
Cook, Australia 53 F5
Cook, B., Chile 80 H3
Cook, Mt., N.Z. 51 K3
Cook Inlet, U.S.A. . . 60 C4
Cook Is., Pac. Oc. . . 57 J11
Cook Strait, N.Z. . . . 51 J5
Cookeville, U.S.A. . . 69 G3
Cookhouse, S. Africa 48 E4
Cookstown, Australia 54 B4
Cookstown, U.K. . . . 13 B5
Cookstown □, U.K. . . 13 B5
Cooktown, Australia . 54 B4
Coolabah, Australia . 55 E4
Cooladdi, Australia . . 55 D4
Coolah, Australia . . . 55 E4
Coolamon, Australia . 55 E4
Coolangatta, Australia 55 D5
Coolgardie, Australia 53 F3
Coolibah, Australia . . 52 C5
Coolidge, U.S.A. . . . 73 K8
Coolidge Dam, U.S.A. 73 K8
Cooma, Australia . . . 55 F4
Coonabarabran,
  Australia 55 E4
Coonamble, Australia 55 E4
Coonana, Australia . . 53 F3
Coondapoor, India . . 36 N9
Coongie, Australia . . 55 D3
Coongoola, Australia 55 D4
Cooninie, L., Australia 55 D2
Cooper, U.S.A. 71 J7
Cooper →, U.S.A. . . 69 J6
Cooper Cr. →,
  Australia 55 D2
Cooperstown, N. Dak.,
  U.S.A. 70 B5
Cooperstown, N.Y.,
  U.S.A. 68 D8
Coorabie, Australia . . 53 F5
Coorabulka, Australia 54 C3
Coorow, Australia . . 53 E2
Cooroy, Australia . . . 55 D5
Coos Bay, U.S.A. . . . 72 E1
Cootamundra,
  Australia 55 E4
Cootehill, Ireland . . . 13 B4
Cooyar, Australia . . . 55 D5
Cooyeena, Australia . 55 C2
Cope, U.S.A. 70 F3

Copenhagen =
  København,
  Denmark 9 J12
Copiapó, Chile 80 B2
Copiapó →, Chile . . 80 B2
Copley, Australia . . . 55 E2
Copp L., Canada . . . 64 A6
Copper Center, U.S.A. 60 B5
Copper Cliff, Canada 62 C3
Copper Harbor, U.S.A. 68 B2
Coppermine, Canada 60 B8
Coppermine →,
  Canada 60 B8
Coquet →, U.K. . . . 10 B6
Coquilhatville =
  Mbandaka, Zaïre . . 46 D3
Coquille, U.S.A. 72 E1
Coquimbo, Chile . . . 80 C2
Corabia, Romania . . 17 G12
Coracora, Peru 78 G4
Coral Gables, U.S.A. . 69 N5
Coral Harbour, Canada 61 B11
Coral Sea, Pac. Oc. . 56 J7
Corato, Italy 20 D7
Corbin, U.S.A. 68 G3
Corby, U.K. 11 E7
Corby Glen, U.K. . . . 11 E7
Corcoran, U.S.A. . . . 73 H4
Corcubión, Spain . . . 19 A1
Cordele, U.S.A. 69 K4
Cordell, U.S.A. 71 H5
Córdoba, Argentina . 80 C4
Córdoba, Spain 19 D3
Córdoba, Sierra de,
  Argentina 80 C4
Cordon, Phil. 33 A6
Cordova, Ala., U.S.A. 69 J2
Cordova, Alaska,
  U.S.A. 60 B5
Corella →, Australia 54 B3
Corfield, Australia . . 54 C3
Corfu = Kérkira,
  Greece 21 E8
Corigliano Cálabro,
  Italy 20 E7
Coringa Is., Australia 54 B4
Corinna, Australia . . 54 G4
Corinth = Kórinthos,
  Greece 21 F10
Corinth, U.S.A. 69 H1
Corinth, G. of =
  Korinthiakós Kólpos,
  Greece 21 E10
Corinto, Brazil 79 G10
Cork, Ireland 13 E3
Cork □, Ireland 13 E3
Cork Harbour, Ireland 13 E3
Cormack L., Canada . 64 A4
Cormorant, Canada . 65 C8
Cormorant L., Canada 65 C8
Cornell, U.S.A. 70 C9
Corner Brook, Canada 63 C8
Corning, Ark., U.S.A. 71 G9
Corning, Calif., U.S.A. 72 G2
Corning, Iowa, U.S.A. 70 E7
Corning, N.Y., U.S.A. 68 D7
Cornwall, Canada . . 62 C5
Cornwall □, U.K. . . . 11 G3
Corny Pt., Australia . 55 E2
Coro, Venezuela . . . 78 A5
Coroatá, Brazil 79 D10
Corocoro, Bolivia . . 78 G5
Coroico, Bolivia . . . 78 G5
Coromandel, N.Z. . . 51 G5
Coromandel Coast,
  India 36 N12
Corona, Australia . . 55 E3
Corona, Calif., U.S.A. 73 K5
Corona, N. Mex.,
  U.S.A. 73 J11
Coronada, U.S.A. . . 73 K5
Coronation, Canada . 64 C6
Coronation Gulf,
  Canada 60 B8
Coronation I., U.S.A. 64 B2
Coronation I.,
  Antarctica 5 C18
Coronation Is.,
  Australia 52 B3
Coronel, Chile 80 D2
Coronel Dorrego,
  Argentina 80 D4
Coronel Pringles,
  Argentina 80 D4
Coronel Suárez,
  Argentina 80 D4
Corowa, Australia . . 55 F4
Corozal, Panama . . . 74 H14
Corpus Christi, U.S.A. 71 M6
Corpus Christi, L.,
  U.S.A. 71 L6
Corque, Bolivia 78 G5
Corrèze □, France . . 18 D4
Corrib, L., Ireland . . 13 C2
Corrientes, Argentina 80 B5
Corrientes □, Peru . 78 D4
Corrientes, C.,
  Colombia 78 B3
Corrientes, C., Mexico 74 C3
Corrigan, U.S.A. . . . 71 K7
Corrigin, Australia . . 53 F2
Corry, U.S.A. 68 E6
Corse, France 18 F8
Corse, C., France . . 20 C3
Corse-du-Sud □,
  France 18 F9
Corsica = Corse,
  France 18 F8
Corsicana, U.S.A. . . 71 J6

Cortez, U.S.A. 73 H9
Cortland, U.S.A. . . . 68 D7
Cortona, Italy 20 C4
Çorum, Turkey 23 F5
Corumbá, Brazil . . . 78 G7
Corumbá de Goiás,
  Brazil 79 G9
Coruña = La Coruña,
  Spain 19 A1
Corvallis, U.S.A. . . . 72 D2
Corvette, L. de la,
  Canada 62 B5
Corydon, U.S.A. . . . 70 E8
Cosenza, Italy 20 E7
Coshocton, U.S.A. . . 68 E5
Cosmo Newberry,
  Australia 53 E3
Costa Blanca, Spain 19 C5
Costa Brava, Spain . 19 B7
Costa del Sol, Spain 19 D3
Costa Dorada, Spain 19 B6
Costa Rica ■,
  Cent. Amer. 75 F8
Costilla, U.S.A. 73 H11
Cotabato, Phil. 33 C6
Cotagaita, Bolivia . . 78 H5
Côte-d'Ivoire = Ivory
  Coast ■, Africa . . 44 G3
Côte-d'Or □, France 18 C6
Coteau des Prairies,
  U.S.A. 70 C6
Coteau du Missouri,
  U.S.A. 70 B4
Côtes-d'Armor □,
  France 18 B3
Côtes-du-Nord =
  Côtes-d'Armor □,
  France 18 B2
Cotonou, Benin . . . 44 G5
Cotopaxi, Ecuador . . 78 D3
Cotswold Hills, U.K. . 11 F5
Cottage Grove, U.S.A. 72 E2
Cottbus, Germany . . 16 C7
Cottingham, U.K. . . 10 D5
Cottonwood, U.S.A. . 73 J7
Cotulla, U.S.A. 71 L5
Coudersport, U.S.A. . 68 E6
Couedic, C. du,
  Australia 55 F2
Coulee City, U.S.A. . 72 C4
Coulman I., Antarctica 5 D11
Coulonge →, Canada 62 C4
Council, Alaska, U.S.A. 60 B3
Council, Idaho, U.S.A. 72 D5
Council Bluffs, U.S.A. 70 E7
Council Grove, U.S.A. 70 F6
Courantyne →,
  S. Amer. 78 B7
Courtenay, Canada . 64 D3
Courtrai = Kortrijk,
  Belgium 15 D3
Coushatta, U.S.A. . . 71 J8
Coutts, Canada 64 D6
Coventry, U.K. 11 E6
Coventry L., Canada . 65 A7
Covilhã, Portugal . . 19 B2
Covington, Ga., U.S.A. 69 J4
Covington, Ky., U.S.A. 68 F3
Covington, Okla.,
  U.S.A. 71 G6
Covington, Tenn.,
  U.S.A. 71 H10
Cowal, L., Australia . 55 E4
Cowan, Canada . . . 65 C8
Cowan, L., Australia 53 F3
Cowan L., Canada . . 65 C7
Cowangie, Australia . 55 D2
Cowarie, Australia . . 55 D2
Cowcowing Lakes,
  Australia 53 F2
Cowdenbeath, U.K. . 12 E5
Cowell, Australia . . . 55 E2
Cowes, U.K. 11 G6
Cowra, Australia . . . 55 E4
Coxim, Brazil 79 G8
Cox's Bazar, Bangla. 37 J17
Cox's Cove, Canada . 63 C8
Cozad, U.S.A. 70 E5
Cozumel, I. de, Mexico 74 C7
Craboon, Australia . . 55 E4
Cracow = Kraków,
  Poland 17 C9
Cracow, Australia . . 55 D5
Cradock, S. Africa . . 48 E4
Craig, Alaska, U.S.A. 64 B2
Craig, Colo., U.S.A. . 72 F10
Craigavon = Lurgan,
  U.K. 13 B5
Craiova, Romania . . 21 B10
Cramsie, Australia . . 54 C3
Cranberry Portage,
  Canada 65 C8
Cranbrook, Tas.,
  Australia 54 G4
Cranbrook, W. Austral.,
  Australia 53 F2
Cranbrook, Canada . 64 D5
Crandon, U.S.A. . . . 70 C10
Crane, Oreg., U.S.A. 72 E4
Crane, Tex., U.S.A. . 71 K3
Crater, L., U.S.A. . . 72 E2
Crateús, Brazil 79 E10
Crato, Brazil 79 E11
Crawford, U.S.A. . . 70 D3
Crawfordsville, U.S.A. 68 E2
Crawley, U.K. 11 F7
Crazy Mts., U.S.A. . 72 C8
Crean L., Canada . . 65 C7
Crécy-en-Ponthieu,
  France 18 A4

Credo

Credo, Australia 53 F3
Cree →, Canada 65 B7
Cree →, U.K. 12 G4
Cree L., Canada 65 B7
Creede, U.S.A. 73 H10
Creighton, U.S.A. 70 D6
Cremona, Italy 20 B4
Cres, Croatia 20 B6
Cresbard, U.S.A. 70 C5
Crescent, Okla., U.S.A. 71 H6
Crescent, Oreg., U.S.A. 72 E3
Crescent City, U.S.A. 72 F1
Cressy, Australia 55 F3
Crested Butte, U.S.A. 73 G10
Creston, Canada 64 D5
Creston, Iowa, U.S.A. 70 E7
Creston, Wash., U.S.A. 72 C4
Crestview, U.S.A. 69 K2
Crete = Kríti, Greece 21 G11
Crete, U.S.A. 70 E6
Creus, C., Spain 19 A7
Creuse □, France 18 C5
Creuse →, France 18 C4
Crewe, U.K. 10 D5
Criciúma, Brazil 80 B7
Crieff, U.K. 12 E5
Crimea = Krymskiy Poluostrov, Ukraine 23 E5
Cristóbal, Panama 74 H14
Crişul Alb →, Romania 17 E10
Crişul Negru →, Romania 17 E10
Crna Gora = Montenegro □, Montenegro 21 C8
Crna Gora, Serbia 21 C9
Crna Reka →, Macedonia 21 D9
Croaghpatrick, Ireland 13 C2
Croatia ■, Europe 20 B7
Crocker, Banjaran, Malaysia 32 C5
Crockett, U.S.A. 71 K7
Crocodile = Krokodil →, Mozam. 49 D5
Crocodile Is., Australia 54 A1
Croix, L. La, Canada 62 C1
Croker, C., Australia 52 B5
Croker I., Australia 52 B5
Cromarty, Canada 65 B10
Cromarty, U.K. 12 D4
Cromer, U.K. 10 E9
Cromwell, N.Z. 51 L2
Cronulla, Australia 55 E5
Crooked →, Canada 64 C4
Crooked →, U.S.A. 72 D3
Crookston, Minn., U.S.A. 70 B6
Crookston, Nebr., U.S.A. 70 D4
Crooksville, U.S.A. 68 F4
Crookwell, Australia 55 E4
Crosby, Minn., U.S.A. 70 B8
Crosby, N. Dak., U.S.A. 65 D8
Crosbyton, U.S.A. 71 J4
Cross →, Canada 65 C9
Cross City, U.S.A. 69 L4
Cross Fell, U.K. 10 C5
Cross L., Canada 65 C9
Cross Plains, U.S.A. 71 J5
Cross Sound, U.S.A. 60 C6
Crossett, U.S.A. 71 J9
Crossfield, Canada 64 C6
Crosshaven, Ireland 13 E3
Crotone, Italy 20 E7
Crow →, Canada 64 B4
Crow Agency, U.S.A. 72 D10
Crow Hd., Ireland 13 E1
Crowell, U.S.A. 71 J5
Crowley, U.S.A. 71 K8
Crown Point, U.S.A. 68 E2
Crows Nest, Australia 55 D5
Crowsnest Pass, Canada 64 D6
Croydon, Australia 54 B3
Croydon, U.K. 11 F7
Crozet Is., Ind. Oc. 35 J4
Cruz Alta, Brazil 80 B6
Cruz del Eje, Argentina 80 C4
Cruzeiro, Brazil 79 H10
Cruzeiro do Sul, Brazil 78 E4
Cry L., Canada 64 B3
Crystal Brook, Australia 55 E2
Crystal City, Mo., U.S.A. 70 F9
Crystal City, Tex., U.S.A. 71 L5
Crystal Falls, U.S.A. 68 B1
Crystal River, U.S.A. 69 L4
Crystal Springs, U.S.A. 71 K9
Csongrád, Hungary 17 E10
Cu Lao Hon, Vietnam 34 G10
Cuamato, Angola 48 B2
Cuamba, Mozam. 47 G7
Cuando →, Angola 47 H4
Cuando Cubango □, Angola 48 B3
Cuangar, Angola 48 B2
Cuanza →, Angola 42 G5
Cuarto →, Argentina 80 C4
Cuba, U.S.A. 73 J10
Cuba ■, W. Indies 75 C9
Cuballing, Australia 53 F2
Cubango →, Africa 48 B3
Cuchi, Angola 47 G3
Cúcuta, Colombia 78 B4
Cudahy, U.S.A. 68 D2
Cuddalore, India 36 P11

Cuddapah, India 36 M11
Cuddapan, L., Australia 54 D3
Cudgewa, Australia 55 F4
Cue, Australia 53 E2
Cuenca, Ecuador 78 D3
Cuenca, Spain 19 B4
Cuenca, Serranía de, Spain 19 C5
Cuernavaca, Mexico 74 D5
Cuernavaca, Morelos, Mexico 74 D5
Cuero, U.S.A. 71 L6
Cuervo, U.S.A. 71 H2
Cuevas del Almanzora, Spain 19 D5
Cuevo, Bolivia 78 H6
Cuiabá, Brazil 79 G7
Cuiabá →, Brazil 79 G7
Cuillin Hills, U.K. 12 D2
Cuillin Sd., U.K. 12 D2
Cuima, Angola 47 G3
Cuito →, Angola 48 B3
Cukai, Malaysia 34 Q16
Culbertson, U.S.A. 70 A2
Culcairn, Australia 55 F4
Culebra, Sierra de la, Spain 19 B2
Culgoa →, Australia 55 D4
Culiacán, Mexico 74 C3
Culion, Phil. 33 B6
Cullarin Ra., Australia 55 E4
Cullen, U.K. 12 D6
Cullen Pt., Australia 54 A3
Cullera, Spain 19 C5
Cullman, U.S.A. 69 H2
Culloden Moor, U.K. 12 D4
Culpeper, U.S.A. 68 F7
Culuene →, Brazil 79 F8
Culver, Pt., Australia 53 F3
Culverden, N.Z. 51 K4
Cumaná, Venezuela 78 A6
Cumberland, Canada 64 D3
Cumberland, Md., U.S.A. 68 F6
Cumberland, Wis., U.S.A. 70 C8
Cumberland →, U.S.A. 69 G2
Cumberland I., U.S.A. 69 K5
Cumberland Is., Australia 54 C4
Cumberland L., Canada 65 C8
Cumberland Pen., Canada 61 B13
Cumberland Plateau, U.S.A. 69 H3
Cumberland Sd., Canada 61 B13
Cumborah, Australia 55 D4
Cumbria □, U.K. 10 C5
Cumbrian Mts., U.K. 10 C4
Cumbum, India 36 M11
Cummins, Australia 55 E2
Cumnock, Australia 55 E4
Cumnock, U.K. 12 F4
Cundeelee, Australia 53 F3
Cunderdin, Australia 53 F2
Cunene →, Angola 48 B1
Cúneo, Italy 20 B2
Cunnamulla, Australia 55 D4
Cupar, Canada 65 C8
Cupar, U.K. 12 E5
Cupica, G. de, Colombia 78 B3
Curaçao, Neth. Ant. 75 E11
Curaray →, Peru 78 D4
Curiapo, Venezuela 78 B6
Curicó, Chile 80 C2
Curitiba, Brazil 80 B7
Currabubula, Australia 55 E5
Currais Novos, Brazil 79 E11
Curralinho, Brazil 79 D9
Currant, U.S.A. 72 G6
Curraweena, Australia 55 E4
Currawilla, Australia 54 D3
Current →, U.S.A. 71 G9
Currie, Australia 54 F3
Currie, Mt., S. Africa 49 E4
Currituck Sd., U.S.A. 69 G8
Curtis, U.S.A. 70 E4
Curtis Group, Australia 54 F4
Curtis I., Australia 54 C5
Curuápanema →, Brazil 79 D7
Curuçá, Brazil 79 D9
Çürüksu Çayı →, Turkey 23 G4
Curup, Indonesia 32 E2
Cururupu, Brazil 79 D10
Curuzú Cuatiá, Argentina 80 B5
Cushing, U.S.A. 71 H6
Cushing, Mt., Canada 64 B3
Custer, U.S.A. 70 D3
Cut Bank, U.S.A. 72 B7
Cuthbert, U.S.A. 69 K3
Cuttaburra →, Australia 55 D3
Cuttack, India 37 J14
Cuvier, C., Australia 53 D1
Cuvier I., N.Z. 51 G5
Cuxhaven, Germany 16 B4
Cuyahoga Falls, U.S.A. 68 E5
Cuyo, Phil. 33 B6
Cuzco, Bolivia 78 H5
Cuzco, Peru 78 F4
Cwmbran, U.K. 11 F4
Cyclades = Kikládhes, Greece 21 F11
Cygnet, Australia 54 G4

Cynthiana, U.S.A. 68 F3
Cypress Hills, Canada 65 D7
Cyprus ■, Asia 38 C2
Cyrenaica, Libya 45 C9
Cyrene = Shaḥḥāt, Libya 45 B9
Czar, Canada 65 C6
Czech Rep. ■, Europe 16 D7
Czeremcha, Poland 17 B11
Częstochowa, Poland 17 C9

D

Da →, Vietnam 34 B8
Da Hinggan Ling, China 31 B7
Da Lat, Vietnam 34 G10
Da Nang, Vietnam 34 D10
Da Qaidam, China 30 C4
Daba Shan, China 31 C5
Dabakala, Ivory C. 44 G4
Dąbie, Poland 16 B7
Dabo, Indonesia 32 E2
Dabola, Guinea 44 F2
Daboya, Ghana 44 G4
Dąbrowa Tarnówska, Poland 17 C10
Dacca = Dhaka, Bangla. 37 H17
Dacca = Dhaka □, Bangla. 37 G17
Dadanawa, Guyana 78 C7
Dade City, U.S.A. 69 L4
Dadra and Nagar Haveli □, India 36 J8
Dadu, Pakistan 36 F5
Daet, Phil. 33 B6
Dagana, Senegal 44 E1
Daghestan Republic □, Russia 23 F8
Dagö = Hiiumaa, Estonia 22 C3
Dagupan, Phil. 33 A6
Dahlak Kebir, Eritrea 40 D3
Dahlonega, U.S.A. 69 H4
Dahod, India 36 H9
Dahomey = Benin ■, Africa 44 G5
Dahra, Senegal 44 E1
Dai-Sen, Japan 29 G6
Daingean, Ireland 13 C4
Daintree, Australia 54 B4
Daiō-Misaki, Japan 29 G8
Dairût, Egypt 45 C11
Daisetsu-Zan, Japan 28 C11
Dajarra, Australia 54 C2
Dakar, Senegal 44 F1
Dakhla, W. Sahara 44 D1
Dakhla, El Wâhât el-, Egypt 45 C10
Dakhovskaya, Russia 23 F7
Dakota City, U.S.A. 70 D6
Đakovica, Serbia 21 C9
Dālaki, Iran 39 D6
Dalälven, Sweden 9 F14
Dalandzadgad, Mongolia 30 B5
Dalarö, Sweden 9 G15
Dālbandīn, Pakistan 36 E4
Dalbeattie, U.K. 12 G5
Dalby, Australia 55 D5
Dalgán, Iran 39 E8
Dalhart, U.S.A. 71 G3
Dalhousie, Canada 63 C6
Dali, China 30 D5
Dalian, China 31 C7
Daliang Shan, China 30 D5
Dāliyat el Karmel, Israel 41 C4
Dalkeith, U.K. 12 F5
Dall I., U.S.A. 64 C2
Dallarnil, Australia 55 D5
Dallas, Oreg., U.S.A. 72 D2
Dallas, Tex., U.S.A. 71 J6
Dalmacija □, Croatia 20 C7
Dalmatia = Dalmacija, Croatia 20 C7
Dalmellington, U.K. 12 F4
Dalnegorsk, Russia 25 E14
Dalnerechensk, Russia 25 E14
Daloa, Ivory C. 44 G3
Dalton, Canada 62 C3
Dalton, Ga., U.S.A. 69 H3
Dalton, Nebr., U.S.A. 70 E3
Dalton Iceberg Tongue, Antarctica 5 C9
Dalvík, Iceland 8 D4
Daly →, Australia 52 B5
Daly L., Canada 65 B7
Daly Waters, Australia 54 B1
Daman, India 36 J8
Dāmaneh, Iran 39 C6
Damanhûr, Egypt 45 B11
Damar, Indonesia 33 F7
Damaraland, Namibia 48 C2
Damascus = Dimashq, Syria 41 B5
Damāvand, Iran 39 C7
Damāvand, Qolleh-ye, Iran 39 C7
Damba, Angola 46 F3
Dāmghān, Iran 39 B7
Damietta = Dumyât, Egypt 45 B11
Damīr Qābū, Syria 38 B4
Dammam = Ad Dammām, Si. Arabia 39 E6
Damoh, India 36 H11

Dampier, Australia 52 D2
Dampier, Selat, Indonesia 33 E8
Dampier Arch., Australia 52 D2
Dana, Indonesia 33 F6
Dana, L., Canada 62 B4
Danbury, U.S.A. 68 E9
Danby L., U.S.A. 73 J6
Dandaragan, Australia 53 F2
Dandeldhura, Nepal 37 E12
Dandeli, India 36 M9
Dandenong, Australia 55 F4
Dandong, China 31 B7
Danforth, U.S.A. 63 C6
Danger Is. = Pukapuka, Cook Is. 57 J11
Danger Pt., S. Africa 48 E2
Dangora, Nigeria 44 F6
Daniel, U.S.A. 72 E8
Daniel's Harbour, Canada 63 B8
Danielskuil, S. Africa 48 D3
Danilov, Russia 22 C7
Dankhar Gompa, India 36 C11
Dannemora, Sweden 9 F14
Dannemora, U.S.A. 68 C9
Dannevirke, N.Z. 51 J6
Dannhauser, S. Africa 49 D5
Dansville, U.S.A. 68 D7
Dante, Somali Rep. 40 E5
Danube →, Europe 21 B13
Danville, Ill., U.S.A. 68 E2
Danville, Ky., U.S.A. 68 G3
Danville, Va., U.S.A. 69 G6
Danzig = Gdańsk, Poland 17 A9
Dao, Phil. 33 B6
Daoud = Aïn Beïda, Algeria 44 A6
Dar es Salaam, Tanzania 46 F7
Dar Mazār, Iran 39 D7
Dar'ā, Syria 41 C5
Dar'ā □, Syria 41 C5
Dārāb, Iran 39 D7
Daraj, Libya 44 B7
Dārān, Iran 39 C6
Dārayyā, Syria 41 B5
Darband, Pakistan 36 B8
Darband, Kūh-e, Iran 39 D8
Darbhanga, India 37 F14
Darby, U.S.A. 72 C6
Dardanelle, U.S.A. 71 H8
Dardanelles = Çanakkale Boğazı, Turkey 21 D12
Dārestān, Iran 39 D8
Dârfûr, Sudan 45 F9
Dargai, Pakistan 36 B7
Dargan Ata, Uzbekistan 24 E7
Dargaville, N.Z. 51 F4
Darién, Panama 74 H14
Darién, G. del, Colombia 78 B3
Darjeeling = Darjiling, India 37 F16
Darjiling, India 37 F16
Dark Cove, Canada 63 C9
Darkan, Australia 53 F2
Darkhazineh, Iran 39 D6
Darling →, Australia 55 E3
Darling Downs, Australia 55 D5
Darling Ra., Australia 53 F2
Darlington, U.K. 10 C6
Darlington, S.C., U.S.A. 69 H6
Darlington, Wis., U.S.A. 70 D9
Darlot, L., Australia 53 E3
Darłowo, Poland 16 A8
Darnah, Libya 45 B9
Darnall, S. Africa 49 D5
Darnley, Australia 54 C3
Darnley B., Canada 60 B7
Darr →, Australia 54 C3
Darrington, U.S.A. 72 B3
Dart →, U.K. 11 G4
Dart, C., Antarctica 5 D14
Dartmoor, U.K. 11 G4
Dartmouth, Australia 54 C3
Dartmouth, Canada 63 D7
Dartmouth, U.K. 11 G4
Dartmouth, L., Australia 55 D4
Darvaza, Turkmenistan 24 E6
Darvel, Malaysia 33 D5
Darwha, India 36 J10
Darwin, Australia 52 B5
Darwin River, Australia 52 B5
Daryoi Amu = Amudarya →, Uzbekistan 24 E6
Dās, U.A.E. 39 E7
Dasht, Iran 39 B8
Dasht →, Pakistan 36 G2
Dasht-e Mārgow, Afghan. 36 D3
Dasseneiland, S. Africa 48 E2
Datia, India 36 G11
Datong, China 31 B6
Datu, Tanjung, Indonesia 32 D3
Datu Piang, Phil. 33 C6
Daugava →, Latvia 22 C4
Daugavpils, Latvia 22 C4
Daulpur, India 36 F10
Dauphin, Canada 65 C8
Dauphin I., U.S.A. 69 K1

Dauphin L., Canada 65 C9
Dauphiné, France 18 D6
Davangere, India 36 M9
Davao, Phil. 33 C7
Davao, G. of, Phil. 33 C7
Davenport, Iowa, U.S.A. 70 E9
Davenport, Wash., U.S.A. 72 C4
Davenport Downs, Australia 54 C3
Davenport Ra., Australia 54 C1
David, Panama 75 F8
David City, U.S.A. 70 E6
Davidson, Canada 65 C7
Davis, U.S.A. 72 G3
Davis Dam, U.S.A. 73 J6
Davis Inlet, Canada 63 A7
Davis Mts., U.S.A. 71 K2
Davis Sea, Antarctica 5 C7
Davis Str., N. Amer. 61 B14
Davos, Switz. 16 E5
Davy L., Canada 65 B7
Dawes Ra., Australia 54 C5
Dawson, Canada 60 B6
Dawson, Ga., U.S.A. 69 K3
Dawson, N. Dak., U.S.A. 70 B5
Dawson, I., Chile 80 G2
Dawson Creek, Canada 64 B4
Dawson Inlet, Canada 65 A10
Dawson Ra., Australia 54 C4
Daxian, China 30 C5
Daxue Shan, China 30 C5
Daylesford, Australia 55 F3
Dayr az Zawr, Syria 38 C4
Daysland, Canada 64 C6
Dayton, Ohio, U.S.A. 68 F3
Dayton, Tenn., U.S.A. 69 H3
Dayton, Wash., U.S.A. 72 C4
Daytona Beach, U.S.A. 69 L5
Dayville, U.S.A. 72 D4
De Aar, S. Africa 48 E3
De Funiak Springs, U.S.A. 69 K2
De Grey, Australia 52 D2
De Grey →, Australia 52 D2
De Kalb, U.S.A. 70 E10
De Land, U.S.A. 69 L5
De Leon, U.S.A. 71 J5
De Pere, U.S.A. 68 C1
De Queen, U.S.A. 71 H7
De Quincy, U.S.A. 71 K8
De Ridder, U.S.A. 71 K8
De Smet, U.S.A. 70 C6
De Soto, U.S.A. 70 F9
De Tour, U.S.A. 68 C4
De Witt, U.S.A. 71 H9
Dead Sea, Asia 41 D4
Deadwood, U.S.A. 70 C3
Deadwood L., Canada 64 B3
Deakin, Australia 53 F4
Deal, U.K. 11 F9
Deal I., Australia 54 F4
Dealesville, S. Africa 48 D4
Dean, Forest of, U.K. 11 F5
Deán Funes, Argentina 80 C4
Dearborn, U.S.A. 62 D3
Dease →, Canada 64 B3
Dease L., Canada 64 B2
Dease Lake, Canada 64 B2
Death Valley, U.S.A. 73 H5
Death Valley Junction, U.S.A. 73 H5
Death Valley Nat. Monument, U.S.A. 73 H5
Deba Habe, Nigeria 44 F7
Debar, Macedonia 21 D9
Debden, Canada 65 C7
Debolt, Canada 64 B5
Deborah East, L., Australia 53 F2
Deborah West, L., Australia 53 F2
Debre Markos, Ethiopia 45 F12
Debre Tabor, Ethiopia 45 F12
Debrecen, Hungary 17 E10
Decatur, Ala., U.S.A. 69 H2
Decatur, Ga., U.S.A. 69 J3
Decatur, Ill., U.S.A. 70 F10
Decatur, Ind., U.S.A. 68 E3
Decatur, Tex., U.S.A. 71 J6
Deccan, India 36 M10
Deception L., Canada 65 B8
Decorah, U.S.A. 70 D9
Dédéagach = Alexandroúpolis, Greece 21 D11
Dédougou, Burkina Faso 44 F4
Dee →, Clwyd, U.K. 10 D4
Dee →, Gramp., U.K. 12 D6
Deep B., Canada 64 A5
Deep Well, Australia 54 C1
Deepwater, Australia 55 D5
Deer →, Canada 65 B10
Deer Lake, Nfld., Canada 63 C8
Deer Lake, Ont., Canada 65 C10
Deer Lodge, U.S.A. 72 C7
Deer Park, U.S.A. 72 C5
Deer River, U.S.A. 70 B8
Deeral, Australia 54 B4
Deerdepoort, S. Africa 48 C4
Defiance, U.S.A. 68 E3
Degeh Bur, Ethiopia 40 F3
Deggendorf, Germany 16 D7

Deh Bīd, Iran 39 D7
Deh-e Shīr, Iran 39 D7
Dehaj, Iran 39 D7
Dehdez, Iran 39 D7
Dehestān, Iran 39 D7
Dehgolān, Iran 38 C5
Dehi Titan, Afghan. 36 C3
Dehibat, Tunisia 44 B7
Dehlorān, Iran 38 C5
Dehnow-e Kūhestān, Iran 39 E8
Dehra Dun, India 36 D11
Dehri, India 37 G14
Deinze, Belgium 15 D3
Dej, Romania 17 E11
Dekese, Zaïre 46 E4
Del Norte, U.S.A. 73 H10
Del Rio, U.S.A. 71 L4
Delano, U.S.A. 73 J4
Delareyville, S. Africa 48 D4
Delavan, U.S.A. 70 D10
Delaware, U.S.A. 68 E4
Delaware □, U.S.A. 68 F8
Delaware →, U.S.A. 68 F8
Delaware B., U.S.A. 67 C12
Delegate, Australia 55 F4
Delft, Neths. 15 B4
Delfzijl, Neths. 15 A6
Delgado, C., Mozam. 46 G8
Delgo, Sudan 45 D11
Delhi, India 36 E10
Delia, Canada 64 C6
Delice →, Turkey 23 G5
Delicias, Mexico 74 B3
Delijān, Iran 39 C6
Dell City, U.S.A. 73 L11
Dell Rapids, U.S.A. 70 D6
Delmiro Gouveia, Brazil 79 E11
Delong, Ostrova, Russia 25 B15
Deloraine, Australia 54 G4
Deloraine, Canada 65 D8
Delphi, U.S.A. 68 E2
Delphos, U.S.A. 68 E3
Delportshoop, S. Africa 48 D3
Delray Beach, U.S.A. 69 M5
Delta, Colo., U.S.A. 73 G9
Delta, Utah, U.S.A. 72 G7
Delungra, Australia 55 D5
Demanda, Sierra de la, Spain 19 A4
Demavand = Damāvand, Iran 39 C7
Demba, Zaïre 46 F4
Dembecha, Ethiopia 45 F12
Dembidolo, Ethiopia 45 G11
Demer →, Belgium 15 D4
Deming, U.S.A. 73 K10
Demini →, Brazil 78 D6
Demopolis, U.S.A. 69 J2
Dempo, Indonesia 32 E2
Den Burg, Neths. 15 A4
Den Haag = 's-Gravenhage, Neths. 15 B4
Den Helder, Neths. 15 B4
Den Oever, Neths. 15 B5
Denain, France 15 D3
Denau, Uzbekistan 24 F7
Denbigh, U.K. 10 D4
Dendang, Indonesia 32 E3
Dendermonde, Belgium 15 C4
Denham, Australia 53 E1
Denham Ra., Australia 54 C4
Denham Sd., Australia 53 E1
Denia, Spain 19 C6
Denial B., Australia 55 E1
Deniliquin, Australia 55 F3
Denison, Iowa, U.S.A. 70 D7
Denison, Tex., U.S.A. 71 J6
Denison Plains, Australia 52 C4
Denizli, Turkey 23 G4
Denman Glacier, Antarctica 5 C7
Denmark, Australia 53 F2
Denmark ■, Europe 9 J10
Denmark Str., Atl. Oc. 4 C6
Denpasar, Indonesia 32 F5
Denton, Mont., U.S.A. 72 C9
Denton, Tex., U.S.A. 71 J6
D'Entrecasteaux, Pt., Australia 53 F2
Denver, U.S.A. 70 F2
Denver City, U.S.A. 71 J3
Deoghar, India 37 G15
Deolali, India 36 K8
Deoria, India 37 F13
Deosai Mts., Pakistan 36 B9
Depot Springs, Australia 53 E3
Deputatskiy, Russia 25 C14
Dera Ghazi Khan, Pakistan 36 D7
Dera Ismail Khan, Pakistan 36 D7
Derbent, Russia 23 F8
Derby, Australia 52 C3
Derby, U.K. 10 E6
Derbyshire □, U.K. 10 E6
Derg →, U.K. 13 B4
Derg, L., Ireland 13 D3
Dergaon, India 37 F19
Dernieres Isles, U.S.A. 71 L9
Derry = Londonderry, U.K. 13 B4
Derryveagh Mts., Ireland 13 B3
Derudub, Sudan 45 E12
Derwent, Canada 65 C6
Derwent →, Derby, U.K. 10 E6

Derwent →, N. Yorks., U.K. . . . 10 D7
Derwent Water, U.K. . . 10 C4
Des Moines, Iowa, U.S.A. 70 E8
Des Moines, N. Mex., U.S.A. 71 G3
Des Moines →, U.S.A. 70 E9
Desaguadero →, Bolivia 78 G5
Deschaillons, Canada 63 C5
Descharme →, Canada 65 B7
Deschutes →, U.S.A. 72 D3
Dese, Ethiopia 40 E2
Desert Center, U.S.A. 73 K6
Deskenatlata L., Canada 64 A6
Desna →, Ukraine . 22 D5
Desolación, I., Chile . 80 G2
Despeñaperros, Paso, Spain 19 C4
Dessau, Germany . . 16 C6
Dessye = Dese, Ethiopia 40 E2
D'Estrees B., Australia 55 F2
Detmold, Germany . . 16 C4
Detour Pt., U.S.A. . . 68 C2
Detroit, Mich., U.S.A. 62 D3
Detroit, Tex., U.S.A. . 71 J7
Detroit Lakes, U.S.A. 70 B7
Deurne, Belgium . . . 15 C4
Deurne, Neths. 15 C5
Deutsche Bucht, Germany 16 A4
Deux-Sèvres □, France 18 C3
Deva, Romania 17 F11
Devakottai, India . . . 36 Q11
Deventer, Neths. . . . 15 B6
Deveron →, U.K. . . 12 D6
Devils Lake, U.S.A. . 70 A5
Devils Paw, Canada . 64 B2
Devizes, U.K. 11 F6
Devon, Canada 64 C6
Devon □, U.K. 11 G4
Devon I., Canada . . . 4 B3
Devonport, Australia . 54 G4
Devonport, N.Z. . . . 51 G5
Devonport, U.K. . . . 11 G3
Dewas, India 36 H10
Dewetsdorp, S. Africa 48 D4
Dewsbury, U.K. . . . 10 D8
Dexter, Mo., U.S.A. . 71 G9
Dexter, N. Mex., U.S.A. 71 J2
Dey-Dey, L., Australia 53 E5
Deyhūk, Iran 39 C8
Deyyer, Iran 39 E6
Dezadeash L., Canada 64 A1
Dezfūl, Iran 39 C6
Dezhneva, Mys, Russia 25 C19
Dhahiriya = Az Ζāhirīyah, Jordan . 41 D3
Dhahran = Az Ζahrān, Si. Arabia 39 E6
Dhaka, Bangla. 37 H17
Dhaka □, Bangla. . . 37 G17
Dhamar, Yemen . . . 40 E3
Dhamtari, India 37 J12
Dhanbad, India 37 H15
Dhangarhi, Nepal . . 37 E12
Dhankuta, Nepal . . . 37 F15
Dhar, India 36 H9
Dharmapuri, India . . 36 N11
Dharwad, India 36 M9
Dharwar, India 36 M9
Dhaulagiri, Nepal . . 37 E13
Dhenkanal, India . . . 37 J14
Dhībān, Jordan 41 D4
Dhidhimotikhon, Greece 21 D12
Dhíkti Óros, Greece . 21 G11
Dhírfis, Greece 21 E10
Dhodhekánisos, Greece 21 F12
Dhrol, India 36 H7
Dhuburi, India 37 F16
Dhule, India 36 J9
Dhut →, Somali Rep. 40 E5
Di Linh, Cao Nguyen, Vietnam 34 G10
Diablo Heights, Panama 74 H14
Diafarabé, Mali 44 F4
Diamantina, Brazil . . 79 G10
Diamantina →, Australia 55 D2
Diamantino, Brazil . . 79 F7
Diamond Harbour, India 37 H16
Diamond Is., Australia 54 B5
Diamond Mts., U.S.A. 72 G6
Diamondville, U.S.A. . 72 F8
Diapaga, Burkina Faso 44 F5
Dibā, Oman 39 E8
Dibaya, Zaïre 46 F4
Dibaya-Lubue, Zaïre . 46 E3
Dibbi, Ethiopia 40 G3
Dibete, Botswana . . 48 C4
Dibrugarh, India . . . 37 F19
Dickinson, U.S.A. . . 70 B3
Dickson, U.S.A. . . . 69 G2
Didiéni, Mali 44 F3
Didsbury, Canada . . 64 C6
Diébougou, Burkina Faso 44 F4
Diefenbaker L., Canada 65 C7
Diego Garcia, Ind. Oc. 35 E6
Diekirch, Lux. 15 E6
Dien Bien, Vietnam . 34 B7
Dieppe, France 18 B4

Dieren, Neths. 15 B6
Dierks, U.S.A. 71 H7
Diest, Belgium 15 D5
Differdange, Lux. . . 15 E5
Digby, Canada 63 D6
Digges, Canada . . . 65 B10
Digges Is., Canada . . 61 B12
Dighinala, Bangla. . . 37 H18
Dighton, U.S.A. . . . 70 F4
Digne, France 18 D7
Digos, Phil. 33 C7
Digranes, Iceland . . 8 C6
Digul →, Indonesia . 33 F9
Dihang →, India . . . 37 F19
Dīhōk, Iraq 38 B3
Dijlah, Nahr →, Asia 38 D5
Dijon, France 18 C6
Dikomu di Kai, Botswana 48 C3
Diksmuide, Belgium . 15 C2
Dikson, Russia 24 B9
Dikwa, Nigeria 45 F7
Dili, Indonesia 33 F7
Dilley, U.S.A. 71 L5
Dilling, Sudan 45 F10
Dillingham, U.S.A. . . 60 C4
Dillon, Canada 65 B7
Dillon, Mont., U.S.A. 72 D7
Dillon, S.C., U.S.A. . 69 H6
Dillon →, Canada . . 65 B7
Dilolo, Zaïre 46 G4
Dilston, Australia . . 54 G4
Dimashq, Syria 41 B5
Dimashq □, Syria . . 41 B5
Dimbaza, S. Africa . . 49 E4
Dimbokro, Ivory C. . 44 G4
Dimboola, Australia . 55 F3
Dîmbovita →, Romania 17 F13
Dimbulah, Australia . 54 B4
Dimitrovgrad, Bulgaria 21 C11
Dimitrovgrad, Russia . 22 D8
Dimmitt, U.S.A. . . . 71 H3
Dimona, Israel 41 D4
Dinagat, Phil. 33 B7
Dinajpur, Bangla. . . 37 G16
Dinan, France 18 B2
Dīnān Āb, Iran 39 C8
Dinant, Belgium . . . 15 D4
Dinara Planina, Croatia 20 B6
Dinard, France 18 B2
Dinaric Alps = Dinara Planina, Croatia . . 20 B6
Dindigul, India 36 P11
Dingle, Ireland 13 D1
Dingle B., Ireland . . 13 D1
Dingo, Australia . . . 54 C4
Dinguiraye, Guinea . 44 F2
Dingwall, U.K. 12 D4
Dinokwe, Botswana . 48 C4
Dinosaur National Monument, U.S.A. 72 F9
Dinuba, U.S.A. 73 H4
Diourbel, Senegal . . 44 F1
Dipolog, Phil. 33 C6
Dir, Pakistan 36 B7
Diré, Mali 44 E4
Dire Dawa, Ethiopia . 40 F3
Dirico, Angola 47 H4
Dirk Hartog I., Australia 53 E1
Dirranbandi, Australia 55 D4
Disa, India 36 G8
Disappointment, C., U.S.A. 72 C1
Disappointment, L., Australia 52 D3
Disaster B., Australia 55 F4
Discovery B., Australia 55 F3
Disko, Greenland . . 4 C5
Disko Bugt, Greenland 4 C5
Disteghil Sar, Pakistan 36 A9
Distrito Federal □, Brazil 79 G9
Diu, India 36 J7
Dīvāndarreh, Iran . . 38 C5
Divide, U.S.A. 72 D7
Dividing Ra., Australia 53 E2
Divinópolis, Brazil . . 79 H10
Divnoye, Russia . . . 23 E7
Diwāl Kol, Afghan. . 36 B5
Dixon, Ill., U.S.A. . . 70 E10
Dixon, Mont., U.S.A. 72 C6
Dixon, N. Mex., U.S.A. 73 H11
Dixon Entrance, U.S.A. 64 C2
Dixonville, Canada . . 64 B5
Diyarbakır, Turkey . . 23 G7
Djado, Niger 45 D7
Djakarta = Jakarta, Indonesia 33 G12
Djamba, Angola . . . 48 B1
Djambala, Congo . . 46 E2
Djanet, Algeria 44 D6
Djawa = Jawa, Indonesia 33 G14
Djelfa, Algeria 44 B5
Djema, C.A.R. 46 C5
Djenné, Mali 44 F4
Djerba, I. de, Tunisia 45 B7
Djerid, Chott, Tunisia 44 B6
Djibo, Burkina Faso . 44 F4
Djibouti, Djibouti . . . 40 E3
Djibouti ■, Africa . . 40 E3
Djolu, Zaïre 46 D4
Djougou, Benin 44 G5
Djoum, Cameroon . . 46 D2
Djourab, Chad 45 E8
Djugu, Zaïre 46 D6
Djúpivogur, Iceland . 8 D6
Dmitriya Lapteva, Proliv, Russia . . . 25 B15
Dnepr →, Ukraine . 23 E5

Dneprodzerzhinsk, Ukraine 23 E5
Dnepropetrovsk, Ukraine 23 E5
Dnestr →, Europe . 23 E5
Dnestrovski = Belgorod, Russia . . 23 D6
Dnieper = Dnepr →, Ukraine 23 E5
Dniester = Dnestr →, Europe 23 E5
Dnipro = Dnepr →, Ukraine 23 E5
Dniprodzherzhynsk = Ukraine 23 E5
Dnipropetrovsk = Dnepropetrovsk, Ukraine 23 E5
Dnyapro = Dnepr →, Ukraine 23 E5
Doba, Chad 45 G8
Dobbyn, Australia . . 54 B3
Doberai, Jazirah, Indonesia 33 E8
Doblas, Argentina . . 80 D4
Dobo, Indonesia . . . 33 F8
Dobreta-Turnu-Severin, Romania 21 B10
Dobruja, Romania . . 17 F14
Dodecanese = Dhodhekánisos, Greece 21 F12
Dodge Center, U.S.A. 70 C8
Dodge City, U.S.A. . 71 G5
Dodge L., Canada . . 65 B7
Dodgeville, U.S.A. . . 70 D9
Dodoma, Tanzania . . 46 F7
Dodsland, Canada . . 65 C7
Dodson, U.S.A. . . . 72 B9
Doetinchem, Neths. . 15 C6
Dog Creek, Canada . 64 C4
Dog L., Man., Canada 65 C9
Dog L., Ont., Canada . 62 C2
Dogger Bank, N. Sea . 6 E6
Dogi, Afghan. 36 C3
Doha = Ad Dawhah, Qatar 39 E6
Dohazari, Bangla. . . 37 H18
Doi, Indonesia 33 D7
Doi Luang, Thailand . 34 C6
Doig →, Canada . . . 64 B4
Dois Irmãos, Sa., Brazil 79 E10
Dokka, Norway 9 F11
Dokkum, Neths. . . . 15 A5
Doland, U.S.A. 70 C5
Dolbeau, Canada . . 63 C5
Dole, France 18 C6
Dolgellau, U.K. 10 E4
Dolgelley = Dolgellau, U.K. 10 E4
Dollart, Neths. 15 A7
Dolomites = Dolomiti, Italy 20 A4
Dolomiti, Italy 20 A4
Dolores, Argentina . . 80 D5
Dolores, U.S.A. . . . 73 H9
Dolores →, U.S.A. . 73 G9
Dolphin, C., Falk. Is. . 80 G5
Dolphin and Union Str., Canada 60 B8
Dombarovskiy, Russia 24 D6
Dombås, Norway . . . 9 E10
Dombes, France . . . 18 D6
Domburg, Neths. . . . 15 C3
Domel I. = Letsôk-aw Kyun, Burma 34 G5
Domeyko, Chile . . . 80 B2
Domfront, France . . 18 B3
Dominica ■, W. Indies 74 M20
Dominican Rep. ■, W. Indies 75 D10
Domo, Ethiopia 40 F4
Domodóssola, Italy . 20 A3
Domville, Mt., Australia 55 D5
Don →, Russia 23 E6
Don →, Gramp., U.K. 12 D6
Don →, S. Yorks., U.K. 10 D7
Don, C., Australia . . 52 B5
Don Benito, Spain . . 19 C3
Donaghadee, U.K. . . 13 B6
Donald, Australia . . . 55 F3
Donalda, Canada . . . 64 C6
Donaldsonville, U.S.A. 71 K9
Donalsonville, U.S.A. 69 K3
Donau →, Austria . . 16 D8
Donauwörth, Germany 16 D5
Doncaster, U.K. . . . 10 D6
Dondo, Angola 46 F2
Dondo, Mozam. . . . 47 H6
Dondo, Teluk, Indonesia 33 D6
Dondra Head, Sri Lanka 36 S12
Donegal, Ireland . . . 13 B3
Donegal □, Ireland . . 13 B4
Donegal B., Ireland . 13 B3
Donets →, Russia . . 23 E7
Donetsk, Ukraine . . 23 E6
Dongara, Australia . . 53 E1
Dongbei, China 31 B7
Dongchuan, China . . 30 D5
Donggala, Indonesia . 33 E5
Dongola, Sudan . . . 45 E11
Dongting Hu, China . 31 D6
Doniphan, U.S.A. . . 71 G9
Dønna, Norway 8 C12
Donna, U.S.A. 71 M5

Donnaconna, Canada 63 C5
Donnelly's Crossing, N.Z. 51 F4
Donnybrook, Australia 53 F2
Donnybrook, S. Africa 49 D4
Donor's Hill, Australia 54 B3
Donostia = San Sebastián, Spain . 19 A5
Doon →, U.K. 12 F4
Dora, L., Australia . . 52 D3
Dora Báltea →, Italy 20 B3
Doran L., Canada . . 65 A7
Dorchester, U.K. . . . 11 G5
Dorchester, C., Canada 61 B12
Dordogne □, France . 18 D4
Dordogne →, France 18 D3
Dordrecht, Neths. . . 15 C4
Dordrecht, S. Africa . 48 E4
Dore, Mts., France . . 18 D5
Doré L., Canada . . . 65 C7
Doré Lake, Canada . 65 C7
Dori, Burkina Faso . . 44 F4
Doring →, S. Africa . 48 E2
Doringbos, S. Africa . 48 E2
Dorion, Canada . . . 62 C5
Dornoch, U.K. 12 D4
Dornoch Firth, U.K. . 12 D4
Dorohoi, Romania . . 17 E13
Döröö Nuur, Mongolia 30 B4
Dorr, Iran 39 C6
Dorre I., Australia . . 53 E1
Dorrigo, Australia . . 55 E5
Dorris, U.S.A. 72 F3
Dorset □, U.K. 11 G5
Dortmund, Germany . 16 C3
Doruma, Zaïre 46 D5
Dorūneh, Iran 39 C8
Dos Bahías, C., Argentina 80 E3
Dosso, Niger 44 F5
Dothan, U.S.A. 69 K3
Douai, France 18 A5
Douala, Cameroon . . 44 H6
Douarnenez, France . 18 B1
Double Island Pt., Australia 55 D5
Doubs □, France . . . 18 C7
Doubs →, France . . 18 C6
Doubtful Sd., N.Z. . . 51 L1
Doubtloo B., N.Z. . . 51 F4
Douentza, Mali 44 F4
Douglas, S. Africa . . 48 D3
Douglas, U.K. 10 C3
Douglas, Alaska, U.S.A. 64 B2
Douglas, Ariz., U.S.A. 73 L9
Douglas, Ga., U.S.A. 69 K4
Douglas, Wyo., U.S.A. 70 D2
Douglastown, Canada 63 C7
Douglasville, U.S.A. . 69 J3
Doumé, Cameroon . . 46 D2
Dounreay, U.K. 12 C5
Dourados, Brazil . . . 80 A6
Douro →, Europe . . 19 B1
Douro Litoral, Portugal 19 B1
Dove →, U.K. 10 E6
Dove Creek, U.S.A. . 73 H9
Dover, Australia . . . 54 G4
Dover, U.K. 11 F9
Dover, Del., U.S.A. . 68 F8
Dover, N.H., U.S.A. . 68 D10
Dover, Ohio, U.S.A. . 68 E5
Dover, Pt., Australia . 53 F4
Dover, Str. of, Europe 18 A4
Dover-Foxcroft, Canada 63 C6
Dovey = Dyfi →, U.K. 11 E4
Dovrefjell, Norway . . 8 E10
Dow Rūd, Iran 39 C6
Dowagiac, U.S.A. . . 68 E2
Dowgha'i, Iran 39 B8
Dowlatābād, Iran . . 39 D8
Down □, U.K. 13 B6
Downey, U.S.A. . . . 72 E7
Downham Market, U.K. 11 E8
Downieville, U.S.A. . 72 G3
Downpatrick, U.K. . . 13 B6
Downpatrick Hd., Ireland 13 B2
Dowsārī, Iran 39 D8
Draa, Oued →, Morocco 44 C2
Drachten, Neths. . . . 15 A6
Dragoman, Prokhod, Bulgaria 21 C10
Draguignan, France . 18 E7
Drain, U.S.A. 72 E2
Drake, Australia . . . 55 D5
Drake, U.S.A. 70 B4
Drake Passage, S. Ocean 5 B17
Drakensberg, S. Africa 49 E4
Dráma, Greece 21 D11
Drammen, Norway . . 9 G11
Drangajökull, Iceland 8 C2
Drau = Drava →, Croatia 21 B8
Drava →, Croatia . . 21 B8
Drayton Valley, Canada 64 C6
Dreux, France 18 B4
Driffield = Great Driffield, U.K. . . . 10 C7
Driggs, U.S.A. 72 E8
Drin →, Bos.-H. . . . 21 B8
Drøbak, Norway . . . 9 G11
Drogheda, Ireland . . 13 C5
Drogobych, Ukraine . 23 E3
Drogobych = Ukraine 23 E3
Drohobych = Ukraine 23 E3
Droichead Nua, Ireland 13 C5

Droitwich, U.K. 11 E5
Drôme □, France . . . 18 D6
Dromedary, C., Australia 55 F5
Dronfield, Australia . 54 C3
Dronten, Neths. . . . 15 B5
Drumheller, Canada . 64 C6
Drummond, U.S.A. . . 72 C7
Drummond I., U.S.A. . 62 C3
Drummond Pt., Australia 55 E2
Drummond Ra., Australia 54 C4
Drummondville, Canada 62 C5
Drumright, U.S.A. . . 71 H6
Druzhina, Russia . . 25 C15
Dryden, Canada . . . 65 D10
Dryden, U.S.A. 71 K3
Drygalski I., Antarctica 5 C7
Drysdale →, Australia 52 B4
Drysdale I., Australia 54 A2
Dschang, Cameroon . 44 G7
Du Bois, U.S.A. . . . 68 E6
Du Quoin, U.S.A. . . 70 G10
Duaringa, Australia . 54 C4
Dubā, Si. Arabia . . . 38 E2
Dubai = Dubayy, U.A.E. 39 E7
Dubawnt →, Canada 65 A8
Dubawnt, L., Canada 65 A8
Dubayy, U.A.E. 39 E7
Dubbo, Australia . . . 55 E4
Dublin, Ireland 13 C5
Dublin, Ga., U.S.A. . 69 J4
Dublin, Tex., U.S.A. . 71 J5
Dublin □, Ireland . . 13 C5
Dublin B., Ireland . . 13 C5
Dubois, U.S.A. 72 D7
Dubovka, Russia . . . 23 E7
Dubréka, Guinea . . . 44 G2
Dubrovnik, Croatia . . 21 C8
Dubrovskoye, Russia . 25 D12
Dubuque, U.S.A. . . . 70 D9
Duchesne, U.S.A. . . 72 F8
Duchess, Australia . . 54 C2
Ducie I., Pac. Oc. . . 57 K15
Duck Cr. →, Australia 52 D2
Duck Lake, Canada . 65 C7
Duck Mountain Prov. Park, Canada . . 65 C8
Dudhi, India 37 G13
Dudinka, Russia . . . 25 C9
Dudley, U.K. 11 E5
Duero = Douro →, Europe 19 B1
Dufftown, U.K. 12 D5
Dugi Otok, Croatia . . 20 B6
Duifken Pt., Australia 54 A3
Duisburg, Germany . 16 C3
Duiwelskloof, S. Africa 49 C5
Dükdamïn, Iran . . . 39 C8
Duke I., U.S.A. 64 C2
Dukhān, Qatar 39 E6
Duki, Pakistan 36 D6
Duku, Nigeria 44 F7
Dulce →, Argentina . 80 C4
Dulf, Iraq 38 C5
Dulit, Banjaran, Malaysia 32 D4
Dululu, Australia . . . 54 C5
Duluth, U.S.A. 70 B8
Dum Duma, India . . 37 F19
Dum Hadjer, Chad . . 45 F8
Dūmā, Lebanon . . . 41 A4
Dūmā, Syria 41 B5
Dumaguete, Phil. . . 33 C6
Dumai, Indonesia . . 32 D2
Dumaran, Phil. 33 B5
Dumas, Ark., U.S.A. . 71 J9
Dumas, Tex., U.S.A. . 71 H4
Dumbarton, U.K. . . . 12 F4
Dumbleyung, Australia 53 F2
Dumfries, U.K. 12 F5
Dumfries & Galloway □, U.K. . . 12 F5
Dumoine →, Canada 62 C4
Dumoine L., Canada . 62 C4
Dumyât, Egypt 45 B11
Dun Laoghaire, Ireland 13 C5
Dun Laoghaire = Dún Laoghaire, Ireland 13 C5
Dunaföldvár, Hungary 17 E9
Dunărea →, Romania 17 F14
Dunay, Russia 28 C6
Dunback, N.Z. 51 L3
Dunbar, Australia . . 54 B3
Dunbar, U.K. 12 E6
Dunblane, U.K. 12 E5
Duncan, Canada . . . 64 D4
Duncan, Ariz., U.S.A. 73 K9
Duncan, Okla., U.S.A. 71 H6
Duncan, L., Canada . 62 B4
Duncan Passage, Ind. Oc. 34 G2
Duncansby Head, U.K. 12 C5
Dundalk, Ireland . . . 13 B5
Dundalk Bay, Ireland 13 C5
Dundas, Canada . . . 62 D4
Dundas, L., Australia 53 F3
Dundas Str., Australia 52 B5
Dundee, S. Africa . . 49 D5
Dundee, U.K. 12 E6
Dundoo, Australia . . 55 D3
Dundrum, U.K. 13 B6
Dundrum B., U.K. . . 13 B6
Dunedin, N.Z. 51 L3
Dunedin, U.S.A. . . . 69 L4
Dunedin →, Canada . 64 B4
Dunfermline, U.K. . . 12 E5
Dungannon, Canada . 62 D3
Dungannon □, U.K. . 13 B5
Dungarvan, Ireland . 13 D4

Dungarvan Bay, Ireland 13 D4
Dungeness, U.K. . . . 11 G8
Dungo, L. do, Angola 48 B2
Dungog, Australia . . 55 E5
Dungu, Zaïre 46 D5
Dunhuang, China . . 30 B4
Dunk I., Australia . . 54 B4
Dunkeld, U.K. 12 E5
Dunkerque, France . 18 A5
Dunkery Beacon, U.K. 11 F4
Dunkirk = Dunkerque, France 18 A5
Dunkirk, U.S.A. . . . 68 D6
Dunkwa, Ghana . . . 44 G4
Dunlap, U.S.A. 70 E7
Dúnleary = Dun Laoghaire, Ireland . 13 C5
Dunmanus B., Ireland 13 E2
Dunmara, Australia . 54 B1
Dunmore, U.S.A. . . 68 E8
Dunmore Hd., Ireland 13 D1
Dunn, U.S.A. 69 H6
Dunnellon, U.S.A. . . 69 L4
Dunnet Hd., U.K. . . 12 C5
Dunning, U.S.A. . . . 70 E4
Dunolly, Australia . . 55 F3
Dunoon, U.K. 12 F4
Dunqul, Egypt 45 D11
Duns, U.K. 12 F6
Dunseith, U.S.A. . . . 70 A4
Dunsmuir, U.S.A. . . 72 F2
Dunstable, U.K. . . . 11 F7
Dunstan Mts., N.Z. . 51 L2
Dunster, Canada . . . 64 C5
Dunvegan L., Canada 65 A7
Dupree, U.S.A. 70 C4
Dupuyer, U.S.A. . . . 72 B7
Durack →, Australia . 52 C4
Durack Ra., Australia 52 C4
Durance →, France . 18 E6
Durango = Victoria de Durango, Mexico . 74 C4
Durango, Spain . . . 19 A4
Durango, U.S.A. . . . 73 H10
Duranillin, Australia . 53 F2
Durant, U.S.A. 71 J6
Durazno, Uruguay . . 80 C5
Durazzo = Durrës, Albania 21 D8
Durban, S. Africa . . 49 D5
Durg, India 37 J12
Durgapur, India . . . 37 H15
Durham, Canada . . . 62 D3
Durham, U.K. 10 C6
Durham, U.S.A. . . . 69 G6
Durham □, U.K. . . . 10 C6
Durham Downs, Australia 55 D4
Durmitor, Montenegro, Yug. . 21 C8
Durness, U.K. 12 C4
Durrës, Albania . . . 21 D8
Durrie, Australia . . . 54 D3
D'Urville, Tanjung, Indonesia 33 E9
D'Urville I., N.Z. . . . 51 J4
Dusa Mareb, Somali Rep. 40 F4
Dushak, Turkmenistan 24 F7
Dushanbe, Tajikistan 24 F7
Dusky Sd., N.Z. . . . 51 L1
Dussejour, C., Australia 52 B4
Düsseldorf, Germany 16 C3
Dutch Harbor, U.S.A. 60 C3
Dutlwe, Botswana . . 48 C3
Dutton →, Australia . 54 C3
Duyun, China 30 D5
Duzdab = Zähedän, Iran 39 D9
Dvina, Sev. →, Russia 22 B7
Dvinsk = Daugavpils, Latvia 22 C4
Dvinskaya Guba, Russia 22 B6
Dwarka, India 36 H6
Dwellingup, Australia 53 F2
Dwight, U.S.A. 68 E1
Dyer, C., Canada . . 61 B13
Dyer Plateau, Antarctica 5 D17
Dyersburg, U.S.A. . . 71 G10
Dyfed □, U.K. 11 E3
Dyfi →, U.K. 11 E4
Dynevor Downs, Australia 55 D3
Dysart, Canada . . . 65 C8
Dzamin Üüd, Mongolia 31 B6
Dzerzhinsk, Belorussia 17 B14
Dzerzhinsk, Russia . 22 C7
Dzhalinda, Russia . . 25 D13
Dzhambul, Kazakhstan 24 E8
Dzhankoi, Ukraine . . 23 E5
Dzhardzhan, Russia . 25 C12
Dzhetygara, Kazakhstan 24 D7
Dzhezkazgan, Kazakhstan 24 E7
Dzhikimde, Russia . . 25 D13
Dzhizak, Uzbekistan . 24 E7
Dzhugdzur, Khrebet, Russia 25 D14
Dzhungarskiye Vorota = Dzhungarskiye Vorota, Kazakhstan 30 B3
Dzungaria = Junggar Pendi, China 30 B3
Dzungarian Gates = Dzhungarskiye Vorota, Kazakhstan 30 B3
Dzuumod, Mongolia . 30 B5

E

Eabamet, L., Canada . 62 B2
Eads, U.S.A. 70 F3
Eagle, U.S.A. 72 G10
Eagle →, Canada 63 B8
Eagle Butt, U.S.A. . . . 70 C4
Eagle Grove, U.S.A. . . 70 D8
Eagle L., Calif., U.S.A. 72 F3
Eagle L., Maine, U.S.A. 63 C6
Eagle Lake, U.S.A. . . . 71 L6
Eagle Nest, U.S.A. . . . 73 H11
Eagle Pass, U.S.A. . . . 71 L4
Eagle Pt., Australia . . 52 C3
Eagle River, U.S.A. . . 70 C10
Ealing, U.K. 11 F7
Earaheedy, Australia . 53 E3
Earl Grey, Canada . . . 65 C8
Earle, U.S.A. 71 H9
Earlimart, U.S.A. 73 J4
Earn →, U.K. 12 E5
Earn, L., U.K. 12 E4
Earnslaw, Mt., N.Z. . . 51 L2
Earth, U.S.A. 71 H3
Easley, U.S.A. 69 H4
East Angus, Canada . . 63 C5
East B., U.S.A. 71 L10
East Bengal, Bangla. . 37 G17
East Beskids =
Východné Beskydy,
Europe 17 D10
East C., N.Z. 51 G7
East Chicago, U.S.A. . 68 E2
East China Sea, Asia . 31 C7
East Coulee, Canada . 64 C6
East Falkland, Falk. Is. 80 G5
East Grand Forks,
U.S.A. 70 B6
East Helena, U.S.A. . . 72 C8
East Indies, Asia 33 E6
East Jordan, U.S.A. . . 68 C3
East Lansing, U.S.A. . 68 D3
East Liverpool, U.S.A. 68 E5
East London, S. Africa 49 E4
East Main = Eastmain,
Canada 62 B4
East Orange, U.S.A. . . 68 E8
East Pacific Ridge,
Pac. Oc. 57 J17
East Pakistan =
Bangladesh ■, Asia 37 H17
East Pine, Canada . . . 64 B4
East Pt., Canada 63 C7
East Point, U.S.A. . . . 69 J3
East Retford, U.K. . . . 10 D7
East St. Louis, U.S.A. 70 F9
East Schelde → =
Oosterschelde,
Neths. 15 C4
East Siberian Sea,
Russia 25 B17
East Sussex □, U.K. . . 11 G8
East Tawas, U.S.A. . . . 68 C4
East Toorale, Australia 55 E4
Eastbourne, N.Z. 51 J5
Eastbourne, U.K. 11 G8
Eastend, Canada 65 D7
Easter Dal =
Österdalälven →,
Sweden 9 F12
Easter Islands =
Pascua, I. de,
Pac. Oc. 57 K17
Eastern Cr. →,
Australia 54 C3
Eastern Ghats, India . 36 N11
Eastern Group = Lau
Group, Fiji 51 C9
Eastern Group,
Australia 53 F3
Easterville, Canada . . 65 C9
Eastland, U.S.A. 71 J5
Eastleigh, U.K. 11 G6
Eastmain, Canada . . . 62 B4
Eastmain →, Canada 62 B4
Eastman, U.S.A. 69 J4
Easton, Md., U.S.A. . . 68 F7
Easton, Pa., U.S.A. . . . 68 E8
Easton, Wash., U.S.A. 72 C3
Eastport, U.S.A. 63 D6
Eaton, U.S.A. 70 E2
Eatonia, Canada 65 C7
Eatonton, U.S.A. 69 J4
Eau Claire, U.S.A. . . . 70 C9
Ebagoola, Australia . . 54 A3
Ebbw Vale, U.K. 11 F4
Ebeltoft, Denmark . . . 9 H11
Eberswalde, Germany 16 B6
Ebetsu, Japan 28 C10
Eboli, Italy 20 D6
Ebolowa, Cameroon . 46 D2
Ebro →, Spain 19 B6
Ech Cheliff, Algeria . . 44 A5
Echigo-Sammyaku,
Japan 29 F9
Echizen-Misaki, Japan 29 G7
Echo Bay, N.W.T.,
Canada 60 B8
Echo Bay, Ont.,
Canada 62 C3
Echoing →, Canada . 65 B10
Echternach, Lux. 15 E6
Echuca, Australia . . . 55 F3
Ecija, Spain 19 D3
Eclipse Is., Australia . 52 B4
Ecuador ■, S. Amer. . 78 D3
Ed Dâmer, Sudan 45 E11
Ed Debba, Sudan 45 E11
Ed Dueim, Sudan 45 F11
Edah, Australia 53 E2

Edam, Canada 65 C7
Edam, Neths. 15 B5
Eday, U.K. 12 B6
Edd, Eritrea 40 E3
Eddrachillis B., U.K. . . 12 C3
Eddystone, U.K. 11 G3
Eddystone Pt.,
Australia 54 G4
Ede, Neths. 15 B5
Édea, Cameroon 44 H7
Edehon L., Canada . . . 65 A9
Eden, Australia 55 F4
Eden, N.C., U.S.A. . . . 69 G6
Eden, Tex., U.S.A. . . . 71 K5
Eden, Wyo., U.S.A. . . 72 E9
Eden →, U.K. 10 C4
Eden L., Canada 65 B8
Edenburg, S. Africa . . 48 D4
Edendale, S. Africa . . 49 D5
Edenderry, Ireland . . . 13 C4
Edenton, U.S.A. 69 G7
Edenville, S. Africa . . 49 D4
Edge Hill, U.K. 11 E6
Edgefield, U.S.A. 69 J5
Edgeley, U.S.A. 70 B5
Edgemont, U.S.A. . . . 70 D3
Edgeøya, Svalbard . . . 4 B9
Edhessa, Greece 21 D10
Edievale, N.Z. 51 L2
Edina, U.S.A. 70 E8
Edinburg, U.S.A. 71 M5
Edinburgh, U.K. 12 F5
Edirne, Turkey 21 D12
Edithburgh, Australia 55 F2
Edjudina, Australia . . 53 E3
Edmond, U.S.A. 71 H6
Edmonds, U.S.A. 72 C2
Edmonton, Australia . 54 B4
Edmonton, Canada . . 64 C6
Edmund L., Canada . . 65 C10
Edmundston, Canada . 63 C6
Edna, U.S.A. 71 L6
Edna Bay, U.S.A. 64 B2
Edson, Canada 64 C5
Edward →, Australia . 55 F3
Edward, L., Africa . . . 46 E5
Edward I, Canada . . . 62 C2
Edward River,
Australia 54 A3
Edward VII Land,
Antarctica 5 E13
Edwards Plateau,
U.S.A. 71 K4
Edzo, Canada 64 A5
Eekloo, Belgium 15 C3
Effingham, U.S.A. . . . 68 F1
Égadi, Ísole, Italy . . . 20 F5
Eganville, Canada . . . 62 C4
Egeland, U.S.A. 70 A5
Egenolf L., Canada . . 65 B9
Eger = Cheb, Czech. . 16 C6
Eger, Hungary 17 E10
Egersund, Norway . . . 9 G9
Egg L., Canada 65 B7
Eginbah, Australia . . 52 D2
Egmont, C., N.Z. 51 H4
Egmont, Mt., N.Z. . . . 51 H5
Eğridir, Turkey 23 G5
Eğridir Gölü, Turkey . 23 G5
Egvekinot, Russia . . . 25 C19
Egypt ■, Africa 45 C11
Ehime □, Japan 29 H6
Eidsvold, Australia . . 55 D5
Eidsvoll, Norway 9 F11
Eifel, Germany 16 C3
Eigg, U.K. 12 E2
Eighty Mile Beach,
Australia 52 C3
Eil, Somali Rep. 40 F4
Eil, L., U.K. 12 E3
Eildon, L., Australia . . 55 F4
Eileen L., Canada . . . 65 A7
Einasleigh, Australia . 54 B3
Einasleigh →,
Australia 54 B3
Eindhoven, Neths. . . . 15 C5
Eire = Ireland ■,
Europe 13 D4
Eiríksjökull, Iceland . 8 D3
Eirunepé, Brazil 78 E5
Eisenach, Germany . . 16 C5
Eisenerz, Austria 16 E7
Eivissa = Ibiza, Spain 19 C6
Ekalaka, U.S.A. 70 C2
Eketahuna, N.Z. 51 J5
Ekibastuz, Kazakhstan 24 D8
Ekimchan, Russia . . . 25 D14
Ekwan →, Canada . . . 62 B3
Ekwan Pt., Canada . . 62 B3
El Aaiún, W. Sahara . 44 C2
El 'Agrûd, Egypt 41 E3
El Alamein, Egypt . . . 45 B10
El 'Aqaba, W. →,
Egypt 41 E2
El Aricha, Algeria . . . 44 B4
El Arīhā, Jordan 41 D4
El Arish, Australia . . . 54 B4
El 'Arîsh, Egypt 41 D2
El 'Arîsh, W. →,
Egypt 41 D2
El Asnam = Ech
Cheliff, Algeria . . . 44 A5
El Bawiti, Egypt 45 C10
El Bayadh, Algeria . . 44 B5
El Brûk, W. →, Egypt 41 E2
El Buheirat □, Sudan . 45 G11
El Cajon, U.S.A. 73 K5
El Callao, Venezuela . 78 B6
El Campo, U.S.A. 71 L6
El Centro, U.S.A. 73 K6
El Cerro, Bolivia 78 G6

El Cuy, Argentina . . . 80 D3
El Cuyo, Mexico 74 C7
El Daheir, Egypt 41 D3
El Dere, Somali Rep. . 40 G4
El Diviso, Colombia . . 78 C3
El Djouf, Mauritania . 44 E3
El Dorado, Ark., U.S.A. 71 J8
El Dorado, Kans.,
U.S.A. 71 G6
El Dorado, Venezuela 78 B6
El Escorial, Spain . . . 19 B3
El Faiyûm, Egypt 45 C11
El Fâsher, Sudan 45 F10
El Ferrol, Spain 19 A1
El Fuerte, Mexico . . . 74 B3
El Gal, Somali Rep. . . 40 E5
El Geteina, Sudan . . . 45 F11
El Gezira □, Sudan . . 45 F11
El Gîza, Egypt 45 C11
El Goléa, Algeria 44 B5
El Harrach, Algeria . . 44 A5
El Iskandarîya, Egypt 45 B10
El Jadida, Morocco . . 44 B3
El Jebelein, Sudan . . . 45 F11
El Kab, Sudan 45 E11
El Kabrît, G., Egypt . . 41 F2
El Kala, Algeria 44 A6
El Kamlin, Sudan 45 E11
El Kef, Tunisia 44 A6
El Khandaq, Sudan . . 45 E11
El Khârga, Egypt 45 C11
El Khartûm, Sudan . . 45 E11
El Khartûm Bahrî,
Sudan 45 E11
El Kuntilla, Egypt . . . 41 E3
El Laqâwa, Sudan . . . 45 F10
El Mafâza, Sudan . . . 45 F11
El Mahalla el Kubra,
Egypt 45 B11
El Mansûra, Egypt . . 45 B11
El Minyâ, Egypt 45 C11
El Obeid, Sudan 45 F11
El Odaiya, Sudan 45 F10
El Oued, Algeria 44 B6
El Paso, U.S.A. 73 L10
El Portal, U.S.A. 73 H4
El Qâhira, Egypt 45 B11
El Qantara, Egypt . . . 41 E1
El Qasr, Egypt 45 C10
El Quseima, Egypt . . . 41 E3
El Reno, U.S.A. 71 H6
El Saheira, W. →,
Egypt 41 E2
El Salvador ■,
Cent. Amer. 74 E7
El Shallal, Egypt 45 D11
El Suweis, Egypt 45 C11
El Tamarâni, W. →,
Egypt 41 E3
El Thamad, Egypt . . . 41 F3
El Tigre, Venezuela . . 78 B6
El Tîh, G., Egypt 41 F2
El Tina, Khalig, Egypt 41 D1
El Tocuyo, Venezuela 78 B5
El Turbio, Argentina . 80 G2
El Uqsur, Egypt 45 C11
El Vigía, Venezuela . . 78 B4
El Wabeira, Egypt . . . 41 F2
El Wak, Kenya 46 D7
El Wuz, Sudan 45 E11
Elandsvlei, S. Africa . 48 E2
Elat, Israel 41 F3
Elâzığ, Turkey 23 G6
Elba, Italy 20 C4
Elba, U.S.A. 69 K2
Elbasani, Albania . . . 21 D9
Elbe →, Europe 16 B4
Elbert, Mt., U.S.A. . . . 73 G10
Elberta, U.S.A. 68 C2
Elberton, U.S.A. 69 H4
Elbeuf, France 18 B4
Elbing = Elbląg,
Poland 17 A9
Elbląg, Poland 17 A9
Elbow, Canada 65 C7
Elbrus, Asia 23 F7
Elburg, Neths. 15 B5
Elburz Mts. = Alborz,
Reshteh-ye Kühhā-
ye, Iran 39 C7
Elche, Spain 19 C5
Elcho I., Australia . . . 54 A2
Eldon, U.S.A. 70 F8
Eldora, U.S.A. 70 D8
Eldorado, Canada . . . 65 B7
Eldorado, Ill., U.S.A. . 68 G1
Eldorado, Tex., U.S.A. 71 K4
Eldorado Springs,
U.S.A. 71 G8
Eldoret, Kenya 46 D7
Electra, U.S.A. 71 H5
Elefantes →, Mozam. 49 C5
Elektrostal, Russia . . . 22 C6
Elephant Butte Res.,
U.S.A. 73 K10
Elephant I., Antarctica 5 C18
Eleuthera, Bahamas . . 75 C9
Elgin, Canada 63 C8
Elgin, U.K. 12 D5
Elgin, Ill., U.S.A. 68 D1
Elgin, N. Dak., U.S.A. 70 B4
Elgin, Nebr., U.S.A. . . 70 E5
Elgin, Nev., U.S.A. . . . 73 H6
Elgin, Oreg., U.S.A. . . 72 D5
Elgin, Tex., U.S.A. . . . 71 K6
Elgon, Mt., Africa . . . 46 D6
Eliase, Indonesia 33 F8
Elim, S. Africa 48 E2
Elisabethville =
Lubumbashi, Zaïre . 47 G5
Elista, Russia 23 E7

Elizabeth, Australia . . 55 E2
Elizabeth, U.S.A. 68 E8
Elizabeth City, U.S.A. 69 G7
Elizabethton, U.S.A. . 69 G4
Elizabethtown, U.S.A. 68 G3
Elk City, U.S.A. 71 H5
Elk Island Nat. Park,
Canada 64 C6
Elk Lake, Canada . . . 62 C3
Elk Point, Canada . . . 65 C6
Elk River, Idaho, U.S.A. 72 C5
Elk River, Minn., U.S.A. 70 C8
Elkedra, Australia . . . 54 C2
Elkedra →, Australia 54 C2
Elkhart, Ind., U.S.A. . 68 E3
Elkhart, Kans., U.S.A. 71 G4
Elkhorn, Canada 65 D8
Elkhorn →, U.S.A. . . 70 E6
Elkhovo, Bulgaria . . . 21 C12
Elkin, U.S.A. 69 G5
Elkins, U.S.A. 68 F6
Elko, Canada 64 D5
Elko, U.S.A. 72 F6
Ell, L., Australia 53 E4
Ellef Ringnes I.,
Canada 4 B2
Ellendale, Australia . . 52 C3
Ellendale, U.S.A. 70 B5
Ellensburg, U.S.A. . . . 72 C3
Ellenville, U.S.A. 68 E8
Ellery, Mt., Australia . 55 F4
Ellesmere, L., N.Z. . . 51 M4
Ellesmere I., Canada . 4 B4
Ellesmere Port, U.K. . 10 D5
Ellice Is. = Tuvalu ■,
Pac. Oc. 56 H9
Ellinwood, U.S.A. . . . 70 F5
Elliot, Australia 54 B1
Elliot, S. Africa 49 E4
Elliot Lake, Canada . . 62 C3
Elliotdale = Xhora,
S. Africa 49 E4
Ellis, U.S.A. 70 F5
Elliston, Australia . . . 55 E1
Ellisville, U.S.A. 71 K10
Ellon, U.K. 12 D6
Ellore = Eluru, India . 37 L12
Ells →, Canada 64 B6
Ellsworth, U.S.A. 70 F5
Ellsworth Land,
Antarctica 5 D16
Ellsworth Mts.,
Antarctica 5 D16
Ellwood City, U.S.A. . 68 E5
Elma, Canada 65 D9
Elma, U.S.A. 72 C2
Elmali, Turkey 23 G4
Elmhurst, U.S.A. 68 E2
Elmira, U.S.A. 68 D7
Elmore, Australia . . . 55 F3
Eloy, U.S.A. 73 K8
Elrose, Canada 65 C7
Elsas, Canada 62 C3
Elsinore = Helsingør,
Denmark 9 H12
Elsinore, U.S.A. 73 G7
Eltham, N.Z. 51 H5
Elvas, Portugal 19 C2
Elverum, Norway 9 F11
Elvire →, Australia . . 52 C4
Elwood, Ind., U.S.A. . 68 E3
Elwood, Nebr., U.S.A. 70 E5
Elx = Elche, Spain . . 19 C5
Ely, U.K. 11 E8
Ely, Minn., U.S.A. . . . 70 B9
Ely, Nev., U.S.A. 72 G6
Elyria, U.S.A. 68 E4
Emämrüd, Iran 39 B7
Emba, Kazakhstan . . 24 E6
Emba →, Kazakhstan 23 E9
Embarcación,
Argentina 80 A4
Embarras Portage,
Canada 65 B6
Embetsu, Japan 28 B10
Embrun, France 18 D7
Embu, Kenya 46 E7
Emden, Germany 16 B3
Emerald, Australia . . 54 C4
Emerson, Canada . . . 65 D9
Emery, U.S.A. 73 G8
Emi Koussi, Chad . . . 45 E8
Emilia-Romagna □,
Italy 20 B4
Emine, Burgas, Bulgaria . 28 B10
Emmeloord, Neths. . . 15 B5
Emmen, Neths. 15 B6
Emmet, Australia 54 C3
Emmetsburg, U.S.A. . 70 D7
Emmett, U.S.A. 72 E5
Empalme, Mexico . . . 74 B2
Empangeni, S. Africa . 49 D5
Empedrado, Argentina 80 B5
Emperor Seamount
Chain, Pac. Oc. . . . 56 D9
Emporia, Kans., U.S.A. 70 F6
Emporia, Va., U.S.A. . 69 G7
Emporium, U.S.A. . . . 68 E6
Empress, Canada . . . 65 C6
Empty Quarter = Rub'
al Khali, Si. Arabia . 40 D4
Ems →, Germany . . . 16 B3
'En 'Avrona, Israel . . . 41 F3
En Nahud, Sudan . . . 45 F10
Ena, Japan 29 G8
Enana, Namibia 48 B2
Enaratoli, Indonesia . 33 E9
Enard B., U.K. 12 C3
Enare = Inarijärvi,
Finland 8 B19
Encanto, C., Phil. . . . 33 A6

Encarnación, Paraguay 80 B5
Encinal, U.S.A. 71 L5
Encino, U.S.A. 73 J11
Encounter B., Australia 55 F2
Endau →, Malaysia . 34 S16
Ende, Indonesia 33 F6
Endeavour, Canada . . 65 C8
Endeavour Str.,
Australia 54 A3
Enderbury I., Kiribati . 56 H10
Enderby, Canada 64 C5
Enderby I., Australia . 52 D2
Enderby Land,
Antarctica 5 C5
Enderlin, U.S.A. 70 B6
Endicott, N.Y., U.S.A. 68 D7
Endicott, Wash., U.S.A. 72 C5
Endyalgout I., Australia 52 B5
Enewetak Atoll,
Pac. Oc. 56 F8
Enez, Turkey 21 D12
Enfield, U.K. 11 F7
Engadin, Switz. 16 E5
Engaño, C., Phil. 33 A6
Engcobo, S. Africa . . 49 E4
Engels = Pokrovsk,
Russia 22 D8
Engemann L., Canada 65 B7
Enggano, Indonesia . . 32 F2
Enghien, Belgium . . . 15 D4
Engkilili, Malaysia . . 32 D4
England, U.S.A. 71 H9
England □, U.K. 7 E5
Englee, Canada 63 B8
Englehart, Canada . . . 62 C4
Engler L., Canada . . . 65 B7
Englewood, Colo.,
U.S.A. 70 F2
Englewood, Kans.,
U.S.A. 71 G5
English →, Canada . . 65 C10
English Bazar = Ingraj
Bazar, India 37 G16
English Channel,
Europe 11 G6
English River, Canada 62 C1
Enid, U.S.A. 71 G6
Enkhuizen, Neths. . . . 15 B5
Enna, Italy 20 F6
Ennadai, Canada 65 A8
Ennadai L., Canada . . 65 A8
Ennedi, Chad 45 E9
Enngonia, Australia . . 55 D4
Ennis, Ireland 13 D3
Ennis, Mont., U.S.A. . 72 D8
Ennis, Tex., U.S.A. . . . 71 J6
Enniscorthy, Ireland . 13 D5
Enniskillen, U.K. 13 B4
Ennistimon, Ireland . 13 D2
Enns →, Austria 16 D7
Enontekiö, Finland . . 8 B17
Enschede, Neths. 15 B6
Ensenada, Mexico . . . 74 A1
Entebbe, Uganda . . . 46 D6
Enterprise, Canada . . 64 A5
Enterprise, Oreg.,
U.S.A. 72 D5
Enterprise, Utah,
U.S.A. 73 H7
Enugu, Nigeria 44 G6
Enugu Ezike, Nigeria . 44 G6
Enumclaw, U.S.A. . . . 72 C3
Eólie, Ís., Italy 20 E6
Epe, Neths. 15 B5
Épernay, France 18 B5
Ephraim, U.S.A. 72 G8
Ephrata, U.S.A. 72 C4
Épinal, France 18 B7
Epping, U.K. 11 F8
Epukiro, Namibia . . . 48 C2
Equatorial Guinea ■,
Africa 46 D1
Er Rahad, Sudan 45 F11
Er Rif, Morocco 44 A4
Er Roseires, Sudan . . 45 F11
Erāwadī Myit =
Irrawaddy →,
Burma 37 M19
Erbil = Arbîl, Iraq . . . 38 B5
Ercha, Russia 25 C15
Erciyaş Dağı, Turkey . 23 G6
Erebus, Mt., Antarctica 5 D11
Erechim, Brazil 80 B6
Ereğli, Konya, Turkey 23 G5
Ereğli, Zonguldak,
Turkey 23 F5
Eresma →, Spain . . . 19 B3
Erewadi Myitwanya,
Burma 37 M19
Erfenisdam, S. Africa 48 D4
Erfurt, Germany 16 C5
Ergene →, Turkey . . . 21 D12
Ergeni Vozvyshennost,
Russia 23 E7
Eriboll, L., U.K. 12 C4
Érice, Italy 20 E5
Erie, U.S.A. 68 D5
Erie, L., N. Amer. 68 D4
Erigavo, Somali Rep. . 40 E4
Eriksdale, Canada . . . 65 C9
Erimanthos, Greece . . 21 F9
Erimo-misaki, Japan . 28 D11
Eritrea ■, Africa 40 E3
Erlangen, Germany . . 16 D5
Erldunda, Australia . . 54 D1
Ermelo, Neths. 15 B5
Ermelo, S. Africa 49 D4
Ermoúpolis = Síros,
Greece 21 F11
Ernakulam = Cochin,
India 36 Q10
Erne →, Ireland 13 B3

Erne, Lower L., U.K. . 13 B4
Erne, Upper L., U.K. . 13 B4
Ernest Giles Ra.,
Australia 53 E3
Erode, India 36 P10
Eromanga, Australia . 55 D3
Erongo, Namibia 48 C2
Errabiddy, Australia . 53 E2
Erramala Hills, India . 36 M11
Errigal, Ireland 13 A3
Erris Hd., Ireland 13 B1
Erskine, U.S.A. 70 B7
Ertis = Irtysh →,
Russia 24 C7
Erwin, U.S.A. 69 G4
Erzgebirge, Germany . 16 C6
Erzin, Russia 25 D10
Erzincan, Turkey 23 G6
Erzurum, Turkey 23 G7
Es Sahrâ' Esh
Sharqîya, Egypt . . . 45 C11
Es Sînâ', Egypt 45 C11
Esan-Misaki, Japan . . 28 D10
Esashi, Hokkaidō,
Japan 28 B11
Esashi, Hokkaidō,
Japan 28 D10
Esbjerg, Denmark . . . 9 J10
Escalante, U.S.A. 73 H8
Escalante →, U.S.A. . 73 H8
Escambia →, U.S.A. . 69 K2
Escanaba, U.S.A. 68 C2
Esch-sur-Alzette, Lux. 15 E5
Escobal, Panama 74 H14
Escondido, U.S.A. . . . 73 K5
Escuinapa, Mexico . . 74 C3
Escuintla, Mexico . . . 74 E6
Esfahān, Iran 39 C6
Esfideh, Iran 39 C8
Esh Sham = Dimashq,
Syria 41 B5
Esh Shamâlîya □,
Sudan 45 E10
Eshowe, S. Africa . . . 49 D5
Esil = Ishim →,
Russia 24 D8
Esk →, Dumf. & Gall.,
U.K. 12 G5
Esk →, N. Yorks., U.K. 10 C7
Eskifjörður, Iceland . 8 D7
Eskilstuna, Sweden . . 9 G14
Eskimo Pt., Canada . . 65 A10
Eskişehir, Turkey . . . 23 G5
Esla →, Spain 19 B2
Eslāmābād-e Gharb,
Iran 38 C5
Esmeraldas, Ecuador . 78 C3
Espanola, Canada . . . 62 C3
Esperance, Australia . 53 F3
Esperance B., Australia 53 F3
Esperanza, Argentina 80 C4
Espichel, C., Portugal 19 C1
Espinal, Colombia . . . 78 C4
Espinazo, Sierra de =
Espinhaço, Serra do,
Brazil 79 G10
Espinhaço, Serra do,
Brazil 79 G10
Espírito Santo □, Brazil 79 G10
Espungabera, Mozam. 49 C5
Esquel, Argentina . . . 80 E2
Esquina, Argentina . . 80 C5
Essaouira, Morocco . 44 B3
Essen, Belgium 15 C4
Essen, Germany 16 C3
Essendon, Mt.,
Australia 53 E3
Essequibo →, Guyana 78 B7
Essex □, U.K. 11 F8
Esslingen, Germany . 16 D4
Essonne □, France . . 18 B5
Estados, I. de Los,
Argentina 80 G4
Estahbānāt, Iran 39 D7
Estância, Brazil 79 F11
Estancia, U.S.A. 73 J10
Estārm, Iran 39 D8
Estcourt, S. Africa . . . 49 D4
Estelline, S. Dak.,
U.S.A. 70 C6
Estelline, Tex., U.S.A. 71 H4
Esterhazy, Canada . . . 65 C8
Estevan, Canada 65 D8
Estevan Group,
Canada 64 C3
Estherville, U.S.A. . . . 70 D7
Eston, Canada 65 C7
Estonia ■, Europe . . . 22 C4
Estoril, Portugal 19 C1
Estrêla, Serra da,
Portugal 19 B2
Estremadura, Portugal 19 C1
Estrondo, Serra do,
Brazil 79 E9
Esztergom, Hungary . 17 E9
Etadunna, Australia . . 55 D2
Etamamu, Canada . . . 63 B8
Etanga, Namibia 48 B1
Etawah, India 36 F11
Etawah →, U.S.A. . . . 69 H3
Etawney L., Canada . . 65 B9
Ethel Creek, Australia 52 D3
Ethiopia ■, Africa . . . 40 F3
Ethiopian Highlands,
Ethiopia 42 E7
Etive, L., U.K. 12 E3
Etna, Italy 20 F6
Etolin I., U.S.A. 64 B2
Etosha Pan, Namibia . 48 B2
Etowah, U.S.A. 69 H3
Ettrick Water →, U.K. 12 F6

Euboea = Évvoia, Greece ... 21 E11
Eucla Motel, Australia ... 53 F4
Euclid, U.S.A. ... 68 E5
Eucumbene, L., Australia ... 55 F4
Eudora, U.S.A. ... 71 J9
Eufaula, Ala., U.S.A. ... 69 K3
Eufaula, Okla., U.S.A. ... 71 H7
Eufaula, L., U.S.A. ... 71 H7
Eugene, U.S.A. ... 72 E2
Eugowra, Australia ... 55 E4
Eulo, Australia ... 55 D4
Eunice, La., U.S.A. ... 71 K8
Eunice, N. Mex., U.S.A. ... 71 J3
Eupen, Belgium ... 15 D6
Euphrates = Furāt, Nahr al →, Asia ... 38 D5
Eure □, France ... 18 B4
Eure-et-Loir □, France ... 18 B4
Eureka, Canada ... 4 B3
Eureka, Calif., U.S.A. ... 72 F1
Eureka, Kans., U.S.A. ... 71 G6
Eureka, Mont., U.S.A. ... 72 B6
Eureka, Nev., U.S.A. ... 72 G5
Eureka, S. Dak., U.S.A. ... 70 C5
Eureka, Utah, U.S.A. ... 72 G7
Eureka, Mt., Australia ... 53 E3
Euroa, Australia ... 55 F4
Europa, I., Ind. Oc. ... 47 J8
Europa, Picos de, Spain ... 19 A3
Europa, Pta. de, Gib. ... 19 D3
Europa Pt. = Europa, Pta. de, Gib. ... 19 D3
Europe ... 6 F10
Europoort, Neths. ... 15 C4
Eustis, U.S.A. ... 69 L5
Eutsuk L., Canada ... 64 C3
Eva Downs, Australia ... 54 B1
Evale, Angola ... 48 B2
Evans, U.S.A. ... 70 E2
Evans Head, Australia ... 55 D5
Evans L., Canada ... 62 B4
Evanston, Ill., U.S.A. ... 68 D2
Evanston, Wyo., U.S.A. ... 72 F8
Evansville, Ind., U.S.A. ... 68 F2
Evansville, Wis., U.S.A. ... 70 D10
Evaz, Iran ... 39 E7
Eveleth, U.S.A. ... 70 B8
Evensk, Russia ... 25 C16
Everard, L., Australia ... 55 E1
Everard Park, Australia ... 53 E5
Everard Ras., Australia ... 53 E5
Everest, Mt., Nepal ... 37 E15
Everett, U.S.A. ... 72 C2
Everglades, U.S.A. ... 69 N5
Everglades City, U.S.A. ... 69 N5
Everglades Nat. Park, U.S.A. ... 69 N5
Evergreen, U.S.A. ... 69 K2
Everson, U.S.A. ... 72 B2
Evesham, U.K. ... 11 E6
Evinayong, Eq. Guin. ... 46 D2
Évora, Portugal ... 19 C2
Evowghlī, Iran ... 38 B5
Évreux, France ... 18 B4
Évvoia, Greece ... 21 E11
Ewe, L., U.K. ... 12 D3
Ewing, U.S.A. ... 70 D5
Ewo, Congo ... 46 E2
Exaltación, Bolivia ... 78 F5
Excelsior Springs, U.S.A. ... 70 F7
Exe →, U.K. ... 11 G4
Exeter, U.K. ... 11 G4
Exeter, Calif., U.S.A. ... 73 H4
Exeter, Nebr., U.S.A. ... 70 E6
Exmoor, U.K. ... 11 F4
Exmouth, Australia ... 52 D1
Exmouth, U.K. ... 11 G4
Exmouth G., Australia ... 52 D1
Expedition Ra., Australia ... 54 C4
Extremadura □, Spain ... 19 C2
Eyasi, L., Tanzania ... 46 E6
Eyeberry L., Canada ... 65 A8
Eyemouth, U.K. ... 12 F6
Eyjafjörður, Iceland ... 8 C4
Eyrarbakki, Iceland ... 8 E3
Eyre, Australia ... 53 F4
Eyre (North), L., Australia ... 55 D2
Eyre (South), L., Australia ... 55 D2
Eyre Cr. →, Australia ... 55 D2
Eyre Mts., N.Z. ... 51 L2
Eyre Pen., Australia ... 55 E2
Eyvānki, Iran ... 39 C6

F

Fabens, U.S.A. ... 73 L10
Fabriano, Italy ... 20 C5
Facatativá, Colombia ... 78 C4
Fachi, Niger ... 44 E7
Fada, Chad ... 45 E9
Fada-n-Gourma, Burkina Faso ... 44 F5
Faddeyevskiy, Ostrov, Russia ... 25 B15
Fadghāmī, Syria ... 38 C4
Faenza, Italy ... 20 B4
Făgăraș, Romania ... 17 F12
Fagernes, Norway ... 9 F10
Fagersta, Sweden ... 9 F13
Fahlīān, Iran ... 39 D6
Fahraj, Kermān, Iran ... 39 D8

Fahraj, Yazd, Iran ... 39 D7
Fair Hd., U.K. ... 13 A5
Fairbanks, U.S.A. ... 60 B5
Fairbury, U.S.A. ... 70 E6
Fairfax, U.S.A. ... 71 G6
Fairfield, Ala., U.S.A. ... 69 J2
Fairfield, Calif., U.S.A. ... 72 G2
Fairfield, Idaho, U.S.A. ... 72 E6
Fairfield, Ill., U.S.A. ... 68 F1
Fairfield, Iowa, U.S.A. ... 70 E9
Fairfield, Mont., U.S.A. ... 72 C8
Fairfield, Tex., U.S.A. ... 71 K7
Fairford, Canada ... 65 C9
Fairhope, U.S.A. ... 69 K2
Fairlie, N.Z. ... 51 L3
Fairmont, Minn., U.S.A. ... 70 D7
Fairmont, W. Va., U.S.A. ... 68 F5
Fairplay, U.S.A. ... 73 G11
Fairport, U.S.A. ... 68 D7
Fairview, Australia ... 54 B3
Fairview, Canada ... 64 B5
Fairview, N. Dak., U.S.A. ... 70 B2
Fairview, Okla., U.S.A. ... 71 G5
Fairview, Utah, U.S.A. ... 72 G8
Fairweather, Mt., U.S.A. ... 60 C6
Faisalabad, Pakistan ... 36 D8
Faith, U.S.A. ... 70 C3
Faizabad, India ... 37 F13
Fakfak, Indonesia ... 33 E8
Falaise, France ... 18 B3
Falam, Burma ... 37 H18
Falcon Dam, U.S.A. ... 71 M5
Falconara, Canada ... 64 B5
Falkenberg, Sweden ... 9 H12
Falkirk, U.K. ... 12 F5
Falkland Is. ■, Atl. Oc. ... 80 G5
Falkland Is. Dependency □, Atl. Oc. ... 5 B1
Falkland Sd., Falk. Is. ... 80 G5
Falköping, Sweden ... 9 G12
Fall River, U.S.A. ... 68 E10
Fall River Mills, U.S.A. ... 72 F3
Fallbrook, U.S.A. ... 73 K5
Fallon, Mont., U.S.A. ... 72 B2
Fallon, Nev., U.S.A. ... 72 G4
Falls City, Nebr., U.S.A. ... 70 E7
Falmouth, Jamaica ... 74 J16
Falmouth, U.K. ... 11 G2
Falmouth, U.S.A. ... 68 F3
False B., S. Africa ... 48 E2
Falster, Denmark ... 9 J11
Falsterbo, Sweden ... 9 J12
Falun, Sweden ... 9 F13
Famagusta, Cyprus ... 38 C2
Family L., Canada ... 65 C9
Fandriana, Madag. ... 49 C8
Fannich, L., U.K. ... 12 D4
Fannūj, Iran ... 39 E8
Fanny Bay, Canada ... 64 D4
Fano, Italy ... 20 C5
Fanshaw, U.S.A. ... 64 B2
Fao = Al Fāw, Iraq ... 39 D6
Faradje, Zaïre ... 46 D5
Farafangana, Madag. ... 49 C8
Farāh, Afghan. ... 36 C3
Farāh □, Afghan. ... 36 C3
Farahalana, Madag. ... 49 A9
Faranah, Guinea ... 44 F2
Farasān, Jazā'ir, Si. Arabia ... 40 D3
Farasan Is. = Farasān, Jazā'ir, Si. Arabia ... 40 D3
Faratsiho, Madag. ... 49 B8
Fareham, U.K. ... 11 G6
Farewell, C., N.Z. ... 51 J4
Farewell C. = Farvel, Kap, Greenland ... 4 D5
Farghona = Fergana, Uzbekistan ... 24 E8
Fargo, U.S.A. ... 70 B6
Fari'a →, Jordan ... 41 C4
Faribault, U.S.A. ... 70 C8
Farim, Guinea-Biss. ... 44 F1
Farīmān, Iran ... 39 C8
Farina, Australia ... 55 E2
Farmerville, U.S.A. ... 71 J8
Farmington, N. Mex., U.S.A. ... 73 H9
Farmington, Utah, U.S.A. ... 72 F8
Farmville, U.S.A. ... 68 G6
Farnborough, U.K. ... 11 F7
Farne Is., U.K. ... 10 B6
Faro, Brazil ... 79 D7
Faro, Portugal ... 19 D2
Fårö, Sweden ... 9 H15
Faroe Is. = Føroyar, Atl. Oc. ... 7 C4
Farquhar, C., Australia ... 53 D1
Farquhar Is., Seychelles ... 35 F4
Farrars Cr. →, Australia ... 54 D3
Farrāshband, Iran ... 39 D7
Farrell, U.S.A. ... 68 E5
Farrell Flat, Australia ... 55 E2
Farrokhī, Iran ... 39 C8
Farrukhabad-cum-Fatehgarh, India ... 36 F11
Fārs □, Iran ... 39 D7
Fársala, Greece ... 21 E10
Farsund, Norway ... 9 G9
Fartak, Râs, Si. Arabia ... 38 D2
Fārūj, Iran ... 39 B8

Farvel, Kap, Greenland ... 4 D5
Farwell, U.S.A. ... 71 H3
Fasā, Iran ... 39 D7
Fastnet Rock, Ireland ... 13 E2
Fatagar, Tanjung, Indonesia ... 33 E8
Fatehgarh, India ... 36 F11
Fatehpur, Raj., India ... 36 F9
Fatehpur, Ut. P., India ... 37 G12
Fatima, Canada ... 63 C7
Faulkton, U.S.A. ... 70 C5
Faure I., Australia ... 53 E1
Fauresmith, S. Africa ... 48 D4
Fauske, Norway ... 8 C13
Favara, Italy ... 20 F5
Favignana, Italy ... 20 F5
Favourable Lake, Canada ... 62 B1
Fawn →, Canada ... 62 A2
Faxaflói, Iceland ... 8 D2
Faya-Largeau, Chad ... 45 E8
Fayd, Si. Arabia ... 38 E4
Fayette, Ala., U.S.A. ... 69 J2
Fayette, Mo., U.S.A. ... 70 F8
Fayetteville, Ark., U.S.A. ... 71 G7
Fayetteville, N.C., U.S.A. ... 69 H6
Fayetteville, Tenn., U.S.A. ... 69 H2
Fazilka, India ... 36 D9
Fdérik, Mauritania ... 44 D2
Feale →, Ireland ... 13 D2
Fear, C., U.S.A. ... 69 J7
Feather →, U.S.A. ... 72 G3
Featherston, N.Z. ... 51 J5
Fécamp, France ... 18 B4
Fedeshkūh, Iran ... 39 D7
Fehmarn, Germany ... 16 A5
Fehmarn Bælt, Denmark ... 16 A5
Feilding, N.Z. ... 51 J5
Feira de Santana, Brazil ... 79 F11
Feldkirch, Austria ... 16 E4
Felipe Carrillo Puerto, Mexico ... 74 D7
Felixstowe, U.K. ... 11 F9
Felton, U.S.A. ... 10 B6
Femunden, Norway ... 8 E11
Fengjie, China ... 31 C5
Fenit, Ireland ... 13 D2
Fennimore, U.S.A. ... 70 D9
Fenoarivo Afovoany, Madag. ... 49 B8
Fenoarivo Atsinanana, Madag. ... 49 B8
Fens, The, U.K. ... 10 E8
Fenton, U.S.A. ... 68 D4
Fenyang, China ... 31 C6
Feodosiya, Ukraine ... 23 E6
Ferdows, Iran ... 39 C8
Ferfer, Somali Rep. ... 40 F4
Fergana, Uzbekistan ... 24 E8
Fergus, Canada ... 62 D3
Fergus Falls, U.S.A. ... 70 B6
Ferland, Canada ... 62 B2
Fermanagh □, U.K. ... 13 B4
Fermo, Italy ... 20 C5
Fermoy, Ireland ... 13 D3
Fernandina Beach, U.S.A. ... 69 K5
Fernando de Noronha, Brazil ... 79 D12
Fernando Póo = Bioko, Eq. Guin. ... 44 H6
Ferndale, Calif., U.S.A. ... 72 F1
Ferndale, Wash., U.S.A. ... 72 B2
Fernie, Canada ... 64 D5
Fernlees, Australia ... 54 C4
Fernley, U.S.A. ... 72 G4
Ferozepore = Firozpur, India ... 36 D9
Ferrara, Italy ... 20 B4
Ferreñafe, Peru ... 78 E3
Ferriday, U.S.A. ... 71 K9
Ferrol = El Ferrol, Spain ... 19 A1
Ferron, U.S.A. ... 73 G8
Ferryland, Canada ... 63 C9
Fertile, U.S.A. ... 70 B6
Fès, Morocco ... 44 B4
Feshi, Zaïre ... 46 F3
Fessenden, U.S.A. ... 70 B5
Fetlar, U.K. ... 12 A8
Feuilles →, Canada ... 61 C12
Fezzan, Libya ... 45 C8
Ffestiniog, U.K. ... 10 E4
Fianarantsoa, Madag. ... 49 C8
Fianarantsoa □, Madag. ... 49 B8
Fianga, Cameroon ... 45 G8
Fichtelgebirge, Germany ... 16 C6
Ficksburg, S. Africa ... 49 D4
Field, Canada ... 62 C3
Field →, Australia ... 54 C2
Field I., Australia ... 52 B5
Fife □, U.K. ... 12 E5
Fife Ness, U.K. ... 12 E6
Figeac, France ... 18 D5
Figueira da Foz, Portugal ... 19 B1
Figueras, Spain ... 19 A7
Figuig, Morocco ... 44 B4
Fihaonana, Madag. ... 49 B8
Fiherenana, Madag. ... 49 B8
Fiherenana →, Madag. ... 49 C7
Fiji ■, Pac. Oc. ... 51 C8
Filey, U.K. ... 10 C7

Filiatrá, Greece ... 21 F9
Filipstad, Sweden ... 9 G13
Fillmore, Canada ... 65 D8
Fillmore, Calif., U.S.A. ... 73 J4
Fillmore, Utah, U.S.A. ... 73 G7
Findhorn →, U.K. ... 12 D5
Findlay, U.S.A. ... 68 E4
Finger L., Canada ... 65 C10
Fíngóè, Mozam. ... 47 G6
Finistère □, France ... 18 B2
Finisterre, C., Spain ... 19 A1
Finke, Australia ... 54 D1
Finke →, Australia ... 55 D2
Finland ■, Europe ... 9 E19
Finland, G. of, Europe ... 9 G19
Finlay →, Canada ... 64 B3
Finley, Australia ... 55 F4
Finley, U.S.A. ... 70 B6
Finn →, Ireland ... 13 B4
Finnigan, Mt., Australia ... 54 B4
Finniss, C., Australia ... 55 E1
Finnmark fylke □, Norway ... 8 B18
Fiora →, Italy ... 20 C4
Fiq, Syria ... 41 C4
Firat = Furāt, Nahr al →, Asia ... 38 D5
Fire River, Canada ... 62 C3
Firebag →, Canada ... 65 B6
Firedrake L., Canada ... 65 A8
Firenze, Italy ... 20 C4
Firk →, Iraq ... 38 D5
Firozabad, India ... 36 F11
Firozpur, India ... 36 D9
Firūzābād, Iran ... 39 D7
Firūzkūh, Iran ... 39 C7
Firvale, Canada ... 64 C3
Fish →, Namibia ... 48 D2
Fish →, S. Africa ... 48 E3
Fisher, Australia ... 53 F5
Fisher B., Canada ... 65 C9
Fishguard, U.K. ... 11 F3
Fishing L., Canada ... 65 C9
Fitchburg, U.S.A. ... 68 D10
Fitri, L., Chad ... 45 F8
Fitz Roy, Argentina ... 80 F3
Fitzgerald, Canada ... 64 B6
Fitzgerald, U.S.A. ... 69 K4
Fitzmaurice →, Australia ... 52 B5
Fitzroy →, Queens., Australia ... 54 C5
Fitzroy →, W. Austral., Australia ... 52 C3
Fitzroy Crossing, Australia ... 52 C4
Fiume = Rijeka, Croatia ... 20 B6
Fizi, Zaïre ... 46 E5
Flagler, U.S.A. ... 70 F3
Flagstaff, U.S.A. ... 73 J8
Flaherty I., Canada ... 62 A4
Flåm, Norway ... 9 F9
Flambeau →, U.S.A. ... 70 C9
Flamborough Hd., U.K. ... 10 C7
Flaming Gorge Dam, U.S.A. ... 72 F9
Flaming Gorge Res., U.S.A. ... 72 F9
Flamingo, Teluk, Indonesia ... 33 F9
Flanders = West-Vlaanderen □, Belgium ... 15 D3
Flanders = West-Vlaanderen □, Belgium ... 15 D3
Flandre Occidentale = West-Vlaanderen □, Belgium ... 15 D3
Flandre Orientale = Oost-Vlaanderen □, Belgium ... 15 C3
Flandreau, U.S.A. ... 70 C6
Flåsjön, Sweden ... 8 D13
Flat →, Canada ... 64 A3
Flat River, U.S.A. ... 71 G9
Flathead L., U.S.A. ... 72 C6
Flattery, C., Australia ... 54 A4
Flattery, C., U.S.A. ... 72 B1
Flaxton, U.S.A. ... 70 A3
Fleetwood, U.K. ... 10 D4
Flekkefjord, Norway ... 9 G9
Flensburg, Germany ... 16 A4
Flesko, Tanjung, Indonesia ... 33 D6
Flevoland □, Neths. ... 15 B5
Flin Flon, Canada ... 65 C8
Flinders →, Australia ... 54 B3
Flinders B., Australia ... 53 F2
Flinders Group, Australia ... 54 A3
Flinders I., Australia ... 54 F4
Flinders Ras., Australia ... 55 E2
Flinders Reefs, Australia ... 54 B4
Flint, U.K. ... 10 D4
Flint, U.S.A. ... 68 D4
Flint →, U.S.A. ... 69 K3
Flint I., Kiribati ... 57 J12
Flinton, Australia ... 55 D4
Flodden, U.K. ... 10 B5
Floodwood, U.S.A. ... 70 B8
Flora, U.S.A. ... 68 F1

Florala, U.S.A. ... 69 K2
Florence = Firenze, Italy ... 20 C4
Florence, Ala., U.S.A. ... 69 H2
Florence, Ariz., U.S.A. ... 73 K8
Florence, Colo., U.S.A. ... 70 F2
Florence, Oreg., U.S.A. ... 72 E1
Florence, S.C., U.S.A. ... 69 H6
Florence, L., Australia ... 55 D2
Florennes, Belgium ... 15 D4
Florenville, Belgium ... 15 E5
Flores, Indonesia ... 33 F6
Flores I., Canada ... 64 D3
Flores Sea, Indonesia ... 33 F6
Floresville, U.S.A. ... 71 L5
Floriano, Brazil ... 79 E10
Florianópolis, Brazil ... 80 B7
Florida, Uruguay ... 80 C5
Florida □, U.S.A. ... 69 L5
Florida, Straits of, U.S.A. ... 75 C9
Florida Keys, U.S.A. ... 67 F10
Florø, Norway ... 9 F8
Flower's Cove, Canada ... 63 B8
Floydada, U.S.A. ... 71 J4
Fluk, Indonesia ... 33 E7
Flushing = Vlissingen, Neths. ... 15 C3
Flying Fish, C., Antarctica ... 5 D15
Foam Lake, Canada ... 65 C8
Fóggia, Italy ... 20 D6
Fogo, Canada ... 63 C9
Fogo I., Canada ... 63 C9
Foix, France ... 18 E4
Folda, Nord-Trøndelag, Norway ... 8 D11
Folda, Nordland, Norway ... 8 C13
Foleyet, Canada ... 62 C3
Folgefonn, Norway ... 9 F9
Folkestone, U.K. ... 11 F9
Folkston, U.S.A. ... 69 K5
Follett, U.S.A. ... 71 G4
Fond-du-Lac, Canada ... 65 B8
Fond du Lac, U.S.A. ... 70 D10
Fond-du-Lac →, Canada ... 65 B7
Fonseca, G. de, Cent. Amer. ... 74 E7
Fontainebleau, France ... 18 B5
Fontas →, Canada ... 64 B4
Fonte Boa, Brazil ... 78 D5
Fontenay-le-Comte, France ... 18 C3
Fontur, Iceland ... 8 C6
Foochow = Fuzhou, China ... 31 D6
Forbes, Australia ... 55 E4
Ford's Bridge, Australia ... 55 D4
Fordyce, U.S.A. ... 71 J8
Forécariah, Guinea ... 44 G2
Forel, Mt., Greenland ... 4 C6
Foremost, Canada ... 64 D6
Forest, Canada ... 62 D3
Forest City, Iowa, U.S.A. ... 70 D8
Forest City, N.C., U.S.A. ... 69 H5
Forest Grove, U.S.A. ... 72 D2
Forestburg, Canada ... 64 C6
Forestier Pen., Australia ... 54 G4
Forestville, Canada ... 63 C6
Forestville, U.S.A. ... 68 C2
Forez, Mts. du, France ... 18 D5
Forfar, U.K. ... 12 E6
Forks, U.S.A. ... 72 C1
Forlì, Italy ... 20 B5
Forman, U.S.A. ... 70 B6
Formby Pt., U.K. ... 10 D4
Formentera, Spain ... 19 C6
Formia, Italy ... 20 D5
Formosa = Taiwan ■, Asia ... 31 D7
Formosa, Argentina ... 80 B5
Formosa, Serra, Brazil ... 79 F8
Formosa Bay, Kenya ... 46 E8
Føroyar, Atl. Oc. ... 7 C4
Forres, U.K. ... 12 D5
Forrest, Vic., Australia ... 55 F3
Forrest, W. Austral., Australia ... 53 F4
Forrest, Mt., Australia ... 53 D4
Forrest City, U.S.A. ... 71 H9
Forsayth, Australia ... 54 B3
Forster, Australia ... 55 E5
Forsyth, Ga., U.S.A. ... 69 J4
Forsyth, Mont., U.S.A. ... 72 C10
Fort Albany, Canada ... 62 B3
Fort Apache, U.S.A. ... 73 K9
Fort Assiniboine, Canada ... 64 C6
Fort Augustus, U.K. ... 12 D4
Fort Beaufort, S. Africa ... 48 E4
Fort Benton, U.S.A. ... 72 C8
Fort Bragg, U.S.A. ... 72 G2
Fort Bridger, U.S.A. ... 72 F8
Fort Chipewyan, Canada ... 65 B6
Fort Clayton, Panama ... 74 H14
Fort Collins, U.S.A. ... 70 E2
Fort-Coulonge, Canada ... 62 C4
Fort Davis, Panama ... 74 H14
Fort-de-France, Martinique ... 74 N20
Fort de Possel = Possel, C.A.R. ... 46 C3
Fort Defiance, U.S.A. ... 73 J9
Fort Dodge, U.S.A. ... 70 D7

Fort Frances, Canada ... 65 D10
Fort Franklin, Canada ... 60 B7
Fort Garland, U.S.A. ... 73 H11
Fort George, Canada ... 62 B4
Fort Good-Hope, Canada ... 60 B7
Fort Hancock, U.S.A. ... 73 L11
Fort Hertz = Putao, Burma ... 37 F20
Fort Hope, Canada ... 62 B2
Fort Jameson = Chipata, Zambia ... 47 G6
Fort Kent, U.S.A. ... 63 C6
Fort Klamath, U.S.A. ... 72 E3
Fort Lallemand, Algeria ... 44 B6
Fort-Lamy = Ndjamena, Chad ... 45 F7
Fort Laramie, U.S.A. ... 70 D2
Fort Lauderdale, U.S.A. ... 69 M5
Fort Liard, Canada ... 64 A4
Fort Lupton, U.S.A. ... 70 E2
Fort McKenzie, Canada ... 63 A6
Fort Macleod, Canada ... 64 D6
Fort MacMahon, Algeria ... 44 C5
Fort McMurray, Canada ... 64 B6
Fort McPherson, Canada ... 60 B6
Fort Madison, U.S.A. ... 70 E9
Fort Meade, U.S.A. ... 69 M5
Fort Miribel, Algeria ... 44 C5
Fort Morgan, U.S.A. ... 70 E3
Fort Myers, U.S.A. ... 69 M5
Fort Nelson, Canada ... 64 B4
Fort Nelson →, Canada ... 64 B4
Fort Norman, Canada ... 60 B7
Fort Payne, U.S.A. ... 69 H3
Fort Peck, U.S.A. ... 72 B10
Fort Peck Dam, U.S.A. ... 72 C10
Fort Peck L., U.S.A. ... 72 C10
Fort Pierce, U.S.A. ... 69 M5
Fort Pierre, U.S.A. ... 70 C4
Fort Portal, Uganda ... 46 D6
Fort Providence, Canada ... 64 A5
Fort Qu'Appelle, Canada ... 65 C8
Fort Randolph, Panama ... 74 H14
Fort Resolution, Canada ... 64 A6
Fort Rosebery = Mansa, Zambia ... 46 G5
Fort Rupert, Canada ... 62 B4
Fort St. James, Canada ... 64 C4
Fort St. John, Canada ... 64 B4
Fort Sandeman, Pakistan ... 36 D6
Fort Saskatchewan, Canada ... 64 C6
Fort Scott, U.S.A. ... 71 G7
Fort Severn, Canada ... 62 A2
Fort Sherman, Panama ... 74 H14
Fort Shevchenko, Kazakhstan ... 23 F9
Fort-Sibut, C.A.R. ... 45 G8
Fort Simpson, Canada ... 64 A4
Fort Smith, Canada ... 64 B6
Fort Smith, U.S.A. ... 71 H7
Fort Stanton, U.S.A. ... 73 K11
Fort Stockton, U.S.A. ... 71 K3
Fort Sumner, U.S.A. ... 71 H2
Fort Trinquet = Bir Mogrein, Mauritania ... 44 C2
Fort Valley, U.S.A. ... 69 J4
Fort Vermilion, Canada ... 64 B5
Fort Walton Beach, U.S.A. ... 69 K2
Fort Wayne, U.S.A. ... 68 E3
Fort William, U.K. ... 12 E3
Fort Worth, U.S.A. ... 71 J6
Fort Yates, U.S.A. ... 70 B4
Fort Yukon, U.S.A. ... 60 B5
Fortaleza, Brazil ... 79 D11
Forteau, Canada ... 63 B8
Forth →, U.K. ... 12 E5
Forth, Firth of, U.K. ... 12 E6
Fortrose, U.K. ... 12 D4
Fortuna, Calif., U.S.A. ... 72 F1
Fortuna, N. Dak., U.S.A. ... 70 A3
Fortune B., Canada ... 63 C8
Foshan, China ... 31 D6
Fossil, U.S.A. ... 72 D3
Fossilbrook, Australia ... 54 B3
Fosston, U.S.A. ... 70 B7
Foster →, Canada ... 65 B7
Fosters Ra., Australia ... 54 C1
Fostoria, U.S.A. ... 68 E4
Fougamou, Gabon ... 46 E2
Fougères, France ... 18 B3
Foul Pt., Sri Lanka ... 36 Q12
Foula, U.K. ... 12 A6
Foulness I., U.K. ... 11 F8
Foulpointe, Madag. ... 49 B8
Foumban, Cameroon ... 44 G7
Fountain, Colo., U.S.A. ... 70 F2
Fountain, Utah, U.S.A. ... 72 G8
Fourchu, Canada ... 63 C7
Fouriesburg, S. Africa ... 48 D4
Fouta Djalon, Guinea ... 44 F2
Foveaux Str., N.Z. ... 51 M2
Fowey, U.K. ... 11 G3
Fowler, Calif., U.S.A. ... 73 H4
Fowler, Colo., U.S.A. ... 70 F2
Fowler, Kans., U.S.A. ... 71 G4
Fowlers B., Australia ... 53 F5
Fowlerton, U.S.A. ... 71 L5

Fox

Fox →, Canada 65 B10
Fox Valley, Canada .. 65 C7
Foxe Basin, Canada .. 61 B12
Foxe Chan., Canada .. 61 B11
Foxe Pen., Canada .. 61 B12
Foxpark, U.S.A. 72 F10
Foxton, N.Z. 51 J5
Foyle, Lough, U.K. .. 13 A4
Foynes, Ireland 13 D2
Fóz do Cunene, Angola 48 B1
Foz do Gregório, Brazil 78 E4
Foz do Iguaçu, Brazil . 80 B6
Franca, Brazil 79 H9
Francavilla Fontana,
  Italy 21 D7
France ■, Europe 18 C5
Frances, Australia .. 55 F3
Frances →, Canada .. 64 A3
Frances L., Canada .. 64 A3
Franceville, Gabon .. 46 E2
Franche-Comté, France 18 C6
Francistown, Botswana 49 C4
François, Canada 63 C8
François L., Canada .. 64 C3
Franeker, Neths. 15 A5
Frankfort, S. Africa .. 49 D4
Frankfort, Ind., U.S.A. 68 E2
Frankfort, Kans., U.S.A. 70 F6
Frankfort, Ky., U.S.A. . 68 F3
Frankfort, Mich., U.S.A. 68 C2
Frankfurt am Main,
  Germany 16 C4
Frankfurt an der Oder,
  Germany 16 B7
Fränkische Alb,
  Germany 16 D5
Frankland →,
  Australia 53 G2
Franklin, Ky., U.S.A. .. 69 G2
Franklin, La., U.S.A. .. 71 L9
Franklin, N.H., U.S.A. . 68 D10
Franklin, Nebr., U.S.A. 70 E5
Franklin, Tenn., U.S.A. 69 H2
Franklin, Va., U.S.A. .. 69 G7
Franklin, W. Va., U.S.A. 68 F6
Franklin, L., Canada .. 72 F6
Franklin B., Canada .. 60 B7
Franklin D. Roosevelt
  L., U.S.A. 72 B4
Franklin I., Antarctica . 5 D11
Franklin Mts., Canada 60 B7
Franklin Str., Canada . 60 A10
Franklinton, U.S.A. ... 71 K9
Franks Peak, U.S.A. .. 72 E9
Frankston, Australia .. 55 F4
Frantsa Iosifa, Zemlya,
  Russia 24 A6
Franz, Canada 62 C3
Franz Josef Land =
  Frantsa Iosifa,
  Zemlya, Russia .. 24 A6
Fraser →, B.C.,
  Canada 64 D4
Fraser →, Nfld.,
  Canada 63 A7
Fraser, Mt., Australia . 53 E2
Fraser I., Australia ... 55 D5
Fraser Lake, Canada .. 64 C4
Fraserburg, S. Africa .. 48 E3
Fraserburgh, U.K. 12 D6
Fraserdale, Canada ... 62 C3
Fray Bentos, Uruguay . 80 C5
Frazier Downs,
  Australia 52 C3
Fredericia, Denmark .. 9 J10
Frederick, Md., U.S.A. . 68 F7
Frederick, Okla., U.S.A. 71 H5
Frederick, S. Dak.,
  U.S.A. 70 C5
Frederick Sd., U.S.A. . 64 B2
Fredericksburg, Tex.,
  U.S.A. 71 K5
Fredericksburg, Va.,
  U.S.A. 68 F7
Frederickstown, U.S.A. 71 G9
Fredericton, Canada .. 63 C6
Fredericton Junc.,
  Canada 63 C6
Frederikshåb,
  Greenland 4 C5
Frederikshavn,
  Denmark 9 H11
Fredonia, Ariz., U.S.A. 73 H7
Fredonia, Kans., U.S.A. 71 G7
Fredonia, N.Y., U.S.A. . 68 D6
Fredrikstad, Norway .. 9 G11
Freels, C., Canada ... 63 C9
Freeman, U.S.A. 70 D6
Freeport, Bahamas ... 75 B9
Freeport, Canada 63 D6
Freeport, Ill., U.S.A. .. 70 D10
Freeport, N.Y., U.S.A. . 68 E9
Freeport, Tex., U.S.A. . 71 L7
Freetown, S. Leone ... 44 G2
Frégate, L., Canada .. 62 B5
Freiburg, Germany ... 16 E3
Freire, Chile 80 D2
Freising, Germany ... 16 D6
Freistadt, Austria 16 D7
Fréjus, France 18 E7
Fremantle, Australia .. 53 F2
Fremont, Calif., U.S.A. 73 H2
Fremont, Mich., U.S.A. 68 D3
Fremont, Nebr., U.S.A. 70 E6
Fremont, Ohio, U.S.A. 68 E4
Fremont →, U.S.A. ... 73 G8
Fremont, L., U.S.A. ... 72 E9
French Cr. →, U.S.A. . 68 E6
French Guiana ■,
  S. Amer. 79 C8

French Pass, N.Z. 51 J4
French Polynesia ■,
  Pac. Oc. 57 J13
French Terr. of Afars &
  Issas = Djibouti ■,
  Africa 40 E3
Frenchglen, U.S.A. ... 72 E4
Frenchman →,
  N. Amer. 72 B10
Frenchman Butte,
  Canada 65 C7
Frenchman Creek →,
  U.S.A. 70 E4
Fresco →, Brazil 79 E8
Freshfield, C.,
  Antarctica 5 C10
Fresnillo, Mexico 74 C4
Fresno, U.S.A. 73 H4
Fresno Res., U.S.A. .. 72 B9
Frew →, Australia ... 54 C2
Frewena, Australia ... 54 B2
Freycinet Pen.,
  Australia 54 G4
Fria, C., Namibia 48 B1
Frías, Argentina 80 B3
Friedrichshafen,
  Germany 16 E4
Friendly Is. = Tonga ■,
  Pac. Oc. 51 D11
Friesland □, Neths. .. 15 A5
Frijoles, Panama 74 H14
Frío →, U.S.A. 71 L5
Frio, C., Brazil 79 H3
Fritch, U.S.A. 71 H4
Friuli-Venezia Giulia □,
  Italy 20 A5
Frobisher B., Canada . 61 B13
Frobisher B. =
  Iqaluit, Canada ... 61 B13
Frobisher L., Canada . 65 B7
Frohavet, Norway 8 E10
Froid, U.S.A. 70 A2
Fromberg, U.S.A. 72 D9
Frome, U.K. 11 F5
Frome, L., Australia .. 55 E2
Frome Downs,
  Australia 55 E2
Front Range, U.S.A. .. 72 G11
Front Royal, U.S.A. .. 68 F6
Frosinone, Italy 20 D5
Frostburg, U.S.A. 68 F6
Frostisen, Norway ... 8 B14
Frøya, Norway 8 E10
Frunze = Bishkek,
  Kirghizia 24 E8
Frutal, Brazil 79 G9
Frýdek-Místek, Czech. 17 D9
Fuchou = Fuzhou,
  China 31 D6
Fuchū, Japan 29 G6
Fuente Ovejuna, Spain 19 C3
Fuentes de Oñoro,
  Spain 19 B2
Fuerte →, Mexico ... 74 B3
Fuerte Olimpo,
  Paraguay 78 H7
Fuerteventura,
  Canary Is. 44 C2
Fugløysund, Norway . 8 A16
Fuhai, China 30 B3
Fuḥaymī, Iraq 38 C4
Fuji, Japan 29 G9
Fuji-San, Japan 29 G9
Fuji-yoshida, Japan .. 29 G9
Fujian □, China 31 D6
Fujinomiya, Japan ... 29 G9
Fujisawa, Japan 29 G9
Fukien = Fujian □,
  China 31 D6
Fukuchiyama, Japan .. 29 G7
Fukue-Shima, Japan . 29 H4
Fukui, Japan 29 F8
Fukui □, Japan 29 G8
Fukuoka, Japan 29 H5
Fukuoka □, Japan ... 29 H5
Fukushima, Japan ... 28 F10
Fukushima □, Japan . 28 F10
Fukuyama, Japan 29 G6
Fulda, Germany 16 C4
Fulda →, Germany .. 16 C4
Fullerton, Calif., U.S.A. 73 K5
Fullerton, Nebr., U.S.A. 70 E5
Fulton, Mo., U.S.A. .. 70 F9
Fulton, N.Y., U.S.A. .. 68 D7
Fulton, Tenn., U.S.A. . 69 G1
Funabashi, Japan 29 G10
Funchal, Madeira 44 B1
Fundación, Colombia 78 A4
Fundão, Portugal 19 B2
Fundy, B. of, Canada . 63 D6
Funtua, Nigeria 44 F6
Furano, Japan 28 C11
Furāt, Nahr al →,
  Asia 38 D5
Fürg, Iran 39 D7
Furneaux Group,
  Australia 54 G4
Furness, U.K. 10 C4
Furqlus, Syria 41 A6
Fürth, Germany 16 D5
Furukawa, Japan 28 E10
Fury and Hecla Str.,
  Canada 61 B11
Fusagasuga, Colombia 78 C4
Fushun, China 31 B7
Fusong, China 31 B7
Fuxin, China 31 B7
Fuzhou, China 31 D6
Fylde, U.K. 10 D5
Fyn, Denmark 9 J11
Fyne, L., U.K. 12 F3

G

Gabela, Angola 46 G2
Gabès, Tunisia 44 B7
Gabès, G. de, Tunisia 45 B7
Gabon ■, Africa 46 E2
Gaborone, Botswana . 48 C4
Gabrovo, Bulgaria ... 21 C11
Gäbrīk, Iran 39 E8
Gachsār, Iran 39 B6
Gāch Sār, Iran 39 B6
Gachsārān, Iran 39 D6
Gadag, India 36 M9
Gadarwara, India 36 H11
Gadhada, India 36 J7
Gadsden, Ala., U.S.A. 69 H2
Gadsden, Ariz., U.S.A. 73 K6
Gadwal, India 36 L10
Gaffney, U.S.A. 69 H5
Gafsa, Tunisia 44 B6
Gagetown, Canada .. 63 C6
Gagnoa, Ivory C. 44 G3
Gagnon, Canada 63 B6
Gagnon, L., Canada .. 65 A6
Gail, U.S.A. 71 J4
Gainesville, Fla., U.S.A. 69 L4
Gainesville, Ga., U.S.A. 69 H4
Gainesville, Mo.,
  U.S.A. 71 G8
Gainesville, Tex.,
  U.S.A. 71 J6
Gainsborough, U.K. .. 10 D7
Gairdner, L., Australia 55 E2
Gairloch, L., U.K. 12 D3
Galangue, Angola ... 47 G3
Galapagos, Pac. Oc. . 57 H18
Galas →, Malaysia .. 34 Q14
Galashiels, U.K. 12 F6
Galaţi, Romania 21 B13
Galatina, Italy 21 D8
Galax, U.S.A. 69 G5
Galcaio, Somali Rep. . 40 F4
Galdhøpiggen, Norway 9 F10
Galela, Indonesia ... 33 D7
Galesburg, U.S.A. ... 70 E9
Galich, Russia 22 C7
Galicia □, Spain 19 A2
Galilee = Hagalil,
  Israel 41 C4
Galilee, L., Australia . 54 C4
Galilee, Sea of = Yam
  Kinneret, Israel ... 41 C4
Galiuro Mts., U.S.A. . 73 K8
Gallabat, Sudan 45 F12
Gallatin, U.S.A. 69 G2
Galle, Sri Lanka 36 R12
Gállego →, Spain ... 19 B5
Gallegos →,
  Argentina 80 G3
Galley Hd., Ireland .. 13 E3
Gallinas, Pta.,
  Colombia 78 A4
Gallipoli = Gelibolu,
  Turkey 21 D12
Gallípoli, Italy 21 D8
Gallipolis, U.S.A. 68 F4
Gällivare, Sweden ... 8 C16
Galloway, U.K. 12 G4
Galloway, Mull of, U.K. 12 G4
Gallup, U.S.A. 73 J9
Galong, Australia 55 E4
Galoya, Sri Lanka ... 36 Q12
Galty Mts., Ireland .. 13 D3
Galtymore, Ireland .. 13 D3
Galva, U.S.A. 70 E9
Galveston, U.S.A. ... 71 L7
Galveston B., U.S.A. . 71 L7
Gálvez, Argentina ... 80 C4
Galway, Ireland 13 C2
Galway □, Ireland ... 13 C2
Galway B., Ireland ... 13 C2
Gamagori, Japan 29 G8
Gambaga, Ghana 44 F4
Gambela, Ethiopia ... 45 G11
Gambia ■, W. Afr. ... 44 F1
Gambia →, W. Afr. .. 44 F1
Gambier, C., Australia 52 B5
Gambier Is., Australia 55 F2
Gamboma, Congo ... 46 E3
Gamerco, U.S.A. 73 J9
Gamlakarleby =
  Kokkola, Finland .. 8 E17
Gammon →, Canada 65 C9
Gan Jiang →, China . 31 D6
Ganado, Ariz., U.S.A. 73 J9
Ganado, Tex., U.S.A. 71 L6
Gananoque, Canada . 62 D4
Ganaveh, Iran 39 D6
Gäncä = Gyandzha,
  Azerbaijan 23 F8
Gand = Gent, Belgium 15 C3
Ganda, Angola 47 G2
Gandak →, India 37 G14
Gandava, Pakistan ... 36 E5
Gander, Canada 63 C9
Gander L., Canada ... 63 C9
Gandhi Sagar, India . 36 G9
Gandi, Nigeria 44 F6
Ganedidalem = Gani,
  Indonesia 33 E7
Ganga →, India 37 H17
Ganganagar, India ... 36 E8
Gangara, Niger 44 F6
Gangaw, Burma 37 H19
Gangdisê Shan, China 37 D12
Ganges = Ganga →,
  India 37 H17
Gangtok, India 37 F16
Gani, Indonesia 33 E7
Gannett Pk., U.S.A. . 72 E9

Gannvalley, U.S.A. .. 70 C5
Gansu □, China 30 C5
Ganta, Liberia 44 G3
Gantheaume, C.,
  Australia 55 F2
Gantheaume B.,
  Australia 53 E1
Ganyem, Indonesia .. 33 E10
Ganzhou, China 31 D6
Gao Bang, Vietnam .. 34 A9
Gaoua, Burkina Faso . 44 F4
Gaoual, Guinea 44 F2
Gaoxiong, Taiwan ... 31 D7
Gap, France 18 D7
Gar, China 30 C2
Garabogazkol Aylagy
  = Kara Bogaz Gol,
  Zaliv, Turkmenistan 23 F9
Garanhuns, Brazil ... 79 E11
Garawe, Liberia 44 H3
Garber, U.S.A. 71 G6
Garberville, U.S.A. .. 72 F2
Gard →, Somali Rep. 40 F4
Gard □, France 18 D6
Garda, L. di, Italy ... 20 B4
Garde L., Canada 65 A7
Garden City, Kans.,
  U.S.A. 71 G4
Garden City, Tex.,
  U.S.A. 71 K4
Garden Grove, U.S.A. 73 K5
Gardēz, Afghan. 36 C6
Gardiner, U.S.A. 72 D8
Gardner, U.S.A. 68 D10
Gardner Canal, Canada 64 C3
Gardnerville, U.S.A. . 72 G4
Garfield, U.S.A. 72 C5
Gargano, Mte., Italy . 20 D6
Garibaldi Prov. Park,
  Canada 64 D4
Garies, S. Africa 48 E2
Garigliano →, Italy . 20 D5
Garland, U.S.A. 72 F7
Garm, Tajikistan 24 F8
Garmāb, Iran 39 C8
Garmsār, Iran 39 C7
Garner, U.S.A. 70 D8
Garnett, U.S.A. 70 F7
Garoe, Somali Rep. . 40 F4
Garoua, Cameroon .. 45 G7
Garrison, Mont., U.S.A. 72 C7
Garrison, N. Dak.,
  U.S.A. 70 B4
Garrison, Tex., U.S.A. 71 K7
Garrison Res. =
  Sakakawea, L.,
  U.S.A. 70 B3
Garry →, U.K. 12 E5
Garry, L., Canada 60 B9
Garsen, Kenya 46 E8
Garson L., Canada ... 65 B6
Garub, Namibia 48 D2
Garut, Indonesia 33 G12
Garvie Mts., N.Z. 51 L2
Garwa = Garoua,
  Cameroon 45 G7
Gary, U.S.A. 68 E2
Garzê, China 30 C5
Garzón, Colombia ... 78 C3
Gas-San, Japan 28 E10
Gasan,
  Turkmenistan 24 F6
Gascogne, France ... 18 E4
Gascogne, G. de,
  Europe 18 E3
Gascony = Gascogne,
  France 18 E4
Gascoyne →,
  Australia 53 D1
Gascoyne Junc. T.O.,
  Australia 53 E2
Gashaka, Nigeria 44 G7
Gashaua, Nigeria 44 F7
Gaspé, Canada 63 C7
Gaspé, C. de, Canada 63 C7
Gaspé, Pén. de,
  Canada 63 C6
Gaspésie, Parc Prov.
  de la, Canada 63 C6
Gassaway, U.S.A. ... 68 F5
Gastonia, U.S.A. 69 H5
Gastre, Argentina ... 80 E3
Gata, C. de, Spain ... 19 D4
Gata, Sierra de, Spain 19 B2
Gataga →, Canada .. 64 B3
Gateshead, U.K. 10 C6
Gatesville, U.S.A. ... 71 K6
Gâtinais, France 18 B5
Gatineau →, Canada 62 C4
Gatineau, Parc de la,
  Canada 62 C4
Gatun, Panama 74 H14
Gatun, L., Panama ... 74 H14
Gatun Dam, Panama . 74 H14
Gatun Locks, Panama 74 H14
Gatyana, S. Africa ... 49 E4
Gau, Fiji 51 D8
Gauer L., Canada 65 B9
Gauhati, India 37 F17
Gaula →, Norway ... 8 E11
Gausta, Norway 9 G10
Gāvakān, Iran 39 D7
Gāvater, Iran 39 E9
Gāvbandī, Iran 39 E7
Gävleborgs län □,
  Sweden 9 F14
Gawachab, Namibia . 48 D2
Gawilgarh Hills, India 36 J10
Gawler, Australia 55 E2

Gaxun Nur, China ... 30 B5
Gay, Russia 22 D10
Gaya, India 37 G14
Gaya, Niger 44 F5
Gaylord, U.S.A. 68 C3
Gayndah, Australia .. 55 D5
Gaza, Egypt 41 D3
Gaza □, Mozam. 49 C5
Gaza Strip, Egypt 41 D3
Gāzbor, Iran 39 D8
Gaziantep, Turkey ... 23 G6
Gazli, Uzbekistan ... 24 E7
Gcuwa, S. Africa 49 E4
Gdańsk, Poland 17 A9
Gdańska, Zatoka,
  Poland 17 A9
Gdov, Russia 22 C4
Gdynia, Poland 17 A9
Gebe, Indonesia 33 D7
Gebeit Mine, Sudan . 45 D12
Gedaref, Sudan 45 F12
Gede, Tanjung,
  Indonesia 32 F3
Gedser, Denmark ... 9 J11
Geegully Cr. →,
  Australia 52 C3
Geelong, Australia ... 55 F3
Geelvink Chan.,
  Australia 53 E1
Geidam, Nigeria 45 F7
Geikie →, Canada .. 65 B8
Geili, Sudan 45 E11
Geita, Tanzania 46 E6
Gejiu, China 30 D5
Gela, Italy 20 F6
Geladi, Ethiopia 40 F4
Gelderland □, Neths. 15 B6
Geldermalsen, Neths. 15 C5
Geldrop, Neths. 15 C5
Geleen, Neths. 15 D5
Gelehun, S. Leone ... 44 G2
Gelibolu, Turkey 21 D12
Gelsenkirchen,
  Germany 16 C3
Gemas, Malaysia ... 34 S15
Gembloux, Belgium . 15 D4
Gemena, Zaïre 46 D3
Gemerek, Turkey 23 G6
Gemona del Friuli,
  Italy 20 A5
Genale →, Ethiopia . 40 F2
General Acha,
  Argentina 80 D4
General Alvear,
  Buenos Aires,
  Argentina 80 D4
General Alvear,
  Mendoza, Argentina 80 D3
General Artigas,
  Paraguay 80 B5
General Belgrano,
  Argentina 80 D5
General Guido,
  Argentina 80 D5
General Juan
  Madariaga,
  Argentina 80 D5
General La Madrid,
  Argentina 80 D4
General MacArthur,
  Phil. 33 B7
General Martín Miguel
  de Güemes,
  Argentina 80 A4
General Paz, Argentina 80 B5
General Pico,
  Argentina 80 D4
General Pinedo,
  Argentina 80 B4
General Santos, Phil. . 33 C7
General Villegas,
  Argentina 80 D4
Genesee, U.S.A. 72 C5
Genesee →, U.S.A. . 68 D7
Geneseo, Ill., U.S.A. . 70 E9
Geneseo, Kans., U.S.A. 70 F5
Geneva = Genève,
  Switz. 16 E3
Geneva, Ala., U.S.A. . 69 K3
Geneva, N.Y., U.S.A. 68 D7
Geneva, Nebr., U.S.A. 70 E6
Geneva, Ohio, U.S.A. 68 E5
Geneva, L. = Léman,
  Lac, Switz. 16 E3
Geneva, L., U.S.A. .. 68 D1
Genève, Switz. 16 E3
Genil →, Spain 19 D3
Genk, Belgium 15 D5
Gennargentu, Mti. del,
  Italy 20 D3
Gennep, Neths. 15 C5
Genoa = Génova, Italy 20 B3
Genoa, Australia 55 F4
Genoa, U.S.A. 70 E6
Génova, Italy 20 B3
Génova, G. di, Italy .. 20 B3
Gent, Belgium 15 C3
Geographe B.,
  Australia 53 F2
Geographe Chan.,
  Australia 53 D1
Georga, Zemlya,
  Russia 24 A5
George, S. Africa 48 E3
George →, Canada .. 63 A6
George, L., N.S.W.,
  Australia 55 F4
George, L., S. Austral.,
  Australia 55 F3
George, L., W. Austral.,
  Australia 52 D3
George, L., Uganda .. 46 D6
George, L., U.S.A. ... 69 L5

George River = Port
  Nouveau-Québec,
  Canada 61 C13
George Sound, N.Z. .. 51 L1
George Town,
  Malaysia 34 P13
George V Land,
  Antarctica 5 C10
George VI Sound,
  Antarctica 5 D17
George West, U.S.A. . 71 L5
Georgetown, Ont.,
  Canada 62 D4
Georgetown, P.E.I.,
  Canada 63 C7
Georgetown, Gambia 44 F2
Georgetown, Guyana 78 B7
Georgetown, Colo.,
  U.S.A. 72 G11
Georgetown, Ky.,
  U.S.A. 68 F3
Georgetown, S.C.,
  U.S.A. 69 J6
Georgetown, Tex.,
  U.S.A. 71 K6
Georgia □, U.S.A. ... 69 J4
Georgia ■, Asia 23 F7
Georgia, Str. of,
  Canada 64 D4
Georgian B., Canada . 62 C3
Georgievsk, Russia .. 23 F7
Georgina →,
  Australia 54 C2
Georgina Downs,
  Australia 54 C2
Georgiu-Dezh = Liski,
  Russia 23 D6
Gera, Germany 16 C6
Geraardsbergen,
  Belgium 15 D3
Geral, Serra, Brazil .. 80 B7
Geral de Goiás, Serra,
  Brazil 79 F9
Geraldine, U.S.A. ... 72 C8
Geraldton, Australia . 53 E1
Geraldton, Canada .. 62 C2
Gereshk, Afghan. ... 36 D4
Gerik, Malaysia 34 P14
Gering, U.S.A. 70 E3
Gerlach, U.S.A. 72 F4
Germansen Landing,
  Canada 64 B4
Germany ■, Europe . 16 C5
Germiston, S. Africa . 49 D4
Gero, Japan 29 G8
Gerona, Spain 19 B7
Gerrard, Canada 64 C5
Gers □, France 18 E4
Geser, Indonesia 33 E8
Gethsémani, Canada . 63 B7
Gettysburg, Pa., U.S.A. 68 F7
Gettysburg, S. Dak.,
  U.S.A. 70 C5
Getz Ice Shelf,
  Antarctica 5 D14
Gévaudan, France ... 18 D5
Geyser, U.S.A. 72 C8
Geysir, Iceland 8 D3
Ghaghara →, India . 37 G14
Ghana ■, W. Afr. ... 44 G4
Ghanzi, Botswana ... 48 C3
Ghanzi □, Botswana . 48 C3
Gharb el Istiwa'iya □,
  Sudan 45 G10
Ghardaïa, Algeria ... 44 B5
Gharyān, Libya 45 B7
Ghat, Libya 44 D7
Ghaţţī, Si. Arabia ... 38 D3
Ghawdex = Gozo,
  Malta 20 F6
Ghazal, Bahr el →,
  Chad 45 F8
Ghazāl, Bahr el →,
  Sudan 45 G11
Ghazaouet, Algeria .. 44 A4
Ghaziabad, India 36 E10
Ghazipur, India 37 G13
Ghazni, Afghan. 36 C6
Ghazni □, Afghan. .. 36 C6
Ghêlinsor, Somali Rep. 40 F4
Ghent = Gent,
  Belgium 15 C3
Ghizao, Afghan. 36 C4
Ghowr □, Afghan. .. 36 C4
Ghudaf, W. al →, Iraq 38 C4
Ghugus, India 36 K11
Ghūrīān, Afghan. ... 36 B2
Gia Lai = Pleiku,
  Vietnam 34 F10
Gia Nghia, Vietnam . 34 G9
Gian, Phil. 33 C7
Giants Causeway, U.K. 13 A5
Giarabub = Al
  Jaghbūb, Libya ... 45 C9
Giarre, Italy 20 F6
Gibb River, Australia . 52 C4
Gibbon, U.S.A. 70 E5
Gibraltar ■, Europe . 19 D3
Gibraltar, Str. of,
  Medit. 19 E3
Gibson Desert,
  Australia 52 D4
Gibsons, Canada 64 D4
Giddings, U.S.A. 71 K6
Gidole, Ethiopia 45 G12
Giessen, Germany ... 16 C4
Gifān, Iran 39 B8
Gifford Creek, Australia 52 D2
Gifu, Japan 29 G8
Gifu □, Japan 29 G8

Grimshaw

Gigha, U.K. 12 F3
Gijón, Spain 19 A3
Gil I., Canada 64 C3
Gila →, U.S.A. 73 K6
Gila Bend, U.S.A. 73 K7
Gila Bend Mts., U.S.A. 73 K7
Gīlān □, Iran 39 B6
Gilbert →, Australia 54 B3
Gilbert Is., Kiribati 56 G9
Gilbert Plains, Canada 65 C8
Gilbert River, Australia 54 B3
Gilberton, Australia 54 B3
Gilford I., Canada 64 C3
Gilgandra, Australia 55 E4
Gilgit, India 36 B9
Gillam, Canada 65 B10
Gillen, L., Australia 53 E3
Gilles, L., Australia 55 E2
Gillette, U.S.A. 70 C2
Gilliat, Australia 54 C3
Gillingham, U.K. 11 F8
Gilmer, U.S.A. 71 J7
Gilmore, Australia 55 F4
Gilmore, L., Australia 53 F3
Gilmour, Canada 62 D4
Gilroy, U.S.A. 73 H3
Gimbi, Ethiopia 45 G12
Gimli, Canada 65 C9
Gin Gin, Australia 55 D5
Gindie, Australia 54 C4
Gingin, Australia 53 F2
Ginir, Ethiopia 40 F3
Giohar, Somali Rep. 40 G4
Gióna, Óros, Greece 21 E10
Girâfi, W. →, Egypt 41 F3
Girard, U.S.A. 71 G7
Girardot, Colombia 78 C4
Girdle Ness, U.K. 12 D6
Giresun, Turkey 23 F6
Girga, Egypt 45 C11
Giridih, India 37 G15
Girilambone, Australia 55 E4
Girona = Gerona, Spain 19 B7
Gironde □, France 18 D3
Gironde →, France 18 D3
Giru, Australia 54 B4
Girvan, U.K. 12 F4
Gisborne, N.Z. 51 H7
Gisenyi, Rwanda 46 E5
Gitega, Burundi 46 E5
Giuba →, Somali Rep. 40 G3
Giurgiu, Romania 17 G12
Giza = El Gîza, Egypt 45 C11
Gizhiga, Russia 25 C17
Gizhiginskaya Guba, Russia 25 C16
Giżycko, Poland 17 A10
Gjirokastra, Albania 21 D9
Gjoa Haven, Canada 60 B10
Gjøvik, Norway 9 F11
Glace Bay, Canada 63 C8
Glacier B., U.S.A. 64 B1
Glacier Nat. Park, Canada 64 C5
Glacier Park, U.S.A. 72 B7
Glacier Peak, U.S.A. 72 B3
Gladewater, U.S.A. 71 J7
Gladstone, Queens., Australia 54 C5
Gladstone, S. Austral., Australia 55 E2
Gladstone, W. Austral., Australia 53 E1
Gladstone, Canada 65 C9
Gladstone, U.S.A. 68 C2
Gladwin, U.S.A. 68 D3
Gladys L., Canada 64 B2
Gláma, Iceland 8 D2
Glåma →, Norway 9 G11
Glasco, U.S.A. 70 F6
Glasgow, U.K. 12 F4
Glasgow, Ky., U.S.A. 68 G3
Glasgow, Mont., U.S.A. 72 B10
Glastonbury, U.K. 11 F5
Glauchau, Germany 16 C6
Glazov, Russia 22 C9
Gleiwitz = Gliwice, Poland 17 C9
Glen Affric, U.K. 12 D4
Glen Canyon Dam, U.S.A. 73 H8
Glen Canyon Nat. Recreation Area, U.S.A. 73 H8
Glen Coe, U.K. 12 E4
Glen Garry, U.K. 12 D3
Glen Innes, Australia 55 D5
Glen Mor, U.K. 12 D4
Glen Moriston, U.K. 12 D4
Glen Orchy, U.K. 12 E4
Glen Spean, U.K. 12 E4
Glen Ullin, U.S.A. 70 B4
Glenburgh, Australia 53 E2
Glencoe, S. Africa 49 D5
Glencoe, U.S.A. 70 C7
Glendale, Ariz., U.S.A. 73 K7
Glendale, Calif., U.S.A. 73 J4
Glendale, Oreg., U.S.A. 72 E2
Glendive, U.S.A. 70 B2
Glendo, U.S.A. 70 D2
Glenelg, Australia 55 E2
Glenelg →, Australia 55 F3
Glenflorrie, Australia 52 D2
Glengarriff, Ireland 13 E2
Glengyle, Australia 54 C2
Glenmora, U.S.A. 71 K8
Glenmorgan, Australia 55 D4
Glenns Ferry, U.S.A. 72 E6
Glenorchy, Australia 54 G4
Glenore, Australia 54 B3
Glenormiston, Australia 54 C2
Glenreagh, Australia 55 E5
Glenrock, U.S.A. 72 E11
Glenrothes, U.K. 12 E5
Glens Falls, U.S.A. 68 D9
Glenties, Ireland 13 B3
Glenville, U.S.A. 68 F5
Glenwood, Alta., Canada 64 D6
Glenwood, Nfld., Canada 63 C9
Glenwood, Ark., U.S.A. 71 H8
Glenwood, Hawaii, U.S.A. 66 J17
Glenwood, Iowa, U.S.A. 70 E7
Glenwood, Minn., U.S.A. 70 C7
Glenwood Springs, U.S.A. 72 G10
Gliwice, Poland 17 C9
Globe, U.S.A. 73 K8
Głogów, Poland 16 C8
Glorieuses, Is., Ind. Oc. 49 A8
Glossop, U.K. 10 D6
Gloucester, Australia 55 E5
Gloucester, U.K. 11 F5
Gloucester I., Australia 54 B4
Gloucestershire □, U.K. 11 F5
Gloversville, U.S.A. 68 D8
Glovertown, Canada 63 C9
Glückstadt, Germany 16 B4
Gmünd, Austria 16 D7
Gmunden, Austria 16 E6
Gniezno, Poland 17 B8
Gnowangerup, Australia 53 F2
Go Cong, Vietnam 34 G9
Gō-no-ura, Japan 29 H4
Goa, India 36 M8
Goa □, India 36 M8
Goalen Hd., Australia 55 F5
Goalpara, India 37 F17
Goat Fell, U.K. 12 F3
Goba, Ethiopia 40 F2
Goba, Mozam. 49 D5
Gobabis, Namibia 48 C2
Gobi, Asia 31 B6
Gobō, Japan 29 H7
Gochas, Namibia 48 C2
Godavari →, India 37 L13
Godavari Point, India 37 L13
Godbout, Canada 63 C6
Goderich, Canada 62 D3
Godhavn, Greenland 4 C5
Godhra, India 36 H8
Gods →, Canada 65 B10
Gods L., Canada 65 C10
Godthåb, Greenland 61 B14
Godwin Austen = K2, Mt., Pakistan 36 B10
Goeie Hoop, Kaap die = Good Hope, C. of, S. Africa 48 E2
Goéland, L. au, Canada 62 C4
Goeree, Neths. 15 C3
Goes, Neths. 15 C3
Gogama, Canada 62 C3
Gogango, Australia 54 C5
Gogebic, L., U.S.A. 70 B10
Gogra = Ghaghara →, India 37 G14
Goiânia, Brazil 79 G9
Goiás, Brazil 79 G8
Goiás □, Brazil 79 F9
Goio-Ere, Brazil 80 A6
Gojō, Japan 29 G7
Gojra, Pakistan 36 D8
Gokteik, Burma 37 H20
Golan Heights = Hagolan, Syria 41 B4
Goläshkerd, Iran 39 E8
Golchikha, Russia 4 B12
Golconda, U.S.A. 72 F5
Gold Beach, U.S.A. 72 E1
Gold Coast, Australia 55 D5
Gold Coast, W. Afr. 42 F3
Gold Hill, U.S.A. 72 E2
Golden, Canada 64 C5
Golden, U.S.A. 70 F2
Golden B., N.Z. 51 J4
Golden Gate, U.S.A. 72 H2
Golden Hinde, Canada 64 D3
Golden Prairie, Canada 65 C7
Golden Vale, Ireland 13 D3
Goldendale, U.S.A. 72 D3
Goldfield, U.S.A. 73 H5
Goldfields, Canada 65 B7
Goldsand L., Canada 65 B8
Goldsboro, U.S.A. 69 H7
Goldsmith, U.S.A. 71 K3
Goldsworthy, Australia 52 D2
Goldthwaite, U.S.A. 71 K5
Goleniów, Poland 16 B7
Golestānak, Iran 39 D7
Goliad, U.S.A. 71 L6
Golpāyegān, Iran 39 C6
Golspie, U.K. 12 D5
Goma, Rwanda 46 E5
Gomel, Belorussia 22 D5
Gomera, Canary Is. 44 C1
Gómez Palacio, Mexico 74 B4
Gomishān, Iran 39 B7
Gomogomo, Indonesia 33 F8
Gomoh, India 37 H15
Gompa = Ganta, Liberia 44 G3
Gonābād, Iran 39 C8
Gonaïves, Haiti 75 D10
Gonbab-e Kāvūs, Iran 39 B7
Gonda, India 37 F12
Gonder, Ethiopia 45 F12
Gondia, India 36 J12
Gonghe, China 30 C5
Gongolgon, Australia 55 E4
Goniri, Nigeria 45 F7
Gonzales, Calif., U.S.A. 73 H3
Gonzales, Tex., U.S.A. 71 L6
Good Hope, C. of, S. Africa 48 E2
Gooderham, Canada 62 D4
Goodeve, Canada 65 C8
Gooding, U.S.A. 72 E6
Goodland, U.S.A. 70 F4
Goodnight, U.S.A. 71 H4
Goodooga, Australia 55 D4
Goodsoil, Canada 65 C7
Goodsprings, U.S.A. 73 J6
Goole, U.K. 10 D7
Goolgowi, Australia 55 E4
Goomalling, Australia 53 F2
Goombalie, Australia 55 D4
Goondiwindi, Australia 55 D5
Goongarrie, L., Australia 53 F3
Goonyella, Australia 54 C4
Goor, Neths. 15 B6
Gooray, Australia 55 D5
Goose →, Canada 63 B7
Goose L., U.S.A. 72 F3
Gop, India 36 H6
Gorakhpur, India 37 F13
Gordan B., Australia 52 B5
Gordon, U.S.A. 70 D3
Gordon →, Australia 54 G4
Gordon Downs, Australia 52 C4
Gordon L., Alta., Canada 65 B6
Gordon L., N.W.T., Canada 64 A6
Gordonia, S. Africa 48 D3
Gordonvale, Australia 54 B4
Gore, Australia 55 D5
Goré, Chad 45 G8
Gore, Ethiopia 45 G12
Gore, N.Z. 51 M2
Gore Bay, Canada 62 C3
Gorey, Ireland 13 D5
Gorg, Iran 39 D8
Gorgān, Iran 39 B7
Gorgona, I., Colombia 78 C3
Gorinchem, Neths. 15 C4
Gorízia, Italy 20 B5
Gorki = Nizhniy Novgorod, Russia 22 C7
Gorkiy = Nizhniy Novgorod, Russia 22 C7
Gorkovskoye Vdkhr., Russia 22 C7
Görlitz, Germany 16 C7
Gorlovka, Ukraine 23 E6
Gorman, U.S.A. 71 J5
Gorna Oryakhovitsa, Bulgaria 21 C11
Gorno-Altaysk, Russia 24 D9
Gorno Slinkino, Russia 24 C8
Gornyatski, Russia 22 A11
Gornyi, Russia 28 B6
Gorongose →, Mozam. 49 C5
Gorontalo, Indonesia 33 D6
Gort, Ireland 13 C3
Gorzów Wielkopolski, Poland 16 B7
Gosford, Australia 55 E5
Goshen, U.S.A. 68 E3
Goshogawara, Japan 28 D10
Goslar, Germany 16 C5
Gospič, Croatia 20 B6
Gosport, U.K. 11 G6
Gosse →, Australia 54 B1
Göta kanal, Sweden 9 G12
Göteborg, Sweden 9 H11
Göteborgs och Bohus län □, Sweden 9 G11
Gotha, Germany 16 C5
Gothenburg, U.S.A. 70 E4
Gotland, Sweden 9 H15
Gotska Sandön, Sweden 9 G15
Gōtsu, Japan 29 G6
Göttingen, Germany 16 C4
Gottwaldov = Zlin, Czech. 17 D8
Gouda, Neths. 15 B4
Gough I., Atl. Oc. 2 G9
Gouin, Rés., Canada 62 C5
Goulburn, Australia 55 E4
Goulburn Is., Australia 54 A1
Gounou-Gaya, Chad 45 G8
Gouri, Chad 45 E8
Gourits →, S. Africa 48 E3
Gourma Rharous, Mali 44 E4
Gourock Ra., Australia 55 F4
Govan, Canada 65 C8
Governador Valadares, Brazil 79 G10
Gowan Ra., Australia 54 C4
Gowanda, U.S.A. 68 D6
Gowd-e Zirreh, Afghan. 36 E3
Gower, U.K. 11 F3
Gowna, L., Ireland 13 C4
Goya, Argentina 80 B5
Goyder Lagoon, Australia 55 D2
Goyllarisquisga, Peru 78 F3
Goz Beïda, Chad 45 F9
Gozo, Malta 20 F6
Graaff-Reinet, S. Africa 48 E3
Gračac, Croatia 20 B6
Grace, U.S.A. 72 E8
Graceville, U.S.A. 70 C6
Gracias a Dios, C., Honduras 75 E8
Grado, Spain 19 A2
Gradule, Australia 55 D4
Grady, U.S.A. 71 H3
Graénalon, L., Iceland 8 D5
Grafton, Australia 55 D5
Grafton, U.S.A. 70 A6
Graham, Canada 62 C1
Graham, N.C., U.S.A. 69 G6
Graham, Tex., U.S.A. 71 J5
Graham →, Canada 64 B4
Graham Bell, Os., Russia 24 A7
Graham I., Canada 64 C2
Graham Land, Antarctica 5 C17
Graham Mt., U.S.A. 73 K9
Grahamdale, Canada 65 C9
Grahamstown, S. Africa 48 E4
Grain Coast, W. Afr. 42 F2
Grajaú, Brazil 79 E9
Grajaú →, Brazil 79 D10
Grampian □, U.K. 12 D6
Grampian Highlands = Grampian Mts., U.K. 12 E5
Grampian Mts., U.K. 12 E5
Gran Canaria, Canary Is. 44 C1
Gran Chaco, S. Amer. 80 B4
Gran Paradiso, Italy 20 B2
Gran Sasso d'Italia, Italy 20 C5
Granada, Nic. 74 E7
Granada, Spain 19 D4
Granada, U.S.A. 71 F3
Granard, Ireland 13 C4
Granbury, U.S.A. 71 J6
Granby, Canada 62 C5
Grand →, Mo., U.S.A. 70 F8
Grand →, S. Dak., U.S.A. 70 C4
Grand Bahama, Bahamas 75 B9
Grand Bank, Canada 63 C8
Grand Bassam, Ivory C. 44 G4
Grand-Bourg, Guadeloupe 74 M20
Grand Canyon, U.S.A. 73 H7
Grand Canyon National Park, U.S.A. 73 H7
Grand Cayman, Cayman Is. 75 D8
Grand Coulee, U.S.A. 72 C4
Grand Coulee Dam, U.S.A. 72 C4
Grand Falls, Canada 63 C8
Grand Forks, Canada 64 D5
Grand Forks, U.S.A. 70 B6
Grand Haven, U.S.A. 68 D2
Grand I., U.S.A. 68 B2
Grand Island, U.S.A. 70 E5
Grand Isle, U.S.A. 71 L10
Grand Junction, U.S.A. 73 G9
Grand Lac Victoria, Canada 62 C4
Grand Lahou, Ivory C. 44 G3
Grand L., N.B., Canada 63 C6
Grand L., Nfld., Canada 63 C8
Grand L., Nfld., Canada 63 B7
Grand Lake, U.S.A. 72 F11
Grand L., U.S.A. 71 L8
Grand Manan I., Canada 63 D6
Grand Marais, Canada 70 B9
Grand Marais, U.S.A. 68 B3
Grand-Mère, Canada 62 C5
Grand Portage, U.S.A. 62 C2
Grand Rapids, Canada 65 C9
Grand Rapids, Mich., U.S.A. 68 D2
Grand Rapids, Minn., U.S.A. 70 B8
Grand St-Bernard, Col du, Switz. 16 F3
Grand Teton, U.S.A. 72 E8
Grand Valley, U.S.A. 72 G9
Grand View, Canada 65 C8
Grande →, Argentina 80 A3
Grande →, Bolivia 78 G6
Grande →, Bahia, Brazil 79 F10
Grande →, Minas Gerais, Brazil 79 H8
Grande →, U.S.A. 71 N6
Grande, B., Argentina 80 G3
Grande Baie, Canada 63 C5
Grande Baleine, R. de la →, Canada 62 A4
Grande Cache, Canada 64 C5
Grande de Santiago →, Mexico 74 C3
Grande de Santiago →, Nayarit, Mexico 74 C3
Grande-Entrée, Canada 63 C7
Grande Prairie, Canada 64 B5
Grande-Rivière, Canada 63 C7
Grande-Vallée, Canada 63 C6
Grandes-Bergeronnes, Canada 63 C6
Grandfalls, U.S.A. 71 K3
Grandoe Mines, Canada 64 B3
Grandview, U.S.A. 72 C4
Grangemouth, U.K. 12 E5
Granger, Wash., U.S.A. 72 C3
Granger, Wyo., U.S.A. 72 F9
Grangeville, U.S.A. 72 D5
Granite City, U.S.A. 70 F9
Granite Falls, U.S.A. 70 C7
Granite Peak, Australia 53 E3
Granite Pk., U.S.A. 72 D9
Granity, N.Z. 51 J3
Granja, Brazil 79 D10
Granja de Torrehermosa, Spain 19 C3
Granollers, Spain 19 B7
Grant, U.S.A. 70 E4
Grant, Mt., U.S.A. 72 G4
Grant City, U.S.A. 70 E7
Grant I., Australia 52 B5
Grant Range Mts., U.S.A. 73 G6
Grantham, U.K. 10 E7
Grantown-on-Spey, U.K. 12 D5
Grants, U.S.A. 73 J10
Grants Pass, U.S.A. 72 E2
Grantsburg, U.S.A. 70 C8
Grantsville, U.S.A. 72 F7
Granville, France 18 B3
Granville, N. Dak., U.S.A. 70 A4
Granville, N.Y., U.S.A. 68 D9
Granville L., Canada 65 B8
Grapeland, U.S.A. 71 K7
Gras, L. de, Canada 60 B8
Graskop, S. Africa 49 C5
Grass →, Canada 65 B9
Grass Range, U.S.A. 72 C9
Grass River Prov. Park, Canada 65 C8
Grass Valley, Calif., U.S.A. 72 G3
Grass Valley, Oreg., U.S.A. 72 D3
Grasse, France 18 E7
Grassmere, Australia 55 E3
Gravelbourg, Canada 65 D7
's-Gravenhage, Neths. 15 B4
Gravesend, Australia 55 D5
Gravesend, U.K. 11 F8
Grayling, U.S.A. 68 C3
Grayling →, Canada 64 B3
Grays Harbor, U.S.A. 72 C1
Grays L., U.S.A. 72 E8
Grayson, Canada 65 C8
Graz, Austria 16 E7
Greasy L., Canada 64 A4
Great Abaco I., Bahamas 75 B9
Great Artesian Basin, Australia 54 C3
Great Australian Bight, Australia 53 F5
Great Barrier I., N.Z. 51 G5
Great Barrier Reef, Australia 54 B4
Great Basin, U.S.A. 72 G5
Great Bear →, Canada 60 B7
Great Bear L., Canada 60 B7
Great Belt = Store Bælt, Denmark 9 J11
Great Bend, U.S.A. 70 F5
Great Blasket I., Ireland 13 D1
Great Britain, Europe 6 E5
Great Central, Canada 64 D3
Great Dividing Ra., Australia 54 C4
Great Driffield, U.K. 10 C7
Great Falls, Canada 65 C9
Great Falls, U.S.A. 72 C8
Great Fish = Groot Vis →, S. Africa 48 E4
Great Harbour Deep, Canada 63 B8
Great Inagua I., Bahamas 75 C10
Great Indian Desert = Thar Desert, India 36 F7
Great I., Canada 65 B9
Great Karoo, S. Africa 48 E3
Great Lake, Australia 54 G4
Great Ormes Head, U.K. 10 D4
Great Ouse →, U.K. 10 E8
Great Palm I., Australia 54 B4
Great Plains, N. Amer. 66 A6
Great Ruaha →, Tanzania 46 F7
Great Saint Bernard P. = Grand St-Bernard, Col du, Switz. 16 F3
Great Salt Lake, U.S.A. 72 F7
Great Salt Lake Desert, U.S.A. 72 F7
Great Salt Plains Res., U.S.A. 71 G5
Great Sandy Desert, Australia 52 D3
Great Sangi = Sangihe, P., Indonesia 33 D7
Great Slave L., Canada 64 A5
Great Smoky Mts. Nat. Park, U.S.A. 69 H4
Great Stour = Stour →, U.K. 11 F9
Great Victoria Desert, Australia 53 E4
Great Wall, China 31 C5
Great Whernside, U.K. 10 C6
Great Yarmouth, U.K. 10 E9
Greater Antilles, W. Indies 75 D10
Greater London □, U.K. 11 F7
Greater Manchester □, U.K. 10 D5
Greater Sunda Is., Indonesia 32 F4
Gredos, Sierra de, Spain 19 B3
Greece ■, Europe 21 E10
Greeley, Colo., U.S.A. 70 E2
Greeley, Nebr., U.S.A. 70 E5
Green →, Ky., U.S.A. 68 G2
Green →, Utah, U.S.A. 73 G9
Green B., U.S.A. 68 C2
Green Bay, U.S.A. 68 C2
Green C., Australia 55 F5
Green Cove Springs, U.S.A. 69 L5
Green River, U.S.A. 73 G8
Greenbush, U.S.A. 70 A6
Greencastle, U.S.A. 68 F2
Greenfield, Ind., U.S.A. 68 F3
Greenfield, Iowa, U.S.A. 70 E7
Greenfield, Mass., U.S.A. 68 D9
Greenfield, Miss., U.S.A. 71 G8
Greenland ■, N. Amer. 4 C5
Greenland Sea, Arctic 4 B7
Greenock, U.K. 12 F4
Greenore, Ireland 13 B5
Greenore Pt., Ireland 13 D5
Greenough →, Australia 53 E1
Greensboro, Ga., U.S.A. 69 J4
Greensboro, N.C., U.S.A. 69 G6
Greensburg, Ind., U.S.A. 68 F3
Greensburg, Kans., U.S.A. 71 G5
Greensburg, Pa., U.S.A. 68 E6
Greenville, Liberia 44 G3
Greenville, Ala., U.S.A. 69 K2
Greenville, Calif., U.S.A. 72 F3
Greenville, Ill., U.S.A. 70 F10
Greenville, Maine, U.S.A. 63 C6
Greenville, Mich., U.S.A. 68 D3
Greenville, Miss., U.S.A. 71 J9
Greenville, N.C., U.S.A. 69 H7
Greenville, Ohio, U.S.A. 68 E3
Greenville, Pa., U.S.A. 68 E5
Greenville, S.C., U.S.A. 69 H4
Greenville, Tenn., U.S.A. 69 G4
Greenville, Tex., U.S.A. 71 J6
Greenwater Lake Prov. Park, Canada 65 C8
Greenwich, U.K. 11 F8
Greenwood, Canada 64 D5
Greenwood, Miss., U.S.A. 71 J9
Greenwood, S.C., U.S.A. 69 H4
Greenwood, Mt., Australia 52 B5
Gregory, U.S.A. 70 D5
Gregory →, Australia 54 B2
Gregory, L., S. Austral., Australia 55 D2
Gregory, L., W. Austral., Australia 53 E2
Gregory Downs, Australia 54 B2
Gregory L., Australia 52 D4
Gregory Ra., Queens., Australia 54 B3
Gregory Ra., W. Austral., Australia 52 D3
Greifswald, Germany 16 A6
Gremikha, Russia 22 A6
Grenada, U.S.A. 71 J10
Grenada ■, W. Indies 74 Q20
Grenadines, W. Indies 74 Q20
Grenen, Denmark 9 H11
Grenfell, Australia 55 E4
Grenfell, Canada 65 C8
Grenoble, France 18 D6
Grenora, U.S.A. 70 A3
Grenville, C., Australia 54 A3
Grenville Chan., Canada 64 C3
Gresham, U.S.A. 72 D2
Gresik, Indonesia 33 G15
Gretna Green, U.K. 12 F5
Grevenmacher, Lux. 15 E6
Grey →, N.Z. 51 K3
Grey, C., Australia 54 A2
Grey Ra., Australia 55 D3
Grey Res., Canada 63 C8
Greybull, U.S.A. 72 D9
Greymouth, N.Z. 51 K3
Greytown, N.Z. 51 J5
Greytown, S. Africa 49 D5
Gribbell I., Canada 64 C3
Gridley, U.S.A. 72 G3
Griekwastad, S. Africa 48 D3
Griffin, U.S.A. 69 J3
Griffith, Australia 55 E4
Grimari, C.A.R. 45 G9
Grimsby, U.K. 10 D7
Grímsey, Iceland 8 C5
Grimshaw, Canada 64 B5

Grimstad, *Norway* 9 G10
Grinnell, *U.S.A.* 70 E8
Gris-Nez, C., *France* .. 18 A4
Groais I., *Canada* 63 B8
Groblersdal, *S. Africa* 49 D4
Grodno, *Belorussia* ... 22 D3
Grodzisk Wielkopolski,
 Poland 16 B8
Grójec, *Poland* 17 C10
Grong, *Norway* 8 D12
Groningen, *Neths.* 15 A6
Groningen □, *Neths.* .. 15 A6
Groom, *U.S.A.* 71 H4
Groot →, *S. Africa* ... 48 E3
Groot Berg →,
 S. Africa 48 E2
Groot-Brakrivier,
 S. Africa 48 E3
Groot-Kei →,
 S. Africa 49 E4
Groot Vis →, *S. Africa* 48 E4
Groote Eylandt,
 Australia 54 A2
Grootfontein, *Namibia* 48 B2
Grootlaagte →, *Africa* 48 C3
Grootvloer, *S. Africa* . 48 E3
Gros C., *Canada* 64 A6
Gross Glockner,
 Austria 16 E6
Grossenhain, *Germany* 16 C6
Grosseto, *Italy* 20 C4
Groswater B., *Canada* . 63 B8
Groton, *U.S.A.* 70 C5
Grouard Mission,
 Canada 64 B5
Groundhog →,
 Canada 62 C3
Grouse Creek, *U.S.A.* . 72 F7
Groveton, *N.H., U.S.A.* 68 C10
Groveton, *Tex., U.S.A.* 71 K7
Groznyy, *Russia* 23 F8
Grudziądz, *Poland* ... 17 B9
Grundy Center, *U.S.A.* 70 D8
Gruver, *U.S.A.* 71 G4
Gryazi, *Russia* 22 D6
Gryazovets, *Russia* ... 22 D5
Gua, *India* 37 H14
Guadalajara, *Mexico* . 74 C4
Guadalajara, *Spain* .. 19 B4
Guadalcanal,
 Solomon Is. 56 H8
Guadalete →, *Spain* .. 19 D2
Guadalhorce →,
 Spain 19 D3
Guadalquivir →,
 Spain 19 D2
Guadalupe =
 Guadeloupe ■,
 W. Indies 74 L20
Guadalupe, *U.S.A.* ... 73 J3
Guadalupe →, *U.S.A.* 71 L6
Guadalupe, Sierra de,
 Spain 19 C3
Guadalupe Pk., *U.S.A.* 73 L11
Guadarrama, Sierra de,
 Spain 19 B4
Guadeloupe ■,
 W. Indies 74 L20
Guadeloupe Passage,
 W. Indies 74 L19
Guadiana →, *Portugal* 19 D2
Guadix, *Spain* 19 D4
Guafo, Boca del, *Chile* 80 E2
Guaira, *Brazil* 80 A6
Guaitecas, Is., *Chile* . 80 E2
Guajará-Mirim, *Brazil* 78 F5
Guajira, Pen. de la,
 Colombia 78 A4
Gualeguay, *Argentina* 80 C5
Gualeguaychú,
 Argentina 80 C5
Guam ■, *Pac. Oc.* ... 56 F6
Guamúchil, *Mexico* .. 74 B3
Guanahani = San
 Salvador, *Bahamas* 75 C10
Guanajuato, *Mexico* . 74 C4
Guandacol, *Argentina* 80 B3
Guane, *Cuba* 75 C8
Guangdong □, *China* 31 D6
Guangxi Zhuangzu
 Zizhiqu □, *China* . 31 D5
Guangzhou, *China* ... 31 D6
Guanipa →,
 Venezuela 78 B6
Guantánamo, *Cuba* .. 75 C9
Guaporé →, *Brazil* ... 78 F5
Guaqui, *Bolivia* 78 G5
Guarapuava, *Brazil* .. 80 B6
Guarda, *Portugal* 19 B2
Guardafui, C. = Asir,
 Ras, *Somali Rep.* .. 40 E5
Guasdualito, *Venezuela* 78 B4
Guasipati, *Venezuela* . 78 B6
Guatemala, *Guatemala* 74 E6
Guatemala ■,
 Cent. Amer. 74 D6
Guatire, *Venezuela* ... 78 A5
Guaviare □, *Colombia* 78 C4
Guaviare →,
 Colombia 78 C4
Guaxupé, *Brazil* 79 H9
Guayama, *Puerto Rico* 75 D11
Guayaquil, *Ecuador* .. 78 D3
Guayaquil, G. de,
 Ecuador 78 D2
Guaymas, *Mexico* ... 74 B2
Guchil, *Malaysia* 34 P15
Gudbrandsdalen,
 Norway 9 F10
Guddu Barrage,
 Pakistan 36 E6

Gudivada, *India* 37 L12
Gudur, *India* 36 M11
Guecho, *Spain* 19 A4
Guékédou, *Guinea* ... 44 G2
Guelma, *Algeria* 44 A6
Guelph, *Canada* 62 D3
Guéret, *France* 18 C4
Guernica, *Spain* 19 A4
Guernsey, *U.K.* 11 H5
Guernsey, *U.S.A.* 70 D2
Gueydan, *U.S.A.* 71 K8
Gügher, *Iran* 39 D8
Guglionesi, *Italy* 20 C6
Guia Lopes da Laguna,
 Brazil 80 A5
Guiana, *S. Amer.* 76 C4
Guibés, *Namibia* 48 D2
Guidónia-Montecélio,
 Italy 20 C5
Guiglo, *Ivory C.* 44 G3
Guijá, *Mozam.* 49 C5
Guildford, *U.K.* 11 F7
Guilford, *U.S.A.* 63 C11
Guilin, *China* 31 D6
Guilvinec, *France* 18 C1
Guimarães, *Brazil* 79 D10
Guimaras, *Phil.* 33 B6
Guinea ■, *W. Afr.* ... 44 F2
Guinea, Gulf of,
 Atl. Oc. 42 F3
Guinea-Bissau ■,
 Africa 44 F2
Guingamp, *France* ... 18 B2
Güiria, *Venezuela* 78 A6
Guiuan, *Phil.* 33 B7
Guiyang, *China* 30 D5
Guizhou □, *China* ... 30 D5
Gujarat □, *India* 36 H7
Gujranwala, *Pakistan* 36 C9
Gujrat, *Pakistan* 36 C9
Gulbarga, *India* 36 L10
Gulf, The, *Asia* 39 E6
Gulfport, *U.S.A.* 71 K10
Gulgong, *Australia* ... 55 E4
Gull Lake, *Canada* ... 65 C7
Gulshad, *Kazakhstan* 24 E8
Gulu, *Uganda* 46 D6
Gum Lake, *Australia* . 55 E3
Gumlu, *Australia* 54 B4
Gumma □, *Japan* 29 F9
Gummi, *Nigeria* 44 F6
Gumzai, *Indonesia* ... 33 F8
Guna, *India* 36 G10
Gundagai, *Australia* .. 55 F4
Gundih, *Indonesia* ... 33 G14
Gungu, *Zaïre* 46 F3
Gunisao →, *Canada* .. 65 C9
Gunisao L., *Canada* .. 65 C9
Gunnbjørn Fjeld,
 Greenland 4 C6
Gunnedah, *Australia* . 55 E5
Gunningham Cr. →,
 Australia 55 E4
Gunnison, *Colo.,
 U.S.A.* 73 G10
Gunnison, *Utah, U.S.A.* 72 G8
Gunnison →, *U.S.A.* . 73 G9
Gunpowder, *Australia* 54 B2
Guntakal, *India* 36 M10
Guntersville, *U.S.A.* .. 69 H2
Guntur, *India* 37 L12
Gunungapi, *Indonesia* 33 F7
Gunungsitoli,
 Indonesia 32 D1
Gunza, *Angola* 46 G2
Gupis, *Pakistan* 36 A8
Gurdaspur, *India* 36 C9
Gurdon, *U.S.A.* 71 J8
Gurgaon, *India* 36 E10
Gurkha, *Nepal* 37 E14
Gurley, *Australia* 55 D4
Gurun, *Malaysia* 34 P13
Gurupá, *Brazil* 79 D8
Gurupá, I. Grande de,
 Brazil 79 D8
Gurupi, *Brazil* 79 E9
Gurupi →, *Brazil* 79 D9
Guryev = Atyrau,
 Kazakhstan 23 E9
Gusau, *Nigeria* 44 F6
Gusinoozersk, *Russia* 25 D11
Güstine, *U.S.A.* 73 H3
Güstrow, *Germany* ... 16 B6
Gutha, *Australia* 53 E2
Guthalongra, *Australia* 54 B4
Guthrie, *U.S.A.* 71 H6
Guttenberg, *U.S.A.* .. 70 D9
Guyana ■, *S. Amer.* . 78 C7
Guyane française ■ =
 French Guiana ■,
 S. Amer. 79 C8
Guyenne, *France* 18 D4
Guymon, *U.S.A.* 71 G4
Guyra, *Australia* 55 E5
Gwa, *Burma* 37 L19
Gwaai, *Zimbabwe* ... 47 H5
Gwabegar, *Australia* . 55 E4
Gwädar, *Pakistan* ... 36 G3
Gwalia, *Australia* 53 E3
Gwalior, *India* 36 F11
Gwanda, *Zimbabwe* . 47 J5
Gwoebarra B., *Ireland* 13 B3
Gweedore, *Ireland* ... 13 A3
Gwent □, *U.K.* 11 F5
Gweru, *Zimbabwe* ... 47 H5
Gwinn, *U.S.A.* 68 B2
Gwydir →, *Australia* . 55 D4
Gwynedd □, *U.K.* ... 10 E4
Gyandzha, *Azerbaijan* 23 F8
Gyaring Hu, *China* .. 30 C4
Gydanskiy P-ov.,
 Russia 24 C8
Gympie, *Australia* ... 55 D5
Gyöngyös, *Hungary* .. 17 E9
Győr, *Hungary* 17 E8
Gypsum Pt., *Canada* . 64 A6
Gypsumville, *Canada* 65 C9
Gyumri = Kumayri,
 Armenia 23 F7

H

Ha 'Arava →, *Israel* . 41 E4
Haapamäki, *Finland* . 8 E18
Haarlem, *Neths.* 15 B4
Haast →, *N.Z.* 51 K2
Haast Bluff, *Australia* . 52 D5
Hab Nadi Chauki,
 Pakistan 36 G5
Habaswein, *Kenya* ... 46 D7
Habay, *Canada* 64 B5
Habbānīyah, *Iraq* ... 38 C4
Haboro, *Japan* 28 B10
Hachijō-Jima, *Japan* . 29 H9
Hachinohe, *Japan* ... 28 D10
Hachiōji, *Japan* 29 G9
Hadarba, Ras, *Sudan* 45 D12
Hadarom □, *Israel* .. 41 E3
Haddington, *U.K.* ... 12 F6
Hadejia, *Nigeria* 44 F7
Haden, *Australia* 55 D5
Hadera, *Israel* 41 C3
Hadera, N. →, *Israel* 41 C3
Hadhramaut =
 Ḥaḍramawt, *Yemen* 40 D4
Ḥaḍramawt, *Yemen* . 40 D4
Ḥadrānīyah, *Iraq* ... 38 C4
Hadrian's Wall, *U.K.* . 10 C5
Haeju, *N. Korea* 31 C7
Haerhpin = Harbin,
 China 31 B7
Hafar al Bāṭin,
 Si. Arabia 38 D5
Hafizabad, *Pakistan* . 36 C8
Haflong, *India* 37 G18
Hafnarfjörður, *Iceland* 8 D3
Hafun, Ras,
 Somali Rep. 40 E5
Hagalil, *Israel* 41 C4
Hagen, *Germany* 16 C3
Hagerman, *U.S.A.* ... 71 J2
Hagerstown, *U.S.A.* . 68 F7
Hagfors, *Sweden* 9 F12
Hagi, *Iceland* 8 D2
Hagi, *Japan* 29 G5
Hagolan, *Syria* 41 B4
Hagondange-Briey,
 France 18 B7
Hags Hd., *Ireland* ... 13 D2
Hague, C. de la, *France* 18 B3
Hague, The = 's-
 Gravenhage, *Neths.* 15 B4
Haguenau, *France* ... 18 B7
Haifa = Ḥefa, *Israel* 41 C3
Haig, *Australia* 53 F4
Haikou, *China* 31 D6
Ḥā'il, *Si. Arabia* 38 E4
Hailar, *China* 31 B6
Hailey, *U.S.A.* 72 E6
Haileybury, *Canada* . 62 C4
Hailuoto, *Finland* ... 8 D18
Hainan □, *China* 31 E5
Hainaut □, *Belgium* . 15 D4
Haines, *U.S.A.* 72 D5
Haines City, *U.S.A.* .. 69 L5
Haines Junction,
 Canada 64 A1
Haiphong, *Vietnam* .. 30 D5
Haiti ■, *W. Indies* ... 75 D10
Haiya Junction, *Sudan* 45 E12
Haja, *Indonesia* 33 E7
Hajar Bangar, *Sudan* . 45 F9
Hajdúböszörmény,
 Hungary 17 E10
Ḥājjī Muhsin, *Iraq* .. 38 C5
Ḥājjīābād, Eṣfahan,
 Iran 39 C7
Ḥājjīābād, Hormozgān,
 Iran 39 D7
Hajnówka, *Poland* ... 17 B11
Hakansson, Mts., *Zaïre*
Hakken-Zan, *Japan* .. 29 G7
Hakodate, *Japan* 28 D10
Haku-San, *Japan* 29 F8
Hakui, *Japan* 29 F8
Hala, *Pakistan* 36 G6
Halab, *Syria* 38 B3
Halabjah, *Iraq* 38 C5
Halaib, *Sudan* 45 D12
Ḥālat 'Ammār,
 Si. Arabia 38 D3
Halbā, *Lebanon* 41 A5
Halberstadt, *Germany* 16 C5
Halcombe, *N.Z.* 51 J5
Halcon, Mt., *Phil.* ... 33 B6
Halden, *Norway* 9 G11
Haldia, *India* 37 H16
Haldwani, *India* 36 E11
Hale →, *Australia* ... 54 C2
Haleakala Crater,
 U.S.A. 66 H16
Haleyville, *U.S.A.* ... 69 H2
Halfway →, *Canada* .. 64 B4
Haliburton, *Canada* .. 62 C4
Halifax, *Australia* 54 B4
Halifax, *Canada* 63 D7
Halifax, *U.K.* 10 D6
Halifax B., *Australia* . 54 B4
Halifax I., *Namibia* .. 48 D2
Ḥalīl →, *Iran* 39 E8
Hall Beach, *Canada* .. 61 B11
Hall Pt., *Australia* ... 52 C3
Hallands län □,
 Sweden 9 H12
Hällefors, *Sweden* ... 9 G13
Hallett, *Australia* 55 E2
Hallettsville, *U.S.A.* .. 71 L6

Halliday, *U.S.A.* 70 B3
Halliday L., *Canada* .. 65 A7
Hallingdal →, *Norway* 9 F10
Hällnäs, *Sweden* 8 D15
Hallock, *U.S.A.* 65 D9
Halls Creek, *Australia* 52 C4
Halmahera, *Indonesia* 33 D7
Halmstad, *Sweden* ... 9 H12
Halq el Oued, *Tunisia* 45 A7
Hals, *Denmark* 9 H11
Halul, *Qatar* 39 E7
Ḥalvān, *Iran* 39 C8
Hamab, *Namibia* 48 D2
Hamada, *Japan* 29 G6
Hamadān, *Iran* 39 C6
Hamadān □, *Iran* ... 39 C6
Ḥamāh, *Syria* 38 C3
Hamamatsu, *Japan* .. 29 G8
Hamar, *Norway* 9 F11
Hamarøy, *Norway* ... 8 B13
Hambantota, *Sri Lanka* 36 R12
Hamber Prov. Park,
 Canada 64 C5
Hamburg, *Germany* .. 16 B5
Hamburg, *Ark., U.S.A.* 71 J9
Hamburg, *Iowa, U.S.A.* 70 E7
Hame □ = Häme
 lääni □, *Finland* .. 9 F18
Hämeen lääni □,
 Finland 9 F18
Hämeenlinna, *Finland* 9 F18
Hamelin Pool,
 Australia 53 E1
Hameln, *Germany* ... 16 B4
Hamersley Ra.,
 Australia 52 D2
Hamerkaz □, *Israel* .. 41 C3
Hami, *China* 30 B4
Hamilton, *Australia* .. 55 F3
Hamilton, *Bermuda* . 75 A12
Hamilton, *Canada* ... 62 D4
Hamilton, *N.Z.* 51 G5
Hamilton, *U.K.* 12 F4
Hamilton, *Mo., U.S.A.* 70 F8
Hamilton, *Mont.,
 U.S.A.* 72 C6
Hamilton, *N.Y., U.S.A.* 68 D8
Hamilton, *Ohio, U.S.A.* 68 F3
Hamilton, *Tex., U.S.A.* 71 K5
Hamilton →, *Australia* 54 C2
Hamilton Hotel,
 Australia 54 C3
Hamilton Inlet, *Canada* 63 B8
Hamiota, *Canada* 65 C8
Hamlet, *U.S.A.* 69 H6
Hamley Bridge,
 Australia 55 E2
Hamlin = Hameln,
 Germany 16 B4
Hamlin, *U.S.A.* 71 J4
Hamm, *Germany* 16 C3
Hammerfest, *Norway* 8 A17
Hammond, *Ind., U.S.A.* 68 E2
Hammond, *La., U.S.A.* 71 K9
Hammonton, *U.S.A.* . 68 F8
Hampden, *N.Z.* 51 L3
Hampshire □, *U.K.* .. 11 F6
Hampshire Downs,
 U.K. 11 F6
Hampton, *Ark., U.S.A.* 71 J8
Hampton, *Iowa, U.S.A.* 70 D8
Hampton, *S.C., U.S.A.* 69 J5
Hampton, *Va., U.S.A.* 68 G7
Hampton Tableland,
 Australia 53 F4
Hamrat esh Sheykh,
 Sudan 45 F10
Ḥana, *U.S.A.* 66 H17
Hanak, *Si. Arabia* ... 38 E3
Hanamaki, *Japan* ... 28 E10
Hanau, *Germany* 16 C4
Hancock, *Mich., U.S.A.* 70 B10
Hancock, *Minn., U.S.A.* 70 C7
Handa, *Japan* 29 G8
Handa, *Somali Rep.* .. 40 E5
Handan, *China* 31 C6
Handeni, *Tanzania* ... 46 F7
Handwara, *Israel* 41 B3
Haney, *Canada* 64 D4
Hanford, *U.S.A.* 73 H4
Hangayn Nuruu,
 Mongolia 30 B4
Hangchou =
 Hangzhou, *China* . 31 C7
Hangö, *Finland* 9 G17
Hangzhou, *China* 31 C7
Hangzhou Wan, *China* 31 C7
Ḥanīdh, *Si. Arabia* .. 39 E6
Ḥanīsh, *Yemen* 40 E3
Hankinson, *U.S.A.* ... 70 B6
Hanko = Hangö,
 Finland 9 G17
Hanko, *Finland* 9 G17
Hanksville, *U.S.A.* ... 73 G8
Hanle, *India* 36 C11
Hanmer Springs, *N.Z.* 51 K4
Hann →, *Australia* ... 52 C4
Hann, Mt., *Australia* . 52 C4
Hanna, *Canada* 64 C6
Hannaford, *U.S.A.* ... 70 B5
Hannah, *U.S.A.* 70 A5
Hannah B., *Canada* .. 62 B4
Hannibal, *U.S.A.* 70 F9
Hannover, *Germany* . 16 B4
Hanoi, *Vietnam* 30 D5

Hanover = Hannover,
 Germany 16 B4
Hanover, *S. Africa* ... 48 E3
Hanover, *N.H., U.S.A.* 68 D9
Hanover, *Pa., U.S.A.* . 68 F7
Hanover, I., *Chile* ... 80 G2
Hansi, *India* 36 E9
Ḥasanābād, *Iran* 39 C7
Hashimoto, *Japan* ... 29 G7
Hashtjerd, *Iran* 39 C6
Haskell, *Okla., U.S.A.* 71 H7
Haskell, *Tex., U.S.A.* . 71 J5
Hasselt, *Belgium* 15 D5
Hassi Inifel, *Algeria* .. 44 C5
Hassi Messaoud,
 Algeria 44 B6
Hastings I., *Norway* .. 51 H6
Hastings, *U.K.* 11 G8
Hastings, *Mich., U.S.A.* 68 D3
Hastings, *Minn., U.S.A.* 70 C8
Hastings, *Nebr., U.S.A.* 70 E5
Hastings Ra., *Australia* 55 E5
Hat Nhao, *Laos* 34 E9
Hatay = Antalya,
 Turkey 23 G5
Hatch, *U.S.A.* 73 K10
Hatches Creek,
 Australia 54 C2
Hatchet L., *Canada* .. 65 B8
Hateruma-Shima,
 Japan 29 M1
Hatfield P.O., *Australia* 55 E3
Hatgal, *Mongolia* 30 A5
Hathras, *India* 36 F11
Hatia, *Bangla.* 37 H17
Hattah, *Australia* 55 E3
Hatteras, C., *U.S.A.* .. 69 H8
Hattiesburg, *U.S.A.* .. 71 K10
Hatvan, *Hungary* 17 E9
Hau Bon = Cheo Reo,
 Vietnam 34 F10
Haugesund, *Norway* . 9 G8
Haultain →, *Canada* . 65 B7
Hauraki G., *N.Z.* 51 G5
Haut Atlas, *Morocco* . 44 B3
Haut-Rhin □, *France* 18 C7
Haute-Corse □, *France* 18 E9
Haute-Garonne □,
 France 18 E4
Haute-Loire □, *France* 18 D5
Haute-Marne □, *France* 18 B6
Haute-Saône □, *France* 18 C7
Haute-Savoie □,
 France 18 C7
Haute-Vienne □,
 France 18 C4
Hautes-Alpes □,
 France 18 D7
Hauterive, *Canada* ... 63 C6
Hautes Fagnes = Hohe
 Venn, *Belgium* 15 D6
Hautes-Pyrénées □,
 France 18 E4
Hauts-de-Seine □,
 France 18 B5
Hauts Plateaux, *Algeria* 44 A5
Havana = La Habana,
 Cuba 75 C8
Havana, *U.S.A.* 70 E9
Havant, *U.K.* 11 G7
Havasu, L., *U.S.A.* ... 73 J5
Havel →, *Germany* .. 16 B7
Havelange, *Belgium* . 15 D5
Havelock, *N.B., Canada* 63 C6
Havelock, *Ont., Canada* 62 D4
Havelock, *N.Z.* 51 J4
Havelock I., *India* 34 G2
Haverfordwest, *U.K.* . 11 F3
Haverhill, *U.S.A.* 68 D10
Havering, *U.K.* 11 F8
Havlíčkův Brod, *Czech.* 16 D8
Havre, *U.S.A.* 72 B9
Havre-Aubert, *Canada* 63 C7
Havre-St.-Pierre,
 Canada 63 B7
Haw →, *U.S.A.* 69 H6
Hawaii □, *U.S.A.* 66 H16
Hawaii I., *Pac. Oc.* ... 66 J17
Hawaiian Is., *Pac. Oc.* 66 H17
Hawaiian Ridge,
 Pac. Oc. 57 E11
Hawarden, *Canada* .. 65 C7
Hawarden, *U.S.A.* ... 70 D6
Hawea, L., *N.Z.* 51 L2
Hawera, *N.Z.* 51 H5
Hawick, *U.K.* 12 F6
Hawk Junction,
 Canada 62 C3
Hawke B., *N.Z.* 51 H6
Hawker, *Australia* ... 55 E2
Hawkesbury, *Canada* 62 C5
Hawkesbury I., *Canada* 64 C3
Hawkesbury Pt.,
 Australia 54 A1
Hawkinsville, *U.S.A.* . 69 J4
Hawkwood, *Australia* 55 D5
Hawley, *U.S.A.* 70 B6
Hawrān, *Syria* 41 C5
Hawsh Mūssá,
 Lebanon 41 B4
Hawthorne, *U.S.A.* .. 72 G4
Haxtun, *U.S.A.* 70 E3
Hay, *Australia* 55 E3
Hay →, *Australia* 54 C2
Hay →, *Canada* 64 A5
Hay, C., *Australia* 52 B4
Hay L., *Canada* 64 B5
Hay Lakes, *Canada* .. 64 C6
Hay-on-Wye, *U.K.* ... 11 E4
Hay River, *Canada* ... 64 A5
Hay Springs, *U.S.A.* .. 70 D3
Hayachine-San, *Japan* 28 E10
Hayden, *Ariz., U.S.A.* 73 K8
Hayden, *Colo., U.S.A.* 72 F10
Haydon, *Australia* ... 54 B3

Humboldt

Hayes, U.S.A. 70 C4
Hayes →, Canada 65 B10
Haynesville, U.S.A. 71 J8
Hays, Canada 64 C6
Hays, U.S.A. 70 F5
Hayward, U.S.A. 70 B9
Haywards Heath, U.K. 11 F7
Hazafon □, Israel 41 C4
Hazarām, Kūh-e, Iran 39 D8
Hazard, U.S.A. 68 G4
Hazaribag, India 37 H14
Hazelton, Canada 64 B3
Hazelton, U.S.A. 70 B4
Hazen, N. Dak., U.S.A. 70 B4
Hazen, Nev., U.S.A. 72 G4
Hazlehurst, Ga., U.S.A. 69 K4
Hazlehurst, Miss., U.S.A. 71 K9
Hazleton, U.S.A. 68 E8
Hazlett, L., Australia 52 D4
Hazor, Israel 41 B4
Head of Bight, Australia 53 F5
Healdsburg, U.S.A. 72 G2
Healdton, U.S.A. 71 H6
Healesville, Australia 55 F4
Heanor, U.K. 10 D6
Heard I., Ind. Oc. 35 K6
Hearne, U.S.A. 71 K6
Hearne B., Canada 65 A9
Hearne L., Canada 64 A6
Hearst, Canada 62 C3
Heart →, U.S.A. 70 B4
Heart's Content, Canada 63 C9
Heath Pt., Canada 63 C7
Heath Steele, Canada 63 C6
Heavener, U.S.A. 71 H7
Hebbronville, U.S.A. 71 M5
Hebei □, China 31 C6
Hebel, Australia 55 D4
Heber Springs, U.S.A. 71 H9
Hebert, Canada 65 C7
Hebgen, L., U.S.A. 72 D8
Hebrides, U.K. 12 D1
Hebron = Al Khalīl, Jordan 41 D4
Hebron, Canada 61 C13
Hebron, N. Dak., U.S.A. 70 B3
Hebron, Nebr., U.S.A. 70 E6
Hecate Str., Canada 64 C2
Hechi, China 30 D5
Hechuan, China 30 C5
Hecla, U.S.A. 70 C5
Hecla I., Canada 65 C9
Hede, Sweden 8 E12
Hedemora, Sweden 9 F13
Hedley, U.S.A. 71 H4
Heemstede, Neths. 15 B4
Heerde, Neths. 15 B6
Heerenveen, Neths. 15 B5
Heerlen, Neths. 15 D5
Ḥefa, Israel 41 C3
Ḥefa □, Israel 41 C4
Hefei, China 31 C6
Hegang, China 31 B8
Heidelberg, Germany 16 D4
Heidelberg, C. Prov., S. Africa 48 E3
Heidelberg, Trans., S. Africa 49 D4
Heilbron, S. Africa 49 D4
Heilbronn, Germany 16 D4
Heilongjiang □, China 31 B7
Heilunkiang = Heilongjiang □, China 31 B7
Heinola, Finland 9 F19
Heinze Is., Burma 34 E4
Hejaz = Al Ḥijāz, Si. Arabia 40 B2
Hekla, Iceland 8 E4
Hekou, China 30 D5
Helena, Ark., U.S.A. 71 H9
Helena, Mont., U.S.A. 72 C7
Helensburgh, U.K. 12 E4
Helensville, N.Z. 51 G5
Helgoland, Germany 16 A3
Heligoland = Helgoland, Germany 16 A3
Heligoland B. = Deutsche Bucht, Germany 16 A4
Hellendoorn, Neths. 15 B6
Hellevoetsluis, Neths. 15 C4
Hellín, Spain 19 C5
Helmand □, Afghan. 36 D4
Helmand →, Afghan. 36 D2
Helmond, Neths. 15 C5
Helmsdale, U.K. 12 C5
Helper, U.S.A. 72 G8
Helsingborg, Sweden 9 H12
Helsingfors, Finland 9 F18
Helsingør, Denmark 9 H12
Helsinki, Finland 9 F18
Helston, U.K. 11 G2
Helvellyn, U.K. 10 C4
Helwân, Egypt 45 C11
Hemet, U.S.A. 73 K5
Hemingford, U.S.A. 70 D3
Hemphill, U.S.A. 71 K8
Hempstead, U.S.A. 71 K6
Hemse, Sweden 9 H15
Henan □, China 31 C6
Henares →, Spain 19 B4
Henashi-Misaki, Japan 28 D9
Henderson, Ky., U.S.A. 68 G2
Henderson, N.C., U.S.A. 69 G6
Henderson, Nev., U.S.A. 73 H6
Henderson, Pa., U.S.A. 69 H1
Henderson, Tex., U.S.A. 71 J7
Hendersonville, U.S.A. 69 H4
Hendījān, Iran 39 D6
Hendon, Australia 55 D5
Hengelo, Neths. 15 B6
Hengyang, China 31 D6
Henlopen, C., U.S.A. 68 F8
Hennenman, S. Africa 48 D4
Hennessey, U.S.A. 71 G6
Henrietta, U.S.A. 71 J5
Henrietta, Ostrov, Russia 25 B16
Henrietta Maria C., Canada 62 A3
Henry, U.S.A. 70 E10
Henryetta, U.S.A. 71 H6
Hentiyn Nuruu, Mongolia 31 B5
Henty, Australia 55 F4
Henzada, Burma 37 L19
Heppner, U.S.A. 72 D4
Héraðsflói, Iceland 8 D6
Héraðsvötn →, Iceland 8 D4
Herald Cays, Australia 54 B4
Herāt, Afghan. 36 B3
Herāt □, Afghan. 36 B3
Hérault □, France 18 E5
Herbert →, Australia 54 B4
Herbert Downs, Australia 54 C2
Herberton, Australia 54 B4
Hercegnovi, Montenegro, Yug. 21 C8
Herðubreið, Iceland 8 D5
Hereford, U.K. 11 E5
Hereford, U.S.A. 71 H3
Hereford and Worcester □, U.K. 11 E5
Herentals, Belgium 15 C4
Herford, Germany 16 B4
Herington, U.S.A. 70 F6
Herjehogna, Norway 9 F12
Herkimer, U.S.A. 68 D8
Herman, U.S.A. 70 C6
Hermann, U.S.A. 70 F9
Hermannsburg Mission, Australia 52 D5
Hermanus, S. Africa 48 E2
Hermidale, Australia 55 E4
Hermiston, U.S.A. 72 D4
Hermitage, N.Z. 51 K3
Hermite, I., Chile 80 H3
Hermon, Mt. = Ash Shaykh, J., Lebanon 41 B4
Hermosillo, Mexico 74 B2
Hernád →, Hungary 17 E10
Hernandarias, Paraguay 80 B6
Hernando, U.S.A. 71 H10
Herne, Germany 15 C7
Herne Bay, U.K. 11 F9
Herning, Denmark 9 H10
Heroica Nogales = Nogales, Mexico 74 A2
Heron Bay, Canada 62 C2
Herreid, U.S.A. 70 C4
Herrera, Spain 19 D3
Herrick, Australia 54 G4
Herrin, U.S.A. 71 G10
Herstal, Belgium 15 D5
Hertford, U.K. 11 F7
Hertfordshire □, U.K. 11 F7
's-Hertogenbosch, Neths. 15 C5
Hertzogville, S. Africa 48 D4
Herzliyya, Israel 41 C3
Ḥeṣār, Fārs, Iran 39 D6
Ḥeṣār, Markazī, Iran 39 C6
Hesse = Hessen □, Germany 16 C4
Hessen □, Germany 16 C4
Hettinger, U.S.A. 70 C3
Hewett, C., Canada 61 A13
Hexham, U.K. 10 C5
Hexrivier, S. Africa 48 E2
Heydarābād, Iran 39 D7
Heyfield, Australia 55 F4
Heysham, U.K. 10 C5
Heywood, Australia 55 F3
Hialeah, U.S.A. 69 N5
Hiawatha, Kans., U.S.A. 70 F7
Hiawatha, Utah, U.S.A. 72 G8
Hibbing, U.S.A. 70 B8
Hibbs B., Australia 54 G4
Hibernia Reef, Australia 52 B3
Hickory, U.S.A. 69 H5
Hicks, Pt., Australia 55 F4
Hida-Gawa →, Japan 29 G8
Hida-Sammyaku, Japan 29 F8
Hidaka-Sammyaku, Japan 28 C11
Hidalgo del Parral, Mexico 74 B3
Higashiajima-San, Japan 28 F10
Higashiōsaka, Japan 29 G7
Higgins, U.S.A. 71 G4
Higginsville, Australia 53 F3
High Atlas = Haut Atlas, Morocco 44 B3
High I., Canada 63 A7
High Island, U.S.A. 71 L7
High Level, Canada 64 B5
High Point, U.S.A. 69 H6
High Prairie, Canada 64 B5
High River, Canada 64 C6
High Springs, U.S.A. 69 L4
High Tatra = Tatry, Slovakia 17 D10
High Wycombe, U.K. 11 F7
Highbury, Australia 54 B3
Highland □, U.K. 12 D4
Highland Park, U.S.A. 68 D2
Highmore, U.S.A. 70 C5
Highrock L., Canada 65 B7
Hiiumaa, Estonia 22 C3
Ḥijāz □, Si. Arabia 40 C2
Hijo = Tagum, Phil. 33 C7
Hikari, Japan 29 H5
Hiko, U.S.A. 73 H6
Hikone, Japan 29 G8
Hikurangi, N.Z. 51 F5
Hikurangi, Mt., N.Z. 51 H6
Hildesheim, Germany 16 B4
Hill →, Australia 53 F2
Hill City, Idaho, U.S.A. 72 E6
Hill City, Kans., U.S.A. 70 F5
Hill City, Minn., U.S.A. 70 B8
Hill City, S. Dak., U.S.A. 70 D3
Hill Island L., Canada 65 A7
Hillegom, Neths. 15 B4
Hillingdon, U.K. 11 F7
Hillman, U.S.A. 68 C4
Hillmond, Canada 65 C7
Hillsboro, Kans., U.S.A. 70 F6
Hillsboro, N. Dak., U.S.A. 70 B6
Hillsboro, N.H., U.S.A. 68 D10
Hillsboro, N. Mex., U.S.A. 73 K10
Hillsboro, Oreg., U.S.A. 72 D2
Hillsboro, Tex., U.S.A. 71 J6
Hillsdale, U.S.A. 68 E3
Hillside, Australia 52 D2
Hillsport, Canada 62 C2
Hillston, Australia 55 E4
Hilo, U.S.A. 66 J17
Hilversum, Neths. 15 B5
Himachal Pradesh □, India 36 D10
Himalaya, Asia 37 E14
Himatnagar, India 36 H8
Himeji, Japan 29 G7
Himi, Japan 29 F8
Ḥimṣ, Syria 41 A5
Ḥimṣ □, Syria 41 A5
Hinchinbrook I., Australia 54 B4
Hinckley, U.K. 11 E6
Hinckley, U.S.A. 72 G7
Hindmarsh, L., Australia 55 F3
Hindu Kush, Asia 36 B7
Hindubagh, Pakistan 36 D5
Hindupur, India 36 N10
Hines Creek, Canada 64 B5
Hinganghat, India 36 J11
Hingham, U.S.A. 72 B8
Hingoli, India 36 K10
Hinna = Imi, Ethiopia 40 F3
Hinsdale, U.S.A. 72 B10
Hinton, Canada 64 C5
Hinton, U.S.A. 68 G5
Hippolytushoef, Neths. 15 B4
Hirado, Japan 29 H4
Hirakud Dam, India 37 J13
Hiratsuka, Japan 29 G9
Hiroo, Japan 28 C11
Hirosaki, Japan 28 D10
Hiroshima, Japan 29 G6
Hiroshima □, Japan 29 G6
Hisar, India 36 E9
Hisb →, Iraq 38 D5
Ḥismá, Si. Arabia 38 D3
Hispaniola, W. Indies 75 D10
Hīt, Iraq 38 C4
Hita, Japan 29 H5
Hitachi, Japan 29 F10
Hitchin, U.K. 11 F7
Hitoyoshi, Japan 29 H5
Hitra, Norway 8 E10
Ḥiyyon, N. →, Israel 41 E4
Hjalmar L., Canada 65 A7
Hjälmaren, Sweden 9 G13
Hjørring, Denmark 9 H10
Hluhluwe, S. Africa 49 D5
Ho, Ghana 44 G5
Ho Chi Minh City = Phanh Bho Ho Chi Minh, Vietnam 34 G9
Hoa Binh, Vietnam 34 B8
Hoai Nhon, Vietnam 34 E10
Hoare B., Canada 61 B13
Hobart, Australia 54 G4
Hobart, U.S.A. 71 H5
Hobbs, U.S.A. 71 J3
Hobbs Coast, Antarctica 5 D14
Hoboken, Belgium 15 C4
Hobro, Denmark 9 H10
Hoburgen, Sweden 9 H15
Hodaka-Dake, Japan 29 F8
Hodgson, Canada 65 C9
Hódmezővásárhely, Hungary 17 E10
Hodna, Chott el, Algeria 44 A5
Hodonín, Czech. 16 D8
Hoek van Holland, Neths. 15 C4
Hof, Germany 16 C5
Hof, Iceland 8 D6
Höfðakaupstaður, Iceland 8 D3
Hofmeyr, S. Africa 48 E4
Hofsjökull, Iceland 8 D4
Hofsós, Iceland 8 D4
Hōfu, Japan 29 G5
Hogan Group, Australia 54 F4
Hogansville, U.S.A. 69 J3
Hogeland, U.S.A. 72 B9
Hoggar = Ahaggar, Algeria 44 D6
Hohe Rhön, Germany 16 C4
Hohe Venn, Belgium 15 D6
Hohenwald, U.S.A. 69 H2
Hohhot, China 31 B6
Hoi An, Vietnam 34 E10
Hoi Xuan, Vietnam 34 B8
Hoisington, U.S.A. 70 F5
Hōjō, Japan 29 H6
Hokianga Harbour, N.Z. 51 F4
Hokitika, N.Z. 51 K3
Hokkaidō □, Japan 28 C11
Holbrook, Australia 55 F4
Holbrook, U.S.A. 73 J8
Holden, Canada 64 C6
Holden, U.S.A. 72 G7
Holdenville, U.S.A. 71 H6
Holderness, U.K. 10 D7
Holdfast, Canada 65 C7
Holdrege, U.S.A. 70 E5
Holguín, Cuba 75 C9
Hollams Bird I., Namibia 48 C1
Holland, U.S.A. 68 D2
Hollandia = Jayapura, Indonesia 33 E10
Hollidaysburg, U.S.A. 68 E6
Hollis, U.S.A. 71 H5
Hollister, Calif., U.S.A. 73 H3
Hollister, Idaho, U.S.A. 72 E6
Holly, U.S.A. 70 F3
Holly Hill, U.S.A. 69 L5
Holly Springs, U.S.A. 71 H10
Hollywood, Calif., U.S.A. 73 J4
Hollywood, Fla., U.S.A. 69 N5
Holman Island, Canada 60 A8
Hólmavík, Iceland 8 D3
Holmes Reefs, Australia 54 B4
Holmsund, Sweden 8 E16
Holroyd →, Australia 54 A3
Holstebro, Denmark 9 H10
Holsworthy, U.K. 11 G3
Holt, Iceland 8 E4
Holton, Canada 63 B8
Holton, U.S.A. 70 F7
Holtville, U.S.A. 73 K6
Holwerd, Neths. 15 A5
Holy Cross, U.S.A. 60 B4
Holy I., Gwynedd, U.K. 10 D3
Holy I., Northumb., U.K. 10 B6
Holyhead, U.K. 10 D3
Holyoke, Colo., U.S.A. 70 E3
Holyoke, Mass., U.S.A. 68 D9
Holyrood, Canada 63 C9
Homalin, Burma 37 G19
Homand, Iran 39 C8
Hombori, Mali 44 E4
Home B., Canada 61 B13
Home Hill, Australia 54 B4
Homedale, U.S.A. 72 E5
Homer, Alaska, U.S.A. 60 C4
Homer, La., U.S.A. 71 J8
Homestead, Australia 54 C4
Homestead, Fla., U.S.A. 69 N5
Homestead, Oreg., U.S.A. 72 D5
Hominy, U.S.A. 71 G6
Homoine, Mozam. 49 C6
Homs = Ḥimṣ, Syria 41 A5
Homyel = Gomel, Belorussia 22 D5
Hon Chong, Vietnam 34 G8
Honan = Henan □, China 31 C6
Honbetsu, Japan 28 C11
Honda, Colombia 78 B4
Hondeklipbaai, S. Africa 48 E2
Hondo, Japan 29 H5
Hondo, U.S.A. 71 L5
Honduras ■, Cent. Amer. 74 E7
Honduras, G. de, Caribbean 74 D7
Hønefoss, Norway 9 F11
Honey L., U.S.A. 72 F3
Honfleur, France 18 B4
Hong Kong ■, Asia 31 D6
Hongha →, Vietnam 30 D5
Hongjiang, China 31 D5
Hongshui He →, China 31 D5
Honguedo, Détroit d', Canada 63 C7
Hongze Hu, China 31 C6
Honiara, Solomon Is. 56 H7
Honiton, U.K. 11 G4
Honjō, Japan 28 E10
Honolulu, U.S.A. 66 H16
Honshū, Japan 29 G9
Hood, Pt., Australia 53 F2
Hood Mt., U.S.A. 72 D3
Hood River, U.S.A. 72 D3
Hoodsport, U.S.A. 72 C2
Hoogeveen, Neths. 15 B6
Hoogezand, Neths. 15 A6
Hooghly → = Hughli →, India 37 J16
Hook Hd., Ireland 13 D5
Hook I., Australia 54 C4
Hook of Holland = Hoek van Holland, Neths. 15 C4
Hooker, U.S.A. 71 G4
Hooker Creek, Australia 52 C5
Hoopeston, U.S.A. 68 E2
Hoopstad, S. Africa 48 D4
Hoorn, Neths. 15 B5
Hoover Dam, U.S.A. 73 J6
Hope, Canada 64 D4
Hope, Ark., U.S.A. 71 J8
Hope, N. Dak., U.S.A. 70 B6
Hope, L., Australia 55 D2
Hope Pt., U.S.A. 60 B3
Hopedale, Canada 63 A7
Hopefield, S. Africa 48 E2
Hopei = Hebei □, China 31 C6
Hopetoun, Vic., Australia 55 F3
Hopetoun, W. Austral., Australia 53 F3
Hopetown, S. Africa 48 D3
Hopkins, U.S.A. 70 E7
Hopkins, L., Australia 52 D4
Hopkinsville, U.S.A. 69 G2
Hopland, U.S.A. 72 G2
Hoquiam, U.S.A. 72 C2
Hordaland fylke □, Norway 9 F9
Horden Hills, Australia 52 D5
Horlick Mts., Antarctica 5 E15
Horlivka = Gorlovka, Ukraine 23 E6
Hormoz, Iran 39 E7
Hormoz, Jaz. ye, Iran 39 E8
Hormuz Str. of, The Gulf 39 E8
Horn, Austria 16 D7
Horn, Ísafjarðarsýsla, Iceland 8 C2
Horn, Suður-Múlasýsla, Iceland 8 D7
Horn →, Canada 64 A5
Horn, Cape = Hornos, C. de, Chile 80 H3
Horn Head, Ireland 13 A3
Horn I., Australia 54 A3
Horn I., U.S.A. 69 K1
Horn Mts., Canada 64 A5
Hornavan, Sweden 8 C14
Hornbeck, U.S.A. 71 K8
Hornbrook, U.S.A. 72 F2
Horncastle, U.K. 10 D7
Hornell, U.S.A. 68 D7
Hornell L., Canada 64 A5
Hornepayne, Canada 62 C3
Hornos, C. de, Chile 80 H3
Hornsby, Australia 55 E5
Hornsea, U.K. 10 D7
Horobetsu, Japan 28 C10
Horqin Youyi Qianqi, China 31 B7
Horqueta, Paraguay 80 A5
Horse Cr. →, U.S.A. 70 E3
Horse Is., Canada 63 B8
Horsefly L., Canada 64 C4
Horsens, Denmark 9 J10
Horsham, Australia 55 F3
Horsham, U.K. 11 F7
Horten, Norway 9 G11
Horton, U.S.A. 70 F7
Horton →, Canada 60 B7
Horwood, L., Canada 62 C3
Hose, Gunung-Gunung, Malaysia 32 D4
Ḥoseynābād, Khuzestān, Iran 39 C6
Ḥoseynābād, Kordestān, Iran 38 C5
Hoshangabad, India 36 H10
Hoshiarpur, India 36 D9
Hosmer, U.S.A. 70 C5
Hospet, India 36 M10
Hospitalet de Llobregat, Spain 19 B7
Hoste, I., Chile 80 H3
Hot, Thailand 34 C5
Hot Creek Ra., U.S.A. 72 G5
Hot Springs, Ark., U.S.A. 71 H8
Hot Springs, S. Dak., U.S.A. 70 D3
Hotagen, Sweden 8 E13
Hotan, China 30 C2
Hotazel, S. Africa 48 D3
Hotchkiss, U.S.A. 73 G10
Hotham, C., Australia 52 B5
Hoting, Sweden 8 D14
Hottentotsbaai, Namibia 48 D1
Houck, U.S.A. 73 J9
Houffalize, Belgium 15 D5
Houghton, U.S.A. 70 B10
Houghton L., U.S.A. 68 C3
Houghton-le-Spring, U.K. 10 C6
Houhora Heads, N.Z. 51 F4
Houlton, U.S.A. 63 C6
Houma, U.S.A. 71 L9
Houston, Canada 64 C3
Houston, Mo., U.S.A. 71 G9
Houston, Tex., U.S.A. 71 L7
Houtman Abrolhos, Australia 53 E1
Hovd, Mongolia 30 B4
Hove, U.K. 11 G7
Hoveyzeh, Iran 39 D6
Hövsgöl Nuur, Mongolia 30 A5
Howard, Australia 55 D5
Howard, Kans., U.S.A. 71 G6
Howard, S. Dak., U.S.A. 70 C6
Howard I., Australia 54 A2
Howard L., Canada 65 A7
Howe, U.S.A. 72 E7
Howe, C., Australia 55 F5
Howell, U.S.A. 68 D4
Howick, S. Africa 49 D5
Howick Group, Australia 54 A4
Howitt, L., Australia 55 D2
Howley, Canada 63 C8
Howrah = Haora, India 37 H16
Howth Hd., Ireland 13 C5
Hoy, U.K. 12 C5
Høyanger, Norway 9 F9
Hpungan Pass, Burma 37 F20
Hradec Králové, Czech. 16 C7
Hrodna = Grodno, Belorussia 22 D3
Hron →, Slovakia 17 E9
Hrvatska = Croatia ■, Europe 20 B7
Hsenwi, Burma 37 H20
Hsiamen = Xiamen, China 31 D6
Hsian = Xi'an, China 31 C5
Hsinhailien = Lianyungang, China 31 C6
Hsisha Chuntao, Pac. Oc. 32 A4
Hsüchou = Xuzhou, China 31 C6
Hua Hin, Thailand 34 F5
Huacho, Peru 78 F3
Huachón, Peru 78 F3
Huai He →, China 31 C6
Huainan, China 31 C6
Hualapai Pk., U.S.A. 73 J7
Huallaga →, Peru 78 E3
Huambo, Angola 47 G3
Huancabamba, Peru 78 E3
Huancane, Peru 78 G5
Huancapi, Peru 78 F4
Huancavelica, Peru 78 F3
Huancayo, Peru 78 F3
Huang Hai = Yellow Sea, China 31 C7
Huang He →, China 31 C6
Huangshi, China 31 C6
Huánuco, Peru 78 E3
Huaraz, Peru 78 E3
Huarmey, Peru 78 F3
Huascarán, Peru 78 E3
Huasco, Chile 80 B2
Huatabampo, Mexico 74 B3
Huayllay, Peru 78 F3
Hubbard, U.S.A. 71 K6
Hubbart Pt., Canada 65 B10
Hubei □, China 31 C6
Hubli-Dharwad = Dharwad, India 36 M9
Huddersfield, U.K. 10 D6
Hudiksvall, Sweden 9 F14
Hudson, Canada 65 C10
Hudson, Mich., U.S.A. 68 E3
Hudson, N.Y., U.S.A. 68 D9
Hudson, Wis., U.S.A. 70 C8
Hudson, Wyo., U.S.A. 72 E9
Hudson →, U.S.A. 68 E8
Hudson Bay, N.W.T., Canada 61 C11
Hudson Bay, Sask., Canada 65 C8
Hudson Falls, U.S.A. 68 D9
Hudson Mts., Antarctica 5 D16
Hudson Str., Canada 61 B13
Hudson's Hope, Canada 64 B4
Hue, Vietnam 34 D9
Huelva, Spain 19 D2
Huesca, Spain 19 A5
Hugh →, Australia 54 D1
Hughenden, Australia 54 C3
Hughes, Australia 53 F4
Hughli →, India 37 J16
Hugo, U.S.A. 70 F3
Hugoton, U.S.A. 71 G4
Hulla, Nevado del, Colombia 78 C3
Huinca Renancó, Argentina 80 C4
Huize, China 30 D5
Hukawng Valley, Burma 37 F20
Hukuntsi, Botswana 48 C3
Ḥulayfā', Si. Arabia 38 E4
Huld, Mongolia 30 B5
Hull = Kingston upon Hull, U.K. 10 D7
Hull, Canada 62 C4
Hull →, U.K. 10 D7
Hulst, Neths. 15 C4
Hulun Nur, China 31 B6
Humahuaca, Argentina 80 A3
Humaitá, Brazil 78 E6
Humaitá, Paraguay 80 B5
Humansdorp, S. Africa 48 E3
Humbe, Angola 48 B1
Humber →, U.K. 10 D7
Humberside □, U.K. 10 D7
Humbert River, Australia 52 C5
Humble, U.S.A. 71 L8
Humboldt, Canada 65 C7
Humboldt, Iowa, U.S.A. 70 D7
Humboldt, Tenn., U.S.A. 71 H10

Humboldt

Humboldt →, U.S.A. 72 F4
Humboldt Gletscher,
  Greenland 4 B4
Hume, L., Australia 55 F4
Humphreys Pk., U.S.A. 73 J8
Hün, Libya 45 C8
Húnaflói, Iceland 8 D3
Hunan □, China 31 D6
Hundred Mile House,
  Canada 64 C4
Hunedoara, Romania 17 F11
Hungary ■, Europe 17 E9
Hungary, Plain of,
  Europe 6 F9
Hungerford, Australia 55 D3
Hüngnam, N. Korea 31 C7
Hunsberge, Namibia 48 D2
Hunsrück, Germany 16 D3
Hunstanton, U.K. 10 E8
Hunter, U.S.A. 70 B6
Hunter I., Australia 54 G3
Hunter I., Canada 64 C3
Hunter Ra., Australia 55 E5
Hunterville, N.Z. 51 H5
Huntingburg, U.S.A. 68 F2
Huntingdon, Canada 62 C5
Huntingdon, U.K. 11 E7
Huntingdon, U.S.A. 68 E6
Huntington, Ind.,
  U.S.A. 68 E3
Huntington, Oreg.,
  U.S.A. 72 D5
Huntington, Utah,
  U.S.A. 72 G8
Huntington, W. Va.,
  U.S.A. 68 F4
Huntington Beach,
  U.S.A. 73 K5
Huntington Park,
  U.S.A. 73 K4
Huntly, N.Z. 51 G5
Huntly, U.K. 12 D6
Huntsville, Canada 62 C4
Huntsville, Ala., U.S.A. 69 H2
Huntsville, Tex., U.S.A. 71 K7
Huonville, Australia 54 G4
Hupeh = Hubei □,
  China 31 C6
Hūr, Iran 39 D8
Hurley, N. Mex., U.S.A. 73 K9
Hurley, Wis., U.S.A. 70 B9
Huron, U.S.A. 70 C5
Huron, L., N. Amer. 68 C4
Hurricane, U.S.A. 73 H7
Hurunui →, N.Z. 51 K4
Húsavík, Iceland 8 C5
Huskvarna, Sweden 9 H13
Hussar, Canada 64 C6
Hutchinson, Kans.,
  U.S.A. 71 F6
Hutchinson, Minn.,
  U.S.A. 70 C7
Huttig, U.S.A. 71 J8
Hutton, Mt., Australia 55 D4
Huy, Belgium 15 D5
Hvammur, Iceland 8 D3
Hvar, Croatia 20 C7
Hvítá, Iceland 8 D3
Hvítá →, Iceland 8 D3
Hvítárvatn, Iceland 8 D4
Hwang Ho = Huang
  He →, China 31 C6
Hwange, Zimbabwe 47 H5
Hwange Nat. Park,
  Zimbabwe 48 B4
Hyannis, U.S.A. 70 E4
Hyargas Nuur,
  Mongolia 30 B4
Hyden, Australia 53 F2
Hyderabad, India 36 L11
Hyderabad, Pakistan 36 G6
Hyères, France 18 E7
Hyland →, Canada 64 B3
Hyndman Pk., U.S.A. 72 E6
Hyōgo □, Japan 29 G7
Hyrum, U.S.A. 72 F8
Hysham, U.S.A. 72 C10
Hythe, U.K. 11 F9
Hyūga, Japan 29 H5
Hyvinge = Hyvinkää,
  Finland 9 F18
Hyvinkää, Finland 9 F18

I

I-n-Gall, Niger 44 E6
Iaco →, Brazil 78 E5
Iakora, Madag. 49 C8
Ialomiţa →, Romania 21 B12
Iaşi, Romania 17 E13
Iba, Phil. 33 A6
Ibadan, Nigeria 44 G5
Ibagué, Colombia 78 C3
Ibar →, Serbia, Yug. 21 C9
Ibaraki □, Japan 29 F10
Ibarra, Ecuador 78 C3
Iberian Peninsula,
  Europe 6 G5
Iberville, Canada 62 C5
Iberville, Lac d',
  Canada 62 A5
Ibi, Nigeria 44 G6
Ibiá, Brazil 79 G9
Ibicuy, Argentina 80 C5
Ibioapaba, Sa. da,
  Brazil 79 D10
Ibiza, Spain 19 C6
Ibonma, Indonesia 33 E8
Ibotirama, Brazil 79 F10

Ibrāhīm →, Lebanon 41 A4
Ibu, Indonesia 33 D7
Ibusuki, Japan 29 J5
Icá, Peru 78 F3
Içá →, Brazil 78 D5
Içana, Brazil 78 C5
İçel = Mersin, Turkey 23 G5
Iceland ■, Europe 8 D4
Icha, Russia 25 D16
Ich'ang = Yichang,
  China 31 C6
Ichchapuram, India 37 K14
Ichihara, Japan 29 G10
Ichikawa, Japan 29 G9
Ichilo →, Bolivia 78 G6
Ichinohe, Japan 28 D10
Ichinomiya, Japan 29 G8
Ichinoseki, Japan 28 E10
Icy Str., U.S.A. 64 B1
Ida Grove, U.S.A. 70 D7
Ida Valley, Australia 53 E3
Idabel, U.S.A. 71 J7
Idaho □, U.S.A. 72 D6
Idaho City, U.S.A. 72 E6
Idaho Falls, U.S.A. 72 E7
Idaho Springs, U.S.A. 72 G11
Idd el Ghanam, Sudan 45 F9
Iddan, Somali Rep. 40 F4
Idehan, Libya 45 C7
Idehan Marzūq, Libya 45 D7
Idelès, Algeria 44 D6
Idfû, Egypt 45 D11
Ídhi Óros, Greece 21 G11
Ídhra, Greece 21 F10
Idi, Indonesia 32 C1
Idiofa, Zaïre 46 E3
Idlib, Syria 38 C3
Idutywa, S. Africa 49 E4
Ieper, Belgium 15 D2
Ierápetra, Greece 21 G11
Ierzu, Italy 20 E3
'Ifâl, W. al →,
  Si. Arabia 38 D2
Ifanadiana, Madag. 49 C8
Ife, Nigeria 44 G5
Iffley, Australia 54 B3
Ifni, Morocco 44 C2
Iforas, Adrar des, Mali 44 E5
Ifould, L., Australia 53 F5
Igarapé, Brazil 79 H9
Igarapé Açu, Brazil 79 D9
Igarka, Russia 24 C9
Igbetti, Nigeria 44 G5
Iggesund, Sweden 9 F14
Iglésias, Italy 20 E3
Igli, Algeria 44 B4
Igloolik, Canada 61 B11
Ignace, Canada 62 C1
Iguaçu →, Brazil 80 B6
Iguaçu, Cat. del, Brazil 80 B6
Iguaçu Falls = Iguaçu,
  Cat. del, Brazil 80 B6
Iguala, Mexico 74 D5
Igualada, Spain 19 B6
Iguassu = Iguaçu →,
  Brazil 80 B6
Iguatu, Brazil 79 E11
Iguéla, Gabon 46 E1
Iheya-Shima, Japan 29 L3
Ihosy, Madag. 49 C8
Ihotry, L., Madag. 49 C7
Ii, Finland 8 D18
Ii-Shima, Japan 29 L3
Iida, Japan 29 G8
Iijoki →, Finland 8 D18
Iisalmi, Finland 8 E19
Iiyama, Japan 29 F9
Iizuka, Japan 29 H5
Ijebu-Ode, Nigeria 44 G5
IJmuiden, Neths. 15 B4
IJssel →, Neths. 15 B5
IJsselmeer, Neths. 15 B5
Ikaria, Greece 21 F12
Ikeda, Japan 29 G6
Ikela, Zaïre 46 E4
Iki, Japan 29 H4
Ikopa →, Madag. 49 B8
Ilagan, Phil. 33 A6
Ilām, Iran 38 C5
Ilanskiy, Russia 25 D10
Ilbilbie, Australia 54 C4
Ile-à-la-Crosse, Canada 65 B7
Ile-à-la-Crosse, Lac,
  Canada 65 B7
Île-de-France, France 18 B5
Ilebo, Zaïre 46 E4
Ilek, Russia 24 D6
Ilek →, Russia 22 D9
Ilford, Canada 65 B9
Ilfracombe, Australia 54 C3
Ilfracombe, U.K. 11 F3
Ilhéus, Brazil 79 F11
Ili →, Kazakhstan 24 E8
Ilich, Kazakhstan 24 E7
Iliff, U.S.A. 70 E3
Iligan, Phil. 33 C6
Iliodhrómia, Greece 21 E10
Ilion, U.S.A. 68 D8
Ilkeston, U.K. 10 E6
Illampu = Ancohuma,
  Nevada, Bolivia 78 G5
Illana B., Phil. 33 C6
Illapel, Chile 80 C2
Ille-et-Vilaine □, France 18 B3
Iller →, Germany 16 D4
Illimani, Bolivia 78 G5
Illinois □, U.S.A. 67 C9
Illinois →, U.S.A. 67 C8
Ilmen, Oz., Russia 22 C5
Ilo, Peru 78 G4
Iloilo, Phil. 33 B6
Ilorin, Nigeria 44 G5

Ilwaki, Indonesia 33 F7
Imabari, Japan 29 G6
Imaloto →, Madag. 49 C8
Imandra, Oz., Russia 22 A5
Imari, Japan 29 H4
Imbler, U.S.A. 72 D5
imeni 26 Bakinskikh
  Komissarov,
  Azerbaijan 23 G8
imeni 26 Bakinskikh
  Komissarov,
  Turkmenistan 23 G9
Imeni Poliny Osipenko,
  Russia 25 D14
Imeri, Serra, Brazil 78 C5
Imerimandroso,
  Madag. 49 B8
Imi, Ethiopia 40 F3
Imlay, U.S.A. 72 F4
Immingham, U.K. 10 D7
Immokalee, U.S.A. 69 M5
Imola, Italy 20 B4
Imperatriz, Brazil 79 E9
Impéria, Italy 20 C3
Imperial, Canada 65 C7
Imperial, Calif., U.S.A. 73 K6
Imperial, Nebr., U.S.A. 70 E4
Imperial Dam, U.S.A. 73 K6
Imperieuse Reef,
  Australia 52 C2
Impfondo, Congo 46 D3
Imphal, India 37 G18
Imuruan B., Phil. 33 B5
In Belbel, Algeria 44 C5
In Salah, Algeria 44 C5
Ina, Japan 29 G8
Inangahua Junction,
  N.Z. 51 J3
Inanwatan, Indonesia 33 E8
Iñapari, Peru 78 F5
Inari, Finland 8 B19
Inarijärvi, Finland 8 B19
Inawashiro-Ko, Japan 28 F10
Inca, Spain 19 C7
İnce-Burnu, Turkey 23 F5
Inchon, S. Korea 31 C7
Incomáti →, Mozam. 49 D5
Indalsälven →,
  Sweden 8 E14
Indaw, Burma 37 G20
Independence, Calif.,
  U.S.A. 73 H4
Independence, Iowa,
  U.S.A. 70 D9
Independence, Kans.,
  U.S.A. 71 G7
Independence, Mo.,
  U.S.A. 70 F7
Independence, Oreg.,
  U.S.A. 72 D2
Independence Fjord,
  Greenland 4 A6
Independence Mts.,
  U.S.A. 72 F5
India ■, Asia 36 K11
Indian →, U.S.A. 69 M5
Indian Cabins, Canada 64 B5
Indian Harbour,
  Canada 63 B8
Indian Head, Canada 65 C8
Indian Ocean 26 K11
Indiana, U.S.A. 68 E6
Indiana □, U.S.A. 68 E3
Indianapolis, U.S.A. 68 F2
Indianola, Iowa, U.S.A. 70 E8
Indianola, Miss., U.S.A. 71 J9
Indiga, Russia 22 A8
Indigirka →, Russia 25 B15
Indio, U.S.A. 73 K5
Indonesia ■, Asia 32 F5
Indore, India 36 H9
Indramayu, Indonesia 33 G13
Indravati →, India 37 K12
Indre □, France 18 C4
Indre-et-Loire □,
  France 18 C4
Indus →, Pakistan 36 G5
İnebolu, Turkey 23 F5
Ingende, Zaïre 46 E3
Ingham, Australia 54 B4
Ingleborough, U.K. 10 C5
Inglewood, Queens.,
  Australia 55 D5
Inglewood, Vic.,
  Australia 55 F3
Inglewood, N.Z. 51 H5
Inglewood, U.S.A. 73 K4
Ingólfshöfði, Iceland 8 E5
Ingomar, U.S.A. 72 C10
Ingonish, Canada 63 C7
Ingraj Bazar, India 37 G16
Ingrid Christensen
  Coast, Antarctica 5 C6
Inguilec, Ukraine 23 E5
Ingwavuma, S. Africa 49 D5
Inhaca, I., Mozam. 49 D5
Inhafenga, Mozam. 49 C5
Inhambane, Mozam. 49 C6
Inhambane □, Mozam. 49 C5
Inhaminga, Mozam. 47 H7
Inharrime, Mozam. 49 C6
Inharrime →, Mozam. 49 C6
Ining = Yining, China 24 E9
Inírida →, Colombia 78 C5
Inishbofin, Ireland 13 C1
Inishmore, Ireland 13 C2
Inishowen, Ireland 13 A4
Injune, Australia 55 D4
Inklin, Canada 64 B2
Inklin →, Canada 64 B2
Inkom, U.S.A. 72 E7

Inle L., Burma 37 J20
Inn →, Austria 16 D6
Innamincka, Australia 55 D3
Inner Hebrides, U.K. 12 D2
Inner Mongolia = Nei
  Monggol Zizhiqu □,
  China 31 B6
Inner Sound, U.K. 12 D3
Innetalling I., Canada 62 A4
Innisfail, Australia 54 B4
Innisfail, Canada 64 C6
In'no-shima, Japan 29 G6
Innsbruck, Austria 16 E5
Inny →, Ireland 13 C4
Inongo, Zaïre 46 E3
Inoucdjouac, Canada 61 C12
Inowrocław, Poland 17 B9
Inquisivi, Bolivia 78 G5
Inscription, C.,
  Australia 53 E1
Insein, Burma 37 L20
Inta, Russia 22 A11
Interior, U.S.A. 70 D4
Interlaken, Switz. 16 E3
International Falls,
  U.S.A. 70 A8
Interview I., India 34 F2
Inthanon, Ko, Thailand 34 C5
Intiyaco, Argentina 80 B4
Inútil, B., Chile 80 G2
Inuvik, Canada 60 B6
Inveraray, U.K. 12 E3
Inverbervie, U.K. 12 E6
Invercargill, N.Z. 51 M2
Inverell, Australia 55 D5
Inverness, Canada 63 C7
Inverness, U.K. 12 D4
Inverness, U.S.A. 69 L4
Inverurie, U.K. 12 D6
Inverway, Australia 52 C4
Investigator Group,
  Australia 55 E1
Investigator Str.,
  Australia 55 F2
Inya, Russia 24 D9
Inyo Mts., U.S.A. 73 H5
Inyokern, U.S.A. 73 J5
Inza, Russia 22 D8
Iō-Jima, Japan 29 J5
Iola, U.S.A. 71 G7
Iona, U.K. 12 E2
Ione, Calif., U.S.A. 72 G3
Ione, Wash., U.S.A. 72 B5
Ionia, U.S.A. 68 D3
Ionian Is. = Iónioi
  Nísoi, Greece 21 E9
Ionian Sea, Greece 21 E7
Iónioi Nísoi, Greece 21 E9
Íos, Greece 21 F11
Iowa □, U.S.A. 70 D8
Iowa City, U.S.A. 70 E9
Iowa Falls, U.S.A. 70 D8
Ipameri, Brazil 79 G9
Ipatinga, Brazil 79 G10
Ipiales, Colombia 78 C3
Ipin = Yibin, China 30 D5
Ípiros □, Greece 21 E9
Ipixuna, Brazil 78 E4
Ipoh, Malaysia 34 Q14
Ippy, C.A.R. 45 G9
Ipswich, Australia 55 D5
Ipswich, U.K. 11 E9
Ipswich, U.S.A. 70 C5
Ipu, Brazil 79 D10
Iqaluit, Canada 61 B13
Iquique, Chile 78 H4
Iquitos, Peru 78 D4
Irabu-Jima, Japan 29 M2
Iracoubo, Fr. Guiana 79 B8
İrafshān, Iran 39 E9
Iráklion, Greece 21 G11
Iran ■, Asia 39 C7
Iran, Gunung-Gunung,
  Malaysia 32 D4
Iran Ra. = Iran,
  Gunung-Gunung,
  Malaysia 32 D4
Īrānshahr, Iran 39 E9
Irapuato, Mexico 74 C4
Iraq ■, Asia 38 C5
Irbid, Jordan 41 C4
Irbid □, Jordan 41 C5
Irebu, Zaïre 46 E3
Ireland ■, Europe 13 D4
Ireland's Eye, Ireland 13 C5
Iret, Russia 25 C16
Irian Jaya □, Indonesia 33 E9
Iringa, Tanzania 46 F7
Iriomote-Jima, Japan 29 M1
Iriri →, Brazil 79 D8
Irish Republic ■,
  Europe 13 D4
Irish Sea, Europe 10 D3
Irkineyeva, Russia 25 D10
Irkutsk, Russia 25 D11
Irma, Canada 65 C6
Irö-Zaki, Japan 29 G9
Iron Baron, Australia 55 E2
Iron Gate = Portile de
  Fier, Europe 17 F11
Iron Knob, Australia 55 E2
Iron Mountain, U.S.A. 68 C1
Iron Ra., Australia 54 A3
Iron River, U.S.A. 70 B10
Ironbridge, U.K. 11 E5
Ironstone Kopje,
  Botswana 48 D3
Ironton, Mo., U.S.A. 71 G9
Ironton, Ohio, U.S.A. 68 F4
Ironwood, U.S.A. 70 B9

Iroquois Falls, Canada 62 C3
Irrara Cr. →, Australia 55 D4
Irrawaddy □, Burma 37 L19
Irrawaddy →, Burma 37 M19
Irtysh →, Russia 24 C7
Irumu, Zaïre 46 D5
Irún, Spain 19 A5
Irunea = Pamplona,
  Spain 19 A5
Irvine, Canada 65 D6
Irvine, U.K. 12 F4
Irvine, U.S.A. 68 G4
Irvinestown, U.K. 13 B4
Irwin →, Australia 53 E1
Irymple, Australia 55 E3
Isaac →, Australia 54 C4
Isabel, U.S.A. 70 C4
Isabella, Phil. 33 C6
Isabella Ra., Australia 52 D3
Ísafjarðardjúp, Iceland 8 C2
Ísafjörður, Iceland 8 C2
Isahaya, Japan 29 H5
Isangi, Zaïre 46 D4
Isar →, Germany 16 D6
Íschia, Italy 20 D5
Isdell →, Australia 52 C3
Ise, Japan 29 G8
Ise-Wan, Japan 29 G8
Isère □, France 18 D6
Isère →, France 18 D6
Ishigaki-Shima, Japan 29 M2
Ishikari-Gawa →,
  Japan 28 C10
Ishikari-Sammyaku,
  Japan 28 C11
Ishikari-Wan, Japan 28 C10
Ishikawa □, Japan 29 F8
Ishim, Russia 24 D7
Ishim →, Russia 24 D8
Ishinomaki, Japan 28 E10
Ishioka, Japan 29 F10
Ishkuman, Pakistan 36 A8
Ishpeming, U.S.A. 68 B2
Isil Kul, Russia 24 D8
Isiolo, Kenya 46 D7
Isipingo Beach,
  S. Africa 49 E5
Isiro, Zaïre 46 D5
Isisford, Australia 54 C3
İskenderun, Turkey 23 G6
İskenderun Körfezi,
  Turkey 23 G6
Iskut →, Canada 64 B2
Isla →, U.K. 12 E5
Islamabad, Pakistan 36 C8
Island →, Canada 64 A4
Island Falls, Canada 62 C3
Island Falls, U.S.A. 63 C6
Island L., Canada 65 C10
Island Lagoon,
  Australia 55 E2
Island Pond, U.S.A. 68 C10
Islands, B. of, Canada 63 C8
Islay, U.K. 12 F2
Isle aux Morts, Canada 63 C8
Isle of Wight □, U.K. 11 G6
Isle Royale, U.S.A. 70 A10
Isleta, U.S.A. 73 J10
Ismail, Ukraine 23 E4
Ismā'īlīya, Egypt 45 B11
Ismay, U.S.A. 70 B2
Isna, Egypt 45 C11
Isparta, Turkey 23 G5
Íspica, Italy 20 F6
Israel ■, Asia 41 D3
Issyk-Kul, Ozero,
  Kirghizia 24 E8
Istaihah, U.A.E. 39 F7
İstanbul, Turkey 21 D13
Istokpoga, L., U.S.A. 69 M5
Istra, Croatia 20 B5
Istria = Istra, Croatia 20 B5
Itabaiana, Brazil 79 E11
Itaberaba, Brazil 79 F10
Itabira, Brazil 79 G10
Itabuna, Brazil 79 F11
Itaipu Dam, Brazil 80 B6
Itaituba, Brazil 79 D7
Itajaí, Brazil 80 B7
Italy ■, Europe 20 D5
Itampolo, Madag. 49 C7
Itapecuru-Mirim, Brazil 79 D10
Itaperuna, Brazil 79 H10
Itapicuru →, Bahia,
  Brazil 79 F11
Itapicuru →,
  Maranhão, Brazil 79 D10
Itapipoca, Brazil 79 D11
Itaquatiara, Brazil 78 D7
Itaquí, Brazil 80 B5
Itatuba, Brazil 78 E6
Itchen →, U.K. 11 G6
Ithaca = Itháki, Greece 21 E9
Ithaca, U.S.A. 68 D7
Itháki, Greece 21 E9
Ito, Japan 29 G9
Itoigawa, Japan 29 F8
Itonamas →, Bolivia 78 F6
Ittoqqortoormiit =
  Scoresbysund,
  Greenland 4 B6
Ituaçu, Brazil 79 F10
Ituiutaba, Brazil 79 G9
Itumbiara, Brazil 79 G9
Ituna, Canada 65 C8
Iturbe, Argentina 80 A3
Iturup, Ostrov, Russia 25 E15
Ivalo, Finland 8 B19
Ivalojoki →, Finland 8 B19
Ivanhoe, N.S.W.,
  Australia 55 E3

Ivanhoe, W. Austral.,
  Australia 52 C4
Ivanhoe L., Canada 65 A7
Ivano-Frankivsk =
  Ivano-Frankovsk,
  Ukraine 23 E3
Ivano-Frankovsk,
  Ukraine 23 E3
Ivanovo, Belorussia 24 D3
Ivanovo, Russia 22 C7
Ivato, Madag. 49 C8
Ivdel, Russia 22 B11
Iviza = Ibiza, Spain 19 C6
Ivohibe, Madag. 49 C8
Ivory Coast ■, Africa 44 G3
Ivrea, Italy 20 B2
Ivugivik, Canada 61 B12
Iwahig, Phil. 32 C5
Iwaizumi, Japan 28 E10
Iwaki, Japan 29 F10
Iwakuni, Japan 29 G6
Iwamizawa, Japan 28 C10
Iwanai, Japan 28 C10
Iwata, Japan 29 G8
Iwate □, Japan 28 E10
Iwate-San, Japan 28 E10
Iwo, Nigeria 44 G5
Ixiamas, Bolivia 78 F5
Ixopo, S. Africa 49 E5
Iyo, Japan 29 H6
Izegem, Belgium 15 D3
Izena-Shima, Japan 29 L3
Izhevsk, Russia 22 C9
Izmayil = Ismail,
  Ukraine 23 E4
İzmir, Turkey 23 G4
İzmit, Turkey 23 F4
Izra, Syria 41 C5
Izu-Shotō, Japan 29 G10
Izumi-sano, Japan 29 G7
Izumo, Japan 29 G6

J

Jabal Lubnān, Lebanon 41 B4
Jabalpur, India 36 H11
Jabbūl, Syria 38 B3
Jablah, Syria 38 C3
Jablonec, Czech. 16 C7
Jaboatão, Brazil 79 E11
Jaburu, Brazil 78 E6
Jaca, Spain 19 A5
Jacareí, Brazil 80 A7
Jacarèzinho, Brazil 80 A7
Jackman, U.S.A. 63 C5
Jacksboro, U.S.A. 71 J5
Jackson, Australia 55 D4
Jackson, Ala., U.S.A. 69 K2
Jackson, Calif., U.S.A. 72 G3
Jackson, Ky., U.S.A. 68 G4
Jackson, Mich., U.S.A. 68 D3
Jackson, Minn., U.S.A. 70 D7
Jackson, Miss., U.S.A. 71 J9
Jackson, Mo., U.S.A. 71 G10
Jackson, Ohio, U.S.A. 68 F4
Jackson, Tenn., U.S.A. 69 H1
Jackson, Wyo., U.S.A. 72 E8
Jackson, L., U.S.A. 72 E8
Jackson B., N.Z. 51 K2
Jacksons, N.Z. 51 K3
Jacksonville, Ala.,
  U.S.A. 69 J3
Jacksonville, Fla.,
  U.S.A. 69 K5
Jacksonville, Ill., U.S.A. 70 F9
Jacksonville, N.C.,
  U.S.A. 69 H7
Jacksonville, Oreg.,
  U.S.A. 72 E2
Jacksonville, Tex.,
  U.S.A. 71 K7
Jacksonville Beach,
  U.S.A. 69 K5
Jacmel, Haiti 75 D10
Jacob Lake, U.S.A. 73 H7
Jacobabad, Pakistan 36 E6
Jacobina, Brazil 79 F10
Jacques-Cartier, Mt.,
  Canada 63 C6
Jacundá →, Brazil 79 D8
Jadotville = Likasi,
  Zaïre 46 G5
Jādū, Libya 45 B7
Jaén, Peru 78 E3
Jaén, Spain 19 D4
Jaffa = Tel Aviv-Yafo,
  Israel 41 C3
Jaffa, C., Australia 55 F2
Jaffna, Sri Lanka 36 Q12
Jagadhri, India 36 D10
Jagdalpur, India 37 K12
Jagersfontein, S. Africa 48 D4
Jagraon, India 36 D9
Jagtial, India 36 K11
Jaguariaíva, Brazil 80 A7
Jaguaribe →, Brazil 79 D11
Jahrom, Iran 39 D7
Jailolo, Indonesia 33 D7
Jailolo, Selat,
  Indonesia 33 D7
Jaipur, India 36 F9
Jājarm, Iran 39 B8
Jakarta, Indonesia 33 G12
Jakobstad, Finland 8 E17
Jal, U.S.A. 71 J3
Jalalabad, Afghan. 36 B7
Jalapa Enríquez,
  Mexico 74 D5

100

Jalgaon, *Maharashtra,*
  India 36 J10
Jalgaon, *Maharashtra,*
  India 36 J9
Jalibah, *Iraq* 38 D5
Jalna, *India* 36 K9
Jalón →, *Spain* 19 B5
Jalpaiguri, *India* 37 F16
Jaluit I., *Pac. Oc.* 56 G8
Jalūlā, *Iraq* 38 C5
Jamaica ■, *W. Indies* 74 J16
Jamalpur, *Bangla.* . . . 37 G16
Jamalpur, *India* 37 G15
Jamanxim →, *Brazil* 79 D7
Jambe, *Indonesia* 33 E8
Jambi, *Indonesia* 32 E2
Jambi □, *Indonesia* . . 32 E2
James →, *U.S.A.* 70 D6
James B., *Canada* . . . 61 C11
James Ras., *Australia* 52 D5
James Ross I.,
  Antarctica 5 C18
Jamestown, *Australia* 55 E2
Jamestown, *S. Africa* 48 E4
Jamestown, *Ky.,*
  U.S.A. 68 G3
Jamestown, *N. Dak.,*
  U.S.A. 70 B5
Jamestown, *N.Y.,*
  U.S.A. 68 D6
Jamestown, *Tenn.,*
  U.S.A. 69 G3
Jamīlābād, *Iran* 39 C6
Jamkhandi, *India* 36 L9
Jammu, *India* 36 C9
Jammu & Kashmir □,
  India 36 B10
Jamnagar, *India* 36 H7
Jamrud, *Pakistan* 36 C7
Jamshedpur, *India* . . . 37 H15
Jämtlands län □,
  Sweden 8 E12
Jan Kempdorp,
  S. Africa 48 D3
Jan L., *Canada* 65 C8
Jan Mayen, *Arctic* . . . 4 B7
Jand, *Pakistan* 36 C8
Jandaq, *Iran* 39 C7
Jandowae, *Australia* . 55 D5
Janesville, *U.S.A.* . . . 70 D10
Janīn, *Jordan* 41 C4
Januária, *Brazil* 79 G10
Janub Dârfûr □, *Sudan* 45 F9
Janub Kordofân □,
  Sudan 45 F10
Jaora, *India* 36 H9
Japan ■, *Asia* 29 G8
Japan, Sea of, *Asia* . . 28 E7
Japan Trench, *Pac. Oc.* 56 D6
Japen = Yapen,
  Indonesia 33 E9
Japurá →, *Brazil* 78 D5
Jaque, *Panama* 78 B3
Jarābulus, *Syria* 38 B3
Jarama →, *Spain* 19 B4
Jarash, *Jordan* 41 C4
Jargalant = Hovd,
  Mongolia 30 B4
Jarīr, W. al →,
  Si. Arabia 38 E4
Jarosław, *Poland* 17 C11
Jarrahdale, *Australia* . 53 F2
Jarso, *Ethiopia* 45 G12
Jarvis I., *Pac. Oc.* . . . 57 H12
Jarwa, *India* 37 F13
Jāsimīyah, *Iraq* 38 C5
Jasin, *Malaysia* 34 S15
Jāsk, *Iran* 39 E8
Jasło, *Poland* 17 D10
Jasper, *Canada* 64 C5
Jasper, *Ala., U.S.A.* . . 69 J2
Jasper, *Fla., U.S.A.* . . 69 K4
Jasper, *Minn., U.S.A.* . 70 D6
Jasper, *Tex., U.S.A.* . . 71 K8
Jasper Nat. Park,
  Canada 64 C5
Jassy = Iaşi, *Romania* 17 E13
Jászberény, *Hungary* . 17 E9
Jataí, *Brazil* 79 G8
Jatibarang, *Indonesia* 33 G13
Jatinegara, *Indonesia* 33 G12
Játiva, *Spain* 19 C5
Jaú, *Brazil* 79 H9
Jauja, *Peru* 78 F3
Jaunpur, *India* 37 G13
Java = Jawa,
  Indonesia 33 G14
Java Sea, *Indonesia* . 32 E3
Java Trench, *Ind. Oc.* 56 H2
Javhlant = Ulyasutay,
  Mongolia 30 B4
Jawa, *Indonesia* 33 G14
Jay, *U.S.A.* 71 G7
Jaya, Puncak,
  Indonesia 33 E9
Jayanti, *India* 37 F16
Jayapura, *Indonesia* . 33 E10
Jayawijaya,
  Pegunungan,
  Indonesia 33 E9
Jaynagar, *India* 37 F15
Jayrūd, *Syria* 38 C3
Jayton, *U.S.A.* 71 J4
Jazīreh-ye Shif, *Iran* . 39 D6
Jazzīn, *Lebanon* 41 B4
Jean, *U.S.A.* 73 J6
Jean Marie River,
  Canada 64 A4
Jeanerette, *U.S.A.* . . . 71 L9
Jeanette, Ostrov,
  Russia 25 B16
Jebba, *Nigeria* 44 G5

Jebel, Bahr el →,
  Sudan 45 G11
Jedburgh, *U.K.* 12 F6
Jedda = Jiddah,
  Si. Arabia 40 C2
Jędrzejów, *Poland* . . . 17 C10
Jedway, *Canada* 64 C2
Jefferson, *Iowa, U.S.A.* 70 D7
Jefferson, *Tex., U.S.A.* 71 J7
Jefferson, *Wis., U.S.A.* 70 D10
Jefferson, Mt., *Nev.,*
  U.S.A. 72 G5
Jefferson, Mt., *Oreg.,*
  U.S.A. 72 D3
Jefferson City, *Mo.,*
  U.S.A. 70 F8
Jefferson City, *Tenn.,*
  U.S.A. 69 G4
Jeffersonville, *U.S.A.* . 68 F3
Jega, *Nigeria* 44 F5
Jelenia Góra, *Poland* . 16 C7
Jelgava, *Latvia* 9 H17
Jellicoe, *Canada* 62 C2
Jemaja, *Indonesia* . . . 32 D3
Jember, *Indonesia* . . . 33 H15
Jembongan, *Malaysia* 32 C5
Jemeppe, *Belgium* . . . 15 D5
Jena, *Germany* 16 C5
Jena, *U.S.A.* 71 K8
Jenkins, *U.S.A.* 68 G4
Jennings, *U.S.A.* 71 K8
Jennings →, *Canada* 64 B2
Jeparit, *Australia* 55 F3
Jequié, *Brazil* 79 F10
Jequitinhonha, *Brazil* 79 G10
Jequitinhonha →,
  Brazil 79 G11
Jerada, *Morocco* 44 B4
Jerantut, *Malaysia* . . . 34 R15
Jérémie, *Haiti* 75 D10
Jerez de la Frontera,
  Spain 19 D2
Jerez de los
  Caballeros, *Spain* . . 19 C2
Jericho = Arīḥā, *Syria* 38 C3
Jericho = El Arīḥā,
  Jordan 41 D4
Jericho, *Australia* 54 C4
Jerilderie, *Australia* . . 55 F4
Jerome, *U.S.A.* 73 J8
Jersey, *Chan. Is.* 11 H5
Jersey City, *U.S.A.* . . . 68 E8
Jersey Shore, *U.S.A.* . 68 E7
Jerseyville, *U.S.A.* . . . 70 F9
Jerusalem, *Israel* 41 D4
Jervis B., *Australia* . . . 55 F5
Jesselton = Kota
  Kinabalu, *Malaysia* . 32 C5
Jessore, *Bangla.* 37 H16
Jesup, *U.S.A.* 69 K5
Jetmore, *U.S.A.* 71 F5
Jewett, *U.S.A.* 71 K6
Jeyhūnābād, *Iran* 39 C6
Jeypore, *India* 37 K13
Jhal Jhao, *Pakistan* . . 36 F4
Jhalawar, *India* 36 G10
Jhang Maghiana,
  Pakistan 36 D8
Jhansi, *India* 36 G11
Jharsaguda, *India* . . . 37 J14
Jhelum, *Pakistan* 36 C8
Jhelum →, *Pakistan* . 36 D8
Jhunjhunu, *India* 36 E9
Jiamusi, *China* 31 B8
Ji'an, *China* 31 D6
Jiangcheng, *China* . . . 30 D5
Jiangmen, *China* 31 D6
Jiangsu □, *China* 31 C7
Jiangxi □, *China* 31 D6
Jiaxing, *China* 31 C7
Jiayi, *Taiwan* 31 D7
Jibuti = Djibouti ■,
  Africa 40 E3
Jiddah, *Si. Arabia* . . . 40 C2
Jido, *India* 37 E19
Jiggalong, *Australia* . 52 D3
Jihlava, *Czech.* 16 D7
Jihlava →, *Czech.* . . . 16 D8
Jijel, *Algeria* 44 A6
Jijiga, *Ethiopia* 40 F3
Jilin, *China* 31 B7
Jilin □, *China* 31 B7
Jiloca →, *Spain* 19 B5
Jilong, *Taiwan* 31 D7
Jima, *Ethiopia* 45 G12
Jiménez, *Mexico* 74 B4
Jinan, *China* 31 C6
Jindabyne, *Australia* . 55 F4
Jingdezhen, *China* . . . 31 D6
Jinggu, *China* 30 D5
Jinhua, *China* 31 D6
Jining,
  Nei Mongol Zizhiqu,
  China 31 B6
Jining, Shandong,
  China 31 C6
Jinja, *Uganda* 46 D6
Jinnah Barrage,
  Pakistan 36 C7
Jinotega, *Nic.* 74 E7
Jinsha Jiang →, *China* 30 D5
Jinzhou, *China* 31 B7
Jiparaná →, *Brazil* . . . 78 E6
Jipijapa, *Ecuador* 78 D2
Jisr ash Shughūr,
  Syria 38 C3
Jitarning, *Australia* . . 53 F2
Jitra, *Malaysia* 34 N13
Jiu →, *Romania* 17 G11
Jiujiang, *China* 31 D6
Jixi, *China* 31 B8

Jīzān, *Si. Arabia* 40 D3
Jizō-Zaki, *Japan* 29 G6
Joaçaba, *Brazil* 80 B6
João Pessoa, *Brazil* . 79 E12
Joaquín V. González,
  Argentina 80 B4
Jodhpur, *India* 36 F8
Joensuu, *Finland* 22 B4
Jofane, *Mozam.* 49 C5
Joggins, *Canada* 63 C7
Jogjakarta =
  Yogyakarta,
  Indonesia 33 G14
Johannesburg,
  S. Africa 49 D4
John Day, *U.S.A.* 72 D4
John Day →, *U.S.A.* . 72 D3
John H. Kerr Res.,
  U.S.A. 69 G6
John o' Groats, *U.K.* . . 12 C5
John's Ra., *Australia* . 54 C1
Johnson, *U.S.A.* 71 G4
Johnson City, *N.Y.,*
  U.S.A. 68 D8
Johnson City, *Tenn.,*
  U.S.A. 69 G4
Johnson City, *Tex.,*
  U.S.A. 71 K5
Johnson's Crossing,
  Canada 64 A2
Johnston, L., *Australia* 53 F3
Johnston Falls =
  Mambilima Falls,
  Zambia 46 G5
Johnston I., *Pac. Oc.* . 57 F11
Johnstone Str., *Canada* 64 C3
Johnstown, *N.Y.,*
  U.S.A. 68 D8
Johnstown, *Pa., U.S.A.* 68 E6
Johor □, *Malaysia* . . . 34 S16
Johor Baharu,
  Malaysia 34 T16
Joinvile, *Brazil* 80 B7
Joinville I., *Antarctica* 5 C18
Jokkmokk, *Sweden* . . 8 C15
Jökulsá á Bru →,
  Iceland 8 D6
Jökulsá á Fjöllum →,
  Iceland 8 C5
Jolfā,
  Āzarbājān-e Sharqī,
  Iran 38 B5
Jolfā, *Eşfahan, Iran* . . 39 C6
Joliet, *U.S.A.* 68 E1
Joliette, *Canada* 62 C5
Jolo, *Phil.* 33 C6
Jombang, *Indonesia* . 33 G15
Jome, *Indonesia* 33 E7
Jones Sound, *Canada* 4 B3
Jonesboro, *Ark., U.S.A.* 71 H9
Jonesboro, *Ill., U.S.A.* 71 G10
Jonesboro, *La., U.S.A.* 71 J8
Jonesport, *U.S.A.* 63 D6
Jonglei □, *Sudan* 45 G11
Jönköping, *Sweden* . . 9 H13
Jönköpings län □,
  Sweden 9 H13
Jonquière, *Canada* . . 63 C5
Joplin, *U.S.A.* 71 G7
Jordan, *U.S.A.* 72 C10
Jordan ■, *Asia* 41 E5
Jordan →, *Asia* 41 D4
Jordan Valley, *U.S.A.* . 72 E5
Jorhat, *India* 37 F19
Jörn, *Sweden* 8 D16
Jorong, *Indonesia* . . . 32 E4
Jos, *Nigeria* 44 G6
Joseph, *U.S.A.* 72 D5
Joseph, L., *Canada* . . 63 B6
Joseph Bonaparte G.,
  Australia 52 B4
Joseph City, *U.S.A.* . . 73 J8
Jostedal, *Norway* 9 F9
Jotunheimen, *Norway* 9 F10
Jourdanton, *U.S.A.* . . 71 L5
Joussard, *Canada* . . . 64 B5
Juan de Fuca Str.,
  Canada 72 B2
Juan de Nova, *Ind. Oc.* 49 B7
Juan Fernández, Arch.
  de, *Pac. Oc.* 57 L20
Juárez, *Argentina* 80 D5
Juàzeiro, *Brazil* 79 E10
Juàzeiro do Norte,
  Brazil 79 E11
Jubayl, *Lebanon* 41 A4
Jubbah, *Si. Arabia* . . . 38 D4
Jubbulpore =
  Jabalpur, *India* 36 H11
Jubilee L., *Australia* . . 53 E4
Juby, C., *Morocco* . . . 44 C2
Júcar →, *Spain* 19 C5
Juchitán, *Mexico* 74 D5
Judaea = Har Yehuda,
  Israel 41 D3
Judith →, *U.S.A.* 72 C9
Judith Gap, *U.S.A.* . . . 72 C9
Jugoslavia =
  Yugoslavia ■,
  Europe 21 C8
Juiz de Fora, *Brazil* . . 79 H10
Julesburg, *U.S.A.* 70 E3
Juli, *Peru* 78 G5
Julia Cr. →, *Australia* 54 C3
Julia Creek, *Australia* 54 C3
Juliaca, *Peru* 78 G4
Julian, *U.S.A.* 73 K5
Julianehåb, *Greenland* 4 C5
Jullundur, *India* 36 D9
Jumet, *Belgium* 15 D4
Jumilla, *Spain* 19 C5
Jumla, *Nepal* 37 E13

Jumna = Yamuna →,
  India 37 G12
Junagadh, *India* 36 J7
Junction, *Tex., U.S.A.* 71 K5
Junction, *Utah, U.S.A.* 73 G7
Junction B., *Australia* 54 A1
Junction City, *Kans.,*
  U.S.A. 70 F6
Junction City, *Oreg.,*
  U.S.A. 72 D2
Junction Pt., *Australia* 54 A1
Jundah, *Australia* 54 C3
Jundiaí, *Brazil* 80 A7
Juneau, *U.S.A.* 60 C6
Junee, *Australia* 55 E4
Junggar Pendi, *China* 30 B3
Junín, *Argentina* 80 C4
Junín de los Andes,
  Argentina 80 D2
Jūniyah, *Lebanon* 41 B4
Juntura, *U.S.A.* 72 E4
Jupiter →, *Canada* . . . 63 C7
Jur, Nahr el →,
  Sudan 45 G10
Jura = Jura, Mts. du,
  Europe 18 C7
Jura = Schwäbische
  Alb, *Germany* 16 D4
Jura, *U.K.* 12 F3
Jura, Mts. du, *Europe* 18 C7
Jura, Sd. of, *U.K.* 12 F3
Jurado, *Colombia* 78 B3
Juruá →, *Brazil* 78 D5
Juruena →, *Brazil* . . . 78 E7
Juruti, *Brazil* 79 D7
Justo Daract,
  Argentina 80 C3
Jutland = Jylland,
  Denmark 9 H10
Juventud, I. de la,
  Cuba 75 C8
Juwain, *Afghan.* 36 D2
Jūy Zar, *Iran* 38 C5
Jylland, *Denmark* 9 H10
Jyväskylä, *Finland* . . . 8 E18

K

K2, Mt., *Pakistan* 36 B10
Kaap Plateau, *S. Africa* 48 D3
Kaapkruis, *Namibia* . . 48 C1
Kaapstad = Cape
  Town, *S. Africa* 48 E2
Kabaena, *Indonesia* . . 33 F6
Kabala, *S. Leone* 44 G2
Kabale, *Uganda* 46 E6
Kabalo, *Zaïre* 46 F5
Kabambare, *Zaïre* . . . 46 E5
Kabanjahe, *Indonesia* 32 D1
Kabara, *Mali* 44 E4
Kabardino-Balkar
  Republic □, *Russia* . 23 F7
Kabare, *Indonesia* . . . 33 E8
Kabarega Falls,
  Uganda 46 D6
Kabasalan, *Phil.* 33 C6
Kabba, *Nigeria* 44 G6
Kabinakagami L.,
  Canada 62 C3
Kabīr, Zab al →, *Iraq* 38 C4
Kabkabīyah, *Sudan* . . 45 F9
Kabompo →, *Zambia* 47 G4
Kabongo, *Zaïre* 46 F5
Kabra, *Australia* 54 C5
Kabūd Gonbad, *Iran* . 39 B8
Kābul, *Afghan.* 36 B6
Kābul □, *Afghan.* 36 B6
Kabul →, *Pakistan* . . . 36 C8
Kaburuang, *Indonesia* 33 D7
Kabwe, *Zambia* 47 G5
Kachchh, Gulf of, *India* 36 H6
Kachchh, Rann of,
  India 36 H7
Kachin □, *Burma* 37 F20
Kachiry, *Kazakhstan* . 24 D8
Kackar, *Turkey* 23 F7
Kadan Kyun, *Burma* . 34 F5
Kadina, *Australia* 55 E2
Kadiyevka, *Ukraine* . . 23 E6
Kadoka, *U.S.A.* 70 D4
Kadoma, *Zimbabwe* . . 47 H5
Kādugli, *Sudan* 45 F10
Kaduna, *Nigeria* 44 F6
Kaédi, *Mauritania* 44 E2
Kaélé, *Cameroon* 45 F7
Kaesŏng, *N. Korea* . . 31 C7
Kāf, *Si. Arabia* 38 D3
Kafakumba, *Zaïre* . . . 46 F4
Kafan, *Armenia* 23 G8
Kafanchan, *Nigeria* . . 44 G6
Kaffrine, *Senegal* 44 F1
Kafia Kingi, *Sudan* . . . 45 G9
Kafirévs, Ákra, *Greece* 21 E11
Kafue, *Zambia* 47 H5
Kafue →, *Zambia* . . . 47 H5
Kafulwe, *Zambia* 46 F5
Kaga Bandoro, *C.A.R.* 45 G8
Kagan, *Uzbekistan* . . 24 F7
Kagawa □, *Japan* . . . 29 G6
Kagoshima, *Japan* . . . 29 J5
Kagoshima □, *Japan* . 29 J5
Kahak, *Iran* 39 B6
Kahama, *Tanzania* . . . 46 E6
Kahayan →,
  Indonesia 32 E4
Kahemba, *Zaïre* 46 F3
Kahniah →, *Canada* . 64 B4
Kahnūj, *Iran* 39 E8
Kahoka, *U.S.A.* 70 E9

Kahoolawe, *U.S.A.* . . . 66 H16
Kahramanmaraş,
  Turkey 23 G6
Kai, Kepulauan,
  Indonesia 33 F8
Kai Besar, *Indonesia* . 33 F8
Kai Is. = Kai,
  Kepulauan,
  Indonesia 33 F8
Kai-Ketil, *Indonesia* . . 33 F8
Kaiama, *Nigeria* 44 G5
Kaiapoi, *N.Z.* 51 K4
Kaieteur Falls, *Guyana* 78 B7
Kaifeng, *China* 31 C6
Kaikohe, *N.Z.* 51 F4
Kaikoura, *N.Z.* 51 K4
Kaikoura Ra., *N.Z.* . . . 51 J4
Kailua, *U.S.A.* 66 J17
Kaimana, *Indonesia* . 33 E8
Kaimanawa Mts., *N.Z.* 51 H5
Kaingaroa Forest, *N.Z.* 51 H6
Kainji Res., *Nigeria* . . 44 F5
Kaipara Harbour, *N.Z.* 51 G5
Kaipokok B., *Canada* . 63 B8
Kaironi, *Indonesia* . . . 33 E8
Kairouan, *Tunisia* 44 A7
Kaiserslautern,
  Germany 16 D3
Kaitaia, *N.Z.* 51 F4
Kaitangata, *N.Z.* 51 M2
Kaiwi Channel, *U.S.A.* 66 H16
Kajaani, *Finland* 8 D19
Kajabbi, *Australia* 54 B3
Kajana = Kajaani,
  Finland 8 D19
Kajang, *Malaysia* 34 S14
Kajo Kaji, *Sudan* 45 H11
Kaka, *Sudan* 45 F11
Kakabeka Falls, *Canada* 62 C2
Kakamas, *S. Africa* . . 48 D3
Kakamega, *Kenya* . . . 46 D6
Kakanui Mts., *N.Z.* . . . 51 L3
Kake, *Japan* 29 G6
Kakegawa, *Japan* . . . 29 G9
Kakeroma-Jima, *Japan* 29 K4
Kakhovka, *Ukraine* . . . 23 E5
Kakhovskoye Vdkhr.,
  Ukraine 23 E5
Kakinada, *India* 37 L13
Kakisa →, *Canada* . . . 64 A5
Kakisa L., *Canada* . . . 64 A5
Kakogawa, *Japan* . . . 29 G7
Kakwa →, *Canada* . . . 64 C5
Kāl Gūsheh, *Iran* 39 D8
Kāl Safīd, *Iran* 38 C5
Kalabagh, *Pakistan* . . 36 C7
Kalabahi, *Indonesia* . . 33 F6
Kalabáka, *Greece* . . . 21 E9
Kalabo, *Zambia* 47 G4
Kalach, *Russia* 23 D7
Kaladan →, *Burma* . . 37 J18
Kalahari, *Africa* 48 C3
Kalahari Gemsbok Nat.
  Park, *S. Africa* 48 D3
Kālak, *Iran* 39 E8
Kalakamati, *Botswana* 49 C4
Kalakan, *Russia* 25 D12
Kalakh, *Syria* 38 C3
Kalama, *U.S.A.* 72 D2
Kalámata, *Greece* . . . 21 F10
Kalamazoo, *U.S.A.* . . . 68 D3
Kalamazoo →, *U.S.A.* 68 D2
Kalannie, *Australia* . . . 53 F2
Kalántari, *Iran* 39 C7
Kalao, *Indonesia* 33 F6
Kalaotoa, *Indonesia* . 33 F6
Kalasin, *Thailand* 34 D7
Kalat, *Pakistan* 36 E5
Kalāteh, *Iran* 39 B7
Kalāteh-ye-Ganj, *Iran* 39 E8
Kalbarri, *Australia* . . . 53 E1
Kalegauk Kyun, *Burma* 37 M20
Kalemie, *Zaïre* 46 F5
Kalewa, *Burma* 37 H19
Kálfafellsstaður,
  Iceland 8 D6
Kalgan = Zhangjiakou,
  China 31 B6
Kalgoorlie-Boulder,
  Australia 53 F3
Kaliakra, Nos, *Bulgaria* 21 C13
Kalianda, *Indonesia* . . 32 F3
Kalibo, *Phil.* 33 B6
Kalima, *Zaïre* 46 E5
Kalimantan, *Indonesia* 32 E4
Kalimantan Barat □,
  Indonesia 32 E4
Kalimantan Selatan □,
  Indonesia 32 E5
Kalimantan Tengah □,
  Indonesia 32 E4
Kalimantan Timur □,
  Indonesia 32 D5
Kálimnos, *Greece* . . . 21 F12
Kalinin = Tver, *Russia* 22 C6
Kaliningrad, *Russia* . . 22 C6
Kaliningrad, *Russia* . . 22 D3
Kalispell, *U.S.A.* 72 B6
Kalisz, *Poland* 17 C9
Kaliua, *Tanzania* 46 F6
Kalix →, *Sweden* 8 D17
Kalkaska, *U.S.A.* 68 C3
Kalkfeld, *Namibia* . . . 48 C2
Kalkfontein, *Botswana* 48 C3
Kalkrand, *Namibia* . . . 48 C2
Kallsjön, *Sweden* 8 E12
Kalmar, *Sweden* 9 H14
Kalmyk Republic □,
  Russia 23 E8
Kalmykovo,
  Kazakhstan 23 E9
Kalocsa, *Hungary* . . . 17 E9

Kalomo, *Zambia* 47 H5
Kaluga, *Russia* 22 D6
Kalundborg, *Denmark* 9 J11
Kalutara, *Sri Lanka* . . 36 R11
Kalya, *Russia* 22 B10
Kama →, *Russia* 22 C9
Kamaishi, *Japan* 28 E10
Kamaran, *Yemen* 40 D3
Kambalda, *Australia* . 53 F3
Kambarka, *Russia* . . . 22 C9
Kamchatka, P-ov.,
  Russia 25 D16
Kamchatka Pen. =
  Kamchatka, P-ov.,
  Russia 25 D16
Kamen, *Russia* 24 D9
Kamen-Rybolov,
  Russia 28 B6
Kamenets-Podolskiy,
  Ukraine 23 E4
Kamenjak, Rt., *Croatia* 20 B5
Kamenka, *Russia* 22 A7
Kamensk Uralskiy,
  Russia 24 D7
Kamenskoye, *Russia* . 25 C17
Kameoka, *Japan* 29 G7
Kamiah, *U.S.A.* 72 C5
Kamieskroon, *S. Africa* 48 E2
Kamilukuak, L., *Canada* 65 A8
Kamina, *Zaïre* 46 F5
Kaminak L., *Canada* . 65 A9
Kaminoyama, *Japan* . 28 E10
Kamloops, *Canada* . . 64 C4
Kamo, *Japan* 28 F9
Kampala, *Uganda* . . . 46 D6
Kampar, *Malaysia* . . . 34 Q14
Kampar →, *Indonesia* 32 D2
Kampen, *Neths.* 15 B5
Kampot, *Cambodia* . . 34 G8
Kampuchea =
  Cambodia ■, *Asia* . 34 F8
Kampung →,
  Indonesia 33 F9
Kampungbaru =
  Tolitoli, *Indonesia* . . 33 D6
Kamrau, Teluk,
  Indonesia 33 E8
Kamsack, *Canada* . . . 65 C8
Kamskoye Vdkhr.,
  Russia 22 C10
Kamuchawie L.,
  Canada 65 B8
Kamui-Misaki, *Japan* . 28 C10
Kamyanets-Podilskyy
  = Kamenets-
  Podolskiy, *Ukraine* . 23 E4
Kāmyārān, *Iran* 38 C5
Kamyshin, *Russia* . . . 23 D8
Kanaaupscow, *Canada* 62 B4
Kanab, *U.S.A.* 73 H7
Kanab Creek, *U.S.A.* . 73 H7
Kanagi, *Japan* 28 D10
Kanairiktok →,
  Canada 63 A7
Kananga, *Zaïre* 46 F4
Kanarraville, *U.S.A.* . . 73 H7
Kanash, *Russia* 22 C8
Kanawha →, *U.S.A.* . . 68 F4
Kanazawa, *Japan* . . . 29 F8
Kanchanaburi,
  Thailand 34 E5
Kanchenjunga, *Nepal* 37 F16
Kanchipuram, *India* . . 36 N11
Kanda Kanda, *Zaïre* . . 46 F4
Kandahar = Qandahār,
  Afghan. 36 D4
Kandalaksha, *Russia* . 22 A5
Kandalakshkiy Zaliv,
  Russia 22 A5
Kandalu, *Afghan.* 36 E3
Kandangan, *Indonesia* 32 E5
Kandi, *Benin* 44 F5
Kandla, *India* 36 H7
Kandos, *Australia* . . . 55 E4
Kandy, *Sri Lanka* 36 R12
Kane, *U.S.A.* 68 E6
Kane Basin, *Greenland* 4 B4
Kangān, *Fārs, Iran* . . . 39 E7
Kangān, *Hormozgān,*
  Iran 39 E8
Kangar, *Malaysia* 34 N13
Kangaroo I., *Australia* 55 F2
Kangavar, *Iran* 39 C6
Kangean, Kepulauan,
  Indonesia 32 F5
Kangean Is. =
  Kangean, Kepulauan,
  Indonesia 32 F5
Kango, *Gabon* 46 D2
Kangto, *India* 37 F18
Kaniapiskau →,
  Canada 63 A6
Kaniapiskau L., *Canada* 63 B6
Kanin, P-ov., *Russia* . . 22 A8
Kanin Nos, Mys,
  Russia 22 A7
Kanin Pen. = Kanin, P-
  ov., *Russia* 22 A8
Kaniva, *Australia* 55 F3
Kankakee, *U.S.A.* 68 E1
Kankakee →, *U.S.A.* . 68 E1
Kankan, *Guinea* 44 F3
Kanker, *India* 37 J12
Kankunskiy, *Russia* . . 25 D13
Kannapolis, *U.S.A.* . . . 69 H5
Kannauj, *India* 36 F11
Kannod, *India* 36 H10
Kano, *Nigeria* 44 F6
Kan'onji, *Japan* 29 G6
Kanowit, *Malaysia* . . . 32 D4
Kanowna, *Australia* . . 53 F3
Kanoya, *Japan* 29 J5

Kanpetlet, Burma 37 J18
Kanpur, India 36 F12
Kansas □, U.S.A. 70 F6
Kansas →, U.S.A. 70 F7
Kansas City, Kans., U.S.A. 70 F7
Kansas City, Mo., U.S.A. 70 F7
Kansk, Russia 25 D10
Kansu = Gansu □, China 30 C5
Kantang, Thailand .. 34 J5
Kantō □, Japan 29 F9
Kantō-Sanchi, Japan 29 G9
Kanturk, Ireland 13 D3
Kanuma, Japan 29 F9
Kanus, Namibia 48 D2
Kanye, Botswana 48 C4
Kaohsiung = Gaoxiong, Taiwan . 31 D7
Kaohsiung, Taiwan .. 31 D7
Kaokoveld, Namibia . 48 B1
Kaolack, Senegal ... 44 F1
Kapanga, Zaïre 46 F4
Kapchagai, Kazakhstan 24 E8
Kapela, Croatia 20 B6
Kapfenberg, Austria . 16 E7
Kapiri Mposhi, Zambia 47 G5
Kapiskau →, Canada . 62 B3
Kapit, Malaysia 32 D4
Kapiti I., N.Z. 51 J5
Kapoeta, Sudan 45 H11
Kaposvár, Hungary .. 17 E8
Kapps, Namibia 48 C2
Kapuas →, Indonesia 32 E3
Kapuas Hulu, Pegunungan, Malaysia 32 D4
Kapuas Hulu Ra. = Kapuas Hulu, Pegunungan, Malaysia 32 D4
Kapunda, Australia .. 55 E2
Kapuni, N.Z. 51 H5
Kapuskasing, Canada 62 C3
Kapuskasing →, Canada 62 C3
Kaputar, Australia .. 55 E5
Kara, Russia 24 C7
Kara Bogaz Gol, Zaliv, Turkmenistan 23 F9
Kara Kalpak Republic □, Uzbekistan 24 E6
Kara Kum = Karakum, Peski, Turkmenistan 24 F6
Kara Sea, Russia ... 24 B7
Karabutak, Kazakhstan 24 E7
Karachi, Pakistan ... 36 G5
Karad, India 36 L9
Karadeniz Boğazı, Turkey 21 D13
Karaganda, Kazakhstan 24 E8
Karagayly, Kazakhstan 24 E8
Karaginskiy, Ostrov, Russia 25 D17
Karagiye Depression, Kazakhstan 23 F9
Karaikal, India 36 P11
Karaikkudi, India ... 36 P11
Karaj, Iran 39 C6
Karakas, Kazakhstan . 24 E9
Karakitang, Indonesia 33 D7
Karaklis, Armenia ... 23 F7
Karakoram Pass, Pakistan 36 B10
Karakoram Ra., Pakistan 36 B10
Karakum, Peski, Turkmenistan 24 F6
Karalon, Russia 25 D12
Karaman, Turkey ... 23 G5
Karamay, China 30 B3
Karambu, Indonesia . 32 E5
Karamea Bight, N.Z. . 51 J3
Karand, Iran 38 C5
Karanganyar, Indonesia 33 G13
Karasburg, Namibia . 48 D2
Karasino, Russia 24 C9
Karasjok, Norway ... 8 B18
Karasuk, Russia 24 D8
Karasuyama, Japan . 29 F10
Karatau, Kazakhstan . 24 E8
Karatau, Khrebet, Kazakhstan 24 E7
Karawang, Indonesia 33 G12
Karawanken, Europe . 20 A6
Karazhal, Kazakhstan 24 E8
Karbalā, Iraq 38 C5
Karcag, Hungary ... 17 E10
Karda, Russia 25 D11
Kardhítsa, Greece .. 21 E9
Kareeberge, S. Africa 48 E3
Karelian Republic □, Russia 22 A5
Karen, India 34 F2
Kärevändar, Iran ... 39 E9
Kargasok, Russia ... 24 D9
Kargat, Russia 24 D9
Kargil, India 36 B10
Kargopol, Russia ... 22 B6
Kariān, Iran 39 E8
Kariba, Zimbabwe .. 47 H5
Kariba Dam, Zimbabwe 47 H5
Kariba Gorge, Zambia 47 H5
Karibib, Namibia ... 48 C2
Karimata, Kepulauan, Indonesia 32 E3
Karimata, Selat, Indonesia 32 E3

Karimata Is. = Karimata, Kepulauan, Indonesia 32 E3
Karimnagar, India .. 36 K11
Karimunjawa, Kepulauan, Indonesia 32 F4
Karin, Somali Rep. ... 40 E4
Karīt, Iran 39 C8
Kariya, Japan 29 G8
Karkaralinsk, Kazakhstan 24 E8
Karkinitskiy Zaliv, Ukraine 23 E5
Karl-Marx-Stadt = Chemnitz, Germany 16 C6
Karlovac, Croatia ... 20 B6
Karlovy Vary, Czech. . 16 C6
Karlsbad = Karlovy Vary, Czech. 16 C6
Karlsborg, Sweden .. 9 G13
Karlshamn, Sweden . 9 H13
Karlskoga, Sweden .. 9 G13
Karlskrona, Sweden . 9 H13
Karlsruhe, Germany . 16 D4
Karlstad, Sweden ... 9 G12
Karlstad, U.S.A. 70 A6
Karnal, India 36 E10
Karnali →, Nepal ... 37 E12
Karnaphuli Res., Bangla. 37 H18
Karnataka □, India .. 36 N10
Karnes City, U.S.A. . 71 L6
Karnische Alpen, Europe 20 A5
Kärnten □, Austria .. 16 E6
Karonga, Malawi ... 46 F6
Karoonda, Australia . 55 F2
Karora, Sudan 45 E12
Kárpathos, Greece .. 21 G12
Karpinsk, Russia ... 22 C11
Karpogory, Russia .. 22 B7
Kars, Turkey 23 F7
Karsakpay, Kazakhstan 24 E7
Karshi, Uzbekistan .. 24 F7
Karsun, Russia 22 D8
Kartaly, Russia 24 D7
Karufa, Indonesia ... 33 E8
Karumba, Australia .. 54 B3
Karungu, Kenya 46 E6
Karwar, India 36 M9
Kas Kong, Cambodia . 34 G7
Kasai →, Zaïre 46 E3
Kasama, Zambia ... 46 G6
Kasane, Namibia ... 48 B3
Kasanga, Tanzania .. 46 F6
Kasangulu, Zaïre ... 46 E3
Kasaragod, India ... 36 N9
Kasba L., Canada ... 65 A8
Käseh Garān, Iran .. 38 C5
Kasempa, Zambia ... 47 G5
Kasenga, Zaïre 46 G5
Kashabowie, Canada 62 C1
Kāshān, Iran 39 C6
Kashi, China 30 C2
Kashiwazaki, Japan . 29 F9
Kashk-e Kohneh, Afghan. 36 B3
Kāshmar, Iran 39 C8
Kashmir, Asia 36 B10
Kashun Noerh = Gaxun Nur, China . 30 B5
Kasimov, Russia 22 D7
Kasiruta, Indonesia . 33 E7
Kaskaskia →, U.S.A. . 70 G10
Kaskattama →, Canada 65 B10
Kaskinen, Finland ... 8 E16
Kaskö, Finland 8 E16
Kaslo, Canada 64 D5
Kasmere L., Canada . 65 B8
Kasongo, Zaïre 46 E5
Kasongo Lunda, Zaïre 46 F3
Kásos, Greece 21 G12
Kassala, Sudan 45 E12
Kassalā □, Sudan ... 45 E12
Kassel, Germany ... 16 C4
Kassue, Indonesia .. 33 F9
Kastamonu, Turkey . 23 F5
Kastoria, Greece ... 21 D9
Kasulu, Tanzania ... 46 E6
Kasumi, Japan 29 G7
Kasur, Pakistan 36 D9
Kata, Russia 25 D11
Katako Kombe, Zaïre . 46 E4
Katamatite, Australia . 55 F4
Katangi, India 36 J11
Katangli, Russia ... 25 D15
Katha, Burma 37 G20
Katherine, Australia . 52 B5
Kathiawar, India ... 36 H7
Kathithar, India 37 G15
Katima Mulilo, Zambia 48 B3
Katingan = Mendawai →, Indonesia 32 E4
Katiola, Ivory C. ... 44 G3
Katmandu, Nepal ... 37 F14
Katoomba, Australia . 55 E5
Katowice, Poland ... 17 C9
Katrine, L., U.K. 12 E4
Katrineholm, Sweden 9 G14
Katsepe, Madag. ... 49 B8
Katsina, Nigeria ... 44 F6
Katsumoto, Japan .. 29 H4
Katsuura, Japan 29 G10
Katsuyama, Japan .. 29 F8
Kattegatt, Denmark . 9 H11
Katwijk-aan-Zee, Neths. 15 B4
Kauai, U.S.A. 66 H15

Kauai Chan., U.S.A. .. 66 H15
Kaufman, U.S.A. 71 J6
Kaukauna, U.S.A. ... 68 C1
Kaukauveld, Namibia 48 C3
Kaukonen, Finland .. 8 C18
Kauliranta, Finland .. 8 C17
Kaunas, Lithuania .. 22 D3
Kaura Namoda, Nigeria 44 F6
Kautokeino, Norway . 8 B17
Kavacha, Russia 25 C17
Kavalerovo, Russia .. 28 B7
Kavali, India 36 M12
Kavār, Iran 39 D7
Kaválla, Greece 21 D11
Kaw, Fr. Guiana ... 79 C8
Kawagoe, Japan 29 G9
Kawaguchi, Japan .. 29 G9
Kawaihae, U.S.A. ... 66 H17
Kawambwa, Zambia . 46 F5
Kawanoe, Japan 29 G6
Kawardha, India ... 37 J12
Kawasaki, Japan ... 29 G9
Kawene, Canada ... 62 C1
Kawerau, N.Z. 51 H6
Kawhia Harbour, N.Z. 51 H5
Kawio, Kepulauan, Indonesia 33 D7
Kawnro, Burma 37 H21
Kawthaung, Burma .. 34 G5
Kawthoolei = Kawthule □, Burma . 37 L20
Kawthule □, Burma .. 37 L20
Kaya, Burkina Faso .. 44 F4
Kayah □, Burma 37 K20
Kayan →, Indonesia . 32 D5
Kaycee, U.S.A. 72 E10
Kayeli, Indonesia ... 33 E7
Kayenta, U.S.A. 73 H8
Kayes, Mali 44 F2
Kayoa, Indonesia ... 33 D7
Kayrunnera, Australia 55 E3
Kayseri, Turkey 23 G6
Kaysville, U.S.A. ... 72 F8
Kayuagung, Indonesia 32 E2
Kazachinskoye, Russia 25 D11
Kazachye, Russia ... 25 B14
Kazakhstan ■, Asia .. 24 E7
Kazan, Russia 22 C8
Kazan-Rettō, Pac. Oc. 56 E6
Kazanlúk, Bulgaria .. 21 C11
Kazerūn, Iran 39 D6
Kazi Magomed = Kazumba, Zaïre ... 46 F4
Kazuno, Japan 28 D10
Kazym →, Russia ... 24 C7
Ké-Macina, Mali 44 F3
Kéa, Greece 21 F11
Keams Canyon, U.S.A. 73 J8
Kearney, U.S.A. 70 E5
Keban, Turkey 23 G6
Kebnekaise, Sweden . 8 C15
Kebri Dehar, Ethiopia 40 F3
Kebumen, Indonesia . 33 G13
Kechika →, Canada .. 64 B3
Kecskemét, Hungary . 17 E9
Kedgwick, Canada .. 63 C6
Kedia Hill, Botswana 48 C3
Kediri, Indonesia ... 33 G15
Kédougou, Senegal .. 44 F2
Keeley L., Canada .. 65 C7
Keeling Is. = Cocos Is., Ind. Oc. 35 F8
Keelung = Chilung, Taiwan 31 D7
Keene, U.S.A. 68 D9
Keeper Hill, Ireland . 13 D3
Keer-Weer, C., Australia 54 A3
Keetmanshoop, Namibia 48 D2
Keewatin, U.S.A. ... 70 B8
Keewatin □, Canada . 65 A9
Keewatin →, Canada 65 B8
Kefallinía, Greece .. 21 E9
Kefamenanu, Indonesia 33 F6
Keffi, Nigeria 44 G6
Keflavík, Iceland ... 8 D2
Keg River, Canada .. 64 B5
Kegaska, Canada ... 63 B7
Keighley, U.K. 10 D6
Keimoes, S. Africa .. 48 D3
Keith, Australia 55 F3
Keith, U.K. 12 D6
Keith Arm, Canada .. 60 B7
Kejser Franz Joseph Fjord = Kong Franz Joseph Fd., Greenland 4 B6
Kekri, India 36 G9
Kël, Russia 25 C13
Kelang, Malaysia ... 34 R14
Kelantan □, Malaysia 34 P15
Kelantan →, Malaysia 34 N15
Kelibia, Tunisia 45 A7
Kellé, Congo 46 E2
Keller, U.S.A. 72 B4
Kellerberrin, Australia 53 F2
Kellett, C., Canada .. 4 B1
Kellogg, U.S.A. 72 C5
Kelloselkä, Finland . 8 C20
Kells = Ceanannus Mor, Ireland 13 C5
Kélo, Chad 45 G8
Kelowna, Canada ... 64 D5
Kelsey Bay, Canada . 64 C3
Kelso, N.Z. 51 L2
Kelso, U.K. 12 F6
Kelso, U.S.A. 72 C2
Keluang, Malaysia .. 34 S16
Kelvington, Canada . 65 C8

Kem, Russia 22 B5
Kem →, Russia 22 B5
Kema, Indonesia ... 33 D7
Kemano, Canada ... 64 C3
Kemerovo, Russia .. 24 D9
Kemi, Finland 8 D18
Kemi älv = Kemijoki →, Finland 8 D18
Kemijärvi, Finland .. 8 C19
Kemijoki →, Finland 8 D18
Kemmerer, U.S.A. .. 72 F8
Kemmuna = Comino, Malta 20 F6
Kemp L., U.S.A. 71 J5
Kemp Land, Antarctica 5 C5
Kempsey, Australia . 55 E5
Kempt, L., Canada .. 62 C5
Kempten, Germany . 16 E5
Kemptville, Canada . 62 C4
Kendal, Indonesia .. 32 F4
Kendal, U.K. 10 C5
Kendall, Australia .. 55 E5
Kendall →, Australia 54 A3
Kendallville, U.S.A. . 68 E3
Kendari, Indonesia . 33 E6
Kendawangan, Indonesia 32 E4
Kende, Nigeria 44 F5
Kendenup, Australia 53 F2
Kendrapara, India .. 37 J15
Kendrew, S. Africa .. 48 E3
Kendrick, U.S.A. ... 72 C5
Kenedy, U.S.A. 71 L6
Kenema, S. Leone .. 44 G2
Keng Tawng, Burma 37 J21
Keng Tung, Burma .. 37 J21
Kenge, Zaïre 46 E3
Kenhardt, S. Africa . 48 D3
Kenitra, Morocco ... 44 B3
Kenmare, Ireland .. 13 E2
Kenmare, U.S.A. ... 70 A3
Kenmare →, Ireland 13 E2
Kennebec, U.S.A. .. 70 D5
Kennedy Ra., Australia 53 D2
Kennedy Taungdeik, Burma 37 H18
Kennet →, U.K. 11 F7
Kenneth Ra., Australia 52 D2
Kennett, U.S.A. 71 G9
Kennewick, U.S.A. .. 72 C4
Kénogami, Canada .. 63 C5
Kenogami →, Canada 62 B3
Kenora, Canada 65 D10
Kenosha, U.S.A. ... 68 D2
Kensington, Canada . 63 C7
Kensington, U.S.A. . 70 F5
Kensington Downs, Australia 54 C3
Kent, Ohio, U.S.A. .. 68 E5
Kent, Oreg., U.S.A. . 72 D3
Kent, Tex., U.S.A. .. 71 K2
Kent □, U.K. 11 F8
Kent Group, Australia 54 F4
Kent Pen., Canada .. 60 B9
Kentau, Kazakhstan . 24 E7
Kentland, U.S.A. ... 68 E2
Kenton, U.S.A. 68 E4
Kentucky □, U.S.A. . 68 G3
Kentucky →, U.S.A. 68 F3
Kentucky L., U.S.A. . 69 G2
Kentville, Canada .. 63 C7
Kentwood, U.S.A. .. 71 K9
Kentwood, La., U.S.A. 71 K9
Kenya ■, Africa 46 E7
Kenya, Mt., Kenya .. 46 E7
Keokuk, U.S.A. 70 E9
Kepi, Indonesia 33 F9
Kerala □, India 36 P10
Kerama-Rettō, Japan 29 L3
Kerang, Australia .. 55 F3
Keraudren, C., Australia 52 C2
Kerch, Ukraine 23 E6
Kerchoual, Mali 44 E5
Keren, Eritrea 45 E12
Kerguelen, Ind. Oc. . 35 J5
Kericho, Kenya 46 E7
Kerinci, Indonesia .. 32 E2
Kerki, Turkmenistan . 24 F7
Kérkira, Greece 21 E8
Kerkrade, Neths. ... 15 D6
Kermadec Is., Pac. Oc. 56 K10
Kermadec Trench, Pac. Oc. 56 L10
Kermān, Iran 39 D8
Kermān □, Iran 39 D8
Kermānshāh = Bākhtarān, Iran ... 38 C5
Kermit, U.S.A. 71 K3
Kern →, U.S.A. 73 J4
Kerrobert, Canada .. 65 C7
Kerrville, U.S.A. ... 71 K5
Kerry □, Ireland ... 13 D2
Kerry Hd., Ireland .. 13 D2
Kertosono, Indonesia 33 G15
Kerulen →, Asia ... 31 B6
Kerzaz, Algeria 44 C4
Kesagami, Canada ... 62 B4
Kesagami L., Canada 62 B3
Kesennuma, Japan .. 28 E10
Keshit, Iran 39 D8
Keski-Suomen lääni □, Finland 8 E18
Kestell, S. Africa ... 49 D4
Kestenga, Russia ... 22 A5
Keswick, U.K. 10 C4
Ket →, Russia 24 D9
Keta, Ghana 44 G5
Ketapang, Indonesia 32 E4
Ketchikan, U.S.A. .. 60 C6
Ketchum, U.S.A. ... 72 E6

Kettering, U.K. 11 E7
Kettle →, Canada .. 65 B11
Kettle Falls, U.S.A. . 72 B4
Kevin, U.S.A. 72 B8
Kewanee, U.S.A. ... 70 E10
Kewaunee, U.S.A. .. 68 C2
Keweenaw B., U.S.A. 68 B1
Keweenaw Pen., U.S.A. 68 B2
Keweenaw Pt., U.S.A. 68 B2
Key Harbour, Canada 62 C3
Key West, U.S.A. ... 67 F10
Keyser, U.S.A. 68 F6
Keystone, U.S.A. ... 70 D3
Kezhma, Russia 25 D11
Khabarovo, Russia .. 24 C7
Khabarovsk, Russia . 25 E14
Khabr, Iran 39 D8
Khābūr →, Syria ... 38 C4
Khairpur, Pakistan .. 36 F6
Khakhea, Botswana . 48 C3
Khalafābād, Iran ... 39 D6
Khalīlī, Iran 39 E7
Khalkhāl, Iran 39 B6
Khalkís, Greece 21 E10
Khalmer-Sede = Tazovskiy, Russia . 24 C8
Khalmer Yu, Russia . 25 A12
Khalturin, Russia ... 22 C8
Khalūf, Oman 40 C6
Kham Keut, Laos ... 34 C8
Khamas Country, Botswana 48 C4
Khambat, G. of, India 36 J8
Khambhat, India ... 36 H8
Khamir, Iran 39 E7
Khamir, Yemen 40 D3
Khamsa, Egypt 41 E1
Khān Abū Shāmat, Syria 41 B5
Khān Āzād, Iraq ... 38 C5
Khān Mujiddah, Iraq . 38 C4
Khān Shaykhūn, Syria 38 C3
Khān Yūnis, Egypt .. 41 D3
Khānaqin, Iraq 38 C5
Khānbāghī, Iran ... 39 B7
Khandwa, India 36 J10
Khandyga, Russia .. 25 C14
Khāneh, Iran 38 B5
Khanewal, Pakistan . 36 D7
Khaniá, Greece 21 G11
Khanion, Kólpos, Greece 21 G10
Khanka, Ozero, Asia . 25 E14
Khankendy, Azerbaijan 23 G8
Khanty-Mansiysk, Russia 24 C7
Khapcheranga, Russia 25 E12
Kharagpur, India ... 37 H15
Kharan Kalat, Pakistan 36 E4
Kharānaq, Iran 39 C7
Kharda, India 36 K9
Khārga, El Wâhât el, Egypt 45 C11
Khargon, India 36 J9
Khārk, Jazireh, Iran . 39 D6
Kharkiv = Kharkov, Ukraine 23 E6
Kharkov, Ukraine ... 23 E6
Kharovsk, Russia ... 22 C7
Khartoum = El Khartûm, Sudan .. 45 E11
Khasan, Russia 28 C5
Khāsh, Iran 36 E2
Khashm el Girba, Sudan 45 F12
Khaskovo, Bulgaria . 21 D11
Khatanga, Russia .. 25 B11
Khatanga →, Russia 25 B11
Khātūnābād, Iran .. 39 C6
Khatyrka, Russia ... 25 C18
Khaybar, Harrat, Si. Arabia 38 E4
Khāzimiyah, Iraq ... 38 C4
Khed Brahma, India 36 G8
Khemmarat, Thailand 34 D8
Khenāmān, Iran ... 39 D8
Khenchela, Algeria . 44 A6
Khenifra, Morocco .. 44 B3
Kherson, Ukraine .. 23 E5
Kheta →, Russia ... 25 B11
Khilok, Russia 25 D12
Khíos, Greece 21 E12
Khirbat Qanāfār, Lebanon 41 B4
Khiuma = Hiiumaa, Estonia 22 C3
Khiva, Uzbekistan .. 24 E7
Khīyāv, Iran 38 B5
Khlong →, Thailand 34 E5
Khmelnitskiy, Ukraine 23 E4
Khmelnytskyy = Khmelnitskiy, Ukraine 23 E4
Khmer Rep. = Cambodia ■, Asia . 34 F8
Khodzent, Tajikistan 24 E7
Khojak P., Afghan. .. 36 D5
Kholm, Russia 22 C5
Kholmsk, Russia ... 25 E15
Khomas Hochland, Namibia 48 C2
Khomayn, Iran 39 C6
Khon Kaen, Thailand 34 D7
Khong, Cambodia .. 34 E8
Khong →, Laos 34 E9
Khonu, Russia 25 C15
Khoper →, Russia .. 24 C5
Khorāsān □, Iran .. 39 C8
Khorat = Nakhon Ratchasima, Thailand 34 E7

Khorat, Cao Nguyen, Thailand 34 E7
Khorixas, Namibia .. 48 C1
Khorog, Tajikistan .. 24 F8
Khorramābād, Khorāsān, Iran ... 39 C8
Khorramābād, Lorestān, Iran ... 39 C6
Khorrāmshahr, Iran . 39 D6
Khosravī, Iran 39 D6
Khosrowābād, Khuzestān, Iran .. 39 D6
Khosrowābād, Kordestān, Iran .. 38 C5
Khosuyeh, Iran 39 D7
Khouribga, Morocco 44 B3
Khowai, Bangla. ... 37 G17
Khu Khan, Thailand . 34 E8
Khuff, Si. Arabia ... 38 E5
Khūgiānī, Afghan. .. 36 D4
Khulna, Bangla. ... 37 H16
Khulna □, Bangla. .. 37 H16
Khumago, Botswana 48 C3
Khūnsorkh, Iran ... 39 E8
Khūr, Iran 39 C8
Khūrayş, Si. Arabia . 39 E6
Khūrīyā Mūrīyā, Jazā 'ir, Oman 40 D6
Khūsf, Iran 39 C8
Khush, Afghan. 36 C3
Khushab, Pakistan .. 36 C8
Khuzdar, Pakistan .. 36 F5
Khŭzestān □, Iran .. 39 D6
Khvājeh, Iran 38 B5
Khvānsār, Iran 39 D7
Khvor, Iran 39 C7
Khvorgū, Iran 39 E8
Khvormūj, Iran 39 D6
Khvoy, Iran 38 B5
Khyber Pass, Afghan. 36 B7
Kiama, Australia ... 55 E5
Kiamba, Phil. 33 C6
Kiangsi = Jiangxi □, China 31 D6
Kiangsu = Jiangsu □, China 31 C7
Kibangou, Congo ... 46 E2
Kibombo, Zaïre 46 E5
Kibondo, Tanzania .. 46 E6
Kibwesa, Tanzania .. 46 F5
Kibwezi, Kenya 46 E7
Kichiga, Russia 25 D17
Kicking Horse Pass, Canada 64 C5
Kidal, Mali 44 E5
Kidderminster, U.K. . 11 E5
Kidnappers, C., N.Z. . 51 H6
Kidston, Australia .. 54 B3
Kiel, Germany 16 A5
Kiel Kanal = Nord-Ostsee Kanal, Germany 16 A4
Kielce, Poland 17 C10
Kieler Bucht, Germany 16 A5
Kiev = Kiyev, Ukraine 23 C10
Kiffa, Mauritania ... 44 E2
Kifrī, Iraq 38 C5
Kigali, Rwanda 46 E6
Kigoma-Ujiji, Tanzania 46 E5
Kihee, Australia ... 55 D3
Kii-Sanchi, Japan .. 29 G7
Kii-Suidō, Japan ... 29 H7
Kikaiga-Shima, Japan 29 K4
Kikinda, Serbia 21 B9
Kikládhes, Greece .. 21 F11
Kikwit, Zaïre 46 E3
Kilauea Crater, U.S.A. 66 J17
Kilcoy, Australia ... 55 D5
Kildare, Ireland ... 13 C5
Kildare □, Ireland .. 13 C5
Kilgore, U.S.A. 71 J7
Kilimanjaro, Tanzania 46 E7
Kilindini, Kenya ... 46 E7
Kilkee, Ireland 13 D2
Kilkenny, Ireland .. 13 D4
Kilkenny □, Ireland . 13 D4
Kilkieran B., Ireland 13 C2
Killala, Ireland 13 B2
Killala B., Ireland .. 13 B2
Killaloe, Ireland ... 13 D3
Killam, Canada 64 C6
Killarney, Australia . 55 D5
Killarney, Canada .. 62 C3
Killarney, Ireland .. 13 D2
Killarney, Lakes of, Ireland 13 E2
Killary Harbour, Ireland 13 C2
Killdeer, Canada ... 65 D7
Killdeer, U.S.A. 70 B3
Killeen, U.S.A. 71 K6
Killiecrankie, Pass of, U.K. 12 E5
Killin, U.K. 12 E4
Killíni, Greece 21 F10
Killybegs, Ireland .. 13 B3
Kilmarnock, U.K. ... 12 F4
Kilmore, Australia .. 55 F3
Kilosa, Tanzania ... 46 F7
Kilrush, Ireland ... 13 D2
Kilwa Kivinje, Tanzania 46 F7
Kim, U.S.A. 71 G3
Kimaam, Indonesia . 33 F9
Kimba, Australia ... 55 E2
Kimball, Nebr., U.S.A. 70 E3
Kimball, S. Dak., U.S.A. 70 D5
Kimberley, S. Africa . 48 D3
Kimberley Downs, Australia 52 C3
Kimberly, U.S.A. ... 72 E6
Kimry, Russia 22 C6
Kimsquit, Canada .. 64 C3

Kinabalu, Gunong, Malaysia 32 C5
Kinaskan L., Canada .. 64 B2
Kinbasket L., Canada . 64 C5
Kincaid, Canada 65 D7
Kincardine, Canada .. 62 D3
Kinder Scout, U.K. ... 10 D6
Kindersley, Canada .. 65 C7
Kindia, Guinea 44 G2
Kindu, Zaïre 46 E5
Kineshma, Russia 22 C7
King, L., Australia ... 53 F2
King, Mt., Australia .. 54 D4
King City, U.S.A. 73 H3
King Cr. →, Australia 54 C2
King Edward →, Australia 52 B4
King Frederick VI Land = Kong Frederik VI.s Kyst, Greenland ... 4 C5
King George B., Falk. Is. 80 G4
King George I., Antarctica 5 C18
King George Is., Canada 61 C11
King I. = Kadan Kyun, Burma 34 F5
King I., Australia 54 F3
King I., Canada 64 C3
King Leopold Ras., Australia 52 C4
King Sd., Australia .. 52 C3
King William I., Canada 60 B10
King William's Town, S. Africa 48 E4
Kingaroy, Australia .. 55 D5
Kingfisher, U.S.A. ... 71 H6
Kingirbān, Iraq 38 C5
Kingman, Ariz., U.S.A. 73 J6
Kingman, Kans., U.S.A. 71 G5
Kingoonya, Australia . 55 E2
Kings →, U.S.A. 73 H4
Kings Canyon National Park, U.S.A. ... 73 H4
King's Lynn, U.K. 10 E8
Kings Mountain, U.S.A. 69 H5
King's Peak, U.S.A. .. 72 F8
Kingsbridge, U.K. ... 11 G4
Kingsburg, U.S.A. ... 73 H4
Kingscote, Australia .. 55 F2
Kingscourt, Ireland .. 13 C5
Kingsley, U.S.A. 70 D7
Kingsport, U.S.A. 69 G4
Kingston, Canada ... 62 D4
Kingston, Jamaica .. 74 K17
Kingston, N.Z. 51 L2
Kingston, N.Y., U.S.A. 68 E8
Kingston, Pa., U.S.A. 68 E8
Kingston South East, Australia 55 F2
Kingston upon Hull, U.K. 10 D7
Kingston-upon-Thames, U.K. 11 F7
Kingstown, St. Vincent 74 P20
Kingstree, U.S.A. 69 J6
Kingsville, Canada .. 62 D3
Kingsville, U.S.A. ... 71 M6
Kingussie, U.K. 12 D4
Kinistino, Canada ... 65 C7
Kinkala, Congo 46 E2
Kinki □, Japan 29 H8
Kinleith, N.Z. 51 H5
Kinnaird, Canada ... 64 D5
Kinnairds Hd., U.K. .. 12 D7
Kinnarodden, Norway 6 A11
Kinoje →, Canada .. 62 B3
Kinomoto, Japan ... 29 G8
Kinross, U.K. 12 E5
Kinsale, Ireland 13 E3
Kinsale, Old Hd. of, Ireland 13 E3
Kinsha = Chang Jiang →, China .. 31 C7
Kinshasa, Zaïre 46 E3
Kinsley, U.S.A. 71 G5
Kinston, U.S.A. 69 H7
Kintampo, Ghana ... 44 G4
Kintap, Indonesia ... 32 E5
Kintore Ra., Australia 52 D4
Kintyre, U.K. 12 F3
Kintyre, Mull of, U.K. 12 F3
Kinushseo →, Canada 62 A3
Kinuso, Canada 64 B5
Kiosk, Canada 62 C4
Kiowa, Kans., U.S.A. 71 G5
Kiowa, Okla., U.S.A. . 71 H6
Kipahigan L., Canada 65 B8
Kiparissia, Greece .. 21 F9
Kiparissiakós Kólpos, Greece 21 F9
Kipembawe, Tanzania 46 F6
Kipili, Tanzania 46 F6
Kipling, Canada 65 C8
Kippure, Ireland 13 C5
Kipushi, Zaïre 47 G5
Kirensk, Russia 25 D11
Kirgella Rocks, Australia 53 F3
Kirghizia ■, Asia ... 24 E8
Kirghizstan = Kirghizia ■, Asia .. 24 E8
Kirgiziya = Kirghizia ■, Asia 24 E8
Kirgiziya Steppe, Kazakhstan 23 D10
Kiri, Zaïre 46 E3
Kiribati ■, Pac. Oc. .. 56 H10
Kırıkkale, Turkey 23 G5
Kirillov, Russia 22 C6
Kirin = Jilin, China .. 31 B7

Kirin = Jilin □, China 31 B7
Kiritimati, Kiribati ... 57 G12
Kirkcaldy, U.K. 12 E5
Kirkcudbright, U.K. .. 12 G4
Kirkee, India 36 K8
Kirkenes, Norway ... 8 B21
Kirkintilloch, U.K. ... 12 F4
Kirkjubæjarklaustur, Iceland 8 E4
Kirkland, U.S.A. 73 J7
Kirkland Lake, Canada 62 C3
Kırklareli, Turkey ... 21 D12
Kirksville, U.S.A. ... 70 E8
Kirkük, Iraq 38 C5
Kirkwall, U.K. 12 C6
Kirkwood, S. Africa . 48 E4
Kirov = Vyatka, Russia 24 D5
Kirovabad = Gyandzha, Azerbaijan 23 F8
Kirovakan = Karaklis, Armenia 23 F7
Kirovograd, Ukraine . 23 E5
Kirovohrad = Kirovograd, Ukraine 23 E5
Kirovsk, Russia 22 A5
Kirovsk, Turkmenistan 24 F7
Kirovskiy, Russia 25 D16
Kirovskiy, Russia 28 B6
Kirriemuir, U.K. 12 E6
Kirsanov, Russia 22 D7
Kırşehir, Turkey 23 G5
Kirstonia, S. Africa .. 48 D3
Kirthar Range, Pakistan 36 F5
Kiruna, Sweden 8 C16
Kirundu, Zaïre 46 E5
Kirup, Australia 53 F2
Kiryū, Japan 29 F9
Kisangani, Zaïre 46 D5
Kisar, Indonesia 33 F7
Kisaran, Indonesia .. 32 D1
Kisarazu, Japan 29 G9
Kiselevsk, Russia ... 24 D9
Kishanganj, India ... 37 F16
Kishangarh, India ... 36 F7
Kishinev, Moldavia .. 23 E4
Kishiwada, Japan ... 29 G7
Kishtwar, India 36 C9
Kisii, Kenya 46 E6
Kisiju, Tanzania 46 F7
Kiska I., U.S.A. 60 C1
Kiskatinaw →, Canada 64 B4
Kiskittogisu L., Canada 65 C9
Kiskörös, Hungary .. 17 E9
Kiskunfélegyháza, Hungary 17 E9
Kiskunhalas, Hungary 17 E9
Kislovodsk, Russia .. 23 F7
Kiso-Gawa →, Japan 29 G8
Kiso-Sammyaku, Japan 29 G8
Kisofukushima, Japan 29 G8
Kissidougou, Guinea . 44 G2
Kissimmee, U.S.A. .. 69 L5
Kissimmee →, U.S.A. 69 M5
Kississing L., Canada 65 B8
Kisumu, Kenya 46 E6
Kit Carson, U.S.A. ... 70 F3
Kita, Mali 44 F3
Kitab, Uzbekistan ... 24 F7
Kitaibaraki, Japan ... 29 F10
Kitakami, Japan 28 E10
Kitakami-Gawa →, Japan 28 E10
Kitakami-Sammyaku, Japan 28 E10
Kitakata, Japan 28 F9
Kitakyūshū, Japan .. 29 H5
Kitale, Kenya 46 D7
Kitami, Japan 28 C11
Kitami-Sammyaku, Japan 28 B11
Kitchener, Australia . 53 F3
Kitchener, Canada .. 62 D3
Kitega = Gitega, Burundi 46 E5
Kitgum, Uganda 46 D6
Kíthira, Greece 21 F10
Kíthnos, Greece 21 F11
Kitikmeot □, Canada 60 A9
Kitimat, Canada 64 C3
Kitinen →, Finland .. 8 C19
Kitsuki, Japan 29 H5
Kittakittaooloo, L., Australia 55 D2
Kittanning, U.S.A. ... 68 E6
Kittery, U.S.A. 68 D10
Kitui, Kenya 46 E7
Kitwe, Zambia 47 G5
Kivalo, Finland 8 C19
Kivu, Zaïre 46 E5
Kiyev, Ukraine 23 D5
Kiyevskoye Vdkhr., Ukraine 23 D5
Kizel, Russia 22 C10
Kızıl Irmak →, Turkey 23 F6
Kizlyar, Russia 23 F8
Kizyl-Arvat, Turkmenistan 24 F6
Kladno, Czech. 16 C7
Klagenfurt, Austria .. 16 E7
Klaipėda, Lithuania . 22 C3
Klamath →, U.S.A. .. 72 F1
Klamath Falls, U.S.A. 72 E3
Klamath Mts., U.S.A. 72 F2
Klappan →, Canada . 64 B3
Klarälven →, Sweden 9 G13
Klaten, Indonesia ... 33 G14
Klatovy, Czech. 16 D6
Klawak, U.S.A. 64 B2
Klawer, S. Africa 48 E2

Kleena Kleene, Canada 64 C4
Klein, U.S.A. 72 C9
Klein-Karas, Namibia . 48 D2
Klerksdorp, S. Africa . 48 D4
Kletskiy, Russia 24 E5
Klickitat, U.S.A. 72 D3
Klin, Russia 22 C6
Klinaklini →, Canada 64 C3
Klipdale, S. Africa ... 48 E2
Klipplaat, S. Africa .. 48 E3
Kłodzko, Poland 16 C8
Klondike, Canada ... 60 B6
Klouto, Togo 44 G5
Kluane L., Canada .. 60 B6
Klyuchevskaya, Gora, Russia 25 D17
Knaresborough, U.K. . 10 C6
Knee L., Man., Canada 65 B10
Knee L., Sask., Canada 65 B7
Knight Inlet, Canada . 64 C3
Knighton, U.K. 11 E4
Knight's Landing, U.S.A. 72 G3
Knob, C., Australia .. 53 F2
Knockmealdown Mts., Ireland 13 D4
Knokke, Belgium 15 C3
Knóssos, Greece 21 G11
Knox, U.S.A. 68 E2
Knox, C., Canada ... 64 C2
Knox City, U.S.A. ... 71 J5
Knox Coast, Antarctica 5 C8
Knoxville, Iowa, U.S.A. 70 E8
Knoxville, Tenn., U.S.A. 69 H4
Knysna, S. Africa ... 48 E3
Ko Chang, Thailand . 34 F7
Ko Kut, Thailand 34 G7
Ko Phra Thong, Thailand 34 H5
Ko Tao, Thailand 34 G5
Koartac, Canada 61 B13
Koba, Aru, Indonesia 33 F8
Koba, Bangka, Indonesia 32 E3
Kobarid, Slovenia ... 20 A5
Kobayashi, Japan ... 29 J5
Kobdo = Hovd, Mongolia 30 B4
Kōbe, Japan 29 G7
København, Denmark 9 J12
Kōbi-Sho, Japan 29 M1
Koblenz, Germany .. 16 C3
Kobroor, Kepulauan, Indonesia 33 F8
Kocaeli = İzmit, Turkey 23 F4
Kočani, Macedonia 21 D10
Kočevje, Slovenia ... 20 B6
Koch Bihar, India ... 37 F16
Kocheva, Russia 25 D13
Kōchi, Japan 29 H6
Kōchi □, Japan 29 H6
Kochiu = Gejiu, China 30 D5
Kodaikanal, India ... 36 Q10
Kodiak, U.S.A. 60 C4
Kodiak I., U.S.A. 60 C4
Kodiang, Malaysia .. 34 N13
Koes, Namibia 48 D2
Koffiefontein, S. Africa 48 D4
Kofiau, Indonesia ... 33 E7
Koforidua, Ghana ... 44 G4
Kōfu, Japan 29 G9
Koga, Japan 29 F9
Kogaluk →, Canada . 63 A7
Kogan, Australia 55 D5
Koh-i-Bābā, Afghan. . 36 B5
Kohat, Pakistan 36 C7
Kohima, India 37 G19
Kohkīlūyeh va Būyer Aḥmadi □, Iran .. 39 D6
Kohler Ra., Antarctica 5 D15
Kojonup, Australia .. 53 F2
Kojūr, Iran 39 B6
Kokand, Uzbekistan . 24 E8
Kokanee Glacier Prov. Park, Canada ... 64 D5
Kokas, Indonesia ... 33 E8
Kokchetav, Kazakhstan 24 D7
Kokemäenjoki, Finland 9 F16
Kokkola, Finland 8 E17
Koko Kyunzu, Burma . 34 E2
Kokomo, U.S.A. 68 E2
Kokonau, Indonesia . 33 E9
Koksoak →, Canada . 61 C13
Kokstad, S. Africa ... 49 E4
Kokubu, Japan 29 J5
Kokuora, Russia 25 B15
Kola, Indonesia 33 F8
Kola, Russia 22 A5
Kola Pen. = Kolskiy Poluostrov, Russia . 22 A6
Kolaka, Indonesia ... 33 E6
Kolar, India 36 N11
Kolar Gold Fields, India 36 N11
Kolari, Finland 8 C17
Kolayat, India 36 F8
Kolchugino = Leninsk-Kuznetskiy, Russia . 24 D9
Kolda, Senegal 44 F2
Kolding, Denmark ... 9 J10
Kole, Zaïre 46 E4
Kolepom = Yos Sudarso, Pulau, Indonesia 33 F9
Kolguyev, Ostrov, Russia 22 A8
Kolhapur, India 36 L9
Kolín, Czech. 16 C7
Kolmanskop, Namibia 48 D2
Köln, Germany 16 C3
Koło, Poland 17 B9
Kołobrzeg, Poland .. 16 A7

Kolokani, Mali 44 F3
Kolomna, Russia ... 22 C6
Kolomyya, Ukraine .. 23 D4
Kolonodale, Indonesia 33 E6
Kolosib, India 37 G18
Kolpashevo, Russia . 24 D9
Kolpino, Russia 22 C5
Kolskiy Poluostrov, Russia 22 A6
Kolskiy Zaliv, Russia . 22 A5
Kolwezi, Zaïre 46 G5
Kolyma →, Russia .. 25 C17
Kolymskoye, Okhotsko, Russia 25 C16
Komandorskiye Is. = Komandorskiye Ostrova, Russia .. 25 D17
Komandorskiye Ostrova, Russia .. 25 D17
Komárno, Slovakia .. 17 E9
Komatipoort, S. Africa 49 D5
Komatsu, Japan 29 F8
Komatsujima, Japan . 29 H7
Komi Republic □, Russia 22 B10
Kommunarsk, Ukraine 23 E6
Kommunizma, Pik, Tajikistan 24 F8
Komodo, Indonesia . 33 F5
Komono, Congo 46 E2
Komoran, Pulau, Indonesia 33 F9
Komoro, Japan 29 F9
Komotini, Greece ... 21 D11
Kompasberg, S. Africa 48 E3
Kompong Cham, Cambodia 34 F8
Kompong Chhnang, Cambodia 34 F8
Kompong Som, Cambodia 34 G7
Kompong Speu, Cambodia 34 G8
Kompong Thom, Cambodia 34 F8
Komsberg, S. Africa . 48 E3
Komsomolets, Ostrov, Russia 25 A10
Komsomolsk, Russia . 25 D14
Konarhá □, Afghan. .. 36 B7
Konan, Iran 39 D6
Konawa, U.S.A. 71 H6
Konch, India 36 G11
Kondakovo, Russia .. 25 C16
Kondinin, Australia .. 53 F2
Kondoa, Tanzania ... 46 E7
Kondopaga, Russia . 22 B5
Kondratyevo, Russia . 25 D10
Konduga, Nigeria ... 45 F7
Konevo, Russia 22 B6
Kong, Ivory C. 44 G4
Kong, Koh, Cambodia 34 G7
Kong Christian IX.s Land, Greenland .. 4 C6
Kong Christian X.s Land, Greenland .. 4 B6
Kong Franz Joseph Fd., Greenland ... 4 B6
Kong Frederik IX.s Land, Greenland .. 4 C5
Kong Frederik VI.s Kyst, Greenland ... 4 C5
Kong Frederik VIII.s Land, Greenland .. 4 B6
Kong Oscar Fjord, Greenland 4 B6
Konglu, Burma 37 F20
Kongolo, Zaïre 46 F5
Kongor, Sudan 45 G11
Kongsberg, Norway . 9 G10
Kongsvinger, Norway 9 F12
Königsberg = Kaliningrad, Russia 22 D3
Konin, Poland 17 B9
Konjic, Bos.-H. 21 C7
Konkiep, Namibia ... 48 D2
Konosha, Russia 22 B7
Kōnosu, Japan 29 F9
Konotop, Ukraine ... 23 D5
Końskie, Poland 17 C10
Konstanz, Germany . 16 E4
Kont, Iran 39 E9
Kontagora, Nigeria .. 44 F6
Kontum, Vietnam ... 34 E10
Konya, Turkey 23 G5
Konza, Kenya 46 E7
Kookynie, Australia .. 53 E3
Kooline, Australia ... 52 D2
Kooloonong, Australia 55 E3
Koolyanobbing, Australia 53 F2
Koondrook, Australia 55 F3
Koonibba, Australia . 55 E1
Koorawatha, Australia 55 E4
Koorda, Australia ... 53 F2
Kooskia, U.S.A. 72 C6
Kootenay →, Canada 72 B5
Kootenay L., Canada 64 D5
Kootenay Nat. Park, Canada 64 C5
Kootjieskolk, S. Africa 48 E3
Kopaonik, Serbia, Yug. 21 C9
Kópavogur, Iceland .. 8 D3
Koper, Slovenia 20 B5
Kopervik, Norway ... 9 G8
Kopeysk, Russia 24 D7
Kopi, Australia 55 E2
Köping, Sweden 9 G14
Kopparberg, Sweden 9 G13
Kopparbergs län □, Sweden 9 F13
Koppies, S. Africa ... 49 D4

Korab, Macedonia .. 21 D9
Korça, Albania 21 D9
Korce = Korça, Albania 21 D9
Korčula, Croatia 20 C7
Kord Kūy, Iran 39 B7
Kord Sheykh, Iran ... 39 D7
Kordestān □, Iran ... 38 C5
Korea, North ■, Asia . 31 C7
Korea, South ■, Asia . 31 C7
Korea Bay, Korea ... 31 C7
Korea Strait, Asia ... 31 C7
Korhogo, Ivory C. ... 44 G3
Korim, Indonesia ... 33 E9
Korinthiakós Kólpos, Greece 21 E10
Kórinthos, Greece ... 21 F10
Kōriyama, Japan 28 F10
Korla, China 30 B3
Koro, Fiji 51 C8
Koro, Ivory C. 44 G3
Koro, Mali 44 F4
Koro Sea, Fiji 51 C9
Korogwe, Tanzania . 46 F7
Koroit, Australia 55 F3
Koror, Pac. Oc. 33 C8
Körös →, Hungary .. 17 E10
Korraraika, Helodranon' i, Madag. 49 B7
Korsakov, Russia ... 25 E15
Korshunovo, Russia . 25 D12
Korsør, Denmark ... 9 J11
Korti, Sudan 45 E11
Kortrijk, Belgium 15 D3
Koryakskiy Khrebet, Russia 25 C18
Kos, Greece 21 F12
Kosa, Sudan 45 D11
Kościan, Poland 16 B8
Kosciusko, U.S.A. ... 71 J10
Kosciusko, Mt., Australia 55 F4
Kosciusko I., U.S.A. . 64 B2
Kosha, Sudan 45 D11
Kōshetau = Kokchetav, Kazakhstan 24 D7
Koshiki-Rettō, Japan . 29 J4
Kosi-meer, S. Africa . 49 D5
Košice, Slovakia 17 D10
Koslan, Russia 22 B8
Kosovska-Mitrovica, Serbia, Yug. 21 C9
Kostamuksa, Russia . 22 B5
Koster, S. Africa 48 D4
Kōstī, Sudan 45 F11
Kostroma, Russia ... 22 C7
Koszalin, Poland 16 A8
Kota, India 36 G9
Kota Baharu, Malaysia 34 N15
Kota Belud, Malaysia 32 C5
Kota Kinabalu, Malaysia 32 C5
Kota Tinggi, Malaysia 34 T16
Kotaagung, Indonesia 32 F2
Kotabaru, Indonesia . 32 E5
Kotabumi, Indonesia 32 E2
Kotagede, Indonesia 33 G14
Kotamobagu, Indonesia 33 D6
Kotaneelee →, Canada 64 A4
Kotawaringin, Indonesia 32 E4
Kotcho L., Canada .. 64 B4
Kotelnich, Russia ... 22 C8
Kotelnikovo, Russia . 24 E5
Kotelnyy, Ostrov, Russia 25 B14
Kotka, Finland 9 F19
Kotlas, Russia 22 B8
Kotli, Pakistan 36 C8
Kotor, Montenegro, Yug. 21 C8
Kotri, Pakistan 36 G6
Kottayam, India 36 Q10
Kotturu, India 36 M10
Kotuy →, Russia 25 B11
Kotzebue, U.S.A. ... 60 B3
Kouango, C.A.R. 46 C4
Koudougou, Burkina Faso 44 F4
Kougaberg, S. Africa 48 E3
Kouilou →, Congo .. 46 E2
Kouki, C.A.R. 46 C3
Koula Moutou, Gabon 46 E2
Koulen, Cambodia .. 34 F8
Koulikoro, Mali 44 F3
Koumala, Australia .. 54 C4
Koumra, Chad 45 G8
Kounradskiy, Kazakhstan 24 E8
Kountze, U.S.A. 71 K7
Kouroussa, Guinea . 44 F3
Kousséri, Cameroon . 45 F7
Koutiala, Mali 44 F3
Kovdor, Russia 22 A5
Kovel, Ukraine 22 D3
Kovrov, Russia 22 C7
Kowanyama, Australia 54 B3
Kowkash, Canada .. 62 B2
Koyabuti, Indonesia . 33 E10
Koyuk, U.S.A. 60 B3
Koyukuk →, U.S.A. . 60 B4
Koza, Japan 29 L3
Kozáni, Greece 21 D9
Kozhikode = Calicut, India 36 P9
Kozhva, Russia 22 A10
Kpalimé, Togo 44 G5

Kra, Isthmus of = Kra, Kho Khot, Thailand 34 G5
Kra, Kho Khot, Thailand 34 G5
Kra Buri, Thailand ... 34 G5
Kragan, Indonesia .. 33 G14
Kragerø, Norway ... 9 G10
Kragujevac, Serbia, Yug. 21 B9
Krakatau = Rakata, Pulau, Indonesia . 32 F3
Kraków, Poland 17 C9
Kraksaan, Indonesia 33 G15
Kraljevo, Serbia, Yug. 21 C9
Kramatorsk, Ukraine 23 E6
Kramfors, Sweden .. 8 E14
Kranskop, S. Africa .. 49 D5
Krasavino, Russia ... 22 B8
Kraskino, Russia 25 E14
Kraśnik, Poland 17 C11
Krasnoarmeysk, Russia 24 D5
Krasnodar, Russia .. 23 E6
Krasnokamsk, Russia 22 C10
Krasnoperekopsk, Ukraine 23 E5
Krasnorechenskiy, Russia 28 B7
Krasnoselkupsk, Russia 24 C9
Krasnoturinsk, Russia 22 C11
Krasnoufimsk, Russia 22 C10
Krasnouralsk, Russia 22 C11
Krasnovishersk, Russia 22 B10
Krasnovodsk, Turkmenistan 23 F9
Krasnoyarsk, Russia . 25 D10
Krasnyy Luch, Ukraine 23 E6
Krasnyy Yar, Russia . 23 E8
Kratie, Cambodia ... 34 F9
Krau, Indonesia 33 E10
Kravanh, Chuor Phnum, Cambodia . 34 G7
Krefeld, Germany ... 16 C3
Kremenchug, Ukraine 23 E5
Kremenchugskoye Vdkhr., Ukraine ... 23 E5
Kremenchuk = Kremenchug, Ukraine 23 E5
Kremmling, U.S.A. .. 72 F10
Kremnica, Slovakia . 17 D9
Kribi, Cameroon 46 D1
Krishna →, India ... 37 M12
Krishnanagar, India . 37 H16
Kristiansand, Norway 9 G10
Kristianstad, Sweden 9 H13
Kristianstads län □, Sweden 9 H13
Kristiansund, Norway 8 E9
Kristiinankaupunki, Finland 8 E16
Kristinehamn, Sweden 9 G13
Kristinestad, Finland . 8 E16
Kríti, Greece 21 G11
Krivoy Rog, Ukraine . 23 E5
Krk, Croatia 20 B6
Krokodil →, Mozam. 49 D5
Kronobergs län □, Sweden 9 H13
Kronprins Olav Kyst, Antarctica 5 C5
Kronshtadt, Russia .. 22 B4
Kroonstad, S. Africa . 48 D4
Kropotkin, Russia ... 23 E7
Kropotkin, Russia ... 25 D12
Krosno, Poland 17 D10
Krotoszyn, Poland .. 17 C9
Kruger Nat. Park, S. Africa 49 C5
Krugersdorp, S. Africa 49 D4
Kruisfontein, S. Africa 48 E3
Krung Thep = Bangkok, Thailand . 34 F6
Kruševac, Serbia, Yug. 21 C9
Kruzof I., U.S.A. 64 B1
Krymskiy Poluostrov, Ukraine 23 E5
Kryvyy Rih = Krivoy Rog, Ukraine 23 E5
Ksar el Boukhari, Algeria 44 A5
Ksar el Kebir, Morocco 44 B3
Ksar es Souk = Ar Rachidiya, Morocco 44 B4
Kuala, Indonesia ... 32 D3
Kuala Kangsar, Malaysia 34 Q13
Kuala Kerai, Malaysia 34 P15
Kuala Kubu Baharu, Malaysia 34 R14
Kuala Lipis, Malaysia 34 Q15
Kuala Lumpur, Malaysia 34 R14
Kuala Sedili Besar, Malaysia 34 T17
Kuala Terengganu, Malaysia 32 C2
Kualajelai, Indonesia 32 E4
Kualakapuas, Indonesia 32 E4
Kualakurun, Indonesia 32 E4
Kualapembuang, Indonesia 32 E4
Kualasimpang, Indonesia 32 D1
Kuandang, Indonesia 33 D6
Kuangchou = Guangzhou, China . 31 D6
Kuantan, Malaysia .. 34 R16
Kuba, Azerbaijan ... 23 F8
Kuban →, Russia ... 23 E6
Kubokawa, Japan ... 29 H6

Kuchino-eruba-Jima,
  Japan 29 J5
Kuchino-Shima, Japan 29 K4
Kuchinotsu, Japan . . 29 H5
Kucing, Malaysia . . 32 D4
Kuda, India 36 H7
Kudat, Malaysia . . . 32 C5
Kudus, Indonesia . . 33 G14
Kudymkar, Russia . . 24 D6
Kueiyang = Guiyang,
  China 30 D5
Kufstein, Austria . . . 16 E6
Kugong I., Canada . . 62 A4
Küh-e Dīnār, Iran . . 39 D6
Küh-e-Hazārān, Iran 39 D8
Kühak, Iran 36 F3
Kühbonān, Iran . . . 39 D8
Kühestak, Iran 39 E8
Kühīn, Iran 39 C6
Kühīrī, Iran 39 E9
Kühpāyeh, Eşfahan,
  Iran 39 C7
Kühpāyeh, Kermān,
  Iran 39 D8
Kuito, Angola 47 G3
Kuji, Japan 28 D10
Kujū-San, Japan . . . 29 H5
Kukawa, Nigeria . . . 45 F7
Kukerin, Australia . . 53 F2
Kukes, Indonesia . . 33 E8
Kulai, Malaysia . . . 34 T16
Kulasekarappattinam,
  India 36 Q11
Kuldja = Yining, China 30 E9
Kulin, Australia . . . 53 F2
Kulja, Australia . . . 53 F2
Kulm, U.S.A. 70 B5
Kulsary, Kazakhstan . 23 E9
Kulumbura, Australia 52 B4
Kulunda, Russia . . . 24 D8
Külvand, Iran 39 D7
Kulwin, Australia . . . 55 F3
Kulyab, Tajikistan . . 24 F7
Kum Tekei, Kazakhstan 24 E8
Kuma →, Russia . . . 23 F8
Kumagaya, Japan . . 29 F9
Kumai, Indonesia . . . 32 E4
Kumamba, Kepulauan,
  Indonesia 33 E9
Kumamoto, Japan . . 29 H5
Kumamoto □, Japan . 29 H5
Kumanovo,
  Macedonia 21 C9
Kumara, N.Z. 51 K3
Kumarl, Australia . . 53 F3
Kumayri, Armenia . . 23 F7
Kumba, Cameroon . . 44 H6
Kumbakonam, India . 36 P11
Kumbarilla, Australia 55 D5
Kume-Shima, Japan . 29 L3
Kumertau, Russia . . 22 D10
Kumla, Sweden 9 G13
Kumo, Nigeria 44 F7
Kumon Bum, Burma . 37 F20
Kunama, Australia . . 55 F4
Kunashir, Ostrov,
  Russia 25 E15
Kungala, Australia . . 55 D5
Kunghit I., Canada . . 64 C2
Kungrad, Uzbekistan 24 E6
Kungsbacka, Sweden 9 H12
Kungur, Russia 22 C10
Kungurri, Australia . . 54 C4
Kuningan, Indonesia . 33 G13
Kunlong, Burma . . . 37 H21
Kunlun Shan, Asia . . 30 C3
Kunming, China . . . 30 D5
Kununurra, Australia . 52 C4
Kunwarara, Australia . 54 C5
Kunya-Urgench,
  Turkmenistan 24 E6
Kuopio, Finland . . . 8 E19
Kuopion lääni □,
  Finland 8 E19
Kupa →, Croatia . . . 20 B7
Kupang, Indonesia . . 33 F6
Kupyansk, Ukraine . . 23 E4
Kuqa, China 30 B3
Kura →, Azerbaijan . 23 G8
Kuranda, Australia . . 54 B4
Kurashiki, Japan . . . 29 G6
Kurayoshi, Japan . . . 29 G6
Kure, Japan 29 G6
Kurgaldzhino,
  Kazakhstan 24 D8
Kurgan, Russia 24 D7
Kuria Maria Is. =
  Khūrīyā Mūrīyā, Jazā
  'ir, Oman 40 D6
Kuridala, Australia . . 54 C3
Kurigram, Bangla. . . 37 G16
Kuril Is. = Kurilskiye
  Ostrova, Russia . . 25 E15
Kuril Trench, Pac. Oc. 56 C7
Kurilsk, Russia 25 E15
Kurilskiye Ostrova,
  Russia 25 E15
Kurino, Japan 29 J5
Kurmuk, Sudan 45 F11
Kurnool, India 36 M10
Kuro-Shima,
  Kagoshima, Japan . 29 J4
Kuro-Shima, Okinawa,
  Japan 29 M2
Kurow, N.Z. 51 L3
Kurrajong, Australia . 55 E5
Kurri Kurri, Australia . 55 E5
Kursk, Russia 22 D6
Kuršumlija,
  Serbia, Yug. 21 C9
Kuruktag, China . . . 30 B3
Kuruman, S. Africa . . 48 D3

Kuruman →, S. Africa 48 D3
Kurume, Japan 29 H5
Kurunegala, Sri Lanka 36 R12
Kurya, Russia 25 C11
Kusatsu, Japan 29 F9
Kusawa L., Canada . . 64 A1
Kushikino, Japan . . . 29 J5
Kushima, Japan 29 J5
Kushimoto, Japan . . 29 H7
Kushiro, Japan 28 C12
Kushiro →, Japan . . . 28 C12
Kūshk, Iran 39 D8
Kushka, Turkmenistan 24 F7
Küshkī, Īlām, Iran . . . 38 C5
Küshkī, Khorāsān, Iran 39 B8
Kūshkū, Iran 39 E7
Kushtia, Bangla. . . . 37 H16
Kushva, Russia 22 C10
Kuskokwim →, U.S.A. 60 B3
Kuskokwim Bay, U.S.A. 60 C3
Kussharo-Ko, Japan . 28 C12
Kustanay, Kazakhstan 24 D7
Kütahya, Turkey . . . 23 G5
Kutaisi, Georgia . . . 23 F7
Kutaraja = Banda
  Aceh, Indonesia . . 32 C1
Kutch, Gulf of =
  Kachchh, Gulf of,
  India 36 H6
Kutch, Rann of =
  Kachchh, Rann of,
  India 36 H7
Kutno, Poland 17 B9
Kuttabul, Australia . . 54 C4
Kutu, Zaïre 46 E3
Kutum, Sudan 45 F9
Kuujjuaq, Canada . . 61 C13
Kuwait = Al Kuwayt,
  Kuwait 38 D5
Kuwait ■, Asia 38 D5
Kuwana, Japan 29 G8
Kuybyshev = Samara,
  Russia 22 D9
Kuybyshev, Russia . . 24 D8
Kuybyshevskoye
  Vdkhr., Russia . . . 22 C8
Küyeh, Iran 38 B5
Küysanjaq, Iraq . . . 38 B5
Kuyto, Oz., Russia . . 22 B5
Kuyumba, Russia . . . 25 C10
Kuzey Anadolu Dağları,
  Turkey 23 F6
Kuznetsk, Russia . . . 22 D8
Kuzomen, Russia . . . 22 A6
Kvænangen, Norway . 8 A16
Kvarner, Croatia . . . 20 B6
Kvarnerič, Croatia . . 20 B6
Kwabhaca, S. Africa . 49 E4
Kwadacha →, Canada 64 B3
Kwakhanai, Botswana 48 C3
Kwakoegron, Surinam 79 B7
KwaMashu, S. Africa . 49 D5
Kwando →, Africa . . 48 B3
Kwangju, S. Korea . . 31 C7
Kwangsi-Chuang =
  Guangxi Zhuangzu
  Zizhiqu □, China . . 31 D5
Kwangtung =
  Guangdong □, China 31 D6
Kwataboahegan →,
  Canada 62 B3
Kwatisore, Indonesia 33 E8
Kweichow =
  Guizhou □, China . 30 D5
Kwekwe, Zimbabwe . 47 H5
Kwinana New Town,
  Australia 53 F2
Kwoka, Indonesia . . 33 E8
Kyabé, Chad 45 G8
Kyabra Cr. →,
  Australia 55 D3
Kyabram, Australia . . 55 F4
Kyaikto, Burma 34 D4
Kyakhta, Russia . . . 25 D11
Kyancutta, Australia . 55 E2
Kyangin, Burma . . . 37 K19
Kyaukpadaung, Burma 37 J19
Kyaukpyu, Burma . . 37 K18
Kyaukse, Burma . . . 37 J20
Kycen, Russia 25 D11
Kyle Dam, Zimbabwe 47 J6
Kyle of Lochalsh, U.K. 12 D3
Kyneton, Australia . . 55 F3
Kynuna, Australia . . 54 C3
Kyō-ga-Saki, Japan . 29 G7
Kyoga, L., Uganda . . 46 D6
Kyogle, Australia . . . 55 D5
Kyongpyaw, Burma . 37 L19
Kyōto, Japan 29 G7
Kyōto □, Japan 29 G7
Kyrenia, Cyprus . . . 38 C2
Kyrgystan =
  Kirghizia ■, Asia . . 24 E8
Kystatyam, Russia . . 25 C13
Kytal Ktakh, Russia . 25 C13
Kyulyunken, Russia . . 25 C14
Kyunhla, Burma . . . 37 H19
Kyuquot, Canada . . . 64 C3
Kyūshū, Japan 29 H5
Kyūshū □, Japan . . . 29 H5
Kyūshū-Sanchi, Japan 29 H5
Kyustendil, Bulgaria . 21 C10
Kyusyur, Russia 25 B13
Kywong, Australia . . 55 E4
Kyyiv = Kiyev, Ukraine 23 D5
Kyzyl, Russia 25 D10
Kyzyl-Kiya, Kirghizia . 24 E8
Kyzylkum, Peski,
  Uzbekistan 24 E7
Kzyl-Orda, Kazakhstan 24 E7

L

La Asunción,
  Venezuela 78 A6
La Banda, Argentina . 80 B4
La Barge, U.S.A. . . . 72 E8
La Belle, U.S.A. 69 M5
La Biche →, Canada 64 B4
La Boca, Panama . . . 74 H14
La Calera, Chile . . . 80 C2
La Carlota, Argentina 80 C4
La Carolina, Spain . . 19 C4
La Ceiba, Honduras . 74 D7
La Chaux de Fonds,
  Switz. 16 E3
La Chorrera, Panama 74 H14
La Cocha, Argentina . 80 B3
La Conner, U.S.A. . . 72 B2
La Coruña, Spain . . . 19 A1
La Crete, Canada . . . 64 B5
La Crosse, Kans.,
  U.S.A. 70 F5
La Crosse, Wis., U.S.A. 70 D9
La Dorada, Colombia . 78 B4
La Estrada, Spain . . . 19 A1
La Fayette, U.S.A. . . 69 H3
La Follette, U.S.A. . . 69 G3
La Grande, U.S.A. . . 72 D4
La Grange, Ga., U.S.A. 69 J3
La Grange, Ky., U.S.A. 68 F3
La Grange, Tex., U.S.A. 71 L6
La Guaira, Venezuela . 78 A5
La Güera, Mauritania . 44 D1
La Habana, Cuba . . . 75 C8
La Harpe, U.S.A. . . . 70 E9
La Jara, U.S.A. 73 H11
La Junta, U.S.A. . . . 71 F3
La Línea de la
  Concepción, Spain . 19 D3
La Loche, Canada . . 65 B7
La Louvière, Belgium . 15 D4
La Malbaie, Canada . 63 C5
La Mancha, Spain . . 19 C4
La Mesa, Calif., U.S.A. 73 K5
La Mesa, N. Mex.,
  U.S.A. 73 K10
La Moure, U.S.A. . . . 70 B5
La Palma, Canary Is. . 44 C1
La Palma, Panama . . 75 F9
La Palma, Spain . . . 19 D2
La Paragua, Venezuela 78 B6
La Paz, Entre Ríos,
  Argentina 80 C5
La Paz, San Luis,
  Argentina 80 C3
La Paz, Bolivia 78 G5
La Paz, Mexico 74 C2
La Pedrera, Colombia 78 D5
La Perouse Str., Asia . 28 B11
La Pine, U.S.A. 72 E3
La Plant, U.S.A. . . . 70 C4
La Plata, Argentina . . 80 D5
La Porte, U.S.A. . . . 68 E2
La Push, U.S.A. . . . 72 C1
La Quiaca, Argentina . 80 A3
La Reine, Canada . . . 62 C4
La Rioja, Argentina . . 80 B3
La Rioja □, Spain . . . 19 A4
La Robla, Spain . . . 19 A3
La Rochelle, France . 18 C3
La Roda, Spain 19 C4
La Romana, Dom. Rep. 75 D11
La Ronge, Canada . . 65 B7
La Salle, U.S.A. 70 E10
La Sarre, Canada . . . 62 C4
La Scie, Canada . . . 63 C8
La Serena, Chile . . . 80 B2
La Spézia, Italy 20 B3
La Tortuga, Venezuela 75 E11
La Tuque, Canada . . 62 C5
La Unión, Chile 80 E2
La Urbana, Venezuela 78 B5
La Vega, Dom. Rep. . 75 D10
Labe = Elbe →,
  Europe 16 B4
Labé, Guinea 44 F2
Laberge, L., Canada . 64 A1
Labis, Malaysia . . . 34 S16
Laboulaye, Argentina 80 C4
Labrador, Coast of □,
  Canada 63 B7
Labrador City, Canada 63 B6
Lábrea, Brazil 78 E6
Labuan, Pulau,
  Malaysia 32 C5
Labuha, Indonesia . . 33 E7
Labuhan, Indonesia . 33 G11
Labuhanbajo,
  Indonesia 33 F6
Labuk, Telok, Malaysia 32 C5
Labyrinth, L., Australia 55 E2
Labytnangi, Russia . . 22 A12
Lac Allard, Canada . . 63 B7
Lac Bouchette, Canada 63 C5
Lac du Flambeau,
  U.S.A. 70 B10
Lac Édouard, Canada 62 C5
Lac La Biche, Canada 64 C6
Lac la Martre, Canada 60 B8
Lac-Mégantic, Canada 63 C5
Lac Seul, Res., Canada 62 B1
Laccadive Is. =
  Lakshadweep Is.,
  Ind. Oc. 26 J11
Lacepede B., Australia 55 F2
Lacepede Is., Australia 52 C3
Lachine, Canada . . . 62 C5
Lachlan →, Australia 55 E3
Lachute, Canada . . . 62 C5

Lackawanna, U.S.A. . 68 D6
Lacombe, Canada . . 64 C6
Laconia, U.S.A. 68 D10
Lacrosse, U.S.A. . . . 72 C5
Ladakh Ra., India . . 36 C11
Ladismith, S. Africa . 48 E3
Ladoga, L. =
  Ladozhskoye Ozero,
  Russia 22 B5
Ladozhskoye Ozero,
  Russia 22 B5
Lady Grey, S. Africa . 48 E4
Ladybrand, S. Africa . 48 D4
Ladysmith, Canada . . 64 D4
Ladysmith, S. Africa . 49 D4
Ladysmith, U.S.A. . . 70 C9
Lae, Papua N. G. . . . 56 H6
Læsø, Denmark 9 H11
Lafayette, Colo., U.S.A. 70 F2
Lafayette, Ind., U.S.A. 68 E2
Lafayette, La., U.S.A. 71 K9
Lafayette, Tenn.,
  U.S.A. 69 G3
Laferte →, Canada . 64 A5
Lafia, Nigeria 44 G6
Lafleche, Canada . . . 65 D7
Lagan →, U.K. 13 B6
Lagarfljót →, Iceland 8 D6
Lågen →, Norway . . 9 F11
Laghouat, Algeria . . 44 B5
Lagonoy Gulf, Phil. . . 33 B6
Lagos, Nigeria 44 G5
Lagos, Portugal . . . 19 D1
Lagrange, Australia . 52 C3
Lagrange B., Australia 52 C3
Laguna, Brazil 80 B7
Laguna, U.S.A. 73 J10
Laguna Beach, U.S.A. 73 K5
Lagunas, Chile 78 H5
Lagunas, Peru 78 E3
Lahad Datu, Malaysia 33 D5
Lahat, Indonesia . . . 32 E2
Lahewa, Indonesia . . 32 D1
Lahijan, Iran 39 B6
Lahn →, Germany . . 16 C3
Laholm, Sweden . . . 9 H12
Lahontan Res., U.S.A. 72 G4
Lahore, Pakistan . . . 36 D9
Lahti, Finland 9 F18
Lahtis = Lahti, Finland 9 F18
Laï, Chad 45 G8
Lai Chau, Vietnam . . 34 A7
Laidley, Australia . . . 55 D5
Laingsburg, S. Africa 48 E3
Lairg, U.K. 12 C4
Lajere, Nigeria 44 F7
Lajes, Brazil 80 B6
Lakar, Indonesia . . . 33 F7
Lake Andes, U.S.A. . 70 D5
Lake Anse, U.S.A. . . 68 B1
Lake Arthur, U.S.A. . 71 K8
Lake Cargelligo,
  Australia 55 E4
Lake Charles, U.S.A. . 71 K8
Lake City, Colo., U.S.A. 73 G10
Lake City, Fla., U.S.A. 69 K4
Lake City, Iowa, U.S.A. 70 D7
Lake City, Mich., U.S.A. 68 C3
Lake City, Minn.,
  U.S.A. 70 C8
Lake City, S.C., U.S.A. 69 J6
Lake Grace, Australia 53 F2
Lake Harbour, Canada 61 B13
Lake Havasu City,
  U.S.A. 73 J6
Lake King, Australia . 53 F2
Lake Lenore, Canada . 65 C8
Lake Louise, Canada . 64 C5
Lake Mead Nat. Rec.
  Area, U.S.A. 73 J6
Lake Mills, U.S.A. . . 70 D8
Lake Nash, Australia . 54 C2
Lake Providence,
  U.S.A. 71 J9
Lake River, Canada . . 62 B3
Lake Superior Prov.
  Park, Canada 62 C3
Lake Wales, U.S.A. . . 69 M5
Lake Worth, U.S.A. . . 69 M5
Lakefield, Canada . . 62 D4
Lakeland, Australia . . 54 B3
Lakeland, U.S.A. . . . 69 L5
Lakemba, Fiji 51 D9
Lakes Entrance,
  Australia 55 F4
Lakeside, Ariz., U.S.A. 73 J9
Lakeside, Nebr., U.S.A. 70 D3
Lakeview, U.S.A. . . . 72 E3
Lakewood, Colo.,
  U.S.A. 70 F2
Lakewood, N.J., U.S.A. 68 E8
Lakewood, Ohio,
  U.S.A. 68 E5
Laki, Iceland 8 D4
Lakin, U.S.A. 71 G4
Lakitusaki →, Canada 62 B3
Lakonikós Kólpos,
  Greece 21 F10
Lakota, Ivory C. . . . 44 G3
Lakota, U.S.A. 70 A5
Laksefjorden, Norway 8 A19
Lakselv, Norway . . . 8 A18
Lakshadweep Is.,
  Ind. Oc. 26 J11
Lala Ghat, India . . . 37 G18
Lala Ghat, Ethiopia . 45 F12
Lalibela, Spain 19 A1
Lalitapur = Patan,
  Nepal 37 F14

Lamaing, Burma . . . 37 M20
Lamar, Colo., U.S.A. . 70 F3
Lamar, Mo., U.S.A. . 71 G7
Lamas, Peru 78 E3
Lambaréné, Gabon . . 46 E2
Lambasa, Fiji 51 C8
Lambay I., Ireland . . 13 C5
Lambert, U.S.A. . . . 70 B2
Lambert Glacier,
  Antarctica 5 D6
Lamberts Bay,
  S. Africa 48 E2
Lambi Kyun, Burma . 34 G5
Lame, Nigeria 44 F6
Lame Deer, U.S.A. . . 72 D10
Lamego, Portugal . . 19 B2
Lamèque, Canada . . 63 C7
Lameroo, Australia . . 55 F3
Lamesa, U.S.A. 71 J4
Lamía, Greece 21 E10
Lammermuir Hills, U.K. 12 F6
Lamon Bay, Phil. . . . 33 B6
Lamont, Canada . . . 64 C6
Lampa, Peru 78 G4
Lampang, Thailand . . 34 C5
Lampasas, U.S.A. . . 71 K5
Lampedusa, Medit. S. 20 G5
Lampeter, U.K. 11 E3
Lampman, Canada . . 65 D8
Lamprey, Canada . . 65 B10
Lampung □, Indonesia 32 F2
Lamu, Kenya 46 E8
Lamy, U.S.A. 73 J11
Lanai I., U.S.A. 66 H16
Lanak La, India 36 B11
Lanak'o Shank'ou =
  Lanak La, India . . 36 B11
Lanao, L., Phil. 33 C6
Lanark, U.K. 12 F5
Lancang Jiang →,
  China 30 D5
Lancashire □, U.K. . . 10 D5
Lancaster, U.K. 10 C5
Lancaster, Calif., U.S.A. 73 J4
Lancaster, Ky., U.S.A. 68 G3
Lancaster, N.H., U.S.A. 68 C10
Lancaster, Pa., U.S.A. 68 E7
Lancaster, S.C., U.S.A. 69 H5
Lancaster, Wis., U.S.A. 70 D9
Lancaster Sd., Canada 61 A11
Lancer, Canada 65 C7
Lanchow = Lanzhou,
  China 30 C5
Lanciano, Italy 20 C6
Landeck, Austria . . . 16 E5
Landen, Belgium . . . 15 D5
Lander, U.S.A. 72 E9
Lander →, Australia . 52 D5
Landes, France 18 E3
Landes □, France . . . 18 E3
Land's End, U.K. . . . 11 G2
Landsborough Cr. →,
  Australia 54 C3
Landshut, Germany . 16 D6
Landskrona, Sweden . 9 J12
Lanett, U.S.A. 69 J3
Lang Bay, Canada . . 64 D4
Lang Son, Vietnam . . 34 B9
La'nga Co, China . . . 37 D12
Langar, Iran 39 C9
Langara I., Canada . . 64 C2
Langdon, U.S.A. . . . 70 A5
Langeberg, S. Africa . 48 E3
Langeberge, S. Africa 48 D3
Langenburg, Canada . 65 C8
Langholm, U.K. 12 F5
Langjökull, Iceland . . 8 D3
Langkawi, P., Malaysia 34 Q2
Langklip, S. Africa . . 48 D3
Langkon, Malaysia . . 32 C5
Langlade, St- P. & M. . 63 C8
Langlois, U.S.A. . . . 72 E1
Langøya, Norway . . 8 B13
Langres, France . . . 18 C6
Langres, Plateau de,
  France 18 C6
Langsa, Indonesia . . 32 D1
Langtry, U.S.A. 71 L4
Languedoc, France . . 18 E5
Lanigan, Canada . . . 65 C7
Lansdowne, Australia 55 E5
Lansdowne House,
  Canada 62 B2
L'Anse, U.S.A. 62 C2
L'Anse au Loup,
  Canada 63 B8
Lansing, U.S.A. 68 D3
Lanzarote, Canary Is. . 44 C2
Lanzhou, China 30 C5
Lao Cai, Vietnam . . . 34 A7
Laoag, Phil. 33 A6
Laoang, Phil. 33 B7
Laois □, Ireland . . . 13 D4
Laon, France 18 B5
Laona, U.S.A. 68 C1
Laos ■, Asia 34 D8
Lapa, Brazil 80 B7
Lapeer, U.S.A. 68 D4
Lapi = Lapin
  lääni □, Finland . . 8 C19
Lapin lääni □, Finland 8 C19
Lapland = Lappland,
  Europe 8 B18
Lappland, Europe . . . 8 B18
Laptev Sea, Russia . 25 B13
L'Aquila, Italy 20 C5

Lär,
  Āzarbājān-e Sharqī,
  Iran 38 B5
Lār, Fārs, Iran 39 E7
Larache, Morocco . . 44 A3
Laramie, U.S.A. 70 E2
Laramie Mts., U.S.A. . 70 E2
Laranjeiras, Indonesia 33 F6
Larantuka, Indonesia 33 F6
Larap, Phil. 33 B6
Larat, Indonesia . . . 33 F8
Larder Lake, Canada . 62 C4
Laredo, U.S.A. 71 M5
Laredo Sd., Canada . 64 C3
Largs, U.K. 12 F4
Lariang, Indonesia . . 33 E5
Larimore, U.S.A. . . . 70 B6
Lārīn, Iran 39 C7
Lárisa, Greece 21 E10
Larnaca, Cyprus . . . 38 C2
Larne, U.K. 13 B6
Larned, U.S.A. 70 F5
Larrimah, Australia . . 52 C5
Larsen Ice Shelf,
  Antarctica 5 C17
Larvik, Norway 9 G11
Laryak, Russia 24 C8
Las Animas, U.S.A. . . 70 F3
Las Anod, Somali Rep. 40 F4
Las Cascadas, Panama 74 H14
Las Cruces, U.S.A. . . 73 K10
Las Flores, Argentina 80 D5
Las Khoreh,
  Somali Rep. 40 E4
Las Lajas, Argentina . 80 D2
Las Lomitas, Argentina 80 A4
Las Palmas, Canary Is. 44 C1
Las Pipinas, Argentina 80 D5
Las Plumas, Argentina 80 E3
Las Rosas, Argentina . 80 C4
Las Varillas, Argentina 80 C4
Las Vegas, N. Mex.,
  U.S.A. 73 J11
Las Vegas, Nev.,
  U.S.A. 73 H6
Lashburn, Canada . . 65 C7
Lashio, Burma 37 H20
Lassen Pk., U.S.A. . . 72 F3
Last Mountain L.,
  Canada 65 C7
Lastoursville, Gabon . 46 E2
Lastovo, Croatia . . . 20 C7
Latacunga, Ecuador . 78 D3
Latakia = Al
  Lādhiqīyah, Syria . 38 C2
Latchford, Canada . . 62 C4
Latham, Australia . . 53 E2
Latina, Italy 20 D5
Latium = Lazio □, Italy 20 C5
Latouche Treville, C.,
  Australia 52 C3
Latrobe, Australia . . 54 G4
Latrobe, U.S.A. 68 E6
Latvia ■, Europe . . . 22 C3
Lau Group, Fiji 51 C9
Lauchhammer,
  Germany 16 C6
Lauenburg, Germany . 16 B6
Laugarbakki, Iceland . 8 D3
Launceston, Australia 54 G4
Launceston, U.K. . . . 11 G3
Laune →, Ireland . . 13 D2
Launglon Bok, Burma 34 F4
Laura, Australia . . . 54 B3
Laurel, Miss., U.S.A. . 71 K10
Laurel, Mont., U.S.A. 72 D9
Laurencekirk, U.K. . . 12 E6
Laurens, U.S.A. 69 H4
Laurentian Plateau,
  Canada 63 B6
Laurentides, Parc Prov.
  des, Canada 63 C5
Laurie L., Canada . . 65 B8
Laurinburg, U.S.A. . . 69 H6
Laurium, U.S.A. . . . 68 B1
Lausanne, Switz. . . . 16 E3
Laut, Indonesia 32 D3
Laut Ketil, Kepulauan,
  Indonesia 32 E5
Lautoka, Fiji 51 C7
Lauzon, Canada . . . 63 C5
Lava Hot Springs,
  U.S.A. 72 E7
Laval, France 18 B3
Laverne, U.S.A. 71 G5
Laverton, Australia . . 53 E3
Lavrentiya, Russia . . 25 C19
Lávrion, Greece . . . 21 F11
Lavumisa, Swaziland . 49 D5
Lawas, Malaysia . . . 32 D5
Lawele, Indonesia . . 33 F6
Lawn Hill, Australia . . 54 B2
Lawng Pit, Burma . . 37 G20
Lawqah, Si. Arabia . . 38 D4
Lawrence, N.Z. 51 L2
Lawrence, Kans.,
  U.S.A. 70 F7
Lawrence, Mass.,
  U.S.A. 68 D10
Lawrenceburg, Ind.,
  U.S.A. 68 F3
Lawrenceburg, Tenn.,
  U.S.A. 69 H2
Lawrenceville, U.S.A. 69 J4
Lawton, U.S.A. 71 H5
Laxford, L., U.K. . . . 12 C3
Laylán, Iraq 38 C5
Laysan I., Pac. Oc. . . 57 E11
Laytonville, U.S.A. . . 72 G2
Lazio □, Italy 20 C5
Lazo, Russia 28 C6
Le Creusot, France . . 18 C6

Le François, Martinique 74 N21
Le Havre, France 18 B4
Le Mans, France 18 B4
Le Marinel, Zaïre 46 G5
Le Mars, U.S.A. 70 D6
Le Mont-St.-Michel, France 18 B3
Le Moule, Guadeloupe 75 D12
Le Puy, France 18 D5
Le Roy, U.S.A. 71 F7
Le Sueur, U.S.A. 70 C8
Le Tréport, France 18 A4
Le Verdon-sur-Mer, France 18 D3
Lea →, U.K. 11 F7
Lead, U.S.A. 70 C3
Leader, Canada 65 C7
Leadhills, U.K. 12 F5
Leadville, U.S.A. 73 G10
Leaf →, U.S.A. 71 K10
Leakey, U.S.A. 71 L5
Leamington, Canada .. 62 D3
Leamington, U.S.A. .. 72 G7
Leamington Spa = Royal Leamington Spa, U.K. 11 E6
Leandro Norte Alem, Argentina 80 B5
Learmonth, Australia .. 52 D1
Leask, Canada 65 C7
Leavenworth, Kans., U.S.A. 70 F7
Leavenworth, Wash., U.S.A. 72 C3
Lebak, Phil. 33 C6
Lebanon, Ind., U.S.A. 68 E2
Lebanon, Kans., U.S.A. 70 F5
Lebanon, Ky., U.S.A. 68 G3
Lebanon, Mo., U.S.A. 71 G8
Lebanon, Oreg., U.S.A. 72 D2
Lebanon, Pa., U.S.A. 68 E7
Lebanon, Tenn., U.S.A. 69 G2
Lebanon ■, Asia 41 B4
Lebec, U.S.A. 73 J4
Lebomboberge, S. Africa 49 C5
Lebrija, Spain 19 D2
Lebu, Chile 80 D2
Lecce, Italy 21 D8
Lecco, Italy 20 B3
Łęczyca, Poland 17 B9
Ledbury, U.K. 11 E5
Leduc, Canada 64 C6
Lee →, Ireland 13 E3
Leech L., U.S.A. 70 B7
Leedey, U.S.A. 71 H5
Leeds, U.K. 10 D6
Leeds, U.S.A. 69 J2
Leek, U.K. 10 D5
Leesburg, U.S.A. 69 L5
Leesville, U.S.A. 71 K8
Leeton, Australia 55 E4
Leeu Gamka, S. Africa 48 E3
Leeuwarden, Neths. .. 15 A5
Leeuwin, C., Australia 53 F2
Leeward Is., Atl. Oc. . 74 L18
Lefors, U.S.A. 71 H4
Lefroy, L., Australia .. 53 F3
Legal, Canada 64 C6
Leganés, Spain 19 B4
Legazpi, Phil. 33 B6
Legendre I., Australia 52 D2
Leghorn = Livorno, Italy 20 C4
Legnica, Poland 16 C8
Legume, Australia 55 D5
Leh, India 36 B10
Lehututu, Botswana .. 48 C3
Leicester, U.K. 11 E6
Leicestershire □, U.K. 11 E6
Leichhardt →, Australia 54 B2
Leichhardt Ra., Australia 54 C4
Leiden, Neths. 15 B4
Leie →, Belgium 15 C3
Leine →, Germany .. 16 B4
Leinster, Australia 53 E3
Leinster □, Ireland .. 13 C4
Leinster, Mt., Ireland 13 D5
Leipzig, Germany 16 C6
Leiria, Portugal 19 C1
Leisler, Mt., Australia 52 D4
Leith, U.K. 12 F5
Leith Hill, U.K. 11 F7
Leitrim, Ireland 13 B3
Leitrim □, Ireland 13 B3
Leizhou Bandao, China 31 D6
Lek →, Neths. 15 C4
Leksula, Indonesia .. 33 E7
Leland, U.S.A. 71 J9
Leland Lakes, Canada 65 A6
Leleque, Argentina .. 80 E2
Lelystad, Neths. 15 B5
Léman, Lac, Switz. .. 16 E4
Lemhi Ra., U.S.A. .. 72 D7
Lemmer, Neths. 15 B5
Lemmon, U.S.A. 70 C3
Lemoore, U.S.A. 73 H4
Lemvig, Denmark 9 H10
Lena →, Russia 25 B13
Lendeh, Iran 39 D6
Lenggong, Malaysia .. 34 P13
Leninabad = Khodzent, Tajikistan 24 E7
Leninakan = Kumayri, Armenia 23 F7
Leningrad = Sankt-Peterburg, Russia .. 22 C5

Leninogorsk = Ridder, Kazakhstan 24 D9
Leninsk, Russia 23 E8
Leninsk-Kuznetskiy, Russia 24 D9
Leninskoye, Russia .. 25 E14
Lenkoran, Azerbaijan 23 G8
Lenmalu, Indonesia .. 33 E8
Lenoir, U.S.A. 69 H5
Lenoir City, U.S.A. .. 69 H3
Lenora, U.S.A. 70 F4
Lenore L., Canada .. 65 C8
Lens, France 18 A5
Lensk, Russia 25 C12
Lentini, Italy 20 F6
Leoben, Austria 16 E7
Leola, U.S.A. 70 C5
Leominster, U.K. 11 E5
Leominster, U.S.A. .. 68 D10
León, Mexico 74 C4
León, Guanajuato, Mexico 74 C4
León, Nic. 74 E7
León, Spain 19 A3
León, U.S.A. 70 E8
León □, Spain 19 A3
León, Montañas de, Spain 19 A2
Leonardtown, U.S.A. . 68 F7
Leongatha, Australia .. 55 F4
Leonora, Australia .. 53 E3
Léopold II, Lac = Mai-Ndombe, L., Zaïre 46 E3
Leopoldsburg, Belgium 15 C5
Léopoldville = Kinshasa, Zaïre .. 46 E3
Leoti, U.S.A. 70 F4
Leoville, Canada 65 C7
Lépa, L. do, Angola .. 48 B2
Lepel, Belorussia 22 D4
Lepikha, Russia 25 C13
Léré, Chad 45 G7
Leribe, Lesotho 49 D4
Lérida, Spain 19 B6
Lerwick, U.K. 12 A7
Les Cayes, Haiti 75 D10
Les Étroits, Canada .. 63 C6
Les Sables-d'Olonne, France 18 C3
Lesbos = Lésvos, Greece 21 E12
Leshan, China 30 D5
Leshukonskoye, Russia 22 B8
Leskov I., Antarctica . 5 B1
Leskovac, Serbia, Yug. 21 C9
Leslie, U.S.A. 71 H8
Lesopilnoye, Russia .. 28 A7
Lesotho ■, Africa .. 49 D4
Lesozavodsk, Russia 25 E14
Lesse →, Belgium .. 15 D4
Lesser Antilles, W. Indies 75 E12
Lesser Slave L., Canada 64 B5
Lesser Sunda Is., Indonesia 33 F6
Lessines, Belgium .. 15 D3
Lestock, Canada 65 C8
Lesuer I., Australia .. 52 B4
Lésvos, Greece 21 E12
Leszno, Poland 16 C8
Leti, Kepulauan, Indonesia 33 F7
Leti Is. = Leti, Kepulauan, Indonesia 33 F7
Letiahau →, Botswana 48 C3
Leticia, Colombia .. 78 D4
Letjiesbos, S. Africa .. 48 E3
Letlhakeng, Botswana 48 C3
Letpadan, Burma 37 L19
Letpan, Burma 37 K19
Letsók-aw Kyun, Burma 34 G5
Letterkenny, Ireland . 13 B4
Leuser, G., Indonesia 32 D1
Leuven, Belgium 15 D4
Leuze, Hainaut, Belgium 15 D3
Leuze, Namur, Belgium 15 D4
Levan, U.S.A. 72 G8
Levanger, Norway .. 8 E11
Levelland, U.S.A. 71 J3
Leven, U.K. 12 E6
Leven, L., U.K. 12 E5
Leven, Toraka, Madag. 49 A8
Leveque C., Australia 52 C3
Leverkusen, Germany 16 C3
Levin, N.Z. 51 J5
Lévis, Canada 63 C5
Levis, L., Canada 64 A5
Levkás, Greece 21 E9
Levkôsia = Nicosia, Cyprus 38 C2
Lewellen, U.S.A. 70 E3
Lewes, U.K. 11 G8
Lewes, U.S.A. 68 F8
Lewis, U.K. 12 C2
Lewis, Butt of, U.K. .. 12 C2
Lewis Ra., Australia .. 52 D4
Lewis Ra., U.S.A. .. 72 C7
Lewisburg, U.S.A. .. 69 H2
Lewisporte, Canada .. 63 C8
Lewiston, Idaho, U.S.A. 72 C5
Lewiston, Maine, U.S.A. 69 C11
Lewistown, Mont., U.S.A. 72 C9
Lewistown, Pa., U.S.A. 68 E7

Lexington, Ill., U.S.A. 70 E10
Lexington, Ky., U.S.A. 68 F3
Lexington, Miss., U.S.A. 71 J9
Lexington, Mo., U.S.A. 70 F8
Lexington, N.C., U.S.A. 69 H5
Lexington, Nebr., U.S.A. 70 E5
Lexington, Oreg., U.S.A. 72 D4
Lexington, Tenn., U.S.A. 69 H1
Lexington Park, U.S.A. 68 F7
Leyte, Phil. 33 B6
Lhasa, China 30 D4
Lhazê, China 30 D3
Lhokkruet, Indonesia 32 D1
Lhokseumawe, Indonesia 32 C1
Lhuntsi Dzong, India 37 F17
Lianga, Phil. 33 C7
Lianyungang, China .. 31 C6
Liaoning □, China .. 31 B7
Liaoyang, China 31 B7
Liaoyuan, China 31 B7
Liard →, Canada .. 64 A4
Libau = Liepāja, Latvia 22 C3
Libby, U.S.A. 72 B6
Libenge, Zaïre 46 D3
Liberal, Kans., U.S.A. 71 G4
Liberal, Mo., U.S.A. 71 G7
Liberec, Czech. 16 C7
Liberia ■, W. Afr. .. 44 G3
Liberty, Mo., U.S.A. 70 F7
Liberty, Tex., U.S.A. 71 K7
Lîbîya, Sahrâ', Africa 45 C9
Libobo, Tanjung, Indonesia 33 E7
Libode, S. Africa 49 E4
Libonda, Zambia 47 G4
Libourne, France 18 D3
Libramont, Belgium .. 15 E5
Libreville, Gabon 46 D1
Libya ■, N. Afr. 45 C8
Libyan Desert = Lîbîya, Sahrâ', Africa 45 C9
Licantén, Chile 80 D2
Licata, Italy 20 F5
Lichfield, U.K. 10 E6
Lichinga, Mozam. .. 47 G7
Lichtenburg, S. Africa 48 D4
Lida, U.S.A. 73 H5
Lidköping, Sweden .. 9 G12
Liebig, Mt., Australia 52 D5
Liechtenstein ■, Europe 16 E4
Liège, Belgium 15 D5
Liège □, Belgium .. 15 D5
Liegnitz = Legnica, Poland 16 C8
Lienyünchiangshih = Lianyungang, China 31 C6
Lienz, Austria 16 E6
Liepāja, Latvia 22 C3
Lier, Belgium 15 C4
Lièvre →, Canada .. 62 C4
Liffey →, Ireland .. 13 C5
Lifford, Ireland 13 B4
Lifudzin, Russia 28 B7
Lightning Ridge, Australia 55 D4
Liguria □, Italy 20 B3
Ligurian Sea, Italy .. 20 C3
Lihou Reefs and Cays, Australia 54 B5
Lihue, U.S.A. 66 H15
Lijiang, China 30 D5
Likasi, Zaïre 46 G5
Likati, Zaïre 46 D4
Lille, France 18 A5
Lille Bælt, Denmark . 9 J10
Lillehammer, Norway 9 F11
Lillesand, Norway .. 9 G10
Lilleshall, U.K. 11 E5
Lillestrøm, Norway .. 9 G11
Lillian Point, Mt., Australia 53 E4
Lillooet →, Canada 64 D4
Lilongwe, Malawi .. 47 G6
Liloy, Phil. 33 C6
Lima, Indonesia 33 E7
Lima, Peru 78 F3
Lima, Mont., U.S.A. 72 D7
Lima, Ohio, U.S.A. .. 68 E3
Lima →, Portugal .. 19 B1
Limassol, Cyprus .. 38 C2
Limavady, U.K. 13 A5
Limavady □, U.K. .. 13 B5
Limay →, Argentina 80 D3
Limay Mahuida, Argentina 80 D3
Limbang, Brunei 32 D5
Limbe, Cameroon .. 44 H6
Limbri, Australia 55 E5
Limburg, Germany .. 16 C4
Limburg □, Belgium 15 C5
Limburg □, Neths. .. 15 C5
Limeira, Brazil 80 A7
Limerick, Ireland .. 13 D3
Limerick □, Ireland 13 D3
Limestone →, Canada 65 B10
Limfjorden, Denmark 9 H10
Limmen Bight, Australia 54 A2
Limmen Bight →, Australia 54 B2
Límnos, Greece 21 E11
Limoeiro do Norte, Brazil 79 E11
Limoges, France 18 D4
Limón, Costa Rica .. 75 F8
Limon, Panama 74 H14
Limon, U.S.A. 70 F3

Limon B., Panama .. 74 H14
Limousin, France 18 D4
Limpopo →, Africa 49 D5
Limuru, Kenya 46 E7
Linares, Chile 80 D2
Linares, Mexico 74 C5
Linares, Spain 19 C4
Lincoln, Argentina .. 80 C4
Lincoln, N.Z. 51 K4
Lincoln, U.K. 10 D7
Lincoln, Ill., U.S.A. .. 70 E10
Lincoln, Kans., U.S.A. 70 F5
Lincoln, Maine, U.S.A. 63 C6
Lincoln, N. Mex., U.S.A. 73 K11
Lincoln, Nebr., U.S.A. 70 E6
Lincoln Hav = Lincoln Sea, Arctic 4 A5
Lincoln Sea, Arctic .. 4 A5
Lincoln Wolds, U.K. 10 D7
Lincolnshire □, U.K. 10 D7
Lincolnton, U.S.A. .. 69 H5
Lind, U.S.A. 72 C4
Linden, Guyana 78 B7
Linden, U.S.A. 71 J7
Lindesnes, Norway .. 6 D7
Lindi, Tanzania 46 F7
Lindsay, Canada 62 D4
Lindsay, Calif., U.S.A. 73 H4
Lindsay, Okla., U.S.A. 71 H6
Lindsborg, U.S.A. .. 70 F6
Lingayen, Phil. 33 A6
Lingayen G., Phil. .. 33 A6
Lingen, Germany 16 B3
Lingga, Indonesia .. 32 E2
Lingga, Kepulauan, Indonesia 32 E2
Lingga Arch. = Lingga, Kepulauan, Indonesia 32 E2
Lingle, U.S.A. 70 D2
Linguère, Senegal .. 44 E1
Linh Cam, Vietnam . 34 C8
Linhai, China 31 D7
Linhares, Brazil 79 G10
Linköping, Sweden .. 9 G13
Linlithgow, U.K. 12 F5
Linnhe, L., U.K. 12 E3
Lins, Brazil 80 A7
Linton, U.S.A. 70 B4
Linton, Ind., U.S.A. 68 F2
Linton, N. Dak., U.S.A. 70 B4
Linville, Australia .. 55 D5
Linxi, China 31 B6
Linxia, China 30 C5
Linyanti →, Africa .. 48 B4
Linz, Austria 16 D7
Lion, G. du, France 18 E6
Lions, G. of = Lion, G. du, France 18 E6
Lion's Head, Canada 62 D3
Lipa, Phil. 33 B6
Lipari, Is., Italy 20 E6
Lipetsk, Russia 22 D6
Lipovcy Manzovka, Russia 28 B6
Lippe →, Germany .. 16 C3
Lipscomb, U.S.A. .. 71 G4
Liptrap C., Australia 55 F4
Lira, Uganda 46 D6
Liria, Spain 19 C5
Lisala, Zaïre 46 D4
Lisboa, Portugal 19 C1
Lisbon = Lisboa, Portugal 19 C1
Lisbon, U.S.A. 70 B6
Lisburn, U.K. 13 B5
Lisburne, C., U.S.A. 60 B3
Liscannor B., Ireland 13 D2
Lisianski I., Pac. Oc. 56 E10
Lisichansk, Ukraine .. 23 E6
Lisieux, France 18 B4
Liski, Russia 23 D6
Lismore, Australia .. 55 D5
Lismore, Ireland 13 D4
Lisse, Neths. 15 B4
Lista, Norway 9 G9
Lista, Sweden 9 G14
Lister, Mt., Antarctica 5 D11
Liston, Australia 55 D5
Listowel, Canada .. 62 D3
Listowel, Ireland .. 13 D2
Litang, Malaysia .. 33 C5
Litani →, Lebanon 41 B4
Litchfield, Ill., U.S.A. 70 F10
Litchfield, Minn., U.S.A. 70 C7
Lithgow, Australia .. 55 E5
Líthinon, Ákra, Greece 21 G11
Lithuania ■, Europe 22 C4
Litoměřice, Czech. .. 16 C7
Little Barrier I., N.Z. 51 G5
Little Belt Mts., U.S.A. 72 C8
Little Blue →, U.S.A. 70 E6
Little Bushman Land, S. Africa 48 D2
Little Cadotte →, Canada 64 B5
Little Churchill →, Canada 65 B9
Little Colorado →, U.S.A. 73 H8
Little Current, Canada 62 C3
Little Current →, Canada 62 B3
Little Falls, Minn., U.S.A. 70 C7
Little Falls, N.Y., U.S.A. 68 D8
Little Fork →, U.S.A. 70 A8
Little Grand Rapids, Canada 65 C9

Little Humboldt →, U.S.A. 72 F5
Little Karoo, S. Africa 48 E3
Little Lake, U.S.A. .. 73 J5
Little Laut Is. = Laut Ketil, Kepulauan, Indonesia 32 E5
Little Minch, U.K. .. 12 D2
Little Missouri →, U.S.A. 70 B3
Little Namaqualand, S. Africa 48 E2
Little Ouse →, U.K. 11 E8
Little Red →, U.S.A. 71 H9
Little River, N.Z. .. 51 K4
Little Rock, U.S.A. .. 71 H8
Little Sable Pt., U.S.A. 68 D2
Little Sioux →, U.S.A. 70 E6
Little Smoky →, Canada 64 C5
Little Snake →, U.S.A. 72 F9
Little Wabash →, U.S.A. 68 G1
Littlefield, U.S.A. .. 71 J3
Littlefork, U.S.A. .. 70 A8
Littlehampton, U.K. 11 G7
Littleton, U.S.A. 68 C10
Liukang Tenggaja, Indonesia 33 F5
Liuwa Plain, Zambia 47 G4
Liuzhou, China 31 D5
Live Oak, U.S.A. .. 69 K4
Liveringa, Australia 52 C3
Livermore, Mt., U.S.A. 71 K2
Liverpool, U.K. 10 D5
Liverpool, Canada .. 63 D7
Liverpool, U.K. 10 D5
Liverpool Plains, Australia 55 E5
Liverpool Ra., Australia 55 E5
Livingston, Mont., U.S.A. 72 D8
Livingston, Tex., U.S.A. 71 K7
Livingstonia, Malawi 46 G6
Livny, Russia 22 D6
Livonia, U.S.A. 68 D4
Livorno, Italy 20 C4
Livramento, Brazil .. 80 C5
Liwale, Tanzania .. 46 F7
Lizard I., Australia .. 54 A4
Lizard Pt., U.K. 11 H2
Ljubljana, Slovenia 20 A6
Ljungan →, Sweden 8 E14
Ljungby, Sweden .. 9 H12
Ljusdal, Sweden .. 9 F14
Ljusnan = Ljungan →, Sweden 8 E14
Ljusnan →, Sweden 8 E14
Ljusne, Sweden 9 F14
Llancanelo, Salina, Argentina 80 D3
Llandeilo, U.K. 11 F3
Llandovery, U.K. .. 11 F4
Llandrindod Wells, U.K. 11 E4
Llandudno, U.K. .. 10 D4
Llanelli, U.K. 11 F3
Llanes, Spain 19 A3
Llangollen, U.K. .. 10 E4
Llanidloes, U.K. .. 11 E4
Llano, U.S.A. 71 K5
Llano →, U.S.A. .. 71 K5
Llano Estacado, U.S.A. 71 J3
Llanos, S. Amer. .. 78 C4
Lleida = Lérida, Spain 19 B6
Llobregat →, Spain 19 B7
Lloret de Mar, Spain 19 B7
Lloyd B., Australia 54 A3
Lloyd L., Canada .. 65 B7
Lloydminster, Canada 65 C6
Llullaillaco, Volcán, S. Amer. 80 A3
Loa, U.S.A. 73 G8
Loa →, Chile 80 A2
Lobatse, Botswana 48 D4
Lobería, Argentina 80 D5
Lobito, Angola 47 G2
Lobos, Is., Peru 76 C1
Loc Binh, Vietnam 34 B9
Loc Ninh, Vietnam 34 G9
Locarno, Switz. 16 E4
Lochaber, U.K. 12 E4
Lochcarron, U.K. .. 12 D3
Lochem, Neths. 15 B6
Loches, France 18 C4
Lochgelly, U.K. 12 E5
Lochgilphead, U.K. 12 E3
Lochinver, U.K. 12 C3
Lochnagar, Australia 54 C4
Lochy →, U.K. 12 E4
Lock, Australia 55 E2
Lock Haven, U.S.A. 68 E7
Lockeport, Canada .. 63 D6
Lockerbie, U.K. 12 F5
Lockhart, U.S.A. .. 71 L6
Lockhart, L., Australia 53 F2
Lockney, U.S.A. .. 71 H4
Lockport, U.S.A. .. 68 D6
Lod, Israel 41 D3
Lodeinoye Pole, Russia 22 B5
Lodge Grass, U.S.A. 72 D10
Lodgepole, U.S.A. 70 E3
Lodgepole Cr. →, U.S.A. 70 E2
Lodhran, Pakistan .. 36 E7
Lodi, U.S.A. 72 G3
Lodja, Zaïre 46 E4
Lodwar, Kenya 46 D7
Łódź, Poland 17 C10

Loeriesfontein, S. Africa 48 E2
Lofoten, Norway .. 8 B13
Logan, Kans., U.S.A. 70 F5
Logan, Ohio, U.S.A. 68 F4
Logan, Utah, U.S.A. 72 F8
Logan, W. Va., U.S.A. 68 G5
Logan, Mt., Canada 60 B5
Logan Pass, U.S.A. 64 D6
Logansport, Ind., U.S.A. 68 E2
Logansport, La., U.S.A. 71 K8
Logone →, Chad .. 45 F8
Logroño, Spain 19 A4
Lohardaga, India .. 37 H14
Loi-kaw, Burma .. 37 K20
Loimaa, Finland .. 9 F17
Loir →, France 18 C3
Loir-et-Cher □, France 18 C4
Loire □, France 18 D6
Loire →, France .. 18 C2
Loire-Atlantique □, France 18 C3
Loiret □, France .. 18 C5
Loja, Ecuador 78 D3
Loja, Spain 19 D3
Loji, Indonesia 33 E7
Lokandu, Zaïre 46 E5
Lokeren, Belgium .. 15 C3
Lokitaung, Kenya .. 46 D7
Lokka, Finland 8 C19
Løkken Verk, Norway 8 E10
Lokoja, Nigeria 44 G6
Lokolama, Zaïre .. 46 E3
Loliondo, Tanzania 46 E7
Lolland, Denmark .. 9 J11
Lolo, U.S.A. 72 C6
Lom, Bulgaria 21 C10
Loma, U.S.A. 72 C8
Lomami →, Zaïre .. 46 D4
Lombadina, Australia 52 C3
Lombardia □, Italy 20 B3
Lombardy = Lombardia □, Italy 20 B3
Lomblen, Indonesia 33 F6
Lombok, Indonesia 32 F5
Lomé, Togo 44 G5
Lomela, Zaïre 46 E4
Lomela →, Zaïre .. 46 E4
Lometa, U.S.A. 71 K5
Lomié, Cameroon .. 46 D2
Lomond, Canada .. 64 C6
Lomond, L., U.K. .. 12 E4
Lompobatang, Indonesia 33 F5
Lompoc, U.S.A. .. 73 J3
Łomża, Poland 17 B12
Loncoche, Chile .. 80 D2
Londa, India 36 M9
Londiani, Kenya .. 46 E7
London, Canada .. 62 D3
London, U.K. 11 F7
London, Ky., U.S.A. 68 G3
London, Ohio, U.S.A. 68 F4
London, Greater □, U.K. 11 F7
Londonderry, U.K. 13 B4
Londonderry □, U.K. 13 B4
Londonderry, C., Australia 52 B4
Londonderry, I., Chile 80 H2
Londrina, Brazil .. 80 A6
Lone Pine, U.S.A. 73 H4
Long Beach, Calif., U.S.A. 73 K4
Long Beach, Wash., U.S.A. 72 C1
Long Branch, U.S.A. 68 E9
Long Creek, U.S.A. 72 D4
Long Eaton, U.K. .. 10 E6
Long I., Australia .. 54 C4
Long I., Bahamas .. 75 C9
Long I., U.S.A. 68 E9
Long L., Canada .. 62 C2
Long Pine, U.S.A. 70 D5
Long Pt., Canada .. 63 C8
Long Range Mts., Canada 63 C8
Long Reef, Australia 52 B4
Long Str. = Longa, Proliv, Russia .. 4 C16
Long Xuyen, Vietnam 34 G8
Longa, Proliv, Russia 4 C16
Longford, Australia 54 G4
Longford, Ireland .. 13 C4
Longford □, Ireland 13 C4
Longiram, Indonesia 32 E5
Longlac, Canada .. 62 C2
Longmont, U.S.A. 70 E2
Longnawan, Indonesia 32 D4
Longreach, Australia 54 C3
Longton, Australia 54 C4
Longtown, U.K. .. 11 F5
Longview, Canada .. 64 C6
Longview, Tex., U.S.A. 71 J7
Longview, Wash., U.S.A. 72 C2
Lonoke, U.S.A. .. 71 H9
Lons-le-Saunier, France 18 C6
Lookout, C., Canada 62 A3
Lookout, C., U.S.A. 69 H7
Loon →, Alta., Canada 64 B5
Loon →, Man., Canada 65 B8
Loon Lake, Canada 65 C7
Loongana, Australia 53 F4
Loop Hd., Ireland .. 13 D2
Lop Nor = Lop Nur, China 30 B4
Lop Nur, China .. 30 B4
Lopatina, G., Russia 25 D15

Lopez, C.

Lopez, C., Gabon 46 E1
Lopphavet, Norway 8 A16
Lora →, Afghan. 36 D4
Lora, Hamun-i-, Pakistan 36 E4
Lora Cr. →, Australia 55 D2
Lorain, U.S.A. 68 E4
Loralai, Pakistan 36 D6
Lorca, Spain 19 D5
Lord Howe I., Pac. Oc. 56 L7
Lord Howe Ridge, Pac. Oc. 56 L8
Lordsburg, U.S.A. 73 K9
Loreto, Brazil 79 E9
Loreto, Italy 20 C5
Lorient, France 18 C2
Lorn, U.K. 12 E3
Lorn, Firth of, U.K. 12 E3
Lorne, Australia 55 F3
Lorraine, France 18 B7
Lorrainville, Canada 62 C4
Los Alamos, U.S.A. 73 J10
Los Andes, Chile 80 C2
Los Angeles, Chile 80 D2
Los Angeles, U.S.A. 73 K4
Los Angeles Aqueduct, U.S.A. 73 J5
Los Banos, U.S.A. 73 H3
Los Blancos, Argentina 80 A4
Los Hermanos, Venezuela 78 A6
Los Lunas, U.S.A. 73 J10
Los Mochis, Mexico 74 B3
Los Mochis, Sinaloa, Mexico 74 B3
Los Olivos, U.S.A. 73 J3
Los Roques, Venezuela 78 A5
Los Testigos, Venezuela 78 A6
Los Vilos, Chile 80 C2
Loshkalakh, Russia 25 C15
Lošinj, Croatia 20 B6
Lossiemouth, U.K. 12 D5
Lot □, France 18 D4
Lot →, France 18 D4
Lot-et-Garonne □, France 18 D4
Lota, Chile 80 D2
Loṭfābād, Iran 39 B8
Lothair, S. Africa 49 D5
Lothian □, U.K. 12 F5
Loubomo, Congo 46 E2
Loudon, U.S.A. 69 H3
Louga, Senegal 44 E1
Loughborough, U.K. 10 E6
Loughrea, Ireland 13 C3
Loughros More B., Ireland 13 B3
Louis Trichardt, S. Africa 49 C4
Louis XIV, Pte., Canada 62 B4
Louisa, U.S.A. 68 F4
Louisbourg, Canada 63 C8
Louise I., Canada 64 C2
Louiseville, Canada 62 C5
Louisiade Arch., Papua N. G. 56 J7
Louisiana, U.S.A. 70 F9
Louisiana □, U.S.A. 71 K9
Louisville, Ky., U.S.A. 68 F3
Louisville, Miss., U.S.A. 71 J10
Loulé, Portugal 19 D1
Loup City, U.S.A. 70 E5
Lourdes, France 18 E3
Lourdes-du-Blanc-Sablon, Canada 63 B8
Lourenço-Marques = Maputo, Mozam. 49 D5
Louth, Australia 55 E4
Louth, Ireland 13 C5
Louth, U.K. 10 D7
Louth □, Ireland 13 C5
Louvain = Leuven, Belgium 15 D4
Louwsburg, S. Africa 49 D5
Love, Canada 65 C8
Loveland, U.S.A. 70 E2
Lovell, U.S.A. 72 D9
Lovelock, U.S.A. 72 F4
Loviisa = Lovisa, Finland 9 F19
Loving, U.S.A. 71 J2
Lovington, U.S.A. 71 J3
Lovisa, Finland 9 F19
Low Pt., Australia 53 F4
Low Tatra = Nizké Tatry, Slovakia 17 D9
Lowell, U.S.A. 68 D10
Lower Arrow L., Canada 64 D5
Lower California = Baja California, Mexico 74 B2
Lower Hutt, N.Z. 51 J5
Lower L., U.S.A. 72 F3
Lower Lake, U.S.A. 72 G2
Lower Post, Canada 64 B3
Lower Red L., U.S.A. 70 B7
Lower Tunguska = Tunguska, Nizhnyaya →, Russia 25 C9
Lowestoft, U.K. 11 E9
Łowicz, Poland 17 B9
Lowville, U.S.A. 68 D8
Loxton, Australia 55 E3
Loxton, S. Africa 48 E3
Loyalty Is. = Loyauté, Is., N. Cal. 56 K8
Loyang = Luoyang, China 31 C6
Loyauté, Is., N. Cal. 56 K8
Lozère □, France 18 D5
Luachimo, Angola 46 F4
Luacono, Angola 46 G4
Lualaba →, Zaïre 46 D5
Luan Chau, Vietnam 34 B7
Luanda, Angola 46 F2
Luang Prabang, Laos 34 C7
Luangwa, Zambia 47 H6
Luangwa →, Zambia 47 G6
Luanshya, Zambia 47 G5
Luapula →, Africa 46 F5
Luarca, Spain 19 A2
Luashi, Zaïre 46 G4
Luau, Angola 46 G4
Lubalo, Angola 46 F3
Lubang Is., Phil. 33 B6
Lubbock, U.S.A. 71 J4
Lübeck, Germany 16 B5
Lubefu, Zaïre 46 E4
Lubero = Luofu, Zaïre 46 E5
Lubicon L., Canada 64 B5
Lublin, Poland 17 C11
Lubnān, J., Lebanon 41 B4
Lubny, Ukraine 24 D4
Lubuagan, Phil. 33 A6
Lubuk Antu, Malaysia 32 D4
Lubuklinggau, Indonesia 32 E2
Lubuksikaping, Indonesia 32 D2
Lubumbashi, Zaïre 47 G5
Lubutu, Zaïre 46 E5
Lucca, Italy 20 C4
Luce Bay, U.K. 12 G4
Lucea, Jamaica 74 J15
Lucedale, U.S.A. 69 K1
Lucena, Phil. 33 B6
Lucena, Spain 19 D3
Lučenec, Slovakia 17 D9
Lucerne = Luzern, Switz. 16 E4
Lucira, Angola 47 G2
Luckenwalde, Germany 16 B6
Lucknow, India 37 F12
Lüda = Dalian, China 31 C7
Lüderitz, Namibia 48 D2
Ludhiana, India 36 D9
Ludington, U.S.A. 68 D2
Ludlow, U.K. 11 E5
Ludlow, U.S.A. 73 J5
Ludvika, Sweden 9 F13
Ludwigsburg, Germany 16 D4
Ludwigshafen, Germany 16 D4
Luebo, Zaïre 46 F4
Lufira →, Zaïre 46 F5
Lufkin, U.S.A. 71 K7
Luga, Russia 22 C4
Lugano, Switz. 16 E4
Lugansk, Ukraine 23 E6
Lugh Ganana, Somali Rep. 40 G3
Lugnaquilla, Ireland 13 D5
Lugo, Spain 19 A2
Lugoj, Romania 17 F10
Lugovoye, Kazakhstan 24 E8
Luhansk = Lugansk, Ukraine 23 E6
Luiana, Angola 48 B3
Luís Correia, Brazil 79 D10
Luitpold Coast, Antarctica 5 D1
Luiza, Zaïre 46 F4
Luján, Argentina 80 C5
Lukanga Swamp, Zambia 47 G5
Lukenie →, Zaïre 46 E3
Lukolela, Zaïre 46 E3
Łuków, Poland 17 C11
Lule älv →, Sweden 8 D17
Luleå, Sweden 8 D17
Luling, U.S.A. 71 L6
Lulonga →, Zaïre 46 D3
Lulua →, Zaïre 46 E4
Luluabourg = Kananga, Zaïre 46 F4
Lumai, Angola 47 G4
Lumajang, Indonesia 33 H15
Lumbala N'guimbo, Angola 47 G4
Lumberton, Miss., U.S.A. 71 K10
Lumberton, N.C., U.S.A. 69 H6
Lumberton, N. Mex., U.S.A. 73 H10
Lumsden, N.Z. 51 L2
Lumut, Malaysia 34 Q13
Lumut, Tg., Indonesia 32 E3
Lund, U.S.A. 72 G6
Lundazi, Zambia 47 G6
Lundu, Malaysia 32 D3
Lundy, U.K. 11 F3
Lune →, U.K. 10 C5
Lüneburg, Germany 16 B5
Lüneburg Heath = Lüneburger Heide, Germany 16 B5
Lüneburger Heide, Germany 16 B5
Lunenburg, Canada 63 D7
Lunéville, France 18 B7
Lunglei, India 37 H18
Luni, India 36 G8
Luni →, India 36 G7
Luning, U.S.A. 72 G4
Luofu, Zaïre 46 E5
Luoyang, China 31 C6
Luozi, Zaïre 46 E2
Luqa, Malta 20 G6
Luray, U.S.A. 68 F6
Luremo, Angola 46 F3
Lurgan, U.K. 13 B5
Lusaka, Zambia 47 H5
Lusambo, Zaïre 46 E4
Luseland, Canada 65 C7
Lushoto, Tanzania 46 E7
Lusk, U.S.A. 70 D2
Luta = Dalian, China 31 C7
Luton, U.K. 11 F7
Lutong, Malaysia 32 D4
Lutsk, Ukraine 22 D4
Lützow Holmbukta, Antarctica 5 C4
Lutzputs, S. Africa 48 D3
Luverne, U.S.A. 70 D6
Luwuk, Indonesia 33 E6
Luxembourg, Lux. 15 E6
Luxembourg □, Belgium 15 E5
Luxembourg ■, Europe 15 E6
Luxi, China 30 D4
Luxor = El Uqsur, Egypt 45 C11
Luza, Russia 22 B8
Luzern, Switz. 16 E4
Luzhou, China 30 D5
Luziânia, Brazil 79 G9
Luzon, Phil. 33 A6
Lviv = Lvov, Ukraine 23 E3
Lvov, Ukraine 23 E3
Lyakhovskiye, Ostrova, Russia 25 B15
Lyallpur = Faisalabad, Pakistan 36 D8
Lycksele, Sweden 8 D15
Lydda = Lod, Israel 41 D3
Lydenburg, S. Africa 49 D5
Lyell, N.Z. 51 J4
Lyell I., Canada 64 C2
Lyman, U.S.A. 72 F8
Lyme Regis, U.K. 11 G5
Lymington, U.K. 11 G6
Łyna →, Poland 17 A10
Lynchburg, U.S.A. 68 G6
Lynd →, Australia 54 B3
Lynd Ra., Australia 55 D4
Lynden, U.S.A. 72 B2
Lyndhurst, Queens., Australia 54 B3
Lyndhurst, S. Austral., Australia 55 E2
Lyndon →, Australia 53 D1
Lynher Reef, Australia 52 C3
Lynn, U.S.A. 68 D10
Lynn Canal, U.S.A. 64 B1
Lynn Lake, Canada 65 B8
Lynton, U.K. 11 F4
Lynx L., Canada 65 A7
Lyon, France 18 D6
Lyonnais, France 18 D6
Lyons = Lyon, France 18 D6
Lyons, Colo., U.S.A. 70 E2
Lyons, Ga., U.S.A. 69 J4
Lyons, Kans., U.S.A. 70 F5
Lyons, N.Y., U.S.A. 68 D7
Lys = Leie →, Belgium 15 C3
Lysva, Russia 22 C10
Lytle, U.S.A. 71 L5
Lyttelton, N.Z. 51 K4
Lytton, Canada 64 C4
Lyubertsy, Russia 22 C6

M

Ma'adaba, Jordan 41 E4
Maamba, Zambia 48 B4
Ma'ān, Jordan 41 E4
Ma'ān □, Jordan 41 F5
Ma'anshan, China 31 C6
Maarianhamina, Finland 9 F15
Ma'arrat an Nu'mān, Syria 38 C3
Maas →, Neths. 15 C4
Maaseik, Belgium 15 C5
Maassluis, Neths. 15 C4
Maastricht, Neths. 15 D5
Maave, Mozam. 49 C5
Mabel L., Canada 64 C5
Mablethorpe, U.K. 10 D8
Mabrouk, Mali 44 E4
Mabton, U.S.A. 72 C3
Macaé, Brazil 79 H10
McAlester, U.S.A. 71 H7
McAllen, U.S.A. 71 M5
Macamic, Canada 62 C4
Macao = Macau ■, China 31 D6
Macapá, Brazil 79 C8
McArthur →, Australia 54 B2
McArthur, Port, Australia 54 B2
McArthur River, Australia 54 B2
Macau, Brazil 79 E11
Macau ■, China 31 D6
McBride, Canada 64 C4
McCall, U.S.A. 72 D5
McCamey, U.S.A. 71 K3
McCammon, U.S.A. 72 E7
McCauley I., Canada 64 C2
Macclesfield, U.K. 10 D5
McClintock, Canada 65 B10
McClintock Ra., Australia 52 C4
McCloud, U.S.A. 72 F2
McCluer I., Australia 52 B5
M'Clure Str., Canada 4 B2
McClusky, U.S.A. 70 B4
McComb, U.S.A. 71 K9
McConaughy, L., U.S.A. 70 E4
McCook, U.S.A. 70 E4
McCusker →, Canada 65 B7
McDame, Canada 64 B3
McDermitt, U.S.A. 72 F5
Macdonald, L., Australia 52 D4
McDonald Is., Ind. Oc. 35 K6
Macdonnell Ras., Australia 52 D5
McDouall Peak, Australia 55 D1
Macdougall L., Canada 60 B10
MacDowell L., Canada 62 B1
Macduff, U.K. 12 D6
Macedonia = Makedhonia □, Greece 21 D10
Macedonia ■, Europe 21 D9
Maceió, Brazil 79 E11
Macenta, Guinea 44 G3
Macerata, Italy 20 C5
McFarlane →, Canada 65 B7
Macfarlane, L., Australia 55 E2
McGehee, U.S.A. 71 J9
McGill, U.S.A. 72 G6
Macgillycuddy's Reeks, Ireland 13 D2
MacGregor, Canada 65 D9
McGregor, U.S.A. 70 D9
McGregor →, Canada 64 B4
McGregor Ra., Australia 55 D3
Mach, Pakistan 36 E5
Māch Kowr, Iran 39 E9
Machado = Jiparaná →, Brazil 78 E6
Machakos, Kenya 46 E7
Machala, Ecuador 78 D3
Machanga, Mozam. 49 C6
Machattie, L., Australia 54 C2
Machava, Mozam. 49 D5
Machevna, Russia 25 C18
Machias, U.S.A. 63 D6
Machichi →, Canada 65 B10
Machilipatnam, India 37 L12
Machiques, Venezuela 78 A4
Machupicchu, Peru 78 F4
Machynlleth, U.K. 11 E4
McIlwraith Ra., Australia 54 A3
McIntosh, U.S.A. 70 C4
McIntosh L., Canada 65 B8
Macintosh Ra., Australia 53 E4
Macintyre →, Australia 55 D5
Mackay, Australia 54 C4
Mackay, U.S.A. 72 E7
MacKay →, Canada 64 B6
Mackay, L., Australia 52 D4
McKay Ra., Australia 52 D3
McKeesport, U.S.A. 68 E6
Mackenzie, Canada 64 B4
McKenzie, U.S.A. 69 G1
Mackenzie →, Australia 54 C4
Mackenzie →, Canada 60 B6
McKenzie →, U.S.A. 72 D2
Mackenzie Bay, Canada 4 B1
Mackenzie City = Linden, Guyana 78 B7
Mackenzie Highway, Canada 64 B5
Mackenzie Mts., Canada 60 B6
Mackinaw City, U.S.A. 68 C3
McKinlay, Australia 54 C3
McKinlay →, Australia 54 C3
McKinley, Mt., U.S.A. 60 B4
McKinley Sea, Arctic 4 A7
McKinney, U.S.A. 71 J6
Macksville, Australia 55 E5
McLaughlin, U.S.A. 70 C4
Maclean, Australia 55 D5
McLean, U.S.A. 71 H4
McLeansboro, U.S.A. 70 F10
Maclear, S. Africa 49 E4
Macleay →, Australia 55 E5
McLennan, Canada 64 B5
MacLeod, B., Canada 65 A7
McLeod, L., Australia 53 D1
MacLeod Lake, Canada 64 C4
M'Clintock Chan., Canada 60 A9
McLoughlin, Mt., U.S.A. 72 E2
McLure, Canada 64 C4
McMillan L., U.S.A. 71 J2
McMinnville, Oreg., U.S.A. 72 D2
McMinnville, Tenn., U.S.A. 69 H3
McMorran, Canada 65 C7
McMurdo Sd., Antarctica 5 D11
McMurray = Fort McMurray, Canada 64 B6
McNary, U.S.A. 73 J9
MacNutt, Canada 65 C8
Macodoene, Mozam. 49 C6
Macomb, U.S.A. 70 E9
Mâcon, France 18 C6
Macon, Ga., U.S.A. 69 J4
Macon, Miss., U.S.A. 69 J1
Macon, Mo., U.S.A. 70 F8
Macondo, Angola 47 G4
Macoun L., Canada 65 B8
Macovane, Mozam. 49 C6
McPherson, U.S.A. 70 F6
McPherson Ra., Australia 55 D5
Macquarie Harbour, Australia 54 G4
Macquarie Is., Pac. Oc. 56 N7
MacRobertson Land, Antarctica 5 D6
Macroom, Ireland 13 E3
Macroy, Australia 52 D2
Macusse, Angola 48 B3
McVille, U.S.A. 70 B5
Madadeni, S. Africa 49 D5
Madagali, Nigeria 45 F7
Madagascar ■, Africa 49 C8
Madā'in Sālih, Si. Arabia 38 E3
Madama, Niger 45 D7
Madame I., Canada 63 C7
Madaoua, Niger 44 F6
Madaripur, Bangla. 37 H17
Madauk, Burma 37 L20
Madawaska →, Canada 62 C4
Madaya, Burma 37 H20
Madden Dam, Panama 74 H14
Madden Lake, Panama 74 H14
Madeira, Atl. Oc. 44 B1
Madeira →, Brazil 78 D7
Madeleine, Is. de la, Canada 63 C7
Madera, U.S.A. 73 H3
Madha, India 36 L9
Madhya Pradesh □, India 36 H11
Madikeri, India 36 N9
Madill, U.S.A. 71 H6
Madimba, Zaïre 46 E3
Ma'din, Syria 38 C3
Madīnat ash Sha'b, Yemen 40 E3
Madingou, Congo 46 E2
Madirovalo, Madag. 49 B8
Madison, Fla., U.S.A. 69 K4
Madison, Ind., U.S.A. 68 F3
Madison, Nebr., U.S.A. 70 E6
Madison, S. Dak., U.S.A. 70 D6
Madison, Wis., U.S.A. 70 D10
Madison →, U.S.A. 72 D8
Madisonville, Ky., U.S.A. 68 G2
Madisonville, Tex., U.S.A. 71 K7
Madista, Botswana 48 C4
Madiun, Indonesia 33 G14
Madley, U.K. 11 E5
Madras = Tamil Nadu □, India 36 P10
Madras, India 36 N12
Madras, U.S.A. 72 D3
Madre, L., U.S.A. 71 M6
Madre, Sierra, Phil. 33 A6
Madre de Dios →, Bolivia 78 F5
Madre de Dios, I., Chile 80 G1
Madre Occidental, Sierra, Mexico 74 B3
Madre Oriental, Sierra, Mexico 74 C5
Madrid, Spain 19 B4
Madura, Selat, Indonesia 33 G15
Madura Motel, Australia 53 F4
Madurai, India 36 Q11
Madurantakam, India 36 N11
Mae Hong Son, Thailand 34 C5
Mae Sot, Thailand 34 D5
Maebashi, Japan 29 F9
Maesteg, U.K. 11 F4
Maestrazgo, Mts. del, Spain 19 B5
Maevatanana, Madag. 49 B8
Mafeking = Mafikeng, S. Africa 48 D4
Mafeking, Canada 65 C8
Mafeteng, Lesotho 48 D4
Maffra, Australia 55 F4
Mafia I., Tanzania 46 F7
Mafikeng, S. Africa 48 D4
Mafra, Brazil 80 B7
Mafra, Portugal 19 C1
Magadan, Russia 25 D16
Magadi, Kenya 46 E7
Magaliesburg, S. Africa 49 D4
Magallanes, Estrecho de, Chile 80 G2
Magangué, Colombia 78 B4
Magburaka, S. Leone 44 G2
Magdalen Is. = Madeleine, Is. de la, Canada 63 C7
Magdalena, Argentina 80 D5
Magdalena, Bolivia 78 F6
Magdalena, Malaysia 32 D5
Magdalena, U.S.A. 73 J10
Magdalena →, Colombia 78 A4
Magdeburg, Germany 16 B5
Magdelaine Cays, Australia 54 B5
Magee, U.S.A. 71 K10
Magee, I., U.K. 13 B6
Magelang, Indonesia 33 G14
Magellan's Str. = Magallanes, Estrecho de, Chile 80 G2
Magenta, L., Australia 53 F2
Maggiore, L., Italy 20 A3
Magherafelt, U.K. 13 B5
Magnetic Pole (North) = North Magnetic Pole, Canada 4 B2
Magnetic Pole (South) = South Magnetic Pole, Antarctica 5 C9
Magnitogorsk, Russia 22 D10
Magnolia, Ark., U.S.A. 71 J8
Magnolia, Miss., U.S.A. 71 K9
Magog, Canada 63 C5
Magosa = Famagusta, Cyprus 38 C2
Magpie L., Canada 63 B7
Magrath, Canada 64 D6
Maguarinho, C., Brazil 79 D9
Maguse L., Canada 65 A9
Maguse Pt., Canada 65 A10
Magwe, Burma 37 J19
Mahābād, Iran 38 B5
Mahabo, Madag. 49 C7
Mahagi, Zaïre 46 D6
Mahajamba →, Madag. 49 B8
Mahajamba, Helodranon' i, Madag. 49 B8
Mahajanga, Madag. 49 B8
Mahajanga □, Madag. 49 B8
Mahajilo →, Madag. 49 B8
Mahakam →, Indonesia 32 E5
Mahalapye, Botswana 48 C4
Maḥallāt, Iran 39 C6
Māhān, Iran 39 D8
Mahanadi →, India 37 J15
Mahanoro, Madag. 49 B8
Maharashtra □, India 36 J9
Mahasham, W. →, Egypt 41 E3
Mahasolo, Madag. 49 B8
Mahattat ash Shīdīyah, Jordan 41 F4
Mahattat 'Unayzah, Jordan 41 E4
Mahbubnagar, India 36 L10
Maḥḍah, Oman 39 E7
Mahdia, Tunisia 45 A7
Mahé, Seychelles 35 E4
Mahenge, Tanzania 46 F7
Maheno, N.Z. 51 L3
Mahesana, India 36 H8
Mahia Pen., N.Z. 51 H6
Mahilyow = Mogilev, Belorussia 22 D5
Mahnomen, U.S.A. 70 B7
Mahón, Spain 19 C8
Mahone Bay, Canada 63 D7
Mai-Ndombe, L., Zaïre 46 E3
Maicurú →, Brazil 79 D8
Maidenhead, U.K. 11 F7
Maidstone, Canada 65 C7
Maidstone, U.K. 11 F8
Maiduguri, Nigeria 45 F7
Maijdi, Bangla. 37 H17
Maikala Ra., India 37 J12
Main →, Germany 16 D4
Main →, U.K. 13 B5
Main Centre, Canada 65 C7
Maine, France 18 C3
Maine □, U.S.A. 63 C6
Maine →, Ireland 13 D2
Maine-et-Loire □, France 18 C3
Maingkwan, Burma 37 F20
Mainit, L., Phil. 33 C7
Mainland, Orkney, U.K. 12 C5
Mainland, Shet., U.K. 12 A7
Maintirano, Madag. 49 B7
Mainz, Germany 16 D4
Maipú, Argentina 80 D5
Maiquetía, Venezuela 78 A5
Mairabari, India 37 F18
Maitland, N.S.W., Australia 55 E5
Maitland, S. Austral., Australia 55 E2
Maizuru, Japan 29 G7
Majalengka, Indonesia 33 G13
Majene, Indonesia 33 E5
Maji, Ethiopia 45 G12
Major, Canada 65 C7
Majorca = Mallorca, Spain 19 C7
Maka, Senegal 44 F2
Makale, Indonesia 33 E5
Makari, Cameroon 46 B2
Makarikari = Makgadikgadi Salt Pans, Botswana 48 C4
Makarovo, Russia 25 D11
Makasar = Ujung Pandang, Indonesia 33 F5
Makasar, Selat, Indonesia 33 E5
Makasar, Str. of = Makasar, Selat, Indonesia 33 E5
Makat, Kazakhstan 23 E9
Makedhonía □, Greece 21 D10
Makedonija = Macedonia ■, Europe 21 D9
Makena, U.S.A. 66 H16
Makeni, S. Leone 44 G2
Makeyevka, Ukraine 23 E6

Masuda

Makgadikgadi Salt Pans, Botswana 48 C4
Makhachkala, Russia 23 F8
Makhmūr, Iraq 38 C4
Makian, Indonesia 33 D7
Makindu, Kenya 46 E7
Makinsk, Kazakhstan 24 D8
Makiyivka = Makeyevka, Ukraine 23 E6
Makkah, Si. Arabia 40 C2
Makkovik, Canada 63 A8
Makó, Hungary 17 E10
Makokou, Gabon 46 D2
Makoua, Congo 46 E3
Makrai, India 36 H10
Makran Coast Range, Pakistan 36 G4
Maksimkin Yar, Russia 24 D9
Mākū, Iran 38 B5
Makumbi, Zaïre 46 F4
Makunda, Botswana 48 C3
Makurazaki, Japan 29 J5
Makurdi, Nigeria 44 G6
Makūyeh, Iran 39 D7
Makwassie, S. Africa 48 D4
Mal B., Ireland 13 D2
Malabang, Phil. 33 C6
Malabar Coast, India 36 P9
Malabo = Rey Malabo, Eq. Guin. 44 H6
Malacca, Str. of, Indonesia 34 S14
Malad City, U.S.A. 72 E7
Málaga, Spain 19 D3
Malaga, U.S.A. 71 J2
Málaga □, Spain 19 D3
Malaimbandy, Madag. 49 C8
Malakâl, Sudan 45 G11
Malakand, Pakistan 36 B7
Malakoff, U.S.A. 71 J7
Malamyzh, Russia 25 E14
Malang, Indonesia 33 G15
Malanje, Angola 46 F3
Mälaren, Sweden 9 G14
Malargüe, Argentina 80 D3
Malartic, Canada 62 C4
Malatya, Turkey 23 G6
Malawi ■, Africa 47 G6
Malawi, L., Africa 47 G6
Malay Pen., Asia 34 J6
Malaybalay, Phil. 33 C7
Malāyer, Iran 39 C6
Malaysia ■, Asia 32 D4
Malazgirt, Turkey 23 G7
Malbon, Australia 54 C3
Malbooma, Australia 55 E1
Malbork, Poland 17 A9
Malcolm, Australia 53 E3
Malcolm, Pt., Australia 53 F3
Maldegem, Belgium 15 C3
Malden, U.S.A. 71 G10
Malden I., Kiribati 57 H12
Maldives ■, Ind. Oc. 27 J11
Maldonado, Uruguay 80 C6
Malé Karpaty, Slovak Rep. 16 D8
Maléa, Ákra, Greece 21 F10
Malebo, Pool, Africa 42 G5
Malegaon, India 36 J9
Malek Kandī, Iran 38 B5
Malema, Mozam. 47 G7
Malgomaj, Sweden 8 D14
Malha, Sudan 45 E10
Malhão, Sa. do, Portugal 19 D1
Malheur →, U.S.A. 72 D5
Malheur L., U.S.A. 72 E4
Mali ■, Africa 44 E4
Mali →, Burma 37 G20
Mali Kyun, Burma 34 F5
Malik, Indonesia 33 E6
Malili, Indonesia 33 E6
Malin Hd., Ireland 13 A4
Malindi, Kenya 46 E8
Malines = Mechelen, Belgium 15 C4
Maling, Indonesia 33 D6
Malita, Phil. 33 C7
Mallacoota, Australia 55 F4
Mallacoota Inlet, Australia 55 F4
Mallaig, U.K. 12 E3
Mallawi, Egypt 45 C11
Mallorca, Spain 19 C7
Mallow, Ireland 13 D3
Malmberget, Sweden 8 C16
Malmédy, Belgium 15 D6
Malmesbury, S. Africa 48 E2
Malmö, Sweden 9 J12
Malmöhus län □, Sweden 9 J12
Malolos, Phil. 33 B6
Malone, U.S.A. 68 C8
Malozemelskaya Tundra, Russia 22 A9
Malpelo, Colombia 78 C2
Malta, Idaho, U.S.A. 72 E7
Malta, Mont., U.S.A. 72 B10
Malta ■, Europe 20 G6
Maltahöhe, Namibia 48 C2
Malton, U.K. 10 C7
Maluku, Indonesia 33 E7
Maluku □, Indonesia 33 E7
Maluku Sea, Indonesia 33 E6
Malvan, India 36 L8
Malvern, U.S.A. 71 H8
Malvern Hills, U.K. 11 E5
Malvinas, Is. = Falkland Is. ■, Atl. Oc. 80 G5
Malyy Lyakhovskiy, Ostrov, Russia 25 B15
Mama, Russia 25 D12
Mamaia, Romania 17 F14
Mamanguape, Brazil 79 E11
Mamasa, Indonesia 33 E5
Mamberamo →, Indonesia 33 E9
Mambilima Falls, Zambia 46 G5
Mamburao, Phil. 33 B6
Mameigwess L., Canada 62 B2
Mamfe, Cameroon 44 G6
Mammoth, U.S.A. 73 K8
Mamoré →, Bolivia 78 F5
Mamou, Guinea 44 F2
Mamuju, Indonesia 33 E5
Man, Ivory C. 44 G3
Man, I. of, U.K. 10 C3
Man Na, Burma 37 H20
Mana, Fr. Guiana 79 B8
Manaar, G. of = Mannar, G. of, Asia 36 Q11
Manacapuru, Brazil 78 D6
Manacor, Spain 19 C7
Manado, Indonesia 33 D6
Managua, Nic. 74 E7
Manakara, Madag. 49 C8
Manama = Al Manāmah, Bahrain 39 E6
Manambao →, Madag. 49 B7
Manambato, Madag. 49 A8
Manambolo →, Madag. 49 B7
Manambolosy, Madag. 49 B8
Mananara, Madag. 49 B8
Mananara →, Madag. 49 C8
Mananjary, Madag. 49 C8
Manantenina, Madag. 49 C8
Manaos = Manaus, Brazil 78 D7
Manapouri, N.Z. 51 L1
Manapouri, L., N.Z. 51 L1
Manas, China 30 B3
Manas →, India 37 F17
Manassa, U.S.A. 73 H11
Manaung, Burma 37 K18
Manaus, Brazil 78 D7
Manawan L., Canada 65 B8
Manay, Phil. 33 C7
Manbij, Syria 38 B3
Mancelona, U.S.A. 68 C3
Manche □, France 18 B3
Manchegorsk, Russia 22 A5
Manchester, U.K. 10 D5
Manchester, Conn., U.S.A. 68 E9
Manchester, Ga., U.S.A. 69 J3
Manchester, Iowa, U.S.A. 70 D9
Manchester, Ky., U.S.A. 68 G4
Manchester, N.H., U.S.A. 68 D10
Manchester L., Canada 65 A7
Manchuria = Dongbei, China 31 B7
Mand →, Iran 39 D7
Manda, Tanzania 46 G6
Mandabé, Madag. 49 C7
Mandal, Norway 9 G9
Mandalay, Burma 37 J20
Mandale = Mandalay, Burma 37 J20
Mandalī, Iraq 38 C5
Mandan, U.S.A. 70 B4
Mandar, Teluk, Indonesia 33 E5
Mandasor = Mandsaur, India 36 G9
Mandaue, Phil. 33 B6
Mandi, India 36 D10
Mandimba, Mozam. 47 G7
Mandioli, Indonesia 33 E7
Mandla, India 37 H12
Mandoto, Madag. 49 B8
Mandrare →, Madag. 49 D8
Mandritsara, Madag. 49 B8
Mandsaur, India 36 G9
Mandurah, Australia 53 F2
Mandvi, India 36 H6
Mandya, India 36 N10
Maneh, Iran 39 B8
Maneroo, Australia 54 C3
Maneroo Cr. →, Australia 54 C3
Manfalût, Egypt 45 C11
Manfred, Australia 55 E3
Mangalia, Romania 17 G14
Mangalore, India 36 N9
Mangaweka, N.Z. 51 H5
Manggar, Indonesia 32 E3
Manggawitu, Indonesia 33 E8
Mangkalihat, Tanjung, Indonesia 33 D5
Mangla Dam, Pakistan 36 C8
Mangnai, China 30 C4
Mango, Togo 44 F5
Mangoche, Malawi 47 G7
Mangoky →, Madag. 49 C7
Mangole, Indonesia 33 E7
Mangonui, N.Z. 51 F4
Mangueigne, Chad 45 F9
Mangueira, L. da, Brazil 80 C6
Mangum, U.S.A. 71 H5
Mangyshlak Poluostrov, Kazakhstan 24 E6
Manhattan, U.S.A. 70 F6
Manhiça, Mozam. 49 D5
Manhuaçu, Brazil 79 H10
Mania →, Madag. 49 B8
Manica, Mozam. 49 B5
Manica e Sofala □, Mozam. 49 B5
Manicoré, Brazil 78 E6
Manicouagan →, Canada 63 C6
Manifah, Si. Arabia 39 E6
Manifold, Australia 54 C5
Manifold, C., Australia 54 C5
Manigotagan, Canada 65 C9
Manihiki, Cook Is. 57 J11
Manila, Phil. 33 B6
Manila, U.S.A. 72 F9
Manila B., Phil. 33 B6
Manilla, Australia 55 E5
Maningrida, Australia 54 A1
Manipur □, India 37 G18
Manipur →, Burma 37 H19
Manisa, Turkey 23 G4
Manistee, U.S.A. 68 C2
Manistee →, U.S.A. 68 C2
Manistique, U.S.A. 68 C2
Manito L., Canada 65 C7
Manitoba □, Canada 65 B9
Manitoba, L., Canada 65 C9
Manitou, Canada 65 D9
Manitou I., U.S.A. 62 C2
Manitou Is., U.S.A. 68 C2
Manitou L., Canada 63 B6
Manitou Springs, U.S.A. 70 F2
Manitoulin I., Canada 62 C3
Manitowaning, Canada 62 C3
Manitowoc, U.S.A. 68 C2
Manizales, Colombia 78 B3
Manja, Madag. 49 C7
Manjacaze, Mozam. 49 C5
Manjakandriana, Madag. 49 B8
Manjhand, Pakistan 36 G6
Manjil, Iran 39 B6
Manjimup, Australia 53 F2
Manjra →, India 36 K10
Mankato, Kans., U.S.A. 70 F5
Mankato, Minn., U.S.A. 70 C8
Mankayane, Swaziland 49 D5
Mankono, Ivory C. 44 G3
Mankota, Canada 65 D7
Manly, Australia 55 E5
Manmad, India 36 J9
Mann Ras., Australia 53 E5
Manna, Indonesia 32 E2
Mannahill, Australia 55 E3
Mannar, Sri Lanka 36 Q11
Mannar, G. of, Asia 36 Q11
Mannar I., Sri Lanka 36 Q11
Mannheim, Germany 16 D4
Manning, Canada 64 B5
Manning, U.S.A. 69 J5
Manning Prov. Park, Canada 64 D4
Mannington, U.S.A. 68 F5
Mannum, Australia 55 E2
Mano, S. Leone 44 G2
Manokwari, Indonesia 33 E8
Manombo, Madag. 49 C7
Manono, Zaïre 46 F5
Manouane, L., Canada 63 B5
Manresa, Spain 19 B6
Mansa, Zambia 46 G5
Mansel I., Canada 61 B11
Mansfield, Australia 55 F4
Mansfield, U.K. 10 D6
Mansfield, La., U.S.A. 71 J8
Mansfield, Ohio, U.S.A. 68 E4
Mansfield, Wash., U.S.A. 72 C4
Manson Creek, Canada 64 B4
Manta, Ecuador 78 D2
Mantalingajan, Mt., Phil. 32 C5
Manteca, U.S.A. 73 H3
Manteo, U.S.A. 69 H8
Mantes-la-Jolie, France 18 B4
Manthani, India 36 K11
Manti, U.S.A. 72 G8
Mantiqueira, Serra da, Brazil 79 H10
Manton, U.S.A. 68 C3
Mántova, Italy 20 B4
Mänttä, Finland 8 E18
Mantua = Mántova, Italy 20 B4
Manu, Peru 78 F4
Manua Is., Amer. Samoa 51 B14
Manuae, Cook Is. 57 J12
Manuel Alves →, Brazil 79 F9
Manui, Indonesia 33 E6
Manville, U.S.A. 70 D2
Many, U.S.A. 71 K8
Manyara, L., Tanzania 46 E7
Manych-Gudilo, Oz., Russia 23 E7
Manyoni, Tanzania 46 F6
Manzai, Pakistan 36 C7
Manzanares, Spain 19 C4
Manzanillo, Cuba 75 C9
Manzanillo, Mexico 74 D4
Manzano Mts., U.S.A. 73 J10
Manzarīyeh, Iran 39 C6
Manzhouli, China 31 B6
Manzini, Swaziland 49 D5
Mao, Chad 45 F8
Maoke, Pegunungan, Indonesia 33 E9
Maoming, China 31 D6
Mapam Yumco, China 30 C3
Mapia, Kepulauan, Indonesia 33 D8
Mapinhane, Mozam. 49 C6
Maple Creek, Canada 65 D7
Mapleton, U.S.A. 72 D2
Mapuera →, Brazil 78 D7
Maputo, Mozam. 49 D5
Maputo, B. de, Mozam. 49 D5
Maqnā, Si. Arabia 38 D2
Maquela do Zombo, Angola 46 F3
Maquinchao, Argentina 80 E3
Maquoketa, U.S.A. 70 D9
Mar, Serra do, Brazil 80 B7
Mar Chiquita, L., Argentina 80 C4
Mar del Plata, Argentina 80 D5
Maraã, Brazil 78 D5
Marabá, Brazil 79 E9
Maracá, I. de, Brazil 79 C8
Maracaibo, Venezuela 78 A4
Maracaibo, L. de, Venezuela 78 B4
Maracay, Venezuela 78 A5
Marādah, Libya 45 C8
Maradi, Niger 44 F6
Marāgheh, Iran 38 B5
Marāh, Si. Arabia 38 E5
Marajó, I. de, Brazil 79 D9
Marākand, Iran 38 B5
Maralal, Kenya 46 D7
Maralinga, Australia 53 F5
Marama, Australia 55 F3
Marampa, S. Leone 44 G2
Marana, U.S.A. 73 K8
Maranboy, Australia 52 B5
Marand, Iran 38 B5
Maranguape, Brazil 79 D11
Maranhão = São Luís, Brazil 79 D10
Maranhão □, Brazil 79 E9
Maranoa →, Australia 55 D4
Marañón →, Peru 78 D4
Marão, Mozam. 49 C5
Maraş = Kahramanmaraş, Turkey 23 G6
Marathon, Australia 54 C3
Marathon, Canada 62 C2
Marathón, Greece 21 E10
Marathon, U.S.A. 71 K3
Maratua, Indonesia 33 D5
Marāwih, U.A.E. 39 E7
Marbella, Spain 19 D3
Marble Bar, Australia 52 D2
Marble Falls, U.S.A. 71 K5
Marburg, Germany 16 C4
March, U.K. 11 E8
Marche, France 18 C4
Marche □, Italy 20 C5
Marche-en-Famenne, Belgium 15 D5
Marches = Marche □, Italy 20 C5
Marcus I. = Minami-Tori-Shima, Pac. Oc. 56 E7
Marcus Necker Ridge, Pac. Oc. 56 F9
Mardan, Pakistan 36 B8
Mardie, Australia 52 D2
Mardin, Turkey 23 G7
Maree L., U.K. 12 D3
Mareeba, Australia 54 B4
Marek = Stanke Dimitrov, Bulgaria 21 C10
Marek, Indonesia 33 E6
Maremma, Italy 20 C4
Marengo, U.S.A. 70 E8
Marerano, Madag. 49 C7
Marfa, U.S.A. 71 K2
Margaret →, Australia 52 C4
Margaret Bay, Canada 64 C3
Margaret L., Canada 64 B5
Margaret River, Australia 52 C4
Margarita, Panama 74 H14
Margarita, I. de, Venezuela 78 A6
Margaritovo, Russia 28 C7
Margate, S. Africa 49 E5
Margate, U.K. 11 F9
Margelan, Uzbekistan 24 E8
Marguerite, Canada 64 C4
Mari Republic □, Russia 22 C8
Maria I., N. Terr., Australia 54 A2
Maria I., Tas., Australia 54 G4
Maria van Diemen, C., N.Z. 51 F4
Marian L., Canada 64 A5
Mariana Trench, Pac. Oc. 56 F6
Marianao, Cuba 75 C8
Marianna, Ark., U.S.A. 71 H9
Marianna, Fla., U.S.A. 69 K3
Marias →, U.S.A. 72 C8
Ma'rib, Yemen 40 D4
Maribor, Slovenia 20 A6
Marico →, Africa 48 C4
Maricopa, Ariz., U.S.A. 73 K7
Maricopa, Calif., U.S.A. 73 J4
Maricourt, Canada 61 C12
Marīdī, Sudan 45 H10
Marie Byrd Land, Antarctica 5 D14
Marie-Galante, Guadeloupe 75 D12
Mariecourt, Canada 61 B12
Mariehamn, Finland 9 F15
Marienberg, Neths. 15 B6
Marienbourg, Belgium 15 D4
Mariental, Namibia 48 C2
Mariestad, Sweden 9 G12
Marietta, Ga., U.S.A. 69 J3
Marietta, Ohio, U.S.A. 68 F5
Mariinsk, Russia 24 D9
Marília, Brazil 79 H8
Marillana, Australia 52 D2
Marín, Spain 19 A1
Marina Plains, Australia 54 A3
Marinduque, Phil. 33 B6
Marine City, U.S.A. 68 D4
Marinette, U.S.A. 68 C2
Maringá, Brazil 80 A6
Marion, Ala., U.S.A. 69 J2
Marion, Ill., U.S.A. 71 G10
Marion, Ind., U.S.A. 68 E3
Marion, Iowa, U.S.A. 70 D9
Marion, Kans., U.S.A. 70 F6
Marion, Mich., U.S.A. 68 C3
Marion, N.C., U.S.A. 69 H4
Marion, Ohio, U.S.A. 68 E4
Marion, S.C., U.S.A. 69 H6
Marion, Va., U.S.A. 69 G5
Marion, L., U.S.A. 69 J5
Marion I., Ind. Oc. 35 J2
Mariposa, U.S.A. 73 H4
Mariscal Estigarribia, Paraguay 78 H6
Maritime Alps = Maritimes, Alpes, Europe 20 B2
Maritimes, Alpes, Europe 20 B2
Maritsa →, Bulgaria 21 D12
Mariupol, Ukraine 23 E6
Marīvān, Iran 38 C5
Markazī □, Iran 39 C6
Marked Tree, U.S.A. 71 H9
Marken, Neths. 15 B5
Market Drayton, U.K. 10 E5
Market Harborough, U.K. 11 E7
Markham, Mt., Antarctica 5 E11
Markham L., Canada 65 A8
Markovo, Russia 25 C17
Marks, Russia 22 D8
Marksville, U.S.A. 71 K8
Marla, Australia 55 D1
Marlborough, Australia 54 C4
Marlborough Downs, U.K. 11 F6
Marlin, U.S.A. 71 K6
Marlow, U.S.A. 71 H6
Marmagao, India 36 M8
Marmara, Turkey 21 D12
Marmara, Sea of = Marmara Denizi, Turkey 21 D13
Marmara Denizi, Turkey 21 D13
Marmarth, U.S.A. 70 B3
Marmion, Mt., Australia 53 E2
Marmion L., Canada 62 C1
Marmolada, Mte., Italy 20 A4
Marmora, Canada 62 D4
Marne □, France 18 B6
Marne →, France 18 B5
Maroala, Madag. 49 B8
Maroantsetra, Madag. 49 B8
Maromandia, Madag. 49 A8
Marondera, Zimbabwe 47 H6
Maroni →, Fr. Guiana 79 B8
Maroochydore, Australia 55 D5
Maroona, Australia 55 F3
Marosakoa, Madag. 49 B8
Maroua, Cameroon 45 F7
Marovoay, Madag. 49 B8
Marquard, S. Africa 48 D4
Marquesas Is. = Marquises, Is., Pac. Oc. 57 H14
Marquette, U.S.A. 68 B2
Marquises, Is., Pac. Oc. 57 H14
Marracuene, Mozam. 49 D5
Marrakech, Morocco 44 B3
Marrawah, Australia 54 G3
Marree, Australia 55 D2
Marrilla, Australia 52 D1
Marrimane, Mozam. 49 C5
Marromeu, Mozam. 49 B6
Marrowie Cr. →, Australia 55 E4
Marrupa, Mozam. 47 G7
Marsá Matrûh, Egypt 45 B10
Marsá Susah, Libya 45 B9
Marsabit, Kenya 46 D7
Marsala, Italy 20 F5
Marsaxlokk, Malta 20 G6
Marsden, Australia 55 E4
Marseille, France 18 E6
Marseilles = Marseille, France 18 E6
Marsh I., U.S.A. 71 L9
Marsh L., U.S.A. 70 C6
Marshall, Liberia 44 G2
Marshall, Ark., U.S.A. 71 H8
Marshall, Mich., U.S.A. 68 D3
Marshall, Minn., U.S.A. 70 C7
Marshall, Mo., U.S.A. 70 F8
Marshall, Tex., U.S.A. 71 J7
Marshall →, Australia 54 C2
Marshall Is. ■, Pac. Oc. 56 G9
Marshalltown, U.S.A. 70 D8
Marshfield, Mo., U.S.A. 71 G8
Marshfield, Wis., U.S.A. 70 C9
Marshūn, Iran 39 B6
Marstrand, Sweden 9 H11
Mart, U.S.A. 71 K6
Martaban, Burma 37 L20
Martaban, G. of, Burma 37 L20
Martapura, Kalimantan, Indonesia 32 E4
Martapura, Sumatera, Indonesia 32 E2
Marte, Nigeria 45 F7
Martelange, Belgium 15 E5
Martha's Vineyard, U.S.A. 68 E10
Martin, S. Dak., U.S.A. 70 D4
Martin, Tenn., U.S.A. 71 G10
Martin, L., U.S.A. 69 J3
Martinborough, N.Z. 51 J5
Martinique ■, W. Indies 75 E12
Martinique Passage, W. Indies 75 D12
Martinsburg, U.S.A. 68 F7
Martinsville, Ind., U.S.A. 68 F2
Martinsville, Va., U.S.A. 69 G6
Marton, N.Z. 51 J5
Martos, Spain 19 D4
Marudi, Malaysia 32 D4
Ma'ruf, Afghan. 36 D5
Marugame, Japan 29 G6
Marulan, Australia 55 E5
Marunga, Angola 48 B3
Marvast, Iran 39 D7
Marwar, India 36 G8
Mary, Turkmenistan 24 F7
Mary Frances L., Canada 65 A7
Mary Kathleen, Australia 54 C2
Maryborough = Port Laoise, Ireland 13 C4
Maryborough, Queens., Australia 55 D5
Maryborough, Vic., Australia 55 F3
Maryfield, Canada 65 D8
Maryland □, U.S.A. 68 F7
Maryport, U.K. 10 C4
Mary's Harbour, Canada 63 B8
Marystown, Canada 63 C8
Marysvale, U.S.A. 73 G7
Marysville, Canada 64 D5
Marysville, Calif., U.S.A. 72 G3
Marysville, Kans., U.S.A. 70 F6
Marysville, Ohio, U.S.A. 68 E4
Maryvale, Australia 55 D5
Maryville, U.S.A. 69 H4
Marzūq, Libya 45 C7
Masaka, Uganda 46 E6
Masalembo, Kepulauan, Indonesia 32 F4
Masalima, Kepulauan, Indonesia 32 F5
Masamba, Indonesia 33 E6
Masan, S. Korea 31 C7
Masasi, Tanzania 46 G7
Masaya, Nic. 74 E7
Masbate, Phil. 33 B6
Mascara, Algeria 44 A5
Mascarene Is., Ind. Oc. 35 G4
Masela, Indonesia 33 F7
Maseru, Lesotho 48 D4
Mashābih, Si. Arabia 38 E3
Mashhad, Iran 39 B8
Mashīz, Iran 39 D8
Mashkel, Hamun-i-, Pakistan 36 E3
Mashki Chāh, Pakistan 36 E3
Mashonaland Central □, Zimbabwe 49 B5
Mashonaland East □, Zimbabwe 49 B5
Mashonaland West □, Zimbabwe 49 B4
Masi, Norway 8 B17
Masi Manimba, Zaïre 46 E3
Masindi, Uganda 46 D6
Masisea, Peru 78 E4
Masjed Soleyman, Iran 39 D6
Mask, L., Ireland 13 C2
Masoala, Tanjon' i, Madag. 49 B9
Masoarivo, Madag. 49 B7
Masohi, Indonesia 33 E7
Masomeloka, Madag. 49 C8
Mason, U.S.A. 71 K5
Mason City, U.S.A. 70 D8
Masqat, Oman 40 C6
Massa, Italy 20 B4
Massachusetts □, U.S.A. 68 D10
Massaguet, Chad 45 F8
Massakory, Chad 45 F8
Massangena, Mozam. 49 C5
Massawa = Mitsiwa, Eritrea 45 E12
Massena, U.S.A. 68 C8
Massénya, Chad 45 F8
Masset, Canada 64 C2
Massif Central, France 18 D5
Massillon, U.S.A. 68 E5
Massinga, Mozam. 49 C6
Masson I., Antarctica 5 C7
Masterton, N.Z. 51 J5
Mastuj, Pakistan 36 A8
Mastung, Pakistan 36 E5
Masuda, Japan 29 G5

Masvingo

Masvingo, *Zimbabwe* 47 J6
Maşyāf, *Syria* 38 C3
Mataboor, *Indonesia* . 33 E9
Matachewan, *Canada* 62 C3
Matadi, *Zaire* 46 F2
Matagalpa, *Nic.* 74 E7
Matagami, *Canada* . . 62 C4
Matagami, L., *Canada* 62 C4
Matagorda, *U.S.A.* . . . 71 L7
Matagorda B., *U.S.A.* . 71 L6
Matagorda I., *U.S.A.* . 71 L6
Matak, P., *Indonesia* . 32 D3
Matakana, *Australia* . . 55 E4
Matam, *Senegal* 44 E2
Matamoros, *Coahuila,*
Mexico 74 B4
Matamoros,
Tamaulipas, Mexico 74 B5
Ma'ţan as Sarra, *Libya* 45 D9
Matane, *Canada* 63 C6
Matanzas, *Cuba* 75 C8
Matapan, C. =
Taínaron, Ákra,
Greece 21 F10
Matapédia, *Canada* . . 63 C6
Matara, *Sri Lanka* . . 36 S12
Mataram, *Indonesia* . . 32 F5
Matarani, *Peru* 78 G4
Mataranka, *Australia* . 52 B5
Matarma, Râs, *Egypt* . 41 E1
Matatiele, *S. Africa* . . 49 E4
Mataura, *N.Z.* 51 M2
Matera, *Italy* 20 D7
Matheson Island,
Canada 65 C9
Mathis, *U.S.A.* 71 L6
Mathura, *India* 36 F10
Mati, *Phil.* 33 C7
Matima, *Botswana* . . 48 C3
Matiri Ra., *N.Z.* 51 J4
Matlock, *U.K.* 10 D6
Matmata, *Tunisia* . . . 44 B6
Mato Grosso □, *Brazil* 79 F8
Mato Grosso, Planalto
do, *Brazil* 79 G8
Mato Grosso do Sul □,
Brazil 79 G8
Matochkin Shar,
Russia 24 B6
Matosinhos, *Portugal* 19 B1
Matsue, *Japan* 28 D10
Matsumae, *Japan* . . 28 D10
Matsumoto, *Japan* . . 29 F9
Matsusaka, *Japan* . . . 29 G8
Matsuura, *Japan* 29 H4
Matsuyama, *Japan* . . 29 H6
Mattagami →,
Canada 62 B3
Mattancheri, *India* . . 36 Q10
Mattawa, *Canada* . . . 62 C4
Mattawamkeag, *U.S.A.* 63 C6
Matterhorn, *Switz.* . . 16 F3
Matthew's Ridge,
Guyana 78 B6
Mattice, *Canada* 62 C3
Matuba, *Mozam.* . . . 49 C5
Matucana, *Peru* 78 F3
Matun, *Afghan.* 36 C6
Maturín, *Venezuela* . . 78 B6
Mau Ranipur, *India* . . 36 G11
Maud, Pt., *Australia* . 52 D1
Maude, *Australia* . . . 55 E3
Maudin Sun, *Burma* . 37 M19
Mauganj, *India* 37 G12
Maui, *U.S.A.* 66 H16
Maulamyaing =
Moulmein, *Burma* . 37 L20
Maumee, *U.S.A.* 68 E4
Maumee →, *U.S.A.* . . 68 E4
Maumere, *Indonesia* . 33 F6
Maun, *Botswana* . . . 48 B3
Mauna Kea, *U.S.A.* . 66 J17
Mauna Loa, *U.S.A.* . 66 J17
Maungmagan Kyunzu,
Burma 34 E4
Maupin, *U.S.A.* 72 D3
Maurepas L., *U.S.A.* . 71 K9
Maures, *France* 18 E7
Maurice, L., *Australia* 53 E5
Mauritania ■, *Africa* . 44 D3
Mauritius ■, *Ind. Oc.* . 43 J9
Mauston, *U.S.A.* . . . 70 D9
Mavinga, *Angola* . . . 47 H4
Mawk Mai, *Burma* . . 37 J20
Mawlaik, *Burma* . . . 37 H19
Mawquq, *Si. Arabia* . 38 E4
Mawson Coast,
Antarctica 5 C6
Max, *U.S.A.* 70 B4
Maxesibeni, *S. Africa* 49 E4
Maxhamish L., *Canada* 64 B4
Maxixe, *Mozam.* . . . 49 C6
Maxwelton, *Australia* 54 C3
May Downs, *Australia* 54 C4
May Pen, *Jamaica* . . 74 K16
Maya →, *Russia* . . . 25 D14
Mayaguana, *Bahamas* 75 C10
Mayagüez, *Puerto Rico* 75 D11
Mayāmey, *Iran* 39 B7
Maydan, *Iraq* 38 C5
Maydena, *Australia* . . 54 G4
Mayenne, *France* . . . 18 B3
Mayenne →, *France* . 18 C3
Mayer, *U.S.A.* 73 J7
Mayerthorpe, *Canada* 64 C5
Mayfield, *U.S.A.* . . . 69 G1
Mayhill, *U.S.A.* 73 K11
Maykop, *Russia* 23 F7
Maymyo, *Burma* . . . 34 A4

Maynard Hills,
Australia 53 E2
Mayne →, *Australia* . 54 C3
Maynooth, *Ireland* . . 13 C5
Mayo, *Canada* 60 B6
Mayo □, *Ireland* . . . 13 C2
Mayo L., *Canada* . . . 60 B6
Mayon Volcano, *Phil.* 33 B6
Mayor I., *N.Z.* 51 G6
Mayson L., *Canada* . 65 B7
Maysville, *U.S.A.* . . . 68 F4
Mayu, *Indonesia* . . . 33 D7
Mayville, *U.S.A.* 70 B6
Mayya, *Russia* 25 C14
Mazabuka, *Zambia* . . 47 H5
Mazagán = El Jadida,
Morocco 44 B3
Mazagão, *Brazil* . . . 79 D8
Mazán, *Peru* 78 D4
Māzandarān □, *Iran* . 39 B7
Mazarredo, *Argentina* 80 F3
Mazarrón, *Spain* . . . 19 D5
Mazaruni →, *Guyana* 78 B7
Mazatlán, *Mexico* . . . 74 C3
Mazatlán, *Sinaloa,*
Mexico 74 C3
Māzhān, *Iran* 39 C8
Mazinān, *Iran* 39 B8
Mazoe →, *Mozam.* . . 47 H6
Mazurian Lakes =
Mazurski, Pojezierze,
Poland 17 B10
Mazurski, Pojezierze,
Poland 17 B10
Mbabane, *Swaziland* . 49 D5
Mbaïki, *C.A.R.* 46 D3
Mbala, *Zambia* 46 F6
Mbale, *Uganda* 46 D6
Mbalmayo, *Cameroon* 46 D2
Mbamba Bay, *Tanzania* 46 G6
Mbandaka, *Zaire* . . . 46 D3
Mbanza Congo, *Angola* 46 F2
Mbanza Ngungu, *Zaire* 46 F2
Mbarara, *Uganda* . . . 46 E6
Mbashe →, *S. Africa* . 49 E4
Mbeya, *Tanzania* . . . 46 F6
Mbini □, *Eq. Guin.* . . 46 D2
Mbour, *Senegal* 44 F1
Mbout, *Mauritania* . . 44 E2
Mbuji-Mayi, *Zaire* . . . 46 F4
Mbulu, *Tanzania* . . . 46 E7
Mchinji, *Malawi* 47 G6
Mdina, *Malta* 20 G6
Mead, L., *U.S.A.* . . . 73 H6
Meade, *U.S.A.* 71 G4
Meadow, *Australia* . . 53 E1
Meadow Lake, *Canada* 65 C7
Meadow Lake Prov.
Park, *Canada* 65 C7
Meadow Valley
Wash →, *U.S.A.* . . 73 H6
Meadville, *U.S.A.* . . . 68 E5
Meaford, *Canada* . . . 62 D3
Mealy Mts., *Canada* . 63 B8
Meander River, *Canada* 64 B5
Meares, C., *U.S.A.* . . 72 D2
Mearim →, *Brazil* . . 79 D10
Meath □, *Ireland* . . . 13 C5
Meath Park, *Canada* . 65 C7
Meaux, *France* 18 B5
Mebechi-Gawa →,
Japan 28 D10
Mecca = Makkah,
Si. Arabia 40 C2
Mecca, *U.S.A.* 73 K5
Mechelen, *Belgium* . . 15 C4
Mecheria, *Algeria* . . . 44 B4
Mecklenburger Bucht,
Germany 16 A5
Meconta, *Mozam.* . . . 47 G7
Meda, *Australia* 52 C3
Medan, *Indonesia* . . . 32 D1
Medanosa, Pta.,
Argentina 80 F3
Medéa, *Algeria* 44 A5
Medellín, *Colombia* . . 78 B3
Medemblik, *Neths.* . . 15 B5
Mederdra, *Mauritania* 44 E1
Medford, Oreg., *U.S.A.* 72 E2
Medford, Wis., *U.S.A.* 70 C9
Mediaş, *Romania* . . . 17 E12
Medical Lake, *U.S.A.* . 72 C5
Medicine Bow, *U.S.A.* 72 F10
Medicine Bow Pk.,
U.S.A. 72 F10
Medicine Bow Ra.,
U.S.A. 72 F10
Medicine Hat, *Canada* 65 D6
Medicine Lake, *U.S.A.* 70 A2
Medicine Lodge,
U.S.A. 71 G5
Medina = Al Madīnah,
Si. Arabia 40 C2
Medina, N. Dak.,
U.S.A. 70 B5
Medina, N.Y., *U.S.A.* . 68 D6
Medina, Ohio, *U.S.A.* 68 E3
Medina →, *U.S.A.* . . 71 L5
Medina del Campo,
Spain 19 B3
Medina-Sidonia, *Spain* 19 D3
Medinipur, *India* . . . 37 H15
Mediterranean Sea,
Europe 42 C5
Médoc, *France* 18 D3
Medport =
Marsaxlokk, *Malta* . 20 G6
Medstead, *Canada* . . 65 C7
Medveditsa →,
Russia 23 E7

Medvezhi, Ostrava,
Russia 25 B17
Medvezhyegorsk,
Russia 22 B5
Medway →, *U.K.* . . . 11 F8
Meeberrie, *Australia* . 53 E2
Meekatharra, *Australia* 53 E2
Meeker, *U.S.A.* . . . 72 F10
Meerut, *India* 36 E10
Meeteetse, *U.S.A.* . . 72 D9
Mega, *Ethiopia* 45 H12
Mégara, *Greece* . . . 21 F10
Meghalaya □, *India* . 37 G17
Mehr Jān, *Iran* 39 C7
Mehrābād, *Iran* 38 B5
Mehrān, *Iran* 38 C5
Mehriz, *Iran* 39 D7
Mei Xian, *China* 31 D6
Meiganga, *Cameroon* 46 C2
Meiktila, *Burma* . . . 37 J19
Meissen, *Germany* . . 16 C6
Mejillones, *Chile* . . . 80 A2
Meka, *Australia* 53 E2
Mékambo, *Gabon* . . . 46 D2
Mekdela, *Ethiopia* . . 45 F12
Mekhtar, *Pakistan* . . 36 D6
Meknès, *Morocco* . . . 44 B3
Mekong →, *Asia* . . . 34 H9
Mekongga, *Indonesia* 33 E6
Melagiri Hills, *India* . 36 N10
Melaka, *Malaysia* . . 34 S15
Melaka □, *Malaysia* . 34 S15
Melalap, *Malaysia* . . 32 C5
Melanesia, *Pac. Oc.* . 56 H7
Melbourne, *Australia* . 55 F3
Melbourne, *U.S.A.* . . 69 L5
Mélèzes →, *Canada* . 61 C12
Melfi, *Chad* 45 F8
Melfort, *Canada* 65 C8
Melilla, *Morocco* . . . 44 A4
Melita, *Canada* 65 D8
Melitopol, *Ukraine* . . 23 E6
Melk, *Austria* 16 D7
Mellansel, *Sweden* . . 8 E15
Mellen, *U.S.A.* 70 B9
Mellerud, *Sweden* . . . 9 G12
Mellette, *U.S.A.* 70 C5
Melo, *Uruguay* 80 C6
Melolo, *Indonesia* . . 33 F6
Melrose, *N.S.W.,*
Australia 55 E4
Melrose, *W. Austral.,*
Australia 53 E3
Melrose, *U.K.* 12 F6
Melrose, *U.S.A.* 71 H3
Melstone, *U.S.A.* . . . 72 C10
Melton Mowbray, *U.K.* 10 E7
Melun, *France* 18 B5
Melut, *Sudan* 45 F11
Melville, *Canada* . . . 65 C8
Melville, C., *Australia* 54 A3
Melville, L., *Canada* . 63 B8
Melville B., *Australia* . 54 A2
Melville I., *Australia* . 52 B5
Melville I., *Canada* . . 4 B2
Melville Pen., *Canada* 61 B11
Melvin →, *Canada* . . 64 B5
Memba, *Mozam.* . . . 47 G8
Memboro, *Indonesia* . 33 F5
Memel = Klaipeda,
Lithuania 22 C3
Memel, *S. Africa* . . . 49 D4
Memmingen, *Germany* 16 E5
Mempawah, *Indonesia* 32 D3
Memphis, Tenn.,
U.S.A. 71 H10
Memphis, Tex., *U.S.A.* 71 H4
Mena, *U.S.A.* 71 H7
Menai Strait, *U.K.* . . 10 D3
Ménaka, *Mali* 44 E5
Menan = Chao
Phraya →, *Thailand* 34 F6
Menarandra →,
Madag. 49 D7
Menard, *U.S.A.* 71 K5
Menasha, *U.S.A.* . . . 68 C1
Menate, *Indonesia* . . 32 E4
Mendawai →,
Indonesia 32 E4
Mende, *France* 18 D5
Mendip Hills, *U.K.* . . 11 F5
Mendocino, *U.S.A.* . . 72 G2
Mendocino, C., *U.S.A.* 72 F1
Mendota, Calif., *U.S.A.* 73 H3
Mendota, Ill., *U.S.A.* . 70 E10
Mendoza, *Argentina* . 80 C3
Mene Grande,
Venezuela 78 B4
Menen, *Belgium* . . . 15 D3
Menfi, *Italy* 20 F5
Menggala, *Indonesia* 32 E3
Mengzi, *China* 30 D5
Menihek L., *Canada* . 63 B6
Menin = Menen,
Belgium 15 D3
Menindee, *Australia* . 55 E3
Menindee L., *Australia* 55 E3
Meningie, *Australia* . 55 F2
Menominee, *U.S.A.* . . 68 C2
Menominee →,
U.S.A. 68 C2
Menomonie, *U.S.A.* . 70 C9
Menongue, *Angola* . . 47 G3
Mentawai, Kepulauan,
Indonesia 32 E1
Menton, *France* 18 E7
Mentz Dam, *S. Africa* 48 E4
Menzelinsk, *Russia* . . 22 C9
Menzies, *Australia* . . 53 E3

Me'ona, *Israel* 41 B4
Meppel, *Neths.* 15 B6
Mer Rouge, *U.S.A.* . . 71 J9
Merabéllou, Kólpos,
Greece 21 G11
Meramangye, L.,
Australia 53 E5
Meran = Merano, *Italy* 20 A4
Merano, *Italy* 20 A4
Merauke, *Indonesia* . 33 F10
Merbabu, *Indonesia* . 33 G14
Merbein, *Australia* . . 55 E3
Merca, *Somali Rep.* . . 40 G3
Merced, *U.S.A.* 73 H3
Mercedes,
Buenos Aires,
Argentina 80 C5
Mercedes, *Corrientes,*
Argentina 80 B5
Mercedes, San Luis,
Argentina 80 C3
Mercedes, *Uruguay* . 80 C5
Merceditas, *Chile* . . . 80 B2
Mercer, *N.Z.* 51 G5
Mercy C., *Canada* . . 61 B13
Meredith, C., *Falk. Is.* 80 G4
Meredith, L., *U.S.A.* . 71 H4
Merga = Nukheila,
Sudan 45 E10
Mergui Arch. = Myeik
Kyunzu, *Burma* . . 34 G4
Mérida, *Mexico* 74 C7
Mérida, *Spain* 19 C2
Mérida, *Venezuela* . . 78 B4
Mérida, Cord. de,
Venezuela 76 B2
Meriden, *U.S.A.* 68 E9
Meridian, Idaho, *U.S.A.* 72 E5
Meridian, Miss., *U.S.A.* 69 J1
Meridian, Tex., *U.S.A.* 71 K6
Meriruma, *Brazil* . . . 79 C8
Merkel, *U.S.A.* 71 J4
Merksem, *Belgium* . . 15 C4
Mermaid Reef,
Australia 52 C2
Merowe, *Sudan* . . . 45 E11
Merredin, *Australia* . . 53 F2
Merrick, *U.K.* 12 F4
Merrill, Oreg., *U.S.A.* 72 E3
Merrill, Wis., *U.S.A.* . 70 C10
Merriman, *U.S.A.* . . . 70 D4
Merritt, *Canada* 64 C4
Merriwa, *Australia* . . 55 E5
Merriwagga, *Australia* 55 E4
Merry I., *Canada* . . . 62 A4
Merrygoen, *Australia* 55 E4
Merryville, *U.S.A.* . . . 71 K8
Mersa Fatma, *Eritrea* 40 E3
Mersch, *Lux.* 15 E6
Merseburg, *Germany* 16 C5
Mersey →, *U.K.* 10 D5
Merseyside □, *U.K.* . 10 D5
Mersin, *Turkey* 23 G5
Mersing, *Malaysia* . . 34 S16
Merthyr Tydfil, *U.K.* . 11 F4
Mertzon, *U.S.A.* 71 K4
Meru, *Kenya* 46 D7
Mesa, *U.S.A.* 73 K8
Mesgouez, L., *Canada* 62 B4
Meshed = Mashhad,
Iran 39 B8
Meshra er Req, *Sudan* 45 G10
Mesick, *U.S.A.* 68 C3
Mesilinka →, *Canada* 64 B4
Mesilla, *U.S.A.* 73 K10
Mesolóngion, *Greece* 21 E9
Mesopotamia = Al
Jazirah, *Iraq* 38 C5
Mesquite, *U.S.A.* . . . 73 H6
Mess Cr. →, *Canada* 64 B2
Messina, *Italy* 20 E6
Messina, *S. Africa* . . 49 C5
Messina, Str. di, *Italy* 20 E6
Messini, *Greece* . . . 21 F10
Messiniakós Kólpos,
Greece 21 F10
Mesta →, *Bulgaria* . . 21 D11
Meta →, *S. Amer.* . . 78 B5
Metairie, *U.S.A.* 71 L9
Metaline Falls, *U.S.A.* 72 B5
Metán, *Argentina* . . . 80 B4
Metangula, *Mozam.* . 47 G6
Metema, *Ethiopia* . . 45 F12
Methven, *N.Z.* 51 K3
Methy L., *Canada* . . . 65 B7
Metil, *Mozam.* 47 H7
Metlakatla, *U.S.A.* . . 64 B2
Metropolis, *U.S.A.* . . 71 G10
Mettur Dam, *India* . . 36 P10
Metz, *France* 18 B7
Meulaboh, *Indonesia* . 32 D1
Meureudu, *Indonesia* 32 C1
Meurthe-et-Moselle □,
France 18 B7
Meuse □, *France* . . . 18 A6
Meuse →, *Europe* . . 18 A6
Mexborough, *U.K.* . . 10 D6
Mexia, *U.S.A.* 71 K6
Mexiana, I., *Brazil* . . 79 C9
Mexicali, *Mexico* . . . 74 A1
México, *Mexico* 74 D5
México □, *Mexico* . . 74 D5
Mexico ■, *Cent. Amer.* 74 C4
Mexico, G. of,
Cent. Amer. 74 B7
Meymaneh, *Afghan.* . 36 B4
Mezen, *Russia* 22 A7
Mezen →, *Russia* . . . 22 A7
Mezökövesd, *Hungary* 17 E10

Mezötúr, *Hungary* . . 17 E10
Mhow, *India* 36 H9
Miallo, *Australia* 54 B4
Miami, *Ariz., U.S.A.* . 73 K8
Miami, *Fla., U.S.A.* . . 69 N5
Miami, *Tex., U.S.A.* . 71 H4
Miami →, *U.S.A.* . . . 68 F3
Miami Beach, *U.S.A.* . 69 N5
Miamisburg, *U.S.A.* . 68 F3
Miāndowāb, *Iran* . . . 38 B5
Miandrivazo, *Madag.* . 49 B8
Miāneh, *Iran* 38 B5
Mianwali, *Pakistan* . . 36 C7
Miarinarivo, *Madag.* . 49 B8
Miass, *Russia* 22 D11
Michigan □, *U.S.A.* . . 67 B9
Michigan, L., *U.S.A.* . 68 C2
Michigan City, *U.S.A.* 68 E2
Michikamau L., *Canada* 63 B7
Michipicoten, *Canada* 62 C3
Michipicoten I., *Canada* 62 C2
Michurinsk, *Russia* . . 22 D7
Micronesia, Federated
States of ■, *Pac. Oc.* 56 G7
Mid Glamorgan □,
U.K. 11 F4
Mid-Indian Ridge,
Ind. Oc. 35 H6
Midai, P., *Indonesia* . 32 D3
Midale, *Canada* 65 D8
Middelburg, *Neths.* . . 15 C3
Middelburg, C. Prov.,
S. Africa 48 E3
Middelburg, Trans.,
S. Africa 49 D4
Middelwit, *S. Africa* . 48 C4
Middle Alkali L., *U.S.A.* 72 F3
Middle Andaman I.,
India 34 F2
Middle I., *Australia* . . 53 F3
Middle Loup →,
U.S.A. 70 E5
Middleport, *U.S.A.* . . 68 F4
Middlesboro, *U.S.A.* . 67 C10
Middlesboro, *U.S.A.* . 69 G4
Middlesbrough, *U.K.* . 10 C6
Middleton, *Australia* . 54 C3
Middleton, *Canada* . . 63 D6
Middletown, Conn.,
U.S.A. 68 E9
Middletown, N.Y.,
U.S.A. 68 E8
Middletown, Ohio,
U.S.A. 68 F3
Midi, Canal du →,
France 18 E4
Midland, *Canada* . . . 62 D4
Midland, Mich., *U.S.A.* 68 D3
Midland, Tex., *U.S.A.* 71 K3
Midleton, *Ireland* . . . 13 E3
Midlothian, *U.S.A.* . . 71 J6
Midongy,
Tangorombohitr' i,
Madag. 49 C8
Midongy Atsimo,
Madag. 49 C8
Midway Is., *Pac. Oc.* . 56 E10
Midwest, *U.S.A.* 67 B9
Midwest, *U.S.A.* 72 E10
Mie □, *Japan* 29 G8
Międzychód, *Poland* . 16 B7
Międzyrzec Podlaski,
Poland 17 C11
Mienga, *Angola* 48 B2
Miercurea Ciuc,
Romania 17 E12
Mieres, *Spain* 19 A3
Mifraz Hefa, *Israel* . . 41 C4
Migdāl, *Israel* 41 C4
Miguel Alves, *Brazil* . 79 D10
Mihara, *Japan* 29 G6
Mikinai, *Greece* 21 F10
Mikkeli, *Finland* 9 F19
Mikkeli □ = Mikkelin
lääni □, *Finland* . . 8 F20
Mikkelin lääni □,
Finland 8 F20
Mikkwa →, *Canada* . 64 B6
Mikonos, *Greece* . . . 21 F11
Mikun, *Russia* 22 B9
Milaca, *U.S.A.* 70 C8
Milagro, *Ecuador* . . . 78 D3
Milan = Milano, *Italy* . 20 B3
Milan, Mo., *U.S.A.* . . 70 E8
Milan, Tenn., *U.S.A.* . 69 H1
Milang, *Australia* . . . 55 E2
Milano, *Italy* 20 B3
Milâs, *Turkey* 23 G4
Milazzo, *Italy* 20 E6
Milbank, *U.S.A.* 70 C6
Milden, *Canada* 65 C7
Mildura, *Australia* . . . 55 E3
Mileh Tharthār, *Iraq* . 38 C4
Miles, *Australia* 55 D5
Miles, *U.S.A.* 71 K4
Miles City, *U.S.A.* . . . 72 C2
Milestone, *Canada* . . 65 D8
Mileura, *Australia* . . . 53 E2
Milford, Del., *U.S.A.* . 68 F8
Milford, Utah, *U.S.A.* 73 G7
Milford Haven, *U.K.* . 11 F2
Milford Sd., *N.Z.* . . . 51 L1
Milh, Bahr al, *Iraq* . . 38 C4
Miliana, *Algeria* 44 C5
Miling, *Australia* . . . 53 F2
Milk →, *N. Amer.* . . 72 B10
Milk River, *Canada* . . 64 D6
Mill City, *U.S.A.* 72 D2
Mill I., *Antarctica* . . . 5 C8
Mill Lacs, L., *U.S.A.* . 68 B8

Mille Lacs, L. des,
Canada 62 C1
Milledgeville, *U.S.A.* . 69 J4
Millen, *U.S.A.* 69 J5
Miller, *U.S.A.* 70 C5
Millicent, *Australia* . . 55 F3
Millinocket, *U.S.A.* . . 63 C6
Millmerran, *Australia* 55 D5
Mills L., *Canada* . . . 64 A5
Milltown Malbay,
Ireland 13 D2
Millville, *U.S.A.* 68 F8
Millwood Res., *U.S.A.* 71 J8
Milne →, *Australia* . . 54 C2
Milne Inlet, *Canada* . 61 A11
Milnor, *U.S.A.* 70 B6
Milo, *Canada* 64 C6
Mílos, *Greece* 21 F11
Milparinka P.O.,
Australia 55 D3
Milton, *N.Z.* 51 M2
Milton, *U.K.* 12 D4
Milton, Fla., *U.S.A.* . 69 K2
Milton, Pa., *U.S.A.* . . 68 E7
Milton-Freewater,
U.S.A. 72 D4
Milton Keynes, *U.K.* . 11 E7
Miltou, *Chad* 45 F8
Milwaukee, *U.S.A.* . . 68 D2
Milwaukie, *U.S.A.* . . 72 D2
Min Chiang →, *China* 30 D6
Min Jiang →, *China* . 30 D5
Mina, *U.S.A.* 73 G4
Mina Pirquitas,
Argentina 80 A3
Mīnā Su'ud, *Si. Arabia* 39 D6
Mīnā'al Aḥmadī,
Kuwait 39 D6
Mīnāb, *Iran* 39 E8
Minago →, *Canada* . 65 C9
Minaki, *Canada* 65 D10
Minamata, *Japan* . . . 29 H5
Minami-Tori-Shima,
Pac. Oc. 56 E7
Minas, *Uruguay* 80 C5
Minas Basin, *Canada* 63 C7
Minas de Rio Tinto,
Spain 19 D2
Minas Gerais □, *Brazil* 79 G9
Minatitlán, *Mexico* . . 74 D6
Minbu, *Burma* 37 J19
Mindanao, *Phil.* 33 C6
Mindanao Sea = Bohol
Sea, *Phil.* 33 C6
Mindanao Trench,
Pac. Oc. 33 B7
Minden, *Germany* . . 16 B4
Minden, *U.S.A.* 71 J8
Mindiptana, *Indonesia* 33 F10
Mindoro, *Phil.* 33 B6
Mindoro Str., *Phil.* . . 33 B6
Mindouli, *Congo* . . . 46 E2
Mine, *Japan* 29 G5
Minehead, *U.K.* 11 F4
Mineola, *U.S.A.* 71 J7
Mineral Wells, *U.S.A.* 71 J5
Minersville, *U.S.A.* . . 73 G7
Mingan, *Canada* . . . 63 B7
Mingechaurskoye
Vdkhr., *Azerbaijan* . 23 F8
Mingela, *Australia* . . 54 B4
Mingenew, *Australia* . 53 E2
Mingera Cr. →,
Australia 54 C2
Mingin, *Burma* 37 H19
Mingt'iehkaitafan =
Mintaka Pass,
Pakistan 36 A9
Minho, *Portugal* . . . 19 B1
Minho →, *Spain* . . . 19 B1
Minidoka, *U.S.A.* . . . 72 E7
Minigwal, L., *Australia* 53 E3
Minilya, *Australia* . . . 53 D1
Minilya →, *Australia* . 53 D1
Minipi, L., *Canada* . . 63 B7
Mink L., *Canada* . . . 64 A5
Minna, *Nigeria* 44 G6
Minneapolis, Kans.,
U.S.A. 70 F6
Minneapolis, Minn.,
U.S.A. 70 C8
Minnedosa, *Canada* . 65 C9
Minnesota □, *U.S.A.* . 70 C7
Minnie Creek, *Australia* 53 D2
Minnipa, *Australia* . . 55 E2
Minnitaki L., *Canada* . 62 C1
Mino, *Japan* 29 G8
Miño →, *Spain* 19 B1
Minorca = Menorca,
Spain 19 C8
Minore, *Australia* . . . 55 E4
Minot, *U.S.A.* 70 A4
Minsk, *Belorussia* . . 22 D4
Mińsk Mazowiecki,
Poland 17 B11
Mintaka Pass, *Pakistan* 36 A9
Minto, *Canada* 60 B5
Minton, *Canada* 65 D8
Minturn, *U.S.A.* 72 G10
Minusinsk, *Russia* . . 25 D10
Minutang, *India* . . . 37 E20
Minvoul, *Gabon* . . . 46 D2
Mir, *Niger* 45 F7
Mir Kūh, *Iran* 39 E8
Mir Shahdād, *Iran* . . 39 E8
Miraflores Locks,
Panama 74 H14
Miraj, *India* 36 L9
Miram Shah, *Pakistan* 36 C7
Miramar, *Mozam.* . . 49 C6
Miramichi B., *Canada* 63 C7
Miranda, *Brazil* 79 H7

Mountain Home

Miranda de Ebro, Spain 19 A4
Mirando City, U.S.A. 71 M5
Mirani, Australia 54 C4
Mirbāţ, Oman 40 D5
Miri, Malaysia 32 D4
Miriam Vale, Australia 54 C5
Mirim, L., S. Amer. 80 C6
Mirnyy, Russia 25 C12
Mirond L., Canada 65 B8
Mirpur Khas, Pakistan 36 G6
Mirror, Canada 64 C6
Mirzapur, India 37 G13
Mirzapur-cum-Vindhyachal = Mirzapur, India 37 G13
Misawa, Japan 28 D10
Miscou I., Canada 63 C7
Mish'āb, Ra's al, Si. Arabia 39 D6
Mishan, China 31 B8
Mishawaka, U.S.A. 68 E2
Mishima, Japan 29 G9
Miskah, Si. Arabia 38 E4
Miskolc, Hungary 17 D10
Misool, Indonesia 33 E8
Misrātah, Libya 45 B8
Missanabie, Canada 62 C3
Missinaibi →, Canada 62 B3
Missinaibi L., Canada 62 C3
Mission, S. Dak., U.S.A. 70 D4
Mission, Tex., U.S.A. 71 M5
Mission City, Canada 64 D4
Missisa L., Canada 62 B2
Mississagi →, Canada 62 C3
Mississippi □, U.S.A. 67 D9
Mississippi →, U.S.A. 71 L10
Mississippi, Delta of the, U.S.A. 71 L9
Mississippi Sd., U.S.A. 71 K10
Missoula, U.S.A. 72 C6
Missouri □, U.S.A. 70 F8
Missouri →, U.S.A. 70 F9
Missouri Valley, U.S.A. 70 E7
Mistake B., Canada 65 A10
Mistassini →, Canada 63 C5
Mistassini L., Canada 62 B5
Mistastin L., Canada 63 A7
Mistatim, Canada 65 C8
Mistretta, Italy 20 F6
Misty L., Canada 65 B8
Misurata = Misrātah, Libya 45 B8
Mitchell, Australia 55 D4
Mitchell, Ind., U.S.A. 68 F2
Mitchell, Nebr., U.S.A. 70 E3
Mitchell, Oreg., U.S.A. 72 D3
Mitchell, S. Dak., U.S.A. 70 D5
Mitchell →, Australia 54 B3
Mitchell, Mt., U.S.A. 69 H4
Mitchell Ras., Australia 54 A2
Mitchelstown, Ireland 13 D3
Mito, Japan 29 F10
Mitsinjo, Madag. 49 B8
Mitsiwa, Eritrea 45 E12
Mitsukaidō, Japan 29 F9
Mittagong, Australia 55 E5
Mitú, Colombia 78 C4
Mitumba, Chaîne des, Zaïre 46 F5
Mitumba Mts. = Mitumba, Chaîne des, Zaïre 46 F5
Mitwaba, Zaïre 46 F5
Mitzic, Gabon 46 D2
Miyagi □, Japan 28 E10
Miyah, W. el →, Syria 38 C3
Miyake-Jima, Japan 29 G9
Miyako, Japan 28 E10
Miyako-Jima, Japan 29 M2
Miyako-Rettō, Japan 29 M2
Miyakonojō, Japan 29 J5
Miyanoura-Dake, Japan 29 J5
Miyazaki, Japan 29 J5
Miyazaki □, Japan 29 H5
Miyazu, Japan 29 G7
Miyet, Bahr el = Dead Sea, Asia 41 D4
Miyoshi, Japan 29 G6
Mizamis = Ozamiz, Phil. 33 C6
Mizdah, Libya 45 B7
Mizen Hd., Cork, Ireland 13 E2
Mizen Hd., Wick., Ireland 13 D5
Mizoram □, India 37 H18
Mizpe Ramon, Israel 41 E3
Mizusawa, Japan 28 E10
Mjölby, Sweden 9 G13
Mjøsa, Norway 9 F11
Mkomazi →, S. Africa 49 E5
Mkuze, S. Africa 49 D5
Mkuze →, S. Africa 49 D5
Mladá Boleslav, Czech. 16 C7
Mlawa, Poland 17 B10
Mmabatho, S. Africa 48 D4
Mo i Rana, Norway 8 C13
Moa, Indonesia 33 F7
Moab, U.S.A. 73 G9
Moabi, Gabon 46 E2
Moala, Fiji 51 D8
Moalie Park, Australia 55 D3
Moba, Zaïre 46 F5
Mobārakābād, Iran 39 D7
Mobārakīyeh, Iran 39 C6
Mobaye, C.A.R. 46 D4
Mobayi, Zaïre 46 D4
Moberly, U.S.A. 70 F8
Moberly →, Canada 64 B4
Mobile, U.S.A. 69 K1
Mobile B., U.S.A. 69 K2
Mobridge, U.S.A. 70 C4
Mobutu Sese Seko, L., Africa 46 D6
Moçambique, Mozam. 47 H8
Moçâmedes = Namibe, Angola 47 H2
Mochudi, Botswana 48 C4
Mocimboa da Praia, Mozam. 46 G8
Moclips, U.S.A. 72 C1
Mocoa, Colombia 78 C3
Mocuba, Mozam. 47 H7
Modane, France 18 D7
Modder →, S. Africa 48 D3
Modderrivier, S. Africa 48 D3
Módena, Italy 20 B4
Modena, U.S.A. 73 H7
Modesto, U.S.A. 73 H3
Módica, Italy 20 F6
Moe, Australia 55 F4
Moei →, Thailand 34 D5
Moengo, Surinam 79 B8
Moffat, U.K. 12 F5
Mogadishu = Muqdisho, Somali Rep. 40 G4
Mogador = Essaouira, Morocco 44 B3
Mogalakwena →, S. Africa 49 C4
Mogami →, Japan 28 E10
Mogaung, Burma 37 G20
Mogi das Cruzes, Brazil 80 A7
Mogi-Mirim, Brazil 80 A7
Mogilev, Belorussia 22 D5
Mogilev-Podolskiy, Moldavia 23 E4
Mogocha, Russia 25 D12
Mogoi, Indonesia 33 E8
Mogok, Burma 37 H20
Mogumber, Australia 53 F2
Mohács, Hungary 17 F9
Mohales Hoek, Lesotho 48 E4
Mohall, U.S.A. 70 A4
Moḥammadābād, Iran 39 B8
Mohoro, Tanzania 46 F7
Moidart, L., U.K. 12 E3
Mointy, Kazakhstan 24 E8
Moisie, Canada 63 B6
Moisie →, Canada 63 B6
Moïssala, Chad 45 G8
Mojave, U.S.A. 73 J4
Mojave Desert, U.S.A. 73 J5
Mojokerto, Indonesia 33 G15
Mokai, N.Z. 51 H5
Mokhotlong, Lesotho 49 D4
Mokokchung, India 37 F19
Mol, Belgium 15 C5
Molchanovo, Russia 24 D9
Mold, U.K. 10 D4
Moldavia ■, Europe 23 E4
Molde, Norway 8 E9
Moldova ■ = Moldavia ■, Europe 23 E4
Molepolole, Botswana 48 C4
Molfetta, Italy 20 D7
Moline, U.S.A. 70 E9
Moliro, Zaïre 46 F6
Molise □, Italy 20 D6
Mollendo, Peru 78 G4
Mollerin, L., Australia 53 F2
Mölndal, Sweden 9 H12
Molokai, U.S.A. 66 H16
Molong, Australia 55 E4
Molopo →, Africa 48 D3
Molotov = Perm, Russia 22 C10
Moloundou, Cameroon 46 D3
Molson L., Canada 65 C9
Molteno, S. Africa 48 E4
Molu, Indonesia 33 F8
Molucca Sea = Maluku Sea, Indonesia 33 E6
Moluccas = Maluku, Indonesia 33 E7
Moma, Mozam. 47 H7
Mombasa, Kenya 46 E7
Mombetsu, Japan 28 B11
Mompós, Colombia 78 B4
Møn, Denmark 9 J12
Mon →, Burma 37 J19
Mona, Canal de la, W. Indies 75 D11
Monach Is., U.K. 12 D1
Monaco ■, Europe 18 E7
Monadhliath Mts., U.K. 12 D4
Monaghan, Ireland 13 B5
Monaghan □, Ireland 13 B5
Monahans, U.S.A. 71 K3
Monarch Mt., Canada 64 C3
Monastir = Bitola, Macedonia 21 D9
Monastir, Tunisia 45 A7
Moncayo, Sierra del, Spain 19 B5
Mönchengladbach, Germany 16 C3
Monchique, Portugal 19 D1
Monchique, Sa. de, Portugal 19 D1
Monclova, Mexico 74 B4
Moncton, Canada 63 C7
Mondego →, Portugal 19 B1
Mondeodo, Indonesia 33 E6
Mondoví, Italy 20 B2
Mondovi, U.S.A. 70 C9
Mondrain I., Australia 53 F3
Monessen, U.S.A. 68 E6
Monett, U.S.A. 71 G8
Monforte, Portugal 19 C2
Mong Cai, Vietnam 34 B9
Mong Hsu, Burma 37 J21
Mong Kung, Burma 37 J20
Mong Lang, Burma 34 B4
Mong Nai, Burma 37 J20
Mong Pawk, Burma 37 H21
Mong Ton, Burma 37 J21
Mong Wa, Burma 37 J22
Mong Yai, Burma 37 H21
Mongalla, Sudan 45 G11
Mongers, L., Australia 53 E2
Monghyr = Munger, India 37 G15
Mongo, Chad 45 F8
Mongolia ■, Asia 25 E10
Mongororo, Chad 45 F9
Mongu, Zambia 47 H4
Môngua, Angola 48 B2
Monkira, Australia 54 C3
Monkoto, Zaïre 46 E4
Monmouth, U.K. 11 F5
Monmouth, U.S.A. 70 E9
Mono, L., U.S.A. 73 H4
Monópoli, Italy 20 D7
Monqoumba, C.A.R. 46 D3
Monroe, Ga., U.S.A. 69 J4
Monroe, La., U.S.A. 71 J8
Monroe, Mich., U.S.A. 68 E4
Monroe, N.C., U.S.A. 69 H5
Monroe, Utah, U.S.A. 73 G7
Monroe, Wis., U.S.A. 70 D10
Monroe City, U.S.A. 70 F9
Monroeville, U.S.A. 69 K2
Monrovia, Liberia 44 G2
Monrovia, U.S.A. 73 J4
Mons, Belgium 15 D3
Monse, Indonesia 33 E6
Mont-de-Marsan, France 18 E3
Mont-Joli, Canada 63 C6
Mont-Laurier, Canada 62 C4
Mont-St.-Michel, Le = Le Mont-St.-Michel, France 18 B3
Mont Tremblant Prov. Park, Canada 62 C5
Montagu, S. Africa 48 E3
Montagu I., Antarctica 5 B1
Montague, Canada 63 C7
Montague, U.S.A. 72 F2
Montague Ra., Australia 53 E2
Montague Sd., Australia 52 B4
Montalbán, Spain 19 B5
Montaña, Peru 78 E4
Montana □, U.S.A. 66 A5
Montargis, France 18 C5
Montauban, France 18 D4
Montauk, U.S.A. 68 E10
Montbéliard, France 18 C7
Monte Alegre, Brazil 79 D8
Monte Azul, Brazil 79 G10
Monte Bello Is., Australia 52 D2
Monte-Carlo, Monaco 18 E7
Monte Caseros, Argentina 80 C5
Monte Comán, Argentina 80 C3
Monte Sant' Ángelo, Italy 20 D6
Monte Santu, C. di, Italy 20 D3
Monte Vista, U.S.A. 73 H10
Montebello, Canada 62 C5
Montecristi, Ecuador 78 D2
Montego Bay, Jamaica 74 J16
Montejinnie, Australia 52 C5
Montélimar, France 18 D6
Montello, U.S.A. 70 D10
Montemorelos, Mexico 74 B5
Montenegro □, Montenegro 21 C8
Montepuez, Mozam. 47 G7
Monterey, U.S.A. 73 H3
Montería, Colombia 78 B3
Monterrey, Mexico 74 B4
Montes Claros, Brazil 79 G10
Montesano, U.S.A. 72 C2
Montevideo, Uruguay 80 C5
Montevideo, U.S.A. 70 C7
Montezuma, U.S.A. 70 E8
Montgomery = Sahiwal, Pakistan 36 D8
Montgomery, U.K. 11 E4
Montgomery, Ala., U.S.A. 69 J2
Montgomery, W. Va., U.S.A. 68 F5
Monticello, Ark., U.S.A. 71 J9
Monticello, Fla., U.S.A. 69 K4
Monticello, Ind., U.S.A. 68 E2
Monticello, Iowa, U.S.A. 70 D9
Monticello, Ky., U.S.A. 69 G3
Monticello, Minn., U.S.A. 70 C8
Monticello, Miss., U.S.A. 71 K9
Monticello, Utah, U.S.A. 73 H9
Montijo, Spain 19 C2
Montilla, Spain 19 D3
Montluçon, France 18 C5
Montmagny, Canada 63 C5
Montmartre, Canada 65 C8
Montmorency, Canada 63 C5
Monto, Australia 54 C5
Montoro, Spain 19 C3
Montpelier, Idaho, U.S.A. 72 E8
Montpelier, Ohio, U.S.A. 68 E3
Montpelier, Vt., U.S.A. 68 C9
Montpellier, France 18 E5
Montréal, Canada 62 C5
Montreal L., Canada 65 C7
Montreal Lake, Canada 65 C7
Montreuil, France 18 A4
Montreux, Switz. 16 E3
Montrose, U.K. 12 E6
Montrose, U.S.A. 73 G10
Monts, Pte. des, Canada 63 C6
Montserrat ■, W. Indies 74 L19
Monveda, Zaïre 46 D4
Monywa, Burma 37 H19
Monza, Italy 20 B3
Monze, Zambia 47 H5
Monze, C., Pakistan 36 G5
Monzón, Spain 19 B6
Mooi River, S. Africa 49 D4
Moolawatana, Australia 55 D2
Mooliabeenee, Australia 53 F2
Mooloogool, Australia 53 E2
Moomin Cr. →, Australia 55 D4
Moonah →, Australia 54 C2
Moonbeam, Canada 62 C3
Moonda, L., Australia 54 D3
Moonie, Australia 55 D5
Moonie →, Australia 55 D4
Moonta, Australia 55 E2
Moora, Australia 53 F2
Mooraberree, Australia 54 D3
Moorarie, Australia 53 E2
Moorcroft, U.S.A. 70 C2
Moore →, Australia 53 F2
Moore, L., Australia 53 E2
Moore Reefs, Australia 54 B4
Moorefield, U.S.A. 68 F6
Mooresville, U.S.A. 69 H5
Moorfoot Hills, U.K. 12 F5
Moorhead, U.S.A. 70 B6
Mooroopna, Australia 55 F4
Moorreesburg, S. Africa 48 E2
Moose →, Canada 62 B3
Moose Factory, Canada 62 B3
Moose I., Canada 65 C9
Moose Jaw, Canada 65 C7
Moose Jaw →, Canada 65 C7
Moose Lake, Canada 65 C8
Moose Lake, U.S.A. 70 B8
Moose Mountain Cr. →, Canada 65 D8
Moose Mountain Prov. Park, Canada 65 D8
Moose River, Canada 62 B3
Moosehead L., U.S.A. 63 C6
Moosomin, Canada 65 C8
Moosonee, Canada 62 B3
Mopeia Velha, Mozam. 47 H7
Mopipi, Botswana 48 C3
Mopti, Mali 44 F4
Moquegua, Peru 78 G4
Mora, Sweden 9 F13
Mora, Minn., U.S.A. 70 C8
Mora, N. Mex., U.S.A. 73 J11
Moradabad, India 36 E11
Morafenobe, Madag. 49 B7
Moramanga, Madag. 49 B8
Moran, Kans., U.S.A. 71 G7
Moran, Wyo., U.S.A. 72 E8
Moranbah, Australia 54 C4
Morant Pt., Jamaica 74 K17
Morar, L., U.K. 12 E3
Moratuwa, Sri Lanka 36 R11
Morava →, Europe 16 D8
Moravia, U.S.A. 70 E8
Moravian Hts. = Ceskomoravská Vrchovina, Czech. 16 D7
Morawa, Australia 53 E2
Morawhanna, Guyana 78 B7
Moray Firth, U.K. 12 D5
Morbihan □, France 18 C2
Morden, Canada 65 D9
Mordovian Republic □, Russia 22 D7
Mordvinia = Mordovian Republic □, Russia 22 D7
Møre og Romsdal fylke □, Norway 8 E9
Morea, Australia 55 F3
Morea, Greece 6 H10
Moreau →, U.S.A. 70 C4
Morecambe, U.K. 10 C5
Morecambe B., U.K. 10 C5
Moree, Australia 55 D4
Morehead, U.S.A. 68 F4
Morehead City, U.S.A. 69 H7
Morelia, Mexico 74 D4
Morelia, Michoacan, Mexico 74 D4
Morella, Australia 54 C3
Morella, Spain 19 B5
Morena, Sierra, Spain 19 C3
Morenci, U.S.A. 73 K9
Moresby I., Canada 64 C2
Moreton, Australia 54 A3
Moreton I., Australia 55 D5
Morgan, Australia 55 E2
Morgan, U.S.A. 72 F8
Morgan City, U.S.A. 71 L9
Morganfield, U.S.A. 68 G2
Morganton, U.S.A. 69 H5
Morgantown, U.S.A. 68 F6
Morgenzon, S. Africa 49 D4
Morghak, Iran 39 D8
Morice L., Canada 64 C3
Morinville, Canada 64 C6
Morioka, Japan 28 E10
Morlaix, France 18 B2
Mornington, Vic., Australia 55 F4
Mornington, W. Austral., Australia 52 C4
Mornington, I., Chile 80 F1
Mornington I., Australia 54 B2
Moro G., Phil. 33 C6
Morocco ■, N. Afr. 44 B3
Morococha, Peru 78 F3
Morogoro, Tanzania 46 F7
Morombe, Madag. 49 C7
Morón, Cuba 75 C9
Morón de la Frontera, Spain 19 D3
Morondava, Madag. 49 C7
Morotai, Indonesia 33 D7
Moroto, Uganda 46 D6
Morpeth, U.K. 10 B6
Morphou, Cyprus 38 C2
Morrilton, U.S.A. 71 H8
Morrinhos, Brazil 79 G9
Morrinsville, N.Z. 51 G5
Morris, Canada 65 D9
Morris, Ill., U.S.A. 68 E1
Morris, Minn., U.S.A. 70 C7
Morris, Mt., Australia 53 E5
Morrisburg, Canada 62 D4
Morrison, U.S.A. 70 E10
Morristown, Ariz., U.S.A. 73 K7
Morristown, S. Dak., U.S.A. 70 C4
Morristown, Tenn., U.S.A. 69 G4
Morro Bay, U.S.A. 73 J3
Morrumbene, Mozam. 49 C6
Morshansk, Russia 22 D7
Morteros, Argentina 80 C4
Mortes, R. das →, Brazil 79 F8
Mortlake, Australia 55 F3
Morton, Tex., U.S.A. 71 J3
Morton, Wash., U.S.A. 72 C2
Morundah, Australia 55 E4
Moruya, Australia 55 F5
Morvan, France 18 C6
Morven, Australia 55 D4
Morvern, U.K. 12 E3
Morwell, Australia 55 F4
Morzhovets, Ostrov, Russia 22 A7
Moscos Is., Burma 34 F4
Moscow = Moskva, Russia 22 C6
Moscow, U.S.A. 72 C5
Mosel →, Europe 18 A7
Moselle = Mosel →, Europe 18 A7
Moselle □, France 18 B7
Moses Lake, U.S.A. 72 C4
Mosgiel, N.Z. 51 L3
Moshi, Tanzania 46 E7
Moshupa, Botswana 48 C4
Mosjøen, Norway 8 D12
Moskenesøya, Norway 8 C12
Moskenstraumen, Norway 8 C12
Moskva, Russia 22 C6
Moskva →, Russia 22 C6
Mosomane, Botswana 48 C4
Mosquera, Colombia 78 C3
Mosquero, U.S.A. 71 H3
Moss, Norway 9 G11
Moss Vale, Australia 55 E5
Mossaka, Congo 46 E3
Mossbank, Canada 65 D7
Mossburn, N.Z. 51 L2
Mosselbaai, S. Africa 48 E3
Mossendjo, Congo 46 E2
Mossgiel, Australia 55 E3
Mossman, Australia 54 B4
Mossoró, Brazil 79 E11
Mossuril, Mozam. 47 G8
Mossy →, Canada 65 C8
Most, Czech. 16 C6
Mosta, Malta 20 G6
Moşţafāābād, Iran 39 C7
Mostaganem, Algeria 44 A5
Mostar, Bos.-H. 21 C7
Mostardas, Brazil 80 C6
Mosul = Al Mawşil, Iraq 38 B4
Motala, Sweden 9 G13
Motherwell, U.K. 12 F5
Motihari, India 37 F14
Mott, U.S.A. 70 B3
Motueka, N.Z. 51 J4
Motueka →, N.Z. 51 J4
Mouanda, Gabon 46 E2
Mouchalagane →, Canada 63 B6
Moúdhros, Greece 21 E11
Moudjeria, Mauritania 44 E2
Mouila, Gabon 46 E2
Moulamein, Australia 55 F3
Moulins, France 18 C5
Moulmein, Burma 37 L20
Moulton, U.S.A. 71 L6
Moultrie, U.S.A. 69 K4
Moultrie, L., U.S.A. 69 J5
Mound City, Mo., U.S.A. 70 E7
Mound City, S. Dak., U.S.A. 70 C4
Moundou, Chad 45 G8
Moundsville, U.S.A. 68 F5
Mount Airy, U.S.A. 69 G5
Mount Amherst, Australia 52 C4
Mount Angel, U.S.A. 72 D2
Mount Augustus, Australia 52 D2
Mount Barker, S. Austral., Australia 55 F2
Mount Barker, W. Austral., Australia 53 F2
Mount Carmel, U.S.A. 68 F2
Mount Clemens, U.S.A. 62 D3
Mount Coolon, Australia 54 C4
Mount Darwin, Zimbabwe 47 H6
Mount Desert I., U.S.A. 63 D6
Mount Dora, U.S.A. 69 L5
Mount Douglas, Australia 54 C4
Mount Eba, Australia 55 E2
Mount Edgecumbe, U.S.A. 64 B1
Mount Elizabeth, Australia 52 C4
Mount Fletcher, S. Africa 49 E4
Mount Forest, Canada 62 D3
Mount Gambier, Australia 55 F3
Mount Garnet, Australia 54 B4
Mount Hope, N.S.W., Australia 55 E4
Mount Hope, S. Austral., Australia 55 E2
Mount Hope, U.S.A. 68 G5
Mount Horeb, U.S.A. 70 D10
Mount Howitt, Australia 55 D3
Mount Isa, Australia 54 C2
Mount Keith, Australia 53 E3
Mount Larcom, Australia 54 C5
Mount Lofty Ra., Australia 55 F2
Mount McKinley Nat. Park, U.S.A. 60 B5
Mount Magnet, Australia 53 E2
Mount Margaret, Australia 55 D3
Mount Maunganui, N.Z. 51 G6
Mount Molloy, Australia 54 B4
Mount Monger, Australia 53 F3
Mount Morgan, Australia 54 C5
Mount Morris, U.S.A. 68 D7
Mount Mulligan, Australia 54 B3
Mount Narryer, Australia 53 E2
Mount Oxide Mine, Australia 54 B2
Mount Pearl, Canada 63 C9
Mount Perry, Australia 55 D5
Mount Phillips, Australia 52 D2
Mount Pleasant, Iowa, U.S.A. 70 E9
Mount Pleasant, Mich., U.S.A. 68 D3
Mount Pleasant, S.C., U.S.A. 69 J6
Mount Pleasant, Tenn., U.S.A. 69 H2
Mount Pleasant, Tex., U.S.A. 71 J7
Mount Pleasant, Utah, U.S.A. 72 G8
Mount Rainier Nat. Park., U.S.A. 72 C3
Mount Revelstoke Nat. Park, Canada 64 C5
Mount Robson Prov. Park, Canada 64 C5
Mount Sandiman, Australia 53 D2
Mount Shasta, U.S.A. 72 F2
Mount Sterling, Ill., U.S.A. 70 F9
Mount Sterling, Ky., U.S.A. 68 F4
Mount Surprise, Australia 54 B3
Mount Vernon, Australia 52 D2
Mount Vernon, Ind., U.S.A. 70 F10
Mount Vernon, N.Y., U.S.A. 68 E9
Mount Vernon, Ohio, U.S.A. 68 E4
Mount Vernon, Wash., U.S.A. 72 B2
Mountain City, Nev., U.S.A. 72 F6
Mountain City, Tenn., U.S.A. 69 G5
Mountain Grove, U.S.A. 71 G8
Mountain Home, Ark., U.S.A. 71 G8
Mountain Home, Idaho, U.S.A. 72 E6

Mountain Iron

Mountain Iron, U.S.A. 70 B8
Mountain Park, Canada 64 C5
Mountain View, Ark., U.S.A. 71 H8
Mountain View, Calif., U.S.A. 73 H2
Mountainair, U.S.A. 73 J10
Mountmellick, Ireland 13 C4
Moura, Australia 54 C4
Moura, Brazil 78 D6
Mourdi, Dépression du, Chad 45 E9
Mourdiah, Mali 44 F3
Mourilyan, Australia 54 B4
Mourne →, U.K. 13 B4
Mourne Mts., U.K. 13 B5
Mouscron, Belgium 15 D3
Moussoro, Chad 45 F8
Moutohara, N.Z. 51 H6
Moutong, Indonesia 33 D6
Moville, Ireland 13 A4
Moy →, Ireland 13 B3
Moyale, Kenya 40 G2
Moyamba, S. Leone 44 G2
Moyen Atlas, Morocco 44 B3
Moyle □, U.K. 13 A5
Moyo, Indonesia 32 F5
Moyobamba, Peru 78 E3
Moyyero →, Russia 25 C11
Mozambique = Moçambique, Mozam. 47 H8
Mozambique ■, Africa 47 H7
Mozambique Chan., Africa 49 B7
Mozdok, Russia 23 F7
Mozdūrān, Iran 39 C9
Mozyr, Belorussia 22 D4
Mpanda, Tanzania 46 F6
Mpika, Zambia 47 G6
Mpumalanga, S. Africa 49 D5
Mpwapwa, Tanzania 46 F7
Msaken, Tunisia 45 A7
Msoro, Zambia 47 G6
Mtubatuba, S. Africa 49 D5
Mu Us Shamo, China 31 C5
Muaná, Brazil 79 D9
Muang Chiang Rai, Thailand 34 C5
Muang Lamphun, Thailand 34 C5
Muar, Malaysia 34 S15
Muar →, Malaysia 34 S15
Muarabungo, Indonesia 32 E2
Muaraenim, Indonesia 32 E2
Muarajuloi, Indonesia 32 E4
Muarakaman, Indonesia 32 E5
Muaratebo, Indonesia 32 E2
Muaratembesi, Indonesia 32 E2
Muaratewe, Indonesia 32 E4
Mubarraz = Al Mubarraz, Si. Arabia 39 E6
Mubende, Uganda 46 D6
Mubi, Nigeria 45 F7
Muck, U.K. 12 E2
Muckadilla, Australia 55 D4
Muconda, Angola 46 G4
Mucuri, Brazil 79 G11
Mucusso, Angola 48 B3
Mudanjiang, China 31 B7
Muddy →, U.S.A. 73 H8
Mudgee, Australia 55 E4
Mudjatik →, Canada 65 B7
Mueller Ra., Australia 52 C4
Mufulira, Zambia 47 G5
Mughayrā', Si. Arabia 38 D3
Mugi, Japan 29 H7
Muğla, Turkey 23 G4
Mugu, Nepal 37 E13
Muhammad Qol, Sudan 45 D12
Mühlig Hofmann fjella, Antarctica 5 D3
Mui Bai Bung, Vietnam 34 H8
Mui Ron, Vietnam 34 C9
Muikamachi, Japan 29 F9
Muine Bheag, Ireland 13 D5
Muir, L., Australia 53 F2
Mukah, Malaysia 32 D4
Mukden = Shenyang, China 31 B7
Mukhtuya = Lensk, Russia 25 C12
Mukinbudin, Australia 53 F2
Mukomuko, Indonesia 32 E2
Muktsar, India 36 D9
Mukur, Afghan. 36 C5
Mukutawa →, Canada 65 C9
Mulchén, Chile 80 D2
Mulde →, Germany 16 C6
Mulo Crook, U.S.A. 71 H3
Muleshoe, U.S.A. 71 H3
Mulgathing, Australia 55 E1
Mulgrave, Canada 63 C7
Mulhacén, Spain 19 D4
Mülheim, Germany 16 C4
Mulhouse, France 18 C7
Mull, U.K. 12 E3
Mullaittvu, Sri Lanka 36 Q12
Mullen, U.S.A. 70 D4
Mullengudgery, Australia 55 E4
Mullens, U.S.A. 68 G5
Muller, Pegunungan, Indonesia 32 D4
Mullet Pen., Ireland 13 B1
Mullewa, Australia 53 E2
Mulligan →, Australia 54 C2

Mullin, U.S.A. 71 K5
Mullingar, Ireland 13 C4
Mullins, U.S.A. 69 H6
Mullumbimby, Australia 55 D5
Multan, Pakistan 36 D7
Mulvane, U.S.A. 71 G6
Mulwala, Australia 55 F4
Mumbwa, Zambia 47 H5
Mun →, Thailand 34 E7
Muna, Indonesia 33 F6
München, Germany 16 D5
Munchen-Gladbach = Mönchengladbach, Germany 16 C3
Muncho Lake, Canada 64 B3
Muncie, U.S.A. 68 E3
Muncoonie, L., Australia 54 D2
Mundala, Indonesia 33 E10
Mundare, Canada 64 C6
Munday, U.S.A. 71 J5
Münden, Germany 16 C4
Mundiwindi, Australia 52 D3
Mundo Novo, Brazil 79 F10
Mundrabilla, Australia 53 F4
Mungallala, Australia 55 D4
Mungallala Cr. →, Australia 55 D4
Mungana, Australia 54 B3
Mungbere, Zaïre 46 D5
Munger, India 37 G15
Mungindi, Australia 55 D4
Munhango, Angola 47 G3
Munich = München, Germany 16 D5
Munising, U.S.A. 68 B2
Munku-Sardyk, Russia 25 D11
Muñoz Gamero, Pen., Chile 80 G2
Munroe L., Canada 65 B9
Münster, Germany 16 C3
Munster □, Ireland 13 D3
Muntadgin, Australia 53 F2
Muntok, Indonesia 32 E3
Munyak, Uzbekistan 24 E6
Muon Pak Beng, Laos 34 C6
Muonio, Finland 8 C17
Mupa, Angola 47 H3
Muqdisho, Somali Rep. 40 G4
Mur →, Austria 16 E8
Murakami, Japan 28 E9
Murallón, Cuerro, Chile 80 F2
Muranga, Kenya 46 E7
Murashi, Russia 22 C8
Murayama, Japan 28 E10
Murban, U.A.E. 39 F7
Murchison →, Australia 53 E1
Murchison, Mt., Antarctica 5 D11
Murchison Falls = Kabarega Falls, Uganda 46 D6
Murchison House, Australia 53 E1
Murchison Ra., Australia 54 C1
Murcia, Spain 19 C5
Murcia □, Spain 19 D5
Murdo, U.S.A. 70 D4
Murdoch Pt., Australia 54 A3
Mureş →, Romania 17 E10
Mureşul = Mureş →, Romania 17 E10
Murfreesboro, U.S.A. 69 H2
Murgab, Tajikistan 24 F8
Murgon, Australia 55 D5
Murgoo, Australia 53 E2
Muria, Indonesia 33 G14
Müritz See, Germany 16 B6
Murmansk, Russia 22 A5
Murom, Russia 22 C7
Muroran, Japan 28 C10
Muroto, Japan 29 H7
Muroto-Misaki, Japan 29 H7
Murphy, U.S.A. 72 E5
Murphysboro, U.S.A. 71 G10
Murray, Ky., U.S.A. 69 G1
Murray, Utah, U.S.A. 72 F8
Murray →, Australia 55 F2
Murray →, Canada 64 B4
Murray, L., U.S.A. 69 H5
Murray Bridge, Australia 55 F2
Murray Downs, Australia 54 C1
Murray Harbour, Canada 63 C7
Murraysburg, S. Africa 48 E3
Murree, Pakistan 36 C8
Murrin Murrin, Australia 53 E3
Murrumbidgee →, Australia 55 E3
Murrumburrah, Australia 55 E4
Murrurundi, Australia 55 E5
Mursala, Indonesia 32 D1
Murtle L., Canada 64 C5
Murtoa, Australia 55 F3
Murwara, India 37 H12
Murwillumbah, Australia 55 D5
Mürzzuschlag, Austria 16 E7
Muş, Turkey 23 G7
Mûsa, G., Egypt 45 C11
Musa Khel, Pakistan 36 D6
Musá Qal'eh, Afghan. 36 C4
Musafargarh, Pakistan 36 D7
Musala, Bulgaria 21 C10
Musay'īd, Qatar 39 E6

Muscat = Masqat, Oman 40 C6
Muscat & Oman = Oman ■, Asia 40 C6
Muscatine, U.S.A. 70 E9
Musgrave, Australia 54 A3
Musgrave Ras., Australia 53 E5
Mushie, Zaïre 46 E3
Musi →, Indonesia 32 E2
Muskeg →, Canada 64 A4
Muskegon, U.S.A. 68 D2
Muskegon →, U.S.A. 68 D2
Muskegon Heights, U.S.A. 68 D2
Muskogee, U.S.A. 71 H7
Muskwa →, Canada 64 B4
Muslimiyah, Syria 38 B3
Musmar, Sudan 45 E12
Musoma, Tanzania 46 E6
Musquaro, L., Canada 63 B7
Musquodoboit Harbour, Canada 63 D7
Musselburgh, U.K. 12 F5
Musselshell →, U.S.A. 72 C10
Mussoorie, India 36 D11
Mussuco, Angola 48 B2
Mustang, Nepal 37 E13
Musters, L., Argentina 80 F3
Muswellbrook, Australia 55 E5
Mût, Egypt 45 C10
Mutanda, Mozam. 49 C5
Mutaray, Russia 25 C11
Mutare, Zimbabwe 47 H6
Muting, Indonesia 33 F10
Mutsu, Japan 28 D10
Mutsu-Wan, Japan 28 D10
Muttaburra, Australia 54 C3
Muweilih, Egypt 41 E3
Muxima, Angola 46 F2
Muya, Russia 25 D12
Muzaffarabad, Pakistan 36 B8
Muzaffarnagar, India 36 E10
Muzaffarpur, India 37 F14
Muzhi, Russia 24 C7
Muzon C., U.S.A. 64 C2
Mvuma, Zimbabwe 47 H6
Mwanza, Tanzania 46 E6
Mweelrea, Ireland 13 C2
Mweka, Zaïre 46 E4
Mwenezi, Zimbabwe 47 J6
Mwenga, Zaïre 46 E5
Mweru, L., Zambia 46 F5
Mwinilunga, Zambia 47 G4
My Tho, Vietnam 34 G9
Myanaung, Burma 37 K19
Myanmar = Burma ■, Asia 37 J20
Myaungmya, Burma 37 L19
Mycenae = Mikinai, Greece 21 F10
Myeik Kyunzu, Burma 34 G4
Myingyan, Burma 37 J19
Myitkyina, Burma 37 G20
Mykolayiv = Nikolayev, Ukraine 23 E5
Mymensingh, Bangla. 37 G17
Mynydd Du, U.K. 11 F4
Mýrdalsjökull, Iceland 8 E4
Myroodah, Australia 52 C3
Myrtle Beach, U.S.A. 69 J6
Myrtle Creek, U.S.A. 72 E2
Myrtle Point, U.S.A. 72 E1
Mysore = Karnataka □, India 36 N10
Mysore, India 36 N10
Mytishchi, Russia 22 C6
Myton, U.S.A. 72 F8
Mývatn, Iceland 8 D5
Mzimkulu →, S. Africa 49 E5
Mzimvubu →, S. Africa 49 E4

N

Naab →, Germany 16 D6
Naantali, Finland 9 F17
Naas, Ireland 13 C5
Nababiep, S. Africa 48 D2
Nabari, Japan 29 G8
Nabawa, Australia 53 E1
Nabberu, L., Australia 53 E3
Naberezhnyye Chelny, Russia 24 D6
Nabeul, Tunisia 45 A7
Nabīd, Iran 39 D8
Nabire, Indonesia 33 E9
Nabisipi →, Canada 63 B7
Nablus = Nābulus, Jordan 41 C4
Naboomspruit, S. Africa 49 C4
Nābulus, Jordan 41 C4
Nābulus □, Jordan 41 C4
Naches, U.S.A. 72 C3
Nachingwea, Tanzania 46 G7
Nackara, Australia 55 E2
Naco, U.S.A. 73 L9
Nacogdoches, U.S.A. 71 K7
Nacozari, Mexico 74 A3
Nadiad, India 36 H8
Nadūshan, Iran 39 C7
Nadvoitsy, Russia 22 B5
Nadym, Russia 24 C8
Nadym →, Russia 24 C8

Nafada, Nigeria 44 F7
Naftshahr, Iran 38 C5
Nafud Desert = An Nafūd, Si. Arabia 38 D4
Naga, Phil. 33 B6
Nagagami →, Canada 62 C3
Nagahama, Japan 29 G8
Nagai, Japan 28 E10
Nagaland □, India 37 F19
Nagano, Japan 29 F9
Nagano □, Japan 29 F9
Nagaoka, Japan 29 F9
Nagappattinam, India 36 P11
Nagar Parkar, Pakistan 36 G7
Nagasaki, Japan 29 H4
Nagasaki □, Japan 29 H4
Nagato, Japan 29 G5
Nagaur, India 36 F8
Nagercoil, India 36 Q10
Nagīneh, Iran 39 C8
Nagoorin, Australia 54 C5
Nagornyy, Russia 25 D13
Nagoya, Japan 29 G8
Nagpur, India 36 J11
Nagykanizsa, Hungary 16 E8
Nagykőrös, Hungary 17 E9
Naha, Japan 29 L3
Nahanni Butte, Canada 64 A4
Nahanni Nat. Park, Canada 64 A3
Nahariyya, Israel 38 C2
Nahāvand, Iran 39 C6
Nahlin, Canada 64 B2
Naicam, Canada 65 C8
Nā'ifah, Si. Arabia 40 D5
Nain, Canada 63 A7
Nā'īn, Iran 39 C7
Nainpur, India 36 H12
Naira, Indonesia 33 E7
Nairn, U.K. 12 D5
Nairobi, Kenya 46 E7
Naivasha, Kenya 46 E7
Najafābād, Iran 39 C6
Najibabad, India 36 E11
Najmah, Si. Arabia 39 E6
Nakadōri-Shima, Japan 29 H4
Nakaminato, Japan 29 F10
Nakamura, Japan 29 H6
Nakano, Japan 29 F9
Nakano-Shima, Japan 29 K4
Nakashibetsu, Japan 28 C12
Nakfa, Eritrea 45 E12
Nakhichevan, Azerbaijan 23 G8
Nakhichevan Republic □, Azerbaijan 23 G8
Nakhl, Egypt 41 F2
Nakhl-e Taqī, Iran 39 E7
Nakhodka, Russia 25 E14
Nakhon Phanom, Thailand 34 D8
Nakhon Ratchasima, Thailand 34 E7
Nakhon Sawan, Thailand 34 E6
Nakhon Si Thammarat, Thailand 34 H6
Nakina, B.C., Canada 64 B2
Nakina, Ont., Canada 62 B2
Nakskov, Denmark 9 J11
Naksup, Canada 64 C5
Nal →, Pakistan 36 G4
Nalchik, Russia 23 F7
Nalgonda, India 36 L11
Nallamalai Hills, India 36 M11
Nalón →, Spain 19 A2
Nālūt, Libya 45 B7
Nam Co, China 30 C4
Nam Dinh, Vietnam 34 B9
Nam-Phan, Vietnam 34 G9
Nam Phong, Thailand 34 D7
Nam Tha, Laos 34 B6
Namacunde, Angola 48 B2
Namacurra, Mozam. 49 B6
Namak, Daryācheh-ye, Iran 39 C7
Namak, Kavir-e, Iran 39 C8
Namaland, Namibia 48 C2
Namangan, Uzbekistan 24 E8
Namapa, Mozam. 47 G7
Namaqualand, S. Africa 48 D2
Namber, Indonesia 33 E8
Nambour, Australia 55 D5
Nambucca Heads, Australia 55 E5
Namcha Barwa, China 30 D4
Nameh, Indonesia 32 D5
Namew L., Canada 65 C8
Namib Desert = Namibwoestyn, Namibia 48 C2
Namibe, Angola 47 H2
Namibe □, Angola 48 B1
Namibia ■, Africa 48 C2
Namibwoestyn, Namibia 48 C2
Namlea, Indonesia 33 E7
Namoi →, Australia 55 E4
Nampa, U.S.A. 72 E5
Nampō-Shotō, Japan 29 J10
Nampula, Mozam. 47 H7
Namrole, Indonesia 33 E7
Namse Shankou, China 37 E13
Namsen →, Norway 8 D11
Namsos, Norway 8 D11
Namtay, Russia 25 C13
Namtu, Burma 37 H20
Namu, Canada 64 C3
Namur, Belgium 15 D4

Namur □, Belgium 15 D4
Namutoni, Namibia 48 B2
Namwala, Zambia 47 H5
Nan, Thailand 34 C6
Nanaimo, Canada 64 D4
Nanango, Australia 55 D5
Nanao, Japan 29 F8
Nanching = Nanjing, China 31 C6
Nanchong, China 30 C5
Nancy, France 18 B7
Nanda Devi, India 36 D11
Nandan, Japan 29 G7
Nanded, India 36 K10
Nandewar Ra., Australia 55 E5
Nandi, Fiji 51 C7
Nandurbar, India 36 J9
Nandyal, India 36 M11
Nanga, Australia 53 E1
Nanga-Eboko, Cameroon 46 D2
Nanga Parbat, Pakistan 36 B9
Nangapinoh, Indonesia 32 E4
Nangarhár □, Afghan. 36 B7
Nangatayap, Indonesia 32 E4
Nanjing, China 31 C6
Nanking = Nanjing, China 31 C6
Nankoku, Japan 29 H6
Nanning, China 30 D5
Nannup, Australia 53 F2
Nanping, China 31 D6
Nansei-Shotō = Ryūkyū-rettō, Japan 29 M2
Nansen Sd., Canada 4 A3
Nanticoke, U.S.A. 68 E7
Nanton, Canada 64 C6
Nantong, China 31 C7
Nantucket I., U.S.A. 58 E12
Nanuque, Brazil 79 G10
Nanutarra, Australia 52 D2
Nanyang, China 31 C6
Nanyuki, Kenya 46 D7
Náo, C. de la, Spain 19 C6
Naococane L., Canada 63 B5
Naoetsu, Japan 29 F9
Napa, U.S.A. 72 G2
Napanee, Canada 62 D4
Napier, N.Z. 51 H6
Napier Broome B., Australia 52 B4
Napier Downs, Australia 52 C3
Napier Pen., Australia 54 A2
Naples = Nápoli, Italy 20 D6
Naples, U.S.A. 69 M5
Napo →, Peru 78 D4
Napoleon, N. Dak., U.S.A. 70 B5
Napoleon, Ohio, U.S.A. 68 E3
Nápoli, Italy 20 D6
Nappa Merrie, Australia 55 D3
Naqqāsh, Iran 39 C6
Nara, Japan 29 G7
Nara, Mali 44 E3
Nara □, Japan 29 G8
Nara Visa, U.S.A. 71 H3
Naracoorte, Australia 55 F3
Naradhan, Australia 55 E4
Narasapur, India 37 L12
Narathiwat, Thailand 34 N14
Narayanganj, Bangla. 37 H17
Narayanpet, India 36 L10
Narbonne, France 18 E5
Nardîn, Iran 39 B7
Nardò, Italy 21 D8
Narembeen, Australia 53 F2
Nares Str., Arctic 58 B13
Naretha, Australia 53 F3
Narin, Afghan. 36 A6
Narindra, Helodranon' i, Madag. 49 A8
Narita, Japan 29 G10
Narmada →, India 36 J8
Narodnaya, Russia 22 A10
Narooma, Australia 55 F5
Narrabri, Australia 55 E4
Narrandera, Australia 55 E4
Narraway →, Canada 64 B5
Narrogin, Australia 53 F2
Narromine, Australia 55 E4
Narsimhapur, India 36 H11
Naruto, Japan 29 G7
Narva, Estonia 22 C4
Narvik, Norway 8 B14
Naryan-Mar, Russia 24 A9
Naryilco, Australia 55 D3
Narym, Russia 24 D9
Narymskoye, Kazakhstan 24 E9
Naryn, Kirghizia 24 E8
Nasa, Norway 8 C13
Nasarawa, Nigeria 44 G6
Naseby, N.Z. 51 L3
Naser, Buheirat en, Egypt 45 D11
Nashua, Iowa, U.S.A. 70 D8
Nashua, Mont., U.S.A. 72 B10
Nashua, N.H., U.S.A. 68 D10
Nashville, Ark., U.S.A. 71 J8
Nashville, Ga., U.S.A. 69 K4
Nashville, Tenn., U.S.A. 69 G2
Nasik, India 36 K8
Nasirabad, India 36 F9

Naskaupi →, Canada 63 B7
Nasrīān-e Pā'īn, Iran 38 C5
Nass →, Canada 64 B3
Nassau, Bahamas 75 B9
Nassau, B., Chile 80 H3
Nasser, L. = Naser, Buheirat en, Egypt 45 D11
Nässjö, Sweden 9 H13
Nat Kyizin, Burma 34 E4
Nata, Botswana 48 C4
Natagaima, Colombia 78 C3
Natal, Brazil 79 E11
Natal, Canada 64 D6
Natal, Indonesia 32 D1
Natal □, S. Africa 49 D5
Naţanz, Iran 39 C6
Natashquan, Canada 63 B7
Natashquan →, Canada 63 B7
Natchez, U.S.A. 71 K9
Natchitoches, U.S.A. 71 K8
Nathalia, Australia 55 F4
Nathdwara, India 36 G8
Natimuk, Australia 55 F3
Nation →, Canada 64 B4
National City, U.S.A. 73 K5
Natitingou, Benin 44 F5
Natoma, U.S.A. 70 F5
Natron, L., Tanzania 46 E7
Natuna Besar, Kepulauan, Indonesia 32 D3
Natuna Is. = Natuna Besar, Kepulauan, Indonesia 32 D3
Natuna Selatan, Kepulauan, Indonesia 32 D3
Naturaliste, C., Australia 54 G4
Naubinway, U.S.A. 62 C2
Naumburg, Germany 16 C5
Nā'ūr at Tunayb, Jordan 41 D4
Nauru ■, Pac. Oc. 56 H8
Naushahra = Nowshera, Pakistan 36 B8
Nauta, Peru 78 D4
Nautanwa, India 37 F13
Navajo Res., U.S.A. 73 H10
Navalcarnero, Spain 19 B3
Navan = An Uaimh, Ireland 13 C5
Navarino, I., Chile 80 H3
Navarra □, Spain 19 A5
Navasota, U.S.A. 71 K6
Naver →, U.K. 12 C4
Navoi, Uzbekistan 24 E7
Navojoa, Mexico 74 B3
Navolok, Russia 22 B6
Návpaktos, Greece 21 E9
Návplion, Greece 21 F10
Navsari, India 36 J8
Nawabshah, Pakistan 36 F6
Nawakot, Nepal 37 F14
Nawalgarh, India 36 F9
Náxos, Greece 21 F11
Nāy Band, Iran 39 E7
Nayakhan, Russia 25 C16
Nayoro, Japan 28 B11
Nayyāl, W. →, Si. Arabia 38 D3
Nazareth = Nazerat, Israel 41 C4
Nazas →, Mexico 74 B4
Naze, The, U.K. 11 F9
Nazerat, Israel 41 C4
Nāzik, Iran 38 B5
Nazir Hat, Bangla. 37 H17
Nazko, Canada 64 C4
Nazko →, Canada 64 C4
Ncheu, Malawi 47 G6
Ndalatando, Angola 46 F2
Ndélé, C.A.R. 45 G9
Ndendé, Gabon 46 E2
Ndjamena, Chad 45 F7
Ndjolé, Gabon 46 E2
Ndola, Zambia 47 G5
Neagh, Lough, U.K. 13 B5
Neah Bay, U.S.A. 72 B1
Neale, L., Australia 52 D5
Near Is., U.S.A. 60 C1
Neath, U.K. 11 F4
Nebine Cr. →, Australia 55 D4
Nebit Dag, Turkmenistan 23 G9
Nebraska □, U.S.A. 70 E5
Nebraska City, U.S.A. 70 E7
Nébrodi, Monti, Italy 20 F6
Necedah, U.S.A. 70 C9
Nechako →, Canada 64 C4
Neches →, U.S.A. 71 L8
Neckar →, Germany 16 D4
Necochea, Argentina 80 D4
Needles, U.S.A. 73 J6
Needles, The, U.K. 11 G6
Neemuch = Nimach, India 36 G9
Neenah, U.S.A. 68 C1
Neepawa, Canada 65 C9
Neft-chala = imeni 26 Bakinskikh Komissarov, Azerbaijan 23 G8
Nefta, Tunisia 44 B6
Neftyannyye Kamni, Azerbaijan 23 F9
Negapatam = Nagappattinam, India 36 P11
Negaunee, U.S.A. 68 B2

Negele, Ethiopia 40 F2
Negeri Sembilan □,
  Malaysia 34 S15
Negev Desert =
  Hanegev, Israel .. 41 E3
Negoiul, Vf., Romania 17 F12
Negombo, Sri Lanka . 36 R11
Negotin, Serbia, Yug. 21 B10
Negra Pt., Phil. 33 A6
Negrais, C. = Maudin
  Sun, Burma ... 37 M19
Negro →, Argentina 80 E4
Negro →, Brazil ... 78 D6
Negro →, Uruguay . 80 C5
Negros, Phil. 33 C6
Nehāvand, Iran 39 C6
Nehbandān, Iran ... 39 D9
Nei Monggol
  Zizhiqu □, China . 31 B8
Neidpath, Canada .. 65 C7
Neihart, U.S.A. 72 C8
Neijiang, China 30 D5
Neilton, U.S.A. 72 C2
Neiva, Colombia ... 78 C3
Nejanilini L., Canada . 65 B9
Nekā, Iran 39 B7
Nekemte, Ethiopia .. 45 G12
Neksø, Denmark ... 9 J13
Nelia, Australia 54 C3
Neligh, U.S.A. 70 D5
Nelkan, Russia 25 D14
Nelma, Russia 25 E14
Nellore, India 36 M11
Nelson, Canada 64 D5
Nelson, N.Z. 51 J4
Nelson, U.K. 10 D5
Nelson, U.S.A. 73 J7
Nelson →, Canada . 65 C9
Nelson, C., Australia . 55 F3
Nelson, Estrecho, Chile 80 G2
Nelson Forks, Canada 64 B4
Nelson House, Canada 65 B9
Nelson L., Canada .. 65 B8
Nelspoort, S. Africa . 48 E3
Nelspruit, S. Africa . 49 D5
Néma, Mauritania ... 44 E3
Neman →, Lithuania 22 C3
Nemeiben L., Canada 65 B7
Nemunas =
  Neman →,
  Lithuania 22 C3
Nemuro, Japan 28 C12
Nemuro Kaikyō, Japan 28 C12
Nemuy, Russia 25 D14
Nen Jiang →, China 31 B7
Nenagh, Ireland ... 13 D3
Nenana, U.S.A. 60 B5
Nene →, U.K. 10 E8
Nenjiang, China 31 B7
Nenusa, Kepulauan,
  Indonesia 33 D7
Neodesha, U.S.A. ... 71 G7
Neosho, U.S.A. 71 G7
Neosho →, U.S.A. . 71 H7
Nepal ■, Asia 37 F14
Nepalganj, Nepal ... 37 E12
Nephi, U.S.A. 72 G8
Nephin, Ireland 13 B2
Nerchinsk, Russia .. 25 D12
Nerchinskiy Zavod,
  Russia 25 D12
Néret, L., Canada .. 63 B5
Neretva →, Croatia . 21 C7
Nerva, Spain 19 D2
Nes, Iceland 8 D5
Neskaupstaður, Iceland 8 D7
Ness, L., U.K. 12 D4
Nesttun, Norway ... 9 F8
Netanya, Israel 41 C3
Nète →, Belgium .. 15 C4
Netherdale, Australia . 54 C4
Netherlands ■, Europe 15 C5
Netherlands Antilles ■,
  W. Indies 75 E11
Nettilling L., Canada . 61 B12
Neubrandenburg,
  Germany 16 B6
Neuchâtel, Switz. 16 E3
Neuchâtel, Lac de,
  Switz. 16 E3
Neufchâteau, Belgium 15 E5
Neumünster, Germany 16 A4
Neunkirchen, Germany 16 D3
Neuquén, Argentina . 80 D3
Neuruppin, Germany . 16 B6
Neuse →, U.S.A. ... 69 H7
Neusiedler See,
  Austria 16 E8
Neuss, Germany 15 C6
Neustrelitz, Germany . 16 B6
Neva →, Russia ... 22 C5
Nevada, U.S.A. 71 G7
Nevada □, U.S.A. .. 72 G5
Nevada, Sierra, Spain 19 D4
Nevada, Sierra, U.S.A. 72 G3
Nevada City, U.S.A. . 72 G3
Nevanka, Russia ... 25 D10
Nevers, France 18 C5
Nevertire, Australia . 55 E4
Neville, Canada 65 D7
Nevinnomyssk, Russia 23 F7
Nevis, W. Indies ... 75 D12
Nevyansk, Russia .. 22 C11
New Albany, Ind.,
  U.S.A. 68 F3
New Albany, Miss.,
  U.S.A. 71 H10
New Amsterdam,
  Guyana 78 B7
New Angledool,
  Australia 55 D4
New Bedford, U.S.A. . 68 E10

New Bern, U.S.A. ... 69 H7
New Boston, U.S.A. . 71 J7
New Braunfels, U.S.A. 71 L5
New Brighton, N.Z. . 51 K4
New Britain,
  Papua N. G. 56 H7
New Britain, U.S.A. . 68 E9
New Brunswick, U.S.A. 68 E8
New Brunswick □,
  Canada 63 C6
New Caledonia,
  Pac. Oc. 56 K8
New Castile = Castilla
  La Mancha □, Spain 19 C4
New Castle, Ind.,
  U.S.A. 68 F3
New Castle, Pa., U.S.A. 68 E5
New Cristóbal, Panama 74 H14
New Delhi, India ... 36 E10
New Denver, Canada . 64 D5
New England, U.S.A. . 70 B3
New England Ra.,
  Australia 55 E5
New Forest, U.K. ... 11 G6
New Glasgow, Canada 63 C7
New Guinea, Oceania 56 H5
New Hampshire □,
  U.S.A. 68 D10
New Hampton, U.S.A. 70 D8
New Hanover, S. Africa 49 D5
New Haven, U.S.A. .. 68 E9
New Hazelton, Canada 64 B3
New Hebrides =
  Vanuatu ■, Pac. Oc. 56 J8
New Iberia, U.S.A. .. 71 K9
New Ireland,
  Papua N. G. 56 H7
New Jersey □, U.S.A. 68 E8
New Kensington,
  U.S.A. 68 E6
New Lexington, U.S.A. 68 F4
New Liskeard, Canada 62 C4
New London, Conn.,
  U.S.A. 68 E9
New London, Minn.,
  U.S.A. 70 C7
New London, Wis.,
  U.S.A. 70 C10
New Madrid, U.S.A. . 71 G10
New Meadows, U.S.A. 72 D5
New Mexico □, U.S.A. 66 D5
New Norcia, Australia 53 F2
New Norfolk, Australia 54 G4
New Orleans, U.S.A. . 71 K9
New Philadelphia,
  U.S.A. 68 E5
New Plymouth, N.Z. . 51 H5
New Plymouth, U.S.A. 72 E5
New Providence,
  Bahamas 75 B9
New Radnor, U.K. ... 11 E4
New Richmond, U.S.A. 70 C8
New Roads, U.S.A. .. 71 K9
New Rockford, U.S.A. 70 B5
New Ross, Ireland .. 13 D5
New Salem, U.S.A. .. 70 B4
New Scone, U.K. ... 12 E5
New Siberian Is. =
  Novaya Sibir,
  Ostrov, Russia ... 25 B16
New Siberian Is. =
  Novosibirskiye
  Ostrova, Russia .. 25 B15
New Smyrna Beach,
  U.S.A. 69 L5
New South Wales □,
  Australia 55 E4
New Springs, Australia 53 E3
New Town, U.S.A. .. 70 A3
New Ulm, U.S.A. ... 70 C7
New Waterford,
  Canada 63 C7
New Westminster,
  Canada 64 D4
New York □, U.S.A. . 68 D8
New York City, U.S.A. 68 E9
New Zealand ■,
  Oceania 51 J5
Newala, Tanzania .. 46 G7
Newark, Del., U.S.A. 68 F8
Newark, N.J., U.S.A. 68 E8
Newark, N.Y., U.S.A. 68 D7
Newark, Ohio, U.S.A. 68 E4
Newark-on-Trent, U.K. 10 D7
Newaygo, U.S.A. ... 68 D3
Newberg, U.S.A. ... 72 D2
Newberry, Mich.,
  U.S.A. 68 B3
Newberry, S.C., U.S.A. 69 H5
Newbrook, Canada .. 64 C6
Newburgh, U.S.A. .. 68 E8
Newbury, U.K. 11 F6
Newburyport, U.S.A. 68 D10
Newcastle, Australia . 55 E5
Newcastle, Canada .. 63 C6
Newcastle, S. Africa . 49 D4
Newcastle, U.K. ... 13 B6
Newcastle, U.S.A. .. 70 D2
Newcastle Emlyn, U.K. 11 E3
Newcastle-under-
  Lyme, U.K. 10 D5
Newcastle-upon-Tyne,
  U.K. 10 C6
Newcastle Waters,
  Australia 54 B1
Newdegate, Australia 53 F2
Newell, U.S.A. 70 C3
Newfoundland □,
  Canada 63 B8
Newhalem, U.S.A. .. 64 B3

Newham, U.K. 11 F8
Newhaven, U.K. ... 11 G8
Newkirk, U.S.A. ... 71 G6
Newman, Australia .. 52 D2
Newmarket, Ireland . 13 D3
Newmarket, U.K. ... 11 E8
Newnan, U.S.A. ... 69 J3
Newport, Gwent, U.K. 11 F5
Newport, I. of W., U.K. 11 G6
Newport, Shrops., U.K. 11 E5
Newport, Ark., U.S.A. 71 H9
Newport, Ky., U.S.A. 68 F3
Newport, N.H., U.S.A. 68 D9
Newport, Oreg., U.S.A. 72 D1
Newport, R.I., U.S.A. 68 E10
Newport, Tenn., U.S.A. 69 H4
Newport, Vt., U.S.A. 68 C9
Newport, Wash.,
  U.S.A. 72 B5
Newport Beach, U.S.A. 73 K5
Newport News, U.S.A. 68 G7
Newquay, U.K. 11 G2
Newry, U.K. 13 B5
Newry & Mourne □,
  U.K. 13 B5
Newton, Iowa, U.S.A. 70 E8
Newton, Mass., U.S.A. 68 D10
Newton, Miss., U.S.A. 71 J10
Newton, N.C., U.S.A. 69 H5
Newton, N.J., U.S.A. 68 E8
Newton, Tex., U.S.A. 71 K8
Newton Abbot, U.K. . 11 G4
Newton Boyd,
  Australia 55 D5
Newton Stewart, U.K. 12 G4
Newtonmore, U.K. .. 12 D4
Newtown, U.K. 11 E4
Newtownabbey □,
  U.K. 13 B6
Newtownards, U.K. .. 13 B6
Neya, Russia 22 C7
Neyrīz, Iran 39 D7
Neyshābūr, Iran ... 39 B8
Nezhin, Ukraine ... 23 D5
Nezperce, U.S.A. .. 72 C5
Ngabang, Indonesia . 32 D3
Ngabordamlu,
  Tanjung, Indonesia 33 F8
Ngami Depression,
  Botswana 48 C3
Nganglong Kangri,
  China 37 C12
Nganjuk, Indonesia . 33 G14
Ngaoundéré,
  Cameroon 46 C2
Ngapara, N.Z. 51 L3
Ngawi, Indonesia .. 33 G14
Ngha Lo, Vietnam .. 34 B8
Ngoring Hu, China .. 30 C4
Ngudu, Tanzania ... 46 E6
Nguigmi, Niger 45 F7
Ngukurr, Australia .. 54 A1
Nguru, Nigeria 44 F7
Nha Trang, Vietnam . 34 F10
Nhacoongo, Mozam. . 49 C6
Nhangutazi, L.,
  Mozam. 49 C5
Nhill, Australia 55 F3
Nhulunbuy, Australia 54 A2
Niafounké, Mali 44 E4
Niagara, U.S.A. 68 C1
Niagara Falls, Canada 62 D4
Niagara Falls, U.S.A. 68 D6
Niah, Malaysia 32 D4
Niamey, Niger 44 F5
Niangara, Zaire ... 46 D5
Nias, Indonesia 32 D1
Nibong Tebal,
  Malaysia 34 P13
Nicaragua ■,
  Cent. Amer. 74 E7
Nicaragua, L. de, Nic. 74 E7
Nicastro, Italy 20 E7
Nice, France 18 E7
Niceville, U.S.A. ... 69 K2
Nichinan, Japan ... 29 J5
Nicholasville, U.S.A. 68 G3
Nicholson, Australia . 52 C4
Nicholson →,
  Australia 54 B2
Nicholson Ra.,
  Australia 53 E2
Nicobar Is., Ind. Oc. . 26 J13
Nicola, Canada 64 C4
Nicolet, Canada ... 62 C5
Nicosia, Cyprus ... 38 C2
Nicoya, Pen. de,
  Costa Rica 74 F7
Nidd →, U.K. 10 C6
Niekerkshoop, S. Africa 48 D3
Niemen = Neman →,
  Lithuania 22 C3
Nienburg, Germany . 16 B4
Nieu Bethesda,
  S. Africa 48 E3
Nieuw Amsterdam,
  Surinam 79 B7
Nieuw Nickerie,
  Surinam 79 B7
Nieuwoudtville,
  S. Africa 48 E2
Nieuwpoort, Belgium 15 C2
Nièvre □, France ... 18 C5
Niğde, Turkey 23 G5
Nigel, S. Africa 49 D4
Niger ■, W. Afr. ... 44 E6
Niger →, W. Afr. .. 44 G6
Nigeria ■, W. Afr. .. 44 G6
Nightcaps, N.Z. ... 51 L2
Nii-Jima, Japan ... 29 G9
Niigata, Japan 28 F9
Niigata □, Japan ... 29 F9

Niihama, Japan 29 H6
Niihau, U.S.A. 66 H14
Niimi, Japan 29 G6
Niitsu, Japan 28 F9
Nijil, Jordan 41 E4
Nijkerk, Neths. 15 B5
Nijmegen, Neths. .. 15 C5
Nijverdal, Neths. ... 15 B6
Nik Pey, Iran 39 B6
Nikel, Russia 8 B21
Nikiniki, Indonesia . 33 F6
Nikki, Benin 44 G5
Nikkō, Japan 29 F9
Nikolayev, Ukraine . 23 E5
Nikolayevsk, Russia . 23 D8
Nikolayevsk-na-Amur,
  Russia 25 D15
Nikolskoye, Russia . 25 D17
Nikopol, Ukraine .. 23 E5
Nīkshahr, Iran 39 E9
Nîl, Nahr en →, Africa 45 B11
Nîl el Abyad →,
  Sudan 45 E11
Nîl el Azraq →,
  Sudan 45 E11
Nile = Nîl, Nahr
  en →, Africa ... 45 B11
Niles, U.S.A. 68 E5
Nimach, India 36 G9
Nimbahera, India .. 36 G9
Nîmes, France 18 E6
Nimmitabel, Australia 55 F4
Nimneryskiy, Russia . 25 D13
Nimule, Sudan 46 D6
Ninawá, Iraq 38 B4
Nindigully, Australia 55 D4
Ninemile, U.S.A. ... 64 B2
Nineveh = Nīnawá,
  Iraq 38 B4
Ningaloo, Australia . 52 D1
Ningbo, China 31 D7
Ningjing Shan, China 30 D4
Ningpo = Ningbo,
  China 31 D7
Ningsia Hui A.R. =
  Ningxia Huizu
  Zizhiqu □, China . 30 C5
Ningxia Huizu
  Zizhiqu □, China . 30 C5
Ninh Binh, Vietnam . 34 B8
Ninove, Belgium ... 15 D4
Niobrara, U.S.A. ... 70 D6
Niobrara →, U.S.A. 70 D6
Nioro du Sahel, Mali 44 E3
Niort, France 18 C3
Nipawin, Canada ... 65 C8
Nipawin Prov. Park,
  Canada 65 C8
Nipigon, Canada ... 62 C2
Nipigon, L., Canada . 62 C2
Nipin →, Canada .. 65 B7
Nipishish L., Canada 63 B7
Nipissing, L., Canada 62 C4
Nipomo, U.S.A. ... 73 J3
Niquelândia, Brazil . 79 F9
Nīr, Iran 38 B5
Nirasaki, Japan 29 G9
Nirmal, India 36 K11
Nirmali, India 37 F15
Niš, Serbia, Yug. .. 21 C9
Nişāb, Yemen 40 E4
Nishinomiya, Japan . 29 G7
Nishin'omote, Japan 29 J5
Nishiwaki, Japan ... 29 G7
Niskibi →, Canada . 62 A2
Nisutlin →, Canada 64 A2
Nitchequon, Canada 63 B5
Niterói, Brazil 79 H10
Nith →, U.K. 12 F5
Nitra, Slovakia 17 D9
Nitra →, Slovakia .. 17 E9
Niuafo'ou, Tonga .. 51 B11
Niue, Cook Is. 57 J11
Niut, Indonesia 32 D4
Nivelles, Belgium .. 15 D4
Nivernais, France .. 18 C5
Nixon, U.S.A. 71 L6
Nizamabad, India .. 36 K11
Nizamghat, India .. 37 E19
Nizhne Kolymsk,
  Russia 25 C17
Nizhne-Vartovsk,
  Russia 24 C8
Nizhneangarsk, Russia 25 D11
Nizhnekamsk, Russia 22 C9
Nizhneudinsk, Russia 25 D10
Nizhneyansk, Russia 25 B14
Nizhniy Novgorod,
  Russia 22 C7
Nizhniy Tagil, Russia 22 C10
Nizké Tatry, Slovakia 17 D9
Njombe, Tanzania .. 46 F6
Nkambe, Cameroon . 44 G7
Nkawkaw, Ghana .. 44 G4
Nkhata Bay, Malawi 46 G6
Nkhota Kota, Malawi 47 G6
Nkongsamba,
  Cameroon 44 H6
Nkurenkuru, Namibia 48 B2
Nmai →, Burma ... 37 G20
Noakhali = Maijdi,
  Bangla. 37 H17
Noatak, U.S.A. 60 B3
Nobeoka, Japan ... 29 H5
Noblesville, U.S.A. . 68 E3
Nocera Inferiore, Italy 20 D6
Nocona, U.S.A. ... 71 J6
Noda, Japan 29 G9
Noel, U.S.A. 71 G7
Nogales, Mexico ... 74 A2
Nogales, U.S.A. ... 73 L8

Nōgata, Japan 29 H5
Noggerup, Australia . 53 F2
Noginsk, Russia ... 25 C10
Nogoa →, Australia 54 C4
Noi →, Thailand ... 34 E6
Noirmoutier, I. de,
  France 18 C2
Nojane, Botswana .. 48 C3
Nojima-Zaki, Japan . 29 G9
Nok Kundi, Pakistan . 36 E3
Nokaneng, Botswana 48 B3
Nokhtuysk, Russia .. 25 C12
Nokomis, Canada ... 65 C8
Nokomis L., Canada 65 B8
Nola, C.A.R. 46 D3
Noma Omuramba →,
  Namibia 48 B3
Noman L., Canada . 65 A7
Nome, U.S.A. 60 B3
Nomo-Zaki, Japan . 29 H4
Nonacho L., Canada 65 A7
Nonda, Australia ... 54 C3
Nong Khae, Thailand 34 E6
Nong Khai, Thailand 34 D7
Nongoma, S. Africa . 49 D5
Noonamah, Australia 52 B5
Noonan, U.S.A. ... 70 A3
Noondoo, Australia . 55 D4
Noonkanbah, Australia 52 C3
Noord Brabant □,
  Neths. 15 C5
Noord Holland □,
  Neths. 15 B4
Noordbeveland, Neths. 15 C3
Noordoostpolder,
  Neths. 15 B5
Noordwijk aan Zee,
  Neths. 15 B4
Nootka, Canada ... 64 D3
Nootka I., Canada .. 64 D3
Nóqui, Angola 46 F2
Noranda, Canada .. 62 C4
Nord □, France 18 A5
Nord-Ostsee Kanal,
  Germany 16 A4
Nord-Trøndelag
  fylke □, Norway . 8 D12
Nordaustlandet,
  Svalbard 4 B9
Nordegg, Canada .. 64 C5
Nordhausen, Germany 16 C5
Nordkapp, Norway . 8 A18
Nordkapp, Svalbard . 4 A9
Nordkinn =
  Kinnarodden,
  Norway 6 A11
Nordland fylke □,
  Norway 8 D12
Nordrhein-
  Westfalen □,
  Germany 16 C3
Nordvik, Russia ... 25 B12
Norembega, Canada 62 C3
Norfolk, Nebr., U.S.A. 70 D6
Norfolk, Va., U.S.A. . 68 G7
Norfolk □, U.K. 10 E9
Norfolk Broads, U.K. 10 E9
Norfolk I., Pac. Oc. . 56 K8
Norfork Res., U.S.A. 71 G8
Norilsk, Russia 25 C9
Norley, Australia ... 55 D3
Norma, Mt., Australia 54 C3
Normal, U.S.A. 70 E10
Norman, U.S.A. ... 71 H6
Norman →, Australia 54 B3
Norman Wells, Canada 60 B7
Normanby →,
  Australia 54 A3
Normandie, France . 18 B4
Normandin, Canada 62 C5
Normandy =
  Normandie, France 18 B4
Normanhurst, Mt.,
  Australia 53 E3
Normanton, Australia 54 B3
Norquay, Canada .. 65 C8
Norquinco, Argentina 80 E2
Norrbotten □, Sweden 8 C17
Norrby, Sweden ... 8 D15
Nørresundby, Denmark 9 H10
Norris, U.S.A. 72 D8
Norristown, U.S.A. . 68 E8
Norrköping, Sweden 9 G14
Norrland, Sweden .. 8 E13
Norrtälje, Sweden .. 9 G15
Norseman, Australia 53 F3
Norsk, Russia 25 D14
North Adams, U.S.A. 68 D9
North America 58 F10
North Andaman I.,
  India 34 F2
North Battleford,
  Canada 65 C7
North Bay, Canada . 62 C4
North Belcher Is.,
  Canada 62 A4
North Bend, Canada 64 D4
North Bend, U.S.A. . 72 E1
North Berwick, U.K. 12 E6
North Canadian →,
  U.S.A. 71 H7
North Cape =
  Nordkapp, Norway 8 A18
North Cape =
  Nordkapp, Svalbard 4 A9
North C., N.Z. 51 F4
North Caribou L.,
  Canada 62 B1
North Carolina □,
  U.S.A. 69 H5
North Channel, Canada 62 C3

North Channel, U.K. . 12 G3
North Chicago, U.S.A. 68 D2
North Dakota □, U.S.A. 70 B5
North Dandalup,
  Australia 53 F2
North Down □, U.K. . 13 B6
North Downs, U.K. .. 11 F8
North East Frontier
  Agency = Arunachal
  Pradesh □, India .. 37 E19
North Esk →, U.K. . 12 E6
North European Plain,
  Europe 6 D11
North Foreland, U.K. 11 F9
North Henik L., Canada 65 A9
North I., N.Z. 51 H5
North Knife →,
  Canada 65 B10
North Korea ■, Asia . 31 C7
North Lakhimpur, India 37 F19
North Las Vegas,
  U.S.A. 73 H6
North Loup →, U.S.A. 70 E5
North Magnetic Pole,
  Canada 4 B2
North Minch, U.K. .. 12 C3
North Nahanni →,
  Canada 64 A4
North Ossetian
  Republic □, Russia . 23 F7
North Pagai, I. = Pagai
  Utara, Indonesia . 32 E2
North Palisade, U.S.A. 73 H4
North Platte, U.S.A. . 70 E4
North Platte →,
  U.S.A. 70 E4
North Pt., Canada .. 63 C7
North Pole, Arctic .. 4 A
North Portal, Canada 65 D8
North Powder, U.S.A. 72 D5
North Rhine
  Westphalia □ =
  Nordrhein-
  Westfalen □,
  Germany 16 C3
North Ronaldsay, U.K. 12 B6
North
  Saskatchewan →,
  Canada 65 C7
North Sea, Europe .. 6 D6
North Sentinel I., India 34 G2
North Sporades =
  Voríai Sporádhes,
  Greece 21 E10
North Sydney, Canada 63 C7
North Taranaki Bight,
  N.Z. 51 H5
North Thompson →,
  Canada 64 C4
North Tonawanda,
  U.S.A. 68 D6
North Truchas Pk.,
  U.S.A. 73 J11
North Twin I., Canada 62 B3
North Tyne →, U.K. 10 C5
North Uist, U.K. ... 12 D1
North Vancouver,
  Canada 64 D4
North Vernon, U.S.A. 68 F3
North Wabasca L.,
  Canada 64 B6
North Walsham, U.K. 10 E9
North West C.,
  Australia 52 D1
North West Christmas
  I. Ridge, Pac. Oc. . 57 G11
North West Frontier □,
  Pakistan 36 B8
North West Highlands,
  U.K. 12 D3
North West River,
  Canada 63 B7
North West
  Territories □,
  Canada 60 B9
North York Moors,
  U.K. 10 C7
North Yorkshire □,
  U.K. 10 C6
Northallerton, U.K. .. 10 C6
Northam, S. Africa .. 48 C4
Northampton,
  Australia 53 E1
Northampton, U.K. .. 11 E7
Northampton, U.S.A. 68 D9
Northampton Downs,
  Australia 54 C4
Northamptonshire □,
  U.K. 11 E7
Northcliffe, Australia . 53 F2
Northern Circars, India 37 L13
Northern Indian L.,
  Canada 65 B9
Northern Ireland □,
  U.K. 13 B5
Northern Light, L.,
  Canada 62 C1
Northern Marianas ■,
  Pac. Oc. 56 F6
Northern Territory □,
  Australia 52 D5
Northfield, U.S.A. .. 70 C8
Northland □, N.Z. .. 51 F4
Northome, U.S.A. .. 70 B7
Northport, Ala., U.S.A. 69 J2
Northport, Mich.,
  U.S.A. 68 C3
Northport, Wash.,
  U.S.A. 72 B5
Northumberland □,
  U.K. 10 B5

Northumberland, C.,
  Australia 55 F3
Northumberland Is.,
  Australia 54 C4
Northumberland Str.,
  Canada 63 C7
Northwich, U.K. 10 D5
Northwood, Iowa,
  U.S.A. 70 D8
Northwood, N. Dak.,
  U.S.A. 70 B6
Norton, U.S.A. 70 F5
Norton Sd., U.S.A. .. 60 B3
Norwalk, Conn., U.S.A. 68 E9
Norwalk, Ohio, U.S.A. 68 E4
Norway ■, Europe ... 8 E11
Norway House,
  Canada 65 C9
Norwegian Sea,
  Atl. Oc. 4 C8
Norwich, U.K. 10 E9
Norwich, U.S.A. 68 D8
Noshiro, Japan 28 D10
Nosok, Russia 24 B9
Noss Hd., U.K. 12 C5
Nossob →, S. Africa 48 D3
Nosy Bé, Madag. ... 47 G9
Nosy Boraha, Madag. 49 B8
Nosy Mitsio, Madag. 47 G9
Nosy Varika, Madag. 49 C8
Notigi Dam, Canada 65 B9
Notikewin →, Canada 64 B5
Noto, Italy 20 F6
Notre-Dame, Canada 63 C7
Notre Dame B.,
  Canada 63 C8
Notre Dame de
  Koartac = Koartac,
  Canada 61 B13
Notre Dame d'Ivugivic
  = Ivugivik, Canada 61 B12
Nottaway →, Canada 62 B4
Nottingham, U.K. ... 10 E6
Nottinghamshire □,
  U.K. 10 D7
Nottoway →, U.S.A. 68 G7
Notwane →,
  Botswana 48 C4
Nouâdhibou,
  Mauritania 44 D1
Nouâdhibou, Ras,
  Mauritania 44 D1
Nouakchott, Mauritania 44 E1
Nouméa, N. Cal. ... 56 K8
Noupoort, S. Africa . 48 E3
Nouveau Comptoir,
  Canada 62 B4
Nouvelle-Calédonie =
  New Caledonia ■,
  Pac. Oc. 56 K8
Nova Casa Nova, Brazil 79 E10
Nova Cruz, Brazil .. 79 E11
Nova Friburgo, Brazil 79 H10
Nova Gaia =
  Cambundi-Catembo,
  Angola 46 G3
Nova Iguaçu, Brazil . 79 H10
Nova Iorque, Brazil . 79 E10
Nova Lima, Brazil .. 79 G10
Nova Lisboa =
  Huambo, Angola . 47 G3
Nova Mambone,
  Mozam. 49 C6
Nova Scotia □, Canada 63 C7
Nova Sofala, Mozam. 49 C5
Nova Venécia, Brazil . 79 G10
Novara, Italy 20 B3
Novaya Ladoga, Russia 22 B5
Novaya Lyalya, Russia 24 D7
Novaya Sibir, Ostrov,
  Russia 25 B16
Novaya Zemlya, Russia 24 B6
Nové Zámky, Slovakia 17 D9
Novgorod, Russia ... 22 C5
Novgorod-Severskiy,
  Ukraine 22 D5
Novi Sad, Serbia, Yug. 21 B8
Novo Remanso, Brazil 79 E10
Novoataysk, Russia .. 24 D9
Novocherkassk, Russia 23 E7
Novokachalinsk, Russia 28 B6
Novokazalinsk,
  Kazakhstan 24 E7
Novokuybyshevsk,
  Russia 22 D8
Novokuznetsk, Russia 24 D9
Novomoskovsk, Russia 22 D6
Novorossiysk, Russia 23 F6
Novorybnoye, Russia 25 B11
Novoshakhtinsk,
  Russia 23 E6
Novosibirsk, Russia . 24 D9
Novosibirskiye
  Ostrova, Russia .. 25 B15
Novotroitsk, Russia . 24 D6
Novouzensk, Russia . 24 D8
Novska, Croatia 20 B7
Novvy Port, Russia .. 24 C8
Now Shahr, Iran 39 B6
Nowbarān, Iran 39 C6
Nowghāb, Iran 39 C8
Nowgong, India 37 F18
Nowra, Australia ... 55 E5
Nowshera, Pakistan . 36 B8
Nowy Sącz, Poland . 17 D10
Nowy Tomyśl, Poland 16 B8
Noxon, U.S.A. 72 C6
Noyes I., U.S.A. ... 64 B2
Nsanje, Malawi 47 H7
Nsawam, Ghana 44 G4
Nsukka, Nigeria 44 G6

Nu Jiang →, China .. 30 D4
Nu Shan, China 30 D4
Nubian Desert =
  Nûbîya, Es Sahrâ En,
  Sudan 45 D11
Nûbîya, Es Sahrâ En,
  Sudan 45 D11
Nuboai, Indonesia .. 33 E9
Nueces →, U.S.A. .. 71 M6
Nueltin L., Canada .. 65 A9
Nueva Imperial, Chile 80 D2
Nueva Rosita, Mexico 74 B4
Nuéve de Julio,
  Argentina 80 D4
Nuevitas, Cuba 75 C9
Nuevo, G., Argentina 80 E4
Nuevo Laredo, Mexico 74 B5
Nugget Pt., N.Z. ... 51 M2
Nuhaka, N.Z. 51 H6
Nukey Bluff, Australia 55 E2
Nukheila, Sudan ... 45 E10
Nuku'alofa, Tonga .. 51 E11
Nukus, Uzbekistan .. 24 E6
Nulato, U.S.A. 60 B4
Nullagine →,
  Australia 52 D3
Nullarbor, Australia . 53 F5
Nullarbor Plain,
  Australia 53 F4
Numalla, L., Australia 55 D3
Numan, Nigeria 45 G7
Numata, Japan 29 F9
Numazu, Japan 29 G9
Numbulwar, Australia 54 A2
Numfoor, Indonesia . 33 E8
Numurkah, Australia . 55 F4
Nunaksaluk I., Canada 63 A7
Nuneaton, U.K. 11 E6
Nunivak, U.S.A. 60 B3
Nunkun, India 36 C10
Nunspeet, Neths. ... 15 B5
Nûrâbâd, Iran 39 E8
Nuremburg =
  Nürnberg, Germany 16 D5
Nurina, Australia ... 53 F4
Nuriootpa, Australia . 55 E2
Nürnberg, Germany . 16 D5
Nurran, L. = Terewah,
  L., Australia 55 D4
Nurrari Lakes,
  Australia 53 E5
Nusa Barung,
  Indonesia 33 H15
Nusa Kambangan,
  Indonesia 33 G13
Nusa Tenggara
  Barat □, Indonesia 32 F5
Nusa Tenggara
  Timur □, Indonesia 33 F6
Nusaybin, Turkey ... 23 G7
Nushki, Pakistan ... 36 E5
Nutak, Canada 61 C13
Nutwood Downs,
  Australia 54 B1
Nuuk = Godthåb,
  Greenland 61 B14
Nuwakot, Nepal ... 37 E13
Nuweveldberge,
  S. Africa 48 E3
Nuyts, C., Australia . 53 F5
Nuyts Arch., Australia 55 E1
Nxau-Nxau, Botswana 48 B3
Nyah West, Australia 55 F3
Nyahanga, Tanzania . 46 E6
Nyahururu, Kenya .. 46 D7
Nyaingentanglha Shan,
  China 30 D3
Nyâlâ, Sudan 45 F9
Nyandoma, Russia .. 22 B7
Nyangana, Namibia . 48 B3
Nyarling →, Canada 64 A6
Nyasa, L. = Malawi, L.,
  Africa 47 G6
Nyazepetrovsk, Russia 22 C10
Nybro, Sweden 9 H13
Nyda, Russia 24 C8
Nyeri, Kenya 46 E7
Nyíregyháza, Hungary 17 E10
Nykarleby, Finland .. 8 E17
Nykøbing, Denmark . 9 J11
Nyköping, Sweden .. 9 G14
Nylstroom, S. Africa . 49 C4
Nymagee, Australia . 55 E4
Nynäshamn, Sweden 9 G14
Nyngan, Australia ... 55 E4
Nysa, Poland 17 C8
Nysa →, Europe ... 16 B7
Nyssa, U.S.A. 72 E5
Nyurba, Russia 25 C12
Nzega, Tanzania .. 46 E6
N'Zérékoré, Guinea . 44 G3
Nzeto, Angola 46 F2

O

Ō-Shima, Nagasaki,
  Japan 29 G4
Ō-Shima, Shizuoka,
  Japan 29 G9
Oacoma, U.S.A. ... 70 D5
Oahe Dam, U.S.A. . 70 C4
Oahe L., U.S.A. ... 70 C4
Oahu, U.S.A. 66 H16
Oak Creek, U.S.A. . 72 F10
Oak Harbour, U.S.A. 72 B2
Oak Hill, U.S.A. ... 68 G5
Oak Park, U.S.A. .. 68 E2
Oak Ridge, U.S.A. . 69 G3
Oakan-Dake, Japan . 28 C12

Oakbank, Australia .. 55 E3
Oakdale, Calif., U.S.A. 73 H3
Oakdale, La., U.S.A. . 71 K8
Oakengates, U.K. .. 10 E5
Oakes, U.S.A. 70 B5
Oakey, Australia ... 55 D5
Oakham, U.K. 10 E7
Oakland, Calif., U.S.A. 73 H2
Oakland, Oreg., U.S.A. 72 E2
Oakland City, U.S.A. 68 F2
Oakley, Idaho, U.S.A. 72 E7
Oakley, Kans., U.S.A. 70 F4
Oakover →, Australia 52 D3
Oakridge, U.S.A. ... 72 E2
Oamaru, N.Z. 51 L3
Oates Land, Antarctica 5 C11
Oatman, U.S.A. 73 J6
Oaxaca, Mexico ... 74 D5
Ob →, Russia 24 C7
Oba, Canada 62 C3
Obama, Japan 29 G7
Oban, U.K. 12 E3
Obbia, Somali Rep. . 40 F4
Obed, Canada 64 C5
Oberhausen, Germany 16 C3
Oberlin, Kans., U.S.A. 70 F4
Oberlin, La., U.S.A. . 71 K8
Oberon, Australia ... 55 E4
Obi, Kepulauan,
  Indonesia 33 E7
Obi Is. = Obi,
  Kepulauan,
  Indonesia 33 E7
Óbidos, Brazil 79 D7
Obihiro, Japan 28 C11
Obilatu, Indonesia .. 33 E7
Obo, C.A.R. 46 C5
Oboyan, Russia 24 D4
Obozerskaya, Russia 24 C5
Observatory Inlet,
  Canada 64 B3
Obshchi Syrt,
  Kazakhstan 6 E16
Obskaya Guba, Russia 24 C8
Obuasi, Ghana 44 G4
Ocala, U.S.A. 69 L4
Ocaña, Spain 19 C4
Ocanomowoc, U.S.A. 70 D10
Ocate, U.S.A. 71 G2
Occidental, Cordillera,
  Colombia 78 C3
Ocean City, U.S.A. . 68 F8
Ocean I. = Banaba,
  Kiribati 56 H8
Ocean Park, U.S.A. . 72 C1
Oceanside, U.S.A. .. 73 K5
Ochil Hills, U.K. ... 12 E5
Ochre River, Canada . 65 C9
Ocilla, U.S.A. 69 K4
Ocmulgee →, U.S.A. 69 K4
Oconee →, U.S.A. . 69 K4
Oconto, U.S.A. 68 C2
Oconto Falls, U.S.A. 68 C1
Octave, U.S.A. 73 J7
Ocumare del Tuy,
  Venezuela 78 A5
Ōda, Japan 29 G6
Ódáðahraun, Iceland . 8 D5
Odate, Japan 28 D10
Odawara, Japan ... 29 G9
Odda, Norway 9 F9
Oddur, Somali Rep. . 40 G3
Odei →, Canada ... 65 B9
Odendaalsrus,
  S. Africa 48 D4
Odense, Denmark .. 9 J11
Oder →, Germany . 16 B7
Odesa = Odessa,
  Ukraine 23 E5
Odessa, Ukraine . . . 23 E5
Odessa, Tex., U.S.A. 71 K3
Odessa, Wash., U.S.A. 72 C4
Odiakwe, Botswana . 48 C4
Odienné, Ivory C. .. 44 G3
Odintsovo, Russia .. 22 C6
O'Donnell, U.S.A. .. 71 J4
Odorheiu Secuiesc,
  Romania 17 E12
Odra →, Poland ... 16 B7
Odžak, Bos.-H. 21 B8
Odzi, Zimbabwe ... 49 B5
Oeiras, Brazil 79 E10
Oelrichs, U.S.A. ... 70 D3
Oelwein, U.S.A. ... 70 D9
Oenpelli, Australia .. 52 B5
Ofanto →, Italy ... 20 D7
Offa, Nigeria 44 G5
Offaly □, Ireland ... 13 C4
Offenbach, Germany . 16 C4
Ofotfjorden, Norway . 8 B14
Ōfunato, Japan 28 E10
Oga, Japan 28 E9
Oga-Hantō, Japan .. 28 E9
Ogahalla, Canada .. 62 B2
Ōgaki, Japan 29 G8
Ogallala, U.S.A. ... 70 E4
Ogasawara Gunto,
  Pac. Oc. 56 E6
Ogbomosho, Nigeria 44 G5
Ogden, Iowa, U.S.A. 70 D8
Ogden, Utah, U.S.A. 72 F7
Ogdensburg, U.S.A. 68 C8
Ogeechee →, U.S.A. 69 K5
Oglio →, Italy 20 B4
Ogmore, Australia .. 54 C4
Ogoki, Canada 62 B2
Ogoki L., Canada .. 62 B2
Ogoki Res., Canada . 62 B2
Ogooué →, Gabon . 46 E1

Ogowe = Ogooué →,
  Gabon 46 E1
Ohai, N.Z. 51 L2
Ohakune, N.Z. 51 H5
Ohanet, Algeria ... 44 C6
Ohata, Japan 28 D10
Ohey, Belgium 15 D5
Ohio □, U.S.A. 68 E3
Ohio →, U.S.A. ... 68 G1
Ohre →, Czech. ... 16 C7
Ohridsko, Jezero,
  Macedonia 21 D9
Ohrigstad, S. Africa . 49 C5
Oil City, U.S.A. 68 E6
Oise □, France 18 B5
Ōita, Japan 29 H5
Ōita □, Japan 29 H5
Oiticica, Brazil 79 E10
Ojai, U.S.A. 73 J4
Ojiya, Japan 29 F9
Ojos del Salado, Cerro,
  Argentina 80 B3
Oka →, Russia 24 D5
Okaba, Indonesia .. 33 F9
Okahandja, Namibia . 48 C2
Okahukura, N.Z. ... 51 H5
Okanagan, L., Canada 64 C5
Okandja, Gabon ... 46 E2
Okanogan, U.S.A. .. 72 B4
Okanogan →, U.S.A. 72 B4
Okaputa, Namibia .. 48 C2
Okara, Pakistan ... 36 D8
Okarito, N.Z. 51 K3
Okaukuejo, Namibia . 48 B2
Okavango Swamps,
  Botswana 48 B3
Okaya, Japan 29 F9
Okayama, Japan ... 29 G6
Okayama □, Japan . 29 G6
Okazaki, Japan 29 G8
Okeechobee, U.S.A. 69 M5
Okeechobee, L., U.S.A. 69 M5
Okefenokee Swamp,
  U.S.A. 69 K4
Okehampton, U.K. .. 11 G3
Okha, Russia 25 D15
Okhotsk, Russia ... 25 D15
Okhotsk, Sea of, Asia 25 D15
Okhotskiy Perevoz,
  Russia 25 C14
Okhotsko Kolymskoye,
  Russia 25 C16
Oki-Shotō, Japan .. 29 F6
Okiep, S. Africa ... 48 D2
Okinawa □, Japan .. 29 L3
Okinawa-Guntō, Japan 29 L3
Okinawa-Jima, Japan 29 L4
Okino-erabu-Shima,
  Japan 29 L4
Oklahoma □, U.S.A. 71 H6
Oklahoma City, U.S.A. 71 H6
Okmulgee, U.S.A. .. 71 H7
Okolona, U.S.A. ... 71 H10
Okrika, Nigeria 44 H6
Oktabrsk, Kazakhstan 23 E10
Oktyabrskiy, Russia . 22 D9
Oktyabrskoye, Russia 24 C7
Oktyabrskoy
  Revolyutsii, Os.,
  Russia 25 B10
Oktyabrskoye, Russia 24 C7
Okuru, N.Z. 51 K2
Okushiri-Tō, Japan . 28 C9
Okwa →, Botswana 48 C3
Ola, U.S.A. 71 H8
Ólafsfjörður, Iceland . 8 C4
Ólafsvík, Iceland ... 8 D2
Olancha, U.S.A. ... 73 H4
Öland, Sweden 9 H14
Olary, Australia 55 E3
Olathe, U.S.A. 70 F7
Olavarría, Argentina . 80 D4
Ólbia, Italy 20 D3
Old Castile = Castilla y
  Leon □, Spain ... 19 B3
Old Castle, Ireland . 13 C4
Old Cork, Australia . 54 C3
Old Crow, Canada .. 60 B6
Old Fletton, U.K. .. 11 E7
Old Fort →, Canada 65 B6
Old Town, U.S.A. .. 63 D6
Old Wives L., Canada 65 C7
Oldbury, U.K. 11 F5
Oldenburg, Germany 16 B4
Oldenzaal, Neths. .. 15 B6
Oldham, U.K. 10 D5
Oldman →, Canada 64 D6
Olds, Canada 64 C6
Olean, U.S.A. 68 D6
Olekma →, Russia . 25 C13
Olekminsk, Russia .. 25 C13
Olenegorsk, Russia . 22 A5
Olenek, Russia 25 C12
Olenek →, Russia .. 25 B13
Oléron, I. d', France 18 D3
Oleśnica, Poland ... 17 C8
Olga, Russia 25 E14
Olga, L., Canada ... 62 C4
Olga, Mt., Australia . 53 E5
Olifants →, Africa .. 49 C5
Olifantshoek, S. Africa 48 D3
Ólimbos, Óros, Greece 21 D10
Olinda, Brazil 79 E12
Oliveira, Brazil 79 H10
Olivenza, Spain ... 19 C2
Oliver, Canada 64 D5
Oliver L., Canada .. 65 B8
Ollagüe, Chile 78 H5
Olney, Ill., U.S.A. .. 68 F1
Olney, Tex., U.S.A. . 71 J5
Olomane →, Canada 63 B7
Olomouc, Czech. ... 16 D7

Olonets, Russia 22 B5
Olongapo, Phil. 33 B6
Olovo, Bos.-H. 21 B8
Olovo, Yugoslavia .. 21 B8
Olovyannaya, Russia 25 D12
Oloy →, Russia ... 25 C16
Olsztyn, Poland ... 17 B10
Olt →, Romania ... 17 G13
Olteniţa, Romania .. 17 F13
Olton, U.S.A. 71 H3
Olympia, Greece ... 21 F9
Olympia, U.S.A. ... 72 C2
Olympic Mts., U.S.A. 72 C2
Olympic Nat. Park,
  U.S.A. 72 C2
Olympus, Mt. =
  Ólimbos, Óros,
  Greece 21 D10
Olympus, Mt., U.S.A. 72 C2
Om →, Russia 24 D8
Ōma, Japan 28 D10
Ōmachi, Japan 29 F8
Omae-Zaki, Japan .. 29 G9
Ōmagari, Japan ... 28 E10
Omagh, U.K. 13 B4
Omagh □, U.K. ... 13 B4
Omaha, U.S.A. 70 E7
Omak, U.S.A. 72 B4
Oman ■, Asia 40 C6
Oman, G. of, Asia .. 39 E8
Omaruru, Namibia .. 48 C2
Omaruru →, Namibia 48 C1
Omate, Peru 78 G4
Ombai, Selat,
  Indonesia 33 F7
Omboué, Gabon ... 46 E1
Ombrone →, Italy .. 20 C4
Omdurmân, Sudan . 45 E11
Ometepec, Mexico . 74 D5
Ominato, Japan ... 28 D10
Omineca →, Canada 64 B4
Omitara, Namibia .. 48 C2
Ōmiya, Japan 29 G9
Ommen, Neths. ... 15 B6
Omo →, Ethiopia .. 45 G12
Omolon →, Russia . 25 C16
Omono-Gawa →,
  Japan 28 E10
Omsk, Russia 24 D8
Omsukchan, Russia . 25 C16
Ōmu, Japan 28 B11
Ōmura, Japan 29 H4
Omuramba
  Omatako →,
  Namibia 47 H4
Ōmuta, Japan 29 H5
Onaga, U.S.A. 70 F6
Onalaska, U.S.A. .. 70 D9
Onamia, U.S.A. ... 70 B8
Onancock, U.S.A. .. 68 G8
Onang, Indonesia .. 33 E5
Onaping L., Canada 62 C3
Onavas, Mexico ... 74 B3
Onawa, U.S.A. 70 D6
Onaway, U.S.A. ... 68 C3
Oncócua, Angola .. 48 B1
Onda, Spain 19 C5
Ondangua, Namibia . 48 B2
Ondjiva, Angola ... 48 B2
Ondo, Nigeria 44 G5
Öndörhaan =
  Vladivkavkaz, Russia 23 F7
Ore Mts. = Erzgebirge,
  Germany 16 C6
Örebro, Sweden ... 9 G13
Örebro län □, Sweden 9 G13
Oregon, U.S.A. 70 D10
Oregon □, U.S.A. .. 72 E3
Oregon City, U.S.A. 72 D2
Orekhovo-Zuyevo,
  Russia 22 C6
Orel, Russia 22 D6
Orem, U.S.A. 72 F8
Orenburg, Russia .. 22 D10
Orense, Spain 19 A2
Orepuki, N.Z. 51 M1
Øresund, Europe ... 9 H12
Orford Ness, U.K. .. 11 E9
Orhon Gol →,
  Mongolia 30 A5
Orient, Australia ... 55 D3
Oriental, Cordillera,
  Colombia 78 B4
Orihuela, Spain ... 19 C5
Orinoco →,
  Venezuela 78 B6
Orissa □, India 37 K14
Oristano, Italy 20 E3
Oristano, G. di, Italy 20 E3
Orizaba, Mexico ... 74 D5
Orizaba, Veracruz,
  Mexico 74 D5
Orkanger, Norway . 8 E10
Orkla →, Norway .. 8 E10
Orkney, S. Africa .. 48 D4
Orkney □, U.K. ... 12 C6
Orkney Is., U.K. ... 12 C6
Orland, U.S.A. 72 G2
Orlando, U.S.A. ... 69 L5
Orléanais, France .. 18 C4
Orléans, France ... 18 C4
Orléans, I. d', Canada 63 C5
Ormara, Pakistan .. 36 G4
Ormoc, Phil. 33 B6
Ormond, N.Z. 51 H6
Ormond Beach, U.S.A. 69 L5
Orne □, France 18 B4
Örnsköldsvik, Sweden 8 E15
Orocué, Colombia .. 78 C4
Orogrande, U.S.A. . 73 K10
Oromocto, Canada . 63 C6
Oroqen Zhiqi, China 31 A7
Oroquieta, Phil. ... 33 C6

Orós, Brazil 79 E11
Orotukan, Russia ... 25 C16
Oroville, Calif., U.S.A. 72 G3
Oroville, Wash., U.S.A. 72 B4
Orroroo, Australia .. 55 E2
Orsha, Belorussia .. 22 D5
Orsk, Russia 22 D10
Orşova, Romania ... 17 F11
Ortegal, C., Spain .. 19 A2
Orthez, France 18 E3
Ortigueira, Spain ... 19 A2
Ortles, Italy 20 A4
Ortón →, Bolivia .. 78 F5
Ortona, Italy 20 C6
Orūmïyeh, Iran 38 B5
Orūmïyeh, Daryācheh-ye, Iran 38 B5
Oruro, Bolivia 78 G5
Oruzgān □, Afghan. . 36 C5
Orvieto, Italy 20 C5
Orwell →, U.K. 11 E9
Oryakhovo, Bulgaria . 21 C10
Ōsa, Russia 22 C10
Osage, Iowa, U.S.A. . 70 D8
Osage, Wyo., U.S.A. 70 D2
Osage →, U.S.A. .. 70 F9
Osage City, U.S.A. . 70 F7
Ōsaka, Japan 29 G7
Osawatomie, U.S.A. 70 F7
Osborne, U.S.A. ... 70 F5
Osceola, Ark., U.S.A. 71 H10
Osceola, Iowa, U.S.A. 70 E8
Oscoda, U.S.A. 68 C4
Ösel = Saaremaa, Estonia 22 C3
Osh, Kirghizia 24 E8
Oshawa, Canada ... 62 D4
Oshkosh, Nebr., U.S.A. 70 E3
Oshkosh, Wis., U.S.A. 70 C10
Oshnovïyeh, Iran .. 38 B5
Oshogbo, Nigeria .. 44 G5
Oshtorïnän, Iran ... 39 C6
Oshwe, Zaïre 46 E3
Osijek, Croatia 21 B8
Osipenko = Berdyansk, Ukraine 23 E6
Osizweni, S. Africa . 49 D5
Oskaloosa, U.S.A. . 70 E8
Oskarshamn, Sweden 9 H14
Oskélanéo, Canada . 62 C4
Öskemen = Ust-Kamenogorsk, Kazakhstan 24 E9
Oslo, Norway 9 G11
Oslob, Phil. 33 C6
Oslofjorden, Norway . 9 G11
Osmanabad, India .. 36 K10
Osmaniye, Turkey .. 23 G6
Osnabrück, Germany 16 B4
Osorio, Brazil 80 B6
Osorno, Chile 80 E2
Osoyoos, Canada .. 64 D5
Ospika →, Canada . 64 B4
Osprey Reef, Australia 54 A4
Oss, Neths. 15 C5
Ossa, Mt., Australia . 54 G4
Óssa, Óros, Greece . 21 E10
Ossabaw I., U.S.A. . 69 K5
Ossining, U.S.A. ... 68 E9
Ossokmanuan L., Canada 63 B7
Ossora, Russia 25 D17
Ostend = Oostende, Belgium 15 C2
Österdalälven →, Sweden 9 F12
Östergötlands län □, Sweden 9 G13
Östersund, Sweden . 8 E13
Østfold fylke □, Norway 9 G11
Ostfriesische Inseln, Germany 16 B3
Ostrava, Czech. 17 D9
Ostróda, Poland ... 17 B9
Ostrołęka, Poland .. 17 B10
Ostrów Mazowiecka, Poland 17 B10
Ostrów Wielkopolski, Poland 17 C8
Ostrowiec-Świętokrzyski, Poland 17 C10
Ōsumi-Kaikyō, Japan 29 J5
Ōsumi-Shotō, Japan 29 J5
Osuna, Spain 19 D3
Oswego, U.S.A. ... 68 D7
Oswestry, U.K. 10 E4
Otago □, N.Z. 51 L2
Otago Harbour, N.Z. 51 L3
Ōtake, Japan 29 G6
Otaki, N.Z. 51 J5
Otaru, Japan 28 C10
Otaru-Wan = Ishikari-Wan, Japan 28 C10
Otavalo, Ecuador .. 78 C3
Otavi, Namibia 48 B2
Otchinjau, Angola .. 48 B1
Othello, U.S.A. 72 C4
Otira Gorge, N.Z. .. 51 K3
Otis, U.S.A. 70 E3
Otjiwarongo, Namibia 48 C2
Otoineppu, Japan .. 28 B11
Otorohanga, N.Z. .. 51 H5
Otoskwin →, Canada 62 B2
Otosquen, Canada . 65 C8
Otranto, Italy 21 D8
Otranto, C. d', Italy . 21 D8
Otranto, Str. of, Italy . 21 D8
Otse, S. Africa 48 D4
Ōtsu, Japan 29 G7
Ōtsuki, Japan 29 G9

Ottawa = Outaouais →, Canada 62 C5
Ottawa, Canada ... 62 C4
Ottawa, Ill., U.S.A. . 70 E10
Ottawa, Kans., U.S.A. 70 F7
Ottawa Is., Canada . 61 C11
Otter →, U.K. 11 G4
Otter Rapids, Ont., Canada 62 B3
Otter Rapids, Sask., Canada 65 B8
Ottosdal, S. Africa . 48 D4
Ottoshoop, S. Africa 48 D4
Ottumwa, U.S.A. .. 70 E8
Oturkpo, Nigeria .. 44 G6
Otway, B., Chile ... 80 G2
Otway, C., Australia . 55 F3
Otwock, Poland ... 17 B10
Ou →, Laos 34 B7
Ou-Sammyaku, Japan 28 E10
Ouachita →, U.S.A. 71 K9
Ouachita, L., U.S.A. 71 H8
Ouachita Mts., U.S.A. 71 H7
Ouadâne, Mauritania 44 D2
Ouadda, C.A.R. ... 45 G9
Ouagadougou, Burkina Faso 44 F4
Ouahran = Oran, Algeria 44 A4
Ouallene, Algeria .. 44 D5
Ouanda Djallé, C.A.R. 45 G9
Ouango, C.A.R. ... 46 D4
Ouargla, Algeria ... 44 B6
Ouarzazate, Morocco 44 B3
Oubangi →, Zaïre . 46 E3
Ouddorp, Neths. ... 15 C3
Oude Rijn →, Neths. 15 B5
Oudenaarde, Belgium 15 D3
Oudtshoorn, S. Africa 48 E3
Ouessant, I. d', France 18 B1
Ouesso, Congo 46 D3
Ouest, Pte., Canada 63 C7
Ouezzane, Morocco 44 B3
Ouidah, Benin 44 G5
Ouida = Oujda, Morocco 44 B4
Oujeft, Mauritania . 44 D2
Ouled Djellal, Algeria 44 B6
Oulu, Finland 8 D18
Oulu = Oulun lääni □, Finland ... 8 D19
Oulujärvi, Finland .. 8 D19
Oulujoki →, Finland 8 D18
Oulun lääni □, Finland 8 D19
Oum Chalouba, Chad 45 E9
Ounguati, Namibia . 48 C2
Ounianga-Kébir, Chad 45 E9
Ounianga Sérir, Chad 45 E9
Our →, Lux. 15 E6
Ouray, U.S.A. 73 G10
Ourense = Orense, Spain 19 A2
Ouricuri, Brazil 79 E10
Ouro Prêto, Brazil .. 79 H10
Ourthe →, Belgium 15 D5
Ouse, Australia 54 G4
Ouse →, E. Susx., U.K. 11 G8
Ouse →, N. Yorks., U.K. 10 D7
Outaouais →, Canada 62 C5
Outardes →, Canada 63 C6
Outer Hebrides, U.K. 12 D1
Outer I., Canada ... 63 B8
Outjo, Namibia 48 C2
Outlook, Canada ... 65 C7
Outlook, U.S.A. ... 70 A2
Ouyen, Australia ... 55 F3
Ovalau, Fiji 51 C8
Ovalle, Chile 80 C2
Ovar, Portugal 19 B1
Overflakkee, Neths. 15 C4
Overijssel □, Neths. 15 B6
Overpelt, Belgium .. 15 C5
Overton, U.S.A. ... 73 H6
Övertorneå, Sweden 8 C17
Ovid, U.S.A. 70 E3
Oviedo, Spain 19 A3
Ovruch, Ukraine ... 24 D3
Owaka, N.Z. 51 M2
Owase, Japan 29 G8
Owatonna, U.S.A. . 70 C8
Owbeh, Afghan. ... 36 B3
Owego, U.S.A. 68 D7
Owen Sound, Canada 62 D3
Owendo, Gabon ... 46 D1
Owens L., U.S.A. .. 73 H5
Owensboro, U.S.A. 68 G2
Owensville, U.S.A. . 70 F9
Owl →, Canada ... 65 B10
Owo, Nigeria 44 G6
Owosso, U.S.A. ... 68 D3
Owyhee, U.S.A. ... 72 F5
Owyhee →, U.S.A. 72 E5
Owyhee, L., U.S.A. 72 E5
Ox Mts., Ireland .. 13 B3
Oxelösund, Sweden 9 G14
Oxford, N.Z. 51 K4
Oxford, U.K. 11 F6
Oxford, Miss., U.S.A. 71 H10
Oxford, N.C., U.S.A. 69 G6
Oxford, Ohio, U.S.A. 68 F3
Oxford L., Canada . 65 C9
Oxfordshire □, U.K. 11 F6
Oxley, Australia ... 55 E3
Oxnard, U.S.A. 73 J4
Oxus = Amudarya →, Uzbekistan 24 E6
Oya, Malaysia 32 D4
Oyama, Japan 29 F9
Oyem, Gabon 46 D2
Oyen, Canada 65 C6

Oykel →, U.K. 12 D4
Oymyakon, Russia .. 25 C15
Oyo, Nigeria 44 G5
Ōyūbari, Japan 28 C11
Ozamiz, Phil. 33 C6
Ozark, Ala., U.S.A. . 69 K3
Ozark, Ark., U.S.A. . 71 H8
Ozark, Mo., U.S.A. . 71 G8
Ozark Plateau, U.S.A. 71 G9
Ozarks, L. of the, U.S.A. 70 F8
Ozona, U.S.A. 71 K4

P

P.K. le Roux Dam, S. Africa 48 E3
Pa-an, Burma 37 L20
Pa Sak →, Thailand 34 E6
Paamiut = Frederikshåb, Greenland 4 C5
Paarl, S. Africa 48 E2
Paatsi →, Russia .. 8 B20
Paauilo, U.S.A. 66 H17
Pab Hills, Pakistan . 36 F5
Pabna, Bangla. 37 G16
Pacaja →, Brazil .. 79 D8
Pacaraima, Sierra, Venezuela 78 C6
Pacasmayo, Peru .. 78 E3
Pachpadra, India .. 36 G8
Pachuca, Mexico .. 74 C5
Pacific, Canada ... 64 C3
Pacific-Antarctic Ridge, Pac. Oc. 57 M16
Pacific Grove, U.S.A. 73 H3
Pacific Ocean, Pac. Oc. 57 G14
Pacitan, Indonesia . 33 H14
Padaido, Kepulauan, Indonesia 33 E9
Padang, Indonesia . 32 E2
Padang Endau, Malaysia 34 S16
Padangpanjang, Indonesia 32 E2
Padangsidempuan, Indonesia 32 D1
Paddockwood, Canada 65 C7
Paderborn, Germany 16 C4
Padloping Island, Canada 61 B13
Pádova, Italy 20 B4
Padre I., U.S.A. 71 M6
Padstow, U.K. 11 G3
Padua = Pádova, Italy 20 B4
Paducah, Ky., U.S.A. 68 G1
Paducah, Tex., U.S.A. 71 H4
Paeroa, N.Z. 51 G5
Pafúri, Mozam. 49 C5
Pag, Croatia 20 B6
Pagadian, Phil. 33 C6
Pagai Selatan, P., Indonesia 32 E2
Pagai Utara, Indonesia 32 E2
Pagalu = Annobón, Atl. Oc. 43 G4
Pagastikós Kólpos, Greece 21 E10
Pagatan, Indonesia . 32 E5
Page, Ariz., U.S.A. . 73 H8
Page, N. Dak., U.S.A. 70 B6
Pago Pago, Amer. Samoa 51 B13
Pagosa Springs, U.S.A. 73 H10
Pagwa River, Canada 62 B2
Pahala, U.S.A. 66 J17
Pahang □, Malaysia 34 R15
Pahang →, Malaysia 34 R16
Pahiatua, N.Z. 51 J5
Pahokee, U.S.A. ... 69 M5
Pahrump, U.S.A. .. 73 H6
Paia, U.S.A. 66 H16
Paignton, U.K. 11 G4
Päijänne, Finland .. 9 F18
Pailin, Cambodia .. 34 F7
Painan, Indonesia . 32 E2
Painesville, U.S.A. . 68 E5
Paint Hills = Nouveau Comptoir, Canada . 62 B4
Paint L., Canada ... 65 B9
Paint Rock, U.S.A. 71 K5
Painted Desert, U.S.A. 73 J8
Paintsville, U.S.A. . 68 G4
País Vasco □, Spain 19 A4
Paisley, Canada ... 62 D3
Paisley, U.K. 12 F4
Paisley, U.S.A. 72 E3
Paita, Peru 78 E2
Pak Lay, Laos 34 C6
Pakaraima Mts., Guyana 78 B6
Pakistan ■, Asia ... 36 E4
Pakistan, East = Bangladesh ■, Asia 37 H17
Pakokku, Burma ... 37 J19
Pakse, Laos 34 E8
Paktïā □, Afghan. .. 36 C6
Pala, Chad 45 G8
Palacios, U.S.A. 71 L6
Palagruža, Croatia . 20 C7
Palam, India 36 K10
Palamós, Spain ... 19 B7
Palampur, India ... 36 C10
Palana, Australia .. 54 F4
Palana, Russia 25 D16
Palanan, Phil. 33 A6
Palanan Pt., Phil. .. 33 A6
Palangkaraya, Indonesia 32 E4

Palani Hills, India .. 36 P10
Palanpur, India 36 G8
Palapye, Botswana . 48 C4
Palatka, Russia 25 C16
Palatka, U.S.A. 69 L5
Palau = Belau ■, Pac. Oc. 56 G5
Palauk, Burma 34 F5
Palawan, Phil. 32 C5
Palayankottai, India 36 Q10
Paleleh, Indonesia . 33 D6
Palembang, Indonesia 32 E2
Palencia, Spain ... 19 A3
Palermo, Italy 20 E5
Palestine, Asia 41 D4
Palestine, U.S.A. .. 71 K7
Paletwa, Burma ... 37 J18
Palghat, India 36 P10
Palgrave, Mt., Australia 52 D2
Pali, India 36 G8
Palisade, U.S.A. ... 70 E4
Palitana, India 36 J7
Palk Bay, Asia 36 Q11
Palk Strait, Asia ... 36 Q11
Palkānah, Iraq 38 C5
Palla Road = Dinokwe, Botswana 48 C4
Palm Beach, U.S.A. 69 M6
Palm Is., Australia . 54 B4
Palm Springs, U.S.A. 73 K5
Palma, Mozam. 46 G8
Palma →, Brazil ... 79 F9
Palma, B. de, Spain 19 C7
Palma de Mallorca, Spain 19 C7
Palmares, Brazil ... 79 E11
Pálmas, G. di, Italy 20 E3
Palmdale, U.S.A. .. 73 J4
Palmeira dos Índios, Brazil 79 E11
Palmeirinhas, Pta. das, Angola 46 F2
Palmer, U.S.A. 60 B5
Palmer →, Australia 54 B3
Palmer Arch., Antarctica 5 C17
Palmer Lake, U.S.A. 70 F2
Palmer Land, Antarctica 5 D18
Palmerston, N.Z. .. 51 L3
Palmerston North, N.Z. 51 J5
Palmetto, U.S.A. .. 69 M4
Palmi, Italy 20 E6
Palmira, Colombia . 78 C3
Palmyra = Tudmur, Syria 38 C3
Palmyra, U.S.A. ... 70 F9
Palmyra Is., Pac. Oc. 57 G11
Palo Alto, U.S.A. .. 73 H2
Palopo, Indonesia . 33 E6
Palos, C. de, Spain 19 D5
Palouse, U.S.A. ... 72 C5
Palparara, Australia 54 C3
Palu, Indonesia ... 33 E5
Palu, Turkey 23 G7
Paluan, Phil. 33 B6
Pama, Burkina Faso 44 F6
Pamanukan, Indonesia 33 G12
Pamekasan, Indonesia 33 G15
Pamirs, Tajikistan .. 24 F8
Pamlico →, U.S.A. 69 H7
Pamlico Sd., U.S.A. 69 H8
Pampa, U.S.A. 71 H4
Pampa de las Salinas, Argentina 80 C3
Pampanua, Indonesia 33 E6
Pampas, Argentina . 80 D4
Pampas, Peru 78 F4
Pamplona, Colombia 78 B4
Pamplona, Spain .. 19 A5
Pampoenpoort, S. Africa 48 E3
Pana, U.S.A. 70 F10
Panaca, U.S.A. ... 73 H6
Panaitan, Indonesia 33 G11
Panaji, India 36 M8
Panamá ■, Cent. Amer. 75 F9
Panamá, Panama .. 74 H14
Panamá, G. de, Panama 75 F9
Panama Canal, Panama 74 H14
Panama City, U.S.A. 69 K3
Panamint Ra., U.S.A. 73 J5
Panão, Peru 78 E3
Panarukan, Indonesia 33 G15
Panay, Phil. 33 B6
Panay, G., Phil. 33 B6
Pancake Ra., U.S.A. 73 G6
Pančevo, Serbia, Yug. 21 B9
Pancorbo, Paso, Spain 19 A4
Pandan, Phil. 33 B6
Pandegelang, Indonesia 33 G12
Pandharpur, India . 36 L9
Pando, Uruguay ... 80 C5
Pando, L. = Hope, L., Australia 55 D2
Panevézys, Lithuania 22 C9
Panfilov, Kazakhstan 24 E8
Pang-Long, Burma . 37 H21
Pang-Yang, Burma . 37 H21
Pangalanes, Canal des, Madag. 49 C8
Pangani, Tanzania . 46 F7
Pangfou = Bengbu, China 31 C6
Pangkah, Tanjung, Indonesia 33 G15
Pangkajene, Indonesia 33 E5

Pangkalanbrandan, Indonesia 32 D1
Pangkalanbuun, Indonesia 32 E4
Pangkalansusu, Indonesia 32 D1
Pangkalpinang, Indonesia 32 E3
Pangkoh, Indonesia 32 E4
Pangnirtung, Canada 61 B13
Pangrango, Indonesia 33 G12
Panguitch, U.S.A. .. 73 H7
Pangutaran Group, Phil. 33 C6
Panhandle, U.S.A. . 71 H4
Panjgur, Pakistan .. 36 F4
Panjim = Panaji, India 36 M8
Panjinad Barrage, Pakistan 36 E7
Panna, India 36 G12
Panorama, Brazil .. 80 A6
Pantar, Indonesia .. 33 F6
Pante Macassar, Indonesia 33 F6
Pantelleria, Italy ... 20 F5
Pánuco, Mexico ... 74 C5
Panyam, Nigeria .. 44 G6
Paola, U.S.A. 70 F7
Paonia, U.S.A. 73 G10
Paoting = Baoding, China 31 C6
Paot'ou = Baotou, China 31 B6
Paoua, C.A.R. 45 G8
Pápa, Hungary 17 E8
Papakura, N.Z. 51 G5
Papantla, Mexico .. 74 C5
Papar, Malaysia ... 32 C5
Papien Chiang = Da →, Vietnam 34 B8
Paposo, Chile 80 B2
Papua New Guinea ■, Oceania 56 H6
Papudo, Chile 80 C2
Papun, Burma 37 K20
Papunya, Australia . 52 D5
Pará = Belém, Brazil 79 D9
Pará □, Brazil 79 D8
Paraburdoo, Australia 52 D2
Paracatu, Brazil ... 79 G9
Paracel Is. = Hsisha Chuntao, Pac. Oc. 32 A4
Parachilna, Australia 55 E2
Parachinar, Pakistan 36 C7
Paradip, India 37 J15
Paradise, U.S.A. ... 72 C6
Paradise →, Canada 63 B8
Paradise Valley, U.S.A. 72 F5
Parado, Indonesia . 33 F5
Paragould, U.S.A. . 71 G9
Paragua →, Venezuela 78 B6
Paraguaçu, Brazil .. 79 F11
Paraguaná, Pen. de, Venezuela 78 A4
Paraguarí, Paraguay 80 B5
Paraguay ■, S. Amer. 80 A5
Paraguay →, Paraguay 80 B5
Paraíba = João Pessoa, Brazil 79 E12
Paraíba □, Brazil .. 79 E11
Paraíba do Sul →, Brazil 79 H10
Parainen, Finland .. 9 F17
Parak, Iran 39 E7
Parakou, Benin ... 44 G5
Paramaribo, Surinam 79 B7
Paramushir, Ostrov, Russia 25 D16
Paran →, Israel ... 41 E4
Paraná, Argentina . 80 C4
Paraná, Brazil 79 F9
Paraná □, Brazil ... 80 A6
Paraná →, Argentina 80 C5
Paranaguá, Brazil .. 80 B7
Paranaíba →, Brazil . 79 H8
Paranapanema →, Brazil 80 A6
Paranapiacaba, Serra do, Brazil 80 A7
Parang, Jolo, Phil. . 33 C6
Parang, Mindanao, Phil. 33 C6
Paratinga, Brazil ... 79 F10
Paratoo, Australia . 55 E2
Parattah, Australia . 54 G4
Parbhani, India 36 K10
Parchim, Germany . 16 B5
Pardes Hanna, Israel 41 C3
Pardo →, Bahia, Brazil 79 G11
Pardo →, Mato Grosso, Brazil 79 H8
Pardo →, São Paulo, Brazil 79 H9
Pardubice, Czech. . 16 C7
Pare, Indonesia 33 G15
Parecis, Serra dos, Brazil 78 F7
Pareh, Iran 38 B5
Paren, Russia 25 C17
Parent, Canada ... 62 C5
Parent, L., Canada . 62 C4
Parepare, Indonesia 33 E5
Parguba, Russia ... 22 B5
Pariaguán, Venezuela 78 B6
Pariaman, Indonesia 32 E2
Parigi, Java, Indonesia 33 G13
Parigi, Sulawesi, Indonesia 33 E6

Parika, Guyana 78 B7
Parima, Serra, Brazil 78 C6
Parinari, Peru 78 D4
Parîng, Romania ... 17 F11
Parintins, Brazil ... 79 D7
Pariparit Kyun, Burma 37 M18
Paris, Canada 62 D3
Paris, France 18 B5
Paris, Idaho, U.S.A. 72 E8
Paris, Ky., U.S.A. .. 68 F3
Paris, Tenn., U.S.A. 69 G1
Paris, Tex., U.S.A. . 71 J7
Paris, Ville de □, France 18 B5
Pariti, Indonesia ... 33 F6
Park City, U.S.A. .. 72 F8
Park Falls, U.S.A. .. 70 C9
Park Range, U.S.A. 72 G10
Park Rapids, U.S.A. 70 B7
Park River, U.S.A. . 70 A6
Park Rynie, S. Africa 49 E5
Parka Bandar, Iran 39 E8
Parker, Ariz., U.S.A. 73 J6
Parker, S. Dak., U.S.A. 70 D6
Parker Dam, U.S.A. 73 J6
Parkersburg, U.S.A. 68 F5
Parkerview, Canada 65 C8
Parkes, Australia .. 55 E4
Parkside, Canada .. 65 C7
Parkston, U.S.A. .. 70 D5
Parksville, Canada . 64 D4
Parma, Italy 20 B4
Parma, U.S.A. 72 E5
Parnaguá, Brazil .. 79 F10
Parnaíba, Piauí, Brazil 79 D10
Parnaíba, São Paulo, Brazil 79 G8
Parnaíba →, Brazil 79 D10
Parnassós, Greece . 21 E10
Pärnu, Estonia 22 C3
Paroo →, Australia 55 E3
Páros, Greece 21 F11
Parowan, U.S.A. .. 73 H7
Parral, Chile 80 D2
Parramatta, Australia 55 E5
Parrett →, U.K. .. 11 F5
Parris I., U.S.A. ... 69 J5
Parrsboro, Canada . 63 C7
Parry Is., Canada .. 4 B2
Parry Sound, Canada 62 C3
Parshall, U.S.A. ... 70 B3
Parsnip →, Canada 64 B4
Parsons, U.S.A. ... 71 G7
Parsons Ra., Australia 54 A2
Paru →, Brazil 79 D8
Paruro, Peru 78 F4
Parvān □, Afghan. . 36 B6
Parvatipuram, India 37 K13
Parys, S. Africa ... 48 D4
Pas-de-Calais □, France 18 A5
Pasadena, Calif., U.S.A. 73 J4
Pasadena, Tex., U.S.A. 71 L7
Pasaje, Ecuador ... 78 D3
Pascagoula, U.S.A. 71 K10
Pascagoula →, U.S.A. 71 K10
Pasco, Canada 72 C4
Pasco, Cerro de, Peru 78 F3
Pascua, I. de, Pac. Oc. 57 K17
Pasfield L., Canada 65 B7
Pashmakli = Smolyan, Bulgaria 21 D11
Pasir Mas, Malaysia 34 N15
Pasir Putih, Malaysia 34 P15
Pasirian, Indonesia 33 H15
Paskūh, Iran 39 E9
Pasley, C., Australia 53 F3
Pasni, Pakistan ... 36 G3
Paso de Indios, Argentina 80 E3
Paso Robles, U.S.A. 73 J3
Paspébiac, Canada 63 C6
Passage West, Ireland 13 E3
Passau, Germany . 16 D6
Passero, C., Italy .. 20 F6
Passo Fundo, Brazil 80 B6
Passos, Brazil 79 H9
Pastaza →, Peru .. 78 D3
Pasto, Colombia .. 78 C3
Pasuruan, Indonesia 33 G15
Patagonia, Argentina 80 F3
Patagonia, U.S.A. . 73 L8
Patambar, Iran 39 D9
Patan, India 36 H8
Patan, Nepal 37 F14
Patani, Indonesia .. 33 D7
Patchewollock, Australia 55 F3
Patchogue, U.S.A. 68 E9
Patea, N.Z. 51 H5
Pategi, Nigeria 44 G6
Patensie, S. Africa . 48 E3
Paternò, Italy 20 F6
Pateros, U.S.A. ... 72 B4
Paterson, U.S.A. .. 68 E8
Paterson Ra., Australia 52 D3
Pathankot, India .. 36 C9
Pathfinder Res., U.S.A. 72 E10
Pati, Indonesia 33 G14
Patiala, India 36 D10
Patkai Bum, India . 37 F19
Pátmos, Greece ... 21 F12
Patna, India 37 G14
Patos, L. dos, Brazil 80 C6
Patos de Minas, Brazil 79 G9
Patquía, Argentina . 80 C3
Pátrai, Greece 21 E9
Pátraikós Kólpos, Greece 21 E9
Patrocínio, Brazil .. 79 G9
Pattani, Thailand .. 34 N14

Patten, U.S.A. 63 C6
Patterson, Calif., U.S.A. 73 H3
Patterson, La., U.S.A. . 71 L9
Patti, Italy 20 E6
Patuakhali, Bangla. . 37 H17
Pau, France 18 E3
Pauillac, France . . . 18 D3
Pauini →, Brazil . . . 78 D6
Pauk, Burma 37 J19
Paul I., Canada . . . 63 A7
Paulis = Isiro, Zaïre . 46 D5
Paulistana, Brazil . . 79 E10
Paullina, U.S.A. . . . 70 D7
Paulo Afonso, Brazil . 79 E11
Paulpietersburg, S. Africa 49 D5
Pauls Valley, U.S.A. . 71 H6
Pāveh, Iran 38 C5
Pavia, Italy 20 B3
Pavlodar, Kazakhstan . 24 D8
Pavlograd, Ukraine . . 23 E6
Pavlovo, Russia . . . 22 C7
Pavlovo, Russia . . . 25 C12
Pavlovsk, Russia . . . 23 D7
Pawhuska, U.S.A. . . . 71 G6
Pawnee, U.S.A. 71 G6
Pawnee City, U.S.A. . 70 E6
Pawtucket, U.S.A. . . 68 E10
Paxton, Ill., U.S.A. . . 68 E1
Paxton, Nebr., U.S.A. . 70 E4
Paya Bakri, Malaysia . 34 S15
Payakumbuh, Indonesia 32 E2
Payette, U.S.A. . . . 72 D5
Payne Bay = Bellin, Canada 61 B13
Payne L., Canada . . . 61 C12
Paynes Find, Australia 53 E2
Paynesville, U.S.A. . . 70 C7
Paysandú, Uruguay . . 80 C5
Payson, Ariz., U.S.A. . 73 J8
Payson, Utah, U.S.A. . 72 F8
Paz, B. la, Mexico . . 74 C2
Pāzanān, Iran 39 D6
Pazardzhik, Bulgaria . 21 C11
Pe Ell, U.S.A. 72 C2
Peace →, Canada . . 64 B6
Peace Point, Canada . 64 B6
Peace River, Canada . 64 B5
Peach Springs, U.S.A. . 73 J7
Peak, The = Kinder Scout, U.K. 10 D6
Peak Downs, Australia 54 C4
Peak Downs Mine, Australia 54 C4
Peak Hill, N.S.W., Australia 55 E4
Peak Hill, W. Austral., Australia 53 E2
Peak Ra., Australia . . 54 C4
Peake, Australia . . . 55 F2
Peake Cr. →, Australia 55 D2
Peale Mt., U.S.A. . . . 73 G9
Pearl →, U.S.A. . . . 71 K10
Pearl City, U.S.A. . . . 66 H16
Pearsall, U.S.A. . . . 71 L5
Pearse I., Canada . . . 64 C2
Peary Land, Greenland 4 A6
Pease →, U.S.A. . . . 71 H5
Pebane, Mozam. . . . 47 H7
Pebas, Peru 78 D4
Peč, Serbia, Yug. . . . 21 C9
Pechenga, Russia . . . 22 A5
Pechora →, Russia . 22 A9
Pechorskaya Guba, Russia 22 A9
Pecos, U.S.A. 71 K3
Pecos →, U.S.A. . . . 71 L3
Pécs, Hungary 17 E9
Pedder, L., Australia . 54 G4
Peddie, S. Africa . . . 49 E4
Pedirka, Australia . . 55 D2
Pedra Azul, Brazil . . 79 G10
Pedreiras, Brazil . . . 79 D10
Pedro Afonso, Brazil . 79 E9
Pedro Juan Caballero, Paraguay 80 A5
Pedro Miguel Locks, Panama 74 H14
Peebinga, Australia . . 55 E3
Peebles, U.K. 12 F5
Peekskill, U.S.A. . . . 68 E9
Peel, U.K. 10 C3
Peel →, Australia . . 55 E5
Peel →, Canada . . . 60 B6
Peera Peera Poolanna L., Australia . . . 55 D2
Peers, Canada 64 C5
Pegasus Bay, N.Z. . . 51 K4
Pegu, Burma 37 L20
Pegu Yoma, Burma . . 37 K19
Pehuajó, Argentina . . 80 D4
Peip'ing = Beijing, China 31 C6
Peixe, Brazil 79 F9
Pekalongan, Indonesia 33 G13
Pekan, Malaysia . . . 34 R16
Pekanbaru, Indonesia 32 D2
Pekin, U.S.A. 70 E10
Peking = Beijing, Beijing, China . . . 31 C6
Peking = Beijing, Beijing, China . . . 31 C6
Pelabuhan Kelang, Malaysia 34 S14
Pelabuhan Ratu, Teluk, Indonesia 33 G12
Pelabuhanratu, Indonesia 33 G12
Pelaihari, Indonesia . 32 E4

Peleaga, Romania . . 17 F11
Pelée, Mt., Martinique 74 N20
Pelee, Pt., Canada . . 62 D3
Pelee I., Canada . . . 62 D3
Peleng, Indonesia . . 33 E6
Pelham, U.S.A. 69 K3
Pelican L., Canada . . 65 C8
Pelican Narrows, Canada 65 B8
Pelican Rapids, Canada 65 C8
Pelkosenniemi, Finland 8 C19
Pella, S. Africa 48 D2
Pella, U.S.A. 70 E8
Pelly →, Canada . . . 60 B6
Pelly Bay, Canada . . 61 B11
Pelly L., Canada . . . 60 B9
Peloponnese = Pelopónnisos □, Greece 21 F10
Pelopónnisos □, Greece 21 F10
Peloro, C., Italy . . . 20 E6
Pelorus Sd., N.Z. . . . 51 J4
Pelotas, Brazil 80 C6
Pelvoux, Massif de, France 18 D7
Pemalang, Indonesia . 33 G13
Pematangsiantar, Indonesia 32 D1
Pemba I., Tanzania . . 46 F7
Pemberton, Australia . 53 F2
Pemberton, Canada . . 64 C4
Pembina, U.S.A. . . . 65 D9
Pembina →, U.S.A. . 65 D9
Pembine, U.S.A. . . . 68 C2
Pembino, U.S.A. . . . 70 A6
Pembroke, Canada . . 62 C4
Pembroke, U.K. . . . 11 F3
Pembroke, U.S.A. . . 69 J5
Pen-y-Ghent, U.K. . . 10 C5
Peña de Francia, Sierra de, Spain 19 B2
Peñalara, Pico, Spain . 19 B4
Penang = Pinang, Malaysia 34 P13
Penápolis, Brazil . . . 80 A6
Peñarroya-Pueblonuevo, Spain 19 C3
Peñas, C. de, Spain . . 19 A3
Penas, G. de, Chile . . 80 F2
Pench'i = Benxi, China 31 B7
Pend Oreille →, U.S.A. 72 B5
Pend Oreille, L., U.S.A. 72 C5
Pendembu, S. Leone . 44 G2
Pender B., Australia . 52 C3
Pendleton, U.S.A. . . 72 D4
Penedo, Brazil 79 F11
Penetanguishene, Canada 62 D4
Pengalengan, Indonesia 33 G12
Penguin, Australia . . 54 G4
Peniche, Portugal . . . 19 C1
Penicuik, U.K. 12 F5
Penida, Indonesia . . 32 F5
Peninsular Malaysia □, Malaysia 34 Q15
Penmarch, Pte. de, France 18 C1
Penn Yan, U.S.A. . . . 68 D7
Pennant, Canada . . . 65 C7
Penner →, India . . . 36 M12
Pennines, U.K. 10 C5
Pennsylvania □, U.S.A. 68 E6
Penny, Canada 64 C4
Penola, Australia . . . 55 F3
Penong, Australia . . 53 F5
Penrith, Australia . . 55 E5
Penrith, U.K. 10 C5
Pensacola, U.S.A. . . 69 K2
Pensacola Mts., Antarctica 5 E1
Pense, Canada 65 C8
Penshurst, Australia . 55 F3
Penticton, Canada . . 64 D5
Pentland, Australia . . 54 C4
Pentland Firth, U.K. . 12 C5
Pentland Hills, U.K. . 12 F5
Penylan L., Canada . . 65 A7
Penza, Russia 22 D8
Penzance, U.K. 11 G2
Penzhino, Russia . . . 25 C17
Penzhinskaya Guba, Russia 25 C17
Peoria, Ariz., U.S.A. . 73 K7
Peoria, Ill., U.S.A. . . 70 E10
Pera Hd., Australia . . 54 A3
Perabumilih, Indonesia 32 E2
Perak □, Malaysia . . 34 P14
Percé, Canada 63 C7
Perche, France 18 B4
Percival Lakes, Australia 52 D4
Percy Is., Australia . . 54 C5
Perdido, Mte., Spain . 19 A6
Perdu, Mt. = Perdido, Mte., Spain 19 A6
Pereira, Colombia . . 78 C3
Perekerten, Australia . 55 E3
Perenjori, Australia . . 53 E2
Pereyaslav Khmelnitskiy, Ukraine 23 D5
Pergamino, Argentina 80 C4
Perham, U.S.A. . . . 70 B7
Perhentian, Kepulauan, Malaysia 34 P15
Péribonca →, Canada 63 C5
Péribonca, L., Canada 63 B5
Perico, Argentina . . . 80 A3

Périgord, France . . . 18 D4
Périgueux, France . . . 18 D4
Perijá, Sierra de, Colombia 78 B4
Perlas, Arch. de las, Panama 75 F9
Perlis □, Malaysia . . 34 N13
Perm, Russia 22 C10
Pernambuco = Recife, Brazil 79 E12
Pernambuco □, Brazil 79 E11
Pernatty Lagoon, Australia 55 E2
Peron, C., Australia . . 53 E1
Peron Is., Australia . . 52 B5
Peron Pen., Australia . 53 E1
Perow, Canada 64 C3
Perpendicular Pt., Australia 55 E5
Perpignan, France . . 18 E5
Perry, Fla., U.S.A. . . 69 K4
Perry, Ga., U.S.A. . . 69 J4
Perry, Iowa, U.S.A. . . 70 E7
Perry, Maine, U.S.A. . 69 C12
Perry, Okla., U.S.A. . 71 G6
Perryton, U.S.A. . . . 71 G4
Perryville, U.S.A. . . . 71 G10
Persia = Iran ■, Asia . 39 C7
Persian Gulf = Gulf, The, Asia 39 E6
Perth, Australia . . . 53 F2
Perth, Canada 62 D4
Perth, U.K. 12 E5
Perth Amboy, U.S.A. . 68 E8
Peru, Ill., U.S.A. . . . 70 E10
Peru, Ind., U.S.A. . . 68 E2
Peru ■, S. Amer. . . . 78 E3
Peru-Chile Trench, Pac. Oc. 57 K20
Perúgia, Italy 20 C5
Pervomaysk, Ukraine . 23 E5
Pervouralsk, Russia . 22 C10
Pésaro, Italy 20 C5
Pescara, Italy 20 C6
Peshawar, Pakistan . 36 B7
Peshtigo, U.S.A. . . . 68 C2
Pesqueira, Brazil . . . 79 E11
Petah Tiqwa, Israel . . 41 C3
Petaling Jaya, Malaysia 34 R14
Petaluma, U.S.A. . . 72 G2
Petange, Lux. 15 E5
Petauke, Zambia . . . 47 G6
Petawawa, Canada . . 62 C4
Peter I.s Øy, Antarctica 5 C16
Peter Pond L., Canada 65 B7
Peterbell, Canada . . . 62 C3
Peterborough, Australia 55 E2
Peterborough, Canada 61 D12
Peterborough, U.K. . . 11 E7
Peterhead, U.K. . . . 12 D7
Petermann Bjerg, Greenland 58 B17
Petersburg, Alaska, U.S.A. 64 B2
Petersburg, Ind., U.S.A. 68 F2
Petersburg, Va., U.S.A. 68 G7
Petersburg, W. Va., U.S.A. 68 F6
Petford, Australia . . 54 B3
Petit Bois I., U.S.A. . . 69 K1
Petit-Cap, Canada . . 63 C7
Petit Lac Manicouagan, Canada 63 B6
Petitcodiac, Canada . 63 C6
Petite Baleine →, Canada 62 A4
Petite Saguenay, Canada 63 C5
Petitsikapau, L., Canada 63 B6
Petlad, India 36 H8
Peto, Mexico 74 C7
Petone, N.Z. 51 J5
Petoskey, U.S.A. . . . 68 C3
Petra, Jordan 41 E4
Petra, Ostrova, Russia 4 B13
Petra Velikogo, Zaliv, Russia 28 C5
Petrich, Bulgaria . . . 21 D10
Petrograd = Sankt-Peterburg, Russia . 22 C5
Petrolândia, Brazil . . 79 E11
Petrolia, Canada . . . 62 D3
Petrolina, Brazil . . . 79 E10
Petropavlovsk, Kazakhstan 24 D7
Petropavlovsk-Kamchatskiy, Russia 25 D16
Petrópolis, Brazil . . . 79 H10
Petroşani, Romania . . 17 F11
Petrovaradin, Serbia, Yug. 21 B8
Petrovsk, Russia . . . 22 D8
Petrovsk-Zabaykalskiy, Russia 25 D11
Petrozavodsk, Russia . 22 B5
Petrus Steyn, S. Africa 49 D4
Petrusburg, S. Africa . 48 D4
Peureulak, Indonesia . 32 D1
Pevek, Russia 25 C18
Pforzheim, Germany . 16 D4
Phagwara, India . . . 36 D9
Phala, Botswana . . . 48 C4
Phalodi, India 36 F8
Phan Rang, Vietnam . 34 G10
Phan Thiet, Vietnam . 34 G10
Phangan, Ko, Thailand 34 H6
Phangnga, Thailand . 34 H5
Phanh Bho Ho Chi Minh, Vietnam . . 34 G9

Phatthalung, Thailand 34 J6
Phelps, U.S.A. 70 B10
Phelps L., Canada . . 65 B8
Phenix City, U.S.A. . 69 J3
Phet Buri, Thailand . 34 F5
Phetchabun, Thailand 34 D6
Phetchabun, Thiu Khao, Thailand . . 34 E6
Phetchaburi = Phet Buri, Thailand . . 34 F5
Phichai, Thailand . . 34 D6
Phichit, Thailand . . 34 D6
Philadelphia, Miss., U.S.A. 71 J10
Philadelphia, Pa., U.S.A. 68 E8
Philip, U.S.A. 70 C4
Philippeville, Belgium 15 D4
Philippi L., Australia . 54 C2
Philippines ■, Asia . . 33 B6
Philippolis, S. Africa . 48 E4
Philippopolis = Plovdiv, Bulgaria . 21 C11
Philipsburg, U.S.A. . . 72 C7
Philipstown, S. Africa 48 E3
Phillip I., Australia . . 55 F4
Phillips, Tex., U.S.A. . 71 H4
Phillips, Wis., U.S.A. . 70 C9
Phillipsburg, U.S.A. . 70 F5
Phillott, Australia . . 55 D4
Philomath, U.S.A. . . 72 D2
Phitsanulok, Thailand 34 D6
Phnom Dangrek, Thailand 34 E8
Phnom Penh, Cambodia 34 G8
Phnom Thbeng, Cambodia 34 F8
Phoenix, U.S.A. . . . 73 K7
Phoenix Is., Kiribati . 56 H10
Phong Saly, Laos . . 34 B7
Phosphate Hill, Australia 54 C2
Phra Chedi Sam Ong, Thailand 34 E5
Phra Nakhon Si Ayutthaya, Thailand 34 E6
Phrae, Thailand . . . 34 C6
Phrao, Thailand . . . 34 C5
Phu Doan, Vietnam . 34 B8
Phu Loi, Laos 34 B7
Phu Ly, Vietnam . . . 34 B8
Phuket, Thailand . . 34 J5
Phumiphon, Khuan, Thailand 32 A1
Piacenza, Italy 20 B3
Pialba, Australia . . . 55 D5
Pian Cr. →, Australia 55 E4
Piapot, Canada . . . 65 D7
Piatra Neamţ, Romania 17 E13
Piauí □, Brazil 79 E10
Piave →, Italy 20 B5
Piazza Ármerina, Italy 20 F6
Pibor Post, Sudan . . 45 G11
Pica, Chile 78 H5
Picardie, France . . . 18 B5
Picardy = Picardie, France 18 B5
Picayune, U.S.A. . . . 71 K10
Pichilemu, Chile . . . 80 C2
Pickerel L., Canada . 62 C1
Pickle Lake, Canada . 62 B1
Pico Truncado, Argentina 80 F3
Picton, Australia . . . 55 E5
Picton, Canada . . . 62 D4
Picton, N.Z. 51 J5
Pictou, Canada . . . 63 C7
Picture Butte, Canada 64 D6
Picún Leufú, Argentina 80 D3
Pidurutalagala, Sri Lanka 36 R12
Piedmont = Piemonte □, Italy . 20 B2
Piedmont, U.S.A. . . 69 J3
Piedmont Plateau, U.S.A. 69 J5
Piedras, R. de las →, Peru 78 F5
Piedras Negras, Mexico 74 B4
Piedras Negras, Coahuila, Mexico . 74 B4
Piemonte □, Italy . . 20 B2
Pierce, U.S.A. 72 C6
Pierre, U.S.A. 70 C4
Piet Retief, S. Africa . 49 D5
Pietarsaari = Jakobstad, Finland . 8 E17
Pietermaritzburg, S. Africa 49 D5
Pietersburg, S. Africa 49 C4
Pietrosul, Romania . . 17 E12
Pietrosul, Romania . . 17 E13
Pigeon, U.S.A. 68 D4
Piggott, U.S.A. 71 G9
Pigüe, Argentina . . . 80 D4
Pikes Peak, U.S.A. . . 70 F2
Piketberg, S. Africa . 48 E2
Pikeville, U.S.A. . . . 68 G4
Pikwitonei, Canada . 65 B9
Pila, Brazil 79 E11
Pilar, Brazil 79 E11
Pilar, Paraguay 80 B5
Pilas Group, Phil. . . . 33 C6
Pilcomayo →, Paraguay 80 B5
Pilibhit, India 36 E11
Pilica →, Poland . . . 17 C10
Pilos, Greece 21 F9
Pilot Mound, Canada 65 D9
Pilot Point, U.S.A. . . 71 J6
Pilot Rock, U.S.A. . . 72 D4

Pilsen = Plzeň, Czech. 16 D6
Pima, U.S.A. 73 K9
Pimba, Australia . . . 55 E2
Pimenta Bueno, Brazil 78 F6
Pimentel, Peru 78 E3
Pinang, Malaysia . . 34 P13
Pinar del Río, Cuba . 75 C8
Pincher Creek, Canada 64 D6
Pinchi L., Canada . . 64 C4
Pinckneyville, U.S.A. . 70 F10
Pińczów, Poland . . . 17 C10
Pindar, Australia . . . 53 E2
Pindiga, Nigeria . . . 44 G7
Pindos Óros, Greece . 21 E9
Pindus Mts. = Pindos Óros, Greece . . . 21 E9
Pine →, Canada . . . 65 B7
Pine, C., Canada . . . 63 C9
Pine Bluff, U.S.A. . . 71 H8
Pine City, U.S.A. . . . 70 C8
Pine Falls, Canada . . 65 C9
Pine Pass, Canada . . 64 B4
Pine Point, Canada . . 64 A6
Pine Ridge, U.S.A. . . 70 D3
Pine River, Canada . . 65 C8
Pine River, U.S.A. . . 70 B7
Pinega →, Russia . . 22 B8
Pinehill, Australia . . 54 C4
Pinerolo, Italy 20 B2
Pinetop, U.S.A. . . . 73 J9
Pinetown, S. Africa . 49 D5
Pinetree, U.S.A. . . . 72 E11
Pineville, Ky., U.S.A. . 69 G4
Pineville, La., U.S.A. . 71 K8
Ping →, Thailand . . 34 E6
Pingaring, Australia . 53 F2
Pingdingshan, China . 31 C6
Pingdong, Taiwan . . 31 D7
Pingelly, Australia . . 53 F2
Pingliang, China . . . 30 C5
Pingrup, Australia . . 53 F2
Pingxiang, China . . . 30 D5
Pinhel, Portugal . . . 19 B2
Pini, Indonesia 32 D1
Piniós →, Greece . . 21 E10
Pinjarra, Australia . . 53 F2
Pink →, Canada . . . 65 B8
Pinnacles, U.S.A. . . 73 H3
Pinnaroo, Australia . 55 F3
Pinos Pt., U.S.A. . . . 73 H3
Pinrang, Indonesia . . 33 E5
Pinsk, Belorussia . . 22 D4
Pintados, Chile . . . 78 H5
Pintumba, Australia . 53 F5
Pinyug, Russia 22 B8
Pioche, U.S.A. 73 H6
Piombino, Italy . . . 20 C4
Pioner, Os., Russia . . 25 B10
Piorini, L., Brazil . . . 78 D6
Piotrków Trybunalski, Poland 17 C9
Pipestone, U.S.A. . . 70 D6
Pipestone →, Canada 62 B2
Pipestone Cr. →, Canada 65 D8
Pipmuacan, Rés., Canada 63 C5
Pippingarra, Australia 52 D2
Piqua, U.S.A. 68 E3
Piquiri →, Brazil . . . 80 A6
Pīr Sohrāb, Iran . . . 39 E9
Piracicaba, Brazil . . 80 A7
Piracuruca, Brazil . . 79 D10
Piraiévs, Greece . . . 21 F10
Piraiévs = Piraiévs, Greece 21 F10
Pirané, Argentina . . 80 B5
Pirapora, Brazil . . . 79 G10
Pírgos, Greece 21 F9
Pirineos, Spain . . . 19 A6
Piripiri, Brazil 79 D10
Pirot, Serbia, Yug. . . 21 C10
Piru, Indonesia . . . 33 E7
Pisa, Italy 20 C4
Pisagua, Chile 78 G4
Pisco, Peru 78 F3
Písek, Czech. 16 D7
Pishan, China 30 C2
Pising, Indonesia . . 33 F6
Pistóia, Italy 20 C4
Pistol B., Canada . . . 65 A10
Pisuerga →, Spain . . 19 B3
Pitarpunga, L., Australia 55 E3
Pitcairn I., Pac. Oc. . 57 K14
Pite älv →, Sweden . 8 D16
Piteå, Sweden 8 D16
Piteşti, Romania . . . 21 B11
Pithapuram, India . . 37 L13
Pithara, Australia . . 53 F2
Pitlochry, U.K. 12 E5
Pitt I., Canada 64 C3
Pittsburg, Kans., U.S.A. 71 G7
Pittsburg, Tex., U.S.A. 71 J7
Pittsburgh, U.S.A. . . 68 E6
Pittsfield, Ill., U.S.A. . 70 F9
Pittsfield, Mass., U.S.A. 68 D9
Pittsworth, Australia . 55 D5
Pituri →, Australia . . 54 C2
Piura, Peru 78 E2
Pizzo, Italy 20 E7
Placentia, Canada . . 63 C9
Placentia B., Canada . 63 C9
Placerville, U.S.A. . . 72 G3
Plain Dealing, U.S.A. 71 J8
Plainfield, U.S.A. . . 68 E8
Plains, Kans., U.S.A. . 71 G4

Plains, Mont., U.S.A. . 72 C6
Plains, Tex., U.S.A. . 71 J3
Plainview, Nebr., U.S.A. 70 D6
Plainview, Tex., U.S.A. 71 H4
Plainville, U.S.A. . . . 70 F5
Plainwell, U.S.A. . . . 68 D3
Plakhino, Russia . . . 24 C9
Plankinton, U.S.A. . . 70 D5
Plano, U.S.A. 71 J6
Plant City, U.S.A. . . 69 M4
Plaquemine, U.S.A. . 71 K9
Plasencia, Spain . . . 19 B2
Plaster Rock, Canada 63 C6
Plastun, Russia . . . 28 B8
Plata, Río de la, S. Amer. 80 C5
Platani →, Italy . . . 20 F5
Plateau du Coteau du Missouri, U.S.A. . 70 B4
Platí, Ákra, Greece . . 21 D11
Plato, Colombia . . . 78 B4
Platte, U.S.A. 70 D5
Platte →, U.S.A. . . . 70 F7
Platteville, U.S.A. . . 70 E2
Plattsburg, U.S.A. . . 68 C9
Plattsmouth, U.S.A. . 70 E7
Plauen, Germany . . 16 C6
Playgreen L., Canada 65 C9
Pleasant Bay, Canada 63 C7
Pleasant Hill, U.S.A. . 70 F7
Pleasanton, U.S.A. . . 71 L5
Pleasantville, U.S.A. . 68 F8
Pleiku, Vietnam . . . 34 F10
Plenty →, Australia . 54 C2
Plenty, B. of, N.Z. . . 51 G6
Plentywood, U.S.A. . 70 A2
Plesetsk, Russia . . . 22 B7
Plessisville, Canada . 63 C5
Pletipi L., Canada . . 63 B5
Pleven, Bulgaria . . . 21 C11
Plevlja, Montenegro, Yug. . 21 C8
Płock, Poland 17 B9
Ploieşti, Romania . . 21 B12
Plonge, Lac la, Canada 65 B7
Plovdiv, Bulgaria . . . 21 C11
Plummer, U.S.A. . . . 72 C5
Plumtree, Zimbabwe . 47 J5
Plymouth, U.K. . . . 11 G3
Plymouth, Ind., U.S.A. 68 E2
Plymouth, N.C., U.S.A. 69 H7
Plymouth, Wis., U.S.A. 68 D2
Plynlimon = Pumlumon Fawr, U.K. 11 E4
Plzeň, Czech. 16 D6
Po →, Italy 20 B5
Po Hai = Bo Hai, China 31 C6
Pobeda, Russia . . . 25 C15
Pobedino, Russia . . 25 E15
Pobedy Pik, Kirghizia 24 E8
Pocahontas, Ark., U.S.A. 71 G9
Pocahontas, Iowa, U.S.A. 70 D7
Pocatello, U.S.A. . . . 72 E7
Pocomoke City, U.S.A. 68 F8
Poços de Caldas, Brazil 79 H9
Podgorica, Montenegro, Yug. . 21 C8
Podkamennaya Tunguska →, Russia 25 C10
Podolsk, Russia . . . 22 C6
Podor, Senegal . . . 44 E1
Podporozhy, Russia . 22 B5
Pofadder, S. Africa . 48 D2
Pogamasing, Canada 62 C3
Pogranitšnyi, Russia . 28 B5
Poh, Indonesia . . . 33 E6
Pohnpei, Pac. Oc. . . 56 G7
Poinsett, C., Antarctica 5 C8
Point Edward, Canada 62 D3
Point Pedro, Sri Lanka 36 Q12
Point Pleasant, U.S.A. 68 F4
Pointe-à-la Hache, U.S.A. 71 L10
Pointe-à-Pitre, Guadeloupe 74 L20
Pointe Noire, Congo . 46 E2
Poisonbush Ra., Australia 52 D3
Poitiers, France . . . 18 C4
Pojoaque Valley, U.S.A. 73 J11
Pokaran, India 36 F7
Pokataroo, Australia . 55 D4
Pokrovsk, Russia . . 22 D8
Pokrovsk, Russia . . 25 C13
Polacca, U.S.A. . . . 73 J8
Polan, Iran 39 E9
Poland ■, Europe . . 17 C10
Polatsk = Polotsk, Belorussia 22 C4
Polcura, Chile 80 D2
Polden Hills, U.K. . . 11 F5
Polesye, Belorussia . 22 D4
Polevskoy, Russia . . 22 C11
Polewali, Indonesia . 33 E5
Poli, Cameroon . . . 46 C2
Polillo Is., Phil. . . . 33 B6
Políyiros, Greece . . 21 D10
Pollachi, India 36 P10
Pollock, U.S.A. . . . 70 C4
Polnovat, Russia . . 24 C7
Polo, U.S.A. 70 E10
Polotsk, Belorussia . 22 C4
Polson, U.S.A. 72 C6
Poltava, Ukraine . . . 23 E5
Polunochnoye, Russia 22 B11

Polyarny, Russia 22 A5
Polynesia, Pac. Oc. .. 57 H11
Polynésie française
  = French
  Polynesia ■, Pac. Oc. 57 J13
Pombal, Brazil 79 E11
Pombal, Portugal ... 19 C1
Pomeroy, Ohio, U.S.A. 68 F4
Pomeroy, Wash.,
  U.S.A. 72 C5
Pomona, U.S.A. 73 J5
Pompano Beach,
  U.S.A. 69 M5
Pompeys Pillar, U.S.A. 72 D10
Ponape = Pohnpei,
  Pac. Oc. 56 G7
Ponask, L., Canada . 62 B1
Ponass L., Canada .. 65 C8
Ponca, U.S.A. 70 D6
Ponca City, U.S.A. .. 71 G6
Ponce, Puerto Rico .. 75 D11
Ponchatoula, U.S.A. . 71 K9
Poncheville, L., Canada 62 B4
Pond Inlet, Canada .. 61 A12
Pondicherry, India .. 36 P11
Ponds, I. of, Canada . 63 B8
Ponferrada, Spain ... 19 A2
Ponnani, India 36 P9
Ponnyadaung, Burma 37 J19
Ponoka, Canada 64 C6
Ponorogo, Indonesia . 33 G14
Ponoi, Russia 22 A7
Ponoi →, Russia ... 22 A7
Ponoka, Canada 64 C6
Ponta Grossa, Brazil . 80 B6
Ponta Pora, Brazil .. 80 A5
Pontarlier, France .. 18 C7
Pontchartrain, L.,
  U.S.A. 71 K9
Ponte Nova, Brazil .. 79 H10
Pontedera, Italy 20 C4
Pontefract, U.K. 10 D6
Ponteix, Canada 65 D7
Pontevedra, Spain .. 19 A1
Pontiac, Ill., U.S.A. . 70 E10
Pontiac, Mich., U.S.A. 68 D4
Pontian Kecil, Malaysia 34 T16
Pontianak, Indonesia . 32 E3
Pontic Mts. = Kuzey
  Anadolu Dağları,
  Turkey 23 F6
Pontine Is. = Ponziane,
  Isole, Italy 20 D5
Pontine Mts. = Kuzey
  Anadolu Dağları,
  Turkey 23 F6
Ponton →, Canada . 64 B5
Pontypool, U.K. 11 F4
Pontypridd, U.K. ... 11 F4
Ponziane, Isole, Italy . 20 D5
Poochera, Australia .. 55 E1
Poole, U.K. 11 G6
Pooley I., Canada .. 64 C3
Poona = Pune, India . 36 K8
Pooncarie, Australia . 55 E3
Poopelloe L., Australia 55 E3
Poopó, L. de, Bolivia . 78 G5
Popanyinning,
  Australia 53 F2
Popayán, Colombia .. 78 C3
Poperinge, Belgium . 15 D2
Popigay, Russia 25 B12
Popilta, L., Australia . 55 E3
Popio L., Australia .. 55 E3
Poplar, U.S.A. 70 A2
Poplar →, Man.,
  Canada 65 C9
Poplar →, N.W.T.,
  Canada 64 A4
Poplar Bluff, U.S.A. . 71 G9
Poplarville, U.S.A. .. 71 K10
Popocatepetl, Mexico 74 D5
Popocatépetl, Volcán,
  Mexico 74 D5
Popokabaka, Zaïre .. 46 F3
Porbandar, India ... 36 J6
Porcher I., Canada .. 64 C2
Porcupine →, Canada 65 B8
Porcupine →, U.S.A. 60 B5
Pori, Finland 9 F16
Porjus, Sweden 8 C15
Porkkala, Finland .. 9 G18
Porlamar, Venezuela . 78 A6
Poronaysk, Russia .. 25 E15
Poroshiri-Dake, Japan 28 C11
Porpoise B., Antarctica 5 C9
Porretta, Passo di, Italy 20 B4
Porsangen, Norway . 8 A18
Port Adelaide,
  Australia 55 E2
Port Alberni, Canada . 64 D4
Port Alfred, Canada . 63 C5
Port Alfred, S. Africa . 48 E4
Port Alice, Canada .. 64 C3
Port Allegany, U.S.A. 68 E6
Port Allen, U.S.A. .. 71 K9
Port Alma, Australia . 54 C5
Port Angeles, U.S.A. . 72 B2
Port Antonio, Jamaica 74 J17
Port Aransas, U.S.A. 71 M6
Port Arthur, Australia 54 G4
Port Arthur, U.S.A. .. 71 L8
Port au Port B., Canada 63 C8
Port-au-Prince, Haiti . 75 D10
Port Augusta, Australia 55 E2
Port Augusta West,
  Australia 55 E2
Port Austin, U.S.A. . 62 D3
Port Bergé Vaovao,
  Madag. 49 B8
Port Blair, India 34 G2
Port Blandford, Canada 63 C9

Port Bradshaw,
  Australia 54 A2
Port Broughton,
  Australia 55 E2
Port Burwell, Canada . 62 D3
Port-Cartier, Canada . 63 B6
Port Chalmers, N.Z. . 51 L3
Port Chester, U.S.A. . 68 E9
Port Clements, Canada 64 C2
Port Clinton, U.S.A. . 68 E4
Port Colborne, Canada 62 D4
Port Coquitlam,
  Canada 64 D4
Port Curtis, Australia . 54 C5
Port Darwin, Australia 52 B5
Port Darwin, Falk. Is. . 80 G5
Port Davey, Australia . 54 G4
Port Dickson, Malaysia 34 S14
Port Douglas, Australia 54 B4
Port Edward, Canada . 64 C2
Port Elgin, Canada .. 62 D3
Port Elizabeth,
  S. Africa 48 E4
Port Ellen, U.K. 12 F2
Port en Bessin, France 18 B3
Port Erin, I. of Man . 10 C3
Port Essington,
  Australia 52 B5
Port Etienne =
  Nouâdhibou,
  Mauritania 44 D1
Port Fairy, Australia . 55 F3
Port-Gentil, Gabon .. 46 E1
Port Gibson, U.S.A. . 71 K9
Port Glasgow, U.K. .. 12 F4
Port Harcourt, Nigeria 44 H6
Port Hardy, Canada .. 64 C3
Port Harrison =
  Inoucdjouac, Canada 61 C12
Port Hawkesbury,
  Canada 63 C7
Port Hedland, Australia 52 D2
Port Henry, U.S.A. .. 68 C9
Port Hood, Canada .. 63 C7
Port Hope, Canada .. 62 D4
Port Huron, U.S.A. .. 68 D4
Port Isabel, U.S.A. .. 71 M6
Port Jefferson, U.S.A. 68 E9
Port Kelang =
  Pelabuhan Kelang,
  Malaysia 34 S14
Port Kembla, Australia 55 E5
Port Kenny, Australia 55 E1
Port-la-Nouvelle,
  France 18 E5
Port Laoise, Ireland . 13 C4
Port Lavaca, U.S.A. . 71 L6
Port Lincoln, Australia 55 E2
Port Loko, S. Leone . 44 G2
Port Louis, Mauritius . 35 G4
Port Lyautey = Kenitra,
  Morocco 44 B3
Port MacDonnell,
  Australia 55 F3
Port Macquarie,
  Australia 55 E5
Port Maria, Jamaica . 74 J17
Port Mellon, Canada . 64 D4
Port-Menier, Canada . 63 C7
Port Moresby,
  Papua N. G. 56 H6
Port Mouton, Canada 63 D7
Port Musgrave,
  Australia 54 A3
Port Nelson, Canada . 65 B10
Port Nolloth, S. Africa 48 D2
Port Nouveau-Québec,
  Canada 61 C13
Port O'Connor, U.S.A. 71 L6
Port of Spain,
  Trin. & Tob. 74 S20
Port Orchard, U.S.A. . 72 C2
Port Orford, U.S.A. . 72 E1
Port Pegasus, N.Z. .. 51 M1
Port Perry, Canada .. 62 D4
Port Phillip B.,
  Australia 55 F3
Port Pirie, Australia . 55 E2
Port Radium = Echo
  Bay, Canada 60 B8
Port Renfrew, Canada 64 D4
Port Roper, Australia . 54 A2
Port Rowan, Canada . 62 D3
Port Safaga = Bûr
  Safâga, Egypt ... 45 C11
Port Said = Bûr Sa'îd,
  Egypt 45 B11
Port St. Joe, U.S.A. . 69 L3
Port St. Johns,
  S. Africa 49 E4
Port-St.-Louis-du-
  Rhône, France ... 18 E6
Port Sanilac, U.S.A. . 62 D3
Port Saunders, Canada 63 B8
Port Shepstone,
  S. Africa 49 E5
Port Simpson, Canada 64 C2
Port Stanley = Stanley,
  Falk. Is. 80 G5
Port Stanley, Canada . 62 D3
Port Sudan = Bûr
  Sûdân, Sudan ... 45 E12
Port Talbot, U.K. 11 F4
Port Townsend, U.S.A. 72 B2
Port-Vendres, France . 18 E5
Port Vladimir, Russia . 22 A5
Port Wakefield,
  Australia 55 E2
Port Washington,
  U.S.A. 68 D2
Port Weld, Malaysia . 34 Q13

Portachuelo, Bolivia .. 78 G6
Portadown, U.K. 13 B5
Portage, U.S.A. 70 D10
Portage La Prairie,
  Canada 65 D9
Portageville, U.S.A. . 71 G10
Portalegre, Portugal . 19 C2
Portales, U.S.A. 71 H3
Portarlington, Ireland 13 C4
Porter L., N.W.T.,
  Canada 65 A7
Porter L., Sask.,
  Canada 65 B7
Porterville, S. Africa . 48 E2
Porterville, U.S.A. .. 73 H4
Porthcawl, U.K. 11 F4
Porthill, U.S.A. 72 B5
Portile de Fier, Europe 17 F11
Portimão, Portugal .. 19 D1
Portland, N.S.W.,
  Australia 55 E4
Portland, Vic., Australia 55 F3
Portland, Maine, U.S.A. 63 D5
Portland, Mich., U.S.A. 68 D3
Portland, Oreg., U.S.A. 72 D2
Portland, I. of, U.K. . 11 G5
Portland B., Australia 55 F3
Portland Bill, U.K. .. 11 G5
Portland Prom.,
  Canada 61 C12
Portlands Roads,
  Australia 54 A3
Portneuf, Canada ... 63 C5
Porto, Portugal 19 B1
Pôrto Alegre, Brazil . 80 C6
Porto Amboim =
  Gunza, Angola ... 46 G2
Pôrto de Móz, Brazil . 79 D8
Porto Empédocle, Italy 20 F5
Pôrto Esperança, Brazil 78 G7
Pôrto Franco, Brazil . 79 E9
Pôrto Mendes, Brazil . 80 A6
Pôrto Murtinho, Brazil 78 H7
Pôrto Nacional, Brazil 79 F9
Porto Novo, Benin .. 44 G5
Porto Santo, Madeira 44 B1
Pôrto Seguro, Brazil . 79 G11
Pôrto Tórres, Italy .. 20 D3
Pôrto União, Brazil .. 80 B6
Pôrto Válter, Brazil . 78 E4
Porto Vecchio, France 18 F8
Pôrto Velho, Brazil .. 78 E6
Portoferraio, Italy ... 20 C4
Portola, U.S.A. 72 G3
Portoscuso, Italy ... 20 E3
Portoviejo, Ecuador . 78 D2
Portpatrick, U.K. ... 12 G3
Portree, U.K. 12 D2
Portrush, U.K. 13 A5
Portsmouth, Domin. . 74 M20
Portsmouth, U.K. ... 11 G6
Portsmouth, N.H.,
  U.S.A. 68 D10
Portsmouth, Ohio,
  U.S.A. 68 F4
Portsmouth, Va.,
  U.S.A. 68 G7
Portsoy, U.K. 12 D6
Porttipahta, Finland . 8 B19
Portugal ■, Europe . 19 C2
Portuguese-Guinea =
  Guinea-Bissau ■,
  Africa 44 F2
Portumna, Ireland .. 13 C3
Porvenir, Chile 80 G2
Porvoo = Borgå,
  Finland 9 F18
Posadas, Argentina .. 80 B5
Posht-e-Badam, Iran . 39 C7
Poso, Indonesia 33 E6
Posse, Brazil 79 F9
Possel, C.A.R. 46 C3
Possession I.,
  Antarctica 5 D11
Post, U.S.A. 71 J4
Post Falls, U.S.A. ... 72 C5
Poste Maurice Cortier,
  Algeria 44 D5
Postmasburg, S. Africa 48 D3
Postojna, Slovenia .. 20 B6
Potchefstroom,
  S. Africa 48 D4
Poteau, U.S.A. 71 H7
Poteet, U.S.A. 71 L5
Potenza, Italy 20 D6
Poteriteri, L., N.Z. .. 51 M1
Potgietersrus, S. Africa 49 C4
Poti, Georgia 23 F7
Potiskum, Nigeria .. 44 F7
Potomac →, U.S.A. . 68 F7
Potosí, Bolivia 78 G5
Pototan, Phil. 33 B6
Potrerillos, Chile ... 80 B3
Potsdam, Germany .. 16 B7
Potsdam, U.S.A. ... 68 C8
Potter, U.S.A. 70 E3
Pottstown, U.S.A. .. 68 E8
Pottsville, U.S.A. ... 68 E8
Pottuvil, Sri Lanka .. 36 R12
Pouce Coupé, Canada 64 B4
Poughkeepsie, U.S.A. 68 E9
Poulaphouca Res.,
  Ireland 13 C5
Poulsbo, U.S.A. 72 C2
Pouso Alegre, Brazil . 79 F7
Povenets, Russia ... 22 B5
Poverty B., N.Z. ... 51 H7
Póvoa de Varzim,
  Portugal 19 B1
Powassan, Canada .. 62 C4
Powder →, U.S.A. .. 70 B2
Powder River, U.S.A. 72 E10

Powell, U.S.A. 72 D9
Powell, L., U.S.A. ... 73 H8
Powell River, Canada 64 D4
Powers, Mich., U.S.A. 68 C2
Powers, Oreg., U.S.A. 72 E1
Powers Lake, U.S.A. . 70 A3
Powys □, U.K. 11 E4
Poyang Hu, China .. 31 D6
Poyarkovo, Russia .. 25 E13
Požarevac,
  Serbia, Yug. 21 B9
Poznań, Poland 16 B8
Pozo Almonte, Chile . 78 H5
Pozoblanco, Spain .. 19 C3
Prachin Buri, Thailand 34 E6
Prachuap Khiri Khan,
  Thailand 34 G5
Prado, Brazil 79 G11
Prague = Praha,
  Czech. 16 C7
Praha, Czech. 16 C7
Praid, Romania 17 E12
Prainha, Amazonas,
  Brazil 78 E6
Prainha, Pará, Brazil . 79 D8
Prairie, Australia ... 54 C3
Prairie →, U.S.A. .. 71 H5
Prairie City, U.S.A. . 72 D4
Prairie du Chien,
  U.S.A. 70 D9
Prairies, Canada ... 60 C9
Prapat, Indonesia ... 32 D1
Prata, Brazil 79 G9
Prato, Italy 20 C4
Pratt, U.S.A. 71 G5
Prattville, U.S.A. ... 69 J2
Pravia, Spain 19 A2
Praya, Indonesia ... 32 F5
Preeceville, Canada . 65 C8
Prelate, Canada 65 C7
Premier, Canada ... 64 B3
Premont, U.S.A. ... 71 M5
Prentice, U.S.A. ... 70 C9
Prenzlau, Germany . 16 B6
Preobrazheniye, Russia 28 C6
Prepansko Jezero,
  Macedonia 21 D9
Preparis North
  Channel, Ind. Oc. . 34 E2
Preparis South
  Channel, Ind. Oc. . 34 E2
Přerov, Czech. 17 D8
Prescott, Canada ... 62 D4
Prescott, Ariz., U.S.A. 73 J7
Prescott, Ark., U.S.A. 71 J8
Preservation Inlet, N.Z. 51 M1
Presho, U.S.A. 70 D4
Presidencia Roque
  Saenz Peña,
  Argentina 80 B4
Presidente Epitácio,
  Brazil 79 H8
Presidente Hermes,
  Brazil 78 F6
Presidente Prudente,
  Brazil 79 H8
Presidio, U.S.A. 71 L2
Prespa, L. = Prepansko
  Jezero,
  Macedonia 21 D9
Presque Isle, U.S.A. . 63 C6
Prestbury, U.K. 11 F5
Presteigne, U.K. ... 11 E5
Preston, U.K. 10 D5
Preston, Idaho, U.S.A. 72 E8
Preston, Minn., U.S.A. 70 D8
Preston, Nev., U.S.A. 72 G6
Preston, C., Australia 52 D2
Prestonpans, U.K. .. 12 F6
Prestwick, U.K. 12 F4
Pretoria, S. Africa .. 49 D4
Préveza, Greece ... 21 E9
Prey-Veng, Cambodia 34 G8
Pribilof Is., Bering S. . 4 D17
Příbram, Czech. 16 D7
Price, U.S.A. 72 G8
Price I., Canada 64 C3
Prichard, U.S.A. ... 69 K1
Prieska, S. Africa ... 48 D3
Priest L., U.S.A. 72 B5
Priest River, U.S.A. . 72 B5
Priestly, Canada ... 64 C3
Prikaspiyskaya
  Nizmennost, Asia . 23 E8
Prilep,
  Macedonia 21 D9
Priluki, Ukraine 23 D5
Prime Seal I., Australia 54 G4
Primrose L., Canada . 65 C7
Prince Albert, Canada 65 C7
Prince Albert, S. Africa 48 E3
Prince Albert Mts.,
  Antarctica 5 D11
Prince Albert Nat. Park,
  Canada 65 C7
Prince Albert Pen.,
  Canada 60 A8
Prince Albert Sd.,
  Canada 60 A8
Prince Alfred, C.,
  Canada 4 B1
Prince Charles I.,
  Canada 61 B12
Prince Charles Mts.,
  Antarctica 5 D6
Prince Edward I. □,
  Canada 63 C7
Prince Edward Is.,
  Ind. Oc. 35 J2
Prince George, Canada 64 C4
Prince of Wales, C.,
  U.S.A. 58 C3

Prince of Wales I.,
  Australia 54 A3
Prince of Wales I.,
  Canada 60 A10
Prince of Wales I.,
  U.S.A. 64 B2
Prince Patrick I.,
  Canada 4 B2
Prince Regent Inlet,
  Canada 4 B3
Princess Charlotte B.,
  Australia 54 A3
Princess May Ras.,
  Australia 52 C4
Princess Royal I.,
  Canada 64 C3
Princeton, Canada .. 64 D4
Princeton, Ill., U.S.A. 70 E10
Princeton, Ind., U.S.A. 68 F2
Princeton, Ky., U.S.A. 68 G2
Princeton, Mo., U.S.A. 70 E8
Princeton, N.J., U.S.A. 68 E8
Princeton, W. Va.,
  U.S.A. 68 G5
Principe, I. de, Atl. Oc. 42 F4
Principe Chan., Canada 64 C2
Principe da Beira,
  Brazil 78 F6
Prineville, U.S.A. ... 72 D3
Prins Harald Kyst,
  Antarctica 5 D4
Prinsesse Astrid Kyst,
  Antarctica 5 D3
Prinsesse Ragnhild
  Kyst, Antarctica .. 5 D4
Priozersk, Russia ... 22 B5
Pripet = Pripyat →,
  Europe 22 D5
Pripet Marshes =
  Polesye, Belorussia 22 D4
Pripyat →, Europe .. 22 D5
Pripyat Marshes =
  Polesye, Belorussia 22 D4
Priština, Serbia, Yug. . 21 C9
Privas, France 18 D6
Privolzhskaya
  Vozvyshennost,
  Russia 23 D8
Prizren, Serbia, Yug. . 21 C9
Probolinggo, Indonesia 33 G15
Proddatur, India 36 M11
Progreso, Mexico ... 74 C7
Prokopyevsk, Russia . 24 D9
Prome = Pyè, Burma 37 K19
Prophet →, Canada . 64 B4
Propriá, Brazil 79 F11
Proserpine, Australia . 54 C4
Prosser, U.S.A. 72 C4
Prostějov, Czech. ... 16 D8
Proston, Australia ... 55 D5
Protection, U.S.A. .. 71 G5
Provence, France ... 18 E6
Providence, Ky., U.S.A. 68 G2
Providence, R.I., U.S.A. 68 E10
Providence Bay,
  Canada 62 C3
Providence Mts.,
  U.S.A. 73 J6
Providencia, I. de,
  Colombia 75 E8
Provideniya, Russia . 25 C19
Provins, France 18 B5
Provo, U.S.A. 72 F8
Provost, Canada ... 65 C6
Prud'homme, Canada 65 C7
Pruszków, Poland .. 17 B10
Prut →, Romania .. 17 F14
Prydz B., Antarctica . 5 C6
Pryluky = Priluki,
  Ukraine 23 D5
Pryor, U.S.A. 71 G7
Przemyśl, Poland ... 17 D11
Przeworsk, Poland .. 17 C11
Przhevalsk, Kirghizia . 24 E8
Pskov, Russia 22 C4
Puán, Argentina ... 80 D4
Pucallpa, Peru 78 E4
Pudozh, Russia 22 B6
Pudukkottai, India .. 36 P11
Puebla, Mexico 74 D5
Puebla, Puebla, Mexico 74 D5
Pueblo, U.S.A. 70 F2
Pueblo Hundido, Chile 80 B2
Puelches, Argentina . 80 D3
Puelén, Argentina ... 80 D3
Puente Alto, Chile .. 80 C2
Puente-Genil, Spain . 19 D3
Puerco →, U.S.A. .. 73 J10
Puerto Aisén, Chile . 80 F2
Puerto Ayacucho,
  Venezuela 78 B5
Puerto Barrios,
  Guatemala 74 D7
Puerto Bermejo,
  Argentina 80 B5
Puerto Bermúdez, Peru 78 F4
Puerto Bolívar,
  Ecuador 78 D3
Puerto Cabello,
  Venezuela 78 A5
Puerto Cabezas, Nic. . 75 E8
Puerto Carreño,
  Colombia 78 B5
Puerto Chicama, Peru 78 E3
Puerto Coig, Argentina 80 G3
Puerto Cortés,
  Honduras 74 D7
Puerto Cumarebo,
  Venezuela 78 A5
Puerto de Santa María,
  Spain 19 D2

Puerto del Rosario,
  Canary Is. 44 C2
Puerto Deseado,
  Argentina 80 F3
Puerto Heath, Bolivia . 78 F5
Puerto La Cruz,
  Venezuela 78 A6
Puerto Leguízamo,
  Colombia 78 D4
Puerto Lobos,
  Argentina 80 E3
Puerto Madryn,
  Argentina 80 E3
Puerto Maldonado,
  Peru 78 F5
Puerto Montt, Chile . 80 E2
Puerto Morelos,
  Mexico 74 C7
Puerto Natales, Chile . 80 G2
Puerto Páez, Venezuela 78 B5
Puerto Pinasco,
  Paraguay 80 A5
Puerto Pirámides,
  Argentina 80 E4
Puerto Plata,
  Dom. Rep. 75 D10
Puerto Princesa, Phil. 33 C5
Puerto Quellón, Chile 80 E2
Puerto Rico ■,
  W. Indies 75 D11
Puerto Sastre,
  Paraguay 78 H7
Puerto Suárez, Bolivia 78 G7
Puerto Wilches,
  Colombia 78 B4
Puertollano, Spain ... 19 C3
Pueyrredón, L.,
  Argentina 80 F2
Pugachev, Kazakhstan 22 D8
Puget Sd., U.S.A. ... 72 C2
Púglia □, Italy 20 D7
Pügünzi, Iran 39 E8
Puigcerdá, Spain ... 19 A6
Pukaki L., N.Z. 51 L3
Pukapuka, Cook Is. .. 57 J11
Pukatawagan, Canada 65 B8
Pukekohe, N.Z. 51 G5
Pulaski, N.Y., U.S.A. . 68 D7
Pulaski, Tenn., U.S.A. 69 H2
Pulaski, Va., U.S.A. . 68 G5
Pulicat, L., India 36 N12
Pullman, U.S.A. 72 C5
Pulog, Phil. 33 A6
Pumlumon Fawr, U.K. 11 E4
Puna, Bolivia 78 G5
Puná, I., Ecuador ... 78 D2
Punakha, Bhutan ... 37 F16
Punata, Bolivia 78 G5
Punch, India 36 C9
Pune, India 36 K8
Punjab □, India 36 D9
Punjab □, Pakistan . 36 D9
Puno, Peru 78 G4
Punta Alta, Argentina 80 D4
Punta Arenas, Chile . 80 G2
Punta de Díaz, Chile . 80 B2
Punta Gorda, U.S.A. . 69 M5
Puntabie, Australia .. 55 E1
Puntarenas, Costa Rica 75 F8
Punto Fijo, Venezuela 78 A4
Punxsutawney, U.S.A. 68 E6
Puquio, Peru 78 F4
Pur →, Russia 24 C8
Purace, Vol., Colombia 78 C3
Puralia = Puruliya,
  India 37 H15
Purbeck, Isle of, U.K. 11 G5
Purcell, U.S.A. 71 H6
Puri, India 37 K14
Purmerend, Neths. .. 15 B4
Purnia, India 37 G15
Pursat, Cambodia ... 34 F7
Purukcahu, Indonesia 32 E4
Puruliya, India 37 H15
Purus →, Brazil ... 78 D6
Purwakarta, Indonesia 33 G12
Purwodadi, Jawa,
  Indonesia 33 G14
Purwodadi, Jawa,
  Indonesia 33 G13
Purwokerto, Indonesia 33 G13
Purworejo, Indonesia 33 G14
Pusan, S. Korea 31 C7
Pushchino, Russia .. 25 D16
Pushkino, Russia ... 23 D8
Putahow L., Canada . 65 B8
Putao, Burma 37 F20
Putaruru, N.Z. 51 H5
Puthein Myit →,
  Burma 37 M19
Putignano, Italy 20 D7
Puting, Tanjung,
  Indonesia 32 E4
Putorana, Gory, Russia 25 C10
Puttalam, Sri Lanka . 36 Q11
Putten, Neths. 15 B5
Puttgarden, Germany 16 A5
Putumayo →,
  S. Amer. 78 D5
Putussibau, Indonesia 32 D4
Puy-de-Dôme, France 18 D5
Puy-de-Dôme □,
  France 18 D5
Puyallup, U.S.A. ... 72 C2
Püzeh Rīg, Iran 39 E8
Pweto, Zaïre 46 F5
Pwllheli, U.K. 10 E3
Pya-ozero, Russia .. 22 A5
Pyapon, Burma 37 L19
Pyasina →, Russia . 25 B9
Pyatigorsk, Russia .. 23 F7
Pyè, Burma 37 K19

Pyinmana, Burma . . . 37 K20
P'yŏngyang, N. Korea 31 C7
Pyote, U.S.A. 71 K3
Pyramid L., U.S.A. . . 72 G4
Pyrénées, Europe 18 E4
Pyrénées-
Atlantiques □,
France 18 E3
Pyrénées-Orientales □,
France 18 E5
Pyu, Burma 37 K20

Q

Qaanaaq = Thule,
Greenland 4 B4
Qachasnek, S. Africa . 49 E4
Qādib, Yemen 40 E5
Qa'el Jafr, Jordan . . . 41 E5
Qa'emābād, Iran 39 D9
Qā'emshahr, Iran . . . 39 B7
Qahremānshahr, Iran =
Bākhtarān, Iran . . 38 C5
Qaidam Pendi, China . 30 C4
Qajarīyeh, Iran 39 D6
Qal'at al Akhḍar,
Si. Arabia 38 E3
Qal'at Sukkar, Iraq . . 38 D5
Qal'eh Darreh, Iran . . 38 B5
Qal'eh Shaharak,
Afghan. 36 B4
Qamar, Ghubbat al,
Yemen 40 D5
Qamdo, China 30 C4
Qamruddin Karez,
Pakistan 36 D6
Qandahār, Afghan. . . 36 D4
Qandahār □, Afghan. . 36 D4
Qapān, Iran 39 B7
Qaqortoq =
Julianehåb,
Greenland 4 C5
Qâra, Egypt 45 C10
Qaraghandy =
Karaganda,
Kazakhstan 24 E8
Qārah, Si. Arabia . . . 38 D4
Qareh →, Iran 38 B5
Qareh Tekān, Iran . . . 39 B6
Qarqan He →, China 30 C3
Qarshi = Karshi,
Uzbekistan 24 F7
Qartabā, Lebanon . . . 41 A4
Qaryat al Gharab, Iraq 38 D5
Qaryat al 'Ulyā,
Si. Arabia 38 E5
Qasr 'Amra, Jordan . . 38 D3
Qaşr-e Qand, Iran . . . 39 E9
Qasr Farâfra, Egypt . 45 C10
Qatanā, Syria 41 B5
Qatar ■, Asia 39 E6
Qaṭlīsh, Iran 39 B8
Qattâra, Munkhafed el,
Egypt 45 C10
Qattâra Depression =
Qattâra, Munkhafed
el, Egypt 45 C10
Qawām al Ḥamzah,
Iraq 38 D5
Qāyen, Iran 39 C8
Qazaqstan =
Kazakhstan ■, Asia 24 E7
Qazvin, Iran 39 B6
Qena, Egypt 45 C11
Qeqertarsuaq = Disko,
Greenland 4 C5
Qeqertarsuaq =
Godhavn, Greenland 4 C5
Qeshlāq, Iran 38 C5
Qeshm, Iran 39 E8
Qezi'ot, Israel 41 E3
Qibâ', Si. Arabia 38 E5
Qila Safed, Pakistan . 36 E2
Qila Saifullāh, Pakistan 36 D6
Qilian Shan, China . . 30 C4
Qingdao, China 31 C7
Qinghai □, China . . . 30 C4
Qinghai Hu, China . . 30 C5
Qingjiang, China 31 C6
Qinhuangdao, China . 31 C6
Qinzhou, China 30 D5
Qiqihar, China 25 E13
Qiraîya, W. →, Egypt 41 E3
Qiryat Ata, Israel . . . 41 C4
Qiryat Gat, Israel . . . 41 D3
Qiryat Mal'akhi, Israel 41 D3
Qiryat Shemona, Israel 41 B4
Qiryat Yam, Israel . . . 41 C4
Qitai, China 30 B3
Qojūr, Iran 38 B5
Qom, Iran 39 C6
Qomsheh, Iran 39 D6
Qoostanay = Kustanay,
Kazakhstan 24 D7
Qu Xian, China 31 D6
Quairading, Australia . 53 F2
Qualeup, Australia . . . 53 F2
Quambatook, Australia 55 F3
Quambone, Australia . 55 E4
Quamby, Australia . . . 54 C3
Quan Long, Vietnam . 34 H8
Quanah, U.S.A. 71 H5
Quandialla, Australia . 55 E4
Quang Ngai, Vietnam . 34 E10
Quang Yen, Vietnam . 34 B9
Quanzhou, China 31 D6
Quaraí, Brazil 80 C5
Quartzsite, U.S.A. . . . 73 K6

Quatsino, Canada . . . 64 C3
Quatsino Sd., Canada . 64 C3
Qūchān, Iran 39 B8
Queanbeyan, Australia 55 F4
Québec, Canada 63 C5
Québec □, Canada . . . 63 B6
Queen Alexandra Ra.,
Antarctica 5 E11
Queen Charlotte,
Canada 64 C2
Queen Charlotte Is.,
Canada 64 C2
Queen Charlotte Str.,
Canada 64 C3
Queen Elizabeth Is.,
Canada 58 B10
Queen Mary Land,
Antarctica 5 D7
Queen Maud G.,
Canada 60 B9
Queen Maud Land,
Antarctica 5 D3
Queen Maud Mts.,
Antarctica 5 E13
Queens Chan.,
Australia 52 C4
Queenscliff, Australia . 55 F3
Queensland □,
Australia 54 C3
Queenstown, Australia 54 G4
Queenstown, N.Z. . . . 51 L2
Queenstown, S. Africa 48 E4
Queimadas, Brazil . . . 79 F11
Quela, Angola 46 F3
Quelimane, Mozam. . . 47 H7
Quelpart = Cheju Do,
S. Korea 31 C7
Quemado, N. Mex.,
U.S.A. 73 J9
Quemado, Tex., U.S.A. 71 L4
Quequén, Argentina . . 80 D5
Querétaro, Mexico . . . 74 C4
Querétaro, Querétaro,
Mexico 74 C4
Quesnel, Canada . . ! . 64 C4
Quesnel →, Canada . . 64 C4
Quesnel L., Canada . . 64 C4
Questa, U.S.A. 73 H11
Quetico Prov. Park,
Canada 62 C1
Quetta, Pakistan 36 D5
Quezon City, Phil. . . . 33 B6
Qufār, Si. Arabia 38 E4
Qui Nhon, Vietnam . . 34 F10
Quibaxe, Angola 46 F2
Quibdo, Colombia . . . 78 B3
Quiberon, France 18 C2
Quick, Canada 64 C3
Quiet L., Canada 64 A2
Quilán, C., Chile 80 E2
Quilengues, Angola . . 47 G2
Quilimari, Chile 80 C2
Quilino, Argentina . . . 80 C3
Quill L., Canada 65 C8
Quilla, C., Canada . . . 64 A5
Quime, Bolivia 78 G5
Quimilí, Argentina . . . 80 B4
Quimper, France 18 B1
Quimperlé, France . . . 18 C2
Quincy, Calif., U.S.A. . 72 G3
Quincy, Fla., U.S.A. . . 69 K3
Quincy, Ill., U.S.A. . . 70 F9
Quincy, Mass., U.S.A. 68 D10
Quincy, Wash., U.S.A. 72 C4
Quines, Argentina . . . 80 C3
Quinga, Mozam. 47 H8
Quintanar de la Orden,
Spain 19 C4
Quintanar de la Sierra,
Spain 19 B4
Quintero, Chile 80 C2
Quinyambie, Australia 55 E3
Quipungo, Angola . . . 47 G2
Quirindi, Australia . . . 55 E5
Quissanga, Mozam. . . 47 G8
Quitilipi, Argentina . . 80 B4
Quitman, Ga., U.S.A. . 69 K4
Quitman, Miss., U.S.A. 69 J1
Quitman, Tex., U.S.A. 71 J7
Quito, Ecuador 78 D3
Quixadá, Brazil 79 D11
Qumbu, S. Africa 49 E4
Quneitra, Syria 41 B4
Quoin I., Australia . . . 52 B4
Quoin Pt., S. Africa . . 48 E2
Quondong, Australia . 55 E3
Quorn, Australia 55 E2
Quqon = Kokand,
Uzbekistan 24 E8
Qurnat as Sawdâ',
Lebanon 41 A5
Qûs, Egypt 45 C11
Qusaybah, Iraq 38 C4
Quseir, Egypt 45 C11
Qūshchī, Iran 38 B5
Quthing, Lesotho 49 E4
Qūṭīābād, Iran 39 C6
Qyzylorda = Kzyl-Orda,
Kazakhstan 24 E7

R

Raahe, Finland 8 D18
Raasay, U.K. 12 D2
Raasay, Sd. of, U.K. . 12 D2
Raba, Indonesia 33 F5
Rába →, Hungary . . . 17 E9
Rabat, Malta 20 G6
Rabat, Morocco 44 B3

Rabaul, Papua N. G. . 56 H7
Rabbit →, Canada . . 64 B3
Rabbit Lake, Canada . 65 C7
Rabbitskin →, Canada 64 A4
Rābor, Iran 39 D8
Race, C., Canada 63 C9
Rach Gia, Vietnam . . 34 G8
Racine, U.S.A. 68 D2
Radama, Nosy, Madag. 49 A8
Radama, Saikanosy,
Madag. 49 A8
Rădăuţi, Romania . . . 17 E12
Radford, U.S.A. 68 G5
Radisson, Canada . . . 65 C7
Radium Hot Springs,
Canada 64 C5
Radnor Forest, U.K. . 11 E4
Radom, Poland 17 C11
Radomir, Bulgaria . . . 21 C10
Radomsko, Poland . . . 17 C9
Radstock, U.K. 11 F5
Radstock, C., Australia 55 E1
Radville, Canada 65 D8
Rae, Canada 64 A5
Rae Bareli, India 37 F12
Rae Isthmus, Canada . 61 B11
Raeren, Belgium 15 D6
Raeside, L., Australia . 53 E3
Raetihi, N.Z. 51 H5
Rafaela, Argentina . . 80 C4
Rafah, Egypt 41 D3
Rafai, C.A.R. 46 D4
Rafḥā, Si. Arabia 38 D4
Rafsanjān, Iran 39 D8
Raft Pt., Australia . . . 52 C3
Ragachëv, Belarus . . 17 B16
Ragama, Sri Lanka . . 36 R11
Ragged, Mt., Australia 53 F3
Raglan, Australia . . . 54 C5
Raglan, N.Z. 51 G5
Ragusa, Italy 20 F6
Raha, Indonesia 33 E6
Rahad al Bardi, Sudan 45 F9
Rahaeng = Tak,
Thailand 34 D5
Raḥimah, Si. Arabia . . 39 E6
Rahimyar Khan,
Pakistan 36 E7
Rāhjerd, Iran 39 C6
Raichur, India 36 L10
Raigarh, India 37 J13
Raijua, Indonesia . . . 33 F6
Railton, Australia . . . 54 G4
Rainbow Lake, Canada 64 B5
Rainier, U.S.A. 72 C2
Rainier, Mt., U.S.A. . . 72 C3
Rainy L., Canada 65 D10
Rainy River, Canada . 65 D10
Raippur, India 37 J12
Raj Nandgaon, India . 37 J12
Raja, Ujung, Indonesia 32 D1
Raja Ampat,
Kepulauan,
Indonesia 33 E7
Rajahmundry, India . . 37 L12
Rajajooseppi, Finland . 8 B20
Rajang →, Malaysia . 32 D4
Rajapalaiyam, India . . 36 Q10
Rajasthan □, India . . 36 F8
Rajasthan Canal, India 36 E8
Rajgarh, India 36 G10
Rajkot, India 36 H7
Rajpipla, India 36 J8
Rajshahi, Bangla. . . . 37 G16
Rajshahi □, Bangla. . 37 G16
Rakaia, N.Z. 51 K4
Rakaia →, N.Z. 51 K4
Rakan, Ra's, Qatar . . 39 E6
Rakata, Pulau,
Indonesia 32 F3
Rakitnoye, Russia . . . 28 B7
Rakops, Botswana . . . 48 C3
Raleigh, U.S.A. 69 H6
Raleigh B., U.S.A. . . . 69 H7
Ralls, U.S.A. 71 J4
Ram →, Canada . . . 64 A4
Rām Allāh, Jordan . . . 41 D4
Ram Hd., Australia . . 55 F4
Ramanathapuram,
India 36 Q11
Ramanetaka, B. de,
Madag. 49 A8
Ramat Gan, Israel . . . 41 C3
Ramatlhabama,
S. Africa 48 D4
Rambipuji, Indonesia . 33 H15
Ramea, Canada 63 C8
Ramechhap, Nepal . . 37 F15
Ramelau, Indonesia . . 33 F7
Ramgarh, Bihar, India 37 H14
Ramgarh, Raj., India . 36 F7
Rāmhormoz, Iran . . . 39 D6
Ramîan, Iran 39 B7
Ramingining, Australia 54 A2
Ramla, Israel 41 D3
Ramnad =
Ramanathapuram,
India 36 Q11
Ramona, U.S.A. 73 K5
Ramore, Canada 62 C3
Ramotswa, Botswana . 48 C4
Rampur, India 36 E11
Rampur Hat, India . . . 37 G15
Ramree Kyun =
Ramree
Kyun, Burma 37 K18
Ramree Kyun, Burma 37 K18
Rāmsar, Iran 39 B6
Ramsey, U.K. 10 C3
Ramsgate, U.K. 11 F9
Ramtek, India 36 J11

Ranaghat, India 37 H16
Ranau, Malaysia 32 C5
Rancagua, Chile 80 C2
Rancheria →, Canada 64 A3
Ranchester, U.S.A. . . 72 D10
Ranchi, India 37 H14
Randers, Denmark . . . 9 H11
Randfontein, S. Africa 49 D4
Randolph, U.S.A. 72 F8
Råne älv →, Sweden . 8 D17
Rangaunu B., N.Z. . . . 51 F4
Rangeley, U.S.A. 68 C10
Rangely, U.S.A. 72 F9
Ranger, U.S.A. 71 J5
Rangia, India 37 F17
Rangiora, N.Z. 51 K4
Rangitaiki →, N.Z. . . 51 G6
Rangitata →, N.Z. . . 51 K3
Rangkasbitung,
Indonesia 33 G12
Rangon →, Burma . . 37 L20
Rangoon, Burma 37 L20
Rangpur, Bangla. . . . 37 G16
Rani Bennur, India . . 36 M9
Raniganj, India 37 H15
Raniwara, India 36 G8
Rāniyah, Iraq 38 B5
Ranken →, Australia . 54 C2
Rankin, U.S.A. 71 K4
Rankin Inlet, Canada . 60 B10
Rankins Springs,
Australia 55 E4
Rannoch, L., U.K. . . . 12 E4
Rannoch Moor, U.K. . 12 E4
Ranobe, Helodranon' i,
Madag. 49 C7
Ranohira, Madag. . . . 49 C8
Ranomafana,
Toamasina, Madag. 49 B8
Ranomafana, Toliara,
Madag. 49 C8
Ranong, Thailand . . . 34 H5
Rānsa, Iran 39 C6
Ransiki, Indonesia . . . 33 E8
Rantau, Indonesia . . . 32 E5
Rantauprapat,
Indonesia 32 D1
Rantemario,
Indonesia 33 E5
Rantoul, U.S.A. 68 E1
Rapa, Pac. Oc. 57 K13
Rāpch, Iran 39 E8
Rapid →, Canada . . . 64 B3
Rapid City, U.S.A. . . . 70 D3
Rapid River, U.S.A. . . 68 C2
Rapides des Joachims,
Canada 62 C4
Rarotonga, Cook Is. . . 57 K12
Ra's al 'Ayn, Syria . . 38 B4
Ra's al Khaymah,
U.A.E. 39 E8
Ra's al-Unuf, Libya . . 45 B8
Ra's an Naqb, Jordan 41 F4
Ras Bânâs, Egypt . . . 45 D12
Ras Dashen, Ethiopia 45 F12
Râs Timirist,
Mauritania 44 E1
Rasa, Punta, Argentina 80 E4
Rashad, Sudan 45 F11
Rashîd, Egypt 45 B11
Rasht, Iran 39 B6
Rason L., Australia . . 53 E3
Rasra, India 37 G13
Rat Buri, Thailand . . . 34 F5
Rat Is., U.S.A. 60 C1
Rat River, Canada . . . 64 A6
Ratangarh, India 36 E9
Raṭāwī, Iraq 38 D5
Rath Luirc, Ireland . . 13 D3
Rathdrum, Ireland . . . 13 D5
Rathenow, Germany . 16 B6
Rathkeale, Ireland . . . 13 D3
Rathlin, U.K. 13 A5
Rathlin O'Birne I.,
Ireland 13 B3
Ratlam, India 36 H9
Ratnagiri, India 36 L8
Raton, U.S.A. 71 G2
Rattray Hd., U.K. . . . 12 D7
Ratz, Mt., Canada . . . 64 B2
Raub, Malaysia 34 R14
Raufarhöfn, Iceland . 8 C6
Raukumara Ra., N.Z. . 51 H6
Rauma, Finland 9 F16
Raurkela, India 37 H14
Rausu-Dake, Japan . . 28 B12
Ravānsar, Iran 38 C5
Rāvar, Iran 39 D8
Ravenna, Italy 20 B5
Ravenna, U.S.A. 70 E5
Ravensburg, Germany 16 E5
Ravenshoe, Australia . 54 B4
Ravensthorpe,
Australia 53 F3
Ravenswood, Australia 54 C4
Ravenswood, U.S.A. . 68 F5
Ravi →, Pakistan . . . 36 D7
Rawalpindi, Pakistan . 36 C8
Rawāndūz, Iraq 38 B5
Rawdon, Canada 62 C5
Rawene, N.Z. 51 F4
Rawlinna, Australia . . 53 F4
Rawlins, U.S.A. 72 F10
Rawlinson Ra.,
Australia 53 D4
Rawson, Argentina . . 80 E3
Ray, U.S.A. 70 A3
Ray, C., Canada 63 C8
Rayadurg, India 36 M10
Rayagada, India 37 K13
Raychikhinsk, Russia . 25 E13

Rāyen, Iran 39 D8
Raymond, Canada . . . 64 D6
Raymond, U.S.A. 72 C2
Raymondville, U.S.A. . 71 M6
Raymore, Canada . . . 65 C8
Rayne, U.S.A. 71 K8
Rayong, Thailand . . . 34 F6
Rayville, U.S.A. 71 J9
Raz, Pte. du, France . 18 B1
Razan, Iran 39 C6
Razdolnoye, Russia . . 28 C5
Razeh, Iran 39 C6
Razgrad, Bulgaria . . . 21 C12
Ré, I. de, France 18 C3
Reading, U.K. 11 F7
Reading, U.S.A. 68 E8
Realicó, Argentina . . . 80 D4
Ream, Cambodia 34 G7
Rebecca, L., Australia 53 F3
Rebi, Indonesia 33 F8
Rebiana, Libya 45 D9
Rebun-Tō, Japan . . . 28 B10
Recherche, Arch. of
the, Australia 53 F3
Recife, Brazil 79 E12
Recklinghausen,
Germany 15 C7
Reconquista, Argentina 80 B5
Recreo, Argentina . . . 80 B3
Red →, N. Amer. . . . 70 A6
Red →, U.S.A. 71 K9
Red Bay, Canada . . . 63 B8
Red Bluff, U.S.A. . . . 72 F2
Red Bluff L., U.S.A. . 71 K3
Red Cliffs, Australia . 55 E3
Red Cloud, U.S.A. . . . 70 E5
Red Deer, Canada . . . 64 C6
Red Deer →, Alta.,
Canada 65 C6
Red Deer →, Man.,
Canada 65 C8
Red Deer L., Canada . 65 C8
Red Indian L., Canada 63 C8
Red Lake, Canada . . . 65 C10
Red Lake Falls, U.S.A. 70 B6
Red Lodge, U.S.A. . . 72 D9
Red Oak, U.S.A. 70 E7
Red Rock, Canada . . . 62 C2
Red Rock, L., U.S.A. . 70 E8
Red Rocks Pt.,
Australia 53 F4
Red Sea, Asia 40 C2
Red Sucker L., Canada 65 C10
Red Tower Pass =
Turnu Rosu Pasul,
Romania 17 F12
Red Wing, U.S.A. . . . 70 C8
Redbridge, U.K. 11 F8
Redcar, U.K. 10 C6
Redcliff, Canada 65 C6
Redcliffe, Australia . . 55 D5
Redcliffe, Mt., Australia 53 E3
Reddersburg, S. Africa 48 D4
Redding, U.S.A. 72 F2
Redditch, U.K. 11 E6
Redfield, U.S.A. 70 C5
Redknife →, Canada . 64 A5
Redlands, U.S.A. 73 K5
Redmond, Australia . . 53 F2
Redmond, U.S.A. 72 D3
Redon, France 18 C2
Redonda, Antigua . . . 74 L19
Redondela, Spain . . . 19 A1
Redondo, Portugal . . 19 C2
Redondo Beach, U.S.A. 73 M8
Redrock Pt., Canada . 64 A5
Redruth, U.K. 11 G2
Redvers, Canada 65 D8
Redwater, Canada . . . 64 C6
Redwood City, U.S.A. 73 H2
Redwood Falls, U.S.A. 70 C7
Ree, L., Ireland 13 C4
Reed, L., Canada 65 C8
Reed City, U.S.A. . . . 68 D3
Reeder, U.S.A. 70 B3
Reedley, U.S.A. 73 H4
Reedsburg, U.S.A. . . . 70 D9
Reedsport, U.S.A. . . . 72 E1
Reefton, N.Z. 51 K3
Refugio, U.S.A. 71 L6
Regensburg, Germany 16 D6
Réggio di Calábria,
Italy 20 E6
Réggio nell' Emilia,
Italy 20 B4
Regina, Canada 65 C8
Rehoboth, Namibia . . 48 C2
Rehovot, Israel 41 D3
Rei-Bouba, Cameroon 45 G7
Reichenbach, Germany 16 C6
Reid, Australia 53 F4
Reid River, Australia . 54 B4
Reidsville, U.S.A. . . . 69 G6
Reigate, U.K. 11 F7
Reims, France 18 B6
Reina Adelaida, Arch.,
Chile 80 G2
Reinbeck, U.S.A. 70 D8
Reindeer →, Canada . 65 B8
Reindeer I., Canada . . 65 C9
Reindeer L., Canada . 65 B8
Reinga, C., N.Z. 51 F4
Reinosa, Spain 19 A3
Reitz, S. Africa 49 D4
Reivilo, S. Africa 48 D3
Rekinniki, Russia 25 C17
Reliance, Canada 65 A7
Remarkable, Mt.,
Australia 55 E2
Rembang, Indonesia . 33 G14
Remeshk, Iran 39 E8
Remich, Lux. 15 E6
Remscheid, Germany . 16 C4
Rendsburg, Germany . 16 A4

Rene, Russia 25 C19
Renfrew, Canada 62 C4
Renfrew, U.K. 12 F4
Rengat, Indonesia . . . 32 E2
Renkum, Neths. 15 C5
Renmark, Australia . . 55 E3
Rennell Sd., Canada . 64 C2
Renner Springs T.O.,
Australia 54 B1
Rennes, France 18 B3
Reno, U.S.A. 72 G4
Reno →, Italy 20 B5
Renovo, U.S.A. 68 E7
Rensselaer, U.S.A. . . 68 E2
Renton, U.S.A. 72 C2
Republic, Mich., U.S.A. 68 B2
Republic, Wash.,
U.S.A. 72 B4
Republican →, U.S.A. 70 F6
Republican City, U.S.A. 70 E5
Repulse Bay, Canada . 61 B11
Requena, Peru 78 E4
Requena, Spain 19 C5
Reserve, Canada 65 C8
Reserve, U.S.A. 73 K9
Resht = Rasht, Iran . . 39 B6
Resistencia, Argentina 80 B5
Reşiţa, Romania 17 F10
Resolution I., Canada . 61 B13
Resolution I., N.Z. . . . 51 L1
Ressano Garcia,
Mozam. 49 D5
Reston, Canada 65 D8
Réthímnon, Greece . . 21 G11
Réunion ■, Ind. Oc. . . 43 J9
Reutlingen, Germany . 16 D4
Reval = Tallinn,
Estonia 22 C3
Revda, Russia 22 C10
Revelstoke, Canada . . 64 C5
Revilla Gigedo, Is.,
Pac. Oc. 57 F16
Revillagigedo I., U.S.A. 64 B2
Rewa, India 37 G12
Rewari, India 36 E10
Rexburg, U.S.A. 72 E8
Rey, Iran 39 C6
Rey Malabo, Eq. Guin. 44 H6
Reykjahlíð, Iceland . . 8 D5
Reykjanes, Iceland . . 8 E2
Reykjavík, Iceland . . . 8 D3
Reynolds, Canada . . . 65 D9
Reynolds Ra., Australia 52 D5
Reynosa, Mexico 74 B5
Rezvān, Iran 39 E8
Rhayader, U.K. 11 E4
Rheden, Neths. 15 B6
Rhein, Canada 65 C8
Rhein →, Europe . . . 15 C6
Rheine, Germany 16 B3
Rheinland-Pfalz □,
Germany 16 C3
Rhin = Rhein →,
Europe 15 C6
Rhine = Rhein →,
Europe 15 C6
Rhineland-Palatinate □
= Rheinland-Pfalz □,
Germany 16 C3
Rhinelander, U.S.A. . . 70 C10
Rhode Island □, U.S.A. 68 E10
Rhodes = Ródhos,
Greece 21 F13
Rhodesia =
Zimbabwe ■, Africa 47 H5
Rhodope Mts. =
Rhodopi Planina,
Bulgaria 21 D11
Rhodopi Planina,
Bulgaria 21 D11
Rhön = Hohe Rhön,
Germany 16 C4
Rhondda, U.K. 11 F4
Rhône □, France 18 D6
Rhône →, France . . . 18 E6
Rhum, U.K. 12 E2
Rhyl, U.K. 10 D4
Rhymney, U.K. 11 F4
Riachão, Brazil 79 E9
Riasi, India 36 C9
Riau □, Indonesia . . . 32 D2
Riau, Kepulauan,
Indonesia 32 D2
Riau Arch. = Riau,
Kepulauan,
Indonesia 32 D2
Ribadeo, Spain 19 A2
Ribatejo, Portugal . . . 19 C1
Ribble →, U.K. 10 C5
Ribe, Denmark 9 J10
Ribeirão Prêto, Brazil 79 H9
Riberalta, Bolivia . . . 78 F5
Riccarton, N.Z. 51 K4
Rice Lake, U.S.A. . . . 70 C9
Rich Hill, U.S.A. 71 F7
Richards Bay, S. Africa 49 D5
Richards L., Canada . 65 B7
Richardson →,
Canada 65 B6
Richardson, U.S.A. . . 70 B3
Richey, Australia 53 F2
Richey, U.S.A. 70 B2
Richfield, Idaho, U.S.A. 72 E6
Richfield, Utah, U.S.A. 73 G8
Richibucto, Canada . . 63 C7
Richland, Ga., U.S.A. . 69 J3
Richland, Oreg., U.S.A. 72 D5
Richland, Wash.,
U.S.A. 72 C4
Richland Center, U.S.A. 70 D9

Richlands, *U.S.A.* 68 G5
Richmond, *N.S.W.,*
  Australia 55 E5
Richmond, *Queens.,*
  Australia 54 C3
Richmond, *N.Z.* 51 J4
Richmond, *S. Africa* . . 49 D5
Richmond, *U.K.* 10 C6
Richmond, *Calif.,*
  U.S.A. 72 H2
Richmond, *Ind., U.S.A.* 68 F3
Richmond, *Ky., U.S.A.* . 68 G3
Richmond, *Mo., U.S.A.* 70 F8
Richmond, *Tex., U.S.A.* 71 L7
Richmond, *Utah,*
  U.S.A. 72 F8
Richmond, *Va., U.S.A.* . 68 G7
Richmond Ra.,
  Australia 55 D5
Richmond-upon-
  Thames, *U.K.* 11 F7
Richton, *U.S.A.* 69 K1
Richwood, *U.S.A.* 68 F5
Ridder, *Kazakhstan* . . 24 D9
Ridgedale, *Canada* . . . 65 C8
Ridgeland, *U.S.A.* 69 J5
Ridgelands, *Australia* . 54 C5
Ridgetown, *Canada* . . 62 D3
Ridgway, *U.S.A.* 68 E6
Riding Mountain Nat.
  Park, *Canada* 65 C8
Ridley, Mt., *Australia* . 53 F3
Ried, *Austria* 16 D6
Riet →, *S. Africa* 48 D3
Rieti, *Italy* 20 C5
Rifle, *U.S.A.* 72 G10
Rifstangi, *Iceland* 8 C5
Rig Rig, *Chad* 45 F7
Riga, *Latvia* 22 C3
Riga, G. of = Rīgas
  Jūras Līcis, *Latvia* . 22 C3
Rīgān, *Iran* 39 D8
Rīgas Jūras Līcis,
  Latvia 22 C3
Rigby, *U.S.A.* 72 E8
Rigestān □, *Afghan.* . . 36 D4
Riggins, *U.S.A.* 72 D5
Rigolet, *Canada* 63 B8
Riihimäki, *Finland* . . . 9 F18
Riiser-Larsen-halvøya,
  Antarctica 5 C4
Rijeka, *Croatia* 20 B6
Rijn →, *Neths.* 15 B4
Rijssen, *Neths.* 15 B6
Rijswijk, *Neths.* 15 B4
Rikuzentakada, *Japan* 28 E10
Riley, *U.S.A.* 72 E4
Rimah, Wadi ar →,
  Si. Arabia 38 E4
Rimbey, *Canada* 64 C6
Rímini, *Italy* 20 B5
Rîmnicu Sărat,
  Romania 17 F13
Rîmnicu Vîlcea,
  Romania 21 B11
Rimouski, *Canada* . . . 63 C6
Rinca, *Indonesia* 33 F5
Rinconada, *Argentina* 80 A3
Ringkøbing, *Denmark* 9 H10
Ringling, *U.S.A.* 72 C8
Ringvassøy, *Norway* . 8 B15
Rinia, *Greece* 21 F11
Rinjani, *Indonesia* . . . 32 F5
Rio Branco, *Brazil* . . . 78 E5
Rio Branco, *Uruguay* . 80 C6
Rio Claro, *Trin. & Tob.* 74 S20
Río Colorado,
  Argentina 80 D4
Río Cuarto, *Argentina* 80 C4
Rio das Pedras,
  Mozam. 49 C6
Rio de Janeiro, *Brazil* 79 H10
Rio de Janeiro □,
  Brazil 79 H10
Rio do Sul, *Brazil* 80 B7
Río Gallegos,
  Argentina 80 G3
Rio Grande, *Argentina* 80 G3
Rio Grande, *Brazil* . . . 80 C6
Rio Grande →, *U.S.A.* 71 N6
Rio Grande City, *U.S.A.* 71 M5
Río Grande del
  Norte →, *N. Amer.* 67 E7
Rio Grande do
  Norte □, *Brazil* . . . 79 E11
Rio Grande do Sul □,
  Brazil 80 B6
Rio Largo, *Brazil* 79 E11
Río Mulatos, *Bolivia* . 78 G5
Río Muni = Mbini □,
  Eq. Guin. 46 D2
Rio Negro, *Brazil* 80 B7
Rio Verde, *Brazil* 79 G8
Rio Vista, *U.S.A.* 72 G3
Riobamba, *Ecuador* . . 78 D3
Ríohacha, *Colombia* . 78 A4
Riosucio, *Caldas,*
  Colombia 78 B3
Riosucio, *Choco,*
  Colombia 78 B3
Riou L., *Canada* 65 B7
Ripon, *U.S.A.* 71 H10
Ripon, *U.K.* 10 C6
Ripon, *U.S.A.* 68 D1
Rishā', *W. ar →,*
  Si. Arabia 38 E5
Rishiri-Tō, *Japan* 28 B10
Rishon le Ziyyon, *Israel* 41 D3
Rison, *U.S.A.* 71 J8
Risør, *Norway* 9 G10
Ritchies Archipelago,
  India 34 F2

Ritzville, *U.S.A.* 72 C4
Rivadavia, *Chile* 80 B2
Rivera, *Uruguay* 80 C5
Riverhead, *U.S.A.* . . . 68 E9
Riverhurst, *Canada* . . 65 C7
Riverina, *Australia* . . . 53 E3
Rivers, *Canada* 65 C8
Rivers, L. of the,
  Canada 65 D7
Rivers Inlet, *Canada* . 64 C3
Riversdale, *S. Africa* . 48 E3
Riverside, *Calif., U.S.A.* 73 K5
Riverside, *Wyo., U.S.A.* 72 F10
Riversleigh, *Australia* 54 B2
Riverton, *Australia* . . . 55 E2
Riverton, *Canada* 65 C9
Riverton, *N.Z.* 51 M1
Riverton, *U.S.A.* 72 E9
Riviera, *Europe* 16 F4
Riviera di Levante, *Italy* 20 B3
Riviera di Ponente,
  Italy 20 C2
Rivière-à-Pierre,
  Canada 63 C5
Rivière-au-Renard,
  Canada 63 C7
Rivière-du-Loup,
  Canada 63 C6
Rivière-Pentecôte,
  Canada 63 C6
Rivne = Rovno,
  Ukraine 23 D4
Rivoli B., *Australia* . . . 55 F3
Riyadh = Ar Riyāḍ,
  Si. Arabia 40 C4
Rize, *Turkey* 23 F7
Rizzuto, C., *Italy* 20 E7
Rjukan, *Norway* 9 G10
Roag, L., *U.K.* 12 C2
Roanne, *France* 18 C6
Roanoke, *Ala., U.S.A.* 69 J3
Roanoke, *Va., U.S.A.* 68 G6
Roanoke →, *U.S.A.* . 69 H7
Roanoke I., *U.S.A.* . . 69 H8
Roanoke Rapids,
  U.S.A. 69 G7
Robbins I., *Australia* . 54 G4
Robe →, *Australia* . . . 52 D2
Robe →, *Ireland* 13 C2
Robert Lee, *U.S.A.* . . . 71 K4
Roberts, *U.S.A.* 72 E7
Robertson, *S. Africa* . 48 E2
Robertson I., *Antarctica* 5 C18
Robertson Ra.,
  Australia 52 D3
Robertsport, *Liberia* . 44 G2
Robertstown, *Australia* 55 E2
Roberval, *Canada* . . . 63 C5
Robeson Chan.,
  Greenland 4 A4
Robinson →,
  Australia 54 B2
Robinson Ra., *Australia* 53 E2
Robinson River,
  Australia 54 B2
Robinvale, *Australia* . 55 E3
Roblin, *Canada* 65 C8
Roboré, *Bolivia* 78 G7
Robson, Mt., *Canada* . 64 C5
Robstown, *U.S.A.* . . . 71 M6
Roca, C. da, *Portugal* . 19 C1
Rocas, I., *Brazil* 79 D12
Rocha, *Uruguay* 80 C6
Rochdale, *U.K.* 10 D5
Rochefort, *Belgium* . . 15 D5
Rochefort, *France* . . . 18 D3
Rochelle, *U.S.A.* 70 E10
Rocher River, *Canada* 64 A6
Rochester, *Canada* . . 64 C6
Rochester, *U.K.* 11 F8
Rochester, *Ind., U.S.A.* 68 E2
Rochester, *Minn.,*
  U.S.A. 70 C8
Rochester, *N.H., U.S.A.* 68 D10
Rochester, *N.Y., U.S.A.* 68 D7
Rock →, *Canada* 64 A3
Rock Hill, *U.S.A.* 69 H5
Rock Island, *U.S.A.* . . 70 E9
Rock Rapids, *U.S.A.* . 70 D6
Rock Springs, *Mont.,*
  U.S.A. 72 C10
Rock Springs, *Wyo.,*
  U.S.A. 72 F9
Rock Valley, *U.S.A.* . . 70 D6
Rockdale, *U.S.A.* 71 K6
Rockefeller Plateau,
  Antarctica 5 E14
Rockford, *U.S.A.* 70 D10
Rockglen, *Canada* . . . 65 D7
Rockhampton,
  Australia 54 C5
Rockhampton Downs,
  Australia 54 B2
Rockingham, *Australia* 53 F2
Rockingham B.,
  Australia 54 B4
Rockingham Forest,
  U.K. 11 E7
Rocklake, *U.S.A.* 70 A5
Rockland, *Idaho,*
  U.S.A. 72 E7
Rockland, *Maine,*
  U.S.A. 63 D6
Rockland, *Mich., U.S.A.* 70 B10
Rockmart, *U.S.A.* . . . 69 H3
Rockport, *Mo., U.S.A.* 70 E7
Rockport, *Tex., U.S.A.* 71 L6
Rockville, *U.S.A.* 68 F7

Rockwall, *U.S.A.* 71 J6
Rockwell City, *U.S.A.* . 70 D7
Rockwood, *U.S.A.* . . . 69 H3
Rocky Ford, *U.S.A.* . . 70 F3
Rocky Gully, *Australia* 53 F2
Rocky Lane, *Canada* . 64 B5
Rocky Mount, *U.S.A.* . 69 H7
Rocky Mountain
  House, *Canada* . . . 64 C6
Rocky Mts., *N. Amer.* 64 C4
Rockyford, *Canada* . . 64 C6
Rod, *Pakistan* 36 E3
Rødbyhavn, *Denmark* 9 J11
Roddickton, *Canada* . 63 B8
Roderick I., *Canada* . . 64 C3
Rodez, *France* 18 D5
Ródhos, *Greece* 21 F13
Rodney, C., *N.Z.* 51 G5
Rodriguez, *Ind. Oc.* . . 35 F5
Roe →, *U.K.* 13 A5
Roebourne, *Australia* . 52 D2
Roebuck B., *Australia* 52 C3
Roebuck Plains,
  Australia 52 C3
Roermond, *Neths.* . . . 15 C5
Roes Welcome Sd.,
  Canada 61 B11
Roeselare, *Belgium* . . 15 D3
Rogagua, L., *Bolivia* . 78 F5
Rogaland fylke □,
  Norway 9 G9
Rogers, *U.S.A.* 71 G7
Rogers City, *U.S.A.* . . 68 C4
Rogerson, *U.S.A.* . . . 72 E6
Rogersville, *U.S.A.* . . 69 G4
Roggan River, *Canada* 62 B4
Roggeveldberge,
  S. Africa 48 E3
Rogoaguado, L.,
  Bolivia 78 F5
Rogue →, *U.S.A.* 72 E1
Rohri, *Pakistan* 36 F6
Rohtak, *India* 36 E10
Roi Et, *Thailand* 34 D7
Rojas, *Argentina* 80 C4
Rojo, C., *Mexico* 74 C5
Rokan →, *Indonesia* . 32 D2
Rokeby, *Australia* . . . 54 A3
Rolândia, *Brazil* 80 A6
Rolette, *U.S.A.* 70 A5
Rolla, *Kans., U.S.A.* . . 71 G4
Rolla, *Mo., U.S.A.* . . . 71 G9
Rolla, *N. Dak., U.S.A.* 70 A5
Rolleston, *Australia* . . 54 C4
Rollingstone, *Australia* 54 B4
Roma, *Australia* 55 D4
Roma, *Italy* 20 D5
Roma, *Sweden* 9 H15
Roman, *Romania* 17 E13
Roman, *Russia* 25 C12
Romang, *Indonesia* . . 33 F7
Români, *Egypt* 41 E1
Romania ■, *Europe* . . 21 B11
Romblon, *Phil.* 33 B6
Rome = Roma, *Italy* . 20 D5
Rome, *Ga., U.S.A.* . . . 69 H3
Rome, *N.Y., U.S.A.* . . 68 D8
Romney, *U.S.A.* 68 F6
Romney Marsh, *U.K.* . 11 F8
Romorantin-Lanthenay,
  France 18 C4
Romsdalen, *Norway* . 8 E10
Rona, *U.K.* 12 D3
Ronan, *U.S.A.* 72 C6
Roncador, Serra do,
  Brazil 79 F8
Ronceverte, *U.S.A.* . . 68 G5
Ronda, *Spain* 19 D3
Rondane, *Norway* . . . 9 F10
Rondônia □, *Brazil* . . 78 F6
Rondonópolis, *Brazil* . 79 G8
Rong, Koh, *Cambodia* 34 G7
Ronge, L. la, *Canada* . 65 B7
Ronne Ice Shelf,
  Antarctica 5 D18
Ronsard, C., *Australia* 53 D1
Ronse, *Belgium* 15 D3
Roodepoort, *S. Africa* 49 D4
Roof Butte, *U.S.A.* . . . 73 H9
Roorkee, *India* 36 E10
Roosendaal, *Neths.* . . 15 C4
Roosevelt, *Minn.,*
  U.S.A. 70 A7
Roosevelt, *Utah, U.S.A.* 72 F8
Roosevelt →, *Brazil* . 78 E6
Roosevelt, Mt., *Canada* 64 B3
Roosevelt I., *Antarctica* 5 D12
Roosevelt Res., *U.S.A.* 73 K8
Roper →, *Australia* . . 54 A2
Ropesville, *U.S.A.* . . . 71 J3
Roraima □, *Brazil* . . . 78 C6
Roraima, Mt.,
  Venezuela 78 B6
Rørketon, *Canada* . . . 65 C9
Røros, *Norway* 8 E11
Rosa, *Zambia* 46 F6
Rosa, Monte, *Europe* . 16 F3
Rosalia, *U.S.A.* 72 C5
Rosario, *Argentina* . . 80 C4
Rosário, *Brazil* 79 D10
Rosario, *Mexico* 74 C3
Rosario, *Paraguay* . . . 80 A5
Rosario de la Frontera,
  Argentina 80 B4
Rosário do Sul, *Brazil* 80 C6
Rosas, *Spain* 19 A7
Rosas, G. de, *Spain* . . 19 A7
Roscoe, *U.S.A.* 70 C5
Roscommon, *Ireland* . 13 C3
Roscommon, *U.S.A.* . 68 C3
Roscommon □, *Ireland* 13 C3

Roscrea, *Ireland* 13 D4
Rose →, *Australia* . . . 54 A2
Rose Blanche, *Canada* 63 C8
Rose Harbour, *Canada* 64 C2
Rose Pt., *Canada* 64 C2
Rose Valley, *Canada* . 65 C8
Roseau, *Domin.* 74 M20
Roseau, *U.S.A.* 70 A7
Rosebery, *Australia* . . 54 G4
Rosebud, *U.S.A.* 71 K6
Roseburg, *U.S.A.* . . . 72 E2
Rosedale, *Australia* . . 54 C5
Rosedale, *U.S.A.* 71 J9
Rosemary, *Canada* . . 64 C6
Rosenberg, *U.S.A.* . . . 71 L7
Rosenheim, *Germany* 16 E6
Rosetown, *Canada* . . 65 C7
Rosetta = Rashîd,
  Egypt 45 B11
Roseville, *U.S.A.* 72 G3
Rosewood, *N. Terr.,*
  Australia 52 C4
Rosewood, *Queens.,*
  Australia 55 D5
Roshkhvār, *Iran* 39 C8
Rosignol, *Guyana* . . . 78 B7
Roskilde, *Denmark* . . 9 J12
Roslavl, *Russia* 22 D5
Roslyn, *Australia* 55 E4
Rosmead, *S. Africa* . . 48 E4
Ross, *Australia* 54 G4
Ross, *N.Z.* 51 K3
Ross I., *Antarctica* . . 5 D11
Ross Ice Shelf,
  Antarctica 5 E12
Ross L., *U.S.A.* 72 B3
Ross-on-Wye, *U.K.* . . 11 F5
Ross Sea, *Antarctica* . 5 D11
Rossan Pt., *Ireland* . . 13 B3
Rossburn, *Canada* . . . 65 C8
Rossignol, L., *Canada* 62 B5
Rossignol Res., *Canada* 63 D6
Rossland, *Canada* . . . 64 D5
Rosslare, *Ireland* 13 D5
Rosso, *Mauritania* . . . 44 E1
Rossosh, *Russia* 23 D6
Rossport, *Canada* . . . 62 C2
Røssvatnet, *Norway* . 8 D13
Rossville, *Australia* . . 54 B4
Rosthern, *Canada* . . . 65 C7
Rostock, *Germany* . . . 16 A6
Rostov, *Russia* 22 C6
Rostov, *Russia* 23 E6
Roswell, *U.S.A.* 71 J2
Rosyth, *U.K.* 12 E5
Rotan, *U.S.A.* 71 J4
Rothaargebirge,
  Germany 16 C4
Rother →, *U.K.* 11 G8
Rotherham, *U.K.* 10 D6
Rothes, *U.K.* 12 D5
Rothesay, *Canada* . . . 63 C6
Rothesay, *U.K.* 12 F3
Roti, *Indonesia* 33 F6
Roto, *Australia* 55 E4
Rotoroa, L., *N.Z.* 51 J4
Rotorua, *N.Z.* 51 H6
Rotorua, L., *N.Z.* 51 H6
Rotterdam, *Neths.* . . . 15 C4
Rottnest I., *Australia* . 53 F2
Rottumeroog, *Neths.* . 15 A6
Rottweil, *Germany* . . . 16 D4
Rotuma, *Fiji* 56 J9
Roubaix, *France* 18 A5
Rouen, *France* 18 B4
Rouleau, *Canada* 65 C8
Round Mt., *Australia* . 55 E5
Round Mountain,
  U.S.A. 72 G5
Roundup, *U.S.A.* 72 C9
Rousay, *U.K.* 12 B5
Roussillon, *France* . . 18 E5
Rouxville, *S. Africa* . . 48 E4
Rouyn, *Canada* 62 C4
Rovaniemi, *Finland* . . 8 C18
Rovereto, *Italy* 20 B4
Rovigo, *Italy* 20 B4
Rovinj, *Croatia* 20 B5
Rovno, *Ukraine* 23 D4
Rovuma →, *Tanzania* 46 G8
Row'ān, *Iran* 39 C6
Rowena, *Australia* . . . 55 D4
Rowley Shoals,
  Australia 52 C2
Roxas, *Phil.* 33 B6
Roxboro, *U.S.A.* 69 G6
Roxborough Downs,
  Australia 54 C2
Roxburgh, *N.Z.* 51 L2
Roy, *Mont., U.S.A.* . . . 72 C9
Roy, *N. Mex., U.S.A.* . 71 H2
Roy Hill, *Australia* . . . 52 D2
Royal Leamington Spa,
  U.K. 11 E6
Royan, *France* 18 D3
Rtishchevo, *Russia* . . 22 D7
Ruacaná, *Angola* 48 B1
Ruahine Ra., *N.Z.* . . . 51 H6
Ruapehu, *N.Z.* 51 H5
Ruapuke I., *N.Z.* 51 M2
Ruâq, W. →, *Egypt* . . 41 F2
Rub' al Khali,
  Si. Arabia 40 D4
Rubh a' Mhail, *U.K.* . . 12 F2
Rubha Hunish, *U.K.* . . 12 D2
Rubicone →, *Italy* . . . 20 B5
Rubio, *Venezuela* . . . 78 B4
Rubtsovsk, *Russia* . . . 24 D9
Ruby, L., *U.S.A.* 72 F6
Ruby Mts., *U.S.A.* . . . 72 F6

Rudall →, *Australia* . . 52 D3
Rudnichnyy, *Russia* . . 22 C9
Rudnogorsk, *Russia* . 25 D11
Rudnyy, *Kazakhstan* . 24 D7
Rudolf, Ostrov, *Russia* 24 A6
Rudyard, *U.S.A.* 68 B3
Rufa'a, *Sudan* 45 F11
Rufiji →, *Tanzania* . . . 46 F7
Rufino, *Argentina* . . . 80 C4
Rufisque, *Senegal* . . . 44 F1
Rugby, *U.K.* 11 E6
Rugby, *U.S.A.* 70 A5
Rügen, *Germany* 16 A6
Ruhr →, *Germany* . . . 16 C3
Ruidosa, *U.S.A.* 71 L2
Ruidoso, *U.S.A.* 73 K11
Rujm Tal'at al
  Jamā'ah, *Jordan* . . 41 E4
Rukwa L., *Tanzania* . . 46 F6
Rulhieres, C., *Australia* 52 B4
Rum Jungle, *Australia* 52 B5
Rumāḥ, *Si. Arabia* . . . 38 E5
Rumania =
  Romania ■, *Europe* 21 B11
Rumaylah, *Iraq* 38 D5
Rumbalara, *Australia* . 54 D1
Rumbêk, *Sudan* 45 G10
Rumford, *U.S.A.* 68 C10
Rumoi, *Japan* 28 C10
Rumsey, *Canada* 64 C6
Rumula, *Australia* . . . 54 B4
Runanga, *N.Z.* 51 K3
Runaway, C., *N.Z.* . . . 51 G6
Runcorn, *U.K.* 10 D5
Rungwa, *Tanzania* . . . 46 F6
Runton Ra., *Australia* 52 D3
Ruoqiang, *China* 30 C3
Rupa, *India* 37 F18
Rupat, *Indonesia* 32 D2
Rupert →, *Canada* . . . 62 B4
Rupert House = Fort
  Rupert, *Canada* . . . 62 B4
Rurrenabaque, *Bolivia* 78 F5
Rusape, *Zimbabwe* . . 47 H6
Ruschuk = Ruse,
  Bulgaria 21 C11
Ruse, *Bulgaria* 21 C11
Rushden, *U.K.* 11 E7
Rushford, *U.S.A.* 70 D9
Rushville, *Ill., U.S.A.* . 70 E9
Rushville, *Ind., U.S.A.* 68 F3
Rushville, *Nebr., U.S.A.* 70 D3
Rushworth, *Australia* . 55 F4
Russas, *Brazil* 79 D11
Russell, *Canada* 65 C8
Russell, *U.S.A.* 70 F5
Russell L., *Man.,*
  Canada 65 B8
Russell L., *N.W.T.,*
  Canada 64 A5
Russellkonda, *India* . . 37 K14
Russellville, *Ala.,*
  U.S.A. 69 H2
Russellville, *Ark.,*
  U.S.A. 71 H8
Russellville, *Ky., U.S.A.* 69 G2
Russia ■, *Eurasia* . . . 25 C11
Russkaya Polyana,
  Kazakhstan 24 D8
Russkoye Ustie, *Russia* 4 B15
Rustavi, *Georgia* 23 F8
Rustenburg, *S. Africa* 48 D4
Ruston, *U.S.A.* 71 J8
Ruteng, *Indonesia* . . . 33 F6
Ruth, *U.S.A.* 72 G6
Rutherglen, *U.K.* 12 F4
Rutland I., *India* 34 G2
Rutland Plains,
  Australia 54 B3
Rutledge →, *Canada* . 65 A6
Rutledge L., *Canada* . 65 A6
Rutshuru, *Zaire* 46 E5
Ruurlo, *Neths.* 15 B6
Ruwais, *U.A.E.* 39 E7
Ruwenzori, *Africa* . . . 46 D5
Ružomberok, *Slovakia* 17 D9
Rwanda ■, *Africa* . . . 46 E5
Ryan, L., *U.K.* 12 G3
Ryazan, *Russia* 22 D6
Ryazhsk, *Russia* 22 D7
Rybache, *Kazakhstan* 24 E9
Rybachiy Poluostrov,
  Russia 22 A5
Rybinsk, *Russia* 22 C6
Rybinskoye Vdkhr.,
  Russia 22 C6
Ryde, *U.K.* 11 G6
Rye, *U.K.* 11 G8
Rye →, *U.K.* 10 C7
Rye Patch Res., *U.S.A.* 72 F4
Ryegate, *U.S.A.* 72 C9
Rylstone, *Australia* . . 55 E4
Ryōthu, *Japan* 28 E9
Rypin, *Poland* 17 B9
Ryūgasaki, *Japan* . . . 29 G10
Ryūkyū Is. = Ryūkyū-
  rettō, *Japan* 29 M2
Ryūkyū-rettō, *Japan* . 29 M2
Rzeszów, *Poland* 17 C10
Rzhev, *Russia* 22 C5

S

Sa Dec, *Vietnam* 34 G8
Sa'ādatābād, *Fārs, Iran* 39 D7
Sa'ādatābād, *Kermān,*
  Iran 39 D7
Saale →, *Germany* . . . 16 C5
Saar →, *Europe* 16 D3

Saarbrücken, *Germany* 16 D3
Saaremaa, *Estonia* . . 22 C3
Saariselkä, *Finland* . . 8 B20
Saarland □, *Germany* 15 E7
Sab 'Bi'ār, *Syria* 38 C3
Saba, *W. Indies* 74 K18
Sabadell, *Spain* 19 B7
Sabah □, *Malaysia* . . . 32 C5
Sabanalarga, *Colombia* 78 A4
Sabang, *Indonesia* . . . 32 C1
Sabará, *Brazil* 79 G10
Sabarania, *Indonesia* 33 E9
Sábáudia, *Italy* 20 D5
Sabhah, *Libya* 45 C7
Sabie, *S. Africa* 49 D5
Sabinal, *U.S.A.* 71 L5
Sabinas, *Mexico* 74 B4
Sabinas Hidalgo,
  Mexico 74 B4
Sabine →, *U.S.A.* 71 L8
Sabine L., *U.S.A.* 71 L8
Sabine Pass, *U.S.A.* . . 71 L8
Sabkhet el Bardawîl,
  Egypt 41 D2
Sablayan, *Phil.* 33 B6
Sable, C., *Canada* . . . 63 D6
Sable, C., *U.S.A.* 67 E10
Sable I., *Canada* 63 D8
Sabolev, *Russia* 25 D16
Sabrina Coast,
  Antarctica 5 C9
Sabulubek, *Indonesia* 32 E1
Sabzevār, *Iran* 39 B8
Sabzvārān, *Iran* 39 D8
Sac City, *U.S.A.* 70 D7
Sachigo →, *Canada* . . 62 A2
Sachigo, L., *Canada* . . 62 B1
Saco, Maine, U.S.A.* . . 69 D10
Saco, Mont., U.S.A.* . . 72 B10
Sacramento, *U.S.A.* . . 72 G3
Sacramento →,
  U.S.A. 72 G3
Sacramento Mts.,
  U.S.A. 73 K11
Sádaba, *Spain* 19 A5
Sadani, *Tanzania* 46 F7
Sadao, *Thailand* 34 N13
Sadd el Aali, *Egypt* . . 45 D11
Sado, *Japan* 28 E9
Sadon, *Burma* 37 G20
Şafājah, *Si. Arabia* . . . 38 E3
Säffle, *Sweden* 9 G12
Safford, *U.S.A.* 73 K9
Saffron Walden, *U.K.* . 11 E8
Safi, *Morocco* 44 B3
Şafīābād, *Iran* 39 C6
Safid Dasht, *Iran* 39 C6
Safid Kūh, *Afghan.* . . . 36 B3
Safwān, *Iraq* 38 D5
Saga, *Indonesia* 33 E8
Saga, *Japan* 29 H5
Saga □, *Japan* 29 H5
Sagae, *Japan* 28 E10
Sagala, *Mali* 44 F3
Sagar, *India* 36 M9
Saginaw, *U.S.A.* 68 D4
Saginaw B., *U.S.A.* . . 68 D4
Sagīr, Zab as →, *Iraq* 38 C4
Saglouc, *Canada* 61 B12
Sagres, *Portugal* 19 D1
Sagua la Grande, *Cuba* 75 C8
Saguache, *U.S.A.* . . . 73 G10
Saguenay →, *Canada* 63 C5
Sagunto, *Spain* 19 C5
Sahagún, *Spain* 19 A3
Saham al Jawlān,
  Syria 41 C4
Sahand, Kūh-e, *Iran* . . 38 B5
Sahara, *Africa* 44 D5
Saharan Atlas =
  Saharien, Atlas,
  Algeria 44 B5
Saharanpur, *India* . . . 36 E10
Saharien, Atlas,
  Algeria 44 B5
Sahasinaka, *Madag.* . 49 C8
Sahiwal, *Pakistan* . . . 36 D8
Şahneh, *Iran* 38 C5
Sahtaneh →, *Canada* 64 B4
Sahuarita, *U.S.A.* 73 L8
Şa'id Bundas, *Sudan* . 45 G9
Saïda, *Algeria* 44 B5
Saïdābād, *Kermān,*
  Iran 39 D7
Saïdābād, *Semnān,*
  Iran 39 B7
Sa'idiyeh, *Iran* 39 B6
Saidpur, *Bangla.* 37 G16
Saidu, *Pakistan* 36 B8
Saigon = Phanh Bho
  Ho Chi Minh,
  Vietnam 34 G9
Saijō, *Japan* 29 H6
Saikhoa Ghat, *India* . . 37 F19
Saiki, *Japan* 29 H5
Sailolof, *Indonesia* . . 33 E8
Şa'in Dezh, *Iran* 38 B5
St. Abb's Head, *U.K.* . 12 F6
St. Alban's, *Canada* . . 63 C8
St. Albans, *U.K.* 11 F7
St. Albans, *Vt., U.S.A.* 68 C9
St. Albans, *W. Va.,*
  U.S.A. 68 F5
St. Alban's Head, *U.K.* 11 G5
St. Albert, *Canada* . . . 64 C6
St. Andrew's, *Canada* 63 C8
St. Andrews, *U.K.* . . . 12 E6
St. Ann B., *Canada* . . 63 C7
St. Anthony, *Canada* . 63 B8
St. Anthony, *U.S.A.* . . 72 E8
St. Arnaud, *Australia* . 55 F3

St. Arthur, *Canada*	63	C6
St. Asaph, *U.K.*	10	D4
St-Augustin-Saguenay, *Canada*	63	B8
St. Augustine, *U.S.A.*	69	L5
St. Austell, *U.K.*	11	G3
St.-Barthélemy, I., *W. Indies*	74	K19
St. Bee's Hd., *U.K.*	10	C4
St. Boniface, *Canada*	65	D9
St. Bride's, *Canada*	63	C9
St. Brides B., *U.K.*	11	F2
St.-Brieuc, *France*	18	B2
St. Catharines, *Canada*	62	D4
St. Catherines I., *U.S.A.*	69	K5
St. Catherine's Pt., *U.K.*	11	G6
St. Charles, *Ill., U.S.A.*	68	E1
St. Charles, *Mo., U.S.A.*	70	F9
St. Christopher = St. Kitts, *W. Indies*	74	K19
St. Christopher-Nevis ■, *W. Indies*	74	K19
St. Clair, L., *Canada*	62	D3
St. Claude, *Canada*	65	D9
St. Cloud, *Fla., U.S.A.*	69	L5
St. Cloud, *Minn., U.S.A.*	70	C7
St-Coeur de Marie, *Canada*	63	C5
St. Cricq, C., *Australia*	53	E1
St. Croix, *Virgin Is.*	75	D12
St. Croix →, *U.S.A.*	70	C8
St. Croix Falls, *U.S.A.*	70	C8
St. David's, *Canada*	63	C8
St. David's, *U.K.*	11	F2
St. David's Head, *U.K.*	11	F2
St.-Denis, *France*	18	B5
St.-Denis, *Réunion*	35	G4
St. Elias, Mt., *U.S.A.*	60	B5
St. Elias Mts., *Canada*	64	A1
St.-Étienne, *France*	18	D6
St. Eustatius, *W. Indies*	74	K19
St-Félicien, *Canada*	62	C5
St.-Flour, *France*	18	D5
St. Francis, *U.S.A.*	70	F4
St. Francis →, *U.S.A.*	71	H9
St. Francis, C., *S. Africa*	48	E3
St. Francisville, *U.S.A.*	71	K9
St-Gabriel-de-Brandon, *Canada*	62	C5
St. Gallen = Sankt Gallen, *Switz.*	16	E4
St. George, *Australia*	55	D4
St. George, *Canada*	63	C6
St. George, *S.C., U.S.A.*	69	J5
St. George, *Utah, U.S.A.*	73	H7
St. George, C., *Canada*	63	C8
St. George, C., *U.S.A.*	69	L3
St. George Ra., *Australia*	52	C4
St-Georges, *Belgium*	15	D5
St. George's, *Canada*	63	C8
St-Georges, *Canada*	63	C5
St-Georges, *Fr. Guiana*	79	C8
St. George's, *Grenada*	74	Q20
St. George's B., *Canada*	63	C8
St. Georges Basin, *Australia*	52	C4
St. George's Channel, *U.K.*	13	E6
St. Georges Hd., *Australia*	55	F5
St. Gotthard P. = San Gottardo, Paso del, *Switz.*	16	E4
St. Helena, *U.S.A.*	72	G2
St. Helena ■, *Atl. Oc.*	2	E9
St. Helena B., *S. Africa*	48	E2
St. Helens, *Australia*	54	G4
St. Helens, *U.K.*	10	D5
St. Helens, *U.S.A.*	72	D2
St. Helier, *U.K.*	11	H5
St-Hubert, *Belgium*	15	D5
St-Hyacinthe, *Canada*	62	C5
St. Ignace, *U.S.A.*	68	C3
St. Ignace I., *Canada*	62	C2
St. Ignatius, *U.S.A.*	72	C6
St. Ives, *Cambs., U.K.*	11	E7
St. Ives, *Corn., U.K.*	11	G2
St. James, *U.S.A.*	70	D7
St-Jean, *Canada*	62	C5
St-Jean →, *Canada*	63	B7
St-Jean, L., *Canada*	63	C5
St. Jean Baptiste, *Canada*	65	D9
St-Jean-Port-Joli, *Canada*	63	C5
St-Jérôme, *Qué., Canada*	62	C5
St Jérôme, *Qué., Canada*	63	C5
St. John, *Canada*	63	C6
St. John, *Kans., U.S.A.*	71	G5
St. John, *N. Dak., U.S.A.*	70	A5
St. John →, *N. Amer.*	63	C6
St. John, C., *Canada*	63	C8
St. John's, *Antigua*	74	K20
St. John's, *Canada*	63	C9
St. Johns, *Ariz., U.S.A.*	73	J9
St. Johns, *Mich., U.S.A.*	68	D3
St. John's →, *U.S.A.*	69	K5
St. Johnsbury, *U.S.A.*	68	C9
St. Joseph, *La., U.S.A.*	71	K9
St. Joseph, *Mich., U.S.A.*	68	D2
St. Joseph, *Mo., U.S.A.*	70	F7
St. Joseph →, *U.S.A.*	68	D2
St. Joseph, I., *Canada*	62	C3
St. Joseph, L., *Canada*	62	B1
St-Jovite, *Canada*	62	C5
St. Kilda, *N.Z.*	51	L3
St. Kitts, *W. Indies*	74	K19
St. Kitts-Nevis = St. Christopher-Nevis ■, *W. Indies*	74	K19
St. Laurent, *Canada*	65	C9
St-Laurent, *Fr. Guiana*	79	B8
St. Lawrence, *Australia*	54	C4
St. Lawrence, *Canada*	63	C8
St. Lawrence →, *Canada*	63	C6
St. Lawrence, Gulf of, *Canada*	63	C7
St. Lawrence I., *U.S.A.*	60	B3
St. Leonard, *Canada*	63	C6
St. Lewis →, *Canada*	63	B8
St-Lô, *France*	18	B3
St-Louis, *Senegal*	44	E1
St. Louis, *Mich., U.S.A.*	68	D3
St. Louis, *Mo., U.S.A.*	70	F9
St. Louis →, *U.S.A.*	70	B8
St. Lucia ■, *W. Indies*	74	P21
St. Lucia, L., *S. Africa*	49	D5
St. Lucia Channel, *W. Indies*	74	N21
St. Lunaire-Griquet, *Canada*	63	B8
St-Malo, *France*	18	B2
St-Marc, *Haiti*	75	D10
St. Maries, *U.S.A.*	72	C5
St-Martin, *W. Indies*	74	J18
St. Martin, L., *Canada*	65	C9
St. Martins, *Canada*	63	C6
St. Martinsville, *U.S.A.*	71	K9
St. Mary Pk., *Australia*	55	E2
St. Marys, *Australia*	54	G4
St. Mary's, *U.K.*	11	H1
St. Marys, *U.S.A.*	68	E6
St. Mary's, C., *Canada*	63	C9
St. Mary's B., *Canada*	63	C9
St. Marys Bay, *Canada*	63	D6
St-Mathieu, Pte., *France*	18	B1
St. Matthews, I. = Zadetkyi Kyun, *Burma*	34	H5
St-Maurice →, *Canada*	62	C5
St. Michael's Mount, *U.K.*	11	G2
St.-Nazaire, *France*	18	C2
St. Neots, *U.K.*	11	E7
St. Niklass = Sint Niklaas, *Belgium*	15	C4
St.-Omer, *France*	18	A5
St-Pacome, *Canada*	63	C6
St-Pamphile, *Canada*	63	C6
St. Pascal, *Canada*	63	C6
St. Paul, *Canada*	64	C6
St. Paul, *Minn., U.S.A.*	70	C8
St. Paul, *Nebr., U.S.A.*	70	E5
St. Paul, I., *Ind. Oc.*	35	H6
St. Paul I., *Canada*	63	C7
St. Peter, *U.S.A.*	70	C8
St. Peter Port, *Chan. Is.*	11	H5
St. Peters, *N.S., Canada*	63	C7
St. Peters, *P.E.I., Canada*	63	C7
St. Petersburg = Sankt-Peterburg, *Russia*	22	C5
St. Petersburg, *U.S.A.*	69	M4
St.-Pierre, *St- P. & M.*	63	C8
St. Pierre, *Seychelles*	35	E3
St-Pierre, L., *Canada*	62	C5
St.-Pierre et Miquelon □, *St- P. & M.*	63	C8
St.-Quentin, *France*	18	B5
St. Regis, *U.S.A.*	72	C6
St. Sebastien, Tanjon'i, *Madag.*	49	A8
St-Siméon, *Canada*	63	C6
St. Stephen, *Canada*	63	C6
St. Thomas, *Canada*	62	D3
St. Thomas, *Virgin Is.*	75	D12
St-Tite, *Canada*	62	C5
St-Tropez, *France*	18	E7
St. Truiden = Sint Truiden, *Belgium*	15	D5
St.-Valéry-sur-Somme, *France*	18	A4
St. Vincent, G., *Australia*	55	F2
St. Vincent & the Grenadines ■, *W. Indies*	74	Q20
St. Vincent Passage, *W. Indies*	74	P21
St-Vith, *Belgium*	15	D6
Ste-Agathe-des-Monts, *Canada*	62	C5
Ste-Anne de Beaupré, *Canada*	63	C5
Ste-Anne-des-Monts, *Canada*	63	C6
Ste. Genevieve, *U.S.A.*	70	G9
Ste-Marguerite →, *Canada*	63	B6
Ste.-Marie, *Martinique*	74	N20
Ste-Marie de la Madeleine, *Canada*	63	C5
Ste.-Rose, *Guadeloupe*	74	L20
Ste. Rose du Lac, *Canada*	65	C9
Saintes, *France*	18	D3
Saintes, I. des, *Guadeloupe*	74	M20
Saintonge, *France*	18	D3
Saipan, *Pac. Oc.*	56	F6
Sairang, *India*	37	H18
Sairecábur, Cerro, *Bolivia*	80	A3
Saitama □, *Japan*	29	F9
Sajama, *Bolivia*	78	G5
Sak →, *S. Africa*	48	E3
Sakai, *Japan*	29	G7
Sakaide, *Japan*	29	G6
Sakaiminato, *Japan*	29	G6
Sakākah, *Si. Arabia*	38	D4
Sakakawea, L., *U.S.A.*	70	B3
Sakami, L., *Canada*	62	B4
Sakarya = Adapazan, *Turkey*	23	F5
Sakarya →, *Turkey*	23	F5
Sakashima-Guntō, *Japan*	29	M2
Sakata, *Japan*	28	E9
Sakeny →, *Madag.*	49	C8
Sakha = Yakut Republic □, *Russia*	25	C13
Sakhalin, *Russia*	25	D15
Sakhalinskiy Zaliv, *Russia*	25	D15
Sakon Nakhon, *Thailand*	34	D8
Sakrivier, *S. Africa*	48	E3
Sakuma, *Japan*	29	G8
Sakurai, *Japan*	29	G7
Sala, *Sweden*	9	G14
Sala-y-Gómez, *Pac. Oc.*	57	K17
Salaberry-de-Valleyfield, *Canada*	62	C5
Saladillo, *Argentina*	80	D5
Salado →, *Buenos Aires, Argentina*	80	D5
Salado →, *La Pampa, Argentina*	80	D3
Salado →, *Santa Fe, Argentina*	80	C4
Salaga, *Ghana*	44	G4
Sālah, *Syria*	41	C5
Salālah, *Oman*	40	D5
Salamanca, *Chile*	80	C2
Salamanca, *Spain*	19	B3
Salamanca, *U.S.A.*	68	D6
Salāmatābād, *Iran*	38	C5
Salamis, *Greece*	21	F10
Salar de Atacama, *Chile*	80	A3
Salar de Uyuni, *Bolivia*	78	H5
Salatiga, *Indonesia*	33	G14
Salavat, *Russia*	22	D10
Salaverry, *Peru*	78	E3
Salawati, *Indonesia*	33	E8
Salayar, *Indonesia*	33	F6
Salcombe, *U.K.*	11	G4
Saldaña, *Spain*	19	A3
Saldanha, *S. Africa*	48	E2
Saldanha B., *S. Africa*	48	E2
Sale, *Australia*	55	F4
Salé, *Morocco*	44	B3
Salekhard, *Russia*	22	A12
Salem, *India*	36	P11
Salem, *Ind., U.S.A.*	68	F2
Salem, *Mass., U.S.A.*	68	D10
Salem, *Mo., U.S.A.*	71	G9
Salem, *N.J., U.S.A.*	68	F8
Salem, *Ohio, U.S.A.*	68	E5
Salem, *Oreg., U.S.A.*	72	D2
Salem, *S. Dak., U.S.A.*	70	D6
Salem, *Va., U.S.A.*	68	G5
Salerno, *Italy*	20	D6
Salford, *U.K.*	10	D5
Salida, *U.S.A.*	66	C5
Salima, *Malawi*	47	G6
Salina, *Italy*	20	E6
Salina, *U.S.A.*	70	F6
Salina Cruz, *Mexico*	74	D5
Salinas, *Brazil*	79	G10
Salinas, *Ecuador*	78	D2
Salinas, *U.S.A.*	73	H3
Salinas →, *U.S.A.*	73	H3
Salinas Ambargasta, *Argentina*	80	B4
Salinas Grandes, *Argentina*	80	B4
Saline →, *Ark., U.S.A.*	71	J8
Saline →, *Kans., U.S.A.*	70	F6
Salinópolis, *Brazil*	79	D9
Salisbury = Harare, *Zimbabwe*	47	H6
Salisbury, *Australia*	55	E2
Salisbury, *U.K.*	11	F6
Salisbury, *Md., U.S.A.*	68	F8
Salisbury, *N.C., U.S.A.*	69	H5
Salisbury Plain, *U.K.*	11	F6
Salkhad, *Jordan*	41	C5
Sallisaw, *U.S.A.*	71	H7
Salmās, *Iran*	38	B5
Salmo, *Canada*	64	D5
Salmon, *U.S.A.*	72	D7
Salmon →, *Canada*	64	C4
Salmon →, *U.S.A.*	72	D5
Salmon Arm, *Canada*	64	C5
Salmon Falls, *U.S.A.*	72	E6
Salmon Gums, *Australia*	53	F3
Salmon Res., *Canada*	63	C8
Salmon River Mts., *U.S.A.*	72	D6
Salo, *Finland*	9	F17
Salome, *U.S.A.*	73	K7
Salonica = Thessaloníki, *Greece*	21	D10
Salonta, *Romania*	17	E10
Salsk, *Russia*	23	E7
Salso →, *Italy*	20	F5
Salt →, *U.S.A.*	73	K7
Salt Creek, *Australia*	55	F2
Salt Fork →, *U.S.A.*	71	G6
Salt Lake City, *U.S.A.*	72	F8
Salta, *Argentina*	80	A3
Saltcoats, *U.K.*	12	F4
Saltee Is., *Ireland*	13	D5
Saltfjorden, *Norway*	8	C13
Salthólmavík, *Iceland*	8	D3
Saltillo, *Mexico*	74	B4
Saltillo, *Coahuila, Mexico*	74	B4
Salto, *Uruguay*	80	C5
Salton Sea, *U.S.A.*	73	K6
Saltpond, *Ghana*	44	G4
Saltville, *U.S.A.*	68	G5
Saluda →, *U.S.A.*	69	H5
Salûm, *Egypt*	45	B10
Salûm, Khâlig el, *Egypt*	45	B10
Saluzzo, *Italy*	20	B2
Salvador, *Brazil*	79	F11
Salvador, *Canada*	65	C7
Salvador, L., *U.S.A.*	71	L9
Salween →, *Burma*	37	L20
Salyany, *Azerbaijan*	23	G8
Salyersville, *U.S.A.*	68	G4
Salzburg, *Austria*	16	E6
Salzburg □, *Austria*	16	E6
Salzgitter, *Germany*	16	B5
Sam Neua, *Laos*	34	B8
Sam Ngao, *Thailand*	34	D5
Sam Rayburn Res., *U.S.A.*	71	K7
Sama, *Russia*	24	C7
Sama de Langreo, *Spain*	19	A3
Samagaltai, *Russia*	25	D10
Samales Group, *Phil.*	33	C6
Samani, *Japan*	28	C11
Samar, *Phil.*	33	B7
Samara, *Russia*	22	D9
Samaria = Shômrôn, *Jordan*	41	C4
Samarinda, *Indonesia*	32	E5
Samarkand = Samarqand, *Uzbekistan*	24	F7
Samarqand, *Uzbekistan*	24	F7
Sāmarrā, *Iraq*	38	C4
Sambalpur, *India*	37	J14
Sambar, Tanjung, *Indonesia*	32	E4
Sambas, *Indonesia*	32	D3
Sambava, *Madag.*	49	A9
Sambhal, *India*	36	E11
Sambhar, *India*	36	F9
Sambor, *Cambodia*	34	F9
Sambre →, *Europe*	15	D4
Same, *Tanzania*	46	E7
Samnah, *Si. Arabia*	38	E3
Sámos, *Greece*	21	F12
Samothráki, *Greece*	21	D11
Sampacho, *Argentina*	80	C4
Sampang, *Indonesia*	33	G15
Sampit, *Indonesia*	32	E4
Sampit, Teluk, *Indonesia*	32	E4
Samsun, *Turkey*	23	F6
Samui, Ko, *Thailand*	34	H6
Samut Prakan, *Thailand*	34	F6
Samut Sakhon, *Thailand*	34	F6
Samut Songkhram →, *Thailand*	34	F6
San, *Mali*	44	F4
San →, *Poland*	17	C10
San Agustin, C., *Phil.*	33	C7
San Ambrosio, *Pac. Oc.*	57	K20
San Andreas, *U.S.A.*	72	G3
San Andres, I. de, *Caribbean*	75	E8
San Andres Mts., *U.S.A.*	73	K10
San Andrés Tuxtla, *Mexico*	74	D5
San Angelo, *U.S.A.*	71	K4
San Antonio, *N. Mex., U.S.A.*	73	K10
San Antonio, *Tex., U.S.A.*	71	L5
San Antonio →, *U.S.A.*	71	L6
San Antonio, C., *Argentina*	80	D5
San Antonio, C., *Cuba*	74	C8
San Antonio Oeste, *Argentina*	80	E4
San Augustine, *U.S.A.*	71	K7
San Benito, *U.S.A.*	71	M6
San Bernardino, *U.S.A.*	73	J5
San Bernardino Str., *Phil.*	33	B6
San Bernardo, *Chile*	80	C2
San Bernardo, I. de, *Colombia*	78	B3
San Blas, C., *U.S.A.*	69	L3
San Borja, *Bolivia*	78	F5
San Carlos, *Argentina*	80	C3
San Carlos, *Chile*	80	D2
San Carlos, *Phil.*	33	B6
San Carlos, *U.S.A.*	73	K8
San Carlos, *Amazonas, Venezuela*	78	C5
San Carlos, *Cojedes, Venezuela*	78	B5
San Carlos de Bariloche, *Argentina*	80	E2
San Carlos del Zulia, *Venezuela*	78	B4
San Carlos I., *U.S.A.*	73	K8
San Clemente, *U.S.A.*	73	K5
San Clemente I., *U.S.A.*	73	K4
San Cristóbal, *Argentina*	80	C4
San Cristóbal, *Mexico*	74	D6
San Cristóbal, *Venezuela*	78	B4
San Diego, *Calif., U.S.A.*	73	K5
San Diego, *Tex., U.S.A.*	71	M5
San Diego, C., *Argentina*	80	G3
San Felipe, *Chile*	80	C2
San Felipe, *Venezuela*	78	A5
San Felíu de Guíxols, *Spain*	19	B7
San Félix, *Pac. Oc.*	57	K20
San Fernando, *Chile*	80	C2
San Fernando, *La Union, Phil.*	33	A6
San Fernando, *Pampanga, Phil.*	33	A6
San Fernando, *Spain*	19	D2
San Fernando, *Trin. & Tob.*	74	S20
San Fernando, *U.S.A.*	73	J4
San Fernando de Apure, *Venezuela*	78	B5
San Fernando de Atabapo, *Venezuela*	78	C5
San Francisco, *Argentina*	80	C4
San Francisco, *U.S.A.*	73	H2
San Francisco →, *U.S.A.*	73	K9
San Francisco de Macorís, *Dom. Rep.*	75	D10
San Francisco del Monte de Oro, *Argentina*	80	C3
San Gil, *Colombia*	78	B4
San Gottardo, Paso del, *Switz.*	16	E4
San Ignacio, *Bolivia*	78	G6
San Ignacio, *Paraguay*	80	B5
San Ildefonso, C., *Phil.*	33	A6
San Javier, *Argentina*	80	C4
San Javier, *Bolivia*	78	G6
San Joaquin →, *U.S.A.*	73	G3
San Jorge, B. de, *Mexico*	74	A2
San Jorge, G., *Argentina*	80	F3
San Jorge, G. de, *Spain*	19	B5
San José, *Bolivia*	78	G6
San José, *Costa Rica*	75	F8
San José, *Guatemala*	74	E6
San José, *Phil.*	33	A6
San Jose, *U.S.A.*	73	H3
San Jose →, *U.S.A.*	73	J10
San Jose de Buenavista, *Phil.*	33	B6
San José de Jáchal, *Argentina*	80	C3
San José de Mayo, *Uruguay*	80	C5
San José de Ocune, *Colombia*	78	C4
San José del Guaviare, *Colombia*	78	C4
San Juan, *Argentina*	80	C3
San Juan, *Phil.*	33	B6
San Juan, *Puerto Rico*	75	D11
San Juan →, *Nic.*	75	E8
San Juan →, *U.S.A.*	73	H8
San Juan, C., *Eq. Guin.*	46	D1
San Juan Bautista, *U.S.A.*	73	H3
San Juan Capistrano, *U.S.A.*	73	K5
San Juan de los Morros, *Venezuela*	78	B5
San Juan Mts., *U.S.A.*	73	H10
San Julián, *Argentina*	80	F3
San Justo, *Argentina*	80	C4
San Leandro, *U.S.A.*	73	H2
San Lorenzo, *Ecuador*	78	C3
San Lorenzo, *Peru*	78	F3
San Lorenzo, Mt., *Argentina*	80	F2
San Lucas, *Bolivia*	78	H5
San Lucas, C., *Mexico*	74	C2
San Luis, *Argentina*	80	C3
San Luis, *U.S.A.*	73	H11
San Luis Obispo, *U.S.A.*	73	J3
San Luis Potosí, *Mexico*	74	C4
San Marcos, *U.S.A.*	71	L6
San Marino ■, *Europe*	20	C5
San Martín, L., *Argentina*	80	F2
San Mateo, *U.S.A.*	73	H2
San Matías, *Bolivia*	78	G7
San Matías, G., *Argentina*	80	E4
San Miguel, *El Salv.*	74	E7
San Miguel, *U.S.A.*	73	J3
San Miguel →, *Bolivia*	78	F6
San Miguel de Tucumán, *Argentina*	80	B3
San Narciso, *Phil.*	33	A6
San Nicolás de los Arroyas, *Argentina*	80	C4
San Nicolas I., *U.S.A.*	73	K4
San-Pédro, *Ivory C.*	44	H3
San Pedro →, *U.S.A.*	73	K8
San Pedro de las Colonias, *Mexico*	74	B4
San Pedro de Lloc, *Peru*	78	E3
San Pedro de Macorís, *Dom. Rep.*	75	D11
San Pedro del Paraná, *Paraguay*	80	B5
San Pedro Sula, *Honduras*	74	D7
San Rafael, *Argentina*	80	C3
San Rafael, *Calif., U.S.A.*	72	H2
San Rafael, *N. Mex., U.S.A.*	73	J10
San Ramón de la Nueva Orán, *Argentina*	80	A4
San Remo, *Italy*	20	C2
San Roque, *Argentina*	80	B5
San Rosendo, *Chile*	80	D2
San Saba, *U.S.A.*	71	K5
San Salvador, *Bahamas*	75	C10
San Salvador, *El Salv.*	74	E7
San Salvador de Jujuy, *Argentina*	80	A4
San Sebastián, *Argentina*	80	G3
San Sebastián, *Spain*	19	A5
San Simon, *U.S.A.*	73	K9
San Valentin, Mte., *Chile*	80	F2
San Vicente de la Barquera, *Spain*	19	A3
San Ygnacio, *U.S.A.*	71	M5
Sana', *Yemen*	40	D3
Sana →, *Bos.-H.*	20	B7
Sanaga →, *Cameroon*	44	H6
Sanana, *Indonesia*	33	E7
Sanandaj, *Iran*	38	C5
Sanco Pt., *Phil.*	33	C7
Sancti-Spíritus, *Cuba*	75	C9
Sand →, *S. Africa*	49	C5
Sand Springs, *U.S.A.*	71	G6
Sanda, *Japan*	29	G7
Sandakan, *Malaysia*	32	C5
Sandan = Sambor, *Cambodia*	34	F9
Sanday, *U.K.*	12	B6
Sanders, *U.S.A.*	73	J9
Sanderson, *U.S.A.*	71	K3
Sandfly L., *Canada*	65	B7
Sandgate, *Australia*	55	D5
Sandía, *Peru*	78	F5
Sandnes, *Norway*	9	G8
Sandness, *U.K.*	12	A7
Sandoa, *Zaïre*	46	F4
Sandomierz, *Poland*	17	C10
Sandover →, *Australia*	54	C2
Sandoway, *Burma*	37	K19
Sandpoint, *U.S.A.*	72	B5
Sandringham, *U.K.*	10	E8
Sandspit, *Canada*	64	C2
Sandstone, *Australia*	53	E2
Sandusky, *Mich., U.S.A.*	62	D3
Sandusky, *Ohio, U.S.A.*	68	E4
Sandviken, *Sweden*	9	F14
Sandwich, C., *Australia*	54	B4
Sandwich B., *Canada*	63	B8
Sandwich B., *Namibia*	48	C1
Sandwip Chan., *Bangla.*	37	H17
Sandy Bight, *Australia*	53	F3
Sandy, *Queens., Australia*	54	C5
Sandy C., *Tas., Australia*	54	G3
Sandy Cr. →, *U.S.A.*	72	F9
Sandy L., *Canada*	62	B1
Sandy Lake, *Canada*	62	B1
Sandy Narrows, *Canada*	65	B8
Sanford, *Fla., U.S.A.*	69	L5
Sanford, *N.C., U.S.A.*	69	H6
Sanford →, *Australia*	53	E2
Sanford Mt., *U.S.A.*	60	B5
Sanga →, *Congo*	46	E3
Sanga-Tolon, *Russia*	25	C15
Sangamner, *India*	36	K9
Sangar, *Russia*	25	C13
Sangasangadalam, *Indonesia*	32	E5
Sangeang, *Indonesia*	33	F5
Sanger, *U.S.A.*	73	H4
Sanggau, *Indonesia*	32	D4
Sangihe, Kepulauan, *Indonesia*	33	D7
Sangihe, P., *Indonesia*	33	D7
Sangkapura, *Indonesia*	32	F4
Sangli, *India*	36	L9
Sangmélina, *Cameroon*	46	D2
Sangonera →, *Spain*	19	D5
Sangre de Cristo Mts., *U.S.A.*	71	G2
Sangudo, *Canada*	64	C6
Sāniyah, *Iraq*	38	C4
Sanjo, *Japan*	28	F9
Sankt Gallen, *Switz.*	16	E4
Sankt Moritz, *Switz.*	16	E4

Sankt-Peterburg, Russia 22 C5
Sankuru →, Zaïre ... 46 E4
Sanlúcar de Barrameda, Spain . 19 D2
Sanmenxia, China .. 31 C6
Sanming, China .. 31 D6
Sannaspos, S. Africa . 48 D4
Sannicandro Gargánico, Italy .. 20 D6
Sannieshof, S. Africa . 48 D4
Sannin, J., Lebanon .. 41 B4
Sanok, Poland ... 17 D11
Sanquhar, U.K. .. 12 F5
Santa Ana, Bolivia .. 78 F5
Santa Ana, Ecuador . 78 D2
Santa Ana, El Salv. .. 74 E7
Santa Ana, U.S.A. .. 73 K5
Santa Barbara, U.S.A. 73 J4
Santa Catalina, G. of, U.S.A. ... 73 K5
Santa Catalina I., U.S.A. ... 73 K4
Santa Catarina □, Brazil ... 80 B7
Santa Clara, Cuba .. 75 C9
Santa Clara, Calif., U.S.A. ... 73 H3
Santa Clara, Utah, U.S.A. ... 73 H7
Santa Clotilde, Peru .. 78 D4
Santa Coloma de Gramanet, Spain . 19 B7
Santa Cruz, Argentina 80 G3
Santa Cruz, Bolivia .. 78 G6
Santa Cruz, Phil. ... 33 B6
Santa Cruz, U.S.A. .. 73 H2
Santa Cruz →, Argentina ... 80 G3
Santa Cruz de Tenerife, Canary Is. .. 44 C1
Santa Cruz do Sul, Brazil ... 80 B6
Santa Cruz I., Solomon Is. ... 56 J8
Santa Cruz Is., U.S.A. 73 K4
Santa Elena, Ecuador . 78 D2
Santa Eugenia, Pta., Mexico ... 74 B1
Santa Fe, Argentina .. 80 C4
Santa Fe, U.S.A. .. 73 J11
Santa Filomena, Brazil 79 E9
Santa Inés, I., Chile .. 80 G2
Santa Isabel = Rey Malabo, Eq. Guin. . 44 H6
Santa Isabel, Argentina 80 D3
Santa Isabel, Brazil .. 79 F8
Santa Lucia Range, U.S.A. ... 73 J3
Santa Maria, Brazil .. 80 B6
Santa Maria, U.S.A. .. 73 J3
Santa María →, Mexico ... 74 A3
Santa Maria da Vitória, Brazil ... 79 F10
Santa Maria di Leuca, C., Italy .. 21 E8
Santa Marta, Colombia 78 A4
Santa Marta, Sierra Nevada de, Colombia ... 78 A4
Santa Maura = Levkás, Greece ... 21 E9
Santa Monica, U.S.A. . 73 K4
Santa Rita, U.S.A. .. 73 K10
Santa Rosa, La Pampa, Argentina ... 80 D4
Santa Rosa, San Luis, Argentina ... 80 C3
Santa Rosa, Bolivia .. 78 F5
Santa Rosa, Brazil .. 80 B6
Santa Rosa, Calif., U.S.A. ... 72 G2
Santa Rosa, N. Mex., U.S.A. ... 71 H2
Santa Rosa de Copán, Honduras ... 74 E7
Santa Rosa I., Calif., U.S.A. ... 73 K3
Santa Rosa I., Fla., U.S.A. ... 69 K2
Santa Rosa Ra., U.S.A. 72 F5
Santa Vitória do Palmar, Brazil .. 80 C6
Santai, China ... 30 C5
Santana, Coxilha de, Brazil ... 80 C5
Santana do Livramento, Brazil .. 80 C5
Santander, Spain ... 19 A4
Santaquin, U.S.A. ... 72 G8
Santarém, Brazil ... 79 D8
Santarém, Portugal .. 19 C1
Santiago, Brazil ... 80 B6
Santiago, Chile ... 80 C2
Santiago →, Peru ... 78 D3
Santiago de Compostela, Spain . 19 A1
Santiago de Cuba, Cuba ... 75 D9
Santiago de los Cabelleros, Dom. Rep. ... 75 D10
Santiago del Estero, Argentina ... 80 B4
Santo Amaro, Brazil . 79 F11
Santo Ângelo, Brazil . 80 B6
Santo Antônio, Brazil 79 G7
Santo Corazón, Bolivia 78 G7
Santo Domingo, Dom. Rep. 75 D11

Santo Tomás, Peru .. 78 F4
Santo Tomé, Argentina 80 B5
Santo Tomé de Guayana = Ciudad Guayana, Venezuela 78 B6
Santoña, Spain ... 19 A4
Santos, Brazil ... 80 A7
Santos Dumont, Brazil 80 A8
Sanza Pombo, Angola 46 F3
São Anastácio, Brazil . 80 A6
São Bernado de Campo, Brazil 79 H9
São Borja, Brazil ... 80 B5
São Carlos, Brazil 80 A7
São Cristóvão, Brazil . 79 F11
São Domingos, Brazil . 79 F9
São Francisco, Brazil . 79 G10
São Francisco →, Brazil ... 79 F11
São Francisco do Sul, Brazil ... 80 B7
São Gabriel, Brazil .. 80 C6
São João del Rei, Brazil ... 79 H10
São João do Araguaia, Brazil ... 79 E9
São João do Piauí, Brazil ... 79 E10
São José do Rio Prêto, Brazil ... 80 A7
São Leopoldo, Brazil . 80 B6
São Lourenço, Brazil . 79 H9
São Lourenço →, Brazil ... 79 G7
São Luís, Brazil ... 79 D10
São Marcos →, Brazil 79 G9
São Marcos, B. de, Brazil ... 79 D10
São Mateus, Brazil .. 79 G11
São Paulo, Brazil ... 80 A7
São Paulo □, Brazil .. 80 A7
São Paulo, I., Atl. Oc. 2 D8
São Roque, C. de, Brazil ... 79 E11
São Sebastião, I. de, Brazil ... 80 A7
São Tomé, Atl. Oc. .. 42 F4
São Tomé & Principe ■, Africa . 43 F4
São Vicente, C. de, Portugal ... 19 D1
Saône →, France .. 18 D6
Saône-et-Loire □, France ... 18 C6
Saonek, Indonesia ... 33 E7
Saparua, Indonesia .. 33 E7
Sapele, Nigeria ... 44 G6
Sapelo I., U.S.A. ... 69 K5
Saposoa, Peru ... 78 E3
Sapporo, Japan ... 28 C10
Sapudi, Indonesia ... 33 G16
Sapulpa, U.S.A. ... 71 G7
Saqqez, Iran ... 38 B5
Sar Dasht, Iran ... 39 C6
Sar Gachineh, Iran .. 39 D6
Sar Planina, Macedonia ... 21 C9
Saráb, Iran ... 38 B5
Sarabadi, Iraq ... 38 C5
Sarada →, India ... 37 F12
Saragossa = Zaragoza, Spain ... 19 B5
Saraguro, Ecuador .. 78 D3
Sarajevo, Bos.-H. ... 21 C8
Saran, G., Indonesia . 32 E4
Saranac Lake, U.S.A. . 68 C8
Sarandí del Yi, Uruguay ... 80 C5
Sarandí Grande, Uruguay ... 80 C5
Sarangani B., Phil. .. 33 C7
Sarangani Is., Phil. .. 33 C7
Sarangarh, India ... 37 J13
Saransk, Russia ... 22 D8
Sarapul, Russia ... 22 C9
Sarasota, U.S.A. ... 69 M4
Saratoga, U.S.A. ... 72 F10
Saratoga Springs, U.S.A. ... 68 D9
Saratov, Russia ... 22 D8
Saravane, Laos ... 34 E9
Sarawak □, Malaysia . 32 D4
Sarbāz, Iran ... 39 E9
Sarbīsheh, Iran ... 39 C8
Sarda = Sarada →, India ... 37 F12
Sardalas, Libya ... 44 C7
Sardarshahr, India .. 36 E9
Sardegna □, Italy ... 20 E3
Sardinia = Sardegna, Italy ... 20 E3
Sárdūīyeh = Dar Mazār, Iran ... 39 D8
Sargent, U.S.A. ... 70 E5
Sargodha, Pakistan .. 36 C8
Sarh, Chad ... 45 G8
Sārī, Iran ... 39 B7
Sarikei, Malaysia ... 32 D4
Sarina, Australia ... 54 C4
Sarita, U.S.A. ... 71 M6
Sark, Chan. Is. ... 11 H5
Sarlat-la-Canéda, France ... 18 D4
Sarles, U.S.A. ... 70 A5
Sarmi, Indonesia ... 33 E9
Sarmiento, Argentina . 80 F3
Sarnia, Canada ... 62 D3
Sarny, Ukraine ... 22 D4
Sarolangun, Indonesia 32 E2
Saronikós Kólpos, Greece ... 21 F10
Saros Körfezi, Turkey 21 D12
Sarpsborg, Norway .. 9 G11

Sarre = Saar →, Europe 16 D3
Sarro, Mali ... 44 F3
Sartène, France ... 20 D3
Sarthe □, France 18 C4
Sarthe →, France ... 18 C3
Sartynya, Russia ... 24 C7
Sarvestān, Iran ... 39 D7
Saryshagan, Kazakhstan 24 E8
Sasabeneh, Ethiopia . 40 F3
Sasaram, India ... 37 G14
Sasebo, Japan ... 29 H4
Saser, India ... 36 B10
Saskatchewan □, Canada ... 65 C7
Saskatchewan →, Canada ... 65 C8
Saskatoon, Canada .. 65 C7
Saskylakh, Russia ... 25 B12
Sasolburg, S. Africa . 48 D4
Sasovo, Russia ... 22 D7
Sassandra, Ivory C. .. 44 H3
Sassandra →, Ivory C. ... 44 H3
Sássari, Italy ... 20 D3
Sassnitz, Germany .. 16 A6
Sata-Misaki, Japan .. 29 J5
Satadougou, Mali ... 44 F2
Satanta, U.S.A. ... 71 G4
Satara, India ... 36 L8
Satilla →, U.S.A. ... 69 K5
Satka, Russia ... 22 C10
Satmala Hills, India .. 36 J9
Satna, India ... 37 G12
Sátoraljaújhely, Hungary ... 17 D11
Satpura Ra., India ... 36 J10
Satsuna-Shotō, Japan 29 K5
Satu Mare, Romania . 17 E11
Satui, Indonesia ... 32 E5
Satun, Thailand ... 34 N13
Saturnina →, Brazil . 78 F7
Sauda, Norway ... 9 G9
Sauðarkrókur, Iceland . 8 D4
Saudi Arabia ■, Asia . 40 B3
Sauer →, Germany .. 15 E6
Saugerties, U.S.A. ... 68 D9
Sauk Centre, U.S.A. .. 70 C7
Sauk Rapids, U.S.A. . 70 C7
Sault Ste. Marie, Canada ... 62 C3
Sault Ste. Marie, U.S.A. ... 68 B3
Saumlaki, Indonesia . 33 F8
Saumur, France ... 18 C3
Saunders C., N.Z. ... 51 L3
Saunders I., Antarctica 5 B1
Saunders Point, Australia ... 53 E4
Saurbær, Borgarfjarðarsýsla, Iceland ... 8 D3
Saurbær, Eyjafjarðarsýsla, Iceland ... 8 D4
Sauri, Nigeria ... 44 F6
Saurimo, Angola ... 46 F4
Sava →, Serbia, Yug. 21 B9
Savage, U.S.A. ... 70 B2
Savage I. = Niue, Cook Is. ... 57 J11
Savai'i, W. Samoa ... 51 A12
Savalou, Benin ... 44 G5
Savanna, U.S.A. ... 70 D9
Savanna la Mar, Jamaica ... 74 J15
Savannah, Ga., U.S.A. 69 J5
Savannah, Mo., U.S.A. 70 F7
Savannah, Tenn., U.S.A. ... 69 H1
Savannah →, U.S.A. . 69 J5
Savannakhet, Laos .. 34 D8
Savant L., Canada ... 62 B1
Savant Lake, Canada . 62 B1
Savanur, India ... 36 M9
Savé, Benin ... 44 G5
Save →, Mozam. .. 49 C5
Säveh, Iran ... 39 C6
Savelugu, Ghana ... 44 G4
Savoie □, France ... 18 D7
Savona, Italy ... 20 B3
Savonlinna, Finland .. 22 B4
Sawahlunto, Indonesia 32 E2
Sawai, Indonesia ... 33 E7
Sawai Madhopur, India 36 F10
Sawara, Japan ... 29 G10
Sawatch Mts., U.S.A. . 73 G10
Sawel Mt., U.K. ... 13 B4
Sawmills, Zimbabwe . 47 H5
Sawu, Indonesia ... 33 F6
Sawu Sea, Indonesia . 33 F6
Saxby →, Australia .. 54 B3
Say, Niger ... 44 F5
Sayabec, Canada ... 63 C6
Sayán, Peru ... 78 F3
Sayan, Vostochnyy, Russia ... 25 D10
Sayan, Zapadnyy, Russia ... 25 D10
Saydā, Lebanon ... 41 B4
Sayhut, Yemen ... 40 D5
Saynshand, Mongolia 31 B6
Sayre, Okla., U.S.A. . 71 H5
Sayre, Pa., U.S.A. ... 68 E7
Sazan, Albania ... 21 D8
Sāzava →, Czech. ... 16 D7
Sazin, Pakistan ... 36 B8

Scandia, Canada 64 C6
Scandinavia, Europe . 8 E12
Scapa Flow, U.K. ... 12 C5
Scarborough, Trin. & Tob. ... 74 R21
Scarborough, U.K. .. 10 C7
Scebeli, Wabi →, Somali Rep. ... 40 G3
Scenic, U.S.A. ... 70 D3
Schaffhausen, Switz. . 16 E4
Schagen, Neths. ... 15 B4
Schefferville, Canada . 63 B6
Schelde →, Belgium . 15 C4
Schenectady, U.S.A. . 68 D9
Scheveningen, Neths. . 15 B4
Schiedam, Neths. ... 15 C4
Schiermonnikoog, Neths. ... 15 A6
Schio, Italy ... 20 B4
Schleswig, Germany . 16 A4
Schleswig-Holstein □, Germany ... 16 A4
Schofield, U.S.A. ... 70 C10
Schouten, Australia .. 54 G4
Schouten Is. = Supriori, Kepulauan, Indonesia ... 33 E9
Schouwen, Neths. ... 15 C3
Schreiber, Canada ... 62 C2
Schuler, Canada ... 65 C6
Schumacher, Canada . 62 C3
Schurz, U.S.A. ... 72 G4
Schuyler, U.S.A. ... 70 E6
Schwäbische Alb, Germany ... 16 D4
Schwaner, Pegunungan, Indonesia ... 32 E4
Schwarzwald, Germany ... 16 D4
Schweinfurt, Germany 16 C5
Schweizer-Reneke, S. Africa ... 48 D4
Schwerin, Germany .. 16 B5
Schwyz, Switz. ... 16 E4
Sciacca, Italy ... 20 F5
Scilla, Italy ... 20 E6
Scilly, Isles of, U.K. .. 11 H1
Scioto →, U.S.A. ... 68 F4
Scobey, U.S.A. ... 70 A2
Scone, Australia ... 55 E5
Scoresbysund, Greenland ... 4 B6
Scotia, U.S.A. ... 72 F1
Scotia Sea, Antarctica 5 B18
Scotland, U.S.A. ... 70 D6
Scotland □, U.K. ... 12 E5
Scotland Neck, U.S.A. 69 G7
Scott, C., Canada ... 64 C3
Scott City, U.S.A. ... 70 F4
Scott Glacier, Antarctica ... 5 C8
Scott I., Antarctica ... 5 C11
Scott Inlet, Canada .. 61 A12
Scott Is., Canada ... 64 C3
Scott L., Canada ... 65 B7
Scott Reef, Australia . 52 B3
Scottburgh, S. Africa . 49 E5
Scottsbluff, U.S.A. .. 70 E3
Scottsboro, U.S.A. .. 69 H2
Scottsburg, U.S.A. .. 68 F3
Scottsdale, Australia . 54 G4
Scottsville, U.S.A. ... 69 G2
Scottville, U.S.A. ... 68 D2
Scranton, U.S.A. ... 68 E8
Scunthorpe, U.K. ... 10 D7
Scusciuban, Somali Rep. ... 40 E5
Scutari = Üsküdar, Turkey ... 21 D13
Seabrook, L., Australia 53 F2
Seaford, U.S.A. ... 68 F8
Seaforth, Canada ... 62 D3
Seagraves, U.S.A. ... 71 J3
Seal →, Canada ... 65 B10
Seal Cove, Canada ... 63 C8
Seal L., Canada ... 63 B7
Sealy, U.S.A. ... 71 L6
Searchlight, U.S.A. ... 73 J6
Searcy, U.S.A. ... 71 H9
Searles L., U.S.A. ... 73 J5
Seaside, U.S.A. ... 72 D2
Seaspray, Australia .. 55 F4
Seattle, U.S.A. ... 72 C2
Sebastopol = Sevastopol, Ukraine 23 F5
Sebastopol, U.S.A. .. 72 G2
Sebewaing, U.S.A. .. 68 D4
Sebha = Sabhah, Libya ... 45 C7
Sebuku, Indonesia .. 32 E4
Sebuku, Teluk, Malaysia ... 32 D5
Sechelt, Canada ... 64 D4
Sechura, Desierto de, Peru ... 78 E2
Secretary I., N.Z. ... 51 L1
Secunderabad, India . 36 L11
Sedalia, U.S.A. ... 70 F8
Sedan, Australia ... 55 E2
Sedan, France ... 18 B6
Sedan, U.S.A. ... 71 G6
Seddon, N.Z. ... 51 J5
Seddonville, N.Z. ... 51 J4
Sedeh, Fārs, Iran ... 39 D7

Sedeh, Khorāsān, Iran 39 C8
Sederot, Israel ... 41 D3
Sedgewick, Canada .. 64 C6
Sedhiou, Senegal ... 44 F1
Sedley, Canada ... 65 C8
Sedova, Pik, Russia .. 24 B6
Sedro Woolley, U.S.A. 72 B2
Seeheim, Namibia ... 48 D2
Seekoei →, S. Africa 48 E4
Seg-ozero, Russia ... 22 B5
Segamat, Malaysia .. 34 S15
Seget, Indonesia ... 33 E8
Segezha, Russia ... 22 B5
Ségou, Mali ... 44 F3
Segovia = Coco →, Cent. Amer. ... 75 E8
Segovia, Spain ... 19 B3
Segre →, Spain ... 19 B6
Séguéla, Ivory C. ... 44 G3
Seguin, U.S.A. ... 71 L6
Segura →, Spain ... 19 C5
Seh Qal'eh, Iran ... 39 C8
Sehitwa, Botswana .. 48 C3
Sehore, India ... 36 H10
Seiland, Norway ... 8 A17
Seiling, U.S.A. ... 71 G5
Seinäjoki →, Finland . 8 E17
Seine →, France ... 18 B4
Seine-et-Marne □, France ... 18 B5
Seine-Maritime □, France ... 18 B4
Seine-St.-Denis □, France ... 18 B5
Seistan, Iran ... 39 D9
Sekayu, Indonesia ... 32 E2
Sekondi-Takoradi, Ghana ... 44 H4
Sekuma, Botswana .. 48 C3
Selah, U.S.A. ... 72 C3
Selama, Malaysia ... 34 P13
Selangor □, Malaysia 34 R14
Selaru, Indonesia ... 33 F8
Selby, U.K. ... 10 D6
Selby, U.S.A. ... 70 C4
Selden, U.S.A. ... 70 F4
Sele →, Italy ... 20 B7
Selemdzha →, Russia 25 D13
Selenga = Selenge Mörön →, Asia . 30 A5
Selenge Mörön →, Asia ... 30 A5
Seletan, Tg., Indonesia 32 E4
Selfridge, U.S.A. ... 70 B4
Sélibabi, Mauritania . 44 E2
Seligman, U.S.A. ... 73 J7
Selima, El Wâhât el, Sudan ... 45 D10
Selinda Spillway, Botswana ... 48 B3
Selkirk, Canada ... 65 C9
Selkirk, U.K. ... 12 F6
Selkirk I., Canada ... 65 C9
Selkirk Mts., Canada . 64 C5
Sells, U.S.A. ... 73 L8
Selma, Ala., U.S.A. .. 69 J2
Selma, Calif., U.S.A. . 73 H4
Selma, N.C., U.S.A. . 69 H6
Selmer, U.S.A. ... 69 H1
Selpele, Indonesia ... 33 E8
Selsey Bill, U.K. ... 11 G7
Selu, Indonesia ... 33 F8
Selva, Argentina ... 80 B4
Selvas, Brazil ... 78 E5
Selwyn, Australia ... 54 C3
Selwyn L., Canada ... 65 A8
Selwyn Ra., Australia 54 C3
Seman →, Albania .. 21 D8
Semarang, Indonesia 33 G14
Semau, Indonesia ... 33 F6
Semeru, Indonesia ... 33 H15
Semey = Semipalatinsk, Kazakhstan ... 24 D9
Seminoe Res., U.S.A. . 72 E10
Seminole, Okla., U.S.A. 71 H6
Seminole, Tex., U.S.A. 71 J3
Semiozernoye, Kazakhstan ... 24 D7
Semipalatinsk, Kazakhstan ... 24 D9
Semirara Is., Phil. ... 33 B6
Semisopochnoi, U.S.A. 60 C2
Semitau, Indonesia .. 32 D4
Semiyarskoye, Kazakhstan ... 24 D8
Semmering Pass, Austria ... 16 E7
Semnān, Iran ... 39 C7
Semnān □, Iran ... 39 C7
Semois →, Europe .. 15 E4
Semporna, Malaysia . 33 D5
Semuda, Indonesia .. 32 E4
Sen →, Cambodia .. 34 F8
Senā, Iran ... 39 D6
Sena Madureira, Brazil 78 E5
Senador Pompeu, Brazil ... 79 E11
Senai, Malaysia ... 34 T16
Senaja, Malaysia ... 32 C5
Senanga, Zambia ... 48 B3
Senatobia, U.S.A. ... 71 H10
Sendai, Kagoshima, Japan ... 29 J5
Sendai, Miyagi, Japan 28 E10
Sendai-Wan, Japan .. 28 E10
Seneca, Oreg., U.S.A. 72 D4
Seneca, S.C., U.S.A. . 69 H4
Seneca Falls, U.S.A. . 68 D7
Seneca L., U.S.A. ... 68 D7
Senegal ■, W. Afr. .. 44 F2
Senegal →, W. Afr. . 44 E1

Senegal →, W. Afr. . 44 E1
Senegambia, Africa . 42 E2
Senekal, S. Africa ... 49 D4
Senge Khambab = Indus →, Pakistan 36 G5
Sengkang, Indonesia 33 E6
Senhor-do-Bonfim, Brazil ... 79 F10
Senigállia, Italy ... 20 C5
Senj, Croatia ... 20 B6
Senja, Norway ... 8 B14
Senlis, France ... 18 B5
Senmonorom, Cambodia ... 34 F9
Sennâr, Sudan ... 45 F11
Senneterre, Canada .. 62 C4
Sens, France ... 18 B5
Senta, Serbia, Yug. .. 21 B9
Sentinel, U.S.A. ... 73 K7
Sentolo, Indonesia .. 33 G14
Seo de Urgel, Spain . 19 A6
Seoul = Sŏul, S. Korea 31 C7
Separation Point, Canada ... 63 B8
Sepīdān, Iran ... 39 D7
Sepone, Laos ... 34 D9
Sept-Îles, Canada ... 63 B6
Sequim, U.S.A. ... 72 B2
Sequoia Nat. Park, U.S.A. ... 73 H4
Seraing, Belgium ... 15 D5
Seram, Indonesia ... 33 E7
Seram, Kepulauan, Indonesia ... 33 E8
Seram Sea, Indonesia 33 E7
Serang, Indonesia ... 33 G12
Serasan, Indonesia .. 32 D3
Serbia □, Yugoslavia 21 C9
Serdobsk, Russia ... 22 D7
Seremban, Malaysia . 34 S14
Serenje, Zambia ... 47 G6
Sereth = Siret →, Romania ... 17 F14
Sergino, Russia ... 24 C7
Sergipe □, Brazil ... 79 F11
Sergiyev Posad, Russia 22 C6
Seria, Brunei ... 32 D4
Serian, Malaysia ... 32 D4
Seribu, Kepulauan, Indonesia ... 32 F3
Seringapatam Reef, Australia ... 52 B3
Sermata, Indonesia .. 33 F7
Serny Zavod, Turkmenistan ... 24 F6
Serov, Russia ... 22 C11
Serowe, Botswana ... 48 C4
Serpentine, Australia . 53 F2
Serpentine Lakes, Australia ... 53 E4
Serpukhov, Russia .. 22 D6
Sérrai, Greece ... 21 D10
Serrezuela, Argentina 80 C3
Serrinha, Brazil ... 79 F11
Sertânia, Brazil ... 79 E11
Serua, Indonesia ... 33 F8
Serui, Indonesia ... 33 E9
Serule, Botswana ... 48 C4
Sesepe, Indonesia ... 33 E7
Sesfontein, Namibia . 48 B1
Sesheke, Zambia ... 48 B3
Setana, Japan ... 28 C9
Sète, France ... 18 E5
Sete Lagôas, Brazil .. 79 G10
Sétif, Algeria ... 44 A6
Seto, Japan ... 29 G8
Setonaikai, Japan ... 29 G6
Settat, Morocco ... 44 B3
Setté-Cama, Gabon .. 46 E1
Setting L., Canada ... 65 B9
Settle, U.K. ... 10 C5
Settlement Pt., Bahamas ... 69 M6
Setúbal, Portugal ... 19 C1
Setúbal, B. de, Portugal ... 19 C1
Seulimeum, Indonesia 32 C1
Sevan, Ozero, Armenia 23 F8
Sevastopol, Ukraine . 23 F5
Seven Emu, Australia 54 B2
Seven Sisters, Canada 64 C3
Severn →, Canada .. 62 A2
Severn →, U.K. ... 11 F5
Severn L., Canada ... 62 B1
Severnaya Zemlya, Russia ... 25 B10
Severnyye Uvaly, Russia ... 22 C8
Severo-Kurilsk, Russia 25 D16
Severo-Yeniseyskiy, Russia ... 25 C10
Severodvinsk, Russia 22 B6
Severomorsk, Russia . 22 A5
Sovorouralsk, Russia . 22 B10
Sevier →, U.S.A. ... 73 G7
Sevier L., U.S.A. ... 73 G7
Sevilla, Spain ... 19 D3
Seville = Sevilla, Spain 19 D3
Seward, Alaska, U.S.A. 60 B5
Seward, Nebr., U.S.A. 70 E6
Seward Pen., U.S.A. . 60 B3
Sewer, Indonesia ... 33 F8
Sexsmith, Canada ... 64 B5
Seychelles ■, Ind. Oc. 27 K9
Seyðisfjörður, Iceland . 8 D7
Seydvān, Iran ... 38 B5
Seymchan, Russia ... 25 C16
Seymour, Australia .. 55 F4
Seymour, S. Africa .. 49 E4

Seymour, Ind., U.S.A. 68 F3
Seymour, Tex., U.S.A. 71 J5
Seymour, Wis., U.S.A. 68 C1
Sfax, Tunisia 45 B7
Sfîntu Gheorghe,
Romania 21 B11
Shaanxi □, China .. 31 C5
Shaba □, Zaïre 46 F4
Shabunda, Zaïre .. 46 E5
Shache, China 30 C2
Shackleton Ice Shelf,
Antarctica 5 C8
Shackleton Inlet,
Antarctica 5 E11
Shādegān, Iran 39 D6
Shadrinsk, Russia .. 24 D7
Shafter, Calif., U.S.A. 73 J4
Shafter, Tex., U.S.A. 71 L2
Shaftesbury, U.K. .. 11 F5
Shahba, Syria 41 C5
Shahdād, Iran 39 D8
Shahdadkot, Pakistan 36 F5
Shahgarh, India 36 F6
Shāhhāt, Libya 45 B9
Shahjahanpur, India 36 F11
Shahr Kord, Iran ... 39 C6
Shāhrakht, Iran 39 C9
Shahrig, Pakistan .. 36 D5
Shaikhabad, Afghan. 36 B6
Shajapur, India 36 H10
Shakawe, Botswana 48 B3
Shakhty, Russia ... 23 E7
Shakhunya, Russia . 22 C8
Shaki, Nigeria 44 G5
Shakopee, U.S.A. .. 70 C8
Shala, L., Ethiopia . 45 G12
Shaluli Shan, China 30 C4
Shām, Iran 39 E8
Shamāl Dârfûr □,
Sudan 45 E10
Shamāl Kordofân □,
Sudan 45 F10
Shamattawa, Canada 65 B10
Shamattawa →,
Canada 62 A2
Shamil, Iran 39 E8
Shāmkūh, Iran 39 C8
Shamo = Gobi, Asia 31 B6
Shamo, L., Ethiopia 45 G12
Shamokin, U.S.A. .. 68 E7
Shamrock, U.S.A. .. 71 H4
Shamva, Zimbabwe . 47 H6
Shan □, Burma 37 J21
Shāndak, Iran 39 D9
Shandong □, China 31 C6
Shanghai, China ... 31 C7
Shangqiu, China ... 31 C6
Shangrao, China ... 31 D6
Shangshui, China .. 31 C6
Shaniko, U.S.A. ... 72 D3
Shannon, Greenland 4 B7
Shannon, N.Z. 51 J5
Shannon →, Ireland 13 D2
Shansi = Shanxi □,
China 31 C6
Shantar, Ostrov
Bolshoy, Russia ... 25 D14
Shantou, China 31 D6
Shantung =
Shandong □, China 31 C6
Shanxi □, China ... 31 C6
Shaoguan, China ... 31 D6
Shaoxing, China ... 31 C7
Shaoyang, China ... 31 D6
Shapinsay, U.K. .. 12 B6
Shaqra', Si. Arabia . 38 E5
Shaqrā', Yemen ... 40 E4
Shari, Japan 28 C12
Sharjah = Ash
Shāriqah, U.A.E. .. 39 E7
Shark B., Australia . 53 E1
Sharon, U.S.A. 68 E4
Sharon Springs, U.S.A. 70 F4
Sharp Pt., Australia . 54 A3
Sharpe L., Canada .. 65 C10
Sharq el Istiwa'iya □,
Sudan 45 G11
Sharya, Russia 22 C8
Shashi, Botswana .. 49 C4
Shashi, China 31 C6
Shasta, Mt., U.S.A. . 72 F2
Shasta L., U.S.A. .. 72 F2
Shatt al'Arab →, Iraq 39 D6
Shattuck, U.S.A. ... 71 G5
Shaunavon, Canada 65 D7
Shaw →, Australia . 52 D2
Shaw I., Australia .. 54 C4
Shawano, U.S.A. ... 68 C1
Shawinigan, Canada 62 C5
Shawnee, U.S.A. ... 71 H6
Shaybārā, Si. Arabia 38 E3
Shaykh Sa'īd, Iraq . 38 C5
Shcherbakov =
Rybinsk, Russia .. 22 C6
Shchuchiosk,
Kazakhstan 24 D8
Shebele = Scebeli,
Wabi →,
Somali Rep. 40 G3
Sheboygan, U.S.A. . 68 D2
Shediac, Canada ... 63 C4
Sheelin, L., Ireland . 13 C4
Sheep Haven, Ireland 13 A4
Sheerness, U.K. ... 11 F8
Sheet Harbour, Canada 63 D7
Sheffield, U.K. 10 D6
Sheffield, Ala., U.S.A. 69 H2
Sheffield, Tex., U.S.A. 71 K4
Sheho, Canada 65 C8
Shekhupura, Pakistan 36 D8
Shelburne, N.S.,
Canada 63 D6

Shelburne, Ont.,
Canada 62 D3
Shelburne B., Australia 54 A3
Shelby, Mich., U.S.A. 68 D2
Shelby, Mont., U.S.A. 72 B8
Shelby, N.C., U.S.A. 69 H5
Shelbyville, Ill., U.S.A. 70 F10
Shelbyville, Ind.,
U.S.A. 68 F3
Shelbyville, Tenn.,
U.S.A. 69 H2
Sheldrake, Canada .. 63 B7
Shelikhova, Zaliv,
Russia 25 D16
Shell Lake, Canada .. 65 C7
Shell Lakes, Australia 53 E4
Shellbrook, Canada .. 65 C7
Shellharbour, Australia 55 E5
Shelling Rocks, Ireland 13 E1
Shelton, U.S.A. 72 C2
Shenandoah, Iowa,
U.S.A. 70 E7
Shenandoah, Pa.,
U.S.A. 68 E7
Shenandoah, Va.,
U.S.A. 68 F6
Shenandoah →,
U.S.A. 68 F7
Shendam, Nigeria .. 44 G6
Shendî, Sudan 45 E11
Shensi = Shaanxi □,
China 31 C5
Shenyang, China ... 31 B7
Sheopur Kalan, India 36 G10
Shepparton, Australia 55 F4
Sherborne, U.K. ... 11 G5
Sherbro I., S. Leone . 44 G2
Sherbrooke, Canada 63 C5
Sheridan, Ark., U.S.A. 71 H8
Sheridan, Wyo., U.S.A. 72 D10
Sherman, U.S.A. ... 71 J6
Sherridon, Canada .. 65 B8
Sherwood, N. Dak.,
U.S.A. 70 A4
Sherwood, Tex., U.S.A. 71 K4
Sherwood Forest, U.K. 10 D6
Sheslay, Canada ... 64 B2
Sheslay →, Canada . 64 B2
Shethanei L., Canada 65 B9
Shetland □, U.K. .. 12 A7
Shetland Is., U.K. .. 12 A7
Sheyenne, U.S.A. .. 70 B5
Sheyenne →, U.S.A. 70 B6
Shibām, Yemen 40 D4
Shibata, Japan 28 F9
Shibecha, Japan ... 28 C12
Shibetsu, Japan ... 28 B11
Shibogama L., Canada 62 B2
Shibushi, Japan 29 J5
Shickshock Mts. =
Chic-Chocs, Mts.,
Canada 63 C6
Shido, Japan 29 G7
Shiel, L., U.K. 12 E3
Shield, C., Australia . 54 A2
Shiga □, Japan 29 G8
Shigaib, Sudan 45 E9
Shihchiachuang =
Shijiazhuang, China 31 C6
Shijiazhuang, China . 31 C6
Shikarpur, Pakistan . 36 F6
Shikoku □, Japan .. 29 H6
Shikoku-Sanchi, Japan 29 H6
Shilabo, Ethiopia .. 40 F3
Shiliguri, India 37 F16
Shilka, Russia 25 D12
Shilka →, Russia .. 25 D13
Shillelagh, Ireland . 13 D5
Shillong, India 37 G17
Shilo, Jordan 41 C4
Shimabara, Japan .. 29 H5
Shimada, Japan ... 29 G9
Shimane □, Japan .. 29 G6
Shimanovsk, Russia 25 D13
Shimizu, Japan 29 G9
Shimodate, Japan .. 29 F9
Shimoga, India 36 N9
Shimonoseki, Japan 29 H5
Shimpur Rapids,
Angola 48 B2
Shin, L., U.K. 12 C4
Shin-Tone →, Japan 29 G10
Shinano →, Japan . 29 F9
Shindand, Afghan. . 36 C3
Shingleton, U.S.A. . 62 C2
Shingū, Japan 29 H7
Shinjō, Japan 28 E10
Shinshār, Syria ... 41 A5
Shinyanga, Tanzania 46 E6
Shiogama, Japan .. 28 E10
Shiojiri, Japan 29 F9
Ship I., U.S.A. 71 K10
Shiping, China 30 D5
Shipki La, India ... 36 D11
Shippegan, Canada 63 C7
Shippensburg, U.S.A. 68 E7
Shiprock, U.S.A. ... 73 H9
Shiqma, N. →, Israel 41 D3
Shir Kūh, Iran 39 D7
Shiragami-Misaki,
Japan 28 D10
Shirakawa, Fukushima,
Japan 29 F10
Shirakawa, Gifu, Japan 29 F8
Shirane-San, Gumma,
Japan 29 F9
Shirane-San,
Yamanashi, Japan . 29 G9
Shiraoi, Japan 28 C10
Shīrāz, Iran 39 D7

Shire →, Africa 47 H7
Shiretoko-Misaki,
Japan 28 B12
Shiriya-Zaki, Japan . 28 D10
Shiroishi, Japan ... 28 E10
Shīrvān, Iran 39 B8
Shirwa, L. = Chilwa,
L., Malawi 47 H7
Shivpuri, India 36 G10
Shizuoka, Japan ... 29 G9
Shizuoka □, Japan . 29 G9
Shkoder = Shkodra,
Albania 21 C8
Shkodra, Albania .. 21 C8
Shkumbini →,
Albania 21 D8
Shmidta, O., Russia . 25 A10
Shō-Gawa →, Japan 29 F8
Shoal Lake, Canada . 65 C8
Shōdo-Shima, Japan 29 G7
Shoeburyness, U.K. . 11 F8
Sholapur = Solapur,
India 36 L9
Shologontsy, Russia . 25 C12
Shōmrōn, Jordan .. 41 C4
Shoshone, U.S.A. .. 72 E6
Shoshone L., U.S.A. 72 D8
Shoshone Mts., U.S.A. 72 G5
Shoshong, Botswana 48 C4
Shoshoni, U.S.A. .. 72 E9
Show Low, U.S.A. .. 73 J9
Shreveport, U.S.A. . 71 J8
Shrewsbury, U.K. .. 10 E5
Shrirampur, India .. 37 H16
Shropshire □, U.K. . 11 E5
Shuangliao, China .. 31 B7
Shuangyashan, China 31 B8
Shuicheng, China .. 30 D5
Shule, China 30 C2
Shumagin Is., U.S.A. 60 C4
Shumikha, Russia .. 24 D7
Shungnak, U.S.A. .. 60 B4
Shūr →, Iran 39 D7
Shūr Āb, Iran 39 C6
Shūr Gaz, Iran 39 D8
Shūrāb, Iran 39 C8
Shūrjestān, Iran ... 39 D7
Shurugwi, Zimbabwe 47 H6
Shūsf, Iran 39 D9
Shūshtar, Iran 39 D6
Shuswap L., Canada . 64 C5
Shūzū, Iran 39 D7
Shwebo, Burma ... 37 H19
Shwegu, Burma ... 37 G20
Shweli →, Burma .. 37 H20
Shymkent = Chimkent,
Kazakhstan 24 E7
Shyok, India 36 B11
Shyok →, Pakistan . 36 B9
Si Kiang = Xi
Jiang →, China .. 31 D6
Si-ngan = Xi'an, China 31 C5
Si Racha, Thailand . 34 F6
Siahan Range, Pakistan 36 F4
Siaksrindrapura,
Indonesia 32 D2
Sialkot, Pakistan .. 36 C9
Siam = Thailand ■,
Asia 34 D6
Siantan, P., Indonesia 32 D3
Siāreh, Iran 39 D9
Siargao, Phil. 33 C7
Siasi, Phil. 33 C6
Siau, Indonesia ... 33 D7
Šiauliai, Lithuania .. 22 C3
Sibasa, S. Africa ... 49 C5
Sibay, Russia 22 D10
Sibayi, L., S. Africa . 49 D5
Šibenik, Croatia ... 20 C6
Siberia, Russia 4 D13
Siberut, Indonesia . 32 E1
Sibi, Pakistan 36 E5
Sibil, Indonesia ... 33 E10
Sibiti, Congo 46 E2
Sibiu, Romania 21 B11
Sibley, Iowa, U.S.A. . 70 D7
Sibley, La., U.S.A. . 71 J8
Sibolga, Indonesia . 32 D1
Sibsagar, India 37 F19
Sibu, Malaysia 32 D4
Sibuco, Phil. 33 C6
Sibuguey B., Phil. . 33 C6
Sibutu, Phil. 33 D5
Sibutu Passage,
E. Indies 33 D5
Sibuyan, Phil. 33 B6
Sibuyan Sea, Phil. . 33 B6
Sicamous, Canada . 64 C5
Sichuan □, China .. 30 C5
Sicilia, Italy 20 F6
Sicily = Sicilia, Italy . 20 F6
Sicuani, Peru 78 F4
Siddipet, India 36 K11
Sidéradougou,
Burkina Faso 44 F4
Sîdi Barrâni, Egypt . 45 B10
Sidi-bel-Abbès, Algeria 44 A4
Sidlaw Hills, U.K. .. 12 E5
Sidley, Mt., Antarctica 5 D14
Sidmouth, U.K. ... 11 G4
Sidmouth, C., Australia 54 A3
Sidney, Canada 64 D4
Sidney, Mont., U.S.A. 70 B2
Sidney, N.Y., U.S.A. 68 D8
Sidney, Nebr., U.S.A. 70 E3
Sidney, Ohio, U.S.A. 68 E3
Sidoarjo, Indonesia . 33 G15
Sidon = Saydā,
Lebanon 41 B4
Sidra, G. of = Surt,
Khalīj, Libya 45 B8

Siedlce, Poland 17 B11
Siegen, Germany ... 16 C4
Siem Reap, Cambodia 34 F7
Siena, Italy 20 C4
Sierra Blanca, U.S.A. 73 L11
Sierra Blanca Pk.,
U.S.A. 73 K11
Sierra City, U.S.A. . 72 G3
Sierra Colorada,
Argentina 80 E3
Sierra Gorda, Chile . 80 A3
Sierra Leone ■, W. Afr. 44 G2
Sifnos, Greece 21 F11
Sifton, Canada 65 C8
Sifton Pass, Canada 64 B3
Sighetu-Marmatiei,
Romania 17 E11
Sighişoara, Romania 17 E12
Sigli, Indonesia ... 32 C1
Siglufjörður, Iceland . 8 C4
Sigsig, Ecuador ... 78 D3
Sigtuna, Sweden .. 9 G14
Sigüenza, Spain ... 19 B4
Siguiri, Guinea 44 F3
Sigurd, U.S.A. 73 G8
Sihanoukville =
Kompong Som,
Cambodia 34 G7
Sikar, India 36 F9
Sikasso, Mali 44 F3
Sikeston, U.S.A. ... 71 G10
Sikhote Alin, Khrebet,
Russia 25 E14
Sikhote Alin Ra. =
Sikhote Alin,
Khrebet, Russia .. 25 E14
Síkinos, Greece ... 21 F11
Sikkani Chief →,
Canada 64 B4
Sikkim □, India ... 37 F16
Sikotu-Ko, Japan .. 28 C10
Sil →, Spain 19 A2
Silchar, India 37 G18
Silcox, Canada 65 B10
Siler City, U.S.A. .. 69 H6
Silesia = Śląsk, Poland 16 C8
Silgarhi Doti, Nepal . 37 E12
Silghat, India 37 F18
Silifke, Turkey 23 G5
Siliguri = Shiliguri,
India 37 F16
Siling Co, China ... 30 C3
Silistra, Bulgaria .. 21 B12
Siljan, Sweden 9 F13
Silkeborg, Denmark 9 H10
Sillajhuay, Cordillera,
Chile 78 G5
Siloam Springs, U.S.A. 71 G7
Silsbee, U.S.A. 71 K7
Silva Porto = Kuito,
Angola 47 G3
Silver City, Panama . 74 H14
Silver City, N. Mex.,
U.S.A. 73 K9
Silver City, Nev.,
U.S.A. 72 G4
Silver Cr. →, U.S.A. 72 E4
Silver Creek, U.S.A. . 68 D6
Silver Lake, U.S.A. . 72 E3
Silver Streams,
S. Africa 48 D3
Silverton, Colo., U.S.A. 73 H10
Silverton, Tex., U.S.A. 71 H4
Silvies →, U.S.A. . 72 E4
Simanggang, Malaysia 32 D4
Simard, L., Canada . 62 C4
Simbirsk, Russia .. 22 D8
Simcoe, Canada ... 62 D3
Simcoe, L., Canada . 62 D4
Simenga, Russia .. 25 C11
Simeulue, Indonesia 32 D1
Simferopol, Ukraine 23 F5
Simikot, Nepal 37 E12
Simla, India 36 D10
Simmie, Canada ... 65 D7
Simojärvi, Finland . 8 C19
Simojoki →, Finland 8 D18
Simonette →, Canada 64 B5
Simonstown, S. Africa 48 E2
Simpang, Malaysia . 34 Q13
Simplon Pass =
Simplonpass, Switz. 16 E4
Simplonpass, Switz. 16 E4
Simpson Desert,
Australia 54 D2
Simunjan, Malaysia . 32 D4
Simushir, Ostrov,
Russia 25 E16
Sinabang, Indonesia 32 D1
Sinadogo, Somali Rep. 40 F4
Sinai = Es Sînâ', Egypt 45 C11
Sinai, Mt. = Mûsa, G.,
Egypt 45 C11
Sinai Peninsula, Egypt 41 F2
Sinaloa de Levya,
Mexico 74 B3
Sīnāwan, Libya ... 44 B7
Sincelejo, Colombia 78 B3
Sinclair, U.S.A. ... 72 F10
Sinclair Mills, Canada 64 C4
Sincorá, Serra do,
Brazil 79 F10
Sind □, Pakistan .. 36 F6
Sind Sagar Doab,
Pakistan 36 D7
Sindangan, Phil. ... 33 C6
Sindangbarang,
Indonesia 33 G12
Sines, Portugal ... 19 D1
Singa, Sudan 45 F11
Singapore ■, Asia . 34 T16

Singapore, Straits of,
Asia 34 T17
Singaraja, Indonesia 32 F5
Singida, Tanzania .. 46 E6
Singitikós Kólpos,
Greece 21 D10
Singkaling Hkamti,
Burma 37 G19
Singkawang, Indonesia 32 D3
Singleton, Australia . 55 E5
Singleton, Mt.,
N. Terr., Australia . 52 D5
Singleton, Mt.,
W. Austral., Australia 53 E2
Singora = Songkhla,
Thailand 34 J6
Sinî □, Egypt 41 F2
Sinjai, Indonesia .. 33 F6
Sinjār, Iraq 38 B4
Sinkat, Sudan 45 E12
Sinkiang Uighur =
Xinjiang Uygur
Zizhiqu □, China . 30 B3
Sinni →, Italy 20 D7
Sinnuris, Egypt ... 45 C11
Sinop, Turkey 23 F6
Sinskoye, Russia .. 25 C13
Sint Niklaas, Belgium 15 C4
Sint Truiden, Belgium 15 D5
Sintang, Indonesia . 32 D4
Sinton, U.S.A. 71 L6
Sintra, Portugal ... 19 C1
Siocon, Phil. 33 C6
Sioma, Zambia 48 B3
Sion, Switz. 16 E3
Sioux City, U.S.A. . 70 D6
Sioux Falls, U.S.A. . 70 D6
Sioux Lookout, Canada 62 B1
Siping, China 31 B7
Sipiwesk L., Canada 65 B9
Sipora, Indonesia .. 32 E1
Siquijor, Phil. 33 C6
Sir Edward Pellew
Group, Australia . 54 B2
Sir Graham Moore Is.,
Australia 52 B4
Siracusa, Italy 20 F6
Sirajganj, Bangla. .. 37 G16
Sīrdān, Iran 39 B6
Siret →, Romania . 17 F14
Sirohi, India 36 G8
Sironj, India 36 G10
Síros, Greece 21 F11
Sirsa, India 36 E9
Sisak, Croatia 20 B7
Sisaket, Thailand .. 34 E8
Sishen, S. Africa .. 48 D3
Sisipuk L., Canada . 65 B8
Sisophon, Cambodia 34 F7
Sisseton, U.S.A. .. 70 C6
Sīstān va
Balūchestān □, Iran 39 E9
Sisters, U.S.A. 72 D3
Sitapur, India 37 F12
Siteki, Swaziland .. 49 D5
Sitges, Spain 19 B6
Sitka, U.S.A. 60 C6
Sitoti, Botswana .. 48 C3
Sittang Myit →,
Burma 37 L20
Sittard, Neths. 15 C5
Sittwe, Burma 37 J18
Siuri, India 37 H15
Sīvand, Iran 39 D7
Sivas, Turkey 23 G6
Sivomaskinskiy, Russia 22 A11
Sivrihisar, Turkey .. 23 G5
Sîwa, Egypt 45 C10
Siwalik Range, Nepal 37 F13
Siwan, India 37 F14
Sizewell, U.K. 11 E9
Sjælland, Denmark . 9 J11
Sjumen = Šumen,
Bulgaria 21 C12
Skagafjörður, Iceland 8 D4
Skagastølstindane,
Norway 9 F9
Skagerrak, Denmark 9 H10
Skagway, U.S.A. ... 64 B1
Skaidi, Norway 8 A18
Skara, Sweden 9 G12
Skaraborgs län □,
Sweden 9 G12
Skardu, Pakistan .. 36 B9
Skeena →, Canada . 64 C2
Skeena Mts., Canada 64 B3
Skegness, U.K. ... 10 D8
Skeldon, Guyana .. 78 B7
Skellefte älv →,
Sweden 8 D16
Skellefteå, Sweden . 8 D16
Skelleftehamn,
Sweden 8 D16
Skerries, The, U.K. . 10 D3
Skibbereen, Ireland . 13 E2
Skiddaw, U.K. 10 C4
Skien, Norway 9 G10
Skierniewice, Poland 17 C10
Skikda, Algeria ... 44 A6
Skipton, Australia . 55 F3
Skipton, U.K. 10 D5
Skirmish Pt., Australia 54 A1
Skíros, Greece 21 E11
Skive, Denmark ... 9 H10
Skjálfandafljót →,
Iceland 8 D5
Skjálfandi, Iceland . 8 C5
Skoghall, Sweden .. 9 G12
Skopje,
Macedonia 21 C9
Skövde, Sweden ... 9 G12

Skovorodino, Russia . 25 D13
Skowhegan, U.S.A. . 63 D6
Skownan, Canada .. 65 C9
Skudeneshavn,
Norway 9 G8
Skull, Ireland 13 E2
Skunk →, U.S.A. .. 70 E9
Skwierzyna, Poland . 16 B7
Skye, U.K. 12 D2
Skykomish, U.S.A. . 72 C3
Skyros = Skíros,
Greece 21 E11
Slamet, Indonesia .. 32 F3
Slaney →, Ireland .. 13 D5
Sląsk, Poland 16 C8
Slate Is., Canada .. 62 C2
Slatina, Romania .. 21 B11
Slaton, U.S.A. 71 J4
Slave →, Canada .. 64 A6
Slave Coast, W. Afr. 44 F4
Slave Lake, Canada 64 B6
Slave Pt., Canada .. 64 A5
Slavgorod, Russia .. 24 D8
Slavkov, Czech. ... 16 D8
Slavyanka, Russia .. 28 C5
Slavyansk, Ukraine . 23 E6
Sleaford, U.K. 10 E7
Sleaford B., Australia 55 E2
Sleat, Sd. of, U.K. . 12 D3
Sleeper Is., Canada . 61 C11
Sleepy Eye, U.S.A. . 70 C7
Slemon L., Canada . 64 A5
Slidell, U.S.A. 71 K10
Sliedrecht, Neths. . 15 C4
Slieve Aughty, Ireland 13 C3
Slieve Bloom, Ireland 13 C4
Slieve Donard, U.K. . 13 B6
Slieve Gullion, Ireland 13 B5
Slieve Mish, Ireland . 13 D2
Slievenamon, Ireland 13 D4
Sligo, Ireland 13 B3
Sligo □, Ireland ... 13 B3
Sligo B., Ireland ... 13 B3
Slite, Sweden 9 H15
Sliven, Bulgaria ... 21 C12
Slobodskoy, Russia . 22 C9
Slocan, Canada 64 D5
Slochteren, Neths. . 15 A6
Slough, U.K. 11 F7
Slovak Rep. ■, Europe 17 D9
Slovakian Ore Mts. =
Slovenské
Rudohorie, Slovakia 17 D9
Slovenia ■, Europe . 20 B6
Slovenija =
Slovenia ■, Europe 20 B6
Slovenská Republika
= Slovak Rep. ■,
Europe 17 D9
Slovenské Rudohorie,
Slovakia 17 D9
Slovyansk =
Slavyansk, Ukraine . 23 E6
Sluis, Neths. 15 C3
Slurry, S. Africa ... 48 D4
Slyne Hd., Ireland . 13 C1
Slyudyanka, Russia . 25 D11
Smalltree L., Canada 65 A7
Smara, Morocco ... 44 B3
Smartt Syndicate Dam,
S. Africa 48 E3
Smeaton, Canada .. 65 C8
Smederevo,
Serbia, Yug. 21 B9
Smidovich, Russia . 25 E14
Smiley, Canada 65 C7
Smith, Canada 64 B6
Smith →, Canada .. 64 B3
Smith Arm, Canada 60 B7
Smith Center, U.S.A. 70 F5
Smith Sund,
Greenland 4 B4
Smithburne →,
Australia 54 B3
Smithers, Canada .. 64 C3
Smithfield, S. Africa . 49 E4
Smithfield, N.C., U.S.A. 69 H6
Smithfield, Utah,
U.S.A. 72 F8
Smiths Falls, Canada 62 D4
Smithton, Australia . 54 G4
Smithtown, Australia 55 E5
Smithville, U.S.A. .. 71 K6
Smoky →, Canada . 64 B5
Smoky Bay, Australia 55 E1
Smoky Falls, Canada 62 B3
Smoky Hill →, U.S.A. 70 F6
Smoky Lake, Canada 64 C6
Smøla, Norway 8 E10
Smolensk, Russia .. 22 D5
Smolikas, Óros, Greece 21 D9
Smolyan, Bulgaria . 21 D11
Smooth Rock Falls,
Canada 62 C3
Smoothstone L.,
Canada 65 C7
Smyrna = İzmir,
Turkey 23 G4
Snaefell, U.K. 10 C3
Snæfellsjökull, Iceland 8 D2
Snake →, U.S.A. .. 72 C4
Snake I., Australia . 55 F4
Snake L., Canada .. 65 B7
Snake River Plain,
U.S.A. 72 E7
Sneek, Neths. 15 A5
Sneeuberge, S. Africa 48 E3
Snizort, L., U.K. ... 12 D2
Snøhetta, Norway . 8 E10

Snohomish, U.S.A. 72 C2
Snow Hill, U.S.A. 68 F8
Snow Lake, Canada 65 C8
Snowbird L., Canada 65 A8
Snowdon, U.K. 10 D3
Snowdrift, Canada 65 A6
Snowdrift →, Canada 65 A6
Snowflake, U.S.A. 73 J8
Snowshoe Pk., U.S.A. 72 B6
Snowtown, Australia 55 E2
Snowville, U.S.A. 72 F7
Snowy →, Australia 55 F4
Snowy Mts., Australia 55 F4
Snyder, Okla., U.S.A. 71 H5
Snyder, Tex., U.S.A. 71 J4
Soahanina, Madag. 49 B7
Soalala, Madag. 49 B8
Soanierana-Ivongo, Madag. 49 B8
Soap Lake, U.S.A. 72 C4
Sobat, Nahr →, Sudan 45 G11
Sobral, Brazil 79 D10
Soc Trang, Vietnam 34 H8
Soch'e = Shache, China 30 C2
Sochi, Russia 23 F6
Société, Is. de la, Pac. Oc. 57 J12
Society Is. = Société, Is. de la, Pac. Oc. 57 J12
Socompa, Portezuelo de, Chile 80 A3
Socorro, Colombia 78 B4
Socorro, U.S.A. 73 J10
Socotra, Ind. Oc. 40 E5
Soda L., U.S.A. 73 J5
Soda Plains, India 36 B11
Soda Springs, U.S.A. 72 E8
Söderhamn, Sweden 9 F14
Söderköping, Sweden 9 G14
Södermanlands län □, Sweden 9 G14
Södertälje, Sweden 9 G14
Sodiri, Sudan 45 F10
Sodo, Ethiopia 45 G12
Soekmekaar, S. Africa 49 C4
Soest, Neths. 15 B5
Sofia = Sofiya, Bulgaria 21 C10
Sofia →, Madag. 49 B8
Sofiiski, Russia 25 D14
Sofiya, Bulgaria 21 C10
Sōfu-Gan, Japan 29 K10
Sogamoso, Colombia 78 B4
Sogār, Iran 39 E8
Sogn og Fjordane fylke □, Norway 9 F9
Sogndalsfjøra, Norway 9 F9
Sognefjorden, Norway 9 F8
Soh, Iran 39 C6
Sohâg, Egypt 45 C11
Soignies, Belgium 15 D4
Soissons, France 18 B5
Sōja, Japan 29 G6
Sokhumi = Sukhumi, Georgia 23 F7
Sokodé, Togo 44 G5
Sokol, Russia 22 C7
Sokółka, Poland 17 B11
Sokolo, Mali 44 F3
Sokoto, Nigeria 44 F6
Sol Iletsk, Russia 22 D10
Solano, Phil. 33 A6
Solapur, India 36 L9
Soledad, U.S.A. 73 H3
Soledad, Venezuela 78 B6
Solent, The, U.K. 11 G6
Solfonn, Norway 9 F9
Soligalich, Russia 22 C7
Solikamsk, Russia 22 C10
Solila, Madag. 49 C8
Solimões = Amazonas →, S. Amer. 79 C9
Solingen, Germany 15 C7
Sollefteå, Sweden 8 E14
Sóller, Spain 19 C7
Sologne, France 18 C4
Solok, Indonesia 32 E2
Solomon, N. Fork →, U.S.A. 70 F5
Solomon, S. Fork →, U.S.A. 70 F5
Solomon Is. ■, Pac. Oc. 56 H7
Solon, China 31 B7
Solon Springs, U.S.A. 70 B9
Solor, Indonesia 33 F6
Solothurn, Switz. 16 E3
Soltānābād, Khorāsān, Iran 39 C8
Soltānābād, Khorāsān, Iran 39 B8
Soltānābād, Markazī, Iran 39 C6
Solunska Glava, Macedonia 21 D9
Solvay, U.S.A. 68 D7
Solvychegodsk, Russia 22 B8
Solway Firth, U.K. 10 C4
Solwezi, Zambia 47 G5
Sōma, Japan 28 F10
Somali Rep. ■, Africa 40 F4
Somalia ■ = Somali Rep. ■, Africa 40 F4
Sombor, Serbia, Yug. 21 B8
Sombrerete, Mexico 74 C4
Sombrero, Anguilla 75 D12
Somers, U.S.A. 72 B6
Somerset, Canada 65 D9
Somerset, Colo., U.S.A. 73 G10
Somerset, Ky., U.S.A. 68 G3
Somerset □, U.K. 11 F5
Somerset East, S. Africa 48 E4
Somerset I., Canada 60 A10
Somerset West, S. Africa 48 E2
Somerton, U.S.A. 73 K6
Someş →, Romania 17 E11
Sommariva, Australia 55 D4
Somme □, France 18 B5
Somport, Puerto de, Spain 19 A5
Son La, Vietnam 34 B7
Sondags →, S. Africa 48 E4
Sønderborg, Denmark 9 J10
Søndre Strømfjord, Greenland 61 B14
Sonepur, India 37 J13
Song Cau, Vietnam 34 F10
Songea, Tanzania 46 G7
Songhua Jiang →, China 31 B8
Songkhla, Thailand 34 J6
Songpan, China 30 C5
Sonipat, India 36 E10
Sonmiani, Pakistan 36 G5
Sono →, Brazil 79 E9
Sonora, Calif., U.S.A. 73 H3
Sonora, Tex., U.S.A. 71 K4
Sonora →, Mexico 74 B2
Sonsonate, El Salv. 74 E7
Soochow = Suzhou, China 31 C7
Sopi, Indonesia 33 D7
Sopot, Poland 17 A9
Sop's Arm, Canada 63 C8
Sør-Rondane, Antarctica 5 D4
Sør-Trøndelag fylke □, Norway 8 E10
Sorata, Bolivia 78 G5
Sorel, Canada 62 C5
Soreq, N. →, Israel 41 D3
Soria, Spain 19 B4
Sorkh, Kuh-e, Iran 39 C8
Sorocaba, Brazil 80 A7
Sorochinsk, Russia 22 D9
Sorong, Indonesia 33 E8
Soroti, Uganda 46 D6
Sørøya, Norway 8 A17
Sørøysundet, Norway 8 A17
Sorrento, Australia 55 F3
Sorrento, Italy 20 D6
Sorsele, Sweden 8 D14
Sorsogon, Phil. 33 B6
Sortavala, Russia 22 B5
Soscumica, L., Canada 62 B4
Sosnogorsk, Russia 22 B9
Sosnovka, Russia 25 D11
Sosnowiec, Poland 17 C9
Sosva, Russia 22 C11
Souanké, Congo 46 D2
Soúdhas, Kólpos, Greece 21 G11
Sŏul, S. Korea 31 C7
Sound, The = Øresund, Europe 9 H12
Sound, The, U.K. 11 G3
Sources, Mt. aux, Lesotho 49 D4
Soure, Brazil 79 D9
Souris, Man., Canada 65 D8
Souris, P.E.I., Canada 63 C7
Souris →, Canada 70 A5
Sousa, Brazil 79 E11
Sousel, Brazil 79 D8
Sousse, Tunisia 45 A7
South Africa ■, Africa 48 E3
South Aulatsivik I., Canada 63 A7
South Australia □, Australia 55 E2
South Baldy, U.S.A. 73 J10
South Bend, Ind., U.S.A. 68 E2
South Bend, Wash., U.S.A. 72 C2
South Boston, U.S.A. 69 G6
South Branch, Canada 63 C8
South Brook, Canada 63 C8
South Carolina □, U.S.A. 69 J5
South Charleston, U.S.A. 68 F5
South China Sea, Asia 32 C4
South Dakota □, U.S.A. 70 C5
South Downs, U.K. 11 G7
South East C., Australia 54 G4
South East Is., Australia 53 F3
South Esk →, U.K. 12 E5
South Foreland, U.K. 11 F9
South Fork →, U.S.A. 72 C7
South Gamboa, Panama 74 H14
South Georgia, Antarctica 5 B1
South Glamorgan □, U.K. 11 F4
South Haven, U.S.A. 68 D2
South Henik, L., Canada 65 A9
South Honshu Ridge, Pac. Oc. 56 E6
South Horr, Kenya 46 D7
South I., N.Z. 51 L3
South Invercargill, N.Z. 51 M2
South Knife →, Canada 65 B10
South Korea ■, Asia 31 C7
South Loup →, U.S.A. 70 E5
South Magnetic Pole, Antarctica 5 C9
South Milwaukee, U.S.A. 68 D2
South Molton, U.K. 11 F4
South Nahanni →, Canada 64 A4
South Natuna Is. = Natuna Selatan, Kepulauan, Indonesia 32 D3
South Orkney Is., Antarctica 5 C18
South Pagai, I. = Pagai Selatan, P., Indonesia 32 E2
South Pass, U.S.A. 72 E9
South Pittsburg, U.S.A. 69 H3
South Platte →, U.S.A. 70 E4
South Pole, Antarctica 5 E
South Porcupine, Canada 62 C3
South River, Canada 62 C4
South Ronaldsay, U.K. 12 C6
South Sandwich Is., Antarctica 5 B1
South Saskatchewan →, Canada 65 C7
South Seal →, Canada 65 B9
South Sentinel I., India 34 G2
South Shetland Is., Antarctica 5 C18
South Shields, U.K. 10 C6
South Sioux City, U.S.A. 70 D6
South Taranaki Bight, N.Z. 51 H5
South Thompson →, Canada 64 C4
South Twin I., Canada 62 B4
South Tyne →, U.K. 10 C5
South Uist, U.K. 12 D1
South West Africa = Namibia ■, Africa 48 C2
South West C., Australia 54 G4
South Yorkshire □, U.K. 10 D6
Southampton, Canada 62 D3
Southampton, U.K. 11 G6
Southampton, U.S.A. 68 E9
Southampton I., Canada 61 B11
Southbridge, N.Z. 51 K4
Southend, Canada 65 B8
Southend-on-Sea, U.K. 11 F8
Southern Alps, N.Z. 51 K3
Southern Cross, Australia 53 F2
Southern Hills, Australia 53 F3
Southern Indian L., Canada 65 B9
Southern Ocean, Antarctica 5 C6
Southern Pines, U.S.A. 69 H6
Southern Uplands, U.K. 12 F5
Southport, Australia 55 D5
Southport, U.K. 10 D4
Southport, U.S.A. 69 J6
Southwest C., N.Z. 51 M1
Southwold, U.K. 11 E9
Soutpansberg, S. Africa 49 C4
Sovetsk, Russia 22 C3
Sovetsk, Russia 22 C8
Sovetskaya Gavan, Russia 25 E15
Soviet Union = Commonwealth of Independent States ■, Eurasia 25 D11
Soweto, S. Africa 49 D4
Sōya-Kaikyō = La Perouse Str., Asia 28 B11
Sōya-Misaki, Japan 28 B10
Soyo, Angola 46 F2
Sozh →, Belorussia 22 D5
Spa, Belgium 15 D5
Spain ■, Europe 19 C4
Spalding, Australia 55 E2
Spalding, U.K. 10 E7
Spalding, U.S.A. 70 E5
Spaniard's Bay, Canada 63 C9
Spanish, Canada 62 C3
Spanish Fork, U.S.A. 72 F8
Spanish Town, Jamaica 74 K17
Sparks, U.S.A. 72 G4
Sparta = Spárti, Greece 21 F10
Sparta, Ga., U.S.A. 69 J4
Sparta, Wis., U.S.A. 70 D9
Spartanburg, U.S.A. 69 H4
Spárti, Greece 21 F10
Spartivento, C., Calabria, Italy 20 F7
Spartivento, C., Sard., Italy 20 E3
Spassk-Dalniy, Russia 25 E14
Spátha, Ákra, Greece 21 G10
Spatsizi →, Canada 64 B3
Spearfish, U.S.A. 70 C3
Spearman, U.S.A. 71 G4
Speers, Canada 65 C7
Speightstown, Barbados 74 P22
Spence Bay, Canada 60 B10
Spencer, Idaho, U.S.A. 72 D7
Spencer, Iowa, U.S.A. 70 D7
Spencer, Nebr., U.S.A. 70 D5
Spencer, W. Va., U.S.A. 68 F5
Spencer, C., Australia 55 F2
Spencer B., Namibia 48 D1
Spencer G., Australia 55 E2
Spences Bridge, Canada 64 C4
Spenser Mts., N.Z. 51 K4
Sperrin Mts., U.K. 13 B5
Spessart, Germany 16 C4
Spey →, U.K. 12 D5
Speyer, Germany 16 D4
Spinazzola, Italy 20 D7
Spirit Lake, U.S.A. 72 C5
Spirit River, Canada 64 B5
Spiritwood, Canada 65 C7
Spithead, U.K. 11 G6
Spitzbergen = Svalbard, Arctic 4 B8
Split, Croatia 20 C7
Split L., Canada 65 B9
Splügenpass, Switz. 16 E4
Spofford, U.S.A. 71 L4
Spokane, U.S.A. 72 C5
Spoleto, Italy 20 C5
Spooner, U.S.A. 70 C9
Sporyy Navolok, Mys, Russia 24 B7
Spragge, Canada 62 C3
Sprague, U.S.A. 72 C5
Sprague River, U.S.A. 72 E3
Spratly I., S. China Sea 32 C4
Spray, U.S.A. 72 D4
Spree →, Germany 16 B6
Spremberg, Germany 16 C7
Spring City, U.S.A. 72 G8
Spring Mts., U.S.A. 73 H6
Spring Valley, U.S.A. 70 D8
Springbok, S. Africa 48 D2
Springdale, Canada 63 C8
Springdale, Ark., U.S.A. 71 G7
Springdale, Wash., U.S.A. 72 B5
Springer, U.S.A. 71 G2
Springerville, U.S.A. 73 J9
Springfield, N.Z. 51 K3
Springfield, Colo., U.S.A. 71 G3
Springfield, Ill., U.S.A. 70 F10
Springfield, Mass., U.S.A. 68 D9
Springfield, Mo., U.S.A. 71 G8
Springfield, Ohio, U.S.A. 68 F4
Springfield, Oreg., U.S.A. 72 D2
Springfield, Tenn., U.S.A. 69 G2
Springfontein, S. Africa 48 E4
Springhill, Canada 63 C7
Springhouse, Canada 64 C4
Springhurst, Australia 55 F4
Springs, S. Africa 49 D4
Springsure, Australia 54 C4
Springvale, Queens., Australia 54 C3
Springvale, W. Austral., Australia 52 C4
Springville, N.Y., U.S.A. 68 D6
Springville, Utah, U.S.A. 72 F8
Springwater, Canada 65 C7
Spur, U.S.A. 71 J4
Spurn Hd., U.K. 10 D8
Spuzzum, Canada 64 D4
Squamish, Canada 64 D4
Square Islands, Canada 63 B8
Squires, Mt., Australia 53 E4
Sragen, Indonesia 33 G14
Srbija = Serbia □, Yugoslavia 21 C9
Sre Umbell, Cambodia 34 G7
Sredinny Ra. = Sredinnyy Khrebet, Russia 25 D16
Sredinnyy Khrebet, Russia 25 D16
Sredne Tambovskoye, Russia 25 D14
Srednekolymsk, Russia 25 C16
Srednevilyuysk, Russia 25 C13
Sretensk, Russia 25 D12
Sri Lanka ■, Asia 36 R12
Srikakulam, India 37 K13
Srinagar, India 36 B9
Staaten →, Australia 54 B3
Staðarhólskirkja, Iceland 8 D3
Stadlandet, Norway 8 E8
Stadskanaal, Neths. 15 A6
Stafafell, Iceland 8 D6
Staffa, U.K. 12 E2
Stafford, U.K. 10 E5
Stafford, U.S.A. 71 G5
Staffordshire □, U.K. 10 E5
Staines, U.K. 11 F7
Stakhanov = Kadiyevka, Ukraine 23 E6
Stalingrad = Volgograd, Russia 23 E7
Staliniri = Tskhinvali, Georgia 23 F7
Stalino = Donetsk, Ukraine 23 E6
Stalinogorsk = Novomoskovsk, Russia 22 D6
Stalybridge, U.K. 10 D5
Stamford, Australia 54 C3
Stamford, U.K. 11 E7
Stamford, Conn., U.S.A. 68 E9
Stamford, Tex., U.S.A. 71 J5
Stamps, U.S.A. 71 J8
Stanberry, U.S.A. 70 E7
Standerton, S. Africa 49 D4
Standish, U.S.A. 68 D4
Stanford, U.S.A. 72 C8
Stanger, S. Africa 49 D5
Stanislav = Ivano-Frankovsk, Ukraine 23 E3
Stanke Dimitrov, Bulgaria 21 C10
Stanley, Australia 54 G4
Stanley, N.B., Canada 63 C6
Stanley, Sask., Canada 65 B8
Stanley, Falk. Is. 80 G5
Stanley, Idaho, U.S.A. 72 D6
Stanley, N. Dak., U.S.A. 70 A3
Stanley, Wis., U.S.A. 70 C9
Stanovoy Khrebet, Russia 25 D13
Stanovoy Ra. = Stanovoy Khrebet, Russia 25 D13
Stansmore Ra., Australia 52 D4
Stanthorpe, Australia 55 D5
Stanton, U.S.A. 71 J4
Staples, U.S.A. 70 B7
Stapleton, U.S.A. 70 E4
Star City, Canada 65 C8
Stara Planina, Bulgaria 21 C10
Stara Zagora, Bulgaria 21 C11
Staraya Russa, Russia 22 C5
Starbuck I., Kiribati 57 H12
Staritsa, Russia 22 C5
Starke, U.S.A. 69 K4
Starkville, Colo., U.S.A. 71 G2
Starkville, Miss., U.S.A. 69 J1
Starogard, Poland 17 B9
Start Pt., U.K. 11 G4
Staryy Kheydzhan, Russia 25 C15
Staryy Oskol, Russia 22 D6
State College, U.S.A. 68 E7
Staten, I. = Estados, I. de Los, Argentina 80 G4
Statesboro, U.S.A. 69 J5
Statesville, U.S.A. 69 H5
Staunton, Ill., U.S.A. 70 F10
Staunton, Va., U.S.A. 68 F6
Stavanger, Norway 9 G8
Staveley, N.Z. 51 K3
Stavelot, Belgium 15 D5
Staveren, Neths. 15 B5
Stavern, Norway 9 G11
Stavropol, Russia 23 E7
Stawell, Australia 55 F3
Stawell →, Australia 54 C3
Steamboat Springs, U.S.A. 72 F10
Steele, U.S.A. 70 B5
Steelton, U.S.A. 68 E7
Steelville, U.S.A. 71 G9
Steen River, Canada 64 B5
Steenkool = Bintuni, Indonesia 33 E8
Steenwijk, Neths. 15 B6
Steep Pt., Australia 53 E1
Steep Rock, Canada 65 C9
Stefanie L. = Chew Bahir, Ethiopia 45 H12
Stefansson Bay, Antarctica 5 C5
Steiermark □, Austria 16 E7
Steinbach, Canada 65 D9
Steinfort, Lux. 15 E5
Steinkjer, Norway 8 E11
Steinkopf, S. Africa 48 D2
Stellarton, Canada 63 C7
Stellenbosch, S. Africa 48 E2
Stendal, Germany 16 B5
Stensele, Sweden 8 D14
Stepanakert = Khankendy, Azerbaijan 23 G8
Stephan, U.S.A. 70 A6
Stephens Creek, Australia 55 E3
Stephens I., Canada 64 C2
Stephenville, Canada 63 C8
Stephenville, U.S.A. 71 J5
Stepnoi = Elista, Russia 23 E7
Stepnyak, Kazakhstan 24 D8
Steppe, Asia 26 E9
Sterkstroom, S. Africa 48 E4
Sterling, Colo., U.S.A. 70 E3
Sterling, Ill., U.S.A. 70 E10
Sterling, Kans., U.S.A. 70 F5
Sterling City, U.S.A. 71 K4
Sterlitamak, Russia 22 D10
Stettin = Szczecin, Poland 16 B7
Stettler, Canada 64 C6
Steubenville, U.S.A. 68 E5
Stevens Point, U.S.A. 70 C10
Stevenson L., Canada 65 C9
Stewart, B.C., Canada 64 B3
Stewart, N.W.T., Canada 60 B6
Stewart, C., Australia 54 A1
Stewart, I., Chile 80 G2
Stewart I., N.Z. 51 M1
Stewiacke, Canada 63 C7
Steynsburg, S. Africa 48 E4
Steyr, Austria 16 D7
Steytlerville, S. Africa 48 E3
Stigler, U.S.A. 71 H7
Stikine →, Canada 64 B2
Stilfontein, S. Africa 48 D4
Stillwater, N.Z. 51 K3
Stillwater, Minn., U.S.A. 70 C8
Stillwater, Okla., U.S.A. 71 G6
Stillwater Ra., U.S.A. 72 G4
Stilwell, U.S.A. 71 H7
Štip, Macedonia 21 D10
Stirling, Australia 54 B3
Stirling, Canada 64 D6
Stirling, U.K. 12 E5
Stirling Ra., Australia 53 F2
Stockerau, Austria 16 D8
Stockett, U.S.A. 72 C8
Stockholm, Sweden 9 G15
Stockport, U.K. 10 D5
Stockton, Calif., U.S.A. 73 H3
Stockton, Kans., U.S.A. 70 F5
Stockton, Mo., U.S.A. 71 G8
Stockton-on-Tees, U.K. 10 C6
Stoke on Trent, U.K. 10 D5
Stokes Bay, Canada 62 C3
Stokes Pt., Australia 54 G3
Stokes Ra., Australia 52 C5
Stokkseyri, Iceland 8 E3
Stokksnes, Iceland 8 D6
Stolac, Bos.-H. 21 C7
Stolbovaya, Russia 25 C16
Stolbovoy, Ostrov, Russia 25 D17
Stonehaven, U.K. 12 E6
Stonehenge, Australia 54 C3
Stonewall, Canada 65 C9
Stony L., Canada 65 B9
Stony Rapids, Canada 65 B7
Stony Tunguska = Podkamennaya Tunguska →, Russia 25 C10
Stora Lulevatten, Sweden 8 C15
Stora Sjöfallet, Sweden 8 C15
Storavan, Sweden 8 D15
Store Bælt, Denmark 9 J11
Store Creek, Australia 55 E4
Støren, Norway 8 E11
Storlulea = Stora Lulevatten, Sweden 8 C15
Storm B., Australia 54 G4
Storm Lake, U.S.A. 70 D7
Stormberge, S. Africa 48 E4
Stormsrivier, S. Africa 48 E3
Stornoway, U.K. 12 C2
Storsjön, Sweden 8 E12
Storuman, Sweden 8 D14
Stoughton, Canada 65 D8
Stour →, Dorset, U.K. 11 G5
Stour →, Here. & Worcs., U.K. 11 E5
Stour →, Kent, U.K. 11 F9
Stour →, Suffolk, U.K. 11 F9
Stourbridge, U.K. 11 E5
Stout, L., Canada 65 C10
Stowmarket, U.K. 11 E9
Strabane, U.K. 13 B4
Strabane □, U.K. 13 B4
Strahan, Australia 54 G4
Stralsund, Germany 16 A6
Strand, S. Africa 48 E2
Strangford L., U.K. 13 B6
Stranraer, U.K. 12 G3
Strasbourg, Canada 65 C8
Strasbourg, France 18 B7
Strasburg, U.S.A. 70 B4
Stratford, Canada 62 D3
Stratford, N.Z. 51 H5
Stratford, Calif., U.S.A. 73 H4
Stratford, Tex., U.S.A. 71 G3
Stratford-upon-Avon, U.K. 11 E6
Strath Spey, U.K. 12 D5
Strathalbyn, Australia 55 F2
Strathclyde □, U.K. 12 F4
Strathcona Prov. Park, Canada 64 D3
Strathmore, Australia 54 B3
Strathmore, Canada 64 C6
Strathmore, U.K. 12 E5
Strathnaver, Canada 64 C4
Strathpeffer, U.K. 12 D4
Strathroy, Canada 62 D3
Strathy Pt., U.K. 12 C4
Stratton, U.S.A. 70 F3
Straumnes, Iceland 8 C2
Strawberry Res., U.S.A. 72 F8
Strawn, U.S.A. 71 J5
Streaky B., Australia 55 E1
Streaky Bay, Australia 55 E1
Streator, U.S.A. 70 E10
Streeter, U.S.A. 70 B5
Strelka, Russia 25 D10
Strezhevoy, Russia 24 C8
Strómboli, Italy 20 E6
Stromeferry, U.K. 12 D3
Stromness, U.K. 12 C5
Ströms vattudal, Sweden 8 D13

Strömstad, *Sweden* .. 9 G11
Strömsund, *Sweden* . 8 E13
Stronsay, *U.K.* 12 B6
Stronsburg, *U.S.A.* ... 70 E6
Stroud, *U.K.* 11 F5
Stroud Road, *Australia* 55 E5
Struer, *Denmark* 9 H10
Strumica,
　Macedonia 21 D10
Struthers, *Canada* ... 62 C2
Struthers, *U.S.A.* 68 E5
Stryker, *U.S.A.* 72 B6
Strzelecki Cr. →,
　Australia 55 D2
Stuart, *Fla., U.S.A.* .. 69 M5
Stuart, *Nebr., U.S.A.* . 70 D5
Stuart →, *Canada* ... 64 C4
Stuart Bluff Ra.,
　Australia 52 D5
Stuart L., *Canada* ... 64 C4
Stuart Ra., *Australia* . 55 D1
Stull, L., *Canada* 62 B1
Stung Treng,
　Cambodia 34 F8
Stupart →, *Canada* .. 65 B10
Sturgeon B., *Canada* . 65 C9
Sturgeon Bay, *U.S.A.* 68 C2
Sturgeon Falls, *Canada* 62 C4
Sturgeon L., *Alta.,*
　Canada 64 B5
Sturgeon L., *Ont.,*
　Canada 62 B1
Sturgis, *Mich., U.S.A.* 68 E3
Sturgis, *S. Dak., U.S.A.* 70 C3
Sturt Cr. →, *Australia* 52 C4
Sturt Creek, *Australia* 52 C4
Stutterheim, *S. Africa* 48 E4
Stuttgart, *Germany* .. 16 D4
Stuttgart, *U.S.A.* 71 H9
Stykkishólmur, *Iceland* 8 D2
Styria = Steiermark □,
　Austria 16 E7
Suakin, *Sudan* 45 E12
Subang, *Indonesia* ... 33 G12
Subansiri →, *India* .. 37 F18
Subayhah, *Si. Arabia* 38 D3
Subi, *Indonesia* 32 D3
Subotica, *Serbia, Yug.* 21 A8
Success, *Canada* 65 C7
Suceava, *Romania* ... 17 E13
Suchan, *Russia* 28 C6
Suchou = Suzhou,
　China 31 C7
Süchow = Xuzhou,
　China 31 C6
Suck →, *Ireland* 13 C3
Sucre, *Bolivia* 78 G5
Sud, Pte. →, *Canada* . 63 C7
Sud-Ouest, Pte. du,
　Canada 63 C7
Sudan, *U.S.A.* 71 H3
Sudan ■, *Africa* 45 E11
Sudbury, *Canada* 62 C3
Sudbury, *U.K.* 11 E8
Südd, *Sudan* 45 G11
Sudeten Mts. =
　Sudety, *Europe* ... 16 C8
Sudety, *Europe* 16 C8
Sudirman,
　Pegunungan,
　Indonesia 33 E9
Sueca, *Spain* 19 C5
Suez = El Suweis,
　Egypt 45 C11
Suez, G. of = Suweis,
　Khalîg el, *Egypt* .. 45 C11
Suffield, *Canada* 65 C6
Suffolk, *U.S.A.* 68 G7
Suffolk □, *U.K.* 11 E9
Sugar City, *U.S.A.* ... 70 F3
Sugluk = Saglouc,
　Canada 61 B12
Suhâr, *Oman* 39 E8
Suihua, *China* 31 B7
Suir →, *Ireland* 13 D4
Sukabumi, *Indonesia* . 33 G12
Sukadana, *Kalimantan,*
　Indonesia 32 E3
Sukadana, *Sumatera,*
　Indonesia 32 F3
Sukagawa, *Japan* ... 29 F10
Sukaraja, *Indonesia* .. 32 E4
Sukarnapura =
　Jayapura, *Indonesia* 33 E10
Sukhona →, *Russia* .. 22 C6
Sukhumi, *Georgia* ... 23 F7
Sukkur, *Pakistan* 36 F6
Sukkur Barrage,
　Pakistan 36 F6
Sukumo, *Japan* 29 H6
Sukunka →, *Canada* . 64 B4
Sula, Kepulauan,
　Indonesia 33 E7
Sulaiman Range,
　Pakistan 36 D6
Sülär, *Iran* 39 D6
Sulawesi □, *Indonesia* 33 E6
Sulawesi Sea,
　Indonesia 33 D6
Sulima, *S. Leone* 44 G2
Sulina, *Romania* 17 F14
Sulitälma, *Sweden* ... 8 C14
Sulitjelma, *Norway* .. 8 C14
Sullana, *Peru* 78 D2
Sullivan, *Ill., U.S.A.* .. 70 F10
Sullivan, *Ind., U.S.A.* . 68 F2
Sullivan, *Mo., U.S.A.* . 70 F9
Sullivan Bay, *Canada* 64 C3
Sullivan I. = Lambi
　Kyun, *Burma* 34 G5
Sulphur, *La., U.S.A.* . 71 K8

Sulphur, *Okla., U.S.A.* 71 H6
Sulphur Pt., *Canada* .. 64 A6
Sulphur Springs,
　U.S.A. 71 J7
Sulphur Springs
　Draw →, *U.S.A.* .. 71 J4
Sultan, *Canada* 62 C3
Sultanpur, *India* 37 F13
Sultsa, *Russia* 22 B8
Sulu Arch., *Phil.* 33 C6
Sulu Sea, *E. Indies* .. 33 C6
Suluq, *Libya* 45 B9
Sulzberger Ice Shelf,
　Antarctica 5 D10
Sumalata, *Indonesia* . 33 D6
Sumatera □, *Indonesia* 32 D2
Sumatra =
　Sumatera □,
　Indonesia 32 D2
Sumatra, *U.S.A.* 72 C10
Sumba, *Indonesia* ... 33 F5
Sumba, Selat,
　Indonesia 33 F5
Sumbawa, *Indonesia* . 32 F5
Sumbawa Besar,
　Indonesia 32 F5
Sumbe, *Angola* 46 G2
Sumburgh Hd., *U.K.* . 12 B7
Sumedang, *Indonesia* 33 G12
Šumen, *Bulgaria* 21 C12
Sumenep, *Indonesia* . 33 G15
Sumgait, *Azerbaijan* . 23 F8
Summer L., *U.S.A.* .. 72 E3
Summerland, *Canada* 64 D5
Summerside, *Canada* 63 C7
Summersville,
　U.S.A. 68 F5
Summerville, *Ga.,*
　U.S.A. 69 H3
Summerville, *S.C.,*
　U.S.A. 69 J5
Summit Lake, *Canada* 64 C4
Summit Pk., *U.S.A.* .. 73 H10
Sumner, *U.S.A.* 70 D8
Sumoto, *Japan* 29 G7
Šumperk, *Czech.* ... 16 D8
Sumqayit = Sumgait,
　Azerbaijan 23 F8
Sumter, *U.S.A.* 69 J5
Sumy, *Ukraine* 23 D5
Sun City, *U.S.A.* 73 K7
Sunagawa, *Japan* ... 28 C10
Sunart, L., *U.K.* 12 E3
Sunburst, *U.S.A.* ... 72 B8
Sunbury, *Australia* .. 55 F3
Sunbury, *U.S.A.* 68 E7
Sunda, Selat,
　Indonesia 32 F3
Sunda Is., *Indonesia* . 26 K14
Sunda Str. = Sunda,
　Selat, *Indonesia* .. 32 F3
Sundance, *U.S.A.* ... 70 C2
Sundarbans, The, *Asia* 37 J16
Sundargarh, *India* ... 37 H14
Sundays →
　Sondags →,
　S. Africa 48 E4
Sunderland, *U.K.* ... 10 C6
Sundre, *Canada* 64 C6
Sundridge, *Canada* .. 62 C4
Sundsvall, *Sweden* .. 8 E14
Sungai Patani,
　Malaysia 34 P13
Sungaigerong,
　Indonesia 32 E2
Sungailiat, *Indonesia* . 32 E3
Sungaipakning,
　Indonesia 32 D2
Sungaipenuh,
　Indonesia 32 E2
Sungaitiram, *Indonesia* 32 E5
Sungari = Songhua
　Jiang →, *China* .. 31 B8
Sungei Siput, *Malaysia* 34 Q14
Sungguminasa,
　Indonesia 33 F5
Sunghua Chiang =
　Songhua Jiang →,
　China 31 B8
Sunnyside, *Utah,*
　U.S.A. 72 G8
Sunnyside, *Wash.,*
　U.S.A. 72 C3
Sunnyvale, *U.S.A.* .. 73 H2
Sunray, *U.S.A.* 71 G4
Suntar, *Russia* 25 C12
Suoyarvi, *Russia* 22 B5
Supai, *U.S.A.* 73 H7
Supaul, *India* 37 F15
Superior, *Ariz., U.S.A.* 73 K8
Superior, *Mont., U.S.A.* 72 C6
Superior, *Nebr., U.S.A.* 70 E5
Superior, *Wis., U.S.A.* 70 B8
Superior, L., *N. Amer.* 62 C2
Suphan Buri, *Thailand* 34 E6
Supriori, Kepulauan,
　Indonesia 33 E9
Süq Suwayq,
　Si. Arabia 38 E3
Sûr, *Lebanon* 41 B4
Sur, Pt., *U.S.A.* 73 H3
Sura →, *Russia* 22 C8
Surabaja = Surabaya,
　Indonesia 33 G15
Surabaya, *Indonesia* . 33 G15
Surakarta, *Indonesia* . 33 G14
Surat, *Australia* 55 D4
Surat, *India* 36 J8
Surat Thani, *Thailand* 34 H5
Suratgarh, *India* 36 E8
Sûre = Sauer →,
　Germany 15 E6
Surgut, *Russia* 24 C8

Suriapet, *India* 36 L11
Surigao, *Phil.* 33 C7
Surin, *Thailand* 34 E7
Surinam ■, *S. Amer.* 79 C7
Suriname □, *S. Amer.* 79 C7
Suriname →,
　Surinam 79 B7
Surrey □, *U.K.* 11 F7
Surt, *Libya* 45 B8
Surt, Khalîj, *Libya* .. 45 B8
Surtsey, *Iceland* 8 E3
Suruga-Wan, *Japan* . 29 G9
Susa, *Italy* 20 B2
Susaki, *Japan* 29 H6
Süsangerd, *Iran* 39 D6
Susanino, *Russia* ... 25 D15
Susanville, *U.S.A.* ... 72 F3
Susquehanna →,
　U.S.A. 68 F7
Susques, *Argentina* . 80 A3
Sussex, *Canada* 63 C6
Sussex, E. □, *U.K.* .. 11 G8
Sussex, W. □, *U.K.* . 11 G7
Sustut →, *Canada* .. 64 B3
Susuman, *Russia* ... 25 C15
Susunu, *Indonesia* .. 33 E8
Sutherland, *S. Africa* 48 E3
Sutherland, *U.S.A.* .. 70 E4
Sutherland Falls, *N.Z.* 51 L1
Sutherlin, *U.S.A.* ... 72 E2
Sutlej →, *Pakistan* .. 36 E7
Sutton, *U.S.A.* 70 E6
Sutton →, *Canada* .. 62 A3
Sutton in Ashfield,
　U.K. 10 D6
Suttor →, *Australia* . 54 C4
Suttsu, *Japan* 28 C10
Suva, *Fiji* 51 D8
Suva Planina,
　Serbia, Yug. 21 C10
Suvorov Is. =
　Suwarrow Is.,
　Cook Is. 57 J11
Suwałki, *Poland* 17 A11
Suwannee →, *U.S.A.* 69 L4
Suwanose-Jima, *Japan* 29 K4
Suwarrow Is., *Cook Is.* 57 J11
Suwayq aş Şuqban,
　Iraq 38 D5
Suweis, Khalîg el,
　Egypt 45 C11
Suzdal, *Russia* 22 C7
Suzhou, *China* 31 C7
Suzu, *Japan* 29 F8
Suzu-Misaki, *Japan* . 29 F8
Suzuka, *Japan* 29 G8
Svalbard, *Arctic* 4 B8
Svalbarð, *Iceland* ... 8 C6
Svanvik, *Norway* 8 B21
Svappavaara, *Sweden* 8 C16
Svartisen, *Norway* .. 8 C12
Svay Rieng, *Cambodia* 34 G8
Svealand □, *Sweden* . 9 G13
Sveg, *Sweden* 8 E13
Svendborg, *Denmark* 9 J11
Sverdlovsk =
　Yekaterinburg,
　Russia 22 C11
Sverdrup Is., *Canada* . 4 B3
Svetlaya, *Russia* 28 A9
Svir →, *Russia* 22 B5
Svishtov, *Bulgaria* ... 21 C11
Svobodnyy, *Russia* .. 25 D13
Svolvær, *Norway* ... 8 B13
Swabian Alps =
　Schwäbische Alb,
　Germany 16 D4
Swainsboro, *U.S.A.* . 69 J4
Swakopmund, *Namibia* 48 C1
Swale →, *U.K.* 10 C6
Swan Hill, *Australia* . 55 F3
Swan Hills, *Canada* . 64 C5
Swan L., *Canada* ... 65 C8
Swan River, *Canada* . 65 C8
Swanage, *U.K.* 11 G6
Swansea, *Australia* .. 55 F5
Swansea, *U.K.* 11 F4
Swartberge, *S. Africa* 48 E3
Swartmodder, *S. Africa* 48 D3
Swartruggens,
　S. Africa 48 D4
Swastika, *Canada* ... 62 C3
Swatow = Shantou,
　China 31 D6
Swaziland ■, *Africa* . 49 D5
Sweden ■, *Europe* . 9 H13
Sweet Home, *U.S.A.* 72 D2
Sweetwater, *U.S.A.* . 71 J4
Sweetwater →,
　U.S.A. 72 E10
Swellendam, *S. Africa* 48 E3
Świdnica, *Poland* ... 16 C8
Świebodzin, *Poland* . 16 B7
Swift Current, *Canada* 65 C7
Swiftcurrent →,
　Canada 65 C7
Swilly, L., *Ireland* ... 13 A4
Swindle, I., *Canada* .. 64 C3
Swindon, *U.K.* 11 F6
Swinemünde =
　Świnoujście, *Poland* 16 B7
Świnoujście, *Poland* . 16 B7
Switzerland ■, *Europe* 16 E4
Swords, *Ireland* 13 C5
Sydney, *Australia* ... 55 E5
Sydney, *Canada* 63 C7
Sydney Mines, *Canada* 63 C7
Sydprøven, *Greenland* 4 C5

Sydra G. of = Surt,
　Khalîj, *Libya* 45 B8
Syktyvkar, *Russia* ... 22 B9
Sylacauga, *U.S.A.* .. 69 J2
Sylarna, *Sweden* ... 8 E12
Sylhet, *Bangla.* 37 G17
Sylvan Lake, *Canada* 64 C6
Sylvania, *U.S.A.* 69 J5
Sylvester, *U.S.A.* ... 69 K4
Sym, *Russia* 24 C9
Synnott Ra., *Australia* 52 C4
Syracuse, *Kans., U.S.A.* 71 F4
Syracuse, *N.Y., U.S.A.* 68 D7
Syrdarya →,
　Kazakhstan 24 E7
Syria ■, *Asia* 38 C3
Syul'dzhyukyor, *Russia* 25 C12
Syzran, *Russia* 22 D8
Szczecin, *Poland* ... 16 B7
Szczecinek, *Poland* . 16 B8
Szechwan =
　Sichuan □, *China* . 30 C5
Szeged, *Hungary* ... 17 E10
Székesfehérvár,
　Hungary 17 E9
Szekszárd, *Hungary* . 17 E10
Szentes, *Hungary* ... 17 E10
Szolnok, *Hungary* .. 17 E10
Szombathely, *Hungary* 16 E8

T

Tabacal, *Argentina* ... 80 A4
Tabaco, *Phil.* 33 B6
Ţâbah, *Si. Arabia* ... 38 E4
Tabarka, *Tunisia* 44 A6
Ţabas, *Khorāsān, Iran* 39 C9
Ţabas, *Khorāsān, Iran* 39 C8
Tabatinga, Serra da,
　Brazil 79 F10
Tabāzīn, *Iran* 39 D8
Taber, *Canada* 64 D6
Tablas, *Phil.* 33 B6
Table B. = Tafelbaai,
　S. Africa 48 E2
Table B., *Canada* ... 63 B8
Table Mt., *S. Africa* . 48 E2
Tableland, *Australia* . 52 C4
Tabletop, Mt., *Australia* 54 C4
Tábor, *Czech.* 16 D7
Tabora, *Tanzania* ... 46 F6
Tabou, *Ivory C.* 44 H3
Tabrīz, *Iran* 38 B5
Tabuaeran, *Pac. Oc.* 57 G12
Tabûk, *Si. Arabia* ... 38 D3
Tacheng, *China* 30 B3
Tacloban, *Phil.* 33 B6
Tacna, *Peru* 78 G4
Tacoma, *U.S.A.* 72 C2
Tacuarembó, *Uruguay* 80 C5
Tademaït, Plateau du,
　Algeria 44 C5
Tadjoura, *Djibouti* ... 40 E3
Tadmor, *N.Z.* 51 J4
Tadoule, L., *Canada* . 65 B9
Tadoussac, *Canada* . 63 C6
Tadzhikistan =
　Tajikistan ■, *Asia* . 24 F8
Taegu, *S. Korea* 31 C7
Taejŏn, *S. Korea* ... 31 C7
Tafalla, *Spain* 19 A5
Tafelbaai, *S. Africa* .. 48 E2
Tafermaar, *Indonesia* 33 F8
Tafihān, *Iran* 39 D7
Taft, *Iran* 39 D7
Taft, *Phil.* 33 B7
Taft, *Calif., U.S.A.* .. 73 J4
Taft, *Tex., U.S.A.* ... 71 M6
Taga Dzong, *Bhutan* 37 F16
Taganrog, *Russia* ... 23 E6
Tagbilaran, *Phil.* 33 C6
Tagish, *Canada* 64 A2
Tagish L., *Canada* ... 64 A2
Tagliamento →, *Italy* 20 B5
Taguatinga, *Brazil* .. 79 F10
Tagum, *Phil.* 33 C7
Tagus = Tejo →,
　Europe 19 C1
Tahakopa, *N.Z.* 51 M2
Tahan, Gunong,
　Malaysia 34 Q15
Tahat, *Algeria* 44 D6
Tāherī, *Iran* 39 E7
Tahiti, *Pac. Oc.* 57 J13
Tahoe, L., *U.S.A.* ... 72 G3
Tahoe City, *U.S.A.* .. 72 G3
Tahoua, *Niger* 44 F6
Tahta, *Egypt* 45 C11
Tahulandang,
　Indonesia 33 D7
Tahuna, *Indonesia* .. 33 D7
Taï, *Ivory C.* 44 G3
T'aichung = Taizhong,
　Taiwan 31 D7
Taieri →, *N.Z.* 51 M3
Taihape, *N.Z.* 51 H5
Tailem Bend, *Australia* 55 F2
Taimyr, Poluostrov,
　Russia 25 B11
Tain, *U.K.* 12 D4
Tainan, *Taiwan* 31 D7
Taínaron, Ákra, *Greece* 21 F10
T'aipei = Taibei,
　Taiwan 31 D7
T'aipei, *Taiwan* 31 D7
Taiping, *Malaysia* ... 34 Q13

Taitao, Pen. de, *Chile* 80 F2
Taivalkoski, *Finland* .. 8 D20
Taiwan ■, *Asia* 31 D7
Taíyetos Óros, *Greece* 21 F10
Taiyiba, *Israel* 41 C4
Taiyuan, *China* 31 C6
Taizhong, *Taiwan* ... 31 D7
Ta'izz, *Yemen* 40 E3
Tajikistan ■, *Asia* ... 24 F8
Tajima, *Japan* 29 F9
Tajo = Tejo →,
　Europe 19 C1
Tajrīsh, *Iran* 39 C6
Tājūrā, *Libya* 45 B7
Tak, *Thailand* 34 D5
Takāb, *Iran* 38 B5
Takachiho, *Japan* ... 29 H5
Takada, *Japan* 29 F9
Takahagi, *Japan* 29 F10
Takaka, *N.Z.* 51 J4
Takamatsu, *Japan* .. 29 G7
Takaoka, *Japan* 29 F8
Takapuna, *N.Z.* 51 G5
Takasaki, *Japan* 29 F9
Takatsuki, *Japan* ... 29 G7
Takaungu, *Kenya* ... 46 E7
Takayama, *Japan* ... 29 F8
Take-Shima, *Japan* .. 29 J5
Takefu, *Japan* 29 G8
Takengon, *Indonesia* 32 D1
Takeo, *Cambodia* ... 34 G8
Takeo, *Japan* 29 H5
Tākestān, *Iran* 39 C6
Taketa, *Japan* 29 H5
Takikawa, *Japan* ... 28 C10
Takla L., *Canada* 64 B3
Takla Landing, *Canada* 64 B3
Takla Makan =
　Taklamakan Shamo,
　China 26 F12
Taklamakan Shamo,
　China 26 F12
Taku →, *Canada* ... 64 B2
Takum, *Nigeria* 44 G6
Tal Halāl, *Iran* 39 D7
Tala, *Uruguay* 80 C5
Talara, *Peru* 78 D2
Talas, *Kirghizia* 24 E8
Talâta, *Egypt* 41 E1
Talaud, Kepulauan,
　Indonesia 33 D7
Talaud Is. = Talaud,
　Kepulauan,
　Indonesia 33 D7
Talavera de la Reina,
　Spain 19 C3
Talawana, *Australia* . 52 D3
Talayan, *Phil.* 33 C6
Talbot, C., *Australia* . 52 B4
Talbragar →,
　Australia 55 E4
Talca, *Chile* 80 D2
Talcahuano, *Chile* ... 80 D2
Talcher, *India* 37 J14
Taldy Kurgan =
　Taldyqorghan =
　Taldy
　Kurgan, *Kazakhstan* 24 E8
Taldyqorghan = Taldy
　Kurgan, *Kazakhstan* 24 E8
Talesh, *Iran* 39 B6
Talesh, Kūhhā-ye, *Iran* 39 B6
Tali Post, *Sudan* 45 G11
Taliabu, *Indonesia* .. 33 E6
Talibon, *Phil.* 33 B6
Talihina, *U.S.A.* 71 H7
Taling Sung, *Thailand* 34 E5
Taliwang, *Indonesia* . 32 F5
Tall 'Asūr, *Jordan* ... 41 D4
Tall Kalakh, *Syria* ... 41 A5
Talladega, *U.S.A.* ... 69 J2
Tallangatta, *Australia* 55 F4
Tallarook, *Australia* .. 55 F4
Tallering Pk., *Australia* 53 E2
Tallinn, *Estonia* 22 C3
Tallulah, *U.S.A.* 71 J9
Talodi, *Sudan* 45 F11
Taltal, *Chile* 80 B2
Taltson →, *Canada* . 64 A6
Talwood, *Australia* .. 55 D4
Talyawalka Cr. →,
　Australia 55 E3
Tama, *U.S.A.* 70 E8
Tamale, *Ghana* 44 G4
Tamano, *Japan* 29 G6
Tamanrasset, *Algeria* 44 D6
Tamar →, *U.K.* 11 G3
Tamarang, *Australia* . 55 E5
Tamashima, *Japan* .. 29 G6
Tamaské, *Niger* 44 F6
Tambacounda,
　Senegal 44 F2
Tambelan, Kepulauan,
　Indonesia 32 D3
Tambellup, *Australia* 53 F2
Tambo, *Australia* 54 C4
Tambo de Mora, *Peru* 78 F3
Tambohorano, *Madag.* 49 B7
Tambora, *Indonesia* . 32 F5
Tambov, *Russia* 22 D7
Tambuku, *Indonesia* . 33 G15
Tamburâ, *Sudan* 45 G10
Tâmchekket,
　Mauritania 44 E2
Tamega →, *Portugal* 19 B1
Tamenglong, *India* .. 37 G18
Tamgak, Mts., *Niger* 44 E6
Tamil Nadu □, *India* . 36 P10
Tammerfors =
　Tampere, *Finland* . 9 F17
Tammisaari, *Finland* . 9 F17

Tamo Abu,
　Pegunungan,
　Malaysia 32 D5
Tampa, *U.S.A.* 69 M4
Tampa B., *U.S.A.* ... 69 M4
Tampere, *Finland* ... 9 F17
Tampico, *Mexico* ... 74 C5
Tampin, *Malaysia* ... 34 S15
Tamrida = Qādib,
　Yemen 40 E5
Tamu, *Burma* 37 G19
Tamworth, *Australia* . 55 E5
Tamworth, *U.K.* 11 E6
Tana, *Norway* 8 A20
Tana →, *Kenya* 46 E8
Tana →, *Norway* ... 8 A20
Tana, L., *Ethiopia* ... 45 F12
Tanabe, *Japan* 29 H7
Tanafjorden, *Norway* . 8 A20
Tanahbala, *Indonesia* 32 E1
Tanahgrogot,
　Indonesia 32 E5
Tanahjampea,
　Indonesia 33 F6
Tanahmasa, *Indonesia* 32 E1
Tanahmerah,
　Indonesia 33 F10
Tanakura, *Japan* 29 F10
Tanami, *Australia* ... 52 C4
Tanami Desert,
　Australia 52 C5
Tanana, *U.S.A.* 60 B4
Tanana →, *U.S.A.* .. 60 B4
Tananarive =
　Antananarivo,
　Madag. 49 B8
Tánaro →, *Italy* 20 B3
Tanbar, *Australia* ... 54 D3
Tandag, *Phil.* 33 C7
Tandaué, *Angola* 48 B2
Tandil, *Argentina* ... 80 D5
Tandil, Sa. del,
　Argentina 80 D5
Tando Adam, *Pakistan* 36 G6
Tandou L., *Australia* . 55 E3
Tane-ga-Shima, *Japan* 29 J5
Taneatua, *N.Z.* 51 H6
Tanen Tong Dan,
　Burma 34 D5
Tanezrouft, *Algeria* .. 44 D5
Tanga, *Tanzania* 46 F7
Tanganyika, L., *Africa* 46 F6
Tanger, *Morocco* ... 44 A3
Tangerang, *Indonesia* 33 G12
Tanggula Shan, *China* 30 C4
Tangier = Tanger,
　Morocco 44 A3
Tangkak, *Malaysia* .. 34 S15
Tangorin P.O.,
　Australia 54 C3
Tangshan, *China* 31 C6
Tanimbar, Kepulauan,
　Indonesia 33 F8
Tanimbar Is. =
　Tanimbar,
　Kepulauan,
　Indonesia 33 F8
Tanjay, *Phil.* 33 C6
Tanjore = Thanjavur,
　India 36 P11
Tanjung, *Indonesia* .. 32 E5
Tanjungbalai,
　Indonesia 32 D1
Tanjungbatu,
　Indonesia 32 D5
Tanjungkarang
　Telukbetung,
　Indonesia 32 F3
Tanjungpandan,
　Indonesia 32 E3
Tanjungpinang,
　Indonesia 32 D2
Tanjungpriok,
　Indonesia 33 G12
Tanjungredeb,
　Indonesia 32 D5
Tanjungselor,
　Indonesia 32 D5
Tannu-Ola, *Russia* .. 25 D10
Tanout, *Niger* 44 F6
Tanta, *Egypt* 45 B11
Tantung = Dandong,
　China 31 B7
Tanunda, *Australia* .. 55 E2
Tanzania ■, *Africa* .. 46 F6
Tanzilla →, *Canada* . 64 B2
Taolanaro, *Madag.* .. 49 D8
Taos, *U.S.A.* 73 H11
Taoudenni, *Mali* 44 D4
Taourirt, *Morocco* ... 44 B4
Tapa Shan = Daba
　Shan, *China* 31 C5
Tapah, *Malaysia* 34 Q14
Tapajós →, *Brazil* .. 79 D8
Tapaktuan, *Indonesia* 32 D1
Tapanui, *N.Z.* 51 L2
Tapauá →, *Brazil* .. 78 E6
Tapeta, *Liberia* 44 G3
Tapi →, *India* 36 J8
Tapirapecó, Serra,
　Venezuela 78 C6
Tappahannock, *U.S.A.* 68 G7
Tapuaenuku, Mt., *N.Z.* 51 J4
Tapul Group, *Phil.* ... 33 C6
Taqtaq, *Iraq* 38 C5
Taquari →, *Brazil* ... 78 G7
Tara, *Australia* 55 D5
Tara, *Russia* 24 D8
Tara →,
　Montenegro, Yug. 21 C8
Tara →, *Russia* 24 D8

Tarabagatay, Khrebet, Kazakhstan . . . 24 E9
Tarābulus, Lebanon . . 41 A4
Tarābulus, Libya . . . 45 B7
Tarakan, Indonesia . . 32 D5
Taralga, Australia . . . 55 E4
Tarama-Jima, Japan . 29 M2
Taranaki □, N.Z. . . . 51 H5
Taranga Hill, India . . 36 H8
Táranto, Italy 20 D7
Táranto, G. di, Italy . 20 D7
Tarapacá, Colombia . . 78 D5
Tararua Ra., N.Z. . . . 51 J5
Tarauacá, Brazil 78 E4
Tarauacá →, Brazil . . 78 E5
Tarawera, N.Z. 51 H6
Tarawera, L., N.Z. . . . 51 H6
Tarbat Ness, U.K. . . . 12 D5
Tarbela Dam, Pakistan 36 B8
Tarbert, Strath., U.K. . 12 F3
Tarbert, W. Isles, U.K. 12 D2
Tarbes, France 18 E4
Tarboro, U.S.A. 69 H7
Tarbrax, Australia . . . 54 C3
Tarcoola, Australia . . 55 E1
Tarcoon, Australia . . . 55 E4
Taree, Australia 55 E5
Tarentaise, France . . . 18 D7
Tarfaya, Morocco . . . 44 C2
Tarifa, Spain 19 D3
Tarija, Bolivia 80 A4
Tariku →, Indonesia 33 E9
Tarim Basin = Tarim Pendi, China . . 30 B3
Tarim He →, China . 30 C3
Tarim Pendi, China . . 30 B3
Taritatu →, Indonesia 33 E9
Tarka →, S. Africa . 48 E4
Tarkastad, S. Africa . 48 E4
Tarkhankut, Mys, Ukraine 23 E5
Tarko Sale, Russia . . . 24 C8
Tarkwa, Ghana 44 G4
Tarlac, Phil. 33 A6
Tarlton Downs, Australia 54 C2
Tarma, Peru 78 F3
Tarn □, France 18 E5
Tarn →, France 18 D4
Tarn-et-Garonne □, France 18 D4
Tarnów, Poland 17 C10
Tarnowskie Góry, Poland 17 C9
Taroom, Australia . . . 55 D4
Taroudannt, Morocco 44 B3
Tarpon Springs, U.S.A. 69 L4
Tarragona, Spain . . . 19 B6
Tarrasa, Spain 19 B7
Tarshiha = Me'ona, Israel 41 B4
Tarso Emissi, Chad . . 45 D8
Tarsus, Turkey 23 G5
Tartagal, Argentina . . 80 A4
Tartu, Estonia 22 C4
Ţarţūs, Syria 38 C2
Tarumizu, Japan 29 J5
Tarutao, Ko, Thailand 34 J5
Tarutung, Indonesia . 32 D1
Tasawāh, Libya 45 C7
Taschereau, Canada . 62 C4
Taseko →, Canada . 64 C4
Tash-Kumyr, Kirghizia 24 E8
Tashauz, Turkmenistan 24 E6
Tashi Chho Dzong = Thimphu, Bhutan . 37 F16
Tashkent, Uzbekistan . 24 E7
Tashtagol, Russia . . . 24 D9
Tasikmalaya, Indonesia 33 G13
Tåsjön, Sweden 8 D13
Taskan, Russia 25 C16
Tasman B., N.Z. 51 J4
Tasman Mts., N.Z. . . . 51 J4
Tasman Pen., Australia 54 G4
Tasman Sea, Pac. Oc. 56 L8
Tasmania □, Australia 54 G4
Tasu Sd., Canada . . . 64 C2
Tatar Republic □, Russia 22 C9
Tatarsk, Russia 24 D8
Tateyama, Japan 29 G9
Tathlina L., Canada . . 64 A6
Tathra, Australia . . . 55 F4
Tatinnai L., Canada . . 65 A9
Tatnam, C., Canada . . 65 B10
Tatra = Tatry, Slovakia 17 D10
Tatry, Slovakia 17 D10
Tatsuno, Japan 29 G7
Tatta, Pakistan 36 G5
Tatuí, Brazil 80 A7
Tatum, U.S.A. 71 J3
Tat'ung = Datong, China 31 B6
Tatvan, Turkey 23 G7
Taubaté, Brazil 80 A7
Tauern, Austria 16 E6
Taumarunui, N.Z. . . . 51 H5
Taumaturgo, Brazil . . 78 E4
Taung, S. Africa 48 D3
Taungdwingyi, Burma 37 J19
Taunggyi, Burma . . . 37 J20
Taungup, Burma 37 K19
Taungup Pass, Burma 37 K19
Taungup Taunggya, Burma 37 K18
Taunton, U.K. 11 F4
Taunton, U.S.A. 68 E10
Taunus, Germany . . . 16 C4
Taupo, N.Z. 51 H5
Taupo, L., N.Z. 51 H5
Tauranga, N.Z. 51 G6
Tauranga Harb., N.Z. . 51 G6

Taurianova, Italy 20 E7
Taurus Mts. = Toros Dağlan, Turkey . . 23 G5
Tavda, Russia 24 D7
Tavda →, Russia . . 24 D7
Taveta, Tanzania . . . 46 E7
Taveuni, Fiji 51 C9
Tavira, Portugal . . . 19 D2
Tavistock, U.K. 11 G3
Tavoy, Burma 34 E5
Taw →, U.K. 11 F3
Tawas City, U.S.A. . . 68 C4
Tawau, Malaysia . . . 32 D5
Tawitawi, Phil. 33 B6
Tay →, U.K. 12 E5
Tay, L., Australia . . . 53 F3
Tay, L., U.K. 12 E4
Tay, Firth of, U.K. . . 12 E5
Tay Ninh, Vietnam . . 34 G9
Tayabamba, Peru . . . 78 E3
Taylor, Canada 64 B4
Taylor, Nebr., U.S.A. . 70 E5
Taylor, Tex., U.S.A. . 71 K6
Taylor Mt., U.S.A. . . 73 J10
Taylorville, U.S.A. . . 70 F10
Taymā, Si. Arabia . . 38 E3
Taymyr, Oz., Russia . 25 B11
Taymyr, Poluostrov, Russia 25 B11
Tayport, U.K. 12 E5
Tayshet, Russia 25 D10
Tayside □, U.K. 12 E5
Taytay, Phil. 33 B5
Taz →, Russia 24 C8
Taza, Morocco 44 B4
Tāzah Khurmātū, Iraq 38 C5
Tazawa-Ko, Japan . . 28 E10
Tazin L., Canada . . . 65 B7
Tazovskiy, Russia . . . 24 C8
Tbilisi, Georgia 23 F7
Tchad = Chad ■, Africa 45 E8
Tchad, L., Chad 45 F7
Tch'eng-tou = Chengdu, China . . 30 C5
Tchentlo L., Canada . 64 B4
Tchibanga, Gabon . . 46 E2
Tch'ong-k'ing = Chongqing, China . 30 D5
Te Anau, L., N.Z. . . . 51 L1
Te Aroha, N.Z. 51 G5
Te Awamutu, N.Z. . . 51 H5
Te Kuiti, N.Z. 51 H5
Te Puke, N.Z. 51 G6
Te Waewae B., N.Z. . 51 M1
Tea Tree, Australia . . 54 C1
Teague, U.S.A. 71 K6
Tebakang, Malaysia . 32 D4
Tébessa, Algeria . . . 44 A6
Tebicuary →, Paraguay 80 B5
Tebingtinggi, Indonesia 32 D1
Tecuci, Romania . . . 17 F13
Tecumseh, U.S.A. . . 68 D4
Tedzhen, Turkmenistan 24 F7
Tees →, U.K. 10 C6
Teesside, U.K. 10 C6
Tefé, Brazil 78 D6
Tegal, Indonesia . . . 33 G13
Tegelen, Neths. 15 C6
Tegid, L. = Bala, L., U.K. 10 E4
Tegina, Nigeria 44 F6
Tegucigalpa, Honduras 74 E7
Tehachapi, U.S.A. . . 73 J4
Tehachapi Mts., U.S.A. 73 J4
Tehrān, Iran 39 C6
Tehuantepec, Mexico 74 D5
Tehuantepec, G. de, Mexico 74 D5
Tehuantepec, Istmo de, Mexico 74 D6
Teifi →, U.K. 11 E3
Teign →, U.K. 11 G4
Teignmouth, U.K. . . . 11 G4
Tejo →, Europe . . . 19 C1
Tekamah, U.S.A. . . . 70 E6
Tekapo, L., N.Z. 51 K3
Tekeli, Kazakhstan . . 24 E8
Tekirdağ, Turkey . . . 21 D12
Tekkali, India 37 K14
Tekoa, U.S.A. 72 C5
Tel Aviv-Yafo, Israel . 41 C3
Tel Lakhish, Israel . . 41 D3
Tel Megiddo, Israel . . 41 C4
Tela, Honduras 74 D7
Telanaipura = Jambi, Indonesia 32 E2
Telavi, Georgia 23 F8
Telegraph Creek, Canada 64 B2
Telemark fylke □, Norway 9 G10
Teles Pires →, Brazil 78 E7
Telescope Peak, U.S.A. 73 H5
Telford, U.K. 10 E5
Télimélé, Guinea . . . 44 F2
Telkwa, Canada . . . 64 C3
Tell City, U.S.A. . . . 68 G2
Tellicherry, India . . . 36 P9
Telluride, U.S.A. . . . 73 H10
Telom →, Malaysia 34 Q14
Telpos Iz, Russia . . . 22 B10
Telsen, Argentina . . . 80 E3
Teluk Anson, Malaysia 34 Q14
Teluk Betung = Tanjungkarang Telukbetung, Indonesia 32 F3

Teluk Intan = Teluk Anson, Malaysia . . 34 Q14
Telukbutun, Indonesia 32 D3
Telukdalem, Indonesia 32 D1
Tema, Ghana 44 G5
Temanggung, Indonesia 33 G14
Temax, Mexico 74 C7
Temba, S. Africa . . . 49 D4
Tembeling →, Malaysia 34 Q15
Teme →, U.K. 11 E5
Temecula, U.S.A. . . . 73 K5
Temerloh, Malaysia . 34 R15
Temir, Kazakhstan . . 24 E6
Temirtau, Kazakhstan 24 D8
Temirtau, Russia . . . 24 D9
Témiscaming, Canada 62 C4
Temma, Australia . . . 54 G3
Temora, Australia . . . 55 E4
Tempe, U.S.A. 73 K8
Temple, U.S.A. 71 K6
Temple B., Australia . 54 A3
Templemore, Ireland . 13 D4
Templeton →, Australia 54 C2
Temuco, Chile 80 D2
Temuka, N.Z. 51 L3
Tenaha, U.S.A. 71 K7
Tenali, India 36 L12
Tenasserim, Burma . . 34 F5
Tenasserim □, Burma 34 F5
Tenby, U.K. 11 F3
Tendaho, Ethiopia . . 40 E3
Tenerife, Canary Is. . . 44 C1
Teng →, Burma 34 B5
Tengah □, Indonesia 33 E6
Tengah Kepulauan, Indonesia 32 F5
Tengchong, China . . 30 D4
Tenggara □, Indonesia 33 E6
Tenggarong, Indonesia 32 E5
Tengiz, Ozero, Kazakhstan 24 D7
Tenkasi, India 36 Q10
Tenke, Zaïre 46 G5
Tenkodogo, Burkina Faso 44 F4
Tennant Creek, Australia 54 B1
Tennessee □, U.S.A. . 67 C9
Tennessee →, U.S.A. 68 G1
Tennille, U.S.A. 69 J4
Tenom, Malaysia . . . 32 C5
Tenryū-Gawa →, Japan 29 G8
Tent L., Canada 65 A7
Tenterfield, Australia . 55 D5
Teófilo Otoni, Brazil . 79 G10
Tepa, Indonesia 33 F7
Tepic, Mexico 74 C4
Teplice, Czech. 16 C6
Ter Apel, Neths. 15 B7
Téra, Niger 44 F5
Teraina, Kiribati . . . 57 G11
Téramo, Italy 20 C5
Terang, Australia . . . 55 F3
Terek →, Russia . . . 23 F8
Terengganu □, Malaysia 34 Q16
Teresina, Brazil 79 E10
Terewah, L., Australia 55 D4
Terhazza, Mali 44 D3
Teridgerie Cr. →, Australia 55 E4
Termez = Termiz, Uzbekistan 24 F7
Térmoli, Italy 20 C6
Ternate, Indonesia . . 33 D7
Terneuzen, Neths. . . 15 C3
Terney, Russia 25 E14
Terni, Italy 20 C5
Ternopol, Ukraine . . 23 D3
Terowie, N.S.W., Australia 55 E4
Terowie, S. Austral., Australia 55 E2
Terrace, Canada 64 C3
Terrace Bay, Canada . 62 C2
Terracina, Italy 20 D5
Terralba, Italy 20 E3
Terranova = Ólbia, Italy 20 D3
Terrassa = Tarrasa, Spain 19 B7
Terre Haute, U.S.A. . 68 F2
Terrebonne B., U.S.A. 71 L9
Terrell, U.S.A. 71 J6
Terrenceville, Canada 63 C9
Terrick Terrick, Australia 54 C4
Terry, U.S.A. 70 B2
Terschelling, Neths. . 15 A5
Teruel, Spain 19 B5
Tervola, Finland . . . 8 C18
Teryaweyna L., Australia 55 E3
Tešanj, Bos.-H. . . . 21 B7
Teshio, Japan 28 B10
Teshio-Gawa →, Japan 28 B10
Tesiyn Gol →, Mongolia 30 A4
Teslin, Canada 64 A2
Teslin →, Canada . . 64 A2
Teslin L., Canada . . . 64 A2
Tessalit, Mali 44 D5
Tessaoua, Niger . . . 44 F6
Test →, U.K. 11 F6

Tetachuck L., Canada 64 C3
Tetas, Pta., Chile . . . 80 A2
Tete, Mozam. 47 H6
Teteven, Bulgaria . . . 21 C11
Tethul →, Canada . . 64 A6
Teton →, U.S.A. . . . 72 C8
Tétouan, Morocco . . 44 A3
Tetovo, Macedonia . . . 21 C9
Tetuán = Tétouan, Morocco 44 A3
Tetyukhe Pristan, Russia 28 B7
Teuco →, Argentina 80 B4
Teulon, Canada 65 C9
Teun, Indonesia 33 F7
Teutoburger Wald, Germany 16 B4
Tevere →, Italy 20 D5
Teverya, Israel 41 C4
Teviot →, U.K. 12 F6
Tewantin, Australia . 55 D5
Tewkesbury, U.K. . . . 11 F5
Texada I., Canada . . 64 D4
Texarkana, Ark., U.S.A. 71 J8
Texarkana, Tex., U.S.A. 71 J7
Texas □, Australia . . 55 D5
Texas □, U.S.A. . . . 71 K5
Texas City, U.S.A. . . 71 L7
Texel, Neths. 15 A4
Texhoma, U.S.A. . . . 71 G4
Texline, U.S.A. 71 G3
Texoma, L., U.S.A. . 71 J6
Thaba Nchu, S. Africa 48 D4
Thaba Putsoa, Lesotho 49 D4
Thabana Ntlenyana, Lesotho 49 D4
Thabazimbi, S. Africa 49 C4
Thai Hoa, Vietnam . . 34 C8
Thai Nguyen, Vietnam 34 B8
Thailand ■, Asia . . . 34 D6
Thailand, G. of, Asia . 34 G6
Thakhek, Laos 34 D8
Thal, Pakistan 36 C7
Thala La, Burma . . . 37 E20
Thallon, Australia . . . 55 D4
Thame →, U.K. . . . 11 F6
Thames, N.Z. 51 G5
Thames →, Canada . 62 D3
Thames →, U.K. . . 11 F8
Thane, India 36 K8
Thanet, I. of, U.K. . . 11 F9
Thang Goo, Vietnam 34 E10
Thangoo, Australia . . 52 C3
Thangool, Australia . 54 C5
Thanh Hoa, Vietnam 34 C8
Thanh Pho Ho Chi Minh = Phanh Bho Ho Chi Minh, Vietnam 34 G9
Thanjavur, India . . . 36 P11
Thar Desert, India . . 36 F7
Tharad, India 36 G7
Thargomindah, Australia 55 D3
Tharrawaddy, Burma 37 L19
Tharthar, W. →, Iraq 38 C4
Thásos, Greece 21 D11
Thatcher, Ariz., U.S.A. 73 K9
Thatcher, Colo., U.S.A. 71 G2
Thaton, Burma 37 L20
Thaungdut, Burma . . 37 G19
Thayer, U.S.A. 71 G9
Thayetmyo, Burma . . 37 K19
Thazi, Burma 37 J20
The Alberga →, Australia 55 D2
The Coorong, Australia 55 F2
The Dalles, U.S.A. . . 72 D3
The English Company's Is., Australia 54 A2
The Frome →, Australia 55 D2
The Grampians, Australia 55 F3
The Hague = 's-Gravenhage, Neths. 15 B4
The Hamilton →, Australia 55 D2
The Macumba →, Australia 55 D2
The Neales →, Australia 55 D2
The Officer →, Australia 53 E5
The Pas, Canada . . . 65 C8
The Rock, Australia . 55 F4
The Salt L., Australia 55 E3
The Stevenson →, Australia 55 D2
The Warburton →, Australia 55 D2
Thebes = Thívai, Greece 21 E10
Thedford, U.S.A. . . . 70 E4
Theebine, Australia . 55 D5
Thekulthili L., Canada 65 A7
Thelon →, Canada . 65 A8
Theodore, Australia . 54 C5
Thermaïkos Kólpos, Greece 21 D10
Thermopolis, U.S.A. . 72 E9
Thermopylae P., Greece 21 E10

Thessalía □, Greece . 21 E9
Thessalon, Canada . 62 C3
Thessaloniki, Greece . 21 D10
Thessaloniki, Gulf of = Thermaïkos Kólpos, Greece 21 D10
Thessaly = Thessalía □, Greece 21 E9
Thetford, U.K. 11 E8
Thetford Mines, Canada 63 C5
Theunissen, S. Africa 48 D4
Thevenard, Australia . 55 E1
Thibodaux, U.S.A. . . 71 L9
Thicket Portage, Canada 65 B9
Thief River Falls, U.S.A. 70 A6
Thiel Mts., Antarctica 5 E16
Thiérache, France . . . 18 B5
Thies, Senegal 44 F1
Thika, Kenya 46 E7
Thikombia, Fiji 51 B9
Thimphu, Bhutan . . 37 F16
Þingvallavatn, Iceland 8 D3
Thionville, France . . 18 B7
Thíra, Greece 21 F11
Thirsk, U.K. 10 C6
Thisted, Denmark . . 9 H10
Thistle I., Australia . . 55 F2
Thívai, Greece 21 E10
Thlewiaza →, Man., Canada 65 B8
Thlewiaza →, N.W.T., Canada 65 A10
Thoa →, Canada . . 65 A7
Thomas, Okla., U.S.A. 71 H5
Thomas, W. Va., U.S.A. 68 F6
Thomas, L., Australia 55 D2
Thomaston, U.S.A. . 69 J3
Thomasville, Ala., U.S.A. 69 K2
Thomasville, Ga., U.S.A. 69 K3
Thomasville, N.C., U.S.A. 69 H5
Thompson, Canada . 65 B9
Thompson, U.S.A. . . 73 G9
Thompson →, Canada 64 C4
Thompson →, U.S.A. 70 F8
Thompson Falls, U.S.A. 72 C6
Thompson Landing, Canada 65 A6
Thompson Pk., U.S.A. 72 F2
Thomson's Falls = Nyahururu, Kenya 46 D7
Thon Buri, Thailand . 34 F6
Þórisvatn, Iceland . . 8 D4
Þorlákshöfn, Iceland 8 E3
Thornaby on Tees, U.K. 10 C6
Þórshöfn, Iceland . . 8 C6
Thouin, C., Australia 52 D2
Thrace = Thráki □, Greece 21 D11
Thráki □, Greece . . . 21 D11
Three Forks, U.S.A. . 72 D8
Three Hills, Canada . 64 C6
Three Hummock I., Australia 54 G3
Three Lakes, U.S.A. . 70 C10
Three Points, C., Ghana 44 H4
Three Rivers, Australia 53 E2
Three Rivers, U.S.A. . 71 L5
Three Sisters, U.S.A. . 72 D3
Throssell, L., Australia 53 E3
Throssell Ra., Australia 52 D3
Thubun Lakes, Canada 65 A6
Thuin, Belgium . . . 15 D4
Thule, Greenland . . . 4 B4
Thun, Switz. 16 E3
Thunder B., U.S.A. . . 68 C4
Thunder Bay, Canada 62 C2
Thung Song, Thailand 34 H5
Thunkar, Bhutan . . . 37 F17
Thüringer Wald, Germany 16 C6
Thurles, Ireland . . . 13 D4
Thurloo Downs, Australia 55 D3
Thursday I., Australia 54 A3
Thurso, Canada 62 C4
Thurso, U.K. 12 C5
Thurston I., Antarctica 5 D16
Thutade L., Canada . 64 B3
Thylungra, Australia . 55 D3
Thysville = Mbanza Ngungu, Zaïre . . 46 F2
Tia, Australia 55 E5
Tian Shan, China . . . 30 B3
Tianjin, China 31 C6
Tianshui, China 30 C5
Tiaret, Algeria 44 A5
Tiassalé, Ivory C. . . . 44 G4
Tibati, Cameroon . . . 45 G7
Tiber = Tevere →, Italy 20 D5
Tiber Res., U.S.A. . . 72 B8
Tiberias = Teverya, Israel 41 C4
Tiberias, L. = Yam Kinneret, Israel . . 41 C4
Tibesti, Chad 45 D8
Tibet = Xizang □, China 30 C3
Tibnī, Syria 38 C3
Tibooburra, Australia 55 D3

Tiburón, Mexico . . . 74 B2
Tichît, Mauritania . . 44 E3
Ticino →, Italy 20 B3
Ticonderoga, U.S.A. . 68 D9
Tiddim, Burma 37 H18
Tidjikja, Mauritania . 44 E2
Tidore, Indonesia . . . 33 D7
Tiel, Neths. 15 C5
Tiel, Senegal 44 F1
Tielt, Belgium 15 D3
Tien Shan, Asia . . . 26 E11
Tien-tsin = Tianjin, China 31 C6
T'ienching = Tianjin, China 31 C6
Tienen, Belgium . . . 15 D4
Tientsin = Tianjin, China 31 C6
Tierra Amarilla, U.S.A. 73 H10
Tierra de Campos, Spain 19 A3
Tierra del Fuego, I. Gr. de, Argentina . 80 G3
Tiétar →, Spain . . . 19 C2
Tieyon, Australia . . . 55 D1
Tiffin, U.S.A. 68 E4
Tiflis = Tbilisi, Georgia 23 F7
Tifton, U.S.A. 69 K4
Tifu, Indonesia 33 E7
Tigil, Russia 25 D16
Tignish, Canada . . . 63 C7
Tigre →, Peru 78 D4
Tigris = Dijlah, Nahr →, Asia . . 38 D5
Tigyaing, Burma . . . 37 H20
Tih, Gebel el, Egypt . 45 C11
Tijuana, Mexico . . . 74 A1
Tikamgarh, India . . 36 G11
Tikhoretsk, Russia . . 23 E7
Tikrīt, Iraq 38 C4
Tiksi, Russia 25 B13
Tilamuta, Indonesia . 33 E6
Tilburg, Neths. 15 C5
Tilbury, Canada . . . 62 D3
Tilbury, U.K. 11 F8
Tilden, Nebr., U.S.A. . 70 D6
Tilden, Tex., U.S.A. . 71 L5
Tilichiki, Russia . . . 25 C17
Till →, U.K. 10 B5
Tillabéri, Niger 44 F5
Tillamook, U.S.A. . . 72 D2
Tillsonburg, Canada . 62 D3
Tílos, Greece 21 F12
Tilpa, Australia 55 E3
Tilsit = Sovetsk, Russia 22 C3
Tilt →, U.K. 12 E5
Timagami L., Canada 62 C3
Timanskiy Kryazh, Russia 22 A9
Timaru, N.Z. 51 L3
Timbedgha, Mauritania 44 E3
Timber Lake, U.S.A. . 70 C4
Timboon, Australia . 55 F3
Timbuktu = Tombouctou, Mali . 44 E4
Timimoun, Algeria . . 44 C5
Timişoara, Romania . 17 F10
Timmins, Canada . . 62 C3
Timok →, Serbia, Yug. 21 B10
Timon, Brazil 79 E10
Timor, Indonesia . . . 33 F7
Timor □, Indonesia . 33 F7
Timor Sea, Ind. Oc. . 52 B4
Tinaca Pt., Phil. . . . 33 C7
Tindouf, Algeria . . . 44 C3
Tingo Maria, Peru . . 78 E3
Tinjoub, Algeria . . . 44 C3
Tinkurrin, Australia . 53 F2
Tinnevelly = Tirunelveli, India . . 36 Q10
Tinnoset, Norway . . 9 G10
Tinogasta, Argentina . 80 B3
Tínos, Greece 21 F11
Tintinara, Australia . 55 F3
Tioman, Pulau, Malaysia 34 S17
Tipongpani, India . . 37 F19
Tipperary, Ireland . . 13 D3
Tipperary □, Ireland 13 D4
Tipton, U.K. 11 E5
Tipton, Calif., U.S.A. 73 H4
Tipton, Ind., U.S.A. . 68 E2
Tipton, Iowa, U.S.A. 70 E9
Tiptonville, U.S.A. . 71 G10
Tīrān, Iran 39 C6
Tirana, Albania 21 D8
Tiranë = Tirana, Albania 21 D8
Tiraspol, Moldavia . 23 E4
Tirat Karmel, Israel . . 41 C3
Tirebolu, Turkey . . . 23 F6
Tiree, U.K. 12 E2
Tîrgovişte, Romania . 21 B11
Tîrgu-Jiu, Romania . 17 F11
Tîrgu Mureş, Romania 17 E12
Tirich Mir, Pakistan . 36 A7
Tirodi, India 36 J11
Tirol □, Austria . . . 16 E5
Tirso →, Italy 20 E3
Tiruchchirappalli, India 36 P11
Tirunelveli, India . . . 36 Q10
Tirupati, India 36 N11
Tiruvannamalai, India 36 N11
Tisa →, Serbia, Yug. 17 F10
Tisdale, Canada . . . 65 C8
Tishomingo, U.S.A. . 71 H6
Tisza = Tisa →, Hungary 17 E10

Tit-Ary, Russia 25 B13
Titicaca, L., S. Amer. . 78 G5
Titograd = Podgorica,
  Montenegro, Yug. . 21 C8
Titov Veles,
  Macedonia 21 D9
Titovo Užice,
  Serbia, Yug. 21 C8
Titule, Zaïre 46 D5
Titusville, Fla., U.S.A. 69 L5
Titusville, Pa., U.S.A. . 68 E6
Tivaouane, Senegal . 44 F1
Tiverton, U.K. 11 G4
Tívoli, Italy 20 D5
Tizi-Ouzou, Algeria . 44 A5
Tiznit, Morocco 44 C3
Tjeggelvas, Sweden . 8 C14
Tjirebon = Cirebon,
  Indonesia 33 G13
Tlaxcala, Mexico ... 74 D5
Tlaxiaco, Mexico ... 74 D5
Tlell, Canada 64 C2
Tlemcen, Algeria ... 44 B4
Tmassah, Libya 45 C8
Toad →, Canada ... 64 B4
Toamasina, Madag. . . 49 B8
Toamasina □, Madag. 49 B8
Toay, Argentina 80 D4
Toba, Japan 29 G8
Toba Kakar, Pakistan . 36 D6
Tobago, W. Indies .. 74 R21
Tobelo, Indonesia ... 33 D7
Tobermorey, Australia 54 C2
Tobermory, Canada .. 62 C3
Tobermory, U.K. 12 E2
Tobin, L., Australia .. 52 D4
Tobin L., Canada ... 65 C8
Toboali, Indonesia .. 32 E3
Tobol, Kazakhstan .. 24 D7
Tobol →, Russia ... 24 D7
Toboli, Indonesia ... 33 E6
Tobolsk, Russia 24 D7
Tobruk = Tubruq,
  Libya 45 B9
Tocantinópolis, Brazil 79 E9
Tocantins □, Brazil . 79 F9
Tocantins →, Brazil . 79 D9
Toccoa, U.S.A. 69 H4
Tochigi, Japan 29 F9
Tochigi □, Japan ... 29 F9
Tocopilla, Chile 80 A2
Tocumwal, Australia . 55 F4
Tocuyo →, Venezuela 78 A5
Todd →, Australia . . 54 C2
Todeli, Indonesia ... 33 E6
Todenyang, Kenya .. 46 D7
Todos os Santos, B.
  de, Brazil 79 F11
Tofield, Canada 64 C6
Tofino, Canada 64 D3
Tofua, Tonga 51 D11
Tōgane, Japan 29 G10
Togba, Mauritania .. 44 E2
Togian, Kepulauan,
  Indonesia 33 E6
Togliatti, Russia ... 22 D8
Togo ■, W. Afr. 44 G5
Tōhoku □, Japan ... 28 E10
Toinya, Sudan 45 G10
Tojikiston =
  Tajikistan ■, Asia . 24 F8
Tojo, Indonesia 33 E6
Tōjō, Japan 29 G6
Tokachi-Dake, Japan . 28 C11
Tokachi-Gawa →,
  Japan 28 C11
Tokaj, Hungary 17 D10
Tokala, Indonesia ... 33 E6
Tōkamachi, Japan .. 29 F9
Tokanui, N.Z. 51 M2
Tokar, Sudan 45 E12
Tokara-Rettō, Japan . 29 K4
Tokarahi, N.Z. 51 L3
Tokashiki-Shima,
  Japan 29 L3
Tokelau Is., Pac. Oc. . 56 H10
Tokmak, Kirghizia .. 24 E8
Toko Ra., Australia .. 54 C2
Tokong, Malaysia ... 34 P13
Tokoro-Gawa →,
  Japan 28 B12
Tokuno-Shima, Japan 29 L4
Tokushima, Japan .. 29 G7
Tokushima □, Japan . 29 H7
Tokuyama, Japan .. 29 G5
Tōkyō, Japan 29 G9
Tolaga Bay, N.Z. ... 51 H7
Tolbukhin, Bulgaria . 21 C12
Toledo, Spain 19 C3
Toledo, Ohio, U.S.A. . 68 E4
Toledo, Oreg., U.S.A. . 72 D2
Toledo, Wash., U.S.A. 72 C2
Toledo, Montes de,
  Spain 19 C3
Tolga, Algeria 44 B6
Toliara, Madag. ... 49 C7
Toliara □, Madag. .. 49 C8
Tolima, Colombia .. 78 C3
Tolitoli, Indonesia .. 33 D6
Tolleson, U.S.A. ... 73 K7
Tolo, Zaïre 46 E3
Tolo, Teluk, Indonesia 33 E6
Tolosa, Spain 19 A4
Toluca, Mexico 74 D5
Tom Burke, S. Africa . 49 C4
Tom Price, Australia . 52 D2
Tomah, U.S.A. 70 D9
Tomahawk, U.S.A. .. 70 C10
Tomakomai, Japan .. 28 C10
Tomar, Portugal 19 C1
Tomaszów
  Mazowiecki, Poland 17 C9

Tombé, Sudan 45 G11
Tombigbee →, U.S.A. 69 K2
Tombouctou, Mali .. 44 E4
Tombstone, U.S.A. .. 73 L8
Tombua, Angola ... 48 B1
Tomelloso, Spain ... 19 C4
Tomingley, Australia . 55 E4
Tomini, Indonesia ... 33 D6
Tomini, Teluk,
  Indonesia 33 E6
Tomkinson Ras.,
  Australia 53 E4
Tommot, Russia 25 D13
Tomnavoulin, U.K. .. 12 D5
Tomsk, Russia 24 D9
Tonalea, U.S.A. 73 H8
Tonantins, Brazil ... 78 D5
Tonasket, U.S.A. ... 72 B4
Tonawanda, U.S.A. . 68 D6
Tonbridge, U.K. 11 F8
Tondano, Indonesia . 33 D6
Tonekābon, Iran ... 39 B6
Tonga ■, Pac. Oc. .. 51 D11
Tonga Trench, Pac. Oc. 56 J10
Tongaat, S. Africa .. 49 D5
Tongareva, Cook Is. . 57 H12
Tongatapu, Tonga .. 51 E11
Tongchuan, China .. 31 C5
Tongeren, Belgium .. 15 D5
Tonghua, China 31 B7
Tongking, G. of =
  Tonkin, G. of, Asia . 30 E5
Tongobory, Madag. . 49 C7
Tongoy, Chile 80 C2
Tongres = Tongeren,
  Belgium 15 D5
Tongsa Dzong, Bhutan 37 F17
Tongue, U.K. 12 C4
Tongue →, U.S.A. . 70 B2
Tonk, India 36 F9
Tonkin = Bac Phan,
  Vietnam 34 A8
Tonkin, G. of, Asia .. 30 E5
Tonlé Sap, Cambodia 34 F8
Tono, Japan 28 E10
Tonopah, U.S.A. ... 73 G5
Tønsberg, Norway .. 9 G11
Tooele, U.S.A. 72 F7
Toompine, Australia . 55 D3
Toonpan, Australia .. 54 B4
Toora, Australia 55 F4
Toora-Khem, Russia . 25 D10
Toowoomba, Australia 55 D5
Top-ozero, Russia .. 22 A5
Topeka, U.S.A. 70 F7
Topki, Russia 24 D9
Topley, Canada 64 C3
Topock, U.S.A. 73 J6
Topolobampo, Mexico 74 B3
Toppenish, U.S.A. .. 72 C3
Toraka Vestale, Madag. 49 B7
Torata, Peru 78 G4
Torbay, Canada 63 C9
Torbay, U.K. 11 G4
Tordesillas, Spain .. 19 B3
Torfajökull, Iceland . 8 E4
Torgau, Germany ... 16 C6
Torhout, Belgium ... 15 C3
Tori-Shima, Japan .. 29 J10
Torino, Italy 20 B2
Torit, Sudan 45 H11
Tormes →, Spain .. 19 B2
Tornado Mt., Canada . 64 D6
Torne älv →, Sweden 8 D18
Torneå = Tornio,
  Finland 8 D18
Torneträsk, Sweden . 8 B15
Tornio, Finland 8 D18
Tornionjoki →,
  Finland 8 D18
Tornquist, Argentina . 80 D4
Toro, Cerro del, Chile 80 B3
Toro, Pta., Panama .. 74 H14
Toroníios Kólpos,
  Greece 21 D10
Toronto, Australia .. 55 E5
Toronto, Canada ... 62 D4
Toronto, U.S.A. ... 68 E5
Toropets, Russia ... 22 C5
Tororo, Uganda ... 46 D6
Toros Dağları, Turkey 23 G5
Torquay, Canada ... 65 D8
Torquay, U.K. 11 G4
Tôrre de Moncorvo,
  Portugal 19 B2
Torre del Greco, Italy 20 D6
Torrelavega, Spain .. 19 A3
Torremolinos, Spain . 19 D3
Torrens, L., Australia . 55 E2
Torrens Cr. →,
  Australia 54 C4
Torrens Creek,
  Australia 54 C4
Torréon, Coahuila,
  Mexico 74 B4
Torres, Mexico 74 B2
Torres Strait, Australia 56 H6
Torres Vedras,
  Portugal 19 C1
Torrevieja, Spain ... 19 D5
Torrey, U.S.A. 73 G8
Torridge →, U.K. .. 11 G3
Torridon, L., U.K. .. 12 D3
Torrington, Conn.,
  U.S.A. 68 E9
Torrington, Wyo.,
  U.S.A. 70 D2
Tortosa, Spain 19 B6
Tortosa, C., Spain .. 19 B6

Torūd, Iran 39 C7
Toruń, Poland 17 B9
Tory I., Ireland 13 A3
Tosa, Japan 29 H6
Tosa-Shimizu, Japan . 29 H6
Tosa-Wan, Japan ... 29 H6
Toscana □, Italy ... 20 C4
Toshkent = Tashkent,
  Uzbekistan 24 E7
Tostado, Argentina .. 80 B4
Tosu, Japan 29 H5
Totak, Russia 22 C7
Totma, Russia 22 C7
Totnes, U.K. 11 G4
Totten Glacier,
  Antarctica 5 C8
Tottenham, Australia . 55 E4
Tottori, Japan 29 G7
Tottori □, Japan ... 29 G7
Touba, Ivory C. 44 G3
Toubkal, Djebel,
  Morocco 44 B3
Tougan, Burkina Faso 44 F4
Touggourt, Algeria .. 44 B6
Tougué, Guinea 44 F2
Toul, France 18 B6
Toulepleu, Ivory C. . 44 G3
Toulon, France 18 E6
Toulouse, France ... 18 E4
Toummo, Niger 45 D7
Toungoo, Burma ... 37 K20
Tourane = Da Nang,
  Vietnam 34 D10
Tourcoing, France .. 18 A5
Tournai, Belgium ... 15 D3
Tournon, France ... 18 D6
Tours, France 18 C4
Touwsrivier, S. Africa 48 E3
Towada, Japan 28 D10
Towada-Ko, Japan .. 28 D10
Towamba, Australia . 55 F4
Towanda, U.S.A. ... 68 E7
Towang, India 37 F17
Tower, U.S.A. 70 B8
Towerhill Cr. →,
  Australia 54 C3
Towner, U.S.A. 70 A4
Townsend, U.S.A. .. 72 C8
Townshend I.,
  Australia 54 C5
Townsville, Australia . 54 B4
Towson, U.S.A. 68 F7
Toya-Ko, Japan ... 28 C10
Toyah, U.S.A. 71 K3
Toyahvale, U.S.A. .. 71 K3
Toyama, Japan 29 F8
Toyama □, Japan .. 29 F8
Toyama-Wan, Japan . 29 F8
Toyohashi, Japan .. 29 G8
Toyokawa, Japan .. 29 G8
Toyonaka, Japan ... 29 G7
Toyooka, Japan ... 29 G7
Toyota, Japan 29 G8
Tozeur, Tunisia 44 B6
Trabzon, Turkey ... 23 F6
Tracadie, Canada .. 63 C7
Tracy, Calif., U.S.A. . 73 H3
Tracy, Minn., U.S.A. . 70 C7
Tradovoye, Russia .. 28 C6
Trafalgar, C., Spain . 19 D2
Trail, Canada 64 D5
Trainor L., Canada .. 64 A4
Tralee, Ireland 13 D2
Tralee B., Ireland .. 13 D2
Tramore, Ireland ... 13 D4
Tran Ninh, Cao
  Nguyen, Laos ... 34 C7
Trancas, Argentina .. 80 B3
Trang, Thailand ... 34 J5
Trangahy, Madag. .. 49 B7
Trangan, Indonesia . 33 F8
Trangie, Australia .. 55 E4
Trani, Italy 20 D7
Tranoroa, Madag. .. 49 C8
Transantarctic Mts.,
  Antarctica 5 E12
Transcaucasia =
  Zakavkazye, Asia . 23 F7
Transcona, Canada . 65 D9
Transilvania, Romania 21 B11
Transkei □, S. Africa 49 E4
Transvaal □, S. Africa 48 D4
Transylvania =
  Transilvania,
  Romania 21 B11
Transylvanian Alps,
  Romania 6 F10
Trápani, Italy 20 E5
Trapper Peak, U.S.A. 72 D6
Traralgon, Australia . 55 F4
Tras os Montes e Alto
  Douro, Portugal .. 19 B2
Trasimeno, L., Italy . 20 C5
Trat, Thailand 34 F7
Traveller's L., Australia 55 E3
Travers, Mt., N.Z. .. 51 K4
Traverse City, U.S.A. 68 C3
Travnik, Bos.-H. ... 21 B7
Trayning, Australia .. 53 F2
Trébbia →, Italy ... 20 B3
Trebinje, Bos.-H. .. 21 C8
Třebon, Czech. 16 D7
Tredegar, U.K. 11 F4
Tregaron, U.K. 11 E4
Tregrosse Is., Australia 54 B5
Tréguier, France ... 18 B2
Treherne, Canada .. 65 D9

Trekveld, S. Africa .. 48 E2
Trelew, Argentina .. 80 E3
Trelleborg, Sweden . 9 J12
Tremonton, U.S.A. .. 72 F7
Tremp, Spain 19 A6
Trenche →, Canada 62 C5
Trenggalek, Indonesia 33 H14
Trenque Lauquen,
  Argentina 80 D4
Trent →, U.K. 10 D7
Trentino-Alto Adige □,
  Italy 20 A4
Trento, Italy 20 A4
Trenton, Canada ... 62 D4
Trenton, Mo., U.S.A. . 70 E8
Trenton, N.J., U.S.A. . 68 E8
Trenton, Nebr., U.S.A. 70 E4
Trenton, Tenn., U.S.A. 71 H10
Trepassey, Canada . 63 C9
Tres Arroyos,
  Argentina 80 D4
Três Corações, Brazil 79 H9
Três Lagoas, Brazil . 79 H8
Tres Montes, C., Chile 80 F1
Tres Puentes, Chile . 80 B2
Tres Puntas, C.,
  Argentina 80 F3
Três Rios, Brazil ... 79 H10
Treungen, Norway .. 9 G10
Treviso, Italy 20 B5
Triabunna, Australia . 54 G4
Tribulation, C.,
  Australia 54 B4
Tribune, U.S.A. 70 F4
Trichinopoly =
  Tiruchchirappalli,
  India 36 P11
Trichur, India 36 P10
Trida, Australia 55 E4
Trier, Germany 16 D3
Trieste, Italy 20 B5
Triglav, Slovenia ... 20 A5
Trikkala, Greece ... 21 E9
Trikora, Puncak,
  Indonesia 33 E9
Trim, Ireland 13 C5
Trincomalee, Sri Lanka 36 Q12
Trindade, Bolivia ... 78 F6
Trindade, I., Atl. Oc. . 2 F8
Trinidad, Bolivia ... 78 F6
Trinidad, Colombia .. 78 B4
Trinidad, Cuba 75 C9
Trinidad, Uruguay .. 80 C5
Trinidad, U.S.A. ... 71 G2
Trinidad, I., Argentina 80 D4
Trinidad & Tobago ■,
  W. Indies 74 S20
Trinity, Canada 63 C9
Trinity →, Calif.,
  U.S.A. 72 F2
Trinity →, Tex.,
  U.S.A. 71 L7
Trinity B., Canada .. 63 C9
Trinity Mts., U.S.A. . 72 F4
Trinkitat, Sudan ... 45 E12
Trion, U.S.A. 69 H3
Tripoli = Tarābulus,
  Lebanon 41 A4
Tripoli = Tarābulus,
  Libya 45 B7
Tripolis, Greece ... 21 F10
Tripp, U.S.A. 70 D6
Tripura □, India ... 37 H17
Tristan da Cunha,
  Atl. Oc. 2 F9
Trivandrum, India .. 36 Q10
Trnava, Slovakia ... 17 D8
Trochu, Canada ... 64 C6
Trodely I., Canada .. 62 B4
Troglav, Croatia ... 20 C7
Troilus, L., Canada .. 62 B5
Trois-Pistoles, Canada 63 C6
Trois-Rivières, Canada 62 C5
Troitsk, Russia 24 D7
Troitsko Pechorsk,
  Russia 22 B10
Trölladyngja, Iceland 8 D5
Trollhättan, Sweden . 9 G12
Tromelin I., Ind. Oc. . 35 F4
Troms fylke □, Norway 8 B15
Tromsø, Norway ... 8 B15
Tronador, Argentina . 80 E2
Trondheim, Norway . 8 E11
Trondheimsfjorden,
  Norway 8 E11
Troon, U.K. 12 F4
Tropic, U.S.A. 73 H7
Trossachs, The, U.K. 12 E4
Trostan, U.K. 13 A5
Trotternish, U.K. ... 12 D2
Troup, U.S.A. 71 J7
Trout →, Canada .. 64 A5
Trout L., N.W.T.,
  Canada 64 A4
Trout L., Ont., Canada 65 C10
Trout Lake, U.S.A. .. 62 C2
Trout River, Canada . 63 C8
Trouville-sur-Mer,
  France 18 B4
Trowbridge, U.K. ... 11 F5
Troy, Ala., U.S.A. .. 69 K3
Troy, Idaho, U.S.A. . 72 C5
Troy, Kans., U.S.A. . 70 F7
Troy, Mo., U.S.A. .. 70 F9
Troy, Mont., U.S.A. . 72 B6
Troy, N.Y., U.S.A. .. 68 D9
Troy, Ohio, U.S.A. .. 68 E3
Troyes, France 18 B6
Trucial States = United
  Arab Emirates ■,
  Asia 39 F7

Truckee, U.S.A. ... 72 G3
Trujillo, Honduras .. 74 D7
Trujillo, Peru 78 E3
Trujillo, Spain 19 C3
Trujillo, U.S.A. 71 H2
Trujillo, Venezuela .. 78 B4
Truk, Pac. Oc. 56 G7
Trumann, U.S.A. ... 71 H9
Trumbull, Mt., U.S.A. 73 H7
Truro, Canada 63 C7
Truro, U.K. 11 G2
Truslove, Australia . 53 F3
Truth or
  Consequences,
  U.S.A. 73 K10
Trutnov, Czech. ... 16 C7
Tryon, U.S.A. 69 H4
Tsaratanana, Madag. 49 B8
Tsaratanana, Mt. de,
  Madag. 49 A8
Tsau, Botswana ... 48 C3
Tselinograd,
  Kazakhstan 24 D8
Tsetserleg, Mongolia . 30 B5
Tshabong, Botswana 48 D3
Tshane, Botswana .. 48 C3
Tshela, Zaïre 46 E2
Tshesebe, Botswana 49 C4
Tshikapa, Zaïre 46 F4
Tshofa, Zaïre 46 F5
Tshwane, Botswana . 48 C3
Tsigara, Botswana .. 48 C4
Tsihombe, Madag. .. 49 D8
Tsimlyansk Res. =
  Tsimlyanskoye
  Vdkhr., Russia ... 23 E7
Tsimlyanskoye Vdkhr.,
  Russia 23 E7
Tsinan = Jinan, China 31 C6
Tsineng, S. Africa .. 48 D3
Tsinghai = Qinghai □,
  China 30 C4
Tsingtao = Qingdao,
  China 31 C7
Tsinjomitondraka,
  Madag. 49 B8
Tsiroanomandidy,
  Madag. 49 B8
Tsivory, Madag. ... 49 C8
Tskhinvali, Georgia . 23 F7
Tsna →, Russia ... 22 D7
Tsodilo Hill, Botswana 48 B3
Tsolo, S. Africa ... 49 E4
Tsomo, S. Africa ... 49 E4
Tsu, Japan 29 G8
Tsu L., Canada 64 A6
Tsuchiura, Japan .. 29 F10
Tsugaru-Kaikyō, Japan 28 D10
Tsumeb, Namibia .. 48 B2
Tsumis, Namibia ... 48 C2
Tsuruga, Japan ... 29 G8
Tsurugi-San, Japan . 29 H7
Tsuruoka, Japan ... 28 E9
Tsushima, Gifu, Japan 29 G8
Tsushima, Nagasaki,
  Japan 29 G4
Tual, Indonesia 33 F8
Tuam, Ireland 13 C3
Tuamotu Arch. =
  Tuamotu Is., Pac. Oc. 57 J13
Tuamotu Is., Pac. Oc. 57 J13
Tuamotu Ridge,
  Pac. Oc. 57 K14
Tuao, Phil. 33 A6
Tuapse, Russia 23 F6
Tuatapere, N.Z. ... 51 M1
Tuba City, U.S.A. .. 73 H8
Tuban, Indonesia .. 33 G15
Tubarão, Brazil ... 80 B7
Tûbâs, Jordan 41 C4
Tubau, Malaysia ... 32 D4
Tübingen, Germany . 16 D4
Tubruq, Libya 45 B9
Tubuai Is., Pac. Oc. . 57 K12
Tucacas, Venezuela . 78 A5
Tuchodi →, Canada 64 B4
Tucson, U.S.A. 73 K8
Tucumcari, U.S.A. .. 71 H3
Tucupita, Venezuela . 78 B6
Tucuruí, Brazil 79 D9
Tudela, Spain 19 A5
Tudmur, Syria 38 C3
Tudor, L., Canada .. 63 A6
Tuen, Australia 55 D4
Tugela →, S. Africa 49 D5
Tuguegarao, Phil. .. 33 A6
Tugur, Russia 25 D14
Tukangbesi,
  Kepulauan,
  Indonesia 33 F6
Tukarak I., Canada . 62 A4
Tukayyid, Iraq 38 D5
Tükrah, Libya 45 B9
Tuktoyaktuk, Canada 60 B6
Tukuyu, Tanzania .. 46 F6
Tula, Mexico 74 C5
Tula, Russia 22 D6
Tulancingo, Mexico . 74 C5
Tulare, U.S.A. 73 H4
Tulare Lake Bed,
  U.S.A. 73 K4
Tularosa, U.S.A. ... 73 K10
Tulbagh, S. Africa .. 48 E2
Tulcán, Ecuador ... 78 C3
Tulcea, Romania ... 21 B13
Tulemalu L., Canada 65 A9
Tûleh, Iran 39 C7
Tuli, Indonesia 33 E6
Tuli, Zimbabwe ... 47 J5

Tulia, U.S.A. 71 H4
Tülkarm, Jordan ... 41 C4
Tullahoma, U.S.A. .. 69 H2
Tullamore, Australia . 55 E4
Tullamore, Ireland .. 13 C4
Tulle, France 18 D4
Tullibigeal, Australia 55 E4
Tullow, Ireland 13 D4
Tully, Australia 54 B4
Tulmaythah, Libya .. 45 B9
Tulmur, Australia .. 54 C3
Tulsa, U.S.A. 71 G7
Tulsequah, Canada . 64 B2
Tulua, Colombia ... 78 C3
Tulun, Russia 25 D11
Tulungagung,
  Indonesia 32 F4
Tum, Indonesia 33 E8
Tumaco, Colombia . 78 C3
Tumatumari, Guyana 78 B7
Tumba, L., Zaïre ... 46 E3
Tumbarumba,
  Australia 55 F4
Túmbes, Peru 78 D2
Tumby Bay, Australia 55 E2
Tumeremo, Venezuela 78 B6
Tumkur, India 36 N10
Tummel, L., U.K. ... 12 E5
Tump, Pakistan 36 F3
Tumpat, Malaysia .. 34 N15
Tumu, Ghana 44 F4
Tumucumaque, Serra,
  Brazil 79 C8
Tumut, Australia ... 55 F4
Tumwater, U.S.A. .. 72 C2
Tunbridge Wells, U.K. 11 F8
Tuncurry, Australia . 55 E5
Tunduru, Tanzania .. 46 G7
Tundzha →, Bulgaria 21 D12
Tunga Pass, India .. 37 E19
Tungabhadra →,
  India 36 M11
Tungaru, Sudan ... 45 F11
Tungnafellsjökull,
  Iceland 8 D5
Tungsten, Canada .. 64 A3
Tunguska,
  Nizhnyaya →,
  Russia 25 C9
Tunica, U.S.A. 71 H9
Tunis, Tunisia 44 A7
Tunisia ■, Africa .. 44 B6
Tunja, Colombia ... 78 B4
Tunnsjøen, Norway . 8 D12
Tunungayualok I.,
  Canada 63 A7
Tunuyán,
  Argentina 80 C3
Tunuyán →,
  Argentina 80 C3
Tunxi, China 31 D6
Tuolumne, U.S.A. .. 73 H3
Tuoy-Khaya, Russia . 25 C12
Tūp Āghāj, Iran ... 38 B5
Tupelo, U.S.A. 69 H1
Tupik, Russia 25 D12
Tupinambaranas,
  Brazil 78 D7
Tupiza, Bolivia 80 A3
Tupper, Canada ... 64 B4
Tupper Lake, U.S.A. 68 C8
Tupungato, Cerro,
  S. Amer. 80 C3
Túquerres, Colombia 78 C3
Tura, Russia 25 C11
Turabah, Si. Arabia . 38 D4
Tūrān, Iran 39 C8
Turayf, Si. Arabia .. 38 D3
Turda, Romania ... 17 E11
Turek, Poland 17 B9
Turfan = Turpan,
  China 30 B3
Turgutlu, Turkey ... 23 G4
Turia →, Spain ... 19 C5
Turiaçu, Brazil 79 D9
Turiaçu →, Brazil . 79 D9
Turin = Torino, Italy . 20 B2
Turin, Canada 64 D6
Turkana, L., Africa .. 46 D7
Turkestan, Kazakhstan 24 E7
Turkey ■, Eurasia .. 23 G6
Turkey Creek, Australia 52 C4
Turkmenistan ■, Asia 24 F6
Turks & Caicos Is. ■,
  W. Indies 75 C10
Turku, Finland 9 F17
Turlock, U.S.A. 73 H3
Turnagain →, Canada 64 B3
Turnagain, C., N.Z. . 51 J6
Turneffe Is., Belize .. 74 D7
Turner, Australia ... 52 C4
Turner, U.S.A. 72 B9
Turner Pt., Australia . 54 A1
Turner Valley, Canada 64 C6
Turnhout, Belgium .. 15 C4
Turnor L., Canada .. 65 B7
Tŭrnovo, Bulgaria .. 21 C11
Turnu Măgurele,
  Romania 17 G12
Turnu Rosu Pasul,
  Romania 17 F12
Turon, U.S.A. 71 G5
Turpan, China 30 B3
Turriff, U.K. 12 D6
Tursãq, Iraq 38 C5
Turtle Head I.,
  Australia 54 A3
Turtle L., Canada .. 65 C7
Turtle Lake, N. Dak.,
  U.S.A. 70 B4
Turtle Lake, Wis.,
  U.S.A. 70 C8

Vermilion

Turtleford, *Canada* 65 C7
Turukhansk, *Russia* 25 C9
Turun ja Porin lääni □, *Finland* 9 F17
Tuscaloosa, *U.S.A.* 69 J2
Tuscany = Toscana, *Italy* 20 C4
Tuscola, *Ill., U.S.A.* 68 F1
Tuscola, *Tex., U.S.A.* 71 J5
Tuscumbia, *U.S.A.* 69 H2
Tuskar Rock, *Ireland* 13 D5
Tuskegee, *U.S.A.* 69 J3
Tuticorin, *India* 36 Q11
Tutóia, *Brazil* 79 D10
Tutong, *Brunei* 32 D4
Tutrakan, *Bulgaria* 21 B12
Tutshi L., *Canada* 64 B2
Tuttle, *U.S.A.* 70 B5
Tuttlingen, *Germany* 16 E4
Tutuala, *Indonesia* 33 F7
Tutuila, *Amer. Samoa* 51 B13
Tuva Republic □, *Russia* 25 D10
Tuvalu ■, *Pac. Oc.* 56 H9
Tuxpan, *Mexico* 74 C5
Tuxtla Gutiérrez, *Mexico* 74 D6
Tuy, *Spain* 19 A1
Tuy Hoa, *Vietnam* 34 F10
Tuya L., *Canada* 64 B2
Tuyen Hoa, *Vietnam* 34 D9
Tūysarkān, *Iran* 39 C6
Tuz Gölü, *Turkey* 23 G5
Ţūz Khurmātū, *Iraq* 38 C5
Tuzla, *Bos.-H.* 21 B8
Tver, *Russia* 22 C6
Tweed →, *U.K.* 12 F7
Tweed Heads, *Australia* 55 D5
Tweedsmuir Prov. Park, *Canada* 64 C3
Twentynine Palms, *U.S.A.* 73 J5
Twillingate, *Canada* 63 C9
Twin Bridges, *U.S.A.* 72 D7
Twin Falls, *U.S.A.* 72 E6
Twin Valley, *U.S.A.* 70 B6
Twisp, *U.S.A.* 72 B3
Two Harbors, *U.S.A.* 70 B9
Two Hills, *Canada* 64 C6
Two Rivers, *U.S.A.* 68 C2
Twofold B., *Australia* 55 F4
Tychy, *Poland* 17 C9
Tyler, *U.S.A.* 67 D7
Tyler, *Minn., U.S.A.* 70 C6
Tyler, *Tex., U.S.A.* 71 J7
Tynda, *Russia* 25 D13
Tyne →, *U.K.* 10 C6
Tyne & Wear □, *U.K.* 10 C6
Tynemouth, *U.K.* 10 B6
Tyre = Sūr, *Lebanon* 41 B4
Tyrifjorden, *Norway* 9 F11
Tyrol = Tirol □, *Austria* 16 E5
Tyrrell →, *Australia* 55 F3
Tyrrell, L., *Australia* 55 F3
Tyrrell Arm, *Canada* 65 A9
Tyrrell L., *Canada* 65 A7
Tyrrhenian Sea, *Europe* 20 E5
Tysfjorden, *Norway* 8 B14
Tyulgan, *Russia* 22 D10
Tyumen, *Russia* 24 D7
Tywi →, *U.K.* 11 F3
Tywyn, *U.K.* 11 E3
Tzaneen, *S. Africa* 49 C5
Tzukong = Zigong, *China* 30 D5

U

U.S.A. = United States of America ■, *N. Amer.* 66 C7
Uanda, *Australia* 54 C3
Uarsciek, *Somali Rep.* 40 G4
Uato-Udo, *Indonesia* 33 F7
Uatumã →, *Brazil* 78 D7
Uaupés, *Brazil* 78 D5
Uaupés →, *Brazil* 78 C5
Ubá, *Brazil* 79 H10
Ubaitaba, *Brazil* 79 F11
Ubangi = Oubangi →, *Zaïre* 46 E3
Ubauro, *Pakistan* 36 E6
Ube, *Japan* 29 H5
Ubeda, *Spain* 19 C4
Uberaba, *Brazil* 79 G9
Uberlândia, *Brazil* 79 G9
Ubombo, *S. Africa* 49 D5
Ubon Ratchathani, *Thailand* 34 E8
Ubundu, *Zaïre* 46 E5
Ucayali →, *Peru* 78 D4
Uchi Lake, *Canada* 65 C10
Uchiura-Wan, *Japan* 28 C10
Uchur →, *Russia* 25 D14
Ucluelet, *Canada* 64 D3
Uda →, *Russia* 25 D14
Udaipur, *India* 36 G8
Udaipur Garhi, *Nepal* 37 F15
Uddevalla, *Sweden* 9 G11
Uddjaur, *Sweden* 8 D16
Udgir, *India* 36 K10
Udhampur, *India* 36 C9
Udi, *Nigeria* 44 G6
Údine, *Italy* 20 A5
Udmurt Republic □, *Russia* 22 C9
Udon Thani, *Thailand* 34 D7
Udupi, *India* 36 N9
Ueda, *Japan* 29 F9
Uedineniya, Os., *Russia* 4 B12
Uele →, *Zaïre* 46 D4
Uelen, *Russia* 25 C19
Uelzen, *Germany* 16 B5
Ufa, *Russia* 22 D10
Ufa →, *Russia* 22 D10
Ugab →, *Namibia* 48 C1
Ugalla →, *Tanzania* 46 F6
Uganda ■, *Africa* 46 D6
Ugie, *S. Africa* 49 E4
Uglegorsk, *Russia* 25 E15
Ugolyak, *Russia* 25 C13
Ugûn Mûsa, *Egypt* 41 F1
Uhrichsville, *U.S.A.* 68 E5
Uíge, *Angola* 46 F2
Uinta Mts., *U.S.A.* 72 F8
Uitenhage, *S. Africa* 48 E4
Uithuizen, *Neths.* 15 A6
Uji-guntō, *Japan* 29 J4
Ujjain, *India* 36 H9
Újpest, *Hungary* 17 E9
Ujung Pandang, *Indonesia* 33 F5
Uka, *Russia* 25 D17
Uke-Shima, *Japan* 29 K4
Ukerewe I., *Tanzania* 46 E6
Ukhrul, *India* 37 G19
Ukhta, *Russia* 22 B9
Ukiah, *U.S.A.* 72 G2
Ukraine ■, *Europe* 23 E5
Ukwi, *Botswana* 48 C3
Ulaanbaatar, *Mongolia* 25 E11
Ulaangom, *Mongolia* 30 A4
Ulan Bator = Ulaanbaatar, *Mongolia* 25 E11
Ulan Ude, *Russia* 25 D11
Ulcinj, *Montenegro, Yug.* 21 D8
Ulco, *S. Africa* 48 D3
Ulhasnagar, *India* 36 K8
Ulladulla, *Australia* 55 F5
Ullapool, *U.K.* 12 D3
Ullswater, *U.K.* 10 C5
Ulm, *Germany* 16 D4
Ulmarra, *Australia* 55 D5
Ulonguè, *Mozam.* 47 G6
Ulricehamn, *Sweden* 9 H12
Ulster □, *U.K.* 13 B5
Ulungur He →, *China* 30 B3
Ulutau, *Kazakhstan* 24 E7
Ulverston, *U.K.* 10 C4
Ulverstone, *Australia* 54 G4
Ulya, *Russia* 25 D15
Ulyanovsk = Simbirsk, *Russia* 22 D8
Ulyasutay, *Mongolia* 30 B4
Ulysses, *U.S.A.* 71 G4
Umala, *Bolivia* 78 G5
Uman, *Ukraine* 23 E5
Umaria, *India* 37 H12
Umarkot, *Pakistan* 36 G6
Umatilla, *U.S.A.* 72 D4
Umba, *Russia* 22 A5
Umbrella Mts., *N.Z.* 51 L2
Umbria □, *Italy* 20 C5
Ume älv →, *Sweden* 8 E16
Umeå, *Sweden* 8 E16
Umera, *Indonesia* 33 E7
Umkomaas, *S. Africa* 49 E5
Umm ad Daraj, J., *Jordan* 41 C4
Umm al Qaywayn, *U.A.E.* 39 E7
Umm al Qittayn, *Jordan* 41 C5
Umm Bāb, *Qatar* 39 E6
Umm Bel, *Sudan* 45 F10
Umm el Fahm, *Israel* 41 C4
Umm Lajj, *Si. Arabia* 38 E3
Umm Ruwaba, *Sudan* 45 F11
Umnak, *U.S.A.* 60 C3
Umniati →, *Zimbabwe* 47 H5
Umpang, *Thailand* 34 D5
Umpqua →, *U.S.A.* 72 E1
Umtata, *S. Africa* 49 E4
Umuarama, *Brazil* 79 H8
Umzimvubu = Port St. Johns, *S. Africa* 49 E4
Umzinto, *S. Africa* 49 E5
Unac →, *Bos.-H.* 20 B7
Unalaska, *U.S.A.* 60 C3
Uncía, *Bolivia* 78 G5
Uncompahgre Pk., *U.S.A.* 73 G10
Underberg, *S. Africa* 49 D4
Underbool, *Australia* 55 F3
Ungarie, *Australia* 55 E4
Ungarra, *Australia* 55 E2
Ungava B., *Canada* 61 C13
Ungava Pen., *Canada* 61 C12
União da Vitória, *Brazil* 80 B6
Unimak, *U.S.A.* 60 C3
Union, *Miss., U.S.A.* 71 J10
Union, *Mo., U.S.A.* 70 F9
Union, *S.C., U.S.A.* 69 H5
Union, *Mt., U.S.A.* 73 J7
Union City, *Pa., U.S.A.* 68 E6
Union City, *Tenn., U.S.A.* 71 G10
Union Gap, *U.S.A.* 72 C3
Union of Soviet Socialist Republics = Commonwealth of Independent States ■, *Eurasia* 25 D11
Union Springs, *U.S.A.* 69 J3
Uniondale, *S. Africa* 48 E3
Uniontown, *U.S.A.* 68 F6
Unionville, *U.S.A.* 70 E8
United Arab Emirates ■, *Asia* 39 F7
United Kingdom ■, *Europe* 7 E5
United States of America ■, *N. Amer.* 66 C7
Unity, *Canada* 65 C7
Unnao, *India* 37 F12
Unst, *U.K.* 12 A8
Unuk →, *Canada* 64 B2
Uozu, *Japan* 29 F8
Upata, *Venezuela* 78 B6
Upemba, L., *Zaïre* 46 F5
Upernavik, *Greenland* 4 B5
Upington, *S. Africa* 48 D3
Upolu, *W. Samoa* 51 A13
Upper Alkali Lake, *U.S.A.* 72 F3
Upper Arrow L., *Canada* 64 C5
Upper Foster L., *Canada* 65 B7
Upper Hutt, *N.Z.* 51 J5
Upper Klamath L., *U.S.A.* 72 E3
Upper Lake, *U.S.A.* 72 G2
Upper Musquodoboit, *Canada* 63 C7
Upper Red L., *U.S.A.* 70 A7
Upper Sandusky, *U.S.A.* 68 E4
Upper Volta = Burkina Faso ■, *Africa* 44 F4
Uppsala, *Sweden* 9 G14
Uppsala län □, *Sweden* 9 G14
Upstart, C., *Australia* 54 B4
Upton, *U.S.A.* 70 C2
Ur, *Iraq* 38 D5
Uracara, *Brazil* 78 D7
Urakawa, *Japan* 28 C11
Ural, *Australia* 55 E4
Ural →, *Kazakhstan* 23 E9
Ural Mts. = Uralskie Gory, *Russia* 22 C10
Uralla, *Australia* 55 E5
Uralsk, *Kazakhstan* 22 D9
Uralskie Gory, *Russia* 22 C10
Urandangi, *Australia* 54 C2
Uranium City, *Canada* 65 B7
Uranquinty, *Australia* 55 F4
Urawa, *Japan* 29 G9
Uray, *Russia* 24 C7
'Uray'irah, *Si. Arabia* 39 E6
Urbana, *Ill., U.S.A.* 68 E1
Urbana, *Ohio, U.S.A.* 68 E4
Urbino, *Italy* 20 C5
Urbión, Picos de, *Spain* 19 A4
Urcos, *Peru* 78 F4
Urda, *Kazakhstan* 23 E8
Urdzhar, *Kazakhstan* 24 E9
Ure →, *U.K.* 10 C6
Ures, *Mexico* 74 B2
Urfa, *Turkey* 23 G6
Urfahr, *Austria* 16 D7
Urganch = Urgench, *Uzbekistan* 24 E7
Urgench, *Uzbekistan* 24 E7
Uribia, *Colombia* 78 A4
Urk, *Neths.* 15 B5
Urmia = Orūmīyeh, *Iran* 38 B5
Urmia, L. = Orūmīyeh, Daryācheh-ye, *Iran* 38 B5
Uruana, *Brazil* 79 G9
Urubamba, *Peru* 78 F4
Urubamba →, *Peru* 78 F4
Uruçuí, *Brazil* 79 E10
Uruguai →, *Brazil* 80 B6
Uruguaiana, *Brazil* 80 B5
Uruguay ■, *S. Amer.* 80 C5
Uruguay →, *S. Amer.* 80 C5
Urumchi = Ürümqi, *China* 24 E9
Ürümqi, *China* 24 E9
Urup, Os., *Russia* 25 E16
Uryung-Khaya, *Russia* 25 B12
Usa →, *Russia* 22 A10
Uşak, *Turkey* 23 G4
Usakos, *Namibia* 48 C2
Usedom, *Germany* 16 B6
Ush-Tobe, *Kazakhstan* 24 E8
Ushakova, Os., *Russia* 4 A12
Ushant = Ouessant, I. d', *France* 18 B1
Ushibuka, *Japan* 29 H5
Ushuaia, *Argentina* 80 G3
Ushumun, *Russia* 25 D13
Usk →, *U.K.* 11 F5
Üsküdar, *Turkey* 21 D13
Usman, *Russia* 22 D6
Usoke, *Tanzania* 46 F6
Usolye Sibirskoye, *Russia* 25 D11
Uspallata, P. de, *Argentina* 80 C3
Uspenskiy, *Kazakhstan* 24 E8
Ussuri →, *Asia* 28 A7
Ussuriysk, *Russia* 25 E14
Ussurka, *Russia* 28 B6
Ust-Aldan = Batamay, *Russia* 25 C13
Ust Amginskoye = Khandyga, *Russia* 25 C14
Ust-Bolsheretsk, *Russia* 25 D16
Ust Chaun, *Russia* 25 C18
Ust'-Ilga, *Russia* 25 D11
Ust Ilimpeya = Yukti, *Russia* 25 C11
Ust-Ilimsk, *Russia* 25 D11
Ust Ishim, *Russia* 24 D8
Ust-Kamchatsk, *Russia* 25 D17
Ust-Kamenogorsk, *Kazakhstan* 24 E9
Ust-Karenga, *Russia* 25 D12
Ust Khayryuzova, *Russia* 25 D16
Ust-Kut, *Russia* 25 D11
Ust Kuyga, *Russia* 25 B14
Ust Maya, *Russia* 25 C14
Ust-Mil, *Russia* 25 D14
Ust-Nera, *Russia* 25 C15
Ust-Nyukzha, *Russia* 25 D13
Ust Olenek, *Russia* 25 B12
Ust-Omchug, *Russia* 25 C15
Ust Port, *Russia* 24 C9
Ust Tsilma, *Russia* 22 A9
Ust-Tungir, *Russia* 25 D13
Ust Urt = Ustyurt, Plato, *Kazakhstan* 24 E6
Ust Usa, *Russia* 22 A10
Ust Vorkuta, *Russia* 24 C7
Ústí nad Labem, *Czech.* 16 C7
Ustica, *Italy* 20 E5
Ustinov = Izhevsk, *Russia* 22 C9
Ustye, *Russia* 25 D10
Ustyurt, Plato, *Kazakhstan* 24 E6
Usu, *China* 30 B3
Usuki, *Japan* 29 H5
Usumacinta →, *Mexico* 74 D6
Usumbura = Bujumbura, *Burundi* 46 E5
Uta, *Indonesia* 33 E9
Utah □, *U.S.A.* 72 G8
Utah, L., *U.S.A.* 72 F8
Ute Cr. →, *U.S.A.* 71 H3
Utete, *Tanzania* 46 F7
Uthai Thani, *Thailand* 34 E6
Utiariti, *Brazil* 78 F7
Utica, *U.S.A.* 68 D8
Utik L., *Canada* 65 B9
Utikuma L., *Canada* 64 B5
Utrecht, *Neths.* 15 B5
Utrecht, *S. Africa* 49 D5
Utrecht □, *Neths.* 15 B5
Utrera, *Spain* 19 D3
Utsjoki, *Finland* 8 B19
Utsunomiya, *Japan* 29 F9
Uttar Pradesh □, *India* 36 F11
Uttaradit, *Thailand* 34 D6
Uttoxeter, *U.K.* 10 E6
Uudenmaan lääni □, *Finland* 9 F18
Uusikaarlepyy, *Finland* 8 E17
Uusikaupunki, *Finland* 9 F16
Uva, *Russia* 22 C9
Uvalde, *U.S.A.* 71 L5
Uvat, *Russia* 24 D7
Uvinza, *Tanzania* 46 F6
Uvira, *Zaïre* 46 E5
Uvs Nuur, *Mongolia* 30 A4
Uwajima, *Japan* 29 H6
Uyandi, *Russia* 25 C15
Uyuni, *Bolivia* 78 H5
Uzbekistan ■, *Asia* 24 E7
Uzen, *Kazakhstan* 23 F9
Uzerche, *France* 18 D4

V

Vaal →, *S. Africa* 48 D3
Vaal Dam, *S. Africa* 49 D4
Vaalwater, *S. Africa* 49 C4
Vaasa, *Finland* 8 E16
Vaasan lääni □, *Finland* 8 E17
Vác, *Hungary* 17 E9
Vacaville, *U.S.A.* 72 G3
Vach →, *Russia* 24 C8
Vadodara, *India* 36 H8
Vadsø, *Norway* 8 A20
Værøy, *Norway* 8 C12
Váh →, *Slovakia* 17 E9
Vahsel B., *Antarctica* 5 D1
Vaigach, *Russia* 24 B6
Val-de-Marne □, *France* 18 B5
Val-d'Oise □, *France* 18 B5
Val d'Or, *Canada* 62 C4
Val Marie, *Canada* 65 D7
Valahia, *Romania* 21 B11
Valcheta, *Argentina* 80 E3
Valdayskaya Vozvyshennost, *Russia* 22 C5
Valdepeñas, *Spain* 19 C4
Valdés, Pen., *Argentina* 80 E4
Valdez, *U.S.A.* 60 B5
Valdivia, *Chile* 80 D2
Valdosta, *U.S.A.* 69 K4
Vale, *U.S.A.* 72 E5
Valença, *Brazil* 79 F11
Valença do Piauí, *Brazil* 79 E10
Valence, *France* 18 D6
Valencia, *Spain* 19 C5
Valencia, *Venezuela* 78 A5
Valencia □, *Spain* 19 C5
Valencia, Albufera de, *Spain* 19 C5
Valencia, G. de, *Spain* 19 C6
Valencia de Alcántara, *Spain* 19 C2
Valenciennes, *France* 18 A5
Valentia Harbour, *Ireland* 13 E1
Valentia I., *Ireland* 13 E1
Valentim, Sa. do, *Brazil* 79 E10
Valentin, *Russia* 28 C7
Valentine, *Nebr., U.S.A.* 70 D4
Valentine, *Tex., U.S.A.* 71 K2
Valera, *Venezuela* 78 B4
Valier, *U.S.A.* 72 B7
Valjevo, *Serbia, Yug.* 21 B8
Valkeakoski, *Finland* 9 F18
Valkenswaard, *Neths.* 15 C5
Valladolid, *Mexico* 74 C7
Valladolid, *Spain* 19 B3
Valle d'Aosta □, *Italy* 20 B2
Valle de la Pascua, *Venezuela* 78 B5
Vallecas, *Spain* 19 B4
Valledupar, *Colombia* 78 A4
Vallejo, *U.S.A.* 72 G2
Vallenar, *Chile* 80 B2
Valletta, *Malta* 20 G6
Valley City, *U.S.A.* 70 B6
Valley Falls, *U.S.A.* 72 E3
Valleyview, *Canada* 64 B5
Valls, *Spain* 19 B6
Valognes, *France* 18 B3
Valona = Vlóra, *Albania* 21 D8
Valparaíso, *Chile* 80 C2
Valparaiso, *U.S.A.* 68 E2
Vals →, *S. Africa* 48 D4
Vals, Tanjung, *Indonesia* 33 F9
Valsad, *India* 36 J8
Valverde del Camino, *Spain* 19 D2
Van, *Turkey* 23 G7
Van, L. = Van Gölü, *Turkey* 23 G7
Van Alstyne, *U.S.A.* 71 J6
Van Bruyssel, *Canada* 63 C5
Van Buren, *Canada* 63 C6
Van Buren, *Ark., U.S.A.* 71 H7
Van Buren, *Maine, U.S.A.* 69 B11
Van Buren, *Mo., U.S.A.* 71 G9
Van Diemen, C., *N. Terr., Australia* 52 B5
Van Diemen, C., *Queens., Australia* 54 B2
Van Diemen G., *Australia* 52 B5
Van Gölü, *Turkey* 23 G7
Van Horn, *U.S.A.* 71 K2
Van Reenen P., *S. Africa* 49 D4
Van Rees, Pegunungan, *Indonesia* 33 E9
Van Tassell, *U.S.A.* 70 D2
Van Wert, *U.S.A.* 68 E3
Vanavara, *Russia* 25 C11
Vancouver, *Canada* 64 D4
Vancouver, *U.S.A.* 72 D2
Vancouver, C., *Australia* 53 G2
Vancouver I., *Canada* 64 D3
Vandalia, *Ill., U.S.A.* 70 F10
Vandalia, *Mo., U.S.A.* 70 F9
Vanderbijlpark, *S. Africa* 49 D4
Vandergrift, *U.S.A.* 68 E6
Vanderhoof, *Canada* 64 C4
Vanderlin I., *Australia* 54 B2
Vandyke, *Australia* 54 C4
Vänern, *Sweden* 9 G12
Vänersborg, *Sweden* 9 G12
Vang Vieng, *Laos* 34 C7
Vanga, *Kenya* 46 E7
Vangaindrano, *Madag.* 49 C8
Vanguard, *Canada* 65 D7
Vanier, *Canada* 62 C4
Vankarem, *Russia* 25 C18
Vankleek Hill, *Canada* 62 C5
Vanna, *Norway* 8 A15
Vännäs, *Sweden* 8 E15
Vannes, *France* 18 C2
Vanrhynsdorp, *S. Africa* 48 E2
Vanrook, *Australia* 54 B3
Vansbro, *Sweden* 9 F13
Vansittart B., *Australia* 52 B4
Vanua Levu, *Fiji* 51 C8
Vanua Mbalavu, *Fiji* 51 C9
Vanuatu ■, *Pac. Oc.* 56 J8
Vanwyksvlei, *S. Africa* 48 E3
Vanzylsrus, *S. Africa* 48 D3
Var □, *France* 18 E7
Varanasi, *India* 37 G13
Varangerfjorden, *Norway* 8 A20
Varaždin, *Croatia* 20 A7
Varberg, *Sweden* 9 H12
Vardar →, *Macedonia* 21 D10
Varese, *Italy* 20 B3
Variadero, *U.S.A.* 71 H2
Värmlands län □, *Sweden* 9 G12
Varna, *Bulgaria* 21 C12
Värnamo, *Sweden* 9 H13
Varzaneh, *Iran* 39 C7
Vasa, *Finland* 8 E16
Vasa Barris →, *Brazil* 79 F11
Vascongadas = País Vasco □, *Spain* 19 A4
Vasht = Khāsh, *Iran* 36 E2
Vaslui, *Romania* 17 E13
Vassar, *Canada* 65 D9
Vassar, *U.S.A.* 68 D4
Västerås, *Sweden* 9 G14
Västerbottens län □, *Sweden* 8 D14
Västernorrlands län □, *Sweden* 8 E14
Västervik, *Sweden* 9 H14
Västmanlands län □, *Sweden* 9 G14
Vasto, *Italy* 20 C6
Vatnajökull, *Iceland* 8 D5
Vatneyri, *Iceland* 8 D2
Vatoa, *Fiji* 51 D9
Vatoloha, *Madag.* 49 B8
Vatomandry, *Madag.* 49 B8
Vatra-Dornei, *Romania* 17 E12
Vättern, *Sweden* 9 G13
Vaucluse □, *France* 18 E6
Vaughn, *Mont., U.S.A.* 72 C8
Vaughn, *N. Mex., U.S.A.* 73 J11
Vaupés = Uaupés →, *Brazil* 78 C5
Vauxhall, *Canada* 64 C6
Vava'u, *Tonga* 51 D11
Växjö, *Sweden* 9 H13
Vaygach, Ostrov, *Russia* 24 C6
Vechte →, *Neths.* 15 B6
Vedea →, *Romania* 17 G12
Veendam, *Neths.* 15 A6
Veenendaal, *Neths.* 15 B5
Vefsna →, *Norway* 8 D12
Vega, *Norway* 8 D11
Vega, *U.S.A.* 71 H3
Vegafjorden, *Norway* 8 D12
Veghel, *Neths.* 15 C5
Vegreville, *Canada* 64 C6
Vejer de la Frontera, *Spain* 19 D3
Vejle, *Denmark* 9 J10
Velay, Mts. du, *France* 18 D5
Velddrif, *S. Africa* 48 E2
Velebit Planina, *Croatia* 20 B6
Vélez, *Colombia* 78 B4
Vélez Málaga, *Spain* 19 D3
Vélez Rubio, *Spain* 19 D4
Velhas →, *Brazil* 79 G10
Velikaya →, *Russia* 22 C4
Velikaya Kema, *Russia* 28 B8
Veliki Ustyug, *Russia* 22 B8
Velikiye Luki, *Russia* 22 C5
Velikonda Range, *India* 36 M11
Velletri, *Italy* 20 D5
Vellore, *India* 36 N11
Velsen-Noord, *Neths.* 15 B4
Velsk, *Russia* 22 B7
Velva, *U.S.A.* 70 A4
Venado Tuerto, *Argentina* 80 C4
Venda □, *S. Africa* 49 C5
Vendée □, *France* 18 C3
Véneto □, *Italy* 20 B5
Venézia, *Italy* 20 B5
Venézia, G. di, *Italy* 20 B5
Venezuela ■, *S. Amer.* 78 B5
Venezuela, G. de, *Venezuela* 78 A4
Vengurla, *India* 36 M8
Venice = Venézia, *Italy* 20 B5
Venkatapuram, *India* 37 K12
Venlo, *Neths.* 15 C6
Venraij, *Neths.* 15 C5
Ventana, Sa. de la, *Argentina* 80 D4
Ventersburg, *S. Africa* 48 D4
Venterstad, *S. Africa* 48 E4
Ventnor, *U.K.* 11 G6
Ventspils, *Latvia* 9 H16
Ventuarí →, *Venezuela* 78 C5
Ventura, *U.S.A.* 73 J4
Venus B., *Australia* 55 F4
Vera, *Argentina* 80 B4
Vera, *Spain* 19 D5
Veracruz, *Mexico* 74 D5
Veraval, *India* 36 J7
Vercelli, *Italy* 20 B3
Verdalsøra, *Norway* 8 E11
Verde →, *Argentina* 80 E3
Verden, *Germany* 16 B4
Verdigre, *U.S.A.* 70 D5
Verdun, *France* 18 B6
Vereeniging, *S. Africa* 49 D4
Vérendrye, Parc Prov. de la, *Canada* 62 C4
Verga, C., *Guinea* 44 F2
Vergemont, *Australia* 54 C3
Vergemont Cr. →, *Australia* 54 C3
Verkhnevilyuysk, *Russia* 25 C13
Verkhneye Kalinino, *Russia* 25 D11
Verkhniy Baskunchak, *Russia* 23 E8
Verkhoyansk, *Russia* 25 C14
Verkhoyansk Ra. = Verkhoyanskiy Khrebet, *Russia* 25 C13
Verkhoyanskiy Khrebet, *Russia* 25 C13
Verlo, *Canada* 65 C7
Vermilion, *Canada* 65 C6
Vermilion →, *Alta., Canada* 65 C6
Vermilion →, *Qué., Canada* 62 C5

Vermilion, B., U.S.A. . 71 L9
Vermilion Bay, Canada 65 D10
Vermilion Chutes,
Canada 64 B6
Vermilion L., U.S.A. . 70 B8
Vermillion, U.S.A. . . 70 D6
Vermont □, U.S.A. . 68 D9
Vernal, U.S.A. 72 F9
Verner, Canada 62 C3
Verneukpan, S. Africa 48 D3
Vernon, Canada 64 C5
Vernon, U.S.A. 71 H5
Vero Beach, U.S.A. . 69 M5
Véroia, Greece 21 D10
Verona, Italy 20 B4
Veropol, Russia 25 C17
Versailles, France . . 18 B5
Vert, C., Senegal . . . 44 F1
Verulam, S. Africa . . 49 D5
Verviers, Belgium . . 15 D5
Veselovskoye Vdkhr.,
Russia 23 E7
Vesoul, France 18 C7
Vest-Agder fylke □,
Norway 9 G9
Vesterålen, Norway . . 8 B13
Vestfjorden, Norway . 8 C13
Vestfold fylke □,
Norway 9 G11
Vestmannaeyjar,
Iceland 8 E3
Vestspitsbergen,
Svalbard 4 B8
Vestvågøy, Norway . . 8 B12
Vesuvio, Italy 20 D6
Vesuvius, Mt. =
Vesuvio, Italy . . . 20 D6
Veszprém, Hungary . 17 E8
Vetlanda, Sweden . . 9 H13
Vetlugu →, Russia . 24 D5
Vetluga, Belgium . . . 15 C2
Veys, Iran 39 D6
Vezhen, Bulgaria . . . 21 C11
Viacha, Bolivia 78 G5
Viamão, Brazil 80 C6
Viana, Brazil 79 D10
Viana, Portugal 19 C2
Viana do Castelo,
Portugal 19 B1
Vianópolis, Brazil . . 79 G9
Vibank, Canada 65 C8
Viborg, Denmark . . . 9 H10
Vicenza, Italy 20 B4
Vich, Spain 19 B7
Vichy, France 18 C5
Vicksburg, Mich.,
U.S.A. 68 D3
Vicksburg, Miss.,
U.S.A. 71 J9
Viçosa, Brazil 79 E11
Victor, India 36 J7
Victor, U.S.A. 70 F2
Victor Harbor,
Australia 55 F2
Victoria, Canada . . . 64 D4
Victoria, Chile 80 D2
Victoria, Guinea . . . 44 F2
Victoria, Malaysia . . 32 C5
Victoria, Seychelles . 35 E4
Victoria, Kans., U.S.A. 70 F5
Victoria, Tex., U.S.A. . 71 L6
Victoria □, Australia . 55 F3
Victoria →, Australia 52 C4
Victoria, Grand L.,
Canada 62 C4
Victoria, L., Africa . . 46 E6
Victoria, L., Australia . 55 E3
Victoria Beach, Canada 65 C9
Victoria de Durango,
Mexico 74 C4
Victoria Falls,
Zimbabwe 47 H5
Victoria Harbour,
Canada 62 D4
Victoria I., Canada . . 60 A8
Victoria Ld., Antarctica 5 D11
Victoria Res., Canada 63 C8
Victoria River Downs,
Australia 52 C5
Victoria Taungdeik,
Burma 37 J18
Victoria West, S. Africa 48 E3
Victoriaville, Canada . 63 C5
Victorica, Argentina . 80 D3
Victorville, U.S.A. . . 73 J5
Vicuña, Chile 80 C2
Vidalia, U.S.A. 69 J4
Vidin, Bulgaria 21 C10
Vidisha, India 36 H10
Viedma, Argentina . . 80 E4
Viedma, L., Argentina 80 F2
Vien Pou Kha, Laos . 34 B6
Vienna = Wien,
Austria 16 D8
Vienna, U.S.A. 71 G10
Vienne, France 18 D6
Vienne □, France . . . 18 C4
Vienne →, France . . 18 C4
Vientiane, Laos 34 D7
Vierzon, France 18 C5
Vietnam ■, Asia . . . 34 C9
Vigan, Phil. 33 A6
Vigia, Brazil 79 D9
Vigo, Spain 19 A1
Vijayawada, India . . 37 L12
Viking, Canada 64 C6
Vikna, Norway 8 D11
Vikulovo, Russia . . . 24 D8
Vila da Maganja,
Mozam. 47 H7
Vila de João Belo =
Xai-Xai, Mozam. . . 49 D5

Vila do Chibuto,
Mozam. 49 C5
Vila Franca de Xira,
Portugal 19 C1
Vila Gomes da Costa,
Mozam. 49 C5
Vila Machado, Mozam. 47 H6
Vila Real, Portugal . . 19 B2
Vila Real de Santo
António, Portugal . 19 D2
Vila Velha, Brazil . . . 79 H10
Vilaine →, France . . 18 C2
Vilanandro, Tanjona,
Madag. 49 B7
Vilanculos, Mozam. . 49 C6
Vilhelmina, Sweden . 8 D14
Vilhena, Brazil 78 F6
Viliga, Russia 25 C16
Villa Ahumada, Mexico 74 A3
Villa Ángela, Argentina 80 B4
Villa Bella, Bolivia . . 78 F5
Villa Bens = Tarfaya,
Morocco 44 C2
Villa Cisneros =
Dakhla, W. Sahara . 44 D1
Villa Colón, Argentina 80 C3
Villa de María,
Argentina 80 B4
Villa Dolores,
Argentina 80 C3
Villa Hayes, Paraguay 80 A5
Villa María, Argentina 80 C4
Villa Mazán, Argentina 80 B3
Villa Montes, Bolivia . 80 A4
Villa Ocampo,
Argentina 80 B5
Villach, Austria 16 E6
Villagarcía de Arosa,
Spain 19 A1
Villaguay, Argentina . 80 C5
Villahermosa, Mexico 74 D6
Villahermosa, Tabasco,
Mexico 74 D6
Villalba, Spain 19 A2
Villanueva, U.S.A. . . 73 J11
Villanueva de la
Serena, Spain . . . 19 C3
Villarreal, Spain . . . 19 C5
Villarrica, Chile 80 D2
Villarrica, Paraguay . 80 B5
Villarrobledo, Spain . 19 C4
Villavicencio, Colombia 78 C4
Villaviciosa, Spain . . 19 A3
Villazón, Bolivia . . . 80 A3
Ville-Marie, Canada . 62 C4
Ville Platte, U.S.A. . . 71 K8
Villena, Spain 19 C5
Villiers, S. Africa . . . 49 D4
Villisca, U.S.A. 70 E7
Vilna, Canada 64 C6
Vilnius, Lithuania . . 22 D4
Vilskutskogo, Proliv,
Russia 25 B11
Vilvoorde, Belgium . . 15 D4
Vilyuy →, Russia . . 25 C13
Vilyuysk, Russia . . . 25 C13
Viña del Mar, Chile . 80 C2
Vinaroz, Spain 19 B6
Vincennes, U.S.A. . . 68 F2
Vindel älven →,
Sweden 8 E15
Vindeln, Sweden . . . 8 D15
Vindhya Ra., India . . 36 H10
Vineland, U.S.A. . . . 68 F8
Vinh, Vietnam 34 C8
Vinita, U.S.A. 71 G7
Vinkovci, Croatia . . . 21 B8
Vinnitsa, Ukraine . . 23 E4
Vinnytsya = Vinnitsa,
Ukraine 23 E4
Vinton, Iowa, U.S.A. . 70 D8
Vinton, La., U.S.A. . . 71 K8
Viqueque, Indonesia . 33 F7
Virac, Phil. 33 B6
Virago Sd., Canada . 64 C2
Viramgam, India . . . 36 H8
Virden, Canada 65 D8
Vire, France 18 B3
Vírgenes, C., Argentina 80 G3
Virgin →, Canada . . 65 B7
Virgin →, U.S.A. . . . 73 H6
Virgin Is. (British) ■,
W. Indies 75 D12
Virgin Is. (U.S.) ■,
W. Indies 75 D12
Virginia, S. Africa . . 48 D4
Virginia, U.S.A. 70 B8
Virginia □, U.S.A. . . 68 G7
Virginia Beach, U.S.A. 68 G8
Virginia City, Mont.,
U.S.A. 72 D8
Virginia City, Nev.,
U.S.A. 72 G4
Virginia Falls, Canada 64 A3
Virginiatown, Canada 62 C4
Viroqua, U.S.A. 70 D9
Virton, Belgium 15 E5
Virudunagar, India . . 36 Q10
Vis, Croatia 20 C7
Visalia, U.S.A. 73 H4
Visayan Sea, Phil. . . 33 B6
Visby, Sweden 9 H15
Viscount Melville Sd.,
Canada 4 B2
Visé, Belgium 15 D5
Višegrad, Bos.-H. . . 21 C8
Viseu, Brazil 79 D9
Viseu, Portugal 19 B2
Vishakhapatnam, India 37 L13
Viso, Mte., Italy . . . 20 B2
Visokoi I., Antarctica . 5 B1

Vistula = Wisła →,
Poland 17 A9
Vitebsk, Belorussia . 22 C5
Viterbo, Italy 20 C5
Viti Levu, Fiji 51 C7
Vitim, Russia 25 D12
Vitim →, Russia . . . 25 D12
Vitória, Brazil 79 H10
Vitoria, Spain 19 A4
Vitória da Conquista,
Brazil 79 F10
Vitsyebsk = Vitebsk,
Belorussia 22 C5
Vittória, Italy 20 F6
Vittório Véneto, Italy . 20 B5
Vivero, Spain 19 A2
Vizianagaram, India . 37 K13
Vlaardingen, Neths. . 15 C4
Vladikavkaz, Russia . 23 F7
Vladimir, Russia . . . 22 C7
Vladivostok, Russia . 25 E14
Vlieland, Neths. . . . 15 A4
Vlissingen, Neths. . . 15 C3
Vlóra, Albania 21 D8
Vltava →, Czech. . . 16 C7
Vogelkop = Doberai,
Jazirah, Indonesia . 33 E8
Vogelsberg, Germany 16 C4
Vohibinany, Madag. . 49 B8
Vohimarina, Madag. . 49 A9
Vohimena, Tanjon' i,
Madag. 49 D8
Vohipeno, Madag. . . 49 C8
Voi, Kenya 46 E7
Voisey B., Canada . . 63 A7
Vojmsjön, Sweden . . 8 D14
Volborg, U.S.A. 70 C2
Volcano Is. = Kazan-
Rettó, Pac. Oc. . . . 56 E6
Volchayevka, Russia . 25 E14
Volda, Norway 8 E9
Volga →, Russia . . . 23 E8
Volga Hts. =
Privolzhskaya
Vozvyshennost,
Russia 23 D8
Volgodonsk, Russia . 23 E7
Volgograd, Russia . . 23 E7
Volgogradskoye
Vdkhr., Russia . . . 23 D8
Volkhov →, Russia . 22 B5
Volksrust, S. Africa . 49 D4
Vollenhove, Neths. . 15 B5
Volochanka, Russia . 25 B10
Vologda, Russia . . . 22 C6
Vólos, Greece 21 E10
Volsk, Russia 22 D8
Volta →, Ghana . . . 44
Volta, L., Ghana . . . 44 G5
Volta Redonda, Brazil 79 H10
Voltaire, C., Australia . 52 B4
Volterra, Italy 20 C4
Volturno →, Italy . . 20 D5
Volvo, Australia 55 E3
Volzhskiy, Russia . . 23 E7
Vondrozo, Madag. . . 49 C8
Voorburg, Neths. . . 15 B4
Vopnafjörður, Iceland 8 D6
Vorarlberg □, Austria 16 E5
Voríai Sporádhes,
Greece 21 E10
Vorkuta, Russia . . . 22 A11
Voronezh, Russia . . 22 D6
Voroshilovgrad =
Lugansk, Ukraine . 23 E6
Voroshilovsk =
Kommunarsk,
Ukraine 23 E6
Vorovskoye, Russia . 25 D16
Vosges, France 18 B7
Vosges □, France . . 18 B7
Voss, Norway 9 F9
Vostok I., Kiribati . . 57 J12
Votkinsk, Russia . . . 22 C9
Votkinskoye Vdkhr.,
Russia 22 C10
Vouga →, Portugal . 19 B1
Vozhe Oz., Russia . . 22 B6
Voznesenka, Russia . 25 D10
Voznesensk, Ukraine 23 E5
Voznesenye, Russia . 22 B6
Vrangelya, Ostrov,
Russia 25 B19
Vranje, Serbia, Yug. . 21 C9
Vratsa, Bulgaria . . . 21 C10
Vrbas →,
Bos.-H. 21 B7
Vrede, S. Africa 49 D4
Vredefort, S. Africa . 48 D4
Vredenburg, S. Africa 48 E2
Vredendal, S. Africa . 48 E2
Vršac, Serbia, Yug. . . 21 B9
Vryburg, S. Africa . . 48 D3
Vryheid, S. Africa . . 49 D5
Vught, Neths. 15 C5
Vulcan, Canada 64 C6
Vulcan, U.S.A. 68 C2
Vulcano, Italy 20 E6
Vung Tau, Vietnam . . 34 G9
Vyatka, Russia 24 D5
Vyatka →, Russia . . 22 C9
Vyatskiye Polyany,
Russia 22 C9
Vyazemskiy, Russia . 25 E14
Vyazma, Russia . . . 22 C5
Vyborg, Russia 22 B4
Vychegda →, Russia 22 B8
Vychodné Beskydy,
Europe 17 D10
Vyg-ozero, Russia . . 22 B5
Vyrnwy, L., U.K. . . . 10 E4

Vyshniy Volochek,
Russia 22 C5
Vyshza = imeni 26
Bakinskikh
Komissarov,
Turkmenistan . . . 23 G9
Vytegra, Russia 22 B6

W

W.A.C. Bennett Dam,
Canada 64 B4
Wa, Ghana 44 F4
Waal →, Neths. . . . 15 C5
Wabakimi L., Canada . 62 B2
Wabana, Canada . . . 63 C9
Wabasca, Canada . . 64 B6
Wabash, U.S.A. 68 E3
Wabash →, U.S.A. . 68 G1
Wabeno, U.S.A. 68 C1
Wabigoon L., Canada 65 D10
Wabowden, Canada . 65 C9
Wąbrzeźno, Poland . 17 B9
Wabuk Pt., Canada . 62 A2
Wabush, Canada . . . 63 B6
Wabuska, U.S.A. . . . 72 G4
Waco, U.S.A. 71 K6
Waconichi, L., Canada 62 B5
Wad Banda, Sudan . 45 F10
Wad Hamid, Sudan . 45 E11
Wâd Medanî, Sudan . 45 F11
Wadayama, Japan . . 29 G7
Waddeneilanden,
Neths. 15 A5
Waddenzee, Neths. . 15 A5
Wadderin Hill,
Australia 53 F2
Waddington, Mt.,
Canada 64 C3
Waddy Pt., Australia . 55 C5
Wadena, Canada . . . 65 C8
Wadena, U.S.A. 70 B7
Wadesboro, U.S.A. . 69 H5
Wadhams, Canada . 64 C3
Wâdi as Sir, Jordan . 41 D4
Wadi Halfa, Sudan . . 45 D11
Wadsworth, U.S.A. . 72 G4
Wafrah, Si. Arabia . . 38 D5
Wageningen, Neths. . 15 C5
Wager B., Canada . . 61 B11
Wager Bay, Canada . 61 B10
Wagga Wagga,
Australia 55 F4
Waghete, Indonesia . 33 E9
Wagin, Australia . . . 53 F2
Wagon Mound, U.S.A. 71 G2
Wagoner, U.S.A. . . . 71 G7
Wah, Pakistan 36 C8
Wahai, Indonesia . . 33 E7
Wahiawa, U.S.A. . . . 66 H15
Wâhid, Egypt 41 E1
Wahoo, U.S.A. 70 E6
Wahpeton, U.S.A. . . 70 B6
Waiau →, N.Z. 51 K4
Waibeem, Indonesia . 33 E8
Waigeo, Indonesia . . 33 E8
Waihi, N.Z. 51 G5
Waihou →, N.Z. . . . 51 G5
Waikabubak, Indonesia 33 F5
Waikari, N.Z. 51 K4
Waikato →, N.Z. . . . 51 G5
Waikerie, Australia . . 55 E2
Waikokopu, N.Z. . . . 51 H6
Waikouaiti, N.Z. . . . 51 L3
Waimakariri →, N.Z. 51 K4
Waimate, N.Z. 51 L3
Waingapu, Indonesia 33 F6
Wainganga →, India 36 K11
Wainuiomata, N.Z. . 51 J5
Wainwright, Canada . 65 C6
Wainwright, U.S.A. . 60 A3
Waiouru, N.Z. 51 H5
Waipara, N.Z. 51 K4
Waipawa, N.Z. 51 H6
Waipiro, N.Z. 51 H7
Waipu, N.Z. 51 F5
Waipukurau, N.Z. . . 51 J6
Wairakei, N.Z. 51 H6
Wairarapa, L., N.Z. . 51 J5
Wairoa, N.Z. 51 H6
Waitaki →, N.Z. . . . 51 L3
Waitara, N.Z. 51 H5
Waitsburg, U.S.A. . . 72 C5
Waiuku, N.Z. 51 G5
Wajima, Japan 29 F8
Wajir, Kenya 46 D8
Wakasa, Japan 29 G7
Wakasa-Wan, Japan . 29 G7
Wakatipu, L., N.Z. . . 51 L2
Wakaw, Canada . . . 65 C7
Wakayama, Japan . . 29 G7
Wakayama-ken □,
Japan 29 H7
Wake Forest, U.S.A. . 69 H6
Wake I., Pac. Oc. . . . 56 F8
Wakefield, N.Z. 51 J4
Wakefield, U.K. 10 D6
Wakefield, U.K. 70 B10
Wakeham Bay =
Maricourt, Canada . 61 C12
Wakema, Burma . . . 37 L19
Wakkanai, Japan . . . 28 B10
Wakkerstroom,
S. Africa 49 D5
Wakool, Australia . . 55 F3
Wakool →, Australia 55 F3
Wakre, Indonesia . . 33 E8
Wakuach L., Canada . 63 A6
Wałbrzych, Poland . . 16 C8

Walbury Hill, U.K. . . 11 F6
Walcha, Australia . . 55 E5
Walcheren, Neths. . . 15 C3
Walcott, U.S.A. 72 F10
Waldburg Ra.,
Australia 52 D2
Walden, U.S.A. 72 F10
Waldport, U.S.A. . . . 72 D1
Waldron, U.S.A. 71 H7
Wales □, U.K. 11 E4
Walgett, Australia . . 55 E4
Walgreen Coast,
Antarctica 5 D15
Walhalla, Australia . . 55 F4
Walhalla, U.S.A. . . . 65 D9
Walker, U.S.A. 70 B7
Walker L., Man.,
Canada 65 C9
Walker L., Qué.,
Canada 63 B6
Walker L., U.S.A. . . . 72 G4
Walkerston, Australia 54 C4
Wall, U.S.A. 70 C3
Walla Walla, U.S.A. . 72 C4
Wallabadah, Australia 54 B3
Wallace, Idaho, U.S.A. 72 C6
Wallace, N.C., U.S.A. 69 H7
Wallace, Nebr., U.S.A. 70 E4
Wallaceburg, Canada 62 D3
Wallachia = Valahia,
Romania 21 B11
Wallal, Australia . . . 55 E4
Wallal Downs,
Australia 52 C3
Wallambin, L.,
Australia 53 F2
Wallaroo, Australia . 55 E2
Wallasey, U.K. 10 D4
Wallerawang, Australia 55 E5
Wallhallow, Australia 54 B2
Wallis & Futuna, Is.,
Pac. Oc. 56 J10
Wallowa, U.S.A. . . . 72 D5
Wallowa Mts., U.S.A. 72 D5
Wallsend, Australia . 55 E5
Wallsend, U.K. 10 C6
Wallula, U.S.A. 72 C4
Wallumbilla, Australia 55 D4
Walmsley, L., Canada 65 A7
Walney, I. of, U.K. . . 10 C4
Walnut Ridge, U.S.A. 71 G9
Walsall, U.K. 11 E6
Walsenburg, U.S.A. . 71 G2
Walsh, U.S.A. 71 G3
Walsh →, Australia . 54 B3
Walsh P.O., Australia 54 B3
Waltham Station,
Canada 62 C4
Waltman, U.S.A. . . . 72 E10
Walvisbaai, S. Africa 48 C1
Wamba, Zaïre 46 D5
Wamego, U.S.A. . . . 70 F6
Wamena, Indonesia . 33 E9
Wamsasi, Indonesia . 33 E7
Wana, Pakistan 36 C6
Wanaaring, Australia 55 D3
Wanaka, N.Z. 51 L2
Wanaka L., N.Z. . . . 51 L2
Wanapiri, Indonesia . 33 E9
Wanapitei L., Canada 62 C3
Wanbi, Australia . . . 55 E3
Wandarrie, Australia 53 E2
Wandoan, Australia . 55 D4
Wang Saphung,
Thailand 34 D6
Wanga, Indonesia . . 33 E8
Wanganella, Australia 55 F3
Wanganui, N.Z. 51 H5
Wangaratta, Australia 55 F4
Wangary, Australia . 55 E2
Wangerooge, Germany 16 B3
Wangiwangi, Indonesia 33 F6
Wanless, Canada . . 65 C8
Wanxian, China 31 C5
Wapakoneta, U.S.A. . 68 E3
Wapato, U.S.A. 72 C3
Wapawekka L., Canada 65 C8
Wapikopa L., Canada 62 B2
Wapsipinicon →,
U.S.A. 70 E9
Warangal, India 36 L11
Waratah, Australia . . 54 G4
Waratah B., Australia 55 F4
Warburton, Vic.,
Australia 55 F4
Warburton,
W. Austral., Australia 53 E4
Warburton Ra.,
Australia 53 E4
Ward, N.Z. 51 J5
Ward →, Australia . 55 D4
Ward Cove, Canada . 64 B2
Warden, S. Africa . . 49 D4
Wardha, India 36 J11
Wardha →, India . . 36 K11
Wardlow, Canada . . 64 C6
Ware, Canada 64 B3
Warialda, Australia . . 55 D5
Warkopi, Indonesia . 33 E8
Warley, U.K. 11 E6
Warm Springs, U.S.A. 73 G5
Warman, Canada . . . 65 C7
Warmbad, Namibia . 48 D2
Warmbad, S. Africa . 49 C4
Warnambool Downs,
Australia 54 C3
Warnemünde,
Germany 16 A6

Warner, Canada . . . 64 D6
Warner Mts., U.S.A. . 72 F3
Warner Robins, U.S.A. 69 J4
Waroona, Australia . 53 F2
Warracknabeal,
Australia 55 F3
Warragul, Australia . 55 F4
Warrawagine, Australia 52 D3
Warrego →, Australia 55 E4
Warrego Ra., Australia 54 C4
Warren, Australia . . 55 E4
Warren, Ark., U.S.A. . 71 J8
Warren, Mich., U.S.A. 68 D4
Warren, Minn., U.S.A. 70 A6
Warren, Ohio, U.S.A. 68 E5
Warren, Pa., U.S.A. . 68 E5
Warrenpoint, U.K. . . 13 B5
Warrensburg, U.S.A. 70 F8
Warrenton, S. Africa 48 D3
Warrenton, U.S.A. . . 72 C2
Warrenville, Australia 55 D4
Warri, Nigeria 44 G6
Warrina, Australia . . 55 D2
Warrington, U.K. . . . 10 D5
Warrington, U.S.A. . 69 K2
Warrnambool,
Australia 55 F3
Warroad, U.S.A. . . . 70 A7
Warsa, Indonesia . . 33 E9
Warsaw = Warszawa,
Poland 17 B10
Warsaw, U.S.A. 68 E3
Warszawa, Poland . . 17 B10
Warta →, Poland . . 16 B7
Warthe = Warta →,
Poland 16 B7
Waru, Indonesia . . . 33 E8
Warwick, Australia . . 55 D5
Warwick, U.K. 11 E6
Warwick, U.S.A. . . . 68 E10
Warwickshire □, U.K. 11 E6
Wasatch Ra., U.S.A. . 72 F8
Wasbank, S. Africa . 49 D5
Wasco, Calif., U.S.A. 73 J4
Wasco, Oreg., U.S.A. 72 D3
Waseca, U.S.A. 70 C8
Wasekamio L., Canada 65 B7
Wash, The, U.K. . . . 10 E8
Washburn, N. Dak.,
U.S.A. 70 B4
Washburn, Wis., U.S.A. 70 B9
Washim, India 36 J10
Washington, D.C.,
U.S.A. 68 F7
Washington, Ga.,
U.S.A. 69 J4
Washington, Ind.,
U.S.A. 68 F2
Washington, Iowa,
U.S.A. 70 E9
Washington, Mo.,
U.S.A. 70 F9
Washington, N.C.,
U.S.A. 69 H7
Washington, Pa.,
U.S.A. 68 E5
Washington, Utah,
U.S.A. 73 H7
Washington □, U.S.A. 72 C3
Washington, Mt.,
U.S.A. 68 C10
Washington I., U.S.A. 68 C2
Wasian, Indonesia . . 33 E8
Wasior, Indonesia . . 33 E8
Waskaiowaka, L.,
Canada 65 B9
Waskesiu Lake, Canada 65 C7
Wassenaar, Neths. . 15 B4
Waswanipi, Canada . 62 C4
Waswanipi, L., Canada 62 C4
Watampone,
Indonesia 33 E6
Water Park Pt.,
Australia 54 C5
Water Valley, U.S.A. . 71 H10
Waterberge, S. Africa 49 C4
Waterbury, U.S.A. . . 68 E9
Waterbury L., Canada 65 B8
Waterford, Ireland . . 13 D4
Waterford □, Ireland . 13 D4
Waterford Harbour,
Ireland 13 D5
Waterhen L., Man.,
Canada 65 C9
Waterhen L., Sask.,
Canada 65 C7
Waterloo, Belgium . . 15 D4
Waterloo, Canada . . 62 D3
Waterloo, S. Leone . . 44 G2
Waterloo, Ill., U.S.A. 70 F9
Waterloo, Iowa, U.S.A. 70 D8
Watersmeet, U.S.A. . 70 B10
Waterton-Glacier Int.
Peace Park, U.S.A. 72 B7
Watertown, N.Y.,
U.S.A. 68 D8
Watertown, S. Dak.,
U.S.A. 70 C6
Watertown, Wis.,
U.S.A. 70 D10
Waterval-Boven,
S. Africa 49 D5
Waterville, Maine,
U.S.A. 63 D6
Waterville, Wash.,
U.S.A. 72 C3
Watervliet, U.S.A. . . 68 D9
Wates, Indonesia . . 33 G14
Watford, U.K. 11 F7
Watford City, U.S.A. . 70 B3
Wathaman →,
Canada 65 B8

Watheroo, Australia . 53 F2
Watkins Glen, U.S.A. . 68 D7
Watling I. = San
  Salvador, Bahamas 75 C10
Watonga, U.S.A. . . 71 H5
Watrous, Canada . . 65 C7
Watrous, U.S.A. . . 71 H2
Watsa, Zaïre 46 D5
Watseka, U.S.A. . . 68 E2
Watson, Australia . . 53 F5
Watson, Canada . . 65 C8
Watson Lake, Canada 64 A3
Watsonville, U.S.A. . 73 H3
Wattiwarriganna
  Cr. →, Australia . 55 D2
Watuata = Batuata,
  Indonesia 33 F6
Watubela, Kepulauan,
  Indonesia 33 E8
Watubela Is. =
  Watubela,
  Kepulauan,
  Indonesia 33 E8
Waubay, U.S.A. . . 70 C6
Waubra, Australia . . 55 F3
Wauchope, Australia . 55 E5
Wauchula, U.S.A. . . 69 M5
Waugh, Canada . . . 65 D9
Waukarlycarly, L.,
  Australia 52 D3
Waukegan, U.S.A. . . 68 D2
Waukesha, U.S.A. . . 68 D1
Waukon, U.S.A. . . 70 D9
Wauneta, U.S.A. . . 70 E4
Waupaca, U.S.A. . . 70 C10
Waupun, U.S.A. . . 70 D10
Waurika, U.S.A. . . 71 H6
Wausau, U.S.A. . . 70 C10
Wautoma, U.S.A. . . 70 C10
Wauwatosa, U.S.A. . 68 D2
Wave Hill, Australia . 52 C5
Waveney →, U.K. . . 11 E9
Waverley, N.Z. . . . 51 H5
Waverly, Iowa, U.S.A. 70 D8
Waverly, N.Y., U.S.A. 68 D7
Wavre, Belgium . . . 15 D4
Wâw, Sudan 45 G10
Wâw al Kabir, Libya . 45 C8
Wawa, Canada . . . 62 C3
Wawanesa, Canada . 65 D9
Waxahachie, U.S.A. . 71 J6
Way, L., Australia . . 53 E3
Wayabula Rau,
  Indonesia 33 D7
Wayatinah, Australia . 54 G4
Waycross, U.S.A. . . 69 K4
Wayne, Nebr., U.S.A. 70 D6
Wayne, W. Va., U.S.A. 68 F4
Waynesboro, Ga.,
  U.S.A. 69 J4
Waynesboro, Miss.,
  U.S.A. 69 K1
Waynesboro, Pa.,
  U.S.A. 68 F7
Waynesboro, Va.,
  U.S.A. 68 F6
Waynesburg, U.S.A. . 68 F5
Waynesville, U.S.A. . 69 H4
Waynoka, U.S.A. . . 71 G5
Wazirabad, Pakistan . 36 C9
We, Indonesia . . . 32 C1
Weald, The, U.K. . . 11 F8
Wear →, U.K. . . . 10 C6
Weatherford, Okla.,
  U.S.A. 71 H5
Weatherford, Tex.,
  U.S.A. 71 J6
Weaverville, U.S.A. . 72 F2
Webb City, U.S.A. . . 71 G7
Webster, S. Dak.,
  U.S.A. 70 C6
Webster, Wis., U.S.A. 70 C8
Webster City, U.S.A. . 70 D8
Webster Groon, U.S.A. 70 F9
Webster Springs,
  U.S.A. 68 F5
Weda, Indonesia . . 33 D7
Weda, Teluk, Indonesia 33 D7
Weddell I., Falk. Is. . 80 G4
Weddell Sea,
  Antarctica 5 D1
Wedderburn, Australia 55 F3
Wedgeport, Canada . 63 D6
Wee Waa, Australia . 55 E4
Weed, U.S.A. . . . 72 F2
Weemelah, Australia . 55 D4
Weenen, S. Africa . . 49 D5
Weert, Neths. 15 C5
Weifang, China . . . 31 C6
Weimar, Germany . . 16 C5
Weipa, Australia . . 54 A3
Weir →, Australia . . 55 D4
Weir →, Canada . . 65 B10
Weir River, Canada . 65 B10
Weiser, U.S.A. . . . 72 D5
Wejherowo, Poland . 17 A9
Welbourn Hill,
  Australia 55 D1
Welch, U.S.A. . . . 68 G5
Welkom, S. Africa . . 48 D4
Welland, Canada . . 62 D4
Welland →, U.K. . . 10 E7
Wellesley Is., Australia 54 B2
Wellin, Belgium . . . 15 D5
Wellingborough, U.K. . 11 E7
Wellington, Australia . 55 E4
Wellington, Canada . 62 D4
Wellington, N.Z. . . 51 J5
Wellington, S. Africa . 48 E2
Wellington, Shrops.,
  U.K. 10 E5

Wellington, Somst.,
  U.K. 11 G4
Wellington, Colo.,
  U.S.A. 70 E2
Wellington, Kans.,
  U.S.A. 71 G6
Wellington, Nev.,
  U.S.A. 72 G4
Wellington, Tex.,
  U.S.A. 71 H4
Wellington, I., Chile . 80 F1
Wellington, L.,
  Australia 55 F4
Wells, Norfolk, U.K. . 10 E8
Wells, Somst., U.K. . 11 F5
Wells, Minn., U.S.A. . 70 D8
Wells, Nev., U.S.A. . 72 F6
Wells, L., Australia . 53 E3
Wells Gray Prov. Park,
  Canada 64 C4
Wellsboro, U.S.A. . . 68 E7
Wellsville, Mo., U.S.A. 70 F9
Wellsville, N.Y., U.S.A. 68 D7
Wellsville, Ohio, U.S.A. 68 E5
Wellsville, Utah, U.S.A. 72 F8
Wellton, U.S.A. . . . 73 K6
Wels, Austria 16 D7
Welshpool, U.K. . . . 11 E4
Wem, U.K. 10 E5
Wenatchee, U.S.A. . 72 C3
Wenchi, Ghana . . . 44 G4
Wenchow = Wenzhou,
  China 31 D7
Wendell, U.S.A. . . 72 E6
Wendesi, Indonesia . 33 E8
Wendover, U.S.A. . . 72 F6
Wenlock →, Australia 54 A3
Wenshan, China . . 30 D5
Wensu, China . . . 30 B3
Wentworth, Australia . 55 E3
Wenut, Indonesia . . 33 E8
Wenzhou, China . . 31 D7
Weott, U.S.A. . . . 72 F2
Wepener, S. Africa . 48 D4
Werda, Botswana . . 48 D3
Werder, Ethiopia . . 40 F4
Weri, Indonesia . . . 33 E8
Werribee, Australia . 55 F3
Werrimull, Australia . 55 E3
Werris Creek, Australia 55 E5
Wersar, Indonesia . . 33 E8
Weser →, Germany . 16 B4
Wesiri, Indonesia . . 33 F7
Wesley Vale, U.S.A. . 73 J10
Wesleyville, Canada . 63 C9
Wessel, C., Australia . 54 A2
Wessel Is., Australia . 54 A2
Wessington Springs,
  U.S.A. 70 C5
West, U.S.A. 71 K6
West B., U.S.A. . . . 71 L10
West Baines →,
  Australia 52 C4
West Bend, U.S.A. . . 68 D1
West Bengal □, India 37 H15
West Bookids –
  Západné Beskydy,
  Europe 17 D9
West Branch, U.S.A. . 68 C3
West Bromwich, U.K. . 11 E5
West Cape Howe,
  Australia 53 G2
West Chester, U.S.A. . 68 F8
West Columbia, U.S.A. 71 L7
West Des Moines,
  U.S.A. 70 E8
West Falkland, Falk. Is. 80 G4
West Fjord =
  Vestfjorden, Norway 8 C13
West Frankfort, U.S.A. 70 G10
West Glamorgan □,
  U.K. 11 F4
West Helena, U.S.A. . 71 II9
West Ice Shelf,
  Antarctica 5 C7
West Memphis, U.S.A. 71 H9
West Midlands □, U.K. 11 E6
West Monroe, U.S.A. . 71 J8
West Nicholson,
  Zimbabwe 47 J5
West Palm Beach,
  U.S.A. 69 M5
West Plains, U.S.A. . 71 G9
West Pt. = Ouest, Pte.,
  Canada 63 C7
West Pt., Australia . . 55 F2
West Point, Ga., U.S.A. 69 J3
West Point, Miss.,
  U.S.A. 69 J1
West Point, Nebr.,
  U.S.A. 70 E6
West Point, Va., U.S.A. 68 G7
West Road →,
  Canada 64 C4
West Rutland, U.S.A. . 68 D9
West Schelde =
  Westerschelde →,
  Neths. 15 C3
West Siberian Plain,
  Russia 26 C11
West Sussex □, U.K. . 11 G7
West-Terschelling,
  Neths. 15 A5
West Virginia □, U.S.A. 68 F5
West-Vlaanderen □,
  Belgium 15 D3
West Wyalong,
  Australia 55 E4
West Yellowstone,
  U.S.A. 72 D8

West Yorkshire □, U.K. 10 D6
Westall Pt., Australia . 55 E1
Westbrook, Maine,
  U.S.A. 69 D10
Westbrook, Tex., U.S.A. 71 J4
Westbury, Australia . 54 G4
Westby, U.S.A. . . . 70 A2
Western Australia □,
  Australia 53 E2
Western Ghats, India . 36 N9
Western Isles □, U.K. . 12 D1
Western Sahara ■,
  Africa 44 D2
Western Samoa ■,
  Pac. Oc. 51 A13
Westernport, U.S.A. . 68 F6
Westerschelde →,
  Neths. 15 C3
Westerwald, Germany 16 C3
Westhope, U.S.A. . . 70 A4
Westland Bight, N.Z. . 51 K3
Westlock, Canada . . 64 C6
Westmeath □, Ireland 13 C4
Westminster, U.S.A. . 68 F7
Westmorland, U.S.A. . 73 K6
Weston, Malaysia . . 32 C5
Weston, Oreg., U.S.A. 72 D4
Weston, W. Va., U.S.A. 68 F5
Weston I., Canada . . 62 B4
Weston-super-Mare,
  U.K. 11 F5
Westport, Ireland . . 13 C2
Westport, N.Z. . . . 51 J3
Westport, U.S.A. . . 72 C1
Westray, Canada . . 65 C8
Westray, U.K. . . . 12 B6
Westree, Canada . . 62 C3
Westville, Ill., U.S.A. . 68 E2
Westville, Okla., U.S.A. 71 G7
Westwood, U.S.A. . . 72 F3
Wetar, Indonesia . . 33 F7
Wetaskiwin, Canada . 64 C6
Wetteren, Belgium . . 15 D3
Wetzlar, Germany . . 16 C4
Wewaka, U.S.A. . . 71 H6
Wexford, Ireland . . 13 D5
Wexford □, Ireland . 13 D5
Wexford Harbour,
  Ireland 13 D5
Weyburn, Canada . . 65 D8
Weyburn L., Canada . 64 A5
Weymouth, Canada . 63 D6
Weymouth, U.K. . . . 11 G5
Weymouth, C.,
  Australia 54 A3
Whakatane, N.Z. . . 51 G6
Whale →, Canada . . 63 A6
Whale Cove, Canada . 65 A10
Whales, B. of,
  Antarctica 5 D12
Whalsay, U.K. . . . 12 A8
Whangamomona, N.Z. 51 H5
Whangarei, N.Z. . . 51 F5
Whangarei Harb., N.Z. 51 F5
Wharfe →, U.K. . . . 10 D6
Wharfedale, U.K. . . 10 C5
Wharton, U.S.A. . . 71 L6
Wheatland, U.S.A. . . 70 D2
Wheaton, U.S.A. . . 70 C6
Wheeler, Oreg., U.S.A. 72 D2
Wheeler, Tex., U.S.A. 71 H4
Wheeler →, Canada . 65 B7
Wheeler Pk., N. Mex.,
  U.S.A. 73 H11
Wheeler Pk., Nev.,
  U.S.A. 73 G6
Wheeling, U.S.A. . . 68 E5
Whernside, U.K. . . 10 C5
Whidbey I., U.S.A. . . 64 B4
Whiskey Gap, Canada 64 D6
Whiskey Jack L.,
  Canada 65 B8
Whistloduck Cr. →,
  Australia 54 C2
Whitby, U.K. 10 C7
White →, Ark., U.S.A. 71 J9
White →, Colo.,
  U.S.A. 72 F9
White →, Ind., U.S.A. 68 F2
White →, S. Dak.,
  U.S.A. 70 D5
White, L., Australia . 52 D4
White B., Canada . . 63 B8
White Bear Res.,
  Canada 63 C8
White Bird, U.S.A. . . 72 D5
White Butte, U.S.A. . 70 B3
White City, U.S.A. . . 70 F6
White Cliffs, Australia 55 E3
White Deer, U.S.A. . 71 H4
White Hall, U.S.A. . . 70 F9
White I., N.Z. 51 G6
White L., U.S.A. . . . 71 L8
White Mts., Calif.,
  U.S.A. 73 H4
White Mts., N.H.,
  U.S.A. 67 B12
White Nile = Nîl el
  Abyad →, Sudan . 45 E11
White Otter L., Canada 62 C1
White Pass, Canada . 64 B1
White River, Canada . 62 C2
White River, S. Africa 49 D5
White River, U.S.A. . 70 D4
White Russia =
  Belorussia ■, Europe 22 D4
White Sea = Beloye
  More, Russia . . . 22 A6
White Sulphur Springs,
  Mont., U.S.A. . . . 72 C8

White Sulphur Springs,
  W. Va., U.S.A. . . 68 G5
Whitecliffs, N.Z. . . . 51 K3
Whitecourt, Canada . 64 C5
Whiteface, U.S.A. . . 71 J3
Whitefish, U.S.A. . . 72 B6
Whitefish L., Canada . 65 A7
Whitefish Pt., U.S.A. . 68 B3
Whitegull, L., Canada 63 A7
Whitehall, Mich.,
  U.S.A. 68 D2
Whitehall, Mont.,
  U.S.A. 72 D7
Whitehall, N.Y., U.S.A. 68 D9
Whitehall, Wis., U.S.A. 70 C9
Whitehaven, U.K. . . 10 C4
Whitehorse, Canada . 64 A1
Whitehorse, Vale of,
  U.K. 11 F6
Whitemark, Australia . 54 G4
Whitemouth, Canada . 65 D9
Whitesboro, U.S.A. . 71 J6
Whiteshell Prov. Park,
  Canada 65 C9
Whitetail, U.S.A. . . 70 A2
Whiteville, U.S.A. . . 69 H6
Whitewater, U.S.A. . 68 D1
Whitewater Baldy,
  U.S.A. 73 K9
Whitewater L., Canada 62 B2
Whitewood, Australia 54 C3
Whitewood, Canada . 65 C8
Whitfield, Australia . 55 F4
Whithorn, U.K. . . . 12 G4
Whitianga, N.Z. . . . 51 G5
Whitmire, U.S.A. . . 69 H5
Whitney, Canada . . 62 C4
Whitney, Mt., U.S.A. . 73 H4
Whitstable, U.K. . . . 11 F9
Whitsunday I.,
  Australia 54 C4
Whittlesea, Australia . 55 F4
Whitwell, U.S.A. . . 69 H3
Wholdaia L., Canada . 65 A8
Whyalla, Australia . . 55 E2
Whyjonta, Australia . 55 D3
Wiarton, Canada . . 62 D3
Wibaux, U.S.A. . . . 70 B2
Wichita, U.S.A. . . . 71 G6
Wichita Falls, U.S.A. . 71 J5
Wick, U.K. 12 C5
Wickenburg, U.S.A. . 73 K7
Wickepin, Australia . 53 F2
Wickham, C., Australia 54 F3
Wicklow, Ireland . . 13 D5
Wicklow □, Ireland . 13 D5
Wicklow Hd., Ireland . 13 D5
Widgiemooltha,
  Australia 53 F3
Widnes, U.K. 10 D5
Wieliczka, Poland . . 17 D10
Wieluń, Poland . . . 17 C9
Wien, Austria 16 D8
Wiener Neustadt,
  Austria 16 E8
Wierden, Neths. . . . 15 B6
Wiesbaden, Germany . 16 C4
Wigan, U.K. 10 D5
Wiggins, Colo., U.S.A. 70 E2
Wiggins, Miss., U.S.A. 71 K10
Wight, I. of □, U.K. . . 11 G6
Wigtown, U.K. . . . 12 G4
Wigtown B., U.K. . . 12 G4
Wilber, U.S.A. . . . 70 E6
Wilberforce, C.,
  Australia 54 A2
Wilburton, U.S.A. . . 71 H7
Wilcannia, Australia . 55 E3
Wildrose, U.S.A. . . 70 A3
Wildwood, U.S.A. . . 68 F8
Wilge →, S. Africa . 49 D4
Wilhelm II Coast,
  Antarctica 5 C7
Wilhelmshaven,
  Germany 16 B4
Wilhelmstal, Namibia 48 C2
Wilkes Barre, U.S.A. . 68 E8
Wilkesboro, U.S.A. . 69 G5
Wilkie, Canada . . . 65 C7
Wilkinson Lakes,
  Australia 53 E5
Willamina, U.S.A. . . 72 D2
Willandra Billabong
  Creek →, Australia 55 E4
Willapa, B., U.S.A. . 72 C2
Willard, N. Mex.,
  U.S.A. 73 J10
Willard, Utah, U.S.A. . 72 F7
Willcox, U.S.A. . . . 73 K9
Willemstad, Neth. Ant. 75 E11
Willeroo, Australia . 52 C5
William →, Canada . 65 B7
William Creek,
  Australia 55 D2
Williambury, Australia 52 D2
Williams, Australia . 53 F2
Williams Lake, Canada 64 C4
Williamsburg, Ky.,
  U.S.A. 69 G3
Williamsburg, Va.,
  U.S.A. 68 G7
Williamson, U.S.A. . 68 G4
Williamsport, U.S.A. . 68 E7
Williamston, U.S.A. . 69 H7
Williamstown,
  Australia 55 F3
Williamsville, U.S.A. . 71 G9
Willis Group, Australia 54 B5
Williston, S. Africa . . 48 E3
Williston, Fla., U.S.A. 69 L4

Williston, N. Dak.,
  U.S.A. 70 A3
Williston L., Canada . 64 B4
Willits, U.S.A. . . . 72 G2
Willmar, U.S.A. . . . 70 C7
Willow Bunch, Canada 65 D7
Willow L., Canada . . 64 A5
Willow Lake, U.S.A. . 70 C6
Willow Springs, U.S.A. 71 G8
Willowlake →,
  Canada 64 A4
Willowmore, S. Africa 48 E3
Willows, Australia . . 54 C4
Willows, U.S.A. . . . 72 G2
Willowvale = Gatyana,
  S. Africa 49 E4
Wills, L., Australia . . 52 D4
Wills Cr. →, Australia 54 C3
Wills Point, U.S.A. . . 71 J7
Willunga, Australia . 55 F2
Wilmette, U.S.A. . . 68 D2
Wilmington, Australia 55 E2
Wilmington, Del.,
  U.S.A. 68 F8
Wilmington, Ill., U.S.A. 68 E1
Wilmington, N.C.,
  U.S.A. 69 H7
Wilmington, Ohio,
  U.S.A. 68 F4
Wilpena Cr. →,
  Australia 55 E2
Wilsall, U.S.A. . . . 72 D8
Wilson, U.S.A. . . . 69 H7
Wilson →, Queens.,
  Australia 55 D3
Wilson →,
  W. Austral., Australia 52 C4
Wilson Bluff, Australia 53 F4
Wilsons Promontory,
  Australia 55 F4
Wilton, U.K. 11 F6
Wilton →, Australia . 54 B1
Wilton →, Australia . 54 A1
Wiltshire □, U.K. . . 11 F6
Wiltz, Lux. 15 E5
Wiluna, Australia . . 53 E3
Wimmera →,
  Australia 55 F3
Winburg, S. Africa . . 48 D4
Winchester, U.K. . . 11 F6
Winchooter, Idaho,
  U.S.A. 72 C5
Winchester, Ind.,
  U.S.A. 68 E3
Winchester, Ky., U.S.A. 68 G3
Winchester, Tenn.,
  U.S.A. 69 H2
Winchester, Va., U.S.A. 68 F6
Wind →, U.S.A. . . 72 E9
Wind River Range,
  U.S.A. 72 E9
Windau = Ventspils,
  Latvia 9 H16
Windber, U.S.A. . . 68 E6
Windermere, L., U.K. . 10 C5
Windfall, Canada . . 64 C5
Windflower L., Canada 64 A5
Windhoek, Namibia . 48 C2
Windom, U.S.A. . . 70 D7
Windorah, Australia . 54 D3
Window Rock, U.S.A. 73 J9
Windrush →, U.K. . . 11 F6
Windsor, Australia . . 55 E5
Windsor, N.S., Canada 63 D7
Windsor, Nfld., Canada 63 C8
Windsor, Ont., Canada 62 D3
Windsor, U.K. . . . 11 F7
Windsor, Colo., U.S.A. 70 E2
Windsor, Mo., U.S.A. 70 F8
Windsor, Vt., U.S.A. . 68 D9
Windsorton, S. Africa 48 D3
Windward Is.,
  W. Indies 74 P20
Windy L., Canada . . 65 A8
Winefred L., Canada . 65 B6
Winfield, U.S.A. . . . 71 G6
Wingate Mts., Australia 52 B5
Wingen, Australia . . 55 E5
Wingham, Australia . 55 E5
Wingham, Canada . . 62 D3
Winifred, U.S.A. . . 72 C9
Winisk, Canada . . . 62 A2
Winisk →, Canada . 62 A2
Winisk L., Canada . . 62 B2
Wink, U.S.A. 71 K3
Winkler, Canada . . 65 D9
Winlock, U.S.A. . . . 72 C2
Winneba, Ghana . . 44 G4
Winnebago, U.S.A. . 70 D7
Winnebago L., U.S.A. 68 D1
Winnecke Cr. →,
  Australia 52 C5
Winnemucca, U.S.A. . 72 F5
Winnemucca, L.,
  U.S.A. 72 F4
Winner, U.S.A. . . . 70 D5
Winnett, U.S.A. . . . 72 C9
Winnfield, U.S.A. . . 71 K8
Winnibigoshish L.,
  U.S.A. 70 B7
Winning, Australia . . 52 D1
Winnipeg, Canada . . 65 D9
Winnipeg →, Canada 65 C9
Winnipeg, L., Canada 65 C9
Winnipeg Beach,
  Canada 65 C9
Winnipegosis, Canada 65 C9
Winnipegosis L.,
  Canada 65 C9
Winnsboro, La., U.S.A. 71 J9
Winnsboro, S.C.,
  U.S.A. 69 H5

Winnsboro, Tex.,
  U.S.A. 71 J7
Winokapau, L., Canada 63 B7
Winona, Miss., U.S.A. 71 J10
Winona, Wis., U.S.A. 70 C9
Winooski, U.S.A. . . 68 C9
Winschoten, Neths. . 15 A7
Winslow, U.S.A. . . 73 J8
Winston-Salem, U.S.A. 69 G5
Winter Garden, U.S.A. 69 L5
Winter Haven, U.S.A. 69 M5
Winter Park, U.S.A. . 69 L5
Winters, U.S.A. . . . 71 K5
Winterset, U.S.A. . . 70 E7
Winterswijk, Neths. . 15 C6
Winterthur, Switz. . . 16 E4
Winthrop, Minn.,
  U.S.A. 70 C7
Winthrop, Wash.,
  U.S.A. 72 B3
Winton, Australia . . 54 C3
Winton, N.Z. 51 M2
Winton, U.S.A. . . . 69 G7
Wirral, U.K. 10 D4
Wirrulla, Australia . . 55 E1
Wisbech, U.K. . . . 10 E8
Wisconsin □, U.S.A. . 70 C10
Wisconsin →, U.S.A. 70 D9
Wisconsin Dells, U.S.A. 70 D10
Wisconsin Rapids,
  U.S.A. 70 C10
Wisdom, U.S.A. . . . 72 D7
Wishaw, U.K. 12 F5
Wishek, U.S.A. . . . 70 B5
Wisła →, Poland . . 17 A9
Wismar, Germany . . 16 B5
Wisner, U.S.A. . . . 70 E6
Witbank, S. Africa . . 49 D4
Witdraai, S. Africa . . 48 D3
Witham →, U.K. . . 10 D7
Withernsea, U.K. . . 10 D8
Witney, U.K. 11 F6
Witnossob →,
  Namibia 48 D3
Witten, Germany . . 15 C7
Wittenberg, Germany 16 C6
Wittenberge, Germany 16 B5
Wittenoom, Australia 52 D2
Wkra →, Poland . . 17 B10
Wlingi, Indonesia . . 33 H15
Włocławek, Poland . 17 B9
Wodonga, Australia . 55 F4
Woëvre, France . . . 18 B6
Wokam, Indonesia . 33 F8
Wolf →, Canada . . 64 A2
Wolf Creek, U.S.A. . 72 C7
Wolf L., Canada . . 64 A2
Wolf Point, U.S.A. . . 70 A2
Wolfe I., Canada . . 62 D4
Wolfsburg, Germany 16 B5
Wolin, Poland . . . 16 B7
Wollaston, Is., Chile . 80 H3
Wollaston L., Canada 65 B8
Wollaston Pen.,
  Canada 60 B8
Wollogorang, Australia 54 B2
Wollongong, Australia 55 E5
Wolmaransstad,
  S. Africa 48 D4
Wolseley, Australia . 55 F3
Wolseley, Canada . . 65 C8
Wolseley, S. Africa . 48 E2
Wolstenholme, C.,
  Canada 58 C12
Wolvega, Neths. . . 15 B6
Wolverhampton, U.K. 11 E5
Wonarah, Australia . 54 B2
Wondai, Australia . . 55 D5
Wongalarroo L.,
  Australia 55 E3
Wongan Hills,
  Australia 53 F2
Wongawol, Australia . 53 E3
Wonosari, Indonesia . 33 G14
Wŏnsan, N. Korea . . 31 C7
Wonthaggi, Australia . 55 F4
Woocalla, Australia . 55 E2
Wood Buffalo Nat.
  Park, Canada . . . 64 B6
Wood Is., Australia . 52 C3
Wood L., Canada . . 65 B8
Wood Lake, U.S.A. . 70 D4
Woodah, I., Australia 54 A2
Woodanilling, Australia 53 F2
Woodburn, Australia . 55 D5
Woodenbong,
  Australia 55 D5
Woodend, Australia . 55 F3
Woodgreen, Australia 54 C1
Woodland, U.S.A. . . 72 G3
Woodlands, Australia 52 D2
Woodpecker, Canada 64 C4
Woodridge, Canada . 65 D9
Woodroffe, Mt.,
  Australia 53 E5
Woodruff, Ariz., U.S.A. 73 J8
Woodruff, Utah, U.S.A. 72 F8
Woods, L., Australia . 54 B1
Woods, L., Canada . 63 B6
Woods, L. of the,
  Canada 65 D10
Woodstock, Queens.,
  Australia 54 B4
Woodstock,
  W. Austral., Australia 52 D2
Woodstock, N.B.,
  Canada 63 C6
Woodstock, Ont.,
  Canada 62 D3
Woodstock, U.K. . . 11 F6
Woodstock, U.S.A. . 70 D10

Woodsville

Woodsville, U.S.A. 68 C9
Woodville, N.Z. 51 J5
Woodville, U.S.A. 71 K7
Woodward, U.S.A. 71 G5
Woolamai, C., Australia 55 F4
Woolgoolga, Australia 55 E5
Woombye, Australia 55 D5
Woomera, Australia 55 E2
Woonsocket, R.I., U.S.A. 68 E10
Woonsocket, S. Dak., U.S.A. 70 C5
Wooramel, Australia 53 E1
Wooramel →, Australia 53 E1
Wooroloo, Australia 53 F2
Wooster, U.S.A. 68 E5
Worcester, S. Africa 48 E2
Worcester, U.K. 11 E5
Worcester, U.S.A. 68 D10
Workington, U.K. 10 C4
Worksop, U.K. 10 D6
Workum, Neths. 15 B5
Worland, U.S.A. 72 D10
Worms, Germany 16 D4
Wortham, U.S.A. 71 K6
Worthing, U.K. 11 G7
Worthington, U.S.A. 70 D7
Wosi, Indonesia 33 E7
Wou-han = Wuhan, China 31 C6
Wour, Chad 45 D8
Wousi = Wuxi, China 31 C7
Wowoni, Indonesia 33 E6
Woy Woy, Australia 55 E5
Wrangel I. = Vrangelya, Ostrov, Russia 25 B19
Wrangell, U.S.A. 60 C6
Wrangell I., U.S.A. 64 B2
Wrangell Mts., U.S.A. 60 B5
Wrath, C., U.K. 12 C3
Wray, U.S.A. 70 E3
Wrekin, The, U.K. 10 E5
Wrens, U.S.A. 69 J4
Wrexham, U.K. 10 D4
Wright, Canada 64 C4
Wright, Phil. 33 B7
Wrightson, Mt., U.S.A. 73 L8
Wrigley, Canada 60 B7
Wrocław, Poland 16 C8
Września, Poland 17 B8
Wu Jiang →, China 30 D5
Wubin, Australia 53 F2
Wuhan, China 31 C6
Wuhsi = Wuxi, China 31 C7
Wuhu, China 31 C6
Wukari, Nigeria 44 G6
Wuliaru, Indonesia 33 F8
Wuluk'omushih Ling, China 30 C3
Wulumuchi = Ürümqi, China 24 E9
Wum, Cameroon 44 G7
Wunnummin L., Canada 62 B2
Wuntho, Burma 37 H19
Wuppertal, Germany 16 C3
Wuppertal, S. Africa 48 E2
Wurung, Australia 54 B3
Würzburg, Germany 16 D4
Wusuli Jiang = Ussuri →, Asia 28 A7
Wutongqiao, China 30 D5
Wuwei, China 30 C5
Wuxi, China 31 C7
Wuxing, China 31 C7
Wuyi Shan, China 31 D6
Wuzhong, China 30 C5
Wuzhou, China 31 D6
Wyaaba Cr. →, Australia 54 B3
Wyalkatchem, Australia 53 F2
Wyandotte, U.S.A. 68 D4
Wyandra, Australia 55 D4
Wyangala Res., Australia 55 E4
Wyara, L., Australia 55 D3
Wycheproof, Australia 55 F3
Wye →, U.K. 11 F5
Wyemandoo, Australia 53 E2
Wymondham, U.K. 11 E7
Wymore, U.S.A. 70 E6
Wynbring, Australia 55 E1
Wyndham, Australia 52 C4
Wyndham, N.Z. 51 M2
Wyndmere, U.S.A. 70 B6
Wynne, U.S.A. 71 H9
Wynnum, Australia 55 D5
Wynyard, Australia 54 G4
Wynyard, Canada 65 C8
Wyola, L., Australia 53 E5
Wyoming □, U.S.A. 66 B5
Wyong, Australia 55 E5
Wytheville, U.S.A. 68 G5

X

Xai-Xai, Mozam. 49 D5
Xainza, China 30 C3
Xangongo, Angola 48 B2
Xánthi, Greece 21 D11
Xapuri, Brazil 78 F5
Xau, L., Botswana 48 C3
Xenia, U.S.A. 68 F4
Xhora, S. Africa 49 E4
Xhumo, Botswana 48 C3
Xi Jiang →, China 31 D6
Xiaguan, China 30 D5
Xiamen, China 31 D6
Xi'an, China 31 C5
Xiang Jiang →, China 31 D6
Xiangfan, China 31 C6
Xiangtan, China 31 D6
Xianyang, China 31 C5
Xiao Hinggan Ling, China 31 B7
Xichang, China 30 D5
Xieng Khouang, Laos 34 C7
Xigazê, China 30 D3
Xinavane, Mozam. 49 D5
Xing'an, China 31 D6
Xingu →, Brazil 79 D8
Xining, China 30 C5
Xinjiang Uygur Zizhiqu □, China 30 B3
Xinxiang, China 31 C6
Xique-Xique, Brazil 79 F10
Xisha Qundao = Hsisha Chuntao, Pac. Oc. 32 A4
Xixabangma Feng, China 37 E14
Xizang □, China 30 C3
Xuanhua, China 31 B6
Xuzhou, China 31 C6

Y

Yaamba, Australia 54 C5
Yaapeet, Australia 55 F3
Yabelo, Ethiopia 45 H12
Yablonovy Khrebet, Russia 25 D12
Yablonovy Ra. = Yablonovy Khrebet, Russia 25 D12
Yabrūd, Syria 41 B5
Yacheng, China 31 E5
Yacuiba, Bolivia 80 A4
Yadgir, India 36 L10
Yadkin →, U.S.A. 69 H5
Yagodnoye, Russia 25 C15
Yagoua, Cameroon 46 B3
Yahk, Canada 64 D5
Yahuma, Zaïre 46 D4
Yaita, Japan 29 F9
Yakima, U.S.A. 72 C3
Yakima →, U.S.A. 72 C3
Yakovlevka, Russia 28 B6
Yaku-Shima, Japan 29 J5
Yakut Republic □, Russia 25 C13
Yakutat, U.S.A. 60 C6
Yakutsk, Russia 25 C13
Yala, Thailand 34 N14
Yalbalgo, Australia 53 E1
Yalboroo, Australia 54 C4
Yalgoo, Australia 53 E2
Yalinga, C.A.R. 45 G9
Yalleroi, Australia 54 C4
Yalobusha →, U.S.A. 71 J9
Yalong Jiang →, China 30 D5
Yalta, Ukraine 23 F5
Yalutorovsk, Russia 24 D7
Yam Ha Melaḥ = Dead Sea, Asia 41 D4
Yam Kinneret, Israel 41 C4
Yamada, Japan 29 H5
Yamagata, Japan 28 E10
Yamagata □, Japan 28 E10
Yamaguchi, Japan 29 G5
Yamaguchi □, Japan 29 G5
Yamal, Poluostrov, Russia 24 B8
Yamal Pen. = Yamal, Poluostrov, Russia 24 B8
Yamanashi □, Japan 29 G9
Yamantau, Gora, Russia 22 D10
Yamba, N.S.W., Australia 55 D5
Yamba, S. Austral., Australia 55 E3
Yambah, Australia 54 C1
Yambarran Ra., Australia 52 C5
Yâmbiô, Sudan 45 H10
Yambol, Bulgaria 21 C12
Yamdena, Indonesia 33 F8
Yame, Japan 29 H5
Yamethin, Burma 37 J20
Yamma-Yamma, L., Australia 55 D3
Yamoussoukro, Ivory C. 44 G3
Yampa →, U.S.A. 72 F9
Yampi Sd., Australia 52 C3
Yamuna →, India 37 G12
Yamzho Yumco, China 30 D4
Yana →, Russia 25 B14
Yanac, Australia 55 F3
Yanagawa, Japan 29 H5
Yanai, Japan 29 H6
Yanaul, Russia 22 C10
Yanbu 'al Baḥr, Si. Arabia 38 F3
Yancannia, Australia 55 E3
Yanco Cr. →, Australia 55 F4
Yandal, Australia 53 E3
Yandanooka, Australia 53 E2
Yandaran, Australia 54 C5
Yandoon, Burma 37 L19
Yangambi, Zaïre 46 D4
Yangch'ü = Taiyuan, China 31 C6
Yangi-Yer, Kazakhstan 24 E7
Yangon = Rangoon, Burma 37 L20
Yangquan, China 31 C6
Yangtze Kiang = Chang Jiang →, China 31 C7
Yangzhou, China 31 C6
Yanhee Res., Thailand 34 D5
Yanji, China 31 B7
Yankton, U.S.A. 70 D6
Yanna, Australia 55 D4
Yanqi, China 30 B3
Yantabulla, Australia 55 D4
Yantai, China 31 C7
Yao, Chad 45 F8
Yaoundé, Cameroon 44 H7
Yap I., Pac. Oc. 56 G5
Yapen, Indonesia 33 E9
Yapen, Selat, Indonesia 33 E9
Yappar →, Australia 54 B3
Yaqui →, Mexico 74 B2
Yar-Sale, Russia 24 C8
Yaraka, Australia 54 C3
Yaransk, Russia 22 C8
Yardea P.O., Australia 55 E2
Yare →, U.K. 11 E9
Yarensk, Russia 22 B8
Yarí →, Colombia 78 D4
Yarkand = Shache, China 30 C2
Yarkhun →, Pakistan 36 A8
Yarmouth, Canada 63 D6
Yarmūk →, Syria 41 C4
Yaroslavl, Russia 22 C6
Yarqa, W. →, Egypt 41 F2
Yarra Yarra Lakes, Australia 53 E2
Yarraden, Australia 54 A3
Yarraloola, Australia 52 D2
Yarram, Australia 55 F4
Yarraman, Australia 55 D5
Yarranvale, Australia 55 D4
Yarras, Australia 55 E5
Yarrowmere, Australia 54 C4
Yartsevo, Russia 25 C10
Yasawa Group, Fiji 51 C7
Yasinski, L., Canada 62 B4
Yasothon, Thailand 34 E8
Yass, Australia 55 E4
Yates Center, U.S.A. 71 G7
Yathkyed L., Canada 65 A9
Yatsushiro, Japan 29 H5
Yauyos, Peru 78 F3
Yavari →, Peru 78 D4
Yavatmal, India 36 J11
Yavne, Israel 41 D3
Yawatahama, Japan 29 H6
Yayama-Rettō, Japan 29 M1
Yazd, Iran 39 D7
Yazd □, Iran 39 D7
Yazoo →, U.S.A. 71 J9
Yazoo City, U.S.A. 71 J9
Yding Skovhøj, Denmark 9 J10
Ye Xian, China 31 C6
Yealering, Australia 53 F2
Yebyu, Burma 37 M21
Yecla, Spain 19 C5
Yeeda, Australia 52 C3
Yeelanna, Australia 55 E2
Yegros, Paraguay 80 B5
Yehuda, Midbar, Israel 41 D4
Yei, Sudan 45 H11
Yekaterinburg, Russia 22 C11
Yekaterinodar = Krasnodar, Russia 23 E6
Yelanskoye, Russia 25 C13
Yelarbon, Australia 55 D5
Yelets, Russia 22 D6
Yelizavetgrad = Kirovograd, Ukraine 23 E5
Yell, U.K. 12 A7
Yell Sd., U.K. 12 A7
Yellow Sea, China 31 C7
Yellowhead Pass, Canada 64 C5
Yellowknife, Canada 64 A6
Yellowknife →, Canada 64 A6
Yellowstone →, U.S.A. 70 B3
Yellowstone L., U.S.A. 72 D8
Yellowstone National Park, U.S.A. 72 D8
Yellowtail Res., U.S.A. 72 D9
Yelvertoft, Australia 54 C2
Yemen ■, Asia 40 E3
Yenangyaung, Burma 37 J19
Yenbo = Yanbu 'al Baḥr, Si. Arabia 38 F3
Yenda, Australia 55 E4
Yenisey →, Russia 24 B9
Yeniseysk, Russia 25 D10
Yeniseyskiy Zaliv, Russia 24 B9
Yenyuka, Russia 25 D13
Yeo, L., Australia 53 E3
Yeola, India 36 J9
Yeovil, U.K. 11 G5
Yeppoon, Australia 54 C5
Yerbent, Turkmenistan 24 F6
Yerbogachen, Russia 25 C11
Yerevan, Armenia 23 F7
Yerilla, Australia 53 E3
Yermak, Kazakhstan 24 D8
Yermakovo, Russia 25 D13
Yermo, U.S.A. 73 J5
Yerofey Pavlovich, Russia 25 D13
Yershov, Russia 23 D8
Yerushalayim = Jerusalem, Israel 41 D4
Yes Tor, U.K. 11 G4
Yeso, U.S.A. 71 H2
Yessey, Russia 25 C11
Yeu, I. d', France 18 C2
Yevpatoriya, Ukraine 23 E5
Yeysk, Russia 23 E6
Yezd = Yazd, Iran 39 D7
Yi 'Allaq, G., Egypt 41 E2
Yiannitsa, Greece 21 D10
Yibin, China 30 D5
Yichang, China 31 C6
Yichun, China 31 B7
Yilehuli Shan, China 31 A7
Yinchuan, China 30 C5
Yindarlgooda, L., Australia 53 F3
Yingkou, China 31 B7
Yining, China 24 E9
Yinmabin, Burma 37 H19
Yinnietharra, Australia 52 D2
Yishan, China 30 D5
Yíthion, Greece 21 F10
Yiyang, China 31 D6
Ylitornio, Finland 8 C17
Ylivieska, Finland 8 D18
Ynykchanskiy, Russia 25 C14
Yoakum, U.S.A. 71 L6
Yog Pt., Phil. 33 B6
Yogyakarta, Indonesia 33 G14
Yoho Nat. Park, Canada 64 C5
Yokadouma, Cameroon 46 D2
Yokkaichi, Japan 29 G8
Yoko, Cameroon 45 G7
Yokohama, Japan 29 G9
Yokosuka, Japan 29 G9
Yokote, Japan 28 E10
Yola, Nigeria 45 G7
Yonago, Japan 29 G6
Yonaguni-Jima, Japan 29 M1
Yonezawa, Japan 28 F10
Yong Peng, Malaysia 34 T16
Yonibana, S. Leone 44 G2
Yonkers, U.S.A. 68 E9
Yonne □, France 18 C5
Yonne →, France 18 B5
York, Australia 53 F2
York, U.K. 10 D6
York, Ala., U.S.A. 69 J1
York, Nebr., U.S.A. 70 E6
York, Pa., U.S.A. 68 F7
York, C., Australia 54 A3
York, Kap, Greenland 4 B4
York Sd., Australia 52 B4
Yorke Pen., Australia 55 E2
Yorkshire Wolds, U.K. 10 D7
Yorkton, Canada 65 C8
Yorktown, U.S.A. 71 L6
Yornup, Australia 53 F2
Yoron-Jima, Japan 29 L4
Yos Sudarso, Pulau, Indonesia 33 F9
Yosemite National Park, U.S.A. 73 H4
Yoshkar Ola, Russia 22 C8
Yotvata, Israel 41 F4
Youbou, Canada 64 D4
Youghal, Ireland 13 E4
Youghal B., Ireland 13 E4
Young, Australia 55 E4
Young, Canada 65 C7
Younghusband, L., Australia 55 E2
Younghusband Pen., Australia 55 F2
Youngstown, Canada 65 C6
Youngstown, U.S.A. 68 E5
Yoweragabbie, Australia 53 E2
Yozgat, Turkey 23 G5
Ypres = Ieper, Belgium 15 D2
Ypsilanti, U.S.A. 68 D4
Yreka, U.S.A. 72 F2
Ysleta, U.S.A. 73 L10
Ystad, Sweden 9 J12
Ysyk-Köl = Issyk-Kul, Ozero, Kirghizia 24 E8
Ythan →, U.K. 12 D7
Ytyk-Kel, Russia 25 C14
Yu Jiang →, China 31 D6
Yu Shan, Taiwan 31 D7
Yuan Jiang →, China 31 D6
Yuba City, U.S.A. 72 G3
Yūbari, Japan 28 C10
Yūbetsu, Japan 28 B11
Yucatán □, Mexico 74 C7
Yucatán, Canal de, Caribbean 74 C7
Yucatán, Península de, Mexico 74 D7
Yucatan Str. = Yucatán, Canal de, Caribbean 74 C7
Yucca, U.S.A. 73 J6
Yuci, China 31 C6
Yudino, Russia 24 D7
Yuendumu, Australia 52 D5
Yugoslavia ■, Europe 21 C8
Yukon →, N. Amer. 60 B3
Yukon Territory □, Canada 60 B6
Yukti, Russia 25 C11
Yukuhashi, Japan 29 H5
Yule →, Australia 52 D2
Yuma, Ariz., U.S.A. 73 K6
Yuma, Colo., U.S.A. 70 E3
Yumen, China 30 C4
Yundamindra, Australia 53 E3
Yungas, Bolivia 78 G5
Yunnan □, China 30 D5
Yunta, Australia 55 E2
Yur, Russia 25 D14
Yurgao, Russia 24 D9
Yuribei, Russia 24 B8
Yurimaguas, Peru 78 E3
Yushu, China 30 C4
Yuxi, China 30 D5
Yuzawa, Japan 28 E10
Yuzhno-Sakhalinsk, Russia 25 E15
Yvelines □, France 18 B4
Yvetot, France 18 B4

Z

Zaandam, Neths. 15 B4
Zabaykalskiy, Russia 25 E12
Zabid, Yemen 40 E3
Zābol, Iran 39 D9
Zābolī, Iran 39 E9
Zabrze, Poland 17 C9
Zacapa, Guatemala 74 E7
Zacatecas, Mexico 74 C4
Zacoalco, Mexico 74 C4
Zadar, Croatia 20 B6
Zadetkyi Kyun, Burma 34 H5
Zafarqand, Iran 39 C7
Zafra, Spain 19 C2
Żagań, Poland 16 C7
Zagazig, Egypt 45 B11
Zāgheh, Iran 39 C6
Zagorsk = Sergiyev Posad, Russia 22 C6
Zagreb, Croatia 20 B7
Zāgros, Kuhhā-ye, Iran 39 C6
Zagros Mts. = Zāgros, Kuhhā-ye, Iran 39 C6
Zāhedān, Fārs, Iran 39 D7
Zāhedān, Sīstān va Balūchestān, Iran 39 D9
Zahlah, Lebanon 41 B4
Zaïre ■, Africa 46 E4
Zaïre →, Africa 46 F2
Zaječar, Serbia 21 C10
Zakamensk, Russia 25 D11
Zakavkazye, Asia 23 F7
Zākhū, Iraq 38 B4
Zákinthos, Greece 21 F9
Zalingei, Sudan 45 F9
Zambeze →, Africa 47 H7
Zambezi = Zambeze →, Africa 47 H7
Zambezi, Zambia 47 G4
Zambia ■, Africa 47 G5
Zamboanga, Phil. 33 C6
Zamora, Mexico 74 D4
Zamora, Spain 19 B3
Zamość, Poland 17 C11
Zanaga, Congo 46 E2
Zandvoort, Neths. 15 B4
Zanesville, U.S.A. 68 F4
Zangābād, Iran 38 B5
Zanjan, Iran 39 B6
Zanjān □, Iran 39 B6
Zante = Zákinthos, Greece 21 F9
Zanthus, Australia 53 F3
Zanzibar, Tanzania 46 F7
Zaouiet El-Kala = Bordj Omar Driss, Algeria 44 C6
Zaouiet Reggane, Algeria 44 C5
Zapadnaya Dvina, Russia 24 D4
Zapadnaya Dvina →, Belorussia 22 C3
Západné Beskydy, Europe 17 D9
Zapala, Argentina 80 D2
Zapata, U.S.A. 71 M5
Zapolyarnyy, Russia 22 A5
Zaporizhzhya = Zaporozhye, Ukraine 23 E6
Zaporozhye, Ukraine 23 E6
Zaragoza, Spain 19 B5
Zaragoza □, Spain 19 B5
Zarand, Kermān, Iran 39 D8
Zarand, Markazī, Iran 39 C6
Zaranj, Afghan. 36 D2
Zāreh, Iran 39 C6
Zarembo I., U.S.A. 64 B2
Zaria, Nigeria 44 F6
Zarneh, Iran 38 C5
Zarqā' →, Jordan 41 C4
Zarrīn, Iran 39 C7
Zaruma, Ecuador 78 D3
Żary, Poland 16 C7
Zarzis, Tunisia 45 B7
Zashiversk, Russia 25 C15
Zaskar Mts., India 36 C10
Zastron, S. Africa 48 E4
Zavāreh, Iran 39 C7
Zavitinsk, Russia 25 D13
Zavodovski, I., Antarctica 5 B1
Zawiercie, Poland 17 C9
Zāwiyat al Bayḍā, Libya 45 B9
Zāyā, Iraq 38 C5
Zayarsk, Russia 25 D11
Zaysan, Kazakhstan 24 E9
Zaysan, Oz., Kazakhstan 24 E9
Zayü, China 30 D4
Zduńska Wola, Poland 17 C9
Zeballos, Canada 64 D3
Zebediela, S. Africa 49 C4
Zeebrugge, Belgium 15 C3
Zeehan, Australia 54 G4
Zeeland □, Neths. 15 C3
Zeerust, S. Africa 48 D4
Zefat, Israel 41 C4
Zeil, Mt., Australia 52 D5
Zeila, Somali Rep. 40 E3
Zeist, Neths. 15 B5
Zeitz, Germany 16 C6
Zelenograd, Russia 22 C6
Zelzate, Belgium 15 C3
Zémio, C.A.R. 46 C5
Zemun, Serbia 21 B9
Zerbst, Germany 16 C6
Zeya, Russia 25 D13
Zeya →, Russia 25 D13
Zghartā, Lebanon 41 A4
Zhailma, Kazakhstan 24 D7
Zhambyl = Dzhambul, Kazakhstan 24 E8
Zhangjiakou, China 31 B6
Zhangye, China 30 C5
Zhangzhou, China 31 D6
Zhanjiang, China 31 D6
Zhanyi, China 30 D5
Zhaotong, China 30 D5
Zhayyq = Ural →, Kazakhstan 23 E9
Zhdanov = Mariupol, Ukraine 23 E6
Zhejiang □, China 31 D7
Zheleznodorozhny, Russia 22 B9
Zheleznogorsk-Ilimskiy, Russia 25 D11
Zhengzhou, China 31 C6
Zhigansk, Russia 25 C13
Zhitomir, Ukraine 23 D4
Zhlobin, Belorussia 22 D5
Zhokhova, Ostrov, Russia 25 B16
Zhongdian, China 30 D4
Zhumadian, China 31 C6
Zhupanovo, Russia 25 D16
Zhytomyr = Zhitomir, Ukraine 23 D4
Zīārān, Iran 39 B6
Zibo, China 31 C6
Zielona Góra, Poland 16 C7
Zierikzee, Neths. 15 C3
Zigey, Chad 45 F8
Zigong, China 30 D5
Ziguinchor, Senegal 44 F1
Žilina, Slovak Rep. 17 D9
Zillah, Libya 45 C8
Zima, Russia 25 D11
Zimbabwe ■, Africa 47 H5
Zinder, Niger 44 F6
Zion Nat. Park, U.S.A. 73 H7
Zipaquirá, Colombia 78 C4
Zitundo, Mozam. 49 D5
Ziway, L., Ethiopia 45 G12
Zlatograd, Bulgaria 21 D11
Zlatoust, Russia 22 C10
Zlin, Czech. 17 D8
Zlītan, Libya 45 B7
Zmeinogorsk, Kazakhstan 24 D9
Znojmo, Czech. 16 D8
Zoar, S. Africa 48 E3
Zobeyrī, Iran 38 C5
Zomba, Malawi 47 H7
Zongo, Zaïre 46 D3
Zonguldak, Turkey 23 F5
Zorra Island, Panama 74 H14
Zorritos, Peru 78 D2
Zouar, Chad 45 D8
Zouérate, Mauritania 44 D2
Zoutkamp, Neths. 15 A6
Zrenjanin, Serbia 21 B9
Zuetina, Libya 45 B9
Zufar, Oman 40 D5
Zug, Switz. 16 E4
Zuid-Holland □, Neths. 15 C4
Zuidhorn, Neths. 15 A6
Zula, Eritrea 45 E12
Zumbo, Mozam. 47 H6
Zungeru, Nigeria 44 G6
Zuni, U.S.A. 73 J9
Zunyi, China 30 D5
Zurbātīyah, Iraq 38 C5
Zürich, Switz. 16 E4
Zutphen, Neths. 15 B6
Zuwārah, Libya 45 B7
Zūzan, Iran 39 C8
Zverinogolovskoye, Russia 24 D7
Zvishavane, Zimbabwe 47 J6
Zvolen, Slovak Rep. 17 D9
Zwettl, Austria 16 D7
Zwickau, Germany 16 C6
Zwolle, Neths. 15 B6
Zwolle, U.S.A. 71 K8
Zymoetz →, Canada 64 C3
Żyrardów, Poland 17 B10
Zyryanka, Russia 25 C16
Zyryanovsk, Kazakhstan 24 E9

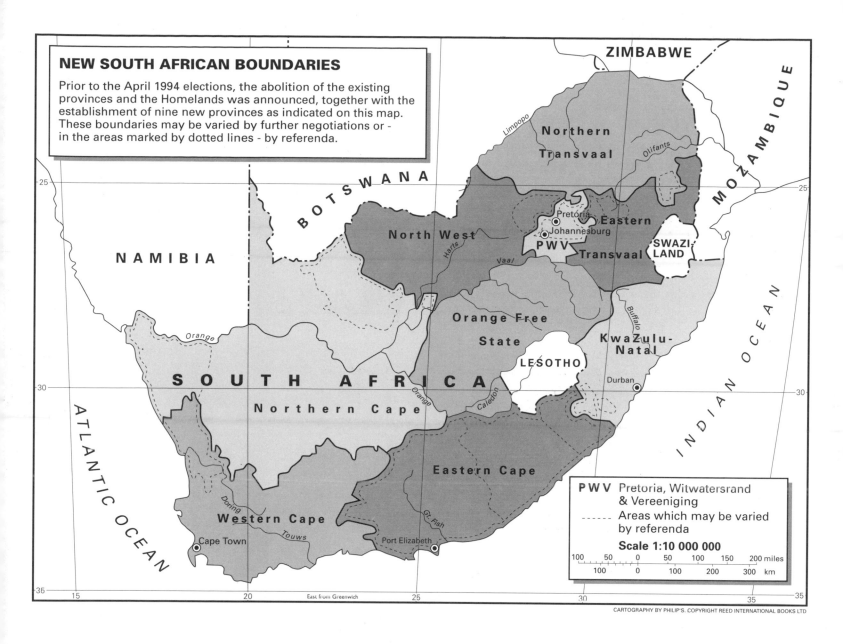

NEW SOUTH AFRICAN BOUNDARIES

Prior to the April 1994 elections, the abolition of the existing provinces and the Homelands was announced, together with the establishment of nine new provinces as indicated on this map. These boundaries may be varied by further negotiations or - in the areas marked by dotted lines - by referenda.

ZIMBABWE

MOZAMBIQUE

BOTSWANA

NAMIBIA

Limpopo

Olifants

Northern Transvaal

North West

Pretoria
Johannesburg
PWV
Eastern
Transvaal

SWAZI-LAND

Harts

Vaal

Orange Free State

KwaZulu-Natal

Buffalo

LESOTHO

Durban

INDIAN OCEAN

Orange

S O U T H   A F R I C A

Northern Cape

Caledon

Orange

Eastern Cape

ATLANTIC OCEAN

Doring

Touws

Western Cape

Gt. Fish

Cape Town

Port Elizabeth

PWV Pretoria, Witwatersrand & Vereeniging

- - - - - Areas which may be varied by referenda

Scale 1:10 000 000

| 100 | 50 | 0 | 50 | 100 | 150 | 200 miles |
| 100 | 0 | 100 | 200 | 300 km |

East from Greenwich

25

30

35

15

20

25

30

35

CARTOGRAPHY BY PHILIP'S. COPYRIGHT REED INTERNATIONAL BOOKS LTD

KEY TO WORLD MAP PAGES

NORTH AMERICA

SOUTH AMERICA

AFRIC

PACIFIC OCEAN 56-57

PACIFIC OCEAN

ATLANTIC OCEAN

Arctic Circle

Tropic of Cancer

Equator

Tropic of Capricorn

4

8

12

13

10-11

18

19

60-61

64-65

62-63

72-73

70-71

68-69

66

74-75

78-79

80